Comprehensive Clinical Psychology

Comprehensive Clinical Psychology

Editors-in-Chief

Alan S. Bellack
The University of Maryland at Baltimore, MD, USA

Michel Hersen
Pacific University, Forest Grove, OR, USA

Volume 2

PROFESSIONAL ISSUES

Volume Editor

Arthur N. Wiens
Oregon Health Sciences University, Portland, OR, USA

1998

AN IMPRINT OF ELSEVIER SCIENCE

AMSTERDAM—LAUSANNE—NEW YORK—OXFORD—SHANNON—SINGAPORE—TOKYO

Elsevier Science Ltd., The Boulevard, Langford Lane, Kidlington, Oxford, OX5 1GB, UK

First edition 1998

Library of Congress Cataloging-in-Publication Data
Comprehensive clinical psychology / editors-in-chief. Alan S. Bellack, Michel Hersen. —1st ed.
p. cm.
Includes indexes.
Contents: v. 1. Foundations / volume editor, Eugene Walker — v. 2. Professional issues / volume editor, Arthur N. Wiens — v. 3. Research and Methods / volume editor, Nina R. Schooler — v. 4. Assessment / volume editor, Cecil R. Reynolds — v. 5. Children & adolescents / volume editor, Thomas Ollendick — v. 6. Adults / volume editor, Paul Salkovskis — v. 7. Clinical geropsychology / volume editor, Barry Edelstein — v. 8. Health psychology / volume editors, Derek W. Johnston and Marie Jonhston — v. 9. Applications in diverse populations / volume editor, Nirbhay N. Singh — v. 10. Sociocultural and individual differences / volume editor, Cynthia D. Belar — v. 11. Indexes.
1. Clinical psychology. I. Bellack, Alan S. II. Hersen, Michel.
[DNLM: 1. Psychology, Clinical. WM 105 C737 1998]
RC467.C597 1998
616.89--dc21
DNLM/DLC
for Library of Congress 97-50185
CIP

British Library Cataloguing in Publication Data
A catalogue record for this book is available from the British Library.

ISBN 0-08-042707-3 (set : alk. paper)
ISBN 0-08-043141-0 (Volume 2)

∞™ The paper used in this publication meets the minimum requirements of the American National Standard for Information Sciences—Permanence of Paper for Printed Library Materials, ANSI Z39.48–1984.

Typeset by Bibliocraft, Dundee, UK.
Printed and bound in Great Britain by BPC Wheatons Ltd., Exeter, UK.

Contents

Introduction to *Comprehensive Clinical Psychology*

Co-Editors-in-Chief

Alan S. Bellack and Michel Hersen

Background

Clinical psychology is a relatively new field. While its roots can be traced back to at least the late nineteenth century, its evolution as a distinct academic discipline and profession dates only to the Second World War. The first 20 years of this postwar period saw steady, albeit nonspectacular, growth. Based substantially in the United States and Europe during this period, the study of clinical psychology developed as an alternative to medical school and psychiatry for many students interested in clinical service careers or the scientific study of human behavior. Postgraduate training was conducted exclusively in large university psychology departments within a strict scientist–practitioner model. The total number of Ph.D. candidates admitted to graduate school programs each year was relatively small; there were fewer than 50 accredited programs in the United States during much of this period, each admitting only 5–10 students. The number of new Ph.D.'s produced each year was substantially less, as many students failed to complete the rigorous scientific requirements of these elite programs. Career opportunities were similarly delimited, due in no small part to restraints on clinical practice imposed by psychiatrists and other physicians. The dominant form of psychotherapy was psychoanalysis, and psychologists were either excluded from psychoanalytic institutes or trained only as lay analysts who were proscribed from clinical practice. Few jurisdictions awarded licenses for independent practice, and psychologists generally were not reimbursed for their activities unless they worked under the direction of a physician. A sizable minority of clinical psychologists followed their mentors into university positions, teaching and conducting research. The majority, who were more interested in clinical service, opted for work in large psychiatric or Veterans Administration hospitals, where the modal activity was psychological testing; verbal psychotherapy was provided at the discretion of medical supervisors. A gradually increasing number of psychologists elected to be in private practice, where there was a greater professional autonomy. Medical hegemony over services for psychiatric disorders was even greater in Europe and Latin America.

The last 30 years has witnessed a massive change in the profession, stimulated by a number of scientific, clinical, and economic factors. Psychoanalysis gradually fell out of favor due to a dearth of data on its effectiveness and a desire for shorter term treatments that were not the primary purview of psychiatrists. First, client-centered therapy and then behavior therapy emerged as brief, highly effective alternatives. The former was entirely a product of clinical psychology, and was the intellectual and technical forebear of the current mandate for empirical evaluation of psychotherapies.

Carl Rogers, his colleagues, and students were the first to demonstrate the feasibility of careful, objective evaluation of the therapy process as well as outcome. While behavior therapy owes much of its legacy to psychiatrists such as Joseph Wolpe, it was substantially a product of academic psychologists searching for an approach with a strong scientific underpinning (in this case learning theory) that could be subjected to rigorous scientific scrutiny. Early behavior therapy emerged simultaneously in the UK and the US: in the UK psychologists such as Hans Eysenck based their work on Pavlov and classical conditioning, while in the US researchers were following Skinner and operant conditioning theories. The two schools merged with cognitive therapy, developed largely by Beck and Ellis through the 1960s, when the limitations of behavior therapy in isolation became apparent, particulary with depressed patients, and cognitive-behavior therapy is now widely practised.

Behavior therapy and cognitive-behavior therapy have not only proven themselves to be effective with a broad array of disorders, they have since been shown to be very successful alternatives to pharmacotherapy as well. Notably, behavior therapy was able to produce significant changes in populations that had previously been warehoused as untreatable, including people with physical and developmental disabilities and schizophrenia. Many of the most important contributions to the behavior therapies came from the UK, The Netherlands, South Africa, Australia, and Scandinavia, providing a tremendous stimulus for the development of clinical psychology globally. The availability of cost-effective, scientifically sound nonmedical treatments has decreased the medical monopoly of psychiatric/mental health services around the world and fostered the evolution of clinical psychology as a legally sanctioned helping profession, as well as a prestigious scientific discipline.

Scientific advances in our understanding of the brain and the role of psychosocial factors in physical health and illness have led to the development of two other rapidly growing subspecialties of clinical psychology: neuropsychology and health psychology. Novel assessment and treatment technologies in these two areas have created professional opportunities for clinical psychologists in medical schools, general medical hospitals, and other nonpsychiatric settings. Clinical psychologists can now be found conducting research and providing services in departments of neurology and neurosurgery, medicine, cardiac surgery, pediatrics, anesthesiology, oncology, and other medical specialty areas, as well as in the traditional psychiatric settings. They increasingly serve as directors of governmental agencies and service facilities. They comprise a large percentage of research grant recipients in the US, Canada, and the UK, and sit on prestigious government and foundation review boards. In fact the field has earned sufficient public recognition that it now has the somewhat dubious distinction of having clinical psychologists as lead characters on television shows and in cinema.

Stimulated, in part, by these exciting developments in scientific progress and clinical creativity, the field has grown geometrically in the past two decades. Psychology is now the second leading undergraduate major in the US and is increasingly popular elsewhere in the world as well. There are now more than 175 doctoral programs in the United States, each admitting many more students per annum than the 5–10 that has been typical of traditional scientist–practitioner Ph.D. programs over the past 25 years. Some of these schools have entering classes as large as 200 per year. Moreover, along with the professional school movement, which began in the 1970s, a new degree, the Psy.D. (or Doctorate in Psychology), is regularly being offered as an alternative to the Ph.D. Basically a professional rather than an academic degree, the Psy.D. is reflective of the local practitioner–scientist model rather than the scientist–practitioner.

Yet another trend in the field is the proliferation of master's level psychologists, specifically trained to carry out some of the more mundane functions formerly implemented by doctoral level psychologists. Indeed, each year in the United States alone 10 000 new master's level psychologists graduate from university programs. The financial and programmatic implication of such large numbers is obvious.

Statistics are not readily available about the size of the profession in all regions of the globe, but anecdotal evidence supports the hypothesis that the field is growing worldwide. As previously indicated, behavioral and cognitive-behavioral therapies owe a substantial debt to scientists and clinicians from Europe, Australia, and South Africa. There are now enough cognitive-behavior therapists to support national societies in most Western European countries, as well as Asia, Australia, and Latin America. Many of the most important developments in the psychosocial treatment of severe and persistent mental illness in the last decade have come from the United Kingdom, Australia, Switzerland, and Germany. Psychologists in Scandinavia, the United Kingdom, and the Netherlands have played a central role in the development of cognitive-behavioral treatments for anxiety and depression, and there have also been notable contributions from these regions to health psychology. As the hold of psychoanalytic therapies on psychiatric treatment in Europe continues its inevitable decline, there will be increasing opportunities for clinical psychologists to provide shorter term behavioral and cognitive-behavioral treatments. In addition, exciting developments are also emerging from Japan, China, and other countries in the Pacific rim. It seems likely that the global influence of regional approaches and thinking will lead to a more multicultural and universal psychology than has been the case in the past.

The scientific and clinical literatures have burgeoned along with the number of clinical psychologists in the world. This has been an era of rapid growth of knowledge and increasing specialization. General topics, such as psychological assessment, clinical child psychology, and psychotherapy, that used to merit only one or two graduate courses to establish expertise, have expanded and are subdivided to the extent that circumscribed specialty areas, such as neuropsychology, geropsychology, behavioral pediatrics, or cognitive-behavior therapy for depression can each require postdoctoral training. Consequently, hundreds of undergraduate, graduate, and professional level texts are published each year. Specialty journals abound. Where a few key generalist journals such as the *Journal of Consulting and Clinical Psychology* used to represent the entire field, each subdiscipline now has multiple journals, and there are both national journals (e.g., the *British Journal of Clinical Psychology*, the *British Journal of Health Psychology*, the *Australian Journal of Cognitive and Behavioral Therapy*) and journals representing specific populations or disorders (e.g., *Addictive Behaviors*, *Journal of Family Violence*, *Journal of Clinical Geropsychology*), or domains of practice (e.g., *Journal of Clinical Psychology in Medical Setting*). Specialization has made it difficult for professionals to keep abreast of developments within their immediate areas of expertise, and impossible for them to be conversant with the literature in other areas. Moreover, given the plethora of choices, it is also virtually impossible for either students or professionals to know where to find the most accurate, up-to-date information in most areas.

The combination of a large and increasing number of students and professionals, and rapidly growing scientific and clinical literature, makes this a particularly appropriate time for *Comprehensive Clinical Psychology*. This multivolume work encompasses the entire field, and represents a single source of information on the scientific status of clinical psychology and its subspecialties, on theory, and on clinical techniques. The work covers the history of the field, and current thinking about training, professional standards and practices, and sociocultural factors in mental health and illness.

Genesis of Comprehensive Clinical Psychology

Following preliminary conceptual discussions between Elsevier Science and Alan S. Bellack at several international conferences in 1994, Michel Hersen was asked to join as Co-Editor-in-Chief. The first official planning meeting for the project took place in June 1995. In addition to Elsevier Science staff, Alan S. Bellack and Michel Hersen invited Tom Ollendick, Nina Schooler, and Warren Tryon to serve as consultants. At that meeting, the philosophical and international scope of the project was agreed upon and established, with the scientific underpinnings of the field identified as the model. The objective here was to ensure that chapters reflect our core knowledge and that the material stand the test of time.

At that meeting, we also underscored that since clinical psychology was now an international discipline, the work should reflect contributions at the cross-cultural level, with chapters solicited from eminent psychologists worldwide. Although it was acknowledged that the United States was in the forefront of the field, the work could not simply represent the American perspective but to the extent possible would represent diversity at its best. Consistent with the international perspective, at the initial planning meeting, the importance of having an Honorary International Editorial Advisory Board comprised of international representatives was acknowledged, and the 10 specific volumes to comprise *Comprehensive Clinical Psychology* were identified. Preliminary outlines for each volume were developed and volumes editors were considered.

The international perspective was to be reflected at a tripartite level. First, diversity among editors and contributors for their respective volumes was selected as a goal. Second, chapters in each volume were designed to reflect diversity by providing the reader with worldwide examples, not simply the Anglo-Saxon view. Of course, where basic facts and principles were the same, there was no need to present regional diversity. Third, and related to the first two parts, the Honorary International Editorial Advisory Board provided us with an international perspective on overall organization and specifics for the individual volumes.

Between June and October 1995, Alan S. Bellack and Michel Hersen, in consultation with Elsevier Science, invited the ten volume editors to assume their positions, and a meeting of the Editors-in-Chief, the ten volume editors (C. Eugene Walker, Arthur N. Wiens, Nina R. Schooler, Cecil R. Reynolds, Thomas Ollendick, Paul Salkovskis, Barry Edelstein, Marie Johnston and Derek W. Johnston, Nirbhay N. Singh, and Cynthia D. Belar), and Elsevier Science staff was convened in October of that year. At that meeting, each of the volume editors presented his or her conception of the relevant volume, and the nature of coverage and particular contributors was discussed at length. Most of all the philosophical underpinnings of the work were stressed so as to insure intervolume consistency.

Subsequent to the October 1995 meeting, the enormous work to bring this project to fruition began, with potential authors invited to contribute, manuscripts reviewed, and then edited. Were it not for the wonders of electronic communication, a project of this scope would not have been possible, especially given the international aspects involved. A lengthy series of checks and balances was instituted to guarantee the quality and excellence of each contribution. The volume editor first approved each contributor's chapter outline, followed by editing and approval of the text. This process frequently required several revisions. The Co-Editor-in-Chief then reviewed each chapter for scope, level, and overlap, but only after the volume editor had first verified the accuracy of references cited. After the Co-Editor-in-Chief's labors, the manuscript was reviewed by Elsevier staff for format, writing style, reference checking, and other technical issues.

Aims and Scope

The final organization and contents of the work evolved over a series of discussions between the Editors-in-Chief, the volume editors, and Elsevier Science. It was comparatively easy to select the primary domains that needed to be covered: history, treatment, assessment, research, training, and professional issues. It was also comparatively easy to identify the first two-thirds, or so, of specific topics that required chapter-length coverage: treatment of the primary *DSM/ICD* disorders, basic research strategies, standard assessment techniques, etc. However, organizing the vast set of requisite topics into coherent volumes, determining which topics warranted independent chapters, and assigning page limits to individual chapters proved to be daunting. Two broad organizational themes immediately suggested themselves: a focus on core themes or techniques across populations vs. integrated coverage of populations. For example, the former would have entailed volumes on treatment modalities, such as behavior therapy, as they are applied to children and adults, while the latter would call for separate volumes on children and adults that covered diverse approaches. To complicate matters, some topics, such as Research Methods and Professional Issues, do not lend themselves to breakdown by population, and others, such as Behavioral Medicine, do not lend themselves to a breakdown by themes or techniques. Volume length was also an important factor, making some content-based solutions less practical than others. For example, we determined that treatment should receive more attention than assessment; a strict population-based solution would have led to separate short volumes on assessment of adults and children. Ultimately, we opted for an organizational structure that balanced practical considerations with our collective prediction about how the individual volumes would be used. While it was different earlier in the development of the field, we believe that the current trend is for people to be more organized around populations than techniques. Hence, more people are likely to pick up and cross-reference a single volume on children or the elderly than a volume on Behavior Therapy. Our strategy for identifying chapter length topics and associated page limits is more difficult to explain. Once again, we relied on our collective judgement, honed by negotiation. In rough order, priority was given to topics that had established empirical literatures, that were deemed to be "important," that had broad interest, and that were likely to be at least as important in the next decade. Page limits were determined substantially by estimates of the first two criteria. We began with an overall target for the entire work and minimums and maximums for volumes, and then worked backwards to divide up the allotted pages among the chapters designated for each volume. Given that no scheme will please everyone, we are confident that the organization of the work adequately reflects the field now and in the foreseeable future.

Under the careful aegis of the outstanding group of experts comprising the Honorary International Editorial Advisory Board, 10 leading international scholars were selected to edit the 10 specific volumes.

Volume 1 (*Foundations*), edited by C. Eugene Walker, provides a complete overview of the basic foundations of clinical psychology, with special emphasis on the relationship between clinical psychology and other fields of science. Beginning with a brief history of clinical psychology, as well as a look at its current scientific status, this informative volume covers such topics as the biological bases of clinical psychology, elucidating research in genetics, psychobiology, psychopharmacology, and the use of animal models in human mental health problems; clinical psychology in the behavioral sciences, including anthropology, epidemiology, sociology, and research psychology; and the major systems and theories that are used in clinical psychology. The volume also describes various techniques for library research and information retrieval in psychology.

Volume 2 (*Professional Issues*), edited by Arthur W. Wiens, focuses on the professional, legal, and ethical issues that are relevant to clinical psychology. The volume addresses the various educational and training programs available, such as doctoral study, internship training, and postdoctoral residency programs, and reviews the accreditation of these programs. Also highlighted are the various international government guidelines for registration, certification, and licensing, including a discussion of the advantages of specialty recognition and practice certificates. The volume concludes with a look at ethical and legal guidelines in the management of clinical psychology practices, national healthcare policies, and advocacy efforts for government support for practitioners.

Volume 3 (*Research and Methods*), edited by Nina R. Schooler, explores the function of research in clinical psychology. The volume begins with an in-depth look at research approaches, including the use of descriptive studies, single case designs, observational methods, and other methods of analysis. The volume goes on to explore a broad range of topics that have been the focus of research, such as test development and validation, personality assessment, clinical interventions, and service evaluations and outcomes. Finally, various statistical techniques are reviewed, including descriptive and inferential statistics, factor analysis, and sampling and generalizability.

Volume 4 (*Assessment*), edited by Cecil R. Reynolds, provides valuable information on the development and role of assessment in clinical practice, analyzing such topics as psychometrics; taxonomic, functional, and actuarial approaches to diagnosis; and specific instruments, techniques, and procedures. Chapters also review the range of assessment techniques and procedures used in clinical practice, with emphasis on intelligence, neuropsychological, personality, projective, computer-assisted, therapeutic, and forensic assessment. The volume concludes with a review of legal guidelines and regulations in the use of psychological testing.

Volume 5 (*Children & Adolescents: Clinical Formulation & Treatment*), edited by Thomas Ollendick, draws on the experience and research of leading scientists and clinicians from Australia, Canada, Israel, the United Kingdom, and the United States to present state-of-the-art information on all aspects of child psychology and psychiatry, with special attention given to the psychopathology, assessment, treatment, and prevention of childhood behavioral disorders. The volume highlights the developmental-contextual framework used in the clinical formulation of these disorders, as well as process and outcome issues in treatment. Various theoretical perspectives are also reviewed, including applied behavior analysis, family systems therapy, play therapy, and pharmacologic therapy. In the final section, all of the major childhood disorders found in the *DSM* and *ICD* are described, with information on their prevalence, etiology, assessment, and treatment. This section also analyzes the empirical status of the various therapies used for treatment of childhood disorders.

Volume 6 (*Adults: Clinical Formulation & Treatment*), edited by Paul Salkovskis, provides valuable insights into the basis of the psychological theories and interventions used for behavioral and emotional problems and reviews how to integrate clinical skills with these theories. Various treatment approaches are addressed, such as cognitive therapy, family therapy, and Humanistic/Rogerian/Gestalt approaches, as well as the issues related to treatments, including stress management, arousal reduction methods, suicidal behavior, and specific issues in working with groups. The final section details specific problem areas and disorders, ranging from such universally recognized problems as gambling and substance abuse to more specific disorders such as post-traumatic stress, depression, obsessive-compulsive, and the various phobias. Each chapter in the volume emphasizes approaches that have an empirical basis.

Volume 7 (*Clinical Geropsychology*), edited by Barry Edelstein, addresses the emerging field of clinical psychology in the aging population. The volume begins with a review of this area of research, presenting important epidemiological information. The volume then offers a detailed look at issues that range from analyzing physiological and cognitive aspects to cognitive changes and specific neurological disorders common among older adults. Specific topics covered include sexuality, bereavement, anxiety, substance abuse, and schizophrenia. Each chapter presents a summary of clinical research and its practical application. Voids in the knowledge base are also noted, along with recommendations for the direction of future investigations. The volume also addresses management problems, such as incontinence, wandering, and aggressive behavior, and reviews the various mental healthcare systems available in different countries.

Volume 8 (*Health Psychology*), edited by Derek W. Johnston and Marie Johnston, provides a comprehensive overview of the development and application of clinical health psychology. Beginning with a discussion of training, assessment, and measurement issues, this volume analyzes the key behaviors that either affect or are related to health. Topics covered include stress and disease, the experience of illness, and behavior that can affect the neuroendocrine, cardiovascular, and immune systems. The volume also provides a detailed analysis of specific clinical problems and their psychological aspects and interventions. These include cancer, diabetes, epilepsy, disfigurement, and smoking.

Volume 9 (*Applications in Diverse Populations*), edited by Nirbhay N. Singh, covers the broad spectrum of diverse issues that clinical psychologists typically face in their work. Four sections outline the various psychological aspects found in different populations, as well as methods for assessment, diagnostic information, and interventions useful with these different groups. Section I focuses on select child, adolescent, and adult populations, including those with developmental disorders, learning disabilities, and mental retardation. Section II is devoted to various types of families and their issues, including families of individuals with HIV or AIDS, families of alcoholics, and families of children with serious emotional disturbances. Section III covers victims of violence and abuse, including child sexual abuse. Section IV examines perpetrators of violence and abuse, including sex offenders and issues of domestic violence.

Volume 10 (*Sociocultural and Individual Differences*), edited by Cynthia D. Belar, covers cross-cultural psychopathology and interventions. Chapters examine such select topics as gender, sexual orientation, socioeconomic status, religions, and training for clinical psychologists. The volume also provides valuable insights into the use of clinical psychology in different parts of the world, as well as personality assessment across international settings.

Given the scope and detail of *Comprehensive Clinical Psychology*, Volume 11 is devoted to: (i) a Name Index, (ii) a Subject Index, (iii) a List of Contributors, and (iv) a list of the Contents of All Volumes. The Name Index is an accumulation of all the authors who are cited in text in the reference sections throughout the entire work. The Subject Index, consisting of more than 40 000 entries, is a consolidation of all the individual volume subject indexes. It is presented in word-by-word alphabetical sequence with a maximum of three levels of heading. Terminology in the index is based on standard internationally recognized sources. Cross-references are provided to assist the user to locate preferred terms and terms of related interest.

Acknowledgments

To produce a tome of this magnitude requires an enormous number of individuals with unique talents working in concert. To begin with, we applaud the herculean efforts of our driving force and friend at Elsevier Science, Barbara Barrett. We also gratefully acknowledge the efforts of two other publishing editors at Elsevier Science, Susan Hanscom and David Hoole, who provided guidance and encouragement along the way. We are particularly thankful for the exceptionally hard work of Angela Greenwell and her staff in Oxford, who made sure that all tasks were implemented reasonably on time and who orchestrated the day-to-day management of this huge undertaking. Next, we thank our eminent volume editors, who had the difficult job of soliciting, tracking, and editing manuscripts for their respective volumes. Similarly, we thank the Honorary International Editorial Advisory Board for their excellent input in developing the outline for the work and suggestions as to potential international contributors. Of course, we owe a great deal to the individual contributors who agreed to share their expertise with us in a timely fashion. Finally, we are most appreciative of our own editorial assistants, Sonia McQuarters and Burt G. Bolton, who repeatedly have provided us with the kind of support that makes all of this a possibility.

HONORARY INTERNATIONAL EDITORIAL ADVISORY BOARD

Preface

Volume 2 focuses on the interfaces of education and training in clinical psychology, professional practice, protection of the public, and needs of society. The individual chapters that address the interfaces are presented in seven broad categories. Consistent with the international perspective of *Comprehensive Clinical Psychology*, the authors invited to contribute chapters in each of the categories are from different countries around the world.

Education and Training in Clinical Psychology

Chapter 2.01 is written by Professor Ingrid Lunt, a former president of the European Federation of Professional Psychologists' Association (EFPPA). Her chapter covers some of the history and emerging trends in education and training for clinical psychology primarily, but not exclusively, within the European Union. She reports that in 1997 there were 15 member states, covering most of the western European countries (excluding Iceland, Norway, and Switzerland). Of particular interest is Professor Lunt's observation that the countries of Europe have very different histories which, in turn, are reflected in differences in training and practice within clinical psychology. The European countries remain quite different among regional groupings, that is, the Nordic countries, the United Kingdom (where training has much in common with the United States), the German speaking countries, and a southern European group.

Clinical psychology emerged as a recognizable profession at different times in different countries. In the United Kingdom the formation of the National Health Service (NHS) in 1948 provided considerable impetus to the development of the profession. The development of behavior therapy led to clinical psychologists developing a therapeutic role, in addition to their established role in psychological assessment, and in the 1960s they became recognized clinical practitioners in their own right. In the Nordic countries clinical psychology also developed in the 1940s and early 1950s. Clinical psychology progressed through broad phases, as in the United Kingdom, with a phase focusing on diagnostic examination and testing of individual patients, a phase focusing on therapeutic work involving mainly psychotherapy, and a phase focusing on indirect work with other professional groups through techniques such as consultation and training. In Spain, clinical psychology has a shorter history and is generally acknowledged to have emerged in the 1970s, whereas in Italy and Greece it emerged in the 1960s.

Interestingly, psychological activity within the mental health field is becoming increasingly differentiated in European countries. Three task forces of EFPPA, focusing on clinical psychology, health psychology, and psychotherapy, have drawn up a model defining overlap and separate areas of activity within the health field, with corresponding commonalities and differences in education and training. Such differentiation appears quite similar to the development of specialties in psychology in the United States (see chapters by Drs. Kerry Hamsher, Walter Pryzwansky, and Tommy Stigall).

Professor Qicheng Jing and Dr. Peicheng Hu (Chapter 2.07) chronicle that Chinese psychology has a long past but a short history. Some 2000 years ago there were descriptions of psychological thought in which it was supposed that some diseases could lead to emotions of anger, happiness, pensiveness, sadness, and fear; and that these, in turn, could cause damage to the liver, heart, spleen, lungs, and kidneys. The beginning of modern Chinese psychology dates to 1917 when the first psychological laboratory was established at Peking University. The first department of psychology was established at Nanking Teachers College in 1920. The first department of medical psychology was established at Beijing Medical College in 1979. The term "medical psychology" was introduced via the former Soviet Union in the 1950s, and is still used in China. At present, as the authors indicate, the difference between clinical psychology and medical psychology is small, but a proposal to replace the term "medical psychology" with "clinical psychology" has been rejected to date.

Professor Jing and Dr. Hu suggest that the practice of "clinical psychology" encompasses the following: (i) medical psychology in medical schools, (ii) psychiatry in mental hospitals, (iii) psychological counseling in universities and schools, and (iv) clinics providing psychological counseling and psychotherapy in society. Medical students study "medical psychology" as a requirement. Most "medical psychologists" are trained in medicine and receive additional training in psychology. They have prescription rights in hospitals. Most psychiatrists in China consider themselves to be also medical psychologists.

Historically, after 1949 China followed a pattern of development in science similar to that in the Soviet Union. In all medical and biological sciences, Pavlov's theory of conditioned reflexes was taken as the starting point. The behavioral approach was the dominant methodology in clinical psychology. Then, during the period of the Chinese Cultural Revolution (1966–1976) psychology was attacked as a "pseudoscience," a bourgeois discipline imported from the West. The Chinese Psychological Society was dissolved and Chinese psychologists were sent to factories and farms in remote parts of the country to do physical labor and for thought reform. Subsequently, psychology was rehabilitated and again recognized as a scientific discipline. The Chinese Mental Health Association was inaugurated in 1985. Several years later, the Beijing Municipal Bureau of Health published standards for the ratings of hospitals. To achieve the highest rating, a hospital had to provide psychological counseling and psychotherapy in its related departments. Due to this government mandate, psychological counseling and psychotherapy soon became widely used in Chinese hospitals.

Educators in psychology from a number of countries have generally agreed that psychology, in addition to being a scientific discipline, is a profession. In the introduction to his chapter (Chapter 2.05), Dr. Paul Nelson describes professions as characterized by a differentiated and dynamic body of knowledge; a system of disciplined methods of inquiry and practice through which that body of knowledge is challenged, expanded or modified, and applied; and a core of shared values and attitudes that together speak to a sense of integrity and social responsibility. Professions are characterized as well by a sense of self-discipline and self-regulation, governed by standards of practice and ethical principles in accordance with which their members are subject to peer review.

Dr. Nelson goes on to say that the foundation of any profession is the requisite education and training that leads to the entry level of practice. Consistent with the disciplinary principles just stated, it is the responsibility of a profession to establish education, training, credentialing, and practice standards or guidelines.

That clinical psychology is a dynamic and evolving body of knowledge in the United States is well documented by Dr. Lynn Rehm (Chapter 2.02). In the introduction to his chapter he points out that clinical psychology, throughout its history, has been involved in a continuing battle of borders and territory with academic disciplines and professional rivals. The scope of clinical psychology's practice has expanded in competition with neighbors outside of and within psychology. He traces the history of clinical psychology from its beginning, accepted as dating from 1896 when Lightner Witmer opened a psychology clinic at the University of Pennsylvania. The history of clinical psychology in the United States is also chronicled in a series of training conferences beginning with the "Boulder Conference" which was convened in Boulder, Colorado in 1945. The Boulder Conference report is best known for setting forth the scientist–professional model of training for both research and practice.

A number of subsequent training conferences have attempted to keep up with the changing world of clinical psychology. Dr. Rehm reports on 11 conferences, the most recent one being the 1994 National Conference on Postdoctoral Education and Training in Psychology which essentially confirmed the importance of education and training across the entire lifetime of a professional psychologist. Dr. Rehm considers a variety of current themes in clinical training in the United States that must be addressed in the further evolution of clinical psychology. These themes include, in part: defining a core curriculum, pressures to extend training, overproduction of psychologists, multiple levels of training, industrialization of health care, and biological trends in treatment.

Dr. Sanford Pederson (Chapter 2.03) addresses the issue of possible overproduction of psychologists in his chapter on internship education and training in professional psychology. It has been evident for several years that in the United States there are larger numbers of students seeking professional psychology internships than there are available internship positions. Psychology continues to be the most popular undergraduate major and this has meant ever greater numbers of students seeking admission to doctoral training programs in professional psychology. Issues of supply and demand are considered further in Chapters 2.35 and 2.36.

Postdoctoral education and training in clinical psychology, another level of training, is discussed by Dr. Kerry Hamsher (Chapter 2.04). In its broadest definition, such training could refer to all education and training beyond the doctoral degree. However, many specific programs have been developed to address many specialty and subspecialty areas in psychology. Dr. Hamsher presents an overview of organizing for education, credentialing, and accreditation in clinical neuropsychology.

Registration, Certification, and Licensure of Psychologists

Registration, certification, and licensure of psychologists is at the interface of psychology and society, that is, what psychology wants and needs to evolve as a profession, and what society wants from psychologists and the concomitant privileges it wishes to accord psychologists. Who should, and will, ultimately determine psychology's destiny? What limitations should psychology accept from the societies in which psychologists practice? What are the knowledge limitations of psychologists' practices and how should they be acknowledged? Psychologist practitioners in the United States must acknowledge that the "profession" of psychology is not the same as the "science" of psychology; therefore, in the interim, practitioners must assume responsibility for helping individuals in a society even in the absence of a verified scientific database.

Professor Frank McPherson (Chapter 2.06) suggests that it is difficult to describe the legal status of clinical psychology in Europe because: the situation is rapidly changing, detailed accounts of regulations are not readily available, and major differences exist among the European nations in regard to how laws protect clinical psychologists. He makes the interesting observation that, although differences in regulation might seem unsurprising in view of the political divisions which have existed between European nations throughout much of the history of professional psychology, the general political ideology of a nation appears to have had little effect. Thus, the earliest European nations with laws regulating the practice of psychology included some which, at the time had either left- or right-wing authoritarian regimes and others which then, as now, were parliamentary democracies. Ironically, as Professor McPherson points out, a nation which no longer exists, the German Democratic Republic, was, in 1967, the first European nation to regulate clinical psychology.

The development of standards and the regulation of the practice of clinical psychology in China is described by Professor Jing and Dr. Hu (Chapter 2.07); in India by Dr. Santosh K. Verma (Chapter 2.08); and in Latin America by Dr. Hector Fernández-Alvarez (Chapter 2.09). These authors describe the great heterogeneity and size of their countries or regions and the relatively recent development of psychology as an independent discipline.

Dr. Craig Schoon (Chapter 2.10) discusses the political theory of regulatory processes in the professions from a generic perspective. One underlying ideal of regulation, which might be termed "libertarian," holds that the public is entitled to maximum liberty in personal decisions regarding the purchase of products and services, including such services as health care and those that may affect their financial well-being. A converse "totalitarian" ideal reflects a belief that the state is best suited to make decisions regarding the production of goods and the provision of services. Under the latter model, regulatory control of the means of production and delivery of services is deemed to be in the best interests of the public. The need for this control rests on the public's presumed inability to make informed decisions. In a democracy such as the United States, the public's interests are balanced between trusting the public to make its own choices and the responsibility of the state to protect the health and welfare of its citizens. Licensure has spread broadly across many professions in the United States; states currently regulate over 1000 professions.

Other chapters in this section on the registration, certification, and licensure of psychologists discuss steps in the development of a credentialing program. Drs. I. Leon Smith and Sandra Greenberg (Chapter 2.11) suggest that after a strategic credentialing analysis (see Schoon, Chapter 2.10), a practice analysis should be done to define the critical performance areas and the underlying knowledge, skills, or abilities of practitioners. Such a practice analysis is described in Chapter 2.11; the analysis provides a picture of what practicing psychologists in the United States and Canada know and do and provides a database for policymaking in regard to education, certification, and accreditation. It also contributes to the development of two major assessment tools for credentialing. The first of these is the Examination for Professional Practice of Psychology (EPPP), an objective test which is being used routinely by licensure boards in the United States and Canada (Dr. Gerald Rosen, Chapter 2.12). The second is the oral examination for licensure which is also used routinely in the United States and Canada and probably by regulatory bodies around the world. Dr. Diane Hill (Chapter 2.13) discusses efforts to enhance the reliability and validity of the oral examination. Drs. Stephen DeMers (Chapter 2.14) and Stephan Jern (Chapter 2.15) discuss current and future credentialing issues in the United States and in the Scandinavian countries, respectively.

Finally, to move beyond initial certification or licensure for practice, Drs. David Rodgers and Edward Bourg (Chapters 2.16 and 2.17) discuss the issues of continuing competency assurance in practice over a professional career. Dr. Rodgers points out that various professional groups have embraced the concept of "recredentialing" to periodically reassess practice competency and to identify incompetent practitioners whose services are hazardous to the public and damaging to the reputation of all professionals. He carefully analyzes the concept and how difficult it is to implement it validly and goes on to review various other mechanisms for protecting the public: for example, market forces, codes of conduct, litigation, and peer review and pressure. Dr. Bourg notes that an essential element of a profession is the commitment that its practitioners stay knowledgeable about developments in their given field of practice and that this commitment to lifelong learning has been a hallmark of clinical psychology in the

United States. The term "continuing education" generally refers to education for the professional learner and currently is used to describe a very large array of adult learning experiences. Many of the state licensing boards in the United States have continuing education requirements that must be met before a psychologist's license will be renewed.

Specialty Recognition and Practice Certificates

In Chapter 2.01, Professor Lunt notes that psychological activity within the mental health field is becoming increasingly differentiated in European countries, leading to the formation of task forces in EFPPA to study similarities and differences in clinical psychology, health psychology, and psychotherapy. In the United States it is also recognized that knowledge and practice skills in psychology have expanded and become increasingly differentiated and that no one psychologist is a master of all of the practice areas of psychology. Psychologists have assumed that practice specialty identification and recognition of individual psychologist specialists is a direct professional service to the public, helping individual citizens identify those psychologists who have the education and training to help them with a particular problem. Many citizens are already familiar with the model of specialization in medicine so that the concept is not foreign to them.

There are many issues for psychologists to consider in establishing, developing, and/or maintaining specialty certification programs. A major issue to consider is the rationale for the development of specialties. For example, is the profession of psychology concerned with quality assurance, financial advantages, recognition of advances in technology or knowledge, or conformity with government regulation or intervention? What methods should a profession use to define the breadth and depth of its individual specialties? How are turf battles resolved within and across the professions? What should be the relationship between specialty certification and licensure? What should be the bases for determining specialty eligibility requirements, and should specialty certifications be time-dated? Who should have the responsibility to see that the specialist's expert knowledge is constantly updated?

Professor Paul Martin (Chapter 2.18) suggests caution in using the word "specialist." When used in the context of the discipline of psychology, "clinical" is viewed as one among a number of specialties. On the other hand, clinical psychology covers a broad domain, and specialties within clinical psychology are often recognized: for example, mental health, health psychology, child clinical psychology, and adolescent psychology. Are the latter specialties or subspecialties? Some clinical psychologists see health psychology, for example, as a subspecialty of clinical psychology, while some health psychologists see clinical psychology as a subspecialty of health psychology!

Dr. Stigall (Chapter 2.19) describes the Commission for the Recognition of Specialties and Proficiencies in Professional Psychology (CRSPPP) which was established by the American Psychological Association (APA) Council of Representatives in February 1995. Implicit in the Council's action was recognition of the need to bring some order into the conceptualization of specialties and to communicate more effectively with the general public about the nature and scope of psychological practice. Dr. Stigall goes on to say that specialization can be thought of either as the division of human labor for increased efficiency, or the organization of knowledge. After due deliberation, CRSPPP developed the definition of a specialty in psychology as follows:

> A specialty is a defined area of psychological practice which requires advanced knowledge and skills acquired through an organized sequence of education and training. The advanced knowledge and skills specific to a specialty are obtained subsequent to the acquisition of core scientific and professional foundations in psychology.

Dr. Stigall observes that, in addition to pursuing its work of reviewing petitions for specialty recognition, this Commission must also contend with important conceptual and philosophical issues among which are questions about the nature and purpose of professional specialization, and an evolving quest for a conceptual model—a taxonomy for specialties and proficiencies.

Recognition of individual psychologists

Three chapters are devoted to the recognition of individual psychologists' expertise for practice. Dr. Walter Pryzwansky (Chapter 2.20) describes the development and activities of the American Board of Professional Psychology (ABPP) which, since 1947, has awarded diplomas to individual psychologists who practice in various specialty areas of psychology. A diploma assures the public that the specialists designated by the ABPP have successfully completed an approved doctoral program, and an examination by professional peers designed to assess the knowledge, skills, and experience required to provide high-quality psychological services in that specialty.

Dr. Kris Ludwigsen (Chapter 2.21) suggests that one of the primary issues which has marked the coming of age of clinical psychology as an independent health care profession is the attainment of hospital practice privileges to allow independent admission, treatment, and discharge privileges of the most acute and disturbed patients. Psychologists' roles within hospitals have extended from salaried staff to independent contractors to attending or consulting staff. Psychologists have held the salaried positions of hospital administrator and assistant administrator, state hospital superintendent, and hospital owner. Beginning in 1957, clinical psychologists on the faculty of the University of Oregon Medical School were recognized as full members of the medical staff of its university hospital. In 1978, after psychologists obtained similar recognition at six other university hospitals, and following three years of legislative efforts, California was the first state to grant statutory permission for hospitals to include psychologists on the medical staff and to accord them admitting and attending privileges. Currently, psychologists have full privileges in a large number of medical school hospitals and the medical staff of community hospitals. Dr. Ludwigsen describes in detail the privileges and obligations that attend hospital staff membership.

Dr. John Hall (Chapter 2.22) describes the structure of professional regulatory procedures in the United Kingdom where today some professions are regulated by Acts of Parliament and others by Royal Charter. The British Psychological Society was incorporated by Royal Charter in 1965, and now sets standards for professional education and maintains a register of Chartered Psychologists. A major factor in the practice regulation of all UK health care professions is the NHS. It is the principal employer of nearly all categories of such professionals. Consequently, it is estimated that for clinical psychology probably not more than 5% of the national practitioner resource is available privately. The clinical component of training of nearly all health care professionals takes place in NHS settings, linked in most cases to universities, with funding of training supported at least partially in some way by central government, so there is a degree of integration of training systems with service delivery systems.

Ethical, Legal, and Practice Guidelines in Practice

Ethical decision making has always been expected of health care professionals. The APA also recognized the need for a formal ethics code to define standards of practice, educate members regarding professional values, and provide an avenue to address complaints of unethical conduct. The APA developed its first ethics code in 1953. It represented a key element in the structuring of psychology as an independent profession. The importance of ethical decision making has increased with the complexities of technology, societal structures and the development of the public conscience through the public media. Now various professional associations, licensing jurisdictions, and the courts monitor professional practice.

Dr. Cynthia Sturm (Chapter 2.23), writing about the APA code, says that ethical behavior represents a personal lifelong commitment, a responsibility to colleagues and the profession of psychology, and a pledge to uphold the public trust. She further acknowledges that psychologists must renew their knowledge of ethical standards of behavior throughout their careers, inasmuch as professional values evolve over time. She recognizes that the APA code of ethics grows out of the context of an industrialized culture but believes that there are commonalities in ethics that may extend across international boundaries. Further, the evolution of information technology will permit greater opportunities for an international dialogue within psychology regarding the use of psychological science and practice to benefit the global society.

Dr. Norma Simon (Chapter 2.24) describes how the American Association of State Psychology Boards (AASPB) established a Model Licensure Committee in 1987 to develop an AASPB Code of Conduct that could be used as the basis for disciplinary action by licensure boards. The committee wanted to develop a code that would fill the problematic legal gaps that it felt existed due to the aspirational nature of the then Canadian Psychological Association and APA ethics codes, and the need for licensure boards to say definitively what was required of a licensed psychologist. Ambiguity was to be eliminated wherever possible. Dr. Simon indicates that the AASPB code was a trail blazer in defining and sharpening the "shalls" and "shall nots" for psychologists, and she highlights the distinctive features of the code in her chapter.

Legal considerations

Randolph Reaves, Esquire, an attorney and the Executive Officer for the Association of State and Provincial Psychology Boards (ASPPB), concludes his chapter (Chapter 2.25) with the observation that the interaction of law and psychology is a constant, never-ending process. Psychologists are required to know, understand, and follow the requirements imposed by statute and regulation. To be successful they must understand the potential liabilities for unethical, incompetent, or illegal practice. His chapter is on legal considerations in the practice of psychology, and he details laws and legal case precedents regarding: (i) the regulation of the practice of psychology, (ii) the business of practicing psychology and, (iii) civil, criminal, and license related liability. The content of his chapter is required knowledge for all

North American psychologists and will probably be read with great interest by clinical psychologists around the world.

Practice guidelines

In the United States, practice guidelines have been proposed by the APA and by other professional organizations. Consistent with this evolution of thought and practice, Dr. Manfred Meier (Chapter 2.26) designed his contribution to this volume to assist psychologists in using psychological tests in a professionally and ethically responsible manner, consistent with published guidelines and standards. He further calls attention to the fact that a three profession interorganizational group has been writing an expanded *Standards for Educational and Psychological Testing* to be published soon and he expects that this document will encourage an even more deliberate application of test standards to all major types of test-related psychological evaluations.

Dr. Peter Nathan (Chapter 2.27) addresses the issues of critical pathways, practice guidelines, and empirically validated procedures. He traces the evolution of research on the outcomes of psychosocial treatment from the 1950s to the present and thus to his conclusion that research has now yielded empirically validated psychosocial treatments for a wide range of disorders. He clearly challenges the assumption that all psychotherapies are more or less effective.

Dr. William Kelleher (Chapter 2.28) starts his chapter with a brief review of the new practice paradigm of "evidence-based medicine" which is being promoted as an international model of practice. He thinks that the medical endorsement of this concept for the practice of health care delivery seems especially noteworthy and timely as increased focus is being placed today on the relevance of the scientist–practitioner model in clinical psychology. His chapter reviews other current factors encouraging evidence-based practice, for example, professional ethics and commitment to quality patient care. He also reviews barriers against such practice, for example, the belief by some that various psychotherapies are equivalent in effectiveness of psychotherapy. He believes that advances in computer technology, clinical information management systems, and medicine's movement in the evidence-based practice direction are now supporting evidence-based practice in clinical psychology.

The Management of Practice in Clinical Psychology

Certainly in the United States, particularly in the past decade, there have been major changes in how health and mental health services are funded, organized, and delivered. There has been increasing recognition among clinicians and citizens in general that there is major overlap in physical and mental health. All over Europe professionalization of psychology has been taking place, often catalyzed by clinical psychologists interacting with public health organizations in order to guarantee a high level of psychological expertise. Official registers of psychologists have been developed in many countries.

Dr. Harry van der Vlugt (Chapter 2.29) reviews principal practice settings for clinical psychologists in various European countries. His review of employment of psychologists in The Netherlands is quite detailed inasmuch as this is his home country. However, he also reviews related information for many other European countries ranging from Belgium and Switzerland to the Czech Republic. Overall, he sees that the kind of work which psychologists are doing is diversifying rapidly, although the majority of psychologists work in health-related areas. He thinks that in many countries psychologists are still an extension of physicians but increasingly psychology is being recognized as a specialty in its own right and psychologists are being paid directly through the health system and health insurance. He also describes an increase in private practice.

A popular automobile advertising slogan in the United States says, "This is not your father's Oldsmobile." The same theme is relevant to the chapter by Dr. Donald Weinstein (Chapter 2.30) on establishing and maintaining a clinical practice in the United States. His chapter is designed to expose the reader to the enormous potential available to a psychologist along with the techniques for the maintenance and survival of an independent practice in the 1990s and beyond. The practice he describes is not that of the solo practitioner who sees a succession of individual patients in a day or week. First of all, what he describes is a group practice with multiple providers: male and female staff, child and adult therapists, and assessors and therapists with interest and expertise around varying presenting problems. He also engages multiple consultants and advisors: for example, accountants, attorneys, insurance agents.

Dr. Weinstein states that the successful independent practitioner must use a strong, workable general philosophy in making decisions. He describes the following for himself:

> For the first five years that I was in practice, I maintained the belief that I was a psychologist running a small business. At about that point, I began to recognize and enjoy the reality that I was a businessman with a doctorate in psychology, running a complex business. Very early I recognized that I could not do this on my own. One characteristic of the entrepreneurial process is seeing and seizing opportunities. A general

> business philosophy needs to be developed that drives and directs the practice so that the psychologist can remain proactive. To be reactive and attempt to play catch-up will typically leave you behind.

He believes that opportunities for practice abound and that the exciting aspect of change and expansion is learning new skills, meeting new people, and creating new business opportunities. He asserts that there is no question that due to outside forces our profession is dynamic and our practices must be prepared to change. To stick with what we used to do because we thought it was a good idea and it was the "right thing" may not pay the mortgage.

Dr. Mark McMinn (Chapter 2.31) presents thoughts on technology in practice and also the theme that the contemporary practice of psychology requires a prudent balance of the traditional and the new. Specifically, he refers to communication with patients where rapid technological advances have propelled psychologists into other spheres of communication than just face-to-face interpersonal interactions. He thinks that technological changes will continue at an accelerating pace and calls for psychologists to keep abreast of technological advances and to appreciate their implications for practice.

His chapter is divided into three general headings. The first describes well-established practice technologies and under this heading he describes computerized office management. The second section describes partially established practice technologies which include computerized assessment tools, interviewing, therapy, electronic mail, and the maintenance of clinical databases. The third general heading includes emerging practice technologies which he believes to be teleconferencing, global networking environments, and virtual reality. A promising current development is expert system-based computer-assisted training programs that utilize artificial intelligence technology to model the decision-making processes of experts in a particular subspecialty. Dr. McMinn thinks that appropriate and effective technological methods promise to enhance learning for students while simultaneously equipping them with technological skills to enter the changing mental health marketplace.

National Health Care Policies and Clinical Psychology

This section is best introduced by referring to Chapter 2.32 written by Dr. Pierre Ritchie and Professor Henry Edwards on the evolution of Canada's health care system and its implications for the practice of psychology as a health profession. They assert that the rapid pace of health care reform will continue into the twenty-first century and that the policy elements which will shape Canada's health care system from 1997 to 2020 are increasingly clear. Future health policy will be driven by a greater emphasis on a systems orientation and fiscal sustainability. As a result, there will be more focus on defining the services to be funded rather than on simply funding providers. Given the traditional strong emphasis on funding physicians, this change potentially allows for the emergence of a larger number of health service providers, especially in primary care. Organized psychology in Canada is working vigorously to ensure the inclusion of psychologists in a reformed primary care system, which the authors also discuss. In the public sector, Canada will almost certainly remain a "single-payer" system. Evidence-based decision making (see also Chapter 2.28) is regarded as a key element in making the future health care system appropriate to meeting health needs and in controlling costs.

With reference to credentialing, Dr. Ritchie and Professor Edwards think that mobility of psychologists will emerge as a central topic for organized psychology in Canada, the United States, and Mexico. Psychologists will also face the challenge of competency-based credentialing; medicine and nursing are already devoting substantial resources to this issue. They conclude their chapter with the thought that, on balance, after a period of sustained evolution, the realistic prospect for Canadian health service psychologists is bright for those who are prepared to adapt to emerging opportunities.

Drs. Patrick DeLeon, Morgan Sammons, Gary VandenBos, and Professor Robert Frank (Chapter 2.33) discuss the changing health care environment in the United States. The authors have both professional and governmental experience and are unusually qualified to discuss the evolution of health care into the twenty-first century. They acknowledge that the United States health care system has undergone tremendous structural changes which have had direct implications for the profession of psychology. Times have been hard for many of the psychologists in solo practice as there has been an unprecedented acceptance of managed care, increasing requirements for professional accountability and the provision of cost-effective services, and a gradual awareness of the clinical potential inherent in technological advances within the communications and computer industries, that is, telehealth. Simultaneously, with the advent of the professional school movement there has been an exponential growth in the number of professional psychologists. The authors challenge the profession to internally decide what are its strengths and where it can best excel with our academic and practice communities working together to address society's needs.

Dr. Clarissa Marques writes on the evolution of managed behavioral health care in the United States (Chapter 2.34). She points to four aspects of the health care delivery system that she believes provided the context for the development of managed behavioral health care. The first is the diversity in the professional categories of providers delivering behavioral health care services and the training associated with each category of provider to provide behavioral health care services. The second is the variety in the therapeutic orientations(s) of the behavioral health care providers even within any given professional category of provider. The third is the variance in the modalities of treatment available for individuals with mental disorders with limited information regarding the metrics to compare the outcome of care by modality. The fourth is the fragmentation in the continuity of care for individuals across levels of care or between providers within the same level of care. She goes on to detail a variety of concepts of managed care.

She also observes that many psychologists have felt that managed care has disadvantaged or "squeezed" them between psychiatrists, who because of their medical training and licensure are uniquely situated to provide medication management and inpatient hospital based services, and other master's prepared therapists, who may be more likely to accept a lower rate of reimbursement than psychologists. The concern seems to stem from the perceived lack of differentiation for psychologists relative to other mental health professionals, with the exception of psychological testing as a distinguishing skill. She believes that the unfortunate aspect of such a discussion is the difficulty that psychologists have in seeing that the training provided to doctoral level psychologists is unique among the mental health professionals, not just for the provision of behavioral health care services, but also for the management of behavioral health care systems. What most psychologists come to learn is that as a professional group we gain the greatest strength in drawing from all of our subspecialty programs: from industrial and organizational psychology for the management of health care delivery systems; from experimental psychology for the methodology needed to assess the outcome of care; from statistical psychology in understanding the meaningfulness of data; from social psychology in understanding the impact of social and family systems on the individual; from developmental psychology in understanding the staging process of human development. Dr. Marques asserts that, as a profession, we have yet to prepare our graduates to embrace the richness of the field and encourage psychologists to apply themselves to all aspects of the health care system. Such an assertion clearly leads into the next subsection.

Supply and demand

Dr. Sanford Pederson has addressed the issue of the possible overproduction of psychologists in his chapter (2.03) on internship training. Supply and demand issues are addressed even more directly in two other chapters in this section.

The first (Chapter 2.35) is by Professor Paul Emmelkamp and Dr. Agnes Scholing who write about demographic characteristics of psychologists and supply and demand issues in The Netherlands. They describe different education and training programs for psychologists and the work settings of clinical psychologists and psychotherapists. After a review of psychologists working in mental health settings and students enrolled in clinical psychology training programs, they conclude that the percentage of female clinical psychologists will increase in the future. This is consistent with the male/female demographic characteristics of new doctoral psychologists in the United States.

Regarding job prospects, they note that in the 1970s it was predicted that the numbers of psychology students would decrease in the ensuing years and that the demands from society would increase. The contrary has proven true. As a consequence, official data from employment offices show increasing numbers of unemployed psychologists. However, they suggest several areas that will require more psychologists in the future: an increasing number of psychologists will be employed in the care of the elderly and in working in penal institutions with juvenile delinquents. By contrast, given the relatively few people addicted to hard drugs in The Netherlands, it is not expected that there will be a need for more psychologists to work with addicts. Similarly, given that few people are HIV positive, there is not likely to be a need for more psychologists in this area.

Dr. Jessica Kohout (Chapter 2.36) notes that the number of psychologists in the health service provider subfields has tripled from 1975 to 1995 in the United States. Demographically, the "face" of professional psychology has also changed in that time period. In the 1970s, a newly graduated clinical psychologist would have been white, male, and in his late twenties. More often than not he would have earned a Ph.D. and would be headed, after licensure, toward academic employment or into independent practice. In contrast, in the late 1990s, the new doctorate is likely to be a woman and white, although the representation of persons of color has inched up over time. Graduates in the late 1990s are somewhat older than were their colleagues two decades before, with the median age of new Ph.D.s in 1995 just over 33 years. Increasingly, new graduates may have earned a Psy.D. degree. The new doctorate is less likely to find as many opportunities for academic employment and independent practice as was the case in the 1970s. Dr. Kohout also points out that no discussion of supply or demand can be meaningful without some reference to the supply of master's-level psychological personnel or to the supply of professionals in mental health fields outside psychology.

When assessing the issue of whether there are too many graduate psychologists, she asserts that it depends on what you define as the appropriate scope of practice. She thinks it is evident that there likely are a sufficient number of psychologists trained to provide mental health services to individual clients in independent practice settings. At the same time there are shortages in areas to which traditionally trained psychologists have not been recruited and to which they are not attracted: for example, rural and frontier areas, urban settings that may appear dangerous, treatment settings for seriously mentally ill or behaviorally disturbed individuals. A common characteristic of these groups of patients, settings, and areas is that they may not fit within the parameters or paradigm of a typical independent practice, and consequently will lack access to services. She suggests that it will be important to urge psychology to expand its perspectives on what constitutes an appropriate scope of practice. She warns that if the educational systems in psychology do not respond by providing training appropriate to the new health care systems and real world problems, there may be too many clinical psychologists. But there is no oversupply if clinical psychologists address the persistent and worsening nature of many of society's ills. She urges that we create a match between the training that students are receiving and the needs of the society. She has some suggestions for future directions in training and scope of practice.

How Does Society View Clinical Psychology?

How the public views psychologists and their relevance in helping to solve public problems is becoming an increasingly important issue for clinical psychologists. In the United States, by the year 2020, over 59 million people will be over 65 years of age. Eighty percent will have at least one chronic illness such as heart disease, arthritis, diabetes, depression, or declining function. The growing proportion of "ethnic minorities" has led to a substantial change in needs for housing, education, urban employment, and so forth. With recognition of the major changes, research programs on the application of psychological science to issues of national urgency such as violence, AIDS, teenage pregnancy, overcrowding, crises in employment, and family relocation need to be continued and new programs developed.

In this section, the authors address issues of how the public views psychologists, national priority needs, and implications for psychologists in the United States and Japan, and the final chapter addresses national advocacy for psychology.

Dr. Raymond Fowler and Ms. Rhea Farberman have contributed two chapters. The first (Chapter 2.37) looks at psychologists' work and the public's perception as a dichotomy. Psychologists work in so many settings that it is difficult to identify all of them. However, many people are aware of psychologists only as professors, researchers, or in their traditional counseling and clinical roles. The authors call attention to the work of psychologists in numerous and varied settings and also to their hidden contributions in such areas as computer technology, understanding the needs and ramifications of a more diverse population, helping to deal with corporate downsizing, and education reform.

Chapter 2.38 by Farberman and Fowler discusses the image of psychology presented by the mass media in the United States. The impact of television and films is unquestioned when one considers that of all American homes with children, 99% own at least one television, and that movies have been a popular form of leisure time entertainment since the 1930s. Many professions' images have been created in the public's mind through their portrayal in film and on television. The authors review a variety of public presentations and conclude that the comical and inaccurate portrayals of mental health providers has created a stereotyped image of the profession and has likely added to the stigma around mental health services. The authors then further describe that in 1995 the APA Council of Representatives directed that the association undertake a national public education campaign designed to communicate the value of psychological services. The campaign is designed to call the public's attention to psychology by linking its services to problems people worry about and then to educate the public about what psychologists do, how psychotherapy works, and the unique training and skills of psychologists.

Dr. Joanne Callan (Chapter 2.39) asserts that, in order to provide leadership and build partnerships with the public, it is imperative that clinical psychologists become well informed on national needs. Four need categories are presented: (i) health care (including mental health); (ii) education; (iii) work and economics; and (iv) families and communities: relationships, systems, and communication. Her presentation of each of these four need categories suggests many problem areas in which clinical psychologists have, or should develop, expertise to help with solutions.

Drs. Shimonaka and Nakazato (Chapter 2.40) focus particularly on the national priority needs of the elderly in Japan. By 1995, Japanese life expectancy had become the highest in the world for 10 consecutive years for men and 11 consecutive years for women. This trend is expected to continue. An important issue facing Japan as an aging society is the change in family structure. The traditional Japanese family system (three generations in one household) started to break down after the Second World War and the "nuclear" family, which had long been common in Western countries, began to take over. The number of people in the younger generation who consider it an obligation to look after their aged parents has been decreasing drastically. The authors discuss the clinical psychological services sought in Japan. While psychological counseling is the most common service, they point out that only a few elderly are taking advantage of these services; this is because revealing a personal psychological problem to a stranger is seen as shameful. Also, they are not used to paying money for such intangible services as counseling.

Finally, Drs. Jill Reich and Nina Levitt (Chapter 2.41) discuss national advocacy for psychology; the specifics of their discussion relate to the United States but the concepts that they develop appear quite universal. Advocacy is a dynamic process which, on the one hand, points out psychology's potential to contribute to areas of national need and, on the other, in so doing further reinforces the need for psychology's contributions to society. The process of advocacy is essentially one of education, that is, working to educate policymakers about the value of the discipline and hence the need or right of the discipline for support, resources, recognition, status, and the like. The authors, more specifically, describe the nature of advocacy in the political process, advocacy in action, and the various advocates who speak on behalf of a discipline. A problem presented by clinical psychology is that it is not well understood by the general public. Some know psychologists as mental health practitioners; others are aware that psychologists are behavioral scientists who conduct research in areas like cognition and neuroscience; and still others remember their psychology professors from undergraduate courses in personality and perception. Inasmuch as advocacy often requires keeping the message simple, only a limited part of psychology will be addressed.

The authors summarize their detailed discussion of advocacy by saying that successful advocacy is a complex, multidimensional process requiring discipline, flexibility, vigilance, and strategic action. It requires ongoing involvement by psychologists who often understand neither the reasons for their participation nor the process. Moreover, all along the way it is necessary to compromise, reducing the chances of getting less than what you at first wanted, but probably concluding with something quite different from what you first set out to accomplish. Perhaps this is the nature of clinical psychology as it continues to evolve into the twenty-first century.

Contributors to Volume 2

Dr. E. F. Bourg
California School of Professional Psychology, Alameda Campus, 1005 Atlantic Avenue, Alameda, CA 94501, USA
56 Ross Circle, Oakland, CA 94618, USA

Dr. J. E. Callan
1028 Santa Florencia, Solana Beach, CA 92075, USA

Dr. P. H. DeLeon
United States Senate, Hart Senate Office Building, Suite 722, Washington DC 20510-1102, USA

Dr. S. T. DeMers
Department of Education and Counseling Psychology, University of Kentucky, Lexington, KY 40506, USA

Professor H. P. Edwards
School of Psychology, University of Ottawa, 120 University, Suite 605D, PO Box 450, Station A, Ottawa, ON K1N 6N5, Canada

Professor P. M. G. Emmelkamp
Department of Clinical Psychology, University of Amsterdam, Roeterstraat 15, 1018 WB Amsterdam, The Netherlands

Ms. R. K. Farberman
American Psychological Association, 750 First Street Northeast, Washington, DC 20002-4242, USA

Dr. H. C. Fernández-Alvarez
AIGLE, Direccion Postal C.C. 135 Suc. 26, (1426) Buenos Aires, Argentina

Dr. R. D. Fowler
American Psychological Association, 750 First Street Northeast, Washington, DC 20002-4242, USA

Professor R. G. Frank
College of Health Professions, University of Florida Health Sciences Center, PO Box 100185, Gainesville, FL 32610-0185, USA

Dr. S. Greenberg
Professional Examination Service, 475 Riverside Drive, Room No. 740, New York, NY 10115-0089, USA

Dr. J. N. Hall
Psychology Department, The Warneford Hospital, Warneford Lane, Headington, Oxford, OX3 7JX, UK

Dr. K. de S. Hamsher
Neuropsychology Clinic, 1218 West Kilbourn Avenue, Suite 415, Milwaukee, WI 53233-1325, USA

Dr. D. S. Hill
Sommerville and Company Inc., The Cairn Building, 727 East 16th Avenue, Denver, CO 80203-2003, USA

Dr. P. Hu
Department of Medical Psychology, Beijing Medical University, Beijing 100083, China

Dr. S. Jern
Department of Education and Psychology, Linköping University, S-581 83 Linköping, Sweden
Fridhemsgatan 10, S-262 53 Ängelholm, Sweden

Professor Q. Jing
Institute of Psychology, Chinese Academy of Sciences, PO Box 1603, Beijing 100012, China

Dr. W. J. Kelleher
Geriatric Institute, Nova Southeastern University, 4800 North State Road 7, Suite B, Fort Lauderdale, FL 33319, USA

Dr. J. L. Kohout
Research Office, Central Programs, American Psychological Association, 750 First Street Northeast, Washington, DC 20002-4242, USA

Dr. N. G. Levitt
Public Policy Office, American Psychological Association, 750 First Street Northeast, Washington, DC 20002-4242, USA

Dr. K. R. Ludwigsen
2213 Buchanan Road, Suite 203, Antioch, CA 94509, USA
Kaiser Foundation Hospital, Martinez-Walnut Creek, CA, USA

Professor I. Lunt
Psychology and Special Needs Group, Institute of Education, University of London, 25 Woburn Square, London, WC1H 0AA, UK

Dr. C. C. Marques
Green Spring Health Services Inc., Suite 500, 5565 Sterrett Place, Columbia, MD 21044-2644, USA

Professor P. R. Martin
Department of Psychology, University of New England, Armidale, New South Wales 2351, Australia

Dr. M. R. McMinn
Department of Psychology, Wheaton College, Wheaton, IL 60187, USA

Professor F. M. McPherson
Tayside Area Clinical Psychology Department, Royal Dundee Liff Hospital, Dundee, DD2 5NF, UK

Dr. M. J. Meier
PO Box 21, Bruce, WI 54819, USA
Condominios Bugambilias, Edificio X-4, Nuevo Vallanta Boulevard y Paseo Cocoterios, Nuevo Vallanta, Nayarit 48300, Mexico

Dr. K. Nakazato
Department of Psychology, Tokyo Metropolitan Institute of Gerontology, 35-2 Sakaecho, Itabashiku, Tokyo 173, Japan

Dr. P. E. Nathan
Department of Psychology, University of Iowa, Iowa City, IA 52242, USA

Dr. P. D. Nelson
Educational Directorate, American Psychological Association, 750 First Street Northeast, Washington, DC 20002-4242, USA

Dr. S. L. Nielsen
Norwegian Psychological Association, Storgata 10 A, 0155 Oslo, Norway

Dr. S. L. Pederson
7171 Southpoint Drive, Dayton, OH 45459, USA
School of Professional Psychology, Wright State University, 9 North Edwin C. Moses Boulevard, Dayton, OH 45407, USA

Dr. W. B. Pryzwansky
School of Education, CB# 3500 Peabody Hall, University of North Carolina at Chapel Hill, Chapel Hill, NC 27599-3500, USA

Dr. R. P. Reaves
Association of State and Provincial Psychology Boards, PO Box 4389, Montgomery, AL 36103-4389, USA

Dr. L. P. Rehm
Department of Psychology, University of Houston, Houston, TX 77204-5341, USA

Dr. J. N. Reich
Education Directorate, American Psychological Association, 750 First Street Northeast, Washington, DC 20002-4242, USA

Dr. P. L.-J. Ritchie
Centre for Psychological Services, School of Psychology, University of Ottawa, 11 Marie Curie Street, PO Box 450, Station A, Ottawa, ON K1N 6N5, Canada

Dr. D. A. Rodgers
2842 Winthrop Road, Shaker Heights, OH 44120-1826, USA

Dr. G. A. Rosen
3435 Central Avenue, Huntingdon Valley, PA 19006, USA

Dr. M. T. Sammons
National Naval Medical Center, US Navy, Bethesda, MD, USA
7840 Oracle Place, Potomac, MD 20854, USA

Dr. A. Scholing
Department of Clinical Psychology, University of Groningen, Academic Hospital, Hanzeplein 1, 9713 EZ Groningen, The Netherlands

Dr. C. G. Schoon
Professional Examination Service, 475 Riverside Drive, Room No. 708, New York, NY 10115-0089, USA

Dr. Y. Shimonaka
Department of Psychology, Tokyo Metropolitan Institute of Gerontology, 35-2 Sakaecho, Itabashiku, Tokyo 173, Japan

Dr. N. P. Simon
2 Garden Place, Pelham Manor, NY 10803, USA

Dr. I. L. Smith
Professional Examination Service, 475 Riverside Drive, Room No. 740, New York, NY 10115-0089, USA

Dr. T. T. Stigall
The Psychology Group, 701 South Acadian Thruway, Baton Rouge, LA 70806-5698, USA

Dr. C. A. Sturm
5441 South West Macadam, Suite 102, Portland, OR 97201, USA

Dr. G. R. VandenBos
Publications and Communications, American Psychological Association, 750 First Street Northeast, Washington, DC 20002-4242, USA

Dr. S. K. Verma
Department of Psychiatry, Postgraduate Institute of Medical Education and Research, Pgimer, Chandigarh 160012, India

Dr. H. van der Vlugt
Department of Psychology, Tilburg University, PO Box 90153, 5000 LE Tilburg, The Netherlands

Dr. D. J. Weinstein
24100 Chagrin Boulevard, Suite 400, Beachwood, OH 44122, USA

Volume Editors

Volume 1: Foundations
Professor C. Eugene Walker, *University of Oklahoma Health Sciences Center, Oklahoma City, OK, USA*

Volume 2: Professional Issues
Professor Arthur N. Wiens, *Oregon Health Sciences University, Portland, OR, USA*

Volume 3: Research and Methods
Professor Nina R. Schooler, *Hillside Hospital, Glen Oaks, NY, USA*

Volume 4: Assessment
Professor Cecil R. Reynolds, *Texas A&M University, College Station, TX, USA*

Volume 5: Children & Adolescents: Clinical Formulation & Treatment
Professor Thomas Ollendick, *Virginia Tech, Blacksburg, VA, USA*

Volume 6: Adults: Clinical Formulation & Treatment
Professor Paul Salkovskis, *University of Oxford, Warneford Hospital, UK*

Volume 7: Clinical Geropsychology
Professor Barry Edelstein, *West Virginia University, Morgantown, WV, USA*

Volume 8: Health Psychology
Professor Derek W. Johnston and Professor Marie Johnston, *University of St. Andrews, UK*

Volume 9: Applications in Diverse Populations
Dr Nirbhay N. Singh, *Virginia Commonwealth University, Richmond, VA, USA*

Volume 10: Sociocultural and Individual Differences
Professor Cynthia D. Belar, *University of Florida Health Sciences Center, Gainesville, FL, USA*

Volume 11: Indexes

2.01
History and Emerging Trends in Education and Training for Clinical Psychology in the European Union

INGRID LUNT
University of London, UK

2.01.1 INTRODUCTION

This chapter covers some of the history and emerging trends in education and training for clinical psychology mainly, but not only, in the European Union (EU). The EU is developing and changing rapidly. In 1997 there are 15 member states, covering most of the western European countries (but not Iceland, Norway, and Switzerland). However, many of the central and eastern European countries have applied for membership, and are working towards criteria which will enable them to join. This will mean an expanded and changed Europe in the not too distant future.

The countries of Europe have very different histories, which are reflected in the development of their professions and, of particular relevance here, in the development of clinical psychology as a profession and the training for the profession. Clearly, increased mobility between students, practitioners, and researchers, and some of the moves within the EU, are having the effect of bringing together some of the trends and achieving greater "convergence," a term used in the EU. Nevertheless, in the field of psychology and its education and training, the European countries remain strikingly different, at least between regional groupings. This chapter will attempt to consider European clinical psychology education and training in its similarities and its differences.

As mentioned, the region of Europe consists both of the EU and nonmember states, many of the latter in eastern Europe and formerly belonging to the Soviet Union. The countries of Europe constitute a very diverse group which may nevertheless be grouped into broad regions with some commonality in education and training patterns. For these purposes, at a very broad level it is possible to identify a Nordic group of countries (the Scandinavian countries), with considerable commonalities in their education and training; the UK, which has much in common with education and training in the USA and other parts of the English-speaking world; the German-speaking countries; and a southern European group. Of course, within these regions, what characterizes Europe is its diversity and the individuality of its countries.

This chapter will, to some extent, use regional groupings in its consideration of clinical psychology education and training. There are a number of models or definitions of the field of clinical psychology, a field which emerged in European countries substantially after World War II. This issue is particularly important as there are moves towards greater mobility following the Treaty of Rome and the European Directives (in particular Directive EC 89/48). Education and training in the different countries follow very different patterns, which are related to the traditions and history of university education in the different countries. Nevertheless, it is possible to distinguish three or four broad patterns or models of education and training. All countries are moving towards increasing specialization and postqualification training.

The chapter will draw substantially on work carried out within the European Federation of Professional Psychologists' Associations (EFPPA), a federation of national psychology associations with 28 member associations (1997) representing all countries of the EU, all other countries in western Europe, and a growing number of member associations from central and eastern Europe. This federation provides a unique opportunity for comparison between the practices of different European countries, and a forum for discussion and debate of important issues.

2.01.2 EMERGENCE OF CLINICAL PSYCHOLOGY

Although there are differences between countries, it is possible to provide a general definition of the field which would be agreeable to all European countries. Clinical psychologists may be defined as psychologists who:

> apply psychology in a clinical context, usually a hospital, medical or community setting, with people (patients or staff) who consider themselves to be in need of a psychological perspective on their lives. In practice, the majority of clinical psychologists contribute to the assessment and treatment of people who see themselves as having psychological problems, such as those with mental health difficulties, but they also work with the handicapped, families, those with learning difficulties, and, more widely, with staff and organisation. (Llewelyn, 1994, p. 115)

In a survey carried out by an EFPPA Task Force on Clinical Psychology, all countries except France agreed with the APA definition of this field.

Clinical psychology emerged as a recognizable profession at different times in different countries. In both the UK and the USA, the two world wars provided a significant impetus to the emergence of this profession, initially through the need to develop psychological tests to recruit suitable personnel. In the UK, the formation of the National Health Service in 1948 provided a considerable impetus to the development of this new profession. In these early days, the role was largely one of laboratory technician administering psychometric and other tests, usually for medical practitioners. However, in the UK the development of behavior therapy led to clinical psychologists developing a therapeutic role, and by the 1960s they had become clinical practitioners in their own right.

Again, in the Nordic countries, clinical psychology emerged substantially after World War II, in the 1940s and early 1950s. The Norwegian Psychological Association was founded in 1934, the Danish Psychological Association in 1947, the Swedish Psychological Association in 1955, and the Finnish Union of Psychologists in 1957. The formation of these psychological associations reflected the emergence in these countries of a profession of psychology, mainly clinical psychology, which has progressed through similar broad major phases as in the UK: a phase focusing on diagnostic examination and testing of individual patients, a phase focusing on therapeutic work involving mainly psychotherapy, a phase focusing on indirect work with other professional groups through techniques such as consultation and training.

In Spain, on the other hand, clinical psychology has a shorter history (Belloch & Olabarria, 1994) and is said to have emerged in the 1970s, along with fundamental changes in Spanish society. Similarly in Italy, clinical psychology as a professional application emerged substantially in the 1960s (Spaltro, 1993) and there remain some tensions over the autonomy and role of clinical psychologists and their relationship with medical practitioners, especially psychiatrists. The Association of Greek Psychologists, founded in 1963, reflects the existence of professional psychology in Greece, although at that time, and until very recently, all clinical psychologists received their training overseas, and the profession was very much dominated by the medical profession (Velli, 1995).

In all European countries, clinical psychologists represent the largest group of psychologists, and have experienced a rapid growth in their number between the 1960s and the 1980s with the expansion of mental health provision and the growing awareness of the contribution of clinical psychology to a wide and diverse range of areas of work (EFPPA, 1997). However, in many European countries the emergence of the specialty of health psychology, with a focus on prevention rather than treatment, and the promotion of health rather than a more therapeutic function, has led to attempts to define and differentiate fields of psychological activity within the mental health field. For example, three EFPPA task forces, focusing on clinical psychology, health psychology, and psychotherapy, have drawn up a model defining overlap and separate areas of activity within the health field, with corresponding commonalities and differences in education and training (EFPPA, 1997).

2.01.2.1 Scientist–Practitoner Model

In the UK, there is a strong commitment to a scientist practitioner model: "the clinical psychologist is first and foremost an 'applied scientist' or 'scientist–practitioner' who seeks to use scientific knowledge to a beneficial end" (Marzillier & Hall, 1990, p. 9). This commitment also characterizes the Nordic countries, which have been influenced substantially by the USA and also by the UK. These countries would sign up to the definition that:

> clinical psychologists share several common attributes. They are psychologists because they have been trained to use the guidelines of knowledge of psychology in their professional work. They are clinicians because they attempt to understand people in their natural complexity and in their continuous adaptive transformations ... they are scientists because they utilise the scientific methods to achieve objectivity and precision in their professional work. Finally they are professionals because they render important human services by helping individuals, social groups and communities to solve psychological problems and improve the quality of life. (Kendall & Norton-Ford, 1982, p. 4)

This model is also espoused by Spanish clinical psychology where Belloch and Olabarria (1994, p. 144) state that clinical psychology training is "very similar to that proposed in the 1940s, in the famous Boulder Conference, organized by the APA." In France, where there is a strong clinical psychoanalytic tradition, there is less of a commitment to the "Boulder" model.

However, some of the problems inherent in the scientist practitioner model, such as bridging "the gap between ... formal training and scientific thinking on the one hand, and the demands of practice on the other" (Raimy, 1950, quoted in Barlow, Hayes, & Nelson, 1984, p. 9) are also evident in some European countries (see Pilgrim & Treacher, 1992, who write, "British training programmes have consistently espoused the scientist–professional model and in so doing have glossed over the difficulties that are inherent to the model," p. 80). The three phases of professional training for psychologists, described by Peterson (1991) as the preprofessional, the scientist professional, and the professional phase appear to be replicated to some extent in European countries, although in the late 1990s all professional training for clinical psychologists is based in universities rather than professional schools, and there are several countries where the education and training is predominantly academic, and is then followed by a separate internship or registration/licenseship phase, usually based in a hospital or clinic.

2.01.3 PATTERNS OF UNIVERSITY EDUCATION AND TRAINING

Europe is characterized by the diversity of its university education systems. For example, the time taken to complete training in the different countries differs, and the degree awarded also varies. Some countries award a diploma or license, others award a degree such as Masters or Doctorate, on completion of professional training as a (clinical) psychologist. Some counries award a general qualification as a professional psychologist, while others award a more specialized qualification, for example, in the field of clinical psychology. However, it is possible (and see below) to state that most countries in Europe require a period of at least five to six years education and training in order to be able to practice as a clinical psychologist, and increasingly they are developing postgraduate qualifications and specialization.

There have been a number of surveys considering patterns of training, carried out mainly by EFPPA task groups (see Section 2.01.5). An early task force on education and training for psychology agreed in 1990 a document entitled *Optimal standards for professional training in psychology* (EFPPA, 1990) (see Appendix 1). Agreed policy in this area, therefore, is a six-year length of education and training, based in a university or other institution of higher education, consisting of a theoretical foundation with some internship, and containing a research element. A more recent task force, which focuses on clinical psychology, compares patterns of education and training in its interim report (EFPPA, 1997). Lunt (1993, 1994) and Newstead and Makinen (1997) have carried out some further comparisons.

As mentioned, most of the countries of western Europe require a similar overall length of time (i.e., between four and six years) for professional qualification as a (clinical) psychologist. The countries vary considerably in issues such as whether there is any practicum or internship within the training or whether this becomes a postgraduate requirement for registration or licensing, and how specialized the training is.

However, it is possible to contrast three different approaches in the EU, and this is particularly the case in relation to how specialized or generic the professional training is. We can distinguish between three general forms of organization in professional training: the "continuous specialist," the "continuous generic," and the "discontinuous specialist" organization; there are, of course, some "mixed mode" (Lunt, 1993; see also Newstead, 1994). Newstead and Makinen (1997) refer to these three forms of organization as the "five year specialist," "five year generalist," and the "three-plus-three" models.

2.01.3.1 The Continuous Specialist Model

In this model, students enroll at the outset on a psychology course which specializes in a single area such as clinical, educational, or organizational psychology. In the EFPPA survey, this model was found in Sweden and Belgium (Newstead, 1994). To an extent, this is the "mixed mode," referred to by Lunt (1993). In a few countries such as The Netherlands with a more "mixed mode," a four to six year program leads to the degree of *Doctorandus* at the same time as the professional title *psycholoog*. This entails a one-year general introduction then a three-year specialization in clinical psychology.

2.01.3.2 The Continuous and Generic Education Model

This is the "five year generalist" model referred to by Newstead and Makinen (1997). Those countries (e.g., the Nordic countries) which have a more continuous and generic training provide a general degree or program in psychology which leads to a qualification to practice as a psychologist (unspecialized). Later specialization and qualification occur on the job. In the EFPPA survey (Newstead, 1994), this is the most frequently found model, found in Austria, Spain, Hungary, Italy, Germany, Switzerland, Denmark, and Norway.

2.01.3.3 Discontinuous and Specialist Education or the Three-plus-three Model

Some countries have a "discontinuous" and "specialist" organization in which students study for three or four years and receive a general qualification in psychology, following which they enroll on a new course (often at a different institution) where they specialize in clinical psychology at Master's or, increasingly, Doctorate level. This model is followed by the UK, Ireland, Malta, and Greece.

These different ways of organizing training in psychology may lead to problems in comparing qualifications across Europe, since a training leading to a qualification to practice as a clinical psychologist, for example, in one country may be either too general or too specific for another European country. In those countries in Europe where the qualification is more generic and where all professional psychology graduates are able to practice in the range of settings as educational, clinical, organizational/industrial psychologists with later specialization occurring on the job and in the specific context, the qualification is likely be too general in comparison with those countries where the basic professional education and training is specialized, and evaluation of equivalence of qualifications is enormously complex.

2.01.4 MOBILITY WITHIN THE EUROPEAN UNION

In the early days of the European Community (EC), a single "common" market within the EC was envisaged in the Treaty of Rome which established the European Economic Community (EEC) in 1957: "Freedom to work anywhere in the European Community is one of the basic rights laid down by the Treaty of Rome." Article 48 of the Treaty provides for the free movement of labor to be achieved by the removal of discrimination, based on nationality, in respect of employment. Article 57 allows for the mutual recognition and coordination of professional qualifications.

In the early stages of the implementation of the Treaty, attempts were made to harmonize qualifications across member countries. Some professions were made subject to their own special or sectoral directive containing agreements on the harmonization (or standardization) across all the member countries of the content of courses, minimum length of study and training, and skills that a graduate in the field should possess. Sectoral directives were agreed for seven professions (doctors, dentists, nurses, midwives, vetinarians, pharmacists, and architects). However, it soon became clear that attempts to harmonize qualifications across member states were immensely complex and time-consuming and the task of agreeing a common curriculum for all EC professionals even in a single field began to look impossible. As McPherson states:

> The slow progress was partly of course due to the technical problems of harmonising what were often quite heterogeneous systems of training and practice. However, possibly the main reason was that free movement and "right of establishment" was a political goal for which few professions expressed much enthusiasm. Many of the negotiations showed a lack of urgency. (McPherson, 1988, p. 354)

With a growing awareness that harmonization of qualifications was an almost impossible task, as every country was required to agree to common content, length, and nature of training, in 1985 the European Commission introduced a new approach to cover other professions to which access is in some way restricted (or regulated) by the state, either by law or through a professional organization and which require at least three years university level training or equivalent. This approach was to be based on equivalence rather than harmonization and on the mutual recognition of qualifications. As Haaksman (1990) put it:

> in comparing study courses and professional skills, equivalence is more important than equality. In other words credentials evaluation should be based on mutual trust and respect rather than suspicion and pedantry ... the acquired skills should be comparable. The thing that matters is: equivalence in its most literal meaning. (Haaksman, 1990, p. 25)

This new approach took the form of the Directive 89/48/EC, entitled Mutual Recognition of Higher Education Diplomas, which applies to any regulated profession for which at least three years higher education level training is required and enables a professional from one member state to become a member of the equivalent profession in another member state without having to requalify. It does this by the principle of mutual recognition which enables suitably qualified professionals to have their qualifications recognized and to use the professional title. The Directive is intended to encourage the free movement of skilled labor around the EU by specifying the basis on which one member state will recognize, or at least evaluate, the professional qualifications awarded by another. It acknowledges that standards and content differ between countries and seeks to establish some equivalence between those trained in the countries of the EU.

This means that a psychologist qualified and recognized in one member state should be able to move and practice in another member state (subject to certain provisos). Implementation of the Directive is in most countries the responsibility of a government department, though unusually, in the UK this responsibility is given to the professional association, the British Psychological Society (BPS), which is the "competent authority" in terms of the Directive, and which therefore has responsibility for evaluating the equivalence of qualifications obtained in other countries.

2.01.5 THE ROLE OF THE EUROPEAN FEDERATION OF PROFESSIONAL PSYCHOLOGISTS" ASSOCIATIONS

EFPPA is a federation of 28 (1997) national European psychology associations which, among other things, has a central role in the development of standards in clinical psychology, in considerations of the implementation of the European Directives and in liaison work with Brussels. EFPPA was formed in 1981 at a time when the matters of mobility and mutual recognition were becoming more pressing, and psychologists and psychology associations of member states realized that a federation would provide a professionally and politically useful way to move forward and to begin to develop common policies in this area. Clinical psychologists, in particular, were faced with the growing prospects of mobility between countries in the EU, and the implications of the Treaty of Rome (see above).

The Federation plays an important role within the EU, and provides an important forum for exchanging information on patterns of education and training, legislation and regulation of psychologists, negotiating with politicians and policy makers, and influencing policy at a European level. It achieves much of its work through its task forces, which are small groups drawn from many European countries and usually focused on a particular topic or subfield within psychology (e.g., the task forces on clinical psychology, education and training, European legal matters). The member associations of EFPPA differ considerably in their nature: some are both scientific and professional organizations, others are traditional "learned societies," yet others operate effectively as trade unions, others are themselves federations of smaller associations within the same country. However, in 1997 all the national member associations include clinical psychologists. The fact that EFPPA is a federation of professional psychology associations means that much of its efforts are spent on clinical psychology and clinical psychologists, and is also the largest group of psychologists within Europe.

As mentioned above, EFPPA has had two task forces on education and training; the Task Force on Education and Training (which reported in 1990) produced the document entitled *Optimal standards for professional training for psychologists* (Appendix 1). In its report, the Task Force stated:

> EFPPA ... fully recognises that the content and form of training in professional psychology in each country will inevitably reflect its own legal, educational and professional traditions. However, to encourage international co-operation among professional psychologists and to assist member associations in their efforts to develop professional training and practice in their own countries, EFPPA is publishing the following statement which describes the optimal standards for training required for independent professional practice. (EFPPA, 1990, p. 1)

This was an attempt to produce a very broad framework with some elements, such as length of training, location in university base, theory and practical application, with which all member associations could agree, or at least would aspire towards. This document provided a very important beginning, although it has no legal status and is nothing more (nor less) than a rather broad goal. As may be seen (Appendix 1), the *Optimal standards* document states that preparation for autonomous practice in psychology should consist of at least two parts (theoretical and skills-based), lasting at least six years, based within a university and containing a research element. If it were possible to ensure these basic standards and level, recognition of qualifications between different countries would become more straightforward. However, in formulating these standards as "optimal" rather than "minimal," EFPPA recognizes that they are aspirational rather than required standards, and that EFPPA has a role in promoting the quality of professional education in clinical psychology across its member associations.

A further Task Force on the Evaluation of Curricula, formed in 1991, is carrying out a study of curriculum documentation in psychology and detailed interviews in different universities across Europe, in order to compare the different curricula in psychology of some universities in a number of European countries so as to increase an awareness and understanding of common and different areas in psychology education and training. The aims of the study are:

> to study the way in which psychology is taught in a range of institutions in different countries; to determine commonalities in training; to investigate the feasibility of laying down minimal standards for the accreditation of psychology curricula across Europe; to provide a basis for determining equivalence of psychology qualifications in European countries. (EFPPA, 1990, p. 1)

Newstead (1994) made a preliminary report of the work of this task force. As Newstead and Makinen (1997) have pointed out, there is considerable similarity and agreement between different countries over basic psychological theory. The differences appear particularly in the more professional domain, and in particular over how specialized the basic education is and what model of practice is adopted.

A third task force focuses specifically on clinical psychology (EFPPA, 1997) and aims to compare training and practice in clinical psychology across EFPPA member countries. This task force has carried out a questionnaire survey of clinical psychology practice and training across European countries, and has collaborated with task forces in the fields of health psychology and psychotherapy in an attempt to define the field.

2.01.6 TRAINING ROUTES IN THE DIFFERENT MEMBER STATES OF THE EUROPEAN UNION

In order to compare training routes in the different countries in Europe, and by definition therefore all the member states of the European Union, EFPPA set up a Task Force in Clinical Psychology in 1995. This Task Force has collected a substantial amount of data through a questionnaire exploring education and training routes and clinical psychology practice.

Most of the countries in the EU have considerable overlap in the content of the psychology curriculum, at least for the first three years of study, when universities in most countries provide a foundation in mainly theoretical areas of psychology. The Curriculum Task Force study (Newstead, 1994) identifies the percentage of time spent on different areas of psychology in the first three years of study (psychonomics, biological, social, developmental, individual differences, theory, methodology, applied psychology, project/thesis, professional placement). There was considerable agreement in the percentages of time spent on these different areas of the curriculum, except for one difference in that a few countries included a professional placement during this phase, while the majority left this until a later stage in the education and training. Some examples of different types of education and training routes will illustrate differences in patterns. It is in the second phase (the second two or three years) of professional qualification that there are substantial differences between European countries, specifically both in how specialized or general is the training, and the model of practice developed in the training period. There are also considerable differences in the nature and mode of professional training of clinical skills, and the nature of the internship or clinical placements undertaken.

2.01.6.1 The Nordic Countries (Denmark, Finland, Sweden)

Denmark has two universities offering education and training in clinical psychology, Finland has six, while Sweden has five. In these countries, the training period is at least five years, and the degree awarded is the degree of Candidate of Psychology, which in turn qualifies for postgraduate studies aiming at the degree of Licentiate and Doctor of Philosophy. In Finland every year about 180 students begin studying psychology as a main subject, making a total of around 1200 students of psychology in Finland (Saari, 1995). In all the Nordic countries postgraduate specialization is being developed, and increasingly required in order to practice as a clinical psychologist. In Finland, for example, specialist qualifications have existed since 1992 at the licentiate degree level in the areas of psychotherapy, health psychology, educational psychology, neuropsychology, and the psychology of work and organizations.

2.01.6.2 The United Kingdom

In the UK there are three phases of professional training: undergraduate (Bachelors), postgraduate (Masters and Doctorate) and postqualification. Clinical psychologists are qualified by obtaining first a Bachelors degree in psychology (of the breadth and standard determined by the BPS which accredits all courses); then a Doctorate in Clinical Psychology (DClinPsy), a professional doctorate taking three years and based in a university, which includes substantial internship or supervised practice in at least the three prescribed areas of clinical practice: adult mental health, child mental health, learning difficulties. The BPS has considerable control in determining the content and nature of psychology that qualifies for professional training. It defines the theoretical foundation, and also the professional training, through controlling the criteria for entry to the Register of Chartered Psychologists. This is a voluntary register which guarantees the qualifications of clinical psychologists and their undertaking to abide by the Code of Conduct and disciplinary procedures of the BPS.

There are about 18 universities where it is possible to study the final three years (doctoral level) to become a clinical psychologist, although there are over 100 universities where the undergraduate (Bachelors) degree in psychology is offered. It should be noted that in the UK, where psychology is one of the most popular subjects of study for school leavers aged

18, only 20% of those who achieve a Bachelors degree in psychology continue to become professional psychologists, and the number of training places in clinical psychology is determined by the National Health Service and is very restricted.

2.01.6.3 Ireland

Ireland follows the same pattern of training as the UK, though it awards two-year Masters degrees as the final qualification for clinical psychologists; there are two universities offering clinical psychology training in Ireland. Both in the UK and in Ireland there has been a model of qualification provided by the BPS which existed as a form of inservice training, studying for the qualification while working as an assistant clinical psychologist on a form of internship. This has been largely superseded by university-based courses.

2.01.6.4 Greece

In Greece, four universities offer degrees in psychology, and are developing two-year Masters programs for clinical psychology.

2.01.6.5 France

Training for clinical psychologists takes five years, progressing through the general Diploma which is awarded after two years, the License after the third year, and the DESS after the fifth year.

2.01.6.6 Spain

In Spain there are 12 faculties of psychology and a somewhat larger number of departments of psychology. Clinical psychology education consists of two cycles, a core general program lasting at least two years, and an advanced more specialist program lasting at least two years. This leads to a qualification to practice (*licendiado en psicologo*), although the license through the Colegio Oficial de Psicologos, which was formed in 1979, requires the five year degree in psychology and a period of supervised practice or internship for the title of *psicologo*. However, postgraduate training is being developed at both Magister and Doctoral level, with specializations which include clinical psychology (Belloch & Ollabaria, 1994; Prieto, 1991).

2.01.7 DEMOGRAPHIC FEATURES OF CLINICAL PSYCHOLOGISTS

In many countries psychology has become one of, if not, the most popular subjects to study at university. The majority of students studying psychology aspire to become clinical psychologists, and for this reason, in many European countries there is an oversupply of qualified practitioners. Some countries operate so-called *numerus clausus*, either at the start of the psychology study, or during the study. This controls the numbers in training. In the UK where specialist training in clinical psychology is funded by the National Health Service, where the vast majority of clinical psychologists work, the number of "trainee" posts is strictly limited and is planned according to staffing needs in the different regions of the country. In other countries where there is a tradition of predominantly private practice in clinical psychology, there are large numbers of qualified psychologists unable to find work. In all European countries, the ratio of female to male students is between 3:1 and 6:1; leaving the profession in danger of becoming an almost feminized profession in the future (Schorr & Saari, 1995). There has also been some difficulty in many countries in recruiting students from the range of ethnic groups represented in Europe's increasingly multiethnic population. This clearly has implications for the clinical treatment of different client groups.

2.01.8 FUTURE ISSUES

The main issue continues to be mobility of clinical psychologists and evaluation of equivalence. In the late 1990s each country retains its own distinctive pattern of qualification. There are fears that moves to a more common pattern of qualification could lead to a reduction in standards or length of study period; all countries have succeeded in developing the level and length of training of clinical psychology qualification, and moves which threaten this are keenly resisted. On the other hand, evaluation of equivalence is a complex and time-consuming task, and one which may ultimately militate against the spirit of the EU and its directives on free movement. The EU and its Commission has a policy on free movement, and therefore encourages any moves to facilitate this. Some professions have developed an informal "common platform" which is a standard of qualification that is agreed across all EU member states. This is under discussion within EFPPA, although any detailed standard, for example, a European diploma, will be extremely complex and controversial. It remains the case that clinical psychologists in some countries are almost a separate profession with separate education and training (from other psychologists) whereas in other countries they have a specialization from a generic psychology qualification. This major difference shows no sign of reducing.

A further issue concerns the teaching of professional issues and ethical issues. For some countries the qualification in clinical psychology is mainly academic, with little internship or professional experience, while in others the education required clearly specifies supervised practice through internship. As ethical issues become increasingly important, EFPPA has been concerned to develop education in this area, both through the use of exemplar ethical dilemmas, and through a common agreement among European countries that a certain coverage in this area is essential. This is difficult for those countries with a more purely academic approach to the professional training.

As new fields of practice in the health field evolve, in particular health psychology, there is a difficulty in defining the scope of the field of clinical psychology and its training. For example, in some countries it has been said that there may no longer be a field of clinical psychology, since there are strong moves towards health psychology and a focus on preventive work. These new areas, in particular health psychology, have worked out their own curriculum and pattern of education (and EFPPA's task force in this area has played a key role in this); however, the countries differ in the extent and nature of their specialisms within the health field. In one respect psychologists working within the health system could be said to be becoming more generic, while on the other hand there are increasing specializations within this field of work.

2.01.9 SUMMARY

This chapter has presented some broad commonalities and differences in education and training for clinical psychologists in the EU, and highlighted some of the implications for mobility and evaluation of equivalence. It has described some of the work and functions of EFPPA in this respect, and attempted to identify some present and future issues for clinical psychology educators in Europe. As the number of clinical psychologists increases, and the question of mobility becomes more pressing, there will be increasing attempts to develop more common frameworks and standards for education in this field; the challenge is to achieve a balance between allowing individual countries their own autonomy (subsidiarity, as it is called), and developing more common agreed frameworks within which individual countries develop their own patterns of education and training.

2.01.10 APPENDIX 1: EFPPA OPTIMAL STANDARDS FOR PROFESSIONAL TRAINING

EFPPA is an organization of national associations of psychology, the great majority of which represent both the scientific and the professional community.

At its General Assembly held in Luxembourg, September 14–16, 1990, EFPPA fully recognised that the content and form of training in professional psychology in each country will inevitably reflect its own legal, educational, and professional traditions.

However, to encourage international cooperation among professional psychologists and to assist member associations in their efforts to develop professional training and practice in their countries, EFPPA is publishing the following statement which describes the optimal standards for training required for autonomous professional practice.

Member associations which subscribe to these optimal standards are encouraged to work towards their achievement.

1. Preparation for autonomous practice of psychology comprises at least two components: a core programme and an advanced professional training in psychology.

The core programme is concerned with the knowledge and skills relating to psychology as a scientific discipline and is common to all branches and specialisms within psychology.

In the advanced component the student will acquire the knowledge and skills which are necessary for autonomous practice in a chosen field of professional psychology.

At all levels, one should aim at an optimal integration of the core program and the professional training.

2. Both components should be provided within a university or equivalent institute of higher education. In some countries with an established tradition of doing so, professional training may be provided by an affiliated professional school or training programme.

3. Together the two components should last at least six years, with the distribution between the core programme and the advanced training determined by each country, according to national circumstances. However, at least half the time should be devoted to the core programme.

4. All training should be accredited in ways acceptable to the national association.

5. Entry to independent or autonomous professional practice should be restricted to those who have completed both components.

6. The core programme in psychology should provide a broad introduction to psychology. It

should include the traditional subdisciplines in psychology, ranging from the biologically oriented approaches to those that are cognitively and socially oriented and including developmental, methodological, philosophical and ethical issues.

7. Professional training should cover the theoretical knowledge, skills, competencies, and research abilities required in the applied field of psychology as set out below:

Theoretical knowledge

(a) A variety of different theoretical models should be taught because no single model is able to cope satisfactorily with the range of problems that confront the professional psychologist.

(b) Theoretical models must be considered critically so that students are fully aware of their limitations as well as their advantages.

(c) Theoretical teaching needs to be integrated with practice.

Skills and competencies

(a) Substantial practical training is essential.

(b) Practical training should include experience in a variety of settings, methods and approaches. It should include work with individuals, groups, and organizations as well as practice in assessment, program development, and evaluation.

(c) Ethical considerations should be taken into account in training.

(d) Practical training needs to cover communication skills as well as the transmission of psychological skills to others through teaching, supervision and consultation.

(e) Like other aspects of training, practical skills need to be tested and examined.

Research training

(a) Because of the importance of evaluating practices as well as the need to develop new models, techniques, and intervention programs, an appreciation of the methods of applied research is essential.

(b) Students should have the experience of conducting an original and independent research project as part of their training (thesis).

8. National associations have an obligation to ensure that the education and training provided is consistent with their codes of practice and ethical standards.

9. It is recommended that national associations should encourage and promote, keep a record of, and if possible accredit, courses for the training of professional psychologists.

This document was produced by a Task Force on Education and Training in Psychology, consisting of representatives from among the member associations of EFPPA.

Psychological associations in the following countries are member associations of EFPPA (July 1990): Austria, Belgium, Denmark, Finland, France, Germany, Greece, Hungary, Iceland, Italy, Liechtenstein, Luxembourg, The Netherlands, Norway, Poland, Portugal, Spain, Sweden, Switzerland, UK.

Dated July 1990.

2.01.11 APPENDIX 2: MEMBER ASSOCIATIONS OF EFPPA (1997)

Austria, Belgium, Croatia, Cyprus, Denmark, Estonia, Finland, France, Germany, Greece, Hungary, Iceland, Ireland, Italy, Liechtenstein, Luxembourg, Malta, The Netherlands, Norway, Poland, Portugal, Slovakia, Slovenia, Spain, Sweden, Switzerland, Turkey, UK.

2.01.12 APPENDIX 3: BIBLIOGRAPHY

There follows a list of short articles with descriptions of psychology in countries of the European Union.

Austria

Guttmann, G. (1992). Austria. In V. S. Sexton & J. D. Hogan (Eds.), *International psychology: Views from around the world.* Lincoln, NE: University of Nebraska Press.

Belgium

d'Ydewalle, G. (1992). Belgium. In V. S. Sexton & J. D. Hogan (Eds.) *International psychology: Views from around the world.* Lincoln, NE: University of Nebraska Press.

Janssen, P. (1992). The psychological profession in Belgium. *News from EFPPA, 6*(2), 15–19.

Denmark

Foltved, P. (1992). Profile of Danish Psychological Association. *News from EFPPA, 6*(1), 16–18.

Foltved, P. (1995). Professional psychology in Denmark. In A. Schorr & S. Saari (Eds.), *Psychology in Europe* (pp. 15–22). Gottingen, Germany: Hogrefe.

Finland

Legislation on a psychologist's practice: Aims and achievements (1991). *News from EFPPA, 5*(4), 15–17.

Saari, S. (1991). Psychology training in Finland *News from EFPPA, 5*(1), 6–8.

Saari, S. (1992). Profile of Finnish psychology and the Union of Finnish Psychologists. *News from EFPPA, 6*(4), 22–26.

Saari, S. (1995a). The development of psychology in Finland. *News from EFPPA, 9*(2), 4–9.

Saari, S. (1995b). The legalisation of Finnish psychology. In A. Schorr & S. Saari (Eds.), *Psychology in Europe* (pp. 23–34). Gottingen, Germany: Hogrefe.

France

Castro, D., & Denis, M. (1996). Société

Française de Psychologie. *European Psychologist, 1*(2), 149.
Castro, D., & Engelhart, D. (1994). De la formation à la professionalisation. Processus de professionalisation de la psychologie appliquée en France. *European Review of Applied Psychology, 43*(2), 101–112.
Sanches, A. A. (1992). France. In V. S. Sexton & J. D. Hogan (Eds.), *International psychology: Views from around the world.* Lincoln, NE: University of Nebraska Press.
Trognon, A. (1987). France. In A. R. Gilgen & C. K. Gilgen (Eds.), *International handbook of psychology.* Westport, CT: Greenwood Press.
Germany
Graumann, C. F., & Metraux, A. (1992). Federal Republic of Germany. In V. S. Sexton & J. D. Hogan (Eds.), *International psychology: Views from around the world.* Lincoln, NE: University of Nebraska Press.
Schorr, A. (1995). German psychology after reunification. In A. Schorr & S. Saari (Eds.), *Psychology in Europe* (pp. 35–58). Gottingen, Germany: Hogrefe.
Greece
Georgas, J. (1995). Psychology in Greece. In A. Schorr & S. Saari (Eds.), *Psychology in Europe* (pp. 59–76). Gottingen, Germany: Hogrefe.
Velli, T. (1995). Profile of Greece. *News from EFPPA, 9*(1), 20.
Ireland
Brady, T., & McLoone, S. (1992). Ireland. In V. S. Sexton & J. D. Hogan (Eds.), *International psychology: Views from around the world.* Lincoln, NE: University of Nebraska Press.
Italy
Avallone, F. (1994). Training and professional spheres of psychology in France. *European Review of Applied Psychology, 43*(2), 113–121.
Comunian, A.L. (1992). Italy. In V. S. Sexton & J. D. Hogan (Eds.), *International psychology: Views from around the world.* Lincoln, NE: University of Nebraska Press.
Spaltro, E. (1993). Conflicts and developments of Italian psychology. *News from EFPPA, 7*(1), 17–21.
Netherlands
Dijkhuis, J. (1991). Psychologists in The Netherlands: Their training and professional regulations. *News from EFPPA, 5*(2 & 3), 20–22.
Jonkergouw, T. (1991). Profile of the NIP. *News from EFPPA, 5*(4), 23–25.
van Drunen, P. (1995). Professional psychology in the Netherlands. In A. Schorr & S. Saari (Eds.), *Psychology in Europe* (pp. 77–96). Gottingen, Germany: Hogrefe.
van der Ploeg, H. M. (1992). The Netherlands. In V. S. Sexton & J. D. Hogan (Eds.), *International psychology: Views from around the world.* Lincoln, NE: University of Nebraska Press.
Portugal
Pereira, F. (1994). Psychology in Portugal. *News from EFPPA, 8*(3), 22–24.
Pereira, F. (1995). Psychology in Portugal. In A. Schorr & S. Saari (Eds.), *Psychology in Europe* (pp. 97–102). Gottingen, German: Hogrefe.
Spain
Belloch, A., & Olabarria, B. (1994). Clinical psychology: Current status and future prospects. *Applied Psychology: An International Review, 43*(2), 193–211.
Carpentero, H. (1996). Psychology in Spain. *European Psychologist, 1*(1), 71–73.
Prieto, J. M. (1991). Studying psychology in Spain. *News from EFPPA, 5*(4), 18–22.
Tortosa, F. et al. Professional issues in Spanish psychology: Historical profile and present situation. *European Review of Applied Psychology, 43*(2), 123–141.
Yela, M. (1987). Spain. In A. R. Gilgen & C. K. Gilgen (Eds.), *International handbook of psychology.* Westport, CT: Greenwood Press.
Sweden
Persson, H. (1995). Psychology in Sweden. In A. Schorr & S. Saari (Eds.), *Psychology in Europe.* Gottingen, Germany: Hogrefe.
The Swedish Psychological Association (1992). *News from EFPPA, 6*(2), 23–26.
United Kingdom
BPS (1992). The undergraduate curriculum in psychology in the UK. *News from EFPPA, 6*(2), 10–14.
Lindsay, G., & Lunt, I. (1993). Developments in professional psychology in the UK. *News from EFPPA, 7*(2), 3–7.
Lunt, I. (1995a). The training and regulation of psychologists in the United Kingdom. *News from EFPPA, 9*(1), 17–19.
Lunt, I. (1995b). Demographic trends in professional psychology in the United Kingdom. In A. Schorr & S. Saari (Eds.), *Psychology in Europe* (pp. 149–162). Gottingen, Germany: Hogrefe.
Lunt, I., & Lindsay, G. (1993). Professional psychologists in the United Kingdom. *European Review of Applied Psychology, 43*, 91–98.
Newman, C. (1991). Profile of the BPS. *News from EFPPA, 5*(2 & 3), 23.

2.01.13 REFERENCES

Belloch, A., & Olabarria, B. (1994) Clinical psychology: Current status and future prospects. *Applied Psychology: An International Review, 43*(2), 193–211.
EFPPA (1990). *Optimal standards.* Stockholm, Sweden: EFPPA Secretariat
EFPPA (1991). *Task force on evaluation of curriculi: Terms of reference.* Stockholm, Sweden: EFPPA Secretariat.
EFPPA (1997). *Interim report to the General Assembly of EFPPA of Clinical Psychology Task Force.* Stockholm, Sweden: EFPPA Secretariat.

Haaksman, D. (1990). The European Directive and its implications for psychologists, their associations and EFPPA. *News from EFPPA, 4*(1), 24–27.

Kendall, P. C., & Norton-Ford, J. D. (1982). *Clinical psychology. Scientific and professional dimensions.* New York: Wiley.

Llewelyn, S. P. (1994). Assessment and therapy in clinical psychology. In P. Spurgeon, R. Davies, & A. Chapman (Eds.), *Elements of applied psychology* (pp. 115–132). Chur, Switzerland: Harwood.

Lunt, I. (1993). Educational psychology. The European dimension. *Newsletter of the BPS Scottish Division of Educational and Child Psychology, 1,* 1–6.

Lunt, I. (1994). Training and registration of professional psychologists in Europe. Keynote address at First Congress of Psychology, Malta. *News from EFPPA, 8* (3), 10–18.

Marzillier, J. & Hall, J. (1990). *What is clinical psychology?* (2nd ed.). Oxford, UK: Oxford University Press.

McPherson, F. (1988). Psychologists and the EEC. *The Psychologist, 9,* 353–355.

Newstead, S. (1994). The psychology curriculum and the training of psychologists in Europe. *News from EFPPA, 8*(4), 11–14.

Newstead, S., & Makinen, S. (1997). Psychology teaching in Europe. *European Psychologist, 2*(1), 3–10.

Peterson, D. R. (1991). Connection and disconnection of research and practice in the education of professional psychologists. *American Psychologist, 46*(4), 422–429.

Pilgrim, D., & Treacher, A. (1992). *Clinical psychology observed.* London: Routledge.

Prieto, J. M. (1991). Studying psychology in Spain. *News from EFPPA, 5*(4), 18–22.

Raimy, V. C. (Ed.) (1950). *Training in clinical psychology.* New York: Prentice-Hall.

Saari, S. (1995). The development of psychology in Finland. *News from EFPPA, 9*(2), 4–9.

Schorr, A., & Saari, S. (Eds.) (1995). *Psychology in Europe.* Gottingen, Germany: Hogrefe.

Spaltro, E. (1993). Conflicts and developments of Italian psychology. *News from EFPPA, 7*(1), 17–21.

Velli, T. (1995). Profile of Greece. Theoni Velli. *News from EFPPA, 9*(1), 20.

2.02
History and Emerging Trends in Education and Training for Clinical Psychology in the United States

LYNN P. REHM
University of Houston, TX, USA

2.02.1 INTRODUCTION

Clinical psychology celebrated its centennial in 1996. The evolution of the field, over this 100 years plus, has reflected the historical events in each era. In particular, World Wars I and II had major influences on its growth and directions. The stresses and strains that have occurred within psychology generally have steered the profession in one direction or another. Theoretical debates, professional associations, conferences, and the initiatives of individual psychologists have been some of the pushes and pulls that have altered the course of clinical psychology.

Many of the tensions in clinical psychology today can be traced back through history. The position of psychology among academic disciplines and among professional rivals has been a continuing battle of borders and territory. The relationship between clinical psychology and other areas of psychology has similarly been one of growth, interchange, overlap, and jostling for position. The scope of clinical psychology practice has expanded in competition with neighbors outside and inside psychology. The identity of clinical psychology has evolved from these conflicts and debates. The results of all of these influences are manifest in the themes of education and training in clinical psychology today.

In this chapter, I will attempt to review some of the major events influencing clinical psychology in different eras of development (Reisman,

1991)—its beginning years, between the world wars, growth years following World War II and the modern years of professional expansion. I will try to extract some of the themes and issues of education and training that intertwine with the events of those eras.

2.02.2 THE BEGINNING YEARS

The history of scientific psychology is traditionally dated to 1879 when Wilhelm Wundt began a doctoral program to train students in psychology at the University of Leipzig. Wundt had opened his psychology laboratory in 1875, the same year William James established a psychology demonstration laboratory at Harvard. Wundt and James trained many of the early pioneers of psychology in the USA.

The 1880s and 1890s were a period of openings and beginnings for psychology as it became established in American universities. G. Stanley Hall, a student of James, took a position at Johns Hopkins in 1881 and founded the second psychological laboratory there in 1883. In 1887 he founded the *American Journal of Psychology*. Hall became President of Clark University in 1889 and in 1892 he founded the American Psychological Association there and became its first president. James McKeen Cattell, a student of Wundt, took a position at the University of Pennsylvania in 1888 and founded the third psychological laboratory. In the same year, Joseph Jastrow, with a doctorate from Johns Hopkins, took a position at the University of Wisconsin. Cattel and Jastrow were the first psychologists to have the title Professor of Psychology.

The beginning of clinical psychology is traditionally dated to 1896 when Lightner Witmer opened a psychology clinic at the University of Pennsylvania. Witmer obtained his doctorate with Wundt in 1892 and in that year took over the psychological laboratory from Cattel. With the opening of the clinic, Witmer began a training program in the field he came to call "clinical psychology," although he preferred the term "psychological orthogenics." He advocated the "clinical method" of teaching and in 1897 began a summer course in the clinic based on learning from individual clinical cases, the first practicum in clinical psychology. Witmer also founded the journal *The Psychological Clinic* in 1907. Witmer's clinic was devoted to helping children with intellectual and learning difficulties and can be thought of as the first child guidance clinic.

The first decades of the twentieth century saw new service and teaching clinics and new applied training programs open. Carl Seashore and R. L. Sylvester opened a Psychological Clinic at the University of Iowa in 1908 and a similar clinic was opened at Clark University in 1909. Courses in clinical psychology were begun in the same year at the universities of Minnesota and Washington where clinics soon followed.

In 1909 the Juvenile Psychopathic Institute was formed in Chicago to aid the courts in dealing with delinquent children. It was staffed by William Healy, a physician, and Grace Fernald, a psychologist. This was the first true child guidance clinic and clinic outside of a university setting. Henry H. Goddard working as the director of a psychological research laboratory at the Institute for Backward Children in Vineland, New Jersey, began the first internship in psychology at Vineland in 1908 (Reisman, 1991).

Psychological application was largely limited to "mental testing." In the early years this consisted of simple tests of reaction time, and speed and accuracy measures on simple tasks. A number of batteries of such tests were proposed with great optimism that they could be used to predict everything from separating psychiatric cases from retarded cases, to selecting children for school programs, and to guiding people in the choice of vocations. These hopes were soon dashed by the results of studies that found little in the way of reliable differences between groups or of practical predictions that could be made with these measures. At the same time, there was a new direction in measurement as intellectual assessment was taking hold of the USA in the form of various translations and revisions of the French Binet–Simon tests. Intelligence testing became the primary focus of psychological application. While much was going on in the field of psychiatry, such as Emile Kraeplin's first psychiatric text in 1883, and Freud and Brewer's *Studies in Hysteria* in 1895, psychology expressed little interest in psychopathology or psychotherapy. Intellectual testing and remedial teaching were its assessments and interventions.

2.02.2.1 Science and Practice

The opening of Witmer's clinic was not widely celebrated in psychology. Many psychologists felt that application was premature and that psychology should be solely a basic science. Wundt had founded psychology as the scientific study of consciousness. He described the interests of his student Cattell in individual differences as *ganz amerikanishe* (wholly American) as Wundt was interested in universals of experience (Fowler, 1996). The American Psychological Association (APA) was founded to further psychological science, and in 1904 it tightened its membership criteria to require evidence of scientific contributions by new members. This focus on science derived from several concerns. The public image of psychology was mixed with the popular interest in mediums, clairvoyance, mind-reading, and other supernatural phenomena. Joseph Jastrow lamented in his 1901 APA presidential address that in the eyes of the public, "psychologist" was the equivalent of "spook chaser." He devoted great energy to educating the public about the science of psychology, for example, he took a battery of 15 early mental tests to a booth at the Chicago World's Fair in 1893 and showed the public the tests while collecting data on mental and sensory capacities.

William James' highly popular 1890 book, *Principles of Psychology*, recommended practicing psychologically healthy habits. The book was coolly received by academic psychology for the reasons that it was too applied, went beyond empirical fact, and contained too much philosophy and religion. In the academic world, where nearly all psychologists were employed, psychology was trying to establish itself as a separate science apart from philosophy, religion, education, or physiology. At Harvard, William James was Professor of Physiology, and then Professor of Philosophy before he briefly became a Professor of Psychology. While there was much disagreement within psychology about what type of science it should be, it was generally agreed that it was a science that should have its own separate identity. Those who tended toward application were seen as tarnishing this scientific image.

2.02.2.2 Early Curricula

In its early period then, psychology education overlapped with other fields, such as physiology, medicine, philosophy, and pedagogy. From England, Francis Galton added statistical methods such as the correlation coefficient to the scientific methodology of psychology. Graduate education in clinical psychology similarly borrowed from other fields. Witmer recognized an overlap of clinical psychology with other professions. In the 1904–1905 academic year, Witmer arranged for his students to take courses in psychiatry and neuropathology. Witmer's clinic and others like it used the consultation of physicians, social workers, educators, and others. It is noteworthy that psychology in its very beginnings included a doctoral graduate degree. In the USA, universities had only recently been bestowing doctoral degrees at all. Yale was the first to do this in 1861, followed by Harvard in 1872. Johns Hopkins opened in 1876 entirely as a graduate school.

Clinical psychology began to develop its own curricular identity. By 1908, five psychology courses in clinical psychology were offered at the University of Pennsylvania—three in developmental psychology, one in abnormal psychology, and one in mental and physical deficits in school children. From the beginning Witmer saw the clinic as central to the clinical method of teaching. Students were to observe and participate in a scientific study of cases. The identity of clinical psychology was further aided by such events as the publication in 1910 of *The Manual of Mental Tests* by Guy M. Whipple—the first standard, widely-used text on psychological testing. Clinical psychologists were largely mental testers, but with a research point of view. By and large they were employed in universities doing teaching and research, but perhaps also participating in clinics. A few psychologists began getting jobs in research laboratories in various institutions for the retarded or mentally ill, and a few were employed in schools. Psychology, as a new science, and clinical psychology, as a new applied component of psychology, were established and ready to take on new challenges.

2.02.3 THE AFTERMATH OF WORLD WAR I

In World War I the US army adopted psychological testing to process and place troops. The Army Alpha and Beta tests were developed and psychology began to invest itself in the field of mental testing. World War I suddenly and greatly expanded the need for testing and for trained personnel to administer tests. At about the same time, psychological assessment entered the schools on a larger scale with another increased demand for "mental testers." New tests were developed in the intellectual domain and testing expanded into the areas of personality assessment, physiological assessment of emotions, and vocational selection. Psychology struggled with who should give mental tests, as they were given by people with doctorates and masters degrees in psychology, but also by bachelor level psychometrists, teachers, and other professionals.

2.02.3.1 Science and Practice

Training for assessment became a contentious issue within psychology. In World War I, Robert Yerkes, President of the APA, headed up psychology's war efforts in the area of psychological testing. He was criticized by J. E. Wallace Wallin for recruiting experimental psychologists with little training in mental testing (Routh, 1994). Already in 1915, Whipple had proposed in a resolution adopted by APA "that this Association discourages the use of mental tests by those unqualified" (Reisman, 1991, p 115). The dispute about qualifications for testing erupted at the December 1917, APA convention at Carnegie Institute in Pittsburgh. The APA formed a committee on qualifications for testing experts, but it was not enough to please a group of clinical psychologists who met on December 29, 1917 and formed the American Association of Clinical Psychologists with Wallin as president, Leta Hollingsworth as secretary, and six members. This first association of clinical psychologists voted itself out of existence two years later when, with the efforts of Yerkes, they rejoined APA as the Clinical Section. APA agreed to attend to the interests of applied psychology.

The issues of clinical qualifications and APA's attention to practice continued to be sources of friction within APA. In 1921, APA reaffirmed its purpose to advance science and its requirement for research contributions for membership. It recommended certification for "consulting" (applied) psychologists and elimination of the Clinical Section. The certification program was not very successful because of its high standards and the Clinical Section was not eliminated. In 1924 the Clinical Section became the Clinical Division of APA and recommended standards for clinical education including a Ph.D. from an approved graduate school and four years of professional experience including one year in diagnosis. In 1926 APA opened its membership to associate members with a Ph.D. in psychology and employment in the field, but without the scientific publications necessary for full voting members. Within three years, associate members outnumbered full members.

In the 1930s an APA Committee on Standards of Training recommended standards of training for clinical psychology including a Ph.D. and one year of supervised training or a master's degree and one year of training for "assistant psychologists." Pleas were made to APA to set standards for psychological testing. State and local associations of clinical psychologists and consulting psychologists (those in private practice) arose, and in 1937 the Clinical Division of APA dissolved itself and recommended that its members join the new American Association of Applied Psychology with its sections in Clinical Psychology, Consulting Psychology, Educational Psychology, and a few others.

The curriculum of clinical psychology expanded in these decades as new theoretical approaches were introduced. The theories of Freud and his followers grew in influence in the United States at the same time that John D. Watson disseminated his ideas about behaviorism. Watson reinforced the notion that the study of animal learning could lead to applications of principles to humans. Gestalt and phenomenological approaches were being introduced as well. A 1930 textbook in abnormal psychology by H. L. Hollingsworth opened with a series of seven introductory chapters describing theoretical approaches to the topic before addressing any disorders. Psychiatry was going through a new biological era with the introduction of psychosurgery, narcosis therapy, and chemical inductions of seizures, and a parallel interest in biological assessments was popular in psychology. Witmer wrote of "psychochemistry" and offered a course in "Behavior and Metabolism." The nature vs. nurture debate raged with a focus on mental retardation. On the psychology side, nurture gained ground during this era. Psychologists argued about the structure of intelligence, and the debate between Spearman's general factor model and Thorndike's specific factor model was animated.

Psychology expanded in the settings of training, in research, in publication, and in areas of practice as well. In 1915 the first department of applied psychology was established at Carnegie Institute of Technology with Walter Van Dyke Bingham as its chair. Similar programs opened at other universities although the Carnegie Tech department was disbanded in 1924. In 1927 the Harvard Psychology Clinic was opened by psychiatrist Morton Prince who gave the *Journal of Abnormal Psychology* to APA, adding to APA's new publication initiatives. James McKeen Cattell founded the Psychological Corporation in 1921 to publish psychological tests. Child guidance clinics opened around the country with a growing concern about juvenile delinquency. Practice in schools, clinics, institutions, and individual consultation increased in the latter part of this era.

Psychology fought with organized psychiatry over whether psychologists could diagnose mental retardation. Intervention became a larger part of psychological practice, but conflict with psychiatry was largely averted by the convention that psychological interventions were educational in nature and not psychotherapy. Psychological intervention increased with play therapy, group therapy, and specific learning theory based interventions and psychotherapy in general gained credence in the eye of the public. Psychoanalysis was limited in the USA to physicians. Psychology was poised for a new leap into the future with World War II.

2.02.4 WORLD WAR II AND ENTRY INTO THE MODERN ERA OF CLINICAL TRAINING

Just as World War I, World War II had a major impact on clinical psychology. Again testing was employed in the military on a large scale and psychologists were called on to develop, validate, and administer the testing programs. Both the government and the public were coming to view psychotherapy and counseling favorably and these views moved psychology in the direction of training for intervention. In 1941 the National Research Council urged psychiatry and psychology to cooperate for the good of national defense. This action aided the recognition of psychology in the military and muted some of psychiatry's objection to psychologists entering into the psychotherapy role. Estimates of the need for psychotherapists and counselors in the military, veterans services, and state mental health programs led to government funding of graduate education in psychology. By the end of the war, the Veterans Administration (VA) was offering half-time salaries to graduate students in training to work in VA facilities, and the Public Health Service was providing grants to graduate training programs for staff, facilities improvement, and student fellowships in the mental health fields. New training programs were started to meet the need and take advantage of these support programs.

2.02.4.1 Boulder Conference

In 1945 the VA and National Institute of Mental Health (NIMH) asked APA to provide a list of graduate programs that provided appropriate clinical training to justify supporting their students. The APA responded by appointing a Committee on Training in Clinical Psychology chaired by David Shakow. In 1947 this committee issued what became known as the Shakow Report (see Shakow, 1969). The report was expanded in 1949 with some elaborations on suggested curricula for clinical training. The path of clinical psychology now led to one of the major milestones in the history of clinical psychology, the Boulder Conference.

In August 1949 the NIMH sponsored a week-long Conference on Training in Clinical Psychology in Boulder, Colorado. Victor Raimy, a faculty member of the host Department of Psychology at the University of Colorado, reported on the conference in the form of a book (Raimy, 1950). The conference was filled with discussion, debate, and disagreement. Most of the actions taken at the conference were to ratify portions of the Shakow Report. The articulation of a series of consensus positions for clinical psychology was a great accomplishment, even though positions adopted at the conference would continue to be debated for decades to come.

The conference report is best known for setting forth the scientist–practitioner model of training in which students are trained both in research and practice. Raimy (1950) reported that agreement was reached on a statement that "research competence is acquired only by doing research" (p. 88). There were, however, dissenters on both the experimentalist and clinician sides of the issue. The report is very explicit about the idea that the scientist–practitioner model is a model of training, and not a model of practice. It was anticipated that clinical psychologists would work in a variety of settings demanding a variety of roles. Private practice was discouraged by the conferees. Though some schools had dropped the master's degree, the conference recommended research requirements at both a predissertation and dissertation level. Strong training in statistics was recommended on the science side. On the practice side, training in psychotherapy was endorsed, though some lamented the lack of empirical support for psychotherapy. Raimy (p. 93) quotes one anonymous wag as saying "Psychotherapy is an unspecified technique applied to unspecified problems of unpredictable outcome. For this technique we recommend rigorous training." The ethical issue of offering unvalidated techniques was raised.

The doctoral degree was asserted as the level for entry into practice in psychology, affirming earlier recommendations by various groups. Training in testing was specifically discouraged for undergraduates. No decision was made on appropriate training at the master's level, a problem that psychology has never resolved. A four-year program was envisioned with an internship in the third year during which the dissertation topic would be formulated. Dissertations in any area of psychology were deemed acceptable, although research in personality was recommended. After some debate, the group also decided that multiple case studies would be acceptable as a dissertation, although there was no agreement whether a single case study would be appropriate.

Concern was expressed over the relationship between the graduate programs and the federal agencies that were funding them. All agreed that quality assessment and control was the role of the universities and that the agencies should not dictate curriculum. Some noted that the funding of students had some negative effects. The large time commitments that were required of students on VA stipends were making it difficult for students to finish their programs in a timely manner. In addition, the emphasis on VA work was reducing the opportunities to see women and children in practicum or internship. Indeed, psychology's traditional focus on children was in the process of change.

The conference participants agreed that a minimum curriculum should include four core areas:

(i) general psychology, including systematic, experimental, and social psychology;

(ii) clinical psychology and mental hygiene, including broad training in theory, method, and techniques;

(iii) field work with a variety of clinical problems at different levels of responsibility; and

(iv) research and methods of investigation.

However, beyond this minimum the conference favored a diversity of approaches among university departments to prevent the field from stagnating. The conference urged the field to move forward in the areas of accrediting of graduate programs, developing standards for internships, adopting an ethical code, and certification or licensing of individuals. Progress was soon made on these goals.

2.02.4.2 Professional Developments

Accreditation began in 1947 to accommodate the request of the VA to identify high-quality training programs. Forty-two programs that had achieved some level of initial approval were invited to the Boulder Conference. The growth of accredited programs can be seen by the numbers in Table 1. Provisional accreditation was given for a number of years to new programs that did not as yet have track records for their products. In the 1950s internships began to be accredited as well, though the VA was slow to acknowledge the APA accreditation system and for many years VA internships were largely considered outside the accreditation system.

APA adopted its first ethics code for clinical and consulting psychologists in 1951. It was expanded in 1952 to cover all professional psychology and published in 1953. Periodic revisions and amendments to the code occurred in 1958, 1963, 1968, 1977, 1979, 1981, and 1990. The current *Ethical Principles of Psychologists* was finalized in December 1992. The current code covers a wide range of activities in expanded areas of practice such as forensic activities and issues in education and research.

Connecticut was the first state to pass a certification law for psychologists in 1945. The law required a Ph.D. in psychology and one year of experience. Virginia followed in 1946 with a law requiring a Ph.D. and five years of experience. The first licensing law was passed in Georgia in 1951. APA officially favored certification over licensure. Within psychology, some felt that licensure was premature. Outside of psychology licensure was resisted by psychiatry which opposed independent practice by psychologists. It was not until 1977 that Missouri completed the cycle by becoming the last state to pass a psychology licensing law. Because the process was so prolonged, the American Board of Examiners in Professional Psychology (ABEPP) was formed in 1947 to provide a certificate or diploma to clinical, counseling, or industrial psychologists with a doctorate, and five years of experience, who passed a written and an oral examination.

Clinical psychology returned to APA in 1945 when APA expanded its mission statement to advance psychology both as a science and as a profession. With the change, the modern division structure was adopted. In the original plan for 19 divisions, there was to have been a Division 11, the Division of Abnormal Psychology and Psychotherapy, and a Division 12, the Division of Clinical Psychology. The former was to be for the researchers and the latter was to have been a direct continuation of the Clinical Section of the American Association of Applied Psychology. The members reconsidered, however, and formed only one division, 12, with the name the Division of Clinical and Abnormal Psychology. In 1955 it took its present name of the Division of Clinical Psychology. Other organizations pertinent to clinical psychology were formed in the ensuing years. During the early 1950s directors of clinical training programs began meeting at APA conventions and evolved into the Council of University Directors of Clinical Psychology, an organization that advances training by and for clinical directors. The Association of Psychology Internship Centers (APIC) was formed to aid and advance internship programs. APIC later became the Association of Psychology Postdoctoral and Internship Centers (APPIC).

The factions of science and practice continued their disputes in and out of APA in the modern eras. Other organizations were founded because of dissatisfaction with APA. For example, the Psychonomic Society was formed in 1959 as a home for basic researchers. Divisions proliferated in APA to represent ever-expanding and differentiating interests. Some practice divisions

Table 1 Number of APA fully and provisionally accredited doctoral programs by decade.

Year	*Clinical*	*Counseling*	*School*	*Professional/ scientific*
1950–Full	35			
1960–Full	56	26		
1970–Full/ Provisional	73/1	21/1		
1980–Full/ Provisional	112/5	21/6	11/5	3
1990–Full	163	59	38	3
1996–Full	188	68	44	7

formed to serve interests within the clinical psychology community, as with the Psychotherapy Division, 29, and later the Division of Independent Practice, 42. As practitioners gained dominance in APA, science and practice in APA explored division into separate "assemblies" in the late 1980s, but the constitutional amendment that would have split the organization was defeated by the members. APA central office was reorganized around science, practice, public interest, and education constituencies. Practice members were assessed an additional sum to advance professional interests. Another association, the American Psychological Society, was formed with an emphasis on research only. With these changes, relative peace has been maintained in APA in recent years.

In the 1960s, 1970s and 1980s the practice of clinical psychology continued to expand into new areas and to become more differentiated into specialties. Psychological practice became better recognized in law, and better funded by third-party sources. The establishment of community mental health centers in the 1960s opened another source of employment for psychologists and was a sign of the country's acceptance of psychiatric and psychological outpatient treatment. With licensing established, psychologists gained other forms of recognition through state legislation, such as freedom of choice for the public to choose psychologists under insurance plans, and hospital practice in some states. Psychology was recognized for coverage under federal health plans like Champus and Medicaid, and in most private mental health benefit plans.

2.02.4.3 Education and Training

After Boulder there were a number of other training conferences held to keep up with the changing world of practice. Among the most prominent were the following:

(i) Conference on Psychology and Mental Health. Stanford, CA, 1955 (Strother 1956).

(ii) Conference on Graduate Education in Psychology. Miami Beach, FL, 1958 (Roe, 1959).

(iii) Conference on the Professional Preparation of Clinical Psychologists. Chicago, IL 1965 (Hoch, Ross, & Winder, 1966).

(iv) Conference on Levels and Patterns of Professional Training in Psychology. Vail, CO, 1973 (Korman, 1974).

(v) National Conference and Self-Study: Quality in Professional Psychology Training. La Jolla, CA, 1981 (Callan, Peterson, & Stricker, 1986).

(vi) National Conference on the Future of Graduate Education and Training in Professional Psychology. Mission Bay San Diego, CA, 1986 (Bourg et al., 1987).

(vii) Conference on Graduate Training in Psychology, Salt Lake City, UT, 1986 (Bickman, 1987).

(viii) National Conference on Internship Training in Psychology. Gainesville, FL, 1987 (Belar et al., 1987).

(ix) The National Conference on Scientist-Practitioner Education and Training for the Professional Practice of Psychology. Gainesville, FL, 1990 (Assembly of Scientist-Practitioner Psychologists & Department of Clinical and Health Psychology, University of Florida, 1990).

(x) National Conference on Postdoctoral Training in Professional Psychology. Ann Arbor, MI, 1992 (Larsen et al., 1993).

(xi) National Conference on Postdoctoral Education and Training in Psychology. Norman, OK, 1994 (Education Directorate, APA, 1995).

Comparison among the recommendations of these conferences highlights the controversial issues in clinical psychology education and underscores our inability to reach consensus. Whereas the 1949 Boulder Conference had discouraged teaching testing to undergraduates, the 1965 Chicago Conference recommended that practical training for undergraduates including psychological testing and interviewing would be appropriate. In 1986 the Utah Conference reiterated the Boulder idea that undergraduate education was not for practice in psychology. Master's training has been the topic of recommendations by several conferences. The Chicago Conference took a stand against master's training in clinical psychology, but recognized that specific practical skills might be taught to persons who would employ nonpsychological titles at the master's level. The Vail Conference in 1973 was much more favorable towards master's training for practice under supervision. A core curriculum was recommended in outline by the Boulder Conference, and the importance of a core was reiterated by the early conferences thereafter. The 1965 Chicago Conference opined that "the notion of a core curriculum is no longer possible" (Hoch et al., 1966, p. 47). Utah favored a core, and cited the accreditation standards list in 1986, but wanted to leave specification up to departments. The National Council of Schools of Psychology focused their 1986 Mission Bay Conference on issues of a core, and developed a detailed outline of what it should be. Some of the bolder recommendations of the conferences were not acted on by the field. For example, the 1987 Gainesville Internship Conference recommended a two-year internship, and the 1986 Utah Conference recommended that by 1995 free-standing professional schools would no longer be eligible for APA accreditation until they affiliated with a regionally accredited university.

2.02.4.4 The Vail Conference

The Vail Conference deserves special comment because it was a clear milestone for clinical psychology in marking the acceptance of professional schools. The 1973 Conference on Levels and Patterns of Professional Training in Psychology was convened because of growing concerns that the Boulder model of scientist–practitioner training was not meeting the needs of a changing professional world, of society, and of groups of students underrepresented in psychology. By this time, several professional schools and programs in psychology had been initiated. The program at Adelphi founded by Gordon Derner in 1951 was the precursor of this movement. His "scholar–practitioner" program was intended to provide students with a knowledge base that would let them critically read research, but not train them in actually doing research. This program was accredited by the APA in 1957 on appeal. In 1968 the University of Illinois initiated a Psy.D. track in their clinical program under the direction of Donald Peterson. Students in this track took the same course work as the Ph.D. students, but did more in-depth clinical work rather than the usual thesis and dissertation research. In 1969, the California School of Professional Psychology (CSPP) was founded with free-standing campuses in major cities of California. The CSPP, offering a Ph.D., was founded by members of the California Psychological Association who felt the existing programs in the state were not meeting the needs of the public. By the time of the Vail Conference, the National Council of Schools of Professional Psychology (NCSPP) (later to become the National Council of Schools and Programs of Professional Psychology, NCSPPP) had been formed to advance the interests of the professional schools.

The Vail Conference endorsed the new trend in professional training while acknowledging that it should expand upon and not replace scientist–practitioner training and should not exclude the science base of the profession. The conference urged all training programs to become more attuned to the public needs that they are serving, and to incorporate diversity in their training curricula, practicum, target populations, students, and faculty. Affirmative action for women and minorities was urged. The conference also took a strong stand on professional training at multiple levels—Associate of Arts, bachelor's, master's, and doctoral. The master's degree was posed at the journeyman level of practice with the doctorate representing the master level of practice. The conference urged APA to recognize persons with master's degrees as entitled to the title of "psychologist" and to grant full membership to them. The recommendations of the conference fell short of endorsing licensure and independent practice at the master's level. Vail illustrates the fact that training conferences do better at endorsing trends already underway in the field (e.g., professional schools) and do less well at initiating new trends (e.g., official recognition of master's level psychologists).

Finally, the Vail conference envisioned a career ladder or lattice. Psychologists at all levels were to participate in continuing educational development to expand and update their skills and to move up the career ladder. Training programs were encouraged to offer these professional development curricula in the form of flexible, small units of education in ways that would count for career and degree advancement. They envisioned people accumulating continuing education that would lead to the next professional degree up the ladder as well as to new skills across the lattice.

2.02.5 CURRENT THEMES IN CLINICAL TRAINING

Clinical psychology's century of history has bought us a long way from the laboratories, summer practica, and applied teaching clinics of our early days. In 1996 there were about 84 000 professional psychologists licensed in the USA. According to the recent practice analysis conducted by the Association of State and Provincial Psychology Boards, about half of these are clinical psychologists (Greenberg, Smith, & Muenzen, 1995). The 188 accredited doctoral programs in clinical psychology are varied in location (department of psychology, school of education, department of psychiatry, free-standing professional school, professional school within a university, etc.), degree offered (Ph.D., Ed.D., or Psy.D.), size (number of students, faculty, and their ratio), curriculum (required and elective courses, core content, theories and methods emphasized), orientation to science and practice (research and practice experience required), facilities (classrooms, laboratories, and clinics), faculty (orientation, training, areas of expertise, clinical and research activities), and students (admission criteria, goals and orientation). These programs exist in a changing world of public perceptions and needs, market conditions, and the rapid evolution of the health care system. A number of themes go into this mix.

Defining a core curriculum has always been a problem in clinical psychology. We have always been reluctant to be too specific in identifying a core for fear of impinging on the academic freedom and innovation of individual programs. The result, however, is that we are not able to assure the public that a clinical psychologist can be guaranteed to have some minimal competencies. Programs often go in the other direction by trying to be overly inclusive in what they require. The Boulder Conference envisioned a four-year program. Today's students are taking six to seven years or more to complete a doctorate. There are constant pressures to add to the curriculum as new topics become increasingly relevant. How will we include psychopharmacology, mental health law, neuropsychological assessment, human sexuality, cultural diversity, health economics, health administration, and other worthy topics in an already crowded curriculum? In addition, there are pressures to extend training in other ways. Should the internship be one or two years? Most states require two years of experience for licensure. Should not both of these be organized and accredited training experiences? Should the internship come before or after the awarding of the doctorate? Perhaps training programs should maintain quality control over the complete educational experience of their students, including the internship. Perhaps internships should be autonomous in their quality control. An argument can be made that, to parallel other mental health professions, we should award the academic degree and follow it with a residency. The economic consideration that a degree facilitates third-party reimbursement cannot be entirely ignored.

Is the length of training, both academic and internship, justified by the economics of the cost, job market, and income potential? Some believe we are overproducing psychologists. Increasingly clinical psychology faces competition from other mental health providers. Master's level providers are pouring in to the field, providing the same functions as clinical psychologists at lower cost. On the other hand, new markets seem to be opening to clinical psychologists. Health psychology has moved into virtually every medical specialty area. Clinical neuropsychology, sports psychology, the psychology of health promotion, forensic and correctional psychology, outcomes evaluation in managed care, etc., are new and expanding areas of clinical psychological practice. Will the new markets make demand equal to supply?

Psychology in the USA has never been able to solve the problem of multiple levels of training. The traditional position of the APA is that in the US, the doctorate is the entry level for independent practice and people trained at the master's level need supervision. This position has been asserted back to our earliest years, though the reality of education is that we have trained at multiple levels for practice. For the most part, the USA is alone in the doctoral level policy. In most countries of the world, the master's level is the entry practice level for psychology and the doctorate is a specialized teaching and research degree. Even our neighbor Canada seems to be recognizing master's level registration for practice in more of its provinces. Master's level practitioners are flooding the mental health job market under new titles such as "Professional Counselor," "Marriage and Family Therapist," "Substance Abuse Counselor," etc. We in psychology, and particularly in clinical psychology, are providing much of the training for master's level practice, but then we give away regulation and control to newly formed and newly defined disciplines with separate licensing boards and professional organizations. The problem has been recognized for decades and many recommendations have been made (e.g., some bold suggestions by the Vail Conference), but no official position on integrating the field seems to be attainable. Increasingly psychology is also training people at the bachelor's and even the AA level for positions in mental health, such as psychiatric technicians and case managers. No training model has appeared on our horizon to integrate our increasingly multiple levels of training.

How does training in clinical psychology fit into the increasingly large list of specialty and proficiency designations we see in psychology? Where do we fit *vis-à-vis* health psychology—is it a subset of clinical, a subspecialty, a neighbor specialty, or a number of specialties among which clinical is one? Do the traditional specialty designations continue to make sense? Do clinical and counseling psychology overlap more than they differ? How is the public served if we offer services to children under the labels child clinical psychologists, child psychologists, applied developmental psychologists, pediatric psychologists, family psychologists, school psychologists, and clinical school psychologists? Currently within APA, the Council for the Recognition of Specialties and Proficiencies in Professional Psychology is charged with sorting out this terminological mess. The Division of Clinical Psychology has asserted that clinical is a broad general practice specialty or a field, and other health service specialties may be tracks within and/or postdoctoral extensions of doctoral training in clinical psychology. Professional psychology must face this problem with a taxonomy that makes sense for training programs and for the public's ability to know who we are and what we do. Marking out the domains and boundaries of specialties would also help to define core curricula for the specialties.

A dramatic change is underway in our health delivery system in the USA. The industrialization of health care is an apt description for the reorganization of providers, the management of care, the imposition of guidelines, the review of utilization and quality, the measurement of outcomes in care delivery, and the other changes that are occurring daily. "Behavioral health" is being offered by large corporations on a capitated basis to a large number of industries, buying for large numbers of consumers. How is education in clinical psychology responding to these changes? We need to educate ourselves on the changes taking place. We need to train our students in the new systems of care delivery and offer practica in the new health care settings. Health care delivery is becoming more integrated into primary care settings with specialists on call for "one stop shopping." Mental health care is, therefore, returning to a more interdisciplinary practice, and we need to train our students to work in interprofessional settings on teams with a variety of professionals. We need to draw on our measurement skills to train students to implement new methods of outcomes assessment for our services and the services of others. We need to look at our intervention skill training and train students in the delivery of empirically effective methods in cost-efficient modalities. The Division of Clinical Psychology has initiated a project for identifying "Empirically Supported Treatments" (Task Force on the Promotion and Dissemination of Psychological Procedures, 1995). The project has been much debated (for example, a special series of articles is in press in the *Journal of Consulting and Clinical Psychology*), but was intended to call attention within psychology to the need to establish and present to various audiences an evidence base for our interventions. We need to move more of our interventions research out into the field to include evaluations of the effectiveness of treatment in actual care delivery settings. We should give more attention to studying different levels of intervention for problems of different severities. Prevention services should become more important in large-scale coordinated health care delivery systems.

Psychiatry has entered a new era of "medicalization" or "biological psychiatry." The "decade of the brain" has focused research on the biological substrata of behavior and behavior disorders. Psychology education is paralleling this trend. Our students need to be taught the basics of brain and nervous system structure, physiology, chemistry, and function. "Biological bases of behavior," as an element of our curriculum, takes on larger proportions in our core curriculum. Psychopharmacology is now recommended as a content area that should be included in all health service provider curricula in psychology.

A possible extension of this biological trend is the much debated (e.g., special feature of seven articles in the March, 1996 *American Psychologist*, Current Issues: Prescription Privileges) push for prescription privileges for psychologists. On the side favoring prescription privileges is the argument that psychologists should be able to provide full services to consumers and not have to rely on referals for medication. Psychologists may be better able to integrate pharmacotherapy into a psychological perspective and may choose more often not to medicate. Underserved populations may be better served if psychologists can expand their service options. Training seems to be feasible in a relatively short period of time. An increased market share for psychologists is also an important motivation for the move in this direction. On the side opposing prescription privileges for psychologists is the argument that training for prescription privileges fundamentally distorts the educational process away from our traditional expertise in behavior, affect, and cognition. Our traditional expertise is complementary to psychiatry's biological expertise as we have taken over preeminence in the field of psychotherapy. Why compete for pharmacotherapy where we will never have the equivalent basic and applied training to physicians? The debate is evolving in our journals and conventions and in our training programs. It will be resolved in the state legislatures.

The combining of science and practice in the education of clinical psychologists has been a central theme of the last 100 years. Today we recognize a broad spectrum of positions on the issue, with "scholar–practitioner" programs at one end and "clinical scientist" programs at the other. We like to boast that our training in science makes us distinct from other mental health professionals, but empirical demonstration of the difference is difficult. The best mix of science and practice in our training programs will depend on our goals, our preferences, and the evidence of our success. Hopefully our science will continue to inform our practice and help to resolve the many dilemmas we will face in our second century.

2.02.6 REFERENCES

Assembly of Scientist–Practitioner Psychologists & Department of Clinical and Health Psychology, University of Florida (1990). *The National Conference on Scientist-Practitioner Education and Training for the Professional Practice of Psychology*. Gainesville, FL: Author.

Belar, C. D., Bieliauskas, L. A., Larsen, K. G., Mensh, I. N., Poey, K., & Roehlke, H. J. (1987). *Proceedings of the national conference on internship training in psychology*. Baton Rouge, LA: Land & Land Printers.

Bickman, L. (1987). Proceedings of the National Conference on Graduate Education in Psychology, University of Utah, June 13–19, 1987 [special issue]. *American Psychologist*, *42*(12), 1041–1047.

Bourg, E. F., Bent, R. J., Callan, J. E., Jones, N. F., McHolland, J., & Stricker, G. (1987). *Standards and evaluation in the education and training of professional psychologists: Knowledge, attitudes, and skills*. Norman, OK: Transcript Press.

Callan, J. E., Peterson, D. R., & Stricker, G. (1986). *Quality in professional psychology training: National conference and self-study*. LaJolla, CA: National Council of Schools of Professional Psychology.

Education Directorate, American Psychological Association (1995). *Education and training beyond the doctoral degree: Proceedings of the American Psychological Association national conference on postdoctoral education and training in psychology*. Madison, CT: International Universities Press.

Fowler, R. D. (1996, August). *APA and clinical psychology: Past, present and future*. Invited address at the meeting of the American Psychological Association, Toronto, ON.

Greenberg, S., Smith, I. L., & Muenzen, P. M. (1995). *Study of the practice of licensed psychologists in the United States and Canada*. New York: Professional Examination Service.

Hoch, E. L., Ross, A. O., & Winder, C. L. (Eds.) (1966). *Professional preparation of clinical psychologists*. Washington, DC: American Psychological Association.

Hollingsworth, H. L. (1930). *Abnormal psychology*. New York: Ronald Press Company.

Korman, M. (1974). National conference on levels and patterns of professional training in psychology: The major themes. *American Psychologist*, *29*, 441–449.

Larsen, K. G., Belar, C. D., Bieliauskas, L. A., Klepac, R. K., Stigall, T. T., & Zimet, C. N. (1993). *Proceedings: National conference on postdoctoral training in professional psychology*. Baton Rouge, LA: Land & Land Printers.

Raimy, V. (1950). *Training in clinical psychology*. New York: Prentice Hall.

Reisman, J. M. (1991). *A history of clinical psychology* (2nd ed.). New York: Hemisphere Publications.

Report of the Committee on Training in Clinical Psychology of the American Psychological Association Submitted at the Detroit Meeting of the American Psychological Association, September 9–13 (1947). Recommended graduate training program in clinical psychology. *American Psychologist*, *2*, 539–558.

Roe, A. (Ed.) (1959). *Graduate education in psychology* (Report of the Conference on Graduate Education in Psychology sponsored by the Education and Training Board of APA, held at Miami Beach, FL, November 29—December 7, 1958). Washington, DC: American Psychological Association.

Routh, D. K. (1994). *Clinical psychology since 1917: Science, practice and organization*. New York: Plenum Press.

Shakow, D. (1969). *Clinical psychology as a science and profession: A 40-year odyssey*. Chicago, IL: Aldine Publishing.

Strother, C. R. (1956). *Psychology and mental health*. Washington, DC: American Psychological Association.

Task Force on the Promotion and Dissemination of Psychological Procedures (1995). Training in and dissemination of empirically-validated psychological treatments: Report and recommendations. *The Clinical Psychologist*, *48*, 3–23.

2.03
Internship Education and Training in Professional Psychology

SANFORD. L. PEDERSON
Wright State University, Dayton, OH, USA

2.03.1 INTRODUCTION

The internship is the final required formally organized training experience before the awarding of the doctoral degree. It is intended to be a clinical experience that is fully integrated with the doctoral program experience. It is the culmination of three to six years of postgraduate education, and is intended to be the time when all that has been learned is integrated into a new understanding and a new sophistication in clinical thinking and clinical skills.

The internship in clinical psychology has generally been considered the "capstone" of professional training. It is the training experience where the science and practice of psychology, and the learning that has occurred in both the classroom and the clinic, are integrated in an intensive and extensive experience that has as its goal the completion of the fully qualified clinical psychologist. The internship in clinical psychology is typically a full-time experience where the student provides a variety of psychological services under the supervision of a licensed psychologist during the final year of training prior to the awarding of the doctoral degree.

The idea of an "internship" is almost as old as clinical psychology itself. H. H. Goddard developed the first formal internship program at the Vineland Training School in 1908, only 12 years after Lightner Witmer opened his psychology clinic at the University of Pennsylvania in 1896. However, internship training as a formal part of training in clinical psychology did not begin for many years, when formal training programs in clinical psychology were first described (American Psychological Association [APA], 1945). The APA, through the leadership of David Shakow, began the development of criteria for internships in clinical psychology at the same time that it began developing criteria for doctoral programs in psychology (APA, 1947). The APA began formally accrediting independent internships in clinical psychology in 1955. Today there are over 500 internship programs in the USA and Canada (Hall & Cantrell, 1996).

It is generally accepted that the internship is a prerequisite for the professional practice of clinical psychology. The internship is that part of the training of the clinical psychologist where the professional identity is finalized and the new clinician begins to develop a stronger sense of career goals. Given the multitude of training and developmental tasks to be accomplished during the internship, one year is actually quite a brief period of time. In fact, many newer models suggest that an additional postdoctoral training year is either desirable or necessary (Belar et al., 1989; Larsen et al., 1993; Strother, 1956).

Internships have been developed in a wide variety of settings, ranging from the traditional VA hospital and medical school to the university counseling center and the community mental health center. There are even some unusual internships in places such as employee assistance programs. Many newly developing internships are consortia, with several different agencies, often of different types, banding together to pool resources to provide an internship where none of the agencies could do so individually. Consortia also have an advantage of providing a wide range of types of placements for interns, the opportunity to be exposed to a variety of clinical environments. However, consortia are sometimes difficult to coordinate, can suffer from an uneven quality of supervision, can lack a consistent training model and focus, provide fewer opportunities for interactions with other interns, and increase the possibility of an intern "getting lost" in a large system where the training director does not have routine weekly or more frequent contact with interns.

Blom (1995) developed a taxonomy of types of internship settings classified by the range of patients served, the continuum of care provided, and the variety of interventions offered. The first type he describes, class I—comprehensive care settings, serves a wide range of patients across a full continuum of care in a variety of contexts with a variety of interventions. These include veterans affairs medical centers, military medical centers, medical school teaching hospitals, large public and private multispecialty medical centers, and certain consortia that include the full range of types of care settings. The second type, class II—limited care settings, does not offer the full range of opportunities across the three dimensions used. These include psychiatric hospitals, comprehensive community mental health centers, private general hospitals, small public and private hospitals, and children's hospitals. The third type, class III—specialty care settings, focus on a particular class of patients or interventions. These include outpatient mental health clinics, head injury rehabilitation centers, substance abuse programs, and university counseling centers. This taxonomy can be useful when a program of study for an individual is being considered, in light of specific career goals.

While the one year full-time internship remains the most common internship experience, a number of alternative models have also been developed. As new models of doctoral education have been developed, some of the traditional internship concepts have been modified to meet the needs of changing doctoral training programs. Some of the forces that have driven the changes in internship models include the changing demographics of psychology doctoral students and the changing economics of graduate and professional training in psychology, training models that call for greater integration of the classroom and clinic throughout graduate training, and the continuing development of specialty areas in clinical psychology requiring specialized training beyond the internship. These forces have taken what was once a relatively unitary model of internship training and fractionated it into a multiplicity of models.

The half-time two-year internship has been considered an acceptable alternative to the one-year full-time internship since the APA began accrediting independent internships in 1955. It is often seen as a less desirable alternative selected only because of specific practical constraints, such as child care and other family issues, or the lack of availability of full-time internships in cases where students do not see themselves as having geographic mobility. The negative aspects of the half-time internship include the lack of a full-time immersion experience in clinical work, the inability to be present for half of the work of the multidisciplinary team, and the lesser degree of professional socialization and identification.

Additionally, many of the available (but not APA-accredited) half-time internships are without stipends. A wide range of groups and conferences have endorsed the concept that all interns should be compensated at a level appropriate to their training. Kohut and Cooney (1993) found that only 54% of part-time interns received stipends, while 98% of full-time interns received stipends.

In spite of these disadvantages, there is a continuing call for greater numbers of half-time internships in clinical psychology. This is likely due to the need for larger numbers of internship opportunities in specific geographic areas which allow the intern to have other responsibilities at the same time as the internship. However, for internship sites there are few advantages, and indeed a number of disadvantages, to offering half-time positions as opposed to full-time positions.

Some professional schools of psychology have adopted a model of two years of two-thirds time internship integrated with the final year of coursework and the dissertation (Dorken & Cummings, 1977). This model does allow for greater integration of classroom work and clinic work, but also suffers from many of the same disadvantages of the two-year half-time internship model.

Captive internships, internships that are only for students enrolled in a particular doctoral program and are integrated with that doctoral program, may take any of the forms described earlier. The advantages and disadvantages of captive internships have been extensively discussed in the literature. In summary, while the captive internship allows for a consistent educational philosophy and set of quality control standards (Abrams & Brabender, 1993), it also does not provide interns with exposure to other approaches and alternative role models (Fraser & Bent, 1994).

While the primary source of information about internships available in the USA and Canada is the *APPIC Directory* (Hall & Cantrell, 1996), there are a number of specialty listings also available. Cripe (1995) lists doctoral programs, internships, and postdoctoral fellowships in clinical neuropsychology, while Blanchard (1994) lists programs with significant research opportunities for clinical psychology interns. Other specialized societies also offer directories of internship opportunities in their specialty.

There is a wide variety of resources available to aid students in their search for an internship in clinical psychology. Megargee (1997) is currently the most comprehensive guide for the prospective intern, covering academic, practical, and strategic aspects of applying to, interviewing for, and obtaining an internship in clinical psychology. Another text is Levinger and Schefres (1995). Numerous journal articles have been written to advise the potential intern, such as Lopez, Oehlert, and Moberly (1996), Mellott, Arden, and Cho (1996), Plante (1996), and Stewart and Stewart (1996a, 1996b). Workshops are also frequently available at major psychological organization meetings, such as Pederson (1996).

2.03.2 CONCEPTUAL ORIGINS OF THE NEED FOR INTERNSHIP TRAINING

While internships in clinical psychology had existed for many years, the first clear articulation of the need for internship training as a routine part of professional preparation in clinical psychology was in the Report of the Subcommittee on Graduate Internship Training in Psychology (APA, 1945). This committee, chaired by David Shakow, described the characteristics of the clinical psychology intern and the clinical psychology internship program, as well as its relationship to the doctoral degree program.

Early in their report the committee observed that, "It is impossible to consider the problem of internships separately from the other aspects of preparation for clinical psychological practice" (p. 245). So from the earliest beginnings of formalized internship programs in clinical psychology, we see an emphasis on the integration of the work done in the classroom and laboratory with the work done in the clinic. This early model of the internship placed it in the third year of graduate education, after a one-year practicum experience in the second year, and prior to a return to the university to complete the dissertation, partake in cross-disciplinary seminars, and complete any additional needed courses. It should be noted that use of the term "residence appointment" referred to the expectation that the intern would live on the grounds of the internship institution. This was felt to be important, since

"It permits twenty-four hour residency in an atmosphere permeated with a psychology of a living kind and appears to have more potential for the maturation of the personality than almost any other experience ordinarily available to the psychologist" (p. 260). The report closes with a repeated discussion of the need for and ways in which the internship and the academic program be integrated, and some specific recommendations such as the establishment of a standardized internship certificate, and the development of standards for internship centers. It is of historical interest to note that this early report raised the question of whether the Ph.D. or the Psy.D. was the more appropriate degree for the clinical psychologist.

2.03.3 CONFERENCES ADDRESSING INTERNSHIP EDUCATION AND TRAINING

While many conferences have been held that examined the education and training of the clinical psychologist, not all have focused clearly on issues of internship training. The conferences at Chicago (Hoch, Ross, & Winder, 1966), Vail (Korman, 1976), and Utah (Bickman & Ellis, 1990) have focused primarily on issues of curriculum and design of the doctoral degree program, with relatively less emphasis on the internship aspect of clinical psychology education and training. A brief review of those conferences having a significant focus on internship training in clinical psychology follows.

2.03.3.1 Boulder

Much of what may be considered the traditional model of internship training originated at the Boulder Conference. The conference held at Boulder in 1949 (Raimy, 1950) was the first time that a large group of psychologists formally gathered together to answer questions about how clinical psychologists should be trained. The growing need for mental health services, particularly that prompted by the return of soldiers and sailors from World War II, prompted the USA Veterans Administration and the APA to begin to develop formal models for the education and training of clinical psychologists.

The internship was originally conceptualized as a predoctoral experience where the intern was immersed in the activities of a clinical service setting for a full year. It was intended to differ from a clerkship or practicum in several ways. First and foremost, it was a full-time year-long immersion in clinical service activities. It would take place in a multidisciplinary setting, and would be at a training site that was not a part of the student's doctoral degree program. It would be focused on the development of the skill necessary for semi-independent practice through a gradual increase in responsibility and case management. Finally, the internship was intended to be a socialization in the values of the professional practice of clinical psychology.

The traditional model of internship training, as an integral part of the Boulder model of doctoral education, consists of full-time students in a program with primarily full-time faculty. In the Boulder plan, the internship was to be taken in the third year of study, with the student returning to the university in the fourth year to complete the dissertation. This aspect, the third-year internship, has changed over time to where most internships are taken in the fourth or fifth year of graduate study, frequently after dissertation data have at least been collected (Davies, 1987).

The Boulder conference strongly expressed the opinion that science and practice should be integrated throughout the curriculum, and that the academic experience and the internship experience also be closely integrated with each other. It was one of the first of many (frequently unheeded) calls for close working relationship between academic departments and internship agencies.

2.03.3.2 Stanford

The Boulder Conference recommended a follow-up conference be held in five years. In 1955, delegates representing 37 universities and 14 field training agencies met at Stanford University (Strother, 1956). While the focus was less on specific recommendations than the Boulder Conference, the Stanford Conference did call for a four-year academic program followed by a two-year postdoctoral internship. There was also a recommendation that universities and field training agencies provide joint appointments for faculty and staff, so as to enhance integration of the science and practice of clinical psychology. While the structural changes recommended by the Stanford Conference were generally unheeded, there has been movement toward some types of joint appointments in close relationships between universities and field training agencies, including internship agencies.

2.03.3.3 Miami

While the conference held in Miami in 1958 (Roe, Gustad, Moore, Ross, & Skodad, 1959) was concerned with graduate education in psychology in general, not just in clinical, it nonetheless had some specific concerns about the internship in clinical psychology. It was at this conference that some of the earliest conflicts between internship agencies and academic programs began to arise, in addition to an articulation of the frustration involved in attempting to have the internship serve a true integrative function. This concern over integration of science and practice, which the early models suggested was so important, is a theme which can be seen to have continued in a variety of forms to the present day.

2.03.3.4 Gainesville

The internship plays a critical role in the education and training of clinical psychologists. Yet, as a separate educational experience, it has received relatively little attention until the past 10–15 years. While more general conferences on the education and training of clinical psychologists all affirmed the need for an internship that was in some fashion (usually unspecified) integrated with coursework and practicum experiences, it was not until 1987 that there was a national conference devoted exclusively to considering the internship in professional psychology.

The Association of Psychology Postdoctoral and Internship Centers (APPIC) convened a conference in Gainesville, Florida, in 1987 to explore the purpose of the internship and develop models for quality internship training (Belar et al., 1989). To date, this is the only national conference to focus exclusively on internship training. Forty-eight invited delegates representing the full range of internship settings met for four days to consider a number of questions, including (i) the purpose of the internship, (ii) which psychologists need an internship, (iii) when an internship should occur, (iv), the core requirements of internship, (v), the ideal characteristics on an internship program, and (vi) outcome criteria for evaluating internship training programs.

The delegates to this conference articulated a model of internship as a two-year experience, one year predoctoral and one year postdoctoral. The predoctoral year was described as the generalist training year, with the postdoctoral year where specialty training might begin. This more closely approximates the model used in training physicians, one generalist year followed by specialty training. The two-year model is also consistent with most state and provincial licensing requirements (Association of State and Provincial Psychology Boards, ASPPB, 1996). In this, the two-year internship was seen as having the goal of producing an autonomous professional. In many ways, the Gainesville Conference can be seen as setting the stage for the later APPIC-sponsored Ann Arbor Conference on Postdoctoral Training in Professional Psychology.

The Gainesville Conference, while not explicitly affirming the Boulder model of doctoral education, is best seen as a continuation of the development of the traditional internship model. The Gainesville Conference concluded that the internship should occur after completion of all academic program requirements, including the dissertation.

The Gainesville Conference also affirmed that all interns should be paid a stipend, repeated the call for close and cooperative working relationships between the academic department and the internship agency, and agreed upon a core set of experiences for the predoctoral internship year: (i) a variety of methods of assessment and diagnosis; (ii) a variety of interventions/treatments across a variety of problems and diverse populations; (iii) experience with culturally and ethnically diverse populations, but not limited to delivery of direct services; (iv) research and its practical applications; (v) application of empirical skill and critical thinking to professional practice; (vi) professional, legal, and ethical issues; and (vii) introduction to supervision and management of psychological services.

2.03.3.5 Ann Arbor

While focusing particularly on postdoctoral education and training, in many ways the Ann Arbor Conference (Larsen et al., 1993) can be seen as a logical extension of the Gainesville internship conference. Not only were both conferences primary sponsored by APPIC, but the articulation at Ann Arbor of the need for postdoctoral training for all psychologists, not just those choosing a recognized specialty, is the logical extension of the Gainesville two-year internship model.

Both the Gainesville and Ann Arbor conferences clearly stated that all internship training should occur in sites accredited by the APA and/or the Canadian Psychological Association. The delegates to both Gainesville and Ann Arbor (there was considerable overlap of delegates between the two conferences) clearly felt that all training in professional psychology should take place within the context of programs that had the commitment to quality education and training to submit their programs as candidates for accreditation by the appropriate body. The statement that completion of an accredited internship should be a prerequisite for accredited postdoctoral training was an outgrowth of that philosophy.

2.03.3.6 Orlando

In 1997, APPIC and APA jointly prepared a major national conference to examine issues of supply and demand throughout the professional lifespan of psychologists. What follows is a summary of the reasons for this conference and the plans for its execution, drawn from Pederson (1997).

It has been becoming increasingly clear that there are larger numbers of students seeking professional psychology internships than there are available internship positions. While the number of professional psychology internship positions continues to grow, the number of students seeking internships appears to be increasing even more rapidly. In the late 1990s there is no reason to expect a reversal of this trend to occur soon.

The positive employment outlook for new doctorates in professional psychology has waned. Other areas of psychology have been suffering similar shrinkage in traditional employment for some time. While reliable data sources often lag somewhat behind the rapid change of current events, a multitude of anecdotal and trend evidence suggests that the new doctoral psychologist has a more difficult time finding employment than was previously so, and that salaries are decreasing. In some areas this shrinkage has been dramatic.

There have been numerous efforts to examine parts of the changing practice marketplace picture, such as the APA Presidential Task Force on Training for Managed Care Settings, the APA Division 42 project on Training and Education for Work with Managed Care, the work on Managed Care and Training currently being done by the Center for Mental Health Services, and the APA Board of Educational Affairs Task Force in Education and Training in Professional Psychology. There have been, of course, numerous conferences on training models for doctoral education, internship training, and postdoctoral training and education, such as the Boulder, Vail, Gainesville, Ann Arbor, and Norman Conferences, to name only a few. However, the work of all these separate groups needs to be brought together and placed in the context of other, broader questions, to take a comprehensive and future-oriented look at where psychology is going as a discipline and as a profession.

Psychology continues to be the most popular undergraduate major. This trend will probably continue to increase. This means even greater numbers of students seeking admission to doctoral training programs in professional psychology. We are seeing ever-increasing numbers of new professional psychology doctoral programs opening in an effort to fill this market demand for training in professional psychology. This, too, is likely to continue.

As the size of government at all levels continues to decrease, the amount of public money dedicated to psychology will continue to dwindle. This decrease has been and will continue to be seen in education, research, and professional services, indeed for the entire discipline of psychology, not just for professional psychology and not just for those involved in the education and training of professional psychologists. The effects are being felt first in the education and training community and in the practice community, but those effects are, and will continue to effect, the entire career span of psychologists. Even if we could somehow magically create enough internships for all those seeking them today, we would still have a shortfall as the number of students in training continues to increase. If that increase is continually met, we will soon be overpopulated with psychologists who are competing not only with each other but with the larger and ever increasing numbers of master's level practitioners in a variety of disciplines, including our own.

We are entering a crucial phase in the development of psychology as a discipline and as a profession. Psychology as a discipline is less than 150 years old, and just 100 years old as a profession. We are now seeing the ending of the first major expansion of the discipline and profession that occurred in concert with a wide gamut of social changes following World War II. Before psychology collapses under its own weight, we must take a critical look at where we are going, and what changes need to be made. Models of education and training, models of scientific employment, and models of practice that have served the field so well are beginning to no longer serve the needs either of psychology or of society effectively. We can continue to allow the situation to develop in a fashion that is controlled by forces largely external to psychology, or we can have a hand in determining our own destiny.

As market forces drive more and more of the discipline and profession of psychology, we must look at what we are doing educationally to prepare the next generation of psychologists for the twenty-first century and beyond. The demand for training is increasing while the competition to provide services of all kinds is also increasing. Steps must be taken to correct the many imbalances of supply and demand that exist throughout the career span of the psychologist, before these many imbalances overwhelm us.

Clearly, the answers to these questions cannot be developed in a single conference. In fact, it is unlikely that even all the necessary questions can be formulated at a single conference. Rather, this conference should be seen as an initial stage in a process with which we may be occupied for many years. While the many training conferences that have been held have looked at training models as they "should be," we must begin to look at training and employment as they are driven by a market economy.

Approximately 50 delegates representing 17 national psychology organizations from the USA and Canada and 50 delegates at-large convened in Orlando, Florida, on November 12–16, 1997. The delegates developed answers to a set of questions concerning what psychology's response should be to the changing nature of clinical psychological practice, with the increasing influence of economic and marketing factors. The questions fall into four basic groups, those concerned with entry into professional training and the early preparation of the professional psychologist, those concerned with the transition to internship, those concerned with the early career experiences, and those concerned with later career and exit issues. The responses to these questions included a thorough response, concrete and specific recommendations, and a plan for implementation which will include a time frame, recommended responsible parties, and challenges to implementation. It is hoped that this structure will provide an answer to the problem observed by Laughlin and Worley (1991) that many psychology conferences take place and offer visionary solutions, but those solutions are infrequently actually implemented. The full conference proceedings will be published in 1998.

2.03.4 RESEARCH ON INTERNSHIP EDUCATION AND TRAINING IN CLINICAL PSYCHOLOGY IN THE LATE 1990s

Stedman (in press) provides an excellent review of the literature to date on internship training in clinical psychology. Stedman divided the current literature into several categories:

> The Gainesville Conference, general characteristics of internship programs, interns preparation for internship, intern selection process, supervision of interns, evaluation of interns, management of impaired interns, reflections of interns on their internship experience, and finally, consideration of the internship director. (p. 3)

Much of the work reviewed by Stedman is either of a purely theoretical nature, or of restricted applicability to a particular setting or type of setting. Stedman calls for more empirical research on the nature of internship training, the numbers of students and sites, and alternative models of internship training.

While there has always been generalized agreement within the clinical psychology training community about the need for an internship, the term is surprisingly absent from most state and provincial licensing laws. Only 10 states (no Canadian provinces) make reference to an "internship" requirement. While all such laws require "supervised experience," most do not require an "internship" (ASPPB, 1996). There is a clear difference between these two types of experiences, although it may be a difficult distinction for lawmakers to grasp. That distinction is that an internship is a planned programmatic series of clinical and classroom experiences under supervision that is designed to develop the skills and abilities of the individual intern, whereas supervised experience is just that, experience that is supervised, without the planned, programmatic, or didactic aspects of an internship program.

2.03.5 FOUNDING AND DEVELOPMENT OF THE ASSOCIATION OF PSYCHOLOGY POSTDOCTORAL AND INTERNSHIP CENTERS

In 1968, a group of medical school psychologists consisting of Elton Ash, Ronald Fox, David Kemp, Robert Martin, and Arthur Wiens met to form what was then called the Association of Psychology Internship Centers (APIC). APIC was initially developed to attempt to bring some order to the chaotic way in which students and internships were matched to each other. The first set of "rules" was developed to begin to provide common dates of notification and negotiation.

In 1972 APIC published its first *Directory* of internship programs, listing 90 programs (Fox, 1972). Growth was rapid. By the 5th Edition of the *Directory* there were 261 programs listed. In 1989 APIC was the first national organization to develop standards for postdoctoral programs in professional psychology. In 1991, APIC changed its name to APPIC (Association of Psychology Postdoctoral and Internship Centers) to reflect its growing involvement in postdoctoral training. Today there are 534 internship programs and 77 postdoctoral programs who are members of APPIC and listed in the *APPIC Directory* (Hall & Cantrell, 1996).

It is generally accepted that APPIC Membership Criteria (see Section 2.03.5.1) define what is (and therefore what is not) an internship in psychology. It can therefore be fairly stated that the *APPIC Directory* lists almost all legitimate internship programs in clinical psychology. Note that there exist one or two APA-accredited doctoral programs that include captive internship programs meeting APPIC membership criteria that are not actually members of APPIC.

Probably the most influential and controversial aspect of APPIC policy has been the Uniform Notification Day Policies (formally known as "Policies on Offers and Acceptances"). It is this procedure that has governed the matching of intern applicants and intern positions in the USA and Canada since the mid-1970s.

Simply stated, the policies state that internships may not offer internship positions nor request, accept, or use information from applicants about their relative rankings of internship sites until the second Monday in February (Uniform Notification Day, UND). As currently construed, UND lasts for four hours, from 9 a.m. Central Time to 1 p.m. Central Time. This latest iteration is one of a string of policy changes shortening the time from its original week, down to one and a half days for many years, now to one-half day. Of course the advent of computer matching of applicants and internships may reduce this time to a few nanoseconds.

In 1986 APIC began the development of a body to enforce its policies, and the APPIC Standards and Review Committee was born. Since this time, APPIC has issued numerous private sanctions, and has publicly censured and placed on probation three of its member programs for violation of its Policy on Offers and Acceptances. Increasingly as the number of applicants has continued to outstrip the number of available positions, there have been increasing informal complaints of widespread violations of APPIC policy. The bulk of the reputed violations concern the APPIC policy that states that internship sites may not ask applicants where the internship site ranks for them, the so-called "first choice" issue. In spite of the increase in informal secondhand, thirdhand (and more remote) complaints, the number of complaints actually filed with the APPIC Standards and Review Committee has decreased. Some attribute this to a fear of later retaliation against either the student or the student's doctoral program, whether real or only feared.

Since the mid-1980s, APPIC has increasingly moved toward a much more active advocacy role. APPIC is now seen as the organization that speaks to the interests of and standards for experiential professional psychology education and training at both the doctoral and postdoctoral levels. It has addressed issues of internship funding, the critical importance of the internship in the preparation of clinical psychologists, and is beginning to address broad issues of supply and demand not only for training in clinical psychology but also markets for psychological services. Many of the future directions discussed later in this chapter are arising out of specific APPIC initiatives. A more complete history of APPIC may be found in Stedman (1989) and Pederson (1993a).

2.03.5.1 APPIC Membership Criteria

These membership criteria for doctoral psychology internship programs were revised in 1994; internships that are accredited by the APA or the Canadian Psychological Association are recognized as meeting APPIC doctoral membership criteria. All others must meet all of the following criteria (i.e., 1 through 14 below) and are reviewed for adherence to the criteria every three years.

1. A psychology internship is an organized training program that, in contrast to supervised experience or on-the-job training, is designed to provide the intern with a planned, programmed sequence of training experiences. The primary focus and purpose is assuring breadth and quality of training.
2. The internship agency has a clearly designated doctoral level staff psychologist who is responsible for the integrity and quality of the training program, actively licensed (certified or registered) by the State Board of Examiners in the jurisdiction where the program exists, and present at the training facility a minimum of 20 hours a week.
3. The internship training agency staff consists of at least two full time equivalent doctoral level psychologists who serve as primary supervisors, who are actively licensed (certified or registered) by the State Board of Examiners in the jurisdiction where the program exists.
4. Intern supervision is provided by staff members of the internship agency or by qualified affiliates of that agency who carry clinical responsibility for the cases being supervised. At least two hours per week of regularly scheduled individual supervision are provided by one or more doctoral level licensed psychologists (regardless of whether the internship is completed in one year or two). Supervision is provided with the specific intent of dealing with psychological services rendered directly by the intern.
5. The internship provides training in a range of psychological assessment and intervention activities conducted directly with the recipients of psychological services.
6. At least 25% of the trainee's time is in face-to-face psychological services to patients/clients.

7. The internship must provide at least two hours per week in didactic activities such as case conferences, seminars, inservice training, or grand rounds.

8. Internship training is at post-clerkship, post-practicum, and post-externship level, and precedes the granting of the doctoral degree.

9. The internship agency has a minimum of two full time equivalent interns at the internship level of training during any period of training. These interns must be on site and in training at the time of initial application for APPIC membership.

10. The internship level psychology trainees have a title such as "Intern," "Resident," "Fellow," or other designation of trainee status.

11. The internship agency has a written statement or brochure which provides a clear description of the nature of the training program, including the goals and content of the internship and clear expectations for quantity and quality of the trainee's work, and is made available to prospective interns.

12. Internship programs have documented due process procedures for interns which are given to interns at the beginning of the training period.

13. The internship experience (minimum 1500 hours) must be completed in no less than nine months and no more than 24 months.

14. APPIC member programs are required to issue a certificate of internship completion which includes the word "Psychology" to all interns who have successfully completed the program.

(*APPIC Membership Criteria*. Copyright 1996, Association of Psychology Postdoctoral and Internship Centers. Reprinted with permission.)

2.03.6 DATA ON NUMBERS OF PROGRAMS AND INTERNS IN THE USA AND CANADA IN 1997

There were, during the 1996–1997 training year, a total of 534 agencies providing 2431 full-time internship positions in APPIC-member programs. Of these, 411 agencies were accredited by either the APA or Canadian Psychological Association, and those agencies provided 2070 full-time positions. There were an additional 65 half-time and 76 unpaid positions at these agencies, making a total of 2572 positions available in the USA and Canada (Hall & Cantrell, 1996). The number of internship positions has been rising or held steady for the past eight years (Pederson, 1995).

One major problem is that there is no data source in 1997 on the total number of students enrolled in doctoral programs in clinical, counseling, and school psychology in the USA and Canada. While there is some suggestion that the number of graduate students seeking internships has begun to outpace the growth in the number of internship positions, the magnitude of the problem is unknown (Pederson, 1995, 1997). As the data suggesting that the imbalance between the number of internship positions and the number of students increases, there is an increasing call for some national action on this issue (Pederson, 1997).

2.03.7 CONTINUING ISSUES UNDER DISCUSSION

2.03.7.1 Prerequisites for Internship Appointment

Prior to 1993, there was much confusion in the field of clinical psychology as to what constituted a "practicum hour." Building on the work of several other groups and with the cooperation of the Council of Chairs of Training Councils, APPIC published the first uniform definition of a practicum hour and a standard form on which to report those hours. The definition essentially revolves around the clock hour as the basic unit, and the separation of direct, face-to-face provision of services from indirect service and other training activities. It also defines practicum hours as those receiving academic credit, not work experience prior to or concurrent with doctoral training in clinical psychology.

There remains no universal agreement on the ideal number of practicum hours; statements of 400–2000 hours have been heard in various quarters. Normative data on the actual numbers of practicum hours obtained by clinical psychology graduate students prior to internship is conspicuously lacking.

Given the tremendous diversity of internship settings, it is highly unlikely that any additional standardization of prerequisites for internship will occur at any time soon. Some sites require completion of two years of graduate study, some require three years, some require a completed dissertation, some require a completed dissertation proposal. Some internship sites may require preparation in specific assessment and intervention techniques, while others may be much more flexible.

2.03.7.2 Uniform Requirement and Uniform Applications

For many years graduate students and graduate degree programs have been asking that the process of applying to internships be simplified, in particular by a uniform application form. APPIC began studying the possible adoption of a uniform application in 1991. The US Department of Veterans Affairs (VA), began such a project in 1994 for use by its internship programs. APPIC built upon the initial structure of the VA application and developed an APPIC Uniform Internship Application in 1997. Use of this application is restricted to APPIC-member internships, and its use is optional for APPIC members. The APPIC Uniform Internship Application is available from the APPIC World Wide Web Site at http://www.appic.org.

2.03.7.3 Uniform Notification Day and Computer Matching

Since its inception in the early 1970s, the APPIC Uniform Notification Day for Internship Offers and Acceptances has been controversial. A variety of different methods and different amounts of time have been used, with full satisfaction of all parties concerned still an elusive goal. Stedman (1989) provides a historical review of these various procedures and their outcomes.

Computerized matching of internships and interns has been considered since the 1970s (Pederson, 1993b). The first APPIC vote on computer matching was on the proposal of Briggs (1984), which was defeated. Later, Pederson and Blom (1988) presented another proposal, this time with a somewhat different matching algorithm which allowed for greater flexibility on the part of internship sites in ranking their choices. In 1989–1990, APPIC conducted the Pilot Study of a Computerized Internship Matching Program (Zimet, Blom, Pederson, & Klepac, 1991). Due to the voluntary nature of participation in the Pilot Study, a complete data set was not obtained, which led to many positions and applicants for whom matches could not be determined. Due to the state-of-the-art of computer systems at the time, and the volunteer staffing of the project, there were also a variety of procedural difficulties. This system was also rejected in voting by the APPIC membership.

More recently, APPIC surveys have suggested that a majority of internship directors now favor a computerized matching system, and the APPIC Board of Directors has appointed a committee to obtain proposals for a professional operated system based on the algorithm of Pederson and Blom (1988) to present to the membership for a vote as early as 1998. Although funding of the project remains an important issue, it is anticipated that a computerized matching system will likely be in place and in operation by 2000 at the latest.

2.03.8 FUNDING FOR INTERNSHIP EDUCATION AND TRAINING

2.03.8.1 Present and Future Prospects

Funding for internship programs in clinical psychology has traditionally come from one type or another of government funding either directly or indirectly. Indeed, the earliest formal paid internships in clinical psychology were offered by the US Veterans Administration, which played a key role in the development of standards for clinical psychology education and training (Laughlin & Worley, 1991). A variety of other federal, state, and local government agencies have housed many internship programs. As the size of government in the USA continues to decrease at all levels, this pattern is rapidly changing. Clinical psychology internship training is being caught in the industrialization of health care, and beginning to suffer as a result.

Many long-established government funded internship programs have closed entirely, some due to the closing of their host institutions. More privately funded internships are opening, but these are often under strong pressure to demonstrate their cost-effectiveness. As many managed care companies are beginning to refuse to pay for services provided by nonlicensed personnel, psychology internship programs are seeing a significant decrease in revenue in many locales. This has led to a variety of possible systemic strategies on the part of the training community, including the possibility of seeking changes in state and provincial licensing laws to provide for a limited licensure for interns. Some believe that this would be an easier process if the internship were to occur after receipt of the doctoral degree. Others fear that moving the internship to the postdoctoral year without a simultaneous change in licensing laws requiring an internship would lead to most psychologists not obtaining this additional training if it was not required by either doctoral programs or licensing laws.

2.03.9 FUTURE DIRECTIONS

While much of the future of clinical psychology internship training may well be established at the November 1997 Orlando conference, there are a number of directions upon which it is safe to speculate. Let us begin with a few relatively obvious ones. The managed care movement will continue to grow in both size and influence. The days of one-person private practice will be over, and almost all psychologists will be employed by some kind of company or agency. Some of these companies may be larger group partnerships, but the cottage industry days will be far behind. The impact of this on training will be slight at first, but will grow larger as financial issues begin to outweigh clinical concerns. Training directors will be forced to ever-increasing efforts to show how their internships and postdoctoral programs are cost-effective for the organization. Many programs will close when they are unable to convince their business-oriented companies that training pays off financially. Public sector training such as VA, state, and county hospitals will become even more financially pressed, and downsizing will continue. Postdoctoral training will expand to provide specialty training to fill niche markets. Specialization will also begin to occur earlier and earlier in the training sequence, as we are already seeing in some fields such as health psychology and neuropsychology.

Short-term and highly marketable treatment programs focused on acute problems will predominate in both practice and training. Training programs without training in several of these types of marketable skills will be hard-pressed to recruit quality interns unless they are research-based programs training faculty rather than practitioners. Marketable will not necessarily imply empirically validated effectiveness, but rather documented "customer satisfaction." This will force clinical psychologists, in their training and practice, to attend more to what patients *say* they want rather than what we think they need.

The impact of technology, of distance learning, and telehealth is difficult to estimate at this time. While distance learning is growing, there is a good deal of informal discussion about its appropriateness for clinical training. The increasing focus on serving the needs of rural populations may foster greater development of psychological service delivery via telecommunications, and hence the supervision of psychological services and the training of clinical psychologists via telecommunications.

One thing that will not change, and probably never will, is the human interaction between student and teacher. Since ancient times when a school was a log with a teacher at one end and a student at the other, the importance of the relationship between those with knowledge to share and those seeking that knowledge has thankfully remained little changed.

2.03.10 SUMMARY

Internship training in clinical psychology is defined and discussed, and the history and conceptual origins of the need for internship training in clinical psychology are explored. The major conferences devoted in whole or part to questions of internship training are reviewed, including a conference to be held in 1997 that may well have a major impact on the future of internship training in clinical psychology. The relevant literature is reviewed, and it is noted that there are many critical areas where empirical data is lacking. The history of the APPIC is presented, as are the APPIC membership criteria and data on the current numbers of interns and internship positions in the USA and Canada. Several current issues are explored, including the development by APPIC of a standardized internship application, and the possible adoption of a computerized internship matching system. The current and future funding of internship training in clinical psychology is discussed. Finally, possible future directions and issues in internship training are examined.

2.03.11 REFERENCES

Abrams, J. C., & Brabender, V. (1993, January). *A captive-consortium internship model in a Psy.D. program.* Paper presented at the Conference of the National Association of Schools of Professional Psychology, La Jolla, CA.

American Psychological Association (1945). Subcommittee report on graduate internship training in psychology. *Journal of Consulting Psychology, 9,* 243–266.

American Psychological Association (1947). Recommended graduate training program in clinical psychology. *American Psychologist, 2,* 539–558.

Association of State and Provincial Psychology Boards (1996). *Handbook of licensing and certification requirements for psychologists in North America.* Montgomery, AL: Author.

Belar, C. D., Bieliauskas, L. A., Larsen, K. G., Mensh, I. N., Poey, K., & Roehlke, H. J. (Eds.) (1989). *Proceedings of the National Conference on Internship Training in Psychology.* Washington, DC: Association of Psychology Internship Centers.

Bickman, L., & Ellis, H. (Eds.) (1990). *Preparing psychologists for the 21st century.* Proceedings of the National Conference on Graduate Education in Psychology. Hillsdale, NJ: Erlbaum.

Blanchard, J. J. (1994). *Directory of research opportunities for clinical psychology interns.* Albuquerque, NM: Society for a Science of Clinical Psychology.

Blom, B. E. (1995). Internship Settings. In G. K. Zammit & J. W. Hull (Eds.), *Guidebook for clinical psychology interns* (pp. 27–52). New York: Plenum.

Briggs, D. (1984) Proposal for a centralized computer internship matching system. *APIC Newsletter, 9,* 11–15.

Cripe, L. (1995). Listing of training programs in clinical neuropsychology. *The Clinical Neuropsychologist, 9,* 327–398.

Davies, R. M. (1987). Demise of the third year internship: The changing role of the internship in graduate training. *Professional Psychology: Research & Practice, 18,* 481–484.

Dorken, H., & Cummings, N. A. (1977). A school of psychology as innovation in professional education: The California School of Professional Psychology. *Professional Psychology, 8,* 129–148.

Fox, R. (1972). *Directory of internship programs in psychology.* Los Angeles: Association of Psychology Internship Centers.

Fraser, J. S., & Bent, R. J. (1994, January). *Reshaping predoctoral internships in the age of professional school training.* Paper presented at the Conference of the National Council of Schools of Professional Psychology, La Jolla, CA.

Hall, R. G., & Cantrell, P. J. (1996). *APPIC directory: Internship and postdoctoral programs in professional psychology* (25th ed.). Washington, DC: Association of Psychology Postdoctoral and Internship Centers.

Hoch, E. L., Ross, A. O., & Winder, C. L. (Eds.) (1969). *Professional preparation of clinical psychologists.* Washington, DC: American Psychological Association.

Kohut, J., & Cooney, B. (1993). *Internship data.* Paper presented at the Conference of the National Council of Schools of Professional Psychology, New Orleans, LA.

Korman, M. (1976). *Levels and patterns of professional training in psychology.* Washington, DC: American Psychological Association.

Larsen, K. G., Belar, C. D., Bieliauskas, L. A., Klepac, R. K., Stigall, T. T., & Zimet, C. N. (1993). *Proceedings of the National Conference on Postdoctoral Training in Professional Psychology.* Washington, DC: Association of Psychology Postdoctoral and Internship Centers.

Laughlin, P. R., & Worley, J. L. (1991). Roles of the American Psychological Association and the Veterans Administration in the development of internships in psychology. *American Psychologist, 46,* 430–436.

Levinger, C., & Schefres, I. (1995). *Everything you need to know to get a psychology internship.* Los Angeles: Internship Publishers.

Lopez, S. J., Oehlert, M. E., & Moberly, R. L. (1996). Selection criteria for American Psychological Association-Accredited internship programs: A survey of training directors. *Professional Psychology: Research and Practice, 27,* 518–520.

Megargee, E. I. (1997) *Megargee's guide to obtaining a psychology internship* (3rd ed.) Muncie, IN: Accelerated Development.

Mellott, R. N., Arden, I. A., & Cho, M. E. (1996). Preparing for the internship: Tips for the prospective applicant. *Professional Psychology: Research and Practice, 27,* 190–196.

Pederson, S. L. (Ed.) (1993a). 25th Anniversary Special Issue (Special Issue). *APPIC Newsletter, 19*(1).

Pederson, S. L. (1993b). The history of computerized internship matching in APPIC. *APPIC Newsletter, 19,* 56–58.

Pederson, S. L. (1995). *Supply and demand for internships in professional psychology: A preliminary report.* Unpublished manuscript prepared for the Council of Chairs of Training Councils.

Pederson, S. L. (1996, August). Overview of the internship application, interviewing, and selection process. In S. L. Pederson (Chair), *Applying and interviewing for professional psychology internships.* Symposium conducted at the meeting of the American Psychological Association, Toronto, Ontario, Canada.

Pederson, S. L. (1997). Supply and demand: Training and employment opportunities in professional psychology. *APPIC Newsletter, 22*(5), 25–27.

Pederson, S. L., & Blom, B. E. (1988). A proposal for a computerized APIC National Intern Matching Program. *APIC Newsletter, 13,* 53–64.

Plante, T. G. (1996). Ten principles of success for psychology trainees embarking on their careers. *Professional Psychology: Research and Practice, 27,* 304–307.

Raimy, V. C. (Ed.) (1950). *Training in clinical psychology.* New York: Prentice-Hall

Roe, A., Gustad, J. W., Moore, B. V., Ross, S., & Skodak, M. (Eds.) (1959). *Graduate education in psychology.* Washington, DC: American Psychological Association.

Stedman, J. M. (1989). The history of the APIC selection process. *APIC Newsletter, 14,* 35–43.

Stedman, J. M. (in press). What we know about predoctoral internship training: A review. *Professional Psychology: Research and Practice.*

Stewart, A. E., & Stewart, E. A. (1996a). Personal and practical considerations in selecting a psychology internship. *Professional Psychology: Research and Practice, 27,* 295–303.

Stewart, A. E., & Stewart, E. A. (1996b). A decision-making technique for choosing a psychology internship. *Professional Psychology: Research and Practice, 27,* 521–526.

Strother, C. R. (1956) *Psychology and mental health.* Washington, DC: American Psychological Association.

Zimet, C. Z., Blom, B. E., Pederson, S. L., & Klepac, R. K. (1990). *The Results of the APIC Pilot Study of the Computerized Internship Matching Program.* Symposium conducted at the meeting of the American Psychological Association, Boston.

2.04
Postdoctoral Education and Training in Clinical Psychology

KERRY de S. HAMSHER
Neuropsychology Clinic, Milwaukie, WI, USA

2.04.1 INTRODUCTION

In its broadest definition, postdoctoral education and training in clinical psychology can refer to all education and training beyond the doctoral degree. This was, in fact, the theme of a national conference convened in 1994, to develop a broad scope of issues related to postgraduate education and training for the discipline of psychology in the twenty-first century (American Psychological Association [APA], 1995). Delegates to the conference focused on six general issues: (i) models for education and training beyond the doctoral degree; (ii) societal needs, changing demographics, and national policies; (iii) expanding knowledge and skills base; (iv) impact of changing technology; (v) evaluation and lifelong learning; and (vi) funding.

2.04.1.1 Models for Education and Training Beyond the Doctoral Degree

The following types of postdoctoral education and training were presented as an initial concept for consideration:

(i) *Formal organized program.* These programs are comprised of specific goals, specified duration of training, specified methods, and have stated criteria for evaluation.

(ii) *Individualized mentorship program.* This program, also known as the apprenticeship model, is one in which the postdoctoral trainee works for one to three years under the direction of an active, established psychologist (mentor) in an adequate learning environment and carries out an organized program of a focused nature. Such mentorships are typically found in research and occasionally in practice and teaching programs.

(iii) *Individualized supervision program.* In this program the emphasis is on individualized supervision of the trainee. It is often used to provide advanced training in a given area of practice such as interpersonal therapy. Individual supervision is required; reading and/or didactic course work may be required and training may be for one or two years. A second type of individual supervision of the trainee's experience by a licensed psychologist may be required for state licensure purposes.

(iv) *Sabbatical/paid leave*. This is institution-sponsored faculty development time, usually involving a range of educational activities designed and proposed by the recipient and ranging from one or two months to one year.

(v) *Continuing education*. Continuing education is the hallmark of lifelong learning. It provides the opportunity for updating the psychologist's knowledge in a given area and expanding it in light of new knowledge derived from other sources (e.g., other disciplines). It can be both formal and informal.

(vi) *Faculty/staff development, peer consultation, and self-study*. This is usually more informal and less systematic than the other forms described above.

This taxonomy has subsequently been adopted by the APA Council of Representatives for the field of psychology (Table 1).

2.04.2 FIFTY YEARS OF EVOLUTION

Early generations of clinical psychologists were considered educated and trained in the specialty of clinical psychology upon receiving their doctoral degrees. Over the years, the need for postdoctoral education for professional practice gradually became more apparent when it was clear that new opportunities for service required specialized training and that critical social needs required trained specialists. Recommendations for supervised training beyond the doctoral degree have been made for at least 50 years.

(i) *Boulder*. In August 1949, a conference supported by the National Institute of Mental Health (NIMH) convened at Boulder, Colorado, to consider the training of clinical psychologists. Seventy-one representatives from training universities, mental health agencies, and allied profession participated (Raimy, 1950). The participants encouraged broad professional training in clinical psychology, leaving more specialization to postdoctoral experience.

(ii) *Stanford*. In August 1955, again with NIMH support, a conference on Education and Training for Psychological Contributions to Mental Health was held at Stanford University. The deciding factor leading to the conference was the rapid growth within the previous three or four years of the mental hygiene movement and the realization that this movement was going to have a far-reaching effect on psychology. The institute strongly favored efforts to define a common core of professional training that would constitute basic preparation for various special fields. The participants suggested that some special training could be included in a predoctoral program, but full competence in any specialty would undoubtedly require some postdoctoral training (Strother, 1956).

(iii) *Miami*. The Miami conference participants (Roe, Gustad, Moore, Ross, & Skodak, 1959) discussed issues of specialization in psychological practice and talked about the gradual development of a two-year internship to follow the doctoral degree. The model of a two-year, supervised period of field training before subspecialty or general practice is not new and it has stood the test of time. It is today the modal preparation period before licensure and practice.

(iv) *Chicago*. Participants in the Chicago conference (Hoch, Ross, & Winder, 1966) differentiated postgraduate and postdoctoral training. Postgraduate training was thought necessary for individuals with doctorates in other specialties who wished to become clinical psychologists. After much debate about postdoctoral training, the conference endorsed the statement that: "Although postdoctoral training is desirable for all clinical specialists, it is deemed essential for those anticipating independent professional practice and also for those who are to teach and supervise in clinical specialty courses" (Hoch et al., 1966, p. 47). It was also agreed that the postdoctoral program should never serve to compensate for deficiencies in training at the predoctoral level. The conferees wished that professional preparation be a continuous, integrated sequence with postdoctoral training, building on predoctoral preparation.

(v) *Menninger Postdoctoral Conference*. An interest group in postdoctoral clinical training was formed in 1958 to provide a forum for the exchange of ideas among psychologists interested in seeking or offering programs of supervised clinical experience beyond the doctoral degree. The efforts of this group to mount a national conference came to fruition on May 18–21 1972, when 42 psychologists representing postdoctoral training facilities, university departments of psychology, the Veterans Administration, APA, NIMH, and doctoral and postdoctoral trainees met at the Menninger Foundation to share their thoughts and experiences (Weiner, 1973). Attendees shared information and raised concerns about current and future postdoctoral education; they developed few policy statements.

(vi) *Gainesville Internship Conference*. The National Conference on Internship Training in Psychology (Belar et al., 1989) proposed that the traditional one year internship be expanded to two year's experience: the first year at doctoral level and the second at postdoctoral level. Two years of supervised

Table 1 Taxonomy to describe postdoctoral education (for practice, research, and teaching in psychology).

	Models					
Variables	*Formal programs*	*Individual mentorship*	*Individual supervision*	*Continuing education*	*Sabbatical/paid leave*	*Faculty development, peer consultation, and self-study*
Orientation/target population	Practice, research, teaching	Research	Practice	Practice, research, teaching	Research, teaching	Practice, research, teaching
Purpose	Specialization, respecialization	Specialized research	Advanced practice competencies	Update/renew knowledge	New knowledge, consolidation of knowledge	Update, confirm, and share knowledge
Content	Clinical competence, advanced research, teaching competence	Individual focus	Clinical care readings	Selected topic areas	Individually tailored	Selected topic areas
Duration	1–2 years	1–3 years	1–5 years	1 day–2 weeks	3–12 months	*ad hoc*
Funding	Institutional, governmental	Institutional, governmental	Institutional, self	Self	Institutional, self	Self
Evaluation/competency	Stated criteria	Stated criteria	Established criteria	Examination	Self-evaluation products	Self-evaluation

experience was deemed necessary to produce an autonomously functioning professional psychologist. In general, the Gainesville conference resulted in a raising of standards for the training of professional psychologists. It codified the contemporary status of the postdoctoral year and asserted the need for organized quality control over this aspect of professional training.

(vii) *NIMH*. The NIMH has received policy recommendations from the National Conference on Implementing Public–Academic Linkages for Clinical Training in Psychology (Callan, Johnson, Leon, Magrab, & Meyers, 1990). Regarding postdoctoral education and training, the conferees suggested that a variety of postdoctoral fellowships should be developed for training focused on priority populations, one to two years for clinical service and administrative training, and two to three years for combined clinical service and research training. Continuity of training experience between the university, internship and postdoctoral facilities was also suggested to ensure that training focused on the actual needs of priority populations and on high-quality services.

(viii) *Ann Arbor*. The National Conference on Postdoctoral Training in Psychology was convened in Ann Arbor in 1992 by the APA, the Association of State and Provincial Psychology Boards (ASPPB), and the Association of Psychology Postdoctoral and Internship Centers (APPIC) (Belar et al., 1993). Its purpose was to develop specific postdoctoral training criteria for students, training programs, and credentialing authorities. Postdoctoral training consisting of one year full-time (or two year half-time) was recommended for psychologists who wanted to teach, conduct research, or to practice. Various structural, supervisory, context, content, and evaluation issues were considered and the conference report was essentially the first detailed APA policy statement regarding postdoctoral training. These conference criteria were subsequently modified by the Inter-organizational Council for Accreditation of Postdoctoral Programs in Psychology (IOC) (see below) and served as the background material for the drafting of the APA's Committee on Accreditation (CoA) accreditation criteria for postdoctoral programs.

(ix) *Norman, Oklahoma*. The 1994 APA National Conference on Postdoctoral Education and Training in Psychology has already been alluded to above (APA, 1995). This was a conference that addressed education and training beyond the doctoral degree very broadly. It was designed for teachers, researchers, and practitioners in psychology.

2.04.3 GROWTH OF FORMAL POSTDOCTORAL PROGRAMS

Alexander (1995) attempted to identify postdoctoral programs in existence in 1960–1962. He reported that, excluding VA installations offering postdoctoral internships, perhaps 22 institutions were offering continuing one or two year programs of study, with an additional 10 that had trained students sporadically over the years as the occasion arose. Eight programs were located in medial schools and five others in private clinical facilities. Most of the remainder were found in joint hospital, clinical, or medical school settings. One program was founded in a school for exceptional children, and one in a university department of psychology. Irving Weiner (1968) identified 46 postdoctoral programs in clinical psychology in 1967 that were (i) designed for psychologists with a degree from an APA-approved doctoral program, (ii) administered and directed principally by psychologists, and (iii) focused primarily on education for advanced professional competence rather than on in-service or on-the-job training.

Wiens (1993) reported on a tabulation of postdoctoral training programs that were listed in various sources in 1990–1991. The largest number was gleaned from *The APA Monitor* from January to December 1991. Other sources of information were the *APPIC Directory*, the *Division of Health Psychology Directory*, and the *Clinical Neuropsychology Directory*. The combined listings totaled 388 postdoctoral training sites which were accommodating 694 trainees. Tabulation of additional listings for 1991 yielded a total of approximately 500 sites.

The listing of postdoctoral training sites was an effort to create greater awareness of the number and variety of postdoctoral education and training opportunities. It was also an effort to encourage discussion of establishing mechanisms for credentialing or accrediting programs that meet established guidelines for training in one or another specialty area.

2.04.4 ORGANIZING FOR EDUCATION, CREDENTIALING, AND ACCREDITATION: THE CLINICAL NEUROPSYCHOLOGY EXAMPLE

In the 1980s, the APA Task Force on Scope and Criteria of Accreditation recommended that the accreditation of education and training programs should be expanded to cover postdoctoral residency programs beginning in the four traditional fields: clinical, counseling, school, and industrial–organizational psychology. Mention was made of eventually turning attention to emerging specialties and, in a footnote to this, clinical neuropsychology was mentioned. By this time a postdoctoral residency in clinical neuropsychology had become the traditional preparation within the specialty. There had been a history of such going back to at least the 1960s. Clinical neuropsychology had obtained a division within APA in 1980. This Division 40 cooperated with the International Neuropsychological Society in its Task Force on Education, Accreditation, and Credentialing. The first of the INS-Division 40 Joint Task Force reports (Meier, 1981) called for the development of board certification in clinical neuropsychology. Just as the APA had sponsored and initially funded the development of the American Board of Professional Psychology (ABPP) to provide board certification for all of psychology beginning in 1947, the APA Division of Clinical Neuropsychology followed suit in sponsoring the American Board of Clinical Neuropsychology which was incorporated in 1981. Board certification examinations under the aegis, scrutiny, and supervision of the ABPP were accomplished in 1984. Subsequently, the INS-Division 40 Task Force reissued guidelines for the doctoral, predoctoral internship, and postdoctoral residency levels of education and training within the specialty. Listings of such programs which self-asserted compliance with the respective guidelines were published (Cripe, 1988).

In 1988, a special meeting was called and held in Iowa City, in conjunction with a meeting of the Midwest Neuropsychology Group. The premise presented was that clinical neuropsychology now had in place all the prerequisite bodies and published guidelines that needed to exist prior to the initiation of accreditation, or so it was thought at that time. At this point the APA had taken no steps to accredit residency programs in the traditional fields, let alone even recognize clinical neuropsychology as a specialty. Directors of residency programs in clinical neuropsychology within contiguous Midwestern states (Iowa, Michigan, Minnesota, Wisconsin, and eventually Illinois and Ohio), agreed to form an organization the purpose of which was to develop mechanisms for the accreditation of residency programs in the specialty of clinical neuropsychology. The Midwest Neuropsychology Consortium of Postdoctoral Programs in Clinical Neuropsychology (MNC) considered itself a working group which would be kept small until accreditation mechanisms were in place, at which time it was planned to expand so as to accept programs within North America. Building on the published guidelines (INS-Division 40 Task Force on Education, Accreditation, and Credentialing, 1986, 1987), the MNC began work on elaborating standards for a residency program, the curriculum, standardization of application materials, deadlines and notification dates and policies. Early informal inquiries had failed to find an independent organization interested in providing oversight of the anticipated accreditation activities. However, after the MNC field tested its policies, procedures, and materials for accreditation, and was about to commence official accreditation site visits in 1991, Manfred Meier (1981) captured the interest of the ABPP in this endeavor.

The ABPP agreed to become involved in accreditation but it would not do so alone. The ABPP called for the development of the Interorganizational Council for Accreditation of Postdoctoral Programs in Psychology (IOC) and an inaugural meeting was held in Minneapolis, Minnesota, in September 1991. Representatives came from the Education Directorate, the Board of Educational Affairs, the Accreditation Office and the Executive Counsel of the APA, along with the Canadian Psychological Association, the National Register of Health Service Providers in Psychology (NRHSPP), the Canadian Register of Health Service Providers in Psychology, the ASPPB, the APPIC, and the National Council of Schools of Professional Psychology (NCSPP). Among these major organizations, all but the NCSPP maintained its membership on the IOC. It was determined that the specialties would be represented by the association of directors of residency programs within the specialty, if such existed; otherwise, a representative of the ABPP member board for the specialty would fulfill this role. This occasioned the MNC to enact its planned expansion and it evolved into the Association of Postdoctoral Programs in Clinical Neuropsychology (APPCN). The APPCN financially supported the representative of clinical neuropsychology to the IOC. The IOC met two to three times a year. Organizational conflicts and debates over concepts dominated the early agenda of the IOC. For example, although the APA asserted proprietary rights concerning accreditation, at that time only the specialty of clinical neuropsychology was positioned to have its residency programs evaluated for accreditation and the APA did not recognize clinical neuropsychology as a specialty (nor a number of other putative specialties which already had been recognized by ABPP). Another issue of key importance to the specialties in professional psychology, and the subject of spirited debate, was the procedure by which standards for education and training in the specialties would be recognized and adopted so that the corollary accreditation criteria could be established.

The APA eventually began a process to address this problem. Authorization was obtained to explore mechanisms by which the APA could come to officially recognize new specialties. The outcome was the formation of the Commission for the Recognition of Specialties and Proficiencies in Professional Psychology (CRSPPP). The CRSPPP worked through considerable developmental issues, along with defining its policies and procedures. After the successful completion of a demonstration project, the CRSPPP was fully commissioned by the APA Council of Representatives in 1995. The Division of Clinical Neuropsychology then officially petitioned the CRSPPP for specialty recognition and presented their application for review. In 1996, the Council of Representatives approved the CRSPPP recommendation, and clinical neuropsychology became the first new specialty to be recognized in professional psychology.

Meanwhile, the IOC decided to postpone consideration of specialty issues in accreditation and proceeded with the generation of guidelines for the accreditation of generic postdoctoral residencies. Generic programs refer to education and training programs that occur after completion of the doctoral program and the predoctoral internship. They are intended to advance the competencies of the residents in a general fashion but do not lead to qualification for the practice of any specialty within professional psychology. Stimulating this process was the National Conference on Postdoctoral Training in Professional Psychology, held in Ann Arbor in 1992 (Belar et al., 1993), which was described above. Building on the APA's guidelines for the accreditation of internship programs, the conference prepared a draft of guidelines for generic residencies. Later, this document was presented to the IOC and APA's Committee on Accreditation (CoA). The Conference on Education and Training Beyond the Doctoral Degree (APA, 1995) held in Norman, Oklahoma in 1994, laid down a foundation of thought about postdoctoral education, thereby providing a broad context for further work on these issues. This conference assembled data and considered possible ramifications and implications from the growth and expansion of residency education and training programs and other changes in professional psychology. One of the recommendations to come from this conference was to move the predoctoral internship to a postdoctoral experience. This policy proposal was endorsed by Council of Graduate Departments of Psychology (COGDOP) in 1997.

Upon completion of the Joint Task Force with Division 40, the INS divorced itself from further involvement in professional matters. That is, the INS was an international, multidisciplinary scientific society and it was realized that its composition was not wellsuited for such matters. Although the INS would remain generally interested in, and supportive of, education in neuropsychology, it also recognized it did not have the resources to assist all of its represented disciplines in all the countries of its membership.

Like other scientific disciplines and practice specialties, the history of neuropsychology in the USA was in part imprinted with a growing number of organizations (Benton, 1987). The INS helped to give birth to Division 40, Division 40 helped to give birth to the ABCN. In accordance with Division 40 guidelines, and in parallel with what became the standard in medicine, the APPCN required that the directors of residency programs be board certified within the specialty. In addition to these kindred, psychologist groups, a multidisciplinary interest group arose which was especially concerned with continuing education and practice matters, that is, the National Academy of Neuropsychology (NAN).

Based on the work of the IOC, which incorporated many of the points raised by the National Conference on Postdoctoral Training in Professional Psychology (Belar et al., 1993), the Conference on Education and Training Beyond the Doctoral Degree (APA, 1995), and ensuing collaboration, the Committee on Accreditation in 1996 adopted the Guidelines and Principles for Accreditation and developed the Accreditation Operating Procedures for Postdoctoral Programs (Committee on Accreditation, 1997; Office of Program Consultation and Accreditation, 1997).

By 1993, clinical neuropsychology's participation in the IOC led to two stirring realizations. First, in order to secure the extension of accreditation to its specialty residency programs, the APPCN would have to seek and obtain general acceptance of their guidelines within the specialty profession. Second, the specialty profession had become so highly differentiated as to reach the point when some form of reintegration appeared necessary in order to achieve the first realization. To this end, proposals calling for an integration of organizations were unanimously approved by the boards of directors of both ABCN and APPCN, as well as by the executive committee of the Division of Clinical Neuropsychology. However, two years elapsed with no concrete action having been taken. To precipitate events, the chief officers of the ABCN, APPCN, Division 40, NAN, and the INS were invited to discuss the proposal to which most had agreed. All agreed to take up the cause of this orphaned brainchild, that is, that a metaorganization of the major organizations within clinical neuropsychology should be established. The title of the Clinical Neuropsychology Synarchy (CNS) was adopted. This erstwhile rare word, synarchy, meaning governance through joint sovereignty, was deemed apropos in its renascent application.

With unanimous accord, the CNS articulated two fundamental positions. These were that clinical neuropsychology was only a specialty and not a proficiency and that there should be but one board certification agency within the specialty. Upon the formation of the CNS it was immediately apparent there were important organizational gaps within the specialty which would become glaring when consideration turned to reissuing integrated guidelines for education and training in clinical neuropsychology. In consequence, the CNS issued a call for two organizing meetings, both of which were held in conjunction with the North American meetings of the INS. In 1996, this led to the formation of the Association for Doctoral Education in Clinical Neuropsychology (ADECN); in 1997, the Association for Internship Centers in Clinical Neuropsychology (AITCN) was brought into existence. Starting before the formation of the latter group, a planning committee of the CNS undertook preparations to bring about the Houston Conference on Specialty Education and Training in Clinical Neuropsychology. The Houston conference was successfully concluded in September of 1997. From this conference it was established that, from this time onward, a residency would become a necessary component in the education and training of a clinical neuropsychologist, and that the beginning of this specialty path began in doctoral programs in professional psychology.

In August of 1996, the declaration of the APA Council of Representatives affirming the CRSPPP recommendation for APA to recognize the specialty of clinical neuropsychology removed a major obstacle to accreditation in clinical neuropsychology and other specialties. Consequently, completion of the formative work for the recognition and representation of the specialties in the accreditation process was the paramount issue before the IOC at its November, 1996 meeting In that meeting the major regulatory organizations proposed the formation of a Council of Specialties (CoS) and charged it with various roles and tasks including that of recognizing, standardizing and interfacing specialty standards for education and training with the accreditation criteria for use by the CoA. In earlier sessions of the IOC, the specialty representatives persuasively argued that the form and content of the specialty residency would essentially define the nature of the specialist. Therefore, it must be made practicable for the psychological specialties to exert their sovereignty and carry out their responsibility to design and refine their own fates on a continuing basis. In support of the CoS, each specialty seeking accreditation of their education and training programs was instructed to form their own synarchy or specialty council, to which at least the following specialty-specific organizations were to be invited to participate: the ABPP member board (i.e., the board certifying agency within the specialty), the corresponding ABPP academy (to represent publically recognized qualified practitioners of the specialty), the APA division or divisions relating to the specialty, and representation of the educators, be they at the doctoral, internship, or residency levels of education and training (as befit the individual specialty). When formed, these specialty councils will become responsible for selecting their representatives to the CoS. The CoS also was charged with the responsibility to facilitate the resolution of disputes that may develop about interspecialty boundaries. The potential for such becomes particularly germane to the CoS when they may affect the accreditation of postdoctoral specialty programs in professional psychology, the recognition of specialties, or the certification of specialists.

It was through many years of preparation and organization that clinical neuropsychology earned the privilege (albeit with tribulations) to blaze a trail, clearing the way for other specialties of psychology to continue their maturation. Of course, this was not without capitalizing upon the developments and experiences of these other specialties in psychology as well as those in medicine. Nor could these advancements have taken place were it not for an audience of prepared minds in professional psychology. It is for this we must be especially grateful for the series of national conferences, dating back to that seminal meeting in Boulder, Colorado, which framed many of the questions, and the subsequent chorus of responses delivered by the collectives of wisdom convened over the past 50 years.

2.04.5 FUTURE

Uncertainties about how the structure of services will unfold in the health care and mental health arenas and how the education of doctoral-level health care professionals will be financially supported in the future place a haze on the horizon of professional psychology. Be that as it may, at least some imperatives can be seen clearly in the foreground. The first of these, of course, is funding. In order to provide quality residency programs in professional psychology, these programs must obtain stable and sufficient funding to support the educational activities of these programs, their residents and faculty. In the current state of flux, a number of deleterious factors are in play. Among these is the pressure from the managed care industry to take over the direction of health care services. In some instances, this has entailed the pounding of the square peg of professional health care services into the round hole of a manufacturing model often favored by some of the business-minded interlopers. The restriction or denial of services for the purposes of short-term financial gains by some third party insurers, their difficulty in considering and assessing the financial impact of services that lie beyond the year's end, and ways to factor-in the quality of life of the insured into the balance sheet are problems that eventually must be overcome.

The organizational structure of accreditation for professional psychology programs is overdue for a re-evaluation and redeployment. Presently it is housed within the membership organization of the APA. Has this become an historical anachronism? The CA is operating on an old model which some may feel is outdated. For example, the final decision on accreditation is principally decided by the committee as a whole on which there is no specific representation of the specialties at the postdoctoral level. Furthermore, in the methods by which the committee's decision to deny the accreditation of a seemingly inadequate program may be overturned, there is no representation of the principal stakeholders. The field of medicine that has probably worked on these problems longer than any other health care profession. In medicine, the overarching authority for accreditation is based on an interorganizational model. This is a model that psychology must consider if other goals, as described below, are to be achieved. A seedling for such a model may exist in the goals and aspirations of the Council of Credentialing Organizations in Professional Psychology (CCOPP). One goal of the CCOPP is to seek an integration of credentialing, accreditation, and other regulatory functions within professional psychology. Furthermore, at some point in the future, consideration of those aspects of the North American Free Trade Agreement (NAFTA) pertaining to professional credentialing and recognition will come into play.

As advanced and specialty education and training at the postdoctoral level unfolds, there will need to be a greater specification and integration of education and training programs at the doctoral, internship and postdoctoral residency levels. Also, if the internship is moved to the postdoctoral stage in the educational sequence, then coordination between internship and residency programs shall be required. In addition, provision must be made for subspecialization through joint residency or postdoctoral fellowship programs in the forthcoming conceptual model for education and training in professional psychology, and the accreditation thereof.

It would be short-sighted if the planning of the new model were to stop short at the point of a resident's departure from postgraduate education. The expected products of these education and training programs, i.e., the knowledge and competencies envisaged to be gained through such, must be coordinated with board certification standards for the individual practitioner in the specialties. At the same time, work must begin on the further considerations that will emerge down stream in the life of a practitioner in professional psychology. These include the timely application of recertification standards within the board-certified specialties and possibly in the relicensing of the general practitioner. To achieve this, mechanisms to plan for, entrain, and steer continuing educational programs in specified directions for the generalist as well as the specialist must be explicated. How the provision for, and approval of, the continuing education of the specialist within their specialty is yet to be proposed. Whatever this may be, the continuing education of the specialist and the periodic board recertification standards to be applied to them must dovetail. Obviously, there must be some parallel between the available curriculum for continuing education, the contemporary standards to be applied to the accreditation of doctoral, internship and residency programs, and the contemporary board certification standards applied to these programs' graduates.

Advancements in the science and profession of psychology, changes in the health care arena, and their interactions call for built-in adaptive capacities in this new model. Such flexibility, however, can no longer be provided through the absence of standards and their enforcement in professional psychology. Instead, mechanisms for prospective planning, rapid and coordinated communication of such changes, and their incorporation into the regulatory activities of professional psychology will need to become the modus operandi as we enter the twenty-first century. It is difficult to foresee how these necessary evolutionary milestones can be achieved without the acceptance and development of a synarchy drawn from the principal constituent organizational components of professional psychology as a whole.

2.04.6 REFERENCES

Alexander, I. E. (1995). Postdoctoral training in clinical psychology. In B. B. Wolman (Ed.), *Handbook of clinical psychology* (pp. 1415–1426). New York: McGraw-Hill.

American Psychological Association (1995). *Education and training beyond the doctoral degree: Proceedings of the American Psychological Association National Conference on Postdoctoral Education and Training in Psychology.* Washington, DC: Author.

Belar, C. D., Bieliauskas, L. A., Larsen, K. G., Mensh, I. N., Poey, K., & Roehlke, H. J. (1989). National conference on internship training in psychology. *American Psychologist, 44,* 60–65.

Belar, C. D., Bieliauskas, L. A., Klepac, R. K., Larsen, K. G., Stigall, T. T., & Zimet, C. N. (1993). National conference on postdoctoral training in professional psychology. *American Psychologist, 48,* 1284–1289.

Benton, A. (1987). Evolution of a clinical specialty. *The Clinical Neuropsychologist, 1,* 5–8.

Callan, J. E., Johnson, D. L., Leon, G. R., Magrab, P. R., & Myers, H. F. (1990). *Policy recommendations from the national conference on implementing public–academic linkages for clinical training in psychology.* Washington, DC: National Institute of Mental Health.

Committee on Accreditation (1997). *The annual report of the committee on accreditation 1996: In the spirit of the new era.* Washington, DC: American Psychological Association.

Cripe, L. (1988). Listing of training programs in clinical neuropsychology 1987. *The Clinical Neuropsychologist, 2,* 13–24.

Hoch, E. L., Ross, A. O., & Winder, C. L. (1966). *Professional preparation of clinical psychologists.* Washington, DC: American Psychological Association.

INS-Division 40 Task Force on Education, Accreditation, and Credentialing (1986). Guidelines for postdoctoral training in clinical neuropsychology. *Newsletter 40*(4), 4.

INS-Division 40 Task Force on Education, Accreditation, and Credentialing (1987). Reports of the INS-Division 40 Task Force on Education, Accreditation, and Credentialing: Guidelines for doctoral training programs in clinical neuropsychology. *The Clinical Neuropsychologist, 1,* 29–34.

Meier, M. J. (1981, September). Report of the Task-Force on Education, Accreditation, and Credentialing of the International Neuropsychological Society. *The INS Bulletin,* 5–10.

Office of Program Consultation and Accreditation (1997). *Book 1: Guidelines and principles for accreditation of programs in professional psychology; Book 2: Accreditation operating procedures of the Committee on Accreditation.* Washington, DC: American Psychological Association.

Raimy, V. C. (1950). *Training in clinical psychology.* New York: Prentice-Hall.

Roe, A., Gustad, J. W., Moore, B. V., Ross, S., & Skodak, M. (1950). *Graduate education in psychology.* Washington, DC: American Psychological Association.

Strother, C. R. (1956). *Psychology and mental health.* Washington, DC: American Psychological Association.

Weiner, I. B. (1968). Postdoctoral training in clinical psychology. *American Psychologist, 23,* 374–377.

Weiner, I. B. (1973). *Postdoctoral education in clinical psychology.* Topeka, KS: Menninger Foundation.

Wiens, A. N. (1993). Postdoctoral education–training for specialty practice: Long anticipated, finally realized. *American Psychologist, 48,* 415–422.

2.05
Accreditation of Education and Training Programs: Its Role in Shaping a Profession

PAUL D. NELSON
American Psychological Association, Washington, DC, USA

2.05.1 THE PROFESSIONS, ACCREDITATION, AND PUBLIC ACCOUNTABILITY

In his annual report to the American Psychological Association (APA), writing as the Association's Executive Secretary, Sanford (1951) spoke about the qualities of a "good profession," suggesting their application to the field of psychology. A most fundamental quality of the professions, Sanford advanced, is a sense of social responsibility. A quarter of a century later, Peterson (1976a) invited our attention again to the characteristics of a profession, challenging us to think about the extent to which they are manifest in psychology, advancing towards that quality of an applied discipline. On all accounts, most will agree that psychology, in addition to being a scientific discipline, is a profession.

Professions are characterized by a differentiated and dynamic body of knowledge; a system of disciplined methods of inquiry and practice through which that body of knowledge is challenged, expanded or modified, and applied; and a core of shared values and attitudes that together speak to a sense of integrity and social responsibility. Professions are characterized as well by a sense of self-discipline and self-regulation, governed by standards of practice and ethical principles in accordance with which their members are subject to peer review.

The foundation of any profession is the requisite education and training that leads to entry level of practice. Consistent with the disciplinary principles just stated, it is the responsibility of a profession to establish education, training, credentialing, and practice standards or guidelines (Drum & Hall, 1993;

Merton, 1969). It must also ensure the validity of those standards or guidelines through regular, periodic evaluation (Kane, 1982; Koocher, 1979; Sechrest & Chatel, 1987; Stevenson & Norcross, 1987).

Typically, it is through accreditation that professions set the standards for education and training leading to their entry level of practice. As a self-regulatory, peer review process, accreditation serves to assess and publicly certify the quality of professional education and training relative to those standards. In so doing, accreditation models the self-critical and peer review qualities expected of professionals in the review of their practice. Thus, it might be argued, accreditation is a link between professional training and practice (Nelson & Aletky, 1987) beyond its value in certifying the quality of education and training for entry level into the profession. In these ways, accreditation and the professions are linked inextricably by a common orientation to public accountability, a sense of social responsibility.

The emphasis on foundational education and training in the professions is not intended to suggest that early inservice and lifelong career experiences in professional service, or their attendant continuing professional education and training programs are of little consequence in shaping the profession. It is at the foundational education and training level in any profession, however, that the qualities characteristic of a competent professional take root. It is at this level that students must be prepared in values and attitude as well as in knowledge and skills for lifelong learning in the discipline.

This chapter reflects on the developmental history of psychology as a scientific discipline and how that development in response to public need led to accreditation activities and the early seeds of a profession by the mid-twentieth century. In addressing these issues, the author intends to illustrate how accreditation has functioned as a forum in some instances, and a lightning rod in others, for national debate of professional education and training issues among and between psychologists within and outside the academy. Through this process, the accreditation standards reflect the thinking of psychologists about the goals and principles of professional education and training, the models or philosophies of training through which those ends are to be achieved, answers to the questions "what constitutes an appropriate curriculum?" and "what competencies do we expect of our graduates?" In the final analysis, the process of accreditation serves a public accountability function for the profession and the higher education community.

2.05.2 THE CONTEXT FOR ACCREDITATION IN THE PROFESSIONS

The early development of clinical psychology training in the scientific laboratory of a research university was not an accident of history, but rather an event consistent with changes that were taking place in leading research universities in the US at the same time. With the chartering of land-grant colleges and universities (Christy & Williamson, 1992), the turn of the nineteenth century was a period during which even the private research universities were conscious of their mission not only to create and disseminate knowledge within the community of scholars but to apply that knowledge to the benefit of society, a public service mission ... an element of mission on which the professions are founded.

Indeed, professional education and training through the universities was a natural conduit for this element of mission to society, perhaps exemplified best at the time of Lightner Witmer's laboratory clinic (Brotemarkle, 1947) by the transformation that was underway in American medical education (Starr, 1982). Drawing upon the scientific traditions of the great German universities, the seeds of modern, science-based medical education were sown in the likes of Johns Hopkins University, Harvard University, and the University of Pennsylvania in the late nineteenth century.

It was not only the university's role in bringing science to bear on medical education that was significant, however, but equally important was the university's alignment with teaching hospitals that served indigent populations of the community and those even from outside the local community whose health was at risk of being impaired by uncommon disease, the latter being the focus of medical research. Thus, in theory at least, alignment of the classroom, laboratory, and clinic afforded medical students first-hand clinical experience and involvement in medical research under the supervision of qualified faculty and clinical scientists. Prior to that time, and even subsequent thereto for some years, medical education was virtually without national standards. Entrepreneurial apprenticeships in the community were common as a way to receive clinical training, and medical schools were comparably without a standard curriculum or metric by which to gauge quality.

This was the background against which the medical profession carried out with support of the Carnegie Foundation a major assessment of its education and training practices, leading to an overhaul of American medical education and training in the early years of the twentieth century (Flexner, 1925). In addition to setting national standards, the profession developed procedures by which to review periodically each medical school, resulting in what was the earliest form of specialized accreditation applied to professional education and training. Within the first few decades of the twentieth century, accreditation practices were also applied to the professions of dentistry, law, and engineering. Now, there is no profession of note in American society without an accreditation process applied to its foundational, entry-level education, and training programs. Accreditation, despite its frailties, has had a profound influence on professional education and training and therefore upon the professions themselves (Young, Chambers, & Kells, 1983).

For reason of developmental differences between medicine and clinical psychology as science-based professional disciplines, accreditation in psychology was not to be implemented, let alone conceived, for another 50 years from the time of Witmer's initial training clinic. At the turn of the nineteenth century, psychology had no identity as a profession. It was a relatively new science, in search of an identity distinct from its parent bodies of philosophy and the physiological sciences. Although its applications began early in the likes of Witmer's clinic at the University of Pennsylvania and another applied laboratory run by Munsterberg and his students at Harvard focused on industrial work problems (Stern, 1917), most developments in the discipline of psychology at that time were of theoretical and scientific significance apart from practical applications.

Applications of psychology outside the university laboratory were stimulated by the involvement of academic psychologists in the nation's service during World War I (Yerkes, 1918). While the decades between the two world wars witnessed more applications of psychology to a broader array of social problems, even advancing major theoretical and methodological schools of thought as reflected in the work of Kurt Lewin and his colleagues (Marrow, 1969), the vast majority of psychologists in the US remained employed primarily in colleges and universities as teachers and researchers, devoted to advancing the science of psychology. Indeed, feeling disfranchised by their academic colleagues whose leadership and values pervaded the APA, the minority of psychologists whose primary employment was outside the academy during those years, psychologists providing primarily clinical and consulting services, formed their own national association in the 1930s, the American Association of Applied Psychology (AAAP).

Although the AAAP and APA were reunified by events of World War II, there remained a sense of skepticism that such unity would last (Hunt, 1975). It didn't, entirely. Nearly 50 years subsequent to the AAAP development, the American Psychological Society (APS) was formed to allow those whose commitments were primarily to science in the university, by then the minority of APA members, to have their own national association (though many remained members of APA too). Throughout it all, the APA remains the largest national association of psychologists with the broadest array of interests and identities across the science and profession of psychology.

In the context of this chapter, the point of these observations is to document how the tensions resulting from disparate value orientations and perspectives between those whose commitment first and foremost has been to advance psychology as a science and those whose comparable priorities have been to advance psychology as a profession, referred to by some as "the two cultures of psychology," have been a central force operative in this discipline in the twentieth century (Albee, 1970; Chein, 1966; Fernberger, 1932; Kimble, 1984; Shakow, 1978; Sheridan, 1990; Tryon, 1963). It is a force that has played a significant role in the foundational education and training for psychology as a profession and in the accreditation process which was to come, following World War II.

2.05.3 ACCREDITATION IN PSYCHOLOGY: THE ADVENT OF A PROFESSION

It was for reasons of public service and accountability that accreditation practices were applied initially to graduate education and training in psychology. With the return of veterans following World War II, and the shortage of doctoral-level clinical psychologists to provide the psychological services needed in Veterans Administration hospitals and other government agencies, the Veterans Administration, followed shortly by the US Public Health Service, requested of the APA Board of Directors in December 1945 a list of education institutions possessing facilities adequate for training clinical psychologists. The idea behind this request was that public funds would be directed in support of those programs that were appropriately qualified to carry out such training. The APA accepted this responsibility and assigned it to the Committee on Graduate and Professional Training which had been gathering data on graduate training in psychology (Sears, 1946).

This was a significant development in the history of psychology. It represented recognition by the public of the worth and need for professional services of psychologists trained at the doctoral level, based upon their demonstrated competence in a myriad of roles of public service during World War II. Furthermore, it represented a public invitation for the profession to accept responsibility for evaluating its education and training programs preparatory for entry-level practice. It was the dawn of a new era in psychology, one in which psychology would flourish not only as a science but also as a profession. In the decade prior to World War II, two-thirds or more of the new doctoral graduates in psychology each year found primary employment in academic settings (Clark, 1957). In the years following World War II, this was to change. Now, in the late 1990s, approximately the same proportion of doctoral graduates in psychology that once found primary employment in academic settings find primary employment in applied, professional service settings outside the academy (APA Research Office, 1997a).

The result of the APA's action in response to the Veterans Administration and US Public Health Service was a report one year later on clinical training facilities in psychology departments at 40 universities, the first published account of quality in education and training for practice in clinical psychology. The Committee on Graduate and Professional Training cautioned readers that the criteria it developed to evaluate quality of training in these academic departments were not necessarily the only possible criteria and that their application to diverse institutions could be problematic. Then it added:

> If accreditation continues to be desirable for the profession, new criteria will gradually develop. . . . The present criteria must be viewed only as steps along the way; they are useful for measuring one stage in a type of professional training that is changing and growing every year. (Sears, 1947, p. 204)

The project was based on the application of published criteria for professional education and training through the process of peer review. With the additional involvement of the graduate departments, university administrations, and clinical program faculties in an analysis (self-study) of their capabilities and needs relative to the criteria, the project was the harbinger of accreditation in psychology.

It was important enough a development, moreover, for the APA Board of Directors to authorize appointment of a special committee on Training in Clinical Psychology in March 1947, the tasks of which would be to: (i) develop formal recommendations for education and training standards in clinical psychology for academic institutions and field service agencies that provide internship and practicum training; (ii) to study and visit the institutions that provide this training, preparing a report on each; and (iii) to maintain communication with other national associations or committees having related missions or interests.

The new committee was chaired by David Shakow and presented its recommendations on clinical training in psychology at the annual meeting of the APA in September 1947. Approved by the APA Council of Representatives, the recommendations became the first official accreditation standards and criteria for psychology (APA Committee on Training in Clinical Psychology, 1947). A year later, the committee published its first report of the outcomes of its review of clinical psychology programs in operation at that time, a process that included site visits by members of the Committee and others who assisted (APA Committee on Training in Clinical Psychology, 1948). Clinical psychology training programs in 36 universities were listed as the initial accredited programs under the new criteria.

From the beginning, it was clear that the committee was sensitive to the importance of the university's involvement in the accreditation review process, and that the procedures for such review should be valid for the purposes intended without being unduly burdensome on either the universities or the Committee. The Committee also understood that the profession of psychology was in its infancy and that education and training for the profession must be afforded opportunity to develop along different lines, even perhaps different philosophies in time. To wit, the committee set forth its stated purpose as follows:

> Our aims are . . . to achieve general agreement on the goals of training and encourage experimentation on methods of achieving these goals and to suggest ways of establishing high standards in a setting of flexibility and reasonable freedom. We also hold that the goals should not be determined by special situations and special demands, but should be oriented toward the question of what is the best training in clinical psychology. (APA Committee on Training in Clinical Psychology, 1947, p. 543)

Even with this broad goal, however, in its first year or two of visiting and evaluating university programs in clinical psychology, the committee discovered that any enthusiasm for accreditation that may have emanated from the APA leadership during that time was not shared universally among university department chairs and others of the academic institutions responsible for the training of psychologists. Shakow and his committee colleagues shared their experience with the accreditation process by reflecting:

> During our visits to universities, we have found attitudes towards the committee's work which varied all the way from those of hearty acceptance, confidence, and appreciation, to those of honest conviction that the committee is a usurper of power and authority and, that by the use of its power and its methods, does damage to the work of graduate departments.
>
> We are convinced of the importance of setting standards and evaluating performance in clinical training—in fact we see this process as inevitable if clinical psychology is to establish itself soundly and be a credit to psychology as a whole. We have set up criteria and administered procedures in ways that seemed best; we are neither satisfied that they are perfect nor persuaded that they are dangerous or ineffective. It is natural that there should be differences of opinion in the Association regarding the goals and techniques we have accepted. Both these differences and our own convictions are still matters of opinion rather than demonstrated fact. (APA Committee on Training in Clinical Psychology, 1949, pp. 340–341)

In sharing this early experience and in their prophesy of the future, the Shakow committee correctly anticipated tensions and challenges that were to characterize the accreditation of professional education and training programs in the decades ahead. As the Sears committee before it had partially forecast, Shakow's committee also envisioned that the process of accrediting programs in professional (clinical) psychology would change over time with regard to the criteria and procedures developed. They knew, in addition, that without a foundation of broad goals and principles to guide the accreditation process, the criteria and procedures in effect at any time could be misapplied, misunderstood, or otherwise impotent. Most important, being of a scientific discipline themselves, they knew how important it would be to evaluate outcomes of graduate professional education programs and of the accreditation process itself. That task was their legacy to future generations of accreditors.

2.05.4 GOALS AND PRINCIPLES OF PROFESSIONAL EDUCATION AND TRAINING

Given the history of this discipline and its state of development at the time of the Shakow committee's work, it is understandable that their approach to developing foundational education and training standards for clinical psychology was guided by the following considerations:

> We are cognizant of the great difficulties which the shift from an academic to a professional program involves in a university setting. We recognize that this change must take much effort and time and that even were it possible to set up a fairly fixed schedule of training, such a step would at present be both premature and ill-advised because of the great need for experimentation in ways of implementing a sound program. We are therefore emphasizing the goals and principles of what we consider a desirable program rather than attempting to lay out a detailed blueprint. (APA Committee on Training in Clinical Psychology, 1947, pp. 539–540)

In an account of the history of graduate professional education and training in psychology (Sheridan, Matarazzo, & Nelson, 1995), two major concerns were noted as the principal focus of debates on accreditation over the past 50 years. One is whether and how education and training in the science and clinical practice of psychology can coexist in one program. The other salient issue has been whether accreditation, with its externally-imposed standards and criteria, inherently violates or otherwise compromises the spirit of innovation and free inquiry that is *sine qua non* of the academy and, in the case of psychology, its science faculty and students.

Certainly the goals set forth by Shakow and his colleagues were sufficiently broad, recommending high standards but with flexibility of perspective to accommodate different ways by which those standards could be achieved. Still, the committee needed a bridge or transfer function by which to link the broad goals of accreditation to the development of standards for professional education and training and the process by which the attainment of those standards could be measured. The bridge they found in the earlier work of Flexner (1925, p. 176):

> . . . the medical school cannot expect to produce fully trained doctors; it can at most hope to equip students with a limited amount of knowledge, to train them in the method and spirit of scientific medicine and to launch them with a momentum that will make them active learners-observers, readers, thinkers, and experimenters—for years to come . . .

to which Shakow and his colleagues added:

> If we substitute clinical psychology for medicine, this statement expresses the essential point which we wish to make in this report. (APA Committee on training in Clinical Psychology, 1947, p. 540)

From this base the Shakow committee set forth the following (paraphrased) principles to serve as standards of professional education and training in psychology and to guide the development of accreditation criteria by which the attainment of those standards could be measured:

(i) A clinical psychologist must first and foremost be a psychologist ... having a point of view and core of knowledge and training which is common to all psychologists.

(ii) Education for the doctorate in clinical psychology should be as rigorous and extensive as that for the traditional doctorate ... combining academic and clinical training.

(iii) Preparation should be broad; it should be directed to research and professional goals, not to narrow technical goals ... with psychologists as a research worker emphasized.

(iv) There should be training in: (a) general psychology; (b) psychodynamics of behavior; (c) diagnostic methods; (d) research methods; (e) related disciplines; and (f) therapy.

(v) Programs should be concerned mainly with basic courses and principles rather than multiple courses in technique, with advanced courses requiring knowledge from earlier courses.

(vi) Courses should be scrutinized for their content rather than judged by their titles. Equally important is ... the quality of the teaching and the integration of courses.

(vii) Instruction should be organized around a careful integration of theory and practice, of academic and field work, by persons representing both aspects (of training).

(viii) Throughout all years of graduate work the student should have contact, both direct and indirect, with clinical (and normal) material ... allowing a range of experience.

(ix) The atmosphere of training should encourage the increase of student maturity, a sense of responsibility for patients and clients, and excitement about psychological problems.

(x) There should be opportunity to study with students of other disciplines ... to acquire a sense of modesty and to learn the value of teamwork in research and service.

(xi) Throughout training there should be an emphasis on the research implications of phenomena being addressed ... with the set to ask "how," "why," "what is the evidence?"

(xii) In addition to the research implications of data, students need to develop a sensitivity to the social implications ... not only to the individual patient or client but to society. (APA Committee on Training in Clinical Psychology, 1947, pp. 543–545).

In the criteria developed for review of programs, these principles were embellished with extensive guidelines and precautions about academic and clinical training, including the year of internship required for completion of doctoral training in clinical psychology. The most important feature of the committee's work, however, was establishing the foundation of broad goals and guiding principles for professional education and training in psychology at the doctoral level. These goals and principles have stood the test of time and remain in effect, essentially, as the foundation upon which the current accreditation guidelines and related program review procedures are based (Committee on Accreditation, 1996).

These principles of education and training in professional psychology reflect more than the thinking of small committees. They have been endorsed and reaffirmed, perhaps in modified form to reflect the development of the field, in each of the past five decades by national conferences of psychologists, educators, and practitioners, convened for different purposes at different times. The first of those was the 1949 Boulder Conference with its focus on clinical training (Raimy, 1950); the most recent on graduate education broadly was the 1987 Utah Conference (Bickman & Ellis, 1990).

2.05.5 MODELS OR PHILOSOPHIES OF PROFESSIONAL EDUCATION AND TRAINING

Conceptually, it is through a model or philosophy of education and training that educators translate their broad, more abstract goals and principles of education and training to a pedagogical plan by which the learning process and attainment of education and training goals can be realized. While there are many ways in which this can be done in programs of professional psychology, perhaps the most salient parameter of conceptualization historically has been that which ties the "model of training" to psychology's two cultures, science and practice. This is not surprising in the context of psychology's history.

While many resolutions about graduate education in clinical psychology were articulated at the Boulder Conference, and concerns were aired about the new accreditation process, most remembered from that conference over the years was its endorsement of the Shakow committee principles and what became known as the "scientist–practitioner" or "scientist–professional" model of education and training in clinical psychology. The spirit of the "scientist–practitioner" philosophy or model, however, had been expressed a few years earlier. An APA committee chaired by Robert Yerkes, in planning for the future of the association, had professed "that the development of psychology as a science and practice should proceed in close relation; and that the scientists of the profession should welcome technological developments and aid and encourage them" (Boring et al., 1942, p. 624).

Subsequent to the Boulder conference, the "scientist–practitioner" model was reinforced at other national conferences on professional education (Hoch, Ross, & Winder, 1966) and graduate education (Roe, Gustad, Moore, Ross, & Skodak, 1959), as well as by national conferences focused on the preparation of school psychologists (Cutts, 1955) and counseling psychologists (Thompson & Super 1964). The model itself was the focus of a conference (Belar & Perry, 1991). How, if at all, science and practice inform each other has been a fundamental issue in the development of psychology as a science-based profession (Barlow, 1981; Belar, 1990) and remains a question of philosophical and pragmatic importance (Stricker, 1997).

The "scientist–practitioner" model has been implemented in different ways among doctoral programs over the years (Henry, 1984). Among accredited programs, there are some that truly achieve an integration of research and practice in the thinking and activities of students and faculty. In others espousing the same model, some with more emphasis on practice, some with more emphasis on science, and some with equal emphasis on both, there is at times bifurcation of the two domains and their respective faculties. It remains, nonetheless, the most commonly espoused model of training among accredited programs today. Indeed, some argue that there is no need for alternative training models (Perry, 1979).

Not all have argued that point, however (Fox, Barclay, & Rodgers, 1982; Peterson, 1976b, 1991; Sechrest, 1990), nor did the delegates of the 1973 Vail Conference (Korman, 1973). Although several of the issues raised at that conference had been discussed at earlier conferences or had been the focus of APA committee work during the 1960s, the Vail Conference clearly endorsed the idea of a professional degree in psychology, the Psy.D. degree, and the value of professional schools of psychology, in addition to the traditional academic Ph.D. degree granted by universities in recognition of scholarly achievement in a discipline.

The model more in keeping with this orientation to professional education and training has been most commonly labeled "professional-scholar" or "practitioner-scholar," connoting an emphasis on preparation for professional practice with the scholarly perspective and habits of an inquiring mind appropriate to the clinical practitioner. The orientations of the practitioner of a profession, and therefore fundamental to professional education and training, it is argued, are different from the orientations of science and scientists (Peterson & Peterson, 1997). Comparative analyses of accredited programs across the spectrum of models reveal differences in admission requirements, acceptance rates, financial assistance, and theoretical orientation (Mayne, Norcross, & Sayette, 1994), activity patterns among students and faculty, as well as time to degree (Gaddy, Charlot-Swilley, Nelson, & Reich, 1995), and differences in professional activity and perspective about their work among graduates (Conway, 1988; Peterson, 1985).

A second theme advanced by the Vail Conference was the need for professional psychologists to be educated and trained with a sensitivity to and understanding of individual and cultural diversity in human lives, a theme consistent with the growing awareness and demographic projections of the ethnic, racial, and cultural diversity of American society and the importance of that fact for psychological research and services. That theme was to become even more pronounced during the 1980s, with considerations of human diversity expanded as well to include sensitivity to issues of gender, sexual orientation, disabilities, and religion. These developments were an expression of the profession's increasing sense of social responsibility in response to events of society during one of the most turbulent decades in US history.

Among the concerns was the perceived public need for many more psychologists to provide mental health services than could be prepared through traditional university academic departments, the corresponding need for their training to be focused on professional issues of practice as well as on the foundational principles set forth earlier by the Shakow committee, and the need for psychologists to have a personal and professional sensitivity to the qualities of individual and cultural diversity that characterize populations requiring psychological services. The accreditation criteria rewritten and approved in the late 1970s recognized and included these two major Vail Conference outcomes, expressing them in the form of goals and principles (American Psychological Association, 1979).

2.05.6 ACCREDITATION STANDARDS: CURRICULUM AND COMPETENCE CONTROVERSY

Another national working conference during the 1970s that influenced the way in which the

1979 accreditation criteria were written was one focused on education and credentialing in psychology (Wellner, 1978). The issue of particular concern at the conference was how psychology as a discipline can be distinguished from other disciplines often confused with psychology by the public. Of particular concern to some was the observation that those having a doctoral degree in psychology do not achieve that academic status through a common curriculum.

Historically, most graduate students in doctoral programs of psychology had a common core of learning experiences including basic textbooks in their first year or two of study (Matarazzo, 1987). If this was the case at least through the 1950s or 1960s, however, it was due to the fact that it made sense to individual faculties over the years and not because graduate departments of psychology endorsed as policy a nationally standardized core curriculum as such. As Ericksen (1958, p. 58) put it, following a survey of graduate department faculties on the value of a core curriculum: "It is quite apparent that we value variability, experimentation, and educational freedom far more than we value conformity and standardization."

While this value remains strong among ranks of the academy, it was to pose serious problems by the 1970s for licensing boards of examiners in psychology, especially in clarifying formal distinctions between the educational qualifications of psychologists and those of licensure applicants having graduated from other than psychology departments or programs. By this time, in clinical psychology, the numbers of programs of different models were increasing and, with an expanding body of psychological knowledge, there were varied curriculum options for students even at times in the same program. Although psychology had always taken pride in its scientific base and the corollary research training expected of those who would be recipients of the doctoral degree, this argument of psychology's distinction from seemingly related disciplines failed to convince the critics and in some instances could not be substantiated in graduate education and training for all licensure candidates.

The result of the 1976 conference on education and credentialing in psychology was the development of a foundational curriculum for the scientific discipline of psychology, the presence of which in a graduate program of study would allegedly designate that program as one in psychology. In did not specify what courses, textbooks, or other media of learning were to be required, but rather the substantive areas of the scientific discipline in which all students of professional psychology at least must demonstrate competence at a graduate level of understanding. The curriculum areas to serve as a foundation for understanding psychology as a scientific discipline were: history of the discipline; research methods and statistics; ethics and professional issues; and each of biological, cognitive-affective, social, and individual bases of behavior. They were incorporated in the accreditation criteria of the late 1970s, with the additional requirement of the core applied areas of competency, such as psychodiagnostics, psychological assessment, intervention procedures, consultation, and program evaluation (American Psychological Association, 1979).

These were not new curriculum foundations for graduate professional education in psychology, of course; they had been articulated in one form or another in the earlier criteria developed by the Shakow committee and in the criteria revised in the early 1970s at which time emphasis was placed on diversity of program models and the evaluation of program quality in the context of a program's chosen model (American Psychological Association, 1973). What seemed most important, however, was the consensus about curriculum areas achieved among those representing the perspectives of accreditation and credentialing in professional psychology. As a consequence, the core curriculum areas included in the accreditation criteria (American Psychological Association, 1979) were those also adopted as "designation criteria" by the Association of State and Provincial Psychology Boards and the National Register of Health Service Providers in Psychology in carrying out their individual psychologist credentialing review functions. The notion was that these curriculum criteria would clarify operationally whether or not an applicant for licensure or other certification as a psychologist had in fact completed a doctoral program in psychology, as distinct from another discipline (Council for the National Register of Health Service Providers in Psychology, 1997). It was clearly the expectation that the accreditation process would ensure at least some standardization in the curriculum areas in which all students in accredited professional psychology programs would be expected to demonstrate competence, if not identical coursework or other experience. Was that objective achieved? The answer to this question resides in the mind of the beholder, to be sure.

Certainly the implementation of accreditation criteria revised in the late 1970s did not result in programs having a standard curriculum at the course and textbook level or in the form of a standard lock-step curriculum plan, nor was that intended. On the other hand, graduates of accredited programs performed better than graduates of unaccredited programs on examination for licensure as a psychologist, much of the examination being based on these foundational areas of curriculum (McGaha & Minder, 1993; Ross, Holzman, Handal, & Gilner, 1991). Moreover, in a practice analysis survey of licensed psychologists conducted by the Professional Examination Service on behalf of the Association of State and Provincial Psychology Boards, most practitioners rated the foundational curriculum areas cited in the accreditation criteria as being at least moderately important and useful in their practice (Greenberg, Smith, & Muenzen, 1996).

While not altogether surprising, a disappointing exception to that finding was the observation among licensed practitioners that their training in "research and evaluation" seemed to be less important and used less frequently in practice than other substantive areas of the discipline's scientific foundations. When considered in the context of criticism previously targeted to graduate training in research methods and measurement (Aiken et al., 1990; Lambert, 1991), this finding raises significant questions about the one area of competence in which psychology traditionally took pride and differentiated its graduates from the professional service providers of other disciplines.

2.05.7 STORM WARNINGS IN ACCREDITATION: TIME FOR CHANGE OF HEADING

The emphasis on core curriculum issues of the 1970s and 1980s was one over which the accreditors were challenged on the one hand by their academic colleagues and on the other by their colleagues in practice, the former predominantly advocating against such a requirement imposed by the accreditors and the latter predominantly in favor of such. Academicians charged that the accreditation process was characterized by what some referred to as a "checklist mentality" having nothing to do with quality of professional education and training. This allegation within psychology was not unlike the charge against other accrediting bodies of the time that their concerns were focused mostly on resources and structures of education, not on the quality of outcomes.

Other concerns about the quality of training in clinical psychology, particularly, were raised with regard to the conceptual orientations (Albee, 1970, 1983; Levy, 1984; Sarason, 1981). At yet another level of criticism, there were those calling for something akin to the "Flexner report" to revamp the curriculum in professional psychology (Strickland, 1985) over concern that by allowing so many different models and programs of psychology to develop there was no standard quality of outcome. A set of core curriculum requirements and clinical competencies shared by all who complete professional education and training, some argued, is the hallmark of a profession (Fox, 1982, 1994; Fox, Kovacs, & Graham, 1985).

Together, the academicians and the practitioners each wanted a more active voice in the accreditation process. There were overtures made about alternative accrediting bodies for different types of programs and questions raised as in decades before about the necessity of accreditation. Whatever concerns about professional education and training were at issue in public debate at meetings of psychologists, the problems cited could most always be laid at the feet of the accreditation process. It was not a quiet time! This period of turbulence for accreditation in psychology had historical roots at least 50 years in the making. If accreditation applied to its professional education and training programs was to have even a chance of addressing constructively the various forces of tension that have been a part of the discipline's history, clearly needed was a different form of organization and operating procedures for the accrediting body itself.

The national context for change in accreditation was also right at the time, for psychology had not been alone in its dilemma by the mid-1980s. Criticism of accreditors and their procedures of quality assessment was gaining momentum in most professions and was being directed at the regional accreditors of postsecondary education institutions as well. The issue of "who controls the accreditors" and related matters of public accountability in accreditation and higher education in general provided a national context in the late 1980s for considerable change in American accreditation circles (Millard, 1991). Higher education institutions themselves were not exempt from public criticism during the same period over concerns for public accountability (Bok, 1990; Ewell, 1994; Wilshire, 1990).

In an effort to bring psychology educators and practitioners together around these issues, a significant development was the convening in 1988 of an *ad hoc* group, the Joint Council on Professional Education in Psychology (JCPEP). The report produced two years later by that group was an integrative summary of the thinking and recommendations generated by different national conferences in the 1980s, national organizations of psychology educators and practitioners, and the mid-1980s work of the APA Task Force on Scope and Criteria for

Accreditation (Stigall et al., 1990). Perhaps most important in developing the report and its recommendations was the strong degree of consensus that had been reached by constituencies that theretofore had often been at variance in their views about accreditation and its role in professional education and training. It was in effect a precursor of what was to be a new accreditation body, the members of which were to represent much the same diversity of constituencies as had the task force.

Thus, following three years of negotiation, a newly constituted Committee on Accreditation was commissioned, a multiorganizational body that would represent the different perspectives of educators, practitioners, and publics served by professional education and training in psychology and the process of accreditation by which the quality of those programs is assessed and certified (Sheridan, Matarazze, & Nelson, 1995). The Committee on Accreditation would be responsible not only for the quality assesment of programs in professional education and training, but also for the formulation and promulgation of accreditation policies and procedures (American Psychological Association, 1991).

The new Committee on Accreditation set to work in the fall of 1992 on a major self-study of its own. The outcome three years later, following more than a year of iterative public comment on earlier drafts of proposed changes, was the unanimous approval by the committee members of a new set of guidelines and procedures for the accreditation of programs in professional psychology (Committee on Accreditation, 1996). Although compromises were necessary along the way, and anyone could find some aspect of the guidelines and procedures with which to quarrel, all major national organizations representing psychologist educators and practitioners signed on, having had ample opportunity to participate in the process that led to the final guidelines.

In setting about its task of designing new accreditation guidelines, the Committee on Accreditation surveyed all communities affected by accreditation to assess their concerns about accreditation and ideas of how it could be improved. The committee also learned from the experiences of other groups convened during the 1980s to propose solutions to some of the problems that had been experienced in accreditation. In addition to national conferences on graduate and professional education and training, significant among those efforts had been the meta self-study process initiated by the National Council of Schools and Programs in Professional Psychology (NCSPP) whose annual conferences and resulting resolutions about professional education and training have been summarized (Peterson, Peterson, Abrams, & Stricker, 1997).

2.05.8 OUTCOMES OF ACCREDITATION: ISSUES OF PUBLIC ACCOUNTABILITY

Most important, reflecting the wisdom of the Shakow committee nearly 50 years earlier, the new accreditation guidelines were framed by a set of guiding principles for professional education and training and a set of goals that recognized simultaneously the needs and values of the academy in its role and those of the profession in being publicly accountable. As its predecessor accrediting body 20 years earlier had seen fit to do (American Psychological Association, 1973), the new committee developed guidelines that would assess program quality in the context of a program's publicly stated education and training goals and objectives. Programs are to demonstrate how they expect to achieve those ends in terms of the resources available to them, their chosen curriculum plan (including clinical training), and the types of competencies they expect of their program graduates.

These curriculum and competency outcomes are framed at a general level in terms of foundational areas of training in psychology as a science and applied (health/human service) discipline. A particularly critical addition to these constructs, however, is the objective of developing in students "attitudes essential for life-long learning, scholarly inquiry, and professional problem-solving as psychologists in the context of an evolving body of scientific and professional knowledge" (Committee on Accreditation, 1996, p. 6).

The most significant departure from earlier accreditation standards and criteria for doctoral and internship programs, however, is the public accountability standard that "the program demonstrates a commitment to excellence through self-study, which assures that its goals and objectives are met, enhances the quality of professional education and training obtained by its students, and contributes to the fulfillment of its sponsor institution's mission" (Committee on Accreditation, 1996, pp. 9, 16).

Moreover, in demonstrating that they meet this standard, accredited programs must demonstrate through this self-study analysis effectiveness in achieving their goals and objectives, and the procedures they have in place to make program adjustments in their goals, resources, and education and training structures that may be deemed necessary by the outcomes analyses conducted. In addition, doctoral programs are expected to evaluate the appropriateness of their goals, objectives, training model, and curriculum in the context of: (i) the sponsor institution's mission and goals; (ii) local, regional, and national needs for psychological services; (iii) national standards of practice; (iv) the evolving scientific and professional knowledge basis of practice; and (v) its graduates' job placements and career paths. Internship programs are accountable in analogous ways. These are aspects of public accountability, the need for which has never been greater.

Accountability to students preparing for careers in psychology is a matter to which graduate programs must be sensitive, given the cost of education and training and the changing employment market for graduates. This matter has become a focus of considerable concern in fields of science (Tobias, Chubin, & Aylesworth, 1995). For science careers in psychology, this concern prompted the APA to form a task force in 1996, the purpose of which was to develop information about career opportunities for research psychologists in other than traditional academic departments, an update on the work of a comparable task force appointed a decade earlier (Klatzky, Alluisi, Cook, Forehand, & Howell, 1985).

There is likewise a changing market of employment in the health and human services areas for psychologists, reflected in the trend away from independent practice and what has been historically a predominant identification with mental health services towards employment in multidisciplinary settings responsible for primary and tertiary care in the full range of health services (APA Research Office, 1997; Glueckauf, Frank, Bond, & McGrew, 1996; Stone et al., 1987). The requirement that psychologists be able to function effectively with professionals of other disciplines on clinical or other forms of problem-solving teams is not a new employment outcome for psychologists of course. It was perceived indeed to be the form of employment most useful for clinical psychologists at the time of the Shakow committee's work. They referred to the professional person as one who "learns the techniques and importance of the group attack on problems: how best to work with other professional groups for the benefit of the individual client and the frequent necessity of identifying himself with a group even broader than his own professional group, namely, the 'team'" (APA Committee on Training in Clinical Psychology, 1947, pp. 556–557).

Beyond the ability to function as part of a multidisciplinary team, psychologists employed in healthcare services in the 1990s also need to understand their role and the potential contributions that they can make in an environment characterized by organized care systems that are operated on a cost-control basis (Friedman, Sobel, Myers, Caudill, & Benson, 1995; Groth-Marnat & Edkins, 1996). This requires some additional professional knowledge and skills, but also adaptation of the foundational knowledge and skills traditional to broadly-trained clinical psychologists to a different service delivery model from that since the 1960s. Psychologists have considerably more to contribute than they have in the maintenance of health and prevention of illness and injury, a major theme of the managed-care era. In that same vein, psychologists have much to contribute to public health services, through the applications of psychological knowledge to shaping and evaluating public policies on education, health, and other human services (Lorion, Iscoe, DeLeon, & VandenBos, 1996).

All things need to be considered in a continuously changing employment market; however, graduates best prepared will be those whose education and training exemplifies the principles of breadth and foundational competencies that Shakow and his committee first articulated, principles that remain in effect in the 1990s. These competencies must include the critical-thinking, problem-solving skills that psychologists bring to bear on problems of human behavior, the types of skills to which psychology's adaptiveness to changing employment markets of the past have been attributed. Indeed, despite the concerns of students and others about the future employment market for psychologists, the graduates of accredited professional education and training programs in psychology are employed in a myriad of settings appropriate to their professional training (Gaddy, Charlot-Swilley, Nelson, & Reich, 1995), also reflected in the diversity of settings in which clinical psychology graduate students take internship training (Sheridan et al., 1995). Thus, the significant increase in numbers of clinical psychologists since the 1960s attributable to the increase in professional schools of psychology (Strickland, 1985) has been accompanied by an increase in the types of settings and roles in which psychologists function. The question at hand is whether this pattern will continue.

Although the answer to this question lies in the future, there are early career employment indicators among graduates of doctoral programs in psychology that bear close monitoring in the years immediately ahead. Within a year of graduation, for example, while unemployment rates remain low, they have increased slightly and graduates are requiring somewhat more time to find initial employment than their counterparts a few years earlier. The proportion of graduates entering postdoctoral residency or fellowship positions is increasing, a pattern that bears closer examination, and proportionately more graduates report that their knowledge and skills are somewhat underutilized in their primary employment settings than was true for earlier years (APA Research Office, 1997a, 1997b; Kohout & Wicherski, 1993; Wicherski & Kohout, 1995).

Much of this undoubtedly reflects the changing market for all. Nonetheless, they should not go unheeded, especially by those who prepare students for the future, the educators. The question "Are graduate departments responsible for the marketability of their graduates?" was one posed of participants at the national conference on graduate education in psychology in the late 1980s (Grosslight, 1990), a question just as timely in the late 1990s. Through the accreditation process, professional education and training programs are expected to evaluate the effectiveness of their graduates. The test for the accreditors is the extent to which they hold accredited programs accountable to such expectations and what effect that has on professional education and training in psychology and the outcomes thereof.

"The real answer to the question 'Shall we evaluate?' lies somewhere in the future," the Shakow committee stated (APA Committee on Training in Clinical Psychology, 1949, p. 341). That future is now! Professional programs of education and training in psychology, their host institutions, the profession, the students and graduates of the programs, and the other publics served by all of the preceding shall be the evaluators. All of these vital perspectives are ensured formal representation on the accrediting body in psychology, for the first time in the 50 years of psychology's experience with accreditation. Thus, the accreditation process serves as a forum through which outcomes of professional education and training, and those of the accreditation process itself, can be assessed and evaluated against standards of public accountability—the hallmark of a profession.

2.05.9 REFERENCES

Aiken, L. S., West, S. G., Sechrest, L., Reno, R. R., Roediger, H. L. III, Scarr, S., Kazdin, A. E., & Sherman, S. J. (1990). Graduate training in statistics, methodology, and measurement in psychology. *American Psychologist, 45,* 721–734.

Albee, G. (1970). The uncertain future of clinical psychology. *American Psychologist, 25,* 1071–1080.

Albee, G. (1983). Preventing psychopathology and promoting human potential. *American Psychologist, 37,* 1043–1060.

American Psychological Association (1973). *Criteria for accreditation.* Washington, DC: APA.

American Psychological Association (1979). *Criteria for Accreditation.* Washington, DC: APA.

American Psychological Association (1991). *Policies for accreditation governance.* Washington, DC: APA.

APA Committee on Training in Clinical Psychology (1947). Recommended graduate training programs in clinical psychology. *American Psychologist, 2,* 539–558.

APA Committee on Training in Clinical Psychology (1948). Clinical training facilities: 1948. *American Psychologist, 3,* 317–318.

APA Committee on Training in Clinical Psychology (1949). Doctoral training programs in clinical psychology: 1949. *American Psychologist, 4,* 331–341.

APA Research Office (1997a). Preliminary results: 1995 doctorate employment survey. *Personal communication.* Washington, DC: APA.

APA Research Office (1997b). Full-time employment settings in 1995 for APA members awarded Ph.D.s in clinical psychology in 1985 and 1990. *Personal communication.* Washington, DC: APA.

Barlow, D. H. (1981). On the relation of clinical research to clinical practice: current issues, new directions. *Journal of Consulting and Clinical Psychology, 49,* 147–155.

Belar, C. D. (1990). Continued integration of scientific and practitioner graduate education in psychology. In L. Bickman & H. Ellis (Eds.), *Preparing psychologists for the 21st century: proceedings of the national conference on graduate education in psychology* (pp. 285–299). Hillsdale, NJ: Erlbaum.

Belar, C. D., & Perry, N. W., Jr. (Eds.) (1991). *Proceedings of the national conference on scientist-practitioner education and training for the professional practice of psychology.* Sarasota, FL: Professional Resource Press.

Bickman, L. J., & Ellis, H. (Eds.) (1990). *Preparing Psychologists for the 21st century: proceedings of the national conference on graduate education in psychology.* Hillsdale, NJ: Erlbaum.

Bok, D. (1990). *Universities and the future of America.* Durham, NC: Duke University Press.

Boring, E. G., Bryan, A. I., Doll, E. A., Elliot, R. M., Hilgard, C., Stone, P., & Yerkes, M. (1942). First report of the subcommittee on survey and planning for psychology. *Psychological Bulletin, 39,* 619–630.

Brotemarkle, R. A. (1947). Fifty years of clinical psychology: 1896–1946. *Journal of Consulting Psychology, 11,* 1–4.

Chein, I. (1966). Some sources of divisiveness among psychologists. *American Psychologist, 21,* 333–342.

Christy, R. D., & Williamson, L. (Eds.) (1992). *A century of service: land-grant colleges and universities, 1890–1990.* New Brunswick, NJ: Transaction Publishers.

Clark, K. E. (1957). *America's psychologists: a survey of a growing profession.* Washington, DC: APA.

Committee on Accreditation (1996). *Guidelines and principles for accreditation of programs in professional psychology.* Washington, DC: APA.

Conway, J. B. (1988). Differences among clinical psychologists: scientists, practitioners, and scientist-practitioners. *Professional Psychology: Research and Practice, 19,* 642–655.

Council for the National Register of Health Service Providers in Psychology (1997). *National Register of Health Service Providers in Psychology* (12th ed., pp. 3–4). Washington, DC: CNRHSP.

Cutts, N. (Ed.) (1955). *School psychologists at mid-century: a report of the Thayer Conference on the functions, qualifications, and training of school psychologists.* Washington, DC: APA.

Drum, D. J., & Hall, J. E. (1993). Psychology's self-regulation and the setting of professional standards. *Applied & Preventive Psychology, 2,* 151–161.

Ericksen, S. C. (1958). The core curriculum is a dependent variable. *American Psychologist, 13,* 56–58.

Ewell, P. T. (1994). A matter of integrity: accountability and the future of self-regulation. *Change, 26,* 24–29.

Fernberger, S. W. (1932). History of the American Psychological Association. *Psychological Bulletin, 29,* 1–89.

Flexner, A. (1925). *Medical education.* New York: Macmillan.

Fox, R. E. (1982). The need for reorientation of clinical psychology. *American Psychologist, 37,* 1051–1057.

Fox, R. E. (1994). Training psychologists for the twenty-first century. *American Psychologist, 49,* 200–206.

Fox, R. E., Barclay, A. G., & Rodgers, D. A. (1982). The foundations of professional psychology. *American Psychologist, 37,* 306–312.

Fox, R. E., Kovacs, A. L., & Graham, S. R. (1985). Proposals for a revolution in the preparation and regulation of professional psychologists. *American Psychologist, 40,* 1042–1050.

Friedman, R., Sobel, D., Myers, P., Caudill, M., & Benson, H. (1995). Behavioral medicine, clinical health psychology, and cost offset. *Health Psychology, 14,* 509–518.

Gaddy, C. D., Charlot-Swilley, D., Nelson, P. D., & Reich, J. N. (1995). Selected characteristics of accredited programs in psychology: a review of outcomes. *Professional Psychology: Research and Practice, 26,* 507–513.

Glueckauf, R. L., Frank, R. G., Bond, G. R., & McGrew, J. H. (Eds.) (1996). *Psychological practice in a changing health care system.* New York: Springer.

Greenberg, S., Smith, I. L., & Muenzen, P. M. (1996). *Study of the practice of licensed psychologists in the United States and Canada.* New York: Professional Examination Service.

Grosslight, J. (Ed.) (1990) Are graduate departments responsible for the marketability of their graduates? In L. Bickman and H. Ellis (Eds.), *Preparing psychologists for the 21st century* (pp. 163–173). Hillsdale, NJ: Erlbaum.

Groth-Marnat, G., & Edkins, G. (1996). Professional psychologists in general health care settings: a review of the financial efficacy of direct treatment interventions. *Professional Psychology: Research and Practice, 27,* 161–174.

Henry, B. (1984). The future of clinical training: forward into the past. *The Clinical Psychologist, Winter,* 25–26.

Hoch, E. L., Ross, A. O., & Winder, C. L. (Eds.) (1966). *Professional preparation of clinical psychologists.* Washington, DC: APA.

Hunt, W. A. (1975). Clinical psychology in 1944–45. *Journal of Clinical Psychology, 31,* 173–178.

Kane, M. T. (1982). The validity of licensure examinations. *American Psychologist, 37,* 911–918.

Kimble, G. A. (1984). Psychology's two cultures. *American Psychologist, 39,* 833–839.

Klatzky, R. L., Alluisi, E. A., Cook, W. A., Forehand, G. A., & Howell, W. C. (1985). Experimental psychologists in industry: perspectives of employers, employees, and educators. *American Psychologist, 40,* 1031–1037.

Kohout, J., & Wicherski, M. (1993). *1991 doctorate employment survey.* Washington, DC: APA.

Koocher, G. P. (1979). Credentialing in psychology: close encounters with competence? *American Psychologist, 34,* 696–702.

Korman, M. (Ed.) (1973). *Levels and patterns of professional training in psychology.* Washington, DC: American Psychological Association.

Lambert, N. M. (1991). The crisis in measurement literacy in psychology and education. *Educational Psychologist, 26,* 23–35.

Levy, L. H. (1984). The metamorphosis of clinical psychology. *American Psychologist, 39,* 486–494.

Lorion, R. P., Iscoe, I., DeLeon, P. H., & VandenBos, G. R. (Eds.) (1996). *Psychology and public policy: balancing public service and professional need.* Washington, DC: APA.

Marrow, A. J. (1969). *The practical theorist: the life and works of Kurt Lewin.* New York: Basic Books.

Matarazzo, J. D. (1987). There is only one psychology, no specialties, but many applications. *American Psychologist, 42,* 893–903.

Mayne, T. J., Norcross, J. C., & Sayette, M. A. (1994). Admission requirements, acceptance rates, and financial assistance in clinical psychology programs. *American Psychologist, 49,* 806–811.

McGaha, S., & Minder, C. (1993). Factors influencing performance on the Examination for Professional Practice in Psychology (EPPP). *Professional Psychology: Research and Practice, 24,* 107–109.

Merton, R. K. (1969). The functions of the professional association. *American Journal of Hospital Pharmacy, 26,* 636–641.

Millard, R. M. (1991). *Today's myths and tomorrow's realities.* San Francisco: Jossey-Bass.

Nelson, P. D., & Aletky, P. J. (1987). Accreditation: a link between training and practice. In B. A. Edelstein & E. S. Berler (Eds.), *Evaluation and accountability in clinical training* (pp. 231–252). New York: Plenum.

Perry, N. W., Jr. (1979). Why clinical psychology does not need alternative training models. *American Psychologist, 34,* 603–611.

Peterson, D. R. (1976a). Is psychology a profession? *American Psychologist, 31,* 572–583.

Peterson, D. R. (1976b). Need for the Doctor of Psychology degree in professional psychology. *American Psychologist, 31,* 792–798.

Peterson, D. R. (1985). Twenty years of practitioner training in psychology. *American Psychologist, 40,* 441–451.

Peterson, D. R. (1991). Connection and disconnection of research and practice in the education of professional psychologists. *American Psychologist, 46,* 422–429.

Peterson, D. R., & Peterson, R. L. (1997). Ways of knowing in a profession: towards an epistemology for the education of professional psychologists. In D. R. Peterson (Ed.), *Education professional psychologists: history and guiding conceptions.* Washington, DC: APA.

Peterson, R. L., Peterson, D. R., Abrams, J. C., & Stricker, G. (1997). The National Council of Schools and Programs of Professional Psychology education model. *Professional Psychology: Research and Practice, 28,* 373–386.

Raimy, V. C. (Ed.) (1950). *Training in clinical psychology.* New York: Prentice-Hall.

Roe, A., Gustad, J. W., Moore, B. V., Ross, S., & Skodak, M. (Eds.) (1959). *Graduate education in psychology.* Washington, DC: APA.

Ross, M. J., Holzman, L. A., Handal, P. J., & Gilner, F. H. (1991). Performance on the Examination for Professional Practice in Psychology as a function of specialty, degree, administrative housing, and accreditation status. *Professional Psychology: Research and Practice, 22,* 347–350.

Sanford, F. H. (1951). Annual report of the executive secretary: 1951. *American Psychologist, 6,* 664–670.

Sarason, S. B. (1981). An asocial psychology and a misdirected clinical psychology. *American Psychologist, 36,* 827–836.

Sears, R. R. (1946). Graduate training facilities. *American Psychologist, 1,* 135–150.

Sears, R. R. (1947). Clinical training facilities: 1947. *American Psychologist, 2,* 199–205.

Sechrest, L. (1990). A case for separate-but-equal in clinical training. In L. Bickman & H. Ellis (Eds.), *Preparing psychologists for the 21st century: proceedings of the national conference on graduate education in psychology* (pp. 69–75). Hillsdale, NJ: Erlbaum.

Sechrest, L., & Chatel, D. M. (1987). Evaluation and accountability in training for professional psychology: an overview. In B. A. Edelstein & E. S. Berler (Eds.), *Evaluation and accountability in clinical psychology* (pp. 1–7). New York: Plenum.

Shakow, D. (1978). Clinical psychology seen some 50 years later. *American Psychologist, 33,* 148–158.

Sheridan, E. P. (1990). Science versus practice or science and practice? In L. Bickman & H. Ellis (Eds.), *Preparing psychologists for the 21st century: proceedings of the national conference on graduate education in psychology* (pp. 225–230). Hillsdale, NJ: Erlbaum.

Sheridan, E. P., Matarazzo, J. D., & Nelson, P. D. (1995). Accreditation of psychology's graduate professional education and training programs: an historical perspective. *Professional Psychology: Research and Practice, 26,* 386–392.

Starr, P. (1982). *The social transformation of American medicine.* New York: Basic Books.

Stern, W. (1917). Hugo Munsterberg: in memorium. *Journal of Applied Psychology, 1,* 186–188.

Stevenson, J. F. & Norcross, J. C. (1987). Current status to training evaluation in clinical psychology. In B. A. Edelstein & E. S. Berler (Eds.), *Evaluation and accountability in clinical training* (pp. 77–115). New York: Plenum.

Stigall, T. T., Bourg, E. F., Bricklin, P. M., Kovacs, A. L., Larsen, K. G., Lorion, R. P., Nelson, P. D., Nurse, A. R., Pugh, R. W., & Wiens, A. N. (Eds.) (1990). *Report of the Joint Council on Professional Education in Psychology.* Baton Rouge, LA: Land and Land.

Stone, G. C., Weiss, S. M., Matarazzo, J. D., Miller, N. E., Rodin, J., Belar, C. D., Follick, M. J., & Singer, J. E. (Eds.) (1987). *Health psychology: a discipline and a profession.* Chicago: University of Chicago Press.

Stricker, G. (1997) Are science and practice commensurable? *American Psychologist, 52,* 442–448.

Strickland, B. R. (1985). Over the boulder(s) and through the vail. *The Clinical Psychologist, Summer,* 52–56.

Thompson, A. S., & Super, D. E. (Eds.) (1964). *The professional preparation of counseling psychologists.* New York: Columbia University Teachers College Bureau of Publications.

Tobias, S., Chubin, D. E., & Aylesworth, K. (1995). *Rethinking science as a career.* Tucson, AZ: Research Corporation.

Tryon, R. C. (1963). Psychology in flux: the academic-professional bipolarity. *American Psychologist, 18,* 134–143.

Wellner, A. M. (Ed.) (1978). *Education and credentialing in psychology: a proposal for a national commission.* Washington, DC: APA.

Wicherski, M. & Kohout, J. (1995). *1993 doctorate employment survey.* Washington, DC: APA.

Wilshire, B. (1990). *The moral collapse of the university: professionalism, purity, and alienation.* Albany, NY: State University of New York Press.

Yerkes, R. M. (1918). Psychology in relation to the war. *Psychological Review, 25,* 85–115.

Young, K. E., Chambers, C. M., & Kells, H. R. (Eds.) (1983). *Understanding accreditation.* San Francisco: Jossey-Bass.

2.06
The Development of Standards and the Regulation of the Practice of Clinical Psychology in Europe

FRANK M. McPHERSON
Tayside Area Clinical Psychology Department, Dundee, UK

2.06.1 INTRODUCTION

In this chapter, the term "practice" of clinical psychology is used to refer both to independent practice and to salaried employment; "licensing" and "legal regulation" are used interchangeably.

Any attempt to describe the legal status of clinical psychology in Europe faces three major difficulties. First, the situation is developing rapidly. In the three years since 1993, the law in six European nation states (hereafter "nations") has changed and some measure of international regulation has been introduced. New laws are anticipated in several nations before the end of the decade. Second, detailed accounts of the regulations which apply to clinical psychology are available for only a few European nations. Whenever possible, published accounts have been supplemented by unpublished papers and personal communications.

Finally, and probably most important, are the difficulties which result from the major differences which exist between the European nations, in the social role of legal recognition, in the ways in which the law protects clinical psychology, and in the extent of that protection. These differences can be understood only in the context of the formal legal systems and of the informal custom and practice which determine how these laws are applied, as well as of the educational, health care, and employment arrangements of each nation. This context is often difficult for non-nationals to grasp and it is easy to be misled by laws and their provisions which, although superficially similar, have different implications within their nations of origin and, conversely, by arrangements which are less different than, at first sight, they appear.

2.06.2 THE DEVELOPMENT OF REGULATION

2.06.2.1 Historical Overview

Ironically, a nation which no longer exists, the German Democratic Republic, was, in 1967, the first European nation to regulate clinical psychology (McPherson, 1986). By a decade later, seven more had done so, namely, Hungary, Iceland, The Netherlands, Norway, Portugal, Spain, and Sweden (Kjølstad, 1983). By 1996, to that number had been added Austria (Friedlmayer & Rössler, 1995), Belgium (Baneke, 1995), Denmark (Føltved, 1995), Finland (Saari, 1995), France (Matefi & Häring, 1993), Germany (Matefi & Häring, 1993), Greece (Georgas, 1995), Italy (Bonal, 1990; Lombardo, 1990), and the UK (Lunt, 1995).

Although together these account for only about 40% of European nations, they include most of those in which clinical psychology exists as a well-developed profession. The main exceptions are the Czech Republic (Brožek & Hoscovec, 1995), Ireland (Brady & McLoone, 1992), Poland (Toeplitz-Winiewka, 1992), Slovakia (Kováč, 1995), Switzerland (Peel, 1992), and Turkey (Sahin, 1995).

2.06.2.2 Influences on Regulation

In addition to these differences in whether and, if so, when laws were introduced, even more striking differences exist in how regulation has been implemented, as the remainder of the chapter will show. Although there is little documentary evidence, three sets of influences appear to have contributed to this variability.

2.06.2.2.1 Political influences

Although differences in regulation might seem unsurprising, in view of the political divisions which have existed between European nations throughout much of the history of professional psychology (McPherson, 1991), the general political ideology of a nation appears to have had little effect. Thus, the earliest European nations with psychology laws included some which, at the time, had both left and right wing authoritarian regimes and others which then, as now, were parliamentary democracies. Moreover, there are even major differences between nations which politically are often grouped together.

The Nordic nations have been cooperating for many years, as have their psychologists who, in the 1950s, made joint proposals to the Nordic Council (of Governments) for the regulation of psychology. Although these were accepted in 1958 and were implemented by Norway in 1973, by Iceland in 1976 and, partly, by Sweden in 1978, it took until 1993 for Finland (Saari, 1995) and 1994 for Denmark (Føltved, 1995) to regulate psychology and 1994 for Sweden to achieve full title protection (Nevalainen, 1995; Persson, 1995).

Of the three Benelux nations, The Netherlands had a law protecting the title "psychologist" as long ago as 1971, whereas in Belgium there was no such law until 1993, the same year in which "psychologist" lost its protected status in The Netherlands. Luxembourg has no psychology laws (Baneke, 1995; van Drunen, 1995).

More specific political attitudes have undoubtedly affected the process of regulation.

Attempts to introduce laws were often opposed by some psychologists and political groups, especially in the 1960s, on the grounds that they threatened individual rights and freedoms (Saari, 1995). More recently, legislation in some nations has been influenced by the determination of governments to promote consumer protection and free competition. Although this has encouraged legislation, the resulting laws have tended only to protect the title, since this allows the consumer to identify qualified and ethical practitioners. The licensing of specific activities has been opposed, since this would restrict competition (Baneke, 1995).

2.06.2.2.2 *Employment arrangements*

Not unexpectedly, the employment and reimbursement arrangements in the health care system of a nation appear to have a significant influence on regulation. Legislation, for example, in 1993 in The Netherlands and Finland, has often been in the context of reforms in the health care system and, as will be discussed later, the influence of employers and insurance companies on the development of postqualification training has been significant.

In the UK, the "social recognition" of clinical psychology provided by the National Health Service (NHS) has been a major reason why there is as yet no full legal protection of any relevant title (McPherson, 1983). Traditionally, the great majority of UK clinical psychologists have been salaried employees of the NHS and, until recently, there has been very little independent practice. The British Psychological Society (BPS) influenced NHS disciplinary procedures and the entry requirements which, in turn, determined the form, duration, and content of UK clinical psychology training. For as long as the NHS remained the monopoly employer and accepted BPS advice, there was little perceived need for additional, legal protection, either for clinical psychologists themselves, or for their patients. The recent renewal of interest in full statutory legislation follows a period of health care reform, which has seen the possibility of greater diversity in employment arrangements within the NHS, along with an increased role for the private and independent provision of services.

The NHS has also influenced the breadth of clinical training obtained in the UK, which is greater than elsewhere in Europe. Although willing to set entry standards, the NHS has been reluctant to approve specialty credentialing, so that a clinical psychologist employed by the NHS is eligible to work with any category of patient and clinical problem. This, in turn, has caused the BPS to ensure that trainee clinical psychologists obtain experience with all the main NHS client groups.

2.06.2.2.3 *Influence of the profession*

The role of the national associations of psychology often appears to have been crucial. Historical accounts of the progress towards legal regulation in some nations emphasize the importance of the political lobbying carried out by the national associations over many years. These accounts also note their role, once political agreement had been reached, in influencing the technical aspects of regulation, such as training requirements and practice arrangements. Where there have been several, competing psychology associations within a nation, or where there has been disagreement about training or practice, legal regulation often appears to have been delayed.

2.06.3 CURRENT STATE OF LEGAL REGULATION

2.06.3.1 Nature of the Laws Regulating Clinical Psychology

There are very wide variations in the legal means by which psychology is regulated in the different European nations. Laws relating to psychology are of four, general types.

First, the unauthorized use of a university degree and title is probably illegal under the criminal or civil legal codes of all European nations; in some, these degree titles enable the user to be identified as having studied psychology.

Second, there are laws which are specific to the title or practice of psychology. Nations with such laws include Austria (1990), Belgium (1993), Denmark (1993), France (1985), Germany (1985), Greece (1979), Hungary (1974), Iceland (1976), Italy (1989), Norway (1973), Portugal (1972), and Sweden (1978 and 1994).

Third, in some nations, the regulation of psychology is included in more general provisions. For example, the 1979 law in Spain was enacted under an older law applying to the regulation of academic disciplines (Prieto & Avila, 1994) and, in 1993 in Finland and The Netherlands, the protection of titles resulted from laws applying to all health care professionals (Saari, 1995; Baneke, 1995).

Finally, in the absence of regulation obtained by Government-sponsored legislation, the national associations of psychologists of several nations—including Germany, The

Netherlands, and the UK—confer titles on their members which they protect by the use of civil laws.

2.06.3.2 Scope of the Laws

Although, for most nations, the laws protecting psychology apply to the whole range of professional psychology activities, for some nations the protection is limited in scope. In Sweden, "psychologist" (Persson, 1995) and in Austria, "clinical psychologist" and "health psychologist" (Friedlmayer & Rössler, 1995) are protected only within the health system, as will be "clinical psychologist" in The Netherlands when the 1993 law is fully implemented (Baneke, 1995; van Drunen, 1995). The Finnish law is interesting: it defines *all* registered psychologists as health care professionals, thus extending to other branches of the profession the protection of title which exists within the health system (Saari, 1995).

2.06.3.3 Regulatory Bodies

Probably in every nation in which there are laws, other than France (Matefi and Häring, 1993), there is a regulatory body for psychology. However, no two European nations have the same arrangements.

One way in which they differ is the extent to which the body is specific to psychology. In Spain and the UK, authority to regulate the profession has been delegated to the national associations of psychologists. Thus, in Spain a Colegia Oficial formed by Parliament with the agreement of the Crown, exists to organize a group of professional experts who share the same academic credentials. It provides a self-governing institution, to which the state delegates power to regulate the work of its members. The Colegia Oficial de Psicólogos (COP) was formed in 1979 to undertake these responsibilities for psychology (Prieto & Avila, 1994). Likewise, in the UK the BPS was given authority by the Crown to set up a voluntary register of its own members and to award and protect the title "chartered psychologist" and several specialist variations (Lunt, 1995).

By contrast, several nations have a psychology board established by the relevant law. Thus, in Belgium, the Psychologists Commission was set up by the Crown (Baneke, 1995). (The term "by the Crown" should be explained. In several European nations with constitutional monarchies, Parliament passes the laws necessary for regulating a profession, but the regulatory body that is set up acts on behalf of the Crown—king or queen—partly to protect the profession from direct political influence.) In Denmark, a nine member board includes representatives of the relevant government departments and the municipalities (Føltved, 1995). In Italy, regional councils are responsible for holding registers of recognized psychologists and for monitoring their professional activities, while a national council is responsible for developing codes of conduct, accrediting private training institutions and recommending scales of fees, for example, to insurance companies (Bonal, 1990; Lombardo, 1990).

In other countries, some or all aspects of regulation are the responsibility of a body with a remit for the wider health care system, such as a government ministry.

A second difference concerns the two main functions of a regulatory board, to grant licenses to individual applicants and to enforce a disciplinary procedure. For some nations, these are done by the same body, although usually with some internal division of function. Elsewhere, in particular where licenses are awarded by a body with a remit wider than psychology, a different agency is in charge of disciplinary matters. In Norway, the licensing of psychologists is done by the Ministry of Health, while the Central Health Authority (CHA) has the power to revoke a psychologist's license, in accordance with the Psychologists Law (Kjølstad, 1995). In Sweden, the National Board of Health and Welfare authorizes the title and the Medical Responsibility Board is concerned with the regulation of professional conduct (Persson, 1995). In Finland, these are the responsibilities, respectively, of the Ministry of Social Affairs and Health and of the National Board of Medicolegal Affairs (Saari, 1995).

2.06.3.4 Laws Protecting a Title

The most common form of legal recognition in Europe is that which protects the use of a designated title. Four different arrangements can be identified.

First, there is the protection of the university degree. Those used by psychology graduates in some European nations are common to several disciplines, for example, *doctoraandus* (*drs*) in The Netherlands. Often, however, they are specific to psychology, for example, *diplom-psychologe* in Germany, *lic. psych.* in the French-speaking parts of Switzerland (although the more general *lic. phil.* is used in the German-speaking cantons) and *cand. psych.* in Denmark. These laws provide limited title protection, in that they indicate that the user has obtained a university degree in psychology.

Second, in all but one of the nations with psychology laws—Portugal being the exception—a professional title is given some measure of legal protection. In most, the protection is of the generic "psychologist," or some equivalent, which does not identify particular specialties within professional psychology. This is the case in Finland, Germany, Iceland, Italy, Norway, and Spain, among other nations. Although "licensed psychologist" was protected in Sweden for many years, there were no restrictions on the use of "psychologist" until 1994 (Persson, 1995). In The Netherlands, the protection which had existed for *psycholoog* since 1971 was abolished by the 1993 law which, however, introduced a protected specialist title (Baneke, 1995; van Drunen, 1995).

There are variations within some nations. Although, in Switzerland, "psychologist" is not protected at federal level (Peel, 1992), it seems that protection exists in some of the component cantons (Matelfi & Häring, 1993). Under the recent law in bilingual Belgium, there are two protected titles, *psycholoog* in the Dutch-speaking parts and *psychologue* in the French-speaking regions (Baneke, 1995).

Third, in several nations, protection is given to a specialist title, usually in addition to the generic "psychologist," although in Austria only "clinical psychologist" and "health psychologist" are protected. In France, *psychologue* can be used alone, but also with a qualifying adjective, for example, indicating clinical specialization. Denmark protects *psykolog,* but those with an additional two years of supervised clinical experience may also apply to use *autoriseret psykolog* (Føltved, 1995). In The Netherlands, the 1993 law created a fully protected title for clinical psychologists, *klinisch psycholoog* (Baneke, 1995). Hungary specifies different levels of training for psychologists and for specialist, clinical psychologists (Pléh, 1991) and a similar law, which has existed in Greece since 1979, has recently been implemented (Georgas, 1995).

Finally, some national associations of psychology confer titles which attract limited protection. Thus, in 1966, the Nederlands Instituut van Psychologen (NIP) introduced the title *NIP klinisch psycholoog* for use by those members who had undergone a period of clinical training and supervised experience specified by NIP. This will continue to be used until the 1993 law is fully in force. To compensate for the loss of protection for *psycholoog,* NIP recently introduced the title *NIP psycholoog* for those of its members who have the relevant *drs* degree and further experience. These NIP titles are protected by patent and trademark (van Drunen, 1995). The German association for professional psychologists, the Berufsverband Deutscher Psychologen (BDP), has a similar arrangement which enables members who have obtained the *diplom-psycholog* and further training and experience to refer to themselves as "BDP clinical psychologists." The Norsk Psykologforening in Norway, in addition to the legally-protected generic title, authorizes the use of a more restricted title by clinical psychologists who have met their additional criteria (Kløve, 1992).

2.06.3.5 Laws Regulating the Practice of Clinical Psychology

To practice any branch of psychology in Spain, it is legally necessary to be a member of the COP (Rodriguez Sutil, 1995) and, in Portugal, to obtain a license from the Ministry of Work, although there appear to be no sanctions for noncompliance (Pereira, 1995).

Entry into the field of health care appears, in some nations, to be restricted to licensed practitioners, although the scope of these restrictions is not always clear. Elsewhere, although there may be no formal restrictions, informal agreements ensure that only licensed psychologists are employed. Where there are restrictions, they tend always to apply, wholly or mainly, to the field of public health. Where they affect independent practice, it is normally in connection with Government-supported insurance companies which, in some nations, will reimburse the fees only of psychologists with the appropriate, protected title. The nations which, by whatever means, most stringently restrict entry into health care to licensed psychologists, are Austria, Finland, Hungary, Norway, and Sweden.

Within the field of health care, there are few examples of laws which explicitly permit or prohibit clinical psychologists from performing specific activities. The Austrian law defines the activities associated with clinical psychology (Friedlmeyer & Rössler, 1995). In Norway, when the 1973 Psychologists Law was passed, other laws were amended so that psychologists were excluded from regulations to combat charlatans and could use hypnosis in the treatment of illness (Kløve, 1992). The recent law in Finland states that "only a licensed professional is entitled to perform the tasks belonging to the said profession and to use the title in question," but it is not yet clear to what extent the application of the law will result in any specific activities being held to be exclusive to psychologists (Saari, 1995).

Psychotherapy is outside the scope of this chapter. However, the situation in brief is that, in some nations, psychotherapy is regarded as a profession in its own right and is regulated independently. In some of these, clinical psychology training allows registration also as a psychotherapist whereas, in others, additional training is required. In several other nations, in which psychotherapy is regarded as an activity to be carried out by members of more generic professions, special practising licenses are required. In most of these, clinical psychologists are eligible for these licenses but, in at least one, psychotherapy can be practised only under the (usually nominal) supervision of a medical practitioner. In some nations, including the UK, there are no regulations.

2.06.4 EDUCATIONAL AND TRAINING REQUIREMENTS NECESSARY FOR LEGAL RECOGNITION

2.06.4.1 Structure of Training

In Greece, Hungary, and the UK, the structure of clinical psychology training is somewhat similar to that in North America, with the university phase being discontinuous, consisting of two separate degree courses. The first of these is concerned with the scientific bases of psychology, while the second is a program of academic, research, and practical studies in the clinical applications of psychology. Hitherto, these latter programs have led to masters degrees, the term "doctoral level" training having no meaning in Europe, where the Ph.D. and its equivalents are awarded only for research. An exception is the UK, where, in the last few years, universities have begun awarding doctoral degrees (usually *doctor of clinical psychology*) on completion of the second degree.

Elsewhere in Europe, the arrangements are quite different. Potential clinical psychologists take a single degree, which normally makes them eligible for licensing as a qualified professional psychologist, although in some nations a further period of practical training and experience is necessary (McPherson, 1991, 1992).

2.06.4.2 Length of Training

The minimum length of training necessary for legal registration, as defined in the relevant laws of each nation, often underestimates the actual time spent by many clinical psychology students before becoming licensed. In many European nations, individual students are given considerable freedom to determine the length of their university studies and, although governments are making strenuous efforts to curtail this freedom, the average time taken may be two or more years longer than the period specified in the relevant curriculum or law.

In most of those nations which legally protect the generic title "psychologist," the minimum period of training prior to licensing is five years: this is the case in Belgium, France, Spain, and Portugal, although in Sweden it is six years—five of study, followed by one year of supervised practice—and in Norway it is between six and seven years (McPherson, 1991, 1992).

Where the protection is of "clinical psychologist," or some other specialist title, the prescribed minimum time is usually longer. Thus, in Denmark, although a five year training leads to the protected *psykolog,* a further two years of supervised practice are required to become an *autorisiret psykolog*. (Føltved, 1995). In Austria, seven years are necessary, in a single degree, as they are in Hungary, although in a five-year first degree, followed by a two-year clinical training period (László & Pléh, 1992). In The Netherlands, eligibility for *klinisch psycholoog* requires four years of inservice training and experience, subsequent to the four year *drs* (Baneke, 1995; van Drunen, 1995). The UK title *chartered clinical psychologist* is awarded after a minimum of six years, three spent on the first (*bachelors*) degree and three on a graduate (*postgraduate* in UK parlance) clinical training course (Lunt, 1995).

2.06.4.3 Academic Content of Training

There are difficulties in comparing the educational requirements necessary to obtain a protected title. Published curricula are potentially misleading, because of wide variations between nations in the relative time typically devoted to formal instruction and to private study. Internationally, there is an absence of agreed definitions of terms such as "supervised experience," "credit hours," and "year of study" and of a system of on-site inspection and peer review, to establish the relationship between what is described and what is done in practice.

In many nations, because of decrees by the national government, or the influence of the profession, there is considerable similarity between different universities in the content of psychology degrees. In some, however, the traditional autonomy of universities remains, so that big differences exist in the curricula which lead to the protected title, thus allowing few generalizations to be made about the "typical" content of training.

2.06.4.3.1 The science of psychology

In those nations in which clinical psychology training involves two separate degree courses, the first (e.g., leading in the UK to the *bachelors* degree) is wholly or mainly devoted to studies in the scientific discipline of psychology. Hence, it covers all or most of the following topics: the biological bases of behavior; perception, learning, and memory; thinking and language; personality, intelligence, and individual differences; social psychology; developmental psychology; research design and quantitative methods; and specialist areas. A research dissertation will also normally be required (McPherson, 1991).

In those nations in which potential clinical psychologists study for a single degree, these topics are usually included during the first semesters, lasting two or three years (McPherson, 1991, 1992).

2.06.4.3.2 The academic bases of clinical psychology

Where training is discontinuous, the academic teaching in clinical psychology and related topics takes place during the course of studies leading to the second, specialist degree in clinical psychology, which is devoted almost exclusively to these subjects.

Where there is a single degree, all potential clinical psychologists take academic courses relevant to clinical psychology during the later semesters. However, there are major differences between nations in the extent to which specialization is possible at this stage.

In particular, in the Nordic nations, all students receive an education in the academic bases, not only of clinical psychology, but also of other branches of professional, applied psychology. Thus, in Norway, the 1987 revision of the standards for the *cand. psychol.* degree require that at least four semesters should be devoted to studying five applied disciplines: namely, school and educational psychology, organizational and occupational psychology, medical and health psychology, community psychology, and clinical psychology. In Denmark, after five "scientific bases" semesters, students spend four semesters studying organizational, educational, and clinical psychology, among other topics. In Finland and Sweden there is also no specialization, with all students undertaking more or less the same courses. Some other nations also expose students to a broad education in professional psychology; thus, in Spanish universities, the second cycle of studies, of between two and three years, includes clinical and educational psychology and the psychology of groups and organizations.

In some other nations, a much greater degree of specialization is possible. In Germany, students are often able to spend their last two or three years studying only one branch of professional, applied psychology—usually clinical, educational, or organizational psychology. Roughly similar arrangements also exist in The Netherlands, Belgium, Italy, and France, although the range and content of the optional specializations vary greatly.

2.06.4.4 Practical Training and Experience

There are major differences between nations in the amount and in the scope of clinical training and experience required of potential clinical psychologists, before they are eligible for the protected title. There are also differences in the stage of the training process at which the experience is obtained. There are three main types of arrangement.

First, in most of the nations in which training is continuous, all the practical training and experience necessary for licensing is carried out during the program leading to the single degree. In some of these, in particular where the profession appears to have had a significant influence on the university curricula, this practicum period is substantial. Elsewhere, however, universities have historically been seen as providing the educational bases for professional training, rather than the training itself, which is thus normally carried out after graduation and hence also after licensing (McPherson, 1992). The minimum practicum period therefore varies greatly. Norway requires four months of practical training and eight months of practical experience. In Finland, there is a supervised practicum of six months and, in Belgium, one which occupies four days weekly for at least seven months. In Sweden, in addition to undertaking a practicum, all students must receive personal therapy. Elsewhere, practical training can be much shorter. In some German universities, only two, six-week periods are required and, in some Spanish universities, only approximately 90 hours.

Second, the main period of supervised training and experience can occur after completion of the single degree. In Denmark, at least two years of such supervised experience are necessary before *autoriseret psykolog* status is granted and Italy and Sweden require a one year internship before the trainee is eligible for licensing.

Finally, where training is discontinuous, the bulk of the program for the second degree is given over to clinical training and supervised practice. The greatest breadth of experience is provided in the UK where, to become a *chartered clinical psychologist,* trainees must have undertaken five supervised and assessed clinical placements, each of at least 65 days: with adults with psychological disorders, with children and adolescents, with people with a learning disability (mental handicap), with older adults, and in another, more specialized area of the trainee's own choice. In the other nations with this structure, trainees obtain experience with fewer client groups—seldom, for example, with people with a learning disability—but often for longer periods.

2.06.4.5 Postqualification Training

Postqualification training and experience, that is, obtained after a clinical psychologist has been licensed, is very much more important in some European nations than, for example, in North America. As described above, the protected generic title can often be obtained without the clinical psychologist having received a significant amount of specialized, clinically relevant education, or practical clinical training. Some years ago, this began to be recognized as a problem. Psychologists who had been licensed and who wished to work as clinicians, found that they required substantial, additional specialist training, both to be acceptable to employers in the health sector and to have marketable skill in independent practice. Also, potential employers and clients, insurance companies concerned with the reimbursement of fees for clinical psychology assessment and treatment, and others who wished to identify psychologists with appropriate clinical skills, found that the generic titles were not helpful. Several solutions to this problem have been attempted.

Possibly the most satisfactory solution has been to introduce protected specialist titles. In The Netherlands, "psychologist" is being replaced with "clinical psychologist" as the legally protected title. Another solution, adopted by several nations, is to have, in addition to the generic title, a legally protected specialist title, available after programs of advanced training. The example of Denmark has already been noted and both Finland and Sweden are implementing lengthy programs, on topics such as psychotherapy, health psychology, and neuropsychology, which will form the basis of postregistration specialty licensing. It was an awareness of the limitations of generic licensing which persuaded Austria to protect two specialist titles, "health psychologist" and "clinical psychologist."

In the absence of protected specialist titles, several national associations arranged their own, advanced programs of study in clinical psychology, leading to a qualification approved by themselves. As noted above, such qualifications have achieved quasilegal status: that is, the title can usually be protected in the civil courts and—usually as the result of lengthy negotiation by the association—is used by employers and by insurance companies to determine eligibility for employment or reimbursement of fees. One of the most extensive programs is that leading to the title "specialist clinical psychologist," awarded by the Norwegian Psychological Association. This requires some five years of postlicensing experience, in at least two settings, including work with both adults and children and at least two years spent as a full-time employee in one setting; a minimum of two hours of supervision per week for two years is specified, along with attendance at courses and workshops. This title qualifies clinical psychologists to be appointed to certain senior posts in the health service and has implications for reimbursement of insurance (Kløve, 1992). Two other examples include: (i) the postqualification title "NIP clinical psychologist," awarded in The Netherlands since 1966, but which will be replaced by the fully protected "clinical psychologist" established by the 1993 law, although the training requirements will continue to be determined largely by NIP (Baneke, 1995); and (ii) the specialist title "BDP clinical psychologist," awarded by the German association, which also has implications for employment and reimbursement. Both require between four and six years of part-time study.

Elsewhere, employers have organized their own training programs, to supplement the training of licensed psychologists. The former German Democratic Republic had an elaborate system of training and regulation, which enabled clinical psychologists to have equal legal status to medical doctors (Kossakowski, 1992). In Spain, a system of internship, Psicólogo Interno Residente (PIR), has been developed by the Ministries of Education and Health, analogous to that for medical graduates. Psychologists who are already registered with the COP spend three years on supervised placements in the public health system (Belloch & Olabarría, 1994).

In several nations, the need was met by private organizations, which developed very many training programs, dedicated to teaching specific clinical skills, usually psychotherapeutic procedures. Some of these are very extensive, lasting several years and involving academic teaching as well as supervised practice. Clinically relevant courses with a more academic orientation are offered by universities, in particular in France and Spain. Often, this additional training does no more than increase the marketability of clinical psychologists in independent practice. However, in Germany, the major health insurance companies have agreed to reimburse the fees only of those clinical psychologists who have undergone specified training, for example, in psychoanalytic or behavioral psychotherapy.

Because many of these programs take place after the clinical psychologist has been licensed, they are not usually subject to scrutiny or control, either by the official regulatory body, or by the relevant national association of psychologists. This has led to anxieties about the quality of training. Some national associations have therefore developed an informal system of accrediting the courses run by private organizations and universities. In nations in which there is no other protection of title or practice, for example, Turkey (Sahin, 1995), this accreditation is seen as a first step towards full legal regulation.

2.06.5 DISCIPLINARY ARRANGEMENTS

The disciplinary arrangements which apply in most of Europe are broadly similar to those in North America, in that licensed clinical psychologists are subject to the criminal and civil law, to the codes of ethics and conduct of their professional bodies, and to the regulations of the relevant licensing authorities. However, the detailed procedures vary greatly.

The range of different bodies involved in regulating conduct in the various European nations has previously been outlined. In those in which clinical psychologists are regulated as health care professionals, both the legal requirements and the penalties imposed appear to be more stringent than elsewhere. Thus, in Finland, the clinical psychologist is *legally* bound, among other things: (i) to apply generally approved and empirically tested procedures in accordance with his/her training; (ii) to maintain and improve the skills required for the practice of the profession (although employers are also legally required to allow him/her to attend any necessary training); (iii) to be aware of the regulations and statutes covering professional conduct; (iv) to create and keep confidential patient records; and (v) to provide assistance to anyone in need of urgent treatment. The penalty for failing to maintain the confidentiality prescribed by law can be six months imprisonment (Saari, 1995).

In most of the nations which legally regulate clinical psychology, the national association has a formal code of ethics which usually appears to have at least some role in disciplinary proceedings, although in some, for example, Norway, the relevant law also includes statements about prohibited conduct (Kjølstad, 1995). However, there appear to be no codes of conduct in use which are as specific and detailed as that produced by the Association of State and Provincial Psychology Boards (see Chapter 24, this volume), and anecdotal evidence suggests that some existing codes are not helpful in disciplinary proceedings.

2.06.6 INTERNATIONAL REGULATION

2.06.6.1 The European Union

The international influences on the legal regulation of clinical psychology in Europe derive from the European Union (EU), formerly the European Economic Community (EEC). Since 1994, EU provisions for the mutual recognition of professional qualifications have also applied to some of the member nations of the European Free Trade Association (EFTA). In 1996, the EU and EFTA nations—collectively referred to as the European Economic Association (EEA)—to which these provisions applied were: Austria, Belgium, Denmark, Finland, France, Germany, Greece, Iceland, Ireland, Italy, Luxembourg, The Netherlands, Norway, Portugal, Spain, Sweden, and the UK.

One aim of the EU is to create a "common market" of professions and occupations, by removing barriers to free movement. The legislative means of achieving this is the "Directive," which is binding on member nations in relation to the required results, although the means of achieving them maybe decided by each nation (McPherson, 1989).

The initial approach was "sectorial," with a separate Directive for each profession. This required member nations to guarantee, for that profession, the mutual recognition of qualifications and the "right of establishment," in other words, that an EU national, trained in one member nation, would have his/her qualifications accepted in any other member nation in which he/she wished to work. Directives were issued only after a significant amount of "harmonization" of training had been achieved, so that each sectorial Directive was able to specify, for the EU as a whole, a common set of minimum training requirements for entry into the profession.

However, progress was very slow and, although work was begun on over 50 Directives, by the early 1980s only seven—mainly concerning health professions—had been implemented. Although this was partly due to the technical problems of harmonizing what were often quite heterogeneous training arrangements, delays were mainly due to a lack of urgency: free movement was a political goal, for which few professions expressed enthusiasm (Orzark, 1983; McPherson, 1989).

The EU lost patience with these delays and adopted a "horizontal" approach, with a single Directive which applied to all professions and occupations which required at least three years of university training. This "general system for the recognition of higher education diplomas" was published in draft form in 1985 and took effect, as Directive 89/48/EEC, in January 1993.

2.06.6.2 General Directive 89/48/EEC

Psychology had not been subject to a sectorial Directive because, in the words of one EU official to the author, "psychology training is so diverse that free movement should not be encouraged." The horizontal Directive applies only to those professional activities which are regulated and, although no definition is given, the clear intention is that the term "regulation" should be defined very broadly. Hence, in many EEA member nations, the Directive covers all clinical psychology practice, both salaried and independent; in all others, at least some aspects are affected.

The Directive is concerned with members of a profession ("migrants") who move from one EEA member nation to another (the "host"). Its main provision is to make illegal any attempt to prevent a migrant clinical psychologist from practicing, merely because they had trained in another member nation; it extends not only to direct discrimination, but also to the setting of licensing or employment requirements which are in excess of those demanded of clinical psychologists of the host nation. It permits an aggrieved migrant to use the civil courts of the host nation to take action against an employer, or a regulatory body and, ultimately, to take the case to the European Court of Justice, which has powers which are normally binding on EU member nations.

Unlike its sectorial predecessors, this Directive was not preceded by a period of harmonization and does not specify training requirements. Therefore, it applies regardless of any differences in the training of a migrant and of clinical psychologists of the host nation. Moreover, EU officials emphasize that, when training courses and professional skills are being compared, the *equivalence* of qualifications is more important than their exact equality. However, where differences in training are significant in length or content, after any postqualification experience has been taken into consideration, the Directive does allow the regulatory body of the host to require the migrant, either to complete an "adaptation period" under some measure of supervision, or to take an examination on those academic or professional topics which they have not previously covered. There are strict limits to what can be required (McPherson, 1990a).

2.06.6.3 Effects of the Directive

Thus far, the Directive is having little effect, because few clinical psychologists migrate within the EEA, due to an absence of work opportunities and to language difficulties. There is some movement between the Nordic nations, but the Directive has added little to the common market for psychologists which they have operated for some years.

The exception is the UK, to which there is a significant amount of migration, because there are vacant clinical psychology posts and many EEA clinical psychologists have English as their second language. The least enthusiastic member of the European family of nations has thus done most to implement the Directive and the BPS has established a committee to scrutinize the qualifications of migrants who have applied for registration as *chartered clinical psychologists.* Most are required to undergo additional training and supervised practice, mainly because of their lack of clinical experience with people with learning disabilities (mental handicap) and with older adults.

One area of uncertainty has not yet been addressed. The Directive applies only to mobility within the same profession but, since some nations protect generic and others specialist titles, it is not clear whether the profession is "psychology," "clinical psychology" (and other specialist variants), or both. It has yet to be determined whether a host nation which protects a specialist title can legally decide that, because a particular migrant was, by title and training, a "psychologist," they belong to a different profession, and so the Directive does not apply.

Similarly, the distinction between "clinical psychology" and "psychotherapy" is causing difficulties. Some migrants, although "clinical psychologists" in their own nation, have been refused right of establishment because the host considered that they were actually "psychotherapists," because their training did not contain sufficient psychology. France has criticised the Directive on the grounds that, even with the maximum permitted adaptation period, migrants could practice in France after several years training less than that required of French clinical psychologists. However, this training gap derives not from the five years necessary to obtain the protected title, but from the very long postqualification training which many French clinical psychologists undertake to become psychotherapists.

If these ambiguities are seen by the EU to obstruct the working of the Directive, psychologists in Europe might be required, either by the EU itself or by a court, to clarify their professional structure and to define "core curricula," which would enable clinical psychology to be discriminated objectively, both from other branches of psychology and from psychotherapy.

2.06.7 FUTURE DEVELOPMENTS

2.06.7.1 National Regulation

Over the next few years, some additional nations are likely to enact laws regulating psychology. The national associations of the Czech Republic, Slovakia, Switzerland, Poland, Turkey, Romania, and the UK, among others, have all indicated that laws are being prepared, for which government support is being sought.

As noted above, it appears that the protection provided by generic titles is increasingly being seen as inadequate, in particular in the health field. This might influence which title these new laws will protect and might also lead to existing laws being changed, as they were in The Netherlands, so that specialist titles, obtained after longer, fully regulated training and experience, will be introduced to replace or supplement the generic "psychologist." However, there is no reason to expect that there will be a change in the preference of most governments for protecting the title, rather than the practice, of clinical psychology.

2.06.7.2 International Regulation

There may well be EU Directives, for example, on the application of Value Added Tax to clinical services and on aspects of consumer protection, which will affect clinical psychology. However, in the field of regulation, the main concern of the EU continues to be to remove barriers to mobility and to the right of establishment. It is clear that, in psychology, the barriers are created less by restrictive national laws and regulations than by language and the absence of work opportunities. Thus, any sectorial Directive for psychology which is proposed by the profession would probably be seen by the EU to be unnecessary. Instead, collaboration between universities and practitioners is being encouraged as a means of promoting harmonization in the training and practice of psychologists.

If further legislation is ever thought to be necessary to enable clinical psychologists to become more mobile, a sectorial Directive, to establish the equivalence of national qualifications, is only one possibility. Another approach was pioneered in the 1980s by FEANI, the European federation of national associations of engineers. According to this model, EU nations would set up a European Register, with its own regulatory body and entry requirements and would agree to grant right of establishment to psychologists on the Register (McPherson, 1990b).

2.06.8 REFERENCES

Baneke, R. F. (1995). Benelux, a bundle of contrasts. *News from EFPPA, 9*(1), 10–12.

Belloch, A. & Olabarría, B. (1994). Clinical psychology: Current status and future prospects. *Applied Psychology: An International Review, 43,* 193–211.

Bonal, I. (1990). L'ordre à l'italienne. *Le Journal des Psychologues, 80,* 55–56.

Brady, T. & McLoone, J. (1992). Ireland. In V. S. Sexton & J. D. Hogan (Eds.), *International psychology: Views from around the world.* Lincoln, NE: University of Nebraska Press.

Brožek, J. & Hoscovec, J. (1995). Psychology in the Czech Republic. In A. Schorr and S. Saari (Eds.), *Psychology in Europe. Facts, figures, realities* (pp. 3–14). Seattle, WA: Hogrefe & Huber.

Føltved, P. (1995). Professional psychology in Denmark. In A. Schorr & S. Saari (Eds.), *Psychology in Europe. Facts, figures, realities* (pp. 15–22). Seattle, WA: Hogrefe & Huber.

Friedlmayer, S. & Rössler, E. (1995). Professional identity and public image of Austrian psychologists. In A. Schorr & S. Saari (Eds.), *Psychology in Europe. Facts, figures, realities* (pp. 165–179). Seattle, WA: Hogrefe & Huber.

Georgas, J. (1995). Psychology in Greece. In A. Schorr & S. Saari (Eds.), *Psychology in Europe. Facts, figures, realities* (pp. 59–75). Seattle, WA: Hogrefe & Huber.

Kjølstad, H. (1983). Professional psychologists associations in Europe 1982. *Tidsskrift for Norsk Psykologforening, 20,* 544–549.

Kjølstad, H. (1995). *Disciplining psychologists in Norway.* Paper presented at the First International Congress on Licensure, Certification, and Credentialing, New Orleans, LA.

Kløve, H. (1992). Norway. In V. S. Sexton & J. D. Hogan (Eds.), *International psychology: Views from around the world.* Lincoln, NE: University of Nebraska Press.

Kossakowski, A. (1992). German Democratic Republic. In V. S. Sexton & J. D. Hogan (Eds.), *International psychology: Views from around the world.* Lincoln, NE: University of Nebraska Press.

Kováč, D. (1995). Psychology in Slovakia—Leaving the Iron Curtain behind. In A. Schorr & S. Saari (Eds.), *Psychology in Europe. Facts, figures, realities* (pp. 103–110). Seattle, WA: Hogrefe & Huber.

László, J. & Pléh, C. (1992). Hungary. In V. S. Sexton & J. D. Hogan (Eds.), *International psychology: Views from around the world.* Lincoln, NE: University of Nebraska Press.

Lombardo, G. P. (1990). Formation et rôle du psychologue clinicien en Italie. *Le Journal des Psychologues, 80,* 57–58.

Lunt, I. (1995). The training and regulation of psychologists in the United Kingdom. *News from EFPPA, 9*(1), 17–19.

Matefi, G. & Häring, E. (1993). *Inventory of regulations in the field of psychology in European countries.* Bonn, Germany: BDP.

McPherson, F. M. (1983). The United Kingdom. *International Journal of Psychology, 6,* 27–34.

McPherson, F. M. (1986). The professional psychologist in Europe. *American Psychologist, 41,* 302– 305.

McPherson, F. M. (1989). Psychologists and the European Economic Community. *The Psychologist, 1,* 353–355.

McPherson, F. M. (1990a). Psychologists and the EEC (II). *The Psychologist, 2,* 382–383.

McPherson, F. M. (1990b, November). The regulation of a European profession of clinical psychology. *Clinical Psychology Forum,* 17–19.

McPherson, F. M. (1991). Professional psychology training in Western and Nordic Europe. *Educational and Child Psychology, 8,* 56–63.

McPherson, F. M. (1992). Clinical psychology training in Europe. *British Journal of Clinical Psychology, 31,* 419–428.

Nevalainen, V. (1995). Legal matters in the Nordic countries. *News from EFPPA, 9*(1), 13–14.

Orzark, L. H. (1983). International authority and national regulation. *Law and Human Behavior, 7,* 251–264.

Peel, R. (1992). Suisse: Une psychologie "fédérale"? *Psychologie Europe, 6,* 2–3.

Pereira, F. (1995). Psychology in Portugal. In A. Schorr & S. Saari (Eds.), *Psychology in Europe. Facts, figures, realities* (pp. 97–102). Seattle, WA: Hogrefe & Huber.

Persson, H. (1995). Psychology in Sweden. In A. Schorr & S. Saari (Eds.), *Psychology in Europe. Facts, figures, realities* (pp. 261–272). Seattle, WA: Hogrefe & Huber.

Pléh, C. (1991). Some notes on training psychologists in Hungary. *News from EFPPA, 5*(4), 12–14.

Prieto, J. M. & Avila, A. (1994). Linking certified knowledge to labor markets. *Applied Psychology: An International Review, 43,* 113–130.

Rodriguez Sutil, C. (1995). The situation in Spain and southern European countries. *News from EFPPA, 9(1),* 15–16.

Saari, S. (1995). The legalization of Finnish psychology. In A. Schorr & S. Saari (Eds.), *Psychology in Europe. Facts, figures, realities* (pp. 23–34). Seattle, WA: Hogrefe & Huber.

Sahin, N. H. (1995). Psychology in Turkey—steps towards accreditation. *News from EFPPA, 9(3),* 11–17.

Toeplitz-Winiewka, M. (1992). The Polish Psychological Association. *News from EFPPA, 6*(3), 22–25.

van Drunen, P. (1995). Professional psychology in The Netherlands. In A. Schorr & S. Saari (Eds.), *Psychology in Europe. Facts, figures, realities* (pp. 77–96). Seattle, WA: Hogrefe & Huber.

2.07
The Development of Standards and the Regulation of the Practice of Clinical Psychology in China

QICHENG JING
Chinese Academy of Sciences, Beijing, China
and
PEICHENG HU
Beijing Medical University, China

2.07.1 BRIEF INTRODUCTION OF THE DEVELOPMENT OF CLINICAL PSYCHOLOGY IN CHINA

Chinese psychology has a long past but a short history. Some 2000 years ago, in the first Chinese medical book, *The Yellow Emperors' Inner Classic*, there are many descriptions of psychological thoughts. One concerns the "five phase theory" in which it is supposed that diseases can lead to emotions of anger, happiness, pensiveness, sadness, and fear, and that these, in turn, may cause damage to the liver, heart, spleen, lungs, and kidneys. Hence, it is important to have good emotions to maintain mental health. This example is typical of the basic ideas in Chinese clinical psychology.

In 1917, the first psychological laboratory was established at Peking University. This marked the beginning of modern Chinese psychology. In 1920, the first department of psychology was established at Nanking Teachers' College, and it was quickly followed by departments at the Universities of Peking, Tsinghua, and Fudan. The Chinese Psychological Society (CPS) was established in 1921 and, also around this period, the Chinese Association of Psychological Testing, the Society of Psychoanalysis, and the Society of Mental Health were established. In 1922, an academic psychological journal was begun by Professor Zhang Yaohsiang. By this time, a few Chinese tests were available and some psychologists started to translate Western tests (Jing, 1994).

Professor Ding Zan set up the first clinic of mental health in 1936 (Kan, 1989), and from this time, clinical psychology in China developed at a much faster pace. The Western working pattern of psychiatry, that is, the combined working group of psychiatrists, clinical psychologists, and social workers, was soon introduced in Shanghai, Nanking, Peking, and Changsha. By 1945, the first book on mental health, *Comprehensive mental health* (Ding, 1945), was available.

After the founding of the People's Republic of China in 1949, China followed a similar pattern of development in science to that in the Soviet Union. Pavlov's theory of conditioned reflexes was taken as the starting point in all medical and biological sciences, hence the dominant methodology in clinical psychology was the behavioral approach. In the early 1950s Professor Li Xintian treated patients suffering from neurosis by psychotherapy and obtained good results. This was the first application of psychotherapy to mental patients in the new China.

The Chinese Cultural Revolution began in 1966 and ended in 1976. During this period psychology was attacked as a "pseudoscience," a bourgeois discipline imported from the West. The CPS was dissolved and Chinese psychologists were sent to factories and farms in remote parts of the country to do physical labor and for thought reform. Only after the Cultural Revolution was psychology rehabilitated and recognized as a scientific discipline. The ultraleftist trend of thought in denouncing science was then criticized. Clinical psychology was once again given a scientific stance.

In 1979, the CPS was re-established after the chaos of 10 years of Cultural Revolution. In September 1985, the Chinese Mental Health Association (CMHA) was inaugurated and held its first national congress. From the 1980s, Professor Peng Youfang of Fujian province, Professor Chen Peizhang of Shanxi province, and Professor Wang Xiaodao from Beijing began psychological counseling and practiced psychotherapy in hospitals. Several years later, the Beijing Municipal Bureau of Health published the standards in the ratings of hospitals. To achieve the standard of grade 3A (the highest rating), a hospital had to provide psychological counseling and psychotherapy in its related departments. Thus, due to this government mandate, psychological counseling and psychotherapy soon became widely used in Chinese hospitals.

In Chinese universities, the first counseling center was set up in 1982 at the Huzhou Normal College of Zhejiang province. The Psychometrics and Counseling Service Center at the Beijing Normal University was established in 1985. After that, counseling centers were set up in Beijing, Shanghai, and in the provinces of Shandong, Shanxi, and Hubei. These counseling centers were established at different types of institutions: 6.6% in hospitals, 70.0% in university student clinics, and 23.4% in university departments of psychology, philosophy, or social sciences. According to a survey conducted in 1989 on 126 000 students, some 20% of college students have mental health problems.

Since the late 1970s, China has adopted a new policy of economic reform and opening up to the outside world. It now has one of the highest rates of economic growth in the world, with an average Gross Domestic Product increase of 12% for five years running. The introduction of a market economy based on free competition, and the strong influence of Western culture with the increase in scenes of sex, terror, violence, and crime on television and other media, have resulted in a general moral decline of the younger generation, and an increase in the number of behavioral disorders. The need for clinical psychology is strongly felt.

2.07.2 THE USE OF THE TERMINOLOGY "CLINICAL PSYCHOLOGY" AND "MEDICAL PSYCHOLOGY"

What is psychology in the minds of ordinary Chinese people? With the publicity that psychology has gained through the media in recent years, more and more people have begun to understand that psychology is a scientific discipline. Some people, however, still think that it is a profession of mind reading or which guesses others people's thoughts. Nevertheless, since most psychologists work in institutions of higher learning, they are respected by ordinary people, just like professors in other fields.

The term "medical psychology" was introduced from the former Soviet Union in 1950s, and is still used in China. At present, the difference between clinical psychology and medical psychology is very small. Some psychologists have proposed replacing the term "medical psychology" with "clinical psychology," but this was rejected at the 1995 Annual Conference of Medical Psychology. In the formal documents of Chinese State Education Commission, the term "medical psychology" is used as a branch of psychology, and the term "clinical psychology" is not used at all. This is one of the reasons why the term "clinical psychology" is not as popular as it is in Western countries, although the actual work of medical psychologists is the same as Western clinical psychologists.

Generally speaking, the field of clinical psychology can be divided into four parts:

(i) *Medical psychology in medical schools.* Most medical schools have departments, sections, and research centers in medical psychology. Medical students undertake medical psychology as one of the required courses of the curriculum. There are out-patient departments of psychological counseling and psychotherapy in Chinese general hospitals. Some general hospitals have in-patient departments of psychosomatic diseases. Most medical psychologists are trained in medicine and receive additional training in psychology. They have prescription rights in hospitals. Other medical psychologists are trained in psychology. They do not have prescription rights and this greatly restricts their performance.

(ii) *Psychiatry in mental hospitals.* Most psychiatrists in China also consider themselves to be medical psychologists. They treat mental patients with medication and psychotherapy. They also take part in psychological counseling or psychotherapy outside of the hospital. The leadership and the majority of the membership of CMHA are psychiatrists.

(iii) *Psychological counseling in universities and schools.* The mental health of students has become one of the most important problems in Chinese education. Psychological counseling centers have been set up in several universities and schools. Originally, most of the workers in these centers were part-time staff. But now, with the development of psychological counseling, the educational administration has realized its importance and recruited more full-time staff. Regarding the professional background of the staff members in these counseling centers, some came from psychology or medicine, but most came from other fields; usually they are graduates from the same university or school.

(iv) *Clinics of psychological counseling and psychotherapy in society.* Often, medical psychologists, psychiatrists, and applied psychologists work together to set up a clinic to provide service to the public. Most clinics are supported by the local government, a few are supported by private institutions. Some NGOs (nongovernment organizations), such as the Jinglun Family Science Center, offer free psychological counseling to the public and have a good reputation in society.

Ordinary people in China like to call the medical psychologist the "psychological doctor." A magazine named *Psychological Doctor* was published as a popular science journal. After the establishment of the CMHA, two journals were published under its auspices, namely, the *Journal of Chinese Mental Health* and the *Journal of Chinese Clinical Psychology.* The term "clinical psychology" was used for the first time in a title of an official publication and this marked the beginning of its public use in China.

2.07.3 PROFESSIONALS IN CLINICAL PSYCHOLOGY

During the Third Conference of the CMHA held in 1996, the President of the Association Professor Cheng Xueshi, declared that its membership had reached 20 000. The majority of members came from the medical profession, while only a small part came from psychology and other behavioral science disciplines. Professor Gong Yaoxian from Hunan Medical University made a survey of the constituents of clinical psychologists in 30 provinces and cities (Gong, 1993). This showed that 76.3–87.5% came from the medical profession, whereas only 2.3–8.3% came from psychology. Detailed statistics are shown in Table 1.

Table 1 Professionals in clinical psychology in China.

	Education		*Original profession*			*Training*		
Clinical work	*College*	*Middle school*	*Medicine*	*Psychology*	*Other*	*Ph.D.*	*Master*	*Other*
Testing	1017 (73.6%)	364 (26.4%)	1053 (76.3%)	114 (8.3%)	214 (15.5%)	11 (0.9%)	105 (8.7%)	1091 (90.4%)
Psychotherapy	802 (81.4%)	183 (18.6%)	862 (87.5%)	23 (2.3%)	100 (10.2%)	6 (0.7%)	64 (7.8%)	746 (91.4%)
Counseling	967 (86.2%)	155 (13.8%)	891 (79.4%)	81 (7.2%)	150 (13.4%)	10 (1.1%)	98 (10.0%)	816 (88.3%)

2.07.4 REGULATIONS OF PSYCHOLOGICAL TESTING

In 1992, the CPS drew up the Regulations of Psychological Testing. This included regulations for the use of psychological tests, and the control and management of psychological tests (CPS, 1993a). The definition of a psychological test is "a measurement tool for counseling, appraisal, and forecasting the differentiation of intelligence; for teaching students according to their aptitude; to select talented people; for occupational guidance, and clinical diagnosis." After the Cultural Revolution, psychological testing was rehabilitated and soon became popular in China. Western tests were introduced into China and revised using Chinese norms. Most tests are used in hospitals, but they are also applied in universities and colleges. Child health care institutions use intelligence and behavioral tests for children. Some Chinese tests were also developed, mainly for use in the educational field. The most frequently used Western tests are the WISC, EPQ, WAIS-RC, MMPI, and WPSSI (Gong & Li, 1996). Psychological tests used in the medical field are mainly for clinical diagnosis, counseling, and psychotherapy. Nonprojective tests are widely used, as are rating scales for personality assessment. Projective tests are seldom used (Dai, Deng, Ryan, & Paulo, 1993). The regulations for psychological testing pointed out that every member and organization under the auspices of the CPS has the responsibility to promote the healthy development of psychological testing when engaged in diagnosis, research, and the using and selling of psychological tests.

2.07.4.1 Registration of Psychological Tests

(i) All psychological tests, edited, revised, PS published, or sold by individual members or groups of the CPS must be registered at the Psychological Testing Committee of the Society.

(ii) Standardized tests which are scientifically valid can be approved, registered, classified, cataloged, and published in the official journal of the CPS, the *Acta Psychologica Sinica*.

2.07.4.2 Qualifications of Personnel Using Psychological Tests

(i) A graduate from the department of psychology and who has engaged in psychological testing for more than two years under an experienced supervisor can be approved as a qualified tester.

(ii) One who has taken part in a psychological test training workshop registered and approved by the Committee of Psychological Testing of CPS can be qualified as a tester.

(iii) The certificates of qualification are of two kinds: the certificate for a single test and the certificate for multiple tests.

2.07.4.3 Control and Management of Tests

(i) In any psychological test manual, the instruction, procedure, and user qualifications must be described in detail.

(ii) Anyone who has the qualifications of testing can buy materials of psychological tests with their certificate and is obliged to take good care of the testing materials.

(iii) The test user must strictly follow every rule in the test manual. The user must choose the appropriate tests for diagnosis and for decision making. Records must be kept and made available for examination.

(iv) Any member or institution under the CPS who wants to revise or sell psychological tests published by other authors must obtain the consent from the test author or unit. The organization who wants to print, publish, or sell psychological test materials must register at the Committee of Psychological Testing of the CPS. The buyer must also have the qualifications for using psychological tests.

(v) To guarantee the scientific nature and practical value of the tests, the content of the standardized tests cannot be published in nonprofessional magazines.

2.07.5 REGULATIONS OF PSYCHOLOGICAL COUNSELING AND PSYCHOTHERAPY

Since the late 1970s, after implementing a policy of reform and opening up to the outside world with a market economy, there has been a marked increase in the number of mental disorders (Chen & Xu, 1996). A nationwide survey was conducted in 1994, in universities and hospitals, on the number of cases of the 10 most common mental disorders and the psychotherapies used for their treatment. The results are shown in Table 2 (Gong & Li, 1996).

In October 1992, the "Regulations for Workers of Psychological Counseling and Psychotherapy in Health Systems" was

Table 2 Numbers of cases of psychotherapy and mental disorder.

Mental disorder	*Behavioral*	*Cognitive*	*Supportive*	*Psy-analysis*	*Morita*	*Biofeedback*	*Hypnosis*	*Total*
Compulsion	114 (44.4%)	39 (15.2%)	18 (7.0%)	28 (10.9%)	32 (12.5%)	8 (3.1%)	3 (1.2%)	257
Phobia	88 (42.5%)	39 (18.8%)	16 (7.7%)	21 (10.5%)	14 (6.8%)	8 (3.9%)	5 (2.4%)	207
Anxiety	41 (23.7%)	38 (22.0%)	26 (15.0%)	21 (12.1%)	17 (9.8%)	15 (8.7%)	5 (2.9%)	173
Depression	11 (8.3%)	42 (31.6%)	44 (33.1%)	16 (12.0%)	2 (1.5%)	4 (3.0%)	4 (3.0%)	133
Schizophrenia	30 (32.6%)	8 (8.7%)	36 (39.1%)	11 (12.0%)	2 (2.2%)	3 (3.3%)	0	92
Neurasthenia	5 (6.9%)	15 (20.8%)	28 (38.9%)	5 (6.9%)	7 (9.7%)	6 (8.3%)	1 (1.4%)	72
Sexual disorder	34 (47.2%)	9 (12.5%)	5 (6.9%)	13 (18.3%)	2 (2.8%)	1 (1.4%)	2 (2.8%)	72
Delusion	4 (5.6%)	27 (38.0%)	14 (19.7%)	6 (8.5%)	13 (18.3%)	2 (2.8%)	1 (1.4%)	71
Hysteria	8 (12.1%)	11 (16.7%)	9 (13.6%)	6 (9.1%)	1 (1.5%)	2 (3.0%)	25 (37.9%)	66
Neurosis	12 (22.6%)	11 (20.8%)	13 (24.5%)	6 (11.3%)	4 (7.6%)	1 (1.9%)	1 (1.9%)	53

announced jointly by the CPS and the CMHA (1993). The contents of the regulations are as follows:

2.07.5.1 Qualifications

2.07.5.1.1 Academic credentials

Academic credentials for professional positions of counseling and psychotherapy should be one of the following:

(i) A person who has received a bachelor's degree or a higher degree from a university department of psychology and has been engaged in psychological counseling and psychotherapy.

(ii) A person who has received a bachelor's degree or a higher degree from a medical school and has been engaged in psychological counseling and psychotherapy.

(iii) A person who has received academic credential of professional training in a college approved by the government, and has been engaged in psychological counseling and psychotherapy.

(iv) A person who does not have any of the above academic credentials but has a middle or higher level professional post (assistant professorship or higher) and has received training in psychological counseling and psychotherapy in a national or provincial organization and has been engaged in psychological counseling and psychotherapy.

2.07.5.1.2 Knowledge

Practitioners of psychological counseling and psychotherapy should have knowledge of theories of psychotherapy, general psychology, developmental psychology, neurology, abnormal psychology (or psychiatry), personality psychology, techniques of interview, psychological diagnosis, and psychological testing. Practitioners without a medical background should have additional medical training, such as internal medicine or pediatrics.

2.07.5.1.3 Clinical practice

Any person with the above academic qualifications should engage in psychological counseling and psychotherapy under the supervision of experienced psychotherapists for more than half a year before independent practice.

2.07.5.2 Responsibility

The code of conduct for a practitioner of psychological counseling and psychotherapy necessarily entails the following:

(i) An understanding of the nature of psychological counseling and psychotherapy, and the principle of maintaining the secrecy and rights of the client.

(ii) Collecting the information directly related to the client and understanding the client's needs.

(iii) Keeping a neutral relationship with the client. If there is any overstepping of this relationship, the treatment must be stopped.

(iv) Knowing the limits of service. During the diagnosis, testing, and treatment any demands exceeding the worker's capacity cannot be fulfilled.

(v) Applying the principle that the treatment is to direct the patients or clients to help themselves and to make efforts to improve themselves.

2.07.6 THE CURRICULUM, TRAINER REQUIREMENTS, AND TRAINING PROGRAM IN CLINICAL PSYCHOLOGY

There are different levels of training programs in China: doctoral, master, bachelor, college for professional training, advanced study, short term training, and training by correspondence. Since the 1980s, clinical psychology has become a popular profession with an increasing number of people wishing to study it or wanting to move into it from their original profession.

In May 1979, the first department of medical psychology was set up at Beijing Medical College. In 1980, a formal document from the Ministry of Public Health announced that every medical school should offer a course of medical psychology. This promoted the popularization of medical psychology. From 1985, medical psychology became the required course for medical students in many medical schools. By 1995, there were 34 medical schools (comprising 48.6% of all medical schools) in the country having medical psychology as a required course, and 36 medical schools (51.4%) having medical psychology as selected course (Li, 1995).

Among the 70 medical schools investigated, 26 have set up departments of medical psychology and 44 have placed medical psychology as a division in other departments. For example, in 15 medical schools (21.4%), medical psychology is a division under the psychiatry department; in six (8.6%), medical psychology is a division under the neurology department; and in another six (8.6%) medical psychology belongs to the physiology department. In other schools, medical psychology is combined with medical education, medical management, or social medicine.

The curriculum of the department of medical psychology in medical schools consists of general psychology, physiological psychology, neuropsychology, abnormal psychology, health psychology, psychological counseling, psychotherapy, psychological testing, psychosomatic diseases, and nursing psychology. In most medical schools (74.3%), medical psychology is taught as a complete course, but in some it is taught in two parts, the basic course and the clinical course.

The contents and teaching hours are different according to the different schools. The teaching hours of medical psychology range from 45 to 72 hours. Generally speaking, psychiatry and nursing students study more hours than students from other disciplines. A unified textbook of medical psychology for nationwide use was published in 1991 and remains the textbook for medical students.

There are 11 universities and colleges which enroll postgraduate students for master or doctoral degrees (Li, 1995). In 17 medical schools (24.3%), short term (half or one year) programs are available for further study in medical psychology.

Regarding the medical psychology faculty, 49 medical schools (70%) have full-time professors. On average, there are four teachers in each school. The professional backgrounds of the full-time professors are: 83.3% come from psychiatry, neurology, physiology, pediatrics, or Chinese traditional medicine; 12.2% come from psychology; and 4.5% come from education. Most part-time professors have backgrounds in psychiatry or neurology.

One of the great influences in the development of clinical psychology came from medical education. In the beginning of the 1980s, the "medical model" was a favored topic in the media. Today, the trend is a shift from the biomedical model to a bio-psycho–socio-medical model. This has popularized medical psychology with consequent rapid development.

2.07.7 PSYCHOTHERAPY AND CHINESE TRADITIONAL MEDICINE

Distinct from Western medicine, Chinese traditional medicine has its own principles as a special branch of medical science. There are five principles of Chinese traditional medicine applicable to the treatment of mental disorders (Yan, 1995):

(i) *Principle of Integration.* To cure an illness a holistic approach is necessary. This principle involves the utilization of more than one therapeutic method so that the patient may receive a combination of psychotherapy, physical therapy, occupational therapy, acupuncture, and traditional Chinese herbal preparations.

(ii) *Principle of Education.* This principle places emphasis on helping the patient to understand their illness through direct or indirect explanations of the symptoms, the coping mechanisms, and the causes of mental disturbance. The depth of explanation will depend on the patient's receptiveness, level of education, and desire for insight. Generally speaking, unconscious mechanisms are rarely explored directly, but dreams, art, and even calligraphy may provide useful signs of disease for the therapist.

(iii) *Principle of Mobilization.* Chinese traditional medicine lays stress on inner factors of the patient. This principle involves the process of mobilizing the patient's latent initiative and motivation for cure. The patient is helped to overcome passivity and dependence on the therapist. By mobilization, the patient is to gain self-reliance, assume responsibility for their mental health, and to cope in harmony with society.

(iv) *Principle of "Dredging."* For somatic functions, there are two principles in Chinese traditional medicine: improving blood circulation to relieve stress, and pain relief by dredging. These principles, when applied to mental disorders, refer to the process of uncovering factors which have contributed to the mental disturbance. The term "dredging" implies searching for, and bringing to the surface, obstacles which lie at the bottom of the mind.

(v) *Principle of Unity.* Traditional medicine emphasizes unity between the human being and the universe; psychotherapy deals with the unity and harmony of the patient with his family and the social environment at large.

In ancient Chinese psychology, body and mind are integrated into a single theory and a healthy mind is considered just as important as a healthy body. Psychological health is characterized by a psychological state of equilibrium through mental self-regulation, so that behavior, habits, and desires can be kept under control. This theory of integration of mind and body, which values harmony and equilibrium, is being increasingly mastered by Chinese clinical psychologists in their practice.

2.07.8 CODE OF CONDUCT AND ETHICAL GUIDELINES FOR PSYCHOLOGICAL TESTING, COUNSELING, AND PSYCHOTHERAPY

In December 1992, the CPS issued the "Ethical Guidelines for Workers of Psychological Testing" (CPS, 1993b). Its three main principles are as follows: first, that anyone who uses psychological tests in diagnosis, counseling, and for selection should bear the qualifications approved by the Committee of Psychological Testing of the CPS; second, that the user should obey the principles of scientific objectivity when applying tests; and, finally, that the user should not hinder the subject's normal functions. In particular a practitioner of psychological testing should:

(i) Have responsibility and observe scientific principles, be serious, show caution, and modesty.

(ii) Obey the national laws, and the rules and regulations of psychological testing.

(iii) Provide true and accurate information, when introducing the results and effects of psychological tests, and avoid acting impetuously, making false diagnosis, and causing misunderstanding.

(iv) Show respect for the client's personality and maintain all personal information in secrecy, except when the conditions lead to the harm to others or to society, only then can the practitioner reveal the truth to persons or units involved.

(v) Test strictly according to the requirements of the profession or society; never misuse tests for profit

(vi) Sustain the effectiveness of any tests by maintaining secrecy over any content, material, standard, and norm which are not suitable for publication.

(vii) Discuss the results of tests with clients in a correct way and provide useful help and suggestions. In general, the practitioner should only give the explanation of the test results, not the score of each test item.

(viii) Respect other practitioners and organizations of psychological testing with sincerity, learn from one another, and cooperate with one another.

(ix) Consider the contradiction, when editing, revising, and selling the psychological tests, caused by the distribution of benefits; avoid any detrimental effects to the development of psychological testing.

In October 1993, the CPS and the CMHA jointly published the "Code of Conduct for Psychological Counseling and Psychotherapy" (CPS & CMHA, 1993). This document proposed that the practitioner of psychological counseling and psychotherapy should:

(i) Respect their profession, obey the national laws, and the rules and codes of conduct of medical practice.

(ii) Be willing to help others, share empathy, show seriousness, show respect, care, and understanding to the client.

(iii) Have rich professional knowledge and the ability to interact positively with others in society.

(iv) Maintain emotional stability; specifically, to avoid accepting clients when in a bad emotional condition.

2.07.9 CONTINUING EDUCATION MANDATES

In June 1996, a National Continuing Education Committee of the Health System was established. Rules were laid down for continuing education requirements for medical workers and medical psychologists. The rules pointed out that "every health worker after graduation must take part in continuing education and obtain a score of more than 25 points each year" (Ministry of Public Health, 1996). The score of 25 points consists of two parts. The first part is a score of 5 to 10, the second part of 15 to 20. The first score is the combined result from: the national continuing education program; the ministerial or provincial continuing education program; and participation in international and national conferences. The second score is the combined result from self-study, publication of papers and books, and attending lectures and other activities.

Since the founding of the People's Republic of China in 1949, about 100 educational colleges have been set up for the training of health workers. Since 1978, many professors have been sent abroad as visiting scholars or visiting scientists for further study to acquire new knowledge and to gain experience in an international perspective.

The "Regulations of Continuing Education" was issued by the Ministry of Human Affairs in 1991. This greatly promoted continuing education in China. In 1994, the "Training Center for Psychological Counseling and Psychotherapy" was set up in Beijing Medical University. As well as Chinese lecturers, lecturers from other countries were recruited. To date, some 300 students have graduated from this training center; many have played important roles in the development of clinical psychology throughout the country.

Chinese clinical psychologists are interested in understanding and learning Western clinical psychology. Before 1949, Chinese psychology was greatly influenced by psychology from the US, but after 1949, the Russian Pavlovian psychology became the dominant trend. After the Cultural Revolution, particularly after the initiation of China's economic reform, Western psychology, especially American psychology, again had a profound influence.

Psychology, being both a natural science and a social science, is more influenced by a country's cultural background. Facing the stresses and challenges in the new era of rapid social and economic change, Chinese people are demanding more from clinical psychologists than they can offer. Chinese clinical psychologists have been doing more research in their own environment than trying to relate to Western theories and methodology. Increasingly, Chinese clinical psychologists are advancing their own theories and suggestions to solve indigenous clinical problems.

2.07.10 FUTURE DIRECTIONS OF CHINESE CLINICAL PSYCHOLOGY

With the progress of China's economic reform, there have been great changes in the lives of individuals, as well as society at large. The psychological impact and imbalance caused by these changes can be greatly felt. Demand for clinical psychology, psychological counseling, and psychotherapy is on the increase. This is a moving force for the development of Chinese clinical psychology. Equally, the improved quality of life, together with a decreasing quality of environmental influence, means that there is an increasing need for psychological guidance. Under these circumstances we can foresee the rapid development of clinical psychology in China.

Compared with clinical psychology in the developed countries there is much work to do in the near future. Some of the necessary areas of study are as follows:

(i) In clinical psychology, we should insist upon combining theory with practice, popularizing the discipline, and promoting its development. We should investigate the status of the psychological health of the Chinese people throughout the nation in order to provide a better service to the population. Improving the nation's psychological health is of great importance to China's economic construction and the future of the nation. At the same time, the application of clinical psychology can improve the people's capacity for adjustment to the social change taking place in the country.

(ii) We should work together with medical doctors to prevent psychological and psychosomatic diseases, including neurosis, personality disorder, hypertension, coronary heart disease, diabetes, cancer, and other diseases. Such diseases can be treated from a mental health perspective. We should inform people how to deal with psychosocial problems and to promote physical and psychological health.

(iii) The popularization and education of mental health will eventually help to promote the material and spiritual well-being of the people. Popular science education should be addressed to different age groups and people from different walks of life, in ways and by methods which reach the whole of society.

(iv) Central and local governments will be involved in the procedure of approval of qualifications. We can experiment on government involvement in the big cities first, such as Beijing and Shanghai, and gradually spread to the whole country. On the basis of approval of qualifications, license for psychotherapy should be given to clinical psychologists as a legal certification for practice. Meanwhile, strengthening the training programs for different levels of professionals is an urgent necessity.

2.07.11 REFERENCES

Chen, C. H., & Xu, C. L. (1996). Progress of epidemiology of mental disorder in China. *Chinese Journal of Psychiatry, 29* (2), 113–116.

Chinese Psychological Society (1993a). The regulations for psychological testing. *Acta Psychologica Sinica, 25,* 221–222.

Chinese Psychological Society (1993b). Ethical guidelines for workers of psychological testing. *Acta Psychologica Sinica, 25,* 222.

Chinese Psychological Society & Chinese Mental Health Association (1993). The regulations for workers of psychological counselling and psychotherapy in health systems. *Acta Psychologica Sinica, 25,* 223–224.

Dai, X. Y., Deng, L. X., Ryan, J. J., & Paolo, A. M. (1993). A Survey of psychological tests used in Chinese clinical psychology and comparison with data in the United States. *Journal of Chinese Clinical Psychology, 1,* 47–50.

Ding, Z. (1945). *Comprehensive mental health.* Chongqing, China: Commercial Press.

Gong, Y. X. (1993). The history and present situation of clinical psychology. *Journal of Chinese Clinical Psychology, 1, 1–3.*

Gong, Y. X., & Li, Q. Z. (1996). The investigation of current Chinese clinical psychology and its prospect. *Journal of Chinese Clinical Psychology, 4,* 1–9.

Jing, Q. C. (1994). Psychology in China. In R. J. Corsini (Ed.) *Encyclopedia of psychology* (2nd ed., Vol. 3, pp. 179–182). New York: Wiley.

Kan, D. G. (1989). The need for rapid development of medical psychology in China. *Medical Education, 9,* 30–31.

Li, X. T. (1995). *The establishment of medical psychology teaching and research units in Chinese medical colleges. (Monograph)* Beijing, China: Beijing Medical University Press.

Ministry of Public Health (1996). *The trial credit system in continuing medical education.* (Government Document).

Yan, H. Q. (1995). Psychotherapy and Chinese culture. *Journal of Chinese Mental Health, Supplement 61–62.*

2.08
The Development of Standards and the Regulation of the Practice of Clinical Psychology in India

SANTOSH K. VERMA
Postgraduate Institute of Medical Education and Research, Chandigarh, India

2.08.1 INTRODUCTION

It is said that psychology has a long past but short history. It is understandable, therefore, that an applied branch of psychology—clinical psychology—will have an even shorter history, particularly in a developing country like India. Training in clinical psychology in India began in 1951 at Banaras Hindu University, Varanasi in Uttar Pradesh (Northern India), as a one-year diploma course in clinical psychology. But it took off more certainly in 1956 with a two-year diploma course in Medical and Social Psychology (now a postgraduate Master of Philosophy degree in Clinical Psychology, rather than the original diploma course) at the All India Institute of Mental Health (now called the National Institute of Mental Health and Neuro-Sciences) at Bangalore in Karnataka State (Southern India). The Indian Association of Clinical Psychology (IACP) was formed in 1968 and its official organ, the *Indian Journal of Clinical Psychology*, began in 1974 (Verma, 1984; Verma & Puri, 1986). Highlights of the historical developments of clinical psychology in India, are listed in Table 1.

At present, there are over 600 qualified clinical psychologists who received their training at the National Institute of Mental Health and Neuro-Sciences, Bangalore (338), the

Table 1 Brief highlights of development of clinical psychology in India.

Phase	*Year*	*Comment*
I (before 1950)	1921	Indian Psycho-analytic Society formed (Dr. Girija Shanker Bose)
	1925	Indian Psychological Association formed (Dr. N. N. Sen Gupta)
	1926	*Indian Journal of Psychology* started
	1930	Indian Psychoanalytical Institute for establishing psychoanalysis in practice
	1947	*Samiksha* (official publication of the Indian Psycho-analytical Society) started
		India became independent (of British rule)
II (1950–1970)	1951	Formal training in clinical psychology (one-year course) started at Banaras Hindu University, Varanasi (Uttar Pradesh)
	1956	Diploma in Medical and Social Psychology (two-year course) started at the All India Institute of Mental Health, Bangalore
	1962	Diploma in Medical and Social Psychology (two-year course) started at the Hospital for Mental Diseases, Ranchi
	1968	IACP formed (President: Dr. N. N. Sen; and Hon. General Secretary: Dr. G. G. Prabhu)
III (1971–1990)	1972	Diploma in Medical and Social Psychology started at the BM Institute of Mental Health, Ahmedabad
	1973	Ph.D. in Clinical Psychology started at the Postgraduate Institute of Medical Education and Research, Chandigarh
	1974	*Indian Journal of Clinical Psychology* (official organ of the IACP) started (Editor: Dr. S. K. Verma)
		First Professor of Clinical Psychology appointed (Prof. H. N. Murthy at Bangalore)
	1979	Workshop on training in clinical psychology (sponsored by the World Health Organization and the Indian Association of Clinical Psychologists) held at Bangalore
	1985	*Journal of Personality and Clinical Studies* (official organ of the Delhi Association of Clinical Psychologists) started at Delhi (Editor: Dr. Habib Ahmad)
	1986	Consumer Protection Act (Act no. 68)
	1987	Mental Health Act (Act no. 14) replacing the Indian Lunacy Act, 1912
IV (present phase)	1992	Rehabilitation Council of India Act (Act no. 34)
	1993/94	"Code of Conduct" adopted by the IACP during its Silver Jubilee
	1994	Policy statement of ethical considerations by Indian Council of Medical Research
	1995/96	The Persons with Disabilities Act 1995 (Act no. 1 of 1996)

Central Institute of Psychiatry, Ranchi (210), or the BM Institute of Mental Health, Ahmedabad (12). These locations are situated in the southern, northern, and western parts of India, respectively; this information has been obtained directly from the directors of these institutions.

In addition, there are a number of Ph.D.s in clinical psychology: from Bangalore (39), Ranchi (7), and the Postgraduate Institute of Medical Education and Research, Chandigarh (10); furthermore, there are others who have completed short-term courses, for limited purposes, from these and other centers, for example, in psychodiagnostics, counseling, psychotherapy, behavior therapy, neuropsychology, and projective psychology.

Clinical psychology is being taught at postgraduate (masters) level as a compulsory paper in only three universities, and as an optional paper in another 26 universities, while 27 universities have no such paper (Ramalingaswami, 1980). Each paper at this level, includes a theory/written examination with or without practicals in psychodiagnostic techniques. A formal dissertation is optional but where it exists it may be on any topic, including that of clinical psychology.

Thus, the shortage of trained practitioners in this area is understandable and unlikely to be satisfactorily overcome in the near future. On top of this is the continuous drainage due to the "three Ms" (Prabhu, 1983), that is, *matrimony* (females leaving the profession after marriage), *misplacement* (those leaving the field of clinical psychology for other professions), and *migration* (those seeking opportunities abroad, rather than remaining unemployed or underemployed).

It is not surprising, therefore, that only about half of the 600 qualified clinical psychologists are members of the IACP (IACP, 1995b).

2.08.2 RECOGNITION AND USE OF THE TITLE "CLINICAL PSYCHOLOGIST"

The title "clinical psychologist" is at present gaining increasingly wider recognition and acceptance, although some in India still continue to confuse this with "psychiatrist" or tend to call any applied psychologist clinical psychologist. Now, there are qualified clinical psychologists working in mental hospitals, general hospitals (in psychiatric, pediatric, neurological, or rehabilitation units), prisons, industry, schools, community clinics (child guidance centers, drug-deaddiction clinics, counseling centers, etc.), military hospitals, selection boards, and research institutes. Some clinical psychologists are also in private practice and they are well accepted by the community at large (Paintal, 1987; Verma, 1982).

The legal position of the profession of clinical psychologists is not completely clear. The Mental Health Act (1987), describes a "clinical psychologist" as a nonofficial member of the Central or State Mental Health Authority. (The author is a member of Chandigarh Mental Health Authority.) Surprisingly, not all State Mental Health Authorities have clinical psychologists on their boards, although there may be psychologists working in some universities, for example, in the Karnataka State. The use of the services of clinical psychologists is also mentioned in this act as one of the minimum legal facilities required for issuing a license to a psychiatric hospital or nursing home. However, the title is neither defined, nor is the necessary qualification described under this act. So, there remains scope for confusions.

Similarly, professionalism is promoted through the recently passed Rehabilitation Council of India Act (1992). The aim of this act is "to provide for the constitution of the Rehabilitation Council of India (RCI) for regulating the training of rehabilitation professionals and the maintenance of a Central Rehabilitation Register and for matters connected therewith or incidental thereto." Its members are appointed by the central government from the ministries of Welfare, Health, and Finance, and also from national bodies such as the University Grants Commission, the Indian Council of Medical Research, State Welfare departments, as well as from private rehabilitation professionals, medical practitioners, and members of parliament. It makes specific mention of "clinical psychologists" as being one of the experts in the rehabilitation professionals field and, like the Mental Health Act, stops just there, without defining this title or listing the qualifications. This is unlike other rehabilitation professionals (e.g., audiologists, speech therapists, hearing aid technicians) whose positions are well defined and their qualifications are listed along with training courses and institutes.

Law Courts in some parts of India, sometimes refer cases directly for the clinical psychologist's opinion in certain medico–legal cases. Special education schools and institutes require and demand intelligence assessment by a clinical psychologist for admission to their schools. Industries require their opinion and advice for selection or promotion as well as settlement disputes, such as, for disability compensation. Cases are also referred by medical boards, psychiatrists, neurologists, pediatricians, neurosurgeons, and speech therapists for different purposes (e.g., for differential diagnosis, counseling, assessment of cognitive functions, assessment of personality conflicts, suitability for different types of therapies, fitness to begin or continue duties after accidents, illness, disability assessments/benefits, income tax rebates). Such referrals are increasing in frequency. Clinical psychologists are also recognized by and invited to serve as mental health professionals, advisors, or experts on the panels of different national research institutes such as the Indian Council of Social Science Research, the Indian Council of Medical Research, the National Council of Educational Research and Training, the National Institute for Mentally Handicapped (NIMH), the National Institute for Visually Handicapped, and the Indian Institute of Criminology and Forensic Science. In fact the founding director of NIMH at Secunderabad happens to be a clinical psychologist. Many senior clinical psychologists (including the author) have served these research institutes for several years now with distinction as advisors, experts, teachers, or evaluators of research projects, and the scope is increasing.

Regarding the use (or misuse) of the title "clinical psychologist," Prabhu (1983) states:

> In India, there is a tendency among those with a Masters' degree or a Doctorate in Psychology to call themselves a *clinical psychologist* and claim they have *some*, *considerable*, *required* or *extensive*

training in clinical psychology. One can emphasize with their enthusiasm but it will be dangerous and unethical to let loose all such claimants to *render service* to society. (p. xi)

One can hardly disagree with this statement but the significant point to note here is the *need* for and *importance* of the title "clinical psychologist"; otherwise few, if any, would have liked to use (or misuse) this title, except for legal purposes, when they have to use it and/or defend it in court.

2.08.3 LEVELS, REGISTRATION, CERTIFICATION, LICENSURE

At the community level there are many interested, intelligent laymen, parents, teachers, and other health professionals, including indigenous faith healers, who use commonsense, keen observation, and insight to help certain kinds of clientele, sometimes with good results too. Some of them have also written books on varied applied aspects and are recognized as "clinical psychologists" by the population at large, even though they have no formal degrees awarded by recognized institutes or universities. Such individuals have always existed, even before the recognized training institutes or universities came into existence.

There are also intelligent laymen who had studied psychology at different levels (graduate and postgraduate levels). They have taken theoretical papers such as applied psychology, abnormal psychology, clinical psychology, personality, and criminal psychology, and subsequently pose as clinical psychologists and work in the community. Some of them might have undertaken short courses in psychodiagnostics, behavior therapy, neuropsychology, counseling, yoga therapy, transcendental meditation, vipassana, or hypnosis, for example, run by some of the recognized schools or universities. They, however, are not fully-fledged clinical psychologists, even though they may be working in the overlapping areas of this helping profession, and even though some of them, at least, are rendering valuable service to the ailing human condition in a country beset with a very limited trained workforce and a large population.

All these are functioning at different levels. At one extreme are fully trained clinical psychologists correctly in position. But, at the other, there are certain untrained or inadequately trained, though intelligent, laymen, psychologists or related professionals who often misuse the title clinical psychologist. Additionally, clinical psychologists are often confused by the media with psychiatrists, psychoanalysts, or even psychologists writing on popular topics. Absence of satisfactory registration, certification, and licensure procedures only increases this confusion.

The IACP defines the term "clinical psychology" as an applied branch of psychology which, drawing heavily from the biological, medical, and social sciences, aims to study systematically all kinds of pathological deviations of human behaviors and preventive (including legal) techniques and measures (IACP, 1995a). It has five classes of individual membership, namely, fellows, professional members, associate members, honorary members, and corresponding members (IACP, 1995b). Only the first two categories are fully qualified as clinical psychologists. The IACP has prepared a list (although incomplete) of qualified professional members and has even issued registration numbers and certificates to some of these qualified clinical psychologists (for a token fee) for practicing purposes. This, however, is not a legal sanction, nor can it prevent others from calling themselves clinical psychologists, and even practicing as such.

Only the RCI (RCI Act, 1992), by virtue of its statutory powers, has been authorized by the Indian government to register with it all those who possess the requisite qualifications of clinical psychologists (however, it is not defined in the schedule published by this council), and issue valid certificates to this effect for practice as one of the "rehabilitation personnels." This, however, is a bone of contention with IACP and opinion is sharply divided amongst the members because it refers to only one of the functions of the clinical psychologists, and it clubs clinical psychologists with lesser trained professions including, audiologists, speech therapists, hearing aid and ear mold technicians, and special education teachers. The latter point has implications for the pay structure of professionals. The result is that very few qualified clinical psychologists bother to register with IACP. The controversy and the fight continues, and so does the demand for a single, separate, independent council for clinical psychologists, covering the entire field of their work.

For obvious reasons, therefore, there is currently no separate licensing system in India covering the entire activities of clinical psychologists.

2.08.4 NECESSARY EDUCATIONAL AND TRAINING QUALIFICATIONS

Both the Mental Health Act of 1987 and the RCI Act of 1992 are, more or less, silent on matters of qualifications. Nevertheless, the IACP Secretariat (Gupta, 1992, 1993) had suggested the educational and training qualifications for clinical psychologists (to be included in their schedule) to the RCI. These recommendations are as follows:

(i) *Educational qualifications*. Either a diploma in Medical and Social Psychology or equivalent Indian or foreign diploma or degree, or a Ph.D. in psychology and at least four years experience of full-time research, training, or practice of clinical psychology in a recognized institution, or a master's degree in psychology with at least seven years of experience of full-time research, training, or practice of clinical psychology in a recognized institution.

(ii) *Training programs*. The principal institutions and their courses are listed in Table 2. However, there are other premier institutions offering a diploma in Medical and Social Psychology, such as the BM Institute of Mental Health, Ahmedabad, and institutions providing for the qualifications of Doctorate in Clinical Psychology, such as the All India Institute of Medical Sciences, New Delhi. These are not included in the official schedule under the RCI Act of 1992. Brief descriptions of the towns and districts in which these institutions are situated are given in Table 3.

Steps are afoot to further modify the qualifications and training programs of the above institutions, restricting them to the degree qualifications from Bangalore and Ranchi only (Gupta, 1994). It is these somewhat contradictory recommendations, made at different periods of time, even by IACP officials, which further add to the prevailing confusion. To the author, these moves seem shortsighted and ill-advised, particularly in view of the shortage of trained professionals and the ever increasing population compared to the training resources available in the country.

2.08.5 SCOPE OF PRACTICE AND PRACTICE STANDARDS

The scope of practice and practice standards are not officially stated or clarified anywhere. They are, however, inherent in the very definition of the term clinical psychology as stated, defined, described, and implied in the IACP constitution and writings of clinical psychologists, presidential addresses, editorials, letters to the editors, and the various seminars on the role and importance of a clinical psychologist in society at large (Ghosh 1977; Misra, 1995; Prabhu, 1983; Ramalingaswami, 1976; Sen, 1975; Sen Mazumdar, 1976; Verma & Pershad, 1980; Verma & Puri 1996).

Whereas the diagnostic role has been emphasized by Ramalingaswami (1976) and the therapeutic role by Sen (1975), Ghosh (1977), Sen Mazumdar (1976), and Misra (1995); Prabhu (1983), on the other hand, has emphasized both roles (a diagnostic-cum-therapeutic role), as well as research in both the areas, depending upon what he calls SCA, that is, the "setting" of the work, the "clients" served, and the "activities" demanded of him, which may vary so widely in India.

The scope of practice is widening, taking in, for example, hospitals (mental hospitals, general hospitals, and private nursing homes in the community), community clinics (child guidance clinics, drug-deaddiction centers, family counseling clinics, marriage counseling clinics, reformatory clinics, observation homes, and orphanages), research institutes, prisons, special education schools, and private practice (part- or full-time practice as clinical psychologist). Surprisingly, however, professionals are as yet silent about practice standards and so it seems is the community at large (Verma & Pershad, 1980; Verma & Puri, 1996).

Table 2 Principal institutions offering courses in clinical psychology.

Institutions	*Courses*
National Institute of Mental Health and Neurosciences, Bangalore	Master of Philosophy in Clinical Psychology (two years) Ph.D. in Clinical Psychology (three years)
Central Institute of Psychiatry Ranchi	Master of Philosophy in Clinical Psychology (two years) Ph.D. in Clinical Psychology (three years)
Postgraduate Institute of Medical Education and Research, Chandigarh	Ph.D. in Clinical Psychology (three years)
Banaras Hindu University, Varanasi	Ph.D. in Clinical Psychology (three years)

Table 3 Main centers of clinical psychology in India.

Ahmedabad	It is the capital of the State of Gujrat and is situated in the west. There is a private business management group which runs the hospital (with no inpatients) and schools for mentally retarded and for normal children, besides many other activities. It is known as BM Institute of Mental Health. A two-year diploma course was started but was discontinued after a few years. It is now replaced by a one-year course in psychodiagnostics and counseling, for limited and circumscribed purposes only
Bangalore	One of the five largest cities of India and situated in the south (in the state of Karnataka), with one of the oldest mental hospitals in the country (the All India Institute of Mental Health, now called the National Institute of Mental Health and Neuro-Sciences). It is here that the two-year diploma course in medical and social psychology was started in a hospital setting. It has one of the largest departments of clinical psychology in the country and has to its credit many of the firsts (such as the first Professor of Clinical Psychology) in the area of clinical psychology
Chandigarh	The Union Territory of Chandigarh is also the capital of two neighboring states, Punjab and Haryana: both lay claim to this "city beautiful," as it is known. It is also a seat of learning with many educational institutions and is situated in northern India. It has a large, general hospital (Nehru Hospital) attached to the Postgraduate Institute of Medical Education and Research (PGIMER) which runs a Ph.D. program (three years) in clinical psychology, besides short-term courses in psychodiagnostics, which is lacking in many north Indian medical colleges and hospitals. It has a drug deaddiction center which runs a continuing education program for the north Indian states. The *Indian Journal of Clinical Psychology* was started here and for its first 10 years the editorial office was here. The PGIMER, together with the All India Institute of Medical Sciences, New Delhi, were formed by an Act of Parliament as "Institutes of Excellence" to serve the ailing population of the country
Delhi	It is the capital city of India and now a State. It is situated in the center of India (earlier it was a Union Territory). It also has a training center for the Ph.D. in clinical psychology, short-term training in neuropsychology is possible and it has a drug deaddiction center within the Department of Psychiatry, All India Institute of Medical Sciences, Delhi
Ranchi	It is the summer capital of the state of Bihar and is situated in north-east India. It has three mental hospitals. It is the second training center where the two-year diploma course in medical and social psychology was started. The Hospital for Mental Diseases (formerly called the "European Mental Hospital" as only European mental patients were admitted under British rule) is now called Central Institute of Psychiatry. Here again, the training was in a mental hospital setting and it is being continued even today
Varanasi	This is a holy city for Hindus and is situated in the north (in the state of Uttar Pradesh). It is one of the oldest cities in India, with three universities and was considered as one of the important seats of learning, even in ancient India. A one-year diploma course in clinical psychology was started, for the first time in India, in a university setting (not hospital setting, although Banaras Hindu University has a medical college and hospital), at a time when psychology was still being taught as part of the curriculum in the Department of Philosophy. The emphasis was then on a psychoanalytical approach. The course was discontinued long before the author joined Banaras Hindu University for a masters degree in psychology in 1960. The start of clinical psychology, thus, was more or less symbolic but indicative of the felt need for such a course

Two related and welcome developments have taken place which are likely to have far-reaching effects in matters of practice standards. One is the Consumer Protection Act (1986), which now also extends over medical services. Rights of patients are now being increasingly recognized and accepted, and the doctor–patient relationship is being seen in a new light. Patients are now considered to be "consumers" of health services. Patients and their relatives can demand and challenge the qualities of the services rendered to them in the Consumer Protection Courts under this act. The second welcome development concerns the "Code of Conduct" recently circulated by the IACP to its members (Gupta, 1993). It is expected that clinical psychologists must possess a minimum degree of competence and should exercise reasonable care in the discharge of their duties. While the first development refers to the legal (external) control, the second is more of an internal and moral one. The first is binding, the second is not, although it is considered desirable. However, as described earlier, only half of trained clinical psychologists are members of the (IACP) and hence it has no legal control over the practice of nonmembers.

The RCI does not cover the entire range of activities of a clinical psychologist, nor has it defined the title clinical psychologist, hence very few clinical psychologists are concerned or registered with it. The Consumer Protection Act is too recent and the schedule of training institutes too incomplete to be commented upon. But it has the potential to have a restraining hand on some of the activities of a clinical psychologist—if considered objectionable—in the future. It has a legal sanction for it. Similarly, the Mental Health Act of 1987 can also impose restrictions but only through the Central or State Mental Health Authorities, which have been formed in some states with clinical psychologists as their nonofficial members. To date, however, they have not been very active but the potential for control is definitely there.

Practice standards for clinical psychologists have not been spelled out very clearly so far. Nevertheless, it cannot be said that there are no provisions for some kind of control over their activities in the light of the two developments described above.

2.08.6 CODE OF CONDUCT AND ETHICS GUIDELINES

During the Silver Jubilee year of IACP (1993/94), a code of conduct (Gupta, 1993) was adopted and circulated among the members. This concerned:

(i) *Professional competence and services.* Interest of the patient is of paramount importance and a clinical psychologist should keep abreast of recent developments in their field.

(ii) *Referrals.* In cases where proper assessment is not possible, the same should be communicated to the referring source and where the need for consultation by a physician psychiatrist or other health professional is felt necessary, the clinical psychologist should do what is necessary at the earliest opportunity.

(iii) *Method of expert opinion.* The clinical psychologist should assume full responsibility of their opinion under all circumstances.

(iv) *Consent for treatment.* Consent should be taken before starting any treatment after explaining to the patient and their available relative, the nature of illness, the method of psychological treatment, and factors associated with its efficacy and the so-called risk factors of the illness.

(v) *Patient welfare.* A clinical psychologist should maintain a high regard for the patient's integrity and welfare and should not take up a case that is not fairly within their competence.

(vi) *Court testimony.* A clinical psychologist should refrain from any bias or prejudice and their comments should be based upon the test findings and their observations.

(vii) *Confidentiality.* The information elicited from the patient and their relatives should not be disclosed to anyone other than concerned coprofessional(s) or, an appropriate authority; the clinical psychologist should not allow test material to be taken out of the clinic or laboratory, except for purposes of teaching and training students.

The IACP constitution suggests that membership may be terminated for any breach of the code of conducts. Nothing, however, is firmly laid down. Currently, the clinical psychologist is legally free to practice their profession even if IACP membership is terminated.

Pershad (1977) talks about professional ethics in psychological testing. The Indian Psychological Association constituted a National Test Commission in 1975 but appointed no clinical psychologist to its board. In addition, some training and research institutes (such as the Postgraduate Institute of Medical Education and Research, Chandigarh or the All India Institute of Medical Sciences) have their own Ethics Committees to screen all research projects, including Masters and Ph.D. theses, originating from that institute and involving human subjects. The Indian Council of Medical Research (ICMR) has put forward certain guidelines for consideration by such research institutes (ICMR circular dated September 1994). These cover such matters as the adequate protection of the rights and welfare of human subjects, whether risks are outweighed by potential benefits, adequate informed consent, the competence of the investigators, and the adequate provision of peer support.

The RCI Act (1992) has provisions for stricter punishments, for example, "imprisonment for a term which may extend to one year or with a fine which may extend to one thousand rupees or both" if individuals act in contravention of any of its provisions. However, so far these provisions exist on paper only. It has not even defined the term rehabilitation, although it mentions which certain professions fall under its provisions. The only disability covered in this Act, that may interest a clinical psychologist is of mental retardation.

However, the Persons with Disabilities Act (1995) which covers equal opportunities, protection of rights, and full participation, has defined disability (including both mental retardation and mental illness), persons with disabilities (with not less than 40% of any disability) and rehabilitation (a process aimed at enabling persons with disabilities to reach and maintain their optimal physical, sensory, intellectual, psychiatric, or sociofunctional level). This act was passed to give effect to the Proclamation on the Full Participation and Equality of the People with Disabilities in the Asian and Pacific Region, for which a meeting was held in Beijing on December 1–5, 1992, and to which India was also a signatory. Unlike the other acts mentioned earlier, there is no direct mention of clinical psychology under this act but the provision is there for rules and standards or required facilities to be provided or maintained in any institutions for persons with disabilities, to be framed by the state government. A certificate by the clinical psychologist to the degree of disability in a person with disabilities is also acceptable under this act.

A clinical psychologist under this act will have some legal control over their activities and, indirectly, shall be required to maintain certain minimum standards.

2.08.7 CONTINUING EDUCATION MANDATES

Although nothing is mandatory regarding continuing education for clinical psychologists, many nevertheless, of their own volition, do join workshops, seminars, or continuing education programs as trainees, participants, observers, or resource persons (Verma & Puri, 1996). For example, continuing education programs are being run at the National Institute of Mental Health and Neuro-Sciences, Bangalore, for those students who qualified before 1974 (Prabhu, 1983). The areas of reeducation include psychodiagnostics, behavior therapy, psychotherapy, stress management, neuropsychological assessments, depression, anxiety, mental retardation, family therapy, projective psychology, and cognitive psychology. These programs are often funded by premier national institutions such as the ICMR, the University Grants Commission, or the Indian Council of Social Science Research and conducted at any training and research institute including universities. Although this is done on a priority basis it is done as a result of an individual's initiative and is never mandatory. Joining such opportunities is easy, as is ignoring them.

Up-to-date knowledge is considered desirable although not mandatory (Verma & Puri, 1996). The IACP code of conduct (Gupta, 1993) refers to the need for a clinical psychologist to keep abreast of the latest developments in the field to enable him to provide efficient and effective services to the sick and needy. However, many such developments are controversial and expert opinion is clearly strongly divided on some of them, with the result that no firm opinion about their requirement has yet been expressed (Verma & Puri, 1996). The desirability of attending at least one of the courses in an area of one's choice, is, however, not questioned. It is the mode of regulation of the rules that has not yet been worked out to general satisfaction.

Here again, it is the absence of proper registration that sets the limits to any effort at improving the quality of services through these programs. There is no authority that can demand it and seek its compliance by all Indian clinical psychologists.

2.08.8 FUTURE DIRECTIONS

Some senior clinical psychologists have expressed their opinions through their writings (mainly in the *Indian Journal of Clinical Psychology*), presidential addresses, and talks in various national forums, seminars, workshops, or symposia on the future of clinical psychology in India (Ghosh, 1977; Mishra, 1995; Prabhu, 1983; Ramalingaswami, 1976; Sen, 1975; Sen Mazumdar, 1976; Verma & Puri, 1996).

Minimum acceptable standards have been suggested for postgraduate level with at least two years full-time diagnostic-cum-therapeutic work in supervised training (preferably an MPhil in clinical psychology) and three years supervised research (Ph.D. in clinical psychology); in short this involves a seven year training program after graduation (Prabhu, 1983). Is it possible to reduce this "wastage" of time, effort, and money by "catching them young" and providing stepwise training in clinical psychology in a well-organized manner?

The need for a separate registration of clinical psychologists, covering the entire practice of this specialty and not only for one or more aspects of the field, has been strongly felt and is being continually advocated at various national and regional forums (Prabhu, 1983; Verma & Puri, 1996). This demand is now gaining ground.

The horizons of the field are expanding and new challenges are arising (Paintal, 1987; Verma, 1982). The emphasis on different types of role for individuals, with different interests and aptitudes, working in different settings, and for different needs of the population served, has often been made (Prabhu, 1983), but not so well organized or accepted (Verma & Puri, 1996). Many clinical psychologists have strong biases in favor of or against some of these roles, which further complicates the issues. Obviously, there cannot be an ideal role model for all such professionals.

Other issues include the numbers leaving the profession, the problems of selection criteria, the point of entry into the training program, the duration and contents of the training program itself (Prabhu, 1983), the need for emphasis on codes of conduct (Gupta, 1993; Verma & Puri, 1996), and on the continuing education mandate (Verma & Puri, 1996).

However, the central and most critical issue remains that of the registration and certification of clinical psychologists by a governmental agency with full statutory powers, such as the Medical Council of India (Verma & Puri, 1996). This seems a distant goal but, in fact, it lies at the root of many problems facing this relatively young profession in India.

2.08.9 SUMMARY

Three points can be made:

(i) Clinical psychology, as an applied branch of psychology, is now being increasingly recognized, accepted, and respected, although it is relatively young and there are not many clinical psychologists in India when considered with respect to the vast population (Prabhu, 1983; Verma & Puri, 1996). There is a limited number of training centres, and there is a continuous loss of trained personnel due to migration, marriage, and misplacement (Prabhu, 1983).

(ii) In the absence of proper registration, the statutory requirements in terms of proper training, the continuous education mandate, an enforceable code of conduct, and practice standards are absent. There is nothing to stop anyone calling himself or herself a clinical psychologist. Although there is no separate, independent council of clinical psychologists with statutory powers, the term is recognized by the Mental Health Act of 1987 and the RCI Act of 1992. Medico–legal cases are sometimes directly referred by courts of law to the clinical psychologists (Verma & Pershad, 1980; Verma & Puri, 1996), and certificates issued by them regarding the degree of mental disability are accepted for legal purposes (Persons with Disabilities Act, 1995). At the same time there are greater legal responsibilities towards patient care and quality of service rendered since the Consumer Protection Act of 1986 come into force.

(iii) Again, on the positive side, there is an active association (the IACP) together with its official organ (the *Indian Journal of Clinical Psychology*). There are active professional members and training programs in addition to regular annual conferences in different parts of the country (Verma, 1984; Verma & Puri, 1996). There is now a greater tolerance of each other's viewpoints, a flexibility in overall approach to mental health problems, and an acceptance of the differing roles that a clinical psychologist can take depending upon the setting, the population served, and the activities required of him (Prabhu, 1983). Opportunities for creative innovations in different settings are there for the young clinical psychologist with enough potential and enthusiasm (Prabhu, 1983). The future is bright indeed for participants in this fast-expanding field.

ACKNOWLEDGMENTS

The author is grateful to the Director and to the Head of the Department of Psychiatry, Postgraduate Institute of Medical Education and Research, Chandigarh, for permission to write this chapter, and to the many senior clinical psychologists of the country, including the office bearers of the Indian Association of Clinical Psychologists, for providing and helping in the collection of the necessary material for this chapter, whose names are too numerous to be included here. Help and information from various training institutes, including the National Institute of Mental Health and Neuro-Sciences, Bangalore, the Central Institute of Psychiatry, Ranchi, the BM Institute of Mental Health, Ahmedabad, and the Rehabilitation Council of India, New Delhi, is gratefully acknowledged. Last, but not least, my thanks to Mr Alok Verma, computer programmer, for preparing this chapter in the prescribed manner.

2.08.10 REFERENCES

The Consumer Protection Act (1986). *Act no. 68 of 1986*. New Delhi: Government of India.

Ghosh, A. (1977). Role of a clinical psychologist: a psychiatrist's point of view (Letter to the editor). *Indian Journal of Clinical Psychology*, *4*, 198–199.

Gupta, S. C. (1992, November). Letter sent to Rehabilitation Council of India, New Delhi and copy circulated among members of IACP. Lucknow, India.

Gupta, S. C. (1993). *Code of conduct* (adopted by IACP, circulated to its members). Lucknow, India: IACP Secretariate.

Gupta, S. C. (1994, October 10). Circular to members of IACP. Lucknow, India: IACP Secretariate.

Indian Association of Clinical Psychologists (1995a). *Amended Constitution of Indian Association of Clinical Psychologist*. Jaipur, India: IACP Secretariate.

Indian Association of Clinical Psychologists (1995b). *Membership list*. Jaipur, India: IACP Secretariate.

Indian Council of Medical Research (1994, September). *Policy statement of ethical considerations involved in research on human subjects*. (Circulated to all the important research institutes in India). New Delhi, India: ICMR.

The Mental Health Act (1987). (*Act no. 14 of 1987*) with State Mental Health Rules (1990) and Central Mental Health Authority Rules (1990). Delhi, India: Law Publishers (India).

Mishra, H. (1995). Clinician clinical psychologist (Editorial). *Indian Journal of Clinical Psychology, 22*, i–ii.

Paintal, H. K. (1987). Expanding horizons for clinical psychologists in India. *Indian Journal of Clinical Psychology, 14*, 5–7.

Pershad, D. (1977). Professional ethics in psychological testing. *ISPT Journal of Research, 1*, 65–68.

Persons with Disabilities Act (1995). (*Act no. 1 of 1996*. Equal opportunities, protection of rights and full participation Act) Published in *The Gazette of India*, Extraordinary, Part II, Section 1, January 1, 1996.

Prabhu, G. G. (1983) Clinical psychology: Then and now. *Indian Journal of Clinical Psychology, 10*, i–xvi.

Ramalingaswami, P. (1976). Clinical psychology in India: Need for a new perspective. *Indian Journal of Clinical Psychology, 3*, 53–58.

Ramalingaswami, P. (1980). *Psychology in India: Challenges and opportunities*, Delhi, India: Prachi Publications.

Rehabilitation Council of India Act (1992) *Act no. 34 of 1992*. Published in *The Gazette of India*, Part II, Section 1, no. 56, September 2, 1992.

Sen, N. N. (1975). Clinical psychology in the eighties (Editorial). *Indian Journal of Clinical Psychology, 2*, i–iv.

Sen Mazumdar, D. P. (1976). A profession in search of its image (Editorial). *Indian Journal of Clinical Psychology, 3*, 1–4.

Verma, S. K. (1982). The field of clinical psychology in India (Editorial). *Indian Journal of Clinical Psychology, 9*, i–ii.

Verma, S. K. (1984). Indian Journal of Clinical Psychology: The first ten years. *Indian Journal of Clinical Psychology, 11*, 11–20.

Verma, S. K., & Pershad, D. (1980). Psychological referrals in a psychiatric unit of a general hospital. *Indian Journal of Clinical Psychology, 7*, 157–162.

Verma, S. K., & Puri, A. (1996). Clinical psychology in India. In *Proceedings of Asian and Indian Academy of Applied Psychology Conference*, Aligarh Muslim University, India.

2.09 Clinical Psychology in Latin America

HÉCTOR C. FERNÁNDEZ-ALVAREZ
AIGLE, Buenos Aires, Argentina

2.09.1 INTRODUCTION

Latin America is a vast geopolitical region, a territory stretching from south of the Rio Grande to the Strait of Magellan, made up of a heterogeneous group of nations forged under the cultural influence of Western European countries with a Latin heritage. Within its boundaries can also be found a few smaller areas which were created under the cultural influence of Danish and British colonizers. Due not only to these circumstances, but also to the varying living conditions in some countries, there are a few lingering doubts regarding exact borders. However, it is generally agreed that Latin America is a subcontinent made up of more than 30 countries and inhabited by some 500 million people. In 1970 the urban population amounted to 58% of the total population. By 1980 it had reached 65% and it is expected to be 77% in the year 2000. Its people are grouped into various regions and subregions: Mexico and Central America, the Caribbean and the Antilles Islands, and South America (which is, in turn divided among Brazil, the Andean nations, and the Southern Cone countries). Some countries, such as Brazil and Mexico, have very large populations (150 and 100 million inhabitants, respectively), while other nations are small both geographically and demographically.

Latin American countries have important common cultural traits, such as similarity in language (with Spanish and Portuguese predominating), religion (mostly Catholic), and the political system of their governments (republican democracies), as well as harsh socioeconomic conditions throughout most of the subcontinent. But there are a few exceptions, such as Cuba, which has had a clearly different social–political form of government since the 1960s. On the other hand, Puerto Rico is an Associate State of the USA, and Mexico is more and more closely linked to the other countries of North America and, consequently, more detached from the countries of Central America to which it is joined by historical and ethnic reasons. For some, Puerto Rico and Mexico are, precisely, the two countries with the closest cultural affinity to the USA (Díaz-Guerrero, 1995), but this is not an opinion unanimously held among psychologists in those countries.

However, there are also great differences within Latin America stemming from the social makeup, ethnic roots, and migratory currents which influenced each region. Since the period of the Conquest (1492), the continent has been exposed to successive waves of cultural invasion. The indigenous people showed greater resistance to acculturation in some areas, such as Mexico and Peru, but they could not prevent being assimilated. One of the results of this process was heavy crossbreeding between white settlers and native inhabitants creating the mestizo or Creole race. This, nevertheless, did not occur without cruel practices of wiping out native populations. In central Mexico, for example, the indigenous population declined from an estimated 25 million people in the year 1519 to just one million in 1605. In other countries, such as Chile and especially Argentina, the aboriginal population was reduced to extremely low levels, so much so that the general population today owes its makeup to successive waves of immigrants from the European continent. In another context, a significant flow of black Africans made their way to Brazil and some islands of the Caribbean where today they account for a large number of the inhabitants of those nations.

During the nineteenth-century, the cultural influence of the USA had a major impact, especially in the central zone and the Caribbean, while European influence predominated in the south. The weight of those cultures made themselves strongly felt in the nations of the continent as a whole, influencing the development of psychology. Therefore, it is impossible to speak of "a single" Latin American psychology. Instead, it can be said that there are various developments in accordance with the different regions and countries. Nevertheless, it cannot be categorically said that there has not been a Latin American psychology. The following are its most common traits:

(i) The development of psychology as an independent discipline is something relatively recent; universities began to provide courses after the Second World War. Therefore, the regulations concerning practicing the various disciplines in general, and clinical psychology in particular, only began to be implemented in recent years. An important consequence of this is, that the average age of Latin American professionals is very young and there is a scarcity of resources with specialized training.

(ii) The evolution of Latin American psychology reflects the strong impact of the psychology coming from other regions. Its development has depended on developments in the USA and Europe. The weight of North American psychology was felt strongest in certain regions like Mexico, Central America, the Caribbean, and northern Andean nations. European influence, mainly French and German, was stronger in the southern part of the continent. European psychology also had a more decisive influence in the clinical area, whereas for years the US influence was greater in other fields. The developments of the discipline in the former Soviet Union had some influence in several countries between the 1960s and 1990s, especially in Cuba, where it contributed both to university study programs and also scientific and professional practices.

(iii) Psychology in general, and clinical psychology in particular, has been mostly oriented according to practical and professional needs. Research has been scarce and has concentrated in the areas of greatest transference and application. In addition, a significant number of psychologists exercise clinical psychology as a private practice, some as their principal activity, others as a complement to another field (Marin, Kennedy, & Boyce, 1987).

(iv) The model of psychology developed in Latin America was oriented not only towards the practical, but also granted significant importance to the social and community aspects in all fields of application. In its search it oriented theory and methodology towards the use of instruments that reflected significant social commitment. (Montero, 1994).

(v) The cultural diversity led to a marked interest in the ethnopsychological developments in the various fields of application. Clinical psychology was not excluded from this process, either in the field of psychopathology or therapy. Studies in this area are perhaps insufficient, but they indicate specific concern among many psychologists on the continent.

Latin American psychologists maintain exchanges through various organizations, each corresponding to different fields of the discipline. But the Interamerican Society of Psychology (SIP) has contributed most to facilitating such exchange. This society was founded in December 1951 in Mexico during the Fourth International Congress on Mental Health. It held its first congress in 1953 in Santo Domingo (Dominican Republic) and has been holding congresses every two years since. The SIP has facilitated access to information and debate on the core aspects of the discipline, while at the same time promoting a dialogue not only among the psychologists of the continent, but also with their colleagues in North America. It has workgroups organized in each specialty, one of which is focused on the area of clinical psychology.

In this Chapter, the following aspects of the practice are dealt with: education, legal matters, fields of application, professional practice, ethical questions, publications, and future directions. Examples are selected from some of the countries which are sufficiently representative of each case. An exhaustive presentation, contemplating the situation in each country, is not possible in the available space.

2.09.2 EDUCATION: TRAINING AND SPECIALIZATION COURSES

During the first half of the twentieth-century, psychological studies were part of medical science or, more frequently, philosophical studies. During this period, drawing on the arrival of numerous European thinkers, developments in psychology were oriented towards two traditional tendencies: psychoanalysis and psychometry (Ardila, 1986; Marin et al. 1987), benefiting from the cultural permeability of the continent.

Teaching psychology in universities as an independent scientific discipline began in some countries in the 1940s, and it took hold throughout the following decade. Guatemala (1946), Colombia (1947), Chile (1948), Brazil (1953), Peru (1955), Argentina (1956), and Venezuela (1956) were the first countries to offer a degree in psychology. By the mid-1970s, those studies had spread throughout the continent. Most courses were offered by state universities, but there were some cases of nonstate university centers, for example, institutes related to religious organizations, such as Universidad de Santo Tomás, Cuba or the Pontificia Universidade Católica de Rio de Janeiro, Brazil.

In 1974, the Latin American Conference on Psychology Training (held in Bogotá, Colombia) was organized for the purpose of discussing the basic course requirements for the career in the continent and to agree on merging university policies on training psychologists (Klappenbach & Paves, 1994; Vilanova, 1993). The conference conclusions pointed to the advantage of a comprehensive basic education and the need for training to take into account both scientific and professional considerations. As will be seen further on, what really happened was somewhat different: orientation in the career and the discipline were mostly directed towards practical and applied aspects. The conference also recommended striving to make psychology an independent field of study within the university, which in fact took place not long afterwards. The original idea to hold similar encounters in the future did not happen. Instead, activities were carried out within the congresses organized by the SIP, especially since the late 1980s. That has been the venue for presenting the efforts undertaken within América Latina Formación Académica, a cooperation program between Europe and Latin America aimed at making studies in psychology at universities in Latin America compatible. In that context, the ideal studies profile for training psychologists was defined as meeting the following principles: (i) a balance between systematization and flexibility, (ii) a balance between commitment to knowledge and commitment to professionalization, (iii) a command of the various research methods and techniques, and (iv) the acquisition of the theoretical and practical capabilities and sufficient skills and techniques to measure, assess, diagnose, and develop assessment, intervention and prevention programs in the various fields of applied psychology.

For many years, very few university centers taught psychology; it was taught exclusively in state or religious institutions. This situation has changed dramatically since 1970. New private and nonreligious universities throughout the continent are now offering courses in psychology. This has helped to diversify the education offered and to create different professional models. Although resisted for many years, especially in the countries most dependent on the European model, new models finally took hold. As a result of this process, the number of centers offering studies in psychology multiplied, reflecting varying degrees of academic and scientific quality. This drew a lot of criticism, but was also a valuable incentive to increase control and regulation mechanisms for the practice, so necessary at the time. In some countries, such as Chile, the number of institutions providing these studies grew exponentially in just a few years. In 1996, both Brazil and Mexico had one hundred universities offering studies in psychology. Such a large number of educational establishments in the field poses a difficult task of coordination and regulation. In Mexico, that task was given to the Consejo Nacional para la Enseñanza e Investigación en Psicología.

As a result of this process, there has been significant growth in the number of students choosing this discipline, most of them women, according to the general trend of professionals registered in the continent over the past several years. Psychology education in Cuba has been quite different from the rest of the continent. University education is public and study plans are closely linked to government education and health policy. For many years, the basic education curriculum in psychology included developing substantial skills in strategic areas and strict knowledge of dialectical materialism (Mitjans Martínez, 1987). Changes in the world political map have produced modifications in that training emphasis but the teaching continues to strive for student training to be heavily oriented towards community needs.

The degrees in psychology given by Latin American universities basically comprise undergraduate course studies which normally last four to five years. At present there is an important trend oriented toward reforming course studies to adjust them to a four-year program in basic studies followed by postgraduate studies toward a master or doctorate as an essential requirement for exercising the profession. Those studies usually include orientations in various fields, the most common being: educational, labor, organizational, forensic, and clinical psychology. A significant percentage of students choose clinical psychology, especially in certain countries like Mexico, Brazil, Uruguay, and Argentina. In Argentina, clinical psychology has been the overwhelming orientation for many years, and psychology came to be considered practically synonymous with clinical psychology.

Clinical courses usually include experience in healthcare centers like psychiatric hospitals, general hospitals, community centers for health prevention and promotion, and other related areas. Students tend to have access to a wide scope of practice during training at government public assistance centers or private centers dedicated to specialized practices. Several universities have their own healthcare centers used for training students. Founded in 1957, the Clinical Psychological Office of the Universidad de San Marcos in Lima, Peru is probably the oldest psychology care center organized by an academic institution for treating its own staff and, at the same time, meeting the needs of the general public. Other interesting examples are the Centro de Servicios Psicológicos of the Universidad Autónoma de Mexico (UNAM), founded in 1981 (Benavidez Torres & Nuñez Obando, 1983), the Centro Asistencial de la Universidad Central de Caracas and the Clinical-Escuela of the Pontifícia Universidade Católica de Campinas in Campinas, Brazil. But the model of university-run centers is still in a minority, partly due to budgetary reasons and partly because of the operational difficulties they pose.

In all cases, however, learning technologies has been a priority over fomenting research. Also contributing to that is the fact that many countries have few full-time professors. In fact, professors frequently divide their time between teaching and academic pursuits, and professional activities outside the realm of the university. But this is not the case in all countries. The prevailing practice in Puerto Rico and Brazil, for example, is very different.

The degree universities most frequently grant is Psychologist or Licensure in Psychology. This degree usually authorizes practicing any field of the profession, including clinical practice. Therefore, graduates can make diagnoses, provide psychological treatments, and carry out tasks in community mental health assistance. Despite that, psychologists interested in working in the clinical field usually receive specialized training in order to compete in the labor market. Although not a formal requirement, this is considered necessary in order to obtain the qualifications for social and professional recognition. When it was not duly formalized, this training was provided in public health centers, private training centers, and by professional associations rather than in universities. In general, it reflected a specific theoretical model or focus. Most followed the schools of behavioral change or psychoanalysis. Other important contributions to the education of clinical psychologists came from the fields of psychiatry and sociology. Psychiatrists played a large role in the teaching throughout many years, but this influence has declined considerably since 1980.

Until recently, psychologists interested in postgraduate studies attended courses at universities in the USA and Europe. Mexico was one of the first countries to offer postgraduate studies through the UNAM which, starting in 1958, organized three different programs, including one in the clinical area. The University of Puerto Rico was also one of the first institutions (1965) to offer postgraduate studies, as was the Pontificia Universidade Catolica de Rio de Janeiro, Brazil (1966). After this, postgraduate programs in clinical psychology began to be offered in Guatemala (Universidad Francisco Marroquín, 1975), Argentina (Universidad de Belgrano, 1975), Colombia (Universidad de Santo Tomás, 1977) and Costa Rica (Universidad de Costa Rica, 1979). Brazil also created the Post-Graduate Studies Program in Clinical Psychology at the Pontifícia Universidade Católica de Sao Paulo, which has offered a masters program since 1976 and doctoral studies starting in 1982. The general goals are the study of psychic reality in its component processes, its sociocultural conditions, its crises and transformations. Since 1980 there has been a major shift in this aspect, with numerous postgraduate courses becoming available. Today, most countries offer postgraduate (masters and doctors) programs in psychology.

Part of the education and training of psychologists usually includes supervision of their work. However, until the mid-1970s psychiatrists tended to perform that task. There were two reasons for this: the strength of the medical profession in mental health administration and the newness of the specialty which limited the experience of psychologists. Since the mid-1970s this situation has changed a great deal, and psychologists have become supervisors at all levels of mental health care.

2.09.3 LEGAL ASPECTS AND REGULATIONS

The creation of university level psychology studies did not mean immediate legal recognition. Legislation authorizing the practice of the profession came many years later. Before that, clinical psychologists saw their activity regulated within the laws governing medicine and their role was mainly limited to being assistants to psychiatrists. Brazil is acknowledged as the pioneer in drawing up a legal body which recognized psychology as an independent profession. In 1962 Law 4119 was passed and Article 13 established that: "The use of psychological methods and techniques for the purpose of (i) psychological diagnosis, (ii) professional orientation and selection, (iii) psychopedagogical guidance, and (iv) solution of adjustment problems shall be considered the exclusive functions of psychologists." The same legal body recognized the following as specializations in this discipline: educational psychology, clinical psychology, and labor applied psychology (Conselho Regional de Psicología, 1996).

The situation of legal recognition began to change in the mid-1970s. Legal recognition and qualification of psychologists was approved in several countries: Venezuela (1975), Colombia (1983), Puerto Rico (1983), Argentina (1985), and Bolivia (1987). In Colombia, Law 58, passed in 1983, recognizes psychology as an independent profession, regulating its exercise throughout the country in all its specialties. Article 11 of the law establishes that

> the functions of a person holding a degree in psychology include, among others, the use of psychological methods and techniques in pursuit of the following objectives: basic and applied research, teaching, psychological diagnosis, psychological treatment, vocational and professional orientation and selection, analysis and modification of individual or group behavior, and psychological prophylaxis. (Pérez-Gómez, 1990)

In Puerto Rico that same year, Law 96 regulated the practice of psychology in all its fields, authorizing "the diagnosis and application of principles, methods and procedures in order to understand, predict, influence or change behavior." In most countries, certification of clinical psychologists is granted by the health and/or education ministries. In some cases, such as Costa Rica and Venezuela, it includes registration in social security and social insurance services.

The legal recognition of psychology as a profession led to the establishment of professional organizations which, depending on the country, were called Association, Society, or College of Psychologists. Some societies group professionals in general or by specialty. For example, in Mexico, Rodríguez and Jurado Cárdenas (1986) speak of the existence of eight associations in the field of clinical psychology. In some countries, belonging to such an entity is an essential requirement to be able to practice the profession. Costa Rica saw the birth of the profession when Law 1977 created the College of Professional Psychologists, which also allowed specialization in clinical psychology. In a similar way, the Peruvian decree law of 1980 approved the creation of the College of Psychologists for the purpose of regulating the practice and assuring it is exercised in accordance with the Code of Professional Ethics. The functions of those entities have been mostly related to promoting all aspects of the discipline and, especially defending the professional working rights of their members. Several efforts have been made to set up a continent-wide federation grouping the various national entities. That has not yet been achieved in a consistent way, probably due to existing differences between regions.

As stated above, certification to practice clinical psychology is normally obtained on receiving a university degree. But this situation is undergoing great change at present. Several countries are quickly beginning to regulate new requirements for exercising the profession, which in practice means establishing the obligation of doing postgraduate studies. Following the US model, a new law in Puerto Rico stipulated that as from 1994 it is necessary to have a doctoral degree to practice clinical psychology. The reason for this requirement is grounded on the fact that clinical psychology is closely linked to health (Alvarez & Velez-Pastrana, 1995). In many countries, psychologists' associations and organizations have been promoting the creation of commissions linked to the certification of the clinical specialization with requirements in addition to possessing a degree in psychology. In Chile, for example, in 1995, the Comisión Nacional de Acreditación de Psicólogos Clínicos issued a set of rules which establishes, among the necessary certification criteria, the requirement of having completed postgraduate studies with proper supervision of practice.

Until recently, since clinical psychologists did not have to take courses to keep themselves up-to-date in the specialty, only the pressure coming from the law of supply and demand acted as a motivation for professionals to seek additional training. But in 1970, UNESCO called attention to the need to promote "permanent education" as a fundamental principle in education policy. The growth in scientific exchange through regional organizations and international events was a powerful factor which helped to create a new attitude in this respect. This development could change the conditions for teaching and training clinical psychologists, fostering continuing education, training, specialization, and updating modalities (Miranda, 1987).

2.09.4 AREAS OF APPLICATION

Clinical psychology in Latin America found fertile ground for its development in some areas, especially in the field of psychotherapy and community mental health. Psychotherapy came on the scene very early and throughout the twentieth-century has undergone continuous evolution. Among the developing regions, Latin America is the region where psychotherapy found its most propitious environment. This field has also felt the strong influence of the USA and Europe, as can be clearly seen upon examining the development of the main approaches to treatment.

2.09.4.1 Psychoanalysis

The extraordinary expansion of psychoanalysis in the Southern Cone is well known. The Asociación Psicoanalítica Argentina, founded in 1942, was the venue of some of the most significant theoretical contributions in the field. It came to have a great number of members, among them renowned international figures. Its official publication, the *Revista de Psicoanálisis* journal, begun in 1943, is one of the most prestigious publications in psychoanalysis. A division within that organization, which took place in the 1970s, led to the creation of an alternative body, the Asociacíon Psicoanalítica de Buenos Aires, with its publication *Psicoanálisis*. Both associations, which number some 1000 members each, are recognized by the International Psychoanalytical Association (IPA). After a few years of discord, the two associations have developed a constructive relationship in recent years. As an indication of the international importance of Argentine psychoanalysis, it is worth mentioning that the last president of the IPA was an Argentinian.

Different variants with strong followings arose throughout the evolution of psychoanalysis in Argentina, most significant among them being the followers of the Kleinian model. Since the mid-1970s the prevailing orientation has been that of Jacques Lacan's followers, who introduced his teachings in various places, including hospitals and universities. The phenomenon of Lacanism in Buenos Aires spread not only to the rest of the country but was disseminated throughout Latin America. The huge exodus of Argentine psychoanalysts in the second half of the 1970s contributed decisively in this regard, paving the way for continental meetings where the so-called Lacanamerican movement was furthered. An important base for that movement had been earlier established in Caracas, Venezuela. In the 1990s this school of thought has made headway in several countries of the continent, from countries with large populations like Brazil, to smaller ones such as Ecuador where a Centro de Estudios Freudianos was organized within the Universidad Católica de Guayaquil.

Brazilian tradition in psychoanalysis, taken as a whole, is rich and best seen in Rio de Janeiro. Other centers of note include Sao Paulo, Porto Alegre, and Bahia. Several associations represent this orientation in Brazil, which also has several important publications, such as the prestigious *Journal de Psicoanalise*. The journal published by the influential Asociación Psicoanalítica Uruguaya is also well-known. There too, for many years, psychoanalysis was a synonym for psychological treatment. This orientation has also undergone important developments in the rest of the continent, especially in Colombia, Venezuela, Chile, and Peru, countries which also have duly recognized psychoanalytical associations. In Panama the most relevant orientation was that of the object relations theory. Mexico has a very particular situation, reflecting great changes over time. Very powerful in Mexico in the 1950s under the influence of Frommian thought, psychoanalysis gradually fell from its zenith in the following decades. But it still has an important base there with influential organizations such as the Asociación Psicoanalítica Mexicana and the Asociación Mexicana de Psicoterapia Psicoanalítica. On a continental level, the organization of the psychoanalytical movement is best represented in the Federación de América Latina, founded in 1965 on the basis of its predecessor, Confederación de Psicoanálisis de América Latina.

2.09.4.2 Behavioral Analysis and Change

Behaviorism advanced along two paths: behavioral analysis (related to experimental aspects) and behavioral modification (linked to therapeutic aspects). Its greatest influence was felt in Mexico and in the countries of Central America and the Caribbean. But it also carried powerful weight in Venezuela, Colombia, and the countries along the Pacific. Likewise, it had numerous followers in Brazil, headquarters of a solid organization of professionals: the Sociedad Brasilera de Terapia Comportamental. In 1996 the society organized a meeting at the Universidad de Campinas which was attended by over 1000 therapists.

The importance of its development in Mexico has been seen at various levels: in the education of significant contingents of clinical psychologists, in eminent publications, and in numerous transcendental scientific events. The dominating model was the application of different therapeutic strategies derived from Skinnerian thought. One of the distinguished centers for work has been the Departamento de Psicología y Medicina de Rehabilitación de la Universidad Veracruzana, the venue of the First Annual Symposium on Behavioral Change held in 1971. Later development of this movement in Mexico shows many similarities with the movement which took place in the same theory in the US, where there was a significant movement toward the development of new procedures based on a behavioral–cognitive approach.

Important developments in behavioral change have taken place in other countries of the continent. In the Caribbean, Puerto Rico is one of the countries where most work has been carried out; another is the Dominican Republic. Guatemala and Costa Rica stand out among the nations of Central America. There have also been vigorous developments in Venezuela and Peru, grouped around organizations like the Asociación Venezolana para el Avance de las Ciencias del Comportamiento and the Sociedad de Análisis y Modificación del Comportamiento de Perú. Its evolution in Colombia was doubly significant. Not only was it a center for important activity but it was also where the Asociación Latinoamericana de Análisis y Modificación de Conducta (ALAMOC) was created. ALAMOC's periodical congresses bring together most of the specialists in the region. Its last congress was held in La Paz, Bolivia. This group has also been responsible for publications in this field.

2.09.4.3 The Humanistic Movement

The different orientations that tend to group themselves under this name are well represented in many countries of the continent, with significant representations in Peru, Chile, and Mexico. The client-centered Rogerian approach, has important representatives, highlighting the work carried out by the group at the Universidad Iberoamericana de Mexico. The last Latin American congress of this orientation was held in La Paz, Bolivia. Another approach within this school, the gestalt therapy, has made important advances in countries like Argentina, Brazil, Uruguay, Peru, Mexico, and Chile. The movement has achieved prominent status in Chile, where much of the specialized literature in Spanish is published. The last international congress of this orientation was held in Buenos Aires, Argentina.

2.09.4.4 Psychodrama

The Federación Latinoamericana of this orientation, currently headquartered in Asunción, Paraguay, groups numerous institutions and therapists from several countries throughout the continent. Argentina has been the forerunner of psychodrama but the greatest number of therapists and institutions are found in Brazil, especially in the north. In this country, it is the Federación de Psicodrama, which groups several associations in the country and has around 3000 members. Among the other countries with important developments in this field, special mention should be given to Mexico, which has a very active group in this specialty.

2.09.4.5 Systemic Therapy

A more recent development, dating from the early 1980s, systemic therapy has found strong followings in Argentina, Brazil, Chile,

Colombia, Ecuador, Mexico, Puerto Rico, Uruguay, and Venezuela. For the most part, developments in this field are branches of US models, having found great acceptance in society in a short period of time. There are numerous national associations promoting local and regional meetings and producing several publications providing information on advances in the discipline on the continent.

2.09.4.6 Cognitive Therapy

This is probably the newest therapeutic orientation in the field of psychotherapy. It is currently in a phase of full expansion, especially in Argentina, Chile, Brazil, and Mexico. The first regional meeting is being planned and hopes to bring together the experience of several countries. But the best indication of the rapid growth in importance of this approach is the fact that Mexico has been chosen as the venue for the World Congress on Cognitive Therapy in 1998.

2.09.4.7 Other Approaches

In addition to smaller scale developments of other specific approaches, there are three important trends in the panorama of Latin American psychotherapy which merit special mention. One of them, with a long history, is the broad movement of group therapy. Reflecting that importance, the international association in this specialty has chosen Buenos Aires to host its congress. Second, the importance family therapy has acquired should also be noted. The main developments in this field came from, but are not limited to, systemic therapy. A monographic issue of the *Revista Interamericana de Psicología* provides up-to-date information on developments in this field (Bernal & Alvarez, 1989).

Finally, the role of psychotherapy in Latin American is highly significant in its support of the integration movement (Fernández-Alvarez, 1992). The first signs of interest in this area go back to the early 1980s. But this tendency gained greater momentum throughout the 1990s, especially as the result of the activity of some groups of professionals, among the most important being, the Fundación AIGLE headquartered in Buenos Aires, Argentina, and Centro Científico de Desarrollo Psicológico in Santiago, Chile.

Community mental health is a field where a great deal of work and creativity has taken place on the continent as a result of a combination of the pressing needs of the population and the high level of social commitment of many Latin American scientists and professionals (especially psychologists). Literature on this topic emphasizes that numerous and varied pilot programs in community mental health have arisen in Latin America (Levav, 1992). Many of these projects were experimental and almost always implemented in urban areas.

Psychologists joined the interdisciplinary teams which put those programs into practice. Pointed examples include the Mental Health Project in Barrio Santa Eduviges, Tegucigalpa, Honduras; the Centro de Atención Psicosocial de Ciudad Sandino, Nicaragua; and the mental health program in the community of Curundú, Panama. Some of these projects have been collaborations with university institutions, such as the Centro de Asistencia a la Comunidad of the Universidad de Rosario in Argentina, which was created in 1984 with three areas of activity: mental health care, education, and social prevention. Its objectives include the creation of a community health center and a network of social work and health promotion, in addition to providing education and professional training.

The mental health programs started on the continent share some common characteristics. These projects sponsor preventive and health promotion activities, particularly through work in schools and other grassroots community organizations. In most of the projects, special importance is given to solving problems with a marked psychosocial bias. The greatest number of programs involving clinical psychologists are in the areas of mental health care and rehabilitation of persons suffering from severe mental disorders, alcoholism, and drug abuse, as well as broaching problems related to violence and crime. The 1990s have seen a great deal of effort being directed to the fight against AIDS. The available professional resources are usually scarce, requiring fast and intensive training courses. In many cases, as a means of multiplying the preventive effects, emphasis is placed on creating self-help groups.

2.09.5 EXERCISING THE PROFESSION

Practicing clinical psychology is conditioned by three overriding factors: (i) the economic limitations of the continent and of each region, (ii) the power of the physician in general, especially that of the psychiatrist, and (iii) the struggle between the different clinical–theoretical orientations. For years, Latin American psychologists found many job opportunities due to the favorable relation between the number of professionals available and existing job supply. The latter centered round two large sectors: on one hand, work in government institutions, especially those in the area of education and health which proposed the implementation of community programs; and, on the other hand, in public and private practices dedicated to the diagnosis and treatment of mental disorders. The number of psychologists working in state health institutions has increased from the 1970s. Taking Costa as an example, its work there was divided between practices in psychiatric hospitals and general hospitals, planning and programming health policies (including preventive activities) and healthcare activities in urban areas (Campos, 1991).

The work of psychologists in government programs has obviously been dependent on the changing conditions which occur in each country. In brief periods of time the economy of many countries in the continent have undergone great fluctuations which affected their social policies. Nonetheless, for a long time the governments of the region have promoted social service plans which favored setting up community action programs. The intensification of the socioeconomic crisis in Latin America in recent years has had a negative impact on state programs. State reforms and low budgets have made it difficult for governments to carry on significant public assistance and community action plans. This has grown worse due to cutbacks in foreign aid granted by international cooperation agencies.

The activity of psychologists in mental health services has been covered through various sources of financing. Hospital services care for the neediest sectors of the population, which in some countries amount to a very large number of people. Health insurance plans run by trade unions and powerful institutions cover the healthcare needs of their members. Other sectors of the population, belonging to the middle and upper-middle strata, choose private health care. More recently, prepaid health insurance plans have appeared as an alternative for covering some mental health needs. The job panorama for psychologists in this field has been growing worse because of two factors: first, the huge growth in the number of professionals, owing to the rise in university graduates, producing a negative balance between supply and demand. This did not happen in Cuba because the professional training of psychologists has been planned by the government in line with the employment needs of the country. Second, less funds have been available in society because of the economic crisis already mentioned.

The institutions in charge of mental health administration began to intervene heavily in planning services, usually with the primary aim of changing the cost/benefit ratio with an eye toward lowering service costs. They encouraged short-term therapy methods and reduced the number of professionals working in private practice. As a result of this, professionals saw their earnings dwindle. In addition, there has been a steady rise in the unemployment rate. At present, there is no managed mental healthcare policy in Latin America as has been gradually implemented in the USA, but steps being taken seem to be moving in that direction. World globalization makes it possible to suppose that the transfer of policies from dominant societies to dependent societies will take place rapidly. Regardless, such change must necessarily adapt to the peculiarities of the new scenario.

2.09.6 ETHICAL QUESTIONS

As the process of regulating the practice made headway at all levels, a growing number of codes of ethics and ethics tribunals began to work at regulating practice standards. Qualification of the profession is usually accompanied by a code of ethics. Professional associations—psychologists colleges in most countries—are entrusted with the task of ensuring that ethical norms are met. In this sense, practice standards are regulated by peers, based on the legal prescriptions and rules current in each country. The users or consumers of psychological services should resort to ordinary courts when they believe they have been injured by a practicing professional.

There are codes of ethics in all countries with many principles in common, strongly inspired by the practicing standards of the American Psychological Association. As an example, Panama's code, drawn up in 1992, describes ethical principles in the following areas: responsibility, competence, legal and moral norms, public statements, confidentiality, people's welfare, professional relations, assessment techniques, research with human participants, and the care and use of animals in research. In accordance with the 1984 law in Honduras governing the College of Psychologists, the Norms of Professional Ethics in effect are aimed at orienting the exercise of psychology as a profession according to the duties which psychologists must fulfill in relation to their patients, colleagues, and society as a whole.

2.09.7 PUBLICATIONS

Even though great efforts have been made in the continent to provide a flow of biographical material, these efforts have often been frustrated by the lack of continuity in the publications, mostly due to economic difficulties. However, some journals have managed to appear regularly and maintain their level of excellence throughout the years, such as the already mentioned *Revista de Psicoanálisis.* Among the oldest publications, the following are worth mentioning: *Arquivos Brasileiros de Psicologia* (Brazil, founded in 1949); *Acta Psiquiátrica y Psicológica de América Latina* (Argentina, 1954); *Revista del Hospital Psiquiátrico de La Habana* (Cuba, 1959); *Revista Interamericana de Psicologi/a* (Interamerican Society of Psychology, 1967); and *Revista Latinoamericana de Psicología* (Colombia, 1969).

These publications contain articles covering various fields of psychology, including clinical psychology. There are also specialized publications reflecting a significant example of the work of Latin American clinical psychologists, such as: *Avances en Psicología Clínica Latinoamericana* (Colombia); *Revista Argentina de Clínica Psicológica* (Argentina); *Terapia Psicológica* (Chile); and *Salud Mental* (México)

There is also a substantial number of publications on various specific approaches.

2.09.8 FUTURE DIRECTIONS

According to World Bank data (1993), in 1990, Latin America had an average per capita income of US$2190 dollars. But it was also one of the three regions in the world with negative economic growth since 1980. The profound crisis that has been afflicting the region will require psychologists to come up with creative answers to respond to an already very visible paradox: a population with greater needs which must be helped with fewer resources.

An overview of the evolution of psychology in Latin America indicates that its most positive aspects have been the high social significance of its practices and the important theoretical and technological development it has achieved despite only counting on scarce resources. The most negative aspects are related to the weakness of culturally specific proposals, because the models and instruments used were mostly imported from other regions. This was felt most in the rural areas where the population groups with greatest ethnic singularity live. For the upcoming years, scientists foresee an increase in demographic displacement towards urban centers, which will probably be accompanied by the creation of human settlements with difficult living conditions. This leads to expectations of significant growth in substance abuse, violence, and other social pathologies which will require doubling the efforts made in community aid activities.

The most urgent aspects on which the future development of clinical psychology in the region should focus are: (i) emphasizing cultural values at all levels of development; (ii) legalizing regulations governing the profession, with specifications regarding certification, supervision of practices, and requirements for continuing professional education; (iii) consolidating postgraduate studies and specialization training programs; (iv) fomenting research at all levels, without ignoring the importance of developing new technology; and (v) being increasingly accurate in designing community action programs with an eye toward more efficiency.

2.09.9 REFERENCES

Alvarez, V. & Velez-Pastrana, M. C. (1995). La profesión de la psicología en Puerto Rico. *Revista Latinoamericana de Psicología, 27,* 175–185.

Ardila, R. (1986). *La psicología en América Latina. Pasado, presente y futuro.* Méxieco: Siglo XXI.

Benavidez Torres, J. Y., & Nuñez Obando, R. (1983). *Una década de la facultad de psicología: 1973–1983.* México: UNAM.

Bernal, G., & Alvarez, A. I. (1989). Psicología y terapia familiar desde Latinoamérica. *Revista Interamericana de Psicología, 23.*

Campos, G. A. (1991). La psicología clínica en las instituciones de salud costarricense. *Revista Costarricense de Psicología, 9*(18), 59–72.

Conselho Regional De Psicologia (1996). *Manual do CRP—06 1996.* Sao Paulo, Brazil: Conselho Regional de Psicologia.

Díaz-Guerrero, R. (1995). Origins and development of Mexican Etnopsychology. *World Psychology, 1,* 49–67.

Fernández-Alvarez, H. (1992). *Fundamentos de un modelo integrativo de psicoterapia.* Buenos Aires, Argentina: Paidós.

Klappenbach, H. A., & Pavesi, P. (1994). Una historia de la psicología en Latinoamérica. *Revista Latinoamericana de Psicología, 26,* 445–482.

Levav, I. (1992). *Temas de salud mental en la comunidad.* Washington, DC: Organizacíon Panamericana de la Salud.

Marin, G., Kennedy, S., & Boyce, B. C. (1987). *Latin American Psychology: a guide to research and training.* Washington, DC: American Psychological Association.

Miranda, R. (1987). La educacíon continua en la enseñanza superior. *Enseñanza e Investigacíon en Psicología, 13,* 13–23.

Mitjans Martínez, A. (1987). *La formación del psicólogo en Cuba.* La Habana, Cuba: Facultad de Psicología.

Montero, M. (1994). *Psicología social comunitaria.* Guadalajara, México: Universidad de Guadalajara.

Pérez-Gómez, A. (1990). *Hacia el siglo XXI: La psicología como ciencia y como profesión en Colombia.* Bogotá, Colombia: Universidad de Los Andes.

Rodríguez, M. A., & Jurado Cárdenas, S. (1986). Las Asociaciones Profesionales de Psicólogos en México. *Revista Mexicana de Psicología, 3,* 197–202.

Vilanova, A. R. (1993). La formación de psicólogos en Iberoamérica. *Acta Psiquiátrica y Psicológica de América Latina, 39,* 193–205.

World Bank (1993). *Informe sobre el desarrollo mundial 1993.* Washington, DC: World Bank.

2.10 Guidelines for the Development, Use, and Interpretation of Credentialing Examinations

CRAIG G. SCHOON
Professional Examination Service, New York, NY, USA

2.10.1 INTRODUCTION

This chapter presents a discussion of the purpose and function of guidelines and standards for the development, use, and evaluation of licensure and certification programs. A brief history of the regulatory process in the professions is presented, including a discussion of the theory, purpose, and function of credentialing as a regulatory procedure. Then, the need for standards and guidelines in the development, use, and evaluation of licensure and certification examinations is examined, with an emphasis on how guidelines and standards serve as aids in meeting the needs and expectations of stakeholders in the credentialing process.

2.10.1.1 History of Regulatory Processes in the Professions

2.10.1.1.1 The political theory of regulation

One underlying ideal of regulation, which might be termed "libertarian," holds that the public is entitled to maximum liberty in personal decisions regarding the purchase of products and services, including such services as healthcare and those that may affect their financial well-being. The ideal extends the same liberty to professionals wishing to provide services and products, thus maximizing freedom to practice along with freedom to choose. Accordingly, a libertarian ideal would minimize regulation of services and products by government, since, in theory, regulation could restrict the range of products and services that the public may choose from (Friedman, 1962).

A converse "totalitarian" ideal reflects a belief that the state is best suited to make decisions regarding the production of goods and the provision of services. Under such a model, control of the means of production and of the delivery of services is deemed to be in the best interests of the public. The need for this control rests on the public's presumed inability to make correct decisions, either due to lack of sufficient facts upon which to make a rational choice, or because those who produce products and provide services wish to limit the ability to make decisions that may endanger their interests.

In a democracy such as that of the USA, the public's interests are balanced between trust in the public's freedom to make its own choices and the responsibility of the state to protect the health and welfare of its citizens. It is in a democracy that the struggle between the libertarian and the totalitarian ideals takes place. To what extent is the government responsible for limiting the public's choices so that the public's health, welfare, and safety are protected? To what extent should the public be free to choose as they wish, and to experience the consequences of their choices? The issue of regulation of professional practice has been at the center of this debate (Friedman, 1962).

The conflict between consumer freedom and government regulation of professional practice is well summarized in a publication by the Association of State and Provincial Psychology Boards (ASPPB) (1990), the body responsible for the licensing of psychologists in the USA and Canada:

> The laws are intended to protect the public by limiting licensure to those persons who are qualified to practice psychology as defined by state and provincial [Canadian] law. The legal basis for licensure lies in the right of the state to enact legislation to protect its citizens. *Caveat emptor*, or "buyer beware," is felt to be an unsound maxim when the "buyer" of services cannot be sufficiently well informed to beware, and hence states have enacted regulatory boards to license qualified practitioners. A professional board is a state or provincial agency acting to protect the public, not serve the profession.

The regulation of professional practice, then, makes the assumption that the citizens of the USA are not sufficiently able to make decisions regarding the purchase of services that affect their health, safety, and welfare, either because they lack sufficient information or because the government has a responsibility to exert some influence on the selection of qualified practitioners—a benevolent form of *in loco parentis*. From this perspective, the cost of making a wrong decision is considered too great: the loss of life, health, safety, or welfare are decision outcomes against which the public must be protected.

The debate regarding the pros and cons of regulation takes several forms. On the libertarian side, it is argued that regulation severely restricts consumer choice by limiting the supply of practitioners to those who meet regulatory requirements. In a recent issue of the *Wall Street Journal*, licensure of cabdrivers was listed as one of the main causes of the decrease in quality of life for New Yorkers, due to both the limitation of the number of cabs operating and the fare increases resulting from the limited competition.

From the libertarian perspective, regulation of professional practice is viewed as government interference in the market operating to the advantage of those who are licensed, since a licensed professional can charge more for services because of this limitation of competition. The libertarian perspective may also presume the existence of explicit strategies by practitioners to exploit state regulation laws that restrict entry into professional practice, thereby increasing the economic advantage to those who meet regulatory requirements.

On the regulation side of the argument are those who believe that the protective function of regulation is ill-served by the political process. According to this perspective, professions may unduly influence legislators to enact regulatory laws that lack genuine benefit to the public. Practice-regulation laws, to be truly effective, should regulate only those professions where malpractice will harm the public's health, welfare, and safety. Those espousing this model further hold that too many professions have achieved regulated status, including professions characterized by little or no capacity to cause harm to the public. Examples of this from the literature include such statements as, "Some of the more unusual professions regulated in at least one state include: Babcock testers, bankruptcy salespersons, wire rope inspectors, lime vendors, mussel fishers, pheasant club operators, safe mechanics, apprentice scalers, resident and non-resident sea moss rakers, tree injectors, weather modifiers, livestock weighers, lightening rod installers, hemp growers, endless chain agents, and egg brokers" (Brinegar, 1990); and "What individuals in these occupations actually do and why regulation is needed may not always be comprehensible" (Schmitt, 1995, p. 8).

This chapter explores how psychologists and others in the measurement community may contribute to this debate by developing measurement and evaluation standards and guidelines applying to the development, use, and evaluation of the decision goals held by stakeholders of the regulation process. As psychologists and measurement specialists, our goal is to provide a scientific structure to frame the debate over practice regulation. Our assumption is that debate in a democracy is an essential tool by which the citizens of a country evaluate and assess those products, services, and governments which best meet their needs and expectations. Published standards and guidelines help to facilitate this evaluation process, so that the public's interests may be met.

2.10.1.1.2 A brief history of regulation

The medical profession was the first to be regulated by law in the USA, with Virginia being the first state to enact regulations restricting the practice of medicine (in 1639), followed by Massachusetts (1649) and New York (1665). The wording of the first regulation statutes points toward public protection as their purpose. Thus, in Massachusetts, the law indicated that the activities of the following individuals should be regulated: "Chirugeons, Midwives, Physitians or others [who were] imployed at any time about the bodye of men, women or children, for preservation of life, or health" (Shryock, 1967, p. 1).

After passage of these initial laws regulating the practice of medicine, regulation by law of professional practice declined until, by the mid-1850s, virtually no state was engaged in regulation of any profession, including medicine. By that time, it was assumed that those who chose to practice medicine were adequately trained by existing educational institutions, who mounted effective efforts to reinforce and promote such a belief among legislators. The same held true for the legal profession; by 1840, almost anyone who wished to practice law could do so by engaging in an apprenticeship controlled by the profession itself.

The regulation of professional practice reemerged in the latter part of the nineteenth century, spurred by state medical societies who were concerned about low standards of education and training in new medical schools. The lobbying of state medical societies for regulation was effective, with Texas being the first state to establish a state examining board in 1873. Licensure of medical practice then spread throughout all states, with New Hampshire being the last state to license the practice of physicians in 1915.

Today, licensure has spread broadly across many professions. The Council of State Governments reports that states currently regulate over 1000 professions (Brinegar, 1990). The concern has been over the inflation of regulation. As Schmitt reports:

> In the immediate past, the emphasis was on licensure, licensure, and more licensure without the appearance of much regard for whether the laws were necessary to protect the public from harm or quackery. Any profession that could get the support of a senator or representative had an excellent chance of obtaining licensure status. In fact, licensing legislation may have been based not so much on logic, but rather on who introduced the bill, who the lobbyist was, and how much financial backing was available. (Schmitt, 1995, p. 9)

2.10.1.2 Forms of Mandatory and Voluntary Practice Regulation

The three vehicles that are commonly employed to regulate professions are practice control (licensure), government and voluntary title control (certification), and registration. In 1977 the US Department of Health, Education, and Welfare defined licensure as:

> the process by which an agency of government grants permission to an individual to engage in a given occupation upon finding that the applicant has attained the minimal degree of competency necessary to ensure that the public health, safety, and welfare will be reasonably well protected.

This definition remains in effect today, and licensure laws are enforced through the police power of individual states. State laws also specify the prerequisites for obtaining licensure status. An individual proven in a court of law to be practicing medicine without a state license is subject to imprisonment.

Government title control establishes specific legal criteria governing the use of a given occupational or professional title. This practice does not restrict the practice of the profession, but rather restricts the titles a practitioner may use. For example, while a Certified Public Accountant (CPA) is a practitioner who has met standards established by the state, nonCPAs may, nonetheless, practice accounting. Consumers of accounting services may use the title to select a practitioner who has achieved established and explicit standards of education, experience, and achievement on standardized examinations. Government title certification is used, then, to provide useful consumer information to the users of title-protected professions.

Voluntary title control, usually known as certification, may be undertaken by professions or trades that wish to establish standards signifying the attainment of specified levels of education, experience, and achievement. Practitioners who voluntarily meet such standards are certified as having attained them by their profession or trade group. Thus, many physician groups certify areas of specialty practice in medicine.

In this chapter, we will refer to the activities involved in all forms of regulation, both mandatory and voluntary, as credentialing. McCready (1982, p. 74) indicates that:

> Credentialing is a generic term that subsumes licensing, certification, registration, and institutional licensure by the states, as well as standards of competence where no licensure is required and certification by private organizations where it is required for practice by reference in state law.

2.10.1.3 The Impact of the Credentialing Process

Credentialing decisions are "high-stakes" decisions. In addition to receiving substantial economic and social benefits, those who are credentialed may be charged with a legal responsibility to engage in practice that does not harm the public. The cost associated with this liability is considerable, as are the consequences of malpractice or unethical behavior. Likewise, substantial expense has already accrued to an individual who is denied a credential. The financial and time investment in preparation for the profession is forfeited, and the economic, social, and psychological consequences of failure to receive a credential may be very significant. Along with the implied benefit to the public of valid credentialing decisions, the credentialing process entails a public cost associated with restriction of the number of practitioners, with its accompanying increase in the cost of the services provided. All of these consequences indicate the high-stakes nature of credentialing decisions.

Credentialing outcomes exert an impact on a host of stakeholders, including the public, the members of the professions, professional associations, educational institutions, membership associations, legislators, members of state boards, testing organizations, standard setting organizations, and others. Given the significance of this impact, stakeholders desire a credentialing system that meets their needs and expectations, and that may be characterized as reasonable, rational, fair, and scientific.

In the USA, stakeholders of credentialing systems may seek to influence the credentialing process through available political and social channels. Thus, members of a profession will utilize the political process to promote the interests of their profession, seeking introduction of appropriate legislation as well as working through their professional associations. Likewise, other stakeholders of credentialing may also access appropriate channels for pursuing their particular interests in credentialing outcomes. For example, the public may seek, through its political representatives, to enact credentialing systems that genuinely meet their stated public-protection objectives, while public-interest organizations such as Fair Test and the Citizens Advocacy Center may be used to promote public interests and to ensure that needs and expectations are met.

2.10.1.4 The Role of Standards and Guidelines

To the extent that the stakeholders of credentialing call for outcomes that are reasonable, rational, fair, and scientific, they use standards and guidelines as an important means of evaluating credentialing programs. The *Standards for Educational and Psychological Testing*, published by the American Educational Research Association, the American Psychological Association, and the National Council on Measurement in Education (AERA, APA,

NCME) states the following regarding the purpose of the *Standards*:

> Educational and psychological testing has also been the target of extensive scrutiny, criticism, and debate both outside and within the professional testing community. The most frequent criticisms are that tests play too great a role in the lives of students and employees and that tests are biased and exclusionary. In consideration of these and other criticisms, the *Standards* is intended to provide a basis for evaluating the quality of testing practices as they affect the various parties involved. (AERA, APA, NCME, 1985, p. 1)

In general, then, to the extent that a given credentialing program has a significant impact (economic, physical well-being, status and/or class membership) on the stakeholders affected by that policy (the public, members of the profession, educational institutions, foundations, etc.), stakeholders will call for evidence that the selection policy is reasonable, rational, fair, and based on scientific principles. Moreover, the greater the impact of the credentialing decision on stakeholders, the greater the potential for challenges to the credentialing program's outcomes, and therefore the more rigorous the evidence required in support of the policy. According to Schoon and Smith (1996a):

> The evidence a credentialing organization provides to support its policy decisions is a function of the expectations of its stakeholders. Consequently, if an organization considers an independent standard setting body such as the National Commission for Certifying Agencies (NCCA) as one of its stakeholders, the credentialing organization will try to follow and meet the NCCA standards and guidelines. Also, an organization whose stakeholders include the scientific measurement community will most likely adhere to the *Standards for Educational and Psychological Testing* (AERA et al., 1985). These independent standards require that considerable evidence be provided to support the reasonableness, rationality, fairness, and scientific foundation of a credentialing program. (pp. 6–7)

2.10.2 PRIMARY STAGES IN THE DEVELOPMENT, USE, INTERPRETATION, AND EVALUATION OF CREDENTIALING PROGRAMS

There are several published standards and guidelines relevant to the development, use, interpretation, and evaluation of credentialing programs. These include the *Standards for Educational and Psychological Testing* (1985), jointly issued by AERA, APA, and NCME; the *Guidelines for Computer-Based Tests and Interpretations* (1988), issued by the APA; the *Principles for the Validation and Use of Personnel Selection Procedures* (1987), issued by the APA Division of Industrial–Organizational Psychology; the *Principles of Fairness: An Examining Guide for Credentialing Boards* (1993), issued by the Council on Licensure, Enforcement, and Regulation and the National Organization for Competency Assurance; the *ETS Standards for Quality and Fairness* (1987), issued by the Educational Testing Service; the *Development, Administration, Scoring and Reporting of Credentialing Examinations: Recommendations for Board Members* (1993), issued by the Council on Licensure, Enforcement and Regulation; the *NCCA Guidelines for Certification Approval* (1991), issued by the National Commission for Certifying Agencies; the Americans with Disabilities Act (1990); the *Uniform Guidelines on Employee Selection Procedures* (1978), issued by the Equal Employment Opportunity Commission, Civil Service Commission, US Department of Labor, and US Department of Justice; and the *Guidelines for the Development, Use, and Evaluation of Licensure and Certification Programs* (1995), published by the Professional Examination Service (PES). These standards and guidelines address the means by which reasonable, rational, fair, and scientific credentialing decisions can be made, either explicitly as standards address specifically to credentialing issues, or implicitly as generic principles applicable to all measurement situations.

The PES *Guidelines for the Development, Use, and Evaluation of Licensure and Certification Programs* (the PES *Guidelines*) (1995) surveys the documents mentioned above and incorporates into a single publication the standards, guidelines, and principles as they are applied to credentialing programs. The PES *Guidelines* assume as a guiding principle the perspective offered by Messick (1989) that validity is a unitary concept that can be termed "construct validity," a concept that encompasses the evidential and consequential bases of test interpretation and test use.

Messick was critical of the *Standards for Educational and Psychological Testing* (AERA et al., 1985) from several perspectives. He points out that the *Standards* encourage the perception that, in many situations, only one kind of validity evidence suffices for establishing the validity of the assessment tool (Messick, 1989, p. 92). This has led, for example, to an over-reliance on establishing content validity as the sole means of demonstrating the validity of credentialing examinations (Popham, 1978). Messick also criticized the *Standards* for its lack of emphasis on the unitary nature of validity, and particularly for its failure to address the value implications of test interpretation and the social consequences of test use, as aspects of construct validity. As our summary of the theory and history of credentialing has indicated, credentialing is rife with value implications and social consequences. Messick believes that these issues must be addressed if credentialing outcomes are to be adequately evaluated in relation to stakeholder needs and expectations.

The PES *Guidelines* incorporate Messick's validation perspective as the theoretical foundation for the development, use, and evaluation of credentialing examinations. The perspective taken in the PES *Guidelines* is that the meaning and purpose of a credentialing program should be explicitly stated in what may be termed a statement of credentialing mission. This explicit statement constitutes a "theory of credentialing" whose meaning and consequences may be rationally tested.

The process of evaluating credentialing programs is not only a scientific issue, but a political and social activity as well. Thus, a comprehensive evaluation cannot rest solely on, say, a correlation coefficient, or the judgment of a content expert. A correlation coefficient or an expert judgment arises from, and must be interpreted within, the social, political, and scientific context of our culture. Again, Messick (1995) states that:

> validity, reliability, comparability, and fairness are not just measurement principles, they are social values that have meaning and force outside of measurement whenever evaluative judgments and decisions are made. As a salient social value, validity assumes both a scientific and a political role that can by no means be fulfilled by a simple correlation coefficient between test scores and a purported criterion ... or by expert judgments that test content is relevant to the proposed test use. (p. 742)

Messick goes on to state that validity constitutes an evaluative summary of both evidential and consequential outcomes of score interpretation and use. The PES *Guidelines* accept this perspective and suggest specific measures that will assist organizations in addressing evidential and consequential validation issues.

2.10.2.1 Conducting a Strategic Credentialing Analysis

According to this perspective, the statement of an organization's credentialing mission is the foundation of the program's validity edifice. The PES *Guidelines* suggest, therefore, that the initial stage consists of a complete "strategic credentialing analysis," leading to the formulation of a statement of the credentialing mission; such an analysis should address the following issues: (i) the legal status of the credentialing organization, especially if the organization is classified as not-for-profit, in which case credentialing activities may be an element in the justification of exemption from taxation; (ii) the purpose of the credential and how credentialing outcomes will protect and/or inform the public or benefit the members of a profession; (iii) the theory of credentialing, which describes how the credentialing program will be conducted to effect credentialing decisions, and its hypothesized outcomes; (iv) the key stakeholders of the organization and how the stated credentialing mission will serve their needs and expectations; (v) the key values and philosophy of the organization; and (vi) what makes the organization's credentialing mission unique within the context of other credentialing activities within the same profession.

2.10.2.1.1 Define legal status of credentialing organizations

The legal status of a credentialing organization has a direct relation to the purpose of a credentialing effort. Thus, if the credential involves licensure, then the credential's purpose is stated by constitutional and state law to involve the protection of the public's health, safety, and welfare. Validation efforts in regard to licensure examinations, then, must be related to the extent to which the health, safety, and welfare of the public is served. As Messick (1995) states:

> Broadly speaking ... validity is an inductive summary of both the existing evidence for, and the potential consequences of, score interpretation and use. Hence, what is to be validated is not the test or observation device as such but the inferences derived from test scores or other indicators—inferences about score meaning or interpretation and about the implications for action that the interpretation entails. (p. 13)

It is clear, then, that the legal purpose of licensure is to protect the public health, safety, and welfare, and that validation activities must relate to that legal purpose.

2.10.2.1.2 Define purpose of the credential

Similarly, many credentialing organizations are classified legally as nonprofit corporations, and their nonprofit status implies a social purpose, as stated in the laws governing tax-exempt status. As a nonprofit entity, the organization pays no taxes on any excess revenue exceeding operating expenses. Hence, as an entity supported by public tax dollars, the nonprofit organization must adopt a mission that benefits the public, either directly or indirectly. For example, organizations organized as 501(c)(3) corporations, which are termed "charitable" in the tax code, must have an explicitly stated mission to serve the public good. Several testing organizations—including American College Testing, Educational Testing Service, the PES, and the National Board of Medical Examiners—have been granted 501(c)(3) status, and thus are required by law to have a stated public service mission. Holding 501(c)(3) status is also not uncommon among professional organizations.

Most professional certification and membership organizations are organized under a status known as a 501(c)(6) corporation. According to tax law, such organizations are called "business leagues," and their purpose is to serve the interests of the profession. Thus, although they are granted nonprofit status because the promotion of professional interests has been deemed to be in the best interest of the public, credentialing organizations are not legally bound to promote public health, safety, and welfare as an explicit purpose of their certification activities. Some of these organizations may define the purpose of certification as a means of denoting attainment of established performance standards within their profession. The implication of voluntary certification, then, does not necessarily include a benefit to the public; rather, its purpose may be to promote the interests of the profession, a mission that is in accord with the legally stated function of 501(c)(6) organizations (Hopkins, 1992). Alternately, some voluntary credentials denote competence in practice areas that do impact public health or safety; in these cases sponsoring organizations may incorporate such a claim into their statement-of-purpose examples.

As we have seen, an explicit statement of the purpose of a credential is essential to establishing the grounds for evaluating the outcomes of a credentialing program with respect to its stated intention. This explicit statement constitutes a pledge that a credentialing program's purpose is clearly stated and open to public scrutiny and evaluation. For example, it is not uncommon for critics of regulation (Dawes, 1994; Friedman, 1962; Shimberg, Esser, & Kruger 1973) to discredit the assumed purpose of licensure to protect the public. One chapter in Dawes' book, *House of cards: Psychology and psychotherapy built on myth* (1994) is entitled, "LICENSING: The Myth of Protecting the Public." Most authors who are critical of licensure deny that the true purpose of licensure is to protect the public; rather, they believe that its purpose is to promote the interests of the profession.

The function of standards and guidelines in this debate is to suggest that the credentialing body state publicly the purpose of a credential, thereby rendering the program open to evaluation and appraisal in terms of the evidence that can be accumulated in support of the stated purpose. Open declarations of the purpose of a credential contribute to an open and evidence-based debate on the more scientific question of whether or not the credentialing outcomes are in accord with their stated intention.

2.10.2.1.3 Define theory of credentialing

The PES *Guidelines* suggest that the statement of the purpose of the credential be supported by a description of the theory of credentialing that underlies the statement of purpose. By a "theory of credentialing" is meant a description of the assumptions underlying the credentialing program. For example, most credentialing programs require specified amounts or types of education, experience, supervision, performance on examinations, and character verification, and the organization usually assumes (hypothesizes) that the standards applied to each of the "credentialing variables" relates to the desired credentialing outcome. To become a licensed psychologist, for example, a candidate must attain:

> a doctoral degree in psychology from an approved program, or the equivalent as determined by the board. ... One or two years supervised experience in a setting approved by the board. ... Demonstration of relevant knowledge through passing an objective written examination ... citizenship, age, and other requirements, as well as requiring evidence of good moral character. (ASPPB, undated, pp. 2–3)

The hypotheses underlying credentialing criteria such as these are that the required performance standards for each variable relate to the knowledge, skills, abilities, and character necessary for minimum competence at the entry level, in the practice of a profession. The PES *Guidelines* suggest that the requisites for credentialing be stated as testable hypotheses, in the form of a credentialing theory, and that the desired outcomes be hypothesized so that objective evaluation of the credentialing outcomes can be conducted.

Schoon and Smith (1996a, 1996b) contend that each of the variables in a credentialing selection system (Cronbach, 1980) should be associated with a rationally established performance standard. Rather than placing sole emphasis on the setting a rational passing point for a credentialing program's written examination, (rational in that it relates to the purpose of the credential, for example, selecting minimally competent candidates), the establishment of rational and explicit standards should also be extended to requisite education, experience, character verification, and any other relevant criteria. Each of the requirements for these variables should relate specifically to the stated purpose of the credentialing program. In this regard, Friedman (1962) believes that the amount of education required for attainment of a credential is often only marginally related to a licensure program's stated purpose of protecting the public. He argues, in the case of medicine, that the educational-plus-experience model places emphasis on excellence to a far greater extent than would be required to produce physicians capable of serving the public competently. The position of the PES *Guidelines* is that such questions can be framed as empirical issues related to the purpose and theory of the credential, which should be addressed to meet the needs of an organization's stakeholders.

2.10.2.1.4 Define key stakeholders of the credentialing organization

Accordingly, the PES *Guidelines* suggest the conduct of a "stakeholder analysis" is to describe those to whom the credentialing organization has an obligation, or upon whom the credential has a significant impact. The PES *Guidelines* (1.4, p. 21) encourage a stakeholder analysis with the goal that those affected by the outcomes of a program's credentialing decisions should be systematically included in the formulation, design, and implementation of the policy underlying the establishment of the credentialing program.

2.10.2.1.5 Define key values and philosophy of the organization

Messick (1989), as we have seen, believes that, included in the construct validity paradigm, are the value implications and social consequences of test interpretation and test use. In keeping with this concept, the PES *Guidelines* recommend that a credentialing organization "Describe the key values and philosophy of the organization as they relate to the credentialing mission" (1.5, p. 21). Given that credentialing outcomes can have a significant, high-stakes impact on the lives of their stakeholders, relevant values might include accuracy, reasonableness, rationality, fairness, due process, timeliness, honesty, openness, responsiveness, and sensitivity to stakeholder feedback. By publicly subscribing to values that are relevant to the needs and expectations of its stakeholders, a credentialing organization facilitates external evaluation of the extent to which these values have been incorporated into credentialing policy.

Messick (1989) argues that measurement of any kind, and the associated outcomes of that measurement, take place within a given value perspective. Outcomes will be interpreted within that value perspective, and may well serve one value perspective rather than another. Thus, making the organization's particular value perspective explicit is an important element in determining the overall "meaning" of the credentialing program and its intended outcomes, and including effort to include perspectives of all stakeholders will provide the value context within which the outcomes of a credentialing program may be evaluated.

2.10.2.1.6 Define what makes the credential unique within the context of other credentialing activities within the same professions

The PES *Guidelines* recommend, as part of the strategic credentialing analysis, that an organization describes what makes the credential unique within the context of other related credentials. For example, in many professions, there may be competing or closely related credentials. For the sake of making clear to stakeholders the credential's precise purpose, the organization must clearly distinguish it from others. This can be done in terms of the theory of credentialing, by specifying differences in such requirements as education, experience, previous credentials, or types of examinations passed, by delineating any difference in the stated purpose of the credentials. Again, the purpose of credentialing should be to enlighten, not to confuse, those holding a stake in the credential, while achieving the intended result of the credentialing decisions made.

2.10.2.2 Conducting an Occupational Practice Analysis

After the credentialing mission has been established, conducting an occupational practice analysis is the initial step in generating empirical evidence relating to the theory of credentialing stated in the strategic credentialing analysis. As such, the occupational practice analysis enumerates, through traditional scientific means, the *constructs* underlying credential performance, that is, needed levels of education and experience; previous credentials; knowledge, ability, and skill levels; and character traits essential to successfully meeting standards desired to obtain the credential.

With regard to validation of credentialing examinations, it has been stated that, "the problem is not one of evaluating tests, it is one of developing and validating hypotheses" (Guion, 1976, p. 791). This hypothesis-testing approach to credentialing program—embodied initially in the conduct of an occupational practice analysis—holds that:

> The answer with respect to applied hypotheses is the same as for substantive or scientific hypotheses, namely, from the implications of construct theories. In applied instances, of course, these would typically be construct theories of performance domains as well as construct theories of the critical aspects of performance that it would be important to diagnose, certify, or predict in connection with applied decision making. Thus, domain constructs and criterion constructs—that is, the knowledge, skills, cognitive processes, personal attributes, or whatever that are entailed in successful domain performance—provide a rational basis for selecting attributes that are representative of the domain or likely to be predictive of criterion success. Construct theories of each identified attribute then serve to guide test construction and test evaluation. Furthermore, the construct theory of the performance domain also affords a rational basis for appraising the meaning and adequacy of the criterion measures themselves. (Messick, 1989, p. 64)

A critical outcome of this scientific approach is the generation of a "construct-referenced" test, rather than a traditional "criterion-referenced" examination. Here, the goal is to utilize the constructs enumerated in the occupational practice analysis as the basis of examinations which, once administered, generate construct-valid scores. It is this type of result that will: "maximize the meaningfulness of score interpretation and minimize construct-irrelevant test variance. The resulting construct-valid scores then provide empirical components for a rationally defensible prediction system and rational components for empirically informed decision making" (Messick, 1989, p. 65).

As pointed out by Schoon and Smith (1996b), the occupational performance analysis is the foundation of the entire credentialing program, and should be used to establish performance standards for all the variables in the theory of credentialing that relate to the credentialing selection system:

> Individuals who establish performance standards should have a thorough understanding of the conceptual foundations of the credential, and should have as much evidence as possible regarding the behaviors they will be designating as defining credentialed status. One important source of data is the occupational practice analysis, job analysis, or role delineation. Those establishing performance standards should have a thorough understanding of the practice analysis, since its goal is to define performances critical to the definition of credentialed behavior and to delineate the knowledge, abilities, and skills that underlie these performances. The statements in the analysis relate directly to the task of establishing performance standards that are reasonable, rational, fair, and relevant to the behavior to be credentialed. The practice analysis should also address the amount of education and experience necessary to acquire the knowledge and skill required for successful performance at the specified performance level of the credential; the practice analysis is, therefore, relevant to the establishment of performance standards for all the variables in the credentialing selection system. (p. 154)

Although there is no single standard method for conducting an occupational practice analysis, commonly used approaches include evaluations by committees of experts in the profession, reviews of work logs, observations of practice, interviews with practitioners, and surveys of practice (Schoon, 1985). Often, more than one of these approaches is used to generate information, so that the constructs generated from one source can be checked against the constructs generated from another (Knapp & Knapp, 1995). The methodologies used to generate data for the occupational practice analysis should be described in detail to facilitate replication of the procedures used at a later date, or by an independent investigator or agency.

Inclusion of all affected stakeholders in the definition of the constructs to be assessed in a credentialing program will contribute to the validity of the credentialing decisions made, and ensure support and acceptance of the credential.

Generating a representative sample of credential stakeholders is described in the PES *Guidelines*, as follows:

> Describe the rationale for selecting the participants in the data collection process, including committee members, practitioners, educators, or others who are identified as legitimate sources for the data that will comprise the occupational practice analysis. Care should be taken to represent all the major areas of practice within the occupation and to achieve a distribution among all geographical areas and practice settings where practice may differ in scope or emphasis (e.g., urban vs. rural, differing educational levels).

> Describe the source of recommendations for participants in the process, and how and by whom final selections of participants were made, including who was not selected and for what reasons. All sampling procedures used to select participants must be described, along with the goal of the sampling process. (2.3, p. 26)

> The purpose of the validation process is to: (a) generate data on the criticality, importance, and frequency of all elements in the practice analysis; (b) indicate if any performance domains, tasks, or Knowledge-ability-skills (KSAs) were overlooked or incorrectly included; and (c) determine if the analysis accurately portrays those behaviors that are critical to the purpose of the credential, and thereby to protecting and/or informing the public and/or promoting the profession. It is necessary to thoroughly describe the procedures used to collect and analyze the validation data, including sampling techniques, rating scales, open-ended responses, or other means of evaluating the practice analysis data. (2.4, p. 26)

Generation of appropriate validation data is essential in building the measurement and hypothesis-testing structure of a sound credentialing program. The analysis of this data will explicate the logical connections that link the constructs derived from the practice analysis with each assessment tool, and the assessment tools with the theory of how credentialing decisions are made to accomplish the mission of the organization.

Specifically, the validation data must be analyzed: (i) to determine what constructs can and should be assessed to accomplish the objectives of the credentialing program; (ii) to identify the assessment tools required to produce construct-relevant scores that can be used to make valid and rational credentialing decisions; (iii) to generate the test specifications for each assessment instrument; and (iv) to generate the instructions to be used by experts in developing the response formats (e.g., multiple-choice examination or clinical simulations) that will best link the construct-related assessment tools to the constructs enumerated in the occupational practice analysis.

2.10.2.3 Developing Assessment Tools

2.10.2.3.1 Develop assessment tools that achieve the credentialing mission of the organization

In a "selection system" (Cronbach, 1980), all variables used to make selection decisions are included as "tests" or "assessment tools." Most of the focus of standards and guidelines has been on explicitly designated assessments such as written examinations, practical examinations, and clinical simulations; these assessment tools are expected to meet the highest technical and psychometric standards when used in high-stakes testing activities such as credentialing. If we consider credentialing, however, to be a selection system, then each selection variable in that system should receive scrutiny in relation to relevant guidelines or standards. Thus, we have made the case that a credentialing organization should, as a first step in the credentialing process, list all the variables in the credentialing selection system, such as education, experience, supervisors ratings, or character references. These variables comprise, in their relationships and structure, a theory of credentialing. Hence, in discussing the standards and guidelines relevant to the development of assessment tools for a credentialing program, our focus will be on the entire array of variables used to make a credentialing decision. This perspective is in accord with the concept of a coherent credentialing selection system, each element of which should be based on a firm scientific and policy foundation.

The general goal statement for developing credentialing assessment tools, then, can be stated as follows:

> Develop an assessment program that achieves the credentialing mission by utilizing data from the strategic credentialing analysis and the occupational practice analysis. Assessment tools should include all formats for decision-making, including such factors as amount of education required for the credential, amount of experience required, supervision documentation, recommendations, or graduation from accredited schools or training programs. The assessment selection system should follow from the theory of credentialing and provide evidence that can be used in the validation of that theory. (PES *Guidelines*, p. 29)

2.10.2.3.2 Describe the credentialing theory in terms of the assessment tools that will be used to implement the theory

Development of the assessment tools for a credentialing selection system should follow logically from the list of selection variables that constitute the theory of credentialing; this listing will have acquired an empirical foundation via the occupational practice analysis. For example, if the practice analysis indicates that the knowledge, skills, and abilities required to practice at the entry level of a profession require a high school education, then using attainment of a college degree as a selection criterion would be considered overly restrictive, that is, such a tool would yield a selection ratio that exceeds the estimated base rate of entry-level competence required for safe practice.

The theory of credentialing and the occupational practice analysis will also address the predicted outcomes of application of the credentialing selection system, and each selection tool should be rationalized in terms of its place in the credentialing selection system. Only selection variables relevant to desired selection outcomes should be included in the credentialing selection system. In terms of the PES *Guidelines*:

> Describe the theory for the assessments that will constitute the tools to be used to make credentialing decisions. This theory should describe the rationale for the amount of education required for the credential, the amount of experience, supervision, or other achievements, and the reasons for using particular assessment formats, such as multiple-choice examinations, clinical simulations, computer-based examinations, practical examinations, oral interviews, or in-basket exercises. The description should include the rationale that links performance on each assessment tool to the theory of credentialing and to the occupational practice analysis. (3.1.1, p. 29)

2.10.2.3.3 ***Build assessment tools from validated test specifications***

The assessment tools that are hypothesized to achieve the credentialing mission are constructed according to the "test specifications" that are the end product of the occupational practice analysis. The test specifications establish a logical connection between the response formats of the assessment tools and the constructs derived from the occupational practice analysis. For example, in the case of a written examination, each item must be judged for its relevance to producing the desired credentialing outcome. In addition, affirmative response must be generated to questions regarding the linkage between the item and the construct it is to measure. For example, after identifying an item in a psychology licensing examination as associated with the construct Competence in Diagnosing Mental Pathology, we could then ask, "Does this item provide information relevant to the construct in question?"

Generally, the initial construction of assessment tools proceeds from test specifications to format generation based on judgments of the logical connection between response formats and the constructs to be measured. The nature of these judgments will relate to the type of outcome decisions that are to be made with the assessment tool. According to Messick (1989):

> As a starting point, when an existing test is to be evaluated for its applicability to a particular job, judgments by job incumbents, supervisors, or other experts could be obtained for the extent to which the test specifications match the importance dimension for the job. Better yet, at a more detailed level, each test item could be judged for the extent to which the knowledge and skills tapped are pertinent to the marker tasks that define the job-importance dimensions [Rosenfeld, Thornton & Skurnick, 1986]. At a more global or molar level with respect to the job, each test item could be judged as to whether or not it taps knowledge or skill that is essential to overall job performance; more globally with respect to an ability or skill test, each of the specific job tasks could be judged as to whether the tested skill is essential for that task performance [Lawshe, 1975]. (p. 69)

2.10.2.3.4 ***Build assessment tools that meet the needs and expectations of one's stakeholders***

Judgments about the applicability of assessment tools to the purpose of the credential should be made by the stakeholders identified in the stakeholder analysis conducted as part of the strategic credentialing analysis, and all stakeholders significantly affected by the credentialing outcomes should be represented. For example, an organization's theory of credentialing may state that credentialing outcomes will be valid indicators of entry-level competence, and that this outcome is not intended to be biased against any minority group. Such a statement would be supported by evidence that minority representatives judged the test formats relevant to hypothesized construct domains and established that the formats were not biased against minority candidates. The actual outcome of the assessment tool regarding bias would have to be subjected to empirical test.

In general, if the stakeholders of the credential demand that the credentialing program be based on procedures that are rational, reasonable, fair, accurate, and scientific, then all response formats should be judged by stakeholders for such criteria as: (i) adherence to standards for item construction and review; (ii) adherence to guidelines for sensitivity review that seek to eliminate language that is sexist, racist, or discriminatory in any way toward any group of candidates; (iii) adherence to guidelines for clarity, accuracy, and consistency; (iv) assurance that test manuals give instructions that are clear, simple, accurate, and complete; and (v) assurance that candidates are not in any way adversely affected by the typography, layout, format, or response method of the examination (3.3.2, p. 33).

2.10.2.3.5 ***Set performance standards for the assessment tools***

Setting performance standards for assessment tools is the critical means of linking the assessment tool to the theory of credentialing outcomes. The assessment tool in and of itself is simply a means of gathering response information regarding construct domain performance. That information is then accessed in reference to a performance standard which is theorized to produce selection outcomes that are in accord with the organization's theory of credentialing (Schoon & Smith, 1996b).

The method used to establish performance standards for the assessment tools included in the credentialing selection system should be described in detail, including the size and composition of the group of experts used to establish the standards, the hypotheses linking expert judgments with desired credentialing outcomes, the method used to obtain expert judgments that will be in accord with the desired outcomes, and the psychometric theory, if any, underlying the standard setting method applied to the assessment tool.

The stakeholder analysis conducted previously again becomes useful in choosing a representative group of stakeholders to comprise standard setting groups. Omission of an important stakeholder group may place the credibility of the credentialing program at risk. If a group of stakeholders that are significantly affected by the outcomes of the credentialing decision are not included in setting the performance standards, this group can claim, with justification, that their needs and expectations were not met by the credential. If the ultimate stakeholder of licensing examinations, the public, are not included in setting performance standards, such a claim could result in the elimination of the credentialing program. Although a public representative may not be qualified to make expert judgments about an issue such as construct relevance, or the probability that a minimally competent candidate would pass a given item, the representative would be capable of assessing whether the process employed to make such judgments is in keeping with the interests of a consumer of the credentialing outcomes.

It is the position of the PES *Guidelines* that establishing performance standards is as much an issue of credentialing policy as it is a purely psychometric exercise. Because credentialing outcomes take place within the value structure of our culture, they have significant social effects. Accordingly, the expert judges that establish performance standards should be versed in the organization's theory of credentialing, the credentialing mission, and the results of the occupational practice analysis. As stated in the PES *Guidelines*:

> Once the committee members have adequate familiarity with the mission, theory, and occupational practice analysis, they should be presented with a description of the standard setting methodology. The exact manner of presenting the methodology must be described so that it can be presented to an organization's stakeholders, replicated, and evaluated. The mission and goals of the credentialing program must be clearly described in relation to each of the selection variables for which a standard will be established. Questions for discussion should be recorded, along with a summary of the discussion held. These questions, and the summary of the discussion, should be public documents that could be made available to the public and to all relevant stakeholders of the credential. (3.1.3, p. 31)

The above guidelines apply to each variable in the credentialing selection system. For example, in terms of the amount of education required to attain a credential, the type and amount of education needed, and for what purpose; this should be presented in the theory of credentialing. The "performance standard" established for requisite education should be set by the credentialing organization's stakeholders, and these stakeholders should be versed in the theory of credentialing as it applies to education, with the goal that the amount of education required for a credential is neither more nor less than that required for the intended credentialing outcomes.

Critics of credentialing (Friedman, 1962; Pew Report, 1995) have indicated that the amount of education required to be eligible for licensing in many professions is not adequately related to actual entry-level practice requirements, and is therefore not a valid "assessment tool" in the credentialing selection system. Their charge is that, if the outcomes of educational selection were validated against entry-level requirements, then "excellence" would seem to have been the performance standard rather than "minimal competence." To apply scrutiny only to written examinations, then, ignores the validation of all the other assessment tools in the credentialing assessment system.

2.10.2.4 Conducting Validation Analyses

2.10.2.4.1 ***Conduct validation analyses that address the evidential and consequential basis of test interpretation and test use***

The validation of a credentialing program consists of evaluation of the adequacy and appropriateness of the inferences and actions that follow from the program's credentialing decisions. According to Messick (1989):

> Validity is an integrated evaluative judgment of the degree to which empirical evidence and theoretical rationales support the adequacy and appropriateness of inferences and action based on test scores or other modes of assessmentelan inductive summary of both the existing evidence for and the potential consequences of score interpretation and use. Hence, what is to be validated is not the test or observation device as such but the inferences derived from test scores or other indicators—inferences about score meaning or interpretation and about the implications for action that the interpretation entails. (p. 13)

(i) Conduct validation analyses that address the evidential basis of test use

The starting point for construct validation of a credentialing selection system is the collection of inductive evaluations of the hypotheses stated in the theory of credentialing. The processes of conducting an occupational analysis, developing test specifications, and developing assessment tools from these specifications have typically been evaluated for adequacy only in terms of their content validity. This approach tends to focus on the assessment tool, in and of itself, as valid, without consideration of the decision outcomes produced by the use of the tool in a credentialing program. This has been particularly true of credentialing, where the role of content validity has been justified as the only validity that, in essence, can be achieved (Popham, 1978).

Messick (1989) criticizes this contention, which underlies some portions of the *Standards for Educational and Psychological Testing* (AERA et al., 1985), stating that:

> The major problem here is that so-called content validity is focused upon test *forms* rather than test *scores*, upon *instruments* rather than measurements [italics added] ... because validity, reliability, comparability, and fairness are not just measurement principles, they are social values that have meaning and force outside of measurement, whenever evaluative judgments and decisions are made. As a salient social value, validity assumes both a scientific and a political role that can by no means be fulfilled by a simple correlation coefficient between test scores and a purported criterion ... or by expert judgments that test content is relevant to the proposed test use. (pp. 41–42)

The problem with many content-validation approaches is that they fail to focus on the nature of the functional relationship being validated. Validation, and most scientific activity, can be seen as the evaluation of observations concerning variables that are hypothesized to be related in some functional way. In the case of content validity, the functionally related variables are the content of the assessment tools and the domain of reference, or construct domains specified in the occupational analysis. Content validation of credentialing examinations, then, focuses on ensuring that an empirically verifiable relationship exists between the content of assessment tools and the constructs of the occupational analysis, as indicated earlier in this chapter. These studies, however, should constitute not the end, but rather the commencement of the validation of a credentialing program.

The PES *Guidelines* suggest that the matrix of correlations amongst the variables comprising the theory of credentialing will provide evaluative information regarding the adequacy and appropriateness of a theory of credentialing. Examples of hypotheses are:

(i) There will be a significant correlation between grades obtained in school and performance on the written credentialing examination.

(ii) There will be a significant positive correlation between grades obtained in the school-based clinical training and performance on a clinical simulation examination required for credentialing.

(iii) There will be a significant correlation between the amount of education received and performance on examinations for credentialing.

(iv) Experience, as measured by supervisor ratings, will correlate positively with both school performance and performance on credentialing examinations.

Correlational findings in regard to these hypotheses will provide evidence regarding the theory of credentialing from which they emerged. For example, if no positive relationship exists between school performance and performance on the credentialing examination, what is the implication for the hypothesis that education provides the necessary skills and abilities necessary to practice the profession? Are the essential KSAs not being taught? Are schools too selective, so that there is restriction of range to the extent that a positive correlation could not occur (indicating that the performance standard established for entry into and graduation from school may not be adequately related to required performance at the entry level).

Evidence in relation to the hypotheses embodied in the theory of credentialing can be obtained readily and inexpensively, and such evidence can have significant implications for both the theory and the policy that stems therefrom. Gathering evidence regarding these assumptions and hypotheses will contribute significantly toward the interpretive meaning of the credentialing assessment tools and, therefore, of the credential and its supporting theory.

The PES *Guidelines* (4.1.7, p. 40) also recommend that concurrent validation studies be undertaken to investigate the relationship between performance on credentialing assessment tools and on outcome measures such as practical examinations, oral examinations, supervisors' ratings, or other outcome measures. Such studies, even though they may not meet the scientific requirements for criterion-related validation, can contribute to the interpretive meaning of the variables comprising the theory of credentialing. For example, state credentialing boards in several professions have constructed practical examinations, which may be administered in addition to a mandated written examination, to achieve enhanced measurement of critical skills and abilities. In some states, for example, veterinary medicine boards have constructed practical examinations involving hands-on skills and abilities in diagnosing and treating animals. These boards have established criteria for minimally acceptable performance for entry-level practice of veterinary medicine.

In cases such as this, where multiple assessment instruments are in use, correlational studies on different types of examinations can be undertaken to good effect. Taking the veterinary medicine example, one could hypothesize that there would be positive significant correlations amongst the written, clinical simulation and practical examinations, but that the correlation between the clinical simulation and the practical examination results should be higher than that between the written examination and the practical examination. The findings of correlational studies such as this have considerable implications for the development, use, and interpretation of the national and state credentialing examinations, and on the credentialing theory for the veterinary profession (Jones & Schoon, 1993; Jones, Schoon, & Lovler, 1994).

In the area of professional licensure, the conduct of genuine outcome studies is impeded by the fact that failing candidates do not enter the profession. Nonetheless, concurrent validation studies of licensure programs can and should be conducted for the evaluative evidence they provide in reference to the adequacy and appropriateness of the theory of credentialing. In the area of voluntary certification, however, the lack of a control group does not, in theory, preclude effective criterion-predictive studies. In this case, were the theory of credentialing to hypothesize that certified practitioners will perform more effectively than their noncertified counterparts, or that certified individuals will produce enhanced outcomes relating to client health, safety, and welfare, these studies can be conducted with full methodological justification. Such hypothesized claims can be scientifically examined, since both certified and noncertified individuals can practice the profession, and their practice outcomes on the same patient populations could be measured for predicted differences. Indeed, such studies should be conducted by certification organizations if their theory of credentialing states that certification benefits the public health, safety, and welfare.

(ii) Conduct validation analyses that address the evidential basis of test interpretation

Because of the high-stakes outcomes of credentialing examinations, and because validation entails the evaluation of the inferences and actions resulting from credentialing decisions, the PES *Guidelines* suggest that an organization:

> Conduct studies that gather evidence regarding the appropriate interpretation of the outcomes of assessment tool use in the credentialing selection system. The evidence gathered should support the stated purpose of the credentialing program, as described in the strategic credentialing analysis and credentialing mission statement. Studies should be conducted for each of the assessment tools in the assessment selection system, with the intention of providing evidence that each contributes to making credentialing decisions consistent with the credentialing mission. (4.2, p. 41)

As we have seen, such studies may be difficult to conduct in the case of licensing examinations. However, these studies may be possible in the case of certification programs. For example, assume that the purpose of a given certification program is to promote the profession by recognizing voluntarily acquired expertise. This program might adopt hypotheses concerning expected correlates to attaining certification, including higher pay, more responsible positions within the same practice setting, higher supervisors' ratings (as measured with blind ratings regarding certified status), and enhanced client satisfaction with practice outcomes. All these hypotheses can and should be examined to provide support or counter-support to the stated purpose of the credential and, therefore, to this organization's theory of credentialing. Studies such as this are recommended in PES *Guidelines* which state:

> Evaluate performance standards in reference to the degree that empirical evidence and theoretical rationales support the adequacy and appropriateness of inferences and actions made as a result of implementation of the standards. The inferences and actions made are credentialing decisions; these decisions should be evaluated in the context of the adopted theory of credentialing, and the predictions and inferences that flow from that theory. (4.2.5, p. 43)

(iii) Conduct validation analyses that address the consequential basis of test use

Messick (1989) makes a very strong case that the value and social consequences of score-based actions must be evaluated as part of the validity evidence provided in support of a measurement theory. The outcomes of a selection system such as credentialing are highly value-laden, and are characterized by substantial social impact. To ignore the value implications of credentialing decisions, and the social outcomes of these decisions, risks the alienation of one's stakeholders and, therefore, support for the program. The measurement issue here is that, to the extent that a credentialing program's stakeholders require evidence that the process is rational, reasonable, fair, and scientific, the sponsoring organization is obligated to demonstrate that the credentialing decisions made are reasonable, rational, fair, and scientific, and it is neither unduly reflective of a given set of values nor biased against minority groups.

Many critics of licensure (Dawes, 1994; Friedman, 1962; Shimburg, 1991) charge that the values of members of the profession are paramount in arriving at licensure decisions, and that licensure programs are used to protect the economic and social interests of professional groups, rather than the interests of the public. The essential charge, then, is that the licensure program addresses the values of one stakeholder group (the members of a profession) to the detriment of other stakeholder groups (the public). The PES *Guidelines* summarize these recommendations:

> Analyze and interpret the value implications of licensing and certification programs. (4.3, p. 44),

and:

> The intended and unintended social consequences of making credentialing decisions should be addressed. The investigation of the consequences and side effects of credentialing decisions is a critical aspect of the validation of the use of tests to make those decisions. Of particular importance is the investigation of any adverse impact that results from the application of an organization's credentialing decision rules; any adverse impact must be examined to see whether it is the result of test invalidity, or of the valid application of the decision rules that constitute the organization's policies. (4.4, p. 45)

2.10.2.5 Minimize Construct-irrelevant Variance and Construct-underrepresentation

The PES *Guidelines* contain a number of specific guidelines aimed at ongoing procedures to eliminate or minimize the two sources of threats to construct validity, construct-irrelevant variance and construct-underrepresentation. On the one hand, construct-irrelevant variance occurs when "the test contains excess reliable variance that is irrelevant to the interpreted construct" (Messick, 1989, p. 34). Construct-underrepresentation, on the other hand, occurs when a test fails to measure enough of the primary construct being measured.

The two major sources of construct-irrelevant variance occur under conditions where tests are either too easy or too difficult in relation to the actual abilities of the candidate population. For example, tests may be too easy for "test-wise" candidates, who can spot the correct answer as a result of improper item construction. Or, a test may be too hard for reasons irrelevant to the construct being measured, perhaps because it requires verbal skills in excess of those required for minimally competent performance, or problem solving skills that exceed those required for performance that would be adequate to protect the public. In either case, to ensure that credentialing decisions are reasonable, rational, accurate, fair, and scientific, we must take steps on an ongoing basis to eliminate or minimize these two sources of error.

In general, procedures must be followed that will ensure that test items have been thoroughly edited to eliminate faulty item construction, inappropriate reading levels, biased language, or language that discriminates against minority groups. In addition, examinations must be printed in print large enough so that candidate visual acuity is not a factor in test scores. Test instructions must be clear and simple, so that verbal intelligence or problem solving skills greater than those required for entry-level competence are not influencing test scores. Tests must be administered under standardized conditions so that certain candidates are neither advantaged or disadvantaged as a result of administration conditions.

Maintaining the security of examination materials is essential to eliminating construct-irrelevant variance: a candidate who obtains a high score because they have access to examination content is obtaining a score that is not relevant to their abilities or skills. Examination instructions and eligibility information should be thorough, accessible, and written at the same reading level required for the examination, in order to prevent score misinterpretation as a result of irrelevant factors.

In conclusion, the score reports generated must not create confusion among users of the scores or the candidates who receive them. Confusion in score interpretation can lead to the establishment of performance standards that are not related to the genuine requirements for minimal competency or to the performance standard established by the credentialing organization. Thus, a construct is interpreted correctly only to the extent that the scores for that construct lead to desired outcomes. Mistakes in scoring or in score interpretation can and do cause errors that affect false-positive and false-negative credentialing decisions, and hence lead to score-based actions that are not in accord with an organization's theory of credentialing.

2.10.2.6 Conduct an Ongoing Program of Research, Evaluation, and Policy Appraisal

Credentialing programs take place through the policies of the organization. In this chapter, we have recommended that credentialing policy be based on a theory of credentialing that results in a statement of credentialing purpose, or credentialing mission. The initial policies of a credentialing organization, or the policies that exist at any point in time for that organization, will reflect the theory of credentialing either implicitly or explicitly. The final section of the PES *Guidelines* recommends that credentialing organizations conduct an ongoing program of research, evaluation, and policy appraisal; that they obtain feedback obtained through such studies for use in reevaluating the credentialing theory and how that theory is realized in credentialing policy; and that they establish ongoing dialogue with stakeholders to share the results of these studies and to obtain their appraisals of the organization's efforts to meet their needs and expectations.

A program of constant evaluation and policy appraisal demonstrates the credentialing organization's commitment to providing a credentialing program that is rational, reasonable, fair, accurate, and scientific. The PES *Guidelines* suggest that this program address such issues as: (i) currentness of the occupational practice analysis; (ii) appropriateness of assessment tools; (iii) implications of already-conducted validity studies, as well as plans for additional studies to test credentialing hypotheses; (iv) maintenance of the constant search for sources of construct-irrelevant variance or construct-underrepresentation; and (v) evaluation and reevaluation of the organization's credentialing policy in light of the finding of this research program.

2.10.3 CONCLUSION

Credentialing, a form of measurement characterized by high-stakes consequences, is situated in the political context of the USA. As such, it embodies the values of our culture and has significant social impact on majority and minority groups. Credentialing has many stakeholders, and each stakeholder group's values and interests exert influence upon the process. The role of standards and guidelines is to frame the dialogue among these groups, such that evidence in support of each perspective is presented clearly and effectively.

Standards and guidelines for credentialing cannot attempt to resolve all issues; rather, they provide the tools whereby evidence can be collected and evaluated, and decisions made, in a rational, reasonable, fair, and scientific manner. Measurement professionals need to bear in mind this role as facilitator of objective, unbiased discussion, evaluation, and appraisal. As Messick (1989) concludes:

> When confronted with media controversy, judicial review, or legal dispute, test specialists are often thrown off balance and frequently filter evidence through their own social values without weighting alternative value perspectives. The impact of social values on the interpretation of evidence is difficult to avoid in any event. However, the effect is less variable or idiosyncratic if the evidence is interpreted in the context not only of personal values and the values of others, but of technical standards to guide professional judgment as well. Because validity is the one essential justification for test interpretation and use, professional judgments about testing should be guided by validity principles in particular and by the broader testing Standards [AERA et al., 1985] in general. However, to be credible, these validity principles and testing standards must be applied sensibly in practice and communicated sensibly to nonprofessional participants in the public debate [Kleinman & Farley, 1985]. This strategy is predicated on the assumption that "scientific argument and political argument differ in degree rather than kind, science having a longer time horizon, more homogeneous participants, and more appeal to formal reasoning [Cronbach, 1988, pp. 6–7]." (p. 91)

2.10.4 REFERENCES

American Association of State Psychology Boards. *Entry requirements for Professional Practice in Psychology: A guide for student and faculty (undated, obtained in 1990).* Association of State and Provincial Psychology Boards, Montgomery, AL.

American Education Research Association, American Psychological Association, and National Council on Measurement in Education (1985). *Standards for educational and psychological testing.* Washington, DC: American Psychological Association.

American Psychological Association (1988). *Guidelines for computer-based tests and interpretations.* Washington, DC: Author.

American Psychological Association, Division of Industrial–Organizational Psychology (1987). *Principles for the validation and use of personnel selection procedures* (3rd ed.). College Park, MD: Author.

Americans with Disabilities Act (1990). 42 USCA 12101 *et seq.* (Also: 56 Fed. Reg. 35734, 56 Fed. Reg. 35694, 56 Fed. Reg. 35592, 56 Fed. Reg. 36731).

Brinegar, P. (Ed.) (1990). *Occupational and professional regulations in the states: A comprehensive compilation.* Lexington, KY: The National Clearinghouse on Licensure, Enforcement, and Regulation.

Council on Licensure, Enforcement and Regulations (1993). *Development, administration, scoring and reporting of credentialing examinations: Recommendations for board members.* Lexington, KY: Author.

Council on Licensure, Enforcement, and Regulation and the National Organization for Competency Assurance. (1993). *Principles of fairness: An examining guide for credentialing boards.* Lexington, KY: Author.

Cronbach, L. J. (1980). Validity on parole: How can we go straight? New directions for testing and measurement: Measuring achievement over a decade. *Proceedings of the 1979 ETS Invitational Conference*, 99–108. San Francisco: Jossey-Bass.

Cronbach, L. J. (1988). Five perspectives on validation argument. In H. H. Wainer and H. Braun (Eds.), *Test validity* (pp. 3–17). Hillsdale, NJ: Erlbaum.

Dawes, R. (1994). *House of cards: Psychology and psychotherapy built on myth.* New York: Free Press.

Educational Testing Service (1987). *ETS standards for quality and fairness.* Princeton, NJ: Author.

Equal Employment Opportunity Commission, Civil Service Commission, US Department of Labor and US Department of Justice (1978, August 25). *Uniform guidelines on employee selection procedures.* Fed. Reg., 43, (166), 38290–38315.

Friedman, M. (1962). *Capitalism and freedom.* Chicago: University of Chicago Press.

Guion, R. M. (1976). Recruiting, selection, and job placement. In M. D. Dunnene (Ed.), *Handbook of industrial and organization psychology* (pp. 777–828). Chicago: Rand McNally.

Hopkins, B. R. (1992). *The law of tax-exempt organizations* (6th ed.). New York: Wiley.

Jones, J. P., & Schoon, C. G. (1993, April). *An examination of the predictive value of two objective measures in veterinary medicine.* Paper presented at the annual meeting of the American Educational Research Association, Atlanta, GA.

Jones, J. P., Schoon, C. G., & Lovler, R. L. (1994, April). *An examination of the underlying constructs measured by three credentialing examinations in veterinary medicine.* Paper presented at the annual meeting of the American Educational Research Association, New Orleans, LA.

Kleiman, L. S., & Farley, R. H. (1985). The implications of professional and legal guidelines for court decisions involving criterion-related validity: A review and analysis. *Personnel Psychology, 38,* 803–833.

Knapp, I. E., & Knapp, L. G. (1995). Practice Analysis: Building the foundation for validity. In J. C. Imapara (Ed.), *Licensure testing: Purposes, procedures, and practices* (pp. 93–116). Lincoln, NE: University of Nebraska, Buros Institute of Mental Measurements.

Lawshe, C. H. (1975). A quantitative approach to content validity. *Personnel Psychology, 28,* 563–575.

McCready, L. A. (1982, Fall). Emerging healthcare occupations: The system under siege. *Health Care Management Reviews,* 71–76.

Messick, S. (1989). Validity. In R. L. Linn (Ed.), *Educational measurement* (3rd ed., pp. 13–103). New York: American Council on Education & Macmillan.

Messick, S. (1995). Validity of psychological assessment: Validation of inferences from persons' responses and performances as scientific inquiry into score meaning. *American Psychologist, 50,* 741–749.

National Commission for Certifying Agencies (1991). *NCCA Guidelines for certification approval.* Washington, DC: Author.

Pew Report. Report of the Taskforce on Healthcare Workforce Regulation (1995). *Reforming health care workforce regulations: Policy considerations for the 21st century.* San Francisco: Pew Health Professions Commission.

Popham, W. J. (1978). *Criterion-referenced measurement.* Englewood Cliffs, NJ: Prentice-Hall.

Professional Examination Service (1995). *Guidelines for the development, use, and evaluation of licensure and certification programs.* New York: Author.

Rosenfeld, M., Thornton, R. F., & Skurnick, L. (1986). *Analysis of the professional functions of teachers: Relationships between job functions and the NTE Core Battery.* Princeton, NJ: Educational Testing Service.

Schmidt, K. L. (1995). What is Licensure? In J. C. Imapara (Ed.), *Licensure testing: Purposes, procedures, and practices* (pp. 1–34). Lincoln, NE: University of Nebraska, Buros Institute of Mental Measurements.

Schoon, C. G. (1985). Methods for defining and assessing professional competence [Special Issue: The Measure of Competence]. *Professional Practice of Psychology, 6*(1), 144–155.

Schoon, C. G., & Smith, I. L. (1996a). In A. H. Browning, A. C. Bugbee, & M. A. Mullins (Eds.), *Certification: A NOCA handbook* (pp. 149–190). Washington, DC: National Organization for Competency Assurance.

Schoon, C. G., & Smith, I. L. (1996b). Guidelines for credentialing programs. *Professional Education Research Quarterly, 17* (4), 6–9.

Shimberg, B. (1991). *Regulation in the public interest: Myth or reality?* (Resource Briefs, 91–1). Lexington, KY: The Council on Licensure, Enforcement, and Regulation.

Shimberg, B., Esser, B. F., & Kruger, D. H. (1973). *Occupational licensing: Practices and policies.* Washington, DC: Public Affairs Press.

Shyrock R. H. (1967). *Medical Licensing in America, 1650–1965.* Baltimore: The Johns Hopkins University Press.

US Department of Health, Education and Welfare (1977). *Credentialing health manpower.* Washington, DC: Author.

2.11
Defining Constructs Underlying the Practice of Psychology in the United States and Canada

I. LEON SMITH and SANDRA GREENBERG
Professional Examination Service, New York, NY, USA

2.11.1 INTRODUCTION

The process of establishing content validity, as described in Chapter 11 of the 1985 revision of the *Standards for Educational and Psychological Testing* (the *Standards*) published by the American Educational Research Association (AERA), the American Psychological Association (APA), and the National Council on Measurement in Education (NCME), emphasizes the need to conduct a practice analysis to ensure that the knowledge, skills, or abilities assessed in credentialing initiatives are limited to those required for competent performance and that they serve a public protection function. According to contemporary theorists like Messick (1989,1995), content validity is one aspect of a comprehensive theory of construct validity. From Messick's perspective, the meaning and interpretation of test scores is established on the basis of many different types of empirical investigations, of which a practice analysis is but one example. This view is consistent with the thinking of Schoon and Smith (1996), who suggest that a practice analysis is the second of six stages in the development, use, and evaluation of licensure examination programs, and immediately follows the conduct of a strategic credentialing analysis which is addressed by Schoon in Chapter 10, this volume.

Although there is no standard way to conduct a practice analysis, common strategies used to define the critical performance areas and the underlying knowledge, skills, or abilities include the use of a committee of subject-matter experts, the compilation of worker logs, observations of practice, and interviews with practitioners (Knapp & Knapp, 1995). In general, it is best to collect practice data from more than one source, as a way of confirming or supplementing the data obtained from other sources. The resulting definition of practice can then be validated by collecting ratings from a representative sample of practitioners. The validation process generates data on the criticality, importance, and frequency of the elements in the practice definition which can be used to evaluate the completeness and appropriateness of the performance areas and the associated knowledge, skills, or abilities. Analysis of the validation data also leads to the development of test specifications supporting examination development activities and to the preparation of instructions for developing the test questions. The outcomes of a practice analysis, then, become the primary basis by which a sponsor of a national licensure program such as the Association of State and Provincial Psychology Boards (ASPPB), formerly the American Association of State Psychology Boards, establishes and defends the content validity of its credentialing initiative.

ASPPB maintains a research program on the Examination for Professional Practice in Psychology (EPPP) consistent with the procedures described above and with the content validity emphasis articulated in the *Standards*. For more information on ASPPB's research program, See Rosen (1991). For a brief history of the origins of the psychology licensing program, the reader is referred to Chapter 10, this volume. Finally, information on EPPP test performance, candidate background information, pass/fail statistics, and the impact of test preparation services on candidate performance is provided by Rosen in Chapter 12, this volume.

ASPPB's research includes three steps: (i) the conduct of a study of professional practice, (ii) the development of revised test specifications based on the study of practice, and (iii) the independent verification that the items and/or forms of the EPPP reflect the test specifications in a representative and fair manner and are consistent with the generic philosophy underlying the EPPP.

Since the mid-1970s, ASPPB has conducted two sets of investigations, each associated with these three steps. ASPPB contracted with Professional Examination Service (PES) to initiate the first set of studies (Richman, 1982). PES conducted an investigation aimed at clarifying the content most appropriate for the EPPP. On the basis of the study, ASPPB developed a new EPPP content outline. All items in the ASPPB item bank were recorded to incorporate the clarified information on the role and knowledge statements. An additional content validation study was conducted under contract to PES (Smith, 1984) to check on the clarity of the new content outline, the quality of the items, and the correspondence between the content categories in the test outline and the items.

ASPPB contracted with the Educational Testing Service to initiate the second set of studies (Rosenfield, Shimberg, & Thornton, 1983). Using existing resources and expert judgments, Rosenfeld et al. created an inventory consisting of 59 responsibilities, 61 procedures, techniques, and resources, and 49 knowledge areas, including ethical/legal considerations and defining the work of professional psychologists. Licensed psychologists in the USA and Canada rated the inventory in terms of time spent, importance, level of application, and level of judgment exercised.

Subsequently, revised test specifications were developed under contract to PES (Rosen & Mirone, 1986). The procedures called for an integration of the results of the job analysis conducted by Rosenfeld et al. (1983) with the findings of the earlier study completed by Richman (1982). All items in the ASPPB item bank were reclassified on the basis of the categories in the new test specifications. ASPPB contracted with PES (Hambleton & Smith, 1988) to conduct a content validity study to provide an independent check that the first two forms of the EPPP based on the new test specifications reflected these specifications, and that the items were free of any unintended content bias with regard to ethnicity, gender, and age. Finally, ASPPB funded PES (Smith & Greenberg, 1991) to address selected recommendations made as part of an audit of the EPPP examination program conducted by the State of California (Werner, 1989). The knowledge, skill, and application statements in the test specifications were augmented with specific topics or elements of practice, the interpretation of the responsibilities was clarified, and guidelines were prepared to facilitate development and classification of items.

The practice analysis study reported herein was conducted by PES under contract with ASPPB and initiated the third comprehensive set of investigations to examine what licensed psychologists in the USA and Canada do and know in order to ensure the continued content validity of the EPPP (Greenberg, Smith, & Muenzen, 1996).

2.11.2 METHOD

2.11.2.1 Committee Structure

The practice analysis study was conducted in collaboration with a five-member Practice Analysis Advisory Committee (PAAC) and a 12-member task force of subject-matter experts appointed by the PAAC on the basis of nominations received from ASPPB's Board of Directors, the Examination Development Committee, and the PAAC. The members of the PAAC represented key decision-makers in ASPPB; in part, they were responsible for guiding aspects of the licensure program, including examination development and validation efforts. The members of the task force represented psychologists in different major areas of practice, including new and emerging specialties.

2.11.2.2 Structure and Development of the Draft Delineations of the Practice of Psychology

Process- and content-based approaches were implemented to study the practice of licensed psychologists in the USA and Canada. Process- and content-based approaches to practice analysis are appropriate for professions such as psychology in which the primary professional behaviors are cognitive in nature (Schoon, 1985).

A process-based approach was used because it provides a structure for describing contemporary practice—that is, for identifying what psychologists do—and because it facilitates the development of examination items in a practice-related framework. The process-based approach comprises the delineation of roles and associated responsibilities performed by psychologists.

Roles represent constructs described by major categories of activities. For example, the role of Direct Service was identified and defined as the provision and/or administration of psychological services to clients, patients, and/or organizations in the areas of problem definition, need assessment, and diagnosis; and the design, implementation, and evaluation of interventions.

Responsibilities represent the specific activities that psychologists perform within each role. For example, to observe, interview, and gather information from the patient/client/organization and related sources (e.g., relevant others, written records, referral source) in order to identify the problems/needs and their contexts, is one responsibility performed in connection with the Direct Service role.

A content-based approach was used because it provides a structure for identifying a comprehensive listing of the critical knowledge that psychologists need in order to perform the responsibilities identified as part of professional practice. The content-based approach provides a user-friendly template for giving feedback to candidates and communicating summary results of EPPP performance to universities, professional schools, and training programs. The content-based approach comprises the delineation of content areas and associated knowledge statements.

Content areas represent constructs described by categories of knowledge used by psychologists in the performance of responsibilities. For example, Biological Bases of Behavior a content area encompassing knowledge of neuroscience, the physiological bases of behavior and illness, and psychopharmacology.

Knowledge statements represent organized bodies of information associated with specific content areas and are necessary in the performance of responsibilities. For example, knowledge of basic neuroscience (e.g., neuroanatomy, neurophysiology, neurochemistry) and clinical neuroscience (e.g., brain–behavior relationships, neurological syndromes and their contribution to cognitive and emotional status and behavior), is a knowledge statement that describes information subsumed in the Biological Bases of Behavior content area.

2.11.2.3 Refining the Delineations of the Practice of Psychology

The following data methods were implemented to supplement and evaluate the structure and content of the draft delineations initially developed by the task force: (i) a sample of 25 licensed psychologists completed a practice log designed to elicit a list of professional responsibilities performed by psychologists; (ii) a sample of 40 licensed psychologists participated in a critical incidents interview in which participants were asked to reflect upon incidents in which they felt particularly effective and particularly ineffective in their practice and to identify the knowledge which made a difference to the outcome; (iii) job descriptions and supervisor's rating forms were collected from members of the PAAC, the task force, and the participants in both the practice log recording and the critical incidents interviews; and (iv) a sample of 29 licensed psychologists completed an independent review of the draft delineations.

The task force and the PAAC used the information in preparing the final delineations. Table 1 presents the roles and the number of associated responsibilities in the process-based delineation, and the content areas and the number of associated knowledge statements in the content-based delineation. A complete copy of the delineations is given in the appendix to this chapter (see Section 2.11.5).

2.11.2.4 Development of a Survey of Practice

In order to validate the process- and content-based delineations, a survey of the practice of psychology was developed for dissemination to licensed psychologists in the USA and Canada. Rating scales were designed to collect data on the roles and responsibilities performed by licensed psychologists and the content areas and knowledge required for practice. A two-part pilot test of the survey was conducted to identify question defects such as ambiguous items and cognitive difficulties in forming answers to questions. First, a sample of 38 licensed psychologists completed the survey via a mail review and evaluated each section to identify any unclear elements. Then, a second sample of four licensed psychologists completed a mail review of the survey and were debriefed in an in-depth telephone interview regarding the cognitive distinctions they made among the rating scales and the scale points associated with the rating scales (Bolton, 1993).

The results of the two-part pilot test were used to refine the process- and content-based delineations, the instructions, and the rating scales. The final survey document, entitled the "Survey of the Practice of Psychology" (the Survey), included six sections. Section One used a set of three rating scales to elicit information about the roles performed in the practice of psychology. Survey respondents were asked to rate the roles in regard to three questions:

(i) How important was the role to *your practice* as a psychologist during the past year?

(ii) What percentage of *your work time* was devoted to each role during the past year?

(iii) How critical is performing the role *protecting the patient/client/public* from harm?

Section Two used a similar set of rating scales to elicit information about the responsibilities in the practice of psychology associated with each role. Survey respondents were asked to rate the responsibilities in regard to three questions:

(i) How important was the performance of the responsibility to *your practice* as a psychologist during the past year?

(ii) How *frequently* have *you* performed this responsibility during the past year?

(iii) How critical is performing the responsibility to *protecting the patient/client/public* from harm?

Section Three elicited information about the content areas—or categories of knowledge—that psychologists use in practice. Survey respondents were asked to rate the content areas in regard to three questions:

(i) How important was the content area to *your practice* as a psychologist during the past year?

(ii) How *frequently* have *you* called upon knowledge from the content area in your practice during the past year?

(iii) How critical is the content area to *protecting the patient/client/public* from harm?

Section Four elicited information about the knowledge that is associated with the content areas and is needed to perform the responsibilities. Survey respondents were asked to rate the knowledge statements in regard to three questions:

(i) What level best represents *your use* of this knowledge in your practice?

(ii) At what point should the knowledge be *acquired* by psychologists?

(iii) How critical is possessing the knowledge to *protecting the patient/client/public* from harm?

Section Five elicited information about the demographic and professional background of respondents with respect to their work in

Table 1 Process- and content-based delineations of the practice of psychology.

Role	*Number of responsibilities*
Direct Service	11
Outreach and Consultation	10
Academic Preparation and Professional Development	8
Research and Evaluation	10
Content area	*Number of knowledge statements*
Biological Bases of Behavior	6
Cognitive-Affective Bases of Behavior	6
Social and Multicultural Bases of Behavior	11
Growth and Lifespan Development	8
Assessment and Diagnosis	14
Treatment/Intervention	11
Research and Evaluation	5
Ethical/Legal/Professional Issues	5

psychology, such as primary and secondary employment setting, practice area, theoretical orientation, specialization or respecialization, and specialty certification; and with respect to demographic variables, such as education, sex, disability, and race or ethnicity.

Section Six solicited qualitative comments wherein respondents were requested to describe any professional responsibilities they perform or knowledge they call upon that was not included in the survey. Most importantly, respondents were asked to comment upon what they believe to be the long-range changes occurring in the practice of psychology.

2.11.2.5 Sampling Plan

The sampling plan for the dissemination of the Survey was designed to (i) generate a sample of 7500 licensed psychologists from those jurisdictions in the USA and Canada that employed the EPPP as an element in the credentialing process, and (ii) ensure the representation of licensed psychologists at or near the entry level of the profession. A minimum of 60 licensed psychologists were sampled from each jurisdiction using the EPPP, regardless of the size of the jurisdiction, and recently licensed psychologists, operationally defined as having been licensed in 1989 or later, were oversampled in every jurisdiction.

The sampling plan included three different data sources: (i) ASPPB-member boards, (ii) the APA Membership Database, and (iii) the Canadian Register of Health Service Providers in Psychology (Canadian Register). In general, the majority of the sample of recent licensees was drawn directly from the ASPPB-member boards using a systematic random sampling technique, and the majority of the sample of less-recent licensees was drawn from the remaining two sources using a systematic random sampling technique.

2.11.2.6 Conduct of the Survey

The conduct of the Survey was designed to yield a high rate of return. Accordingly, the plan involved three carefully timed sequential mailings to the survey recipients as well as one telephone follow-up to a sample of nonrespondents (Dillman, 1978).

(i) Potential participants received a letter describing the nature and scope of the project and inviting their participation in the data collection efforts. Recipients who declined to participate or who were no longer active in the profession were requested to call collect so as to be eliminated from the sample. Potential survey recipients in the three Canadian provinces where the French-language version of the EPPP was offered received an English/French bilingual version of the letter and a postage-paid return postcard for requesting a French-language version of the survey.

(ii) Approximately two weeks later, all remaining potential members of the sample received an English- or French-language survey packet, as appropriate. The survey packet contained: a covering letter reviewing the purpose and importance of the data collection, and assuring the recipients about the confidentiality of the responses; a survey and a postage-paid return envelope; and a postage-paid tracking postcard to be returned, indicating return or nonreturn of the completed survey. As a follow-up, each member of the sample received an English- or French-language reminder/thank-you postcard, as appropriate.

(iii) Subsequently, each member of the sample *not* returning a tracking postcard received a second and then a third survey packet. The packets were identical to the first except that the covering letter identified the recipient as not previously returning a completed survey. In addition, the letter informed recipients of ways to obtain the results of the study. The letter in the third packet urged the recipients to respond so that their own practice might be reflected in ASPPB's picture of contemporary practice. Follow-up reminder/thank-you postcards were sent to all members of the sample who received the second and third survey packets.

(iv) Approximately four weeks after the final mailing, a telephone/mail survey of 250 non-responders was conducted to estimate the potential impact of nonresponse bias.

2.11.3 SUMMARY OF RESULTS

2.11.3.1 Survey Response Rate

The return rate for completed Surveys from eligible participants was 60%, which is considered excellent for surveys of this type (Knapp & Knapp, 1995). Consistent with the sampling plan, every ASPPB-member jurisdiction was represented in the returns, and recently licensed psychologists were overrepresented in proportion to their representation in the population.

2.11.3.2 Professional Background and Demographic Descriptions

(i) More than two-thirds of the US and Canadian respondents indicated that their primary employment setting fell within the general category of human-service settings (including individual independent practice and group psychological practice), whereas about 20% indicated that their primary employment setting was an educational institution/school system.

(ii) US respondents were most likely to have earned a doctoral degree, including the doctorate of psychology degree, as their highest degree in psychology. Canadian respondents were equally likely to have earned either a master's degree or a doctoral degree as their highest degree in psychology.

(iii) Recently licensed US respondents were more likely to have earned a degree from a free-standing school of professional psychology than were less recently licensed respondents. Few Canadian respondents earned degrees from free-standing schools of professional psychology.

(iv) More than one half of the US and Canadian respondents indicated clinical psychology as their major area of training; counseling was reported as the major area of training by about 20% of the US respondents and 15% of the Canadian respondents.

(v) In both the USA and Canada, more respondents indicated clinical child psychology and clinical neuropsychology as their current major area of practice than had trained in those areas.

(vi) In both the USA and Canada, about one-half of respondents described their primary theoretical orientation as cognitive/behavioral or behavioral. In the USA, about one-quarter of the respondents described their primary theoretical orientation as psychodynamic, and no more than 8% identified any one other primary theoretical orientation. In Canada, approximately equal numbers described their primary theoretical orientation as psychodynamic and existential/humanistic (both 18%), and no more than 6% identified any one other primary theoretical orientation.

(vii) About one-quarter of the US respondents and approximately 15% of the Canadian respondents indicated that they had participated in a postdoctoral specialization or respecialization program.

(viii) More than one-half of US and Canadian recently licensed respondents were female, compared to about 40% of the less recently licensed US and Canadian respondents.

(ix) About 93% of the US respondents and 89% of the Canadian respondents indicated they were Caucasian/White. American-Indian or Alaskan Native, Asian or Pacific Islander, Black or African-American, and Hispanic/Latino psychologists were represented among the respondents.

(x) Selected comparisons of professional background and demographic variables indicated that the current sample was representative of the populations of licensed psychologists included in the APA Membership Database and the Canadian Register.

(xi) The results of the respondent/nonrespondent survey revealed few differences in key background and demographic variables.

2.11.3.3 Results Related to the Delineations

Preliminary statistical analyses of the Importance, Time/Frequency, and Criticality ratings indicated that there were few differences in the results of the respondent/nonrespondent survey, or in the ratings of recently vs. less recently licensed respondents and US versus Canadian respondents. Accordingly, the ratings of all the respondents on the roles and responsibilities, and on the content areas and knowledge statements were combined for final data analysis in connection with the development of profiles of practice and revised test specifications for the EPPP. Readers are encouraged to review the appendix to this chapter (see Section 2.11.5) for a complete description of the roles and responsibilities, and the content areas and knowledge statements. These elements comprise the components of the test specifications.

2.11.3.3.1 Process-based delineation

(i) Roles

The Direct Service role was rated most important to the practice of the respondents and most critical to the protection of the patient/client/public from harm. Respondents spent about 70% of their time in that role.

(a) The Direct Service role was rated as moderately to very important to the practice of the respondents; in fact, nearly 90% of the ratings were at scale point three, indicating that the role was very important to the practice of the respondents, and the associated standard deviation was the smallest of any role and in connection with any rating scale. The remaining roles—Outreach and Consultation, Academic/Professional Development, Research and Evaluation—were rated as minimally to moderately important to their practice.

(b) The mean Time ratings indicated that respondents spent two-thirds of their time in the Direct Service role, and one-third of their time in all other roles. However, the magnitude of the standard deviations associated with the mean Time ratings indicated a great deal of variability in the practice patterns of the respondents.

(c) All four delineated roles were rated as moderately to highly critical to the protection of the patient/client/public from harm.

(d) In general, the Importance and Time ratings on the roles varied more than the Criticality ratings; respondents consistently rated the roles as moderately to highly critical to the protection of the patient/client/public, regardless of their own professional practice patterns.

(e) The ratings of the roles by respondents representing various major areas of practice demonstrated some similarities and differences. For example, in terms of the Importance rating scale, the ratings were generally similar in regard to the Direct Service role, but somewhat dissimilar in regard to the Academic Preparation and Professional Development role and the Research and Evaluation role.

(ii) Responsibilities

The Importance, Frequency, and Criticality ratings of the responsibilities were generally consistent with the Importance, Time, and Criticality ratings of the associated roles; thus, the respondents rated the responsibilities associated with the Direct Service role as most important to their practice, most frequently performed, and most critical to the protection of the patient/client/public from harm. In general, the Importance and Frequency ratings on the responsibilities varied more than the Criticality ratings.

(a) Respondents rated virtually all the responsibilities as moderately to highly critical to the protection of the patient/client/public from harm, regardless of their own professional practice patterns.

(b) One responsibility associated with the Direct Service role—to provide direct service in a manner consistent with professional and ethical standards and guidelines, and state/provincial and national laws and regulations—was rated highest of any responsibility on the Importance, Frequency, and Criticality rating scales. Within the Outreach and Consultation role, a similar responsibility—to provide education and consultation in a manner consistent with current professional and ethical standards and guidelines, and state/provincial and national laws and regulations—was rated highest on the same three rating scales.

(c) The ratings of the responsibilities by respondents representing various major practice areas demonstrated similarities and differences. Respondents in various major areas of practice displayed a greater degree of consensus in their Criticality ratings than in their Importance and Frequency ratings.

2.11.3.3.2 Content-based delineation

(i) Content areas

The Treatment/Intervention and Ethical/Legal/Professional Issues content areas were rated most important to the practice of the respondents and most critical to the protection of the patient/client/public from harm; the knowledge base associated with the Treatment/Intervention content area was called upon most frequently by the respondents.

(a) The ratings of the content areas indicated that all areas—except Research and

Evaluation—were moderately to very important to the practice of the respondents and were called upon moderately to very frequently.

(b) All content areas—including Research and Evaluation—were rated as moderately to highly critical to the protection of the patient/client/public from harm.

(c) In general, the Criticality ratings of the respondents were somewhat higher than the Importance ratings.

(d) The ratings of the content areas by respondents in different major areas of practice were generally similar. The respondents in different major areas of practice displayed a great degree of similarity in what content areas they considered critical to the protection of the patient/client/public from harm, even though they varied considerably in their ratings of what content areas are important to and frequently performed in their own practice.

(ii) Knowledge statements

About 85% of the respondents used 51 of the 66 knowledge statements either at the recognition/recall or the apply/interpret/integrate level, and about the same percentage of respondents rated 61 of the 66 knowledge statements as necessary to be acquired at some point in time—either primarily before or after licensure. Finally, the Criticality ratings indicated that 43 of the 66 knowledge statements were rated moderately to highly critical to the protection of the patient/client/public from harm. Other key findings were as follows:

(a) Of the 15 knowledge statements rated by a majority of the respondents as not used or not supported for acquisition, 12 were in two content areas—Assessment and Diagnosis, and Treatment/Intervention.

(b) With few exceptions, the ratings of the knowledge statements by respondents representing various major areas of practice were similar. However, respondents in various major areas of practice were least similar in their ratings of knowledge statements associated with the two content areas, Assessment and Diagnosis and Treatment/Intervention.

2.11.3.4 Qualitative Results

About two-thirds of the respondents identified long-range changes occurring in the practice of the profession, especially those that may affect the knowledge required of licensed psychologists in the future. The following summary characterizes the unique and the common areas of change identified by the US and Canadian respondents:

(i) More than one-quarter of the US respondents commented on the impact of the shift from independent practice to managed care. Respondents described their concerns regarding the constraints of managed care, for example, the focus on brief, solution-oriented therapy; the ethical dilemmas posed around issues such as confidentiality, privacy, the termination of therapy, and the move to outpatient rather than inpatient treatment; the reliance on computer-based assessment and diagnosis; the requirements for quality assurance and outcomes-based assessment; and the focus on the business aspects of practice, including the entrepreneurial management and administration of practice.

(ii) Nearly one-quarter of the US respondents and somewhat fewer of the Canadian respondents commented on the increased emphasis on the biological bases of behavior in clinical practice.

(iii) More than 10% of the US respondents and somewhat fewer of the Canadian respondents commented on the redefinition of the practitioner as a primary healthcare provider or as a case manager supervising other allied health practitioners responsible for direct services.

(iv) Nearly 10% of the US and Canadian respondents commented on one or more of the following shifts toward (a) a more multiculturally diverse patient/client population, (b) a larger geriatric patient/client population, and (c) a more severely disturbed (and violent) society. Each of these trends is associated with a specific knowledge base.

(v) Approximately 10% of the Canadian respondents described the shift from employment within the government-sponsored healthcare system to independent practice and/or employee-assistance programs, in contrast to the move in the US from independent practice to managed care.

Both US and Canadian respondents identified the following types of knowledge and skills as needed in the future:

(i) Knowledge regarding the biological bases of behavior, brief treatments and/or solution-oriented therapeutic techniques, hypnotherapy, forensic psychology, employee-assistance programs, quality assurance procedures, outcomes-based assessment, and specialties in psychology.

(ii) Professional skills associated with consulting and/or working in interdisciplinary collaborative teams, procedures to integrate aspects of spirituality into therapy; sensitivity skills to handle the increasingly diverse patient/client population, and self-assessment skills to recognize one's strengths and limits.

(iii) Generic skills, such as computer skills, for managerial and professional aspects of practice, business skills for developing and administering a practice, and marketing skills for surviving in practice.

2.11.3.5 Process- and Content-based Profiles of Practice

Preliminary statistical analyses revealed that among the Importance, Time/Frequency, and Criticality scales, the latter two ratings contributed maximum independent information to a description or profile of practice. Accordingly, a process-based profile was developed by combining the Criticality and Time/Frequency ratings associated with the roles and responsibilities, and a content-based profile was developed by combining the Criticality and Frequency ratings associated with the content areas, as well as the Criticality and Acquisition ratings associated with the knowledge statements which were rank-ordered from most critical and appropriate to be acquired before licensure, to least critical and not necessary at any point in practice.

In the case of the process-based profile, the largest element related to the Direct Service role (about 70%); the remaining three roles contributed less than 30% to the overall profile of the critical activities performed by licensed psychologists. With respect to the content-based profile, seven of eight content areas each contributed between 11% and 16% to the profile, while one content area—Research and Evaluation—made a smaller contribution (6%) to the profile. The Ethical, Legal, and Professional Issues content area included three of the 10 highest-ranked knowledge statements; the Growth and Lifespan Development, Assessment and Diagnosis, and Treatment/Intervention content areas each included two of the 10 highest-ranked knowledge statements; and the Biological Bases of Behavior content area included one of the 10 highest-ranked knowledge statements.

2.11.3.6 Development of Test Specifications

A systematic review of the results related to the process- and content-based profiles of practice was conducted by a specially constituted ASPPB Test Specifications Panel. The following recommendations were prepared to ensure that the EPPP would reflect the responsibilities performed by licensed psychologists making the greatest contribution to the protection of the patient/client/public from harm; emphasize the knowledge needed by licensed psychologists that serves the public protection function of regulation; and address the issue of developing a generic examination for psychologists.

(i) The use of the content areas and knowledge statements as the primary organizing structure for the test specifications and feedback to the candidates.

(ii) The adoption of percentage weights for the eight content areas.

(iii) The use of a hierarchical weighting for each knowledge statement, indicating the degree to which related questions might be included in each version of the EPPP. In order of priority, the system incorporated the Criticality ratings and the Acquisition ratings for the knowledge statements.

(iv) The revision of eight knowledge statements, including additions, deletions, and modifications of the examples included as part of the knowledge statements; and the elimination of three knowledge statements via the incorporation of the related examples into other knowledge statements.

(v) The use of the roles and responsibilities as an organizing structure for item-writing initiatives and examination assembly.

(vi) The adoption of percentage weights for the four roles and associated responsibilities;

(vii) The use of a classification system by which: (a) test items would be identified by role, responsibility, content area, and knowledge statement; and (b) forms of the EPPP would be constructed so as to reflect the content- and process-based weights in the test specifications.

2.11.4 CONCLUSIONS

The analysis of the practice of psychology reported in this chapter provides a picture of what licensed psychologists in the USA and Canada know and do. However, it is apparent from the descriptions of the short- and long-range changes occurring in the practice of the profession that frequent reviews and updates are needed to ensure that the picture of practice—and the content of the EPPP—continue to reflect contemporary practice. Rapid changes in the delivery of healthcare services mandated by the move to managed care in the USA and to nongovernment-sponsored employment in Canada may require an expanded knowledge base. Similarly, the changing gender base of the profession and the shifts in the client base, along with the move to increased interdisciplinary collaboration may impact the required knowledge base.

Accordingly, future practice analysis initiatives may require: (i) the periodic, but frequent monitoring of specific settings and/or specialties undergoing rapid changes in practice, (ii) the study of professional relationships among intra- and interdisciplinary team members, and (iii) qualitative and quantitative outcome studies of practice as well as investigations of the perceptions of employers and the public regarding the demands of practice and the value and meaning of the licensure credential in psychology. The outcomes of these kinds of studies will be very useful in the continuous process of re-examining and re-evaluating the role and function of regulation in our society (Interprofessional Workgroup on Health Professions Regulation, 1996; Pew Health Professions Commission, 1995).

The analysis of practice provides a database for policy-making in regard to education, certification, and accreditation initiatives in professional psychology. The results of the analysis should be reviewed by those responsible for: college, university, and professional school curricula; training programs; continuing education, in-service education; the development and implementation of specialty certification initiatives; and the accreditation of school, internship, and residency training programs.

Finally, the results of the current analysis should be viewed in the context of practice in other nations and/or political entities. The implementation and/or emergence of the North Atlantic Free Trade Agreement, the General Agreement on Trade and Tariffs, and the European Union indicates the appropriateness of a global perspective and the need to understand the commonalities and differences in practice and in the regulation of psychology around the world that could be provided by the conduct of international studies of practice (ASPPB, 1996).

2.11.5 APPENDIX

2.11.5.1 Roles and Definitions

Direct Service. The provision and/or administration of psychological services to clients, patients, and/or organizations in the areas of problem definition, need assessment, and diagnosis; and the design, implementation, and evaluation of interventions.

Outreach and Consultation. The preparation, presentation, and coordination of educational programs, and/or the dissemination of information or the provision of expertise to a variety of audiences.

Academic Preparation and Professional Development. The development, implementation, and administration of education programs for psychologists, including teaching, supervision, and curricula.

Research and Evaluation. The development and/or participation in any investigation and/or the use of results to expand or refine knowledge or to improve programs and services.

2.11.5.1.1 Responsibilities related to direct service

(i) Make and/or receive referrals.

(ii) Coordinate service delivery with other psychologists and professionals (e.g., health professionals, managed care systems, organizational personnel, schools, community groups, and other outside agencies).

(iii) Observe, interview, and gather information from patient/client/organization and related sources (e.g., relevant others, written records, referral source) to identify the problems/needs and their contexts.

(iv) Develop assessment procedures and/or instruments (e.g., behavioral analyses, structured interviews, work samples, performance tests) for the assessment of relevant characteristics of individuals, groups, jobs, organizations, educational and social institutions, and/or environments

(v) Select, administer, and score norm-referenced, standardized, or other instruments for the assessment of relevant characteristics of individuals, groups, jobs, organizations, educational and social institutions, and/or environments.

(vi) Evaluate and integrate results of information-gathering and assessment processes with scientific/professional knowledge to formulate/reformulate working hypotheses, diagnoses, and intervention recommendations.

(vii) Plan, design, and implement intervention programs (e.g., define goals and objectives, identify appropriate intervention targets and strategies).

(viii) Monitor and evaluate efficacy of interventions/programs, and modify as appropriate.

(ix) Document and/or communicate assessment results, intervention recommendations, progress, and outcomes.

(x) In administering a professional practice—design, implement, and monitor quality assurance, quality control, risk management, and/or other procedures.

(xi) Provide direct service in a manner consistent with current professional and ethical standards and guidelines, and state/provincial and national laws and regulations.

2.11.5.1.2 Responsibilities related to outreach and consultation

(i) Prepare/present/coordinate health promotion programs or workshops (e.g., smoking cessation, parenting, anger control management, informational programs on community psychological services/resources).

(ii) Prepare/present/coordinate prevention and/or early intervention programs for at-risk populations (e.g., substance abuse prevention, HIV–AIDS education, community programs for the elderly).

(iii) Prepare/present/coordinate classes, seminars, or workshops for clients, family and significant others, personnel in school systems, medical and allied healthcare personnel, human resource personnel, and/or the general public.

(iv) Provide expertise to and/or serve on local/state/provincial/federal agencies (e.g., community outreach program, jurisdictional licensing board, legal system).

(v) Provide expertise to and/or serve on local/state/provincial, national or international professional psychology organizations (e.g., APA and Canadian Psychological Association (CPA), American Psychological Society, ASPPBs, Society for Industrial and Organizational Psychology).

(vi) Disseminate knowledge of psychology and its value to the general public.

(vii) Provide consultation regarding design, methodology, statistical analysis, and/or significance of reported data and conclusions of a research or evaluation study.

(viii) Provide expertise to and/or serve on site-specific patient-care, education-related, or research-related committees (e.g., program accreditation, Institutional Review Board, Quality Assurance Committee).

(ix) Establish and maintain intra- and interdisciplinary collaborative relationships, within institutional settings and with other professionals.

(x) Provide education and consultation in a manner consistent with current professional and ethical standards and guidelines, and state/provincial and national laws and regulations.

2.11.5.1.3 Responsibilities related to academic preparation and professional development

(i) Prepare/present/coordinate classes, seminars, or workshops for undergraduates, pre- and postdoctoral students, and professional psychologists.

(ii) Develop/administer/coordinate pre- and postdoctoral practicum, internship, and fellowship programs in human services settings.

(iii) Develop/administer/coordinate undergraduate, pre- and postdoctoral, and continuing education programs in professional psychology.

(iv) Supervise pre- and postdoctoral students and professional practitioners to enhance service delivery.

(v) Supervise and advise undergraduates and pre- and postdoctoral students on research/evaluation (e.g., honors thesis, dissertation).

(vi) Provide mentoring for undergraduates, pre- and postdoctoral students, and/or professional psychologists.

(vii) Provide training in a manner consistent with current professional and ethical standards and guidelines, and state/provincial and national laws and regulations.

(viii) Participate in professional self-development and continuing education designed to enhance professional and personal knowledge and skills.

2.11.5.1.4 Responsibilities related to research and evaluation

(i) Critically review and appraise existing literature with regard to study design, methodology, method of analysis, and generalizability of results and conclusions.

(ii) Use the existing knowledge base to formulate clear research/evaluation questions or to guide intervention or program development.

(iii) Engage in research in a manner that ensures protection of human and/or animal rights, adhering to current professional and ethical standards/guidelines, and jurisdictional and national laws/regulations.

(iv) Formulate research/program evaluation hypotheses, and design appropriate methods to conduct the study.

(v) Collect and analyze data using appropriate methods of analysis (e.g., qualitative, quantitative).

(vi) Report research findings and implications according to professionally accepted standards.

(vii) Submit research findings to peer review for publication and/or presentation.

(viii) Apply research findings in practice, with awareness of strengths and limitations of application.

(ix) Prepare proposals to funding agencies.

(x) Provide expertise to and/or serve in an editorial capacity on professional journals or other refereed publications, or review proposals to funding agencies.

2.11.5.2 Content Areas and Definitions

Biological Bases of Behavior. Knowledge of neuroscience, the physiological bases of behavior and illness, and psychopharmacology.

Cognitive-Affective Bases of Behavior. Knowledge of cognitive science; theories of learning, memory, motivation, and emotion; and factors that influence an individual's cognitive performance and/or emotional experience.

Social and Multicultural Bases of Behavior. Knowledge of social cognition, social interaction processes, and organizational dynamics; theories of personality; and issues in diversity (multiethnic, multicultural, gender, sexual orientation, and disability).

Growth and Lifespan Development. Knowledge of age-appropriate child, adolescent, and adult development; atypical patterns of development; and the protective and risk factors that influence developmental outcomes for individuals.

Assessment and Diagnosis. Knowledge of psychometrics, assessment models, methods for assessment of individuals and organizations/systems, and diagnostic classification systems and issues.

Treatment/Intervention. Knowledge of individual, group, or organizational interventions for specific concerns/disorders; treatment theories; and consultation models and processes.

Research and Evaluation. Knowledge of research design, methodology, and program evaluation; statistical procedures; and criteria for accurate interpretation of research findings.

Ethical/Legal/Professional Issues. Knowledge of the ethical code, professional standards for practice, legal mandates, guidelines for ethical decision-making, and professional training and supervision.

*2.11.5.2.1 **Knowledge statements related to biological bases of behavior***

(i) Basic neuroscience (e.g., neuroanatomy, neurophysiology, neurochemistry) and clinical neuroscience (e.g., brain–behavior relationships, neurological syndromes and their contribution to cognitive and emotional status and behavior).

(ii) Physiological correlates/determinants of behavior and affect (e.g., symptoms of common psychophysiologic reactions and syndromes, such as hyperventilation, anxiety disorders, depressive disorders, stress reactions, headaches, irritable bowel syndrome).

(iii) Biological bases of the behavior and affect associated with acute and chronic illness (e.g., post-stroke depression, diabetes, AIDS, asthma, chemotherapy, fibromyalgia, hypoglycemia, schizophrenia). Includes knowledge of psychoneuroimmunology.

(iv) Basic psychopharmacology (e.g., medication effects, side-effects, and interactions). Includes knowledge of drug metabolism, drug categories (e.g., anxiolytics, antidepressants, antipsychotics, anticonvulsants), and addictive/dependency potential.

(v) Genetic transmission (e.g., the relationship of dominant and recessive genes) and its role in understanding disorders and their behavioral, emotional, and psychosocial manifestations (e.g., Duchenne's muscular dystrophy, Huntington's disease, Down's syndrome).

(vi) Relationship of stress to biological and psychological functioning, with particular reference to lifestyle and lifestyle modification (e.g., cardiac rehabilitation, smoking cessation).

*2.11.5.2.2 **Knowledge statements related to cognitive-affective bases of behavior***

(i) Cognitive science (e.g., sensation and perception, attention, memory, language and spatial skills, intelligence, information processing, problem-solving, strategies for organizing information).

(ii) Theories and principles of learning (e.g., social learning, classical and operant conditioning, primacy/recency effects).

(iii) Theories of motivation (e.g., need/value approaches, cognitive choice approaches, self-regulation).

(iv) Theories of emotions.

(v) Reciprocal interrelationships among cognitions/beliefs, behavior, affect, temperament, and mood (e.g., healthy functioning, performance anxiety, performance enhancement, job satisfaction, depression).

(vi) Influence of psychosocial factors (e.g., sex differences, family styles and characteristics, academic/occupational success) on beliefs/cognitions and behaviors.

*2.11.5.2.3 **Knowledge statements related to social and multicultural bases of behavior***

(i) Social cognition and perception (e.g., attribution theory and biases, information integration, confirmation bias, person perception, development of stereotypes, racism).

(ii) Social interaction (e.g., interpersonal relationships, aggression, altruism, attraction).

(iii) Group dynamics and organizational structures (e.g., school systems, gang behavior, family systems, group thinking, cultural behavior, conformity, compliance, obedience, persuasion) and social influences on individual functioning.

(iv) Environmental/ecological psychology (e.g., person–environment fit, crowding, pollution, noise).

(v) Theories of personality that describe behavior and the etiology of atypical behavior. Includes knowledge of limitations in existing theories for understanding the effect of diversity (e.g., age, ethnicity, gender).

(vi) Multicultural and multiethnic diversity (e.g., racial/ethnic minorities, gender, age, disability, sexual orientation, religious groups, between- and within-group differences).

(vii) Theories of identity development of multicultural/multiethnic groups (e.g., acculturation theories, racial/ethnic identity).

(viii) Role that race, ethnicity, gender, sexual orientation, disability, and other cultural differences play in the psychosocial, political, and economic development of individuals/groups.

(ix) Sexual orientation issues (e.g., sexual identity, gay/lesbian/bisexual, family issues).

(x) Psychology of gender (e.g., psychology of women, psychology of men, gender identity development).

(xi) Disability and rehabilitation issues (e.g., inclusion, psychological impact of disability).

2.11.5.2.4 Knowledge statements related to growth and lifespan development

(i) Normal growth and development (cognitive, social, personality, moral, emotional, and physical) from conception through old age.

(ii) Normative or age-expected behaviors (e.g., normal age range, individual differences) and how the definition of normative behavior is influenced by culture.

(iii) Risk factors which predict an atypical developmental course (e.g., nutritional deficiencies; healthcare, including prenatal care; availability of social support; adequacy of income and housing; poverty; parental alcohol/drug abuse).

(iv) Interventions to reduce risk factors (e.g., poor healthcare, nutritional deficiencies, violence) and to increase resilience (e.g., protective factors such as caregiving, increased social support) and competence (e.g., skill building) of individuals living in at-risk environments.

(v) Life-event changes that can alter the normal course of development (e.g., injury, trauma, illness, onset of chronic disease or disorder in self or parent, death, divorce).

(vi) Theories of development (e.g., constructivist theory, social learning theory, ecological theory).

(vii) How development is influenced by the organism–environment interaction over time (e.g., understanding the relationship between the behavior of the individual and the social, academic, or work environment).

(viii) Family systems functioning and family stages in life and how these impact on individuals (e.g., family life cycle, parent–adolescent communication, birth of child).

2.11.5.2.5 Knowledge statements related to assessment and diagnosis

(i) Psychometric theory and concepts (e.g., measurement, reliability, validity, item characteristics, test fairness, standardization, norms), and test validation procedures (e.g., criterion, predictive, construct, and content strategies; appropriate measurement standards and legal regulations).

(ii) Assessment models (e.g., psychometric, behavioral, neuropsychological, ecological).

(iii) Tests for the measurement of characteristics of individuals (e.g., social, emotional, and behavioral functioning; cognitive; achievement; aptitude; personality; neuropsychological; vocational interest), and the adaptation of these tests for use with special populations.

(iv) Techniques other than tests (e.g., interviews, surveys, naturalistic and structured behavioral observations, physical status, history/biographical data) for the measurement of characteristics of individuals.

(v) Instruments and methods for the measurement of characteristics of jobs, organizations, educational and other social institutions (e.g., job analysis, job evaluation, need assessment, organizational diagnosis, ecological assessment).

(vi) Methods for evaluating environmental/ecological influences on individuals, groups, or organizations (e.g., organizational frameworks, functional analysis of behavior).

(vii) Criteria for selecting assessment devices/approaches (e.g., cultural appropriateness, utility analysis and cost effectiveness, relevance to referral concern).

(viii) Various classification systems (e.g., *DSM-IV* (*Diagnostic and statistical manual of mental disorders, 4th edition*), AAMR (American Academy of Mental Retardation), ICD (*International classification of diseases*)) for diagnosing client functioning.

(ix) Epidemiology of behavioral disorders, base rates of disorders in clinical or demographic populations, comorbidity among behavioral disorders and with medical disorders.

(x) Theory and techniques for the measurement of client changes (e.g., client tracking, formative and summative evaluation, program evaluation).

(xi) Human imaging principles, uses, and clinical implications (e.g., magnetic resonance imaging, computed tomography scanning, positron emission tomography scanning, electroencephalography, SPECT, single photo-emission computed tomography).

(xii) Human laboratory principles, uses, and clinical implications (e.g., drug screens, screening for genetic disorders).

(xiii) Use of computers and related technology in implementing tests, surveys, and other forms of assessment.

(xiv) Quality assurance measurement techniques.

2.11.5.2.6 Knowledge statements related to treatment/intervention

(i) Treatment planning process, including differential diagnosis and efficacy and outcome data.

(ii) Theories of treatment (e.g., behavioral, cognitive, and cognitive-behavioral approaches; psychodynamic approaches; systems/ecological approaches; humanistic approaches).

(iii) Treatment techniques/interventions for specific concerns or specific populations (e.g., marital and family, group therapy, crisis intervention, play therapy, feminist therapy, approaches to stress management, psychoeducational, time-limited/brief therapy, compensation strategies, culturally appropriate treatments and interventions).

(iv) System theories and system interventions (e.g., change of environment, school system, community interventions, family, job and equipment design, consultation).

(v) Organizational interventions (e.g., organizational development, organizational change, performance enhancement/management).

(vi) Consultation models (e.g., mental health, behavioral, instructional, organizational) and processes (e.g., stages, communication skills).

(vii) Human resource management interventions (e.g., selection, performance appraisal, training).

(viii) Theories of career development and counseling (e.g., career assessment, career counseling techniques).

(ix) Adjunctive and alternative interventions and appropriate referral (e.g., physicians, 12-step programs, psychopharmacology, inpatient or partial hospitalization, support groups).

(x) Service delivery systems (e.g., education, health, mental health, social services, forensics, business, and industry), including the roles of other professionals.

(xi) Quality assurance measurement techniques.

2.11.5.2.7 Knowledge statements related to research and evaluation

(i) Research methods (e.g., sampling, instrumentation, data collection procedures).

(ii) Research design (e.g., hypothesis generation, experimental, quasi-experimental, naturalistic inquiry, group designs, and single-case research).

(iii) Appropriate analytical methods (e.g., qualitative, quantitative, descriptive, inferential; univariate, bivariate, and multivariate; parametric and nonparametric) and interpretation (e.g., causal versus correlational; degree and nature of generalizability).

(iv) Criteria for critical appraisal and utilization of research (e.g., technical adequacy; limitations to generalizations; threats to internal, external, and construct validity).

(v) Program planning and evaluation strategies and techniques (e.g., need assessment, process/implementation evaluation, outcome evaluation).

2.11.5.2.8 Knowledge statements related to ethical/legal/professional issues

(i) APA Ethical Principles of Psychologists and Code of Conduct and/or Canadian Code of Ethics for Psychologists (e.g., confidentiality, research, dual relationships, limits of competence, advertising practices, informed consent, record-keeping).

(ii) Professional standards and guidelines for the practice of psychology (e.g., APA/CPA Standards for Providers of Psychological Services, AERA/APA/NCME Standards for Educational and Psychological Testing. ASPPB Code of Conduct, ASPPB Model Licensure Act, credentialing requirements for advanced specialties and proficiencies, other published guidelines for special populations such as women and minorities).

(iii) Pertinent federal, state and/or provincial laws/statutes that affect psychological practice (e.g., laws and regulations relating to family and child protection, education, disabilities, discrimination, duty to warn and privileged communication, commitment and least restrictive care, continuing education requirements, practice regulations, licensure regulations).

(iv) Ethical decision-making process (e.g., balancing professionalism with entrepreneurship, integration of ethical principles and legal/regulatory standards).

(v) Models and approaches for training and supervision of self and others (e.g., methods for developing and enhancing knowledge and proficiency, continuing education, professional self-management, clinical supervision, peer consultation and supervision).

2.11.6 REFERENCES

American Educational Research Association, American Psychological Association, & National Council on Measurement in Education (1985). *Standards for educa-*

tional and psychological testing. Washington, DC: American Psychological Association.

Association of State and Provincial Psychology Boards (1996). *Regulation of professional psychology: An international resource directory*. Montgomery, AL: Author.

Bolton, R. (1993). Pretesting questionnaires: Content analyses of respondents' concurrent verbal protocols. *Marketing Science*, *12*, 280–303.

Dillman, D. A. (1978). *Mail and telephone surveys: The total design method.* New York: Wiley.

Greenberg, S., Smith, I. L., & Muenzen, P. M. (1996). *Study of the practice of licensed psychologist in the United States and Canada.* Montgomery, AL: Association of State and Provincial Psychology Boards.

Hambleton, R. K., & Smith, I. L. (1988). *Content validity and fairness review of the 1987 forms of the Examination for Professional Practice in Psychology (EPPP) (final report)*. New York: Professional Examination Service.

Interprofessional Workgroup on Health Professions Regulation (1996, November). *Views of the licensure and regulation of healthcare professionals*. Unpublished manuscript.

Knapp, J. E., & Knapp, L. G. (1995). Practice analysis: Building the foundation for validity. In J. C. Impara (Ed.), *Licensure testing: Purposes, procedures, and practices* (pp. 93–116). Lincoln, NE: Buros Institute of Mental Measurements.

Messick, S. (1989). Validity. In R. L. Linn (Ed.), *Educational measurement* (3rd ed., pp. 13–103). New York: Macmillan.

Messick, S. (1995). Validity of psychological assessment: Validation of inferences from persons' responses and performances as scientific inquiry into score meaning. *American Psychologist*, *50*, 741–749.

Pew Health Professions Commission (1995, December). *Reforming healthcare workforce regulation: Policy considerations for the 21st century*. San Francisco, CA: Author.

Richman, S. (1982). *The role delineation study for the Examination for Professional Practice in Psychology (final report)*. New York: Professional Examination Service.

Rosen, G. A. (1991). *Research digest: the Examination for Professional Practice in Psychology*. Montgomery, AL: American Association of State Psychology Boards.

Rosen, G. A., & Mirone, J. A. (1986). *The test specification revision project for the Examination for Professional Practice in Psychology (final report)*. New York: Professional Examination Service.

Rosenfeld, M., Shimberg, B., & Thornton, R. F. (1983). *Job analysis of licensed psychologists in the United States and Canada.* Princeton, NJ: The Educational Testing Service.

Schoon, C. G. (1985). Methods for defining and assessing professional competence. *Professional Practice of Psychology*, *6*(1), 144–155.

Schoon, C. G., & Smith, I. L. (1996, Summer). Guidelines for credentialing programs. *Professions Education Research Quarterly*, *17*(4), 6–9.

Smith, I. L. (1984). *Content validity study of the EPPP item bank*. New York: Professional Examination Service.

Smith, I. L., & Greenberg, S. (1991). *Final report for the EPPP test specifications enhancement project*. New York: Professional Examination Service.

Werner, E. (1989). *Analysis of the validity of the Examination for Professional Practice of Psychology*. Sacramento, CA: California Department of Consumer Affairs.

2.12
An Assessment Tool in Credentialing: The Examination for Professional Practice in Psychology

GERALD A. ROSEN
Sylvan Learning Systems, Philadelphia, PA, USA

2.12.1 INTRODUCTION

The Examination for Professional Practice in Psychology (EPPP) is a 200-item multiple-choice examination owned and developed by the Association of State and Provincial Psychology Boards (ASPPB). It is made available by ASPPB to its members for their use in evaluating candidates for licensure or certification as psychologists. The EPPP is administered semiannually in April and October in paper-and-pencil format by the ASPPB member boards. Examinations are scored by the Professional Examination Service (PES), a not-for-profit testing company. PES also provides technical assistance in the development of items and examinations as well as a variety of support services including printing, shipping, and statistical analyses.

According to the ASPPB:

> The EPPP is intended to evaluate the knowledge that should have been acquired by any candidate who has obtained a doctoral degree in psychology followed by one or two years of postdoctoral experience. Such candidates are expected to have acquired a broad base of knowledge of psychology, regardless of individual specialties. This knowledge, and the candidate's ability to apply it, are assessed through the candidate's responses to objective, multiple-choice questions representative of the field at large. Most candidates with the required academic and experiential preparation should be able to pass the test. (ASPPB, 1995a, p. 3)

2.12.2 CONTENT OF THE EPPP

In its early years, the content of the EPPP was based on a list of subjects determined by the members of the Examination Committee, a panel of psychologists appointed by the Board of Directors of ASPPB. For example, Form 6 covered the following subjects: background knowledge; methodology; clinical; other applications; and professional conduct, affairs, and ethics (Carlson, 1978). By today's standards of test development, this list represents a remarkable mix of extremely broad topics. Such informal methods of test construction were common in the 1960s and persisted well into the next decade in psychology and many other professions with national licensure examination programs. However, as the number of participating psychology licensure boards and candidates increased, and as the USA became a more litigious society, attention was drawn to the issue of enhancing the legal defensibility of the EPPP. In response to that need, ASPPB, known at that time as the American Association of State Psychology Boards, funded a series of studies and development projects in order to produce and enhance formal test specifications for the EPPP.

2.12.2.1 The Role Delineation Study of Professional Psychology

In 1978, ASPPB selected PES to conduct a role delineation study of professional psychology in order to help determine the most appropriate content for the EPPP (Richman, 1982). In the first phase of the study, a blue-ribbon panel of 10 psychologists representing clinical, counseling, industrial/organizational, school, and academic psychology described professional psychology in terms of five performance domains, 19 roles, and 49 knowledge statements. Their work was submitted to a group of 80 selected psychologists who evaluated the elements of the role delineation in terms of importance for entry-level practice and to a group of 90 Fellows of the American Psychological Association (APA) who rated the domains and roles for importance and measurability in a multiple-choice test format. Based on these evaluations, the knowledge statements were discarded and the document was trimmed to four domains of practice and eight professional roles. In 1981, a second panel of well-known psychologists added a fifth domain of practice, combined two of the roles, and wrote 58 new knowledge statements linked to the roles and domains. The revised document was submitted to a sample of over 1000 psychologists, of whom 432 rated the elements on six scales, including, for example, importance for entry-level practice and frequency of performance. The final document was submitted to the ASPPB Board of Directors and Examination Committee. With only minor additional changes, the new test specifications were used to develop Forms 16–25 of the EPPP administered from April 1982 to October 1986. Table 1 contains a summary of the test specifications based on the role delineation study.

The importance of the role delineation study in the history of the EPPP cannot be overestimated. For the first time the examination, which, by 1982, was being administered to over 4000 licensure candidates annually, had a systematically derived content outline; one that changed its focus from broad scientific knowledge to knowledge required for safe and effective practice. Perhaps more significantly, it was the first time in the history of the practice of psychology in the USA that there was a consensus as to what constituted performance as a professional psychologist.

Table 1 Summary of EPPP test specifications: April 1982–October 1986.

Domain I: Techniques for appraising and assessing (25–30%)

Role 1: Select, modify, and use psychological assessment techniques/instruments
Requires knowledge of:

1. Widely used psychological tests
2. Limitations and appropriate uses of techniques of behavioral assessment
3. Limitations and appropriate uses of paper-and-pencil tests
4. Standards for test construction
5. Sources of information about psychological assessment techniques
6. Standards of test administration and release of test information
7. Procedures for assessing presenting problems
8. Behavioral effects of disabilities and mental retardation

Role 2: Interpret and report results of assessments
Requires knowledge of:

1. Standard procedures for reporting test scores
2. Modalities for the communication of results
3. Methods of presentation of recommendations for interventions
4. Statistical issues in the interpretation of test scores
5. Relationships between test results and diagnosis
6. Symptom patterns of major diagnostic categories of psychopathology
7. Effects of major psychotropic drugs
8. Relationships between psychological theories and assessment
9. Social determinants of behavior
10. Signs of organizational effectiveness
11. Techniques for matching abilities, skills, and interests to job specifications

Domain II: Design, implementation, and assessment of intervention (25–30%)

Role 3: Design, implement, and evaluate an intervention plan
Requires knowledge of:

1. Components of an intervention plan
2. Major psychological intervention theories
3. Major psychological intervention techniques
4. Psychotherapy research
5. Demographic and environmental assessment techniques
6. Indications and contraindications for matching clients with interventions
7. Community resources
8. Current educational processes/programs
9. Organizational processes
10. Organizational consultation techniques
11. Techniques for identifying measurable goals
12. Record keeping requirements
13. Forms of pre- and postevaluation
14. Process evaluation
15. Peer review techniques
16. Program evaluation
17. Time-line goals
18. Indicators of client acceptance of interventions

Domain III: Uses of the psychological literature (15%)

Role 4: Interpret and apply general psychological literature
Requires knowledge of:

1. Developmental psychology
2. Individual differences and intelligence
3. Information process and thinking
4. Learning and memory
5. Personality and social behavior
6. Physiological basis of behavior
7. Psychological systems and theories
8. Psychopathology
9. Sensation, perception, motivation, and change
10. Specialty areas (e.g., biofeedback, women, forensic)
11. Specialty areas (e.g., clinical, counseling, school, industrial)

Table 1 (continued)

Domain IV: Techniques of research (15%)

Role 5: Design and implement research
Requires knowledge of:
1. Research designs
2. Experimental artifacts
3. Data presentation
4. Test construction
5. Theories of test construction
6. APA and division 14 standards for test construction and validation
7. Elementary computer technology
8. Statistics

Domain V: Professional and ethical issues (18%)

Role 6: Evaluate activities within the limitations of professional, ethical, and legal statutes
Requires knowledge of:
1. APA Code of Ethics
2. Legal issues

2.12.2.2 The Job Analysis of Licensed Psychologists

Role delineation studies are based upon expert judgments of professional practice roles and responsibilities and the knowledge required for their performance. Job analyses are typically based upon direct observations of and/or interviews with job incumbents. In 1981, in an attempt to assemble this type of direct evidence of what constituted the professional practice of psychology, ASPPB selected Educational Testing Service (ETS) to perform a job analysis of licensed psychologists. The ETS job analysis (Rosenfeld, Shimberg, & Thornton, 1983) began with the development of a job analysis inventory based on the duties and responsibilities of psychologists gathered from a literature search, two advisory committees, and interviews with approximately 100 licensed psychologists. A draft job analysis inventory was field-tested on a sample of 150 licensed psychologists. Data received from 80 respondents were used to produce a final inventory containing three broad areas of practice, 59 responsibilities, and 111 knowledge and technique statements. The inventory was mailed to 2994 licensed psychologists in the USA and Canada. Usable responses were received from 1585 individuals, of which 1307 (82%) were clinical, counseling, school, or industrial psychologists, representing the four major practice areas of licensed psychologists.

Factor analyses of the ratings of the 59 responsibilities were used to produce four job dimensions: research and measurement; intervention; organizational applications; and assessment. Of the 111 knowledge and technique statements, 62 were used by at least half of the respondents in the four major practice areas, and 49 of the 62 were rated as important and frequently used. When these 49 knowledge and technique statements were examined for their correlations with the four dimensions, 38 significant linkages were found. The authors concluded that the 38 knowledge and technique statements represented an important body of psychological knowledge frequently applied by licensed psychologists in the four major practice areas.

It should be noted that the job analysis project did not result in the production of new test specifications for the EPPP. It did, however, produce a wealth of new information about the practice of psychology by licensed psychologists. Based on these findings, the authors offered numerous recommendations for the production of a new EPPP content outline including: (i) review of the linkages between the knowledge and technique statements and the dimensions of practice by an independent panel of experts; (ii) further definition of the knowledge and technique statements in operational terms; and (iii) determination of the best assessment mode (e.g., oral vs. written examination) for each of the knowledge and technique statements. Of particular interest was the investigators' statement that:

> The job analysis study has shown that, despite differences on their work settings, client populations, nature of problems, and techniques used, licensed psychologists, in general, share many common responsibilities and use many of the same knowledge and techniques in their work.(p. IX-2)

This statement, and the data upon which it rested, served as the justification for the continued development of the EPPP as an examination measuring broad, general knowledge of psychology. Table 2 contains a summary of the ETS job analysis findings.

2.12.2.3 The Test Specifications Revision Project

In 1985, ASPPB selected PES to undertake a project to produce revised test specifications for the EPPP (Rosen & Mirone, 1986). To accomplish this task, data from the two previous studies, the role delineation and the job analysis, were used. The methodology of the study was similar to the role delineation. A panel of 25 experts representing the four major areas of professional psychology produced an initial document consisting of six dimensions of practice, 58 responsibilities, and 58 knowledge and applications statements. The selection of these particular elements was based on the panel's ratings of professional level, importance, public protection, and most appropriate assessment method. The 58 responsibilities showed considerable overlap and were subsequently reduced to nine by a process of combining and rewording. The 58 knowledge and technique statements were linked to the nine responsibilities. The panel was unable to link nine of the knowledge and applications statements, and thus their number was reduced to 49.

In the final phase of the project, a second panel of experts reduced the number of dimensions from six to five, linked the nine roles to the five dimensions, confirmed the linkages of the knowledge and applications statements to the responsibilities, and, through a process relying on their pooled judgments, provided weights for the dimensions and responsibilities. As a result, the EPPP had a new set of test specifications based on a role delineation, a job analysis, and an extended review by two additional representative panels of experts. Table 3 contains a summary of the revised EPPP test specifications used to develop Forms 26–46 administered from April 1987 to October 1996.

2.12.2.4 The Test Specifications Enhancement Project

In 1990, ASPPB selected PES to conduct a small project, suggested by Werner (1989), to review the EPPP test specifications, examine the accuracy of item classifications, and provide recommendations for improving the effectiveness of the test development process (Smith & Greenberg, 1991). The project used a representative panel of psychologists to review the accuracy of classification of a sample of 176 items, draft recommendations for a set of test construction quality control procedures, and suggest clarifications to the wordings of the dimensions, responsibilities, and knowledge and application statements. Of the 176 items reviewed, 94% were found to be classified correctly. Incorrectly classified items were reclassified or dropped from the item bank. The review of the test specifications resulted in the minor rewording of one dimension and several of the responsibilities and knowledge and application statements. Finally, a set of guidelines was submitted to the Examination Committee for its use in the test development process. While the test specifications enhancement project did not result in any significant changes to the EPPP test specifications or the examination development process, its findings lent significant credibility to both.

2.12.2.5 The Study of the Practice of Licensed Psychologists in the USA and Canada

In 1993, ASPPB requested that PES conduct an analysis of the practice of licensed psychologists in the USA and Canada. Developing a new set of test specifications for the EPPP was only one of the purposes of the study. The others were: (i) to update the list of responsibilities and knowledge required for safe and effective professional practice by licensed psychologists; (ii) to provide a basis for communicating the contemporary role of the licensed psychologist to the public and third-party healthcare payers regarding the scope of professional psychological practice; and (iii) to identify current and emerging practice areas for reviewing educational curricula, schools, training programs, continuing education programs, and specialty recognition initiatives (Greenberg, Smith, & Muenzen, 1995).

The project was conducted in collaboration with a five-member oversight committee and a 12-member representative panel of psychologists. The oversight committee was responsible for policy decisions, selecting the members of the panel, and performing reviews of draft and final survey and practice delineation documents. The panel produced the draft and final practice delineations and reviewed data analyses and results. They also selected the subject-matter experts who took part in the complementary data collection activities.

The practice analysis produced five roles with four groups of underlying responsibilities, and

Table 2 Summary of the findings of the ETS job analysis study.

Dimension I: Research and measurement

Responsibilities:
1. Determine research design for a study
2. Analyze data
3. Observe, record, or collect data
4. Prepare written reports of research
5. Develop methods of assessing critical variables
6. Identify methods of assessing critical variables
7. Define questions to be answered
8. Identify the problem to be studied
9. Develop proposals for research studies
10. Evaluate relevant literature
11. Adhere to guidelines for the conduct of research
12. Assist others in understanding the implications of research findings
13. Keep abreast of professional and scientific developments
14. Serve as an expert witness

Knowledge and techniques:
1. Data collection techniques
2. Test construction
3. Validity concepts
4. Reliability concepts
5. Test fairness
6. Research and experimental design
7. Basic statistics
8. Advanced statistics
9. Sampling theory
10. Criterion measures

Dimension II: Intervention

Responsibilities:
1. Plan intervention strategies
2. Discuss alternative courses of action
3. Set realistic goals
4. Obtain informed consent
5. Provide assistance on personal/organizational problems
6. Recommend services of other professionals
7. Maintain liaison with other service providers
8. Monitor and evaluate effectiveness of interventions
9. Modify intervention strategy

Knowledge and techniques:
1. Interviewing techniques
2. Observational techniques
3. Stress management techniques
4. Conflict management techniques
5. Consultation techniques
6. Human growth and development
7. Learning
8. Personality
9. Individual differences
10. Perception
11. Intelligence
12. Ethical guidelines
13. Specialty guidelines

Dimension III: Organizational applications

Responsibilities:
1. Evaluate the physical and technological environment
2. Evaluate the human resource needs of the organization
3. Conduct cost-benefit analyses
4. Provide assistance in modifying programs or systems

Table 2 (continued)

Knowledge and techniques:
1. Decision-making strategies
2. Learning
3. Motivation
4. Cognition
5. Reliability concepts
6. Organizational morale

Dimension IV: Assessment

Responsibilities:
1. Select instruments, techniques, or procedures
2. Administer and score instruments, techniques, or procedures
3. Interpret and evaluate results
4. Integrate assessment data with other information
5. Prepare a report of findings and diagnosis/problem definition

Knowledge and techniques:
1. Group tests of mental ability
2. Diagnostic tests
3. Tests of social maturity
4. Measures of self-concept
5. Standardized test procedures
6. Personality
7. Motivation
8. Perception
9. Cognition
10. Intelligence
11. Test construction
12. Test scores and norms
13. Strengths and limitations of assessment procedures
14. Validity concepts
15. Reliability concepts
16. Factors affecting test performance
17. Coaching and practice
18. Test fairness

eight content areas each with an underlying group of knowledge statements. The roles included direct service, outreach and consultation, academic preparation and professional development, research and evaluation, and other. The responsibilities were grouped under four of these headings: direct service (e.g., plan, design, and implement intervention programs); outreach and consultation (e.g., disseminate knowledge of psychology and its value to the general public); academic preparation and professional development (e.g., provide mentoring to students and/or professional psychologists); and research and evaluation (e.g., apply research findings to practice). The eight content areas were: assessment and diagnosis; biological bases of behavior; cognitive–affective bases of behavior; ethical/legal/professional issues; growth and lifespan development; research and evaluation; social and multicultural bases of behavior; and treatment/intervention. Only the eight content areas are weighted for test construction purposes. The roles and responsibilities are used primarily as an aid in the item development process (K. Midkiff, PES, personal communication, August 21, 1996). For a complete description of the practice analysis project and the content areas and knowledge statements contained in the test specifications now used to develop the EPPP see Chapter 11, this volume.

Comparisons with previous versions of the test specifications reveal some interesting changes. First, the specifications now contain subject-matter areas (i.e., content areas) from psychology as an academic discipline (e.g., biological bases of behavior, growth and lifespan development). The two earlier versions essentially confined themselves to a strict practice-related format. Practice relatedness is important for legal defensibility because it helps to ensure that an examination will only contain

Table 3 Summary of EPPP test specifications: April 1987–October 1996.

Dimension I: Problem definition/diagnosis (26%)

Responsibility 1: Conduct interviews, observe and gather information from client/patient and relevant others
Requires knowledge of:
1. Techniques of behavioral assessment
2. Theories and principles useful in identifying patient needs and problems
3. Factors affecting behavior
4. Symptoms of common physical diseases and psychophysiological reactions and syndromes
5. Effects of major psychotropic drugs and common prescription drugs on behavior, affect, and cognition

Responsibility 2: Select, administer, and score instruments and techniques and interpret results
Requires knowledge of:
1. Techniques for testing and/or measuring relevant characteristics
2. Concepts relating to tests and measurement

Responsibility 3: Organize and evaluate collected information, plan for additional information as needed, and formulate a working hypothesis
Requires knowledge of:
1. Techniques of data organization
2. The APA's *Diagnostic and statistical manual of mental disorders* (1997) Fourth edition

Dimension II: Design, implementation, and assessment of interventions (26%)

Responsibility 4: Design, conduct, and evaluate interventions and programs to promote effective functioning
Requires knowledge of:
1. Intervention techniques
2. Attitude and value formation and modification techniques

Dimension III: Research (17.5%)

Responsibility 5: Design and implement research and report conclusions and recommendations
Requires knowledge of:
1. Methods of inquiry
2. Research design
3. Experimental artifacts
4. Statistics

Dimension IV: Professional, ethical, and legal issues (16.5%)

Responsibility 6: Take steps to ensure adherence to professional, governmental, and judicial guidelines and regulations for professional and scientific activities
Requires knowledge of:
1. Ethical, professional, and legal issues

Dimension V: Applications to social systems (14%)

Responsibility 7: Develop, conduct, evaluate, and modify intervention strategies and programs designed to promote effective functioning within the social system
Requires knowledge of:
1. Factors affecting the quality of work life
2. Performance evaluation and/or appraisal methods
3. Consultation models and techniques
4. Work sample and other performance tests
5. Decision making strategies
6. Factors affecting the morale of social systems
7. Organizational structures and processes
8. Group dynamics

Responsibility 8: Evaluate the physical, technological, and social environments of the system
Requires knowledge of:
1. Evaluation techniques for physical, technological, and social environments

Responsibility 9: Evaluate the human resource needs of the system
Requires knowledge of:
1. Techniques for the evaluation of human resource needs

items requiring knowledge related to safe and effective practice. However, there is no reason why content areas cannot also be included in practice-related test specifications, as long as the relationship to practice has been demonstrated. Furthermore, the inclusion of content areas helps make the test specifications more meaningful to licensure candidates because these terms are much closer to those used by them as descriptors of what they have learned.

While the new test specifications document continues the ASPPB policy of ensuring that the EPPP is based on current practice, it is not without some potential problems. Although many of the problematic features appear in the unweighted portions of the test specifications, they are still worth noting and are potentially important. For example, the category "other" listed among the five roles seems particularly unfortunate. It is defined as job-related knowledge which is not role specific, but no responsibilities or knowledge statements have been delineated for it. Such "waste-basket" categories can serve as a tempting means of using items that do not properly fit the test specifications. That is, if a item cannot be correctly classified, it can always be put in the "other" category and used anyway. Also, it is arguably the case that the test specifications contain some elements that are not appropriate to entry-level practice. Possibly problematic is the role, academic preparation and professional development, which includes the development, implementation, and administration of educational programs for psychologists. Another element in this category is content area 4, knowledge statement 8, which specifies models and approaches for training and supervision of self and others. Finally, some of the content areas of the test specifications could benefit from clearer wording. For example, "growth and lifespan development" might be better termed "developmental bases of behavior," making it parallel with several other categories.

2.12.3 CONSTRUCTION, ADMINISTRATION, AND SCORING OF THE EPPP

2.12.3.1 Item Development

The EPPP is constructed from a bank of items developed and maintained by PES. Approximately four times per year, PES conducts an item-writing workshop in a different region of the USA or Canada. Licensed psychologists and, occasionally, advanced graduate students are invited to participate. PES supplies instructional materials and item-writing assignments to participants in advance of the workshop. The participants are asked to write a specified number of items prior to the workshop. Most of the time spent during the meeting consists of critical reviews of the previously prepared items. Most items undergo significant revisions and some are discarded. All retained items are checked for accuracy of classification. When these tasks are completed, the remainder of the workshop time is devoted to the writing and review of additional items. Some workshops are specifically targeted to address shortage areas in the item bank.

2.12.3.2 Test Construction

The EPPP is constructed by the Examination Committee with the assistance of PES. The committee meets twice each year in January and June. At the January meeting work is begun on the EPPP form to be administered in October of the same year. The process begins with a draft examination prepared by PES. The draft consists of the previous October's form with approximately 70 items removed, based on a review of item analysis data and item usage information, and between 80 and 90 items added from the EPPP item bank. The committee reviews each item individually and removes or revises items as it sees fit. PES records the instructions of the committee and executes the changes after the meeting. Also, at the January meeting, the committee reviews for a second time the EPPP form to be administered in April of the same year. The April form will have had its first review at the committee's meeting the previous June. Once again, the committee reviews each item individually and makes revisions and deletions. The PES staff record the committee's instructions and keep a tally of the item classifications. After the committee has completed its second review of the April examination form, additional item deletions and substitutions from the item bank are made to bring the examination into conformity with the test specifications. A third and final review of the examination is done by mail after the meeting. The June meeting is identical to January, except that the October form receives a second review and the form for April of the following year is reviewed for the first time.

2.12.3.3 Test Administration

The EPPP is administered by the ASPPB member boards. However, the boards must administer the EPPP in the manner and on the dates specified by ASPPB. This means that all procedures in the Manual of Instructions (PES, 1995a) and all ASPPB policies and procedures must be followed. The examination contains 200, four-option multiple-choice questions and its timed portion is four hours long. The testing session begins with the administration of an optional, nine-item candidate background survey. After the survey has been completed, the test booklets are distributed and the standardized instructions are read to the candidates. The timed portion of the test administration begins immediately thereafter. Candidates with documented disabilities and/or impairments may be tested under nonstandard conditions. Extra testing time is the most common nonstandard condition. However, large-print and Braille examinations are routinely made available. Other special accommodations include readers, signers, and other amanuenses. Some jurisdictions routinely provide extra testing time to candidates who are not native speakers of English. It is the policy of ASPPB to encourage member boards to provide reasonable accommodations to candidates with disabilities or impairments.

2.12.3.4 Scoring

Immediately following test administration, answer sheets are returned to PES for scanning and scoring. Prior to final scoring of the EPPP, PES performs and reviews an item analysis to determine if there are any statistical data that suggest that any of the 200 items may be problematic. This includes miskeyed items, items with no defensible correct answer, and items with more than one defensible correct answer. The results of the item analysis review are discussed with the chairperson and other members of the examination committee. Occasionally, outside experts in a particular subject area are also consulted. Also considered are comments received from examinees. (When tested, candidates are informed that any comments submitted in writing to PES during the two-week period following the examination will be considered in the final scoring process of the EPPP.) Items deemed problematic, if any, are either rekeyed (i.e., have the key corrected) or multiply keyed (i.e., have more than one option scored as correct). EPPP scores are always based on 200 items. Scores are reported by PES to the member boards which, in turn, notify the candidates of their test results and licensure decisions.

It is important to note that all licensure decisions are made by the boards. Neither PES nor ASPPB participate in the licensure decision process. They do, however, provide information that is sometimes used as an aid in the process. For example, along with the examination results, PES supplies a cumulative data table which provides normative information (number, range, mean, and standard deviation), on seven categories of examinees (e.g., all doctoral candidates, doctoral first-time candidates, all masters degree candidates). Many boards continue to use these data for passing score determination. PES also provides an equipercentile equating table that links scores on the just administered form of the EPPP to a base form. The equating table is used by several boards that employ criterion-referenced passing scores. In 1992, ASPPB conducted an investigation into performance on the EPPP, passing score determination procedures of its member boards, and passing scores applied by the boards. As a result of the study, ASPPB formally recommended a uniform passing score of 70% for the EPPP. It was hoped that the use of a uniform passing score by the member boards would enhance the geographical mobility of licensed psychologists by simplifying the process of licensure by endorsement. To date, over 30 boards have adopted the suggested uniform passing score.

2.12.4 CANDIDATE PERFORMANCE ON THE EPPP

Candidate performance on the EPPP has shown remarkable stability over time. For example, EPPP Forms 26–42, administered from April 1987 to April 1995, had an overall mean and standard deviation of 147.9 and 3.0, respectively (PES, 1995b). Scores in the part of the distribution where most passing scores fall, 130–150, are even more stable. It is common for the PES generated equating table to show passing score adjustments of only 0–2 points within this interval of scores.

2.12.4.1 Background Survey Data

ASPPB and PES have graciously made available rarely published data on candidate performance on the EPPP. Specifically, they have provided the numbers, means, and standard deviations of EPPP scores associated with five of the questions on the background survey administered with the EPPP. While most candidates respond to the survey, they are not required to do so. Furthermore, there is no way to verify the accuracy of their responses. Nevertheless, the data, presented in Table 4, clearly provide interesting information on the EPPP and the licensure candidates who sit for it.

For example, graduates of APA accredited programs do better on the EPPP than others. In 1995, 87% of the survey respondents specialized in clinical (57%), counseling (23%), or school (7%) psychology. Indeed, the smallest identified specialization is industrial–organizational psychology (0.5%). This is ironic, given ASPPB's commitment to the representation, some might say overrepresentation, of industrial–organizational psychologists on its expert panels in all its studies of psychological practice. Finally, and it should come as no surprise, the more candidates study for the EPPP the better they tend to do. While there is a slight downturn at the highest level of preparation, the trend is clear. Thus, the best advice for doing well on the EPPP, as with most achievement tests, remains, "study hard!"

2.12.4.2 The Educational Reporting Service

Another source of information on candidate performance on the EPPP is the *Educational Reporting Service: EPPP Performance by Designated Doctoral Programs in Psychology* (ASPPB, 1995b). This listing provides the numbers, means, and standard deviations for

Table 4 1995 EPPP performance data associated with selected background survey response categories.

Response category	*Number*	*Mean*	*SD*
Department awarding highest degree:			
Psychology	4268	144.9	21.1
Educational psychology	997	139.0	21.8
Other	392	137.4	21.4
Graduate of APA accredited program:			
Yes	3000	150.3	19.1
No	770	138.9	21.3
Not applicable	1822	134.0	20.9
Major area of graduate specialization:			
Clinical	3348	146.3	20.9
Counseling	1349	138.2	22.2
School	413	138.5	20.0
Educational	108	137.4	21.7
Developmental	80	145.1	17.3
Community	65	128.5	18.9
Experimental	46	148.0	17.3
Social–personality	34	141.8	20.1
Industrial–organizational	27	143.6	16.0
Other	152	144.0	19.6
Primary professional affiliation:			
Mental health agency	1269	140.9	21.5
Private practice	1016	141.6	21.0
Hospital	830	148.4	20.3
College/university	640	148.2	20.6
School system	501	137.2	21.4
Government	450	141.6	21.7
Medical school/center	266	153.2	17.9
Business	107	133.6	22.7
Research institute	33	150.5	26.6
Other	416	142.8	20.8
Time spent preparing for the EPPP:			
None	47	116.3	26.6
Up to 49 hours	502	129.8	23.9
50–99 hours	1423	142.6	21.6
100–199 hours	1849	147.3	19.7
200 or more hours	1676	144.7	19.4

hundreds of doctoral programs in psychology in the USA and Canada. To be included in the publication a program must meet the requirements for "designation" applied jointly by ASPPB and the Council for the National Register of Health Service Providers in Psychology. The source of the data is candidate self-report at the time of EPPP testing. Tabulations are performed by PES after the October test administration and the publication is revised annually.

2.12.5 RELIABILITY AND VALIDITY OF THE EPPP

2.12.5.1 Reliability

Reliability coefficients (KR_{20}) of EPPP Forms 26–42, administered from April 1987 to April 1995, have ranged from 0.90 to 0.93 (PES, 1995b). Thus, there is little doubt that the EPPP is a reliable instrument. The validity of the EPPP rests primarily upon its content. That is, the EPPP is a valid instrument to the extent that its test specifications are an appropriate representation of the practice of professional psychology and to the extent that test forms accurately represent the test specifications. The above section on EPPP content documents a continuing commitment on the part of ASPPB to study professional practice and to ensure that it is reflected in the test specifications. The mission of the examination committee is to build tests according to the test specifications. The remarkable reliability and stability of candidate performance are indicators of the quality of their work. Other indicators of the validity of the EPPP were seen in Table 4. Where the numbers are large enough to provide stable data, all the major differences in mean scores are in the expected directions.

2.12.5.2 Validity

A digest of EPPP research, including validation research, is published by ASPPB (Rosen, 1991). Included in the document are summaries of criterion-related and content validity studies. The EPPP, like most licensure examinations, has not stimulated a wealth of validation research. Such studies are not easy to conduct. Data are sometimes unavailable for a variety of legal reasons, including confidentiality. Criterion-related validity studies often confirm the obvious, as can, in some cases, be seen in Table 4. Predictive validity studies are essentially impossible to conduct, for practical as well as theoretical reasons, and may be entirely inappropriate for licensure examinations (Rosen, 1986). Content validity studies are of the greatest importance for licensure examinations, but they are relatively costly. Furthermore, because of the need to safeguard the security of examination related materials, they are typically performed by the agency sponsoring or owning the licensure examination, its testing company, or some other carefully selected agent.

2.12.5.2.1 Construct validity

Several researchers have demonstrated that as education in psychology increases, scores on the EPPP increase (Hayes & Mullins, 1978; Hayes & Schreimer, 1978; Terris, 1973). These studies assumed that the Ph.D. represents the highest degree, followed by the other doctorates. While holders of the Ph.D. in psychology continue to outscore others, the gap between them and licensure candidates with Ed.D. and Psy.D. degrees has greatly narrowed in the last decade (PES, 1995b). Other research has demonstrated that among undergraduate majors in psychology, members of honors programs or honorary societies perform better on the EPPP than others (Shrader, 1980). Tipton, Elder, and Ritz (1988) showed that graduates of APA accredited programs outperform graduates of nonaccredited programs. These findings are supported by the background survey data cited above. Kupfersmid and Fiala (1991) demonstrated that EPPP performance of graduates of APA accredited clinical and counseling programs is superior to the performance of graduates of school psychology programs and nonaccredited clinical and counseling psychology programs.

The largest construct validity study of the EPPP was conducted by Hoffman and Aderet (1984) with funding from ASPPB. The authors collected graduate school grades and EPPP scores for 866 psychologists. They discovered that: (i) patterns of mastery of psychology displayed during training were positively correlated with EPPP performance; (ii) candidates from APA accredited programs scored significantly higher than candidates from nonaccredited programs; (iii) EPPP performance was significantly higher for candidates who had been undergraduate psychology majors, particularly among counseling psychology majors; and (iv) candidates with specialties in clinical psychology performed significantly better than candidates from school, counseling, and educational psychology.

2.12.5.2.2 Content validity

As stated above, content-validity studies are the most important part of any validation strategy for licensure examinations. Two such studies of the EPPP are summarized here. Readers desiring more extensive content-validity information on the EPPP are referred to Smith, Hambleton, and Rosen (1988) and Rosen (1991).

Smith (1984) used three panels of experts to review the accuracy of item classifications and rate items for their contribution to the public protection function of the EPPP. The study demonstrated that the EPPP items could be readily classified into the roles in the test outline, although there was less success with knowledge statements. It was noted, however, that knowledge statements were not weighted elements of the test specifications.

Hambleton and Smith (1988) performed a content-validity study of the first two EPPP forms developed with the test specifications adopted in April 1987. Two panels of judges classified 400 items according to the responsibilities and knowledge statements in the test specifications and performed a fairness review of the items. Using an extremely stringent criterion of classification accuracy, the investigators determined that approximately 65% of the items were correctly classified as responsibilities and 52% were correctly classified as knowledge statements. The panelists identified seven items requiring additional review for fairness issues. However, none of these items was found to contain offensive stereotyping. All 400 were deemed appropriate for use on a generic licensure examination.

2.12.6 FUTURE DIRECTIONS FOR THE EPPP

2.12.6.1 Specialty Examinations

While almost all the licensure laws in North America remain relatively general, several states (e.g., Indiana) have adopted new laws which make distinctions between psychologists who are health service providers and others. If this trend continues, one logical consequence will be a growing demand for examinations that also recognize this distinction. It seems reasonable that when such differences are codified into law, different examinations become appropriate for the licensure candidates falling into the different categories. One problem associated with separate examinations has to do with the numbers of candidates who might require specialized examinations. As was shown in Table 4, almost all the EPPP candidates (over 85%) come from clinical, counseling, or school psychology programs. Frankly, there would not be enough candidates to justify the costs involved in developing specialized versions of the EPPP. One possible solution to this problem might be the development of a core examination to be taken by all candidates, with shorter specialty examinations for health service vs. nonhealth service providers in psychology.

2.12.6.2 Overseas Use of the EPPP

ASPPB has maintained a long-standing relationship with the European Federation of Psychology Associations. The two organizations have been exploring the possible use of the EPPP outside North America. In 1994, a version of the EPPP was administered in English in Scandinavia to a small sample of psychologists from the Nordic countries. This effort was part of a pilot project to determine the possible relevance and utility of the EPPP for licensure purposes in Europe. While the outcome of the pilot test has not been made public by ASPPB, it remains an indication of interest in the EPPP. ASPPB routinely receives requests for information about the EPPP from psychological associations and regulatory agencies in other countries. While it is unlikely that forms of the EPPP as administered in North America would be useful in the credentialing of psychologists in other parts of the world, it is clear that ASPPB is the most experienced entity when it comes to the regulation of psychological practice, and has much to share concerning the development and administration of a psychometrically sound licensure examination.

2.12.6.3 Computer Administration of the EPPP

ASPPB has tentative plans to begin computer administration of the EPPP by the year 2001 and has contracted with PES to perform pilot studies to gather information needed to support the decisions that must be made as part of the transition. These decisions bear upon examination equivalence, test security procedures, the psychometric testing model to be employed, and numerous administrative matters that are affected by a conversion from paper-and-pencil to computer-based testing. Moving to computer-administered examinations will remove the burden of test administration from the ASPPB member boards and enhance the standardization of testing conditions across test sites. Depending upon the mode of testing used, candidates may have the opportunity to take examinations by appointment at any of hundreds of locations. Testing may be available year round or during several predetermined testing periods. Scores may be made available to candidates immediately upon completion of the examination or just a few days thereafter. Thus, a major benefit to the candidates will be the increased availability of the examination and faster knowledge of results. This could well expedite hiring, promotions, and salary increases for many psychologists.

2.12.7 SUMMARY

The EPPP is a well-designed and well-constructed examination. Since it was first administered in May 1965 to one licensure candidate in West Virginia, ASPPB has endeavored to effect steady improvement in the EPPP. Those efforts have been most apparent in the years since 1978 when the first comprehensive effort to develop test specifications was undertaken. The improvements to the EPPP test specifications and studies of its content validity have continued on a consistent basis since the first project began. The examination is extremely reliable and has well-documented content validity. The criterion-related validity studies of the EPPP have all produced results that have supported the contention that it is a valid examination. The item development methodology provides an opportunity for psychologists throughout North America to participate in the overall process of test development. The test construction procedures employed by ASPPB, with the support of PES, provide the experts who serve on the ASPPB Examination Committee with the necessary time and opportunity to ensure that each form of the examination is thoughtfully produced and fully representative of the test specifications. In all relevant aspects, the EPPP conforms to the *Standards for Educational and Psychological Testing* (American Educational Research Association, American Psychological Association, & National Council on Measurement in Education, 1985). In short, the EPPP is a reliable and valid instrument that is a highly effective tool for the evaluation of candidates for licensure or certification as psychologists.

2.12.8 REFERENCES

American Educational Research Association, American Psychological Association, & National Council on Measurement in Education (1985). *Standards for educational and psychological testing*. Washington, DC: American Psychological Association.

Association of State and Provincial Psychology Boards (1995a). *Information for candidates: The Examination for Professional Practice in Psychology* (brochure). Montgomery, AL: Author.

Association of State and Provincial Psychology Boards (1995b). *Educational reporting service: EPPP performance by designated doctoral program in psychology*. New York: Professional Examination Service.

Carlson, H. (1978). The AASPB story: The beginnings and first 16 years of the American Association of State Psychology Boards, 1961–1977. *American Psychologist, 33*, 486–495.

Greenberg, S., Smith, I. L., & Muenzen, P. M. (1995). *Study of the practice of professional psychologists in the United States and Canada* (Executive summary). New York: Professional Examination Service.

Hambleton, R. K. & Smith, I. L. (1988). *Content validity and fairness review of the 1987 forms of the Examination for Professional Practice in Psychology (EPPP)*. New York: Professional Examination Service.

Hayes, J. R. & Mullins, D. (1978). Background characteristics of psychologists taking the Examination for Professional Practice in Psychology. *Texas Psychologist, 30*, 1–6.

Hayes, J. R. & Schreimer, R. (1978). Comparison of degree received and performance on the licensing examination. *Psychological Reports, 40*, 42–49.

Hoffman, P. J. & Aderet, A. (1984). *Empirical validity of the EPPP*. Los Altos, CA: COGITAN.

Kupfersmid, J. & Fiala, M. (1991). Comparison of EPPP scores among graduates of varying psychology programs. *American Psychologist, 46*, 534–535.

Professional Examination Service (1995a). *Manual of instructions for the Examination for Professional Practice in Psychology*. New York: Author

Professional Examination Service (1995b). *Annual report on the licensing examination program of the Association of State and Provincial Psychology Boards*. New York: Author.

Richman, S. (1982). *Final report to the American Association of State Psychology Boards on the role delineation study for the Examination for Professional Practice in Psychology*. New York: Professional Examination Service.

Rosen G. A. (1986). A perspective on predictive validity and licensure examinations. *Professional Practice of Psychology, 7*, 116–123.

Rosen, G. A. (1991). *Research digest: The Examination for Professional Practice in Psychology*. Montgomery, AL: Association of State and Provincial Psychology Boards.

Rosen, G. A., & Mirone, J. A. (1986). *Final report of the test specifications revision project*. New York: Professional Examination Service.

Rosenfeld, M., Shimberg, B., & Thornton, R. F. (1983). *Job analysis of licensed psychologists in the United States and Canada*. Princeton, NJ: Educational Testing Service.

Shrader, R. R. (1980). Validation studies on the Examination for Professional Practice in Psychology. *Professional Practice of Psychology, 1*, 23–30.

Smith, I. L (1984). *Content validity study of the AASPB item bank*. New York: Professional Examination Service.

Smith, I. L. & Greenberg, S. (1991). *Final report for the test specifications enhancement project*. New York: Professional Examination Service.

Smith, I. L., Hambleton, R. K., & Rosen, G. A. (1988). Content validity investigations of the Examination for Professional Practice in Psychology. *Professional Practice of Psychology, 9*, 43–80.

Terris, L. D. (1973). The national licensing examination. *Professional Psychology, 4*, 386–391.

Tipton, R. M., Elder, D. D., & Ritz, S. (1988). Performance on the national licensure examination as a function of program specialty and APA accreditation status. *Professional Practice of Psychology, 9*, 81–89.

Werner, E. (1989). *Analysis of the validity of the Examination for Professional Practice in Psychology*. Sacramento, CA: California Department of Consumer Affairs.

2.13
An Assessment Tool in Credentialing: The Oral Examination for Licensure

DIANE S. HILL
Somerville and Company Inc., Denver, CO, USA

2.13.1 INTRODUCTION

The modern history of oral examinations used for credentialing purposes began in 1917 with the first administration of a medical specialty examination. A publication by the American Board of Medical Specialties (Mancall & Bashook, 1995) notes that physicians, like psychologists, have long argued over the viability of oral examinations as part of a credentialing process. At the time of writing, 34 of the 61 North American jurisdictions (Association of State and Provincial Psychology Boards [ASPPB], 1996) that license psychologists use an oral examination as part of a multimodal assessment strategy. Since the field of psychometrics is a domain within the discipline of psychology, we might hope and expect that psychology licensure examinations are beyond reproach. Most psychologists who have endured the rigors of a licensing examination would argue that there is room for improvement.

While this state of affairs is perhaps disappointing for the profession and its practitioners, it should not be all that surprising. Licensing boards have to balance an array of competing legal, technical, cultural, and resource considerations when developing their assessment strategies. Boards adopt a variety of procedures to carry out their gate-keeping function in the service of public protection. At the same time, state, provincial, and federal laws obligate boards not to restrict the rights of professionals to practice their trade. In some states and provinces the political and cultural climate favors an open free market that keeps restrictions to a minimum. In other jurisdictions there is acute awareness and concern over the possibility that incompetents and charlatans will visit harm upon the public. All psychology licensing boards believe in developing reliable and valid assessment procedures. Some have more resources than others with which to do so. Within the context of these often competing concerns and commitments, boards continually strive to carry out their gate-keeping responsibilities with ever-increasing skill and efficacy. Some form of oral examination will, in all likelihood, continue to be part of a multimodal assessment strategy in over one-half of the jurisdictions in North America.

The purpose of this chapter is to serve as an introduction to the use of oral examinations for licensure. It outlines the reasons why boards include the oral examination as a licensing requirement; defines three distinct prototypes; discusses the significant methodological issues; lists some of the pros and cons; and describes future directions. The writer has adapted this manuscript from an earlier manual sponsored by the ASPPB (Hill, Edwards, Crawford, & Warner; 1986). The authors wrote that publication as a guide to best practices for licensing boards that were currently using, or hoped to start using, an oral examination. The purpose of this chapter is to provide university faculty, graduate students, interns, and those preparing for licensure with an overview of what to expect in an oral examination. Those who read this chapter will also be in a better position to encourage their particular jurisdiction to use state-of-the-art assessment procedures when evaluating candidates for licensure.

2.13.2 WHY LICENSING BOARDS USE ORAL EXAMINATIONS

Boards use the oral examination to measure job-relevant knowledge, skills, and personal attributes that they cannot readily address using other assessment modalities. Jurisdictions that include the oral examination do so in combination with other assessment instruments and sources of information as part of a multimodal licensing strategy. The oral examination is particularly useful for boards that wish to observe and evaluate a candidate's understanding of the limits of their own competence. Examiners also value the oral format for the opportunity it affords to observe and rate a candidate's ongoing clinical reasoning. Some oral procedures allow examiners to evaluate the degree of consistency between the candidate's stated theoretical framework, and the application of that framework to clinical issues. Finally, some boards use the oral examination to evaluate the impact of a candidate's personal, emotional, and social functioning on their capacity to provide psychological services.

2.13.3 WHAT IS AN ORAL EXAMINATION?

An oral examination involves a process of verbal interaction between a panel of trained examiners and a candidate for a psychology license. It may be general in content or focus on the candidate's area of specialization, depending on the predetermined objectives of the examination. It does not stand alone as an assessment tool. Rather, it provides information that is supplementary to that derived from a written examination such as the Examination for the Professional Practice of Psychology (EPPP). Examiners assign scores on an oral examination based on their ratings of the candidate's verbal responses. They base their ratings on predetermined criteria.

Candidates in an oral examination respond orally to a series of stimuli, in face-to-face interaction with one or more examiners. While the response format tends to be common to all oral examinations, the manner in which different boards choose to present stimuli may vary. If an applicant applies for licensure in a jurisdiction that uses an oral examination, they can expect the examination to feature one or more of the following procedures.

(i) *Oral questions*. This is the simplest and perhaps most common procedure. Each examiner asks the candidate a series of questions. Boards that use oral examinations differ in the extent to which they favor more or less structure. Some predetermine all questions; others use a partially predetermined set of questions. Some boards prefer to develop questions during the examination itself that are consistent with prescribed themes.

(ii) *Written questions*. Examiners may present prepared questions to the candidate in writing, though the candidate responds orally. This procedure has the advantage of assuring consistency across candidates.

(iii) *Work sample*. At a stated time prior to the examination, the board asks each candidate to submit materials from their caseload. Examiners then formulate questions based on these materials.

(iv) *Case presentation*. The candidate describes one or more cases from their own professional experience.

(v) *Standardized vignette*. The candidate observes a scenario illustrating a relevant situation from the practice of psychology. It may depict a sample of a client's behavior during psychotherapy, or another relevant scenario typically encountered by a licensed psychologist. The candidate may encounter the vignette in written, audio, or video form.

(vi) *Live simulation*. Performers may pose as clients exhibiting various behaviors. The candidate may conduct a clinical interview with "the patient" while the examiners observe. Questions from the examiners follow.

2.13.4 TYPES OF ORAL EXAMINATIONS

In developing their examination procedure, all licensing boards face decisions that require them to balance their concern for protecting the public against the importance of preserving fair trade practices. They must also weigh preferences for flexibility and individual tailoring of an examination against requirements for consistency and standardization. As jurisdictions have addressed these issues, they have adopted procedures that fall into one of three broad categories: (i) the structured oral examination, (ii) the semistructured examination, and (iii) the unstructured examination. While this division into categories is useful, it is also arbitrary, because the degree of structure varies along a continuum. However, in order to develop a clearer picture of the possible approaches to the oral examination, it is useful to compare the three prototypes along the following dimensions:

(i) *Content*. The structured examination consists of predetermined specific questions or standardized stimuli (e.g., scenarios), with specified ratings or scoring criteria for answers. For example, if the scoring system employs a five-point rating scale, the examiners have in front of them sample answers worth five points, three points, and one point, to guide their ratings. There is a set examination format and sequence that does not permit deviations.

The semistructured examination comprises a set of predetermined specific situations that are applicable to groups of candidates (e.g., candidates in clinical psychology, counseling psychology, industrial psychology). Boards also prepare initial questions ahead of time. During the examination, however, the examiners may deviate from these situations and questions, or seek clarification of the candidate's responses.

Boards that use unstructured examinations usually tailor them for each candidate. They prepare examination themes, rather than individual questions, for each candidate, taking into account, for example, his or her academic background, work experience, or theoretical orientation.

(ii) *Content consistency across candidates*. Consistency across candidates is highest in the structured examination and lowest in the unstructured examination. It can be high in the semistructured examination, depending on how the board develops and uses situations and questions. It is highest in the structured examination because every candidate must respond to the same situations and questions, regardless of his or her background or theoretical orientation.

(iii) *Tailoring of questions to the candidate*. The structured examination, does not allow for spontaneous or tailored questions, so that all candidates receive the identical examination. In the semistructured examination, examiners develop tailor-made questions based on the examination blueprint. These questions frequently complement an initial uniform set of questions asked of all candidates. The unstructured examination consists of questions that are specific to each candidate's background, experience, and theoretical approach. Examiners specifically formulate questions for that person around preselected common examination themes.

(iv) *Formulation of questions in view of prior responses*. The structured examination does not allow for questions that derive from a candidate's prior responses. Those who train the examiners instruct them to remember that the quality of a candidate's responses to different questions may vary widely. They make every effort not to allow themselves to be influenced by prior answers when recording their ratings. In semistructured examinations, follow-up questions are appropriate and often essential. The opportunity to follow up on a candidate's response is a significant strength of the unstructured approach. Candidate responses typically lead to further probing from the examiner.

(v) *Scoring*. The structured examination includes specific rating scales for each item. Authors of the examination define anchor points on the rating scale using sample answers for each question. The semistructured examination uses a series of predetermined scoring categories, each with specific rating scales. The scoring categories are broader than the dimensions used for the structured examination. Within each scoring category, there may be both mandatory and suggested areas of questioning. Examiners record ratings independently for each scoring category. In the unstructured examination, examiners rate the candidate's performance on the basis of relatively broad, preselected dimensions (for example, the candidate's awareness of his or her own limits of competence).

(vi) *Examination development costs.* Costs tend to be the highest for the structured examination, relatively high for the semistructured, and lowest for the unstructured examination.

(vii) *Duration.* The structured examination is potentially the shortest, since authors of the examination have preselected the questions and specific scoring criteria, and examiners do not engage in spontaneous interaction with the candidate. The semistructured examination may be of intermediate duration, because it permits unplanned interactions but does not require them. The unstructured examination is potentially the longest, as it is most likely to include spontaneous questions and the examiners may delve into areas suggested by the candidate's previous answers.

(viii) *Decision alternatives.* Theoretically, the decision alternatives are not inherent to any examination format. Each of the three formats may lead to any of the decision alternatives described below. However, the following paragraphs describe the decision alternatives typically associated with each of the three oral examination formats.

The structured examination typically yields a pass or fail decision from the panel of examiners. A prototypical semistructured examination might yield one of the following decisions: pass, fail, or re-examine. Boards reserve this last recommendation for split or unclear decisions. In such cases, they often conduct the re-examination immediately using another panel of examiners.

The unstructured examination yields a recommendation of pass, or defer judgment. In other words, examiners recommend that candidates who do not pass sit for re-examination at some future date. The panel's recommendation stems from the combined overall ratings of the individual examiners with or without preliminary discussion of the individual ratings among examiners.

Regardless of the format of the examination, the examining panel communicates its recommendation to the board following the examination. In all cases, the decision authority rests with the board. The outcome of any oral examination, therefore, is a recommendation to the board by the examining panel.

(ix) *Postexamination feedback to candidates.* In theory, the nature of the postexamination feedback provided to the candidate is independent of the examination format. In practice, somewhat different types of feedback accompany prototypical unstructured, semistructured and structured formats. Following a prototypical structured examination, the candidate typically receives written feedback as numerical subscores on particular items. Because proponents of structured, examinations favor treating all candidates equally, this strategy does not usually allow for qualitative feedback concerning performance during the examination.

After a prototypical semistructured oral examination, candidates may receive feedback either orally or in writing. Boards base their feedback on generic scoring categories (each of which subsumes a number of items or questions), and it is likely to be qualitative rather than numerical. The panel provides feedback after it makes its recommendation. In the unstructured situation, the chair of the examining panel frequently provides verbal feedback to the candidate. The feedback typically consists of qualitative statements about the candidate's strengths and weaknesses, and may include remedial suggestions. Examiners do not provide feedback until they have finalized their recommendation.

(x) *Ratings of relevant personal characteristics of a candidate.* Examining panels may observe and rate personal characteristics of a candidate that are relevant to the practice of psychology. Typically, they use separate rating scales and criteria, even when they are not the object of direct questioning. In the unstructured and semistructured formats, information that the board receives on the candidate's behavior during the examination may warrant direct questioning in this area. Jurisdictions vary in the degree to which they believe that rating of relevant personal characteristics is an appropriate activity for a licensing examination. Those who favor ratings of this type argue that such evaluations are the responsibility of the board and essential for public protection. Those who oppose such ratings argue that lack of objectivity in this type of measurement leaves too much room for examiner bias.

The three types of oral examinations outlined here are prototypes or illustrations rather than descriptions of actual examinations that might be encountered on the road to licensure. In reality, the examination procedures adopted by a particular jurisdiction are a function of historical and cultural precedent, financial resources, and the knowledge, skill, and experience available to apply to the task. Each approach has its advantages. High structure increases ease of computing quantitative psychometric properties, but reduces flexibility, the ability to customize, and spontaneous interaction.

2.13.5 RELIABILITY

"Reliability" refers to consistency of measurement. Indices of reliability compare the proportion of error variance with that of true variance. There are a number of ways of estimating reliability, and examining boards typically apply one or more to their oral examination. Standard 11.3 of the revised *Technical standards for educational and psychological testing* (American Psychological Association [APA], 1985) states that boards should provide estimates of the reliability of licensure or certification decisions.

One study (Novy, Kopel, & Swank, 1996) examined two sources of error variance in the June 1992 administration of the Texas oral examination. This board uses a moderately interactive oral examination based on vignettes that are developed for four different subdisciplines of psychology: clinical, counseling, school, and industrial–organizational. These investigators found that indices of inter-rater reliability were quite high. Only five of the 22 coefficients of agreement calculated fell below 0.85. The authors noted, however, that indices of equivalence across vignettes in the same discipline were less than optimal. Generalizability coefficients that took into account error variance attributable to both raters and vignettes were as follows: clinical, 0.70; counseling, 0.55; and school, 0.65. This small but suggestive study points to a need to attend to equivalency measures in addition to measures of inter-rater reliability when developing oral examinations.

The ASPPB and experts in the field of measurement have, however, taken the position that inter-rater reliability is the most appropriate form of reliability when evaluating oral examinations. The principal purpose in all licensing examinations, including orals, is to arrive at a pass or fail decision concerning each candidate. For this reason, reliability procedures typically focus on the extent to which the examiners reach a final recommendation. This ultimate objective for the licensure process has been used to argue that efforts to establish reliability should focus on examiner's ratings rather than on candidate's responses. The *Technical standards for educational and psychological testing* (APA, 1985, p. 5) define inter-rater reliability as the "consistency of judgments made about people or objects among raters or sets of raters." It is particularly important to assess inter-rater agreement when observational data involve subtle discriminations, as is the case in oral examinations.

Differing perceptions on the part of examiners is the source of error variance that has received the most attention from those interested in oral examinations. To the extent that examination authors and administrators can minimize those disagreements, reliability will increase. The following measures will help to minimize examiner error and increase reliability:

(i) It is important that all examiners are clear about the purpose of the examination. Written guidelines on purposes and procedures are essential.

(ii) Examiners should obtain an outline of appropriate themes, vignettes, or items to ensure that the major elements of the examination are clear and receive appropriate coverage.

(iii) Criteria for scoring should be explicit.

(iv) Two or more examiners should be assigned to each candidate.

(v) Board members need to take responsibility for ensuring that examiners receive training.

(vi) Each examining team should have at least one member who has previous examining experience.

(vii) Board members should monitor the examination sessions by either observing selected sessions or reviewing tape recordings.

(viii) Candidates need to have adequate time to respond to the questions and situations posed in the examination.

2.13.6 VALIDITY

The validity of an assessment instrument refers to the extent to which the test measures what it purports to measure. It tells us what we can infer from test scores. Procedures for determining the validity of a test or examination explore the relationships between performance on the test and other independently observable behaviors. Psychometricians who develop assessment procedures have an array of validation techniques from which to choose. These fall into three distinct but related categories: content-validation procedures, indices of criterion-related validity, and construct-validation strategies. Numerous texts on tests and measurement describe these different methods of assessing the validity of a test. The focus of this discussion is on the content-validation procedures that North American boards are using to answer two questions: (i) Does the test cover a representative sample of the skills and knowledge required for entrance to the independent practice of psychology? (ii) Is performance on the licensing examination reasonably free from the influence of irrelevant variables?

Studies published in the early 1980s (Kane, 1982; Shimberg, 1981) argued convincingly that content validity, rather than criterion-related validity is appropriate for licensing examinations. The validation strategies that apply to personnel selection and those that pertain to licensing are different. Employers often validate personnel selection tests that identify the best among qualified candidates using criterion-related approach. Licensing examinations, in contrast, differentiate between candidates who possess the knowledge, skills, and personal attributes necessary for independent practice, and those who do not. Licensing examinations are most appropriately validated by obtaining evidence of content validity.

The steps that have been taken to create a valid, state-of-the-art national multiple choice examination (the EPPP) can prove helpful to boards interested in developing reliable and valid oral examinations. The process for establishing content validity is a well established one. It is also very costly. It consists of six basic steps: (i) conducting a job analysis, (ii) developing test specifications, (iii) developing a content outline, (iv) constructing an examination blueprint, (v) writing the oral examination proper, and (vi) cross-validating the judgments of the oral examination writers. Other contributors to this volume describe in detail the steps required for developing valid credentialing examinations (see Chapters 10–12 and 14, this volume). The procedure will receive a brief review here to give the reader an idea of the time, money, and expertise necessary to create reliable and valid oral examinations.

(i) *The job analysis.* Over the past 15 years, the ASPPB has commissioned three studies that form the basis for the development of valid credentialing examinations. The Professional Examination Service (PES) has conducted two of them (Greenberg, Smith, & Muenzen, 1995; Richman, 1982), and the Educational Testing Service has conducted one (Rosenfeld, Shimberg, & Thornton, 1983). These job analyses are the source of valuable data concerning what psychologists do on the job and the knowledge and skills necessary for the practice of psychology. Boards committed to developing state-of-the art oral examinations should review these studies as they develop their test specifications. The purpose of the job analysis is to provide a comprehensive description of the roles, responsibilities, and knowledge required for the independent practice of psychology.

(ii) *The table of test specifications.* The PES has also developed two sets of test specifications based on these job analyses. Because these test specifications are based on comprehensive studies of what psychologists do on the job, they also provide an appropriate basis for the development and content validation of other licensing examinations in psychology, including the oral examination. To the extent that jurisdictions view the EPPP and oral examinations as instruments intended to provide complementary but relevant information about candidates for licensing, the content outlines for both instruments would ideally originate from a common table of test specifications.

Once the job analysis and test specifications are complete, the next step is to develop a content outline. Because there is no coordinated effort among jurisdictions to develop oral examinations, each board creates their own. Boards vary considerably in the extent to which they have the resources available to complete steps (iii)–(vi).

(iii) *Developing a content outline.* In order to complete this step, boards need to determine which statements from the table of test specifications they can most appropriately measure using an oral format. The content of the oral examination should complement rather than repeat what other instruments or sources of information already address. For example, one study (Richman, 1982) suggests that the multiple-choice format of the EPPP does not particularly suit the measurement of complex inferences and deductions in decision-making. Boards that use oral examinations would therefore do well to consider including this skill in the content outline of the oral examination.

(iv) *The development of an examination blueprint.* The blueprint is a statement of what any one examination will cover. A given examination typically covers a sample or subset of topics included in the content outline. The sampling procedure will vary depending on the board's purpose in using an oral examination. For example, if a jurisdiction is committed to a generic oral examination, it may first identify statements from the content outline that merit inclusion in every oral examination. Next it may identify the remaining statements to be included through a stratified random sampling procedure. The number of statements selected is a function of practical considerations such as intended format and length of the examination.

Some state boards (e.g., Iowa) use the oral to examine a candidate's knowledge of laws relevant to the practice of psychology. In this case, knowledge and skill statements that relate to jurisprudence are the only statements sampled. Other boards have various rationales for tailoring their examinations to individuals or groups of individuals. The Louisiana board members, for example, believe that it is important to identify for the public a psychologist's particular area of specialization. In this case, the board primarily selects knowledge and skill statements that relate to the candidate's specialty.

(v) *Writing the oral examination.* The next step is to write the oral examination for any given administration. This step consists of writing the themes, scenarios, or questions that correspond to the final examination blueprint. What examination authors write depends both on the nature of the statements that comprise the blueprint and on the format of the oral examination (structured, semistructured, or unstructured). This step includes not only the writing of items, situations, or themes, but also the development of appropriate rating or scoring criteria. Because the writing of items, scenarios, or themes is a judgmental rather than an empirical activity, it should involve licensed psychologists in the process. Ideally, each panel of writers would include members of groups (e.g., ethnic minorities) that the jurisdiction has reason to believe might be at risk of being given an unfair or biased oral examination.

(vi) *Cross-validation of examination writers' judgments.* The task of developing items, situations, or themes that reflect the final blueprint is one which requires judgment. Therefore, a panel of independent experts should determine whether the oral examination as written is an accurate reflection of the blueprint. The board should select this panel on the basis of comparable criteria to those used for the selection of examination writers. Particularly when the review panel includes members of relevant minority groups, this step provides an additional opportunity to ensure that the examination does not include inappropriate biases or potentially discriminatory items.

The procedures described above are well recognized in the field of psychometrics. There is nothing particularly mysterious or technologically difficult about the process of creating content-valid oral examinations. The process of creating a reliable, valid, and multimodal examination strategy that includes an oral examination is not an especially arcane one. However, it is costly in terms of time, money, and expertise. Most boards simply do not have the resources to adopt all the above procedures vigorously. Many boards use some or most of them. However, until there is greater coordination of effort and resources among the psychology licensing boards in North America, many oral examinations will remain less than state-of-the-art. This topic is discussed at greater length in Section 2.13.9.

2.13.7 SCORING

Boards should score all oral examinations using well-defined, pre-established rating criteria. Test authors should provide the examiners with rating sheets that list the dimensions on which they are to rate the candidate's performance. Rating sheets need to include rating scales with verbal descriptors of the points on the scale. The dimensions on which examiners rate the candidate's performance vary depending on the format of the examination. For example, examiners rate performance on a structured examination according to specific rating criteria that they apply to predetermined questions. Raters on an unstructured examination assign ratings along a limited number of relatively broad categories. Examiners may rate performance on a semistructured examination according to both broad and specific criteria, as this approach incorporates elements of the structured and unstructured examinations.

Boards need to decide in advance how to combine these ratings into a judgment about whether or not to license the candidate. For example, a jurisdiction that uses five-point Likert scales may wish to add the scale scores so as to derive a total score, and establish a specified cut-off or passing score. Another jurisdiction may assign more weight to some dimensions than to others. Many combining formulas are possible. The essential point is that the formula is pre-established, with a defensible cut-off point. A cut-off point is defensible to the extent that it demonstrably differentiates between candidates who are ready for independent practice and those who are not.

Finally, for the scoring system employed by any jurisdiction to be defensible, boards need to train examiners in the use of the rating criteria and rating sheets before the examinations begin.

2.13.8 PROS AND CONS OF ORAL EXAMINATIONS

Boards favor oral examinations because they believe that the procedure measures factors that contribute unique information to a certification decision. At least two studies, one in our own profession and one in medicine, suggest that this is the case. PES conducted the first study in the mid-1980s (Rosen & Mirone, 1986). In this investigation, the researchers asked a panel of seven raters to review the 1986 test specifications and to indicate which assessment technique (multiple choice, essay, structured oral, interactive oral, or simulation) most appropriately applies when measuring the knowledge application or skill associated with each statement. The main finding of this pilot project was that the multiple-choice format was less well-suited than others, including the oral examinations, to the measurement of complex inferences and deductions, especially as they relate to decision-making.

More specifically, this small but suggestive study indicates that the oral examination is more appropriate than the multiple-choice format for assessing many of the skills required to define and diagnose problems. Raters favored the oral examination as a tool for measuring a candidate's ability to apply appropriate knowledge to the task of selecting, developing, and interpreting certain diagnostic tests. They also saw the oral examination as superior to a multiple-choice procedure in measuring the candidate's ability to use certain skills, such as stress-management techniques, and apply knowledge of learning, individual differences, or motivation in designing, implementing, and assessing interventions. Finally, raters saw the oral examination as the tool of choice for measuring the ability to apply some kinds of ethical and legal knowledge to the conduct of scientific and professional activities.

More recently, the American Board of Medical Specialties sponsored a symposium on using oral examinations to assess clinical learning. The proceeds from that meeting are available (Mancall & Bashook, 1995) and make informative reading for anyone interested in the use of oral examinations for credentialing purposes. All the papers included in the compendium support the thesis that some form of oral examination is superior to other techniques for assessing a professional's ability to reason and make judgments. One author (Reinhart, 1995) describes a predictive validity study that asked the question: Does the oral examination predict actual performance in a diplomate's own emergency department cases? The investigators developed a standardized method to assess emergency physicians' performances based on their own patient charts. Predictive-validity measures indicated that the correlation between oral examination performance and physician performance on the job was 0.45. Performance on the oral examination was more strongly associated with performance in the emergency department than performance in the written examination. The authors concluded that the oral examination does, in fact, predict physician performance, and that it measures some aspects of performance not assessed by the written examination.

A further study suggested that the oral examination added unique information to the certification decision in the arena of clinical competence, composure when managing a patient, ability to solicit clinical data, and use of consultants. Taken together, these two studies offer valuable insight about where to look for the unique contributions of the oral examination in our own profession. They also suggest some methodological possibilities for investigating the validity of an oral examination over and beyond content validity.

In addition to these empirical studies demonstrating the advantages of the oral format, there are a number of widely held beliefs about the value of the oral examination that await confirmation using more formal research techniques. The two basic questions that studies should address are: (i) Is a particular skill or knowledge demonstrably related to a psychologist's ability to practice independently at an entry level? (ii) Is the skill or knowledge best measured in an oral format?

The list of knowledge and skills that require further investigation includes: (i) interactive skills relevant to the practice of psychology; (ii) consistency between a candidate's theoretical framework and the application of this framework to clinical problems; (iii) the candidate's ability to apply the knowledge and skills of the profession to concrete situations; (iv) the candidate's personal functioning in relation to his or her ability to provide sound psychological services; (v) the candidate's ability to reason and make decisions; and (vi) the candidate's knowledge of the limitation of his or her skills and competence.

Other advantages of the oral examination pertain to one or more of the distinct prototypes described. It is also the case that these advantages are more controversial, and while favored by some may be viewed as problematic by others.

In its unstructured or semistructured formats, the oral examination has the advantage of *flexibility*. Not all jurisdictions, however, would view flexibility as advantageous. Jurisdiction that stress the need to examine all candidates in a consistent manner are likely to consider flexibility a disadvantage. Jurisdictions that tailor parts or all of the examination to individual candidates value the potential flexibility of the oral format. The flexibility of unstructured and semistructured oral examinations gives the following advantages:

(i) The candidate may seek clarification of questions from the examiners.

(ii) The examiners may seek clarification or expansion of answers from the candidate.

(iii) Examination themes or questions can be tailored to the specific background and specific career interests of individual candidates.

(iv) Unusual or seemingly inappropriate responses or comments from a candidate may be followed up by the examiners even when not foreseen before the examination.

(v) The examination may include informal comments from the examiners. For example, the examiners may include certain remarks intended to welcome the candidate to the profession of psychology.

In its structured format, the oral examination offers the potential advantage of *consistency* of measurement across candidates. Jurisdictions that favor giving all candidates the opportunity to demonstrate their competence through the same assessment instrument(s) will probably favor a structured format. This format has the following advantages:

(i) There are specific scoring criteria for all answers. Examination authors develop sample answers that define points on a rating scale in advance. This procedure may reduce error variance in ratings and enhance their objectivity.

(ii) Examiner training may be facilitated by the fact that all examiners learn to rate responses to exactly the same questions.

(iii) Because all candidates are given the identical opportunity to demonstrate competence, there may be less likelihood of charges of unequal or discriminatory treatment by failed candidates.

(iv) Although most jurisdictions have adopted a generic approach to licensing, many offer one or more examinations in different specialty areas. Such jurisdictions, if they wish to employ the structured format, would use the same examination for all candidates in any one specialty area (e.g., clinical psychology), but different examinations across specialty areas.

While the oral examination format offers many advantages, including those described above, it is not without potential measurement and practical shortcomings. The following are important potential limitations, of which users should be aware:

(i) *Measurement limitations or shortcomings*:

(a) Reliability may be below acceptable standards unless well-developed rating scales are used by properly trained raters, and boards calculate and continually work to improve the equivalency coefficients for similar forms of the oral examination.

(b) Allegations of subjectivity or examiner bias are probable unless special precautions are taken to ensure that the examinations are developed and administered in a fair and impartial manner.

(c) Failure to establish and maintain rapport may lead to contamination of examination results if this omission causes undue stress for the candidate.

(ii) *Practical limitations or shortcomings*.

(a) Many knowledge and skill items that are relevant to the practice of psychology are more validly and/or reliably measured by other examination modalities than the oral (e.g., by written examinations such as the EPPP, or by written simulations). Licensing boards should therefore use the oral examination in conjunction with other instruments and sources of data.

(b) The oral examination is human resource intensive, costly, time consuming, and relatively difficult to develop, administer, and score.

The manual published by ASPPB (Hill et al., 1986) argues that the oral examination is the preferred modality for assessing integration and problem solving skills, interpersonal skills, theoretical orientation, personal attributes, and verbal skills. The argument rests on the notion that an examination fulfills its potential only when boards use proper construction, administration and scoring procedures. The authors also note that the national multiple-choice examination (EPPP) is complementary to the oral format in measuring the knowledge and many of the skills required for independent practice. Boards may use the EPPP and the oral examination for complementary purposes, thereby enhancing the validity of the overall assessment process.

2.13.9 FUTURE DIRECTIONS

At present, oral examinations for licensing serve a valuable purpose, but they are not as useful as they might be. The major problems associated with the oral examination derive from the limited resources available to individual boards for their development.

Although the use of oral examinations by licensing boards has become increasingly sophisticated, and will no doubt continue to do so, problem areas remain including the following:

(i) *Lack of reciprocity*. Candidates who have passed an oral examination in one jurisdiction and wish to be licensed in another frequently have to take a new oral examination. Boards could facilitate and enhance the quality and cost-effectiveness of their examinations if jurisdictions with common oral examination objectives cooperated in their development.

(ii) *Duplication of efforts*. At present, each jurisdiction develops its own oral examination. This process is necessarily wasteful of human and financial resources. Boards could reduce such duplication of efforts by jointly developing oral examinations with other jurisdictions that share their examination objectives.

(iii) *Limitations imposed by the licensing acts*. The requirements of psychology licensing acts vary across jurisdictions. In some instances, the act places explicit limitations on the number or types of licensing examinations that a board may use. In most instances, however, common oral examinations could be used across jurisdictions, provided that such examinations are developed through a cooperative effort.

(iv) *Lack of item pools.* At present, few jurisdictions have access to adequate pools of oral examination questions. Such pools are important to the effective use of structured and semistructured oral examinations. Sharing of item pools among jurisdictions with common oral examination objectives and formats represents a potential solution to this problem.

When all is said and done, the fact remains that individual jurisdictions are still responsible for determining their candidate's competence to practice. Solutions to these problems, therefore, will depend on voluntary participation by jurisdictions. There are legitimate obstacles to such cooperation and sharing at present. Among these, the need to maintain the confidentiality of the examination content and specific rating criteria is foremost. Cooperation and sharing are desirable, however, and should be increasingly possible in the not too distant future.

Positive strides in this direction are already in progress. Six North American jurisdictions (Iowa, Kentucky, Manitoba, Missouri, Oklahoma, and Ontario) have signed the North American Reciprocity Agreement. Three boards (Kentucky, Missouri, and Oklahoma) have formed a second consortium and signed the ASPPB Reciprocity Agreement. In order to participate in either of these agreements, a jurisdiction must use an oral examination when it licenses candidates. The purpose of these agreements is to facilitate mobility for psychologists residing in member jurisdictions. Psychologists who wish to move from Iowa to Kentucky, for example, are not required to retake the EPPP or an oral examination. They will only be tested on laws relating to the practice of psychology in their new jurisdiction.

If the trend toward forming agreements designed to remove barriers to mobility continues, jurisdictions may begin to see the wisdom of pooling resources to create more reliable and valid oral examinations. The hope for the near future is that boards with similar objectives will find ways to cooperate in executing the costly and time-consuming steps required to upgrade the reliability and validity of their oral examinations. A longer term solution may well be for the ASPPB to commission an appropriate vendor to develop one or more oral examinations that would be purchased and administered by individual jurisdictions.

2.13.10 REFERENCES

American Psychological Association (1985). *Technical standards for educational and psychological testing.* Washington, DC: Author.

Association of State and Provincial Psychology Boards (1996). *Handbook of licensing and certification requirements for psychologists in North America.* Montgomery, AL: Author.

Greenberg, S., Smith, I. L., & Muenzen, P. M. (1995). *Executive summary: Study of the practice of licensed psychologists in the United States and Canada.* Montgomery, AL: Association of State and Provincial Psychology Boards.

Hill, D. S., Edwards, H. P., Crawford, W., & Warner, J. (1986). *Oral examinations for licensing or certification: A manual for psychology boards.* Montgomery, AL: American Association of State Psychology Boards.

Kane, M. T. (1982). The validity of licensure examinations. *American Psychologist, 37,* 911–918.

Mancall, E. L. (Ed.) (1990). *The oral examination: An historical perspective.* Evanston, IL: American Board of Medical Specialties.

Mancall, E. L., & Bashook, P. G. (Eds.) (1995). *Assessing clinical reasoning: The oral examination and alternative methods.* Evanston, IL: American Board of Medical Specialties.

Novy, D. M., Kopel, K. F., & Swank, P. R. (1996). Psychometrics of oral examinations for psychology licensure: The Texas examination as an example. *Professional Psychology: Research and Practice, 27,* 415–417.

Reinhart, M. A. (1995). Advantages to using the oral examination. In E. L. Mancall & P. G. Bashook (Eds.), *Assessing clinical reasoning: The oral examination and alternative methods* (pp. 31–40). Evanston, IL: American Board of Medical Specialties.

Richman, S. (1982). *Final report to the American Association of State Psychology Boards on the role delineation study for the examination for professional practice in psychology.* New York: Professional Examination Service.

Rosen, G. A., & Mirone, J. A. (1986). *Final report of the test specification project for the Examination for Professional Practice in Psychology.* New York: Professional Examination Service.

Rosenfeld, M., Shimberg, B. S., & Thornton, R. (1983). *Job analysis of licensed psychologists in the United States and Canada: A study of responsibilities and requirements.* Princeton, NJ: Educational Testing Service.

Shimberg, B. S. (1981). Testing for licensure and certification. *American Psychologist, 36,* 1138–1146.

2.14
Credentialing Issues, Current and Future: United States and Canada

STEPHEN T. DeMERS
University of Kentucky, Lexington, KY, USA

2.14.1 INTRODUCTION

This chapter is intended to increase awareness of both the history and the current and future concerns relative to the professional regulation of psychologists in the USA and Canada. The mechanisms of professional regulation include the development of standards for professional preparation, the promulgation of codes of professional conduct and ethics, the adoption of credentialing mechanisms and, finally, the implementation of disciplinary procedures. In the USA and Canada, professional regulation is accomplished through an interplay between professional societies, such as the American (APA) and Canadian (CPA) Psychological Associations, and legislatively mandated regulatory bodies such as psychology licensing boards. This chapter focuses on the role of psychology licensing boards in the regulation of the profession and the current and future issues that licensing boards, licensed psychologists and the public face with respect to the credentialing and discipline of psychologists.

For purposes of brevity, states and provinces are referred to throughout the text as jurisdictions. The term "regulatory body" is used to refer to the legally appointed, elected, or otherwise constituted agency within a jurisdiction to regulate the profession of psychology. In US jurisdictions, the regulatory body is often called the board of psychology, whereas in Canadian jurisdictions, the regulatory body in psychology may be referred to as a register, college, association, corporation, or board.

2.14.2 HISTORICAL PERSPECTIVE ON PSYCHOLOGY LICENSURE

According to *Webster's New World Dictionary* (1986), a profession is described as a calling or vocation involving specialized knowledge, long and intensive preparation, a commitment to public service, and a commitment to high standards of performance and conduct. Numerous authors (Gross, 1978; Newton, 1988; Weissman, 1984), have described the hallmarks of a profession. These include the presence of professional organizations that standardize and advance the development of the field, recognized academic programs that offer degrees documenting the specialized training necessary to competently practice the profession, codes of ethics, and a process whereby entry to the profession is controlled and monitored.

Members of a profession are usually identifiable by a license or certificate issued by a legislatively mandated professional regulatory body. Such regulatory bodies are typically empowered by state or provincial statutes to identify by training, experience, and examination the competent members of the profession, and to discipline incompetent or negligent practitioners in order to protect the public from harm. One of the hallmarks of psychology's emergence as a recognized profession was the passage of psychology licensing laws in states and provinces in the USA and Canada.

Another aspect of regulation is the process of disciplining members of the profession who violate the public trust. Professional associations and regulatory bodies adopt and promulgate ethical standards and codes of professional conduct in psychology (APA, 1992; Association of State and Provincial Psychology Boards [ASPPB], 1991; CPA, 1991) Both professional associations and psychology regulatory boards adjudicate complaints and impose sanctions on those association members and licensed psychologists found guilty of misconduct. The rationale for this professional self-regulation is based on the belief that the average citizen is not competent to judge appropriate professional behavior, and thus professionals should be regulated by their peers.

Although interest in regulation of professions can be traced to ancient times, professional licensing in the USA is a fairly recent phenomenon. A more complete description of the history of psychology regulation is given by Sinclair, Simon, and Pettifor, (1996). In 1888, a landmark US Supreme Court decision (*Dent v. West Virginia*, 1889) legitimized the policing powers of state government over the professions when these powers are used to protect the health and welfare of the public. By 1912, nearly all states and provinces had medical practice acts. The first psychology licensing act was passed in Connecticut in 1945. As for most early psychology laws, the Connecticut law protected the title of "psychologist" but did not preclude others (particularly physicians) from using psychological methods. Ontario passed the first licensing law for psychology in Canada in 1960. By 1977, all states had passed some form of psychology regulation and, in 1990, Prince Edward Island was the last Canadian province to enact a psychology licensing law. Currently there are 61 psychology regulatory boards throughout the USA and Canada including the 50 states, nine provinces, the District of Columbia, and Guam (ASPPB, 1997).

As more states followed Connecticut's lead, there was a growing need for a common standard of training and a common examination to aid the identification of competent psychological practitioners. This need for a common examination was the impetus for the creation of the American Association of State Psychology Boards in 1961. (The organization's name was changed to the Association of State and Provincial Psychology Boards in 1992.) The organization started with representatives from 21 member jurisdictions with licensing laws for psychologists.

The organization's early focus was on the development of a common examination. In 1964, the Association administered the first version (i.e., Form 1) of the Examination for Professional Practice of Psychology (EPPP) to one candidate in Virginia. By the time Form 2 was completed in 1967, it was administered to 122 candidates from 15 states. The EPPP has always been a multiple choice test with items written by an examination committee of content experts across various specialties in psychology. The original EPPP had 150 items, however, this number gradually increased to 200 items where it has remained since 1969. The EPPP has undergone numerous validation studies. Currently, the EPPP is administered twice each year to approximately 5700 candidates in 61 member jurisdictions across the USA and Canada. It is available in both French and English language versions.

The Association has expanded its mission over the years, beyond the examination program to include the development of model licensing laws and an ASPPB Code of Conduct (ASPPB, 1991), development of a disciplinary data system, and an educational program including an annual convention and midwinter meeting, newsletters, publications and other training materials, and programs for members of regulatory bodies.

2.14.3 MISSION OF PSYCHOLOGY REGULATORY BOARDS

As noted earlier, the main purpose of psychology licensing laws is to protect the public from unqualified, incompetent, impaired, or unethical individuals who seek to provide psychological services to the public. Consumer groups and many psychologists themselves misperceive the mission of psychology regulatory boards as focused on protecting the profession. However, the mission, and the activities pursued by boards to accomplish that mission, are clearly focused on protection of the public. Psychology regulatory boards accomplish their mission through two main activities, namely, issuing credentials to qualified and competent practitioners, and investigating complaints against practitioners who are already credentialed. Each of these main activities involves several aspects that are described in more detail in the sections below.

2.14.3.1 Credentialing Qualified Practitioners

Psychology licensing acts are designed to protect the public by identifying and credentialing only those individuals who are qualified and competent to practice psychology safely and ethically. Psychology regulatory boards accomplish this goal by establishing strict standards for educational preparation and supervised experience, and by administering examinations to measure the professional knowledge and skills of the applicant for licensure. Each jurisdiction establishes specific educational requirements for licensure as a psychologist including degree level and type (e.g., Ph.D., Ed.D., Psy.D., M.S., M.A., M.Ed.), program of study (e.g., must be a doctoral degree in psychology), institutional accreditation (e.g., must be regionally accredited in the USA or recognized by Royal Charter in Canada), and specific course content (e.g., program must include courses in professional ethics, research methods, diagnosis and assessment, treatment interventions, etc.).

Similarly, each jurisdiction adopts specific requirements for supervised professional experiences prior to licensure eligibility. For example, one state may require two years of full-time supervised experience, one year of which must be postdoctoral, whereas another may require only one year which may be the predoctoral internship year (ASPPB, 1997). Finally, each jurisdiction also adopts one or more examinations that applicants for licensure must pass at specified levels. Almost all psychology regulatory boards in the USA and Canada use the Examination for Professional Practice in Psychology (EPPP) published by the Association of State and Provincial Psychology Boards (ASPPB) to assess knowledge deemed essential to practice in psychology. The EPPP has been validated over the years through a series of comprehensive job analyses and validation studies. The passing point on the EPPP varies across jurisdictions with most adopting the ASPPB recommended pass point of 70% of the 200 multiple choice items. Some jurisdictions also give oral or written examinations focused on mental health laws, ethics, practice competence, or some combination of these. These so-called complementary exams are typically locally developed, normed or standardized, and scored.

Although the major professional associations such as the APA, CPA, and ASPPB exert considerable influence over members of the profession who serve on licensing boards, the ultimate decisions about setting the educational, supervised experience or examination standards often rests with the legislative body (e.g., state or provincial government) that created and oversees the psychology regulatory board (Retfalvi & Simon, 1996; Wand, 1993). Regulatory boards have the authority and duty to suggest changes in the standards they use, but any party can seek to amend the standards. The final decision about changes to these standards is typically made by a political entity such as a state or provincial legislature and subject to the political forces at work in any locality.

Hence, there is no consistently applied standard of education, supervised experience or examination that is uniform across the USA or Canada. Most psychology licensing acts in the USA require a doctoral degree in psychology for the independent practice of psychology (ASPPB, 1997). A few allow some form of independent practice to persons with a masters degree in psychology and nearly half of the 61 jurisdictions in the USA and Canada allow individuals with masters degrees in psychology to practice as psychological associates under supervision of a licensed psychologist with a doctoral degree (ASPPB, 1997). In Canada, some provinces require standards equivalent to the doctoral standard in most USA states, whereas others grant full independent practice to individuals with masters degrees (Wand, 1993). Also, these educational, supervisory, and examination standards are not static—they change over time as a result of professional association initiatives to raise standards, political opposition to existing standards by some disenfranchized group, or economic forces.

Such diverse and fluctuating requirements for entry into the profession of psychology, both within and across jurisdictions, has resulted in great hardship for licensed psychologists who seek to relocate and find that differences in licensing laws across jurisdictions make them suddenly unacceptable for practice. This same patchwork quilt of licensure standards in psychology has seemed to confuse the public about the training psychologists receive prior to being credentialed to practice. One of the long standing missions of the ASPPB has been to bring greater uniformity across jurisdictions in the standards for licensure so that the public is less confused, and so that practitioners can move more freely across jurisdictions without fear of being denied a license in the new jurisdiction simply because of idiosyncrasies in the new jurisdiction's licensing law.

2.14.3.2 Investigating Complaints

The second major activity that psychology regulatory boards conduct to fulfill their mission is investigating complaints of incompetent or unethical practice against currently licensed practitioners. Each psychology licensing act specifies the grounds for which someone licensed as a psychologist may be disciplined, and the process by which such a charge would be investigated and adjudicated (Reaves, 1996).

Because a license to practice one's profession is clearly a property right of some value and consequence, a governmentally sanctioned process to deny, restrict, or rescind such a license must be conducted with adequate attention to the individual's rights of due process and appeal (Reaves, 1996). In the USA, a psychology regulatory board must provide the following constitutionally specified protections to any individual who is charged with a violation of the licensing act:

(i) adequate notice of the charges against them;

(ii) an opportunity for a fair and impartial hearing;

(iii) an opportunity to confront witnesses against them;

(iv) a decision that is based on the evidence;

(v) a record of the proceedings; and

(vi) some form of appeal or judicial review.

Similar legal protections and processes exist in federal and provincial law in Canada (Reaves, 1996).

Although some complaints are dismissed and others are settled through a negotiated agreement of stipulated conditions of remedy (e.g., mandatory supervision, additional training in ethics, etc.), complaints involving charges of significant misconduct or those charges that are contested are resolved through a hearing process. Before a hearing is scheduled, most jurisdictions in the USA and Canada require that the psychology board must have received a signed, written complaint, conducted an initial investigation of the merits of the charges, notified the psychologist of the specific charges, identified witnesses and subpoenaed documents, and taken any necessary depositions. The hearing itself is conducted in a variety of formats across jurisdictions, depending on local law and the resources available to the regulatory board. In some jurisdictions the hearing is conducted before the regulatory board with the board serving as a panel of inquiry and a decision-making body. In other arrangements, the board is assisted in this process by a hearing officer who serves to rule on motions and arbitrate disputes. In still other situations, the case is heard by the hearing officer alone and a recommendation and transcript of the proceeding is made available to the board which later renders its decision. Following an adverse decision, a psychologist may appeal to a separate legal tribunal (e.g., a circuit court in a state) if they believe they did not receive a fair and impartial hearing of the complaint.

As a result of the hearing, the regulatory board issues its findings of fact and conclusions of law, that is, its findings of what it believes happened and whether such facts constitute a violation of the licensing law. Where a violation is found, the regulatory board may impose an appropriate sanction ranging from a reprimand to a permanent revocation of one's license to practice. Other common sanctions imposed either alone or in combination include suspension of the license, restriction in the type of clients or problem areas addressed (e.g., no children or adolescents because of insufficient expertise with this population, or no forensic evaluations), a return to supervised practice, additional training or education, therapy, restitution of assets, reimbursement of fees, and administrative fines (Reaves, 1996).

According to Peterson (1996), complaints against psychologists have increased substantially since the late 1980s. This may be the result of greater consumer awareness, more vigilant response to complaints from licensing boards, or just better reporting of the same number of complaints that have typically occurred. Since 1983, the ASPPB has maintained a disciplinary data system (DDS) that collects and disseminates summaries of disciplinary actions from its member psychology regulatory boards throughout the USA and Canada. Until 1996, the summary reports of disciplinary actions were disseminated in printed form, first annually, and then quarterly as the number of reports grew. Beginning in 1996, the DDS was placed on-line electronically, whereby jurisdictions could report and retrieve information about disciplinary actions against a specific individual via secured electronic mail, giving regulatory boards immediate and timely access to all disciplinary actions contained in the system.

In a paper (Reaves, 1997) presented at the annual convention of the APA, Randolph Reaves, Executive Director and General

Counsel of the ASPPB, listed the following top 10 reasons for disciplinary action against psychologists in the USA and Canada for the period 1983–1997:

(i) sexual or inappropriate dual relationship with client;

(ii) unprofessional, unethical, or negligent practice;

(iii) fraudulent acts;

(iv) conviction of crime;

(v) inadequate or improper supervision;

(vi) impairment;

(vii) breach of confidentialty;

(viii) improper or inadequate record keeping;

(ix) fraud in application for license; and

(x) failure to comply with continuing education requirements.

According to Reaves (1997), the increase in disciplinary action can be noted through changes in the rate of reporting for several of these categories. For example, in the five years from 1983 to 1988, only 45 psychologists were disciplined for sexual or dual relationships with clients, but in the next 10 years this category increased to a total of 556 actions. Similarly, unprofessional, unethical, or negligent practice jumped from 29 in 1988 to 458 by 1997.

The consequences of being found in violation of the psychology licensing act are not limited to the sanctions imposed by the regulatory board. Reports from the DDS are routinely distributed to other relevant psychology-credentialing or professional associations as well as all regulatory boards (Reaves, 1997). The current distribution list of the DDS includes the ethics committees of the APA, the CPA, the American Board of Professional Psychology (ABPP), the National and Canadian Registers of Health Service Providers in Psychology, and the US Department of Health and Human Services. Given recent government initiatives, media attention and consumer activism, it is quite possible that information from the DDS may soon be made available to the general public through the ASPPB web site as a means for boards to discharge their responsibility to protect the public using modern methods of information dissemination. As a result of such broad distribution, individuals sanctioned by their home board of psychology may find sanctions imposed by other regulatory boards where they hold additional licenses, professional association ethics committees, other credentialing bodies such as the ABPP, or even insurance companies and managed health care providers.

As noted earlier, because psychology regulatory boards are composed of psychologists as well as public advocacy members, many psychologists notified of charges lodged against them expect or hope to receive lenient treatment from their psychologist peers on the board. However, psychologists serving on regulatory boards learn quickly that the role given to them by the legislative act creating the board of psychology requires them to protect the public and not show blind allegiance to the profession.

Furthermore, the rules established to protect the rights of individuals accused of violations necessitates a formal and complete investigation of all complaints, making informal resolution unlikely. However, because the boards of psychology typically decide the issue raised in a complaint, a psychologist unjustly accused can be assured that the panel of individuals who will decide the merits of the complaint is likely to be composed of other psychologists who will understand the conduct of the professional probably better than the average citizen who serves on a civil or criminal jury panel.

2.14.4 CURRENT AND FUTURE ISSUES

A number of challenges to psychology regulation lie ahead, both in the immediate future and the years to come. These challenges include disagreements over the educational standards required to call oneself a psychologist and to practice independently, attempts to redefine the scope of practice regulated by psychology boards (including both expansion of scope of practice to include new areas such as telehealth and prescriptive authority for psychologists, and resistance to encroachments by other professionals into the conduct psychological assessments), and finally, professional and governmental attempts to facilitate the mobility of practitioners both within and between national borders.

2.14.4.1 Educational Standards for Independent Practice

Since the Boulder Conference in 1949 (Raimy, 1950), organized psychology in the USA has espoused the doctoral degree as the entry level for independent practice in psychology. Most licensing laws for psychology passed in both the USA and Canada since Connecticut's first law adopted this doctoral standard in the required education of psychologists for independent practice (Retfalvi & Simon, 1996). A handful of states and provinces adopted the masters degree in psychology, sometimes due to the lack of availability of doctoral level psychologists to fill positions, sometimes due to political forces at work, and sometimes due to concerns about cost, accessibility in rural areas, or other factors. Many colleges and universities continued to prepare individuals at the masters degree level and many early licensing laws contained exemptions from the doctoral standard for state and local government, allowing publicly funded mental health agencies to employ individuals who did not meet the educational requirements for independent practice in that jurisdiction. Also, departments of education in the various American states began credentialing school psychologists for practice in that nation's public schools, and most of these state departments of education adopted a nondoctoral educational standard for independent practice (Fagan & Wise, 1993). All of these factors created a situation where controversy was likely to emerge over the standard for independent practice in psychology.

Such controversy has emerged in recent years in several different ways. Exemptions from licensure requirements for publicly employed psychologists has been challenged by patient advocates, and by professional associations, resulting in the virtual elimination of such exemptions. Individuals with master's degrees credentialed as psychological associates and working under mandatory supervision in jurisdictions allowing for such practice are now seeking to extricate themselves from the supervision requirement by changing licensing laws to allow independent practice with a master's degree. Also, school psychologists with nondoctoral credentials from departments of education are now seeking the right to practice outside the purview of the school without meeting the doctoral standard for independent practice required for such nonschool work in most states. In Canada, several provinces which previously held a doctoral standard similar to the typical state in the USA have rewritten their educational requirements to allow some form of independent practice for individuals trained at the master's-degree level.

Consequently, unlike medicine and law, the profession of psychology in the USA and Canada has never successfully advanced a universally accepted standard of educational preparation for its practitioners. The APA has promulgated standards of accreditation of training programs and model licensing laws, all of which adhere to the doctoral standard (APA, 1995). It remains to be seen if the APA will succeed in maintaining this standard in the years to come.

2.14.4.2 Scope of Practice Issues

Another recent challenge facing psychology has been attempts to expand psychologists' scope of practice into areas such as authority to write pharmaceutical prescriptions and telehealth. In 1997, bills were submitted in several state legislatures in the USA that were designed to amend the psychology licensing act to allow psychologists to write pharmaceutical prescriptions dealing with routine management of mental and behavioral disorders. Early suggestions, that psychologists should seek prescriptive authority, met with considerable resistance within psychology itself. However, recent surveys within the APA have indicated a considerable shift with a majority of practicing psychologists now supporting such authority. Some psychologists who are still opposed cite concerns about practitioners abandoning verbal psychotherapy in favor of writing prescriptions, but most proponents argue that psychologists' extensive training in verbal therapeutic interventions is most likely to result in a balanced and comprehensive treatment regimen should psychologists obtain the ability to prescribe psychoactive medicines as well (Bass, 1996; Deleon & Wiggins, 1996).

For psychology licensing boards, such proposals for change in scope of practice mean opening up licensing laws for amendments to the definition of the practice of psychology. Also, in the legislative arena, a professional group cannot control where the issue will end, resulting in a risk that psychology licensing laws could be altered in unfavorable as well as favorable ways whenever changes in licensing are attempted.

Another aspect of changes in scope of practice involves concerns over the regulation of the practice of psychology and other professions in the age of telecommunications. Licensing laws are premised on the fact that psychological services are delivered in a particular jurisdiction by an individual licensed to practice in that jurisdiction. What happens to regulation when psychological services are delivered to clients via the Internet or other telecommunications system across state, provincial or even national boundaries? If a client feels harmed, to whom do they complain—the board of psychology where they reside, which may have no jurisdiction over an out-of-jurisdiction provider, or the jurisdiction where the provider resides which may feel the activity did not occur in their jurisdiction?

Beyond the complexities of filing complaints, another issue being raised concerns the limits of what constitutes acceptable practice in this medium. Although one can easily think of examples of national or international experts who could and should be available for consultation about rare or specialized cases or topics, should more routine psychotherapy be conducted via electronic bulletin boards for the convenience or benefit of the practitioner or the client. In the absence of any system of national or international licensing, the regulation of psychological services delivered via electronic means is tenuous at best and perhaps nonexistent.

2.14.4.3 Mobility Across Jurisdictions

Given the inconsistency in standards for education and training in psychology across the various states and provinces, and the tendency for most jurisdictions to raise standards for education and supervised experience over time, psychologists licensed in one jurisdiction, particularly those trained perhaps decades earlier, often have difficulty obtaining licenses in new jurisdictions should they choose to relocate. This is true regardless of the fact that the psychologist met all applicable standards at the time they were originally licensed and may have practiced without any disciplinary actions against them for many years. For example, most jurisdictions who are members of ASPPB require 2 years of supervised experience, 1 year of which must be postdoctoral, in order to obtain the initial license to practice. However, such postdoctoral experience was virtually nonexistent as a licensure requirement 20 years previously. Consider, for example, an individual trained and initially licensed 20 years ago, who now wishes to relocate and obtain a license in a jurisdiction that requires a year of postdoctoral supervision.

Most jurisdictions have no mechanism to waive current requirements in such situations because their provisions for reciprocity typically state that the applicant must hold credentials essentially equivalent to the current licensure standards. Regulatory bodies often feel compelled to follow their requirements and procedures rigidly or face challenges from applicants without prior licenses or experience who are also lacking some aspect of qualification and want the board to grant them an exemption or waiver of standards. Obviously, the difference in these situations is that the previously licensed individual has a history of acceptable practice, but bureaucracies often have trouble with recognizing important but perhaps subtle distinctions.

For many years the ASPPB has been pursuing programs designed to facilitate mobility for the benefit of both licensed psychologists and regulatory bodies who are members of the ASPPB. For example, the ASPPB has supported efforts by member jurisdictions to enter into reciprocity agreements. Under the reciprocity agreement approach to mobility, all licensed psychologists in one jurisdiction are eligible for licensure in a cooperating jurisdiction based on evidence of comparable standards in current licensure requirements across jurisdictions. Reciprocity agreements are voluntary arrangements between jurisdictions and, although they are based on comparability in current standards, such agreements require acceptance of all licensed psychologists from a participating jurisdiction regardless of what standards were in place at the time any individual psychologist was originally licensed.

The ASPPB agreement of reciprocity has been in place for several years. However, despite considerable effort and promotion, only eight of 61 member jurisdictions participate. Many jurisdictions do not qualify for the agreement because they do not administer an oral exam, or they do not require a year of postdoctoral supervision. Some jurisdictions do not grant regulatory boards the legal authority to enter into such reciprocity agreements. Finally, despite the fact that many jurisdictions are ineligible or unable to participate in the reciprocity agreement, thousands of individual psychologists in those nonparticipating states and provinces do have the required education, experience and examination performance to meet the standards contained in the reciprocity agreement, but their mobility is not facilitated.

Since 1990, the ASPPB has been working on another more individualized approach to mobility, known as the Certificate of Professional Qualification in Psychology (CPQ) program. This individual certification and credentials bank approach to mobility would offer a repository for licensure-related data and an ASPPB-issued endorsement or certificate to individually licensed psychologists meeting standards for training, examination and professional experience adopted by the ASPPB. ASPPB member jurisdictions would be encouraged to accept holders of the ASPPB certificate as meeting the education, experience and examination requirements for licensure. The individual certification approach to mobility avoids many of the pitfalls that have plagued the widespread adoption of the reciprocity agreement, since it is based on an individual voluntarily demonstrating compliance with ASPPB-recommended standards for mobility.

A central aspect of the CPQ program is creation of an ASPPB credentials bank where individual psychologists can submit evidence of their education, training, experience and examination performance that can be maintained by the ASPPB and accessed as needed. Such a credentials bank will reduce the burdens placed on psychologists and regulatory boards when an experienced psychologist seeks to retrieve and submit evidence of meeting licensure requirements, perhaps long after their training and initial licensure. The CPQ program will be augmented by two other ASPPB services supplying crucial information about applicants for the CPQ, namely the score reporting service and the DDS, each of which offer the most complete repository of information on exam performance and disciplinary data available.

Thus, the CPQ program offers the potential for individual psychologists to deposit their credentials, submit evidence of appropriate education, experience, prior licensure, exam performance, and history of professional discipline to a receiving jurisdiction and avoid the complications and pitfalls of trying to document compliance with current licensure criteria through the traditional initial application procedure. The program is scheduled to begin accepting applications from individual psychologists in August of 1998.

In Canada, pressures from the federal government for free trade across provincial boundaries led to passage of the Agreement on Internal Trade (AIT). Among other things, AIT requires that provinces seek mechanisms and solutions to the problem of inconsistent standards in the regulation of professions across the provinces. The law requires that provinces identify procedures that will allow a professional recognized to practice a profession in one province to be recognized and credentialed for similar work in any other province.

Given the diversity of educational standards for licensing psychologists across the provinces, AIT is forcing Canadian psychology regulatory bodies to revisit their educational standards and make changes. For example, the province of Ontario has held to a doctoral standard for independent practice in psychology, similar to US standards, for many years. In response to AIT, Ontario recently amended their psychology licensing law to allow independent practice of psychological associates at the masters degree level. Thus, Ontario appears to have dealt with AIT by creating a credential for individuals with masters degrees in psychology to practice independently as psychological associates while the title "psychologist" is still reserved for individuals trained at the doctoral level. The full impact of AIT on the regulation of psychology in Canada remains to be seen.

Similar governmental initiatives facilitating free trade, such as the North American Free Trade Agreement (NAFTA) between the USA, Canada, and Mexico, could create even more complex requirements for homogenizing licensing standards for education, supervised experience, and examination across these countries. So far, NAFTA has not trampled on the psychology-credentialing systems that each country has worked hard to develop to meet the needs of its citizens. However, it is not certain how free trade initiatives in the future will affect the regulation of professionals around the world.

2.14.5 CONCLUSIONS

Regulation of individuals to practice psychology in the USA and Canada is a complex and multifaceted process. It involves the interplay of professional associations, legislatively created regulatory bodies, state and provincial governments, and the public. The sole purpose for the passage and continuation of psychology licensing laws is to protect the public from incompetent, or unethical practitioners. When the public (or at least their elected public representatives) lose confidence in the ability of the profession to regulate itself, then psychology licensing laws are either modified or rescinded. Although it may be tempting for the profession to feel that it knows best how to regulate the practice of psychology, the profession must be mindful to educate the public of the reasons underlying its preferred standards and policies, or risk having them rejected by those representing the public's interests.

As modern society changes through technological advances, marketplace forces, and government initiatives, it may be necessary to modify the standards and processes that have been created to regulate the profession of psychology to date. The USA and Canada have been world leaders in the development of credentialing mechanisms and fair and impartial disciplinary proceedings for psychologists. Despite the challenges outlined above, hopefully that leadership can continue for the benefit of the consumers of psychological services and the profession itself.

2.14.6 REFERENCES

American Psychological Association (1992). Ethical principles of psychologists and code of conduct. *American Psychologist, 47*, 1597–1611.

American Psychological Association (1995). *Guidelines and principles for accreditation of professional programs in psychology*. Washington, DC: Author.

Association of State and Provincial Psychology Boards (1991). *ASPPB code of conduct*. Montgomery, AL: Author.

Association of State and Provincial Psychology Boards (1997). *Handbook of licensure and certification requirements in the United States and Canada*. Montgomery, AL: Author.

Bass, L. J. (1996). Future trends. In L. J. Bass, S. T. DeMers, J. R. P. Ogloff, C. Peterson, J. Pettifor, R. P. Reaves, T. Retfalvi, N. P. Simon, C. Sinclair, & R. Tipton (Eds.), *Professional conduct and discipline in psychology* (pp. 143–155). Washington, DC: American

Psychological Association and Montgomery, AL: Association of State and Provincial Psychology Boards.

Canadian Psychological Association (1991). *Canadian code of ethics for psychologists. Revised.* Ottawa, Canada: Author.

Deleon, P. H., & Wiggins, J. G. (1996). Prescription privileges for psychologists. *American Psychologist, 51*(3), 225–229.

Dent v. West Virginia, 129 U.S. 114, 9 St. Ct. 231 (1889).

Fagan, T., & Wise, P. S. (1993). *School psychology: Past, present and future.* New York: Longman.

Gross, S. J. (1978). The myth of professional licensing. *American Psychologist, 11,* 1009–1016.

Newton, L. H. (1988) Lawgiving for professional life: Reflections on the place of the professional code. In A. Flores (Ed.), *Professional ideals.* Belmont, CA: Wadsworth.

Peterson, C. (1996) Common problem areas and their causes resulting in disciplinary actions. In L. J. Bass, S. T. DeMers, J. R. P. Ogloff, C. Peterson, J. Pettifor, R. P. Reaves, T. Retfalvi, N. P. Simon, C. Sinclair, & R. Tipton (Eds.), *Professional conduct and discipline in psychology* (pp. 71–89). Washington, DC: American Psychological Association and Montgomery, AL: Association of State and Provincial Psychology Boards.

Raimy, V. C. (1950). *Training in clinical psychology.* New York: Prentice-Hall.

Reaves, R. P. (1996). Enforcement of codes of conduct by regulatory boards and professional associations. In L. J. Bass, S. T. DeMers, J. R. P. Ogloff, C. Peterson, J. Pettifor, R. P. Reaves, T. Retfalvi, N. P. Simon, C. Sinclair, & R. Tipton (Eds.), *Professional conduct and discipline in psychology* (pp. 101–116). Washington, DC: American Psychological Association and Montgomery, AL: Association of State and Provincial Psychology Boards.

Reaves, R. P. (1997). *Disciplinary actions involving psychologists in the United States and Canada: Top ten reasons.* Paper presented at the annual convention of the American Psychological Association, August, Chicago, IL.

Retfalvi, T., & Simon, N. P. (1996). Licensing, certification, registration, chartering and credentialing. In L. J. Bass, S. T. DeMers, J. R. P. Ogloff, C. Peterson, J. Pettifor, R. P. Reaves, T. Retfalvi, N. P. Simon, C. Sinclair, & R. Tipton (Eds.), *Professional conduct and discipline in psychology* (pp. 39–51). Washington, DC: American Psychological Association and Montgomery, AL: Association of State and Provincial Psychology Boards.

Sinclair, C., Simon, N. P., & Pettifor, J. (1996). History of ethical codes and licensure. In L. J. Bass, S. T. DeMers, J. R. P. Ogloff, C. Peterson, J. Pettifor, R. P. Reaves, T. Retfalvi, N. P. Simon, C. Sinclair, & R. Tipton (Eds.), *Professional conduct and discipline in psychology* (pp. 1–15). Washington, DC: American Psychological Association and Montgomery, AL: Association of State and Provincial Psychology Boards.

Wand, B. (1993). The nature of regulation and entrance criteria. In K. Dobson & D. Dobson (Eds.), *Professional psychology in Canada*(pp. 149–165). Toronto, Canada: Hoegrefe & Huber.

Webster's new world dictionary of American English (1986). New York: Webster's New World.

Weissman, H. N. (1984). Professional standards from the perspective of the sociology of professions. *Professional Psychology: Research and Practice, 15*(4), 471–472.

2.15
Credentialing Issues, Current and Future: Scandinavian Countries

STEFAN JERN
University of Linköping, Sweden

2.15.1 INTRODUCTION

The Scandinavian countries Denmark, Finland, Iceland, Norway, and Sweden make up a cultural unity of 23.5 million people. They have been members of the Nordic Council since 1955, and, with the exception of Iceland and Norway, are member states of the European Union.

The inhabitants of Scandinavia share a common linguistic and cultural background, and their history, political experiences, and geographic closeness have created among them a spirit of Scandinavian cooperation and togetherness. Cooperation in the area of legislation began in the nineteenth century and has resulted in a high degree of harmonization of the legal systems of the region. Examples of early cooperation are the Treaty on Exemption from the Requirements of a Passport (1954) and the Treaty on a Common Labor Market (1954), as well as agreements on cultural cooperation (1975), social security (1982), and the right to practice for licensed professionals in the health systems (1984, not including Iceland).

The Scandinavian countries are developed welfare states with a shared belief in centralism and a high reliance on state control and regulation of, for example, health, social security, educational, and professional systems. As a consequence, since the Second World War Scandinavian professional psychology has developed in a context where training and practice have been influenced to a great degree by government regulations. However, professional organizations have had an important influence on decisions taken by the respective governments. The emergence of standards for training and credentialing systems have in the main followed a common path in the five countries, even though the pace in each may have been different. This chapter outlines the credentialing systems in the Nordic countries. Most examples and specific details given in this chapter are for Swedish conditions, as, in the main, these may be viewed as typical for most of Scandinavia. The number of psychologists in Scandinavia is approximately 15 000 (1996, including students and interns).

As no clear and agreed-upon definitions of licensure or certification exist in Europe, the term "authorization" will be used throughout to cover the means by which credentialing is achieved.

2.15.2 SCANDINAVIAN PROFESSIONAL PSYCHOLOGY: AN OVERVIEW

Compared to the other Scandinavian countries, the emergence of psychology, both as an academic discipline and as a profession, was relatively late in Sweden and Finland. Psychology in Sweden essentially developed after the Second World War, being influenced initially by German Gestalt psychology and later by American psychology as an academic discipline. Psychology as a separate academic discipline and as a professional practice emerged in Denmark and Norway in the 1930s, but did not flourish until the 1960s.

Even though the first professional psychologists in Scandinavia were active in the area of occupational psychology, clinical psychology in Sweden is discussed here as an example to illustrate general developmental trends.

Clinical psychology in Sweden, as in many other European countries, has developed in the context of a national health system run and financed by local and regional authorities. The health-insurance system is comprehensive, general, and has a universal outreach. For this reason the issue of statutory independence of medical supervision and management responsibility has probably become more of a key issue in the development of the profession in Europe than was the case in the USA. There is, however, a small, and now increasing, private sector as well (Jern, 1995).

Clinical psychology in Sweden grew out of clinical practice, initially virtually immune to the influence of academic departments of psychology and psychiatry (Nilsson, 1981).

The first Swedish clinical psychologists with an academic training appeared in the late 1930s in child guidance centers, which later evolved into child and adolescent psychiatric clinics. Within the framework of child psychiatric teamwork, the numbers of these pioneers multiplied to quite an impressive workforce by the early 1950s.

During the 1940s, general psychiatry turned to psychological university institutions for cooperation in diagnostics. Researchers then emerged as visiting consultants in a few university clinics. The clinical psychologist was looked upon as a "learned scholar."

The first positions for clinical psychologists at psychiatric hospitals and clinics opened up in the period between 1950 and 1955, and were mainly seen as the basis of clinical diagnostic laboratories performing psychometric assessment upon a psychiatrist's request. The role was that of "the paramedical assistant."

In the 1960s their duties began to include psychological treatment as well, and the 1970s saw the clinical psychologist enter the psychiatric team as a professional with a full range of skills, including psychotherapy, supervision, program development, and leadership tasks. This is the point where the "clinician–professional" enters the field.

Child and adolescent clinicians in general have been a decade ahead of adult clinicians in all areas of development (Jern, 1979).

2.15.3 ACADEMIC TRAINING OF PSYCHOLOGISTS IN SCANDINAVIA

Academic training of psychologists in Scandinavia is offered at state universities, of which there are three in Denmark, six in Finland, one in Iceland (undergraduate studies only), six in Sweden, and three in Norway. Universities are separate entities with unique charters, but are funded by public means (state taxes). Usually, objectives and curricula for professional training programs in, for example, medicine, law, and psychology, leading to authorization (certification or licensure), have by tradition been strictly regulated by central state authorities, although some local variation has been allowed. The professional associations have set their own standards for training since the mid-1950s, and usually this has had a strong impact on the curricula decided by the central university authorities in all countries. No accreditation systems are in effect as this is alien to the northern European academic tradition. The widespread Boulder model, as a general standard of training was succeeded by the Vail model in the mid-1970s. Today there is a strong move towards professional schools and a pure professional model with some research training, particularly at the newer universities.

Since 1993, each Swedish university has been free to set its own standards, but for psychology a voluntary agreement has been reached to maintain a uniform objective and a flexible system of 11 courses. Entry requirements are set by central authorities, but may vary locally depending on demand and supply. The University of Linköping, which was the last to start a program for the training of psychologists (1995), has developed a different model (problem-based learning), and has local selection and admission procedures.

Training programs are offered within faculties of social science, except for the University of Bergen, Norway, which has a faculty of psychology.

University tuition in Scandinavia is free and most students manage to support themselves on the state student loan system. Since the late 1970s the output in Sweden has been around 300 students per annum, reducing to 150 in the early 1990s. This last figure will more than double during the second half of the 1990s through a doubling of the intake and the addition of one university. These measures have been taken due to an anticipated reduction, by almost half, of the number of psychologists by the year 2010 following retirement of the core body, which comprises psychologists born during and after the Second World War.

In no Scandinavian country is a doctorate needed to become a psychologist. This is in line with the European tradition, where the doctorate degree is considered the first step in a research career. The standards and requirements for attaining a doctorate are generally viewed as too high for professional training, and are in many respects inadequate as the basis for professional practice. The length of training and the academic titles used in the different countries are given in Table 1.

The general model in the Nordic countries involves 4.5–5.5 years of academic training together with a subsequent or partially incorporated internship of 1–2 years" duration, leading to a generic certificate in psychology. The exception to this is Denmark, where a smaller proportion of school psychologists follow an older curriculum. On the northern European continent the same duration and scope of the academic and practical training is usually the rule, but more recent specialization of studies and the subsequent internship has led to the creation of specialized licences or diplomas. In July 1990, the European Federation of Professional Psychologists Association (EFPPA) agreed on optimal standards for professional training in psychology (EFPPA, 1990; Matefi & Häring, 1993), which encompass the generalist as well as the specialized model.

2.15.3.1 Content and Forms of Academic Training in Sweden

Admission to the five-year training program is granted after 12 years of general schooling with a sufficient amount of mathematics, Swedish, and English. This training program is extremely popular, and competition for entrance is very strong, with 16–40 applicants per opening. There is also a requirement of one year's general experience of working life before entrance (Jern, 1995).

The five-year academic training is generic and divided into 11 main courses as shown in Table 2.

Parker (1990), among others, has pointed out the split between academic and applied psychology in Sweden. Certainly this scenario is not unique to Sweden, but it has created specific problems in the training system over the years. The first chair in psychology was established as late as 1948, and the first professor in clinical psychology was appointed as recently as 1983. However, the academic side of Swedish clinical psychology is internationally well known and recognized. With regard to the lack of interaction between academic and applied psychology, Sjöberg (1986) has offered the explanation that, although by the late 1970s research had reached a high standard of methodological refinement, it had little to offer in the way of a metatheory for applied clinical psychology.

Through the establishment of chairs and departments in applied and clinical psychology in the 1970s, the beginning of a remedy was instituted. As the number of experienced professional psychologists has increased, a steady flow of applicants for the doctoral programs has been noted by the universities.

Table 1 Comparison of study time and the academic titles used in Scandinavian countries.

Country	*Training time* (years)	*Title*[a]
Denmark	4.5–5	Cand. psych., Cand. paed. psych.
Finland	6–7	Psykologian Kandidaatti
Iceland	Scandinavian standard[b]	
Norway	6–7	Psych. Cand.
Sweden	5	Psykologexamen[c]

[a]Direct comparisons cannot be made as the longer programs often include at least one year of internship, which in shorter programs is completed after the examination. However, most programs contain one or more periods of practical experience ("practicum") ranging from 8 to 20 weeks of full-time study. [b]The University of Reykjavik offers a three-year undergraduate program, which has to be completed abroad, formerly usually in Denmark, Norway, or Sweden, but now more often in the UK or the USA. [c]Literally "psychologists exam" equivalent to, for example, the "physician's exam" or "dentist's exam." Unfortunately the official English translation on the Swedish certificate reads: "Master of psychology," which might give a false impression if the European Masters degree is set equal to the American MA, which is usually of a more limited scope. The correct translation would probably be Psy.D.

Table 2 General curriculum: psychologist program, Sweden.

Course	*Points*[a] *Lund University*	*Min./max. in six universities*
Introduction	5	5–7
Psychological functions and their biological bases	16	15–20
Humankind in different developmental perspectives	19	17–23
Society, analysis of society, and social psychology	12	10–15
Personality and psychopathology	19	15–20
Assessment and intervention (individuals)	16	16–22
Practicum	15	15–15
Assessment and intervention (groups, organizations, and environment)	38	30–40
Psychotherapy and psychological treatment	25	22–28
Psychological research methodology	15	10–15
Thesis	20	20–20
Individual choice	0	0–10

[a]One point is equivalent to one week's full-time study in the 40-week academic year.

The stipulations for the diplomas in specialist areas of psychology have also intensified the research activities among practitioners, and the split between the academic and applied fields seems to be diminishing.

2.15.3.2 Specialist Training and Certification in Scandinavia

All the Nordic countries, except Iceland, have some type of specialist training following the completion of the authorization. The duration of the training, which is made up of supervision, course work, and a thesis, is usually around five years and is combined with practice in the chosen area of specialization. The certificate of specialization is awarded by the psychological associations (in Norway since 1985, in Denmark since 1994, and in Sweden since 1995). The Finnish system requires the candidate to take a licentiate's degree after having passed a professional program of 80 weeks duration. The degree, is not regulated by the state or by the association. Areas of specialization differ somewhat between countries, but cover clinical psychology, organizational psychology, community psychology, and school psychology, with some subspecializations. The certificate as a specialist is recognized and minimally protected only by the authorities in Norway.

2.15.4 CERTIFICATION SYSTEMS IN SCANDINAVIA

In general, since the 1970s the credentialing systems have moved from professional organizations to state authorities, and they are now a public responsibility in all countries. This applies only to the primary licensure level, however, as systems of specialization have developed within the associations and remain with them. Supervisory bodies controlling the conduct of psychologists with regard to adherence to the principles of sound science and reliable experience are also a part of the public sector, whereas ethical issues are supervised, judged, and decided on by bodies within the ethics boards of the professional organizations, or equivalent professional bodies.

2.15.4.1 Norway

Since 1973, the law has stipulated that no one may present himself or herself as a psychologist unless he or she has acquired the degree of Psykologie Kandidatexamen; can give evidence of an internship of a specified length; and can provide proof of leading a respectable life. The government will appoint a Psychologists Council to counsel the Department of Social Issues in professional matters and issue provisions regulating the practice of psychology. Psychological methods can be (and are) protected by Royal Ordinance. The department can withdraw its authorization of a psychologist if advanced age, a handicapping disease, or chemical abuse make him or her unfit to practice. Withdrawal of authorization can also occur if a psychologist neglects his or her duties or refuses to follow provisions imposed by the public authorities. The decision is not arrived at in a law court but through an administrative procedure. The confidentiality of psychologists is regulated by law.

2.15.4.2 Sweden

From the mid-1950s until 1978, authorization as a psychologist was granted by the Swedish Psychological Association for persons holding an equivalent of the US Ph.D. (filosofie licentiatexamen) in psychology or education and a 1.5-year internship or, for assistant psychologists a BA in psychology, educational psychology, or sociology and six months of practical training under supervision. Persons fulfilling these requirements were awarded a diploma stating that he or she was authorized by the association to practice either as an independent psychologist or as an assistant psychologist.

After a rather short political campaign, and opposed only by parts of the medical and legal professions, in 1978, psychology was included in the Law on Authorization to Practice a Profession within the Health and Medical Services. Licensure requirements involve taking the psychologist's exam and the completion of a one-year internship under supervision (practical training for psychologists [PTP]), with experience from individual and organizational work. Until 1996 the internship had to be completed within the public services, but it can now be done in a private practice setting as well.

The law originally protected the titles "authorized psychologist" and "authorized psychotherapist" and included a provision that the authorized psychotherapist should also state his or her basic training. In 1992 this law was amended with a penal protection for the professional designations "psychologist" and "psychotherapist" when offering healthcare services. The use of these designations outside the healthcare area is not regulated by law, where the protection is of the title "authorized psychologist." Directives and general advice on authorization of psychologists are issued by the Swedish National Board of Health and Welfare, which is also the agency with the right to inspect and control all medical professions. There is no psychologists law, as in Norway, Finland, and Denmark, and no separate psychologists council. With the exception of hypnosis and the practice of certain forms of psychotherapy with some defined groups of patients, there are no regulated or protected psychological fields.

The authorization can be withdrawn on essentially the same grounds as in Norway. This is executed by the Board of Responsibility of the Health Care System (HSAN), which since 1980 has been the supervisory authority for all authorized and unauthorized personnel in the health system. The task of the body is to examine mistakes and neglect in the exercise of medical professions. This is done with special regard to the principles of sound science and reliable experience, whereas ethical considerations usually play a minor role. HSAN can also issue cautions and warnings as administrative decisions. HSAN is a free-standing government authority of eight members appointed by the government for three-year terms. Two members have backgrounds in the medical professions, whereas the others represent various labor unions and the parliament. The chairperson is a judge. Complaints may be filed by patients, relatives of patients, the National Board of Health and Welfare, the Parliamentary Ombudsman, and by the Attorney General (Langton, 1984).

The number of authorized psychologists in Sweden was 6200 in 1994, among a population of 8.8 million inhabitants. This figure includes clinical (2150), educational (800), community, occupational, and organizational psychologists. Of the clinical psychologists, approximately 1000 are in positions within general psychiatry, 800 within child and adolescence, and approximately 200–300 are in neuropsychology/neurology, medical rehabilitation, pediatrics, gynecology/obstetrics, internal medicine, transplantation surgery, addiction units, and pain control centers. Some 100 are self-employed full-time private practitioners. Of the 2150 clinical psychologists, I would estimate that around 1000 run a part-time private practice in addition to their salaried positions, with a mean workload of about 5–10 hours per week. I have not included in these numbers the significant number of clinically related colleagues working in antenatal clinics, nurseries and playschools, or in the areas of mental handicap and social services. There are no clinical psychologists in school psychology.

2.15.4.2.1 Certification of psychotherapists in Sweden

A special issue in Sweden is the certification of psychotherapists; a system which has been in operation since the early 1980s. Originally intended as postgraduate specialization training for psychologists and psychiatrists, the university examination for "psychotherapist" evolved as the basis for a free-standing profession which could also be entered by, for example, social workers, nurses, dentists, clergymen, and others, provided they had completed a 1.5-year postgraduate preparatory course in psychotherapy. The number of authorized psychotherapists has now reached 2600 as shown in Table 3.

Table 3 Number of authorised psychotherapists according to basic training: Sweden (January 1, 1994).

Basic training	*No.*	*%*
Authorized psychologist	1651	63
Social worker	432	17
Authorized physician (psychiatrist)	274	10
Authorized nurse	42	2
Others	200	8
Total	2599	100

The orientation of university training leading to the title "authorized psychotherapist" should be eclectic, but has in practice been overwhelmingly psychoanalytically oriented. Training in group psychotherapy, behavior modification, cognitive therapy, and family therapy can also lead to authorization. Training in these areas is offered by different private institutes, often run by the appropriate professional organization (Jern, 1995).

2.15.4.3 Denmark

Since 1993, Denmark has had a psychologists law protecting the title "psychologist" (restricted to those having earned either of the two university degrees mentioned below) and regulating the entrance to the profession by stipulating the degrees of Candidatus psychologiae or Candidatus paedagogiae et psychologiae supplemented by two-year internship as requirements for authorization.

The Ministry of Social Affairs appoints a Psychologists Council to act as the authorizing and supervisory body of psychologists to serve for a period of four years. Of the nine members of the council, two are appointed by the Danish Psychological Association. Complaints regarding an authorized psychologist should be submitted to the Patients Committee, which is the Danish equivalent of the Swedish HSAN. The committee is authorized to issue cautions and warnings. Withdrawal of authorization as a psychologist is decided in civil courts upon referral from the Psychologists Council. In addition, a psychologist who has shown grave negligence or severe lack of judgement in his or her practice of the profession can be sentenced to a fine or to imprisonment.

2.15.4.4 Finland

A law established in 1994 regulates professions in the health and medical services and gives the conditions for all authorized professionals, including psychologists, which are defined as belonging to a medical profession, irrespective of the area in which they practice. The title "psychologist" is protected, as are the tasks of the profession. The law regulates training criteria, general ethics issues, confidentiality, and continuing education. The supervision of professional conduct is delegated to the Centre for Legal Protection of Patients in The Health Service, which has a standing similar to that of HSAN in Sweden. The sanctions are essentially the same as those of HSAN, but the consequences for a psychologist of being convicted for a felony in a civil court seem to be graver than in other Scandinavian countries.

2.15.4.5 Iceland

Iceland is not part of the Agreement on the Right to Practice for Licensed Professionals in the Health Systems, but protects the title "psychologist" by law. The approximately 130 psychologists in Iceland are supervised by the Ministry of Education.

2.15.5 ETHICS SYSTEMS IN SCANDINAVIA

All Scandinavian psychological associations abide by the Ethical Principles for Scandinavian Psychologists, which were adopted during the period 1987–1991. The associations generally have boards of ethics for supervision of the ethical standard of individual psychologists and standing task forces for policy matters in the ethics area. Final decisions regarding suspension and expulsion are taken by the board of directors and minor sanctions, such as cautions and warnings, are decided on by the board of ethics. In some countries (e.g., Sweden) appeals can be raised to higher levels within the association, such as the board of appeals or the general assembly.

2.15.6 VIOLATIONS OF PRACTICE STANDARDS

The national supervisory boards do not keep open records of filed complaints or decisions, but do in some cases publish yearbooks. The establishment of a national disciplinary databank has been discussed in Sweden. Opposition from the associations and societies of medical doctors has been strong, and no action has been taken by the authorities. As the relevant laws are fairly new in all countries, except Norway and Sweden, data concerning psychologists are scarce at present.

In Sweden early reports (Langton, 1984) indicate that HSAN, files approximately 800 complaints a year, of which approximately 500 concern medical doctors, with around 50 each for nurses and dentists. Approximately 10 psychologists' cases have been filed every year, and of these about seven have been subject to disciplinary measures. Since 1981 not more than five psychologists have had their authorizations withdrawn, which should be compared to a yearly total for all medical professions of between 30 and 40.

The most frequent types of violation are difficult to narrow down from the figures available from HSAN, but a general observation has been that cases concerning child custody, sexual abuse, and psychotherapy increased during the late 1980s and early 1990s. A clearer picture may be arrived at by studying cases filed with and adjudicated by the Swedish Board of Ethics (see Table 4). In the ethics field no disciplinary data banks are kept. According to the statutes of the associations, settled cases should be published regularly in the associations' journals, but for reasons unknown, this rarely occurs.

Violations of practice standards seem to occur mainly in the sensitive fields of social investigations, forensic psychology, and clinical psychology/psychotherapy. The majority of

Table 4 Distribution of filed and adjudicated cases, Swedish Board of Ethics 1983–1995.

	Cases by year (filed/adjudicated)				
Category	*1983–84*	*1985–86*	*1987–88*	*1989–91*	*1992–95*
Social investigations and incest	9/1[a]	17/5[a]	12/5[a]	14/8[a] 10[a]	15/15[a] 13[a]
Clinical psychology and psychotherapy	9/2[a]	15/2[a]	17/2[a]	24/3[c]	20/3[b]
School psychology	4	2	0	4/2[a]	0
Public statements	7	8/1[a]	3	1	1/1[a]
Personal fitness	2	1	0	1	0
Educational activities	0	4	4	1	2/2[a]
Professional relations	0	4	1	4	0
Organizational	1	0	2/1[a]	4/4[a]	1/1[a]
Research	3/1[a]	3/1[a]	0	0	0
Other	0	0	2	0	0
Total	35/4[a]	54/9[a]	41/8[a]	24[a] 53/3[c]	32[a] 39/3[b]

[a]Caution. [b]Warning. [c]Expulsion recommended to the Board of Directors.

cases have been in areas where psychologists act as experts to courts in legal procedures on child custody and sexual abuse, and in clinical settings where psychologists have been accused of improper sexual advances towards clients.

The picture thus overlaps with what has been reported by HSAN, and is probably typical for most of Scandinavia. It has also been noted that, while in the 1980s public concern about psychologists' inappropriate professional conduct was centered around child custody and sexual abuse, in the 1990s this shifted slightly towards an increased concern about psychotherapy including memory recovering techniques, repressed memories, and similar phenomena.

2.15.7 MOBILITY OF PSYCHOLOGISTS AND RECIPROCITY OF LICENSURE

In essence, two different systems apply to the Scandinavian countries: inter-Scandinavian agreements and European Union (EU) regulations.

2.15.7.1 Inter-Scandinavian Agreements and Mobility

The Treaty on a Common Labor Market (1954) and the Agreement on the Right to Practice for Licensed Professionals in the Health Systems (1984) give the rights of free movement and practice to all psychologists in Scandinavia, irrespective of whether or not the psychologist is a citizen of an EU state or not. Every citizen in the Nordic countries is free to reside and work in any of the countries in accordance with the treaty of 1954.

When licensing laws and the regulation of psychology were introduced, the situation became somewhat more complicated and the right for professionals to practice was agreed upon by all Scandinavian countries, except Iceland. This also means that a license, a certification, or an authorization given to a psychologist in one Scandinavian country will be acknowledged by the receiving country as equivalent to its own authorization. Minor requirements for supplementary examination in, for example, social security legislation and language tests are allowed for.

The mobility under this law has been rather slight over the years, with the main movement being from Denmark, which suffers from unemployment problems for psychologists, to Norway, which has a steady shortage of psychologists, especially in the subarctic region. For language reasons, movements to Finland have been negligible, whereas Sweden has had some exchanges with Norway, especially in the border districts. Movement from Denmark to Sweden, and vice versa, is rare. It should be noted that, through the Nordic treaties, Norway became an equal of the other Scandinavian EU member states, in this respect.

2.15.7.2 EU Regulations

The EU Directive 89/48, which covers the free movement of workers between member states of the EU, gives all citizens the right to have their training acknowledged by all member states, provided it has been approved in their own countries.

The directive regulates "vertically" the validity of diplomas and examinations of professionals, with a minimum of three years academic training. The directive covers psychologists, even though EFPPA has striven for a special or "horizontal" directive (like those for medicine and law) covering psychology exclusively. As psychology is not a regulated profession in all member states this is not possible to achieve. The emphasis on issuing directives has diminished under heavy criticism from many member states, and it is now highly unlikely that the vertical directive will be enlarged to encompass psychologists.

The movement of psychologists between the Scandinavian states has not been affected to any great degree by the directive. Its main implication for psychology in Scandinavia at the moment is that it may harmonize the procedures for judging non-EU-trained psychologists' diplomas and licenses. The influx of non-Scandinavian psychologists is low, probably due to language barriers and labor-market requirements.

As the possibilities under the special directive failed to materialize, EFPPA has changed policy, and it is now striving to formulate standards for a "European psychologist" diploma that could be accepted by member states as a "professional passport."

2.15.8 FUTURE DIRECTIONS

The more than 20-year process that has brought about national authorization systems for psychologists in Scandinavia was coordinated initially through a close cooperation of the associations and more recently through EFPPA. The development in Norway has been the guiding principle for this work. The ultimate goal has been national licensing laws, that protect the title and the activities of psychologists, these being administered through a psychologists council under the national health authorities. In this struggle, attempts have been made to create a Nordic psychologists council within the Nordic Council, so far without success. Norway and Denmark have succeeded in creating their own professional bodies within the state administration, whereas resistance has been strong on the political level in Sweden.

2.15.8.1 Continuing Harmonization

The present situation presents a picture of legislation that is both united and divided. With the exception of Iceland, all states protect the title "psychologist" and regulate the training standards for authorization. Finland and Sweden have no psychologist law or psychologists councils and incorporate psychologists in a more general supervisory system for all medical professions. Sweden is also the only country that refuses to protect the activities of psychologists by law. The work on harmonization of legislation will probably continue, and may lead to a further harmonization of the credentialing and supervisory systems in the Nordic countries.

2.15.8.2 Deregulation: Threat or Possibility?

The beginning of an opposing force can be seen in the emergence of national deregulation regarding the professions. For example, in Sweden the attempts to have the control of specialization transferred to the Swedish Board of Health and Welfare may be thwarted by this move. The specialization system of medical doctors was initially a purely professional concern, but in the 1950s it was taken over by the national board. Lately, some aspects of the system have been returned to the professional bodies, and future development in this direction may affect the strivings of psychologists to have their specialities recognized by other professions, the general public, and society at large. It should not be taken for granted, however, that this trend will be entirely negative to the development of professional independence. It may be that the close cooperation between the profession and the public administration can be broken in favor of a more independent standing. If this is to be the case, the issues of a European harmonization of training and credentialing standards through EFPPA will be even more important.

2.15.8.3 Remaining Issues

As a rather young profession, psychology in general has been involved in professional competition to gain its place in society. In clinical psychology this has implied competition with psychiatrists and psychiatric social workers and nurses; in school psychology competition with remedial teachers, welfare officers, and head teachers; and so on in different areas. The battle for certification has been won in Scandinavia, and authorized psychologists are now regarded as belonging to an independent profession, both legally and in the eyes of the public. The relationship with the medical profession, on both an organizational and a daily level, could generally be described as reasonable, and is characterized by mutual respect. However, some problem areas remain, and I will point out a few central ones.

2.15.8.3.1 Access to the national health insurance systems

Clinical psychologists in independent practice can be reimbursed by national health insurance only in Norway. In Sweden this can be done only if the psychologist is also an authorized psychotherapist and the patient has been referred by a physician. This option is open only to the select few who have managed to negotiate a contract with the local health authority. In the other Scandinavian countries no reimbursement is possible. This severely limits free competition with other professions, and the issue will have to be approached on an international level, either within EFPPA or through purely Scandinavian efforts.

2.15.8.3.2 Subordination to the medical systems

As competition within the healthcare market is not free, in order to practice, most clinical psychologists are dependent on positions within the general health system, mostly within psychiatry. This system is legally regulated by the medical profession through the respective National Boards of Health and Welfare, where influential posts and bodies are held by physicians. This has led, for example, to a situation where the medical profession together with administrators has managed to abolish psychological units, departments, and clinics within the hospital system, with the exception of a few university hospitals. Instead, psychologists are incorporated into existing multidisciplinary teams under medical leadership. The phenomenon of being "a guest in somebody else's house" is rather typical for most branches of psychology in Scandinavia. The lack of its own organizational and economic basis within the system seriously hampers development, and perhaps even applied research. However, it must be emphasized that the cooperation with other professions on a daily basis in general carries very few elements of conflict. A possible development that might emerge as a consequence of a common credentialing system and increased autonomy for the profession in Europe is a new emphasis on private and independent practice.

2.15.9 SUMMARY

Since the Second World War, professional psychology in the five Scandinavian countries has evolved in a culturally and linguistically close-knit region, which has been distinguished by remarkable economic and social progress. This has led to a welfare-state framework where a belief in strong, centralized, governmental control of health, social security, and educational systems has been shared by most. All professions have striven to make alliances with governments and supervisory state boards.

Since the 1970s psychology has been regulated by laws and decrees in all Scandinavian countries, except Iceland. The psychological associations have had a strong influence on the training standards and credentialing systems and it might be said that there exists a common Scandinavian training model for psychologists. The professional title is protected in the four major countries and professional activities are protected in all but Sweden. The licensure has full reciprocity within Scandinavia as a result of similar training and credentialing systems, inter-Scandinavian agreements on a common labor market, and the acknowledgement of Nordic licenses in the health field. Directives from the EU have also furthered the free movement of psychologists, but mobility between countries is still low.

The system of control and supervision varies, with two main models having been established: the Danish/Norwegian model, which implies a psychologists law and a psychologists council; and the Swedish/Finnish model, where psychologists are credentialed and supervised by the same body as other medical professions. Goals for the future include creating a common Nordic psychologists council within the Nordic Council in order to further harmonize legislation. It is not clear at the moment if a rising tide of deregulation will lead to a return to authorization and standard setting by the professional associations. Whatever course the development will take, the joint forces of psychologists in Scandinavia and Europe will be needed to defend what has been achieved, and to further future integration of the profession in the region.

2.15.10 REFERENCES

European Federation of Professional Psychologists Association (1990). *EFPPA optimal standards for professional training in psychology* (EFPPA Booklet 3). Bonn, Germany: Berufsverband Deutscher Psychologen.

Jern, S. (1979). The development of clinical psychology: from learned science to professional treatment (in Swedish). *Psykolognytt, 16,* 8–10.

Jern, S. (1995). *Clinical psychology in Sweden today: Problems and prospects.* Paper presented March 18, 1995, at the International Symposium of Clinical Psychology, Nagoya, Japan.

Langton, B. (1984). The law of supervision—the Board of Responsibility of the Health Care System (in Swedish). *Proceedings of the Swedish Society of Physicians, 93*(5), 91–99.

Matefi, G., & Häring, E. (1993). *Inventory of regulations in the field of psychology in European countries.* Bonn, Germany: Berufsverband Deutscher Psychologen.

Nilsson, I. (1981). The history of psychology in Sweden: Laboratories, testing and clinical psychology (in Swedish). *Kritisk Psykologi, 1,* 4–25.

Parker, A. (1990). Towards an international profession of clinical psychology: An Anglo–Swedish perspective. *International Journal of Psychology, 25*(3), 355–370.

Sjöberg, L. (1986). Research directions in psychology (in Swedish). *Swedish research of today.* Stockholm, Sweden: HSFR.

2.16 Recredentialing: Periodic Reassessment of Practice Expertise

DAVID A. RODGERS
Cleveland Clinic Foundation, OH, USA

2.16.1 INTRODUCTION

There is growing discussion of and pressure for formal recredentialing in health services fields (Allred & Steiner, 1994; Bennett & Langdon, 1995; Conn, 1994; Department of Health, Education, & Welfare, 1977; Johanson, 1995; McClennan & Herlihy, 1995; Norcini, 1994; Saunders & Paget, 1994; Wiens, 1983; Wilson, 1993). In psychology, as early as 1973, the American Board of Professional Psychology (ABPP) was considering a recredentialing requirement (Mayfield, 1987; Ross, 1973). In the 1990s, the American Psychological Association (APA) College of Professional Psychology has considered requiring a periodic recredentialing examination for renewal of its proficiency certifications. In medicine, the American Board of Family Practice embraced recredentialing when the board was first formed in 1969, and, by 1993, 16 of the remaining 18 US medical specialty boards had adopted it (Leigh, Young, & Haley, 1993). So have medical specialty groups in other countries (Clunie, 1993; Delahunt, Beer, & Taylor, 1992; Egerton, 1994; Goto, 1994; Phillips & Willis, 1994), nursing specialties (Eagle, 1992; Haag, 1992; Roessler, 1994; Simon, 1992), dental specialties (Allen, 1994; Nelson, 1994), and other health related groups (Chambless et al., 1993; Grim & Grim, 1995; Hasbargen & Culclasure, 1994; Pfister, 1995; Zarowitz et al., 1993). The phenomenon is nevertheless a relatively new one and is not without controversy. Medicine, for example, existed for at least 23 centuries with a defined ethics code, with little or no use of competency-based recredentialing requirements.

The concept of periodic professional recredentialing based on reassessment of practice expertise is highly attractive. Some professionals do not age well. Incompetent professional help is hazardous to the public and damaging to the reputation of all professionals. If credentialing insures competency, then recredentialing should weed out the professionally senescent or irresponsible or lazy who do not maintain their professional expertise over time. Many psychologists would agree with the observation of Sechrest and Chatel that, "Accountability for a profession entails the ability to vouch for the competencies and other desirable characteristics of members of the profession" (1987, p. 2). Periodic reassessment of professional expertise as a requirement for continued credentialing should therefore be a protection both for the public and for the profession.

The foregoing argument seems unassailable except for one critical flaw, the assumption that credentialing, and recredentialing, can insure competency. Even while strongly arguing for recredentialing in their own medical specialty, Bennett and Langdon state a conclusion that almost all who examine the issues carefully eventually reach: "Does [the recredentialing process] measure the ability of any individual to practice medicine? No, it does not" (Bennett & Langdon, 1995, p. 556). While the concept may be sound, the possibility of validly preassessing professional competency may still be remote (Wiens & Dörken, 1986). Without valid assessment procedures, recredentialing based on assessments of uncertain validity tends to be a sham (e.g., Koocher, 1979).

Such complexities warrant a more detailed look at the nature of professional competency and the mechanisms for protecting the public from incompetent practice, as these relate to the issue of recredentialing of professional expertise.

2.16.2 ALTERNATIVE METHODS OF ADDRESSING PROFESSIONAL INCOMPETENCE

The ultimate purpose of recredentialing is to identify professionals who were formerly presumed competent but who may have become incompetent since the last credentialing. Although "recredentialing" by that name may be a relatively new development (see D'Costa, 1986, p. 138), the culture has always had devices for protecting itself from incompetent professionals. That being so, then the question to be asked of the present recredentialing movement is whether or not it improves upon those traditional protections. A brief review of some of the traditional mechanisms is useful, for perspective.

Four ways that performance measures enter into evaluation of professional competency, ways on which the culture has primarily relied in the past, are through: (i) economic factors, (ii) disciplinary regulatory factors, (iii) litigation factors, and (iv) collegial controls by guild structures.

2.16.2.1 Economic

On the economic side, market forces are driven by performance in its most comprehensive sense, such that some degree of professional competence is necessary for professional reputation and economic survival. Maintaining a job or maintaining clients is therefore one form of continuous recredentialing. Indeed, economists might argue that the ultimate criterion of professional expertise *is* economic survival, and the more that economic forces are allowed to operate unencumbered, the more effectively they will serve the public (see Gross, 1978).

2.16.2.2 Regulatory

On the disciplinary regulatory side, professional service that falls below the floor of formally adopted codes of conduct can expose the professional to loss of licensure and privilege of practice. The APA Ethics Code and the Association of State and Provincial Psychology Boards (ASPPB) Code of Conduct are two such measures against which many regulatory groups judge adequacy of professional performance.

2.16.2.3 Litigation

On the litigation side, failure to practice at the level of competence expected of the profession, even though that level is poorly defined and may be capriciously determined by both litigants and jury, can result in malpractice suits. With its impact on both economic status and professional reputation, such litigation not only economically redresses past woes but also to some degree certifies against future professional incompetence and practice.

2.16.2.4 Collegial

On the collegial control side, since each professional's well-being depends heavily on the reputation of his or her profession, collegial groups have a strong interest in preventing colleagues from sullying the profession's image. Since they also have intimate knowledge of the workings of the profession, they are often in an optimal position to exert effective corrective pressure on colleagues who would deviate from acceptable standards. Paradoxically, therefore, self-regulation of a profession can be, and has often proved to be, relatively effective in protecting the public interest. The Hippocratic Oath, originating in the fourth century BC, taken upon joining the ranks of physicians, is often cited as the real beginning of the profession of medicine in the western world, and one of the primary bases for its prospering as a service profession.

Although often effective, professional self-regulation by collegial groups does introduce the dilemma of "the foxes guarding the chicken coop," such that professional protection can be, and often is, placed ahead of public good (Gross, 1978). Especially in the modern era, with an explosion of information resources that tend to undercut the "secret society mystique" that has allowed professionals to claim immunity from public scrutiny and public regulation in the past (Gross, 1978), guild controls have been increasingly replaced with public structures. However, it is worth noting that these public structures are often little more than a giving of legal sanction to the same professionals, appointed to governmental regulatory boards, that would otherwise have sat on professional society ethics boards (see Gross, 1978). This tendency to shift guild control from the collegial organization to the statutory regulatory body has appropriately been called "incestuous" by Matarazzo (1977), but would seem to be a pragmatic first step in the transition to more public accountability.

2.16.3 PROACTIVE VS. RETROACTIVE ACCOUNTABILITY

Neither economic, nor malpractice, nor disciplinary regulatory controls involve a formal demonstration of professional expertise, and all invoke correction only after public injury has occurred. Some form of proactive periodic evaluation, "proactive accountability," that does not depend on prior public injury, would therefore seem to be desirable (Department of Health, Education, & Welfare, 1977; Sechrest & Chatel, 1987). It is, of course, just such proactive accountability that initial credentialing and periodic recredentialing are intended to accomplish, whether the credentialing is in the form of licensure or of special group certification or of guild membership.

Even the requirement for periodic renewal of credential, a requirement that is characteristic of most licensures or certifications or professional group membership, is a process for reviewing the professional's record, to see if specified minimal standards have been maintained. Such renewal is usually based on no more than payment of fees, updating of address, and absence of clear evidence of malfunctioning, such as absence of a felony conviction. In this form, recredentialing has long been a part of professional regulation. In the remainder of this chapter, however, the concept of recredentialing will be reserved for renewal of credential based on some formal assessment of potential for future competency, in the absence of a history of incompetence. It will be differentiated from controls that are predicated on prior occurrence of lack of competency, which are the common bases for disciplinary actions or malpractice suits. The goal of recredentialing is to protect the public from future harm, not to redress past harm.

2.16.4 WHO RECREDENTIALS, FOR WHAT PURPOSE?

Since recredentialing is intended to protect the public by eliminating unqualified applicants who currently hold a qualifying credential and who therefore have not yet demonstrated disqualifying lack of competence, and since failure of the recredentialing process becomes the *de facto* definition of "unqualified," the process can be neither benign nor nonthreatening to the professional (Holmes, 1986). The threat varies considerably, of course, depending on who does the recredentialing and for what purpose. Three such categories of recredentialing can be specified: (i) licensure, (ii) membership of a specialty group, and (iii) retention of a job position. There is a tendency, although not a perfect correlation, for the potential for public protection to increase as threat to the professional increases. Therefore, protection of the public and protection of the professional are often in conflict (Gross, 1978), a fact that greatly influences almost all recredentialing considerations. Both can be profoundly affected by the specific evaluation procedures or standards used, and balancing out these two factors constitutes much of the "art" of developing recredentialing programs.

2.16.4.1 Licensure

Recredentialing for licensure is the most threatening to the professional, because it jeopardizes a major investment of time, effort, and money in a professional career. On the other hand, it is potentially most protective of the public. Without removal of the professional license, some segment of the public will probably continue to be exposed to the services of a presumably incompetent professional. Responsibility for such licensure recredentialing nearly always resides ultimately with a governmental authority rather than with a collegial group. Few professions, and no US or Canadian psychology jurisdiction, now require recredentialing for licensure, except for a mandatory continuing education feature, which may or may not qualify as a true recredentialing measure.

2.16.4.2 Specialty

The issue of what constitutes a recognized psychological specialty, an issue that is much in debate in the APA, is not intended to be raised by this discussion. In this chapter, the term "speciality" is used in its more generic sense to refer to any subgroup of a profession that distinguishes itself by inclusive and exclusive criteria from other members of the profession, and that uses some form of credentialing to identify membership in the subgroup.

Specialty credentialing, and recredentialing when it is undertaken, is usually done by a professional group rather than by a governmental agency. When such is the case, loss of specialty credentialing does not carry loss of career implications to the extent that loss of licensure would. Nevertheless, membership in a specialty board can allow access to job situations or remuneration structures or other professional perquisites that are denied non members, to a degree that can markedly affect professional welfare. Even governmental regulations can reference specialty recognition, giving such recognition the force of law, as though the credentialing were done by a governmental entity, and thereby increasing its professional importance. The threat to the professional of such recredentialing can therefore be high. The fact that the process is usually controlled by the profession itself, and can therefore be more specifically attuned to the concerns of the professionals, can reduce the threat somewhat but may at the same time reduce the assurance that the public interest will be protected (Gross, 1978). For example, it can be used more to assure orthodoxy than to assure competency, or to imply competency without actually assessing professional skills.

Recredentialing for membership in medical specialty boards is becoming common, as has already been noted. While it is still uncommon in psychology specialties, it is being considered in several. The ABPP diplomas and the APA College of Professional Psychology proficiency certificates are two examples already cited.

2.16.4.3 Job

Even though it is less threatening than loss of licensure, recredentialing for job retention poses considerable risk to the professional, representing loss of job security and potential loss of income. It may or may not offer protection to the public, depending largely on the nature of the recredentialing requirements. In the airline industry and some other jobs of high risk potential that require strong and measurable technological skills, recredentialing for retention of job is common practice and relatively effective when based on apparently valid procedures addressing issues of valid public and professional concern. In such situations, the professional's job insecurity is considered secondary to the public interest, and is handled in other ways. For example, airplane pilots can actually purchase loss-of-license insurance.

In psychology, job recredentialing is just beginning to be used. The newest player in the healthcare recredentialing picture is managed care, which may be developing its own recredentialing norms for panel members or other providers with whom it contracts. Such recredentialing may be as much performance based, in terms of history of meeting the demands of management, as it is competency based in terms of reassessment of usually recognized professional skills. As noted, such recredentialing may or may not protect the public. For example, dropping a psychologist from a managed care panel for having too high an average number of therapy sessions per patient, as judged by excessively money-driven norms, might actually harm the public rather than benefit it. Conversely, a managed care structure and most employer oversight situations offer opportunities for objective assessment of professional performance, and therefore could provide more valid assessments of professional competency than can most alternative assessment methods. Except to note that this trend may be the most influential of all factors in the future, data on both the nature and the direction of managed care and other job-retention recredentialing in psychology is sufficiently new that those issues are not reviewed separately in this chapter.

2.16.5 RECREDENTIALING TACTICS

Each of the foregoing categories of recredentialing may have a somewhat different primary emphasis. Licensure primarily protects the public, specialty credentialing primarily protects the integrity and image of the specialty, and job recredentialing primarily selects for whatever skills are deemed critical for the particular job. They nevertheless share a common concern of predicting future professional competency. They therefore tend to draw on a common body of approaches or tactics. The tactics used do much to determine the success of the recredentialing process, the satisfaction of the professionals, and the protection of the public. Four common classes of tactics can be identified: (i) procedural requirements, (ii) knowledge evaluations, (iii) skill demonstration, and (iv) outcome evidence.

2.16.5.1 Procedural Requirements

Recredentialing can be contingent on completion of certain procedures, such as completion of certain educational requirements (e.g. mandatory continuing education), performance of a certain number of critical professional tasks (e.g., log-book record of core procedures done by internal medicine residents (Wigton, 1992)), or consistent conformance to certain standards of practice (e.g., an average of no more than a specified number of therapy sessions per client).

The most common of these procedural requirements in psychology is completion of a defined number of continuing professional education (CPE) credits. The intent is to insure that the professional remains current, by exposure to an adequate amount of the newly emerging information in the field. It is doubtful whether mandatory CPE as currently implemented in most psychology jurisdictions represents an assessment of potential for future competency, however, because almost anyone of almost any level of competence or incompetence could complete the requirements, by simply sitting through the required number of hours of lecture (see Brennan, 1992; Conn, 1994). While mandatory CPE for relicensure is usually not considered to be "recredentialing" in psychology, it is considered to be an adequate basis for recredentialing by others (see Delahunt et al., 1992; Conn, 1994) and is the primary current basis for recredentialing of its certificate holders by the APA College of Professional Psychology.

The literature on mandatory CPE is complex and is beyond the scope of this chapter, except for two relevant observations. First, mandatory CPE requirements that are carefully tailored to the specific demands of professional practice are the most likely to assist in maintenance of professional competency (Conn, 1994; Rodgers, 1989). For example, the requirement to complete an annual "new developments in the field" review course prepared by a select group of specialty experts is likely to be more stimulative of professional competency than are the "catch-as-catch-can" market place driven programs that characterize most mandatory CPE psychology requirements. Such courses would also be more complicated and much more expensive for the credentialing group to prepare (Rodgers, 1989). Second, the primary hazard of mandatory CPE, other than its cost, is that it can give a false sense of security to the public. That outcome may of course please a professional group (Gross, 1978), especially if it relieves the professionals of the anxiety of evaluations that are more uncertain of successful passage.

Procedural requirements other than mandatory CPE are unusual in psychology, but might appropriately be considered, particularly in specialty areas. For example, completion of a certain number of biofeedback assessments and treatment plans might be a useful requirement for a biofeedback group desiring to assure a degree of currency in its techniques. Unless outcomes are monitored, however, no procedural approach that does not contain within it an inherent criterion of competency can assure presence of professional expertise. At worst, it only assures repeated exposure to or experience with bad approaches.

2.16.5.2 Assessments of Knowledge

Assessment of technical knowledge is the most common ingredient of formal assessment of professional skills, at least in psychology (see D'Costa, 1986). This may be so because educational systems have developed so much experience with such assessment. Many of psychology's major credentialing examinations are knowledge based. For example, the Examination for the Professional Practice of Psychology (EPPP), used by all US jurisdictions as a primary basis for professional licensure (Hall, 1987), is an examination of knowledge of the psychological concepts underlying the profession. Knowledge proficiency is also the type of credential offered by the APA College of Professional Psychology. Periodic repassage of a knowledge base evaluation is incorporated into several medical specialty recredentialing programs and is often considered as a possible requirement for recredentialing in psychology areas as well. For example, the APA College of Professional Psychology has debated incorporating such a requirement into at least some phase of its proficiency recredentialing requirements.

For use as reassuring indicators of professional expertise, knowledge base assessments have at least three major limitations. First, knowledge is not synonymous with either skill or competence. Even an elegant textbook knowledge of how to do brain surgery, or how to play basketball, does not safely translate into performance skills. Data supports this conclusion. For an example with even a highly circumscribed activity, a work sample test of anesthesia residents administering a spinal anesthesia correlated only 0.20 (4% of variance) with a multiple-choice knowledge test of the procedure (Howard, 1987).

Second, demonstration of competent knowledge in one information domain does not assure adequate knowledge in a separate critical but unassessed domain (Howard, 1987; Koocher, 1979; Tonesk, 1987). For example, the EPPP assesses a broad universe of information, but falls far short of assessing the specific knowledge that a psychoanalyst or a client-centered therapist or a behavior-modification therapist must draw on daily in order to function effectively within his or her own professional framework.

Third, performance on knowledge-based exams may depend as much on competency in the techniques of assessing the knowledge and on familiarity with the specific vocabulary of the assessment procedure itself as it does on "basic knowledge." Psychology's primary vocabulary is distressingly imprecise, such that words can and do mean different things to different people. For example, what, precisely, is meant by "medical necessity," by "the unconscious," by "emotion," or by "psychotherapy?" Especially in the more precise nuances of professional expertise, such nonstandardized meanings can render the task of truly accurate assessment of knowledge precarious at best and impossible at worst. This problem is compounded when the examination is compressed into such restricted formats as multiple choice options, in which minor differences of interpretation can make significant differences in outcome. Probably reflecting in large part this impact of increasing unfamiliarity with formal test taking and with the conventional vocabulary of the classroom, the American Board of Family Practice recredentialing experience has found a statistically significant systematic decline in examination scores, of up to two standard deviations overall, upon subsequent administrations of its examinations to its experienced practitioners (Leigh et al., 1993). The alternative interpretation seems unlikely, that the family practitioner fresh out of a residency is a substantially more competent and more knowledgeable physician than is the 18-year veteran in the field.

The general conclusion is warranted that knowledge is a necessary, but not a sufficient, ingredient of professional competency. It is part of the professional psychology licensing examination in the USA, but is not the sole basis for licensure, for good reason. If it becomes the sole basis for recredentialing, then such recredentialing can be only a partial, and often misleading, indicator of competency.

2.16.5.3 Skills Demonstration

Like knowledge, skill is a necessary but not sufficient ingredient of competency. Skill is the ability to implement a decision once it is made or to achieve a goal once it is chosen. It is the surgeon's "good hands," the golfer's ability to place the ball near the hole on a shot out of a sand trap, or the client-centered therapist's ability to recognize and reflect the "true feeling" embedded in a client's verbiage. For assessment purposes, skill tends to have a "built-in" quality, such that it can be demonstrated on demand and cannot easily be faked. A candidate can daydream through a CPE lecture or cheat on knowledge-based exams, but cannot fake 90 words a minute on a typing exam or 10 straight baskets from the free-throw line. Carefully constructed, skills assessments can implicitly incorporate knowledge and judgment assessment as well, by requiring skills to be demonstrated in real or simulation situations that require knowledge and judgment of what skills to apply. Such skill assessment is the essential component of airline pilot recredentialing, in which actual performance in handling a plane or a simulator in a situation calling for flying skill combined with flying judgment is observed and evaluated.

When they can be effectively applied, skills-based assessments are attractive recredentialing options. Simulation of real performance situations may allow close assessment of actual performance behavior. The ABPP professional competency examination (Mayfield, 1987; Ross, 1973) and several of the medical specialty board exams, in which the candidate is observed while assessing a real or hypothetical patient or addressing a real or hypothetical clinical problem, are of the skills-assessment type. Some graduate training programs in psychology are incorporating skills assessment into their formal evaluation processes, and nearly all incorporate such assessments informally. Whenever a student is observed role playing a therapy technique or giving a standardized test or is asked to evaluate a projective instrument product in a class discussion or is observed through a one-way mirror while interacting with a client, a skills assessment is being undertaken.

In psychology, there are three limitations to skills assessment as a basis for recredentialing. First, integrity and consistency of application of the skill in real-life situations may differ from that in the test-taking situation. Second, the critical skills necessary for a particular credential must be identified, and such skills are not often either obvious or agreed upon. Third, the valid basis for determining skill competency and the relationship of the skill to actual performance competency should both be unambiguous, and they seldom are.

The first problem, that test behavior may differ from actual clinical behavior, is primarily a problem for performance variables that have differential payoff for the professional within and without the test situation. The motivation for accurately reading a pathology slide probably changes little from test situation to laboratory situation, for example. Unfortunately, many professional psychology skills can be used exploitatively as well as constructively, with one use being demonstrated in an assessment situation and the other in client situations. For example, the exploitation of the therapist–client relationship for sexual or other favors in fact occurs, and would be a clear basis for decredentialing, but would rarely be displayed or observable in an assessment setting. Indeed, a performance evaluation of integrity or other character traits, which require more absolute than relative consistency and over an extended rather than limited time period, and are therefore usually fakable, is almost impossible in a limited test situation. Such traits are nevertheless a critical factor in professional outcome competency.

The solution to the second problem, of what skills to assess, may be obvious for a typist, and perhaps even for a surgeon, but is not for a psychologist. As Sechrest and Chatel have observed: "A major problem for professional psychology is, of course, that we do not really know how to specify what psychologists ought to be able to do, ought in fact to do, and we know even less about how well they ought to be able to do anything" (1987, p. 5). If the generic field of psychology, as Howard (1987) observes, is not easily describable in terms of specific skills, then perhaps subspecialties within psychology are. A skills approach might be useful, for example, in such areas as biofeedback or hypnosis or behavior modification, even if not in generic recredentialing.

The third problem, of criterion for determining the adequacy of a skill, has been especially troublesome in psychology. Many procedural skills in other fields have relatively unambiguous and objective indicators of adequacy. A hairline fracture on radiograph either is detected or is missed. An airplane is either kept within or deviates from a predetermined glide path range. Similar compelling evidence for the appropriateness of a given therapy response or of specific marital counseling advice is generally lacking (Berven, 1987). This dilemma has often been resolved within psychology by relying on the expert judgment of colleagues. If the skill appears adequate to the observer, it is judged adequate. Unfortunately, when there is ambiguity concerning the relationship of the skill to the professional goal, as there often is in psychological practice (Howard, 1987), such an observer-judgment approach is perhaps a better guarantee of orthodoxy than of competence, and as much a measure of the observer as of the observee.

For many purposes, when specific skills are known to play a critical role in professional competency, then skill assessment can be a useful basis for recredentialing. It is being incorporated into most medical specialty board recertification programs. Psychology has not yet identified its critical skills (Stevenson & Norcross, 1987), except possibly in some specialty areas, but perhaps will as it matures more as a profession. While considerably short of a completely valid measure of overall professional competency, the ability of a candidate to demonstrate certain critical professional procedural skills is nevertheless strongly reassuring concerning his or her potential for competency.

2.16.5.4 Outcome Evidence

In terms of public benefit, outcome effectiveness is the ultimate criterion against which all professional expertise is validated (see Berven, 1987; Koocher, 1979). Before such validations can be made, though, outcome effectiveness must itself be reliably measurable (Howard, 1987; Stevenson & Norcross, 1987). In many fields, the outcome produced by the professional services is unambiguous and objectively identifiable. Repair of a broken arm, for example, should result in a reknitted bone and an arm that can be used essentially in the same manner as the same arm before it was broken. Symptomatic relief, such as relief of pain, may be a secondary goal, but is not equivalent to the repair of the break itself.

In psychology, the outcomes achieved are usually ambiguous, and the precision with which they can be either specified or identified is usually far from adequate. Psychology has generally failed, as a profession, to declare what its goals are and what evidence can be used conclusively either to justify or to condemn its actions. Other than client satisfaction, which has been the basis for most psychology professional services (it is also equally the basis, of course, for the services of the drug dealer or the strip teaser), there are almost no agreed upon outcome measures for the effectiveness of psychological work (Sechrest et al., 1987). Should marriage counseling produce divorce, nondivorce? Is symptom relief (e.g., of depression or anxiety) enough, or should hypothetical underlying causes be identified and removed? Should the "cure" address solely the current episode or should it serve as an inoculation against any and all recurrences? Are the psychologist's goals different from or the same as those of a psychiatrist or a social worker addressing the same problem, or indeed do these different disciplines actually address the same problems even when they use the same *ICD-10* (current version of the *International Classification of Diseases*) codes for diagnosis?

Until such basic questions are answered, good outcome measures of professional competence will be almost impossible to specify. Until such outcome measures can be specified, the concept of recredentialing to establish current professional competency is relatively meaningless, because competency will remain undefined. Ultimately, therefore, consideration of the fundamental requirements of effective competency recredentialing requires consideration of the basic nature, goals, and methods of the profession. In no other dimension is the immaturity of the profession of psychology more strongly reflected than in the lack of clarity of these fundamental issues. These issues warrant further attention later in this chapter.

Fields within psychology, such as psychoanalysis, client-centered therapy, behavior modification, and biofeedback therapy, often have more precise concepts of appropriate outcomes for their own areas of practice than does the profession as a whole (Howard, 1987; Tonesk, 1987). This may mean that outcome measures and recredentialing for specialty or proficiency areas is more appropriate than recredentialing for the entire field. Indeed, orthodoxy itself can be an appropriate goal for some groups, such that peer judgment of competency becomes the defining goal of a desirable outcome. With assured orthodoxy, the public protection comes from knowing what to expect, even if not from assurance that a particular outcome will result.

2.16.6 WHAT CONSTITUTES PROFESSIONAL COMPETENCE?

The public's thirst for reassurance, the profession's marketplace competitiveness to satisfy such thirst, and the vested interest of others such as managed care to control professional practice seem to be driving psychology, like medicine and many other professions (e.g., Norcini, 1994), toward recredentialing arrangements. If such is the case, then it would seem wise for the profession to pursue as expeditiously as possible a clear understanding of the goals of the profession, its methods, and the conditions that will contribute best to its future development. Some consideration of these issues as they relate to the recredentialing dilemma follows.

Professional work can be arbitrarily divided into two broad types, practitioner and technological, depending on how the work domain is defined (Rodgers, 1980, 1986). Practitioner work is defined independently of the techniques it uses, by the area of need it addresses. Practitioners may or may not be able to provide a satisfactory solution to the problem they confront, but accept responsibility for it anyway, because it is in their professional domain. Medicine, for example, is defined as that profession which addresses problems of illness, even those illnesses for which it has no cure. Law, similarly, is defined as that profession that addresses legal problems, whether or not the problems have clear legal solutions. Because they must choose methods to fit the given problems, rather than selecting only problems that fit their methods, practitioner professions generally require "unlimited" licenses of practice.

A technology field, in contrast, is defined by its techniques, and limits its scope of work to those problems that fit the technology. A technology field is not expected to address problems for which it lacks a solution. Airplane piloting, for example, is defined by, and limited to, the ability to fly a plane. It does not address any and all transportation needs.

Psychological practice can be of either practitioner or technological type, depending on its focus. For example, the defined and orthodox therapies, such as client centered, psychoanalytic, or behavior modification, are technologies by this conceptualization, being limited to those conditions that are appropriate to the particular approach. Psychologists who specialize exclusively in one or more of these orthodoxies would appropriately be classed as technologists, as that term is here used. In contrast, the clinical psychologist whose office is open to anyone with a psychological problem is a practitioner, even if his or her most common (but not exclusive) method of handling such problems is a particular technological orthodoxy.

In general, technologies lend themselves well to recredentialing approaches, as the evaluation of competency can focus on either the orthodoxy of the professional, by peer judgment of a work sample, or the expected outcome if that is clearly implied by the procedure, such as the relief of phobic symptomatology by a behavior-modification deconditioning regimen. In contrast, practitioner approaches are difficult to assess with competency measures, because they often necessarily address problems of unknown solution with techniques of unknown validity, and routinely address problems of inadequately known solution with techniques known to be only partially effective. Under such circumstances, it is almost impossible on any given trial to divide the variance of either success or failure between an accurate component representing professional skill and other components not reasonably attributable to the work of the professional.

As most psychologists, even specialists in a particular approach, are usually open to assessment and management of problems that may not exactly fit the particular orthodoxy, it is suggested that practitioner work underlies most licensed clinical psychology practice. Understanding the nature and value of such work may therefore further clarify the complexity of the problem of recredentialing in psychology.

2.16.7 PRACTITIONER WORK

2.16.7.1 Addressing a Public-need Domain

As has already been noted, there is little consensus on the proper domain of professional psychology. It has been argued elsewhere (Rodgers, 1981, 1993, 1994) that it should be defined as any problem in human coping effectiveness or personal efficacy. Precise identification of the public needs addressed is ultimately critical for the profession, but is not essential for the material to follow, and is beyond the scope of this chapter.

2.16.7.2 Diagnosis

In practitioner work, the client typically enters the door with a problem for which the solution has not yet been established. The first practitioner act is therefore typically one of diagnosis, that is, determination of the nature of the presenting problem and its relationship to known corrective procedures. Only in the earliest days of the profession could the concept reasonably be held that there was no need for diagnosis, because a single solution (e.g., psychoanalysis, client-centered therapy, behavior modification, etc.) could fit all problems. Most of the profession has given up the hope that the inherent uncertainty of the task which inevitably confronts the practitioner could be converted into the more comfortable certainty of a technological "one size fits all" approach. Diagnosis is therefore necessary, to identify the presenting problem in terms that allow it to be channeled to relevant corrective approaches.

2.16.7.3 Prescription

After diagnosis, the solution to the presenting problem must be determined and recommended. The second practitioner act is therefore typically one of "prescription" of solution. Depending on the nature and clarity of the problem, the solution might be treatment with an orthodox approach, either by the practitioner or by referral to a technical specialist. Often, it is a practical procedure that is designed to deal with the immediate consequences of the problem more than with the problem itself (Rodgers, 1964).

2.16.7.4 Client Supervision

Unfortunately, psychological solutions are seldom as routine as identification of a problem and referral to an appropriate technologist for inevitably effective treatment. Therefore, a third step is usually necessary in practitioner work, and that is to follow the client's progress as corrective steps are tried, modify the diagnosis and treatment plans as necessary, and determine when maximum or optimal benefit has been achieved such that treatment should be discontinued. This third step can be called assuming professional responsibility for the patient, or "client supervision" (see Ohio Administrative Code Section 4732-5-01(B)(1.3)).

The critical dimension in these three essential activities of the practitioner is professional judgment in the face of uncertainty, not application of specific techniques. Indeed, a practitioner could utilize technology "extenders" or referral sources, for psychometrics, for deconditioning, for group therapy, even for individual therapy, and concentrate solely on the professional decision-making of diagnosis and prescription and client supervision, and adequately fulfill all the essential professional requirements of a competent practitioner. The task of assessing the professional expertise of such a professional would then become the task of assessing the adequacy of his or her professional judgment, not his or her skill at carrying out specific procedures. To be sure, such exclusive concentration on judgmental tasks seldom occurs, partially because it is not consistent with the training models used in psychology (but is not inconsistent with those used in medicine), and partially because some of the most useful diagnostic and client management information can come from the interaction associated with treatment or other procedural approaches. Nevertheless, such analysis does suggest that professional judgment, not professional technique, constitutes the *essential* nature of psychological practitioner work.

2.16.8 MATURITY OF THE PROFESSION AND RECREDENTIALING

The maturity of a practitioner field can be measured by the proportion of presenting problems that have clearly defined diagnoses and clearly defined optimal treatment approaches. In this regard, medicine at the turn of the twentieth century is astoundingly mature as compared to medicine at the turn of the nineteenth century. Antibiotics, anesthetics, and exploding biochemical knowledge have converted many formerly ambiguous judgment calls into essentially computer-specifiable exact protocols. When computer certainty can substitute for human judgment, then assessment of the competency of the human judgment is relatively easy and objective. In many of its fields, medicine is approaching that stage of certainty, even in its practitioner areas. As a consequence, effective assessment of competency of professional medical judgment is becoming feasible, perhaps for the first time, and periodic recredentialing based on measuring such effectiveness is becoming tenable.

In this respect, psychology is far from a mature practitioner field. It does not have its own catalog of types of presenting problems, continuing to borrow psychiatry's *DSM-IV* nosology. It does not have workable outcome measures in any substantial area of practice, except possibly measures of symptomatic relief. It has entrenched disputes over appropriate approaches to almost all of the problems that it recognizes as being within its domain, usually along orthodoxy lines of preferred therapies. As previously noted, the profession has not even objectively defined or identified some of its most fundamental concepts. For example, what is "unconscious process?" How does psychotherapy differ from "counseling?" Is "marital counseling" counseling or is it therapy? Is not therapy simply a meaningless term used to describe whatever it is a psychologist does to try to address a client's problems? These areas of confusion or lack of precision are evidence of an immature profession. More importantly, they are evidence that there are few clear-cut objectively definable "correct" judgments for the decisions the practitioner psychologist makes daily (see Berven, 1987, p. 223).

Even conformity to conventional thinking may be wrong, in terms of ideal outcome, when the clear solutions to problems are not known. Within this century, conventional wisdom has called for protracted and ultimately debilitating bed rest following a heart attack, and for radical mastectomy for all breast cancers however small. Under such circumstances, objective, defensible, valid assessment of competent professional judgment is at best difficult and at worst impossible. Therefore, recredentialing decisions based on assessing such competency become precarious (Koocher, 1979).

2.16.9 ADDRESSING THE UNKNOWN

The foregoing analysis is not intended to present a hopelessly dismal picture of the profession of psychology. On the contrary, it is intended to highlight a stage that every developing profession must go through, a stage of considerable uncertainty during which the public may long for reassurance concerning the professional's ability, and may unknowingly seek false security through recredentialing processes that can only minimally address the concerns for which they are designed. The positive aspect of the practitioner approach perhaps needs highlighting.

2.16.9.1 Initial Credentialing

Initial credentialing usually assures that practitioners are extensively trained in the best techniques known to the culture to address the problem areas of the professional domain; have demonstrated a capacity in apprentice roles to function at least minimally effectively; have during education and training and internships, survived many years of close scrutiny by mentors and members of the profession and been found not to display "fatal flaws," characterologic or otherwise, for carrying on the work of the profession; have demonstrated extensive technical knowledge of the field; and have been placed, after licensure, under the ongoing scrutiny of a regulatory board that can at any time measure their performance against a code-of-conduct floor below which their professional work must not fall. In short, the licensed psychologist has been selected to be as knowledgeable as possible about the area and to be unlikely to constitute an unusual hazard to the public, while still being able to render reasonable service. Such a select person usually recognizes and appropriately addresses common problems of known solution. It is the problems of unknown or only partially known solution, but of substantial cultural importance, that raise questions.

2.16.9.2 Practitioner Solution

For these important problems of unknown or ambiguous solution, the question must be raised of how the culture is to address them. To require a guarantee of success is to leave them unaddressed, or to turn them over to dishonest pretenders who falsely guarantee more than they can deliver. The practitioner solution has been to restrict those who can attempt to help such problems to a carefully selected licensed group; to try to limit, by means of protracted training and apprenticeship and a legally enforced code of conduct, the harm that such a select group can do; and then to leave that group free to do the best it can. In other words, the practitioner is deliberately given the freedom to function within a cultural veil of ignorance, because the need is there, and to do what makes the most sense in spite of the ignorance, in the hopes that someone will ultimately lift the veil and allow predictable solutions without creating too much harm in the process.

Those practitioner professions should advance the most rapidly that incorporate strong procedures for progressing through ignorance. This means incorporating procedures that encourage individualized approaches that are outcome driven or at least are outcome assessable in ambiguous areas, and discouraging ones that allow for excessive nonoutcome-driven idiosyncrasy. It also means avoiding procedures that either push too much toward unproved orthodoxy or carry more potential risk than any potential benefit can justify.

In this context, young professions such as psychology can concentrate too hard on proving their adequacy and not hard enough on identifying their inadequacy, and the cultural inadequacy, for dealing with critical problems. Medicine advertises its inability to cure cancer and many other illnesses, and stimulates the research funding to find solutions. Practitioner psychology does not even clearly define the problem domain within which it is willing to contend with the limitations of the present stage of knowledge, seldom admits inability to address a problem, seldom advocates for public support to study its areas of ignorance, seldom identifies clear outcome goals, and often seems more comfortable with technological certainty than with practitioner uncertainty, sometimes thereby becoming a valuable technological extender of a medical practitioner, but blurring its own professional identity and own contributions to lifting the cultural veil of ignorance that cloaks today's unsolved psychological problems.

In the ideal world, the practitioners are a guide through the quicksands of cultural ignorance in their own specialized professional domain, far more than a scientific tour guide over a well-established path. Some (e.g., Stern, 1984) have argued that the practitioner's work should become identical with that of the scientist at this stage, a carefully constructed *in situ* experiment directed toward resolving the problem. This view is disputed by Rodgers, (1964), except insofar as clear outcome goals that allow confirmation/disconfirmation of the professional work inevitably make the work scientific. The primary creed of the practitioner in the face of ignorance is to avoid harm, a commitment that often prevents a definitive scientific test. The next commitment is to deal practically with whatever aspects of the problem lend themselves to being addressed. These steps are often far different from "scientific inquiry," but are critical (Rodgers, 1964). The third step is to function within the accepted standards of the profession, which standards may reflect art more than science but at least reflect a consensus judgment that is safer than individual capriciousness. Finally, if experimental procedures are introduced into the treatment, then these should indeed be approached with the same perspective as a scientist, but this final step may be a rare occurrence in routine practice.

2.16.9.3 Practitioner Recredentialing

It is suggested that dealing with the problems of cultural ignorance is not primarily an individual responsibility, but is the responsibility of the profession as a whole. Adequacy in this role must essentially be judged over time and for the profession, in terms of evidence of successes and failures in the real world and progression toward removing the ignorance. In most practitioner fields, including psychology, competency in this basic role of the practitioner, dealing effectively with important problems under a veil of current ignorance, is essentially unmeasurable by examination, at least by currently practical technology. For this role, high standards of preparation for initial licensure, the influences of professional guild membership and collegial pressures, and the controls of the marketplace, of regulatory board codes of conduct, and of citizen resort to malpractice redress may serve both the public and the profession better than can any feasible recredentialing process, at least until the profession and the field of knowledge which underwrites it matures to the point that a large body of its professional judgment can be effectively reduced to rather precise and agreed upon decision-tree protocols. Recredentialing seems better suited to specialty and job situations in an immature profession than to the general practitioner function.

2.16.10 SUMMARY

Credentialing of expertise in psychology raises many questions and many complexities. Recredentialing conceptually raises many more. In practitioner work, initial credentialing may, appropriately, do more to weed out those at high risk for doing harm and low potential for doing good—the poorly educated, the naïve, the obviously irresponsible, and the professionally unsocialized—than it does to assess and assure current professional expertise. Placing reliance on further experience to sharpen the necessary skills, initial credentialing may set an important floor of reasonable professional training and socialization, but still not guarantee that the essentially untried and newly credentialed practitioner will be immediately effective. Recredentialing, in contrast, has little place unless it directly addresses current professional competency. That, it turns out, is a difficult task in professional psychology and especially in practitioner psychology.

No US or Canadian jurisdiction has yet adopted a competency recredentialing process for the generic or clinical psychology license. The American Board of Professional Psychology, the American Psychological Association College of Professional Psychology, and other specialty or proficiency certifiers within the field have explored competency-based recredentialing procedures, but few if any have adopted them. Therefore, practical experience with such procedures in psychology is lacking. The medical field is gaining experience with recredentialing approaches, however, within their specialty boards. The evidence so far gained suggests that the procedures are feasible in professionally mature specialty areas, are generally demanding and expensive if they attempt to address performance issues, are more easily and defensibly adaptable to procedural and technical than to clinical skills, and are probably more appropriate tools for professional specialty groups than for legal jurisdictions. Examination of the tasks of a professionally immature field such as psychology suggests that control processes other than recredentialing may better serve society and the profession as a whole for the regulation of the practitioner, although recredentialing may be an appropriate approach in technological or specialty areas. The profession's ability to provide valid assurance of professional outcomes competency is currently sufficiently limited in almost all areas of psychology that recredentialing may create more false sense of security than protection for the public. Its primary use in psychology may be to assure orthodoxy or competency in procedural skills or an underlying knowledge base in specialty or proficiency areas.

2.16.11 REFERENCES

Allen, D. L. (1994). A report on compulsory continuing dental education requirements for relicensure. *International Dental Journal, 44*(6), 637–640.

Allred, T. J., & Steiner, L. (1994). Alternate-site testing. Consider the analyst. *Clinics in Laboratory Medicine, 14*(3), 569–604.

Baldwin's Ohio administrative code (Vol. 11) (1997). St. Paul, MN: West Group.

Bennett, W. M., & Langdon, L. O. (1995). Recertification: a challenge to those trained in the "good old days." *American Journal of Kidney Diseases, 26*(3), 556.

Berven, N. L. (1987). Improving evaluation in counselor training and credentialing through standardized simulations. In B. A. Edelstein & E. S. Berler (Eds.), *Evaluation and accountability in clinical training* (pp. 203–229). New York: Plenum.

Brennan, A. (1992). Analysing mandatory continuing education. *Nursing Standard, 6*(42), 29–32.

Chambless, L. E., McMahon, R., Finch, A., Sorlie, P., Heiss, G., Lyles, R., & Wu, K. K. (1993). ARIC hemostasis study—III. Quality control. Atherosclerosis risk in communities. *Thrombosis & Haemostasis, 70*(4), 588–594.

Clunie, G. J. (1993). Postgraduate medical education—comparisons between the United Kingdom and Australia. *Journal of the Royal College of Physicians of London, 27*(2), 154–157.

Conn, R. B. (1994). Continuing clinical chemistry education in the United States. *Clinica Chimica Acta, 232*(1–2), 47–51.

D'Costa, A. G. (1986). The validity of credentialing

examinations. *Evaluation and the Health Professions, 9*(2), 137–169.
Delahunt, B., Beer, I. D., & Taylor, D. E. (1992). Attitudes to specialist recertification: results of a national survey among pathologists. *New Zealand Medical Journal, 105*(947), 493–495.
Department of Health, Education, & Welfare (1977). *Credentialing health manpower* (DHEW Publication No. PHS 77/5005); (NTIS No. HRP-0024664). Washington, DC: DHEW.
Eagle, C. (1992). Anaesthesia and education. *Canadian Journal of Anaesthesia, 39*(2), 158–165.
Egerton, W. S. (1994). Health care delivery system in Australia and its effect on surgical education and training. *World Journal of Surgery, 18*(5), 662–665.
Goto, Y. (1994). Specialist training and certification process for anaesthesiologist in Japan. *Annals of the Academy of Medicine, Singapore, 23*(4), 630–632.
Grim, C. M., & Grim, C. E. (1995). A curriculum for the training and certification of blood pressure measurement for health care providers. *Canadian Journal of Cardiology, 11* (Suppl. H), 38H–42H.
Gross, S. J. (1978). The myth of professional licensing. *American Psychologist, 33*(11), 1009–1016.
Haag, G. P. (1992). Point: retesting should be required for CRNA recertification. *Nurse Anesthesia, 3*(1), 3–5.
Hall, J. E. (1987). Licensure and certification of psychologists. In B. A. Edelstein & E. S. Berler (Eds.), *Evaluation and accountability in clinical training* (pp. 253–281). New York: Plenum.
Hasbargen, J. A., & Culclasure, T. F. (1994). Special Forces Medical Sergeants (18 Delta) recertification. *Military Medicine, 159*(1), 7–9.
Holmes, S. E. (1986). Comments on this special issue. *Evaluation and the Health Professions, 9*(2), 131–136.
Howard, A. (1987). Work samples and simulations in competency evaluation. In B. A. Edelstein & E. S. Berler (Eds.), *Evaluation and accountability in clinical training* (pp. 55–76). New York: Plenum.
Johanson, W. G. (1995). The ABIM recertification program—nearing liftoff. *Chest, 108*(1), 1–2.
Koocher, G. P. (1979). Credentialing in psychology: close encounters with competence? *American Psychologist, 34*(8), 696–702.
Leigh, T. M., Young, P. R., & Haley, J. V. (1993). Performances of family practice diplomates on successive mandatory recertification examinations. *Academic Medicine, 68*(12), 912–919.
Matarazzo, J. D. (1977). Higher education, professional accreditation, and licensure. *American Psychologist, 32*(10), 856–859.
Mayfield, P. N. (1987). Certification of psychologists by the American Board of Professional Psychology. In B. A. Edelstein & E. S. Berler (Eds.), *Evaluation and accountability in clinical training* (pp. 283–297). New York: Plenum.
McClennan, B. L., & Herlihy, C. S. (1995). The continuing competence needs of physicians: a survey of the medical specialty societies. *American Journal of Roentgenology, 165*(4), 789–795.
Nelson, L. P. (1994). American Board of Pediatric Dentistry recertification section examination. *Pediatric Dentistry, 16*(5), 381–382.
Norcini, J. J. (1994). Recertification in the medical specialties. *Academic Medicine, 69*(10 Suppl.), S90–S94.
Pfister, S. M. (1995). Home oxygen therapy: indications, administration, recertification, and patient education. *Nurse Practitioner, 20*(7), 44, 47–52, 54–56.
Phillips, G. D., & Willis, R. J. (1994). Specialist training and examinations in anaesthesia and intensive care in Australia and New Zealand. *Annals of the Academy of Medicine, Singapore, 23*(4), 610–613.
Rodgers, D. A. (1964). In favor of separation of academic and professional training. *American Psychologist, 19*(8), 675–680.
Rodgers, D. A. (1980). The status of psychologists in hospitals: technicians or professionals. *Clinical Psychologist, 33*(4), 5–7.
Rodgers, D. A. (1981). A proposed model psychology licensing law. *Professional Practice of Psychology, 2*(1), 47–71.
Rodgers, D. A. (1986). Psychologists as practitioners, not technicians. In H. Dörken & Associates (Eds.), *Professional psychology in transition: Meeting today's challenges* (pp. 141–173). San Francisco: Jossey-Bass.
Rodgers, D. A. (1989). Mandatory CE solution with teeth: week's retreat at college campus. *Ohio Psychologist, 35*(6), 16–18.
Rodgers, D. A. (1993). When will psychology "psychologize" instead of "medicalize?" *The National Psychologist, March/April, 15.*
Rodgers, D. A. (1994, April 21). *A suggested Nosological Classification System for Clinical Psychology.* Paper presented at the convention of the Ohio Psychological Association, Columbus, OH.
Roessler, G. (1994). Information on certification and recertification of transcultural nurse specialists. *Journal of Transcultural Nursing, 6*(1), 46.
Ross, A. O. (1973). A rejoinder on behalf of ABPP. *American Psychologist, 28*(1), 88–89.
Saunders, N. A., & Paget, N. S. (1994). Maintenance of professional standards and the recertification of physicians. *Journal of Internal Medicine, 236*(4), 363–365.
Sechrest, L., & Chatel, D. M. (1987). Evaluation and accountability in training for professional psychology: an overview. In B. A. Edelstein & E. S. Berler (Eds.), *Evaluation and accountability in clinical training* (pp. 1–37). New York: Plenum.
Simon, A. (1992). Preparation for recertification. *Journal of Post Anesthesia Nursing, 7*(1), 59–61.
Stern, S. (1984). Professional training and professional competence: a critique of current thinking. *Professional Psychology Research and Practice, 15*(2), 230–243.
Stevenson, J. F., & Norcross, J. C. (1987). Current status of training evaluation in clinical psychology. In B. A. Edelstein & E. S. Berler (Eds.), *Evaluation and accountability in clinical training* (pp. 77–115). New York: Plenum.
Tonesk, X. (1987). Clinical evaluation of medical students in US medical schools. In B. A. Edelstein & E. S. Berler (Eds.), *Evaluation and accountability in clinical training* (pp. 183–202). New York: Plenum Press.
Wiens, A. N. (1983). Toward a conceptualization of competency assurance. *Professional Practice of Psychology, 4*(2), 1–15.
Wiens, A. N., & Dörken, H. (1986). Establishing and enforcing standards to assure professional competency. In H. Dörken & Associates (Eds.), *Professional psychology in transition: Meeting today's challenges* (pp. 174–199). San Francisco: Jossey-Bass.
Wigton, R. S. (1992). Training internists in procedural skills. *Annals of Internal Medicine, 116*(12 Pt. 2), 1091–1093.
Wilson, F. C. (1993). Credentialing in medicine. *Annals of Thoracic Surgery, 55*(5), 1345–1348.
Zarowitz, B. J., Vlasses, P. H., Dukes, G. E., Gal, P., Miller, W. A., Porter, W. C., Rush, D. R., Schneider, P., & Talbert, R. L. (1993). Pharmacotherapy specialty certification examination. IV. 1992 results and process modifications, including recertification. The 1992 Specialty Council on Pharmacotherapy, Board of Pharmaceutical Specialties. *Pharmacotherapy, 13*(3), 262–266.

2.17
Continuing Education: Updating of Knowledge and Skills

EDWARD F. BOURG
California School of Professional Psychology, Alameda, CA, USA

2.17.1 INTRODUCTION

An essential element of a profession is that its members embrace the concept of lifelong learning, namely, a commitment to stay knowledgeable about developments in their given field of practice (Peterson, 1976). Continued professional education characterizes mature professions, most importantly, because professions ultimately exist to serve the public welfare and the public has a vested interest in assuring that individual practitioners have up-to-date knowledge and skills. The public has a right to know, for example, that a clinical psychologist treating severe depression is aware of the latest advances in pharmacotherapy for this illness. For almost all practicing psychologists such detailed knowledge could be available only from continuing professional education, since research findings confirming the biological determinants of depression, improved pharmacological treatments for severe depression, and more effective psychosocial treatments of depression are themselves relatively recent.

A commitment to such lifelong learning has been a hallmark of clinical psychology. It is reflected in the proceedings of the various national conferences which have set the standards for education and training in clinical psychology since the late 1940s (Bourg et al., 1987; Korman, 1974; Peterson et al., 1992; Raimy, 1950). The imperative to engage in continued professional education is also reflected in the American Psychological Association (APA) *Ethical Principles of Psychologists and Code of Conduct* (APA, 1992). The enrollment of clinical psychologists in formal continuing education programs, documented in several studies (Brown, Leichtman, Blass, & Fleisher, 1982; McNamara, 1977), is an important method for fulfilling that professional and ethical mandate.

2.17.2 DEFINITION AND SPECIFICATION OF CONTINUING PROFESSIONAL EDUCATION IN CLINICAL PSYCHOLOGY

The term "continuing education" (CE) generally refers to education for the adult learner and currently is used to describe a very large array of adult learning experiences reflected, for example, in the diverse offerings of the "extension division" of major universities. For the professional, an extensive literature around continuing education emphasizing themes such as quality assurance, effectiveness, and methods of teaching has been developed. In the context of a better educated workforce, continuing professional education has been described as follows:

> Education to maintain and improve professional competence is called Continued Professional Education, and is a special subset of the broad field of adult CE. As such it is part of the most rapidly growing segment of American education, one of importance to our society and economy, and one symbolizing profound changes in the way we approach education, work and the relationship between the two. (Hunt, 1992, p. 1)

This chapter about continuing professional education in clinical psychology will consider the major questions within the field for professional psychologists, more specifically clinical psychologists. Although the more general term CE has been the customary nomenclature for such learning experiences, it would enhance public trust for clinical psychology to adopt a more professional referent for these learning experiences. Accordingly, the term "continuing professional education" (CPE) will be used in this chapter except when referring to specific institutional or organizational structures currently designated under the current CE rubric.

CPE has been defined for health care providers by the American Hospital Association (AHA) as follows: " . . . a planned series of activities that enables an individual to acquire the skills, knowledge, and behavior necessary to meet current job requirements or remedy identified deficiencies" (AHA, 1978, p. 2).

Several aspects of this definition are especially relevant for CPE in clinical psychology. First, the emphasis on planning suggests that the individual practitioner should attend CPE programs that fit within the context of a planned self-directed curriculum for development congruent with one's professional life cycle. Also, CPE providers should follow principles of good learning design in developing courses as organized sequences of learning and programs which differentiate the needs of learners. Second, CPE courses should encompass both knowledge-based objectives and skills training; in the field of clinical psychology, as in most professions, insufficient attention has been given to skills training. Finally, the focus on remediation suggests that, for participants and providers alike, considerable attention should be given to cogent, problem-oriented needs assessment.

The concept of lifelong learning for practitioners after the graduate degree includes the whole spectrum of a professional career which now spans 40–50 years of practice. Recently there has been emphasis on specifying a more coherent education and training experience immediately following the doctoral degree (Stewart, Horn, Becker, & Kline, 1993). In a recent survey, a substantial number of postdoctoral programs were identified and described (Wiens & Baum, 1995). Widespread discussion has included a national conference focused on practitioner programs (Association of Psychology Postdoctoral and Internship Centers, 1993); another national conference sponsored by the APA in January 1994, which included discussion and recommendations about postdoctoral education for all practitioner roles (APA, 1995); and the development of criteria and procedures by the APA Committee on Accreditation. In August 1996 the APA Council of Representatives approved criteria for the accreditation of postdoctoral programs for practitioners. "Postdoctoral residency" is the preferred title for these training experiences and in almost all states such postdoctoral training is required for licensure. A professional ethic has clearly evolved in which the basic formal education and training of a professional psychologist in general, and a clinical psychologist in particular, should include the postdoctoral residency. In that sense CPE for clinical psychology really applies to programs of further training after the postdoctoral residency and such programs offered for clinical psychologists in active practice will be the focus of this chapter.

2.17.3 THE EFFECT OF THE EXPONENTIAL GROWTH IN KNOWLEDGE AND EXPANSION OF SKILLS IN CLINICAL PSYCHOLOGY ON CPE

2.17.3.1 The Shrinking Half-life of Graduate Professional Education

The field of clinical psychology flourished in the United States after World War II, partly in response to the need for trained mental health practitioners to deal with the psychological sequelae of combat. The alliance formed among the National Institute of Mental Health, the Veterans Administration, and clinical psychology programs in universities established the basic model for clinical training (Humphreys, 1996). In the years following the war, except for the recent focus on the postdoctoral residency noted above, attention to standards in the education and training of clinical psychologists has been focused primarily on the quality of doctoral programs in clinical psychology.

Yet, given the expansion in knowledge and skills in the field of clinical psychology, the half-life of graduate education is continually shrinking. This concept refers to the estimate that the original body of knowledge learned in a doctoral program will be only one-half as useful in a given period of time, the "half-life," as when the doctorate was originally awarded. In the early 1970s Dubin estimated that the half-life of a doctorate in psychology was 10–12 years (Dubin, 1972). Twenty years later, the participants in the 1994 APA National Conference on Postdoctoral Education and Training in Psychology estimated the half-life of graduate education in psychology to be approximately eight years (APA, 1995). We can expect this trend to continue and lead to greater reliance on CPE across the professional life span of the practitioner. Some authors predict that CPE will eventually become the most important part of the education and training of professionals (Houle, 1980; Hunt, 1992). In the 1993 World Summit on Medical Education, particular emphasis was placed on the importance of continuing education to meet the challenges facing medicine in the twenty-first century: "Continuing Education is the single main process by which medical services can be reorganized, reprogrammed, and made relevant to the contemporary needs of societies" (Walton, 1995, p. 43).

In 1994 the APA sponsored the first national conference broadly focused on postdoctoral education and training in psychology with discussions across the range of roles of psychologists as teachers, researchers, and practitioners. This conference was also inclusive in specifically extending its deliberations to the lifelong education and training of all psychologists. It explicitly included discussion about issues and problems in the CPE of practitioners, including clinical psychologists (APA, 1995) and heralded a shift in emphasis on the paramount "locus" of professional education and training for practitioners. It is easy to imagine that in the not too distant future a relatively senior clinical psychologist will have acquired most of the knowledge and skills used in professional practice through CPE.

2.17.3.2 Differentiation within the Field of Clinical Psychology

A second implication for CPE resulting from the exponential growth in knowledge and the expanding skill base in clinical psychology is increased specialization in professional psychology in general and clinical psychology in particular. Such differentiation is characteristic of well-established professions with an expanding knowledge and skill base, and the demand for innovative opportunities for in-depth CPE programs in which clinical psychologists can learn new specialties and/or subspecialties is a clear consequence. After struggling with the need for standards and procedures to guide this evolution in professional psychology, a consensus has recently been established that further specialization in professional psychology should be guided by a coherent set of policies and procedures. In February 1995 the APA established the Commission for the Recognition of Specialties and Proficiencies in Professional Psychology (CRSPPP) with profound implications for CPE in psychology. One of the CRSPPP standards for seeking recognition as a separate specialty or proficiency is clearly established CPE criteria and programs in a particular field of professional practice. The principles approved for CRSPPP establish three broad parameters for distinguishing among specialties and subspecialties (proficiencies) which have implications for CPE: populations, problems, and theory and techniques.

Not surprisingly, most of the subfields associated with differences in each of these three categories are represented by organized interested groups and/or established divisions within APA. For example, in the area of distinct populations served, applications are likely to be submitted to CRSPPP for specialty or proficiency recognition for women, children, older adults, and ethnic minorities. Many CPE programs are already being offered that directly relate to the specific prevention and treatment needs of each of these populations (Crespi & Rigazio-Digilio, 1992; Myers, Wohlford, Guzman, & Echemendia, 1991; Panayotoff, 1993). As these, and similar areas of practice, continue to evolve and differentiate, more diverse CPE programs will be needed.

Similarly, as psychologically based prevention and treatment programs evolve for both long-standing problems (e.g., serious mental illness) and newer problems (e.g., AIDS), more in-depth CPE programs will be needed (Robiner, Ohnsong, Parker, & Strike, 1994). The APA HOPE program, a "train-the-trainer" CPE effort for the prevention and treatment of AIDS, is a model for an extensive CPE program that can be made available throughout the country for the prevention and treatment of a specific problem. Similarly, a program, jointly sponsored by APA and many state associations, for training a large cadre of psychologists across the country capable of responding in disaster relief teams, is an impressive example of a large-scale CPE program focused on a specific psychological problem of national importance.

Finally, further refinements in more traditional theories (e.g., psychoanalytic, behavioral, or family systems) and newer theoretical subfields (e.g., self-psychology, dialectical behavior therapy, or narrative therapy) will also affect existing CPE programs or spawn new CPE programs for educating and training practitioners. Again, as these or other subfields reach the status of specialties or proficiencies in professional psychology, practitioners will seek CPE programs both to inform themselves as responsible professionals and to seek credentials.

2.17.3.3 CPE for Proficiencies

Both of these motivations have contributed to the recent development of the APA College of Professional Psychology, charged with credentialing individual psychologists in clearly delineated subspecialties or proficiencies. Credentials in these areas are likely to have implications for professional reimbursement in the managed care environment. For example, the College has already established a system for psychologists to qualify for credentials in the field of alcohol and substance abuse. Although the College is itself specifically prohibited from offering CPE programs, CPE providers are already designing programming in this area to assist practitioners in meeting the educational criteria and learning the content specified by the College for both initial certification and periodic recertification. Similar CPE demand and development in other areas in which the College will offer credentialing for proficiencies in professional psychology can be anticipated.

2.17.3.4 CPE for Specialties

Similarly, the various specialties that have *de facto* recognition by the American Boards of Professional Psychology (ABPP) already have elaborate education and training criteria for practitioners who seek credentials in these areas. In the late 1990s ABPP offered diplomate status in nine areas: behavioral psychology, clinical psychology, neuropsychology, counseling psychology, family psychology, forensic psychology, health psychology, industrial organizational psychology, and school psychology. All these specialties and any future specialty area to be recognized by CRSPPP, and any specialty certificate system that recognizes the expertise of individual providers, will need to ensure that CPE programs designed to assist practitioners in such specialty training are provided.

One example of the exponential growth of knowledge and expansion of skills that opens a new avenue for specialized practice in clinical psychology is psychopharmacology. In August 1996, the APA Council of Representatives approved the development of appropriate education and training programs for the authority to prescribe psychotropic medications within an expanded scope of practice for psychologists who are health care providers. Although some general guidelines for such training programs have been promulgated by APA, the development of adequately trained psychologists in such a specialty will call for innovative, carefully sequenced, in-depth CPE programs.

2.17.4 HEALTH CARE REFORM AND CPE

In almost all developed countries the years from the late 1980s have seen a revolution in health care systems that is driven by both political and economic forces. A basic focus in health care reform is the general concern for competent, consistent quality care at a price that immediate payers, such as insurance companies, and intermediate payers, such as employers, are willing to expend (Azzaretto, 1992; Cummings, 1995). The public policy questions surrounding this development are immense. For example, the United States spends more per capita on health care costs than almost any other developed country, and its competitiveness in the evolving global economy is thereby compromised. Also, in an era of fiscal constraint and limited resources, the public must ultimately determine what it is willing to allocate for health care in the context of other pressing economic and social demands.

2.17.4.1 CPE as a Cost Center

These developments impact CPE on a number of levels. First, CPE is itself an integral part of the health care system. As such, in spite of its manifest usefulness in updating health care professionals, CPE must be subject to the same norms of accountability as other health care practices. From the point of view of the managed care company, CPE is a cost center and subject not only to questions of effectiveness in general but cost-effectiveness in particular (Slotnick, Lichtaver, & Raskowski, 1995). With health care reform there is increased emphasis on interdisciplinary practice and therefore a mandate for CPE programs that emphasize such practice. For example, recent studies in the treatment of the seriously mentally ill call for greater interdisciplinary care (Johnson, 1990). Recent breakthroughs in understanding the biological basis for these illnesses and advances in psychopharmacological treatment have led to greater emphasis on collaborative practice between clinical psychologists and psychiatrists as well as primary care physicians, who prescribe the majority of psychotropic medications in the United States (APA, July 1992). Also, the emphasis on case management of clients with a dual diagnosis and the seriously mentally ill calls for closer collaboration with social workers, nurses, and substance abuse counselors.

2.17.4.2 CPE for Expanding Roles in Clinical Psychology

In the evolving health care system, in both the private (including profit and nonprofit organizations) and the public sector, the emphasis on cost-effectiveness associated with managed care encourages the utilization of professionals with less education and training than clinical psychologists to provide direct service. Accordingly, in the context of health care reforms, clinical psychologists are likely to need CPE to broaden their roles beyond the direct provision of mental health services, the activity with which they have become most identified since the late 1960s (Cummings, 1995; Humphreys, 1996).

In order to function in the evolving health care system, many clinical psychologists will need retraining to develop their skills in clinical and administrative supervision, program development and administration, and designing community prevention programs (Broskowski, 1995; Cummings, 1995; Humphreys, 1996). One important role for clinical psychologists in a managed care environment emphasizing cost-effectiveness and accountability will be in the design and implementation of outcome research. Another opportunity to broaden the practice of clinical psychologists may be in the burgeoning field of health psychology, certainly an allied, and many would argue a derivative, field of clinical psychology (Matarazzo, 1987).

Ultimately, clinical psychologists may begin to focus on an even broader spectrum of behaviors and settings which promote health, productivity, quality of life, and a greater sense of community. As this occurs, the need for CPE programs that emphasize the interdisciplinary training of clinical psychologists will expand beyond merely the inclusion of other health care providers. Increasingly those psychologists with specialized training in fields such as neuropsychology and forensic psychology are working with professionals outside the health care field, for example, in the areas of child custody and worker's compensation. Similarly, as clinical psychologists move to more community systems perspectives, they will need to work more collaboratively with other professions such as educators, architects, organizational consultants, and urban planners. CPE programs for clinical psychologists will be required to facilitate such collaboration.

2.17.5 SHAPING CPE FOR THE ACTIVE PRACTITIONER

Based on several important longitudinal studies, psychologists have led the way in clearly differentiating distinct stages in the adult life cycle. Parallel developments have occurred in adult learning theory and application. Providers of CPE for professionals have developed a relatively coherent set of criteria for the adult learner that take account of both adult learning principles and the specific circumstances of the professional work place (Jennett & Swanson, 1994; Mann, 1990; Scott, 1994). For example, for the health care provider relevant criteria include active learning methods, more case specific teaching, and CPE format design which takes into account multiple professional demands (Slotnick et al., 1995).

2.17.5.1 More Sophisticated Needs Assessments

Some principles of adult learning have been incorporated into criteria for CPE programs for clinical psychologists. For example, program offerings based on needs assessments and the specification of learning objectives, both fundamental adult learning practices, have been incorporated in the APA Committee for the Approval of Continuing Education Sponsors (CACES) criteria. Yet, needs assessment for CPE programs for professional psychologists can improve by drawing on both practice and research in CPE in allied health professions. For example, a more complex needs assessment, offering a model for psychology, has recently been conducted by the American Speech, Language, and Hearing Association (L. Phillips and S. Russell, personal communications, August 9, 1996). The goal was to develop CPE courses which clearly distinguished between needs (based on identified problems in practice) and wants (often related to "hot" topics or prominent presenters). This model, utilizing focus groups from the field, recognized that the more traditional method of devising and/or approving CPE programs via a small committee of educators and/or practitioners is inevitably hampered by the scope of their restricted view and decisions based on the limited program submissions that emerge from an "open call" for CPE programs.

2.17.5.2 CPE for the "Reflective Practitioner"

In developing CPE programs for active, especially more senior, practitioners, the concept of the "reflective practitioner" is especially relevant. Schön uses the term to describe a professional making use of a body of knowledge and professional skills in approaching a specific class of society's problems within its domain (Schön, 1983, 1987). This concept has special relevance in clinical psychology in which the major instrument of change is the self and the dictum "healer know thyself" has added meaning.

The reflective practitioner concept is useful in framing a theoretical paradigm for CPE because of the nature of any profession like clinical psychology which is based on science. On the one hand, the basic paradigm of "applied science" is applicable in the sense that applications are based on theory substantiated through research, and practice must inform science by providing the basic clinical datum on which more controlled research studies can be undertaken. On the other hand, given the specific problems individual clients actually present in the complex multifaceted context of the health care system, clinical applications must of necessity "run ahead" of science (Peterson, 1991). Science is pure and allows for absolutes while practice is client-specific, presenting unique issues from case to case. Clinical interventions inevitably involve professional judgment that goes beyond the straightforward application of specific imperatives derived from the science base of psychology. The reflective clinical psychologist is by definition engaged in a continuous professional education paradigm since each client encounter is both a professional service and a subject for continued professional development.

In this context, how does the ongoing learning of the clinical psychology reflective practitioner proceed? Progress in professional knowledge and skills is based on the development of professionals who can reflect across the spectrum of basic values, theory, strategies of intervention, and specific techniques. The first task of the clinical psychologist is always problem setting because they are continually confronted by uniqueness in applying the body of knowledge and skills accumulated. In clinical psychology, the unique features of a case may arise from the larger social, cultural, or familial context which surrounds the client, the specific nature and quality of the presenting problem(s), and/or in the fundamental fact of "individual difference" which every person brings to the clinical encounter; all give rise to conflict and ambiguity with respect to the "correct" intervention.

According to Schön (1987), reflective practitioners move through five stages in their attempt to learn from experience: knowing in action, surprise, reflection in action, the experiment, and reflection on action. Schön developed his ideas with reference to the micro-learning environment of the individual practitioner who is engaged in a continuous process of informal CPE. The concept of the reflective practitioner also has great promise at the macro level of CPE program design and research on the effectiveness of CPE (Fox, 1991; Slotnick et al., 1995). For example, in the context of learning a particular theoretical refinement, intervention strategy, or new technique, reflective clinical psychologists can focus on one or more of the five processes in which they are engaged with specific cases to become more effective in professional judgments and performance: improving one's knowing in action, sharpening one's ability to identify professional surprises, increasing one's effectiveness in reflection in action while caring for the client, designing more effective and appropriate experiments, and improving one's ability to integrate experiences through reflection in action. In designing CPE programs for clinical psychologists, explicit attention can be given to addressing one or more of the five stages in the learning process.

2.17.5.3 Active-learning and Skills-oriented CPE

CPE faculty can also make use of the reflective practitioner paradigm in designing instructional methods to capitalize on this ongoing process by participant learners. While traditional lectures are effective for communicating specific new information, CPE courses are too reliant on traditional knowledge dissemination. Practitioners bring a rich wealth of material from their ongoing reflection process to every CPE course. The literature on CPE across professions is increasingly focusing on a "new paradigm for CPE" which emphasizes more use of active-learning principles and techniques (Moore, Green, Jay, Leist, & Maitland, 1994; Queeney, 1992). Cervero (1988) has suggested a three-step process of allowing the professional first to see, then to try, and then to reflect on the knowledge and skills taught that is more consonant with the practitioner's usual learning style in the practice context. This process facilitates learning through the social construction of professional acumen within a community of practitioners which is both more respectful of and more responsive to the practitioner's felt needs.

Moreover, active-learning instructional methods better capture the complexity involved in any clinical intervention. The practitioner draws from a rich store of basic values, theoretical paradigms, and intervention strategies in making specific technical interventions. Formal CPE programs would be well advised to address more directly the interplay between basic values, theory, intervention strategies, and specific techniques. CPE programs for clinical psychologists are too often focused on theory, whereas most practitioners operate along the more practical end of the spectrum dealing with intervention strategies, specific techniques, and even professional "moves," that is, concrete verbal and nonverbal behaviors (Shapiro & Reiff, 1993). Greater direct relevance to the practitioner's life is gained in courses taught from a problem-based methodological paradigm (Engel et al., 1992; Moore et al., 1994; Slotnick et al., 1995).

2.17.5.4 CPE for Diverse Learning Styles

Finally, in designing programs for active practitioners, more account should be taken of the fact that practitioners bring diverse learning styles and interests to CPE which cut across specific content areas. For example, both gender-based ways of knowing and culturally responsive approaches to learning should be considered in the teaching styles and learning methods utilized (Briscoe, 1990; McGowen & Hart, 1990). Also, clinical services for women and ethnic minority populations need special attention in CPE programs to retrain clinical psychologists in response to changing demographic realities (Lerman & Porter, 1990; Myers et al., 1991).

2.17.6 VARIED AND INNOVATIVE VENUES FOR CPE

2.17.6.1 Informal and Undocumented CPE

It is important to recognize that much important lifelong learning by the active practitioner goes on through informal CPE vehicles. Perhaps the largest informal CPE provider for clinical psychologists in the United States is the APA Office of Publications. Their expansion of computer-assisted learning, through such services as PsycLit and PsycInfo, has greatly eased access to this and related information sources. The APA Office of Publications has launched its first electronic publishing venture with a videotape series teaching psychotherapy skills. Although documentation is scant, clinical psychologists appear to make extensive use of other informal channels of CPE, for example, case supervision provided by senior clinicians, peer supervision groups, in-service training in health care settings, and attendance at professional conferences. The APA CE Programs Office has also provided informal CPE by offering audiotapes of the best-attended sessions at the annual APA Convention.

While some other allied health care professions, for example, pharmacy, provide formal CPE credit for attendance at large conferences and meetings (B. Hammonds, personal communication, August 8, 1996), clinical psychology has exercised more caution with respect to awarding formal CPE credit because of the difficulty in assuring appropriate monitoring. However, many psychologists utilize such forums for informal CPE, thereby gaining access to a broad range of ideas from which they can make more informed decisions regarding future investment in formal CPE study. Smaller, focused conferences are increasingly being deemed appropriate venues for formal CPE credit. For example, clinical psychologists attending the Annual State Leadership Conference, sponsored by the APA Practice Directorate, can gain CPE credit through a carefully planned and monitored system of programs teaching knowledge and skills relevant to contemporary practice.

2.17.6.2 Independent Study CPE

Independent study CPE programs, when carefully planned and monitored, are increasingly available for CPE credit (Woolfort, Lang, Farghaly, Ziemiecki, & Faja, 1991). The APA CE Committee, in conjunction with the APA Office of Publications, has a well-developed independent study program that has grown rapidly since the late 1980s. In 1996, APA's independent study programs expanded to include the Clinician's Research Digest, an abstract of research articles relevant to the practice of clinical psychology. Other CPE providers offer print-based independent study programs, and increasingly, audiotape- and/or videotape-based independent study programs are available. This rapid expansion of independent study programs in clinical psychology will increase exponentially into the twenty-first century with breakthroughs in computer-assisted and distance learning.

2.17.6.3 Teleconference and Videoconference CPE

Some allied health professions have already developed programs based on new technologies (Engel et al., 1992; Hampton, Mazmanian, and Smith, 1994) For example, since the early 1990s the American Speech, Language, and Hearing Association (ASHA) has sponsored a series of national teleconferences, that is, telephone conference calls linking CPE learners across the country. Although this format only allows for limited interactivity in the approximately 40 sites (some accommodating hundreds of participants) selected, it does provide a user-friendly and relatively inexpensive vehicle for disseminating specific new information. ASHA has also pioneered several national videoconferences, concluding that such programming is best done in partnership with established national videoconference vendors in which the association takes primary responsibility for curriculum and faculty, the videoconference expert takes responsibility for all technical logistics, and both share in marketing efforts and profits (S. Russell, personal communication, August 9, 1996).

CPE for other allied health professions is increasingly being provided through preproduced videotapes and over closed circuit television. For example, one for-profit provider has established a national hospital network which delivers ongoing medical education for physicians and nurses in regularly scheduled programming throughout the day. In May 1994 the APA CE Committee and the National Council of Schools and Programs in Professional Psychology pioneered a national CPE videoconference for clinical psychologists on revisions in the newly published *DSM-IV*. This venue proved ideal for delivering such a relatively objective body of information with which all clinical psychologists must be conversant. However, it is not yet clear that clinical psychologists see this vehicle, even with an interactive format, as comparable to face-to-face contact with faculty when dealing with more complex clinical knowledge and skills.

2.17.6.4 Computer-assisted CPE

Another promising new venue for CPE, already being developed in several allied health professions, is the use of computer-assisted learning both through the use of a CD-ROM format or an Internet format that permits regular updating. As noted above, APA has pioneered informal CPE with the CD-ROM format by providing access to a very large data bank in the form of abstracts from a pool of books and articles. With the development of high-end multimedia capability, however, it is clear that we have the capacity to develop sophisticated interactive CPE learning vehicles. In fact, a number of such programs have been developed for undergraduate courses in psychology and for CPE courses in allied health fields (Dillon, 1996). The main obstacle for this venue is that front end production costs are very high and with rapidly changing knowledge and skills, it is difficult to judge whether the expense of such production costs are warranted.

Direct on-line CPE programming through the Internet allows for regular updating of the material presented but production costs, limited access, and lack of sophisticated computer skills by active practitioners is currently problematic. However, the advantages of such a learning vehicle, already being pioneered in some professional certificate programs other than psychology, are clear: (i) no travel time is required; (ii) learning at one's own pace is facilitated; (iii) faculties are capable of both closely monitoring what is being learned by each student and effectively working in both a classroom and tutorial framework simultaneously; (iv) utilization of asynchronous learning with each learner having complete flexibility for presence "in the classroom" when personal and professional availability allow for optimal attention; (v) the possibility of ongoing assessment is maximized when faculties are able to assess and address each individual learner's pace and mastery. Other than planning and production costs, the major disadvantage of such a CPE venue in a field like clinical psychology where subtle verbal and nonverbal cues are so important, is lack of direct face-to-face contact between faculty and learners and among colearners.

2.17.6.5 In-service CPE

Until recently most CPE providers have focused on attracting individual practitioners. With the expansion of managed care in both the private and public sector, doubtless more attention will be given to in-service training (Hargrove, 1992; Marsick, 1990; Presland, 1993). Such programs have the advantage of being both cost-effective and providing the opportunity to attend to individual as well as systemic issues in professional practice. Behavioral health care organizations are now offering such CPE programs for managed care companies who recognize that this training is beneficial for their providers and ultimately their patient subscribers (Lynton, 1992).

2.17.7 QUALITY CONTROL IN CPE: AN INSTRUMENT FOR ENHANCING QUALITY CONTROL IN PRACTICE

CPE will be of increasing importance in clinical psychology because the evolution of the health care system in the developed countries, including the United States, is placing increased emphasis on quality control mechanisms. It is evident that greater accountability will be required of all clinical psychologists (Stricker & Rodriguez, 1988). The three primary methods generally used to ensure competence among professionals are retesting for license renewal, peer review, and mandatory CPE. Of the three methods, the first generally is opposed by professionals and has not been well received in surveys among licensed psychologists (Hellkamp, Imm, & Moll, 1989). Peer review is to some extent incorporated in evolving practice settings, for example, as part of review for hospital privileges for clinical psychologists. CPE, however, is by far the most common method for upgrading the knowledge and skills among health service providers, including clinical psychologists. CPE incorporates peer review, at least in some instructional formats, and provides both an incentive and a structure for maintaining competence in clinical practice.

2.17.7.1 Mandatory CPE

Since the late 1970s the advantages and disadvantages of mandatory continuing professional education (MCPE) have been contested across a broad range of professions. Overall, the practice seems to be clearly gaining acceptance (Garganta, 1989; Phillips 1994b; Queeney & English, 1994) and this has been the trend with licensed psychologists (VandeCreek, Knapp, & Brace, 1990). With a substantial increase in jurisdictions requiring MCPE since the late 1980s, currently 39 of the 61 jurisdictions represented by the Association of State and Provincial Psychology Boards (ASPPB) in the USA and Canada have adopted some form of MCPE and four others are actively considering the practice (ASPPB, 1996). One obvious place to begin assessing quality control in MCPE is to determine what similarities cut across the 39 jurisdictions which have mandated CPE for relicensure; unfortunately there is a wide range of variation among the jurisdictions regarding both the number of hours required for relicensure (10–50 credits per year) and the kind of MCPE activities which various jurisdictions allow under their MCPE relicensure provisions.

A Task Force on Model State and Provincial CE Regulations of the Board of Educational Affairs of the APA, after reviewing the existing statutes, issued the following summary recommendations as a national standard for the USA:

(i) the current modal number of 20 CPE credit hours per year for relicensure is a reasonable guideline for MCPE;

(ii) the APA CACES mechanism for sponsor approval should be recognized by states;

(iii) the current criteria of the APA CACES should be used by jurisdictions which establish independent criteria for CPE approval status;

(iv) the current APA CE Committee criteria (e.g, clearly articulated learning objectives based on adequate needs assessments and assessment of program quality by an independent panel of experts) should be used by jurisdictions which wish to adopt criteria for specific approval of every CPE activity;

(v) a clearinghouse should be established by one or more national organizations responsible for credentialing psychologists in the health care field to foster simplification of tracking compliance with MCPE regulations; and

(vi) participants should maintain their own records of MCPE attendance for some years and regulatory agencies should conduct random audits of such records in assessing compliance with MCPE (APA, October, 1995).

2.17.7.2 Beyond Sponsor Approval to Program Review

Most states accept programs offered by CPE sponsors approved by the APA CACES for licensure renewal. There has been concern, however, during the 1990s about whether a sponsor approval system, however refined the criteria and review process, can sufficiently guarantee the quality of each program offered by approved sponsors. Special concern attends to the practice of cosponsoring activities with institutions which are not part of the sponsor approval system. Although the APA CACES criteria clearly specify involvement in the planning of such activities by the approved cosponsor, it is difficult to monitor compliance. In the context of using MCPE as the major method of assuring quality control among clinical psychology practitioners, this concern has added significance.

One innovative response to this specific concern about reliance on a general sponsor approval system deserves attention and further monitoring. In January 1996, a new MCPE regulation took effect in California requiring that all CPE courses acceptable for relicensure must be individually reviewed and approved by an independent committee established by the Psychology Association Accrediting Agency (Board of Psychology, 1995). The Board of Psychology has revised its regulations to include programs which incorporate an equivalent individual program review process by other professional groups, for example, CE courses sponsored by the APA CE Committee.

One of the major concerns in this new system is the cost and complexity of maintaining such a detailed approval structure. Wisconsin, after maintaining a similar system for some years, moved to the simpler sponsor approval system (A. Pacht, personal communication, August 14, 1996). On the other hand, tighter course by course regulation is under consideration by two other state psychology boards. There is some concern about how well such a system will effectively and fairly control quality across CPE programs. For example, the accrediting agency in California understandably relies heavily on "primary reviewers" of each program and there has been no report about inter-rater reliability.

2.17.8 FUTURE DIRECTIONS: A LONG-TERM RESEARCH AGENDA FOR CPE

One concern raised about MCPE as a measure of assuring quality control is the limited empirical evidence for the effectiveness of CPE in improving the performance of professionals such as clinical psychologists (Phillips, 1994b; Queeney & English, 1994). More importantly, carefully controlled studies have not established that CPE actually improves the health of clients served by clinical psychologists. The effectiveness of CPE in various professions, especially allied health professions, has been a matter of concern over the 1990s. There is, however, growing evidence that CPE does favorably impact performance when CPE programs are well designed according to a sound program development model (Fox 1991; Moore et al., 1994; Phillips, 1994a, 1994b; Raymond, 1991). Moreover, methods for determining program quality are gradually improving as various health care professions work to address the issue of quality assurance in CPE (Newcomer, 1989). A key strategy, albeit an expensive and arduous undertaking, is to simultaneously target various levels in the CPE enterprise in an evaluation process: CPE sponsors, CPE faculty, CPE learning methods, CPE curricula design, learners' acquired knowledge and skills, and improved competence in practice.

In all professions, it is difficult to collect evidence in support of CPE's effect on competence because of the large number of variables affecting performance and the difficulty of designing controlled studies which isolate the impact of specific CPE interventions. Clinical psychology will have to establish a sophisticated research program to determine the effectiveness of CPE. Ultimately the question about CPE's effectiveness will probably have to be addressed in the same way that clinical psychologists addressed the question of psychotherapy's effectiveness. The global question will have to be framed in more specific terms: what kinds of CPE programs are effective for learning what kinds of clinical psychology skills, for what kinds of problems?

2.17.8.1 A Model: Research in Continuing Medical Education

In the health care field, the most impressive research agenda relating to the effectiveness of CPE programs has been undertaken with respect to CPE for physicians (Beaudry, 1989; Davis & Fox, 1994; Davis, Thomson, Oxman, & Haynes, 1995; Fox, Mazamian, & Putnam, 1989; Haynes, Davis, McKibbon, & Tugwell, 1984). A systematic review of the voluminous literature on the effect of Continuing Medical Education (CME), based on a multiyear research project, clearly demonstrated how well advanced the research agenda is on effective CME (Davis et al., 1995). The selection criteria for the study were very strict by current standards in the field of CPE for clinical psychologists: (i) only randomized control trials of CME programs; (ii) clearly replicable educational interventions; (iii) physicians had to be in the majority in the CPE programs included; and (iv) objective measurements of physician performance or health care outcomes had to be present. Using these criteria, the authors selected only 99 studies, which included 160 educational interventions, from an impressive database of over 6000 studies on the broadly defined topic of effective CME programs.

The most effective CME interventions included patient-mediated strategies, peer discussion, audit with feedback, and practice rehearsal. The study concludes that with such carefully controlled and objectively measured CME interventions, physician performance, and to a lesser extent health care outcomes, may be positively altered. The authors emphasize that their selection criteria systematically excluded the results of qualitative research method " ... that would afford additional valuable insights into physician behavioral change" (Davis et al., 1995, p. 703). It should not be surprising, given what clinical psychologists know from learning theory, that the most effective educational interventions emphasized practice-enabling strategies (e.g., role playing), peer discussion, and reinforcing learning methods. Variation in effectiveness was also attributable to motivation, especially to individual readiness to change based on the practitioner's clear perception of a gap between need and current knowledge and skills. In addition, CME programs were more effective in impacting physician performance when barriers to changing behaviors were systematically addressed.

2.17.8.2 Application to a Research Agenda for Clinical Psychology

Probably the most unsettling finding for clinical psychologists from the Davis et al. (1995) study was that relatively short (one day or less) formal CME events generally effected no change. The modal referent for a CPE course in clinical psychology is a one or two day workshop. In fact, the APA CACES criteria for the minimum length of a CE course is one hour, primarily to accommodate CPE programs set in the context of institutional in-service training. However, this negative finding must be interpreted in the context of the strict selection criteria and emphasis on performance enhancement in this specific study. As noted above, many workshops for clinical psychologists are focused on new knowledge and/or theory. Also, an important but limited role of such workshops has been posited in the three-phased learning model developed by Fox et al. (1989): "preparing to change," "making the change," and "solidifying the change." Using this conception, their research in CME found that traditional shorter focused workshops were more useful at the initial and final stage. For actually making performance change, that is, learning new skills, ongoing interaction with peers was essential. This principle is, in fact, incorporated in all specialty training in clinical psychology under the rubric of "supervised professional experience" and widely institutionalized, for example, in the long-standing model for training clinical psychologists in psychoanalysis.

The impressive research agenda for CME programs for physicians described above would need to be adapted to clinical psychology where it may be more difficult to determine such rigorous objective measures of "sound performance." Nevertheless, just as there has been increasing support for empirically validated clinical interventions, a research agenda in CPE for clinical psychology can be envisioned which approximates the standards which have been set by CME program providers and researchers.

2.17.8.3 Key Components of Effective CPE

There does seem to be a clear consensus about criteria which characterize good CPE programs across professions. The International Association for Continuing Education and Training (IACET) has established 10 criteria for the Continuing Education Unit (IACET, 1993). Although these criteria apply across the broad panoply of CE programs sponsored, for example, in large university "extension divisions," the criteria are, in fact, generally reflected in the APA CACES criteria. An eminent consultant on CPE has drawn on these criteria in emphasizing six critical components of effective CPE programs: needs assessment, learning outcomes, qualified CPE faculty, content and instructional methods, demonstration of learning, and program evaluation (Phillips, 1994b). Although these are familiar concepts, the systematic program development model presented relative to these six criteria is very sophisticated and would serve as a helpful guideline for CPE program providers in clinical psychology. For example, in discussing needs assessment, Phillips emphasizes the distinction between need and want. The former is based on clearly identifying the gaps in current knowledge and skills which negatively impact performance. All too often current needs assessment in clinical psychology is simply based on practitioners' "wants," that is, identifying topics in which they are interested. Sophisticated needs assessment is emphasized often as the most important criterion in enhancing effectiveness in CPE (Queeney, 1992; Vanek, Carey, Secic, Jackman, & Fleshler, 1994). In considering qualified CPE faculty, attention is often limited to the qualifications of the faculty with respect to content material but notice should also be taken of the instructor's ability to address the specific needs of adult professional learners (Lynton, 1992; Scott, 1994). Careful attention to these six criteria in controlled studies on CPE would serve as a good starting point for a research agenda on effective CPE programs in clinical psychology.

In an age of cost containment for clinical services one final point is warranted. Those in the educational establishment are understandably committed to the position that more education is better, but for the practitioner CPE can realistically be viewed as a cost center (Slotnick et al., 1995). CPE competes for resources with other aspects of the clinical psychologist's professional and personal life and includes both gains (peer contact, new knowledge and skills, opportunities to gain wisdom from respected practitioners) and costs (enrollment and travel fees, loss of income, unavailability for family contact). More attention must be given to the cost-effectiveness of CPE programs. If the cost of the program is too high for the participant practitioner, whether in financial terms or difficulty of access, there is little likelihood that a CPE program, however well designed, will reach many clinical psychologists. This latter point will be especially important as CPE programs move beyond the mere dissemination of new knowledge in the customary one or two day CPE format to longer term in-depth programs which focus on building skills for more effective clinical practice.

2.17.9 SUMMARY

In this chapter, major future directions in CPE for clinical psychologists have been suggested: continued rapid expansion of knowledge and skills in psychology will demand more CPE as the relative half-life of graduate education continues to diminish; differentiation in the field will continue and specialization and subspecialization will place greater demands on CPE programs that combine the acquisition of knowledge and skills for treating new populations and problems with innovative theories and techniques; the active practitioner will demand greater flexibility and access to CPE and increased utilization by CPE providers of new technology; changes in the health care system focused on greater accountability by clinical psychologists will demand CPE as a predominant method for quality assurance.

Most important, if a chapter on CPE is included in a book on clinical psychology 20 years hence, our field must possess a more coherent body of research on effective CPE programs. That research agenda can build on and complement the work of other health care professions. With thoughtful planning and commitment, it will be difficult but not impossible to disentangle the interaction effects of behavioral change, educational format, practice setting, and the clinical psychology interventions utilized.

In the larger context of changes in the health care system, the industrialization of clinical psychology is here to stay (Cummings, 1995). In a sense, all of the trends noted above are inherently associated with sweeping changes in the delivery of medical services (Walton, 1995). In that context, it will be all the more important to continue the long tradition in clinical psychology which emphasises the need for lifelong learning. There is, however, an important caveat in focusing on the need for CPE exclusively in the context of accountability, an inherently "outer directed" motive. Clinical psychologists also engage in CPE for a combination of psychological factors related to job satisfaction, including sustained interest and excitement, professional affiliation and peer interaction, validation of one's knowledge and skills, and a heightened sense of competence in dealing with troublesome client problems. These psychological factors are some of the major reasons that professionals give for participating in CPE and are the salient variables that many consider in choosing among CPE program options (Slotnick et al., 1995). Even in an industrialized health care system, idealism will be necessary for the health care professional and CPE programs for clinical psychologists will need to continue to appeal to such "inner directed" motives.

2.17.10 REFERENCES

American Hospital Association (1978). *Consideration of legislative mandatory continuing education proposals.* (AHA No. G037 13M–11/78–6474). Chicago: Author.

American Psychological Association (1995). *Education and training beyond the doctoral degree: Proceedings of the American Psychological Association National Conference on Postdoctoral Education and Training in Psychology.* Washington, DC; Author.

American Psychological Association (1992). Ethical principles of psychologists and code of conduct. *American Psychologist. 47*(12), 1597–1611.

American Psychological Association (October, 1995). *Final report of the Board of Educational Affairs Task Force on Developing Model State and Provincial Continuing Education (CE) Regulations.* Washington, DC: Author.

American Psychological Association (July 1992). *Report of the ad hoc task force on psychopharmacology of the American Psychological Association.* Washington, DC: Author.

Association of Psychology Postdoctoral and Internship Centers (1993). *Proceedings of the National Conference on Postdoctoral Training in Psychology, October 27–31, 1992.* Washington, DC: Author.

Association of State and Provincial Psychology Boards (1996). *The handbook of licensure and certification requirements for psychologists in North America.* Montgomery, AL: Author.

Azzaretto, J. F. (1992). Quality control in continuing professional education: Accountability, effectiveness, and regulation. In E. S. Hunt (Ed.), *Professional workers as learners: The scope, problems, and accountability of continuing professional education in the 1990s* (Report No. OR–92–3006). Washington, DC: Office of Educational Research and Improvement. (ERIC Document Reproduction Service No. 350 945).

Beaudry, J. S. (1989). The effectiveness of continuing medical education: A quantitative synthesis. *The Journal of Continuing Education in the Health Professions, 9*(4), 285–307.

Board of Psychology, State of California Department of Consumer Affairs (1995). *Regulations relating to the practice of psychology, 1397.60–1397.69.* Sacramento, CA: Author.

Bourg, E. F., Bent, R. J., Callan, J. E., Jones, N. F., McHolland, J., & Striker, G. (1987). *Standards and evaluation in the education and training of professional psychologists.* Norman, OK: Transcript Press.

Briscoe, D. B. (1990). Community education: A culturally responsive approach to learning. In J. M. Ross-Gordon, L. G. Martin, & D. B. Briscoe (Eds.), *Serving culturally diverse populations. New directions for adult and continuing education. No. 48, Winter 1990: The Jossey-Bass higher and adult education series* (pp. 81–91). San Francisco: Jossey-Bass.

Broskowski, A. T. (1995). The evolution of health care: Implications for the training and careers of psychologists. *Professional Psychology: Research and Practice, 26*(2), 156–162.

Brown, R., Leichtman, S., Blass, T., & Fleisher, E. (1982). Mandated continuing education: Impact on Maryland psychologists. *Professional Psychology: Research and Practice, 13*, 404–411.

Cervero, R. M. (1988). *Effective continuing education for professionals.* San Francisco: Jossey-Bass.

Crespi, T. D., & Rigazio-Digilio, S. A. (1992). Professional development and continuing education: Implications for the school psychologist. *School Psychology International, 13*, 347–355.

Cummings, N. A. (1995). Impact of managed care on employment and training: A primer for survival. *Professional Psychology: Research and Practice, 26*(1), 10–15.

Davis, D. A., & Fox, R. D. (Eds.) (1994). *The physician as learner: Linking research to practice.* Chicago: American Medical Association Press.

Davis, D. A., Thomson, M. A., Oxman, A. D., & Haynes, R. B. (1992). Evidence for the effectiveness of CME: A review of 50 randomized controlled trials. *Journal of the American Medical Association, 268*(9), 1111–1117.

Davis, D. A., Thomson, M. A., Oxman, A. D., & Haynes, R. B. (1995). Changing physician performance: A systematic review of continuing medical education strategies. *Journal of the American Medical Association, 274*(9), 700–705.

Dillon, C. L. (1996). Distance education research and continuing professional education: Reframing questions for the emerging information infrastructure. *The Journal of Continuing Education in the Health Professions, 16*(1), 5–13.

Dubin, S. (1972). Obsolescence or lifelong education: A choice for the professional. *American Psychologist, 7*, 486–498.

Engel, C. E., Browne, E., Nyarango, P., Akor, S., Khwaja, A., Karim, A. A., & Towle, A. (1992). Problem-based learning in distance education: A first exploration in continuing medical education. *Medical Education, 26*(5), 389–401.

Fox, R. D. (1991). New research agendas for CME: Organizing principles for the study of self-directed curricula for change. *The Journal of Continuing Education in the Health Professions, 11*(3), 155–167.

Fox, R. D., Mazamian, P. E., & Putnam, W. E., (Eds.) (1989). *Changing and learning in the lives of physicians.* New York: Praeger.

Garganta, K. J. (1989). *The question of mandatory continuing education for professionals.* Cambridge, MA: Harvard University. (ERIC Document Reproduction Service No. 356 422).

Hampton, C. L., Mazmanian, P. E., & Smith, T. J. (1994). An interactive videoconference: An effective CME delivery system. *The Journal of Continuing Education in the Health Professions, 14*(2), 83–89.

Hargrove, D. S. (1992). Community mental health center staff development for service to special populations. In S. Cooper & T. Lentner (Eds.), *Innovations in community mental health* (pp. 141–169). Sarasota, FL: Professional Resource Books.

Haynes, R. B., Davis, D. A., McKibbon, A., & Tugwell, P. (1984). A critical appraisal of the efficacy of continuing medical education. *Journal of the American Medical Association, 251*(1), 61–64.

Hellkamp, D. T., Imm. P., & Moll, D. (1989). Mandatory continuing education (MCE): Desirable or undesirable? A survey of executive officers of state psychological associations. *Journal of Training & Practice in Professional Psychology, 3*(2), 33–46.

Houle, C. O. (1980). *Continuing learning in the professions.* San Francisco: Jossey-Bass.

Humphreys, K. (1996). Clinical psychologists as psychotherapists: History, future, and alternatives. *American Psychologist, 51*(3), 190–197.

Hunt, E. S. (1992). Introduction: The professional learner as worker. In E. S. Hunt (Ed.), *Professional workers as learners: The scope, problems and accountability of continuing professional education in the 1990s* (Report No. OR-92–3006). Washington, DC: Office of Educational Research and Improvement. (ERIC Document Reproduction Service No. 350 945).

International Association for Continuing Education and

Training (1993). *The continuing education criteria and guidelines*. Washington, DC: Author.

Jenett, P. A., & Swanson, R. W. (1994). Traditional and new approaches to CME: Perceptions of a variety of CME activities. *The Journal of Continuing Education in the Health Professions, 14*(2), 75–82.

Johnson, D. L. (Ed.) (1990). *Service needs of the seriously mentally ill: Training implications for psychology*. Washington, DC: American Psychological Association.

Korman, M. (1974). National conference on levels and patterns of professional training in psychology: The major themes. *American Psychologist, 34*, 696–702.

Lerman, H., & Porter, N. (1990). *Feminist issues in psychotherapy*. New York: Springer.

Lynton, E. A. (1992). Continuing professional education: Comparative approaches and lessons. In E. S. Hunt (Ed.), *Professional workers as learners: The scope, problems and accountability of continuing professional education in the 1990's* (Report No. OR-92–3006). Washington, DC: Office of Educational Research and Improvement (ERIC Document Reproduction Service No. 350 945).

Mann, K. V. (1990). Enhancing learning: How can learning theory help? *The Journal of Continuing Education in the Health Professions, 10*(4), 177–186.

Marsick, V. J. (1990). Human service organizations as communities of learning. In M. Galbreith (Ed.), *Education through community organizations* (pp. 45–54). San Francisco: Jossey-Bass.

Matarazzo, J. D. (1987). There is only one psychology, no specialties, but many applications. *American Psychologist, 42*(10), 893–903.

McGowen, K. R., & Hart, L. E. (1990). Still different after all these years: Gender differences in professional identity formation. *Professional Psychology: Research and Practice, 21*(2), 118–123.

McNamara, J. R. (1977). Patterns of continuing education for Ohio psychologists: A survey of interests and activities (1972–1974). *Professional Psychology, 8*, 368–376.

Moore, D. E., Green, J. S., Jay, S. J., Leist, J. C., & Maitland, F. M. (1994). Creating a new paradigm for CME: Seizing opportunities within the health care revolution. *The Journal of Continuing Education in the Health Professions, 14*(1), 4–31.

Myers, H. F., Wohlford, P., Guzman, L. P., & Echemendia, R. J. (Eds.) (1991). *Ethnic minority perspectives on clinical training and services in psychology*. Washington, DC: American Psychological Association.

Newcomer, K. E. (1989). Techniques for determining program quality. In J. S. Wholey & K. E. Newcomer (Eds.), *Improving government performance: Evaluating strategies for strengthening public agencies and programs. The Jossey-Bass public administration series and the Jossey-Bass management series* (pp. 126–140). San Francisco: Jossey-Bass.

Panayotoff, K. G. (1993). The impact of continuing education on the health of older adults. *Educational Gerontology, 19*, 9–20.

Peterson, D. R. (1976). Is psychology a profession? *American Psychologist, 31*(8), 572–581.

Peterson, D. R. (1991). Connection and disconnection of research and practice in the education of professional psychologists. *American Psychologist, 46*(4), 422–429.

Peterson, R. L., McHolland, J., Bent, R. J., Davis-Russell, E., Edwall, G. E., Maggidson, E., Polite, K., Singer, D. L., & Striker, G. (Eds.) (1992). *The core curriculum in professional psychology*. Washington, DC: American Psychological Association.

Phillips, L. (1994a). *The continuing education guide: The CEU and other professional development criteria*. Dubuque, IA: Kendall/Hunt.

Phillips, L. (1994b). *A study of mandatory continuing education*. Washington, DC: American Psychological Association.

Presland, J. (1993). Planning for continuing professional development. *Educational Psychology in Practice, 8*(4), 225–233.

Queeney, D. S. (1992). Problems of content and delivery in continuing professional education. In E. S. Hunt (Ed.), *Professional workers as learners: The scope, problems and accountability of continuing professional education in the 1990s* (Report No. OR-92–3006). Washington, DC: Office of Educational Research and Improvement (ERIC Document Reproduction Service No. 350 945).

Queeney, D. S., & English, J. K. (1994). *Mandatory continuing education: A status report. Information series, No. 57*. Columbus, OH: Center on Education and Training for Employment. (ERIC Document Reproduction Service No. 372 306).

Raimy, V. C. (Ed.) (1950). *Training in clinical psychology*. New York: Prentice-Hall.

Raymond, M. R. (1991, April). *The effectiveness of continuing education in the health professions: A reanalysis of the literature*. Paper presented at the annual meeting of the American Educational Research Association, San Francisco.

Robiner, W. N., Ohnsong, T. J., Parker, S. A., & Strike, B. (1994). Psychologists' HIV/AIDS experiences, anxiety, knowledge and continuing education: A preliminary report. *The Journal of Continuing Education in the Health Professions, 14*(4), 196–211.

Schön, D. A. (1983). *The reflective practitioner*. New York: Basic Books.

Schön, D. A. (1987). *Educating the reflective practitioner*. San Francisco: Jossey-Bass.

Scott, C. J. (1994). Applied adult learning theory: Broadening traditional CME programs with self-guided, computer-assisted learning. *The Journal of Continuing Education in the Health Professions, 14*(2), 91–99.

Shapiro, S. B., & Reiff, J. (1993). A framework for reflective inquiry on practice: Beyond intuition and experience. *Psychological Reports, 73*, 1379–1394.

Slotnick, H. B., Lichtauer, D. F., & Raskowski, R. R. (1995). Rethinking continuing medical education. *The Journal of Continuing Education in the Health Professions, 15*(1), 8–22.

Stewart, J. A., Horn, D. L., Becker, J. M., & Kline, J. S. (1993). Postdoctoral training in severe mental illness: A model for trainee development. *Professional Psychology: Research and Practice, 24*(3), 286–292.

Stricker, G., & Rodriguez, A. R. (1988). *Handbook of quality assurance in mental health*. New York: Plenum Press.

VandeCreek, L., Knapp, S., & Brace, K. (1990). Mandatory continuing education for licensed psychologists: Its rationale and current implementation. *Professional Psychology: Research and Practice, 21*(2), 135–140.

Vanek, E. P., Carey, W. D., Secic, M., Jackman, D. M., & Fleshler, B. (1994). Value of needs assessment surveys. *The Journal of Continuing Education in the Health Professions, 14*(4), 224–231.

Walton, H. J. (1995). World summit on medical education and continuing education. *The Journal of Continuing Education in the Health Professions, 15*(1), 40–47.

Wiens, A. N., & Baum, C. G. (1995). Characteristics of current postdoctoral programs. In *Education and training beyond the doctoral degree: Proceedings of the American Psychological Association National Conference on Postdoctoral Education and Training in Psychology*. Washington, DC; American Psychological Association.

Woolfort, M. W., Lang, W. P., Farghaly, M. M., Ziemiecki, T. L., & Faja, B. W. (1991). Varying the format of CDE: Practitioners' perceptions of need and usefulness. *The Journal of Continuing Education in the Health Professions, 11*, 215–224.

2.18
Generalist and Specialist Training in Clinical Psychology in Australia

PAUL R. MARTIN
University of New England, Armidale, NSW, Australia

2.18.1 INTRODUCTION

Postgraduate training in clinical psychology in Australia has gone through a dramatic growth period since the 1980s during which time the number of base level courses has doubled and professional doctorates have been introduced at several universities. The rapid change promises to continue into the early twenty-first century so that Australian universities will have a range of training programs that bear little resemblance to the situation in the 1980s.

In preparing this chapter, a questionnaire on clinical training was sent to the heads of all 38 university departments/schools of psychology in Australia. Ultimately, all heads responded, so that this chapter is based on a comprehensive review of current offerings. Sections 2.18.5–2.18.7 report the questionnaire responses.

A word of caution needs to be emphasized with respect to the term "specialist." When used in the context of the discipline of psychology, clinical is viewed as one specialty along with other professional specialties such as counselling, organizational, and educational. On the other hand, clinical psychology covers a broad domain and specialties within clinical psychology are often recognized such as mental health,

health psychology, and child and adolescent psychology. Although it is tempting to call these specialties subspecialties, the problem is that it is debatable with many fields whether they should be identified as a specialty or subspecialty. Some clinical psychologists see health psychology, for example, as a subspecialty of clinical psychology, while some health psychologists see clinical psychology as a subspecialty of health psychology. In this chapter, the term subspecialty will not be used. The meaning of the term specialty should be clear from the context in which it is used and the examples given.

The chapter will begin by developing a context for a discussion of offerings in clinical training. Hence, a brief historical review of training will be presented followed by discussion of the roles of the Australian Psychological Society (APS) and the State and Territory Psychology Registration Boards. This will be followed by an analysis of the various forms of clinical training available in Australia including a consideration of distinctive features. The chapter will conclude with a section on future directions for clinical training.

2.18.2 HISTORY OF EDUCATION AND TRAINING FOR CLINICAL PSYCHOLOGY IN AUSTRALIA

The first universities in Australia were established in the 1850s. The earliest approximation to courses in psychology were taught in philosophy departments and date back to the latter part of the nineteenth century. The first department of psychology in Australia was founded in 1927 at the University of Sydney. This department was followed by departments at the University of Western Australia (UWA) (1930) and the University of New England (1939), or New England University College as it was known at the time.

With respect to the practice of clinical psychology, one of the pioneers was Stanley Porteous, well known for the Maze Test he developed, who established a clinic for subnormal and maladjusted children in Melbourne in 1913 (Taft, 1982). During the 1920s, State governments appointed psychologists in New South Wales, South Australia, Tasmania, and Western Australia (Birnbrauer, 1996). As no Australian universities offered training in clinical psychology during this period, the early practitioners had diverse backgrounds. Elton Mayo in Queensland, for example, was trained as a philosopher, and Ethel Stoneman in Western Australia completed most of her training in the US and Europe.

The growth of professional services in Australia outpaced the provision of appropriate academic training. For many years, three-year graduates were employed as psychologists and the greater part of learning and skills acquisition took place on the job in study groups (Ivison, 1977). In 1949, UWA offered the first systematic training in clinical psychology by way of a one-year full-time fourth year course. This course included nondirective (client-centered) counseling and play therapy, and teaching methods included case work under supervision utilizing one-way screens, group discussion, and role playing. In 1956, this course expanded into a two year full-time postgraduate Diploma in Clinical Psychology (DCP). The University of Sydney established a similar qualification three years later.

The modern era of clinical training in Australia began in 1966 with the introduction of the first masters program. UWA again led the way converting its DCP into the Master of Psychology (Clinical), followed by the University of New South Wales introducing a Master of Psychology (M.Psych.) in 1969. The number of M.Psych. (Clinical) programs increased steadily during the 1970s and 1980s to around 12, and more than doubled during the 1990s.

Although the number of M.Psych. programs has continued to grow, many academics responsible for training in clinical psychology have considered for some time that the masters programs need upgrading to extended programs that will lead to doctoral degrees (Martin, 1989a). The Australian Ph.D. is modeled on the British rather than the North American Ph.D. in that it is a research degree assessed by thesis. It is possible for departments to require students to complete coursework as part of their Ph.D. studies, but typically this is not a significant component of the degree. Through the 1980s Australian universities were opposed to introducing coursework Ph.D.s or professional doctorates as such developments were seen as devaluing the traditional research Ph.D.s. Hence, the only upgraded programs in clinical psychology that were introduced during this period were clinical Ph.D.s or combined M.Psych./Ph.D.s. UWA, for example, established a combined M.Psych./Ph.D. in 1983 whereby students completed all the requirements of both degrees simultaneously except the M.Psych. thesis requirement was replaced by a requirement to complete additional coursework and field placements. Since this time there has been a steady growth in the number of such programs.

The clinical Ph.D.s and combined M.Psych./Ph.D.s essentially upgraded training in clinical psychology by elevating the requirements for the research component of training. Some academics believed that the real need was for increased education in the methods and knowledge base of psychology, and for expanded on-the-job skills training under supervision. The major changes in Australian higher education that began in the late 1980s (National Board of Employment, Education, and Training [NBEET], 1989) created a new environment that provided opportunities for developing innovative programs that met these needs. In 1991, Murdoch University introduced a doctor of psychology (D.Psych.) program that was essentially an extension of their M.Psych. program. The following year UWA established a D.Psych. modeled on Australian medical education which requires six years at university (bachelor of medicine, bachelor of surgery), followed by two years of in-service training, at which point medical practitioners can apply for training programs in the various medical specialties such as neurology, psychiatry, and oncology. Hence, the UWA D.Psych. required applicants to have completed six years at university (bachelors and masters degrees) and two years post-masters supervised experience. The degree was offered in three specialities in clinical psychology: mental health, health psychology, and child and adolescent psychology (Martin, 1993). Only a limited number of D.Psych. programs were set up until 1997 at which time the number increased dramatically.

2.18.3 THE AUSTRALIAN PSYCHOLOGICAL SOCIETY AND ACCREDITATION OF CLINICAL TRAINING PROGRAMS

In 1945, 28 psychologists voted to become an Overseas Branch of the British Psychological Society (O'Neil, 1987). The APS was established as an independent entity in 1965. The *Australian Journal of Psychology* was founded by the Society in 1949 and was joined by the *Australian Psychologist* in 1966. The first edition of the APS Code of Conduct was published in 1968. The APS now has 33 branches and regional groups, 13 interest groups, and over 11 600 members. It has nine Colleges: Clinical Psychologists, Clinical Neuropsychologists, Community Psychologists, Counseling Psychologists, Educational and Developmental Psychologists, Forensic Psychologists, Organisational Psychologists, Sport Psychologists, and Health Psychologists (formed in 1996).

Eligibility criteria for membership of the APS involves the applicant holding an accredited four-year degree in psychology and having undergone a further two years of postgraduate training, either through an accredited university program (i.e., masters or doctorate) or under the supervision of a member of APS. The APS has changed its membership requirements so that from the year 2000, applicants will not be considered eligible under the two years of postgraduate supervised experience rule but will have to complete an accredited university postgraduate program. Eligibility for membership of the Colleges varies. For the College of Clinical Psychologists, applicants are required to have completed an accredited masters degree in clinical psychology followed by two years supervised experience.

The APS first became involved in accreditation of courses in 1972. The accreditation process has changed markedly, however, with the introduction of a new set of guidelines in August 1995 effective from the beginning of 1996 (APS, 1995). These guidelines set out criteria for departments/schools of psychology on the one hand and programs in psychology on the other. The departmental guidelines pertain mainly to staffing and resources. The program guidelines are divided into four sections; three year programs, fourth year programs, professional fifth and sixth year programs, and research higher degree programs. In addition to these general guidelines, each of the Colleges specify guidelines pertaining to the particular College's area of specialty. Clinical psychology programs, for example, have to satisfy the general guidelines for professional fifth and sixth year programs and the guidelines of the College of Clinical Psychologists.

The APS accreditation guidelines emphasize that training should be based on the scientist–practitioner model and specify the following core areas of study:

(i) the systematic study of the mechanisms and etiology of psychological disorders in adults and children;

(ii) the principles and methods of behavioral, psychometric, and clinical assessment of significant psychological problems;

(iii) the principals, procedures, and techniques of psychological intervention and rehabilitation;

(iv) psychopharmacology;

(v) research methods and evaluation;

(vi) health psychology, behavioral medicine, and rehabilitation; and

(vii) ethics and professional standards.

Additional areas of study listed as options include:

(i) neuropsychology;

(ii) forensic psychology;

(iii) sexual dysfunctions;

(iv) interventions with children and families;

(v) working with special groups such as the elderly;
(vi) advanced research and assessment methodology;
(vii) organizational psychology (health administration);
(viii) educational psychology; and
(ix) advanced study of core areas.

The APS accreditation guidelines require students to spend at least 1000 hours completing practicums including a minimum of 400 hours of practical training face to face with clients. Supervision must be provided by clinical psychologists with at least three years of post-masters experience and total contact with supervisors should be at least 200 hours. Students are required to complete three to five practicums external to the university and the practicums must provide students with the experience of dealing with a wide range of clinical problems (acute and chronic), across varying age ranges (child, adult), settings (inpatient/outpatient, community), and using a variety of clinical skills (assessment, treatment, and professional). Practicums typically involve attending the agency for two to three days per week over a period of two to four months.

The APS accreditation guidelines specify that students are required to complete a project which involves collection of original data. The topic of the research must be of direct relevance to the field of clinical psychology, and supervision should be provided by one or more individuals of whom at least one must be from the university department. Research reports are required to be presented in 10 000–15 000 words; and are usually assessed by two examiners who may be members of the university department or external examiners.

All departments of psychology are reviewed in a five-year cycle. The process involves submitting an application followed by a site visit. The review panel conducting the site visit includes a member or nominee of the local State or Territory Psychology Registration Board and representatives from each of the Colleges for which the department offers specialist courses. Site visits last for a minimum of two days and include a meeting with the Vice-Chancellor or nominee, academic and general staff, and students. Also, teaching and research facilities are inspected and examples of students' work, such as theses, are studied. It should by emphasized that the new accreditation guidelines are quite detailed and specific. Also, site visits only developed in the 1980s and 1990s. Accreditation can serve an important role in improving clinical training (Nelson, 1993), and the new APS guidelines and procedures should help achieve this outcome.

2.18.4 STATE AND TERRITORY REGISTRATION ACTS FOR PSYCHOLOGISTS AND SPECIALIST PSYCHOLOGISTS

In 1965, Victoria was the first state to enact a Psychological Practices Act. The other five states and two territories followed with the last act passed in the Australian Capital Territory in 1995. These acts require all practicing psychologists to be registered, and they regulate psychology at a state or territory level via a board which consists usually of psychologists representing different sectors of the profession (e.g., university, health, private practice), a lawyer, a psychiatrist, and a registrar. Most recently enacted legislation includes a representative of consumer interests and this is likely to be a feature of future amendments to acts. The boards report to the Ministers of Health in each state or territory.

Most state and territory registration boards only recognize the title of psychologist. Victoria and Western Australia, however, offer statutory recognition of a range of specialist titles (Wood, 1996). Victoria recognizes clinical, clinical neuropsychological, counseling, educational and developmental, organizational, forensic, sport, and community. Western Australia recognizes the same specialties with the exception of community. Other states and territories are considering recognizing specialist titles.

Eligibility criteria for registration usually involves the applicant holding an accredited four-year degree in psychology and having undergone a further two years of postgraduate training, either through an accredited university program or under the supervision of an experienced registered psychologist. Where specialist titles exist, eligibility for the specialist title is based on whether applicants are eligible for membership of relevant colleges of the APS.

The decision by the APS to require six years of university training for membership by the year 2000 has not been followed by a parallel shift in eligibility criteria by the state and territory registration boards, except for the Northern Territory Psychology Registration Board which will also change to a six-year educational requirement from the year 2000. A survey of the members of the registration boards in all states and territories, however, revealed that an overall majority of members supported increasing the educational requirements for registration to six years (Healy & Franklin, in press). This survey also indicated that a majority of board members favored the introduction of specialist registration. There is a strong move to bring the registration acts of the different states and territories into line with each other but this may take time to achieve.

2.18.5 MASTERS DEGREES: GENERALIST AND SPECIALIST TRAINING

In 1997 there were 25 masters programs in Australia offering training in clinical psychology (see Table 1). Of these programs, 19 were APS accredited with the remaining six too new to qualify for accreditation. Four new masters programs are due to commence in 1998. The nomenclature for most programs is Master of Psychology (Clinical) or Master of Clinical Psychology but some variations exist including Master of Applied Psychology (Clinical), MA (Clinical Psychology), and M.Sc. (Clinical Psychology). Some programs have added health to clinical.

The APS accreditation guidelines state that entry to these programs should be by way of an honors degree in psychology or equivalent, and this seems to be the norm although it was not so in the past (Martin, 1989b). One program has specified the additional requirement of at least one year's professional experience.

The APS accreditation guidelines indicate that masters programs should be constituted as follows: coursework, 40–50%; research, 20–30%; practical placement, 25–30%. In practice, the coursework component varies from 25–59% with a mean of 45%; the research component varies from 19–50% with a mean of 26%; and the practical placement component varies from 17–50% with a mean of 30%. Hence, the means are in line with the APS guidelines but some courses are outside the guidelines. The variability between programs can be seen by comparing three universities who reported the following ratios of coursework–research–practical placements: university A, 56–19–25; university B, 25–50–25; and university C, 25–25–50.

The majority of masters programs are considered to be generalist rather than specialist in orientation. The only exceptions were four programs that indicated a specialty in health psychology and two programs that indicated a specialty in mental health. It is not clear, however, whether these programs had more content in these areas than other programs that did not claim a specialization. When coordinators of masters programs were asked whether there were features of their programs that differentiated them from other programs, some of the responses suggested emphases in particular areas of psychology such as forensic psychology, multicultural psychology, geropsychology, rural psychology, educational/child psychology, and organizational psychology. Most programs adopt a predominantly cognitive-behavioral approach to assessment and treatment, but two programs suggested that they were different by virtue of covering additional theoretical orientations such as psychodynamic, constructionist, and family systems approach.

An example of a masters program is included in Table 2. The table illustrates that the three components of coursework, practicum, and research are represented in each of the four semesters of the program but the balance changes over time. That is, the early part of the program is coursework dominated principally to prepare students for their first practicum but also to help students get started on their research. As the program progresses, the balance changes with coursework steadily decreasing and more time being devoted to practicum and research commitments.

2.18.6 CLINICAL PH.D.s: GENERALIST AND SPECIALIST TRAINING

It is difficult to summarize the situation with respect to clinical Ph.D.s and combined M.Psych./Ph.D.s because of the diversity of arrangements that have been negotiated in different universities. These programs essentially involve students completing most if not all of the requirements for both degrees, more or less simultaneously. In 1997, 14 departments indicated that such programs were available in their university. The number of such programs is debatable, however, as it is obviously possible to complete both degrees at any university that offers both degrees, so the question is only whether special arrangements have been made for completing the two degrees concurrently.

One of the main variations between programs is whether individuals who complete the program successfully take out both degrees or only the higher degree (i.e., Ph.D.). About half the programs award both degrees with the other half acknowledging the completion of the M.Psych. requirements via adding clinical in brackets after Ph.D. or listing the M.Psych. units on the Ph.D. transcript. Programs that award a Ph.D. only need to seek accreditation from the APS for the clinical component of the program. A number of programs have received such accreditation.

Entry requirements for these programs are variable. Some programs simply require an honors degree or equivalent as for M.Psych. programs. Others have elevated this requirement to holding a first class honors and one program requires an M.Psych. or equivalent.

Table 1 Australian universities offering postgraduate training in clinical psychology.

	Master of Psychology			*Clinical Ph.D. or combined M.Psych/Ph.D.*			*Doctor of Psychology*		
University	*Operating 1997*	*APS accredited*	*Planned 1998*	*Operating 1997*	*APS accredited*	*Planned 1998*	*Operating 1997*	*APS accredited*	*Planned 1998*
Adelaide	√	√							
Australian National	√	√		√	√				
Australian Catholic			√						
Bond	√						√		
Charles Sturt	√								
Curtin	√	√		√	√				
Deakin	√	√					√		
Edith Cowan	√			√					
Flinders	√	√		√	√				
Griffith (Nathan)	√	√		√	√				
Griffith (Gold Coast)	√								
James Cook	√	√							
La Trobe	√	√		√	√		√		
Macquarie	√	√		√					
Melbourne	√	√					√		
Monash									√
Murdoch	√	√		√	√		√	√	
New England			√						√
New South Wales	√	√							
Newcastle	√	√							
Queensland	√	√		√	√				
Royal Melbourne IT	√			√					
South Australia	√						√		
Southern Queensland			√						
Sydney	√	√		√	√				
Tasmania	√	√		√	√				
Victoria	√	√					√		
Western Australia	√	√		√	√				
Western Sydney			√						
Wollongong	√	√		√			√	√	
Total	25	19	4	14	10	0	8	2	2

Another variation is to accept applications only from individuals completing M.Psych. programs. The usual arrangement here is for students to transfer into the clinical Ph.D. or combined M.Psych./Ph.D. following successful completion of the first year of the M.Psych. Some programs allow entry via a number of different routes (e.g., direct entry from honors or transfer from M.Psych.).

Traditionally, universities insist on completion of the full Ph.D. requirements for awarding a Ph.D. That is, they will not accept trade-offs along the lines of reducing the scope of research requirements against clinical coursework and placement requirements. More flexibility is shown sometimes with M.Psych. requirements whereby, for example, most universities seem prepared to waive the M.Psych. research requirements if students are completing a Ph.D. concurrently on a clinical topic. Some universities insist, however, on other requirements being added to compensate for dropping the research requirement (e.g., extra coursework and placements). Given that students have to complete the full requirements of a Ph.D., the requirements for clinical Ph.D.s and

Table 2 Outline of the Master of Psychology (Clinical) Program at The University of Western Australia.

Semester	*Year*
One	First
Coursework	Research, evaluation, and accountability I
	Psychotherapy I (general introduction to psychotherapy)
	Clinical problems I (includes psychopathology)
	Child and adult assessment
	Neuropsychology
	Preparation for practicum (includes interviewing and practicum orientation)
	Workshops (four half-day and one full day)
Clinical practicum	Placement in university clinic I (begins half way through semester)
Research	Develop a research topic and find a supervisor
Two	
Coursework	Research, evaluation, and accountability II
	Psychotherapy II (cognitive behavioural therapy)
	Clinical problems II (includes health psychology)
	Workshops (two half day and ten full day)
Clinical practicum	Placement in university clinic II
	External practicum I
Research	Submit a research proposal
Three	Second
Coursework	Case presentations I
	Intellectual disability
	Interventions with children and adolescents
	Family therapy
	Workshops (three half day and one full day)
Clinical practicum	Placement in university clinic III (ends half way through semester)
	External practicum II
Research	Carry out research project
Four	
Coursework	Case presentations II
	Workshops (one half day and five full day)
Clinical practicum	External practicum III
Research	Submit a thesis in form of journal manuscript

Source: Martin (1996a).

combined M.Psych./Ph.D.s are typically research dominated (i.e, at least two-thirds research). One exception is a Ph.D. (Psychotherapy) program that has been established with 50% coursework, 25% research, and 25% practical placements.

Most of these programs do not aim to provide specialist training. Some programs do provide specialist training in areas such as health psychology by means of the M.Psych. component and, of course, the research component focuses on a specific topic and hence may provide some degree of specialist training. The specialist training available in the program therefore depends on the expertise of members of the academic and adjunctive staff as the potential supervisors. The Ph.D. (Psychotherapy) can be conceptualized as a specialist degree, and one program provides training towards a career in academia by means of including training in areas such as teaching, manuscript reviewing, and writing research grant applications.

2.18.7 PROFESSIONAL DOCTORATES: GENERALIST AND SPECIALIST TRAINING

In 1997 there were eight D.Psych. programs in Australia offering training in clinical psychology, six operating for the first time in 1997. A ninth university had a D.Psych. program running but removed it from the statute books. Another two universities are planning to introduce D.Psych. degrees and a third is exploring possibilities. Only two D.Psych. programs are accredited by the APS but they are all likely to be accredited as they incorporate all the requirements of M.Psych. programs.

The degree is referred to generally as a Doctor of Psychology and abbreviated to D.Psych. but one program has the title Doctor of Clinical Psychology and one program uses the abbreviation Psy.D. Direct entry is possible to four programs with an upper second or first class honours degree. A fifth program requires good performance in the first year of the M.Psych. and a sixth program requires good performance during both years of the M.Psych. program. One program offered entry by means of any of the three routes described above. The period for completion of a D.Psych. is generally three years of full-time study but one program requires four years of full-time study.

The APS accreditation guidelines indicate that professional doctorates should be constituted as follows: coursework, 20–30%; research, 40–70%, practical placement, 20–30%. In practice, the coursework component varies from 25 to 39% with a mean of 32%; the research component varies from 33 to 50% with a mean of 43%, and the practical placement component varies from 11 to 33% with a mean of 24%.

Four of the programs did not claim to provide specialist training. One program indicated a specialty in child, adolescent, and family psychology. Another program indicated that students had to choose two of three specialist areas in their third year: health, child, and adult.

2.18.8 THE CONTEXT FOR AUSTRALIAN TRENDS IN CLINICAL TRAINING

Masters degrees in clinical psychology, the entry-level qualification for clinical practice in Australia, have doubled in number since the late 1980s with five more planned for 1998. Placing this trend in an international context, masters level training in clinical psychology in the US has been an issue for more than 30 years as many have argued that this level of training is inadequate for producing fully-fledged scientist–practitioners. Nevertheless, the number of masters programs has increased over time rather than decreased (Edelstein & Brasted, 1991). In contrast, the number of masters programs in the UK has decreased during the 1990s as master of psychology programs have been replaced by doctor of psychology programs (Martin, 1996b).

The increase in masters programs in Australia is probably driven by two main factors. First, the number of universities in Australia doubled between the late 1980s and the late 1990s as a result of legislation converting former teacher training colleges and institutes of technology into universities, and the advent of private universities. Second, the APS changed its membership rules to include the requirement of a higher degree, as noted earlier. This move put pressure on universities to offer professional masters programs as a means of helping their students to gain APS membership. In fact, in an early draft of the current APS accreditation guidelines, the APS stated that only departments offering such programs would be accredited. Although this requirement was removed in later drafts, all departments have been left with the clear impression that they are expected to offer at least one professional masters program.

If the increase in masters programs is large, the increase in doctor of psychology programs is even larger with two programs operating in 1996 against eight programs running in 1997 and two more planned for 1998. Of course, doctor of psychology programs in the US have a history dating back approximately 30 years but the reason for the emergence of the Psy.D. in the US was different from the reason for the emergence of the D.Psych. in Australia. The North American Psy.D. had its origins in clinical psychologists concluding that the Ph.D. was too research dominated to meet the needs of aspirant practitioners (Barlow, Hayes, & Nelson, 1984). The advent of the Australian D.Psych. was based on a desire to upgrade the existing masters programs. Hence, while some North American Psy.D.s have eliminated research training from the curriculum, research is a major component of the Australian D.Psych. representing on average 43% of the degree.

The first doctor of clinical psychology degree was introduced in the UK at about the same time as the D.Psych. in Australia and is usually abbreviated to DClinPsy. Both degrees are extended masters programs but the British DClinPsy is somewhat different in structure to the Australian D.Psych. as the average percentage of the programs devoted to coursework, research, and practical placements is 27%, 26%, and 47%, respectively (Martin, 1996b). Hence, compared to the Australian degree it is more focused on practicums and less on research. The number of DClinPsy programs in the UK has proliferated very rapidly from the first program in 1992 to 17 in 1995 with at least another six in a planning or developmental phase.

One point that stands out from Table 1 is the large number of clinical training programs in Australia. Twenty-five universities are offering clinical training and this number is expected to increase to 30 by 1998. By comparison, the UK has 26 clinical training programs despite the fact that the population of the UK is approximately three times that of Australia. In 1997, 19 universities offered doctoral level training in Australia and by 1998 this number will have risen to 21. In 1989 there were 158 doctoral programs in the US (Edelstein & Brasted, 1991), so that there are approximately twice as many doctoral programs in Australia per capita of population as in the US. The development of doctoral programs in Australia is a particularly important step forward given the data indicating the superior competence of graduates from doctoral programs compared to masters programs (Robiner, Arbisi, & Edwall, 1994).

The impetus for the development of the D.Psych. was the changes in education in Australia discussed earlier (NBEET, 1989). It is relevant to point out that these changes gave rise to a range of professional doctorates being introduced in Australia in addition to the professional doctorates in psychology. In 1996, for example, whilst there were only two D.Psych. programs operating, there were 19 doctor of education degrees (Ed.D.) and 28 other professional doctorates (Shanahan, 1996). Legal/juridical science ($n = 8$) and business administration ($n = 5$) were the second and third most common types of professional doctorate.

The number of Australian universities offering clinical Ph.D.s or combined M.Psych./Ph.D. programs has grown steadily since the early 1980s to 14 programs in the late 1990s. Hence, this option is more common than the D.Psych. and is certainly the preferred option by approximately half the universities offering clinical training. Australian combined programs really have no equivalent in the US as they incorporate the full requirements of a British/Australian, research-only Ph.D. in contrast to North American Ph.D.s which have lesser research requirements due to including coursework and practicum components. Isolated examples of combined programs have existed in the UK for many years but have never been a major provider of clinical training.

2.18.9 DISTINCTIVE FEATURES OF CLINICAL TRAINING IN AUSTRALIA

Comparing clinical training in Australia with clinical training in the US and the UK, a number of impressions arise. First, the Australian system is less diverse in some ways and more diverse in other ways. On the one hand, clinical training in Australia is offered only by university departments of psychology. In contrast, clinical training in the UK has traditionally been offered by university departments of psychology, university departments of psychiatry, jointly by university departments of psychology and psychiatry, and regional or district health authorities in combination with the British Psychological Society. Qualifications in clinical psychology are now awarded through the Open University.

In the US, some clinical training is carried out at professional schools which may or may not be attached to universities. On the other hand, the range of options in clinical training in Australia, that is, M.Psych., D.Psych., clinical Ph.D., and combined M.Psych./Ph.D. is almost certainly broader than the range of options available in the UK and possibly broader than the range of options available in the US.

The most distinctive feature of clinical training in Australia is the consistent commitment to the scientist–practitioner model, and the emphasis on research training which comprises on average 26% of the M.Psych., 43% of the D.Psych., and at least 67% of clinical Ph.D.s. These weightings of the research component of clinical training are greater than are found in the US and the UK. It is easy to see why clinical training in Australia has developed in this way. It reflects, for example, the point made above that clinical training in Australia is based exclusively in university departments of psychology which traditionally place a very high value on research. It also reflects the fact that the profession of clinical psychology, which is likely to favor more emphasis on practicums rather than research, has had relatively little impact on training in Australia compared to other countries. This has occurred for various reasons such as the weak accreditation processes that have operated in Australia in the past (a situation which is, hopefully, changing); and the fact that the profession in Australia is weak and divided compared to some other countries. The latter occurs for many reasons but is related to the small number of clinical psychologists (perhaps 1000–2000 in total) spread across a vast continent, employed by several separate agencies in each of six states and two territories.

What effect has the greater emphasis on research training had? On the positive side, graduates of clinical training programs in Australia seem well satisfied with their research training. A survey by Byrne (1982), for example, reported that research was one of the areas of training that attracted higher adequacy ratings than some other aspects of clinical training. A survey of the profession indicated that 73% of respondents endorsed the length of research training as appropriate and only 25% were dissatisfied with the quality of research training (Martin, 1989b).

The scientist–practitioner model has often been criticized on the grounds that it is an ideal rather than a reality because few clinical psychologists engage in research. A much quoted statement, for example, is the report by Barlow (1980) that the modal number of publications of clinical psychologists in the US was zero despite the majority holding Ph.D.s. It would be nice to believe that the greater emphasis on research in Australian clinical training would result in a higher proportion of clinical psychologists engaging in research. Unfortunately, the survey discussed above suggested that only a minority of clinical psychologists in Australia carried out research even when less stringent criteria than publications were used to index research activity (Martin, 1989b). On the other hand, D.Psych.s and even clinical Ph.D.s have been introduced too recently to gauge their impact on research output, so perhaps a survey of the future will produce more positive findings in terms of research contributions from clinical psychologists in Australia.

2.18.10 FUTURE DIRECTIONS IN CLINICAL TRAINING

In commenting on recent trends in clinical training in the US, Edelstein and Brasted (1991) argued that "the most notable change in the field of clinical psychology in the past two decades has been the shift toward specialization" (p. 51). They went on to state that further specialization in the future was inevitable. The survey results reported in Sections 2.18.5–2.18.7 show little evidence of specialization in Australia even at the doctoral level. A few programs indicated a specialization in health psychology, and there were isolated examples of other specializations such as mental health, child and adolescent, forensic, and geropsychology. Perhaps the lack of specialist training is not surprising as the APS accreditation guidelines allow little freedom for developing specialized programs.

It does seem likely that specialist training in Australia will increase in the future. Much specialist training in the US is accomplished at the postdoctoral level, after generalist training has been completed. As doctoral programs replace masters programs in Australia, postdoctoral training is the next logical step. Professional development activities have never been mandatory in Australia but are now required for continuing membership of the APS Colleges (APS, 1997), and achievement of this important milestone will undoubtedly stimulate developments in postqualification training, many of which will be of a specialist nature.

A significant and unfortunate trend that is emerging in clinical training in Australia is the increased costs for the trainees (Martin, 1996a). Unlike the UK, relatively few clinical students in Australia receive financial support in the form of scholarships or traineeships. In 1988, the federal government introduced the Higher Education Contribution Scheme whereby graduates are required to pay a proportion of the costs of their courses either by means of an upfront (discounted) payment or after graduation by means of a tax levied on their income. During the first few years of the scheme, clinical students were exempted from the tax through government scholarships but after a cutback in the number of available scholarships in 1994, clinical students found themselves liable for the tax. In 1993, the federal government decided to allow universities to charge fees for postgraduate courses. Clinical programs were reluctant to capitalize on this opportunity, but decreased government funding has forced some clinical programs to charge fees and probably most programs will charge fees in the very near future.

It is difficult to predict what effect the introduction of fees will have on clinical training. A decreased demand is possible at least from the financially disadvantaged. Fees may encourage more students to take a break between completing their undergraduate and postgraduate degrees so that they can generate the necessary funds for the latter. More students may opt for part-time study to enable concurrent part-time employment. Students may select programs on more financially-orientated criteria such as which programs will facilitate them earning income whilst studying, and which programs will enable them to gain higher incomes on graduation so that they can repay loans more quickly.

Many changes are taking place in the work environment of clinical psychologists that will impact on clinical training. Traditionally, the majority of clinical psychologists in Australia have worked in the public sector but the size of the public sector is shrinking as the federal and state governments cut spending by privatizing or amalgamating public hospitals and contracting out services. In contrast, private practice is a growth area in psychology and other human service professions. These changes will create challenges for clinical training as practicum supervisors have been drawn typically from the public rather than the private sector, and likewise research has been limited to the public sector. Clinical programs will need to reorientate their training to cater for the changed employment opportunities for graduates.

Other significant developments in the work environment include the move towards "multi-skilling" which is based on the assumption that there are no important differences between psychologists and other health care professionals such as social workers and occupational therapists (Franklin, 1993). Multiskilling has been introduced by federal and state governments, and implications include advertising positions as open to all healthcare professions rather than tied to a particular profession. Budgeting principals have been changed so that funds are allocated for service provision rather than to professionally based departments resulting in professions having to argue for the relative merits of their services. Changes such as these will force clinical training programs to produce graduates who can compete effectively with other health care professionals. Graduates will need to have a clear sense of professional identity and of the unique contribution that clinical psychology can make to the provision of human services. The cautious, critical approach that characterizes the scientific side of the scientist–practitioner model will have to be counterbalanced by the confidence of an established profession with much to offer. Something akin to marketing and promotional skills should become part of every clinical training program.

Finally, it would be inappropriate to conclude a section on future directions without considering the role of technology, given the rapid process of evolution in this field. Technological developments are likely to impact on clinical training in a number of ways. First, computers are used increasingly for psychological assessment and intervention (Bloom, 1992) so that training programs will need to educate students in the use of the new technologies. Second, computers have a number of features that can be used to advantage in training including presenting instructional materials, monitoring students' understanding of the materials, providing students with feedback on their performance, and allowing students to determine the pace and direction of their learning (Kenardy & Adams, 1993). Two approaches to computer-based clinical training have been reported in the literature (Bloom, 1992). One is computer-based clinical consultation in which expert or knowledge based systems are used to assist in assessment and treatment planning. These systems can provide a teaching function by describing the reasoning process that they invoked in reaching decisions. The other approach is simulation of the encounter between the healthcare provider and the client in which the computer is programmed to take the role of the client.

The third contribution of new technology, and perhaps the most exciting, is the role it can play in enhancing distance education and breaking down barriers between universities, not just within national boundaries but also around the world. If it is accepted that there is substantial overlap between clinical training programs even in different countries then similar material is taught in almost 200 doctoral programs each year just in the US, the UK, and Australia, let alone the rest of the world. This is clearly an inefficient system and with most universities experiencing pressure on their resources, alternative models need to be considered. Developments in telecommunications and fiber optics, and the expansion of the World Wide Web and use of email, create opportunities that were not available in the past. Experts in instructional design increasingly are developing distance education materials that facilitate interaction between students and teachers, and the development of skills, rather than simply transmitting information. Hopefully, the future will see the development of high quality clinical teaching materials and units that will be used internationally to the advantage of both teachers and students.

2.18.11 SUMMARY

Clinical psychology training in Australia is entering an exciting phase of its development. The number of programs has increased dramatically and new types of degrees have burst on to the scene. Australia now has a larger number of programs and diverse offerings that are characterized internationally by a strong emphasis on research training. The APS has developed its accreditation principles and processes to the point where they could have an important influence on clinical training, and the advent of mandatory professional development will impact on postqualification clinical training. State and territory legislation related to registration of psychologists needs revision to keep pace with these developments but there are encouraging signs that this process has begun.

The above developments will lead to many challenges. How will an adequate number of clinical supervisors be found given the contraction of the public sector on the one hand and the increased number of trainees needing supervision on the other? Who will employ the expanded group of graduates from these programs? Will the increased financial pressures on students encourage training programs to make changes that will attract students but have detrimental effects such as minimizing training in areas associated with great social need but low financial rewards for clinical psychologists?

The 1990s have been characterized by marked change for clinical training in Australia. The next decade will be even more interesting.

ACKNOWLEDGMENTS

I would like to express my appreciation to all the individuals who completed the questionnaires on which this chapter is partly based.

2.18.12 REFERENCES

Australian Psychological Society (1995). *Accreditation guidelines*. Melbourne, Australia: Author.

Australian Psychological Society (1997). *Professional development handbook*. Melbourne, Australia: Author.

Barlow, D. H. (1980). Behavior therapy: The next decade. *Behavior Therapy, 11,* 315–328.

Barlow, D. H., Hayes, S. C., & Nelson, R. O. (1984). *The scientist practitioner: Research and accountability in clinical and educational settings*. New York: Pergamon.

Birnbrauer, J. S. (1996). The development of clinical psychology. In P. R. Martin & J. S. Birnbrauer (Eds.), *Clinical psychology: Profession and practice in Australia* (pp. 21–51). Melbourne, Australia: Macmillan.

Bloom, B. L. (1992) Computer-assisted psychological intervention: A review and commentary. *Clinical Psychology Review, 12,* 169–197.

Byrne, D. G. (1982). Clinical psychology in Australia: A survey of activities and aspirations. *Australian Psychologist, 17,* 87–96.

Edelstein, B. A., & Brasted, W. S. (1991). Clinical training. In M. Hersen, A. E. Kazdin, & A. S. Bellack (Eds.), *The clinical psychology handbook* (2nd ed., pp. 45–65). New York: Pergamon.

Franklin, J. (1993) Crisis? *The Bulletin of the Australian Psychological Society, 15,* 6–8.

Healy, M., & Franklin, J. (in press). Psychologist registration boards: Views on four and six year education. *Australian Psychologist.*

Ivison, D. J. (1977). Clinical psychology in public service. In M. Nixon & R. Taft (Eds.), *Psychology in Australia: Achievements and prospects* (pp. 175–183). Rushcutters Bay, Australia: Pergamon.

Kenardy, J., & Adams, C. (1993). Computers in cognitive-behaviour therapy. *Australian Psychologist, 28,* 189–194.

Martin, P. R. (1989a). "Specialist" clinical psychologists: Upgrading training in clinical psychology. *Australian Psychologist, 24,* 3–11.

Martin, P. R. (1989b). The scientist–practitioner model and clinical psychology: Time for change? *Australian Psychologist, 24,* 71–92.

Martin, P. R. (1993). The Doctor of Psychology (Clinical) degree at UWA and related developments overseas. *The Bulletin of the Australian Psychological Society, 15,* 12–13.

Martin, P. R. (1996a). Training in clinical psychology. In P. R. Martin & J. S. Bimbrauer (Eds.), *Clinical psychology: Profession and practise in Australia* (pp. 52–76). Melbourne, Australia: Macmillan.

Martin, P. R. (1996b). A survey of doctoral degrees in clinical psychology in the United Kingdom and Australia. *Australian Psychologist, 31,* 191–193.

National Board of Employment, Education, and Training (1989). *Australian graduate studies and higher degrees. Initial report by the Higher Education Council.* Canberra, Australia: Australian Government Publishing Service.

Nelson, P. D. (1993). Improving the clinical training of psychologists: A role for accreditation? In P. Wohlford, H. F. Meyers, & T. Callan (Eds.), *Serving the seriously mentally ill: Public academic linkages in services* (pp. 207–211). Washington, DC: American Psychological Association.

O'Neil, W. (1987). *A century of psychology in Australia.* Sydney, Australia: Sydney University Press.

Robiner, W. N., Arbisi, P., & Edwall, G. E. (1994). The basis of the doctoral degree for psychology licensure. *Clinical Psychology Review, 14,* 227–254.

Shanahan, P. J. (1996). Professional doctorates other than the doctor of education in Australian Universities: Some comparative data. In T. W. Maxwell & P. J. Shanahan (Eds.), *Which way professional doctorates? Context and cases* (pp. 13–28). Armidale, Australia: Faculty of Education, Health, and Professional Studies, University of New England.

Taft, R. (1982). Psychology and its history in Australia. *Australian Psychologist, 17,* 31–39.

Wood, M. M. (1996). Professional affiliations, registration and ethical issues. In P. R. Martin & J. S. Birnbrauer (Eds.), *Clinical psychology: Profession and practice in Australia* (pp. 77–100). Melbourne, Australia: Macmillan.

2.19
Commission for the Recognition of Specialties and Proficiencies in Professional Psychology

TOMMY T. STIGALL
The Psychology Group, Baton Rouge, LA, USA

2.19.1 INTRODUCTION

The Commission for the Recognition of Specialties and Proficiencies in Professional Psychology (CRSPPP) was established by the American Psychological Association (APA) Council of Representatives in February 1995. Implicit in the Council's action was a recognition of the need to bring some order into the conceptualization of specialties and to communicate more effectively with the general public about the nature and scope of psychological practice. In creating this new entity, the APA declared itself open for business in the matter of formally recognizing both practice specialties and proficiencies.

> There shall be a Commission for the Recognition of Specialties and Proficiencies in Profession Psychology. The Commission (a) shall review petitions from petitioning organizations requesting the Association's recognition of a professional specialty or proficiency, and (b) shall establish mechanisms for the periodic evaluation and renewal of such recognition. The Commission shall select from among recognition petitions it reviews those deemed appropriate to recommend to the Council of Representatives as meriting formal

> confirmation. Council shall confirm the recognition of a specialty or proficiency in professional psychology only when such recommendation for recognition shall have been placed before it by the Commission following the completion of an evaluation conducted according to the Commission's procedures. (American Psychological Association, 1996a, Association Rule 90–8)

Thus, the Council delegated responsibility to the Commission for receiving, reviewing and recommending meritorious petitions, while reserving unto itself the final authority to approve any newly proposed specialty or proficiency. At the same time, the Council approved specific criteria and principles for the recognition of specialties and proficiencies. Four historical specialties, clinical, counseling, school, and industrial/organizational psychology, were recognized *de facto*, subject to eventual review and reconfirmation by the normal petitioning process.

By virtue of the fact that the APA College of Professional Psychology previously had been granted authority to examine applicants and certify qualified psychologists in the Treatment of Alcohol and Other Psychoactive Substance Use Disorders, this became the first proficiency of professional psychology to be so recognized. Thereafter, newly proposed proficiencies would have to conform to the CRSPPP review process and be recognized by the Council before they could be considered by the College for the awarding of certificates.

According to the procedures that the Commission would follow, each new or existing specialty and proficiency would be required to submit to review and reconfirmation not less than every seven years. Failure to do so could subject the specialty or proficiency to withdrawal of recognition by APA.

The Commission, as initially constituted, was composed of 13 members, all of whom except for the public member had been appointed to serve on the predecessor Joint Interim Committee for the Identification and Recognition of Specialties and Proficiencies which had been charged with the responsibility to develop recommendations regarding the specialty and proficiency recognition process. (The first commissioners were Cynthia D. Belar, Bruce E. Bennett, Thomas J. Boll [co-chair], Patricia M. Bricklin, Arthur L. Kovacs, Nadine M. Lambert, William P. MacLeod [public member], Joseph D. Matarazzo, Jack K. Plummer, Edward P. Sheridan, Tommy T. Stigall, Arthur N. Wiens, and Jack G. Wiggins, Jr. [co-chair].) Beginning in February 1997, the CRSPPP would be composed of nine commissioners, including one public member who is not to be a psychologist. The remaining eight commissioners must be licensed psychologists and members of the APA. The public member is appointed by the APA Board of Directors. Others are elected by the Council to serve three-year, staggered terms from slates prepared by the following APA governance groups: Board of Educational Affairs, Board of Professional Affairs, Board for the Advancement of Psychology in the Public Interest, and the Committee for the Advancement of Professional Practice.

In addition to pursuing its work of reviewing petitions in light of the definitional criteria and operating procedures under which the Commission operates, the CRSPPP must also contend with important conceptual and philosophical issues. Among these are questions about the nature and purpose of professional specialization and an evolving quest for a conceptual model—a taxonomy for specialties and proficiencies.

2.19.2 NEW SPECIALTIES AND PROFICIENCIES

Specialization can be thought of either as the division of human labor for increased efficiency, or in terms of the organization of knowledge. Both concepts are relevant to an understanding of specialties and proficiencies, as these terms are employed by the CRSPPP, and both are embedded in the following definition, which is incorporated in the APA policy document *Principles for the Recognition of Specialties in Professional Psychology* (American Psychological Association, 1995a):

> A specialty is a defined area of psychological practice which requires advanced knowledge and skills acquired through an organized sequence of education and training. The advanced knowledge and skill specific to a specialty are obtained subsequent to the acquisition of core scientific and professional foundations in psychology. (p. 2)

In addition to the concepts of an organized body of knowledge and the application of this knowledge to practice, the definition emphasizes that the knowledge and skill for specialty practice must be at an advanced level and that it must be acquired in an organized sequence of education and training. A specialty rests on and grows out of the core knowledge and skills of the discipline. It does not supplant or supersede it, but it is distinctive and different from the generic core.

The principles specify 12 criteria that apply in the evaluation of petitions seeking APA recognition of new specialties. Among other things, the criteria stipulate that there must be an identifiable public need for the specialty and that the new specialty must be distinctive, though not necessarily unique, with regard to the three parameters of specialty practice: populations served, problems addressed, and procedures and techniques utilized. For a positive recommendation to be made by the CRSPPP, the petition and supporting documents must be complete and must provide evidence to satisfy all the criteria.

2.19.2.1 Clinical Neuropsychology

In August 1996, the Council of Representatives voted for the first time to recognize a new specialty on the basis of a petition submitted by the APA Division of Clinical Neuropsychology (Division 40). Clinical neuropsychology thus became the fifth specialty in professional psychology officially recognized by the APA (DeLeon, 1997, p. 856). Central to the recognition process is the requirement for a clear and concise definition of the practice of any approved specialty or proficiency. The definition is maintained as a part of the archival record and serves as the basis for communication with the public about the specialized professional services offered by psychologists who are associated with the specialty or proficiency in question. For this purpose, the following definition of clinical neuropsychology was adopted:

> Clinical Neuropsychology is a specialty that applies principles of assessment and intervention based upon the scientific study of human behavior as it relates to normal and abnormal functioning of the central nervous system. The specialty is dedicated to enhancing the understanding of brain–behavior relationships and the application of such knowledge to human problems. (American Psychological Association, 1996, p. 155)

2.19.2.2 Clinical Health Psychology

One year later, in August 1997, the specialty of clinical health psychology was officially recognized by the Council, based on a petition review and favorable recommendation by the CRSPPP. The petition had been prepared by the APA Division of Health Psychology (Division 38). In approving clinical health psychology as the sixth officially recognized specialty in professional psychology, the Council accepted the following definition of this specialty:

> The specialty of Clinical Health Psychology applies scientific knowledge of the interrelationships among behavioral, emotional, cognitive, social and biological components in health and disease to the promotion and maintenance of health; the prevention, treatment and rehabilitation of illness and disability; and the improvement of the health care system. The distinct focus of Clinical Health Psychology is on physical health problems. The specialty is dedicated to the development of high quality services to individuals, families, and health care systems. (American Psychological Association, 1997, p. 158)

In the deliberations of the Council, a controversy arose about the use of the modifier "clinical" in the title of emerging specialties and proficiencies. Proponents argued that the use of "clinical" is necessary to differentiate training programs preparing psychologists for practice from training programs preparing clinical scientists. An opposing point of view held that psychologists who had not neen trained specifically in a clinical psychology program (e.g., counseling psychologists or school psychologists) would be disadvantaged by such terminology. While approving "Clinical Health Psychology" as the title of the new specialty, the Council imposed a moratorium on the recognition of future specialties and proficiencies incorporating "clinical" in the title until "the confusing and problematic meanings surrounding the generic use of the term "clinical" have been addressed and resolved by the APA to the satisfaction of Council" (Council of Representatives, 1997). A special task force was to be appointed by the APA President to address the complex issues involved and report its recommendations to the Council. The task force was to coordinate its activities with the CRSPPP.

2.19.2.3 Biofeedback: Applied Psychophysiology

Biofeedback: Applied Psychophysiology was recognized as a proficiency in professional psychology also at the August 1997 meeting of the Council. But, unlike the petitions for clinical neuropsychology and health psychology, both of which had come from APA divisions, the petition for this new proficiency was submitted from an interdisciplinary organization, The Biofeedback Certification Institute of America. Since 1981, the Institute has certified individual practitioners from various disciplines as proficient in biofeedback. The CRSPPP assumes that proficiencies are not necessarily subsumed by any particular specialty of psychology and they may, in fact, be shared with other disciplines.

> A proficiency is a circumscribed activity in the general practice of professional psychology or one or more of its specialties. The relationship between

> a body of knowledge and a set of skills related to the parameters of practice ... represents the most critical aspect of the definition of a proficiency. (American Psychological Association, 1995b)

Unlike specialties, which must demonstrate their saliency with respect to all three of the essential parameters of practice, proficiencies are required to show that they are distinctive in at least one of the parameters. Emphasis on the procedural and technical aspects of the proficiency can be seen in the official definition of biofeedback: applied psychophysiology:

> Biofeedback refers to a group of therapeutic procedures that use electronic instruments to record and display to the patient information about the ongoing activity of various body processes of which the person is usually unaware. The goal of biofeedback therapy is to help the patient achieve voluntary control over body processes that are normally involuntary or that have become involuntary through accident or disease. Biofeedback is used in the treatment of many medical and psychological disorders. (American Psychological Association, 1997, p. 160)

It is expected that the petition review process will lead to other recommendations for recognition of new specialties and proficiencies. Strong interest has been shown on the part of clinical, counseling, and school psychology in an early submission of petitions for continued recognition on the basis of a formal review by the CRSPPP. Not all petitions reviewed are recommended for recognition. Those that are incomplete or fail to satisfy all the required criteria are returned to the petitioning organization with an explanation of the identified deficiencies. It is left to the petitioning organization whether to revise and resubmit the petition at a later date.

2.19.3 OWNERSHIP OF SPECIALTIES AND PROFICIENCIES

One of the conceptual issues with which the CRSPPP has struggled is that of ownership of specialties and proficiencies. Initial thinking had been that there must be a single administrative organization that would take responsibility for the specialty or proficiency and would continue to oversee the development of this specialized aspect of professional practice. On the advice of legal counsel, and after further deliberation, the CRSPPP has taken a different position on this important question.

The Commission now takes the position that specialties and proficiencies are not owned by any particular membership group or organization, although one or more professional organizations may indeed be closely associated with a particular specialty or proficiency. In spite of the fact that some organization must take responsibility to petition for official APA recognition, it does not follow that APA recognition confers any special status on the petitioning body. For purposes of the APA recognition process, ownership of a specialty or proficiency is assigned to the profession of psychology at large.

It is assumed that there will be at least one organization which will continue to encourage the development of a specialty or proficiency in order to assure its viability. In the event an officially recognized specialty or proficiency should become obsolete or no longer serve a public need, the option for sunsetting comes into play.

2.19.4 GENERAL PRACTICE SPECIALTIES AND SUBSPECIALTIES

The notion of general practice specialties is well established in healthcare and is closely related to the concept of primary care provider. In medicine, internists, family practice physicians, obstetricians, gynecologists, and pediatricians, are often identified in this way. Practice audits in psychology (Greenberg, Smith, & Muenzen, 1996; Rosenfeld, Shimberg, & Thornton, 1983) suggest that the specialties of clinical and counseling psychology, and perhaps school psychology as well, may deserve to be thought of as general practice specialties.

A petition prepared by the APA Division of Clinical Psychology (Division 12) for continued recognition of clinical psychology as a specialty in professional psychology describes the specialty as "the largest general practice specialty providing psychological services in the US and around the world" (Division of Clinical Psychology, 1995, p. 1). The proposed definition of clinical psychology contained in the petition relies on very broad language of the sort that typically is found in the definition of the practice of psychology in state licensing laws. The petition declares, "As a general practice specialty, Clinical Psychology is essentially the equivalent of 'health service provider' in psychology" (p. 2). The petition further asserts that "other health service provider specialties, by and large, have their origins in Clinical Psychology" (p. 2).

The Commission has been receptive to the concept of general practice specialties in professional psychology, including the notion that there could be several such general practice specialties. Thus far, however, the CRSPPP has not addressed the more complex matter of subspecialties or the possible hierarchical relationship among existing and emerging specialties. The development of a formal taxonomy for specialties and proficiencies may eventually prove helpful in establishing a consensus about these matters within the professional community.

2.19.5 RELATIONSHIP OF THE COMMISSION TO OTHER CREDENTIALING BODIES

It is important to understand that the Commission does not credential individual psychologists in practice specialties or proficiencies, those functions being reserved for other appropriate bodies such as state licensing boards, the APA College of Professional Psychology, and the American Board of Professional Psychology (ABPP). The CRSPPP does expect that its decisions and the official recognition of specialties and proficiencies by the APA will inform the activities of credentialing authorities, accreditation bodies, and training institutions, as well as employers and consumers of psychological services.

2.19.5.1 Marketplace Influences

Identification of specialists by appropriate credentialing bodies is a service to the public. The unfettered proliferation of self-declared competencies and the abandonment of definitional criteria to market forces alone is not an acceptable solution to the need for reliable and useful information that will help to guide those persons in need of a psychologist's services.

If one refers to the yellow pages of any metropolitan telephone directory, it is possible to see listed any number of practice areas in association with the advertising of individual psychologists. In the pages of professional journals and trade publications, one can find announcements for all manner of entrepreneurial specialty credentials or certifications; just send in your application and fee. Psychologists seeking to apply for managed care panels are frequently confronted with checklists that they are expected to complete in order to document their areas of specialization. One large managed care company has announced its intention to credential empaneled behavioral health care providers, including psychologists, according to its own list of 13 "specialties" for which specified criteria have been developed. (Merit Behavioral Care Corporation, 1996). The 13 listed specialties are abuse (physical and sexual), addictions, AIDS/HIV, biofeedback, child and adolescent therapy, geriatrics, group therapy, eating disorders, marriage and family therapy, neuropsychological assessment, psychological testing, psychopharmacology, and sexual dysfunction.

It is little wonder that surveys of consumer opinions reveal widespread confusion and lack of knowledge regarding psychology and psychological services (Farberman, 1997). In a free-market economy and free society, it is probably neither possible nor desirable to restrain the free exchange of information about professional and commercial services. But a more uniform system of terminology and definition of specialties and proficiencies in professional psychology should help to improve public understanding about psychological services and increase public confidence in the specialized services that psychologists have to offer.

2.19.5.2 State Licensing Boards

A license to practice psychology issued by the state licensing board is an important, but insufficient, credential to help the consumer identify which kind of psychologist is best qualified to deal with a particular problem. The licensing laws in most jurisdictions are generic, and boards of examiners have relied heavily on ethical guidelines that call upon psychologists to practice in accordance with their documented professional education, training and experience (American Psychological Association, 1992). Beyond this custom, however, a number of states also attempt to regulate specialty practice directly.

A review of state licensing laws (Stigall & Hall, 1998) reveals that the most frequent practice involves separate licensing or certification for school psychologists, typically by the state education agency. The next most frequent occurrence is certification of psychologists as health service providers on the basis of additional qualifications beyond those required for initial licensing. In attempting to identify for the public those psychologists qualified to render health services, licensing boards are following a definitional concept and standard established by the Council for the National Register of Health Service Providers in Psychology (1996).

A few states have sought to license clinical psychologists. In still other states, boards of examiners have taken it upon themselves to develop standards that can be used on a local basis to identify psychologists with special qualifications or areas of practice. Typically, this involves documentation of specified training and supervised experience relevant to a particular specialty or proficiency. The psychologist's special status is registered with the board or, in some instances, a special certificate is issued.

While intended to protect the public, efforts by state licensing boards have been hampered by the absence of clear professional standards regarding specialties and proficiencies in psychology. The result has been largely a patchwork approach, based upon variable standards and interpretations by local authorities. More uniform professional standards applied to specialties and proficiencies should prove useful to officials responsible for administering the licensing and regulatory provisions of state laws. A principal function of the Association of State and Provincial Psychology Boards (ASPPB) has been to promote greater administrative uniformity and consistency across jurisdictions.

2.19.5.3 American Board of Professional Psychology

The organization best known for credentialing specialists in psychology is the American Board of Professional Psychology (ABPP). The ABPP and its predecessor organization, the American Board of Examiners in Professional Psychology, has been examining applicants seeking the ABPP Diploma since 1947. Over the years the number of specialties recognized by the ABPP has grown, so that by 1997 there were 10 separate diplomate categories: behavioral psychology, clinical neuropsychology, clinical psychology, counseling psychology, family psychology, forensic psychology, health psychology, industrial/organizational psychology, psychoanalysis in psychology, and school psychology (ABPP, 1997).

The ABPP diplomate status is intended to signify advanced competence in an area of specialty practice. Eligibility for the ABPP requires licensure as a psychologist and successful performance on the examination conducted by one of the ABPP specialty boards. Additional requirements may be imposed for acceptance by a given specialty.

In the absence of any official external review process for identifying and recognizing specialties, the ABPP has been in the unenviable position of having to make decisions regarding both the recognition of specialties and the credentialing of individual psychologists. Specialty-regulating activities of professional—as opposed to governmental—organizations carry with them an element of antitrust risk, which appears to be directly related to the consolidation of power in a single organization to influence the market for specialty services. For an analysis of the antitrust implications of specialty credentialing and regulation, see Krauss, Ratner, and Sales (1997). With the advent of the CRSPPP, a decision has been reached to concentrate on the ABPP's core function of credentialing specialists, while relying on the APA to exercise the prior function of formally recognizing specialties in professional psychology (J. G. Matarazzo, personal communication, April 25, 1997).

2.19.5.4 National Register of Health Service Providers in Psychology

A voluntary listing of over 15 000 psychologists who have been found to meet the definition of a health service provider in psychology is provided by the *National Register of Health Service Providers in Psychology*. To be listed in the publication, an individual must be licensed for the independent practice of psychology, hold a doctoral degree in psychology, and have completed two years of supervised experience in health services in psychology. One year of experience must be in an organized health service training program or internship, and one year must be postdoctoral. Specific definitional criteria apply to the doctoral program, the internship and the postdoctoral supervised experience. A health service provider in psychology is considered to be "trained and experienced in the delivery of direct, preventive, assessment and therapeutic intervention services to individuals whose growth, adjustment, or functioning is impaired or to individuals who otherwise seek services" (Council for the National Register of Health Service Providers in Pschology, 1996).

As a service to subscribers, the National Register lists up to five areas of expertise for each registrant, along with other identifying information, theoretical orientation, ages or groups targeted, and languages spoken. Registrants may select from a listing of 51 areas of expertise, ranging from "adjustment disorders and relationship problems" to "terminally ill." In order to claim an area of expertise, registrants must document the particular doctoral and postdoctoral education, training, and experience relevant to the claimed expertise. A careful inspection of the listing suggests that most would conform more closely to the concept of proficiency than specialty, as these terms are used by the CRSPPP.

2.19.5.5 APA College of Professional Psychology

With the ascendance of managed care over the past decade, large numbers of psychologists have been confronted with the need to document their qualifications in specific areas of practice in order to meet the requirements imposed by managed care companies and serve on provider panels. This problem was especially acute for those practitioners desiring to provide services to the alcohol and substance abuse population and for whom a generic license to practice psychology was deemed insufficient by the managed care industry. The College of Professional Psychology was therefore established by the APA in 1994 to certify those psychologists who demonstrate that they have mastered the specific knowledge and skill in one or more recognized practice proficiencies.

Since the CRSPPP and the College of Professional Psychology are both integral parts of the APA, formal policies of the organization govern the relationship between the two bodies. Association Rule 130.5 specifies that the College "shall have the authority to issue certificates of proficiency ... from among *recognized* [italics added] practice proficiencies ... subject to ratification by the Council" (American Psychological Association, 1996a, p. 44). The effect of this policy is to restrict the issuance of certificates by the College to that pool of proficiencies already recognized by the Council, based upon prior review and recommendation by the CRSPPP.

Considering the number of petitions for proficiencies that have been submitted to CRSPPP, it is very likely that additional proficiencies will be recognized in the future. At the time of writing, however, only two proficiencies, treatment of alcohol and other psychoactive substance use disorders and biofeedback: applied psychophysiology, had been officially recognized by the APA, and only the former had been developed as a certificate offering by the College.

2.19.5.6 APA Committee on Accreditation

The APA Committee on Accreditation (CoA) is recognized by the US Department of Education as an official accrediting body for professional training programs in psychology. For more than half a century, the APA has implicitly recognized professional specialties through its accreditation of doctoral training programs in clinical, counseling, and school psychology. Accreditation is a voluntary process whereby academic and internship training programs may achieve the APA's imprimatur of approval, based upon a process of self-study and external review. In carrying out this important function, the CoA enjoys unusual autonomy and self-determination in keeping with the requirements of the US Department of Education and APA policy.

More recently, the APA Council has taken steps to expand the scope of accreditation at both the doctoral and postdoctoral levels of training (DeLeon, 1997, p. 857). These changes in accreditation policy and procedures, which have major implications for the development and recognition of specialties in professional psychology, had been anticipated in a report issued some years earlier by the Joint Council on Professional Education in Psychology (JCPEP). Among the resolutions contained in the JCPEP report were the following:

> The JCPEP supports a change in APA policy that would make application for APA accreditation available to all doctoral programs in psychology that publicly declare their intent to educate and train psychologists for practice.
> The JCPEP urges the APA to approve accreditation criteria for postdoctoral residency training that, in addition to providing advanced specialty training, could satisfy the statutory requirements in most jurisdictions for the supervised experience prerequisite to licensure. (Stigall et al., 1990, p. 25)

As new and emerging specialties become recognized by the APA, it is likely that formal postdoctoral education and training will become an integral component of preparation for specialty practice. The CoA will play a key role in developing standards for accreditation of postdoctoral residency training, as well as new doctoral programs in professional psychology. The CRSPPP acknowledges that specialty preparation may incorporate elements of both doctoral and postdoctoral education and training. The criteria for approval of any petition for recognition of a specialty state that "a specialty requires advanced, specialty-specific scientific knowledge," as well as "advanced didactic and experiential preparation that provide the basis for services with respect to the essential parameters of practice" (American Psychological Association, 1995a, p. 4).

2.19.5.7 Council of Credentialing Organizations in Professional Psychology

Individuals contemplating a career in the practice of psychology are confronted with an often bewildering array of educational and credentialing requirements: doctoral education, internship training, postdoctoral supervised experience and licensure as a psychologist, perhaps additional postdoctoral education and training in an area of specialization, specialty examination and certification, and continuing professional education, which may be for the purpose of renewal of license or recertification in one or more practice proficiencies. Each of these domains of professional education, training, or credentialing is overseen by one or more separate administrative bodies. In some instances, these bodies are statutorily based, as in the case of state licensing boards; or they may be part of a professional membership organization, as is true of CRSPPP; or they may be separately incorporated entities such as the National Register and the ABPP.

The need for an interorganizational forum to deliberate and promote more consistent standards and procedures in accreditation and credentialing was recognized by the Joint Interim Committee which had developed the blueprint for the CRSPPP and recommended its creation by the APA. The Council of Credentialing Organizations in Professional Psychology (CCOPP) was established in response to this need. Since 1995, several meetings of representatives from the participating organizations have been held, and plans have been formulated for the future activities of CCOPP.

The mission of the CCOPP is to "provide interorganizational leadership in the integration of policies and procedures for quality and process improvement in designation, accreditation, and certification of training programs, individuals, specialties, and proficiencies in professional psychology" (Council of Credentialing Organizations in Professional Psychology, 1996, p. 1). Participation in the CCOPP is by invitation and in 1996 included representatives from the ABPP, the ASPPB, the National Register, the Canadian Register of Health Service Providers in Psychology, the Canadian Psychological Association, the Association of Psychology Postdoctoral and Internship Centers (APPIC), and from the APA's CRSPPP, the College of Professional Psychology, and the CoA.

An overall goal articulated by the CCOPP is to establish "a seamless credentialing process for professional psychology, one that affords a coherent relationship between individual credentials obtained at different stages and for different purposes in one's professional career" (Council of Credentialing Organizations in Professional Psychology, 1996, p. 2). Other issues with which the CCOPP has been involved are: the development of a database related to credentialing in professional psychology; encouraging the formation of a council of specialties, which would serve in an advisory capacity to the CoA regarding postdoctoral accreditation; and endorsement of a certification proposal advanced by the ASPPB, which is intended to facilitate the interstate mobility of psychologists. The CCOPP has expressed a strong interest in having an opportunity to comment on petitions for the recognition of specialties and proficiencies that come before the CRSPPP.

2.19.6 TOWARD A TAXONOMY OF SPECIALTIES AND PROFICIENCIES

It should be apparent that the specialty and proficiency recognition process followed by the Commission is empirically based. Petitions are initiated by organizations external to the CRSPPP and are evaluated in accordance with established criteria and procedures. Those that are found to meet the criteria are recommended for formal recognition by the APA. At the same time, an element of judgment is always a part of the process, and there are implicit assumptions and biases that cannot altogether be eliminated.

If a formal taxonomy for describing and ordering specialties and proficiencies in professional psychology were available, it could help to make the recognition process more explicit and public. In an effort to move forward with the development of such a taxonomy, the CRSPPP has articulated a number of basic assumptions:

(i) The purpose of identification and recognition of specialties in professional psychology is to promote communication with the general public about psychological services. Our primary audience is not other psychologists.
(ii) Information about specialties in professional psychology must be communicated in language that is easily understood by the general public.
(iii) Specialties are recognized as they are developed by the profession, based upon the advancement of psychological knowledge and identified public need.
(iv) Specialties in professional psychology have the following characteristics: (a) A shared core of scientific and professional knowledge, skill, and attitudes; (b) A distinctive body of knowledge and professional education and training; (c) An education and training sequence consisting of doctoral study, internship, and residency; (d) Assessment, consultation, and treatment or other interventions with individuals, groups, or organizations, tailored for each specialty; (e) Practice proficiencies, which may be subsumed by a given specialty or which may be common to one or more specialties. (Commission for the Recognition of Specialties and Proficiencies in Professional Psychology, 1996)

Based upon these assumptions, the CRSPPP has devised the following rationale and schema for differentiating between general practice specialties and other specialties and proficiencies in professional psychology:

The public will continue to need the services of general practice specialties, such as those of clinical, counseling, school, and industrial/organizational psychology. The general practice specialties include both the common core of knowledge as well as the advanced core of knowledge particular to each specialty. The emergence of new specialties to provide needed psychological services must also be recognized and validated.

1. *General Practice Specialties*
CRSPPP assumes that the majority of professional psychologists are in the general practice of psychology (clinical, counseling, school, and industrial/organizational psychology).

2. *Other Specialties*
The defining criteria for specialties and proficiencies are found in the CRSPPP policy documents. These include problems addressed, populations served, and procedures or technologies employed. All three criteria are required for specialty recognition, and one or more are required for proficiency recognition.

Specialties of professional psychology may evolve from education and training common to one or more general practice specialties, extending that practice with more specialized psychological education, training, and practice competencies, while integrating these elements with relevant scientific knowledge from related disciplines. By comparison, subspecialties can evolve from more intense or focused training and practice within a recognized specialty.

The following groupings are illustrative and not definitive or exhaustive. Other combinations can be conceptualized.

a. Psychology and Neurosciences
- Clinical Neuropsychology
- Pediatric Neuropsychology
- Geriatric Psychology

b. Psychology and Health Sciences
- Clinical Health Psychology
- Pediatric Psychology

c. Psychology and Forensic Sciences
- Correctional Psychology
- Police Psychology

Note: Bulleted titles could emerge as recognized proficiencies, subspecialties, or specialties, depending on their meeting the criteria for specialty or proficiency recognition. (Commission for the Recognition of Specialties and Proficiencies in Professional Psychology, 1966)

A viable taxonomy will require further revision and elaboration of these preliminary elements. Since the evolution of specialties and proficiencies is a dynamic process, any taxonomy must also remain open to change. It is likely that future models will continue to reflect the interplay of empirical and conceptual components. But such robust concepts as general practice specialties, subspecialties, and the grouping of related categories are likely to remain useful in the development of an acceptable taxonomy.

As the knowledge base in the discipline of psychology and related fields continues to expand, it is incumbent on the profession itself to identify for the public both the officially recognized areas of specialized psychological practice and those practitioners qualified to represent themselves as specialists. The specialty and proficiency recognition process established by the APA and administered by the CRSPPP is one indication of the maturing of a responsible profession.

2.19.7 REFERENCES

American Board of Professional Psychology (1997). *Directory of Diplomates*. Columbia, MO: Author.

American Psychological Association (1992). Ethical principles of psychologists and code of conduct. *American Psychologist, 47,* 1597–1611.

American Psychological Association (1995a). *Principles for the recognition of specialties in professional psychology.* Washington, DC: Author.

American Psychological Association (1995b). *Principles for the recognition of proficiencies in professional psychology.* Washington, DC: Author.

American Psychological Association (1996a). *Association rules.* Washington, DC: Author.

American Psychological Association (1996b). *CRSPPP recommendation to recognize clinical neuropsychology as a specialty in professional psychology.* (Council of Representatives Agenda Item No. 13, August 8 and 11, 1996). Washington, DC: Author.

American Psychological Association (1997). *CRSPPP recommendation to recognize specialties and proficiencies in professional psychology* (Council of Representatives Agenda Item No. 11, August 14 and 17, 1997). Washington, DC: Author.

Commission for the Recognition of Specialties and Proficiencies in Professional Psychology (1996). *Minutes of meeting, October 13, 1996.* Washington, DC: American Psychological Association.

Council for the National Register of Health Service Providers in Psychology (1996). *National Register of health service providers in psychology.* Washington, DC: Author.

Council of Credentialing Organizations in Professional Psychology (1996). *Meeting summary, Santa Fe, NM, November 17, 1996.* Washington, DC: American Psychological Association.

Council of Representatives (1997). *Minutes of meeting August 14 and 17, 1997.* Washington, DC: American Psychological Association.

DeLeon, P. H. (1997). Proceedings of the American Psychological Association, Incorporated, for the year 1996: Minutes of the annual meeting of the Council of Representatives, August 8 and 11, 1996, Toronto, Ontario, Canada, and February 21–23, 1997, Washington, DC. *American Psychologist, 52,* 813–868.

Division of Clinical Psychology, American Psychological Association (1995). *Petition for the recognition of a specialty in professional psychology.* Washington, DC: Author.

Farberman, R. K. (1997). Public attitudes about psychologists and mental health care: Research to guide the American Psychological Association Public Education Campaign. *Professional Psychology: Research and Practice, 28,* 128–136.

Greenberg, S., Smith, I. L., & Muenzen, P. M. (1996). *Study of the practice of licensed psychologists in the United States and Canada.* Montgomery, AL: Association of State and Provincial Psychology Boards.

Krauss, D. A., Ratner, J. R., & Sales, B. D. (1997). The antitrust, discrimination, and malpractice implications of specialization. *Applied & Preventive Psychology, 6,* 15–33.

Merit Behavioral Care Corporation (1996). Specialty verification project offers objective criteria for specialist designation. *MBC Spectrum, 2,* 5.

Rosenfeld, M., Shimberg, B., & Thornton, R. F. (1983). *Job analysis of licensed psychologists in the United States and Canada: a study of responsibilities and requirements.* Princeton, NJ: Educational Testing Service.

Stigall, T. T., Bourg, E. F., Bricklin, P. M., Kovacs, A. L., Larsen, K. G., Lorion, R. P., Nelson, P. D., Nurse, A. R., Pugh, R. W., & Wiens, A. N. (Eds.) (1990). *Report of the Joint Council on Professional Education in Psychology.* Baton Rouge, LA: Joint Council on Professional Education in Psychology.

Stigall, T. T., & Hall, J. E. (1998). Licensure and specialization. In B. D. Sales & J. E. Hall (Eds.), *Specialization in psychology.* New York: Plenum.

2.20
Individual Psychologist: Specialty Board Certification

WALTER B. PRYZWANSKY
University of North Carolina at Chapel Hill, NC, USA

2.20.1 INTRODUCTION

The American Board of Professional Psychology (ABPP) is a voluntary professional credentialing organization. As the major, unitary organization in the US certifying specialty practitioners in psychology, ABPP serves the public need by awarding diplomas that certify psychologists who practice in various specialty areas of psychology. Board certification assures the public that the specialists designated by the ABPP have successfully completed an approved doctoral program, and successfully completed an examination process designed to assess the knowledge, skills, and experience required to provide high-quality psychological services in a particular specialty. The goals of ABPP are:

(i) to serve the public welfare by establishing and overseeing standards of specialty credentialing in psychology and, through its Members Boards, to implement examination procedures which lead to the systematic certification of specialists who meet those standards;

(ii) to serve the public by maintaining a registry of those holding diplomas in various specialties recognized by the Board and by providing public information relevant to the quality and access of specialized psychological services;

(iii) to function as a unitary organization with the public, psychology, and other professionals, external groups, regulatory agencies, and its Member Boards;

(iv) to support specialty boards in the development, validation, and administration of examinations to identify qualified practitioners in recognized psychology specialty areas; and

(v) to promote high standards of research, training, and the practice of psychology.

2.20.1.1 ABPP's Role in Specialty Board Certification

2.20.1.1.1 History

Interest in the credentialing of psychologists can be traced back to 1917 when the American Psychological Association (APA) established a committee to certify qualified APA members based upon written and oral examinations. At that time the committee distinguished between two types of practitioners: the *consulting psychologists*, who are competent in administering and interpreting psychological tests, and *clinical psychologists*, who are broadly knowledgeable about psychopathology. Their recommendation was to certify only the former types of psychologists. However, in spite of the establishment of a certification process, very few APA members became certified over the next 10 years, leading APA to abandon this effort (Goodstein, 1988). However, the need for a psychology practice credential continued to be expressed, so that following World War II, when applied psychology services were experiencing rapid growth, the time was ripe for the reconsideration of a system to certify psychologists. For instance, by 1945 only one state licensing law had been adopted and progress on that front did not appear to be imminent. Consequently, the APA facilitated the development of the American Board of Examiners in Professional Psychology (ABEPP), now the ABPP, as a separate and independent credentialing organization in 1947. The purpose of ABPP was to grant certificates of competence to psychologists who passed both generic and specialty examinations in the fields of professional psychology in which they practiced (ABEPP, 1947). The certificates were issued initially for the following specialties: clinical, counseling, and industrial-organizational psychology. Thus, the history of ABPP typically can be read as a reflector of the certification movement in psychology and specialization.

The ABPP national certificate, then, was seen to have the potential to serve as a uniform base for establishing standards for state licensure. But, rather than offer an entry level credential, the ABPP decided to certify only specialists at the highest level of competence. No doubt this decision reflected the potential of the movement for state licensure of psychologists. By 1948, there were three states with such licensing acts and, subsequently, 32 states by 1960. Instead, the ABPP diploma, awarded upon successful completion of an examination, came to represent a standard of excellence and the highest recognition of competence in professional psychology. Applications were accepted for review after the psychologist documented five years of successful practice in professional psychology.

From its inception, ABPP has been involved with credentialing specialties and promoting national standards of training and practice. Consequently, it should be no surprise that nearly from the time of its incorporation ABPP has been petitioned by groups of psychologists claiming to represent a specialty practice area, but for a variety of reasons, those proposals never became fully developed arguments. Meanwhile, the original three existing specialties received some additional validation as practice areas when the process of APA doctoral training program accreditation was instituted. It was not until 20 years later (1967) that a fourth specialty area was added, and then only in conjunction with APA's decision to make available accreditation of doctoral *school psychology* programs.

The four specialties (sometimes referred to as "original," "traditional," or "defacto" specialties in the literature) proceeded to credential psychologists utilizing similar criteria for determining eligibility and for conducting examination processes (Mayfield, 1987). Once the applicant met the eligibility criteria he/she was admitted into candidacy. The next step involved the preparation of a professional work sample which reflected a typical professional service provided by the candidate. The work sample was submitted with a transcript and/or audio/video tape of the session. Following acceptance of the work sample, an oral examination was then scheduled which included a discussion of the work sample, an *in vivo* observation of the candidate with a client, and discussion of ethical and substantive issues related to the "practice" samples and the candidate's specialty area as well as work activity. The basic dimensions of competency that were evaluated were as follows: (i) the effectiveness of the candidates efforts toward constructive intervention based on realistic assessment of the problem presented; (ii) awareness of the relevance of research and theory; and (iii) sensitivity to the ethical implications of professional practice. The examination process was conducted by three diplomates in one of six regions of the nation; the examination usually included one certified psychologist from a specialty other than the declared specialty of the candidate.

The above description covers what has been seen as ABPP's first two historical phases, and it's role in the specialization of the psychology field (Drum & Pryzwansky, in press). The first phase, "identification and clarification of initial specialty practice areas in psychology through intradiscipline consensus," was largely a consensus-seeking process, without specific criteria to differentiate emerging specialties from existing ones. The second phase involved the managing of the certification of specialists within the identified specialties. Thus, the procedures for the examination and certification of advanced competence received the attention of the credentialing organization.

By the late 1970s, the demands for particular specialty recognition began to intensify so that ABPP shifted its focus to this challenge. While committees within APA struggled with the development of principles and criteria for recognition, no formal policy was adopted. Drum and Pryzwansky (in press) note that this period represented a significant phase for the ABPP organization wherein recognition of new and emerging specialties, and incorporation of organizations supporting those specialties, was begun. ABPP explored the development of specialty recognition criteria which included the insurance of competence-based specialty-oriented examinations of clinical judgment. As a result this experience led to two related projects, specialty recognition and accreditation of postdoctoral training programs.

2.20.1.2 ABPP Specialty Recognition

The expansion of the psychologist's services to new work settings, along with the development of knowledge and interventions, resulted in continued and increased petitions to ABPP to facilitate the formal acknowledgment of this development in the field. APA's Board of Professional Affairs committees and task forces had laid the foundation for such a venture by fostering the development of principles and criteria for recognition of specialties in psychology, but no organizational mechanism was forthcoming to operationalize a process of recognition. However, ABPP was able to utilize the work of APA's Subcommittee on Specialization and in 1979 committed itself to establish "specialty examinations in any area of professional psychology where a critical mass of a group of psychologists:

(i) petition for such an area of specialization;

(ii) establish criteria for educational qualification;

(iii) establish criteria for minimum supervised practice;

(iv) establish criteria for examination processes and procedures; and

(v) state willingness to serve as examiners" (Pryzwansky, 1993).

A specialty was defined as an area in the practice of psychology that connotes special competency acquired through an organized sequence of formal education, training, and experience.

Thus, the unique element of ABPP recognition involvement is that the specialty was required to demonstrate its maturity by documenting the fact that a national group of psychologists existed who practiced in the claimed specialty and that financial viability existed to maintain a competency-based examination. What eventually evolved from those initial experiences and the use of existing APA documents was a refinement of guidelines and procedures for the development of an intensive self-study and review by ABPP affirming that standards of affiliation have been met.

The first stage of specialty recognition consists of the documentation of conceptual and practical viability of the applicant specialty. A detailed document is prepared for initial review by the ABPP Standards Committee before full review for recognition is entertained by the Board of Trustees. This document includes six major areas of information. In addition to identification of a credentialing board, information is sought regarding fiscal and long-term stability of the professional specialty. Congruence with ABPP's basic requirements for application must be demonstrated. A separate section of the self-study document includes demographic estimates of the practitioners, their geographic distribution, plus the names and description of predoctoral and/or postdoctoral training programs in the specialty which then completes this section. The "parameters of practices" constitute the third section. Included in this section are descriptions of the typical characteristics of clients and their problems or issues along with the listing of the primary practice settings. A most important section covers the operational definition of the specialty area along with the primary rationale for its recognition and affiliation with ABPP. As noted in the manual, the procedures that the applying Board will use in all their credentialing activities should relate directly to the professional competencies and activities that are defined. Applicant specialty areas are required to define up to 10 basic practice activities in the following professional competency areas: assessment, intervention, consultation, supervision, research and inquiry, consumer protection, and professional development.

Furthermore, the defined practice activities are judged in two ways, that is (i) essential or important but not essential, and (ii) unique vs. shared wherein the practice of other specialties are concerned. Separate sections of the document address how the specialty area has developed education and training standards or guidelines that assure essential activities are learned, as well as the practice standards or guidelines of the specialty. The specialty is required to present a literature review summarizing published research of the past decade on the efficacy of services funded by practitioners in the specialty. Finally, the credentialing activities which will be used in evaluating individual psychologists are solicited. Successful completion of this stage leads to acceptance into the two monitoring phases of affiliation. An implementation plan including final versions of all examination materials, timetable, etc. are then prepared. The specialty board must demonstrate the capacity to administer at least 30 examinations per year. The final phase involves monitoring of all aspects of the specialty boards credentialing process for at least the next two years. This phase includes an ABPP observer at the examination. During this time the specialty area will have full participating rights on the BOT. Successful completion of this phase will result in full affiliation of the Board and the recognition of the psychologists successfully passing these examinations as ABPP Diplomates.

Drum and Pryzwansky (in press) have noted that the recognition system which evolved has led to the identification of two types of specialties. The first type can be referred to as "unbounded" in the sense that some of the original specialties recognized by Psychology and ABPP were broad enough to be considered a professional field. The second type ("bounded") had more circumscribed boundaries with a dependence on the initial specialties in the sense that they have roots in one or more of those traditional specialties. Furthermore, the fact that many of the newer specialties developed and/or are operating within interdisciplinary contexts challenged the training criterion in a psychology specialty definition, and led to some of the founders of the interdisciplinary organizations unable to meet eligibility criteria for this credential. Also, in a related sense, many of the newer specialties have training programs in nonuniversity settings, particularly the postdoctoral areas. Consequently, the designation and/or accreditation system has yet to be fully developed in the psychology field, leaving specialty board organizations as the key to encouraging standards and practice setting guidelines.

As a result of the above described criteria and mechanism for recognition, two specialties were given full recognition and affiliated with ABPP in the mid-1980s: Clinical Neuropsychology (1984) and Forensic Psychology (1985). An updated criteria and procedures recognition and affiliation document evolved which described a three-stage process typically covering three years, *Application Manual for Specialty Affiliation* (ABPP, 1996). In the 1990s four additional specialties were recognized: Family Psychology (1991), Health Psychology (1991), Behavior Psychology (1993), and Psychoanalytic Psychology (1996). It should be noted that the practice activities in any specialty seldom are exclusive to that specialty and that most practice activities are shared with the general practice of professional psychology. The pattern of practice activities, including limiting the scope of practice, and focusing upon more complex or unique problems or technologies, is more relevant in defining a specialty together with advanced education, training, and experience (ABPP, 1996). Brief definitions of each of the 10 specialty boards are as follows:

(i) The American Board of Behavioral Psychology—Applied behavior analysis, cognitive behavior therapy, and cognitive therapy.

(ii) The American Board of Clinical Psychology—Assessment and treatment of mental, physical, emotional, and behavioral disorders.

(iii) The American Board of Clinical Neuropsychology—Evaluation of brain–behavior relationships and the treatment of cognitive, attentional, learning, and memory disorders.

(iv) The American Board of Counseling Psychology—Individual, group, and community interventions for emotional, behavioral, vocational, and mental health problems using preventive, developmental, and remedial approaches, and in the assessment, diagnosis, and treatment of psychopathology.

(v) The American Board of Family Psychology—Intervention and assessment in Family Psychology embracing the total family system including individuals, couples, families, and the intergenerational system.

(vi) The American Board of Forensic Psychology—The practice of psychology as related to law and the legal system.

(vii) The American Board of Health Psychology—The practice of psychology related to health, including the prevention, treatment, and rehabilitation of illness.

(viii) The American Board of Industrial/Organization Psychology—The application of psychology to problems of organizations and individuals/groups in organizational settings.

(ix) The American Board of Psychoanalysis in Psychology—A body of knowledge, a research method, and a treatment technique based on a description of organized unconscious, dynamic mental processes to aid in understanding emotions, attitudes, and belief systems to facilitate more satisfying, secure, and productive living.

(x) The American Board of School Psychology—The facilitation of learning and the promotion of mental health in schools and educational settings.

In addition to these 10 Specialty Boards, two specialty boards are in the second phase of the three-phase process of affiliation with the ABPP. These boards are developing examination materials and credentialing procedures consistent with required standards. The boards should be examining board members and candidates in the near future. The two boards are: The American Board of Group Psychology—The application of general psychological and specific group principles to change, modify, or adapt individual behavior, as well as patterning or modifying the behavior of groups; and The American Board of Rehabilitation Psychology—Assisting the individual with an injury or illness to achieve optional physical, psychological, and interpersonal functioning.

It is interesting to note that while the original four specialties developed at the doctoral level, some of the new or emerging specialties which have been ABPP recognized are clearly postdoctoral in the sense that they build on the doctoral training experience of the "traditional" specialties. Since APA recently established a Commission for the Recognition of Specialties and Proficiencies (DeLeon, 1995), ABPP has suspended its recognition mission to ascertain whether the Commission, speaking for the psychology field, will fill the original need of professional psychologists which prompted ABPP's actions since the late 1980s. Future specialties recognized by the Commission still will be required to validate the fiduciary, conceptual, and practice maturity involved in competency-based credentialing to become ABPP affiliated.

As a result of the ABPP growth in credentialing, structured changes have followed. The examination of each specialty is now developed, monitored, and revised by its respective specialty board. The credential, therefore, has evolved to a specialty board certification recognition of competence. The ABPP maintains minimum standards for applicant eligibility and examination beyond which the Specialty Board may add and/or insure relevance for the specialty. A nonprofit professional credentialing organization, ABPP, currently serves the public need by providing oversight of the certifying of psychologists competent to deliver high-quality services in various specialty areas of psychology.

2.20.1.3 Accreditation of Postdoctoral Training Programs

The emergence of ABPP postdoctoral specialties was a clear indication of the need for a mechanism to acknowledge the education and training standards for the development of competencies in those areas. Consequently, in 1991, ABPP organized the Conference on the Accreditation of Postdoctoral Programs in Psychology which resulted in the formation of the Interorganizational Council for Accreditation of Postdoctoral Programs in Professional Psychology (IOC). Organizations that made up the IOC included ABPP, National Register of Health Service Providers in Psychology, Association of Professional Psychology Internship Council, the Association of State and Provincial Psychology Boards, APA and later its Committee on Accreditation (COA), and representatives from the ABPP Specialty Boards.

The IOC first developed postdoctoral accreditation criteria as well as a Self-Study Document, both of which have subsequently been merged into the APA's COA *Guidelines and Principles for Accreditation of Programs in Professional Psychology*. A joint IOC–COA task force, in addition to addressing merging of documents, has been considering ways for continuing involvement of the IOC representation. Of interest is the requirement that "where postdoctoral residency programs offer education and training in a specialty, the program meets the additional standards promulgated by recognized specialty groups" (IOC, 1994). As a result, when a postdoctoral residency program applying for APA accreditation offers specialty training and requests to be so acknowledged, the entrance requirements must include criteria promulgated by recognized specialty groups.

A Council of Specialties is being formed with the broad aim of developing a general quality assurance process to provide guidance in the development of specialty-specific accreditation standards and self-study documents. Furthermore, such a council could conceivably serve as a mechanism for validating the existence of training standards for a specific specialty, as well as assist the COA in implementing accreditation procedures such as identifying review panels and site visitors for formal involvement in the COA process. Consequently, while much remains to be done in terms of postdoctoral specialty accreditation, significant steps toward the end have been realized.

2.20.2 CURRENT ABPP BOARD CERTIFICATION REQUIREMENTS

2.20.2.1 Eligibility

The purpose of a Specialty Board is to evaluate the qualifications of individual applicants' preparation, experience, knowledge, and competence in a specialty (ABPP, 1995). National in scope, the Specialty Board uniformly implements its policy and procedures in examining psychologists who volunteer to engage in this process. Independently incorporated specialty boards are stable organizations affiliated with ABPP which reflect the current development of the specialty. The individual Boards meet minimum eligibility standards set by the ABPP Board of Trustees, the latter entity serving as a quality control agent in their oversight of the Boards. What follows then is a general description of those minimum standards.

In terms of *education* the applicant psychologist must document that they hold a doctorate in psychology from a regionally accredited institution in the US. In addition the applicant must have had two years of *supervision* in the practice of his or her specialty (one of which may be at the predoctoral level) and three years of *experience*. The experience requirement can be satisfied in two ways. First, the applicant may have completed an accredited postdoctoral in the respective specialty plus one year of pre- or postdoctoral experience. Alternatively, the applicant can document three years of experience, one of which may be predoctoral. Finally, it is required that applicants who provide psychological services of a health care nature will hold a license to practice psychology in the state where he or she practices. The specialty may include additional education, training, and specific experiential criteria in determining eligibility, such as evidence of identification with the specialty, successful completion of a recognized postdoctoral training program, and specific types of practice experience at the postdoctoral level. It is interesting to note the shift from a five-year experience requirement which originally characterized the ABPP, and was a criterion consistent with the concept that certification recognized advanced competency among experienced practitioners in psychology. The addition of six specialties, several of which consider themselves postdoctoral specialties in the sense that specialist training takes place after completion of training in the "traditional" specialties at the doctoral level, has led to an evolution in the role of this credential. While advanced competency is axiomatic in the case of a postdoctoral specialist, *specialty board certification* is a more accurate descriptor of the credential and communicates the essence of the credential clearly both within the profession as well as to other professions and the public.

2.20.2.2 The ABPP Examination Process

Once eligibility has been determined, there are two stages in the examination process. First, the preparation of an acceptable work sample is required which will constitute the basis for one part of the face-to-face oral examination. Specialty Boards have specific guidelines for the development of these materials which should reflect the current practice of the candidate. Appropriate documentation is required. For example, in addition to assessment reports, therapy and/or supervision transcripts, and program evaluation models, the candidate is required to provide an analysis which includes appropriate background data, goals and/or objectives of the activity, relevant theoretical and research scheme, and an evaluative summation including a critique and plans for subsequent follow-up. Audio and/or video tapes of the activity are often included along with other relevant material. The examination proper, then, involves examination of the work sample(s), and may also include an on-site practice sample wherein the examining team can observe the candidate interact under *in vivo* conditions with a live client, or respond to specially prepared videotaped observations of an actual client or an interview conducted with an actual client. The variability noted here reflects the uniqueness of each specialty and the particular avenues of opportunities to assess the clinical practice of the specialty. Furthermore, specialties utilize one or more of several examination models ranging from the assessment center approach, wherein candidates move from station to station, to the more traditional *in vivo* examination approach. All specialty examinations also have an ethics component, again with varying assessment approaches, as well as a component which deals with the substantive content of the specialty.

The evolution from regional examination centers, staffed by representatives from the four traditional specialties, to a national specialty board examination model has facilitated two outcomes. A national board promotes reliability, validity, and consistency objectives in assessment by reducing variability factors which can emerge due to regional emphases. Second, the relevance of content and practice situations is enhanced for the candidate when control of the examination is maintained by the Specialty Board. In turn, the ABPP Board of Trustees serves an oversight function, insuring that fair, sound, and reasonable examinations are conducted, and the examinations themselves are evaluated and updated. This oversight function is assigned to the ABPP Standards Committee which maintains minimum standards and expectations for each of its Specialty Boards, promotes development of the examination process, and facilitates communication and sharing among these Boards with the objective of increasing their relevance for the individual psychologist as well as the profession. The value of any credential, and in particular a competency oriented one, depends on the integrity of the examination.

Finally, ABPP Diplomates, as those holding specialty board certification are called, also are members in their respective specialty Academy. The academies serve as membership organizations promoting continuing education, public service, and advocacy functions for the specialty.

2.20.3 THE ABPP PROFESSIONAL PRACTICE APPRAISAL: SOME EXAMPLES

As noted above, all of the 10 ABPP specialties require candidates to submit examples of typical, relatively current, professional practice activities in the form of a work sample. Following the acceptance of the work sample, an interactive oral examination conducted by three trained psychologist examiners from the candidate's specialty is then conducted. The latter is usually individually administered, although at this time two specialties utilize an assessment center type model of examination. Since state licensure is required of all candidates in practice, those applicants have passed the additional objective examination developed and administered by the Association for State and Provincial Psychology Boards. Only one ABPP specialty, clinical neuropsychology, requires successful completion of an objective examination covering basic content in that specialty. This 100-item written examination contains content covering the lifespan from prenatal development through senescence. The five content categories are (i) neuropsychological assessment; (ii) clinical neuropsychology; (iii) basic and clinical neuroscience; (iv) behavioral (clinical) neurology; and (v) general clinical psychology. The majority of the test items fall within the middle three categories.

What follows are some illustrative descriptions of the process utilized by the three specialties of clinical psychology, clinical neuropsychology, and counseling psychology. Obviously, reference should be made to the credentialing materials of each specialty for a complete and official description of the process.

2.20.3.1 Work Samples

The work sample generally is considered as an example of the candidate's professional practice style and competence in carrying out activities reflective of his/her practice. The Counseling Psychology Board (CP) requires one work sample which must consist of two parts, one of which is focused on assessment and the other on intervention, supplemented by audio and/or video tapes of the sample along with an extensive written documentation. The Clinical Neuropsychology (CN) work sample consists of two cases, each of which must include the neuropsychological evaluation basis and the conceptual basis for the interventions employed, as well as the steps taken to assure an adequate test of the efficacy of the interventions. The case supporting materials are outlined. The Clinical Psychology work sample consists of two videotaped samples of approximately 50 minutes each, one depicting an unrehearsed psychological assessment effort, the other depicting an unrehearsed intervention effort, drawn from recent typical clinical practice. Again, documenting material is specified in each instance.

2.20.3.2 Oral Examination

In terms of the oral examination proper, the same substantive areas are involved and differences exist only in the assessment strategy which is utilized. Counseling Psychology begins the examination with a prerecorded interview with a client constituting an initial intake session (the observed, taped interview must be prepared within 60 days prior to the scheduled oral examination). Following viewing by the examination committee, the candidate will be questioned regarding his/her conclusions to ascertain such information as the understanding of the client and the presenting problem. The work sample, earlier described, is compared and contrasted then with the case. Two additional parts of the examination remain. The candidate is next presented with two written vignettes from which one is chosen, and one or more ways of addressing the presenting problem with appropriate interventions other than individual counseling are presented. Finally, the candidate is asked to discuss the ethical and legal implications of a presented written vignette.

Clinical Neuropsychology begins their oral examination with a fact-finding exercise in which initial neuropsychological consultation in a case is expected. Both a child and adult case are presented for this segment of the examination and the candidate chooses the case and begins to request information on which eventual conclusions are to be made. The work sample is then used as a point of departure for examiners' questions to allow the candidate to demonstrate a reasonable, rational, and defensible approach to patient evaluation, treatment, and report writing. Finally, the candidate is presented with a neuropsychologically related vignette and asked to identify issues. The candidate is asked questions about his/her own professional practices, professional involvement, and research activities.

The Clinical Psychology specialty begins with an examination of the two work sample materials and the professional statement. This segment of the examination is then followed by ethical and legal issues. The candidate is presented with an ethical vignette to review and discuss. This vignette, and the ethical dilemma identified from his/her own practice and presented as part of the candidate's professional statement, will form the context for this segment of the examination.

The above abbreviated examples of examinations from three of the 10 ABPP specialties provide a sample of the competency-based examinations used as part of the ABPP Board certification process. More detailed and current information regarding these three specialties as well as the other ABPP specialties may be obtained by writing to the individual boards at ABPP's Central Office at 2100 East Broadway, Suite 313, Columbia, MO 65201-6082.

2.20.4 PSYCHOLOGISTS AS "HEALTH SERVICES PROVIDERS"

An interesting ABPP development occurred in the early 1970s in response to discussions taking place then regarding national health insurance plans. It was noted that psychologists usually were not included in many of the proposed plans in part due to the fact that insurance carriers had no formal mechanism for determining which credentialed psychologists were qualified to offer health services. Although ABPP credentialed psychologists with a specialty practice, some of those did not offer such services, most notable the large percentage of industrial/organizational psychologists. More relevant to this need to identify psychologists in health services was the fact that state licensure was generic so that it provided no information regarding this question. In large measure as a result of ABPP's credentialing history, the APA Board of Directors specifically requested in 1974 that ABPP establish a National Council for the Register of Health Service Providers in Psychology. The ABPP central office organized such a meeting for the Council in 1974 and funded the organization of the National Register. Further discussions considered the development of "junior diplomate" and the original interest in simply establishing a system of identifying health service providers (HSP) from among all licensed psychologists. The National Register continued its affiliation with ABPP during its start up, but given the demand for a Registry system (7500 applicants in a three-month period), the Council soon evolved into a completely separate organization with the purpose of validating psychologists' credentials as meeting criteria for listing as a health service provider in psychology. Subsequently, some states have added a similar validation from the licensees separate from the license itself.

Most of the ABPP specialties include the basic HSP requirements within the board certification process, and as the psychology credentialing bodies move toward an integrated system for credentialing psychologists, this relationship may become even more apparent. Such systems would include the doctoral internship, postdoctoral training, licensure, listing in the National Register, and ABPP board certification in a specialty; a connection with doctoral and postdoctoral accreditation would complete the system.

2.20.5 THE IMPACT OF BOARD CERTIFICATION ON THE PROFESSION

As the professional has matured so has the ABPP Diplomate evolved as a credential for psychologists. Originally conceived as the practice credential in the absence of state licensure, the ABPP credential then took on the aura of a validation of expertise associated with senior status in a professional and since the late 1980s increasingly is conceptualized as an examination-based endorsement of specialty practice competencies. Clearly, several of the professional psychology specialties (e.g., clinical neuropsychology and forensic psychology) are well along the path leading to the expectation among employers and consumers that attainment of board certification is necessary for practice. Similarly, as the APA continues with the formal process of recognition of specialties (and proficiencies), the natural outcome will require a system for the validation of training and practice in the specialty. Thus, the current ABPP Boards can be viewed as anticipating, if not influencing, the specialization movement within professional psychology. ABPP is the only unitary organization recognized by the profession as certifying specialty practitioners in psychology.

The two aforementioned specialties are increasingly recognized within their practice settings, that is, medically-oriented systems and the judicial system. In addition, the US Department of Defense and the US Public Health Service are committed to implementing pay increments tied to employment longevity within their policies, but implementation has not been realized. At this time two states (MO and OR) recognize psychologists with ABPP board certification employed in the Department of Mental Health system. Over 40 states have a reciprocity type stipulation for psychologists holding the ABPP written into their psychology licensing regulations. Finally, until revision of the APA doctoral program accreditation criteria (1996), which has become "outcome" oriented with less attention to the structure and process of the training program, the qualifications of the directors of the training program ironically have been de-emphasized in a sense so that evidence such as the ABPP credential, or APA Fellow Status, are not mentioned, and thereby no longer encouraged through that mechanism. Discussions regarding accreditation of postdoctoral training in a specialty have noted the importance of the requirement of board certification for the director of the training program.

Another influence of the ABPP certificate subtle as it is, but nevertheless important, concerns the professional development concept in psychological practice. Preparation for the ABPP peer examination has many intangible rewards for psychologists undergoing the activity. The preparation of a work sample leads to a unique structured self-reflection exercise; coupled with the examination process itself the individual psychologist will have experienced activities that contribute to the practitioner's growth and development. The attainment of an independent, rigorous verification that the standards and competencies required in a specialty area were met is an important personal as well as professional reward. Likewise, the continuing upgrading of the examination by the individual boards can lead to and/or reinforce training developments in the specialty. At some future date, when coordination among training programs and accrediting as well as credentialing bodies are better organized, documenting the fact of board certification for graduates can serve as important feedback to the training program and lead to improvement in the quality of professional psychology education and practice.

2.20.6 FUTURE DIRECTIONS

Clearly, activity in the development of tools assessing professional practice will continue and enhance the relevance of the examinations in the respective specialties. The use of the still preferred *in vivo* examinations will no doubt continue to be used as a yardstick against which more cost-effective, increasingly standardized simulated approaches will be tested, approaches which give examiners and candidates more flexibility in dealing with problem-solving scenarios. Also, it is anticipated that computerized assessment alternatives will begin to drop in cost and receive renewed attention. The end result should be even more viable assessment procedures capable of promoting professional development while serving as a measure of competency in practice.

By contrast, the future recognition of specialties will most likely slow in terms of the immediate future, partly to give the applied psychology arena a chance to catch its breath, and partly for the APA process headed by CRSPP to interface with the movements within the credentialing community. At the same time, subspecialities and proficiencies will more than likely continue to grow. Finally, the next decade should bring the realization of a seamless education, training, and accreditation–credentialing system wherein all components are fitted together. The result should be greater protection for the public along with improved service stemming from stronger training programs.

2.20.7 REFERENCES

American Board of Examiners in Professional Psychology (1947). Report of the American Board of Examiners in Professional Psychology. *American Psychologist, 2*(502), 512–517.

American Board of Professional Psychology (1995). *Standards for Boards of the American Board of Professional Psychology*. ABPP.

American Board of Professional Psychology (1996). *Application manual for specialty affiliation*. ABPP.

DeLeon, P. H. (1995). Proceedings of the American Psychological Association, Incorporated, for the Year 1994: Educational Affairs. *American Psychologist, 50*(8), 665–666.

Drum, D. J., & Pryzwansky, W. B. (in press). ABPP and the development of specialization. In B. A. Sales & J. E. Hall (Eds.), *Specialization in psychology*. New York: Plenum.

Goodstein, L. D. (1988). The role of the American Psychological Association in legitimizing the practice of

psychology: A historical perspective. *Professional Practice of Psychology, 9*(1), 1–9.
Mayfield, P. N. (1987). Certification of psychologists by the American Board of Professional Psychology. In B. A. Edelstein & E. S. Berler (Eds.), *Evaluation and accountability in clinical training* (pp. 283–297). New York: Plenum.
Pryzwansky, W. B. (1993). Credentialing in an era of specialties: The ABPP Diplomate. *The Diplomate, 13*(1), 5–7.

2.21
Hospital Staff Membership: United States

KRIS R. LUDWIGSEN
Kaiser Foundation Hospital, Martinez-Walnut Creek, CA, USA

2.21.1 INTRODUCTION

One of the primary issues which has marked the coming of age of clinical psychology as an independent health care profession is the attainment of hospital practice privileges to include independent admission, treatment, and discharge privileges of the most acute and disturbed patients. The clinical role of psychologists in hospitals began in World War II, concurrent with the birth of clinical psychology as a profession. Psychologists initially served as psychodiagnostic consultants evaluating the cognitive, intellectual, and neuropsychological impact of war injuries in Veterans Administration (VA) hospitals with limited responsibilities and expertise. Since then US psychologists have been practicing in state mental hospitals, military hospitals, mental retardation facilities, medical surgical hospitals, chemical dependency facilities, rehabilitation and geriatric facilities, private psychiatric hospitals, VA hospitals, health maintenance organization hospitals, and day treatment centers with some degree of authority. For 50 years, psychologists have been demonstrating their expertise in inpatient care and their value to the hospital as an institution.

2.21.2 PSYCHOLOGISTS' ROLES IN HOSPITALS

Psychologists' roles within hospitals have extended from salaried staff to independent contractors to attending or consulting staff. Psychologists have held the salaried positions of hospital administrator and assistant administrator, state hospital superintendent, and hospital owner. As clinical services director, the psychologist is responsible for overseeing the range of clinical programs and services offered. As director of psychological services, the psychologist determines policies for the psychology staff, oversees training of psychology interns and determines what services salaried psychologists provide within the facility. Psychologists have served as program directors for the adolescent unit, the dual diagnosis program, the day treatment and partial hospitalization programs, as well as quality assurance coordinators. As independent contractors, psychologists have contracted with hospitals to offer, for example, biofeedback, neuropsychological assessment, assertiveness training and anger management groups, groups to manage stress and chronic pain, eating disorders, sexual abuse and incest survivors groups on an ongoing or time-limited basis.

Where consistent with state law, psychologists have held designated medical staff privileges with formal credentialing by the hospital. The Joint Commission for Accreditation of Healthcare Organizations (JCAHO) identifies three levels of medical staff privileges: active staff, courtesy staff, and consulting staff. Both active and courtesy staff may admit patients to the hospital and serve as the primary attending clinician. However, active staff are more involved with the hospital since they have voting privileges within the hospital governance, are required to serve on hospital committees, and are on the call roster to receive emergency referrals. Courtesy staff have the same level of clinical privileges but may not admit more than a specific number of patients per year, are not on the hospital call roster, do not serve on hospital committees, and do not have voting privileges. Consulting staff provide specialty diagnostic or treatment assistance to the attending clinician, such as neurological or neuropsychological assessment, pain management, or biofeedback. Medical staff privileges may be held concurrently with a part-time salaried or independent contractor position.

2.21.3 OBTAINING INDEPENDENT PRIVILEGES

Although it has been a protracted and arduous struggle, psychologists in the USA could not have attained their present extent of hospital privileges prior to passing independent licensure and certification laws which established a certain parity with physicians on an outpatient basis. The hospital practice movement began with several psychologists in various states, military hospitals, and rural areas over the last 30 years, exercising informal privileges in treating patients admitted to the hospital from their own outpatient practices. Collaborating psychiatrists and physicians signed orders and provided informal, collegial support until the former Joint Commission for Accreditation of Hospitals (JCAH) reviewed these procedures and requested that hospitals rescind informal privileges for psychologists. Faced with the possible threat of losing JCAH accreditation, hospitals complied. The JCAH was authorized by the US Department of Health, Education and Welfare to regulate hospitals, and was thereby empowered to promulgate and enforce rules. Founded in 1951 by various physician groups to establish consistent standards for quality of care, for example, how frequently physicians had to see their hospitalized patients, the JCAH was the primary organization accrediting hospitals and health care facilities. The JCAH standards explicitly required physicians to "take medical responsibility for" patients admitted to the hospital with the support of federal statutes and state legislation (Wiggins & Ludwigsen, 1991). The American Psychological Association (APA) and the Association for the Advancement of Psychology (AAP) had petitioned the JCAH for formal status on hospital medical staffs and representation within the JCAH (Zaro, Batchelor, Ginsberg, & Pallak, 1982). However, the decade of struggle by organized psychology did not bear fruit until the AAP notified the Federal Trade Commission (FTC) of the implications of restraint of trade within the health care sector and the FTC determined that professions as well as businesses were subject to antitrust action. Subsequently, hospitals became aware of the antitrust implications of excluding psychologists as a health care profession from hospitals (Bersoff, 1983).

In 1978, after three years of legislative efforts, California was the first state to grant statutory permission for hospitals to include psychologists on the medical staff and to accord them admitting and attending privileges (Enright, Resnick, Ludwigsen, & DeLeon, 1993). Since then, several other states have obtained hospital practice privileges for psychologists. Currently, psychologists have full privileges in various medical schools and are on the medical staff of VA hospitals on a facility-by-facility basis where permitted by state law (Resnick & Morris, 1997).

As psychologists became recognized as health care professionals within hospitals, they began to request guidelines from the APA on hospital practice for psychologists. In response, the APA commissioned *A hospital practice primer for psychologists* (Committee on Professional Practice of the Board of Professional Affairs, 1985) and *Hospital practice advocacy issues* (Committee on Professional Practice of the Board of Professional Affairs, 1988) and adopted the *Guidelines on hospital practice privileges: Credentialing and bylaws* (Resnick, Enright, & Thompson, 1991). Other APA standards relevant to hospital practice are discussed in *Professional liability and risk management* (Bennett, Bryant, VandenBos, & Greenwood, 1990) and *The ethical principles of psychologists and code of conduct* (APA, 1992). Finally, *The psychologist's legal handbook* (Stromberg et al., 1988), discussions of hospital politics (Rozensky, 1991), and of training psychologists for hospital practice (Ludwigsen & Albright, 1994) offer useful guidance to psychologists pursuing independent privileges in hospitals.

Despite the passage of state legislation explicitly permitting hospital privileges for psychologists, the Department of Health Services in California promulgated regulations stating that psychiatrists alone could be responsible for the patient's diagnosis and treatment. In response, a group of independent psychologists filed suit to challenge these regulations as inconsistent with state law. The *CAPP v. Rank* suit was originally upheld by the California Superior Court in 1985, but was appealed with a series of rulings favoring the medical establishment in 1988. The final decision by the California Supreme Court stated that in diagnosis and treatment, psychology and psychiatry are on equal footing where neither is subject to constraints from which the other is free (CAPP v. Rank, 1990).

Faced with the possibility for an antitrust suit asserting discrimination against psychologists as a profession, the JCAH modified its statement on the composition of the medical staff in 1985 to state that the organized medical staff "includes fully licensed physicians and may include other licensed individuals permitted by law and by the hospital to provide patient care independently" (JCAHO, 1992, p.55), and added an APA representative to its oversight committee for mental health care standards in 1988. However, while state psychological associations were mounting campaigns to obtain hospital privileges for psychologists, the JCAH removed staff restrictions, and the *CAPP v. Rank* suit was decided in favor of psychologists practicing independently in hospitals, another barrier to hospital practice emerged. The federal Social Security Administration required physician supervision of nonphysician professionals for hospitals receiving federal reimbursement through Medicare and Medicaid funds (Social Security Administration, 1993). Through the advocacy efforts of the APA the Social Security Acts Amendments of 1994 now guarantees licensed psychologists independent practice and reimbursement for services rendered in a hospital where consistent with state law under the Psychology Services in Hospitals section (Social Security Acts Amendments, 1994).

2.21.4 HOSPITAL BYLAWS

Where state law is permissive, enabling, or silent regarding hospital privileges for psychologists, the next step is to review the current hospital bylaws to determine the appropriate medical staff status of psychologists within the facility. Hospital bylaws are public documents available through the board of directors, the medical staff coordinator or hospital administrator, which define the standards for professional staff membership. Bylaws specify the staff categories available to applicants, and the clinical privileges available within each category (Rozensky, 1997). Modifications are proposed in the Bylaws Committee and then voted upon by the active staff. Changes proposed should be consistent with the wording and principles of practice espoused by the particular hospital's bylaws. Extending the bylaws to enable psychologists to become active, courtesy, or consulting staff members involves a certain degree of research and preparation, for example, on psychologists' current competencies, the role of psychiatrists and other clinicians in the facility, the state nurse practice act, and psychologists' legal scope of practice. Discussions with medical staff colleagues, the Bylaws Committee, the administrator and the board of directors may also be necessary to effect changes in the bylaws. Rozensky (1991) notes that it is more effective to change the rules from within an organization than to challenge them as a newcomer without a full appreciation of the hospital's history regarding the roles of clinical psychologists.

2.21.5 REQUIREMENTS FOR MEDICAL STAFF MEMBERSHIP

Although hospitals are required to be consistent and nondiscriminatory in their policies regarding staff membership, they are not obligated to accept all applicants. Stromberg et al. (1988) note that the entire staff of a hospital or a particular department may be closed to applicants, with appropriate documentation of rationale, if the inpatient facility is inadequate to treat patients likely to be admitted by the applicant, or if the existing staff is sufficient to meet the hospital's needs. Therefore, in applying for privileges, it is important to consider what expertise (e.g., neuropsychology) or benefits (e.g., patient admissions) the practitioner will be contributing towards developing a mutually beneficial relationship with the hospital.

The specific requirements for hospital staff membership differ from hospital to hospital. Stromberg et al. discuss relevant criteria for staff membership including level of education, clinical internships, fellowships or other training, experience, licensure, and current clinical competencies. The American Psychological Association recommends at a minimum: (i) a doctoral degree from a regionally accredited program training psychologists; (ii) state licensure at the independent practice level; and (iii) one year or more of supervised experience in a health care facility with an inpatient component (Resnick et al., 1991). By comparison, the American Psychiatric Association (1986) recommends that privileges be based on verifiable data such as graduation from an accredited medical school, record of postgraduate or specialty training, licensure, specialty board certification, prior experience including previous hospital appointments, letters of recommendation, and lack of malpractice history.

Stromberg et al. note that hospital staff members may be required to carry a certain level of malpractice insurance due to the higher acuity level of hospitalized patients and that privileges may be denied if there are pending or completed professional liability actions or loss of membership or privileges at other inpatient facilities. Privileges may also be denied if there is evidence of significant health impairment, of difficulty in working with others, or if the practitioner's personal style is documented to jeopardize quality of care. Finally, the hospital may determine residential limits for attending staff so that patients can be treated in a timely way in an emergency.

2.21.6 CREDENTIALING AND PRIVILEGING

According to JCAHO standards, all practitioners who treat patients in a hospital must be credentialed whether they are members of the professional staff, independent contractors, or salaried staff. The process of delineation and renewal of clinical privileges is described in the hospital bylaws. Credentialing refers to providing appropriate documentation for the requirements to become a member of the hospital staff. Although the bylaws specify the staff categories available and the clinical privileges available within each, the granting of specific clinical privileges is a separate process from designating a staff category.

Privileging refers to specifying the clinician's scope of practice within each staff category concerning the various patient assessment and treatment procedures. In addition, temporary privileges may be extended relative to an emergency admission, and provisional privileges may be granted to practitioners seeking attending privileges while undergoing the proctoring process.

Credentialing procedures define psychologists, similar to physicians, dentists, and podiatrists, as independent practitioners within the hospital, and define their scope of practice within each inpatient facility. The *JCAHO Accreditation manual for hospitals, 1992* (JCAHO, 1992), Standard MS.2.15, states that apart from the system for granting, renewal, or revision of clinical privileges, the granting of clinical privileges is hospital specific and based on current competence. The hospital may be as specific or general as is practical and necessary. Any limitations on the practitioner's privileges to admit and treat patients should also be specified, for example, that privileges regarding assessment procedures do not include neuropsychological assessment.

Models of privileging for psychologists can be summarized under three categories: privileging by patient categories, privileging by assessment and treatment procedures, and privileging by intensity of containment (Ludwigsen, 1993).

2.21.6.1 Privileging by Patient Categories

In several hospitals, units and programs are organized around the needs of different patient groups, such as children, adolescents, adults, and geriatric patients, as well as chemically dependent, rehabilitation, mentally retarded, eating disorder, and forensic patients. Privileges to treat specific patient categories can be granted based on the psychologist's demonstrated training, experience, and current expertise, and may be considered an extension of defining the psychologist's outpatient specialties.

2.21.6.2 Privileging by Assessment and Treatment Procedures

The privileging process can be conceptualized according to specialized expertise such as cognitive-behavioral therapy, pain management, neuropsychological assessment, biofeedback, clinical hypnosis, and marital and family psychotherapy, which psychologists will be contributing to the hospital. Specialized credentialing standards may be required for neuropsychology, biofeedback, and clinical hypnosis. The APA Division of Clinical Neuropsychology defined the independent practitioner of neuropsychology as having completed two or more years of appropriate supervised training in delivering neuropsychological services in a clinical setting, including a one-year predoctoral internship, postdoctoral training, and clinical neuropsychology experience ("Definition of a clinical neuropsychologist," 1989). Board certification through the American Board of Clinical Neuropsychology further includes a rigorous examination of credentials and clinical competence. The hospital may require documentation of specialized training in biofeedback and clinical hypnosis, for example, certification by the Biofeedback Certification Institute of America or the American Society of Clinical Hypnosis, as appropriate to the community standard of practice and quality of patient care.

2.21.6.3 Privileging by Intensity of Containment

In psychiatric hospitals and state mental hospitals, privileges can be granted for treating patients on the locked unit, the acute care unit, the open unit, and the day treatment unit, based on the assumption that intensifying levels of acuity require greater clinical expertise, as in identifying the potential for and managing suicidal and assaultive behavior. Psychologists applying to admit and treat patients on the locked unit would probably be expected to show documentation of past training and/or experience with suicidal, assaultive, or violent patients, or to complete a period of proctoring on a specified number of acute patients before assuming independent patient care responsibilities. However, many psychologists pursuing admission privileges at such hospitals are requesting the authority to admit and treat suicidal patients from their own practices within an inpatient setting to provide continuity of care.

Proctoring is the most important part of the privileging process because it involves direct observation and evaluation of the prospective staff member's ability to make appropriate and timely assessment and treatment decisions, and to initiate collaborative implementation with the multidisciplinary hospital team. Quarterly proctoring reports are submitted to the Credentials Committee which recommends any changes in staff status after the provisional period. Peer reviews of patient charts may subsequently be used as a basis for recommending recredentialing.

The American Psychiatric Association (1986) states that the ultimate decision regarding who practices in the hospital and what credentials they need for privileges resides with the individual hospital, with quality of patient care as the guiding principle. Recognizing that reviews of psychologists' applications for privileges were often haphazard and conducted by credentials committees having little familiarity with psychologists' training and practice, and that hospitals and medical staffs could be sued for negligent and inappropriate credentialing standards, the APA asserted that the responsibility to ensure quality of patient care must include an orderly, fair, and systematic review of psychologists' credentials. Psychologists must play the major role in delineating clinical privileges, specifying the necessary criteria, reviewing credentials and recommending specific privileges for psychologists, in addition to specifying criteria for renewal of privileges and participating in that process (Resnick et al., 1991). In establishing credentialing and privileging procedures for their discipline at specific inpatient facilities, psychologists should survey APA guidelines, appraise the character and mission of the specific hospital, and review credentialing and privileging procedures for related health care professions.

2.21.7 ETHICAL ISSUES

Linton (1993) and Pope (1990) identify a number of ethical issues of which psychologists entering hospital practice should be cognizant:

(i) Are the lines of clinical responsibility sufficiently clear so that no patient's needs are inadverently overlooked? Is it clear at all times who is responsible for patient management?

(ii) Is the patient adequately protected in the case of suicidal or assaultive impulses or sexual advances from other patients?

(iii) Are clinical decisions made on the basis of the patient's best interests? Psychologists must be sensitive to their responsibility to avoid premature termination of treatment (i.e., patient abandonment) despite the denial of authorization for further treatment by third-party payers. Pope notes that psychologists must also be aware of the financial and political forces that determine a hospital's decisions regarding admission, resource allocation, length of stay, follow-up upon discharge, and the likelihood of readmission in addition to the clinicians' treatment priorities.

(iv) Is the hospital charging appropriately for psychologists' services? In one hospital psychologists' diagnoses were being changed by the billing department to obtain higher reimbursement.

(v) Are there adequate safeguards to protect the patient's confidentiality? Do patients adequately understand who will have access to information about their treatment? Patients may not realize that the details of their private lives can become public knowledge through inpatient records, team meetings, or informal hallway and nursing station "consults." Inpatient treatment is, by its collaborative nature, considerably less confidential than the one-to-one relationship of the outpatient setting. Psychologists must therefore balance the need to discuss and document patient care with protecting potentially harmful details from disclosure. Protecting confidentiality is more difficult for patients in a rural hospital with their interwoven community relationships than in a large hospital in an urban area. The best defense against potential charges is a clear rationale, documented in advance on the patient's chart, concerning the psychologists' decision to include or exclude specific information (Linton, 1993).

(vi) Does the psychologist have the education, training, and experience to carry out clinical responsibilities with the specific patient population? Psychologists must be careful to define their boundaries and limits regarding the kinds of patients, disorders, assessments, therapeutic procedures, and treatment settings they are qualified, by training and experience, to handle, as reinforced by APA ethical guidelines.

(vii) When psychological consultation is requested, as in a medical surgical hospital, does the patient understand the reason for the consultation and provide an informed consent to it?

The hospital milieu is a more political environment than the outpatient psychotherapy setting. Turf issues and rivalries between professions, tensions between administrators and employees, conflicts between practitioners concerning different theoretical orientations or basic values, and competitive struggles for power, income, or recognition are to be expected. To ameliorate potential ethical problems in hospital practice, Linton recommends thinking issues through, consulting with an ethics partner or committee and documenting in advance. Defending oneself after the fact is much easier if sincere attention to and clear recognition of one's limits can be documented through charts, reports, or oral consultations.

2.21.8 MANAGED CARE IN HOSPITAL PRACTICE

In the 1980s, hospitals began to experience pressures toward fiscal accountability and cost containment. Medical costs were increasing at twice and mental health costs at four times the rate of inflation (Wiggins & Ludwigsen, 1991). Since health care in the USA is largely employer based, many employers and third-party payers, including indemnity plans and state and federal health care plans, began searching for ways to lower their escalating costs. Managed care organizations (MCOs) are designed to reduce utilization, for example, through preauthorization and concurrent utilization review, or to reduce costs, for example, through claims review and shifting to less expensive alternatives to hospitalization. With inpatient care consuming some 65–80% of mental health reimbursement, it was inevitable that managed care would target inpatient treatment for intensive monitoring and controls (Broskowski, 1994). To reduce costs, MCOs focused on decreasing the number of admissions and length of stay, utilizing hospitalization primarily for containment and stabilization of, for example, suicidal, assaultive, or psychotic behavior. The patient is discharged after a brief stay to the least restrictive safe setting, such as a day treatment program.

Continuous quality improvement (CQI) approaches have been adapted from manufacturing industry to health care to focus on demonstrating successful treatment outcomes, cost effectiveness, quality control, and consumer/patient satisfaction. They include the adoption of imposed protocol and practice guidelines based on research (Shueman, Troy, & Mayhugh, 1994), for example, for treatment of major depression. Practitioners and hospitals are being treated as contracting health care providers and are being asked to demonstrate accountability to MCOs through treatment outcomes assessment and patient satisfaction.

The draconian measures instituted by MCOs to control costs have resulted in premature discharge from hospitals in some cases; however, legal challenges to MCO decisions have been successfully raised. In *Wickline v. the State of California,* Marshall and Muszynski (1993) note that third-party payers (MCOs) can be held legally accountable when clinically inappropriate decisions result from cost-containment priorities, for example, when appeals made on a patient's behalf for hospital treatment are arbitrarily ignored, unreasonably disregarded, or overridden. The implication of the court's decision is that the priority of cost containment ends when quality of care begins to be compromised. Although managed care has been a largely unregulated industry undergoing considerable growing pains, the second generation of MCOs is focusing on access, demonstrated outcomes, and quality in addition to cost-control.

2.21.9 FUTURE DIRECTIONS

The future of psychology in hospital practice is related to the interaction of several factors: (i) the development of psychology as a profession, including the outcome of advocacy efforts at the federal, state, and local level; (ii) the development of clinical and scientific research; (iii) and the evolution of hospitals within the health care delivery system, and the forces impacting them, such as managed care directives. In contrast to medicine, nursing, and social work, psychology is a relative newcomer to the health care professions practicing in hospitals, and the problem of developing a consistent professional identity is one with which the profession is still struggling. Matarazzo (1977) notes that professions usually begin with haphazard, inconsistent credentialing and proceed through the loose organization of practitioners in an effort to establish the identifying and unique features of the field. This appears to be the current status of psychologists in hospital practice.

Through organized advocacy efforts at the federal, state, and local level, psychologists have broadened their scope of practice to include practicing independently in hospitals. This has required a sustained effort by committed groups of psychologists to overcome varying degrees of resistance, slow progress, entrenched opposition, and interdisciplinary warfare. The legislative issues with the greatest implications for psychologists' autonomy in hospital practice are those supporting independent admitting privileges and prescription privileges. Such privileges are essential to implementing a psychological model of care in contrast to the more traditional disease model. By its nature, the psychological model of treatment is focused on the psychoeducational approach to health management and problems in living, including the prevention, moderation, and amelioration of psychological stress resulting in physical and psychological disorders. Concurrent with psychologists' advocacy efforts, the knowledge basis of the discipline has expanded dramatically, particularly in the areas of health psychology (Sweet, Rozensky, & Tovian, 1991) and primary care. As the most broadly trained mental health professionals, psychologists also have an emerging role in rural hospitals and emergency rooms.

2.21.10 SUMMARY

Psychologists have entered and considerably expanded their clinical roles and responsibilities in hospitals since World War II. In doing so, they have had to confront established professions such as medicine and nursing in demonstrating their clinical expertise and value to the hospital. In order to gain a firm footing within hospitals, psychologists have had to organize and advocate for legal and regulatory changes at the federal, state, and individual hospital level, while simultaneously developing an appropriate professional identity for inpatient practice. As relative newcomers to the hospital, psychologists need to be aware of the complexity of political and organizational issues in pursuing independent privileges or other clinical roles. They must use this knowledge to extend the hospital's bylaws, credentialing, and privileging procedures appropriately for their discipline. In contrast to outpatient practice, patients treated in a hospital are more acute and more clinically complex, and must be treated in collaboration with other members of the treatment team. These factors raise a host of ethical and legal issues which must be carefully considered in a timely manner.

In the USA, hospitals and practitioners are undergoing radical changes in providing health care services, due to the incursion of managed care directives and to related CQI approaches. These changes constitute a health care revolution reminiscent of a quote regarding an earlier revolution: "it was the best of times, it was the worst of times." It requires considerable ingenuity from psychologists to envisage the direction of developments and how best to position themselves, while maintaining the integrity of the philosophy and values of their profession in their work. Nonetheless, the clinical and research developments of the past 50 years have proved that psychologists are innovators with valuable contributions to make in many different venues. As knowledge of the mind–body interaction develops in the healing professions, the value of the psychological treatment model has become increasingly apparent.

Psychologists' training in behavioral approaches to patient care and their research design skills in developing measurable variables to assess outcomes effectiveness are of great value in the current climate of accountability. However, psychologists must recognize, measure, and demonstrate their value to psychiatric, medical–surgical, chemical dependency, geriatric, rehabilitation, and other facilities to assure their inclusion and their autonomy in evolving health care delivery systems.

2.21.11 REFERENCES

American Psychiatric Association (1986). *Credentials and privileges for psychiatrists in hospital-based services.* (Task Force Report No. 24). Washington, DC: Author.

American Psychological Association (1992). The ethical principles of psychologists and code of conduct. *American Psychologist, 47,* 1597–1611.

Bennett, B. E., Bryant, B.K., VandenBos, G.R., & Greenwood, A. (1990). *Professional liability and risk management.* Washington, DC: American Psychological Association.

Bersoff, D. N. (1983). Hospital privileges and the antitrust laws. *American Psychologist, 38,* 1238–1241.

Broskowski, A. (1994). Current mental health care environments: Why managed care is necessary. In R. L. Lowman & R. J. Resnick (Eds.), *The mental health professional's guide to managed care* (pp. 1–18). Washington, DC: American Psychological Association (pp. 1–18).

CAPP v. Rank (1990). 51 Cal.3d 1, 793 P.2d 2.

Committee on Professional Practice of the Board of Professional Affairs (1985). *A hospital practice primer for psychologists.* Washington, DC: American Psychological Association.

Committee on Professional Practice of the Board of Professional Affairs (1988). *Hospital practice advocacy issues.* Washington, DC: American Psychological Association.

Definition of a clinical neuropsychologist (1989). *The Clinical Neuropsychologist, 3,* 22.

Enright, M. F., Resnick, R. J., Ludwigsen, K. R., & DeLeon, P. H. (1993). Hospital practice: Psychology's call to action. *Professional Psychology: Research and Practice, 24,* 135–141.

Joint Commission for Accreditation of Healthcare Organizations (1992). *Accreditation manual for hospitals 1992.* Chicago: Author.

Linton, J. C (1993). Current ethical issues in hospital settings. *Register Report, 19*(1), 9–10.

Ludwigsen, K. R. (1993). Credentialing and privileging issues in hospital practice. *Register Report, 19*(2), 3–6.

Ludwigsen, K. R., & Albright, D. G. (1994). Training psychologists for hospital practice: A proposal. *Professional Psychology: Research and Practice, 25*(3), 241–246.

Marshall, J. W., & Muszynski, I. L. (1993). Legal briefing: Providers should not fear UR entities or court decisions. *Register Report, 19*(2), 7–8, 11.

Matarazzo, J. D. (1977). Higher education, professional accreditation, and licensure. *American Psychologist, 32,* 856–859.

Pope, K. S. (1990). Ethical and malpractice issues in hospital practice. *American Psychologist, 45,* 1066–1070.

Resnick, R. J., Enright, M. F., & Thompson, R. J. (1991). *Guidelines on hospital practice: Credentialing and bylaws.* Washington, DC: American Psychological Association.

Resnick, R. J., & Morris, J. A., Jr. (1997). The history of rural hospital psychology. In J. A. Morris, Jr. (Ed.), *Practicing psychology in rural settings: Hospital privileges and collaborative care.* Washington, DC: American Psychological Association.

Rozensky, R. H. (1991). Psychologists, politics, and hospitals. In J. J. Sweet, R. H. Rozensky, & S. M. Tovian (Eds.), *Handbook of clinical psychology in medical settings* (pp. 59–79). New York: Plenum.

Rozensky, R. H. (1997). Medical staff membership and participation in rural hospitals. In J. A. Morris, Jr. (Ed.), *Practicing psychology in rural settings: Hospital privileges and collaborative care* (pp. 19–36). Washington, DC: American Psychological Association.

Shueman, S. A., Troy, W. G., & Mayhugh, S. L. (1994). Some questions and answers about managed behavioral health care. *Register Report, 20*(1), 1, 6–9.

Social Security Administration (1993). Sec. 1861(e)(4), 42 U.S.C. 1395x (e)(4). Compilation of the Social Security Laws (Committee Print WMCP:103–5). Washington, DC: US Government Printing Office.

Social Security Acts Amendments (1994). Pub. L. No. 103–432, Sec. 104.

Stromberg, C. D., Haggarty, D. J., Leibenluft, R. F., McMillian, M. H., Mishkin, B., Rubin, B. L., & Trilling, H. R. (1988). *The psychologist's legal handbook.* Washington, DC: The Council for the National Register of Health Service Providers in Psychology.

Sweet, J. J., Rozensky, R. H., & Tovian, S. M. (Eds.) (1991). *Handbook of clinical psychology in medical settings.* New York: Plenum.

Wiggins, J. G., & Ludwigsen, K. R. (1991). Marketing psychological services in hospitals. In J. J. Sweet, R. H. Rozensky, & S. M. Tovian (Eds.), *Handbook of clinical psychology in medical settings* (pp. 127–137). New York: Plenum.

Zaro, J. S., Batchelor, W. F., Ginsberg, M. R., & Pallak, M. S. (1982). Psychology and the JCAH: Reflections on a decade of struggle. *American Psychologist, 37,* 1342–1349.

2.22
Individual Psychologists: Professional Registration and Regulatory Procedures in the United Kingdom

JOHN N. HALL
University of Oxford, Warneford Hospital, UK

2.22.1 INTRODUCTION

The origins of regulation of practice of different professions in the UK go back to the medieval craft guilds, when the guilds of individual cities set standards of practice for individual crafts and trades, and by regulating the numbers of apprentices thereby controlled entry to the different trades. In the City of London particularly, a complex system of guilds grew up which was relatively unchallenged until the early nineteenth century. In England at the turn of the nineteenth century only three professions were recognized: the church (meaning the established Church of England), law, and medicine, the latter two of these both having "superior" branches and "inferior" branches, in medicine illustrated by the privileged Royal College of Physicians, and the lowlier apothecaries who existed to meet the need for some medical expertise in poorer areas. The procedure of practice-privileges is antedated by the procedure in the former English voluntary hospitals in the eighteenth and nineteenth centuries of visiting physicians, where respected doctors gave some of their time to the voluntary institutions, and thereby gained both status and advertisement for their skills, available separately on a private fee-paying basis.

From the middle of the nineteenth century there was a rapid growth in the recognition of independent professions; Larson (1977) indicates that of 13 then contemporary professions, 10 had established national associations between 1825 and 1880. The status and rights of emerging professions were confirmed in Britain either by a Royal Charter to the institution concerned, as with the different engineering institutes, or by a specific Act of Parliament, as for medical practitioners through the Medical Act in 1858. The way in which state registration for general nurses in England was finally achieved in 1919, after a battle between the "good-enough" minimal training approach, and the professional high-standards approach, illustrates the power-politics which lay behind the negotiation of professional practice regulation. These same historical issues and processes of the move from apprenticeship to academically justified training, the establishment of status and titles, attempts to protect from competition, the control of training, and the market consequences of under-supply, widely discussed in the sociology of professionalism, should be acknowledged in any discussion of professional practice regulation.

2.22.2 BRITISH PROFESSIONAL REGULATORY PROCEDURES

The legal basis of the present structure of professional regulatory procedures in the UK still rests mostly on the use of Acts of Parliament and of Royal Charters, which apply to the whole country. The larger professions, and those where there is a substantial degree of potential risk, such as pharmacists, are regulated by Act of Parliament, involving careful scrutiny of the proposed legislation by interested parties, and public debate in Parliament of the issues. An Act of Parliament in 1960, for example, created a Council for "Professions Supplementary to Medicine," which registers, for example, physiotherapists as well as radiographers. This Act stipulates a number of medically qualified members of the Council. Legislation is being considered which would release these professions from such heavy medical involvement.

Other professions may be regulated by Royal Charter, where a professional group wishes to have formal recognition of its public standing, but where scarce Parliamentary time is not needed (or available!) because contentious or major issues of public concern are not thought to arise. Bodies set up in this way have a protected right to be consulted on matters of public concern, and to nominate representatives for other public bodies. Despite the archaic name, the procedure for obtaining a charter involves careful legal scrutiny and consultation with other affected public bodies, but does not involve Parliamentary debate. The British Psychological Society (BPS), equivalent in role to the American Psychological Association, was founded in 1901, but was not "incorporated" by Royal Charter until 1965. The objects of the BPS, as set out in the Charter, include "setting a high standard of professional education and knowledge," and "to maintain ... a register of Chartered Psychologists," so that the standards the BPS sets are the nationally accepted professional standards, and the Register of Chartered Psychologists was set up in 1988.

A third category of regulation is essentially self-regulation, where a body sets itself up as a training body, perhaps also setting standards of practice, and is widely recognized and respected for those standards, which are tacitly accepted. A good example is the British Association for Counselling, the main British professional body for counselors, whose accreditation procedure is widely accepted as the standard required for independent practice as a counselor. Other areas of practice may have a number of training bodies, with widely differing standards, and where no one group has established public confidence. An obvious British example are hypnotists, where the yellow pages of any local telephone directory show about 10 different qualifications quoted, although there are respected bodies regulating the practice of hypnosis of those already qualified in a recognized profession of origin.

Since a UK government report of 1971 into the practice of scientology, which recommended legislation to register psychotherapists, a number of proposals have been made to register psychotherapists, including one draft Parliamentary bill, the 1981 Bright Bill. Given the then difficulty in the various psychotherapy bodies agreeing on common standards, this was not pursued, since the position of the government was that it would not support legislation which would have been contentious in the face of such disagreement. However, in 1993 the United Kingdom Council for Psychotherapy was created, which registers psychotherapists under a number of specialized headings, although this procedure is not supported by either an Act of Parliament or Royal Charter.

A major factor in the practice regulation of all UK healthcare professions is the dominance of the National Health Service (NHS), which is the national system of healthcare provision, established in 1948, which includes primary-care medical services as well as secondary-care services. The NHS is the principal employer of nearly all categories of such professions. The clinical component of training of nearly all healthcare professions takes place in NHS settings, linked in most cases to universities, with funding of training supported at least partially in some way by central government, so there is a degree of integration of training systems with service delivery systems.

The practice assumptions of the NHS, as setter of practice standards, and the career structure it offers, have a powerful influence on all private practice. Private practice tends either to be done on a part-time basis associated with a part-time NHS job, or full-time after obtaining substantial NHS experience. Family doctors, or general practitioners (GPs) who are themselves mostly contracted to work for the NHS, are key gatekeepers to private practice, so being known and respected by local GPs is a valuable contributor to successful private practice, at least initially. For professions other than doctors, the proportion of practitioners working wholly or partly outside the NHS varies; there is high demand for private practice podiatry and physiotherapy, for example, but for clinical psychology probably not more than 5% of the national practitioner resource is available privately.

2.22.3 THE PATTERN OF ADMINISTRATIVE AND PROFESSIONAL STRUCTURES IN THE NATIONAL HEALTH SERVICE

Since its inception in 1948, the NHS has gone through a number of organizational changes. Up to 1974 individual hospitals were run by hospital management committees, but since then by health authorities servicing a named area, or latterly district, covering usually a county or major city, with populations typically about 250 000, emphasizing the importance of focusing services on a served population. The then area and district health authorities continued to be organized according to nationally prescribed standard patterns, and clinical psychology services were typically organized as area services, with one clinical psychology service or department providing services to all client groups, including mental health, child, and learning disability services, as well as neurological and general medical services in larger districts.

From the early 1990s the creation of legally autonomous but still state-funded NHS trusts has meant that services are organized more flexibly. The strategic focus of the NHS is now on a primary-care led service, but most clinical psychologists in Britain work in services administered by secondary-care agencies. There are substantial variations in management arrangements for clinical psychologists: services for a number of trusts may be run together as agencies; there may be one central department for a trust; services may be organized as locality services, serving a population of, say, 60 000 people; or services run as a client group/clinical directorate arrangements.

As part of the older centralized system, conditions of service for the NHS in the UK, with a total population of 56 000 000 nationally, were negotiated centrally via what is known as the Whitley Council. This system involved negotiation between the management side, representing both NHS management and with financial input from the Treasury, and the staff side representing the trade unions and professional associations. The Whitley Council has a number of subcommittees concerned with individual staff groupings, and for this purpose clinical psychologists were grouped together with biochemists and physicists in Whitley Professional and Technical Council A, being seen as scientists. This Whitley PTA Council agreed on national grading structures, which until 1990 offered a standard national career progression.

In 1990, a new more flexible grading system was introduced, but the former grade titles are still often used, with higher grade clinical psychologists often being called consultant, specialist head of psychology services, with one such post usually being appointed or recognized as trust head or professional lead. A senior clinical psychologist is appointed within the national Department of Health, and another senior psychologist is a direct adviser to the Chief Medical Officer of the government. While this Whitley system is somewhat cumbersome, it has created a nationally accepted framework for professional standards, and the appointment and grading of psychologists, with a high degree of comparability across the country as compared to the American position. A report originating from national concern about the supply of clinical psychologists (Manpower Planning Advisory Group, 1990), and an overview of British clinical psychology practice (Marzillier & Hall, 1998) together give a good account of the state of clinical psychology in Britain.

2.22.4 EMPLOYMENT CONTRACTS, PRACTICE PRIVILEGES, AND INDEMNITY PROCEDURES

Within the NHS, the trust itself, as the employer, is responsible for all patient care carried out under its authority. The trust, therefore, has a responsibility to assure itself that any staff who come into patient contact are competent to carry out what is expected of them.

For directly employed staff this requirement will be met by thorough checking of qualifications, of professional registration status (and checking of any required annual registration certificates and numbers), and of experience by interview, and by ongoing professional supervision. On appointment, such staff will receive from their employers information about professional practice standards within their trust, and disciplinary procedures of the employing trust if there is any breach of those standards.

Any other staff who come into patient contact, such as university-employed or research-grant funded staff, trainees from other training courses, or foreign visitors, will be required to have an honorary contract, which is both a recognition of their competence, and also covers their work for insurance purposes by the employer's indemnity. An honorary contract will also give information to the person concerned of standards of practice, and usually must name a senior qualified member of the profession concerned who will supervise clinical work. The professional competence standards for an honorary contract then become similar to those expected if the person were acting in a similar capacity as an employee.

A number of private companies offer healthcare services in the UK, and professional staff directly employed by them will be covered by their employer's insurance, and may also be required to possess their own indemnity insurance. The professional standards adopted will be at least those set by the NHS, so the NHS standards do in effect permeate the whole healthcare system in the UK as a minimum. Private hospitals may also offer practice privileges to practitioners, who thereby may use the facilities of the hospital on payment of appropriate charges. Requests for practice privileges are carefully checked and scrutinized, checking carefully the area of practice experience of the person seeking appointment.

To American eyes, British consumers of healthcare may seem either incredibly trusting or stupid, since the level of health-related litigation is extremely low by US standards. UK common law recognizes the principle of "vicarious liability," whereby an employer is responsible for the acts of employees. Practice in the NHS means that it is the employing trust, and not the employee, who is usually sued for professional negligence, with the exception of medical staff. Accordingly there is no requirement for employed clinical psychologists, who do no private practice, to be individually professionally insured. There is no case known to the author of legal damages being awarded against a British clinical psychologist arising out of malpractice, although clinical psychologists have been dismissed from their posts or struck off the Register for malpractice.

Although indemnity insurance is not mandatory for employed psychologists, many clinical psychologists do take out professional insurance, since if a malpractice case is pursued, the interest of the employing trust is to resolve the dispute as quickly and cheaply as possible, and it may therefore settle out of court without attempting any defence of the individual practitioners who thereby may be seen to be at fault. The purpose of the insurance under these circumstances would be to protect the reputation of the clinician, although they were not the defendant in the actual litigation. Any independent practitioner should have indemnity cover, and it is a requirement of the BPS professional ethical code (BPS, 1995) that private clinical psychologists should be so insured. Indemnity insurance is issued by a number of companies, some specializing in therapists more generally, and covers a range of liabilities. As an example, the BPS has links with an insurance scheme, currently offering £1 000 000 cover for any one claim for a premium of £45. Partnerships of psychologists may also be insured. Legal representation is also available through the scheme. The trade union for psychologists also has a legal advice scheme available, but membership of the union does not provide indemnity cover.

2.22.5 BRITISH PSYCHOLOGICAL SOCIETY REGISTRATION PROCEDURES

As already mentioned the BPS maintains a Register of Chartered Psychologists. Registration requires: (i) possessing a first degree (i.e., a bachelors degree with honours) with psychology as a main subject, and which covers the general areas of psychology required by the BPS, and (ii) since obtaining that degree or equivalent, completing a period of study or practice sufficient for practice without supervision for three years full-time, or an equivalent period part-time. Prior to 1990, most British clinical psychology courses lasted three years, with some being for two years. Since 1990, all British clinical psychology training courses have to be of three years full-time duration to meet Whitley Council standards, all courses now conferring doctorates.

Accordingly, on completion of training a clinical psychologists now fulfills both Whitley

Council criteria for employment as a qualified clinical psychologist in the NHS, and BPS criteria for registration. There is a regular accreditation procedure for training courses, conducted by the BPS, ensuring that all courses meet consistent training criteria, and courses will also meet the somewhat varying academic requirements of the university conferring the doctoral degree, usually a Doctor of Clinical Psychology degree. The degree of Doctor of Philosophy has always been in the UK solely a research degree, and not, as in the USA, sometimes a practitioner qualification.

As a condition of registering, chartered psychologists are also required to hold a practicing certificate, issued annually. Exemption may be granted from holding a practice certificate; this applies to retired psychologists, or those not working, or to teachers or researchers in psychology who undertake not to provide any psychological interventions that are held out as being of benefit to others. A member of the public who believes themselves to be in professional contact with a person who holds themselves out to be a chartered psychologist may therefore expect to find their name on the published register, and may ask to see a current practice certificate. By contrast with American practice, it is very rare for UK health professionals to display their academic and professional certificates and diplomas at their place of work.

The chartering regulations make provision for four other specified categories of chartered psychologist, as well as clinical psychologists. There are Chartered Educational Psychologists, Chartered Occupational Psychologists, Chartered Forensic Psychologists, and Chartered Counselling Psychologists. They may use the term C.Psychol. after their name, with an abbreviation to describe which type of chartered psychologist they are, such as C.Couns. Psychol. Professional training courses in the five different branches of applied psychology recognized by the chartering procedure are entirely separate. However, a lateral transfer scheme has been introduced whereby experienced psychologists in other fields may transfer to be recognized as clinical psychologists. This is achieved on a case-by-case analysis of their training and experience, so an individually defined training program is determined, which may include further academic study, research work, and certainly additional supervised clinical experience. On completing the training requirements, they are issued with a "statement of equivalence" from the Committee for the Scrutiny of Individual Clinical Qualifications of the BPS, which then entitles them to work in the NHS.

The total membership of the BPS in 1996 was 21 200, with another 5800 student subscribers. In 1996 there were 8454 chartered psychologists in total, with 3184 full members of the Division of Clinical Psychology, and 1164 full members of the Division of Counselling Psychology.

The legal position in Britain is accordingly that while anyone can continue to call themselves a psychologist, it is possible to sue for misrepresentation if a person described themselves as a chartered psychologist and was offering psychological services. The BPS has prepared the text of a draft Parliamentary bill, and is seeking a Parliamentary sponsor to progress the bill, the passing of which would further protect the public against those misrepresenting themselves as clinical psychologists.

If anyone in receipt of services from a chartered psychologist wishes to complain of the standard of professional service they have received, then the complaints and disciplinary procedure of the BPS will be followed. This has a two-stage process. Minor breaches of the BPS guidelines will be dealt with by a BPS officer. The complaint may then be first considered by an investigatory committee; if they believe a serious professional misdemeanor may have occurred, an investigatory panel may be appointed, to examine the matter further. If a minor offence has taken place, the member may be rebuked or warned. If the circumstances of the complaint suggest that removal from the register may be appropriate, the investigatory panel make a recommendation back to the investigatory committee, who may then set up a disciplinary committee, with external lay membership in addition to senior "Fellows" of the BPS. The last annual report of the BPS, for 1996–1997, showed an increase of 24% of allegations over the previous year, although this still equates to only 127 allegations received.

2.22.6 RECOGNITION OF FOREIGN QUALIFICATIONS BY THE BRITISH PSYCHOLOGICAL SOCIETY

The differing healthcare systems of countries will demand different skills from clinical psychologists: there is no neat definition of clinical psychology practice which travels well from one culture to another. The distinctive requirement of healthcare systems such as that of the UK, where most clinical psychologists work within a public healthcare system requiring services to be offered to a population, is that clinical psychologists should be able to work generically. Accordingly, clinical training requirements are that trainees must complete during their three years four core placements: in adult mental health, children and young people, older people, and learning disability, with an additional fifth specialty placement chosen by the trainee.

Overseas clinical psychologists who wish to work in the UK will follow a process similar to the lateral transfer process already described. On a case by case basis their training will be examined, and a statement of training needs set out. If an overseas clinical psychologist has not had experience in all the above areas, then they may be required to carry out a supervised clinical placement, usually 65 full working days in each area where needed, before a statement of equivalence can be given. Additional academic or research requirements may also be set. Any overseas clinical psychologist wishing to work in the UK is strongly advised to ascertain their status as early as possible, as they cannot be employed in the NHS without a statement of equivalence.

The Treaty of Rome has meant that all member states of the European Community (EC) must agree on common professional standards to bring about movement of labor within the EC. Movement is becoming more common, so that a considerable number of European trained psychologists, especially from The Netherlands and Germany, are seeking work in Britain. The European Federation of Professional Psychologists Associations (EFPPA) exists to promote collaboration between European psychologists, though not all member states of EFPPA are EC members. Given the historical and personal links between the UK and the commonwealth countries, there is a substantial number of clinical psychologists working in Britain who have qualified in such countries, especially Australia, New Zealand, and South Africa, where educational standards and standards of professional training in clinical psychology are close to the British model, unlike Canada where training conforms to the US standard.

Apart from checking professional qualifications, any foreign national, other than an EC citizen, wanting to work in the UK as a qualified clinical psychologist must obtain a work permit. This is obtained on a case-by-case basis by application to the government Department of Employment. Given the shortage of clinical psychologists in Britain, a special fast-track system exists for clinical psychologists to give them accelerated progress through the work permit process.

2.22.7 ADDITIONAL REGISTRATION AND TRAINING PROCEDURES

In general, there are no national legal requirements for additional registration, beyond the base professional registration. Within mental health practice, for example, the nationally accepted professional standards of the main five mental health professions, that is, clinical psychology, occupational therapy, psychiatric nursing, psychiatry, and mental health social work, are such that a formal qualification and experience in any one of these would be taken as evidence of competence to practice, and accordingly there is little incentive for members of any of these professions to have any supplementary registration. The respected Sainsbury Centre for Mental Health (1997) has published proposals for compulsory reaccreditation or licensing in community mental health for all these groups of staff, on a multidisciplinary, practice-related basis. Given that one of the government health ministers of the Labor government elected in 1997 has a strong background in mental health, this may be taken up.

Although a chartered clinical psychologist has little incentive to acquire further formal certification, many clinical psychologists do acquire further formal training and qualifications, in addition to ongoing professional development through workshops, conferences, and local short courses. These may be either in specific forms of psychological treatment, such as the postbasic Oxford Cognitive Therapy training, approved by the BPS, and validated by the University of Oxford, or in healthcare related management skills, such as an MBA. The BPS has a formal process for recognizing postqualification training, through a standing committee on continuing professional development. There are national associations for family therapy, group therapy, and cognitive-analytic therapy, for example, offering postbasic training to well-accepted standards. For clinical psychologists, many of these further qualifications will lead to a postgraduate diploma or masters level degree. Some clinical psychologists do choose to register with the United Kingdom Council for Psychotherapy, but such registration is voluntary.

Clinical psychologists do not have any specified statutory responsibilities or duties under Acts of Parliament, unlike psychiatrists, who have statutory duties with regard to the compulsory detention of patients in a psychiatric hospital under the Mental Health Act 1983. However, under Section 58 of that act they may be required to act as an independent assessor in cases where a patient, already legally detained under the Act, is deemed to require electroconvulsive therapy, for example, and does not give consent. A small number of clinical psychologists also act as mental health commissioners (alongside commissioners from other professional and legal backgrounds), regularly visiting all psychiatric hospitals in the UK and having a duty to inspect the condition of all patients admitted under the Act. The Education Act 1980 provides for the "statementing" of children with special needs, such as those with profound learning disabilities. Any statement is required to include separate statements from a teacher, a doctor, and an educational psychologist, and locally it may be agreed formally that a child clinical psychologist may prepare a psychological statement acceptable for Act purposes. Clinical psychologists in the UK generally are relieved not to have statutory duties, given the burden of being on on-call rotas and the disruption of regular work patterns they involve.

2.22.8 REFERENCES

British Psychological Society (1995). *Ethical code and code of professional practice.* Leicester, UK. Author.

Larson, M. S. (1977). *The rise of professionalism: a sociological analysis.* Berkeley, CA: University of California Press.

Manpower Planning Advisory Group. (1990). *Manpower Planning Advisory Group Report on Clinical Psychology.* London: HMSO.

Marzillier, J. S., & Hall, J. N. (1998). *What is clinical psychology?* Oxford, UK: Oxford University Press.

Sainsbury Centre for Mental Health (1997). *Review of the roles and training of mental health care staff.* London: Author.

2.23
Ethical Principles of Psychologists: United States

CYNTHIA A. STURM
Portland, OR, USA

2.23.1 INTRODUCTION

Psychologists in the USA bear a broad responsibility to conduct themselves professionally to the highest standard. Ethical behavior represents a personal lifelong commitment, a responsibility to colleagues and the profession of psychology, and a pledge to uphold the public trust. The Ethics Code of the American Psychological Association (APA) has evolved as a living document that embodies the ideals, values, and principles of psychological service. The mandatory standards defined in the *Ethical Principles of Psychologists and Code of Conduct* (APA, 1992) function to identify expectations of professional practice, clarify necessary expertise, and ensure protection of the public consumers of psychological services. The profession of psychology in the USA is autonomous from government oversight and supervision by other professions, due to the capacity for self-monitoring through enforcement of the Ethics Code by licensing boards and ethics committees in national and state professional organizations.

2.23.2 AMERICAN PSYCHOLOGICAL ASSOCIATION ETHICS CODE

2.23.2.1 Evolution of the Code

The growth of applied psychology in the USA after World War II led the American Psychological Association, founded in 1892, to recognize the need for a formal ethics code to define standards of practice, educate members regarding professional values, and provide an avenue to address complaints of unethical conduct. An ethical code represented a key element in the structuring of psychology as an independent profession, along with the establishment of graduate training programs, accreditation procedures, and credentialing and licensing mechanisms.

The development of the initial code *Ethical Standards for Psychologists* (APA, 1953) was based upon more than 1000 critical incidents solicited from APA members, reflecting case situations in which psychologists had made decisions with ethical implications. The rationale for this innovative empirical methodology was to create a code with enough relevance and specificity to provide practical guidance to psychologists (Hobbs, 1948). To date there have been six major revisions of the code. The APA Ethics Committee can initiate a revision process based upon the need for changes or additions to the code.

An Ethics Code Task Force was appointed in November 1996 to review the 1992 code and begin the intensive process of another major revision. Elements of the review will include a critical incident survey, a call for comment on the 1992 code, reviews of relevant articles and guidelines, and a legal and case review (APA Ethics Committee, 1995). Draft revisions are published nationally in *The APA Monitor* for review and comment by the APA membership. The last revision process, which produced the 1992 code, spanned six years from initiation to final publication (Canter, Bennett, Jones, & Nagy, 1994). Thus, the Ethics Code, as a living document, continues to evolve to reflect the most current social issues and emerging areas of concern in the psychologist's professional experience.

2.23.2.2 Ethics Education

Graduate training programs are a primary source of education in professional values. Students learn about ethics through coursework, and then apply these principles in supervised clinical practica and internship experience. The importance of formal ethics training has been supported by Handelsman (1986). He asserts that learning ethics by "osmosis," solely in the context of supervised clinical experience, fails to ensure that general ethical theory and reasoning skills can be applied effectively in future clinical contexts.

Psychologists must renew their knowledge of ethical standards of behavior throughout their careers, as professional values evolve over time. For professionals in the workforce, this usually occurs through attending workshops and reviewing relevant APA publications. Journal articles which summarize the educational and adjudicative activities of the APA Ethics Committee are published annually in the *American Psychologist*. The status of evolving standards and guidelines are discussed in *The APA Monitor*, a monthly newspaper. Illustrative casebooks are usually published by the APA after a major revision of the Ethics Code. A comprehensive commentary on the APA Ethics Code by Canter et al. (1994) provides a thorough interpretative analysis of the 1992 code. Current resources on professional, ethical, and policy issues can also be obtained electronically through PsychNet (SM), APA's home page on the World Wide Web.

2.23.2.3 Aspirational Values Underlying the Ethical Principles

Aspirational values are the overarching moral principles that guide ethical decision-making. As ideals, they form the ceiling of expectations regarding professional behavior and offer general guidance across a broad range of situations. Kitchener (1984) summarized five of the fundamental ethical values reflected in human services work. The principle of autonomy emphasizes the promotion of self-determination, freedom of choice, and responsibility for one's own behavior. Nonmaleficence highlights the ethical imperative to avoid or minimize the risk of harm to clients. Beneficence emphasizes the importance of promoting the welfare of others and, more broadly, to contribute to society. The principle of justice encompasses equity, fairness, and nondiscrimination. Finally, fidelity encourages honesty, reliability, and faithfulness to commitments.

Previous versions of the APA Ethics Code mixed aspirational principles with mandatory standards for professional ethical behavior. The structure of the 1992 code changed markedly. The aspirational, nonenforceable values are now in the preamble and general principles introducing the code, and the 102 enforceable Ethical Standards comprise the primary text (APA, 1992). The general principles are summarized below:

(i) *Competence*. This reflects the professional standard of good practice. Psychologists practice only in areas for which they possess adequate education, training, or experience. They recognize that special populations may require specific competencies and take care to protect the welfare of those receiving services when practicing in new areas lacking written standards.

(ii) *Integrity*. Integrity speaks to honesty and fairness in psychologists' professional activities. Statements informing the public regarding credentials, competencies, policies, or services must be accurate and straightforward. Honest self-examination is likewise critical to avoid potential harm to clients from personal limitations or biases which compromise professional effectiveness or objectivity.

(iii) *Professional and scientific responsibility*. This consideration highlights ethical conduct in the psychologist's interactions with other professionals. They must remain watchful of the ethical behavior of colleagues and utilize consultation proactively for themselves.

(iv) *Respect for people's rights and dignity*. These qualities are promoted through advocacy for human rights, privacy, and self-determination. Psychologists maintain awareness of human differences and avoid discrimination.

(v) *Concern for others' welfare*. Psychologists clarify any role conflicts that carry the potential for compromising the best interests of the client. They are aware of the real and perceived power differential in professional relationships and do not take advantage of this.

(vi) *Social responsibility*. In a larger context, psychologists carry a broad responsibility to contribute to the welfare of society and relieve human suffering.

2.23.2.4 Ethical Principles of Psychologists and Code of Conduct

It has been a general criticism of ethics codes that they are too abstract to guide decision-making and behavior in specific situations. Difficulties with enforcement of the 1981 code due to vague language (White v. North Carolina State Board of Examiners of Practicing Psychologists, 1990) led to the need for a major revision with more explicit language and legally enforceable standards (Bersoff, 1994). The 102 ethical standards in the Code of Conduct define unitary ethical concepts in behaviorally specific terms. These are mandatory minimal standards of professional conduct, the floor of ethical behavior. The standards are organized into eight topics: (i) general standards; (ii) evaluation, assessment, or intervention; (iii) advertising and other public statements; (iv) therapy; (v) privacy and confidentiality; (vi) teaching, training supervision, research, and publishing; (vii) forensic activities; and (viii) resolving ethical issues.

In addition to the new structure of the code, important changes were made in several content areas. The concept of "client" has been broadened to describe the professional duty to students, supervisees, employees, and research participants. More attention is given to the reality of overlapping professional roles and multiple relationships. Decision rules are provided to assist psychologists in managing complex professional relationships in order to maintain objectivity, protect the treatment process, and minimize the risk of harm or exploitation to the client. The code requires sensitivity to issues of cultural diversity, human differences, and unfair discrimination. Due to the serious problem of sexual misconduct in the profession (Pope, 1994), stronger language is evident in prohibitions against sexual intimacies with clients, former clients, supervisees, and students. New sections were included on forensic issues and resolution of ethical dilemmas.

More specific guidance in the structuring of the treatment contract and informed consent is provided. Several standards cover the business aspects of psychological practice, such as fees and financial arrangements, barter, and referral practices. Changes regarding advertising and public statements are a response to concerns from the Federal Trade Commission regarding restraint of trade resulting from previous ethical prohibitions about advertising (Koocher, 1994).

Commentaries on the 1992 code highlight its strengths as: (i) attention to cultural diversity, special populations, and individual differences; (ii) pragmatic guidance in structuring individual therapy; (iii) more explicit guidelines regarding multiple relationships; (iv) inclusion of forensic activities; and (v) greater breadth as well as specificity within the standards (Bersoff, 1994). Payton (1994) has criticized the current code for its increased emphasis on the scientific basis of our professional identity and, conversely, the diminished focus on fundamental human rights in the aspirational language of the general principles. Other weaknesses have been noted in the frequent use of qualified or legalistic language, ambiguity, and remaining problems with enforceability (Bersoff, 1994). Concerns have been expressed that steps taken to operationalize the code leave the impression of being protectionistic of the profession (Payton, 1994; Vasquez, 1994). As a result, psychology has lost an inspirational code which strives to promote social responsibility and "stir one to the highest plane of ethical functioning" (Koocher, 1994, p. 361).

2.23.2.5 APA Practice Standards and Guidelines

Various supplemental guidelines and standards of practice have been adopted by the APA or its divisions to further educate psychologists, professional bodies, and courts regarding professional standards. Although not enforceable or mandatory, these policies are utilized by ethics committees and practitioners for important technical guidance. The *General Guidelines for Providers of Psychological Services* (APA, 1987), and *Specialty Guidelines for the Delivery of Services by Clinical Psychologists, Counseling Psychologists, Industrial/Organizational Psychologists and School Psychologists* (APA, 1981), currently under revision, were developed to "define minimum levels of competent professional practices and procedures" (Keith-Spiegel & Koocher, 1985, p. 224). Other clinically relevant standards include *Record Keeping Guidelines* (APA, 1993c) and *Guidelines for Providers of Psychological Services to Ethnic, Linguistic, and Culturally Diverse Populations* (APA, 1993b).

APA guidelines pertaining to assessment include the *Standards for Educational and Psychological Testing* (APA, 1985), which are currently under revision. Complex or specialized areas of practice, such as forensic psychology, often require more specific clarifications by experts in the field. The *Specialty Guidelines for Forensic Psychologists* (Committee on Ethical Guidelines for Forensic Psychologists, 1991), were developed and adopted by the APA Forensic Psychology Division and the American Psychology-Law Society, but have not been adopted by the APA as a whole. The APA has recently adopted the *Guidelines for Child Custody Evaluations and Divorce Proceedings* (APA, 1994), an area of specialization in which ethical complaints are frequently received.

Important standards regarding research include the *Guidelines for Ethical Conduct in the Care and Use of Animals* (APA, 1993a), and the *Ethical Principles in the Conduct of Research with Human Participants* (APA, 1982), now being revised.

The APA Ethics Committee also provides ongoing ethical guidance on specific topics through various policy statements, such as Military Psychologists and Confidentiality (APA, Ethics Committee, 1994, p. 665), "Take home" tests (APA, Ethics Committee, 1994, p. 665), and Services by Telephone, Teleconferencing, and Internet (APA, Ethics Committee, 1996, p. 1285).

2.23.3 REGULATION OF THE PRACTICE OF PSYCHOLOGY

2.23.3.1 State and National Professional Organizations

The APA and the independent state and local psychological associations promote the profession of psychology through advocacy, education, and regulation of members by peer monitoring. Voluntary membership in these professional organizations carries with it the commitment to adhere to the ethical code of the organization. The APA code is typically adopted by the state psychological associations. Other professional societies, such as the American Society for Clinical Hypnosis, Feminist Therapy Institute, American Association for Marriage and Family Therapy, and Association for the Advancement of Behavior Therapy have also developed their own ethics codes (Bass et al., 1996).

National and state ethics committees serve to educate members and respond to and investigate complaints from consumers or other members regarding unprofessional conduct. Ethics committees' rules and procedures define the process of adjudication of complaints against members and the types of sanctions. For less serious violations, which are not likely to have caused harm, committees may respond educatively or with a letter of reprimand. Remedial coursework or clinical supervision may be required. If unethical conduct involves a serious risk of harm to others, more severe sanctions including censure, stipulated resignation of association membership, or expulsion may be used. Unfortunately, due to increasing concerns about liability, many state association ethics committees have suspended their investigatory and adjudicatory functions and now provide primarily educational and consultative services (Nagy, 1996).

State psychological association Professional Standards Review Committees (PSRCs) offer another type of consumer protection. Often focused more specifically upon the review of professional practices and billing, these committees respond to questions raised by providers, consumers, or third-party payers. PSRCs typically function in an advisory role and direct their efforts towards arbitration of complaints (Keith-Spiegel & Koocher, 1985).

2.23.3.2 State Licensure

State licensing boards serve a regulatory function by defining the entry requirements for psychologists who provide services to the public autonomously and use the title of "psychologist." State boards also have legal jurisdiction over those already licensed to monitor and enforce standards of professional conduct. Boards usually adopt either the APA *Ethical Principles of Psychologists and Code of Conduct* (APA, 1992) or the *ASPPB Code of Conduct* (Association of State and Provincial Psychology Boards [ASPPB], 1991). The ASPPB is an organization that assists regulatory boards in the USA and Canada in developing standardized regulatory procedures.

The disciplinary power of licensing boards varies significantly from that of the state association. Only the licensing board can revoke the license to practice, thereby protecting the public from harmful practitioners. State psychological association ethics committees can refer an ethics complaint to the licensing board when a significant risk of harm to others exists through incompetence, sexual misconduct, or professional impairment. It is important to note that many psychologists, such as educators and researchers, have no requirement to be licensed and are therefore exempt from this type of regulation.

2.23.3.3 Informal Peer Monitoring

The 1992 Ethics Code includes a new section on resolving ethical issues, which delineates psychologists' responsibilities when confronted with possible ethical violations by colleagues. If there is uncertainty about a complex ethical issue, consultation with colleagues who have expertise in ethics, as well as state or local psychological association ethics committees may be quite useful (Canter et al., 1994). Informal attempts to resolve potential violations by colleagues are encouraged if the situation is relatively minor and amenable to an educatory intervention. However, in cases of serious misconduct with a risk of harm to others, referral to state or national ethics committees or licensing boards may be a more appropriate action, assuming confidentiality issues can be resolved.

2.23.4 ETHICAL DECISION-MAKING

2.23.4.1 Taking a Proactive Approach

In their classic text, *Ethics in Psychology: Professional Standards and Cases*, Keith-Spiegel and Koocher (1985) advocate a proactive stance of preventing ethical violations through education, sensitization, and self-awareness. Awareness of ethical issues pertinent to each psychologist's scope of professional practice promotes effective self-monitoring. In a survey of 679 APA members, Pope and Vetter (1992) solicited examples of "critical incidents" representing ethical dilemmas that psychologists commonly encounter in their work. The 10 most frequently cited areas of ethical concern were: (i) confidentiality; (ii) blurred, dual, or conflictual relationships; (iii) payment sources, plans, settings, and methods; (iv) academic settings, teaching dilemmas, and concerns about training; (v) forensic psychology; (vi) research; (vii) conduct of colleagues; (viii) sexual issues; (ix) assessment; and (x) questionable or harmful interventions.

The 1992 Ethics Code incorporates specific standards of conduct aimed at preventing or minimizing harm to consumers (Canter et al., 1994). A good practitioner should carefully structure service agreements at the start of the professional relationship, anticipate dilemmas associated with high risk clients or situations, and maintain personal awareness of conflicts or challenges. Experienced clinicians can often quickly identify warning signs at the outset of treatment which may indicate a hidden agenda, or point to a potentially difficult personality style. For example, a treatment referral for a client involved in litigation may be an indirect request for evaluation, under the guise of treatment. Early difficulties in establishing a therapeutic relationship, such as missed appointments, miscommunications, or challenges to usual office procedures may be indicative of a high risk client. Strong emotional reactions to clients should likewise be observed and monitored by clinicians.

The importance of utilizing a formal decision-making model to analyze ethical dilemmas has been emphasized in the literature (Canter et al., 1994; Hill, Glaser, & Harden, 1995; Keith-Spiegel & Koocher, 1985; Kitchener, 1984; Pettifor, 1996). The Canadian Psychological Association (CPA) has incorporated a decision-making model into their ethical code (CPA, 1991). In practice, psychologists must often make ethical decisions during the process of clinical intervention, with minimal opportunity for reflection about alternatives and weighing of potential short-term and long-range consequences. Use of a decision-making framework provides the practitioner a consistent structure to analyze ethical dilemmas, ensure critical factors are not overlooked, and weigh how decisions might affect the rights of various involved parties.

2.23.4.2 Identification of Ethical Dilemmas

Ethically competent practice requires a knowledge of: (i) the current APA Ethics Code and APA practice guidelines and standards; (ii) applicable local, state, and federal laws, including the licensing law; and (iii) institutional or agency rules, regulations, and policies, or contractual obligations (Canter et al., 1994). Ethical awareness involves recognition of an issue as having ethical dimensions or ramifications. Lack of sensitivity may be due to limited clinical experience, practice outside of usual areas of competency, or personal issues which compromise the psychologist's objectivity. Several recent publications have incorporated self-evaluation questions which assist clinicians in reviewing and sensitizing themselves to ethical conflicts in specific areas of practice (Bennett, Bryant, VandenBos, & Greenwood, 1990; Canter et al., 1994; Peterson, 1996).

Analysis of problematic ethical case scenarios must begin with identification of the central issues. A training format developed by the author clarifies five basic areas to consider:

(i) *Clinical context*. This highlights the unique aspects of each case, and may include the initial clinical presentation of the client, diagnostic features, and/or dynamic formulation. In cases of third-party referrals or multiperson therapies, clarification of "who is the client?" may be important. Aspects of human diversity or cultural context should be considered.

(ii) *Ethical issues*. These may include issues of confidentiality, competence to diagnose and treat, sharing of test results, informed consent, role conflicts, boundary issues, or any other issue defined by the Ethics Code.

(iii) *Legal issues*. These must be differentiated from ethical issues. Common legal issues involve privilege, mandatory child and elder abuse reporting, involuntary commitment, situations involving threats of violence to self or others, and billing practices. When the psychologist's ethical duties conflict with the law, steps must be taken to resolve conflicts in a responsible manner while maintaining the highest commitment to the ethics code (Canter et al., 1994). For example, the legal system may subpoena records which include raw test data, placing the psychologist in an ethical–legal dilemma regarding maintaining appropriate confidentiality of test data or protocols (Committee on Legal Issues, APA, 1996). Contractual obligations, for example, with managed care organizations, also represent legal agreements with which psychologists must weigh any competing ethical demands.

(iv) *Moral issues*. These fall beyond the realm of ethical codes and laws. Social issues such as domestic violence, divorce, abortion, gay rights, or physician-assisted suicide are heavily value laden. It is imperative that psychologists avoid any misuse of power or influence and respect the client's rights to self-determination.

(v) *Pragmatic issues*. These encompass the practical aspects of ethical problem-solving. Examples might include a working knowledge of how the legal system acts upon reports of child abuse in a particular community, or the situation in which culturally competent referral resources for a minority client are not readily available.

2.23.4.3 Applying a Decision-making Model

Several authors have outlined rational-evaluative models of ethical decision-making (Canter et al., 1994; CPA, 1991; Kitchener, 1984). Hill, Glaser, and Harden (1995) have added a feeling-intuitive dimension to their feminist model for ethical decision-making, taking into account the emotional reactions of the clinician and the impact upon the therapeutic relationship. These models follow four general steps:

(i) *Generating alternative solutions*. To encourage consideration of multiple solutions, develop at least three potential courses of action.

(ii) *Analysis of each course of action*. For each solution, identify the short-and long-term effects upon the primary client and other affected parties. How does the solution affect the clinician and the treatment relationship? Rank the potential choices.

(iii) *Choice and implementation*. Despite the likelihood that no single option is ideal, a choice of action must be made to implement an ethical path. Avoidance or inaction may be unethical.

(iv) *Evaluation*. A review of the decision process and its consequences is critical. It may be necessary to reengage in the decision-making process if there is still an uncertain or negative outcome.

2.23.5 PROFESSIONAL COMPETENCE

2.23.5.1 Competence: The Cornerstone of Ethics

Competent practice that promotes human welfare and protects clients from harm is the foundation of professional ethics. The boundaries of professional competence are based upon "education, training, supervised experience, or appropriate professional experience" (1992, p. 1600). Professional psychology programs provide an integration of basic science courses with applied training and theory (Tipton, 1996). In the USA, the doctoral degree is considered the most appropriate level of training for entry into independent practice. The APA currently recognizes five areas of professional specialization: clinical, counseling, school, industrial/organizational, and neuropsychology.

The importance of basing judgments upon scientifically and professionally derived knowledge and using empirically founded treatment techniques and assessment measures is highlighted in the Preamble as well as in the Ethical Standards (APA, 1992). Psychologists carry an ongoing responsibility to maintain expertise through keeping current with the professional and scientific literature in their field of activity. The challenge is that "... competence is not a static concept. Rather, it must be evaluated against a changing context of existing knowledge in the field" (Haas & Malouf, 1989, p. 19). Ideally, psychologists make a lifelong commitment to learning and personal growth.

Theoretically, the public is protected from unqualified, incompetent, or unethical practitioners through the state licensure process (Retfalvi & Simon, 1996). Regulatory boards review entry-level academic credentials, supervised internship, and postdoctoral experience. Written and oral examinations cover general psychological knowledge, competence in the candidate's area of specialization, and ethical reasoning. However, enforcement of competence through licensing boards guarantees only minimal levels of knowledge, education, and experience. Cases of gross incompetence may be detected through complaint procedures, but subtle incompetence often goes undetected (Haas & Malouf, 1989).

Although there is agreement that competence is a fundamental expectation, defining competence has proven difficult (Claiborn, 1982). Clear definitions of professional competence or knowledge necessary in areas of specialization are often lacking. Ultimately, the boundaries of competence are self-monitored. The psychologist determines their scope of practice according to their general skills, areas of specialization, and populations commonly treated. Some delivery settings may require specific expertise, such as hospital, rural, forensic, or industrial/organizational practice. Psychologists should be familiar with laws and regulations applicable to their employment settings. Specific clinical competencies and ethical awareness may be required for multiperson therapies such as marital, family, or group interventions (Lakin, 1994). Knowledge of personal strengths and weaknesses is essential in order to monitor one's competence.

Haas and Malouf (1989, p. 16) describe the competent clinician as having the necessary *knowledge*, effective *skills* in applying knowledge, and appropriate *judgment*, or knowing "what to do, how to do it, and when to do it." Overholser and Fine (1990) discuss subtle aspects in defining the boundaries of competence. Inadequate knowledge or misapplication of skills to particular disorders or populations can occur. Relationship skills are essential to an effective treatment relationship. Inability to form a rapport or, conversely, overinvolvement with clients, are examples of subtle forms of incompetence. Personality problems of the therapist may compromise objectivity in evaluation and intervention with clients. Transient stressors such as illness, divorce, or death of a family member, may render the therapist temporarily incompetent.

Issues of human differences are relevant to psychologists in their roles as practitioners, evaluators, teachers, supervisors, researchers, and employers. They must develop the necessary competence to address any differences based upon "age, gender, race, ethnicity, national origin, religion, sexual orientation, disability, language, or socioeconomic status"

(APA, 1992, p. 1601). Cultural competence in testing and assessment practice involves cultural sensitivity and knowledge, a systematic approach to understanding the client as a cultural entity, and methods of service delivery which are culture specific (Dana, 1994). As the practitioner encounters special populations or unique clinical issues for which they lack adequate training, appropriate use of consultation or referral to a more qualified psychologist is warranted.

2.23.5.2 Maintaining and Enhancing Competence

Continuing education, through attendance of formal workshops, clinical and research conferences, or study groups, is critical to update knowledge and skills. Many state licensing boards have adopted mandatory standards for continuing education hours to maintain licensure. In some cases, education hours must cover specific content areas, such as ethics, AIDS education, or child abuse.

Preparation for new areas of practice requires an appropriately thorough study of the literature, completion of relevant academic coursework, training, and supervised experience or ongoing consultation with an expert in the area of specialization.

The APA developed a policy in 1976 for doctoral-level psychologists wishing to change their specialty which outlines formal steps for preparation (APA, 1976). Psychologists must meet the necessary requirements of doctoral training in the new specialty with credit given for requirements previously satisfied. Respecialization in areas involving services in clinical, counseling, or school psychology should include appropriate practicum and internship experience through APA-approved training programs.

2.23.5.3 Professional Impairment

An important aspect of professional competence is managing "personal problems and conflicts" (APA, 1992, p. 1601) which can diminish effectiveness and carry a risk of harm to clients, students, or colleagues. Psychologists must take appropriate steps to prevent serious impairment. Appropriate responses to early signs of personal difficulty include efforts to gain additional support, limiting services, seeking additional consultation or pursuing personal therapy. Ongoing consultation or participation in peer supervision may also benefit the professional by providing mutual support and counteracting isolation.

Professional impairment may be evidenced by absenteeism, diminished work quality, heightened conflicts with co-workers or inappropriate professional boundaries, including sexual exploitation of clients. Impairment is frequently associated with alcohol or drug abuse. Denial is a hallmark of many psychological problems, particularly substance abuse, often precluding self-awareness and intervention as required by the Ethics Code. Impaired judgment can also be associated with burnout, a pattern of emotional exhaustion resulting from chronic demands on physical or emotional resources in the work setting (Freudenberger, 1975).

The Ethics Code encourages psychologists to attempt informal resolution of ethical violations, including addressing potential impairment of colleagues. However, psychologists are often reluctant to confront distressed colleagues. Several state psychological associations have responded to concerns about professional impairment by developing psychologist support committees. The function of these programs is to protect the interests of persons served by psychologists and to assist psychologists in preventing or managing distress so that it does not affect their professional duties.

2.23.6 PROFESSIONAL RELATIONSHIP

2.23.6.1 Client Welfare

The APA Code (1992, p. 1599) "has as its primary goal the welfare and protection of the individuals and groups with whom psychologists work." This fiduciary role requires psychologists always to consider what is in the best interests of the client in making treatment decisions, and maintain safe, beneficial, and objective professional roles. Psychologists must avoid exploitation of those over whom they have supervisory or evaluative authority, such as students, supervisees, research participants, and employees.

The 1992 code emphasizes the importance of sensitivity to issues of human diversity, and "appropriate respect to the fundamental rights, dignity and worth of all people" (APA, 1992, p. 1599). Psychologists must avoid any unfair or discriminatory practices based upon "age, gender, race, ethnicity, national origin, religion, sexual orientation, disability, language, and socioeconomic status" (APA, 1992, p. 1601).

Broader application of ethical duties requires psychologists to be aware of their professional and scientific responsibilities to the greater community and the society as a whole. The importance of societal goals may outweigh individual interests in some clinical situations. Exceptions to confidentiality based upon the duty to protect others in the community is one example. The reality of limited health care finances in the USA raises the dilemma of whether to promote distribution of mental health services according to the needs of the population as a whole, or to advocate for individual needs.

2.23.6.2 Structuring the Professional Relationship

Ethical standards require that psychologists take care at the outset of the therapeutic relationship to discuss with clients significant information about their services. Optimally, the client is actively involved in a mutual process of developing the therapeutic contract.

Treatment providers are encouraged to clarify information in oral or written form that is understandable to the client, and respond to any questions or concerns (Koocher, 1994). Use of standard written office policies has been encouraged for purposes of documentation and effective communication. Such forms usually include basic information such as the professional's qualifications or background, goals and anticipated course of treatment, alternatives to treatment, risks and benefits, confidentiality, and cancellation or missed appointment policies.

Financial arrangements are an essential part of the initial treatment contract. Attention must be paid to matching the client's needs with available resources and identifying any dilemmas at the outset, such as where the treatment needs may exceed the insurance benefits or client's ability to pay (Koocher, 1994).

In psychological assessment situations, psychologists must clearly explain their role as an evaluator. To ensure an objective and unbiased evaluative opinion, the professional must avoid any conflicting or multiple roles. In general, evaluation and treatment roles are mutually exclusive. The code requires that an appropriate explanation of assessment results is provided to the client in understandable language. Any limitations to receiving the results must be identified at the outset.

Services are frequently requested by third parties, such as schools or courts. This may raise ethical dilemmas around potential conflicts of interest between the needs of the payer and the client. It is critical to inform all concerned parties about the nature of the services, responsibilities to each party, and whether evaluative information will be shared or kept confidential.

The increasing involvement of insurers and managed care companies as third parties in monitoring the planning and delivery of mental health services has created further ethical complexities in structuring treatment. Clients must be informed at the outset regarding potential restrictions in reimbursement related to the insurer's definition of "medical necessity" of treatment, requirements to reveal diagnostic and other treatment information to their insurer, and any financial incentives that encourage the practitioner to limit services. From the insurer's perspective, the Ethics Code requires that psychologists provide accurate information regarding the nature of services and charges in reports to third-party payers (APA, 1992). Explanation of the limits of confidentiality is key to the practice of psychotherapy, where personal information is shared with the therapist, as well as for evaluation, where results may be shared with other parties.

2.23.6.3 Informed Consent

The 1992 code emphasizes the importance of obtaining informed consent from clients at the beginning of service. Informed consent requires three elements: (i) the capacity to consent, (ii) adequate knowledge or information regarding the decision, and (iii) voluntariness, without "undue influence" of others. In-person discussion and written documentation of the informed consent process is necessary. Some consider this to be an ongoing process during treatment.

In cases where the client is not capable of giving informed consent, such as with young minors, developmentally disabled, or other severely impaired individuals, the legally authorized guardian should give permission. Populations who are mandated to treatment or evaluation should be carefully evaluated to ensure that their voluntariness has not been compromised.

2.23.6.4 Interruption and Termination of Services

The Ethics Code also delineates the professional's responsibility to provide continuity of care. Anticipation and preparation for potential interruptions to service must be considered by the psychologist to avoid abandonment of the client (Canter et al., 1994). In the event of relocation or discontinuation of practice, illness, or death of a psychologist, steps should be taken to provide for transfer of client records and referral to an appropriate provider. Changes in the client's location or financial status may also interrupt treatment (Vasquez, 1994). For example, financially limited clients who exhaust their insurance coverage, yet remain in need of services must be appropriately referred or continued by the therapist until stabilization or conclusion of treatment. New issues occur in the context of managed care and group practices, where practitioners may leave a practice or panel, and are no longer eligible to provide reimbursable services to a particular client. Whatever the reason, termination of services must always be handled with care and sensitivity.

2.23.7 PRIVACY AND CONFIDENTIALITY

2.23.7.1 Privacy, Privilege, and Confidentiality

The concept of privacy is a personal right based in constitutional law which allows an individual to determine to what extent personal information, thoughts, or feelings will be shared with others (Keith-Spiegel & Koocher, 1985). Confidentiality is an ethical commitment by the psychologist to maintain the privacy of information disclosed in treatment or assessment. It is important to distinguish between the ethical principle of confidentiality and the legal concept of privilege. Privilege refers to the legal right of the client to prevent information shared in certain protected relationships, such as psychotherapy, from being disclosed in court.

2.23.7.2 Limits or Exceptions to Confidentiality

An integral part of structuring professional services is the discussion of the limits of confidentiality and the potential uses of the information gathered in treatment or assessment. Conflicts between ethical and legal standards may be most apparent in this area. Common exceptions to confidentiality include dangerousness to self or others (e.g., suicidality or homicidality), and mandated reporting of suspected child or elder abuse. Required reports to employers, courts, or other third parties may also affect confidentiality. In situations where clients file a malpractice suit against the psychologist, or use their mental status as a legal defense, such actions may serve to waive privilege.

2.23.7.3 Third-party Requests for Information

Voluntary releases to disclose information to others may be given by the client for various purposes, such as communication with other providers, family members, or eligibility for other types of services and benefits. To ensure a valid consent, it is essential to inform the client about the contents of the records to be released and the potential consequences of releasing that information. For example, a therapy client may become involved in divorce litigation and request that the therapist provide case records to support a claim for custody, without realizing that the record as a whole may contain clinical information unfavorable to their legal case. The client's written consent to release information should be documented in the records.

The Ethics Code encourages psychologists to minimize intrusions on privacy by limiting permissible disclosures to information relevant to the purpose of the request. Voluntary disclosure of information to support insurance claims is a common example where the client must agree to release their diagnosis to the insurer in order to get reimbursed for treatment costs. Managed mental health care plans often require extensive information in the process of authorizing treatment, such as the full *Diagnostic and statistical manual of mental disorders, 4th edition* (*DSM-IV*) diagnosis, treatment plans, progress reports, and termination summaries (American Psychiatric Association, 1994). In some reimbursement systems, copies of chart notes are required. Involvement of the client in examining the risks and benefits of disclosure is essential to ensure their rights to make the best choices for themselves.

2.23.7.4 Couple and Family Therapy

A positive change in the 1992 code was the recognition of the ethical complexities involved in multiperson therapies. Group and family therapies differ from dyadic treatment models in important ways, requiring the psychologist to have competence in the technical skills of these modalities and anticipate ethical dilemmas unique to them (Lakin, 1994). In group therapy, the therapist asks group members to respect one another's confidentiality, but pragmatically cannot guarantee that information discussed in session will remain private.

In treatment situations where the couple or family system is the focus, the Ethics Code requires the psychologist to clarify (i) which individuals are being treated as clients, (ii) the role the psychologist will have with each party, and (iii) the ways in which information will be shared for the purposes of treatment or kept confidential from some of the parties (APA, 1992). In family therapy, where members of the system may also be seen in couple or individual sessions, disclosures may not always be held as confidential (Lakin, 1994). A frequent ethical dilemma occurs when parents divorce and later seek access to family treatment records for legal purposes. In family therapy situations where children are not able to give direct consent, the psychologist should provide information at a level understandable to the child, seek their assent and maintain an active consideration of their best interests. Treatment with step-families raises challenging issues regarding the involvement of noncustodial parents in the consent to treatment and their rights to information regarding their children.

2.23.7.5 Documentation and Record Keeping

The primary purpose of the treatment record is to benefit the client. APA Record Keeping Guidelines (APA, 1993c) provide specific guidance regarding the appropriate content, control, maintenance, and retention of records. Federal, state, and local laws may also govern the disposition of records. Thorough documentation should include the client's presenting issues, history, diagnostic formulation, and treatment plan. This clinical information facilitates communication and coordination with other professionals, and continuity of care should the psychologist become unavailable. Psychologists must guard against any misuse of records. For these reasons, sensitive information, speculations, or personal opinions are rarely appropriate in the record (Soisson, VandeCreek, & Knapp, 1987).

Details of informed consent, releases of information, and financial agreements must also be documented. Accurate record keeping is part of the professional's risk management, providing evidence of appropriate treatment and documenting significant decisions, such as steps taken to manage suicide risk (Soisson et al., 1987). A complete and current record permits the psychologist to monitor their own services and participate in external quality assurance reviews.

Recent technological advances in electronic record keeping and computerized databases have greatly impacted issues of privacy of records. Coding to disguise the identity of clients' mental health records is essential when others can access the database without client consent. Protection of privacy is also important when client information is transmitted via facsimile, cellular phones, or electronic mail.

2.23.8 MULTIPLE RELATIONSHIPS

2.23.8.1 Types of Dual Relationships

Multiple or dual relationships occur when a psychologist functions in a professional role concurrently or consecutively with another professional or personal role (Pope, 1991). The Ethics Code acknowledges the inherent power differential in clinical, supervisory, or teaching roles where psychologists have clinical knowledge or evaluative power. Examples of personal roles outside of a service setting include friendships, social involvements, or business relationships. The psychologist should refrain from promising or taking on new roles when any prior relationship creates a risk of harm (APA, 1992). Overlapping relationships can be categorized as sexual, nonsexual, or conflicts of interest (Table 1).

The 1992 Ethics Code is more explicit and restrictive about dual relationships than previous codes. Sexual exploitation in professional relationships is potentially very harmful to the client as well as damaging to the credibility of the profession. Sexual intimacies with current clients, students, or supervisees are expressly prohibited by the code. In the case of former psychotherapy clients, the ban has been extended to at least two years after termination of the professional relationship. Accepting former sexual partners as therapy clients is now also unethical. Psychologists must avoid any type of sexually harassing behavior.

Nonsexual dual relationships are problematic to the extent that the secondary role has the potential to interfere with the fulfillment of the professional's responsibility in the primary role. Sensitivity to any harmful consequences for the client must be the foremost ethical consideration. For example, if a psychologist were asked to perform a cognitive evaluation of an elder in the psychologist's religious community, a potential ethical dilemma is that the professional's objectivity may be compromised by the prior relationship. Despite confidentiality, the client might feel unduly exposed in the future when attending religious functions where the psychologist is present. The psychologist's influence and the client's vulnerability in the professional relationship carry over to the secondary relationship (Barnett, 1996).

Conflicts of interest involve current or preexisting financial and business relationships, or acceptance of gifts or services from clients. In these situations, the self-interest of the psychologist can compromise the fiduciary relationship (Smith & Fitzpatrick, 1995). Because of these issues, the change in the recent code permitting barter with clients in circumstances which can be demonstrated as not exploitative or clinically contraindicated has been controversial (Koocher, 1994).

All of this said, the APA Code acknowledges that multiple relationships may be at times unavoidable or unforseeable. Psychologists who work in small rural or ethnic minority communities, for example, encounter a range of situations in which they may incidentally or intentionally interact with clients in other roles or contexts. Graduate training settings which incorporate teaching, supervisory, collegial, research, and social roles, also tend to create overlapping relationships. Dual relationships

Table 1 Types of dual relationships.

Sexual
Sexual intimacies with clients
during therapy
post-termination
Sexual intimacies with students, supervisees in training
Treatment of former sexual partners
Sexual harassment
Nonsexual
Treatment of students, supervisees, employees, friends, relatives
Research with clients, supervisees, employees, friends, relatives
Mixing evaluative/supervisory and therapeutic roles
Therapeutic and collegial or professional relationships
Post-termination friendship
Social relationships with clients, students, supervisees, research participants, employees
Conflicts of interest
Business/financial relationships with clients
Acceptance of gifts or services

are not always harmful, however, psychologists must be sensitive to their use of power to avoid any exploitation as a result of their position.

2.23.8.2 Professional Boundaries

Psychologists identify difficulties with professional boundaries as a common ethical dilemma (Pope & Vetter, 1992). In clinical settings, a positive therapeutic relationship is the necessary basis for effective treatment interventions. "Proper boundaries provide a foundation for this relationship by fostering a sense of safety and the belief that the clinician will always act in the client's best interest" (Smith & Fitzpatrick, 1995, p. 500). Attention to the maintenance of professional boundaries is ethically imperative so as to: (i) safeguard the client's trust in the professional relationship, (ii) prevent the loss of clinical or evaluative objectivity, and (iii) avoid any risk of harm or exploitation of the client.

Relevant parameters of the therapeutic framework include a defined professional role, agreed upon times and places for treatment, clear financial agreements, and confidential handling of information (Pope, 1994). Boundary violations are departures from accepted practice which place the client or treatment process at risk (Smith & Fitzpatrick, 1995). Examples might include the clinician's self-disclosure of personal problems or opinions, social involvement outside of treatment, inappropriate or sexualized physical contact (e.g., hugging, touching, kissing), or acceptance of gifts or favors. It is always the responsibility of the professional to maintain sound boundaries, even if the client "tests" the relationship by asking for personal involvement. In most cases, boundary violations represent a gratification of the clinician's needs which overshadow the client's best interests, reflect a misuse of professional power or influence, and risk a violation of the client's trust and dependency (Brown, 1994).

2.23.8.3 Sexual Intimacies in Professional Relationships

A general erosion of treatment boundaries often precedes more serious exploitation of clients. For example, Simon (1991) reported that inappropriate therapist self-disclosure is the most common boundary violation shown to be a precursor to therapist–client sexual intimacy. Although the ethical prohibition of sexual intimacies with clients includes a two year post-termination period (APA, 1992), even after this time period the psychologist must demonstrate that the sexual or romantic relationship with the former client does not involve any exploitation. Interpretation of this standard has emphasized a close examination of several risk factors for the former client's vulnerability to exploitation, such as the nature of the therapy, the client's personal history and mental status, and potential adverse impacts on the client or others, which, in essence, make this an almost never rule (Canter et al., 1994).

Several rationales have been discussed in the literature to support a permanent ban on sexual involvement with clients. Some would argue that because of the power imbalance, the client may not be in a position to clearly evaluate the risks of becoming personally involved with a therapist. The existence of transferential aspects of treatment is widely clinically accepted and some courts have recognized the mishandling of the transference in judgments regarding therapist sexual misconduct (Gabbard, 1994). The internal therapist, a positive nondistorted representation of the therapist, may continue to sustain growth and change for the client up to several years post-termination (Pope, 1994). Treatment models which emphasize the ongoing role of the therapist as a consultant throughout the life span also support the preservation of the treatment relationship.

Although the sexual exploitation of clients is a serious problem in the profession, survey data by Pope, Keith-Spiegel, and Tabachnick (1986) found that sexual attraction to clients is actually a common experience that must be differentiated from therapist–client sexual intimacy. Eighty-seven percent of psychotherapists ($n=575$) reported that they had experienced sexual attraction to clients on at least one occasion. It is important for psychologists to acknowledge and understand their sexual feelings in order to prevent acting upon them. Recommended avenues of support for clinicians dealing with feelings of attraction that risk undermining the therapeutic relationship include supervision, professional consultation, peer support, or personal psychotherapy. Proactive steps have been recommended to improve clinical training in the complexities of boundary issues in psychotherapy and the sexual dynamics of clinical relationships (Borys & Pope, 1989; Pope et al., 1986).

Once considered only relevant to treatment settings, attention to the role of boundaries in educational and training settings requires psychologists to consider the supervisee's or student's needs first when making decisions that might impact them. The Ethics Code prohibits sexual relationships with students or supervisees in training, where the psychologist has direct evaluative authority (APA, 1992). The pervasiveness of the power differential in graduate training must be appreciated, as faculty may have ongoing evaluative roles for many years. Teaching and supervising faculty must act as appropriate role models of social and sexual behavior (Hammel, Olkin, & Taube, 1996). Research on student–educator sexual contact suggest a potential modeling effect, in that these students themselves later have greater difficulties with professional boundary violations (Pope, Levenson, & Schover, 1979).

2.23.8.4 Risk Management and Self-care

Understanding risk factors for both the client and professional facilitates a proactive stance towards maintaining therapeutic boundaries. Clients with impulsive, dependent, or borderline features, traumatized populations, especially those with a history of sexual abuse, and chronically ill clients may pose particular challenges in maintaining professional boundaries. Rural settings create higher incidences of overlapping professional and personal roles. Risk factors for the psychologist often involve professional or personal isolation, depression, substance abuse, unresolved personal issues, ongoing stressors, or mental impairment. The code encourages attention to conflicts and personal problems which may impair performance, lead to overidentification with the client, or cause the clinician to reinforce client dependency. Because of the risk of bias involved when multiple relationships occur, the use of supervision or consultation with an expert in ethics to facilitate sound decision-making is encouraged (Canter et al., 1994)

A primary function of professional self-care is to reduce risk factors associated with ethical violations, particularly those involving boundary issues. Some theorize that the therapist's well-being is positively related to the therapeutic outcome (Faunce, 1990), and advocate for self-care as an ethical responsibility (Pettifor, 1996). Optimal self-care for professionals involves physical, emotional, mental, and spiritual dimensions (Faunce, 1990).

Awareness of the impact of professional work is imperative. Although emotional stress cannot always be eliminated, it can be understood and managed. Self-knowledge is important regarding (i) motivations and expectations in professional work, (ii) unresolved personal conflicts, (iii) types of clients one works well with or does not work with effectively, (iv) countertransference reactions, (v) acceptance of limitations, and personal reactions to stress.

Use of specific proactive self-care strategies that help balance personal and professional life such as exercise, leisure activities, and meditation or relaxation, can prevent burnout and promote healthy professional functioning. Psychologists can seek support through professional supervision, personal therapy, or ongoing peer support systems.

2.23.9 FORENSIC ACTIVITIES

2.23.9.1 Forensic Roles

Ethical issues in the forensic activities of psychologists are addressed for the first time in the 1992 code. This addition reflects the apparent increase in forensically related activities of psychologists. Forensic mental health experts serve as consultants to attorneys, provide psychological evaluation, and give expert testimony in judicial settings (Perrin & Sales, 1994). General clinicians may be called into court for testimony, receive subpoenas for records, or provide occasional service to the legal system.

Increasingly, the court system and society are turning to mental health records, seeking factual evidence. Therapy records are being subpoenaed, even at a later date, for legal purposes such as worker's compensation claims, divorce and custody proceedings, and personal injury suits. Some treatment populations, such as abuse victims, carry a high potential for forensic involvement (Walker, 1994). Clinicians need to anticipate with their clients the likelihood of intrusion into the privacy of psychotherapy in such situations. It is critical to separate therapeutic and expert evaluative functions, because of the risk of reaching one-sided conclusions when they are derived solely from therapeutically based observations.

Due to the potential impact of their recommendations, psychologists in expert roles must take care in establishing adequate foundations for their conclusions and, conversely, identify any limitations to their data or the scope of their recommendations. The psychologist must remain independent of economic or professional pressure to modify their opinions. Attorneys may attempt to pressure the psychologist to advocate for their client's position (Canter et al., 1994), such as by asking the psychologist to make stronger statements than are supported by the available data. This highlights an important difference between the adversarial nature of the legal system which promotes advocacy, and the scientific model of psychology which values objectivity.

2.23.9.2 Specialty Guidelines for Forensic Psychologists

Because of the complexities and pitfalls involved in forensic practice, two additional documents have been developed to supplement the Ethics Code. The *Specialty Guidelines for Forensic Psychologists* were developed by a joint Committee on Ethical Guidelines of Division 41 and the American Academy of Forensic Psychology to "improve the quality of forensic psychological services offered to individual clients and the legal system" (Committee on Special Guidelines Forensic Psychologists, 1991, p. 655). They have not been adopted by the APA as a whole.

Competency in forensic psychology includes specialized knowledge in an area of forensic expertise, and interdisciplinary knowledge such as familiarity with the legal setting and the legal and professional standards governing psychologists' roles in the judicial system. Expert knowledge of unique populations, for example, criminal populations, divorcing families, or injured workers, is also critical.

The specialty guidelines provide detailed attention to appropriate methods and procedures for conducting forensic evaluations, objective bases for expert opinions, and the role of the expert witness. As with other psychological services, clarification of the professional role, informed consent, careful attention to confidentiality and privilege issues, and thorough documentation are essential. Because of the potential influence of their opinions, particular care must be taken to ensure the civil rights of the parties involved in legal proceedings.

Child custody evaluations, a specialized area of forensic psychology, are among the most complex assessments that psychologists conduct (Oberlander, 1995), and a frequent basis for ethical complaints to licensing boards and ethics committees. The frequency of high conflict divorce cases in custody evaluation and the seriousness of the potential loss to either parent tends to promote contentiousness by the recipient of services. Because psychologists' recommendations have the potential to influence many lives, keen awareness of the needs and rights of multiple parties and maintaining impartiality are critical. The *Guidelines for Child Custody Evaluations in Divorce Proceedings* (APA, 1994) were developed to provide practitioners and ethics committees with more detailed and consistent standards for competence and practice in this difficult area. The guidelines stress the need for balanced assessment based upon interviews with all relevant parties. Psychologists should refrain from making conclusions regarding parties they did not directly evaluate.

2.23.10 FUTURE DIRECTIONS IN PROFESSIONAL ETHICS

The question "How can psychology contribute more to improving the human condition in the future?" (Farley, 1996, p. 773) reflects the aspirational ideal of professional psychology. Various trends are emerging with potential impact on professional psychology and ethical practice. Growing multicultural awareness within psychology is now influencing training programs (Bass, 1996). Practice issues related to the delivery of culturally competent services and access to services for ethnic and minority populations will be a significant challenge in the future.

Psychologists in the USA are actively pursuing hospital staff privileges which give them the authority to manage patient care in hospital settings. A related development is clinical psychopharmacology, a new field of specialization within professional psychology which is beginning to generate relevant ethical practice guidelines (Buelow & Chafetz, 1996). Prescription privileges for psychologists, allowing psychologists to dispense psychotropic medications, is a controversial role which necessitates careful consideration by the profession. Ethical guidelines must address specific issues of competence, scope of practice, and referral (Buelow & Chafetz, 1996), as well as address the relationship between medical and psychological treatment models.

The growth of managed mental health care in the USA is challenging psychologists to develop new service delivery systems and forge contractual relationships with managed care organizations that also preserve professional autonomy. The impact has been divisive among colleagues who may advocate or oppose the emphasis on shorter-term treatment models that promise cost containment, but are seen by others as rationing of treatment. Confidentiality under such models can be easily compromised by the competing need for documentation and quality assurance. Psychologists must increasingly deal with the legal and business aspects of practice, which must be kept in balance with the therapeutic focus on the relationship with the client.

The editorial article *Ethics in cyberspace* encompasses a wide range of issues and dilemmas resulting from the rapid evolution of information technology, office computerization, electronic communication, and use of the Internet (Koocher, 1996, p. 89). The global impact of the information superhighway on psychology and social systems as a whole is yet to be seen.

2.23.11 SUMMARY

This review of ethical issues in professional psychology in the USA has highlighted the concepts of competence, elements of the professional relationship, confidentiality, and multiple relationships, which form the basis of our professional standards. The aspirational values which inspire professional work seek to enhance the personal freedom and self-determination of clients and promote the broad goals of social welfare. Although commonalities in ethics may extend across international boundaries, our knowledge and practice grows out of the context of an industrialized culture. The evolution of information technology will permit greater opportunities for an international dialogue within psychology regarding the use of psychological science and practice to benefit the global society.

2.23.12 REFERENCES

American Psychiatric Association (1994). *Diagnostic and statistical manual of mental disorders* (4th ed.). Washington, DC: Author.

American Psychological Association (1953). *Ethical standards for psychologists.* Washington, DC: Author.

American Psychological Association (1976). Policy on training for psychologists wishing to change their specialty. Adopted by the Council of Representatives, January 23–25.

American Psychological Association (1981). *Specialty guidelines for the delivery of services by clinical psychologists, counseling psychologists, industrial organizational psychologists, and school psychologists.* Washington, DC: Author.

American Psychological Association (1982). *Ethical principles in the conduct of research with human participants.* Washington, DC: Author.

American Psychological Association (1985). *Standards for Educational and Psychological Testing.* Washington, DC: Author.

American Psychological Association (1987). General guidelines for providers of psychological services. *American Psychologist, 42,* 712–723.

American Psychological Association (1992). Ethical principles of psychologists and code of conduct. *American Psychologist, 47,* 1597–1611.

American Psychological Association (1993a). *Guidelines for ethical conduct in the care and use of animals.* Washington, DC: Author.

American Psychological Association (1993b). Guidelines for providers of psychological services to ethnic, linguistic, and culturally diverse populations. *American Psychologist, 48,* 45–48.

American Psychological Association (1993c). Record keeping guidelines. *American Psychologist, 48,* 984–986.

American Psychological Association (1994). Guidelines for child custody evaluations in divorce proceedings. *American Psychologist, 49,* 677–680.

American Psychological Association, Ethics Committee (1994). Report of the Ethics Committee, 1993. *American Psychologist, 49,* 659–666.

American Psychological Association, Ethics Committee (1995, November). Ethics Committee plan for next review of ethics code. Unpublished plan.

American Psychological Association, Ethics Committee (1996). Report of the Ethics Committee, 1995. *American Psychologist, 51,* 1279–1286.

Association of State and Provincial Psychology Boards. (1991). *ASPPB Code of Conduct.* Montgomery, AL: Author.

Barnett, J. E. (1996). Boundary issues and dual relationships: Where to draw the line? *The Independent Practitioner, 16,* 138–140.

Bass, L. J. (1996). Future trends. In L. J. Bass et al. (Eds.), *Professional conduct and discipline in psychology* (pp. 143–156). Washington, DC: American Psychological Association.

Bass, L. J., DeMers, S. T., Ogloff, J. R., Peterson, C., Pettifor, J. L., Reaves, R. P., Retfalvi, T., Simon, N. P., Sinclair, C., & Tipton, R. M. (1996). *Professional conduct and discipline in psychology.* Washington, DC: American Psychological Association.

Bennett, B. E., Bryant, B. K., VandenBos, G. R., &

Greenwood, A. (1990). *Professional liability and risk management*. Washington, DC: American Psychological Association.

Bersoff, D. N. (1994). Explicit ambiguity: The 1992 Ethics Code as an oxymoron. *Professional Psychology: Research and Practice, 25*, 382–387.

Borys, D. S., & Pope, K. S. (1989). Dual relationships between therapist and client: A national study of psychologists, psychiatrists, and social workers. *Professional Psychology: Research and Practice, 20*, 283–293.

Brown, L. S. (1994). Boundaries in feminist therapy: A conceptual formulation. *Women and Therapy, 15*, 29–38.

Buelow, G. D., & Chafetz, M. D. (1996). Proposed ethical practice guidelines for clinical pharmacopsychology: Sharpening a new focus in psychology. *Professional Psychology: Research and Practice, 27*, 53–58.

Canadian Psychological Association (1991). *Canadian code of ethics for psychologists. Revised.* Ottawa, ON, Canada: Author.

Canter, M. B., Bennett, B. E., Jones, S. E., & Nagy, T. F. (1994). *Ethics for psychologists: A commentary on the APA Ethics Code*. Washington, DC: American Psychological Association.

Claiborn, W. L. (1982). The problem of professional incompetence. *Professional Psychology, 13*, 153–159.

Committee on Ethical Guidelines for Forensic Psychologists (1991). Specialty guidelines for forensic psychologists. *Law and Human Behavior, 15*, 655–665.

Committee on Legal Issues, American Psychological Association (1996). Strategies for private practitioners coping with subpoenas or compelled testimony for client records or test data. *Professional Psychology: Research and Practice, 27*, 245–251.

Dana, R. (1994). Testing and assessment ethics for all persons: Beginning and agenda. *Professional Psychology: Research and Practice, 25*, 349–354.

Farley, F. (1996). From the heart. *American Psychologist, 51*, 772–776.

Faunce, P. S. (1990). The self-care and wellness of feminist therapists. In H. Lerman & N. Porter (Eds.), *Feminist ethics in psychotherapy* (pp. 185–194). New York: Springer.

Freudenberger, H. J. (1975). The staff burn-out syndrome in alternative institutions. *Psychotherapy: Theory, Research and Practice, 12*, 73–82.

Gabbard, G. (1994). Reconsidering the American Psychological Association's policy on sex with former patients: Is it justifiable? *Professional Psychology: Research and Practice, 25*, 329–335.

Haas, L., & Malouf, J. (1989). *Keeping up the good work: A practitioner's guide to mental health ethics*. Sarasota, FL: Professional Resource Exchange.

Hammel, G. A., Olkin, R., & Taube, D. O. (1996). Student–educator sex in clinical and counseling psychology doctoral training. *Professional Psychology: Research and Practice, 27*, 93–97.

Handelsman, M. K. (1986). Problems with ethics training by "osmosis." *Professional Psychology: Research and Practice, 17*, 371–372.

Hill, M., Glaser, K., & Harden, J. (1995). A feminist model for ethical decision-making. In E. J. Rave & C. C. Larsen (Eds.), *Ethical decision-making in therapy* (pp. 18–37). New York: Guilford Press.

Hobbs, N. (1948). The development of a code of ethical standards for psychology. *American Psychologist, 3*, 80–84.

Keith-Spiegel, P., & Koocher, G. P. (1985). *Ethics in psychology: Professional standards and cases*. New York: Random House.

Kitchener, K. S. (1984). Intuition, critical evaluation and ethical principles: The foundation for ethical decisions in counseling psychology. *The Counseling Psychologist, 12*, 43–55.

Koocher, G. P. (1994). The commerce of professional psychology and the new Ethics Code. *Professional Psychology: Research and Practice, 25*, 355–361.

Koocher, G. P. (1996). Editorial: Ethics in cyberspace. *Ethics and Behavior, 6*, 89.

Lakin, M. (1994). Morality in group and family therapies: Multiperson therapies and the 1992 Ethics Code. *Professional Psychology: Research and Practice, 25*, 344–348.

Nagy, T. F. (1996 January/February). Ethics committees: Investigate or educate? *The National Psychologist*, 15–16.

Oberlander, L. (1995). Ethical responsibilities in child custody evaluations: Implications for evaluation methodology. *Ethics and Behavior, 5*, 311–332.

Overholser, J. C., & Fine, M. A. (1990). Defining the boundaries of professional competence: managing subtle cases of clinical incompetence. *Professional Psychology: Research and Practice, 21*, 462–469.

Payton, C. R. (1994). Implications of the 1992 Ethics Code for diverse groups. *Professional Psychology: Research and Practice, 25*, 317–320.

Perrin, G. I., & Sales, B. D. (1994). Forensic standards in the American Psychological Association's new Ethics Code. *Professional Psychology: Research and Practice, 25*, 376–381.

Peterson, C. (1996). Professional conduct and discipline in psychology self-evaluation. In L. J. Bass et al. (Eds.), *Professional conduct and discipline in psychology* (pp. 277–294). Washington, DC: American Psychological Association.

Pettifor, J. L. (1996). Maintaining professional conduct in daily practice. In L. J. Bass et al. (Eds.), *Professional conduct and discipline in psychology* (pp. 91–100). Washington, DC: American Psychological Association.

Pope, K. S. (1991). Dual relationships in psychotherapy. *Ethics and Behavior, 1*, 22–34.

Pope, K. S. (1994). *Sexual involvement with therapists: Patient assessment subsequent therapy, forensics*. Washington, DC: American Psychological Association.

Pope, K. S., Keith-Spiegel, P., & Tabachnick, B. G. (1986). Sexual attraction to clients: The human therapist and the (sometimes) inhuman training system. *American Psychologist, 41*, 147–158.

Pope, K. S., Levenson, H., & Schover, L. R. (1979). Sexual intimacy in psychology training: Results and implications of a national survey. *American Psychologist, 34*, 682–689.

Pope, K. S., & Vetter, V. A. (1992). Ethical dilemmas encountered by members of the American Psychological Association: A nationwide survey. *American Psychologist, 47*, 397–411.

Retfalvi, T., & Simon, N. P. (1996). Licensing, certification, registration, chartering, and credentialing. In L. J. Bass et al. (Eds.), *Professional conduct and discipline in psychology* (pp. 39–52). Washington, DC: American Psychological Association.

Simon, R. I. (1991). Psychological injury caused by boundary violation precursors to therapist–patient sex. *Psychiatric Annals, 21*, 614–619.

Smith, D., & Fitzpatrick, M. (1995). Patient–therapy boundary issues: An integrative review of theory and research. *Professional Psychology: Research and Practice, 26*, 499–506.

Soisson, E. L., VandeCreek, L., & Knapp, S. (1987). Thorough record keeping: A good defense in a litigious era. *Professional Psychology: Research and Practice, 18*, 498–502.

Tipton, R. M. (1996). Education and training. In L. J. Bass et al. (Eds.), *Professional conduct and discipline in psychology* (pp. 17–38). Washington, DC: American Psychological Association.

Vasquez, M. (1994). Implications for the 1992 Ethics Code

for the practice of individual psychotherapy. *Professional Psychology: Research and Practice, 25,* 321–328.

Walker, L. E. (1994). *Abused women and survivor therapy.* Washington, DC: American Psychological Association.

White v. North Carolina State Board of Examiners of Practicing Psychologists; 8810SC1137 North Carolina Court of Appeals, Wake County No. 86-CVS-8131 (Feb. 6, 1990).

2.24
Code of Conduct: Association of State and Provincial Psychology Boards

NORMA P. SIMON
New Hope Guild Training Programs Private Practice, New York, NY, USA

2.24.1 INTRODUCTION

2.24.1.1 Committee Formation

In 1987, the Executive Committee of the American Association of State Psychology Boards (AASPB), the former name of the Association of State and Provincial Psychology Boards (ASPPB), under the leadership of then president Patricia Bricklin, formed a new committee, the Model Licensure Committee (MLC), charged with developing a model code of conduct for the ASPPB and a model act for state/provincial licensure. At that time it was abundantly clear to the 59 member Boards (representing 51 jurisdictions in the USA and eight provinces of Canada) that the American Psychological Association (APA) Model Act for State Licensure for Psychologists lacked certain provisions which the Boards considered important. It was also noted by the Boards at that time that the number of charges brought by patients/clients against psychologists was increasing exponentially. At about that time also, the North Carolina courts were hearing the case of *White v. North Carolina State Board of Examiners of Practicing Psychologists* (1990), in which the judiciary eventually ruled that the Ethical Principles of Psychologists set forth in the preamble to the *APA Code of Ethics* could not be used as the basis for disciplinary action due, at least in part, to its lack of specificity. Consequently, the Executive Committee of the AASPB firmly believed that a more definitive and legally precise document was needed to help guide the various state and provincial jurisdictions in refining their own codes of conduct under which their Boards could act.

When the new MLC first met in 1988, it was informed that the Executive Committee placed a high priority on the MLC's development of a new code of conduct prior to drafting its own version of a model act. Accordingly, this was done.

2.24.2 HISTORY AND PHILOSOPHY OF THE ASPPB CODE OF CONDUCT

Each of the 59 jurisdictions already had some form of a code of conduct arrived at via various methods. They either: (i) referenced the *APA Code of Ethics* (or, in Canada, the Canadian Psychological Association (CPA) *Code of Ethics*) by name; (ii) more or less copied the relevant code of ethics without using its name, if the legal requirements of the jurisdiction did not permit legislation to merely adopt by reference a professional association's code of ethics; (iii) utilized a more or less generic code for all professions in the jurisdiction, with the addition of special provisions for psychology; or (iv) developed an individual code on their own, solely to meet the needs of that jurisdiction. Because the various jurisdictions used such different methods to arrive at their codes, uniformity was impossible.

2.24.2.1 Preparation by Staff

The MLC had asked the AASPB staff to provide the Executive Committee with as many codes of conduct of both the US and Canadian jurisdictions as practicable and, when the MLC began its work, it had 27 codes to review and consider.

When the review was finally completed and a new code drafted, portions of codes from 14 of those jurisdictions were incorporated into the new document.

2.24.2.2 Disparity of Codes

One difficulty the MLC faced initially was the obvious disparity among the many codes of conduct already in use: some were general, some were specific, and some were combinations. The MLC debated long and hard about whether to start their draft of the code by using the most detailed or the most generic among those earlier codes as the basis for developing the new *AASPB Code of Conduct*. After lengthy and occasionally heated discussion, it was decided that, since there were so many codes already in existence, it would be far more efficient for the MLC to adapt and supplement the various existing codes into one cohesive document, rather than to draft their new code without utilizing any of that material.

2.24.2.3 Filling the Legal Gap

From the beginning, and by consensus, the MLC also determined that it did not want to develop a code of conduct that differed greatly from ones that already existed, but rather it wanted to develop a code that would fill the problematic legal gaps then existing due to the aspirational nature of the then Canadian and American Psychological Associations' ethics codes. For this reason, the MLC determined that the *AASPB Code of Conduct* should be brief, to the point, and most definitely not aspirational in nature. The MLC wanted their new code to say, as clearly as possible: "This is required of you," or "This is not acceptable." Ambiguity was to be eliminated wherever possible. Also, the code was to be as positive as possible while remaining crystal clear as to permissible behavior for a psychologist.

2.24.2.4 Living Document

In view of the foregoing, the MLC ultimately decided to start with one of the very detailed codes already in existence and reshape it to contain relevant provisions from other codes, as well as new wording designed to meet all of their requirements. That is what was done and what exists today is intended as a living document, designed to change as times and conditions change and to be further clarified if and when any ambiguity is found to exist.

In some major areas the AASPB code was a trail blazer in defining and sharpening the "shalls" and "shall nots" for psychologists. There were other areas, however, where the new code merely restated, in what the MLC believed to be more precise terms, the material already contained in other codes.

2.24.2.5 New APA Code

After the *ASPPB code of conduct* (ASPPB, 1991) was completed and approved by ASPPB member Boards in October 1990, the APA, aware that their *Code of Ethics* no longer met the legal needs of the various jurisdictions, developed its own *Ethical principles of psychologists and code of conduct* (APA, 1992).

2.24.3 ASPPB CODE

The provisions of the ASPPB code were carefully drafted to possess the following characteristics (ASPPB, 1991, p. 2):

(i) They pertain to the process or technicalities of professional relationships, not to the content of the professional's judgment.

(ii) They pertain to the process or mechanics of the professional relationship, not to the content of the professional judgment itself.

(iii) They are intended primarily to protect the public interest.

(iv) They are as nonintrusive as possible.

(v) They are essentially unambiguous.

(vi) They assure that necessary information will be available for the regulatory board to judge compliance.

(vii) They are sufficient unto themselves without explanatory material.

(viii) They are nonoptional and always pertain; they are coercive and nontrivial.

2.24.3.1 Protection for the Public

The ASPPB believes that its code of conduct differs significantly in function and purpose from the ethics codes of professional associations because the primary purpose of the *ASPPB Code of Conduct* is to protect the public, whereas an organization of professionals necessarily also concerns itself with serving the needs and desires of its own often disparate groups of members. Although a professional association's ethics code may state that the protection of the public is the main function of its code, an association's very existence as a "guild" requires that its code of ethics have a different orientation from that of the ASPPB. This is because the latter was promulgated solely as a guide for, or to be incorporated into, legislation authorizing action by a regulatory body whose *only* purpose is to protect the public. To this date, three jurisdictions—Oklahoma, Maine, and South Carolina—have enacted the entire *ASPPB Code of Conduct* into law. Other jurisdictions have adopted parts of the code (R. Reaves, personal communication, 1996, August 6).

2.24.3.2 Sections of the Code

The overall goal of the committee was to make its code of conduct as simple as possible, both to understand and to follow. The code begins with an introduction, expressing its basic philosophy, followed by a section containing definitions intended to provide clarity and specificity in the use of such commonly used terms as "client," "confidential information," "court order," and "professional relationship."

2.24.3.3 Rules of Conduct

The ASPPB Rules of Conduct, which form the main section of the code, although organized around the same major moral values as other broadly descriptive codes of ethics, imply, though do not expressly state, certain underlying basic tenets of ethically minded psychologists. The headings of the ASPPB Rules of Conduct are: Competence, Impaired Objectivity and Dual Relationships, Client Welfare, Welfare of Supervisees and Research Subjects, Protecting Confidentiality of Clients, Representation of Services, Fees, and Statements, Assessment Procedures, Violation of Law, and

Aiding Illegal Practice. Under these headings, the rules themselves contain many subheadings which include explicit requirements.

2.24.4 DISTINCTIVE PROVISIONS

Reported here are examples of the more significant instances which make the ASPPB code distinctive, and a number of important areas where the ASPPB, APA, and CPA codes are congruent. The ASPPB's thinking was that, once a state board examined both the similarities and the differences between the various codes, each jurisdiction would have a sound basis for using the material to develop a code best suited to its own purposes.

2.24.4.1 Competence

Subsection III.A.3 of the ASPPB code mandates certain behavior by a psychologist when developing competency in an area either new to the individual or to the profession. It states, in part:

> The psychologist ... shall engage in ongoing consultation with other psychologists or relevant professionals and shall seek appropriate education and training in the new area. The psychologist shall inform clients of the innovative nature and the known risks associated with the services, so that the client can exercise freedom of choice regarding such services. (p. 8)

Neither of the other codes specifically requires the psychologist to inform the patient of the innovative nature of a treatment procedure.

2.24.4.2 Formal Opinion

Subsection III.A.5 of the ASPPB code states that: "A psychologist rendering a formal professional opinion about a person, for example about the fitness of a parent in a custody hearing, shall not do so without direct and professional contact with, or a formal assessment of, that person" (p. 8).

This is a stronger statement on the subject than those contained in either the APA or CPA codes. If adopted into law, this would have implications for psychologists who work for managed care companies as case managers, and who routinely make decisions without direct contact with, or formal assessment of, a patient.

2.24.4.3 Record Keeping

Subsection III.A.6.a of the ASPPB code sets forth requirements for more detailed record keeping than is mandated by either of the other codes.

The APA has a record keeping guideline, developed by its Committee on Professional Practices and Standards of the Board of Professional Affairs, in addition to the requirement in its ethics code. However, this more detailed guideline is not part of the APA code. The CPA code is quite general and contains no guidelines for the psychologist as to the requisite content of the records.

The ASPPB code (p. 9) states that the psychologist's records shall contain:

(i) the presenting problem(s) or purpose or diagnosis,

(ii) the fee arrangement,

(iii) the date and substance of each billed or service-count contact or service,

(iv) any test results or other evaluative results obtained and any basic test data from which they were derived,

(v) notation and results of formal consults with other providers, and

(vi) a copy of all test or other evaluative reports prepared as part of the professional relationship.

2.24.4.4 Supervisory Records

Subsection III.A.6.d of the ASPPB code contains a provision requiring supervisors to keep records on supervisory sessions for five years. This is predicated on the acknowledgment that supervisors are generally legally responsible for actions taken by their supervisees, and that having accurate records of the supervision could prove to be quite important to both. Neither of the other codes speaks to this issue.

2.24.4.5 Arrangements in an Emergency

Subsection III.A.7 of the ASPPB code requires the psychologist to make arrangements in case of emergency needs of the patient, should the psychologist be unavailable. The APA code also speaks to this point, but the Canadian code does not mention preplanning for such events. The ASPPB code states, in part: "Continuity of care. The psychologist shall make arrangements for another appropriate professional or professionals to deal with emergency needs of his or her clients, as appropriate, during periods of his or her foreseeable absences from professional availability" (p. 10).

2.24.4.6 Impaired Objectivity and Dual Relationships

Subsection III.B.2.b of the ASPPB code states:

> The psychologist, in interacting with a client or former client to whom the psychologist has at any time within the previous 24 months rendered counseling, psychotherapeutic, or other professional psychological services for the treatment or amelioration of emotional distress or behavioral inadequacy, will not... [followed by three caveats, two of which are also covered in the other codes and will be noted below under the subject of agreements, but the third of which is singular to the ASPPB Code]... enter into a financial or other potentially exploitive relationship with him or her. (p. 11)

The *Canadian code of ethics for psychologists* (CPA, 1991) mentions business interests entered into at the expense of psychologists' clients, which touches on this concern as well.

2.24.4.7 Therapists Making Deals

The MLC had learned of several instances in which therapists had pressured clients to either invest in "deals" involving the therapist or "encouraged" clients to buy items that the therapist was selling. Although these were not as personally harmful as a sexual relationship between therapist and client, the individual client clearly could not make his or her decision as an entirely independent individual. The therapy would be jeopardized because the psychologist would be in a dual relationship with the client and therefore unable to promote the client's welfare in a totally objective manner.

2.24.4.8 Client Welfare

Under client welfare, there are two rules singular to the ASPPB code. Subsection III.C.5 and Subsection 6 of the ASPPB code state: "The psychologist providing services to an individual client shall not induce that client(s) to solicit business on behalf of the psychologist... "; and "The psychologist providing services to a client shall make an appropriate referral of the client to another professional when requested to do so by the client" (p. 12).

The former is covered somewhat in the Testimonials section (3.05) of the APA code which states that psychologists: " ... do not solicit testimonials from current psychotherapy clients or patients or other persons who because of their particular circumstances are vulnerable to undue influence" (p. 8). The CPA code explicitly forbids exploiting a relationship to further the personal, political, or business interests of the psychologist. The specification of the financial prohibition is an important contribution in this code (CPA, 1991).

2.24.4.9 Supervisee Welfare

Again, under Welfare of Supervisees and Research Subjects, Subsection III.D of the ASPPB Code, the inclusion of "financially" as a "shall not" along with "sexually," is new.

2.24.4.10 Major Difference: Law vs. the Code

One of the major differences among the codes appears under Subsection III.E, Protecting Confidentiality of Clients.

Subsection III.E.7 of the ASPPB code states that: "The psychologist may release confidential information upon court order, as defined in Section II of this Code, or to conform with state, federal, or provincial law, rule, or regulation." The code (p. 14) thus clearly states that the law is a higher authority than the *ASPPB Code of Conduct* if provisions of the two are in conflict, whereas both the CPA and APA codes seem to imply that their codes of ethics are above the law. This is a very significant difference and cause for interesting speculation and debate. In this regard, Sinclair (1995) notes how the codes differ as to whether the law or the code shall prevail and that the ASPPB code specifies that the law governs. The other two (in Sinclair's words) "seem to allow for the possibility of some civil disobedience."

2.24.4.11 Confidentiality in Perpetuity

Subsection III.E.12 of the ASPPB code states that: "The psychologist shall continue to treat as confidential information regarding a client after the professional relationship between the psychologist and the client has ceased." This is singular to the ASPPB code (p. 15) and of considerable importance.

2.24.4.12 Display of License

Subsection III.F.1 of the ASPPB code (Representation of Services) is another provision which is contained only in this code, and requires the professional to display a current license. Although this requirement has also been assumed to be a requirement of a number of jurisdictions' codes, it is actually specified in only a few.

2.24.4.13 Violation of Law

Subsection III.I of the ASPPB code (Violations of Law) states that: "The psychologist shall not violate any applicable statute or administrative rule regulating the practice of psychology."

This requirement is specific to this code, although other codes have rules under which this general provision might be assumed.

2.24.5 AREAS OF AGREEMENT

Perhaps the major areas of agreement among all of these codes are those concerning confidentiality in general, dual relationships, and barter. Although the ASPPB code and the 1992 revision of the APA code are more specific than the CPA code, all agree that sexual relationships of any kind during treatment or within two years thereafter (for APA and ASPPB) is not permitted.

2.24.5.1 Post-therapy Time Limit

A great deal of debate occurred at meetings of both the MLC and the APA committees revising the ethics codes in setting time limits. Fourteen jurisdictions require in their administrative codes that two years must elapse before a personal relationship may be initiated. Florida's code states that the psychologist–client relationship is "deemed to continue in perpetuity." Eleven jurisdictions have even made such "sexual misconduct" a criminal offense (R. Reaves, personal communication, 1996, August 6). The ASPPB committee concluded that two years was a legally defensible period of time and so specified. Caveats in both the ASPPB and the APA codes put the burden on the psychologist to prove that the client was not "vulnerable, by reason of emotional or cognitive disorder, to exploitive influence by the psychologist" (ASPPB, 1991, p. 11). Unless the client is proven to not be vulnerable, the prohibition extends indefinitely. The APA code is more detailed than that of the ASPPB in the analysis of what the psychologist would have to prove.

2.24.5.2 Barter

One area under Fees and Statements (ASPPB code Subsection III.F) which is agreed upon by both the ASPPB and the APA codes, but is not mentioned in the CPA code, treats the practice of barter. Although the wording is somewhat different in each of those two codes, both agree that barter can be exploitive and should be avoided. ASPPB's rural psychologists, however, informed the MLC that it is not always possible to avoid barter in their geographical areas, and so have developed ways to safeguard the pride of the client without having the barter become a "dual relationship." One practice was to have the client donate his or her services to a community organization rather than to the psychologist.

2.24.5.3 Other Comments on Similarities

There are many other provisions in which there are slight differences in wording, but substantial agreement in content, among the codes. Sinclair (1996) summarizes the strengths and weaknesses of the codes by stating that:

> the three codes complement one another, serving different purposes and providing both overlapping and singular examples of psychologists' responsibilities. The current versions are attempts by three different bodies of psychologists in Canada and the United States at similar points in time, to define the obligations of psychologists.

2.24.6 CAUSES OF DISCIPLINARY ACTION AND THE DISCIPLINARY DATA BANK

The nature of any code of conduct necessarily flows from the types of complaints that a jurisdiction receives or that an organization finds are being brought against its membership. For example, in earlier APA ethics codes, the references to dual relationships were more general and aspirational than the specific wording regarding sexual relationships with former clients contained in the 1992 *Ethical Principles of Psychologists and Code of Conduct* of the APA as noted below.

Principle 6a of the APA 1989 *Ethical Principles of Psychologists* states:

> Psychologists are continually cognizant of their own needs and of their potentially influential position vis-à-vis persons such as clients, students and subordinates. They avoid exploiting the trust and dependency of such persons. ... Examples of such dual relationships include, but are not limited to, ... sexual intimacies with clients. (p. 393)

The 1992 APA code is far more explicit than its predecessor, as is the ASPPB Code of Conduct.

2.24.6.1 Cause for Changes in the Codes

Changes in the codes of conduct of governmental jurisdictions as well as in the APA and ASPPB Codes, especially regarding dual relationships, were due in large measure to the increasing number of charges brought against psychologists across the country for violating the dual relationship provisions of the existing codes. Because the relevant provision of the code was often phrased in general terms, the ASPPB determined that this essential part of their code needed a definitive clear statement and therefore provided it.

2.24.6.2 Disciplinary Data Bank System

Data collected by the ASPPB Disciplinary Data System in recent years is evidence that these changes were, indeed, needed. Because the ASPPB collects this data, it is able to aid jurisdictions in determining the need to discipline psychologists who violate their codes of conduct in this respect, and the ASPPB also ensures that this information flows across jurisdictional lines so that, if a psychologist has been disciplined in one jurisdiction, all jurisdictions will be informed of this action and be able to react to it. In addition, by having data on the extent to which various areas of the code are being violated, organizations can continue to update their codes to provide more clearly defined rules for the practice of psychology in their jurisdictions.

All of the above depends on maintaining a constantly updated disciplinary data system to house the database for all of the jurisdictions. The ASPPB data bank has been in existence since 1983. The first report on disciplinary actions taken against psychologists by the member Boards was issued on August 15, 1983 (J. Pippin, personal communication, August 21, 1996). However, only since 1995 have the interactive aspects of the database been in place. This allows jurisdictions both to enter data and to check to see if an individual has violated the code in another jurisdiction. The pilot project, which has been in operation serving both small and large jurisdictions and connecting all of them with the ASPPB central office through a secured network, has recently been completed and was a huge success. In the past, two of the problems with the data bank have been the difficulty in collecting the data and convincing the various jurisdictions of the importance of this effort. It was also necessary to convince the jurisdictions of the importance of their supplying the information to the data bank in a timely manner in order to make the system truly useful. With the recent availability of an on-line service, compliance has increased. The ASPPB is now providing access to the system for all member jurisdictions, which was to be completed by October, 1996.

These data, so necessary to help the jurisdictions understand what they may be facing in terms of future disciplinary cases, also inform psychologists where, and what kinds of, education needs to be emphasized in teaching ethics and ethical dilemmas. Table 1 lists the reported disciplinary actions over the 13-year period from August 1983 through July 1996.

2.24.7 FUTURE DIRECTIONS

2.24.7.1 Code Revisions

As the field and practice of psychology change, a number of amendments will need to be made to the *ASPPB code of conduct* and to other organizations' ethics codes. Probably the two most significant developments for the future, and ones that will have huge implications for both professional organizations and licensure boards, are managed care and the Internet. Contracts which mental health providers are being directed to sign with managed care companies are, at least, ethically questionable. The provider is required to hold the company "harmless" and to limit information given to the client/patient, both of which place

Table 1 Reported disciplinary actions for psychologists August 1983–July 1996. Compiled from actions reported to the ASPPB Disciplinary Data System by ASPPB member boards. (Reprinted with the permission of ASPPB.)

Reason for disciplinary action	*Number disciplined*
Sexual/dual relationship with patient	471[a]
Unprofessional/unethical/negligent practice	344[b]
Fraudulent acts	142
Conviction of crimes	105
Inadequate or improper supervision	60[c]
Impairment	52
Breach of confidentiality	45[d]
Improper/inadequate record keeping	41
Fraud in application for license	35
Failure to comply with continuing education requirements	12

[a]When this table was first compiled in January 1988, 45 psychologists had been disciplined for this reason. [b]In 1988 this total was 29. [c]This category doubled between August 1993 and May 1994. [d]There was a 51% increase in this category between August 1993 and May 1994.

the provider in a serious ethical dilemma. This means that organizations and jurisdictions must either change the nature of their codes to accommodate the managed care companies' requirements, or sanction the provider for not adhering more closely to the ethics code or code of conduct of these jurisdictions. New legislation has been introduced in a number of legislatures to remedy some of these problems; however, it will be a long time, if ever, before either the patient or the provider will have the necessary protection once afforded to individuals involved in psychological treatment.

2.24.7.2 New Developments

The Internet, World Wide Web, and other new and exciting communications developments also pose interesting problems for licensing boards. For example, if psychological services are provided by a psychologist on the Internet and a complaint results, which jurisdiction has authority over the provider—the one where the provider lives and works or the one where the client lives; both; or neither? What will happen to the requirement in the ASPPB code mentioned above that the professional has face-to-face contact with the client? What legal changes will be necessary to protect the public while increasing the use and effectiveness of treatment and/or assessment in the new media?

2.24.8 CONCLUSION

All of these codes are in a state of flux (as they should be), so the ways in which they converge and differ will continue to ebb and flow with time. As jurisdictions consider the development or improvement of their laws in this regard, the ASPPB model for a code of conduct should be of considerable assistance in helping each jurisdiction make sound decisions about what it needs to include in a legally defensible document for that jurisdiction. The ASPPB code provides a sound frame of reference for each jurisdiction to consider, because it contains sound, legal language that sets forth clearly and concisely the do's and don'ts governing the appropriate behavior of psychologists necessary to protect the public.

2.24.9 REFERENCES

American Psychological Association (1990). Ethical principles of psychologists (amended June 2, 1989). *American Psychologist, 45*(3). Washington, DC: Author.

American Psychological Association (1992). *Ethical principles of psychologists and code of conduct.* Washington, DC: Author.

Association of State and Provincial Psychology Boards (1991). *Code of conduct.* Montgomery, AL: Author.

Canadian Psychological Association (1991). *Canadian code of ethics for psychologists.* (Revised). Ottawa, ON; Canada: Author.

Sinclair, C. (1995). The Canadian code of ethics for psychologists. *First International Congress of Licensure, Certification, and Credentialling.* Association of State and Provincial Psychology Boards, New Orleans, LA, April.

Sinclair, C. (1996). A comparison of codes of professional conduct and ethics. In Professional Conduct and Discipline in Psychology. American Psychological Association. Washington, DC.

White v. North Carolina State Board of Examiners of Practicing Psychologists, 388 S.E. 2d 148 (N.C. App. 1990).

2.25
Legal Considerations in Practice

RANDOLPH P. REAVES
Association of State and Provincial Psychology Boards, Montgomery, AL, USA

2.25.1 INTRODUCTION

Many books can be and have been written about psychology and its interaction with the field of law. Just deciding where to begin to discuss psychology and law presents a dilemma of considerable proportions. Since the focus of this chapter is the application of law to the practice of psychology, one logical starting place would be the laws that regulate admission to practice the profession in the various US jurisdictions. However, it would probably benefit the reader to first review the meaning of certain words or terms used throughout the chapter.

2.25.2 DEFINITIONS

There are a number of words or terms that appear regularly throughout this chapter and some explanation is in order.

(i) *Agency.* This refers to an administrative body established by Congress or state legislatures to run the government on a day to day basis.

(ii) *Board.* This is often used to refer to the agency that regulates the practice of psychology in each US jurisdiction.

(iii) *Case law.* This is a term that refers to important provisions of judicial opinions that interpret the meaning of statutes or the common law.

(iv) *Certification.* This is the process by which a governmental or nongovernmental agency or association grants authority to use a specified title to an individual who has met predetermined qualifications.

(v) *Licensure.* This is the process by which an agency of government grants permission to an individual to engage in a given occupation upon finding that the applicant has attained the minimal degree of competency necessary to ensure that the public health, safety, and welfare will be reasonably well protected. Since the law establishing a licensed occupation usually sets forth the "scope of practice" covered by the act, licensing laws are often referred to as "practice acts."

(vi) *Regulations.* This is a term used to refer to the rules (or regulations) passed by federal or state agencies under the rule making authority typically delegated to the agency through its enabling legislation. Often the words rules and regulations are used together.

(vii) *Statute.* This refers to a law passed by Congress or a state legislature. Statutes are also referred to as acts or simply laws.

2.25.3 THE REGULATION OF THE PRACTICE OF PSYCHOLOGY

The first statute that legally recognized the practice of the profession was passed in the state of Connecticut in 1945. Over the course of the next 50 years almost every US jurisdiction passed a statute that either regulates the practice of psychology or dictates which individuals are legally entitled to refer to themselves as psychologists. These include all the states, and the District of Columbia, as well as the territories of Guam and Puerto Rico. In 1994, the US Virgin Islands passed a regulatory law. Given the small populations of the remaining US territories, it is entirely possible that the Virgin Islands is the last jurisdiction that will regulate the profession in this country.

2.25.3.1 Statutes Vary Significantly

Not all the statutes referred to above regulate the actual practice of psychology, but they comprise the clear majority. Those jurisdictions that regulate the practice have enacted laws that include a definition of practice and preclude unqualified and unlicensed persons from performing such functions. The definitions, of course, vary considerably. The definition contained in the Association of State and Provincial Psychology Board (ASPPB) (1992) Model Act reads:

> Practice of psychology is defined as the observation, description, evaluation, interpretation, and/or modification of human behavior by the application of psychological principles, methods, or procedures, for the purpose of preventing or eliminating symptomatic, maladaptive, or undesired behavior and of enhancing interpersonal relationships, work and life adjustment, personal effectiveness, behavioral health and mental health. The practice of psychology includes, but is not limited to, psychological testing and the evaluation or assessment of personal characteristics, such as intelligence, personality, abilities, interests, aptitudes, and neuropsychological functioning; counseling, psychoanalysis, psychotherapy, hypnosis, biofeedback, and behavior analysis and therapy; diagnosis and treatment of mental and emotional

disorder or disability, alcoholism and substance abuse, disorders of habit or conduct, as well as of the psychological aspects of physical illness, accident, injury, or disability; and psychoeducational evaluation, therapy, remediation, and consultation. Psychological services may be rendered to individuals, families, groups, organizations, institutions and the public. The practice of psychology shall be construed within the meaning of this definition without regard to whether payment is received for services rendered.

In other jurisdictions "title" acts regulate only the title "psychologist" allowing nonpsychologists to perform functions psychologists perform so long as they use other titles such as "therapist" or "psychotherapists." For example, Colorado Revised Statutes 12–43–216 (1992) Title Use Restriction states:

A psychologist, clinical social worker, marriage and family therapist, or professional counselor may only use the title for which he is licensed under this article. Except as provided in section 12–43–304 (5), no other person shall hold himself out to the public by any title or description of services incorporating the terms "licensed clinical social worker," "clinical social worker," "LCSW," "marriage and family therapist," "LMFT," "professional counselor," "psychologist," "psychology," or "psychological" and he shall not state or imply that he is licensed to practice clinical social work, marriage and family therapy, professional counseling, or psychology. Nothing in this section shall prohibit a person from stating or using the educational degrees which he has obtained.

The viability of "title acts" have been questioned since the decision of the US Court of Appeals for the Eleventh Circuit in *Abrahamson v. Gonzales (1992)*. In this decision this federal court held that denying individuals the right to use the title psychologist while they are legally allowed to perform the functions of a psychologist, violates such practitioners rights to commercial free speech and was unconstitutional. Since the *Abrahamson v. Gonzales (1992)* decision, a number of jurisdictions including Arizona, Florida, Mississippi, and Rhode Island have amended their regulatory statutes in favor of practice acts.

No two psychology regulatory acts are the same, although the pattern of regulation is similar. Most such acts contain definitions, the size and composition of a board of examiners, qualifications for licensure, grounds for disciplinary sanction, renewal requirements and a prohibition against unauthorized practice. Most acts reference some recognized Code of Ethics or Code of Conduct and all include a provision allowing the board to adopt rules and regulations to flesh out the broad parameters of regulatory authority contained in the statute. The boards utilize the rule making process to further define provisions on education, training and other requirements and to detail the everyday operation of the agency.

2.25.3.2 Qualifications for Licensure

One of the major differences among the jurisdictions relates to the level of training required for independent practice. The majority of US jurisdictions require a doctoral degree, although the actual definition of doctoral degree varies among jurisdictions.

Some jurisdictions require a master's degree to qualify for independent practice, however, those jurisdictions comprise a distinct minority that includes North Carolina, Puerto Rico, Vermont, and West Virginia. Many jurisdictions license at both educational levels but require "master's level" psychologists to practice under the supervision of licensed doctoral level psychologists. Titles utilized by these practitioners typically include psychological assistants, associates, and examiners.

Most US jurisdictions issue a generic license entitling the holder of the license to practice psychology. Some states such as Hawaii have chosen to credential only those psychologists that provide health services. Other jurisdictions issue generic licenses and confer health service provider (HSP) designation upon properly qualified practitioners.

There are experience requirements in most US jurisdictions. Typically, two years of supervised experience is required, although the predoctoral year of internship qualifies as a year of experience. Almost every jurisdiction requires passage of the Examination for Professional Practice in Psychology and some form of oral or jurisprudence examination.

At least one jurisdiction, South Carolina, issues licenses in specialty areas, such as clinical, counseling, school, and industrial/organizational psychology. Most jurisdictions, however, recognize individual practitioner's documented areas of competence but do not issue an actual license in the areas or specialties.

School psychology is a recognized specialty in the field and there are many doctoral level school psychologists practicing today. In a few states, which include Ohio and Texas, school psychologists are licensed by the state psychology boards. However, the vast majority of school psychologists do not have doctoral degrees and are not credentialed by boards of psychological examiners, but rather are certified by state boards of education. In most jurisdictions, school psychologists are restricted to practicing within the public school systems and are not allowed to practice independently.

Before closing this section, it should be noted that most psychology regulatory laws contain certain exemptions. These provisions typically exempt individuals in certain practice settings from the application of the statute. It is not unusual for a US jurisdiction to exempt psychologists employed by state or federal governments from meeting the requirements of the regulatory law so long as they only practice psychology within the exempt setting.

It is very important to remember that all psychology boards have rule making powers. These rules can relate to many aspects of practice, from the applicable code of conduct to the length of time records must be retained. Psychologists in every jurisdiction must not only know, but also follow these rules on a regular basis.

2.25.4 THE BUSINESS OF PRACTICING PSYCHOLOGY

Psychologists practicing independently are professionals, but also members of the business community. Like other business people, they are subject to state, federal, and local laws.

2.25.4.1 State Regulation of the Business of Practicing Psychology

Every state, territory, and the District of Columbia have statutes that involve the business practice of psychologists. Some involve reimbursement programs. Others relate to the forms of business practice available to psychologists.

The typical business forms of practice include solo practitioners, partnerships, and professional associations (PAs) or professional corporations (PCs). Many states have passed laws creating a new business entity known as limited liability companies (LLCs). There may be other forms of business practice in some jurisdictions.

Each of these business forms must comply with state and local laws and regulations. Each is required to obtain and renew various business licenses, deduct applicable taxes, and follow all applicable zoning and building laws or codes.

Many states impose restrictions on the corporate practice of professions. It is not unusual for a state statute to forbid stock ownership by nonprofessionals or to prohibit different professionals from holding stock in the same professional corporation. For example,

> **Purpose for which professional corporations may be organized.** Domestic professional corporations may be organized under this article only for the purpose of rendering professional services and services ancillary thereto within a single profession, except that, the same professional corporation or not-for-profit professional corporation may render both medical and dental services, provided that in the case of a professional corporation, at least one shareholder of such professional corporation is a duly licensed medical professional and at least one shareholder is a duly licensed dental professional at the time both services are rendered, and each shareholder is a duly licensed medical or dental professional, or, in the case of a not-for-profit professional corporation, all of the professional services rendered by such corporation are rendered by duly licensed medical professionals and duly licensed dental professionals. (Code of Alabama 1975, Section 10–4–383)

All psychologists that practice independently must choose a form of business practice. It is certainly prudent to consult other knowledgeable professionals such as certified public accountants or attorneys before choosing which business entity to adopt.

2.25.4.2 State Laws that Impact the Practice of Psychology

There are state statutes that impact areas of practice that are not financial in nature. Every jurisdiction has at least one, but probably more, statutes that relate to the confidentiality of patient communications or records. The statutes vary widely and the practitioner must know and understand these legal requirements. For an example of the difference in such confidentiality statutes compare Idaho, Idaho Code §54–2314 (1992) and Oklahoma, Oklahoma Statutes Title 59, §1376 (1993).

> **Privileged communication—confidential relations and communications between psychologist and client.** A person licensed as a psychologist under the provisions of this act cannot, without the written consent of his client, be examined in a civil or criminal action as to any information acquired in the course of his professional services in behalf of the client. The confidential relations and communications between a psychologist and his client are on the same basis as those provided by law between an attorney and client, and nothing in this article shall be construed to require any such privileged communication to be disclosed. (Idaho Code §54–2314(1992))

> **Confidential communications—disclosure—exceptions—threats of patient to self or others.** All communications between a licensed psychologist and

the individual with whom the psychologist engages in the practice of psychology are confidential. At the initiation of the professional relationship the psychologist shall inform the patient of the following limitations to the confidentiality of their communications. No psychologist, colleague, agent or employee of any psychologist, whether professional, clerical, academic or therapeutic, shall disclose any information acquired or revealed in the course of or in connection with the performance of the psychologist's professional services, including the fact, circumstances, findings or records of such services, except under the following circumstances:

1. Pursuant to the provisions of Section 2503 of Title 12 of the Oklahoma Statutes or where otherwise provided by law;
2. Upon express, written consent of the patient;
3. Upon the need to disclose information to protect the rights and safety of self or others if:
   a. the patient presents a clear and present danger to himself and refuses explicitly or by behavior to voluntarily accept further appropriate treatment. In such circumstances, where the psychologist has a reasonable basis to believe that a patient can be committed to a hospital pursuant to Section 5–401 of Title 43A of the Oklahoma Statutes, the psychologist shall have a duty to seek commitment. The psychologist may also contact members of the patient's family, or other individuals if in the opinion of the psychologist, such contact would assist in protecting the safety of the patient.
   b. the patient has communicated to the psychologist an explicit threat to kill or inflict serious bodily injury upon a reasonably identified person and the patient has the apparent intent and ability to carry out the threat. In such circumstances the psychologist shall have a duty to take reasonable precautions. A psychologist shall be deemed to have taken reasonable precautions if the psychologist makes reasonable efforts to take one or more of the following actions:
      (i) communicates a threat of death or serious bodily injury to the reasonably identified person,
      (ii) notifies an appropriate law enforcement agency in the vicinity where the patient or any potential victim resides,
      (iii) arranges for the patient to be hospitalized voluntarily, or
      (iv) takes appropriate steps to initiate proceedings for involuntary hospitalization pursuant to law.
   c. the patient has a history of physical violence which is known to the psychologist and the psychologist has a reasonable basis to believe that there is clear and imminent danger that the patient will attempt to kill or inflict serious bodily injury upon a reasonably identified person. In such circumstances the psychologist shall have a duty to take reasonable precaution. A psychologist shall be deemed to have taken reasonable precautions if the psychologist makes reasonable efforts to take one or more of the following actions:
      (i) communicates a threat of death or serious bodily injury to the reasonably identified person,
      (ii) notifies an appropriate law enforcement agency in the vicinity where the patient or any potential victim resides,
      (iii) arranges for the patient to be hospitalized voluntarily, or
      (iv) takes appropriate steps to initiate proceedings for involuntary hospitalization pursuant to law.
   d. nothing contained in subparagraph (b) of this paragraph shall require a psychologist to take any action which, in the exercise of reasonable professional judgment, would endanger the psychologist or increase the danger to a potential victim or victims, or
   e. the psychologist shall only disclose that information which is essential in order to protect the rights and safety of others;
4. In order to collect amounts owed by the patient for professional services rendered by the psychologist or employees of the psychologist. Provided, the psychologist may only disclose the nature of services provided, the dates of services, the amount due for services and other relevant financial information. If the patient raises as a defense to said action, a substantive assertion concerning the competence of a psychologist or the quality of the services provided, the psychologist may disclose whatever information is necessary to rebut such assertion;
5. In any proceeding brought by the patient against the psychologist and in any malpractice, criminal or license revocation proceeding in which disclosure is necessary or relevant to the claim or defense of the psychologist; or
6. In such situations as shall be defined by the rules and regulations of the Board. (Oklahoma Statutes Title 59, §1376 (1993))

2.25.4.3 State Child and Elderly Abuse Reporting Acts

All states mandate reporting of suspected child abuse. Some states mandate the reporting of suspected abuse of the elderly. Again these statutes vary widely and the competent practitioner must understand the applicable statutes. Compare the wide ranging difference in such laws:

Mandatory reporting.
(a) All hospitals, clinics, sanitariums, doctors, physicians, surgeons, medical examiners, coroners, dentists, osteopaths, optometrists, chiropractors, podiatrists, nurses, school teachers and officials, peace officers, law enforcement officials, pharmacists, social workers, day care workers or employees, mental health professionals or any

other person called upon to render aid or medical assistance to any child, when such child is known or suspected to be a victim of child abuse or neglect, shall be required to report, or cause a report to be made of the same, orally, either by telephone or direct communication immediately followed by a written report, to a duly constituted authority. (Code of Alabama 1975, Section 26–14–3)

Report, duty; time

(a) Except as provided in subdivision (b), any child care custodian, health practitioner, employee of a child protective agency, child visitation monitor, firefighter, animal control officer, or humane society officer who has knowledge of, or observes a child, in his or her professional capacity or within the scope of his or her employment, whom he or she knows or reasonably suspects has been the victim of child abuse, shall report the known or suspected instance of child abuse to a child protective agency immediately or as soon as practically possible by telephone and shall prepare and send a written report thereof within 36 hours of receiving the information concerning the incident. A child protective agency shall be notified and a report shall be prepared and sent even if the child has expired, regardless of whether or not the possible abuse was a factor contributing to the death, and even if suspected child abuse was discovered during an autopsy. For the purposes of this article, "reasonable suspicion" means that it is objectively reasonable for a person to entertain a suspicion, based upon facts that could cause a reasonable person in a like position, drawing when appropriate on his or her training and experience, to suspect child abuse. For the purpose of this article, the pregnancy of a minor does not, in and of itself, constitute a basis of reasonable suspicion of sexual abuse.

(b) Any child care custodian, health practitioner, employee of a child protective agency, child visitation monitor, firefighter, animal control officer, or humane society officer who has knowledge of or who reasonably suspects that mental suffering has been inflicted upon a child or that his or her emotional well-being is endangered in any other way, may report the known or suspected instance of child abuse to a child protective agency.

(c) Any commercial film and photographic print processor who has knowledge of or observes, within the scope of his or her professional capacity or employment, any film, photograph, videotape, negative, or slide depicting a child under the age of 14 years engaged in an act of sexual conduct, shall report the instance of suspected child abuse to the law enforcement agency having jurisdiction over the case immediately, or as soon as practically possible, by telephone, and shall prepare and send a written report of it with a copy of the film, photograph, videotape, negative, or slide attached within 36 hours of receiving the information concerning the incident. As used in this subdivision, "sexual conduct" means any of the following:

(1) Sexual intercourse, including genital–genital, oral–genital, anal–genital, or oral–anal, whether between persons of the same or opposite sex or between humans and animals.

(2) Penetration of the vagina or rectum by any object.

(3) Masturbation for the purpose of sexual stimulation of the viewer.

(4) Sadomasochistic abuse for the purpose of sexual stimulation of the viewer.

(5) Exhibition of the genitals, pubic, or rectal areas of any person for the purpose of sexual stimulation of the viewer.

(d) Any other person who has knowledge of or observes a child whom he or she knows or reasonably suspects has been a victim of child abuse may report the known or suspected instance of child abuse to a child protective agency.

(e) When two or more persons who are required to report are present and jointly have knowledge of a known or suspected instance of child abuse, and when there is agreement among them, the telephone report may be made by a member of the team selected by mutual agreement and a single report may be made and signed by the selected member of the reporting team. Any member who has knowledge that the member designated to report has failed to do so shall thereafter make the report.

(f) The reporting duties under this section are individual, and no supervisor or administrator may impede or inhibit the reporting duties, and no person making a report shall be subject to any sanction for making the report. However, internal procedures to facilitate reporting and apprise supervisors and administrators of reports may be established provided that they are not inconsistent with this article. The internal procedures shall not require any employee required to make reports pursuant to this article to disclose his or her identity to the employer.

(g) A county probation or welfare department shall immediately, or as soon as practically possible, report by telephone to the law enforcement agency having jurisdiction over the case, to the agency given the responsibility for investigation of cases under Section 300 of the Welfare and Institutions Code, and to the district attorney's office every known or suspected instance of child abuse, as defined in Section 11165.6, except acts or omissions coming within subdivision (b) of Section 11165.2, or reports made pursuant to Section 11165.13 based on risk to a child which relates solely to the inability of the parent to provide the child with regular care due to the parent's substance abuse, which shall be reported only to the county welfare department. A county probation or welfare department also shall send a written report thereof within 36 hours of receiving the information concerning the incident to any agency to which it is required to make a telephone report under this subdivision. A law enforcement agency shall immediately, or as soon as practically possible, report by telephone to the agency given responsibility for investigation of cases under Section 300 of the Welfare and Institutions Code and to the district attorney's office every known or suspected instance of child abuse reported to it, except acts or omissions coming within subdivision (b) of Section 11165.2, which shall be reported only to the county welfare department. A law enforcement agency shall report to the county welfare department every known or suspected instance of child abuse reported to it which is alleged to have occurred as a result of the action of a person responsible for the child's welfare, or as the result of the failure of a person responsible for the child's welfare to adequately protect the minor from abuse when the person responsible for the child's welfare knew or reasonably should have known that the minor was in danger of abuse. A law enforcement agency also shall send a written report thereof within 36 hours of receiving the information concerning the incident to any agency to which it is required to make a telephone report under this subdivision. (California Penal Code §11166 (West 1995))

As mentioned, some jurisdictions require psychologists to report suspected abuse of the elderly. An example from Missouri reads:

Report of elder abuse, penalty—false report, penalty—evidence of prior convictions
1. When any physician, medical examiner, coroner, dentist, chiropractor, optometrist, podiatrist, resident intern, nurse, hospital and clinic personnel engaged in examination, care or treatment of persons, or other health practitioner, psychologist, mental health professional, social worker, adult day care center worker, nursing home worker, probation or parole officer, Christian Science practitioner, peace officer or law enforcement official, or other person with responsibility for the care of a person sixty years of age or older has reasonable cause to suspect that such a person has been subjected to abuse or neglect or observes such a person being subjected to conditions or circumstances which would reasonably result in abuse or neglect, he shall immediately report or cause a report to be made to the department in accordance with the provisions of sections 660.250 to 660.295, RSMo. Any other person who becomes aware of circumstances which may reasonably be expected to be the result of or result in abuse or neglect may report to the department.
2. Any person who knowingly fails to make a report as required in subsection 1 of this section is guilty of a class A misdemeanor.
3. Any person who purposely files a false report of elder abuse or neglect shall be guilty of a class A misdemeanor.
4. Every person who has been previously convicted of or pled guilty to making a false report to the department and who is subsequently convicted of making a false report under subsection 3 of this section is guilty of a class D felony.
5. Evidence of prior convictions of false reporting shall be heard by the court, out of the hearing of the jury, prior to the submission of the case to the jury, and the court shall determine the existence of the prior convictions. (Missouri Revised Statutes §565.188 (1993))

2.25.4.4 Federal Laws Impacting the Practice of Psychology

There are many federal laws that relate to the practice of psychology. These laws can probably be lumped into three groups that would include tax law, reimbursement programs, and statutes that protect the confidentiality of patient records.

The Internal Revenue Code mandates that psychologists adhere to the financial requirements of the business side of practice. Deductions for employees income tax withholdings, Federal Insurance Contributions Act (FICA) and Federal Unemployment Tax Act (FUTA) are required.

A whole book could be written regarding the federal programs that provide reimbursement to psychologists and other health care professionals for services provided to covered individuals. Some examples include the Civilian Health Programs for the Uniformed Services (CHAMPUS), Medicare, and Medicaid.

2.25.4.4.1 CHAMPUS

The Civilian Health and Medical Program for the Uniformed Services provides nonmilitary health benefits to active duty military personnel, retired personnel and their dependents, and to dependents of deceased military personnel. Under CHAMPUS, a psychologist can obtain reimbursement for certain services by meeting qualifications and conditions (Reaves, 1996).

2.25.4.4.2 Medicare

In the United States, Medicare is a federally financed health benefits program primarily for persons aged 65 or older (Medicare Act, 1965). Medicare also covers certain disabled individuals. Medicare is administered by the states; however, the Health Care Finance Administration (HCFA), which is part of the United States Department of Health and Human Services, establishes the relevant rules and regulations. Reimbursement for psychologists' services provided to Medicare beneficiaries is severely restricted, although some recent changes allow for reimbursement on a limited basis.

2.25.4.4.3 Medicaid

Medicaid is a medical-assistance program for certain low-income persons in the United States. The Medicaid program is administered by individual states under broad federal guidelines (Medicaid Act, as amended 1984). Unlike Medicare, which is a federally financed and regulated program, Medicaid is financed by a combination of federal and state funds. The rules governing eligibility, the coverage of treatments, services and procedures, and the method and amount of reimbursement vary widely from jurisdiction to jurisdiction.

The importance of Medicaid to psychologists can vary greatly as well, depending on their practice location and their ability to serve the indigent population (Reaves, 1995).

These statutes contain broad provisions that are further defined by agency rule. Psychologists must adhere to these statutes and their attendant rules or run the risk of serious liability.

2.25.4.5 Other State and Federal Laws Impacting the Practice of Psychology

2.25.4.5.1 Freedom of choice

Approximately 40 states and the District of Columbia have freedom of choice laws that prohibit health insurers from restricting the licensed providers from whom an individual may obtain certain psychological services. These laws are important to the practice of psychology because they assure the patient the right to see nonphysician as well as physician mental health care providers. Some of these laws also are referred to as "direct recognition" laws because they afford the consumer the right to have reimbursed services of a specified professional without a prior physician referral. Freedom of choice and direct recognition are distinct concepts, however, and some state laws provide freedom of choice only after physician referral, that is, without direct recognition of psychologists; at least one federal statute complicates this area. The Employee Retirement Insurance Security Act (ERISA) pre-empts such state statutes and makes them inapplicable to health plans covered by this law.

2.25.4.5.2 Laws prohibiting certain billing practices

There are statutes that prohibit certain types of billing practices. These include federal laws against fraud and abuse in the Medicaid and Medicare programs and state laws against theft, kickbacks, fee splitting, fraud, and similar activities. Health care fraud has been identified as a significant contributor to rising health costs in the United States, and therefore, these fraud and abuse laws have been enacted in many jurisdictions as well as at the federal level.

2.25.4.5.3 Laws that involve the legal system

Every day, the number of psychologists called upon to testify in courtrooms grows larger. Psychological testimony is useful and often critical to decisions regarding competency, child custody, and criminal responsibility. There are hundreds of federal and state laws that could impact such testimony such as laws relating to evidence and confidential communications. An effort to discuss such a lengthy body of law is beyond the scope of this chapter.

2.25.4.5.4 Commitment laws

It should be noted that each jurisdiction has its own unique set of statutes and regulations that concern both voluntary and involuntary commitment of the insane or incapacitated. Psychologists are often called upon to express opinions as to whether individuals should or should not be committed to treatment facilities. These laws are by their very nature complex. Psychologists must know and understand such statutes before attempting to testify as experts in such proceedings.

2.25.5 CIVIL, CRIMINAL, AND LICENSE RELATED LIABILITY

2.25.5.1 Civil Liability

This chapter would not be complete without some explanation of the liability that exists for the negligent, incompetent, or illegal practice of the profession. These lawsuits are based on statutes, common law and rapidly expanding case law.

2.25.5.1.1 Failure to warn

There are probably very few members of the psychological community who are not familiar with the name "Tarasoff." Tatiana Tarasoff was a California teenager killed by a young man (Poddar) who was a patient at Cowell Memorial Hospital at the University of California at Berkeley. The killer was examined prior to the crime by a psychologist who recommended that he be committed, by two psychiatrists who concurred with this evaluation and recommendation, and by another psychiatrist, chief of the department, who countermanded the psychologist's recommendation and directed the staff to take no action to confine him.

Without belaboring the facts, the man carried out his previously expressed threat and killed the unknowing victim. One other important, very discouraging fact, is that the psychologist warned the campus police. Three officers took Poddar into custody, but released him because they considered him rational.

The importance of the Tarasoff case is in the conclusions reached by the Supreme Court of California regarding the liability of the psychologist and psychiatrists. That court held that when such a professional determines, or pursuant to the standards of the profession should determine, that a patient presents a serious danger of violence to another, he incurs an obligation to use reasonable care to protect the intended victim from such danger. Further, the discharge of this duty may require the therapist to take one or more various steps depending on the nature of the case, including warning the victim or others likely to apprise the victim of the danger, notifying the police, or taking whatever steps are reasonably necessary under the circumstances. The duty may also extend to other foreseeable persons who may be injured if the threat is carried out, such as a young child of the intended victim.

In another California case, an appellate court upheld a "dangerous patient" exception to the psychotherapist–patient privilege. The psychologist involved had disclosed to two women his fear that both might be harmed by either of two patients. He advised them of communications made in therapy sessions and reflected on audiotape. This court held that the protective privilege ends where the public's peril begins.

The usefulness of this theory of liability is not limited to California; perhaps as many as six or seven other jurisdictions in different parts of the United States have embraced this theory. These now include Colorado (Perreira v. Colorado, 1989), Georgia (Bradley Center Inc. v. Wessner, 1982), Kansas (Durflinger v. Artiles, 1983), Kentucky (Evans v. Morehead Clinic, 1988), Michigan (Davis v. Lhim, 1983/1988), North Carolina, and Texas (Zezulka v. Thapar, 1996). In other states, such as Wisconsin, significant settlements have been reached based on such theories (Lindsey v. Rousseau, 1993). The "duty to warn" can be found in the Restatement(2d) of Torts. Section 315 states:

> There is no duty so to control the conduct of a third person as to prevent him from causing physical harm to another unless:
> (a) a special relation exists between the actor and the third person which imposes a duty upon the actor to control the third person's conduct, or
> (b) a special relation exists between the actor and the other which gives to the other a right to protection.

In 1989, the Arizona Supreme Court adopted a "zone of danger" test as the scope of a psychiatrist's duty to protect third parties. In this case, the foreseeability of the victim was the key (Hamman v. County of Maricopa, 1989). However, it is not a theory that will be easily accepted by many courts in our present conservative era. Similar cases have been lost in Connecticut (Fraser v. US, 1996), Indiana (Webb v. Jarvis, 1990), Iowa (Matter of Estate of Votteler, 1982), Minnesota (Cairl v. State, 1982), and South Carolina (Ellis v. US, 1978), and there are a variety of defenses to such suits.

2.25.5.1.2 Failure to prevent suicide

Many civil lawsuits are brought against psychologists for failing to prevent patients or clients from taking their own lives. The theory of liability is very similar to that in failure to protect cases. A psychologist with a genuine concern for a patient in such conditions should consider options including: therapeutic management of patients; discussing the matter with the patient; warning potential victims; calling police; seeking involuntary commitment of patient, consistent with state laws; referring the patient to a physician or another provider for prescription of medication; seeking assistance of other providers, clergy or friends of the patient; and trying to involve the patient and family or others in conferring and resolving the threating situation.

Record keeping in such cases is essential. Particular care should be given to recording: precisely what the patient said or did bearing on threats of violence; when the therapist learned what; features of the patient's personal history or clinical status that caused the therapist to believe or disbelieve that violence would occur; and exactly what the therapist did to prevent or protect against the threat.

2.25.5.1.3 Failure to protect

Closely akin to "failure to warn" cases are those referred to as "failure to protect" cases. They also are similar to negligent release cases, and both causes of action are typically alleged.

A "failure to protect" case differs from a "failure to warn" case in that the victim in the former is rarely identified or identifiable. Liability is predicated upon the negligence of the provider, which allows the patient access to the victim.

A good example is *Tamsen v. Weber* (1990), in which a patient escaped from the Arizona State Hospital and later abducted a passerby and beat her severely. The litigation later revealed that Traham (the patient) was admitted to the hospital as a danger to himself. While there he attempted suicide. Records that were ultimately produced indicated he was suffering from major depression recurrent with psychotic features and as one expert testified "thinking of killing people."

Nevertheless, the attending psychiatrist granted Traham unsupervised ground privileges. During an unsupervised period on the hospital grounds, he escaped and assaulted Tamsen the next day. The Arizona Court of Appeals held that the psychiatrist owed a duty to protect Tamsen from the violent acts of Traham although Tamsen was not an identifiable victim. Therefore, the alleged negligence in granting unsupervised ground privileges should have gone to a jury on the issue of causation.

An interesting and important case decided in 1994 illustrates how far this liability may extend. In *Almonte v. New York Medical College* (1994), a federal district court refused to dismiss a case against New York Medical College and a professor employed by the college. Both were sued by the parents of a child who was sexually assaulted by a psychiatrist who had trained at the college and had received psychoanalytic training from the individual defendant (Ingram). During the course of his training, the perpetrator (DeMasi) revealed to Ingram that he was a pedophiliac and intended to pursue a career in child psychiatry. The court noted that Ingram, as DeMasi's instructor/analyst, had a measure of control not present in traditional analyst–voluntary patient relationships; he had available to him feasible and not unreasonably burdensome mechanisms for controlling DeMasi. The court also concluded that if no other duty was owed, Ingram had at least the duty to warn or take other steps to protect future patients and therefore the complaint stated a viable claim against Ingram for failure to exercise reasonable care to protect the plaintiffs' son from foreseeable harm.

Some cases that involve harm done by one patient to another might logically fall in this area. A good example is *Halverson v. Pikes Peak Family Counseling and Mental Health Center, Inc.* (1991). Here a patient was sexually assaulted by another patient with a history of violent behavior while she was an inpatient at the facility.

Before leaving this area of liability, it would be prudent to explore the duty to warn or protect foreseeable victims from patients with sexually transmittable diseases. The problem of confidentiality and AIDS poses a dilemma for practitioners. Already a number of physicians have been sued by patients on such theories as negligent infliction of emotional distress when treated by an HIV-positive practitioner who failed to reveal the condition and obtain consent (Faya v. Almaraz, 1993). Many therapists are concerned with the notion that they might be put in the position of having to advise an individual that, should the presence of the HIV virus be revealed to them, they would have no choice but to warn foreseeable victims. That concern is understandable. However, viewing that situation from a purely legal point of view, it easily fits into the failure to warn/protect doctrines.

There is no doubt that an individual who is HIV positive could do considerable harm to an unknowing spouse and/or sexual partner(s). Already there have been numerous successful suits against sexual partners (Kathleen K. v. Robert B., 1984). In many cases, those spouses or partners would be known to the provider and therefore foreseeable victims who could be notified. Arguably, courts will find it easier to uphold a failure to warn (protect) theory in this situation than with a potentially violent person.

A working group on HIV confidentiality at Creighton University Center for Health Policy and Ethics (1991) after conducting a national study on confidentiality in maternal and pediatric HIV, also citing *Tarasoff v. Regents of the University of California* (1976), suggests a formula for decision-making relative to such disclosures:

> When the risk of infection is significant, the identity of the third party is known, warning is likely to be effective in preventing infection, and every reasonable measure to convince the patient to disclose has failed, professionals have a strong ethical obligation to warn those at risk.

At least two courts have agreed. In a 1995 decision, the Alaska Supreme Court found that a physician's disclosure to a husband that his wife had tested positive for the HIV virus was justified in light of the physician's duty to protect third parties from foreseeable exposure to contagious disease. The court described the disclosure as "privileged as a matter of law" (Chizman v. Mackie, 1995). In another 1995 decision, *Reisner v. Regents of the University of California* (1995), the California Court of Appeal held that a third party could sue a physician who failed to advise his girlfriend that she was infected with HIV.

2.25.5.1.4 Failure to properly supervise hospitalized patients

This is another cause of action for negligent conduct. Due to the special relationship which exists between a therapist and a patient, a recognizable duty often arises to protect the patient from himself. Breach of the duty occurs when the therapist does, or more often fails to do something which allows the patient to harm himself. (The reader should note that while many of these cases involve hospitals, invariably the individual providers are also sued.)

A good example of such a supervision case is *Smith v. Rush Presbyterian St. Luke's Medical Centre* (1980), a case in which a young male with "paranoid personality" was admitted to a psychiatric hospital. Following futile attempts to cut his wrists with a pop top, the patient was put on a "suicide risk" list. This classification required observation every 15 min. The patient was also placed in a room with an electrically operated bed and while unobserved, lowered the bed onto his neck and head. The jury verdict was $75 000.

There are a host of such cases and a variety of negligent acts or omissions involved. For instance, there is *Abille v. U.S.* (1980), where a psychiatric patient jumped from an Air Force hospital window. Not only was the patient unattended, but the window had no security device such as a detention screen. In *Pisel v. The Stamford Hospital* (1980), the patient, again unattended, wedged his head into the rails of his bed resulting in brain damage. With *Roesler v. Monora Medical Center* (1978), the patient used a pillowcase to strangle herself and in *Herndobler v. Riveredge Hospital* (1979), an unrestrained patient suffocated herself with a plastic garbage can liner.

There have been a great many cases in which courts have predicated liability on negligent supervision that resulted in injury to other patients. Almost all of these cases involve either rape or other serious physical injuries. Some were perpetrated by other patient, and some involve employees of the various institutions. Of particular concern is *James v. Albergo* (1993), in which an Illinois court held that neither the doctrines of sovereign immunity nor public official immunity barred a lawsuit brought against the professional staff of a state mental institution. In this case, parents alleged that professional personnel at the hospital had misdiagnosed the mental condition of their 5 year old child, recommended his treatment at the hospital, then improperly placed him under the supervision of another minor who eventually committed repeated acts of sexual abuse.

2.25.5.1.5 Negligent release of dangerous patients

Similar to the failure-to-protect type of negligence action is the suit brought for the negligent release of a dangerous patient. Take for instance *Davis v. Lihm* (1983/1988), a Michigan case in which the deceased's 25 year-old son was originally admitted to a state hospital with a diagnosis of paranoid schizophrenia and a history of suicide attempts. Over a 3 year period the patient was admitted and released five more times. His records indicated not only his suicidal tendencies, but the fact that he committed himself to avoid problems at home. Two weeks after his last discharge, his mother was shot and killed by her son while trying to prevent his suicide attempt. The case was tried on both theories, negligent release and failure to warn, and resulted in a jury verdict of $500 000. The case was reversed 5 years later, but on the ground of governmental immunity rather than failure to warn.

A North Carolina case, *Davis v. North Carolina Dept. of Human Resources* (1995), is worth noting. In this negligent release case, the appellate court agreed that liability existed due to the failure of a mental health professional to sufficiently warn a trial judge as to the dangerous nature of a criminal who was committed for such an evaluation.

Negligence in failing to admit suicidal patients or prematurely releasing such patients has also given rise to liability. An example is *Dunn v. Howard University Hospital* (1983), in which a 28 year-old woman was released from an emergency room after a short period of observation. She had been brought to the emergency room by a friend and complained of severe anxiety, depression, and guilt feelings. She also expressed a desire for suicide and self-maiming. The woman had a history of hospitalizations and was previously diagnosed as a manic depressive psychotic. After her release, she jumped to her death. A court later awarded her parents $500 000.

Failure to prevent a patient from escaping from a mental institution can also give rise to liability, particularly if others are injured apprehending the patient. A classic example is *Santangero v. State* (1993), in which two police officers were injured. Evidence in the case revealed that the patient had many previous successful escapes from the institution and that three of those escapes had been accomplished in the same manner. The court agreed that these facts indicated an unreasonable and careless attitude on the part of the state toward the safety of the public as it related to the custody and supervision of the patient. Additionally, the state also violated its regulations by marking the patient as "discharged" 30 days after his escape.

2.25.5.1.6 Negligent prescription of contraindicated drugs

Another cause of action which should be of interest to psychologists, as the movement for prescription privileges grows, is the negligent prescription of contraindicated drugs. This cause of action includes the same elements as other types of professional negligence. It goes without saying that almost every practitioner has a duty to act in a manner that does not cause the patient's condition to worsen. Breach of that duty occurs when the contraindicated drugs, that is, liable to cause the patient harm rather than cure, are prescribed.

A good example of this type of action is *Webb v. Lightburn* (1985), a Colorado suit settled in 1980 for $100 000. In this case the decedent was diagnosed as having a passive–aggressive personality disorder with depressive and hysterical features and a history of drug overdoses. Despite such, and only days after an attempted suicide, the defendant psychiatrist renewed two prescriptions for Seconal. The patient took them all a few days later and died.

Another $100 000 settlement was reached in 1979 in a New York case styled *Haggerty v. New York* (1985). In this case the deceased had been hospitalized previously for suicidal tendencies. On the occasion of his last commitment, Tofranil was prescribed for him, even though his medical records reflected the fact that Tofranil exacerbated his suicidal tendencies. While the ward attendant was asleep, the patient hanged himself with his belt. A similar case is *Greene v. Guarino* (1992). The case involves a substantial settlement for the estate of a man who allegedly committed suicide by ingesting a 30-day supply of an antidepressant. The psychiatrist who prescribed the drug was sued on the theory that he negligently provided a suicidal patient with a toxic amount of the drug.

These are the obvious types of cases, but when dealing with medication of the mentally ill, a number of other areas of potential liability arise. Without spending time outlining them, they include the failure to prescribe adequate antipsychotic medication allowing individuals to cause injury to themselves, an example of which is *Jansen v. University Hospital* (1983).

Another area of concern is the potential for creating a drug dependency. A large verdict resulted in the case of *Badger v. Greenfield* (1981), where a plaintiff produced sufficient proof that his psychiatrist negligently created a drug dependency which later resulted in the loss of significant income when the patient became unable to work. In a more likely scenario giving rise to liability, a physician continued to supply a teenager prescriptions for Preludin and Tuinol allegedly for weight reduction even after it was clear she had become addicted. Despite having promised her parents he would not prescribe for her any more, he did so, and she died of an overdose (Argus v. Scheppegrell, 1985).

Excessive administration of Antabuse has also resulted in liability with large verdicts (Sawyer v. Tauber, 1985), as well as negligent supervision of patients taking such medication (Medi-Stat, Inc. v. Kustunin, 1990). However, the main area of liability, with the largest verdicts, occurs with the improper use of tranquilizers such as Mellaril, Penothiazine, Stelazine, Haldol, and Triavil. A trilogy of cases arising in Iowa (Clites v. State of Iowa, 1982), Colorado (Collins v. Cushner, 1982) and Michigan (Faigenbaum v. Oakland, 1986) indicate that confined patients who develop tardive dyskinesia are the patients who will obtain the most staggering settlements and verdicts. However, for a case involving significant liability when a patient's Haldol dosage was suddenly reduced and damage occurred, see *Leal v. Simon* (1989).

2.25.5.1.7 Failure to report suspected child abuse

Providers should be familiar with mandatory reporting requirements involving suspected child abuse. Occasionally, providers are reluctant to report if the abuse appears to be an isolated event and the abusing parent has sought treatment.

The Missouri Court of Appeals addressed the issue of whether the alleged victim of child abuse could sue two psychologists for failing to comply with the state's Child Abuse Reporting Act. The court held that such a civil suit could not be predicated on the statute since the law did not address the issue of private actions and there was no basis to imply a private right of action since the law did not provide a civil remedy.

However, the court held that the child could bring an action based on common law negligence for failure to warn authorities of the abuse. The court held that the state's public policy favoring protection of children from sexual abuse supports the recognition of a common law duty in this type case. The court limited the right to sue only for failure to warn of specific risks of future harm to readily identifiable victims (Bradley v. Ray, 1995).

2.25.5.1.8 Negligence of auxiliaries

Prior to concluding this section on negligence, it should be noted that very often the person at fault in such cases is not the primary provider, but the staff or clinic auxiliary. The laws of agency and respondent superior require a principal to accept responsibility for the actions of her agents so long as the agent is acting within the scope of her employment.

If the primary provider hires any personnel to assist her in her practice, she must be aware that any negligent acts committed by her assistants will, more than likely, be imputed to her. This situation can be exacerbated if the assistant is not properly qualified, trained or supervised by the primary provider. A classic example is *Andrews v. US* (1984), where a physician's assistant engaged in sexual relations with a female patient under the guise of treatment. Another example is *Doe v. Belmont College* (1992), where a patient sued the counselor's partner, a licensed psychologist, for inadequate supervision and the college that employed both for negligent hiring.

An even better example is *Huntley v. State of New York* (1984), in which a patient at a state psychiatric hospital was permitted to leave the hospital premises and attempted to commit suicide by jumping from the roof of a nearby parking garage. Evidence later revealed that the patient had disclosed her specific suicide plans to a hospital staff member the day before the incident, and the staff member had failed to transmit such information to the staff psychiatrist who controlled the patient's privileges to leave the hospital premises. Auxiliaries should be instructed in writing regarding the confidential nature of patient records. If inappropriate release of such information violates written employee guidelines, liability may not extend to employers.

2.25.5.1.9 *Sexual relations with clients or patients*

Sexual intimacies with clients or patients are forbidden by all recognized codes of conduct. The harm such conduct does to victims has been studied and clearly documented (*Sexual misconduct in the practice of medicine*). Similar to the reactions of women who have been sexually assaulted, female patients tend to feel angry, abandoned, humiliated, mistreated, or exploited by their therapists. Some have even committed suicide (Koren v. Weihs, 1994). The largest civil judgments have been reserved for those professionals that engage in such heinous conduct.

At least one state's highest court has held that a psychologist who initiates sex with a patient can be liable for negligent infliction of emotional distress. In *Corgan v. Muehling* (1991), the Illinois Supreme Court also held that the patient need not allege or prove physical injury to pursue liability under this cause of action. Consent is no defense to this type of malpractice.

Additionally, some cases find that employment facilities are also liable when such conduct occurs. A good example is *Doe v. Samaritan Counseling Center* (1990). In at least two cases, liability attached when the provider engaged in a sexual relationship with the patient's spouse.

2.25.5.1.10 *Public disclosure of confidential information*

A very special relationship exists between therapists and their patients. Confidentiality of communication is the base upon which this relationship exists. Public disclosure of confidential communications can give rise to liability if the substance of the facts revealed is offensive, embarrassing, objectionable, or harmful to the patient's reputation (Horne v. Paton, 1973)

Practitioners should understand the differences in certain legal terms so that they can communicate more effectively with patients who know even less about the provider/patient relationship. The three important terms or concepts are privacy, confidentiality, and privilege. Reasonable definitions are:

(i) *Privacy*. Right to be left alone and to make decisions.

(ii) *Confidentiality*. Reasonable expectations that information will not be divulged.

(iii) *Privilege*. Legal protection against being forced to break the expectation of confidentiality.

Any practitioner would be well advised to make certain that the privilege exists before advising a potential client. The circumstances surrounding the manner in which the information was obtained may destroy the privilege (People v. District Court, County of Adams, 1990). Changing statutes and emerging case law make this a real concern. A good example of this dilemma is *State ex ref. Juvenile Dept. of Lincoln County v. Ashley* (1990), in which the Oregon Supreme Court ruled that the psychotherapist–patient privilege did not apply to communications made during drug counseling. Sometimes a supervising provider assumes the privilege attaches to supervisees, when, in fact, it may not. In many states, legislatures have abolished the privilege in cases involving workers' compensation claims (*Code of Alamaba* 1975, Section 25–5–77). However, a West Virginia physician was chagrined to learn that West Virginia statutes had only abolished the privilege for written medical reports. In *Morris v. Consolidation Coal Co.* (1994), an appellate court held that an injured worker could sue for unauthorized *ex parte* oral communication between the physician and an adversarial party that involved providing confidential information unrelated to written medical reports authorized by W.Va. Code 23-4-7. And, providers should not assume that just because the issue of a party's mental condition is raised in a civil proceeding, it automatically means the privilege has been waived.

Patients should obviously be informed of limitations on confidentiality. Suits can arise in the simplest of circumstances. For example, in *Prince v. St. Francis–St. George Hosp., Inc.* (1985), a provider and clinic were sued when a physician sent an insurance form to the client's husband's employer that indicated she was being treated for alcohol abuse. Suits occasionally are brought for wrongful disclosure when the patient becomes a danger to herself or others. However, at least two courts have recognized the provider's responsibility to warn intended victims and have dismissed suits against providers under the "dangerous patient" exception to the privilege (Mendendez v. Superior Court, 1992). It would also be an excellent idea to review some of the other case law in this area. Several courts have ruled favorably on plaintiffs' claims for invasion of privacy and intentional infliction of emotional distress. Psychologists treating patients suffering from acquired immunodeficiency syndrome should be especially careful and know not only case law but also antidiscrimination laws where such exist.

2.25.5.1.11 Confidentiality in divorce and child custody proceedings

In the area of child custody disputes, mental health professionals should act cautiously. Do not evaluate a minor without the custodial parent's consent. Know your state statutes as regards confidentiality, advise the parent(s) correctly, and document the advice carefully. Counsel defending such a claim should review the cases resolved in favor of defendants, such as *Werner v. Kliewer* (1985), *Jordan v. Kelly* (1984), and *Williams v. Congdon* (1979).

Another case of great significance is *Snow v. Koeppl* (1990), which involves the revelation of allegedly confidential information in a family court case. In this case, the Wisconsin Court of Appeals upheld a trial court's decision to dismiss claims for invasion of privacy and breach of confidentiality. The suit was brought against a psychologist who obtained and delivered to the court excerpts from the plaintiff's earlier counseling records pursuant to a court-ordered psychological evaluation of the plaintiff in a family court action. The appellate court agreed that the psychologist was entitled to absolute immunity.

The reviewing court concluded that a judicial order creating official duties, directly and closely connected to court proceedings, should be broadly construed in favor of the person required to act. Thus a directive to perform a psychological evaluation would be construed to protect the court official from liability for the examination and use of reports of earlier psychological counseling or therapy, since such information bore a general frame of reference and relation to the subject matter of the court's order.

A similar case is *Guity v. Kandilakis* (1991), where a psychologist was ordered by a trial court judge to testify about matters arising during joint counseling sessions with a husband and wife. When the husband later sued the psychologist, the court held that he was immune from suit since the court had ordered him to disclose. Just as important is *Howard v. Drapkin* (1990), in which a disgruntled parent sued a psychologist, hired by both parties to evaluate allegations of sexual abuse, for a custody proceeding. The trial and appellate courts agreed that:

(i) the psychologist was entitled to common-law immunity as a quasi-judicial officer participating in the judicial process; and

(ii) the psychologist was entitled to a statutory privilege for publication in a judicial proceeding.

In an important 1994 case, the Texas Supreme Court held that a mental health professional does not owe a duty to a parent not to negligently misdiagnose a child's condition. The court decided that while a risk of harm to a parent accused of sexual abuse was foreseeable, it was outweighed by the need to allow mental health professionals dealing with the sensitive issue of child abuse to exercise their professional judgment in diagnosing abuse "without the judicial imposition of a countervailing duty to third parties" (Bird v. W. C. W., 1994).

However, also note the case of *Awai v. Kotin* (1993), in which the Colorado Court of Appeals held that court-appointed psychologists were not entitled to absolute immunity from claims that they negligently treated a parent referred to them for evaluation in a divorce/child custody proceeding. The court held that absolute immunity for quasi-judicial functions applied only to those functions intimately related and essential to the judicial decision-making process.

Before leaving this area of potential liability, it would be prudent to review case law abrogating the statutory privilege in parental rights termination cases and divorce litigation. In Alabama, for example, there have been three such cases that give cause for much concern. These cases recognize that privileged communication exists, however, the courts have ruled that the welfare of the child outweighs the need for confidentiality. The New York case of *Matter of W.H.* (1993), a child neglect proceeding, is also instructive.

Mental health professionals should consider requiring patients to acknowledge, in writing, the limitations of confidentiality. Counsel dealing with a case involving alleged breach of confidentiality in US government facilities should review the federal Privacy Act.

2.25.5.1.12 Implanting false memories

One of the most controversial areas in psychology practice is the concept of repressed childhood memories. Much of the increase in the acceptance of this concept is credited to the publication in 1988 of *The courage to heal: A guide for women survivors of child sexual abuse* (Bass & Davis, 1988). Since its publication and other similar books, thousands of women have brought forth claims of childhood sexual abuse that they believed had been repressed due to the trauma involved.

One such case was brought in Ohio and resulted in a multimillion-dollar verdict against the uncle of a 33 year-old woman with such a claim.

In the last five years, serious questions have been raised concerning the validity of the concept of repressed memories. There have been studies demonstrating that people are extremely susceptible to suggestion and misinformation regarding their childhood memories and that memories in general are unreliable. A False Memory Syndrome Foundation has been created, which now has many chapters across the country.

Much of the rise and fall of the false memory concept parallels the similar rise and fall of abuse claims involving satanic cults. The rumors of widely spread satanic cults grew in the late 1970s and early 1980s and were popularized by various Christian evangelical groups and the media. In 1989, the book *Michelle remembers* (Smith & Pazder, 1989) was published and alleged a link between such abuse and repressed memories. In the past few years, there have been a number of events that have called into question the existence of such cults, as well as the validity of recovered memories. These include studies by the Federal Bureau of Investigation (Lanning, K. B.: *Ritual abuse: A law enforcement view or perspective,* 1991) and other publications (Wright, L.: *Remember satan,* 1994).

It will be years, perhaps many years, before the mental health community reaches consensus on these issues. However, there are therapists being sued for allegedly implanting false memories in patients' minds. The first such case was tried in California. In *Ramona v. Ramona* (1994), the jury returned a \$500 000 verdict against therapists the jury believed had, at least, reinforced memories that were false.

While certainly not as publicized as the Ramona case in California, two other courts have held that parents may pursue claims against mental health professionals for allegedly implanting false memories in their children who were patients of the providers. A case published in the federal reporter is *Sullivan v. Cheshier* (1994), in which a psychologist was sued by a patient's parents who alleged the false memory of sexual abuse by her sibling was implanted while the child was under hypnosis.

In reviewing the case, the federal court held that summary dismissal was inappropriate because a genuine issue of material fact existed. The court noted that the parents had conducted an investigation and found no evidence to corroborate the claims. Additionally, the parents produced a witness who denied the truth of the statements and that prior to the hypnosis sessions, the child had never made such claims. The court also noted that after the patient's statements of abuse, she declined all family contacts unless the family members admitted the truth of the statements.

In a 1995 Pennsylvania case, another federal district court held that parents (Tumans) who had paid for their daughter's (Diane) psychiatric treatment could pursue a breach of contract claim against mental health professionals who allegedly implanted false memories of abuse in the patient's mind. The parents had brought their 20 year-old daughter to a clinic (Genesis) to be treated for an eating disorder.

The clinic, a licensed psychologist, and a licensed social worker were sued. The agents of Genesis agreed to treat the young woman but required the parents to separate from their daughter for 2 years. The parents later alleged their daughter was brainwashed when the therapists implanted false memories that her parents were members of a satanic cult that had murdered her twin and sexually abused her. In group therapy sessions, Genesis counselors allegedly told Diane she had been a victim of a satanic cult, and Diane later made the same statements to the group. According to the Tuman's allegations, counselors solicited money from various sources and gave it to Diane to help her hide from her parents, who, according to the complaint, have not seen or heard from her in more than 2 years.

The court agreed that Diane's parents had adequately stated a breach of contract claim in that they alleged that Genesis counselors breached a contractual promise to provide their daughter with adequate care and to properly treat her eating disorder. The court rejected Genesis' contention that the Tumans' complaint was a negligence claim in disguise and should be dismissed.

The court dismissed a claim for negligence against Genesis, holding the entity did not owe a duty of care to Diane's parents. However, it refused to dismiss negligence claims against the counselors, saying it was reasonably foreseeable that the parents of a patient would be harmed by their negligent conduct. The court also declined to dismiss counts alleging defamation, intentional infliction of emotional distress, and misrepresentation, but did dismiss a claim for interference with filial relations, holding that Pennsylvania courts do not recognize such a cause of action (*Tuman v. Genesis Associates,* 1995).

In a 1994 case, *Farris v. Compton* (1994), the District of Columbia Court of Appeals entered an important ruling on the relevant statute of limitations in such cases. This court held that where the plaintiffs have alleged repression of childhood sexual abuse, their claims do not accrue until they have recovered their memories enough to know that they were injured and why.

The case involved two sisters who sued their brother alleging sexual abuse some 25 years earlier. The trial court dismissed the action, and the federal appellate court certified the statute of limitations question to the D.C. Court of Appeals. That court first noted that since the alleged tort had occurred when the plaintiffs were minors, the statute of limitations did not begin to run until they reached majority. At this point, the court found the plaintiffs had repressed memories of the abuse. And, the court concluded, their claims did not accrue until they discovered or should have discovered all of the essential elements of the cause of action.

The court rejected the defendant's contention that defending himself for actions that were admittedly 25 years old would be an unreasonable burden. It also disagreed with the defendant's assertion that an exception to the running of the limitations statute should only be made by the legislature, noting that it was the court's obligation to construe the word "accrues."

And in July 1995, a state district court jury in St. Paul, MN, awarded \$2.4 million to a Minnesota woman who claimed her psychiatrist planted false memories of sexual abuse in her mind. The plaintiff's husband was awarded \$210 000 for loss of consortium. According to a report appearing in the Bureau of National Affairs Health Law Reporter (Vol. 4, 1995), the plaintiff alleged that the psychiatrist told her she must have been repeatedly abused by several relatives and had no memory of such because she suffered from "repression and denial" and could not get better unless she not only remembered the abuse but also relived it and confronted her abusers.

Apparently, the plaintiff broke off relations with her immediate family. Additional allegations included the use of mind altering drugs and coercion, as well as failure to advise the plaintiff of the controversial nature of the treatment or alternatives to it. In January 1996, another St. Paul, MN, jury awarded more than \$2.5 million to another woman who brought similar claims against the same provider. This particular provider faces six more similar lawsuits from former patients (BNA Health Law Reporter, 1996b).

2.25.5.1.13 Other forms of civil liability

There are any number of other forms of civil liability that could be discussed but are limited by space constraints. These, however, do include what is known as a duty to inform, assault and battery, false imprisonment, fraud, and breach of contract.

2.25.5.2 Criminal Liability

Criminal liability is rarely associated with the practice of the mental health professions. However, there are activities that can result in arrest and incarceration. The two major causes of criminal liability are sex with clients and fraudulent billing practices.

2.25.5.2.1 Sexual abuse of patients

A number of states, including California, Colorado, Florida, Georgia, Idaho, Maine, Minnesota, New Hampshire, New Mexico, North Dakota, Texas, and Wisconsin have enacted statutes that make it a crime for a therapist to engage in sex with a client. Michigan has a statute that allows prosecution for sexual intercourse under the pretext of medical treatment. A number of cases, for such offenses as rape and sexual assault, have been tried to successful conclusions for the prosecution.

Wisconsin was the first state to pass a law to criminalize sex between therapist and client, in 1984. Its original law made such activity a Class A misdemeanor. In 1985, Wisconsin upgraded its statute to make sex between therapist and client a felony. That same year, Minnesota passed a law making such conduct a felony.

The Wisconsin statute reads as follows:

> 940.22 Sexual exploitation by therapist; duty to report.
> (2) Sexual contact prohibited. Any person who is or who holds himself or herself out to be a therapist and who intentionally has sexual contact with a patient or client during any ongoing therapist–patient or therapist–client relationship, regardless of whether it occurs during any treatment, con-

> sultation, interview or examination, is guilty of a Class D felony. Consent is not an issue in an action under this subsection. (Wisconsin Statues §940.22 (1985))

The version passed by the Minnesota Legislature reads as follows:

> 609.345 Criminal Sexual Conduct in the Fourth Degree. Subdivision 1. Crime defined. A person who engages in sexual conduct with another person is guilty of criminal sexual conduct in the fourth degree if any of the following circumstances exist:
> ... (h) the actor is a psychotherapist and the complainant is a patient of the psychotherapist and the sexual conduct occurred during the psychotherapy session. Consent by the complainant is not a defense;
> (i) the actor is a psychotherapist and the complainant is a patient or former patient of the psychotherapist and the patient or former patient is emotionally dependent upon the psychotherapist;
> (j) the actor is a psychotherapist and the complainant is a patient or former patient and the sexual contact occurred by means of therapeutic deception. Consent by the complainant is not a defense; ...

According to Schoener, Migrom, Gonsiorek, Luepker, and Conroe (1989) (Minnesota Statutes §609.345 (1985)) in *Psychotherapists' sexual involvement with clients: Invention and prevention,* the first case to be tried in Wisconsin under the 1984 statute involved a doctor of divinity and psychotherapist who allegedly engaged in sex with a female client. The defendant died prior to trial, however, and the case became moot.

However, in 1990, a counselor in Minnesota was convicted of four counts of psychotherapist–patient criminal sexual conduct (State v. Dutton, 1990).

In 1992 the Supreme Court of Colorado considered a constitutional challenge to Section 18–3-405.5(1), 8 B C.R.S. (1988 Supp.), a Colorado statute making sexual penetration of a client by a psychotherapist a class 4 felony. The psychotherapist who was convicted of four counts of aggravated sexual assault under the statute raised a First Amendment challenge.

Colorado's highest court noted that while certain private activities and intimate relationships may qualify for an elevated status of fundamental constitutional rights, the law has never allowed consenting adults simply because they are adults and consent, to engage in any type of sexual behavior of their choice under any circumstances. The court then held that neither a treating psychotherapist nor a client has a fundamental constitutional right to engage in sexual intercourse with the other during the existence of the psychotherapist–client relationship and the statute was therefore not unconstitutional.

The court pointed out the special circumstances inherent in the relationship between psychotherapist and his or her client(s) and held that the state could legitimately protect not only nonconsenting victims of sexual assault but also consenting clients. Due process and equal protection claims were also rejected (Ferguson v. People, 1992).

And, in 1996, a Georgia psychologist was indicted on sexual assault charges for allegedly having sex with a patient while treating her for multiple personality disorder. Several individuals have been successfully prosecuted under the California statute. There are a number of other criminal charges that can result from inappropriate or unlawful sexual contact with patients and colleagues. *Saenz v. Alexander* (1991) is an example of a case in which both criminal and civil liability arose from such conduct.

2.25.5.2.2 ***Fraud and inappropriate billing practices***

Fraud and inappropriate billing practices may also result in criminal liability for mental health professionals. Many have been convicted of fraud or other theft related charges incident to inappropriate or purely illegal billing practices (Marrero v. Dept. of Professional Regulation, 1993).

Virtually every jurisdiction in the US and Canada has laws that prohibit this type of activity. Some are routine criminal statutes that prohibit simple theft, theft by deception, fraud, embezzlement, and the like. Other criminal statutes, enacted to alleviate the abuse within the health care delivery system, are specifically designed for this purpose.

Particular care should be taken when billing the federal government. Often limitations on fees may be found only in obscure federal regulations. Nevertheless, the criminal penalties are serious. In a 1994 prosecution (BNA Health Law Reporter, 1994), a Kansas psychologist was found guilty of soliciting and receiving kickbacks for referring patients and was subject to possible incarceration for 100 years and fines up to $4.75 million. In 1995, a Virginia psychiatric and substance abuse facility pleaded guilty to violating the Medicare and Medicaid anti-kickback statute when it provided improper inducements to prospective patients. Providers' arrangements with the CHAMPUS are now being closely scrutinized. Some cases of inappropriate billing have resulted in serious criminal penalties (US v. Custodio, 1994).

In a 1996 case, a New Mexico psychiatrist learned how serious such matters can be. He was found guilty on 228 counts of submitting false claims to three federal programs. The psychiatrist was not only sentenced to 5 years' probation, but also ordered to repay $700 000 to the federal government and was excluded from the three federal programs (BNA Health Law Reporter, 1996a)

Note that billing activities may involve use of the mail and bring other statutes into play. A number of health care professionals have been convicted of mail fraud for submitting fraudulent reimbursement claims to insurance companies and health plans (US v. Harpster, 1991).

Also note the decision of a New York federal district court, *US v. Willis* (1991). Here the court refused to dismiss a securities fraud indictment against a psychiatrist arising from insider trading on a tip from a patient. Not all such cases result in criminal indictments. In some instances, the federal authorities are willing to forego criminal prosecution, but only after large amounts of money are repaid to the government entities that have been defrauded. In October 1995, a nonprofit drug and alcohol treatment provider in Orlando, FL settled such allegations of falsifying information to the federal government, but only after repaying $500 000.

2.25.5.2.3 Mandatory reporting laws

All mental health professionals should be aware that most mandatory reporting laws include criminal penalties for violators. The possibility of criminal prosecution makes it imperative that every mental health professional familiarizes themself with these statutes and understand the reporting requirements.

2.25.5.2.4 License-related liability

The professional regulatory boards in the various US jurisdictions typically have the legal authority to revoke or suspend professional licenses. In some jurisdictions, that authority rests with a Department of Professional Regulation or some other administrative agency. Regardless of which entity holds the authority, the parameters of such authority will derive from the same statute.

The statute referred to, typically the jurisdiction's "practice act," may contain a reference to a code of conduct or a code of ethics. Violation of the referenced code may be a ground for disciplinary action. For example, the Alabama Psychology Practice Act, *Code of Alabama* 1975, Section 34–26–1 (a)(17) states:

> Violation of the code of ethics adopted in the rules and regulations of the board.

The *Idaho Code* Chapter 23, §54–2305 (1992) provides:

> The board of psychologist examiners shall have the following powers ... (b) To adopt, and, from time to time, revise such rules and regulations not inconsistent with the law as may be necessary to carry into effect the provisions of this act. Such rules and regulations shall include, but not be limited to, (1) a code of ethics for psychologists in the state consistent with the current, and as future amended, ethical standards for psychologists of the American Psychological Association; ...

As these provisions demonstrate, mental health professionals are often legally required to conform their behavior to the dictates of such codes. In many jurisdictions, the relevant code is repeated in full in the board's rules and regulations. However, in others they are simply incorporated by reference. In either case, therapists must know and understand the relevant code as a violation can be grounds for disciplinary action. In some jurisdictions, with some professions, grounds for disciplinary actions will also be found in agency rules and regulations. Woody, in a 1994 study of disciplinary grounds released by the Florida Department of Professional Regulation for the years 1990–1991, 1991–1992, and 1992–1993, found that in that jurisdiction the total number of licensed psychologists averaged 2727 per year. The number of formal complaints averaged 148. Woody's statistics indicate that in the three years studied, 5.3%, 4.6% and 6.7% of licensed psychologists, respectively, had a complaint filed against them (Woody, R. H.: *50 ways to avoid malpractice,* 1988).

2.25.5.2.5 Common reasons for disciplinary action

Over the years, significant data regarding the reasons for license-related liability has been gathered by several organizations, including ASPPB through its Disciplinary Data System. By far the most common cause of disciplinary action is sexual or other dual relationships with patients. However, dual relationships are not the only cause, and in many instances, complaints against psychologists will involve more than one cause for discipline. Table 1 was created by ASPPB in 1995 after careful analysis of its disciplinary data.

During 1993, ASPPB made a concerted effort to convince jurisdictions to release records of disciplinary actions so that an accurate historical database could be created. The jurisdictions

Table 1 Reported disciplinary actions for psychologists: August 1983–July 1996.

Reason for disciplinary action	*Number disciplined*
Sexual/dual relationship with patient	471[a]
Unprofessional/unethical/negligent practice	344[b]
Fraudulent acts	142
Conviction of crimes	105
Inadequate or improper supervision	60[c]
Impairment	52
Breach of confidentiality	45[d]
Fraud in application for license	35
Improper/inadequate record keeping	41
Failure to comply with continuing education requirements	12

[a]When this table was first compiled in January 1988, 45 psychologists had been disciplined for this reason. [b]In 1988, this total was 29. [c]This category more than doubled between August 1993 and January 1996. [d]There was a 50% increase in this category between August 1993 and January 1996.

responded enthusiastically, and during that year, approximately 350 more disciplinary actions were recorded. In 1997, the Disciplinary Data bank holds approximately 1500 names of psychologists whose licenses have been impaired due to negligent, incompetent, unethical, or illegal activities.

There are data banks for other professions. Disciplinary actions against social workers' licenses are being reported to the data bank maintained by the American Association of State Social Work Boards. Actions against psychiatrists' licenses are reported to the National Practitioner Data Bank.

2.25.5.2.6 Less common reasons for disciplinary action

Of the approximately 1500 cases reported to ASPPB the majority fall within the categories listed above. There are, however, many other reasons for disciplinary sanctions and some less common reasons:

(i) failure to make child support payments;
(ii) performing an unrecognized modality (exorcism);
(iii) practicing outside areas of training;
(iv) failure to retain client records;
(v) lack of good moral character;
(vi) assaulting a patient;
(vii) failure to comply with board order;
(viii) lack of professional judgment in communicating personal opinions;
(ix) failure to report suspected child abuse;
(x) use of nude therapy;
(xi) deceptive and misleading advertising of practice;
(xii) misrepresentation of credentials;
(xiii) noncompliance with continuing education requirements.

The number of complaints brought to regulatory boards is rising. Several reasons for the increase exist. Those include the fact that the public is more knowledgeable about the regulatory process, boards are more accessible, and many state ethics committees have abandoned efforts to discipline their memberships (*The National Psychologist,* 1996).

2.25.5.2.7 Disciplinary actions in other professions

Data generated and analyzed by the Federation of State Medical Boards clearly indicate that the number of complaints and disciplinary actions involving physicians and charges of sexual misconduct are rising significantly. It is this author's considered opinion that grounds for disciplinary action against psychiatrists parallel the data generated by the psychology boards. Further, that sexual misconduct, fraudulent billing, and conviction of crimes would clearly be a majority of all cases.

2.25.5.2.8 Mandatory reporting laws

Mental health professionals should be keenly aware of any reporting law relative to knowledge of sexual misconduct by other mental health professionals. A number of states have "whistle blower" statutes, but all are different. Some such laws forbid disclosure without the patient's consent. All such laws have serious repercussions, such as disciplinary action, for failure to follow statutory mandates.

2.25.5.2.9 The complaint process

Virtually all jurisdictions require that complaints concerning psychologists' behavior be in writing. If such a complaint appears valid, an investigation ensues. In some jurisdictions, trained investigators are employed to perform this task. In smaller jurisdictions, a board member may be assigned as an investigating officer.

2.25.5.2.10 Constitutional and statutory protections

Enforcement of these codes involves the application of constitutional and statutory protections. A license to practice is a "property" right that cannot be taken away without due process of law. Therefore, governmental authorities must provide any licensee charged with an infraction at least the following:

(i) adequate notice of the charges;
(ii) an opportunity for a hearing;
(iii) a fair and impartial hearing panel;
(iv) the opportunity to confront and cross-examine adverse witnesses;
(v) a decision based on the evidence;
(vi) a record of the proceedings; and
(vii) some form of judicial review.

These requirements are mandated either by the US Constitution, most state constitutions and/or state statutes. In an effort to standardize procedures among administrative agencies, most have been incorporated in each jurisdictions' administrative procedures act.

2.25.6 CONCLUSION

The interaction of law and psychology is a constant, never ending process. Psychologists are required to know, understand, and follow the requirements imposed by statute and regulation. To be successful they must understand the potential liabilities for unethical, incompetent, or illegal practice. As the foregoing pages illustrate, those requirements and responsibilities are quite significant.

2.25.7 REFERENCES

Abill v. US (1980). 482 F. Supp. 703.
Abrahamson v. Gonzales (1992). 949 F.2d 1567 (11th Cir.).
Almonte v. New York Medical College (1994). 851 F.Supp. 34 (D. Conn.).
Andrews v. US (1984). 732 F.2d 366.
Argus v. Scheppegrell (1985). 472 So.2d 573 (La.).
Association of State and Provincial Psychology Boards (1992). *Model act for licensure of psychologist.* Montgomery, AL: Author.
Association of State and Provincial Psychology Boards (1996). *Handbook of licensing and certification requirements for psychologists in North America.* Montgomery, AL: Author.
Awai v. Kotin (1993). 872 P.2d 1332 (Colo.App.).
Badger v. Greenfield (1981). 24 ATLA L.Rep. 43.
Bass, E., & Davis, L. (1955). *The courage to heal: A guide for women survivors of child sexual abuse.* New York: Harper and Row.
Bird v. W. C. W. (1994). 868 S.W.2d 767 (Tex.).
BNA Health Law Reporter (1994). *3*, 1696.
BNA Health Law Reporter (1995a). *4*, 687.
BNA Health Law Reporter (1995b). *4*, 1266.
BNA Health Law Reporter (1995c). *4*, 1572.
BNA Health Law Reporter (1996a). *5*, 223.
BNA Health Law Reporter (1996b). *5*, 742.
Bradley Center Inc. v. Wessner, Ga., 296 S.E.2d 693.
Bradley v. Ray (1995). 904 S.W.2d 302 (Mo.App. W. D.).
Cairl v. State (1982). 323 N.W. 2d 20 (Minn.).
California Penal Code § 11166 (West 1995).
Chizman v. Mackie, 896 P.2d 196 (Alaska 1995).
Clites v. State of Iowa, Iowa App., 322 N.W.2d 917.
Code of Alabama 1975, Section 10–4–383.
Code of Alabama 1975, Section 25–5–77.
Code of Alabama 1975, Section 26–14–3.
Code of Alabama 1975, Section 34–26–46(a)(17).
Collins v. Cushner (1982, July). 25 ATLA L. Rep. 185.
Colorado Revised Statutes §12–43–216 (1992).
Corgan v. Muehling (1991). 574 N.E. 2d 602 (Ill).
Creighton University Center for Health Policy and Ethics Working Group on HIV Confidentiality (1991). Confidentiality and its limits: ethical guidelines for maternal/pediatric HIV infection. *Creighton Law Review, 25*, 1439–1460.
Davis v. Lhim (1983/1988). 335 N.W. 2d 481 (Mich. App.) (reversed on the ground of immunity in 1988 by the Michigan Supreme Court, 442 N.W. 2d 688).
Davis v. North Carolina Dept. of Human Resources (1995). 465 S.E.2d 2 (N.C. App.).
Doe v. Belmont College (1992). 35 ATLA L. Rep. 148.
Doe v. Samaritan Counseling Center (1990). 791 P.2d 344 (Alaska).
Dunn v. Howard University Hospital (1983). 26 ATLA L. Rep. 232.
Durflinger v. Artiles (1983). 673 P.2d 86 (Kan.).
Ellis v. US 484 F. Supp. 4 (D.C.S.C. 1978).
Evans v. Morehead Clinic, Ky. App., 749 S.W.2d 696.
Faigenbaum v. Oakland Medical Center (1986). 393 N.W. 2d 847 (Mich).
Farris v. Compton (1994). 652 A.2d 49 (D.C.).
Faya v. Almaraz (1993). 620 A.2d 327 (Md.)
Ferguson v. People (1992). 824 P.2d 803 (Colo.).
Fraser v. US (1996). 674 A.2d 811 (Conn.).
Green v. Guarino (1992). 35 ATLA L. Rep. 29.
Guity v. Kandilakis (1991). 821 S.W.2d 595 (Tenn.App.).
Haggerty v. New York (1985). 23 ATLA L. Rep. 285.
Halverston v. Pikes Peak Family Counseling and Mental Health Center, Inc. (1991). 795 P.2d 1352 (Colo.App.).
Hamman v. County of Maricopa (1989). 775 P.2d 1122 (Ariz.).
Herndobler v. Riveredge Hospital (1979). 23 ATLA L.Rep. 139.
Horne v. Patton (1973). 287 So.2d 824 (Ala.).
Howard v. Drapkin (1990). 271 Cal.Rptr. 893 (Cal.App.2 Dist.).
Huntley v. State of New York (1984). 464 N.E. 2d 467 (N.Y.).
Idaho Code § 54–2305 (1992).
Idaho Code § 54–2314 (19) (1992).
In re C.P. (1990). 563 N.E. 2d 1275 (Ind.).
James v. Albergo (1993). 626 N.E. 2d 1137 (Ill.App.).
Jansen v. University Hospital (1983). 26 ATLA L.Rep. 138.
Jordan v. Kelly (1984). 728 F.2d 1.
Kathleen K. v. Robert B. (1984). 198 Cal.Rptr. 273 (Cal.App.).
Koren v. Weihs (1994). 607 N.Y.S. 257 (A.D.1 Dept.).
Lanning, K. B. (1991). *Ritual Abuse: A Law Enforcement View or Perspective*, 15 Child Abuse and Neglect, pp. 171–173.
Leal v. Simon (1989). 542 N.Y.S. 2d 328 (A.D.2 Dept.).

Lindsey v. Rousseau (1993). 36 ATLA L. Rep. 220.
Marrero v. Dept. of Professional Regulation (1993). 662 So.2d 1109 (Fla. App. 1 Dist.).
Matter of Estate of Votteler, Iowa, 327 N.W.2d 759.
Matter of W. H. (1993). 602 N.Y.S.2d 70 (Fam. Ct.).
Medi-Stat, Inc. v. Kustunin (1990). 792 S.W.2d 869 (Ark.).
Mendendez v. Superior Court (1992). 834 P.2d 785 (Cal.App.).
Minnesota Statutes §609.345 (1985).
Missouri Revised Statutes §565.188 (1993).
Morris v. Consolidation Coal Co. (1994). 446 S.E. 2d 648 (W.Va.).
Ohio Revised Code Annotated §4732.12 (Baldwin, 1994).
Oklahoma Statutes Title 59, §1376 (1993).
People v. District Court, County of Adams (1990). 797 P.2d 1259 (Colo.).
Perreira v. Colorado (1989). 768 P.2d 1198 (Colo.).
Pisel v. Stamford Hospital (1980). Conn. 430 A.2d 1.
Prince v. St. Francis-St. George Hosp., Inc. (1985). 484 N.E. 2d 265 (Ohio App.).
Ramona v. Ramona (1994). No. 61898, Cal. Superior Ct.
Reaves, R. P. (1995). *Avoiding liability in the mental health professions*. Montgomery, AL: Publications for Professionals.
Reaves, R. P. (1996). Laws that Affect the Practice of Psychology. In American Psychological Association & Association of State and Provincial Boards (Eds.), *Professional conduct and discipline in psychology* (pp. 109–116). Washington, DC: American Psychological Association.
Reisner v. Regents of the University of California (1995). 37 Cal.Rptr.2d 518 (Ct. App.).
Roesler v. Menora Medical Center (1978). 21 ATLA L. Rep. 327.
Saenz v. Alexander (1991). 854 So.2d 1061 (Fla.App. 1 Dist.).
Santangelo v. State (1993). 601 N.Y.S. 2d 305 (A.D.2 Dept.).
Sawyer v. Tauber (1985). 23 ATLA L.Rep. 277.
Schoener, G. R., Migrom, J. H., Gonsiorek, J. C., Luepker, E. T., & Conroe, R. M. (1989). *Psychotherapists' sexual involvement with clients: Intervention and prevention.* Minneapolis, MN: Walk-In Counseling Center.
Sexual misconduct in the practice of medicine. *Journal of the American Medical Association, 266*(19), 34.
Smith, M., & Pazder, L. (1989). *Michelle remembers* (1991). New York: Pocket Books.
Smith v. Rush Presbyterian St. Luke's Medical Center (1980). 23 ATLA L.Rep. 44.
Snow v. Koeppl (1990). 464 N.W. 2d 215 (Wis.App.).
South Carolina Code Annotated§40–55–180 (Law. Co-op. 1992).
State ex rel. Juvenile Dept. of Lincoln County v. Ashley (1990). 790 P.2d 547 (Or. App.).
State v. Dutton (1990). 450 N.W. 2d 189 (Minn.App.).
Sullivan v. Cheshier (1994). 846 F. Supp. 654 (N.D. Ill.).
Tamsen v. Weber (1990). 802 P.2d 1063 (Ariz. App.).
Tarasoff v. Regents of the University of California (1976). 551 P.2d 334.
The National Psychologist, (1996). *Jan/Feb*, 8.
Tuman v. Genesis Associates (1995). D.C.E. Pa., No.95–0272.
US v. Custodio (1994). 39 F.3d 1121 (C.A. 10 Colo.).
US v. Harpster (1991). 759 F. Supp. 735 (D. Kan.).
US v. Willis (1991). 778 F. Supp. 205 (S.D.N.Y.).
Webb v. Jarvis (1990). 553 N.E. 2d 151 (Ind. App. 1 Dist. 1990).
Webb v. Lightburn (1985). 23 ATLA L.Rep. 285.
Werner v. Kliewer (1985). 710 P.2d 1250 (Kan.).
Williams v. Congdon (1979). 257 S.E.2d 677 (N.C.App.).
Wisconsin Statutes §940.22. (1985).
Woody, R.H. (1988). *50 ways to avoid malpractice*. Sarasota, FL: Professional Resource Exchange.
Wright, L. (1994). *Remember satan*, New York: Knopf.
Zezulka v. Thapar (1996). No. 01–94–01195-CV (Tex. Ct.App., 1st Dist. Jan. 29).

2.26
Responsible Test Use in Clinical Application

MANFRED J. MEIER
University of Minnesota, Twin Cities, MN, USA

2.26.1 INTRODUCTION

This chapter is designed to assist the user of psychological tests in a professionally and ethically responsible manner, consistent with the selected published guidelines and standards. It is intended to identify salient and relevant issues or principles to facilitate the structuring of test use and the interpretation of test data. Therefore, it is hoped to assist graduate students and beginning practitioners in pursuing the goal of maximizing the usefulness of psychological testing and assessment in clinical practice.

Although psychology has been perhaps the foremost discipline in the development and use of formal tests for assessing cognition and behavior, psychological testing and assessment have not always been central to the activities of clinical psychologists. Instead, the importance of psychological testing has varied and for a considerable period of time was even considered to be of relatively little importance in the practice of clinical psychology. After World War II, the practice of psychotherapy became more central, even to the exclusion of psychological testing and assessment for many practicing clinical psychologists. However, over the past 50 years, psychological assessment has assumed greater importance in everyday application, largely as a function of the expansion of assessment activities in clinical neuropsychology and in personality assessment. Despite such cyclical trends, the self-monitoring of responsible practices and the search for effectively applicable standards continues, not only in psychology but in related disciplines as well. Deliberations directed at the development of test standards have been generated by the Joint Committee on Testing Practices which consists of representatives from the American Counseling Association (ACA), the American Psychological Association (APA), the American Speech–Language–Hearing Association (ASLHA), and the National Association of School Psychologists (NASP). Similarly, the Standards for Educational and Psychological Testing (American Psychological Association, 1985) have been revised repeatedly since their inception in 1947 as a result of the cooperative effort of the American Educational Research Association (AERA), the APA, and the National Council on Measurement in Education (NCME). Numerous other organizations have also provided leadership and direction in this extensive domain. It is beyond the scope of this chapter to integrate the many perspectives available in the literature relative to responsible test use. The selective identification of issues and concerns for the present purpose will hopefully orient the interested graduate student or practitioner in clinical psychology to access additional information as needed to establish the responsible practice of clinical psychological assessment.

2.26.1.1 Representative Standards Documents

The Standards for Educational and Psychological Testing (SEPT) reflect understandings reached by consensus on the part of the various organizations that have been involved in their periodic revision since the 1940s. The latest revision is in process and is expected to be made available to the participating organizations some time in 1997 for their ratification. The last previous revision was published in 1985 and was divided into four major sections: Technical Standards for Test Construction and Evaluation; Professional Standards for Test Use; Standards for Particular Applications; and Standards for Administrative Procedures. Of particular relevance for this chapter is Part II, Professional Standards for Test Use, particularly the sections on general principles and clinical testing. The new revision is expected to combine the various specialty chapters into just two chapters: one dealing with educational and the other with psychological testing and assessment issues. The psychological testing component adds material for some of the specialized clinical applications, particularly in relation to neuropsychological and forensic assessments.

Familiarity with this document can be regarded as essential for structuring individual practices in a responsible manner. The many principles promulgated in the standards can be accessed in a more limited and circumscribed manner in the *Responsibilities of Users of Standardized Tests* (RUST) published by the Association for Measurements in Counseling and Education (1991). Such documents provide statements of the collective reflections of many individuals and organizations. Another valuable and systematically organized work is an empirically based product of the Joint Committee on Testing Practices (JCTP, 1988) with representatives of the ACA, the APA, the ASLHA, and the NASP (Eyde et al., 1993). The latter represents the outcome of the work of two committees of the JCTP: the Test User Qualifications Working Group (TUQWG); and the Test User Training Work Group (TUTWG). The resulting study sought to identify the various issues and problems underlying test misuse by means of a database utilizing "critical incidents" detection methods that involved various tests and testing contexts or situations. Such efforts add empirically to the basis for defining, monitoring, and evaluating testing and assessment practice in a given setting or situation. The "critical incident" method isolated a collection of case studies relating to 12 generic test types: educational achievement; employment; group scholastic ability; hearing; individual intelligence; interest; multiple abilities; neuropsychological; personality; projective; readiness; and speech–language. The resulting case book was intended to augment texts and other instructional materials in a graduate curriculum for potential use in the seven assessment contexts from which the case studies were derived: counseling/training; education; employment; general health; mental health; neuropsychology; and speech–language–hearing.

The remainder of this chapter is an attempt to compare the factors yielded by the JCTP study to the test user sequence based on the RUST Statement (Revised 1991). Such a comparison and preliminary integration of those efforts will hopefully provide a foundation for utilizing the new revision of the SEPT 1985 document for the responsible use of psychological and neuropsychological tests in clinical practice.

2.26.2 SUMMARY OF THE JCTP FACTORS

It seems reasonable to assume that the factors derived from the case analyses in the JCTP study will generalize with some adjustments for any dissimilarities across settings and across different purposes of testing. In Eyde et al. (1993), the major factors summarized below also include an account of selected elements that loaded highest on each factor, including those that appear to have the greatest implication for competent test use in general clinical, neuropsychological, and forensic settings.

2.26.2.1 Factor 1: Comprehensive Assessment

This factor reflects the distinction between testing and assessment in applications since it relates to the need to obtain a comprehensive personally relevant database for integration with test score databases to increase the validity of test score-based inferences in the interpretation (Matarazzo, 1990). In addition to medical and psychosocial histories, the comprehensiveness of the assessment requires a working knowledge of the shortcomings of personal qualifications as well as the known limitations of particular tests, consideration of clinical observations during interview and testing, and the possible use of additional tests to confirm or disconfirm inferences that can only be stated as hypotheses (rather than firm conclusions) on the basis of the initial assessment strategy. Comprehensive assessment obviously calls for considerable judgmental elaboration within an empirically sound historical and test score framework.

2.26.2.2 Factor 2: Proper Test Use

This factor appeared to relate to the acceptance of a strong test user responsibility for establishing competence and for the application of a deliberate quality control procedure that reflects an understanding of the multivariate nature of the assessment enterprise. This responsibility includes maintenance of a neutral and objective attitude and the necessary education and training for attaining quality control and the necessary competence for effective assessment practice.

2.26.2.3 Factor 3: Psychometric Knowledge

This factor relates primarily to the knowledge of the technical properties of tests to a depth that permits the user to evaluate the significance of standard errors of measurement, reliability, and validity and to incorporate such knowledge into test interpretation. Considering the vast array of psychological and neuropsychological tests in use, any given clinical practitioner will not ordinarily have a working knowledge of the technical properties of all the available tests. Instead, a typical practitioner will focus on a circumscribed body of tests that are both routinely used and well-understood in terms of applications pertaining to particular referral questions and test purposes. Lacking such knowledge for a particular test would then require additional education and training such as continuing education and formal postdoctoral residency, for example.

2.26.2.4 Factor 4: Maintaining Integrity of Test Results

Although factor 3 also involves the knowledgeable application of psychometric principles, such principles may or may not be effectively applied in the actual interpretation of test results. Thus, this factor relates more to limitations of particular test scores for the purposes being addressed in specific situations or referral contexts. Elements loading highest on this factor include the necessity for avoiding the use of absolute cut-off scores since they do not take into account errors of measurement. Factor 4 reflects the need to correctly apply psychometric knowledge when interpreting a test or test battery in a particular set of circumstances. The necessity for correct application increases as a function of the gravity of any actions that may ultimately be based on test interpretation such as diagnostic, dispositional, and treatment decisions.

2.26.2.5 Factor 5: Accuracy of Scoring

Responsible test use and interpretation obviously depends on the accuracy of the test scores. Psychological test interpretation, accentuated even more in the forensic context, necessitates the establishment of audit procedures in the recording process and periodic checks on score accuracy. Even seemingly minor scoring errors can grossly reduce the validity of inferences derived from individual tests and test battery scores.

2.26.2.6 Factor 6: Appropriate Use of Norms

In a highly diverse society, even norms that have wide applicability need to be understood for their limitations when applied to groups of individuals that were not adequately represented in the normative data for the test or test battery at issue. The effective application of normative data in test interpretation becomes even more crucial as the decisions based on test interpretations, if invalid, may have serious deleterious consequences for the individuals being assessed. Where norms are limited, responsible test use requires extreme caution in the derivation of any conclusions from psychometric data.

2.26.2.7 Factor 7: Interpretive Feedback—Clients/Patients/Referral Sources

Direct interpretive feedback to clients occurs less frequently in clinical settings but is rather routine in counseling situations. The referring professionals (e.g., physicians, attorney) ultimately may interpret the test results to individuals based on the clinical psychological or neuropsychological report. The factor calls for the need for the test interpreter to educate the referring professional to perform this role within the consultation framework or permit the interpreter to assume this role. Interpretive feedback requires the use of language that is readily understood by the recipient and the appreciation of the likely consequences of providing such information to an emotionally disturbed or cognitively impaired individual.

In addition to utilizing the JCTP case book as a means of identifying the more common aspects of test misuse, the case studies for assessing human behavior permit an analysis of the incident for the likely factors involved and the elements that are most likely to be most relevant. Extended to a given clinical practice, problematic incidents, as they are encountered, can be identified by the practitioner and subjected to similar analysis. Such a procedure can also be routinely applied in the context of a psychological test use audit as a periodic check on effectiveness of test use within a practice. Where problematic incidents may occur, peer consultation and review can then be secured in order to avoid such incidents in the future but also to prevent other potentially detrimental incidents from occurring. Deliberate attention to the factors and to their implications for establishing test use guidelines within a given practice should help ensure the effectiveness of the professional in a psychological or neuropsychological assessment role.

2.26.3 IMPLICATIONS OF THE RUST STATEMENT REVISED

It is interesting that the empirically derived factors identified in the JCTP study was anticipated surreptitiously on the basis of the *a priori* deliberations that led to a consensual statement from a committee representing the various divisions and regions of the American Association for Counseling and Development (AACD, 1978). This document was revised subsequently by the Association for Measurements in Counseling and Education (1991). The 1991 statement begins with a consideration of the kinds of decisions made in the counseling situation on the basis, at least in part, of test data. The RUST guidelines emphasize that responsible test use requires a definition of the purposes of testing in determining the information to be obtained and to be interpreted in order to achieve those purposes.

The statement then goes on to address the qualifications of test users, the necessary information for the selection of tests, the conditions favoring the proper test interpretation, and the effective communication of test results by means of interpretative reports to clients, professionals, and other involved parties as appropriate to the counseling situation. Since there is considerable overlap between the issues identified as important to test use in the counseling situation, as compared with the clinical situation, the guidelines may apply to clinical assessments as well. However, the emphasis may vary somewhat in the clinical situation where the purposes may be significantly different, largely as a function of the kinds of referral issues that arise in these respective settings. In the counseling situation, the emphasis is on test use in educational and vocational contexts, although clinical test methods and purposes may also become relevant. In the clinical situation, test use focuses more on referral issues that arise in the mental health, general medical, neurological, and rehabilitation contexts. The remainder of this chapter is an attempt to provide an *a priori* synopsis of the RUST guidelines to be considered, along with the JCTP case book. Such an overview of these documents will hopefully facilitate efforts on the part of clinical practitioners to appreciate and apply the current as well as the anticipated revision of the Standards for Educational and Psychological Testing expected to be published in 1998.

2.26.3.1 Test Decisions

The RUST revision emphasizes the decision issue since the counseling process characteristically is driven by purposes of placement or selection, and the prediction of educational, vocational, some clinical outcomes, and possible negative consequences of decisions. Such purposes are less commonly encountered in the clinical context where description, diagnosis, and the assessment of behavioral change over time as a function of intervention predominate as the more characteristic purposes of testing. Referrals for psychological assessment have traditionally emphasized the establishment of intellectual level with the secondary objectives of providing inferences regarding the individual's ability to participate in psychological and psychiatric interventions, where mental health settings are concerned, and for participating in pre- and postmedical and surgical interventions in nonpsychiatric settings. Similarly, personality assessment is frequently introduced in the generic clinical context as part of a broader strategy to arrive at specific psychiatric diagnoses, treatment plans, and discharge-related dispositional decisions. Clinical neuropsychological assessment constitutes an extension of the use of psychological tests beyond the generic clinical context since the referral issues that define the purposes of the testing require more extensive test batteries and related sophistication in the derivation of valid inferences. The referral issues range from the identification of organic brain change due to a neurogenic process to the differentiation of functional psychiatric from neuropathic and pathophysiologic factors underlying psychological dysfunction. Where organic factors have been implicated, the referral questions may then be extended to prompt the derivation of inferences regarding the probable specific underlying etiological factors and their relative contributions to the pattern of spared and impaired neuropsychological functions that have been identified by means of the test data. The neuropsychological test data are then considered within the broader psychosocial, medical, educational, and vocational data set available at the time of the assessment. Along with etiological considerations, the referral questions may include the need for comment on the likely nature, extent, location, and predicted course of the inferred neurological involvement. Depending upon the ultimate course of the neurological disease process in such instances, the neuropsychological assessment may address the need and a rationale for cognitive and other intervention, including a plan for evaluating the outcome of such interventions and for predicting the long-range course of the individual's psychological and neuropsychological functioning under various assumptions regarding alternatives. Since the tests utilized in generic clinical psychological assessment are characteristically included in a neuropsychological assessment, it is not surprising that competence in neuropsychological assessment requires education and supervised training that includes but also extends well beyond the assessment competence obtained in a traditional, generic clinical predoctoral curriculum (Division 40 Task Force, 1987).

Although clinical decisions are rarely made solely on the basis of the psychological interpretations, such interpretations may weigh heavily within the assessment and intervention framework in the decision process. Even more importantly, psychological test interpretations may play a pivotal role in judicial decisions affecting individuals in both civil and criminal actions.

2.26.3.2 Qualifications of Test Users

It is generally assumed that all psychologists, even at a masters degree level, have had formal course work and supervised training in psychological testing. Programs may vary widely in terms of expectations of graduate students in this domain so that there may not be much uniformity in training opportunities across programs. Even with relatively extensive training, the most expert individuals may not have sufficient knowledge and sets of skills to utilize all instruments available within their practice domain and certainly not for application to all situations in which they may perform test services. The responsibility for judging the relevance and appropriateness of personal, professional qualifications rests fundamentally with the test users as guided by their understanding of professional ethics, personal strengths and limitations, and awareness of the expectations for professional psychologists as proposed by state and national agencies. The latter include credentialing agencies such as state licensure boards, guidelines provided by peers through individual and organizational supportive statements or documents, and commitments to continuing education and advanced study not dictated by statute. When the test users judge that a given assessment challenge exceeds their training and previously supervised experience, they are expected to seek peer consultation and/or initiate referral to another more qualified psychologist. Even technically sound testing, when introduced to address purposes that are not fully understood or that require more expertise for effective application, may result in serious test misuse. Such qualifications include a thorough knowledge of the tests being used, including the selection of particular tests for addressing specific referral questions.

2.26.3.3 Test Selection

After considering the purposes of testing and the conduct of a self-analysis of the necessary knowledge and competence to address the purposes, the professional psychologist is then faced with the selection of tests. This requires a deliberate analysis, based on the test literature, of the most appropriate and valid procedures to be used, any necessary accommodations to meet the needs of individuals who are not represented in the normative population for the test(s) being selected, the evidence favoring psychological constructs underlying the test scores for those tests that are ultimately selected, and the intended use of test interpretation. Thus the appropriateness of the tests selected is a function of the available validity evidence for the use of the test with individuals of the population on which it has been normed, the qualifications of the test user and the likelihood that inferences derived from the test can be stated in probabilistic terms based on the validity evidence for the test. The technical properties of the test should be established and accessible from the test manual and other sources that reflect the technical expectations as achieved by consensus of measurement professionals and as exemplified by the standards for educational and psychological testing and by the assorted codes of fair testing practices.

The selector of tests, therefore, is guided by knowledge of the documented evidence of test score reliability, the adequacy of the norms, the clarity and comprehensibility of the instructions, the test qualities for the population at issue, and the clarity of the scoring criteria and their reliable application. Where individuals of different cultural, racial, ethnic, education, and vocation backgrounds are being compared, the selection of tests should be guided by knowledge of the published norms and any limitations of the norms for application of the test to nonrepresentative individuals and groups. Similarly, bilingualism and language dominance should influence test selection where appropriate. Anyone who has worked in clinical settings will attest to the fact that certain instruments are favored, often (but not always) realistically based on the breadth and depth of the literature pertaining to the use of the test. This also seems to hold true for test batteries in clinical neuropsychological assessment where standard batteries are frequently used. As is the case with widely used individual tests in mental health applications, neuropsychological batteries in widest use tend to have fairly extensive supporting literature. However, as the controversy regarding the use of fixed vs. flexible test batteries continues, there is a growing awareness of the need to justify the particular tests to be used on the basis of relevance for the purposes of testing and the soundness of their psychometric properties for obtaining an adequate data set for drawing valid interpretations.

2.26.3.4 Test Administration

The primary quality issues surrounding test administration involve the necessary environmental circumstances for the encouragement of optimal performances during testing, the importance of administering tests in accord with the standardized instructions and procedures established by the publisher, and the necessity for monitoring examiner as well as examinee behavior to ensure the maintenance of rapport and effective communication. It is essential to inform the examinee with regard to the purpose of the testing and the ultimate use for which the evaluation is being done. Where the professional psychologist is delegating test administration to a trained psychometrist or technician, the responsibility for administration of the tests remains with the supervising psychologist who is also responsible for determining the qualifications of the individual who will actually administer the tests, including previous training and supervised experience, preferably provided under the auspices of an accredited educational institution or training hospital. Where computerized test administration may be concerned, available guidelines should be followed (Green et al. 1984). Whatever the mode of administration, it is necessary to provide a testing environment that is free from distractions and from unpleasant or uncomfortable environmental conditions. Observational data relating to environmental, general health, cognitive or neurological limitations, and emotional variations or deviations should be obtained since such variables may reduce the validity of inferences that will ultimately be derived from the test data. Observations should be systematically recorded and attached to the test score protocol. Interpersonal skills of the test administrator should be applied in a manner that facilitates the performance, within the boundaries set by the test instructions, of the examinee. This consideration underscores the necessity for considerable training and supervised experience of the psychometrist or technician as well as the supervising psychologist.

2.26.3.5 Test Scoring

Minimization of measurement error requires that scoring procedures are accurate and executed in accord with the scoring criteria that have been established for tests in question. This calls for rigorous training of anyone to whom the scoring function may be delegated and the periodic introduction of auditing procedures to establish the reliability of the scorers in a given test use situation. Audit also implies that scored test responses be screened to recognize improbable or grossly distorted (qualitative or quantitative) features of the test data. Such review can also be considered a check on the veracity of the examinee in addition to being part of the test scoring routine. The accuracy of computed raw scores and their conversion to standard scores is fundamental to any immediate or later application.

2.26.3.6 Test Score Interpretation

Test interpretation is a function of the psychologist responsible for deriving inferences from the test results for the purpose of addressing the referral issues that prompted the assessment request. The relevance and meaning of the scores depends upon the interpreter's knowledge of the validity evidence for deriving inferences relating to the construct or constructs underlying the test scores. In turn, the interpretability of the data in light of such knowledge depends upon the reliability of the test scores.

Even when all the assumptions underlying the effective application of a given test are met, such as adequate qualification of the test user, effective test administration, accurate test scoring, and the data are considered sufficiently reliable for subsequent interpretation, it is necessary to acknowledge that all test scores have some degree of error and that no test outcome is likely to be exactly replicable across testings of the same individual or of groups of individuals such as those represented in the available norms for the test. Acknowledgment of error of measurement is essential for moderating the derivation of inferences in test interpretation in a realistic and contextually appropriate manner. Both scorer and test reliabilities need to be considered in the analysis of subtest score differences that are commonly at issue, in general clinical applications, and in neuropsychological assessment.

Utilization of the validity evidence for the test or test battery requires knowledge of the test literature relating to the constructs for the intended use of the test. This places a large burden on the qualifications of the test user as test interpreter and, therefore, requires explicit recognition on the part of the test user of any personal limitations of knowledge and educational/experiential background for the intended use of the test(s) within a particular referral context. The array of inferences derived from tests and test batteries in clinical practice readily become relatively convoluted and complex to a degree that cannot always be justified on the basis of the available literature. Attempts to differentiate tentative inferences (as hypotheses) from firm inferences (as probabilistic conclusions) then become critical considerations in test interpretation. Such distinctions require carefully articulated qualifications in the communication of test interpretations.

It is now widely accepted that the concept of validity is reflected in the inferences derived from tests and is not inherent to the tests *per se* (American Psychological Association, 1985). Test scores are interpreted differently depending upon the purpose for which the test is being applied and the nature and extent of the construct validity evidenced for these inferences within the body of literature that provides the basis for the intended use of the test for a given purpose.

In clinical and clinical neuropsychological applications, tests are used for drawing diagnostic and dispositional inferences, predicting outcomes of various interventions, identifying psychological processes most affected by a psychogenic or a neurogenic condition, monitoring the course of subsequent development after the occurrence of a psychogenic or neurogenic event or process, and for designing interventions that are likely to modify favorably the course of a functional psychiatric or neuropathological process. The many technical and professional issues to be considered in test interpretation are addressed in the SEPT (APA, 1985) that are being revised for publication in 1998.

Accordingly, valid test interpretation depends on the many components of test usage in the formal psychological assessment process. As the ultimate outcome of test usage, communication of the meaning of the test results provides the interface between the professional psychologist and all other users of the information yielded by the assessment process.

2.26.3.7 Communication of Test Results and Interpretations

Tests results and interpretations are ordinarily communicated by means of formal written reports and sometimes by informal oral reports as well. The latter may occur when providing immediate feedback to the referring professional but may also occur upon request either as an incidental or a formal aspect of the referral where the individual being assessed is concerned. Confidentiality of the examinees is characteristically protected by statute so that release of test information must be obtained formally from the examinees or their legal representatives. The consent to release information requires that the examinees be sufficiently informed to make a reasoned judgment with respect to the potential consequences of releasing this information. If examinees are not sufficiently intact to be able to make judgments about the utilization of this information in their best interest, yet remains legally competent, it is the responsibility of the test user to enlist family members and appropriate representatives to facilitate the obtaining of informed consent to be examined and to distribute information regarding the assessment to other individuals.

Assuming the competence to interpret the test results, the professional psychologist is careful to explain concepts imbedded in the inferences derived from test scores, either in the written interpretation or by other reporting means. Inferences are routinely adjusted to incorporate known relationships between various demographic variables and test behaviors. The relative contribution of such variables should be reflected in the inferences or conclusions. All individuals involved in these transactions should be alerted to any limitations of the tests and the assessment as a whole, especially the significance of error of measurement and the potential sources of such errors. Most importantly, where alternative explanations carry even minimal likelihood of being valid, such explanations should be given due consideration in the course of the narrative and weighed in accord with the validity evidence for the test or test battery score/pattern inferences.

The examinee and related interested parties have the right to obtain copies of the materials generated by the assessment process and to challenge the validity of the process itself. It is beyond the purview of this chapter to explore this issue. It arises frequently in the forensic context where considerations relating to the responsible use of tests is of paramount importance and highly subject to formal adversarial challenges.

2.26.4 CONCLUSION

This chapter attempts to identify some developments that have a bearing on the effective and responsible use of psychological and neuropsychological tests in clinical practice. It is intended to orient the professional psychologist to a growing literature that reflects the collective judgment of many of the organizations involved in the development of guidelines for responsible psychological test use. The 1998 version of the Standards for Educational and Psychological Testing is expected to expand significantly on earlier versions and, thereby, to favor even more deliberate application of test standards to all major types of psychological evaluations. The empirical establishment of instances of test misuse using the critical incident technique and the *a priori* deliberation of various organizations has reinforced further the need for the continuously progressive amendation of previous guidelines and standards for psychological test use.

2.26.5 REFERENCES

American Association for Counseling and Development (1978). *Responsibilities of users of standardized tests.* Alexandria, VA: American Association for Counseling and Development.

American Psychological Association (1985). *Standards for educational and psychological testing.* Washington, DC: American Psychological Association.

Association for Measurements in Counseling and Education (1991). *Responsibilities of users of standardized tests.* Alexandria, VA: Association for Measurements in Counseling and Education.

Division 40 Task Force (1987). Reports of the task force on education, accreditation and credentialing. *The Clinical Neuropsychologist, 1*, 22–29.

Eyde, L. D., Robertson, G. J., Krug, S. E., Moreland, K. L., Robertson, A. G., Shewan, C. M., Harrison, P. L., Porch, B. E., Hammer, A. L., & Primoff, E. S. (1993). *Responsible test use: Case studies for assessing human behavior.* Washington, DC: American Psychological Association.

Green, B. F., Bock, R. D., Humphries, L. G., Linn, R. L., & Reckase, M. D. (1984). Technical guidelines for assessing computerized adaptive tests. *Journal of Educational Measurement, 21*(4), 347–360.

Joint Committee on Testing Practices (1988). *Code of fair testing practices in education.* Washington, DC: American Psychological Association.

Matarazzo, J. (1990). Psychological assessment versus psychological testing: Validation from Binet to the school, clinic, and courtroom. *American Psychologist, 45*(9), 999–1017.

2.27
Critical Paths, Practice Guidelines, and Empirically-validated Procedures

PETER E. NATHAN
University of Iowa, Iowa City, IA, USA

2.27.1 INTRODUCTION

The chapter traces the evolution of research on psychosocial treatment outcomes from the 1950s when Hans Eysenck published *The effects of psychotherapy: An evaluation,* which concluded that the psychotherapies of the time were largely ineffective (Eysenck, 1952). In the 1990s, more than 40 years later, advances in outcomes research methodology and the increasing effectiveness of psychosocial treatments have combined to yield empirically-validated psychosocial treatments for a wide range of *DSM-IV* disorders. The chapter also weighs an associated development, the publication of practice guidelines by both the American Psychiatric Association (APA) and the Division of Clinical Psychology of the American Psychological Association. Practice guidelines, like empirically-validated treatments, are controversial, in part because they have the potential to circumscribe the clinical decision-making of mental health professionals. Finally, the chapter considers arguments for and against empirically-validated treatments and practice guidelines, concluding that they represent substantial opportunities for gain for both psychologists and psychiatrists and their patients.

2.27.2 THE EVOLUTION OF EMPIRICALLY-VALIDATED TREATMENTS

Hans Eysenck's 1952 review of psychotherapy effectiveness, updated and extended in 1960 and 1969 (Eysenck, 1960, 1969), was undoubtedly the most important single impetus to the psychosocial treatment research that then unfolded over the ensuing 40 years. Eysenck reached two notable conclusions in his 1952 review. Estimating the spontaneous remission rate of the neuroses, as a benchmark against which to compare the effects of psychotherapy, Eysenck determined that "roughly two-thirds of a group of neurotic patients will recover or improve to a marked extent within about two years of the onset of their illness" (1952, p. 322). On reanalyzing data from Landis (1937) and Denker (1946), Eysenck (1952) also provocatively calculated that "patients treated by means of psychoanalysis improved to the extent of 44%; patients treated eclectically improved to the extent of 64%; patients treated only custodially or by general practitioners improved to the extent of 72%. There thus appears to be an inverse correlation between recovery and psychotherapy" (1952, p. 322). Eysenck's controversial 1952 bottom line, elaborated in 1960 and 1969, was that the psychotherapies in widest use in the 1950s were largely ineffective.

While Eysenck acknowledged that the inadequate methodology of most of the treatment outcome studies of his time required him to qualify his most provocative conclusions, he did not withhold them. Instead, he insisted that his calculations pointed in only one direction: "They fail to prove that psychotherapy, Freudian or otherwise, facilitates the recovery of neurotic patients" (Eysenck, 1952, p. 323).

With a nod to Lewis Carroll's dodo bird, the lead paper at the 1973 annual meeting of the American Psychopathological Association, by Luborsky, Singer, and Luborsky (1976), is titled "Comparative studies of psychotherapies: Is it true that everyone has won and all must have prizes?" Its central premise echoes one Eysenckian theme—that more adequate research methodologies for examining, weighing, and comparing treatment efficacy must be developed before an unencumbered picture of psychotherapy effectiveness is possible. However, contrary to Eysenck and despite the limitations of their methods, these researchers reached a different conclusion about psychotherapy effectiveness:

> Our title implies what I think many of us believe—that all psychotherapies produce some benefits for some patients. What we do not know is whether there are psychotherapies which produce significantly better results and whether certain psychotherapies are especially well suited to certain patients. (Luborsky et al., 1976, p. 3)

Four years after the 1973 meeting of the American Psychopathological Association at which Luborsky and his colleagues shared their conclusions about psychotherapy effectiveness, Smith and Glass (1977) reported on a new statistical procedure called meta-analysis, designed to determine the effectiveness of psychotherapy independently of the shortcomings of the therapy outcome studies of the time. Despite the signal advantages of their new method, Smith and Glass concluded, as had Luborsky and his colleagues, that while psychotherapy is generally effective, it was not possible to differentiate among therapies in effectiveness.

Incorporating almost 400 outcome studies in their meta-analysis, Smith and Glass calculated that "the average study showed a 0.68 standard deviation superiority of the treated group over the control group" (p. 756), which convinced them that psychotherapy works. Of 10 types of therapy evaluated, the average effect size for systematic desensitization was highest, at 0.90, followed by rational-emotive therapy at 0.77, and behavior modification at 0.76. Client-centered therapy achieved an effect size of 0.63, while the effect size for psychodynamic therapy was 0.59. Despite these apparent differences in effect size, however, Smith and Glass could not distinguish among these therapies in effectiveness.

Praised for its substantial sample size and an innovative statistical methodology, Smith and Glass's meta-analysis method was also roundly criticized for the conceptual and methodological spread of the 385 studies included in the analysis, for their agreement with Luborsky et al.'s positive views on the general effects of psychotherapy despite apparently insufficient evidence, and for their unexplained failure to include some of the best-designed behavior therapy outcome studies of the early 1970s in their analysis.

Summarizing the research literature on psychotherapy outcomes published during the decades of the 1950s, 1960s, and 1970s, but emphasizing the voluminous literature of the 1970s, Rachman and Wilson's *The effects of psychological therapy,* published in 1980, reached a distinctly underwhelming assessment of the effectiveness of psychotherapy *ca* 1980:

> Since the First Edition (Rachman, 1971) was published, some slight progress has been made in the attempt to produce evidence to support the claims made on behalf of psychotherapy in general... Nevertheless, it is our view that modest evidence now supports the claim that psychotherapy is capable of producing some beneficial changes—but the negative results still outnumber the positive findings, and both of these are exceeded by reports that are beyond interpretation. (Rachman & Wilson, 1980, p. 259)

In the first edition of the book, Rachman (1971) agreed with Eysenck's earlier judgment that psychotherapy had not been shown to be effective in the 1950s and 1960s. However, by 1980, the improved methodology of outcome research in the 1970s, coupled with advances in behavioral treatment methods, gave Rachman and Wilson reason for guarded optimism.

Also notable in the 1980 volume is Rachman and Wilson's prescient anticipation of cognitive behavior therapy's development into a valuable addition to the therapeutic armamentarium.

Two articles from a 1986 special issue of the *American Psychologist* on psychotherapy outcome research deserve brief mention. In the first of these papers, Howard, Kopta, Krause, and Orlinsky (1986) reported on a successful effort to quantify the dose–effect relationship in psychotherapy. Selecting the therapy session as the dose unit, and the percentage of patients improved as the effect, Howard and his colleagues undertook a "probit analysis" of 15 diverse therapy outcome studies. They reported that "10% to 18% of patients could be expected to have shown some improvement after the first session of psychotherapy, by eight sessions, 48% to 58% of patients would be expected to have measurably improved, (and) about 75% of patients should have shown measurable improvements by the end of six months of once-weekly psychotherapy" (Howard et al., 1986, p. 162). This quantitative determination of a dose–effect relationship for psychotherapy, previously demonstrated for a variety of psychopharmacological treatments, constituted a strong empirical voice of support for psychotherapy in the 1980s.

The title of Stiles, Shapiro, and Elliott's (1986) *American Psychologist* article, "Are all psychotherapies equivalent?," intentionally echoes Luborsky's 1973 review. Starting from the premise that the outcome data to date still "appear to support the conclusion that outcomes of diverse therapies are generally similar," Stiles and his colleagues proceed to explore some possible determinants of the paradox: "outcome equivalence contrasted with content nonequivalence" (Stiles et al., 1986, p. 165). In other words, in the 1980s, prominent clinical scientists were still debating the continuing failure of efforts to differentiate effective from ineffective treatments for specific disorders, although Rachman and Wilson (1980) had previously marshaled strong evidence pointing to the superiority of behavior therapy for a variety of common syndromes.

In 1994, the 180 000 subscribers to *Consumer Reports* were asked a series of questions about their experiences with mental health professionals, physicians, medications, and self-help groups in the largest survey of psychotherapy outcomes. A mail survey of matters of this sensitivity and complexity, a substantially undefined and essentially undiagnosed group of respondents, the absence of an untreated control group, and outcome questions that focused on generalized "improvement" rather than specific outcomes targeted to symptoms all raised concerns about this survey. Most troubling was the very low response rate to the mailed questionnaire, covered in more detail below (*Consumer Reports* Editors, 1996).

The authors of the survey portrayed its principal findings as follows:

(i) Almost half of the respondents whose emotional state was "very poor" or "fairly poor" reported significant improvement following therapy.

(ii) The longer the psychotherapy lasted, the more it helped.

(iii) Psychotherapy alone worked as well as combined psychotherapy and pharmacotherapy; while most persons who took prescribed medication found it helpful, many reported side effects.

As noted above, the study's principal shortcoming was its low response rate: 4100 respondents (slightly > 2%) of the 180 000 subscribers to the magazine reported seeking professional help or joining groups, while only 2900 (ca. 1.5%) reported actually consulting a mental health professional. These numbers are so low they force us to assume that many subscribers with treatment experience decided not to respond to the survey and to hypothesize that more subscribers who felt good about psychotherapy chose to complete the questionnaire than those who did not, thereby skewing the findings in a positive direction. In the absence of data on the universe of *Consumer Reports* subscribers who sought professional help for their emotional problems, this serious design problem cannot be dismissed (*Consumer Reports* Editors, 1996).

While Martin Seligman, a consultant to the project, acknowledged the gap between its methodology and that of other contemporary psychotherapy outcome studies in a 1995 critique of the study (Seligman, 1995), he nonetheless concluded that the *Consumer Reports* survey "complements the (more traditional) efficacy method, and—the best features of these two methods can be combined into a more ideal method that will best provide empirical validation of psychotherapy" (Seligman, 1995, p. 965). Seligman urged his readers to appreciate the difference between efficacy studies—the traditional "gold standard" for judging psychotherapy outcomes—and effectiveness studies, feasibility and clinical utility in the real world, as epitomized by the *Consumer Reports* survey (*Consumer Reports* Editors, 1996).

If efficacy studies show us only part of psychotherapy as a whole, effectiveness studies show us another part. And while it seems likely that the two together reveal more about psychotherapy outcomes than either does separately, we have yet to figure out how to integrate the two. That lesson will only be learned over time and with data from additional studies, which must address the serious methodological problems that prevent us from according the *Consumer Reports* study more credence.

Treatments that work (Nathan & Gorman, 1997) is a comprehensive survey of empirically validated treatments for the full range of *DSM-IV* disorders. Its more than 30 chapters are written largely by the clinical scientists responsible for much of the most consequential treatment outcome research completed during the 1980s and 1990s. The volume offers impressive testimony to additions made, in many instances in the 1990s, in the number of treatments empirically validated for an ever-broader range of the *DSM-IV* disorders. The book also documents gains over the same period in the methodological rigor of the outcome studies on which these judgments were based.

From a handful of somatic treatments for schizophrenia of questionable efficacy in the 1950s, all with devastating side-effects, the chapters of *Treatments that work* on pharmacological treatments for the psychoses reflect the availability in the 1990s, of safer, more effective drug treatments for the most common and disabling psychoses. Just as noteworthy is that a number of the "neuroses," the conditions for whose effective treatment Eysenck despaired in 1950s, can now be treated, with good to excellent outcomes, by pharmacotherapy, often in combination with psychosocial treatments.

The volume also confirms the even greater changes which characterize psychosocial treatments. In 1952, Eysenck could find no evidence of psychotherapy's effectiveness. Now, psychosocial treatments, many of them cognitive-behavioral, have shown clear efficacy for a range of diverse conditions. Moreover, and in many ways just as significantly, psychosocial treatments have now been linked with pharmacological treatments in combined regimens that often demonstrate greater therapeutic effectiveness than either treatment by itself.

In the mid-1990s, it is becoming easier than ever to specify which therapy delivered by which therapist is most effective for which person in which treatment setting. While much progress remains to be made in both outcome methodology and further elaboration of both efficacy and effectiveness, a great deal is already evident.

2.27.3 PRACTICE GUIDELINES

These substantial advances in both outcomes methodology and numbers of empirically-validated treatments have led to an unanticipated consequence: the controversial development of practice guidelines, whose multiple potential uses are now as hotly debated as the efficacy of psychotherapy was in the 1980s.

Pressures on treatment providers to use empirically validated treatments have grown with the identification of more and more of them in the 1990s; the rapid development of managed care (Pallack, 1995) has added to these pressures. For both reasons, several practice guidelines—all having a common goal, the detailed specification of effective treatments for a wide range of syndromes—have appeared. Guidelines developed by the two leading groups of mental health professionals, the APA and Division 12 of the American Psychological Association, are reviewed below.

Essentially identical prefaces introduce the three (APA) practice guidelines published up to 1995. They include the Practice Guidelines for: "the Treatment of Patients with Major Depressive Disorder in Adults" (APA, 1993), "the Treatment of Patients with Bipolar Disorder" (APA, 1994), and "the Treatment of Patients with Substance Use Disorders: Alcohol, Cocaine, Opioids" (APA, 1995). All three explicitly deny the intention "to be construed or to serve as a standard of medical care," because "standards of medical care are determined on the basis of all clinical data available for an individual case and are subject to change as scientific knowledge and technological advance and patterns evolve" (APA, 1993, p. v; 1994, p. iv; 1995, p. 4).

These denials of the use of these psychiatric guidelines as "standards of medical care" are key to understanding a major difference between them and the guideline developed by clinical psychology (Division 12 Task Force, 1995), discussed below. The APA practice guidelines are written to be suggestive rather than prescriptive, in part because they accord substantial weight to clinicians' judgments, not only to the empirical findings. This ambiguity in the role of practice guidelines—when are they suggestive rather than prescriptive and when, if ever, are they prescriptive rather than suggestive—remains a vexing issue, both for those who consult practice guidelines and those who develop them (Grady, 1995; Persons, 1995)

Each psychiatric guideline briefly details disease definition, epidemiology, and natural history, summarizes treatment principles and reviews treatment alternatives at greater length, and concludes with a synopsis of research directions. The coverage of treatment alternatives in these guidelines can best be described as comprehensive but telegraphic.

Persons, Thase, and Crits-Christoph (1996) have claimed that the 1993 guideline for the treatment of major depressive disorder underemphasizes the empirical data on the positive outcomes of several psychosocial treatments and overstates the value of combined psychosocial–pharmacological interventions, thereby reflecting an undervaluation of empirical findings throughout the guideline in favor of "clinical experience" and "clinical judgment."

To help understand how this situation might have come about, the following brief clarification of the use of standards of proof in the 1993 guideline should be considered:

> Definitive standards are difficult to achieve, except in narrow circumstances where multiple replicated studies and wide clinical opinion dictate certain forms of treatment. In other areas much is left to the clinical judgment and expertise of the clinician. (APA, 1993, p. 1)

This apparent willingness to accord "the clinical judgment and expertise of the clinician" equal weight with the empirical findings on treatment outcomes, distinguishes the three APA practice guidelines from the Division 12 Practice Guidelines reviewed. Was "clinical judgment" used consistently as an excuse to favor a psychopharmacological over a psychosocial treatment in the 1993 psychiatric guidelines—or their successors? While that claim cannot be either confirmed or refuted, it can be said that one excellent reason to adopt and use a consistent set of evaluative criteria, as the Division 12 Task Force did, is to avoid any appearance of guild-based bias.

As has been noted, a Task Force of Division 12 of the American Psychological Association published "Training in and dissemination of empirically-validated psychological treatments: report and recommendations" (Division 12 Task Force, 1995). Although the Task Force was constituted "to consider methods for educating clinical psychologists, third party payers, and the public about effective psychotherapies" (p. 3) rather than to develop a set of practice guidelines, its report and recommendations actually constitute a condensed, preliminary set of empirically validated psychosocial treatment guidelines.

Three categories of treatment efficacy are specified: well-established treatments; probably efficacious treatments; and experimental treatments (treatments that have not yet been established as at least probably efficacious). Tables 1 and 2 reproduce the criteria by which the Task Force made these discriminations.

Table 1 Criteria for empirically-validated treatments: well-established treatments.

I. At least two good group design studies, conducted by different investigators, demonstrating efficacy in one or more of the following ways:
A. Superior to pill or psychological placebo or to another treatment.
B. Equivalent to an already established treatment in studies with adequate statistical power.
OR
II. A large series of single case design studies demonstrating efficacy. These studies must have:
A. Used good experimental designs and
B. Compared the intervention to another treatment as in I.A.
Further criteria for both I and II:
III. Studies must be conducted with treatment manuals.
IV. Characteristics of the client samples must be clearly specified.
(Division 12 Task Force, 1995, p. 21)

Table 2 Criteria for empirically-validated treatments: probably efficacious treatments.

I. Two studies showing the treatment is more effective than a waiting list control group.
OR
II. Two studies otherwise meeting the well-established treatment criteria I, III, and IV, but both are conducted by the same investigator.
Or one good study demonstrating effectiveness by these same criteria.
OR
III. At least two good studies demonstrating effectiveness but flawed by heterogeneity of the client samples.
OR
IV. A small series of single-case design studies otherwise meeting the well-established treatment criteria II, III, and IV.
(Division 12 Task Force, 1995, p. 22)

Twenty-two "well-established treatments" for 21 different *DSM-IV* syndromes are identified, as are seven "probably efficacious" treatments for the same number of disorders. With the exception of family education programs for schizophrenia and interpersonal therapy for bulimia and depression, all the "well-established" treatments are behavioral. Similarly, all but the brief psychodynamic therapies listed as "probably efficacious" are behavioral.

The restricted number of empirically-validated treatments listed in the Division 12 Task Force report contrasts sharply with the larger number of diverse treatments endorsed by the

APA (1993, 1994, 1995). As noted above, differences in the standards of proof demanded by the two groups appear to account for this marked difference in number of recommended treatments.

Although the three sets of APA practice guidelines employed a rigorous rating system to reflect the methodological adequacy of the treatment outcome studies reviewed, the willingness of the drafters of these guidelines to include considerations of "clinical practice" and "expert clinical judgment" provided latitude for the inclusion of treatments for which consistently positive findings had not been reported. By contrast, the Division 12 practice guideline was shaped by very specific criteria. While these criteria are not overly demanding, they nonetheless require that studies supporting the efficacy of a treatment meet specific methodological criteria that many other therapy outcome studies have been unable to meet.

Why do behavioral approaches to treatment figure so prominently in these two lists of empirically-validated treatments? One reason is that, as Nathan and Gorman (1997) and others (e.g, Craighead, Kazdin, & Mahoney 1994; Goldfried & Davison, 1994) have suggested, an impressive body of outcome research shows that behavioral treatments can be effective for quite a number of disorders. However, these treatments are also designed to induce the discrete behavioral changes that are the target of many treatment outcome measures; they lend themselves especially well to manualized treatment programs; they are products of the behavioral movement's long history of respect for experimental validation and they tend to induce desired changes within a brief enough duration to fit into the typical, time-limited outcome study. A continuing issue will be whether treatments drawn from traditions not so amenable to accepted outcome research will ultimately be empirically validated when the methodology for doing so has been developed—or whether behavioral treatments will continue to predominate because they achieve positive outcomes other treatments do not.

Prominent psychotherapy researchers, including Garfield (1996), have criticized practice guidelines for being premature by implying greater knowledge of the variables that produce positive change than the state of our knowledge warrants. However, Nathan (1996) believes sufficient progress has been made in developing advanced outcomes methodologies and effective treatments to justify taking a chance and redoubling the efforts made to firmly base clinical practices on the best available empirical findings. Terence Wilson has written with eloquence on behalf of the same point:

> The development and implementation of empirically-validated treatments is seen by many mental health professionals as not only desirable but ethically imperative. It has been commonplace for some time now to emphasize patients' right to treatment and their right to refuse treatment. But patients should (also) have a right to safe and effective treatment. (Wilson, 1995, p. 163)

2.27.4 TRAINING IN EMPIRICALLY-VALIDATED TREATMENTS

The authors of the two sets of practice guidelines write of the importance of integrating training in empirically-validated treatments into training programs for family physicians and mental health professionals. However, a report by the Task Force on Promotion and Dissemination of Psychological Procedures (Crits-Christoph, Frank, Chambless, Brody, & Karp, 1995) revealed that clinical psychology training programs vary from 0 to 96% in the number of empirically-validated psychotherapeutic treatments they teach. Moreover, as Wilson (1995) laments, "underscoring the lack of attention to empirically-validated treatments, the report revealed that more than one-fifth of the programs did not teach anything about 75% or more of the treatment methods listed by the Task Force" (p. 165). Although comparable data for training programs in psychiatry and social work are not available, there is no reason to believe they differ in their degree of commitment to training in empirically-validated treatments.

Beyond the compelling arguments in favor of training in the use of empirically validated treatments from both clinical and ethical perspectives, proponents of doing so also point to an economic justification. In the managed care era of the 1990s, mental health practices that do not have strong empirical support—and do not yield the best possible outcomes—are unlikely to continue to be reimbursed (Barlow, 1994, Broskowski, 1995). Empirical validation of psychological treatments is especially important, Barlow (1994) has observed, since both the public and federal and state policy-makers mistakenly believe that few psychosocial treatments are efficacious. However, as the review of the evolution of empirically-validated treatments in this chapter strongly suggests, many psychological treatments both alone and in combination with drugs are now effective for a wide variety of conditions. Only when these empirical findings are more widely disseminated will patients gain fullest possible access to these treatments.

Wilson (1995) and Persons (1995), supporters of efforts to establish and promote empirically-validated treatments, have assembled some of the reasons empirically validated treatments have not been more widely embraced by mental health professionals. One of the most important factors is the failure of programs training mental health professionals to emphasize empirically-validated therapeutic methods and, conversely, the tendency of these programs to continue to provide training in therapies that lack empirical evidence of efficacy. These authors also cite the paucity of mental health professionals familiar with the empirical data on therapeutic outcomes, the persistent view among many clinicians that all psychotherapies are more or less effective, and the fact that most consumers of mental health services, like most mental health professionals, are not well informed about effective treatments, in further explanation of the relative neglect of empirically-validated treatments.

Since the early 1990s, more scientist-clinicians have begun to acknowledge the contributions empirically-based therapy practice guidelines can make to clinical practice. Clinton, McCormick, and Besteman (1994), Ogles, Lambert, and Sawyer (1995), Schooler (1994), and Schulberg and Rush (1994), among others, have described the diverse benefits therapy practice guidelines could bring. With bulimia nervosa, the focus of much of his clinical research, as an example, Wilson (1995) makes an especially strong case for the widest possible dissemination of empirically validated treatments:

> Moving aggressively in the direction of developing and implementing empirically-validated treatment methods would seem imperative in securing the place of psychological therapy in future health care policy and planning. . . . The development and implementation of empirically-validated treatments is seen by many mental health professionals as not only desirable but ethically imperative. It has been commonplace for some time now to emphasize patients' right to treatment and their right to refuse treatment. But patients should (also) have a right to safe and effective treatment. (Wilson, 1995, p. 163)

2.27.5 MANUALS FOR EMPIRICALLY-VALIDATED TREATMENTS

The decision of the drafters of the Division 12 practice guidelines (Division 12 Task Force, 1995) to include among the criteria for "well-established treatments" that the outcome studies demonstrating their efficacy used treatment manuals recognizes the importance of ensuring that the treatment is delivered as intended in these studies. There is also a growing sentiment among authorities on psychosocial treatment (e.g. Wilson, 1995) that treatment manuals have an important place in every clinician's clinical armamentarium, because they ensure that the treatment provided to the clinician's patients conforms to the standards of the empirically-validated treatment.

For this reason, annotated lists of manuals for empirically-validated treatments have begun to appear. One of the first (Sanderson & Woody, 1995) was a project of the Task Force on Psychological Interventions, a companion group to the Division 12 Task Force on Promotion and Dissemination of Psychological Interventions that developed the Division 12 practice guidelines. To compile their list, Sanderson, Woody, and their colleagues "wrote to leading investigators in the respective areas of treatment research, particularly those whose work formed the basis for judging a particular treatment to be efficacious" (Sanderson & Woody, 1995, p. 7).

The result was an annotated list of treatment manuals, complete with supporting references, for 17 treatments for 13 distinct syndromes: bulimia (cognitive behavioral therapy, interpersonal therapy); chronic headache (behavioral treatment); chronic pain (cognitive behavioral treatment); chronic mental illness (token economy programs); depression (cognitive therapy, interpersonal therapy); discordant couples (behavior therapy); enuresis (behavioral treatment); generalized anxiety disorder (anxiety management, cognitive behavior therapy); obsessive compulsive disorder (behavioral treatment); panic disorder (cognitive therapy); post traumatic stress disorder (cognitive behavioral treatment); social phobia (cognitive behavioral group therapy); and specific phobia (systematic desensitization, exposure therapy).

While the correspondence between this list of treatment manuals and the interventions meeting the Division 12 Task Force criteria for "well-established treatments" is predictably high, the two lists are not identical, although both largely include behavioral and cognitive behavioral interventions. A book has also been published (Van Hasselt & Hersen, 1996) which contains 17 detailed treatment manuals, including many of those identified by Sanderson and Woody (1995).

As noted above, Garfield's criticism of efforts to publicize empirically validated treatments (Garfield 1996) includes concerns about the growing preference for the use of treatment manuals in outcome studies. While Garfield recognizes that the inclusion of treatment manuals in outcome research is designed to buttress the integrity of the therapy being evaluated, he believes that requiring manuals to be employed raises a potentially important problem of external validity:

> The issue raised here is: Are the research findings secured with the use of training manuals directly relevant for the clinical practice of psychotherapy as performed by most practitioners? Whereas the psychotherapists in the research setting are trained and monitored to conform to a specific manual, this clearly is not the case with the average or modal practitioner . . . Consequently, research results based on the use of therapy manuals may have somewhat limited direct relevance for clinical practice. (Garfield, 1996, p. 220)

Garfield also cites Kazdin (1991) who laments the incompleteness of many treatment manuals as well as their failure to reflect the complexity of the therapeutic exchange between patient and therapist, as well as Dobson and Shaw (1988), who ask whether the use of treatment manuals renders research on therapist variables and therapeutic process more difficult.

Wilson (1995) takes issue with these criticisms of the use of treatment manuals both in psychotherapy research and in clinical settings. His advocacy for substantially more widespread use of treatment manuals derives from his conviction that empirically-validated treatments have been substantially undertaught, underpromoted, and underutilized; their wider promulgation, presumably, would be enhanced by an extension of the use of the treatment manuals developed for empirically-validated treatments, whose use would increase the likelihood that the treatment employed was the treatment originally assessed as valid.

2.27.6 FUTURE DIRECTIONS

Practice guidelines are understandably controversial. While the best of them reflect an empirical standard by which the adequacy of a treatment can be judged, they also impose constraints on the decision making of clinicians. Moreover, because they presumably reflect best practices, they will be of interest to managed-care practice monitors, just as they are to clinicians; some managed-care monitors will doubtless use them to assess the quality of practice of individual clinicians, with distinct economic consequences and contrary to the expressed intentions of their developers.

As noted above, concerns have also been raised that considerations other than empirical findings influence the drafters of guidelines. As time goes on and the ultimately corrosive potential of this temptation becomes even more clear, we can hope it will recede as a problem. One solution would be the development of a protocol to guide creators of practice guidelines by setting down a consensus statement of general principles applicable to all syndromes and all treatments. A Task Force of the American Psychological Association has proposed a "Template for developing guidelines: interventions for mental disorders and psychosocial aspects of physical disorders" (American Psychological Association Task Force, 1995). To a substantially greater extent than either the Division 12 or APA practice guidelines, the document explicates key aspects of the processes by which standards of proof ought to be selected and utilized. When further developed, refined, and evaluated, the template might well enable the developers of practice guidelines across the mental health professions to agree on important fundamentals. Above all, such an agreement would lead to establishment of a common set of standards of proof, reducing or eliminating unnecessary and confusing differences among guidelines.

Developed "to assure comprehensiveness and consistency" of practice guidelines, the template has two features especially relevant to this discussion. The first is designed to ensure that the efficacy of a treatment is not judged solely from the results of acceptable outcome studies alone, as important as they are; the nature of the treatment comparisons in those studies are to be considered in this judgment as well. Thus, the drafters of the Division 12 practice guidelines emphasized the adequacy of research designs and the quality of outcomes methodology in reaching their conclusions on efficacious treatments. Adding the nature of the outcome comparison—specifically to no treatment, nonspecific variables in treatment, or treatments known to be effective—provides an additional powerful evaluative dimension. A randomized clinical trial that compares an experimental treatment with one or more established, effective treatments, clearly represents a more powerful test than a randomized clinical trial that compares the experimental treatment to nonrobust comparison treatments or no treatment at all. Clinical scientists have known and generally followed this strategy when possible; making it explicit for consumers of treatment research as well as developers of practice guidelines is the next step.

A second notable feature of the template is the following distinction it draws between the efficacy of an intervention and its effectiveness or clinical utility; the same distinction was also drawn by Seligman (1995) in evaluating the results of the *Consumer Reports* (*Consumer Reports* Editors, 1996) survey:

clinical practice guidelines for behavioral health care (should) be constructed on the basis of two simultaneous considerations or "axes." The first is that guidelines take into consideration a rigorous assessment of scientific evidence with the goal of measuring the efficacy of any given intervention (efficacy). The second axis specifies that guidelines consider the applicability and feasibility of the intervention in the local setting where it is to be proffered (clinical utility). (American Psychological Association Task Force, 1995, p. i)

While a series of well-designed studies might establish the efficacy of an intervention, unless it is effective in real-life clinical settings, it will have little utility.

The clinical utility axis refers to the ability (and willingness) of practitioners to use, and of patients to accept, the treatment in question, and to the range of applicability of that treatment. It reflects the extent to which the intervention, regardless of the efficacy that may or may not have been demonstrated in the clinical research setting, will be effective in the practice setting in which it is to be applied. Among the factors that will be considered under this rubric are the generalizability of administering the intervention in various settings, the feasibility of the intervention across patients and settings, and the costs and benefits associated with the administration of the intervention. (American Psychological Association Task Force, 1995, p. 13)

Up to 1997, the methodology for efficacy studies has been substantially more advanced than that for effectiveness studies. While occasional studies of the generalizability of a treatment have been undertaken (e.g. Finney & Moos, 1997), the methodology for undertaking feasibility and costs and benefits studies requires substantial further development. An important future direction, then, involves the development of research strategies that will undertake effectiveness studies complementary to efficacy studies of the same treatments for the same syndromes.

2.27.7 SUMMARY

The history of systematic efforts to identify empirically-validated treatments for mental disorders is a short one. Only in the 1950s, coincident with Eysenck's influential article, "The effects of psychotherapy: an evaluation" (Eysenck, 1952), was treatment research first subjected to rigorous methodological scrutiny in the effort to distinguish effective from ineffective mental health treatments. Since then, research designs increasingly capable of discriminating efficacious psychosocial and pharmacological treatments have been developed. With Eysenck's 1952 article as a starting point, this chapter reviews several important efforts to distinguish empirically-validated treatments over the past 50 years.

Practice guidelines, reflecting more potent outcomes methodologies and more effective treatments, have been proposed by both the APA and the Division of Clinical Psychology of the American Psychological Association. The guidelines are controversial, however, both because they are new and untested, and because they have the potential to encroach upon the clinical decision-making role that has traditionally been solely the treating clinician's. Differences in the standards of proof on which the psychiatric and psychological practice guidelines rest are explored; they appear to stem from differences in the methodological criteria used to judge outcome studies as well as the degree to which clinical experience and judgment are accorded emphasis.

This review of the current status of empirically-validated treatments, practice guidelines, and standards of proof enables us to anticipate a series of desirable future directions for the continuation of efforts to promote best therapeutic practices among mental health professionals.

2.27.8 REFERENCES

American Psychiatric Association (1993). Practice guideline for the treatment of major depressive disorder in adults. *American Psychiatric Association, 150* (4 Suppl.), 1–26.

American Psychiatric Association (1994). Practice guideline for the treatment of patients with bipolar disorder. *American Journal of Psychiatry, 151* (12 Suppl.), 1–36.

American Psychiatric Association (1995). Practice guideline for the treatment of patients with substance use disorders: alcohol, cocaine, opioids. *American Journal of Psychiatry, 152* (11 Suppl.), 1–59.

American Psychological Association Task Force (1995). *Template for developing guidelines: Interventions for mental disorders and psychosocial aspects of physical disorders*. Washington, DC: Author.

Barlow, D. H. (1994). Psychological intervention in the era of managed competition. *Clinical Psychology: Science and Practice, 1*, 109–122.

Broskowski, A. T. (1995). The evolution of health care: Implications for the training and careers of psychologists. *Professional Psychology: Research and Practice, 26*, 156–162.

Clinton, J. J., McCormick, K., & Besteman, J. (1994). Enhancing clinical practice: The role of practice guidelines. *American Psychologist, 49*, 30–33.

Consumer Reports Editors (1996). Mental health: Does therapy help? *Consumer Reports, 60*, 734–737.

Craighead, L. W., Craighead, W. E., Kazdin, A. E., & Mahoney, M. J. (1994). *Cognitive and behavioral interventions: An empirical approach to mental health problems*. Boston: Allyn & Bacon.

Crits-Christoph, P., Frank, E., Chambless, D. L., Brody, C., & Karp., J. F. (1995). Training in empirically validated treatments: What are clinical psychology students learning? *Professional Psychology: Research and Practice, 26,* 514–522.

Denker, P. (1946). Results of treatment of psychoneuroses by the G.P. *New York State Journal of Medicine, 46,* 2164–2166.

Division 12 Task Force (1995). Training in and dissemination of empirically-validated psychological treatments: Report and recommendations. *The Clinical Psychologist, 48,* 3–23.

Dobson, K. S., & Shaw, B. F. (1988). The use of treatment manuals in cognitive therapy: Experience and issues. *Journal of Consulting and Clinical Psychology, 56,* 673–680.

Eysenck, H. J. (1952) The effects of psychotherapy: an evaluation. *Journal of Consulting Psychology, 16,* 319–324.

Eysenck, H. J. (1960). *Behavior therapy and the neuroses.* Oxford, UK: Pergamon.

Eysenck, H. J. (1969). *The effects of psychotherapy.* New York: Science House.

Finney, J., & Moos, R. (1997). Treatments for alcohol dependence. In P. E. Nathan & J. M. Gorman (Eds.), *Treatments that work.* New York: Oxford University Press.

Garfield, S. L. (1996). Some problems associated with "validated" forms of psychotherapy. *Clinical Psychology: Science and Practice, 3,* 218–229.

Goldfried, M. R., & Davison, G. C. (1994). *Clinical behavior therapy.* New York: Wiley.

Grady, K. E. (1995). Compliance with standards of care: Evidence from medical research. In S. C. Hayes, V. M. Follette, R. M. Dawes, & K. E. Grady (Eds.), *Scientific standards of psychological practice: Issues and recommendations* (pp. 83–91). Reno, NV: Context.

Howard, K. I., Kopta, S. M., Krause, M. S., & Orlinsky, D. E. (1986). The dose–effect relationship in psychotherapy. *American Psychologist, 41,* 159–164.

Kazdin, A. E. (1991). Treatment research: The investigation and evaluation of psychotherapy. In M. Hersen, A. E. Kazdin, & A. S. Bellack (Eds.), *The clinical psychology handbook* (2nd ed., pp. 293–312) New York: Pergamon.

Landis, C. (1937). A statistical evaluation of psychotherapeutic methods. In L. E. Hinsie (Ed.), *Concepts and problems in psychotherapy.* New York: Columbia University Press.

Luborsky, L., Singer, B., & Luborsky, L. (1976). Comparative studies of psychotherapies: Is it true that "everybody has won and all must have prizes"? In R. L. Spitzer & D. F. Klein (Eds.), *Evaluation of psychological therapies* (pp. 3–22). Baltimore: Johns Hopkins University Press.

Nathan, P. E. (1996). Validated forms of psychotherapy may lead to better-validated psychotherapy. *Clinical Psychology: Science and Practice, 3,* 250–254.

Nathan, P. E., & Gorman, J. M. (1997). *Treatments that work.* New York: Oxford University Press.

Ogles, B. M., Lambert, M. J., & Sawyer, J. D. (1995). Clinical significance of the National Institute of Mental Health treatment of depression collaborative research program data. *Journal of Consulting and Clinical Psychology, 63,* 321–326.

Pallack, M. S. (1995). Managed care and outcomes-based standards in the health care revolution. In S. C. Hayes, V. M. Follette, R. M. Dawes, & K. E. Grady (Eds.), *Scientific standards of psychological practice: Issues and recommendations* (pp. 73–77). Reno, NV: Context.

Persons, J. B. (1995). Why practicing psychologists are slow to adopt empirically-validated treatments. In S. C. Hayes, V. M. Follette, R. M. Dawes, & K. E. Grady (Eds.), *Scientific standards of psychological practice: Issues and recommendations* (pp. 141–157). Reno, NV: Context.

Persons, J. B., Thase, M. E., & Crits-Christoph, P. (1996). The role of psychotherapy in the treatment of depression. *Archives of General Psychiatry, 53,* 283–290.

Rachman, S. J. (1971). *The effects of psychological therapy.* Oxford, UK: Pergamon.

Rachman, S. J., & Wilson, G. T. (1980). *The effects of psychological therapy* (2nd enlarged ed.). Oxford, UK: Pergamon.

Sanderson, W. C., & Woody, S. (1995). Manuals for empirically validated treatments. *The Clinical Psychologist, 48,* 7–11.

Schooler, N. R. (1994). Translating treatment research findings into clinical action. *American Journal of Psychiatry, 151,* 1719–1721.

Schulberg, H. C., & Rush, A. J. (1994). Clinical practice guidelines for managing major depression in primary care practice: Implications for psychologists. *American Psychologist, 49,* 34–41.

Seligman, M. E. P. (1995). The effectiveness of psychotherapy: the *Consumer Reports* study. *American Psychologist, 50,* 965–974.

Smith, M. L., & Glass, G. V. (1977). Meta-analysis of psychotherapy outcome studies. *American Psychologist, 32,* 752–760.

Stiles, W. B., Shapiro, D. A., & Elliott, R. (1986). "Are all psychotherapies equivalent?" *American Psychologist, 41,* 165–180.

Van Hasselt, V. B., & Hersen, M. (Eds.) (1996). *Sourcebook of psychological treatment manuals for adult disorders.* New York: Plenum.

Wilson, G. T. (1995). Empirically validated treatments as a basis for clinical practice: Problems and prospects. In S. C. Hayes, V. M. Follette, R. M. Dawes, & K. E. Grady (Eds.), *Scientific standards of psychological practice: Issues and recommendations* (pp. 163–196). Reno, NV: Context.

2.28
Evidence-based Practice in Clinical Psychology

WILLIAM J. KELLEHER
Nova Southeastern University, Fort Lauderdale, FL, USA

2.28.1 INTRODUCTION

2.28.1.1 Definition and Components of "Evidence-based Practice"

Understanding certain rules of evidence is necessary to correctly interpret literature on causation, prognosis, diagnostic tests, and treatment strategy. It follows that clinicians should regularly consult the original literature (and be able to critically appraise the methods and results sections) in solving clinical problems and providing optimal patient care.

At the same time, systematic attempts to record observations in a reproducible and unbiased

> fashion markedly increase the confidence one can have in knowledge about patient prognosis, the value of diagnostic tests, and the efficacy of treatment. In the absence of systematic observation one must be cautious in the interpretation of information derived from clinical experience and intuition, for it may be misleading. (p. 2421)

Interestingly, the above principles are not taken from a clinical psychology treatise detailing the scientist–practitioner model or from a text in applied clinical psychology research design. Although it appears they just as well could have been from the nature of their content. Rather, they were published in the Journal of the American Medical Association (Evidence-based Medicine Working Group, 1992) as basic assumptions for what is refered to as the new paradigm of "Evidence-based medicine." This medical endorsement of the "evidence-based" concept for the practice of health care delivery seems especially noteworthy and timely as increased focus is being placed today on the relevance of the scientist–practitioner model in Clinical Psychology (Montgomery & Ayllon, 1995; O'Sullivan & Quevillon, 1992). What is being touted as new underpinings for the delivery of care by physicians has been advocated as the scientist–practitioner model for the training and practice of clinical psychologists since its pronouncement at the 1949 Boulder Conference (Raimy, 1950). This model's advocacy for the integration of empirical research and clinical psychology practice has been more fully articulated and affirmed in the 1992 National Conference on Scientist–Practitioner Education and Training for the Professional Practice of Psychology (Belar & Perry, 1992). The policy statement from that conference contains principles which are very similar to those detailed above for the model of "evidence-based medicine" and extend these further into specific recommendations for psychology doctoral training programs and the conduct of applied clinical research. What can be taken as a summary statement of that policy statement and the overall scientist–practitioner model follows: "Scientist–practitioner psychologists reflect a research orientation in their practice and a practice relevance in their research" (Belar & Perry, 1992, p. 74).

The concept of evidenced-based practice focuses on the clinical care delivery aspect of the scientist–practitioner model and has two primary components that will be examined in this chapter. In the evidence-based practice of clinical psychology, psychologists' commitment to their profession and to their patients demands an equal commitment to: (i) utilizing evidence-based intervention strategies and protocols that have demonstrated empirical support for the specific clinical problems for which their patients are seeking care, and (ii) employing an ongoing evidence-based patient progress tracking system with empirically supported outcome measures to assess treatment effectiveness. In adhering to both of these components, psychologists will be furthering the growth of their patients and, at the same time, the overall growth of empirical evidence for the practice of psychological intervention.

2.28.1.2 Growth of the Evidence-based Practice Model in Other Disciplines

These two components of evidence-based practice in clinical psychology are very consistent with the assumptions for the medicine counterpart quoted above. The opportunity for evidence-based practice is not unique for one discipline; better that it can be applied across health care disciplines in this age of multi-discipline providers' increasing involvement in the care of the same patient. Within the mental health field, social work has had advocates of an evidence-based model, which has at times been referred to as empirical clinical practice (Jayaratne & Levy, 1979, Witkin, 1991). There have been references in the psychiatric literature of a movement toward evidence-based psychiatry (Goldner & Bilsker, 1995), a concept that might have seemed quite improbable until the 1990s. What explains the growth since the late 1980s in these disciplines of the evidence-based practice concept which clinical psychology has been encouraging within its scientist–practitioner model for years? Why is it in the interest of our patients and our profession that as clinical psychologists we do not decrease our long standing advocacy of evidence-based practice but rather work toward its more consistent and widespread application throughout our discipline? These are two of the major questions to be addressed in this chapter.

2.28.1.3 Organization and Objectives

This review focuses on both components of evidence-based practice in clinical psychology as described above in terms of:

(i) current and projected future key factors encouraging use of the evidence-based practice model;

(ii) historical and current barriers to widespread adoption of the evidence-based practice model;

(iii) professional and technological innovations which have potential for expanding the application of evidence-based practice in mental health care delivery;

(iv) future directions forecasted and recommended for continued development of evidence-based practice; and

(v) a summary of the major supported findings and conclusions.

2.28.2 CURRENT FACTORS ENCOURAGING EVIDENCE-BASED PRACTICE

2.28.2.1 Major Changes in Funding Sources of Health Care

Since the mid-1980s the costs of health care in the United States have been increasing annually four percentage points or more above the rate of inflation (Burlingame, Lambert, Reisinger, Neff, & Mosier, 1995). Over the same period of time the amount spent for mental health care has been increasing at an astoundingly greater rate, with some estimates as high as 30–40% yearly (Giles, 1993). Broskowski (1991) attributes the increase in mental health care utilization to such factors as the growth in numbers of mental health care providers, decreasing stigma of mental health care with popularization in the media, and increased incidence of substance abuse problems. In response to these rapidly and seriously rising costs, private insurance and public agency funding sources for general health and mental health care have made very significant changes in their organization and mechanisms for continuing care coverage.

In the private sector, we have seen the dramatic development and revolutionary growth of managed health care to include employee assistance programs, Health Maintenance Organizations (HMOs), and Preferred Provider Organizations (PPOs). These are the third party payers' answers for dealing with the escalating health and mental health care costs (Foos, Ottens, & Hill, 1991). To illustrate the prevalence of these new forms of care delivery, Montgomery (1988) refers to a 1987 survey which indicated that already 80% of Fortune 500 companies had employee assistance programs for crisis intervention and short-term therapy. Because of this rise in managed care organizations, it has been predicted that by the year 2000 over half the private mental health practitioners will be out of their solo practice and only 5% of the physicians will be practicing independently (Cummings, 1987). Perhaps more to the point of our potential patients' source of funding for their care, it is estimated that in 1992 70% of the US population were receiving their health care by an HMO or other managed care system (Foos et al., 1991).

Given these facts and projected trends, it is necessary for clinical psychologists to be fully aware of the important parameters and to have the professional tools and skills for successful practice in the managed care environment. Much has been documented about the managed care emphases on cost and time efficiency in health care delivery (Giles & Marafiote, 1994; Mirin & Namerow, 1991), professional accountability (Benbenishty & Oyserman, 1995; Ludwigsen & Enright, 1988), utilizing metrics and outcome measures to demonstrate effective treatment (Giles, 1991; Linder, 1991), and preauthorization of a specified treatment plan and duration (Foos et al., 1991). Psychologists practicing from an evidence-based approach are well suited for these requirements as they will offer a detailed and planned treatment protocol which has empirical support and are prepared to work with the patient to monitor their progress regularly with objective measures. The evidence-based concentration on providing the treatment which is known to be successful for what the patient desires is also likely to satisfy the managed care agency's concern for customer satisfaction and keeps the provider very competitive for future referrals. Being as efficient as possible in the time limited therapy format, which tends to characterize empirically supported protocols, allows the evidence-based provider to provide relative savings in cost and time for the managed care agency as well as the patient. This savings potential takes on added significance in the capitation budget system of managed care which will only pay the provider a fixed amount per covered life per month (Giles, 1993).

Since the mid-1980s the public sector has seen dramatic and ongoing cuts in governmental budgets for support of mental health care. This has led to considerable downsizing and mental health providers having "to do more with less." As we have seen, this reduction in funding is occurring during a time of increased requests for services. Similarly, as we have seen for desired evidence-based practice responses to the managed care environment, using empirically supported interventions and system design can hopefully help psychologists and other mental health providers work more efficiently. Providing successful treatment with a time limited course of therapy can provide reinforcement of providers' quality work. This may also indirectly work to offset reportedly increasing community mental health center staff dissatisfaction and stress (Ebben, Bliss, & Perlman, 1991).

2.28.2.2 Professional Ethics and Commitment to Quality Patient Care

As part of their commitment to our patients, psychologists owe it to them to offer and be skilled in those treatments already empirically proven to provide the greatest therapeutic gain in the shortest amount of time. This is a central position of the evidence-based practice model and it touches on what is the ethical thing for psychologists to do when there are known therapy protocols with empirical support for the type of problem their patient is experiencing. Yeaton and Sechrest (1981), refering to what strength of therapy to recommend to a patient, advocate using what they call the "weakest that works" rule of thumb. Eysenck (1994) puts this in perspective perhaps more succinctly, "Where superior, cheaper, and quicker-acting methods of therapy are available, the continued use of expensive, lengthy, and noneffective methods is unethical and contrary to the best traditions of medicine" (p. 491). This scenario applies when there are known intervention strategies that work. As Elliott, Stiles, and Shapiro (1993) point out, when the research evidence is equivocal or not supportive of a particular treatment after controlled study, it is ethical to share that information with a patient who is seeking help for a related problem. Ignoring the positive empirical results supporting a particular treatment should be avoided just as much as making an unjustified blanket recommendation for an unsupported treatment.

As part of their ethical commitment to their patients, psychologists also owe it to them to follow another core principle of evidence-based practice, namely to be objectively tracking the degree of progress they are or are not making in response to treatment (Nelson, 1981). They then know whether to continue, modify, or discontinue treatment procedures and accordingly to do what they can to maintain a high quality of patient service. With the consistent use of outcome measures as the evidence-based practice model recommends, they will then be in the position to also fulfill a commitment to the profession and future potential patients through contributing to the applied clinical psychology research base. This is the scientist–practitioner at work and relates to what David Shakow (1976) believes is a central answer to the question posed in the title of his address to Division 12 of the American Psychological Association, namely, "What is Clinical Psychology?" Another way of capturing this aspect of evidence-based practice was expressed by Benbenishty and Oyserman (1995), "The challenge, therefore, is to collect clinically relevant data systematically, process and analyze it in ways that will inform practice, and to fold these insights back into the daily practice" (p. 312).

2.28.2.3 Empirical Support of Specific Treatment Protocols for Certain Clinical Problems

The scientist–practitioner model has generated numerous controlled studies (including attention/placebo and interorientation comparisons), meta-analyses, case studies, and review articles documenting the effectiveness of certain psychological treatments (Andrews, 1993; Giles, Neims, & Prial, 1993). The American Psychological Association created a task force to examine the research literature to report on the state of empirically supported treatments and to make any recommendations for the further advancement of successful therapy protocols. The findings of this task force have been summarized in a document referred to as the "Chambless Report" (based on the name of the task force chairperson) and it documents treatments found to be effective for many clinical problems, such as anxiety disorders, depression, tension and migraine headaches, marital discord, childhood enuresis, bulimia, tics, and obsessive–compulsive behavior (Task Force on Promotion and Dissemination of Psychological Procedures, 1995).

These empirically proven treatment protocols now make up the core of the current evidence-based practice treatment offerings and without their tested efficacy, psychotherapeutic interventions for their related conditions could not be presented with legitimate and ethical confidence. Many of these have well-developed and detailed protocols including manuals, patient information and workbook materials, monitoring forms, recommended outcome measures, prescribed sequences of therapeutic tasks, and projected program schedules. These supporting materials make it easier for the evidence-based practice provider to be trained in and to duplicate the effective program. However, this report and the treatments found to be effective and worthy of increased application have met with criticism and a lack of widespread distribution (Montgomery & Aylon, 1995). Giles et al. (1993) provide responses to criticisms which have been offered regarding the purported irrelevance of the meta-analyses, methodological deficiencies, and experimenter bias. These are critiques not unique to this body of literature but ones which some believe are actually managed with adequate experimental controls in many of these studies.

2.28.3 BARRIERS AGAINST EVIDENCE-BASED PRACTICE

2.28.3.1 Previous Fee for Service Funding System and Professional Inertia

Historically mental health care has been funded by third party payers according to a fee for service basis (Foos et al., 1991). This had encouraged the practice of treating patients for as long and as intensively as possible, the opposite of the evidence-based practice weakest that works rule of thumb presented earlier. At times, perhaps, this lengthy and intense therapy schedule format was motivated by the therapist's goal to guide the patient to a fully self-actualized state of optimum functioning or in some sense a cure. There is virtually no existing data that any form of therapy has been effective in helping patients achieve such an end-state and that such a therapeutic goal should be the target for intervention. In addition, unfortunately, there has been a lack of financial incentives to change this style of clinical practice but rather strong incentives to keep it going (Cummings, 1987). Bruce Thyer (1995) highlights that not only did this incentive system encourage more lengthy treatments than was necessary but also less concern about tracking progress and adjusting treatment accordingly; irrespective of outcome payment was the same. He observed further,

> Once one has graduated with a professional degree and obtained a state license to practice as a mental health services provider, there are few if any strictures as to what constitutes suitable treatment. Quite literally almost anything goes. (p. 93)

The two components of employing empirically proven protocols and monitoring ongoing measures of patient progress which we have presented as central to the evidence-based practice model were clearly not being encouraged by these fiscal contingencies. With no external pressure or patient outcome data to motivate change, providers were likely to stay with what was familiar to them in their treatment strategies. Again, this is quite inconsistent with evidence-based practice and choosing a therapy protocol not because it feels comfortable for the therapist but because it has been proven to be a right one for the patient. This calls for the therapist to be much more flexible, be open to new and more effective techniques, and to go where the data supports to go.

Unfortunately, the increasing costs generated by this tendency of what Giles (1993) calls the "overprescription of services" contributed to what we have already presented as the managed care revolution in health care delivery. Furthermore, with the discovery of unnecessary or self-serving tests and care being ordered, third party payers developed an increasing loss of faith in health care professionals' judgment, competence, and ethics (Ludwigsen & Enright, 1988). To illustrate some of the consequences of this distrust, we can look at a statement of a medical professional looking in at the mental health care system. John Montgomery (1988), a physician representing Aetna Life & Casualty writes,

> Employers also should be aware of the policies or practices of different treatment facilities. For example, some institutions continue to believe that patients with demonstrated psychological problems usually require a minimum of one full year of treatment. (p. 89)

It appears reasonable to assume that this physician would have a much more positive and trusting response to an evidence-based practice psychologist who was oriented toward offering the treatment that had the best chance of producing successful results for a particular patient in the shortest period of time rather than demanding an excessive minimum amount of time for all patients. Burlingame et al. (1995) propose that given the low ebb in professional trust, it is more critical than ever for providers to document clinical results at the end of treatment as well as by ongoing monitoring of patient progress. This is clearly consistent with the evidence-based practice model.

2.28.3.2 Literature Suggesting an Equivalence of All Psychotherapy

There has been a body of literature which purports an equivalence of all psychotherapeutic approaches to any clinical problem (Bergin & Lambert, 1978; Frank, 1973; Garfield, 1976). Eysenck (1952) wrote one of the first review papers of this type, concluding that psychotherapy has not been proven to have any efficacy. Factors such as the nonspecific placebo effect and spontaneous remission have been offered in defense of Eysenck's and these later reviewers' position. This equivalency conclusion was overlooking the later discovered statistical power and sample size problem and other methodological concerns with interorientation comparisons (Kazdin, 1994). These published conclusions from reviews of the psychotherapy literature could easily have added to the professional inertia described above that experienced providers stay with the therapy techniques for which they had training and felt familiar; after all, it appeared that no other approach would be any more effective for any kind of patient problem.

However, as it can be seen, psychologists now have data to support the efficacy of particular therapy protocols for many different kinds of clinical problems. Even Eysenck (1993, 1994) has modified his conclusions from reviews of the latest literature to note that behavior therapy is effective with a number of conditions. Yet the trend appears to be continuing for therapists to choose empirically undocumented or even contraindicated therapies rather than the empirically proven ones (Montgomery & Ayllon, 1995). Unfortunately, even managed care companies can operate on this outdated equivalency premise and, as a result, fund whoever will provide the equivalent intervention service cheaper, including paraprofessionals with limited training and/or supervision (Giles & Marafiote, 1994). Another misinterpretation possible for managed care system designers from this equivalency assumption was that all mental health patients and problems were equivalent and, therefore, could be successfully managed with the same maximum number of sessions. Given this history and current state of misattributed restrictions on funding, the evidence-base practitioners have their work cut out for them in educating and modifying the managed care community as well as the providers who are still unaware of the advances in empirically supported treatments.

2.28.3.3 The Gap Between Practitioners and Researchers

Clinical researchers (including those demonstrating empirical success with specific treatment protocols) have been criticized for designing their studies or writing their reports without taking into account the realistic clinic caseloads or language to which providers can easily relate (Montgomery & Ayllon, 1995). This contributes to practitioners not consulting or relying on research results for guidance on how to practice (Forsyth & Strong, 1986; Hoshmand & Polkinghorne, 1992). Kordy (1995) presents the conflict between researchers and providers as an interactive one, "Critics blame psychotherapy research for asking the questions which no practitioner is interested in because he/she already knows the answer or doesn't want to know it" (p. 128). Some surveys (Norcross, Prochaska, & Gallagher, 1989) suggest that few providers rely on empirical evidence to guide their practice. Barlow (1981) wrote, "Clinical research has very little or no influence on clinical practice" (p. 147). Needless to say, these observations illustrate the professional habits of a large number of psychologists which were antithetical to the evidence-based practice model. Some (Frank, 1984) went so far as to say that the researcher and the clinician were fundamentally different people and implied that never the twain shall meet. In a related tone, Elliot et al. (1993) refer to the relationship between those who do research and those involved with clinical practice as a dysfunctional one and question whether given this rift any accommodation is possible.

To challenge the notion of separateness and incompatibility of research and practice, Steinmeyer (1994) suggests that scientist–practitioner activity is a much more appropriate term than implying the model is the mark of the person involved. Persons (1993) perceives the reasons for the scientist–practitioner gap to be quite understandable given the different reinforcement contingencies operating on each. Belar and Perry (1992) present in the National Conference of Scientist–Practitioner Education and Training policy statement, "The scientist–practitioner is, by definition, also committed to bridging the gap between scientific foundations and professional practice" (p. 72). They propose that the hyphen between "scientist" and "practitioner" be replaced in future writings by a "~" or an "x" to symbolize integration which they believe is very possible and should be stimulated from the very beginning of psychology doctoral training programs. Related to this, there is further hope of this scientist–practitioner integration generated by the results of such surveys as that of O'Sullivan and Quevillon (1992) which indicate that 98% of doctoral program directors report their programs have always followed, and plan to continue to follow, the Boulder scientist–practitioner training model. The growth of evidence-based practice requires that these graduating psychologists carry this model out into their first clinical positions and beyond. Hopefully, the innovations in technology, applied research methodology, and provider organization, which are reviewed in the next section of this chapter, will help to overcome the barriers discussed in this section and further this growth for self-sustaining progress toward more efficient and effective patient care into the twenty-first century.

2.28.3.4 Limited Dissemination and Training of Empirically Supported Therapy

Many of the more empirically supported treatments are relatively new and have not had widespread dissemination (Andrews, 1993). Many providers, therefore, are not trained in these protocols and have had limited opportunities to pursue this training. This seems to be at least a contributing factor to these effective therapies "not being utilized by even a minority of practitioners" (Giles, 1993) in addition to the barriers for evidence-based practice we have already reviewed. To be more specific, training in these new techniques has had limited availability on a psychology graduate school level as well as in postgraduate or continuing professional education courses. Thyer (1995) comments that snake oil Continuing Education Units are rampant and that, given the limited availability of continuing education credits, the more nonempirically supported treatments are endorsed by professional organizations for Continuing Education credit, the less there will be for the evidence-based therapies.

Professional mental health organizations have been slow to provide official support and impetus for more widespread adoption of the evidence-based practice model and empirically supported treatments. Accreditation standards for academic training and internships tend to omit reference to empirically based treatment. Workshops and training programs in treatments not empirically supported continue to receive support for continuing education credit. Licensing boards are also not addressing the importance of evidence-based practice in their examination and review of professional credentials. All of these organizational behaviors contribute to the contingencies and reinforcement system in which psychology providers serve and as such play a role in the delayed advancement of evidence-based practice.

2.28.3.5 Proliferation and Nonstandardization of Therapeutic Outcome Measures

There has been a proliferation of instruments purported to measure psychological treatment outcome with little effort made to standardize a set of the more valid and reliable metrics for use with particular conditions (Mirin & Namerow, 1991). One review article count totaled over 1400 different measures which have been utilized, with many of these having been designed and employed in a single study (Lambert & Hill, 1994; Lambert, Ogles, & Masters, 1992). This very large number and lack of standardized selection could be contributing to the frequently observed clinical situation of choosing an outcome measure that will not significantly add to the evidence base or, worse yet, will not accurately track the patient's progress. Reportedly, 33% of all US health care institutions are not active in ongoing outcomes research in spite of the staggering number of measures that have been utilized by others (Burlingame et al., 1995).

In addition to this proliferation issue, other factors have been hypothesized as barriers to providers consistently employing outcome measures of their treatment effectiveness. The cost of resources to collect, score, and report the results of these measures in some settings is seen as prohibitive. Some purport that assessing psychotherapy-related change is extremely complex and difficult (Martinovich, Saunders, & Howard, 1996). For example, the selection of measures could well include a variety of change areas and be completed by the patient or significant others. There is widespread disagreement about what types of measures deserve the highest priority with a variety of conceptual schemes and a combination of measures proposed (Elliott, 1992; Lambert et al., 1992; Ryle, 1995). Psychologists committed to evidence-based practice must therefore keep their focus while navigating this maze of metrics with an educated eye for the most relevant, valid, and reliable measures that realistically lend themselves for completion by the patients on a repeating schedule.

In summarizing the current state of affairs in outcome measure selection and the future expansion of the evidence-based practice model, Lambert and Hill (1994) conclude,

> We look forward to the day when researchers can agree on a minimal core outcome battery for measuring change in patients with specific disorders. We are convinced that most of the necessary measures to be included in such batteries already exist.

Indeed, consensus on outcome measures would advance evidence-based practice and the further investigation of which therapies offer the greater potential for patients to achieve their emotional and behavioral goals. In the mean time, it would be wise for providers to make educated choices given the best information available and begin gathering data. The third party payer agencies, as has been presented, want to see the results of such tracking and if the treating psychologists do not make the selection of outcome measures themselves the funding source is likely to fill the void and dictate which metric they expect to see employed. Compared to the third party payer, the psychologist who is functioning as a scientist–practitioner will be in a much better position to choose the instruments sensitive to the most relevant areas of patient change.

2.28.3.6 Growth of Multidisciplinary and Paraprofessional Care Settings

"Perhaps the biggest impediment to collecting useful outcome data is the complex nature of the mental health care delivery system itself"

(Mirin & Namerow, 1991, p. 1009). Since the mid-1980s, there has been a significant increase in demand for mental health care services and a resultant burgeoning of patient caseloads. Managed care has stimulated an increase in patients being treated in settings staffed by practitioners from a variety of health care disciplines and paraprofessionals as well. This type of setting has been touted as offering a better continuum of care than the more traditional single discipline office. However, as a result, it is becoming more difficult pragmatically for providers to monitor each patient's entire record closely and be able to oversee the selection, administration, analysis, and reporting of relevant outcome measures efficiently. This is further complicated by the increasingly complex administrative and fiscal tracking of patients required by their health care insurance companies. Some patients have supplemental insurance plans which need to be addressed in addition to their primary coverage. Therefore, it has become quite difficult for any one provider to organize and manage the tremendous amount of information and data accumulating for his or her patients.

At the same time in these settings, not all the providers, or the health care organization itself, will necessarily share the psychologist's training or inclination to operate within the scientist–practitioner, evidence-based model. Steinmeyer (1994) observes that a lack of differentiation in clinical position requirements among mental health professional disciplines has been developing; what the psychologist, social worker, or psychiatrist can offer is more and more being seen as interchangeable or equivalent. Furthermore, the paraprofessional is being viewed and hired as a cheaper and preferred form of labor who can provide similar or equivalent services as the more expensive psychiatrists, psychologists, and social workers (Cummings, 1987). Thus, the care organization funding the mental health professional could well not be specifically looking for a scientist–practitioner or someone with a psychologist's training and inclination for evidence-based practice. The psychologist working in such a setting will then have to rely much more on his or her own resources and contingencies to pursue and maintain a focus on providing care which is empirically supported and empirically monitored.

This trend away from recognizing the scientific background psychologists and other professionals can bring to the care organization becomes more critical as it is being found that the multidisciplinary continuum of care setting will not always, necessarily, produce effective, or even cost efficient, care. Bickman (1996) reporting on the results of the comprehensive, multidisciplinary Fort Bragg Demonstration Project for children and adolescents states,

> This study raises significant questions about the validity of several widely held beliefs. The cost-effectiveness of the continuum of care has been challenged, as has, more generally, the effectiveness of services as delivered in community settings. (p. 699)

The author further observes that the system of care delivery changes we are seeing with managed care may well improve access and customer satisfaction ratings but "is unlikely to reform clinical outcomes unless it also reforms the actual services delivered. However, there is little research to provide guidance as to what changes in services are required." Therefore, it is concluded that the need for research integrated with practice in the community care delivery setting is much more needed now than ever; unfortunately this is occurring at a time when some organizations are selecting their providers irrespective of their support and training for such evidence-based practice.

This ongoing need for applied clinical research can also be supported by the rapid development observed in brief and packaged therapies in the managed care settings (Foos et al., 1991). As it is being found that "multidisciplinary" does not always lead to more effective and efficient care, so too brief or time limited care may not necessarily result in longer term savings and success. This type of care delivery calls for as much empirical research as has been advocated for the more traditional methods of mental health care. Similarly, an increase in manualized therapy, while it can have advantages for potentially increasing the consistent replication of proven protocols, does not insure positive results and needs to be studied further. Therefore, the opportunities for the scientist–practitioner to be challenged in today's health care environment appear to be increasing but, as has been presented, so too are the potential interferences.

2.28.3.7 Inconsistent Advocacy of Evidence-based Practice for Some Therapy Orientations

Some psychotherapeutic orientations have proponents sending out mixed signals about the relevance and importance of utilizing outcome measures to track treatment effectiveness. For example, consider what is being supported and advocated for the study of psychoanalysis or psychodynamic therapy. From one perspective (Gray, 1996) it is being written that because the desired outcomes of psychoanalysis (i.e., developing a more coherent sense of self, restructuring one's personality, rewriting one's history, or resuming emotional growth) can be unique for the individual patient, "to operationalize these variables for an outcome study may at this time be beyond our technical grasp" (p. 215). This article continues that even writing daily progress notes "violates the core psychoanalytic technique of listening with even-hovering attention." Notes are therefore not likely to be available as a database for review of psychoanalysis. This position certainly does not suggest psychoanalysis and an evidence-based practice orientation are a match even though the title of this article is *Developing Practice Guidelines for Psychoanalysis*. This position, antithetical to evidence-based practice, flies in the face of the work of the Strupp group at Vanderbilt University, the Luborsky group at the University of Pennsylvania, and others who are finding ways to deal with the outcome measure problem in psychoanalysis (Vaughn, Marshall, MacKinnon, & Roose, 1994). Connolly and Strupp (1996) use cluster analysis with patients' writings of reported change to study outcome of psychoanalytic treatment. Luborsky (1995) has changed his position about how viable the integration of research and practice can be. He is now "welcoming the new emphasis on 'grass-roots' research-audit and 'low-tech' investigations aimed at monitoring service delivery and providing information of use to both providers and users of services" (p. 123). This is very close to the research drives practice and practice drives research principle that is underlying evidence-based practice. As consistently or as inconsistently a psychotherapeutic orientation's proponents advocate this position, so may go evidence-based practice for the providers espousing that orientation, whether it be psychoanalytic, behavior, existential, interpersonal, cognitive-behavioral, or other type of therapy.

2.28.4 INNOVATIONS FOR POTENTIAL EVIDENCE-BASED PRACTICE SUPPORT

2.28.4.1 Advances in Computerized Database Technology

There has been a rapid and potentially very valuable growth in the development of clinical information database management systems especially designed for mental health care delivery (Wedding, Topolski, & McGaha, 1995). The better designed of these systems can greatly stimulate the movement toward evidence-based practice through more accurate and efficient computerized processing of the data related to the patient, the provider, the assessment, the treatment, the outcome measures, and many other potentially important variables. As has been presented earlier, the amount of information accumulating and being required to be processed for today's patient in the managed care environment is becoming more than one provider or a group of providers can process, let alone continuously track, analyze, and report in a coherent manner. The computerized information management system can greatly encourage attending to the relevance of a particular treatment for a particular type of patient problem, given that the relevant data can be more easily and clearly visible to all involved. The lessons such a system's utilization allows the providers to learn about effective patient care can be fed back into the system for prescribing such empirically proven therapeutic alternatives with future patients who have similar clinical problems. "The assumption is that sound information could guide program efforts by the results obtained, rather than following practices based on convention or professional ideology" (p. 48). This seems quite in line with the scientist–practitioner concept and a natural for evidence-based practice.

In this age of multidisciplinary provider care delivery settings, the use of a well-designed clinical information management system can also lead to improved communication within the provider network. This in turn could foster more integration of the entire behavioral care community working with a patient and increase overall efficiency and effectiveness (Fessenden & Vogt, 1995). Furthermore, with the emphasis we have seen on fiscal concerns for health care, the cost savings factor of such automated systems should not be ignored. The more comprehensive clinical database package system can also track accounting information and produce billing and other financial reports; and it can do all of this with fewer administrative and accounting errors than noncomputerized systems (Brown, Fraser, & Bendoraitis, 1995). Therefore, what can be good for clinical evidence-based practice can also be very beneficial for the funding system that supports the organization where the care is provided.

Some potential problems, however, need to be addressed and considered with the utilization of a comprehensive clinical information management system. There could be a threat to protecting the patient's confidentiality given that a considerable amount of sensitive information will be residing on a computer hard drive or floppy disk. Obviously, it is critical that appropriate security measures are well-planned and in place from the point of first instaling the system. This will limit the access and processing of all personal information to only those qualified and ethically bound by their profession to preserve the patient's privacy rights. Another important consideration is how the information system is utilized by the organization's administration or personnel office. The clinical value of the system can be undermined if it is used more for managerial control (e.g., personnel utilization review or checking provider productivity) than it is for patient care outcome tracking and reinforcement of staff members' quality work (Binner, 1993).

2.28.4.2 Growth of Provider Networks for Increased Collaboration and Peer Review

As briefly highlighted previously, a variety of different types of provider networks and organizations are being established to maximize efficiency and provide patients with integrated comprehensive care when indicated. These have the potential to allow for easier professional consultation, peer review, and comparison of provider databases to encourage treatment which is responsive to patient progress or lack thereof and is in accord with empirically proven standards of care (Broskowski, 1991). There are descriptions in the literature of such agencies for providers as: psychologists and others in Biodyne (Cummings, 1987), psychiatrists in a professional affiliation group and an HMO virtual group practice (Pomerantz, Liptzin, Carter, & Perlman, 1994, 1995), and psychiatric networks in Canada (Kates, Adsett, Bellissimo, Levine, & Humphrey, 1993). However, as we have seen with the Fort Bragg Demonstration Project results (Bickman, 1996), a network or provider group organization does not by the fact alone of its formation or the breadth of the services it offers insure that effective and efficient treatment will be the results. This would need to be monitored and confirmed through planed empirical evaluation and controled comparisons with other forms of service delivery.

An apparently well-planned and organized model for this type of provider collaboration is that of the Pennsylvania Practice Research Network. This network brings together psychologists who are members of the Pennsylvania Psychological Association (PPA) for several important goals: (i) to design a core assessment battery to measure treatment outcome of all patients treated by PPA psychologists; (ii) to start research based on these assessments as well as patient demographic and diagnostic information to address questions regarding such issues as the nature of the disorders, predictors of outcome, patterns of technique practice, relationships of techniques to outcomes, and overall efficacy of therapy in Pennsylvania, and (iii) to use the network infrastructure "to create other basic and applied therapy research studies among subsets of interested Network member" (T. D. Borkovec, personal communication, May 6, 1996). This network seems to be well on the road to taking the fullest advantage of the significant potential available through a provider organization to further effective patient care. It is the scientist–practitioner model and evidence-based practice in action.

2.28.4.3 New Applied Research Design and Statistical Techniques

We have seen the development of clinical research design and statistical techniques which allow the individual provider or network of providers to contribute to the evidence base for effectiveness of psychotherapy without changing their day-to-day care delivery schedule or caseload (Hoshmand & Polkinghorne, 1992). These techniques and design procedures, if used appropriately, can help narrow the gap and foster the integration of research and practice in clinical psychology and other health care disciplines. Three of the more significant of these developments appear to be: time series methodology (Hayes, 1981), single case study design (Kazdin, 1981), and using measures of clinical significance (Jacobson, Follette, & Revenstorf, 1984; Jacobson & Truax, 1991; Tingey, Lambert, Burlingame, & Hansen, 1996). Time series methodology and case study designs allow for providers to systematically track a single subject or groups of single subjects in a controled study of their response to treatment in comparison to themselves in various conditions of therapy or in a period of no intervention. As Kazdin (1981) notes these designs are not meant to replace experimental research, they "can provide relatively clear information about the impact of treatment" and "probably will continue to contribute greatly to the information available in the field" (p. 191). Measures of clinical significance evaluate the extent to which patients who have received intervention compare with individuals who are functioning well. It could involve analyzing the degree to which the treated patients perform at, or are within, the normative range for a certain type of measure or instrument. Another measure of clinical significance could be to examine whether the individuals who received therapy have made behavioral changes of a certain magnitude and whether they are now significantly improved in their performance rates of this behavior compared to a sample known to be in a dysfunctional group. This type of measure can be seen as getting closer to the bottom line of what patients themselves and third party payers are interested in as outcome results and as such add a significantly important tool to the repertoire of the provider committed to evidence-based practice.

2.28.4.4 Development of Clinical Practice Guidelines

Mental health care disciplines are beginning to follow the lead of medicine and promote the establishment of clinical practice guidelines for particular diagnoses. In medicine, these published guidelines are recommended strategies for the management of patients with a specific clinical condition and are designed to assist the physician with clinical decision-making for choice of medication, clinical tests, prescribed patient activity, and other patient management parameters. In addition, they could indicate the range of what are considered acceptable approaches for diagnosing, managing, and possibly preventing the particular conditions. When applied to mental health care, this practice guideline concept has the potential for clearly highlighting and supporting empirically proven psychotherapeutic protocols for our own profession, referring providers in other disciplines, third party payers, and potential patients. Those programs referred to earlier which have already been found to be effective in empirical research with specific mental health problems would seem to be excellent sources for developing the content of such mental health practice guidelines.

To further illustrate how far this guidelines concept can be stretched and utilized even in the absence of objective empirical evidence consider the proposal of practice guidelines for psychoanalysis previously discussed. Gray (1996) refers to these as "consensus-based practice guidelines" which "codify and integrate existing clinical intelligence and the rich oral tradition in medicine. This makes them better suited than outcome-based parameters for the task of helping the psychiatrist integrate the biospsychosocial aspects of a case" (pp. 213–214). Gray goes on to state that developing guidelines for psychoanalysis on the basis of outcome studies would be "incomplete and difficult to implement." An evidence-based practice orientation would seem to lend itself to finding the development of practice guidelines for conditions with demonstrated treatment effectiveness not as difficult to implement.

2.28.4.5 Innovations for Computerized On-line Information Exchange

Technology has significantly improved for computerized on-line professional literature searches and for staying current with the empirical research literature. Through the use of a computer and a modem, it is no longer necessary to leave the office, travel to a library with adequate medical resources, spend hours going through card catalogs and journal reviews, locating relevant articles, and writing notes on important findings. Now this all can be done very efficiently, accurately, and comprehensively within a few minutes search through the Internet. There is data which suggests that medical students can significantly profit from specific training in how to use these on-line resources, including Medline, in support of the evidence-based medicine model (Evidence-Based Medicine Working Group, 1992). The APA sponsors such an on-line service for searching the mental health literature. Given the potential offered by this technological innovation, it could be said that the evidence-based practitioner has never had it easier.

2.28.5 FUTURE DIRECTIONS AND RECOMMENDATIONS

It appears most likely that the emphases on treatment cost and time efficiency as well as being able to demonstrate clinical effectiveness of therapy will not go away but rather become mandatory for continued mental health care funding. Therefore, the more important and critical becomes the reliance of clinical psychologists on both aspects of the evidence-based practice model, research driving practice and practice driving research. The following recommendations for the different components of the psychological care delivery structure seem worthy of serious consideration and pursuit for more quickly responding to these anticipated requirements and, at the same time, they can contribute to the further growth of evidence-based practice in mental health care. Many of these recommendations are consistent with those from the Chambless Report referred to earlier as well as from the conclusions of similar empirically supported literature reviews such as Thyer (1995).

2.28.5.1 National Psychological Associations

(i) Require training for empirically proven treatments for full accreditation of psychology graduate school and internship programs.

(ii) Publicly endorse treatments which have received empirical support. Actively promote and sponsor workshops in these techniques. Encourage members to become skilled in and utilize these protocols as treatments of choice with their patients who present with related clinical problems.

(iii) Grant continuing education credit only for those workshops offering training in treatments with an established record of empirical support.

(iv) Work with managed care organizations to help them better understand the different parameters (i.e., number and frequency of recommended treatment sessions, other assessment and treatment resources found necessary, etc.) of treatment programs required for different clinical conditions. Educate the administrators of such agencies that not all patients with all mental health conditions have been found to be helped within the same maximum number of allotted sessions.

(v) Organize and sponsor more conferences and symposia similar to the 1993 National Conference on Scientist–Practitioner Education and Training to stimulate more definition and support of the evidence-based practice model.

(vi) Include elements in the organization's code of ethical practice stressing that patients be presented with, as first choice interventions, those strategies that have received empirical support for the type of problem they are seeking help and that providers routinely monitor treatment progress with relevant and validated outcome measures.

(vii) Publish clinical practice guidelines for the conditions that the organization's members have established treatments with empirical support.

2.28.5.2 Clinical Psychology Providers and Researchers

(i) Remain current with applied clinical literature, seeking to be knowledgeable of empirically proven treatments, especially for the type of clinical problems the provider is most commonly requested to treat.

(ii) Obtain training in those empirically proven protocols for clinical problems most frequently encountered. Utilize the protocols, manual, and patient educational or monitoring materials that have already been prepared if they are available for use. This will encourage adherence to the proven techniques and efficiency of effort.

(iii) If not skilled in a proven protocol for the problem with which a patient is presenting, seriously consider referring the patient to a provider (if one is conveniently available) who is trained for such treatment. Explain the circumstances regarding the potential referral to the patient.

(iv) Wherever possible, utilize ongoing objective outcome measures and participate in a clinical information database management system to more easily track ongoing patient progress. Consider reporting illustrative results in a case study or time series format for a professional journal.

(v) Network with other psychologists for participation in a peer review process and possible collaboration in an applied clinical research project. Affiliation with a local hospital may be a mechanism for this type of association.

(vi) Adopt a mind set of therapeutic goals with shorter term sights than the notion of full self-actualization, being oriented toward helping the patient achieve a more adaptive level of functioning and emotional well-being.

(vii) As best as possible, utilize sound clinical judgment in offering treatment for those problems not as yet fully researched. Be systematic in monitoring the results of a treatment plan which has not be adequately tested for that type of clinical condition. Review the data and patient report frequently and be ready to change the direction of therapy as the results are suggesting.

(viii) Research needs to move outside the laboratory and academic settings to study services in the community and clinics where care is more routinely provided. The need has never been as great as it is now for the integration of research and practice.

2.28.5.3 Clinical Psychology Doctoral Training Programs

(i) Follow the guidelines developed at the National Conference on Scientist–Practitioner Education and Training for the Professional Practice of Psychology (Belar & Perry, 1993).

(ii) Recruit faculty who are skilled and experienced in applied clinical research, especially with experience investigating empirical supported treatments, and who support the scientist–practitioner model.

(iii) Offer course work, supervision, and practicum experiences for students to acquire and increase their skills for those treatment protocols with demonstrated treatment effectiveness. Similarly, provide instruction in treatment outcome measure selection and a variety of practical research design techniques, including those for single subject and case study.

(iv) Provide facilities and training for efficiently using the latest technologies in literature reviews and management information systems.

2.28.6 SUMMARY

Evidence-based practice in clinical psychology involves consistently utilizing empirically supported intervention techniques which are proven to be effective for a patient's presenting clinical problem as well as continuously monitoring treatment progress with validated outcome measures. It is consistent with the scientist–practitioner model which since the 1950s has been strongly advocated for clinical psychology training and practice. Given today's managed care environment with its call for cost and time efficiency, accountability, demonstrated results, and customer focus in health care delivery, the need and relevance of the evidence-based practice model have never been greater. This model is also considered very appropriate for today's psychologists to adopt given its consistency with the ethical standards of clinical psychology practice and the significant amount of studies in the professional mental health literature which document the effectiveness of specific treatment protocols for a variety of clinical conditions. These empirically supported treatments are highlighted in the APA Division 12 Task Force Report (1993) commissioned to investigate the effectiveness of psychotherapy literature.

Historically, there have been barriers to the widespread adoption of evidence-based practice and the scientist–practitioner model. These have included: the fee for service funding system, earlier review articles which suggested an equivalence of results for all psychotherapy, a significant gap between those professionals who conducted research and those who delivered patient care, a lack of dissemination and available training for the empirically proven treatments, a tendency for therapists to stay with delivering service in the orientation that felt familiar and not track its real effectiveness for each patient, an overwhelming number of available outcome measures with little standardization of a recommended selection for use, and some inconsistent advocacy of the scientist–practitioner approach within certain therapeutic orientations.

During the 1990s, advances in computer technology, clinical information management systems, and medicine's movement in the evidence-based practice direction are now supporting evidence-based practice in clinical psychology more than ever. National psychological associations, psychology doctoral programs, and individual psychologists can now take full advantage of this prime opportunity to stimulate a more widespread growth of evidence-based practice in clinical psychology by pursuing a variety of recommended actions. Through such action, our profession and our patients can only gain.

2.28.7 REFERENCES

Andrews, G. (1993). The essential psychotherapies. *British Journal of Psychiatry*, *162*, 447–451.

Barlow, D. H. (1981). On the relation of clinical research to clinical practice: Current issues, new directions. *Journal of Consulting and Clinical Psychology*, *49*, 147–155.

Belar, C. D., & Perry, N. W. (1992). National conference on scientist–practitioner education and training for the professional practice of psychology. *American Psychologist*, *47*, 71–75.

Benbenishty, R., & Oyserman, D. (1995). Integrated information systems for human services: A conceptual framework, methodology, and technology. *Computers in Human Services*, *12*, 311–325.

Bergin, A. E., & Lambert, M. J. (1978). The evaluation of therapeutic outcomes. In S. L. Garfield & A. E. Bergin (Eds.), *Handbook of psychotherapy and behavior change* (2nd ed., pp. 16–37). New York: Wiley.

Bickman, L. (1996). A continuum of care: More is not always better. *American Psychologist*, *51*, 689–701.

Binner, P. R. (1993). Information systems and mental health services: Issues for the 90's. *Computers in Human Services*, 47–57.

Broskowski, A. (1991). Current mental health care environments: Why managed care is necessary. *Professional Psychology: Research and Practice*, *22*, 6–14.

Brown, G. S., Fraser, J. B., & Bendoraitis, T. M. (1995). Transforming the future: The coming impact of CIS. *Behavioral Health Management*, *15*, 8–12.

Burlingame, G. M., Lambert, M. J., Reisinger, C. W, Neff, W. M., & Mosier, J. (1995). Pragmatics of tracking mental health outcomes in a managed care setting. *The Journal of Mental Health Administration*, *22*, 226–236.

Connolly, M. B., & Strupp, H. H. (1996). Cluster analysis of patient reported psychotherapy outcomes. *Psychotherapy Research*, *6*, 30–42.

Cummings, N. A. (1987). The future of psychotherapy: One psychologist's perspective. *American Journal of Psychotherapy*, *41*, 349–360.

Ebben, P. A., Bliss, D., & Perlman, B. (1991). Brief report: Problems and issues in community mental health service delivery in the 1990s. *Community Mental Health Journal*, *27*, 225–229.

Elliott, R. (1992). A conceptual analysis of Lambert, Ogles, and Masters's conceptual scheme for outcome assessment. *Journal of Counseling & Development*, *70*, 535–537.

Elliott, R., Stiles, W. B., & Shapiro, D. A. (1993). Are some psychotherapies more equivalent than others? In T. R. Giles (Ed.), *Handbook of effective psychotherapy* (pp. 455–479). New York: Plenum.

Evidence-based Medicine Working Group (1992). Evidence-based medicine: A new approach to teaching the practice of medicine. *Journal of the American Medical Association 268*, 2420–2425.

Eysenck, H. J. (1952). The effects of psychotherapy: An evaluation. *Journal of Consulting Psychology*, *16*, 319–324.

Eysenck, H. J. (1993). Forty years on: The outcome problem in psychotherapy revisited. In T. R. Giles (Ed.), *Handbook of effective psychotherapy* (pp. 3–20). New York: Plenum.

Eysenck, H. J. (1994). The outcome problem in psychotherapy: What have we learned? *Behaviour Research and Therapy*, *32*, 477–495.

Fessenden, R., & Vogt, D. (1995). Speaking the same language: A new approach to documentation. *Behavioral Health Management*, *15*, 22–27.

Foos, J. A., Ottens, A. J., & Hill, L. K. (1991). Managed

mental health: A primer for counselors. *Journal of Counseling & Development*, *69*, 332–336.

Forsyth, D. R., & Strong, S. R. (1986). The scientific study of counseling and psychotherapy: A unificationist view. *American Psychologist*, *41*, 113–119.

Frank, G. (1984). The Boulder model: History, rationale, and critique. *Professional Psychology: Research & Practice*, *15*, 417–435.

Frank, J. D. (1973). *Persuasion and healing*. Baltimore, MD: Johns Hopkins University Press.

Garfield, S. L. (1976). All roads lead to Rome. *Contemporary Psychology*, *21*, 328–329.

Giles, T. R. (1991). Managed mental health care and effective psychotherapy: A step in the right direction? *Journal of Behavior Therapy and Experimental Psychiatry*, *22*, 83–86.

Giles. T. R. (1993). Consumer advocacy and effective psychotherapy: The managed care alternative. In T. R. Giles (Ed.), *Handbook of effective psychotherapy* (pp. 481–488). New York: Plenum.

Giles, T. R., & Marafiote, R. A. (1994). Managed care and psychotherapy outcome: Has the pendulum swung too far? *The Behavior Therapist*, *17*, 239–244.

Giles, T. R., Neims, D. M., & Prial, E. M. (1993). The relative efficacy of prescriptive techniques. In T. R. Giles (Ed.), *Handbook of effective psychotherapy* (pp. 21–39). New York: Plenum.

Goldner, E. M., & Bilsker, D. (1995). Evidence-based psychiatry. *Canadian Journal of Psychiatry*, *40*, 97–101.

Gray, S. H. (1996). Developing practice guidelines for psychoanalysis. *Journal of Psychotherapy Practice and Research*, *5*, 213–227.

Hayes, S. C. (1981). Single case experimental design and empirical clinical practice. *Journal of Consulting and Clinical Psychology*, *49*, 193–211.

Hoshmand, L. T., & Polkinghorne, D. E. (1992). Redefining the science–practice relationship and professional training. *American Psychologist*, *47*, 55–66.

Jacobson, N. S., Follette, W. C., & Revenstorf, D. (1984). Psychotherapy outcome research: Methods for reporting variability and evaluating clinical significance. *Behavior Therapy*, *15*, 336–352.

Jacobson, N. S., & Truax, P. (1991). Clinical significance: A statistical approach to defining meaningful change in psychotherapy research. *Journal of Consulting and Clinical Psychology*, *59*, 12–19.

Jayaratne, S., & Levy, R. L. (1979). *Empirical clinical practice*. New York: Columbia University Press.

Kates, N., Adsett, A., Bellissimo, T., Levine, L., & Humphrey, B. (1993). The Hamilton (McMaster) psychiatric network: The evolution of an integrated network of psychiatric services. *Canadian Journal of Psychiatry*, *38*, 315–318.

Kazdin, A. E. (1981). Drawing valid inferences from case studies. *Journal of Consulting and Clinical Psychology*, *49*, 183–192.

Kazdin, A. E. (1994). Methodology, design, and evaluation in psychotherapy research. In A. E. Bergin & S. L. Garfield (Eds.), *Handbook of psychotherapy and behavior change* (4th ed., pp. 19–71). New York: Wiley.

Kordy, H. (1995). Does psychotherapy research answer the questions of practitoners, and should it? *Psychotherapy Research*, *5*, 128–130.

Lambert, M. J., & Hill, C. E. (1994). Assessing psychotherapy outcomes and processes. In A. E. Bergin & S. L. Garfield (Eds.), *Handbook of psychotherapy and behavior change* (4th ed., pp. 72–113). New York: Wiley.

Lambert, M. J., Ogles, B. M., & Masters, K. S. (1992). Choosing outcome assessment devices: An organizational and conceptual scheme. *Journal of Counseling & Development*, *70*, 527–532.

Linder, J. C. (1991). Outcomes measurement: Compliance tool or strategic initiative? *Health Care Management Review*, *16*, 21–33.

Luborsky, L. (1995). The same and divergent views of "fashions and preoccupations in psychotherapy research." *Psychotherapy Research*, *5*, 118–120.

Ludwigsen, K. R., & Enright, M. F. (1988). The health care revolution: Implications for psychology and hospital practice. *Psychotherapy*, *25*, 424–428.

Martinovich, Z., Saunders, S., & Howard, K. I. (1996). Some comments on "assessing clinical significance". *Psychotherapy Research*, *6*, 124–132.

Mirin, S. M., & Namerow, M. J. (1991). Why study treatment outcome? *Hospital and Community Psychiatry*, *42*, 1007–1013.

Montgomery, J. S. (1988). Shrink mental health care costs. *Personnel Journal*, *67*, 86–91.

Montgomery, R. W., & Ayllon, T. (1995). Matching verbal repertoires: Understanding the contingencies of practice in order to functionally communicate with clinicians. *Journal of Behavior Therapy and Experimental Psychiatry*, *26*, 99–105.

Nelson, R. O. (1981). Realistic dependent measures for clinical use. *Journal of Consulting and Clinical Psychology*, *49*, 168–182.

Norcross, J. C., Prochaska, J., & Gallagher, K. (1989). Clinical psychologists in the 1980s: Theory, research, and practice. *Clinical Psychologist*, *12*, 42–53.

O'Sullivan, J. J., & Quevillon, R. P. (1992). 40 years later is the Boulder model still alive. *American Psychologist*, *47*, 67–70.

Persons, J. (1993). Why are there so few scientist–practitioners? A modest proposal. *The Behavior Therapist*, *16*, 34.

Pomerantz, J. M., Liptzin, B., Carter, A. H., & Perlman, M. S. (1994) The professional affiliation group: A new model for managed mental health care. *Hospital and Community Psychiatry*, *45*, 308–310.

Pomerantz, J. M., Liptzin, B., Carter, A., & Perlman, M. S. (1995). Development and management of a "virtual" group practice: Behavioral clinicians and organizations linked by a capitation contract with an HMO. *Psychiatric Annals*, *25*, 504–508.

Raimy, V. C. (Ed.) (1950). *Training in clinical psychology*. New York: Prentice-Hall.

Ryle, A. (1995). Fashions and preoccupations in psychotherapy research. *Psychotherapy Research*, *5*, 113–117.

Shakow, D. (1976). What is clinical psychology? *American Psychologist*, *31*, 553–560.

Steinmeyer, C. H. (1994). Hypotheses regarding determinants of scientist–practitioner behavior. *The Behavior Therapist*, *17*, 12–13.

Task Force on Promotion and Dissemination of Psychological Procedures (1995). Training in and dissemination of empirically-validated psychological treatments: Report and recommendations. *The Clinical Psychologist*, *48*, 3–23.

Thyer, B. A. (1995). Promoting an empiricist agenda within the human services: An ethical and humanistic imperative. *Journal of Behavior Therapy and Experimental Psychiatry*, *26*, 93–98.

Tingey, R. C., Lambert, M. J., Burlingame, G. M., & Hansen, N. B. (1996). Assessing clinical significance: Proposed extensions to method. *Psychotherapy Research*, *6*, 109–123.

Vaughn, S. C., Marshall, R. D., MacKinnon, R. A. & Roose, S. P. (1994). Current psychotherapy research methodology applied to psychoanalysis: A feasibility study. *Journal of Psychotherapy Practice and Research*, *3*, 334–340.

Wedding, D., Topolski, J., & McGaha, A. (1995). Maintaining the confidentiality of computerized mental health outcome data. *The Journal of Mental Health Administration*, *22*, 237–244.

Witkin, S. L. (1991). Empirical clinical practice: A critical appraisal. *Social Work*, *36*, 158–163.
Yeaton, W. H., & Sechrest, L. (1981). Critical dimensions in the choice of maintenance of successful treatments: Strength, integrity, and effectiveness. *Journal of Consulting and Clinical Psychology*, *49*, 156–167.

2.29 Principal Practice Settings for Clinical Psychologists in European Countries

HARRY VAN DER VLUGT
Tilburg University, The Netherlands

2.29.1 INTRODUCTION

In writing this chapter, several unexpected problems arose. The main problem was how to define a clinical psychologist. Apparently the answer should be a psychologist who works in a clinical setting. But this does not solve the problem because:

(i) Some clinical psychologists work as psychotherapists. In many countries psychotherapists are registered in a separate register including all kinds of psychotherapists with different backgrounds such as social work, theology, psychology, or psychiatry. In other (mostly southern European) countries psychotherapy is considered to be a curative activity which is the privilege of the medical profession.

(ii) Not only psychologists who are officially trained as clinical psychologists work as such in the health system. Many other psychologists work in a clinical setting, for example, child psychologists, psychogerontologists, rehabilitation psychologists, neuropsychologists, health psychologists, and even "orthopedagogues" who hold positions comparable with child psychologists.

(iii) Not all clinical psychologists are members of their national psychological society. The percentage of psychologists who are members of the local societies varies strongly from country to country.

(iv) Due to continuous changes with respect to health services in different countries, the educational systems at the university level are changing as well.

(v) Although there is a tendency within the EC to come to a general ruling with regard to quality of training and a common deontology, so far the differences between countries are that large that globalization is still a pious wish.

Because of the above mentioned problems, the situation in The Netherlands is first highlighted. This is relatively straightforward due to two excellent reviews (Van Drunen, 1995; Brunenberg, Neifmeiger, & Hutschemarker, 1995). From there on other countries in Europe are compared. This comparison is often limited because it is impossible to get the necessary basic information.

2.29.2 THE NETHERLANDS

2.29.2.1 General Historical Background

In 1992 the first century of scientific psychology in The Netherlands was celebrated. The year 1892, when Gerard Heymans established the first psychological laboratory in Groningen, is generally considered the year of its birth. However, it was not until 1921 that psychology became a possible specialization for students of philosophy. At the same time, applied psychology started, especially in the areas of personnel selection and vocational guidance. In 1924, Philips was the first private company to hire a full-time professional psychologist. In 1938, a professional organization of psychologists was founded: the *Nederlandsch Instituut van Practizeerende Psychologen* (Dutch Association of Practising Psychologists, NIPP).

Up to 1940 the NIPP only had 28 members, of whom seven had a medical background. In 1941, by academic statute, psychology was recognized as an independent discipline, and after the war all universities started a full program in psychology. In the early 1950s there were about 100 first-year students in psychology, in the early 1960s more than 250, in the 1970s more than 1000 and in the late 1990s about 2250. This led to a rapid increase in the number of psychologists from 80 in 1945 to about 700 in the early 1960s, about 2500 in the early 1970s, 10 000 in the mid 1980s, and at least 20 000 in the late 1990s; at least 1200 psychologists for every 1 000 000 inhabitants.

Another interesting aspect is the increase of women in psychology. In the mid 1970s only 35% of the graduates were women. In the late 1990s more than 70% of the graduates are women. In the late 1990s the number of men and women in psychology is about the same but in the future women will outnumber men. Also of interest is the number of members of the professional organization NIPP. In the mid 1960s about 80% of psychologists were member of the NIPP but now only about 30% of the psychologists are members.

2.29.2.2 Employment

Until the early 1970s every psychologist could find a job easily. In the 1990s about 80% of graduates find a job within a year. The percentage of unemployment varies per subdiscipline with the lowest unemployment rate for industrial psychologists and an unemployment rate of up to 35% for clinical and child psychology.

The title *psycholoog* used to be protected by law but as of September 1, 1993 its formal protection by law was abandoned.

In November 1993 a law with regard to the professions in individual healthcare (*wet Beroepen in de Individuele Gezondheidszorg* [*Wet Big*]) was accepted by the Dutch government. This law contains rules for a number of professions in individual healthcare with regard to registration, title protection, the kind of activities one is allowed to perform, code of conduct, ethics, and disciplinary procedures.

With regard to the clinical psychologist some specifications are made about official registration as a "Healthcare Psychologist" ("Health Psychologist" by this law is defined as a psychologist who works within the individual healthcare system and contains a larger category than the traditional health psychologist), the specialty of healthcare psychologist, and the educational requirements. A special taskforce was asked to develop specialty requirements with regard to special training and skills for the profession of healthcare psychologist. With the Dutch Psychological Society and the Dutch Pedagogic Society it was agreed that both university tracts should offer the option of becoming a registered healthcare psychologist.

In order to obtain an actual and updated view of the requirements, the kind of work, and the number of psychologists that work within this field, an evaluation was done by the Dutch Center of Mental Health Care (*Nederlands centrum Geestelijke Volksgezondheid,* NcGv). In 1994 it was estimated by the Dutch Central Bureau of Statistics (CBS) that there were about 19 000 psychologists in The Netherlands. A large number of them work within the healthcare systems.

In 1942 the first clinical psychologist was appointed at a hospital under the supervision of a psychiatrist mostly dealing with diagnostics and treatment. Over the years diagnostics and treatment (including psychotherapy) became part of the skills of the clinical psychologist. In 1966 psychologists were allowed to become members of the Dutch Psychotherapy Society (*Nederlandse Vereniging voor Psychotherapie,* NVP).

In the 1970s and 1980s a rapid growth, including a larger differentiation, took place. Clinical psychologists organized themselves within the Dutch Psychological Society (*Nederlands Instituut van Psychologen,* NIP) as a Clinical Psychology section. The number of sections increased due to the increase in differentiations within healthcare. Finally, all these sections were assembled again within the section "Psychologists within Healthcare Systems." With the changes in the healthcare system, resulting in changes in the role of the clinical psychologists, the educational system at the universities also changed. After finishing their specialty in clinical psychology at a university level, graduates had to work for several years under supervision in order to be registered as a clinical psychologist by the Dutch Psychological Society.

In 1982 the university system changed into a two-phase system. It was clear right from the beginning that completion of the first four years of the two-phase system would not guarantee a sufficiently qualified clinical psychologist. At the same time a government held register of psychotherapists was instituted. Special registration requirements for the clinical psychologist were formulated and postdoctoral programs (of four years) for clinical psychologists began. In 1995, 1100 psychologists were registered as clinical psychologists.

2.29.2.3 Employment Settings for Clinical Psychologists

In the late 1990s, psychologists are working within all aspects of the healthcare system, inpatient and outpatient clinics, day care centers, general and mental healthcare, institutions for the mentally handicapped, and so on.

In 1991, Beekman and Heijke estimated the number of psychologists working within the healthcare system by combining data from the CBS, the NIP, and the National Hospital Institute (NZI). This resulted in the overview shown in Table 1.

Another estimate comes from Van Son and Van der Staak (1993). Based upon the figures of the NIP, they estimate that of the 7000 members, about 3000 work within the healthcare system. Of those, 1100 are officially registered as clinical psychologists. On the assumption that 50% of professional psychologists are members of the NIP, 6000 psychologists will be working within the healthcare system.

According to the above-mentioned authors, of the 3000 members of the NIP about 1800 psychologists work in outpatient care and 1000 participate in first-echelon care; about 365 work within rehabilitation centers or nursing homes; about 650 work in psychiatric clinics and rest homes. Institutions for the mentally handicapped, forensic institutions, and general hospitals each employ about 200 clinical psychologists. So by extrapolation (50% membership of the NIP), they arrive at the number of 6000 clinical psychologists.

Table 1 Number of clinical psychologist places within the healthcare system in 1990 (in full-time equivalents of 40 hours).

Inpatient healthcare	
General hospitals	390
Psychiatric hospitals	466
Medical child institutions	12
Medical child day care centers	30
Forensic institutions	40
Nursing homes	59
Institutions for mentally handicapped	145
Institutions for sensory handicapped	13
Subtotal	1155
Outpatient healthcare	
Medical school services	23
Outpatient psychiatric care	800
Institutes for drug addicts	53
Others	12
First-echelon services	245
Subtotal	1133
Forensic	
Prisons	33
Child protection	12
Subtotal	45
Total	2333

As one can see, estimates vary from about 2500 to 6000 clinical psychologists. Because of this large variability in estimates a new estimate was made by a taskforce of the Dutch Center of Mental Health (Brunenberg, Neijmeijer, & Hutschemaekers, 1995).

This review concentrates upon psychologists and pedagogues working within general healthcare, mental healthcare, care for the physically handicapped, care for the mentally handicapped, forensic care, and individual healthcare related private practice.

The psychologists had to meet four criteria: (i) a university education as psychologist or pedagogue, (ii) being employed within the healthcare system, (iii) working within a direct healthcare situation and not as manager, prevention specialist, teacher, or researcher, and (iv) not solely working as a psychotherapist.

First they selected from the membership file of the Dutch Psychological Society all members belonging to the Section of Healthcare ($N=3409$), all members of the Section of Child Psychology ($N=292$), and all members of the Dutch Pedagogic Society ($N=2577$). These 6278 members each received a questionnaire. The second source of information included 1177 institutions in the healthcare setting who were asked to give numbers and names of the psychologists and pedagogues working at their institution. About 53% of the institutions responded, indicating that 1613 psychologists and 679 pedagogues were working there. After eliminating all duplicated names, 7600 questionnaires (4595 psychologists and 3005 pedagogues) were mailed out and 62% responded. For the sake of simplicity from now on differentiation between psychologists and pedagogues will not be made and they will be referred to as clinical psychologists.

Of the 4298 respondents 104 had another form of university education, 1154 were working outside the healthcare system, 326 had other (management, research, teaching) functions within the healthcare system, and 352 worked exclusively as psychotherapists.

The following data are based upon 2362 clinical psychologists working in individual healthcare. Based upon extrapolation (correction for the number of respondents per type of institution), the authors come to an estimate of 4813 clinical psychologists working within the individual healthcare system. This does not include the approximate 15% of clinical psychologists working in private practice (this 15% is based upon individual questionnaires). In total about 5645 clinical psychologists are discussed.

In order to get the whole picture, also included are clinical psychologists with other functions such as management, research, teaching (1320), and also those who work solely as psychotherapists (1030), giving a total of 7383 clinical psychologists working in the individual healthcare system, of whom 62% are females. Table 2 gives a breakdown of clinical psychologists' activities within the healthcare system.

2.29.2.3.1 Employment opportunities

The majority of psychologists have a paid job. About 5% of psychologists have a position as postdoc internship in combination with a paid job. Only 2% have a postdoc internship without a job, 3% work as volunteers.

2.29.2.3.2 Private practice

Approximately 25% of psychologists have some kind of private practice. Of this group, 60% have a private practice exclusively (15% of the total group).

2.29.2.4 Some Final Statements

As of June 1994, 1663 pedagogues and 3310 psychologists worked within the healthcare system. This means that according to the above statistics, within the healthcare system, 200 psychologists and 100 pedagogues are employed per 1 000 000 of the population.

On a yearly basis, about 1000 students complete their psychology studies. Of these, 500 specialize in the health-related areas (clinical and developmental psychology). In the late 1990s, there are about 1000 unemployed psychologists in the health-related area. It is expected that by the year 2001 we will have 4000 unemployed psychologists.

With respect to the *Wet Big* every year (with an optimistic scenario) 160 new places are expected. However, this scenario is based upon the employment situation within the healthcare system. It is as if the NIP is content with the situation in the 1990s and is accepting the status quo. One might wonder if the situation in 1997 is acceptable. Many clinical psychologists complain about the heavy workload they have. Data suggest that only one hour is spent on more than 50% of diagnoses; this is not a very acceptable situation.

Based upon the above analysis and the financial constraints in the first part of the second phase of study (the "healthcare psychologist" part) only 84 people are allowed to enter this new program every year. These students need a paid internship place for two years, so in

Table 2 Comparison of the activities of clinical psychologists within different settings.

	General healthcare	*Mental healthcare*	*Mentally handicapped*	*Physically handicapped*	*Private practice*
Average contract					
Hours per week	27.5	25.9	28.3	21.8	21
Additional job (%)	16.0	20.0		3.0	35
Private practice (%)	12.0	24.0		5.0	
Time distribution (%)					
Client oriented activities	75.0	80.0		80.0	100.0
Diagnostics	25.0	16.0		16.0	13.0
Treatment	18.0	28.0		7.0	44.0
Client rounds	10.0	10.0		15.0	
Guidance	10.0	10.0		11.0	
Advising staff				11.0	
Administration	10.0	10.0		11.0	12.0
Diagnostics (%)					
Interview	44.0	40.0		30.0	70.0
Observation	12.0	23.0		25.0	8.0
Tests	42.0	35.0		41.0	21.0
Others	2.0	2.0			
Types of diagnosis (%)					
Somatopsychological	11.0	2.0		0.0	7.0
Neuropsychological	40.0	12.0		11.0	
Intelligence	8.0	11.0		30.0	5.0
Personality	13.0	26.0		12.0	33.0
Psychopathology	11.0	21.0		8.0	20.0
Social functioning	6.0	11.0		12.0	15.0
Developmental				12.0	
Diagnositc contacts					
Time per contact (mins)	93	92		111	100
Number of contacts	3	3		3	3
Treatment contacts					
Time per contact (mins)	60	42		45	53
Frequency	1/2 mths	1 wk		1 wk	1 wk
Patients per year	53	47		107	33
New contacts per year	93	62		25	42
Average treatment time		11 mths		9 mths	8 mths

total, 168 places are needed. The idea is to train these psychologists in such a way that they have a very broad basic background in the area of the individual healthcare. The only differentiation that is foreseen is between adults and children. After the first part of the second phase, the "health psychologist" will be registered in an official government register. Out of this registered group, around 25% will be allowed to continue for the second part of the second phase to be trained to as specialists in clinical psychology (comparable with medical specialists). How specialized they should be is still a matter of discussion. On the one hand, it is suggested that they should be generalists in terms of clinical psychologist/psychotherapist and on the other hand it is suggested that they should be highly specialized clinical child psychologists, neuropsychologists, health psychologists, psychogerontologists with or without "psycho" therapy qualifications.

2.29.3 COUNTRY-RELATED INFORMATION

For information on the UK see Chapter 22, this volume, and for information on the Scandinavian countries see Chapter 15, this volume.

2.29.3.1 Belgium

Most of the information on Belgium has been forwarded by Bob Cools, Chairman of the Flemish Society for Clinical Psychology.

Clinical psychology is a relative young discipline in Belgium. The first program in clinical psychology started in 1967 at the University of Leuven, followed in 1975 by the University of Gent, and in 1976 by the Free University of Brussels. In 1997, psychology can be studied at seven universities and there are about 5000 psychology students.

The university program has two cycles: *de kandidaturen* (two years) and *de licenties* (three years). During these last three years the student can specialize in clinical psychology. After the *licentie* one is allowed to function professionally as a psychologist.

After the *licentie* there are several opportunities inside or outside the university system for further specialization. A questionnaire by the *Vlaamse Vereniging van Klinisch Psychologen* (Flemish Society for Clinical Psychologists) indicated that out of 481 clinical psychologists, 61% followed an additional specialty in psychotherapy. In the late 1990s, there are about 3000 clinical psychologists in Flanders.

From their foundation, the *Belgische Federatie van Psychologen* (BFP) worked towards a formal recognition of the title *psycholoog* by law. Finally in 1993 the university level *licentiaten in Psychologie* was recognized. However, by 1997 the law had not been put into effect. Protection of the title by law could be considered as the first step toward a fully-fledged status for clinical psychology with appropriate by-laws.

Although clinical psychologists work in the health profession, their five year university education is hardly recognized and their post-graduate training is not recognized at all. They are not allowed to work by themselves in a curative way. Even if their psychological assessment is in some way health related, they are not officially permitted to practice, nor will they be reimbursed by the health authorities.

The title "psychotherapist" is not officially protected. Psychotherapy as a curative activity is considered to be part of the medical profession. Violation of the Royal Degree by a clinical psychologist is an offence which will be submitted to a public prosecutor and is liable to a law suit. A Belgian minister of health labeled clinical psychology as a paramedical discipline. However, the BFP refused to accept this position and claims its own independent status as a scientific discipline in its own right. Legally there is no solution in the foreseeable future for this problem.

2.29.3.1.1 Work setting

Of the above-mentioned 481 interviewed clinical psychologists, a vast majority worked within a health setting, 40% in an intramural, residential setting, 30% in an extramural, outpatient setting, and 20% in private practice. Ten percent work in an educational setting, and 10% work in private business or for a governmental agency. Only 2% work in a research setting. Six percent are unemployed. The employment market is becoming increasingly more competitive and it takes students longer to find a tenured job.

The fact that a licenciate clinical psychologist follows an additional academic track (mostly psychotherapy) appears to be a significant factor in obtaining a job. About 61% of Belgian psychologists follow this additional therapy training.

2.29.3.1.2 Future

The traditional job perception of a clinical psychologist working as a psychotherapist within the health system is still unclear in Belgium. The scattering of all kinds of psychologists in all kinds of different small societies prevents the BFP from extending any political pressure or power. Relatively few (clinical) psychologists are members of the BFP. Because of this current dead-end street situation, it is time for clinical psychologists in Belgium and for the Belgian university system to widen the objectives of clinical psychology towards prevention, health, sport, and geriatrics.

2.29.3.2 Czech Republic

Three universities in the Czech Republic (Charles University in Prague, Masaryk University in Brno, and Palacký University in Olomouc) offer a five-year psychology program. All three universities offer a specialization in clinical psychology.

Psychology in the Czech Republic is still changing as a result of events in its history. According to Brožek and Hoskovec (1995), one can distinguish three periods: (i) From the "victorious February" of 1948 to the end of November 1989. The country was called the Czechoslovak Socialist Republic under the Soviet-controlled totalitarian communism. (ii) From the "Velvet Revolution" of 1989 to December 31, 1992, the end of the Federal Republic of Czechoslovakia. (iii) From January 1, 1993, the date of the emergence of the Czech Republic and Slovakia as separate states. The consequences of this split are not clear yet. There still exists the *Journal Československá*

Psychologie, human contacts still continue, and joint meetings are still held alternating the site between the Czech Republic and Slovakia.

All the psychology associations of the Czech Republic are collective members of the Czech–Moravian Psychological Society, associated with the Academy of Science. The society has about 1700 individual members, representing about one-third of the total number of psychologists in the Czech Republic. The total number of psychologists in the Czech Republic is about 5500. Of the six associations, one is called Association of Clinical Psychologists of Bohemia, Moravia, and Silesia. Psychology is becoming more and more important within the healthcare system. Health services, including mental health services, continue to be available free of charge. In the area of counseling, privatization of services is progressing slowly. In the late 1990s only 25% of the counselors in the field of marital and family counseling have a permit for private practice.

2.29.3.3 France

La Société Française de Psychologie (The French Psychological Society) was founded in 1901 as a scientific society. It was only in December 1991 that practitioners were allowed to join the society, and in 1993 there were approximately 2000 members.

Psychology can be studied at 29 public universities and two private universities in France. The program takes five years and is subdivided in three parts. The first part takes two years and results in a *Diplôme d'Études Universitaires Générales* (DEUG). The second part, which also takes two years, results in a *Licence* or a *Maîtrice*. The third part takes one year and leads to the *Diplôme d'Études Supérieures Spécialsées* (DESS) in Psychology and *Diplôme d'Études Approfondies* (DEA) in Psychology.

The three main fields of practice are clinical psychology, work and organizational psychology, and educational psychology and guidance. The three main fields include many other fields such as psychotherapy, childhood and adolescent psychology, expert evaluation, neuropsychology, social psychology, cognitive psychology, economical psychology, and sport psychology.

Since 1985 the title *psychologue* has been protected by law on a national level enacted by parliament and government.

In 1991 Reyns and Verquerre published a study carried out in 1987. They mailed a questionnaire to all psychologists who obtained their DESS or DEA in 1984–1986. Only 895 psychologists (39%) responded. Of these, 659 (73.6%) were clinical psychologists, 151 (16.9%) were social psychologists, work psychologists, or organizational psychologists, and 85 (9.5%) were research psychologists. The major employers of clinical psychologists are national associations (e.g., Red Cross) (44%), the public sector such as child guidance centers (30.2%), hospitals (19.7%), and private practice (14.3%). The activities of the clinical psychologists were 58% clinical psychology, 32.7% institutional work, 31.1% psychotherapy, 26.9% training, 15.6% selection, and only 5.3% research (because many psychologists were involved with more than one activity this adds up to more than 100%).

Of the interviewed clinical psychologists, the following techniques were used: 59.8% used tests, projective techniques, or graphology; 88.3% used interview techniques; 42.9% used group interviews or group conferences; 5.1% used questionnaires or experiments; 22% used specific therapeutic techniques like psychoanalysis, gestalt therapy, or system therapy; 6.4% used a specific theoretical approach like psychoanalysis or system theory; and 3.5% used role-play techniques or transactional analysis. Of the interviewed clinical psychologists, 23.3% were unemployed, 67.4% had a regular monthly income, and 9.3% had a private practice. This relatively low percentage of clinical psychologists in private practice is due to the fact that there are no regulations in France. The independent clinical psychologist does not get paid by the government or a health insurance system. Because the French consider clinical psychology as a medical activity, and because they are not used to paying for medical activities themselves, it is almost impossible to run a private practice in France.

2.29.3.3.1 Postgraduate training

According to Reyns and Verquerre (1991), 57.5% of clinical psychologists follows some kind of postgraduate training. Approximately 20% of clinical psychologists have a secondary diploma from the third part. Apart from the university program there are many specialty training programs which are mainly complementary. There are programs in psychotherapy, psychoanalysis, psychopedagogics, criminology, sexuality, even graphology. There is an ethical code (*deontologie*) for the members of the *Société Française de la Psychologie*.

Payment is insured either by the state or by the *départments*. The psychological services that are covered by this system are health service (clinical psychology and psychotherapy), *départment* services (clinical psychology, psychotherapy), justice (clinical psychology, psychotherapy, expert evaluation), education (educational psychology, guidance), and private services (clinical psychology, educational psychology, psychotherapy, sometimes organizational psychology).

2.29.3.4 Germany

When looking at the situation of clinical psychology in Germany, one should bear in mind the fact that the reunification between East and West Germany only took place in 1990. The current *Berufsverband Deutscher Psychologen*, BDP (German Association of Professional Psychologists) includes members of the former *Gesellschaft für Psychologie der DDR* (Society of Psychology of the GDR). This information is based upon a representative survey of members of the BDP in 1990/1991 and former members of the GDR in 1991/1992. Of the 10 000 members of the BDP, one-third received a detailed questionnaire and 53.8% responded ($N=1630$), and of the 2500 members of the GDR, one-sixth received a detailed, and for the former East Germany, adapted questionnaire and 37.9% responded ($N=154$). This study was done by Schorr (1995). If we look at the subject sample we do not see any differences with regard to age (all are about an average of 43/44 years of age). However, there is a striking gender difference. Results showed that in the former West Germany the male–female distribution among psychologists was more or less fifty/fifty, in the former East Germany almost 70% were female. Another striking difference was the fact that at the time of the survey no psychologist was in private practice in the former East Germany compared with 27% in the former West Germany.

By comparing the areas of specialization one can see that clinical psychology was the largest specialization in what were West (81.5%) and East (70.9%) Germany. This was followed by work and organizational psychology in the West (11.2%) with only 7.1% in the East; while in the former East Germany, school and educational psychology came second with 16.2% with only 4% in the West.

By comparing the applied fields with each other it was first noticed, as was mentioned before, that 27.1% of the former West German psychologists worked in a private practice, whereas there were none in private practice from the former East Germany. Employment in counseling centers was about the same (18.9% in the former West Germany and 17.8% in the former East Germany). In clinics and rehabilitation clinics, one could see a significantly higher percentage of psychologists in the former East Germany (33.4%) contrary to only 14.3% in the former West Germany. In psychiatry the same kind of significant difference could be seen with 19.1% in the former East Germany and 9.7% in the former West Germany. For alcohol and drug therapy centers, the distribution was 4.6% in the former West Germany and 2.8% in the former East Germany.

If we look at the main tasks of a psychologist it can be seen that what were West and East German psychologists mention counseling and psychotherapy first (respectively 84.6% and 88.3%) followed by psychological assessment which was significantly higher for the former East German psychologists (West 51.1% and East 66.9%) and administrative duties which were significantly higher for psychologists from the former West Germany (West 32% and East 10.4%).

In summary, the above shows that the vast majority of psychologists in the former West and East Germany specialized in clinical psychology and that in the former East Germany about 55.3% of the psychologists were employed within a clinical setting, while in the former West Germany only 28.6% were working in a clinical setting. To what extent the percentage of psychologists in private practice are involved in clinical work remains unclear from this data.

2.29.3.4.1 Aspects of psychological training

(i) Basic training

In Germany there are 37 psychology programs at 36 universities. Each year approximately 6000 students apply to study psychology but only 3300 are accepted. In 1996 there were about 40 000 psychologists; around 6000 unemployed, 41% work in a clinical setting and 19% work independently as therapists or counselors. The whole study program takes six to seven years.

The *Hochschulramengesetz* (new frame law) regulates the general program of 10 semesters, without any specialization. However, many universities have not yet implemented this program. The idea is to add a third stage of around three years to the program, allowing about 5–20% of the *Diplom* students to continue to become "clinical psychologists." The consequence might be depreciation of the *Diplom* and an increase in unemployment which already is 20% for psychologists. This amounts to about 6000 psychologists between the age of 25 and 35 years, of which 60% are women. To date, the title "psychologist" is not protected by law. However, there is a *Berufsordnung für Psychologen* (ethical code) for members of the BDP.

(ii) Postgraduate training and supervision

Psychologists possess, to a surprising extent, further qualifications in addition to their degree in psychology. When quoting only academic qualifications as an example, 25.3% of the former West German psychologists and 10.4% of the former East German psychologists possess an additional qualification. When asked about postgraduate qualifications, qualifications in psychotherapy predominate. More than half of all German psychologists possessed a postgraduate qualification at the time of inquiry. Close to two-thirds of all German psychologists stated that they attended professional training regularly.

Because many psychologists possess a postgraduate training in psychotherapy, they tend to work curatively (not only advising as a counselor). This leads to a conflict of interest with physicians who in the strict sense of the word "curative" were the only ones allowed by the law of 1939 (*Heilpraktiker-Gesetz*) to practice a curative profession. Others are allowed to work in a curative way, however, they do not get paid by the health insurances directly. Psychologists only get paid if their service is requested by a physician. Since physicians are having problems in the job market themselves, they have started practicing psychotherapy themselves, and by doing so, have pushed psychologists out of the market.

In the late 1990s, there are close to 40 000 psychologists in Germany, increasing every year by around 1500. Of those, 41% are working in the clinicial area and 19% work independently as therapists or counselors. This means that only 60% of the psychologists who are trained in clinical psychology find a job in the clinical field. About 20% are unemployed, amounting to about 6000 psychologists between the age of 25 and 35 years old of which 60% is female. Of the 40 000 psychologists only 35% are members of the German Association of Professional Psychologists.

2.29.3.5 Greece

According to James Georgas (1995), when thinking about the history of psychology we should realize that twenty five centuries ago, the ancient Greek philosophers defined and explored the subject, making them the precursors of many theories of modern psychology.

For instance, the concept of empirism led to a school of behaviorism that has dominated psychology in the twentieth century. This concept was originally developed by Protagora, Empéricos, the Stoics, Iamblichos, Plato, and Aristotle. The term *charten agraphon* was employed by Aphrodiseas many centuries before Locke employed its Latin synonym *tabula rasa* (Georgas, 1995).

Among all the ancient Hellenic philosophers, Aristotle is acknowledged as the most accomplished in defining and systematically studying the phenomenon of psychology. However, this chapter deals with modern psychology in modern Greece. The establishment of modern psychology is ironically probably delayed because the philosophers at the University of Athens emphasized the importance of the Greek philosophers to psychology. While in the 1950s and the 1960s psychology separated from philosophy at many American and European universities, it took Greece until 1983 to establish divisions of psychology within departments of philosophy, education, and psychology. In 1987 the first autonomous Department of Psychology was created at the University of Crete. All major Greek universities (i.e., Athens, Thessaloniki, Ioannin, and Crete) now have a department of psychology. These departments run four-year graduate programs leading to a degree called *Ptychio* (Masters degree). In addition, programs leading to the Doctor of Philosophy are awarded at all of these universities.

Because psychology was late in becoming a discipline in itself, one should realize that the majority of Greek psychologists are trained abroad. The largest group has been trained in France, followed by a second group trained in the UK, followed by Germany, the USA, and Canada. One could say that in Greece, psychology is a kaleidoscopic assembly of different theoretical schools and practical applications. The majority of psychologists in Greece (around 800) are members of the Association of Greek Psychologists. Members have to have a degree in psychology at the masters level. A second association was established in 1991, the Hellenic Psychological Society, whose members are university faculty members and psychologists in research centers. The minimum criterion for membership is a Ph.D. in psychology.

A law which licenses psychologists to practice was passed in 1979, regulated by the Ministry of Health and Welfare. However, it only came into force, primarily because of the problems in delineating the specific types of "psychological work" of the three main fields: clinical psychology, educational psychology, and organizational psychology.

Psychologists in Greece work in a variety of settings. By far the largest number are clinical psychologists. The first mental health centers in Greece were established in the 1950s and subsequently the Institute for Child Health and several private mental health centers were also established. Most clinical psychologists are employed in mental health centers. Only few of them combine a full-time position in the mental health or hospital system with a private practice (Georgas, 1995).

2.29.3.6 Italy

Most of the following information is based upon an article by Avallone (1993). In order to understand psychology in Italy one needs some historical background. As in other countries, one might say that experimental psychology started in the second half of the nineteenth century. The first theoretical paper *La psicologia come scienza positiva* by Roberto Ardigò was published in 1870. The first Italian psychological journal appeared in 1905, *Rivista Italiana di Psicologia*, and in 1912 *Psiche-Rivista di studi psicologici.* In 1906, the Fifth International Congress of Psychology took place in Rome and the first three academic chairs were created in Rome, Naples, and Torino. Psychology was introduced in schools and institutions. Mental tests were translated and developed, and in 1910 the Italian Psychological Society was founded. During the first world war in 1915 psychological tests were used to select army personnel, but then the development seemed to stop. The strong influence of the philosophical tradition, but even more due to the influence of the neoidealism (= fascism) and the second world war, negatively influenced the development of science in general and psychology in particular. There also existed an almost traditional dichotomy between pure basic research and applied research resulting in a professional practice without a methodology or theory. It was not until 1971 that one could study psychology in Italy resulting in a graduate degree in psychology. Even in the 1990s the majority of professors in psychology have their primary background in philosophy or medicine. As of 1971 there was a four-year program in psychology, divided into experimental, educational and applied psychology. After the need for a better curriculum became apparent, the four-year program was increased to a five-year program in 1985. At the end of a two-year *propadeuse*, the student studies for another three years in one of the following areas: (i) general and experimental psychology (about 8% of the students); (ii) developmental and educational psychology (15%); (iii) clinical and community psychology (62%); and (iv) work and organizational psychology (15%). Like in other European countries, a stereotypical interest in clinical psychology is seen (Carli, 1987), showing that being a psychotherapist is the ultimate goal of many psychology students.

From 1985 to 1996, the number of universities offering a psychology program increased (Torino, Trieste, Padova, Bologna, Cagliari, Rome, Palermo). In 1996, 11 universities offered a psychology program. Apart from the regular curriculum, Italian universities offer *Corsi di Perfezionamento* allowing students to specialize even further during at least one year. The *Scuolo di Specializzazione* offers a limited number of students to specialize during three or four years in, for example, clinical psychology. The *Dottorato di Ricerca* prepares the student for a research career. Apart from these university programs which are available for a limited number of students, many private programs are available in order to become a psychotherapist in almost any thinkable form of therapy.

In 1989 the State intervened by law, regulating the psychological profession; only psychologists with an academic degree were allowed to be registered in the official register.

Psychotherapists are only registered after an additional four years of university or university equivalent (State recognized) training. Because of this, the new generation of psychologists in Italy can claim a solid base in science for their applied activities.

The major applied area is clinical psychology with many psychologists entering private practice after the State required four-year training. However, many clinical psychologists work for the State, province, and local health units in many health-related structures (being called mental hygiene centers for psychiatric assistance, because Italy had banned all psychiatric hospitals as a result of the antipsychiatry movement).

In Italy, the *Societá Italiana di Psicologia* (SIP) approved its deontological code on September 24, 1981.

2.29.3.7 Portugal

If one looks at the development of psychology in Portugal one should look at the time before and after the democratic revolution in April 1974.

Before the revolution, the State-run universities did not acknowledge psychology as a subject in its own right, it was only a subsidiary course in philosophy. However, several organizations, headed by the Catholic church, created a five-year degree course in psychology in the *Instituto Superior de Psicologia Aplicada* (Higher Institute of Applied Psychology, ISPA), which had evolved from the "Pedagogical Higher Institute" which was founded in 1962. Public universities did not start a psychology program until 1977. Consequently, the majority of certified psychologists claiming a degree in psychology between 1969 and 1982 received their training at the ISPA. These psychologists are assembled in the official but small *Sociedade Portuguesa de Psicólogos* (Portuguese Psychological Society, SPP).

Following the revolution, the proposal to create a psychology course at the public universities was made. In 1977 the psychology course was offered within the framework of the Faculties of the Humanities. A little later the course was offered by the newly created Faculties of Psychology and Educational Sciences (FOCE). In the meantime, psychology degrees were still awarded at the ISPA, which by now was detached from the Catholic founding organizations. At the same time a new *Sindicato Nacional dos Psicólogos* (National Union of Psychologists, SNP) was founded in order to assemble all practitioners of psychology together; those with a psychology degree from ISPA, those with a philosophy degree from State universities, or those with a psychology degree from public universities after 1982.

Rivalry between psychologists from public universities and psychologists from the ISPA resulted in a law recognizing the equality of the ISPA degree with the public university degree. In the context of this competition, the *Associaçâo Portuguesa de licenciados em psicologia* (Association of Psychology Graduates from Public Universities) was established in 1982. The *Associaçâo Portuguesa de Psicólogos* (Portuguese Psychological Society, APP) was also founded.

Once the relationships among psychologists started to improve, members of the Association of Psychology Graduates from Public Universities changed their association into *Associaçâo de Psicologia Portuguesa* (Association of Portuguese Psychologists, APPORT). More recently the Portuguese Society for Clinical Psychology was founded. In 1997 work is in progress to establish the *Ordem dos Psicólogos* (Association of Professional Psychologists). In order to create a single representative body, four of the Portuguese psychological organizations joined forces, thus establishing the "National Board of Psychologists." The purpose of this Board is to draw up the statutes of the "Association of Professional Psychologists."

From the above one can see that the situation is quite complex in Portugal. Because of this it is almost impossible to produce realistic figures and data. There is a rumor that Portugal has about 4000 psychologists, but an estimate of 2500 seems more realistic. In 1996 there were about 3000 undergraduates in psychology. After a five-year program about 600 get their degree every year.

Most psychologists are employed in the educational sector and within organizations in the private sector. The situation with regard to clinical activities is unclear.

The title of "psychologist" is semiprotected. In order to be employed as a psychologist, one has to have an official document called the *carteire profissional* (professional certificate) issued by the Ministry of Work. However, illegal practice does not entail any legal consequences. Hopefully the establishment of the Association of Professional Psychologists will improve this situation (Pereira, 1995).

Four universities offer a psychology program: Lisboa, Porto, Coimbra, and Ispa. The program takes five years and there is a fixed number of entrants.

2.29.3.8 Spain

The current trend in psychology is intervention oriented. This intervention is, due to the specific developments in science in Spain, very technically oriented. In order to understand this development one has to focus upon the scientific dimensions of fundamental psychology in Spain. The emergence of scientific technology became the social justification for psychology as a profession. Standard studies about the history of psychology in Spain usually start with Sénèque, followed by the Renaissance, and ends by analyzing the last 100 years. If we concentrate on the period in which the current discipline of psychology is constructed, we can distinguish two periods.

The first period started at the beginning of the twentieth century until the Civil War (1936–1939). The second period started in the late 1940s to early 1950s, and ended with the Franco regime in the second half of the 1970s. During this period Spain was isolated from the scientific world. The transition to democracy coincided with the start of independent psychology departments. In Spain there exists a rich tradition studying psychological phenomena from a philosophical, medical, historical, and even a literary background. This rich tradition has prevented the modern development of psychology for many years.

As a major event the Spanish psychologists mention the XIe International Psychology Conference planned to take place from September 6 to September 12, 1936 in Madrid. Cajal was president at that time. However, due to the Civil War, the conference was canceled and took place in 1938 in Paris.

The creation of the Spanish Psychological Society started in 1950 and the bylaws were published in 1952. In the following years within the Official College of doctors and licences in philosophy a section of professional psychologists started. In the meantime other psychological associations were created. All these different societies and associations formed the *Colegio Oficial de Psicólogos* (COP) in 1979.

It took until May 1979 that by a Décret Royal psychology became an independent discipline within the university system. Psychology is taught in at least 20 universities and institutions. Within 10 years the number of registered students in psychology increased from about 1000 in 1977 to over 5000 in 1988. The number of doctorates increased from 13 in 1977 to 139 in 1987.

In 1980 the university education in psychology, resulting in a licence, was recognized by law (BOE, April 14, 1980). Each university faculty confers the degree of *Licenciatura en Psicologia* and the COP legally confers the protected title of *Psicologia.* There is still an enormous interest in psychology with more than 39 000 students in 1996 compared to initially 100 students. Currently, there are more than 35 000 psychologists in Spain. The same is true for the Spanish Psychological Societies. The COP and the *Colegi de Cataluña* had about 4500 members in 1981 and now have more than 25 000 members. Spain has probably the highest percentage of psychologists per capita (about 575 psychologists per 1 000 000 inhabitants) in the world.

Because psychology is a young discipline the average age of the Spanish psychologist is quite young. About 30% are below the age of 30, while only 15.4% are older than 40 years. Psychology attracts more women than men (63% women). Of the women the majority prefer to work as school-psychologists or pedagogues (41%), and in traffic and safety psychology 84% of psychologists are female. Clinical psychology is preferred by 37% of the students. Rehabilitation psychology attracts about 18%, while organizational psychology, social psychology, and forensic psychology each attract only less than 10%.

The percentage of unemployment among psychologists is not too bad; only 10.5% vs. 17.3% in the active population and 10.5% vs. 13.6% of the academic population. But this situation will change soon. Among the younger generation of psychologists (younger than 25 years of age), the unemployment rate is high (37.5%). Psychologists have to focus upon new applied areas. There is still an overemphasis in educational psychology, pedagogics, and clinical psychology. This might be the reason why 53.7% of the clinical psychologists work in private practice. More attention should be paid to organizational psychology, social services, justice, and traffic psychology, while there is hardly any interest for environmental, sports, forensic, or military psychology. It is only these new areas that still offer job opportunities.

The first step towards a deontology for Spanish psychologists was set during the first National Psychology Congress in Madrid in 1984, were Alfredo Fierro presented a paper called *Deontological Code* (first draft). Many discussions followed and in 1987 a taskforce of 100 experts got together in Madrid, resulting in a proposal that after elaboration by Alejandro Avila (president) was presented to the Government Board of the *Colegio Oficial de Psicólogos.* The board ratified this proposal.

2.29.3.9 Switzerland

The following observations are based upon a periodically conducted investigation into the employment possibilities for Swiss recent graduates by a working group for academic career counseling (Diem, 1995).

The 1988 sample had a reply rate of 60% and among the 4856 responding graduates, 200 of them were psychologists. Although the unemployment rate for psychologists one year after they graduated is only 5.5% for Swiss standards it is almost twice as high as the average unemployment rate of 3%. Especially when there is an economic recession, like in 1985, the unemployment rate among psychologists was as high as 12%. The major employers for psychologists are universities (20%), social services (42.3%), health services (14.1%), private services like banks and insurance companies (7.9%) and schools, as teachers (7.3%). For 35% of the jobs recently occupied by psychologists, no academic degree was required. Also psychologists are more frequently employed on a part-time basis which is related to the high percentage (68%) of women in psychology (in all other academics an average of 31%). Overall, academic women engage in part-time work (up to 40%), while the figure for men reaches 21%. The higher contingent of women can also explain the lower average income of psychologists. A study by the *Arbeitsgemeinschaft für Akademische Berufsberatung* reveals that women earn about 20% less than men in all employment areas.

The Nationalfond study *La réussite professionnelle des économistes, juristes, médecins et psychologues* (Berberat, Goldschmid, Neirynck-Carton-de-Wiart, Nughes, & Ricci, 1990) gives us some information about the labor market for psychologists. The subject sample comprises 332 psychologists (179 women) who completed their studies at a western Swiss university between 1949 and 1989. It regards exclusively members of the Federation of Swiss Psychologists (*Föderation Schweizer Psychologinnen und Psychologen*, FSP). Almost all of them were employed. Twelve percent worked at Universities or Research Institutions, 30% in education psychology or social services, 21% in private practice, 13% in hospitals and clinics, and 14% in the schools. As one can see these figures differ slightly from the general situation in Switzerland mentioned earlier.

2.29.3.9.1 Clinical psychology in Switzerland

Compared to other countries in Europe, a relatively small percentage (13–14%) of the psychologists are working within the health services. This might be due to the fact that in Switzerland the foundation of clinical psychology was laid by medical doctors. Initially psychologists were only allowed to work with aptitude tests. In the 1950s, psychologists were allowed to enter into psychiatric treatment, initially as diagnostic experts, but later on they increasingly applied themselves to psychopathology (originally a medical discipline). More recently psychotherapy was added to their repertoire. Seen as a whole, the relationship between physicians and clinical psychologists is still largely a dependent one and clinical psychologists tend to represent a marginal group in psychiatric institutions.

In private practice the competition is unequal. Medical doctors' work is entirely compensated by health insurance companies, while psychologists' services are often only partially covered or not compensated at all.

In the research area the picture is totally different. They either work at universities, in research departments of psychiatric clinics, or in clinical research funded by industry. Psychologists' thorough training in methodology is highly respected. Another problem in Switzerland is that the title of "psychologist" is not protected by law.

2.29.4 CONCLUDING REMARKS

Looking over past developments in Europe with regard to psychology in general and clinical psychology in particular, we see some trends emerging. First of all we can see that all over Europe the professionalization of psychology is taking place. Most of the time the professionalization is triggered and catalyzed by clinical psychologists interacting with public health organizations. In order to guarantee a professional high standard of psychological expertise, official registers of psychologists are contrived. Although the need for registration is most strongly felt within the health care services in several countries, this format of registration is extended to all psychologists or for several specializations within psychology.

Another trend we see is that the registration, initially coordinated by national psychological societies, is increasingly done by the official governmental agencies mostly in coordination with the national psychological societies. In some countries the registration leads to protection of the title "psychologist," in other countries only some specialty areas within psychology are registered. Usually registration by law of the title "psychologist" is automatically related to quality control mechanisms.

With regard to education we see an increasing tendency all over Europe to shorten the study time (mostly six to seven-year programs revert to four to five-year programs). In countries where they maintain a longer curriculum, a numerus clausus or numerus fixus is instituted. The consequence of this shortening of the study time is that most studies are considered to be inadequate and/or insufficient. Because of that, additional training programs are developed and required in order to become a registered psychologist. In that case there is always a fixed total with regard to the number of potential candidates who are allowed into this additional postdoctoral training program. So far, a system of continuous education is not officially instituted in Europe.

The kind of work psychologists are doing is diversifying rapidly (e.g., traffic psychology in Spain), but still the majority of psychologists work in health-related areas. In many countries psychologists are still an extension of medical doctors but increasingly it is observable that psychology is recognized as a specialty by its own right, and that the psychologist is paid through the health system and health insurances directly (however, many times only after a referral by a medical doctor).

Next to the increase in the health-related area, we see an increase in private practice: sometimes a single-person practice but often a group practice sometimes even with other health-related professionals. This form of privatization is due to the fact that government institutes hire less people on a tenure basis. Often the official governmental institutions prefer to subcontract special orders/requests to a private organization.

The third area of expansion is in research. The healthcare world, but also (pharmaceutical) industries, are becoming aware of the excellent research training many psychologists in many countries get. This is also one of the few areas where within healthcare there is no competition between medical doctors and psychologists. Psychologists are by virtue of training far better researchers.

I should also say something about the change within clinical psychology itself. It used to be a soft discipline with all "funny" kinds of psychotherapy, and it was hard to prove that they did any good to the clients/patients. But due to financial cut-backs in the more hardcore areas of experimental and research psychology, many experimental, cognitive, psychophysiological, personality, and neuropsychologists showed a clinical inclination/interest which had a strong modifying effect.

All of a sudden assessment became more important, diagnosis was allowed and even mandatory later on, treatment effects were evaluated, theoretical backgrounds were studied, rehabilitation programs and treatment programs were based upon scientific theories from neuroscience, cognitive psychology, or personality psychology.

Although psychology grew in the bosom of philosophy and moved from there into social and educational sciences, by now clinical psychology is becoming a β-science with a very close relationship towards neurosciences.

The above mentioned developments are strongly supported and often initiated by the European Federation of Professional Psychologists Associations (EFPPA). In 1993 Member Associations of the EFPPA were: from Austria the *Berufsverband Österreichischer Psychologen*, from Belgium the *Belgische Federatie van Psychologen—Fédération Belge de Psychologues*, from Denmark the *Dansk Psykologforening*, from Estonia the Union of Estonian Psychologists, from Finland the *Suomen Psykologiitto ry*, from France the *Association Nationale des Organisations de Psychologues*, from Germany the *Berufsverband Deutscher Psychologen*, from Greece the Association of Greek Psychologists, from Hungary the *Magyar Pszichológiai Társaság*, from Iceland the Association of Icelandic Psychology, from Ireland the Psychological Society of Ireland, from Italy the Italian Network of Professional Psychologists' Associations, from Liechtenstein the *Berufsverein der Psychologen Liechtensteins*, from Luxemburg the *Association des Psychologues diplomés*, from Malta the Malta Union of Professional Psychologists, from the Netherlands the *Nederlands Instituut van Psychologen*, from Norway the *Norsk Psykologforening*, from Poland the *Polskie Towarzystwo Psychologiczne*, from Portugal the *Sindicato Nacional dos Psicologos*, from Slovenia the *Drustvo Psihologov Slivenije*, from Spain the *Colegio Oficial de Psicológos*, from Sweden the *Sveriges Psykologförbund*, from Switzerland the *Föderation der Schweizer Psychologen*, from Turkey the Turkish Psychologists Association, from the UK the British Psychological Society, and the Affiliate Member, the Israel Psychological Association.

ACKNOWLEDGMENTS

I would like to thank the quoted authors for their indirect contribution. I hope that, due to limited space, I did not do injustice to the refered articles. Any misquotation is my own responsibility.

2.29.5 REFERENCES

Avallone, F. (1993). Training and professional spheres of psychology in Italy. *European Review of Applied Psychology, 43,* 113–119.

Beekman, T. & Heijke, H. (1991). *Prognoses voor 1990–1995. De arbeidsmarkt voor Klinisch Psychologen* [Prognosis for 1990–1995. The employment market for clinical psychologists]. *De Psycholoog, 26,* 187–193.

Berberat, A. L., Goldschmid, M. L., Neirynck-Carton-de Wiart, I., Nulghes, M. A., & Ricci, J. L. (1990). *La réussite professionelle des économistes, juristes, médecins et psychologues.* Lausanne, Switzerland: Chaire de Pedagogue et Didactique, Ecole Polytechnique Fédérale.

Brožek, J., & Hoscovec, J. (1995). Psychology in the Czech Republic. In A. Schorr & S. Saari (Eds.), *Psychology in Europe* (pp. 3–14). Seattle, WA: Hogrefe & Huber.

Brunenberg, W., Neijmeijer, L., & Hutschemaekers, G. (1995). *Beroep: psycholoog/pedagoog* [Profession: psychologist/pedagogue]. Utrecht, The Netherlands: Nederlands centrum Geestelijke volksgezondheid.

Carli, R. (1987). *Psicologia clinica.* Torino, Italy: Utet.

Diem, M. (1995). Swiss psychologists and the labor market. In A. Schorr & S. Saari (Eds.). *Psychology in Europe* (pp. 125–148). Seattle, WA: Hogrefe & Huber.

Georgas, J. (1995). Psychology in Greece. In A. Schorr & S. Saari (Eds.). *Psychology in Europe* (pp. 59–76). Seattle, WA: Hogrefe & Huber.

Network of the Executive Secretaries of the Members of the European Federation of Professional Psychologists Associations (Ed.) (1993). *Inventory of regulations in the field of psychology in European countries.* [Brochure]. Bonn, Germany: Berufsverband Deutscher Psychologen.

Pereira, F. (1995). Psychology in Portugal. In A. Schorr & S. Saari (Eds.), *Psychology in Europe* (pp. 97–102). Seattle, WA: Hogrefe & Huber.

Reyns, S. & Verquerre, R. (1991). L'insertion professionnelle des psychologues. *Psychologues et Psychologies, 99,* 2–28.

Schorr, A. (1995). German psychology after reunification. In A. Schorr & S. Saari (Eds.), *Psychology in Europe* (pp. 35–58). Seattle, WA: Hogrefe & Huber.

Van Drunen, P. (1995). Professional psychology in The Netherlands. In A. Schorr & S. Saari (Eds.), *Psychology in Europe* (pp. 77–96). Seattle, WA: Hogrefe & Huber.

van Son, M. J. M., & van der Staak, C. P. F. (1993) Inleiding Handboek klinische psychologie [Introduction handbook clinical psychology]. In M. van Son & C. van der Staak (Eds.), *Handboek klinische psychologie.* Houten, The Netherlands: Bohn, Stafleu Van Loghum.

2.30
Establishing and Maintaining a Clinical Practice in the United States

DONALD J. WEINSTEIN
Beachwood, OH, USA

2.30.1 INTRODUCTION

Clearly, there is probably more than one way to develop and maintain a practice during these troubled times in the healthcare arena; what follow are ideas, attitudes, and systems that have worked for one group practice in Ohio. The goal of this chapter is to expose the reader to the enormous potential available to a psychologist along with the techniques for the maintenance and survival of an independent practice in the 1990s. To do that, a historical view or developmental perspective, coupled with a biographical sketch, is taken. The evolution of the practice of psychology may be gleaned elsewhere in these volumes, for example, the evolution from freedom of choice legislation to ERISA to the chapter on managed care, but in this chapter, the reader will discover the need to continually "stroke"—never just to "tread water." The concept of the need for a strong working philosophy along with different processes and "products" will be discussed to illuminate the types of projects and attitudes that have been the driving force for this practice.

2.30.2 CONSIDERATIONS IN ESTABLISHING A PRACTICE

When I initially opened the doors of the practice, a number of considerations, attitudes, and preconceptions drove my decisions.

2.30.2.1 Location(s)

I wanted to be within 30 minutes of population groups to make the office(s) easily accessible.

2.30.2.2 Comprehensive Service Base

I wanted to be a full service health psychology practice provider, enabling the referral source to recognize a mental/behavioral health need, having to only think of one provider. To that end, I knew that I needed male and female staff, child and adult therapists, and assessors and therapists with interest/expertise around varying presenting problems.

2.30.2.3 Comfort and Attractiveness for Me and for the Public

After working at a county hospital with a view of an air shaft from a hospital-green cinder block 12 ft × 12 ft room, I knew that I wanted my "suite of offices" to be pleasant for the staff and clients. My expectation was that the staff and I would be spending a lot of time there and it needed to be comfortable. In addition, I wanted the office to be no more than 10 minutes from home. This allowed me to never miss a dinner with my family and never miss participating in any school or extracurricular function of my children. In addition, I found the unattractiveness of the hospital insulting to the clients.

2.30.2.4 Hours of Service

In the current day and age of two working and volunteering parents, I also believed that it was important to have evening and weekend hours to be able to accommodate clients' work schedules (as long as it was not abusive to the therapist).

2.30.2.5 Overhead Surveillance

I have found that most people do not follow their overheads or pay attention to their costs. I wanted to be able to serve people in their locations with attractive offices at convenient hours, but I also wanted to keep a close eye on costs. These are not necessarily contradictory. Systems (to be described below) were put in place from the start to allow that to happen. Multiple locations do not mean duplication of support staff or equipment.

2.30.2.6 Responsiveness to Caller

Whether the caller was a referral source or a client, I wanted the clinical staff to return calls within three hours. To that extent, everybody was required to carry pagers. When cellular phones became available, the traveling and busiest therapists all were provided with them. Each therapist remained responsible (on call) for their own caseload. For the first 15 years of the practice, I took all after-hours calls not associated with a specific staff person. At this point, the calls are handled by the Director of Clinical Practice. Responsiveness also relates to commitment to the practice, and, therefore, I am not an advocate of part-time employees who work elsewhere. (I have an appreciation of part-time employees who parent the remainder of their time. Barring clinical crises, we attempt to respect their childcare commitments.) Those who work elsewhere invariably will be torn between loyalties if a choice needs to be made. If you have a clinician who works part-time for you and is a school psychologist during the day, the client or referral source may need to speak with this clinician who is not readily available. The practice of psychology, for better or worse, functions on a more immediate, need now basis. In addition, if working part-time elsewhere, issues of multiple malpractice exposure and coverage are a concern.

2.30.2.7 Income Consideration

It should be clear to anyone that when you are earning an income based on a fee-for-service time frame, you are limited in your total gross income by the time you spend. If the overhead is fixed and the office is available, your income can increase if you have somebody else working the space for you. In a solo situation, your income would be vulnerable when you are on vacation or out marketing. If others are providing service and income is being generated, you are still free to go about your life, knowing that money is still being generated. (More will be spent on this later as we discuss contracts for outside service as a method to pay overhead.)

2.30.2.8 Values and Ethics

Do not compromise your values or your ethics for anything or anyone. Do not contract with providers or referral companies (i.e., employee assistance programs (EAPs) or managed care companies) who ask you to do things that you believe are questionable. One managed care company wanted us to submit signed HCFA 1500s to them with no other information other than the subscriber's name filled out. Do not give in to clients who attempt to manipulate you or "the system." I had an adult client's insurance salesman father inform me that his son's benefit plan was bad and that I needed to bill a second session per week instead of just the one he was seen—"who would ever know"—to allow for higher reimbursement and less out of pocket expense.

2.30.3 COMPONENTS OF A PRACTICE

In an effort to orient you to the practice about which you will be reading, let me describe the nature and form of the practice as it currently exists. The author is the sole owner and shareholder of a professional corporation, incorporated under the laws of the State of Ohio in 1978. I was trained as both an experimental and clinical psychologist, and began my career in 1968 as a committed behavioral-oriented therapist (social learning theory *a la* Bandura; cognitive behaviorist *a la* Meichenbaum, Mahoney, etc.). The practice began and remained "health psychology"-oriented (having been trained by William House, Tom Hyde, and Barbara Melamed in the early 1970s). At present, the practice consists of the following divisions or departments.

2.30.3.1 Division of Clinical Practice

This is the division of the practice that delivers clinical services in our outpatient offices. The work performed in these offices may be funded by traditional general indemnity insurance, capitated arrangements that we have had and will continue to have, managed care contracts (either in the form of PPO or EPO as we have with one large Ohio insurer for its HMO product), assessment services to national or local EAPs, etc. This division accounts for 20% of the total fee income generated. At the outset of the practice this unit produced 75% of fee income the remainder being earned by the Division of Mental Retardation and Development Disabilities.

2.30.3.2 Division of Employee Assistance Programs

Marketed as a separate contributing component of the group is a state-wide EAP division that has a number of capitated contracts to provide broad brush EAP services to company employees and eligible family members. Currently, there are seven contracted companies, covering 12 000 lives. This division accounts for 20% of the total fee income generated.

2.30.3.3 Division of Legal Consultation

This division provides psychological consultation to legal referral sources, ranging from public agencies (i.e., workers' compensation, Attorney General's office, Common Pleas or domestic relations courts, Social Security Administration [as a group we do not conduct Bureau of Disability Determination evaluations nor any longer conduct Bureau of Vocational Rehabilitation evaluations], Department of Labor) to attorneys, specializing in various aspects of the law. This division of the practice provides service throughout the state of Ohio and accounts for 20% of the total fee income generated by the group.

2.30.3.4 Division of Mental Retardation and Developmental Disabilities

Believe it or not, this was the core of the practice when it began in 1978 with a grant from the Ohio Office of Developmental Disabilities. To this day, we provide extensive consultative and direct service to facilities—public (state and county agencies) and private not-for-profit agencies—throughout the northern Ohio region. At the time of writing, facilities for the mentally retarded and developmentally disabled are under contract to the practice. When an opportunity became available to provide OBRA-PASARR evaluations, we marketed our services throughout the counties of northern Ohio, and provided coverage to 24 of the counties for this specialized need. This division in the past accounted for 50% of the fee income of the practice, but due to federal and state funding cuts has been reduced drastically to approximately 25%.

2.30.3.5 Division of Long-term Care

Staff are placed in facilities that provide long-term care services to the elderly or disabled. This division of the practice provides service throughout the entire state of Ohio, and has also been made available as a "turnkey" operation to psychologists in other states. One particular group in Utah is up and running with eight contracts since first marketing three months prior to this writing. Our practice provides the direction, forms, manuals, contracts, marketing materials, and more to get the program going, and helps to maintain the momentum in the following months through direct consultation. Within Ohio as a function of Medicare cutbacks I have "sold off" 32 of my contracts and maintained only those eight in the greater Cleveland area to allow for greater profitability resulting from lower overhead to service. This division will vary in its contribution to the total gross fee income dependent upon reimbursement rates and the local fiscal intermediary rate of pay. (On January 1, 1997 the reimbursement rate for Medicare service billed from a Cleveland provider dropped 27%.)

2.30.3.6 Division of Practice Development

The author provides consultation to psychologists nationwide on all facets of practice development and management. Consultation ranges from issues of managed care contracting, capitation, staffing, sale of practice, and long-term care development. This contributes approximately 5% of the gross revenues for the practice.

I believe that it would be helpful to set the stage for the present form of the practice by observing it developmentally. To do this, the reader will be asked to participate in an autobiographical sketch of the practice and owner. Having spent five years as a psychologist on the faculty of Case Western University School of Medicine, Departments of Pediatrics and Psychiatry, I precipitously left in December 1978. At that time, I had a state-funded grant to provide behavioral consultation and treatment to public agencies and citizens with developmental disabilities. The state invited me to take this grant into independent practice and so the doors of the "group" practice opened in December 1978 with money to subsidize the overhead. We began with four clinical staff, one support staff, and 850 square feet of office space divided into two consultation rooms where outpatient psychotherapy was conducted and one waiting room/secretarial area combined, a co-existence that lasted for many years. We began by consulting to six public and private not-for-profit facilities for the mentally retarded and developmentally disabled citizens of northeastern Ohio.

As I write today, the practice has six locations, totaling 7000 square feet where outpatient psychotherapy is conducted (three offices for which I pay the rent, three of which are satellite offices using other's space and staff), and over four dozen contracted facilities where my staff practices psychology, located throughout the entire state of Ohio. The current payroll consists of 35 individuals, 85% of whom are full-time, all of whom are considered "employees" by the Internal Revenue Service (IRS) and hence paid by a W-2. During this period of almost 18 years, the practice has had two statewide capitated contracts (inpatient and outpatient benefits for chemical dependency/substance abuse and mental health) of two years duration, servicing 25 000 members of an HMO, and one regional (northeastern Ohio) capitated contract (outpatient benefit of mental health and chemical dependency/substance abuse only), servicing 45 000 members of an HMO and lasting four years. Currently, the only form of capitation is within one specialized division of the practice, the EAP Division.

2.30.4 GENERAL PHILOSOPHY

You must have a strong, workable general philosophy for making decisions. For the first five years that I was in practice, I maintained the belief that I was a psychologist running a small business. At about that point, I began to recognize and enjoy the reality that I was a businessman with a doctorate in psychology, running a complex business. Very early I recognized that I could not do this on my own. One characteristic of the entrepreneurial process is seeing and seizing opportunities. A general business philosophy needs to be developed that drives and directs the practice so that the psychologist can remain proactive. To be reactive and attempt to play catch-up will typically leave you behind. Much of what has happened to the typical psychology practices (typically solo in days gone by) had been telegraphed ahead of time. Unfortunately psychologists allowed disbelief and denial to blind us while outside forces took control of us, and again we need to react from a defensive posture.

The general philosophy of your business needs to consist of a proactive, organized, goal-oriented cognitive statement(s) that you create. The general philosophy takes thought and planning, and is a vitally important activity for which you must make time as you plan and grow. Within this philosophy is the basis for decisions that need to be made and why they are made, such as deciding on the demographics of the populations to be served. This can be based on the location in which you wish to work (i.e., neighborhood, office-sharing with potential referral source that will help determine your practice, i.e., pediatric practice, internal medical practice, pedi-gi practice, making certain that this arrangement does not violate any Federal laws about the arrangement). For a period of time, we had an Orthodox Jewish social worker in the practice who maintained hours on Sunday. His being with us and his available hours attracted members of the large Orthodox Jewish community in Cleveland. Another decision may be to rent in a nonbarrier free building, but the consequences of that decision should be fully weighed. In many urban and suburban areas, there is the choice of locating on a mass transit/public transportation line or not. All of our managed care credentialing forms inquire about accessibility to public transportation. We always respond in the positive, yet nobody asks what percentage of the client pool utilizes mass transit. We have noted that on average less than one client per month uses a bus. If the choice is to not be on this route, then you are saying something to your potential public and are probably eliminating a segment from your clientele which can be a good decision as long as it is a well thought-out decision.

Most psychologists that I have known over the years have pieced together full-time positions for themselves. Typically, many have had positions on hospital psychiatric services or in psychiatric hospitals. In both settings, the psychologist has more often than not been used as an assessor. One can choose how and where to piece together work. Frequently, daytime school psychologists maintain evening independent practices, each position complimenting the other and rounding out the type of work and the settings for these professionals. I have also known a number of hospital-based, university-affiliated, and government-employed psychologists who maintain part-time independent practices. You can decide on the hours you wish to work and the quantity you wish to work. All of these are directly related to your conscious decision about the work philosophy, the amount of money you wish to earn, and the lifestyle you desire. In some cases, this may be more externally determined than internally. With all of the overhead required by managed care companies (i.e., credentialing, case management, time on the phone, etc.), this part-time private practice venture on the part of psychologists may no longer be viable. When our group first opened in the late 1970s, it was not difficult to fill daytime hours. Now, with two working parents and with managed care companies looking for evening and weekend hours for their subscribers, prizing that as a parameter by which they will choose you as a therapist; as a profession, psychologists tend to be working more evenings and weekends than we might wish. In addition, many of these piece-together clinical positions have allowed for psychologists to maintain nonemployee status (outside subcontractor) with the owner of the practice from whom they office share or sublet space and receive referrals. Many managed care companies will not allow for that arrangement in that they require all providers to be contracted with them individually and, if a member of a group, to be carried on the group malpractice. Therefore, the flexibility of these part-time jobs is being threatened.

As managed care began to remove the freedom of choice of providers for subscribers, much of this decision-making, self-control, and philosophy-setting goals needed to be reassessed; not necessarily thrown out, but realistically reevaluated. As noted more thoroughly below, in the past practitioners could determine their market niche and appeal directly to that specific target niche. With managed care as the predominant referral source for most of the practices that I have surveyed, there is now a new target market to which to appeal, that is to say, the case managers and other controllers from the "dark side" who can now control your client flow.

2.30.5 STRUCTURE/ADVISORS/ STAFFING

It is imperative that the structure and staff of a psychology practice change and mold to the ideas, projects, needs, and circumstances that you create, control, and do not control over time. Market pressures create factors that we do not control; they, too, will affect your staffing needs. I believe that there are a number of givens that are the necessary basis of a viable group practice: advisors/consultants, office manager, support staff, and clinical staff with consideration to level of degree, certification in specialty areas, sex, age, and so on. Each of these will be briefly discussed below.

2.30.5.1 Advisors/Consultants

I strongly believe that to succeed in business you must surround yourself with competent advisors and use them often. Issues of accounting and taxes, corporate structure, employment and labor law, leases (office space, equipment, and automobiles), contracting, Board of Psychology requests (and how to respond appropriately and legally), fiscal structure, and creation of a sensible ledger system (more will become clear as we go on) are the province of other professionals. We can only expect ourselves to know our field (not just "therapy," but the business of psychology) and to know when to use consultants. The Division of Practice Development allows me to interact with psychologists across the USA. It gives me insight into how sparingly our colleagues call on what is available to them—and financially feasible—in the form of business advisors. I frequently see how unaware psychologists are about how and why to use these consultants. The two most frequently needed consultants are accountants and attorneys. Both need to be willing to familiarize themselves with mental health issues, for example, State Board of Psychology (Social Work, etc.) Code of Ethics, regulations, and guidelines. My personal experience has demonstrated that a solo practice or small firm attorney or accountant is perfect for the majority of our needs. My observations have led me to the sound conclusion that we are not good clients for the large firms in that we do not generate enough fees, the rates we are charged are typically too high for our budgets, and we can get the equivalent, if not better, attention elsewhere.

2.30.5.1.1 Accountants

My experience has been that a mid-sized firm of accountants (the one I have used for my entire practice career consists of three partners and 10 additional staff), working closely with my Office Manager, have been able to create general ledger and detailed accounting information to allow me to evaluate the productivity and profit of each division of the practice and each element within. The general ledger that is done in-house functions in such a way as to interface with the information in form and substance that the accountant needs to produce quarterly statements, payroll tax documents, and other financial information that we might wish to utilize. After being in practice for 15 years and having done payroll in-house, I finally switched to a payroll company that prepares the checks and handles the compilation of taxes. With a state-wide business, we need to be paying city tax in multiple locations, and it soon became too complicated and costly to continue to do so in-house. Although it took some time and effort to coordinate and prepare for the transition, the use of an outside service has been cost effective for both my office manager, but more importantly, for my accountant. I believe the importance of that is self-evident.

The availability of cost ledgers, allowing you to evaluate the profitability of a segment of your practice, is a vitally important tool. This is true even if you have only one segment. As you diversify and expand into various market places, you will want to assess the wisdom of continuing in a specific arena and you will need important data to do so. Let me cite three examples: (i) "Yellow Pages" advertising may have gone the way of Edsels and long-term therapy (with all due respect to M. Seligman). With the advent of managed care, the concept of "freedom of choice" has almost disappeared from the subscribers' repertoire of behaviors. There are fewer subscribers allowed to open a phone book and choose a therapist in this day and age. In 1993, over six locations (five different counties, including two different phone companies), I spent \$27 000 in Yellow Page advertising. In 1994, on a rolling basis as the contract year ended, I reduced my cost to \$13 000 and the next year to \$7000. This decision has been driven by the data we collect in the office pertaining to profitability of the money spent in a Yellow Page advertisement. It became evident that we were not paneled providers for many of the potential clients who called from the Yellow Pages and to do so would have involved the creation of another full-time support staff position in addition to continuing advertising all the while managed care companies were dropping their reimbursement rates; talk about unpaid overhead. It was also evident that in some areas callers using the Yellow Pages had the highest no show rate. Also, we began to notice that those individuals who called were those without case managers to guide them, without insurance coverage, and unable to pay our fees. To that extent, it began to feel that the Yellow Pages were no longer a viable source of referrals. With a strong emphasis placed on tracking the intake system within the office (i.e., source of referral, source of payment, number of sessions, total revenue), we could more easily evaluate the profitability of a particular cost center.

Using the same approach, you can assess the profitability of, for example, an office location, contract, or staff person. If you review your goal statement and realize that you want to make a certain predetermined profit or spend only a certain predetermined percentage of income in a specific area, then evaluating the data of cost and income will allow you to make decisions objectively. But only by being true to your philosophy, by keeping an eye to those predetermined goals and percentages will you allow yourself the opportunity to profitably continue in practice. (ii) The second example where financial ledgers were of great value in decision making was in assessing the profitability of multiple locations. As population shifts occur, as employers close or as referral sources change, the initial reason for opening in a certain location may be changing or may have changed. Instead of simply paying rent on an ongoing basis, you will want a system to evaluate the wisdom of staying in a location. One reason for maintaining a location in the absence of "specific site" profitability is to allow you to continue to serve a referral source that refers to your practice in all locations, even if one is not utilized as much. If you recall the general overriding philosophy of making it easy on your referral source, you may serve yourself better by remaining open in a location and not forcing the referral source to differentiate where to use you and where to use another practice. It remains a simple referral process if the referrer can think "psychologist" and think only of you. (iii) The third example is contract profitability. The practice has contracted with a large, for-profit nursing home chain. Of the 16 of their homes that we service two examples of profitability issues need pointing out: (a) one location is a facility smaller in size than our criteria calls for, and (b) three of the facilities are being served by a "less profitable provider" (by virtue of license, we collect less at these sites, but due to geography, we are forced to utilize this person). Both situations are counterbalanced by the desire to service their entire company and, hence, some of the sites may be loss lead item. On balance, the entire nursing home chain is profitable. This can be assessed in your financial feedback established by the accountant and you.

One last thought on the valuable use of an accountant. Frequently throughout your development you will be approached by life/disability insurance salespersons. I submit that most Ph.D. level readers of this paragraph have little ability to evaluate and integrate into your investment strategies the type and amount of insurance needed. It is at this time that your consultant accountant can also be helpful.

2.30.5.1.2 Attorneys

Another consultant of great value is the attorney. My legal needs have varied over the year, but the basic function of an attorney for most practices would include reviewing leases (office space, equipment, cars [do not forget to have first passed the idea of leasing a car by your accountant to see if it is a viable method based on your financial situation, then go to the next and probably more expensive level of advisor], etc); creating employment contracts; contracts for facilities and companies that contract with the practice; discussion with accountant regarding issues of corporate structure, benefits, pension and profit sharing plans, life insurance; and so on. I have had two primary lawyers for the life of the practice. The lawyer I have used for 13 years has functioned as the consultant attorney to the state psychological association's Committee on Ethical Practice: Needless to say, he is well-versed in issues of mental health practice law and, specifically, psychology. I have worked closely with the attorney to minimize the size and language in a legal document to cover all the issues he believes are necessary to protect my best interests and yet to not frighten the other party away. I have found that most psychologists find legal documents daunting and would rather avoid any affiliation rather then feel trapped by a document they feel they do not understand and, hence, avoid.

At one point in my career, 15 years ago, the State Board of Psychology requested a site visit to investigate our compliance with supervision guidelines. My attorney suggested that I request all questions in writing ahead of time and his presence at the site visit. The Board never made that visit. The other attorney I use practices business and tax law in another state, but is well-versed in Federal guidelines and regulations, for example, tax, retirement, insurance. I have, over the years, used him, in conjunction with my accountant, to review life insurance documents prior to purchase. The issues of life and disability insurance being held in or out of a professional corporation has been dealt with by consultation between this attorney and the accountant.

Surprisingly, I have had little use of attorneys as collection agents (I have used three professional collection agencies over the life of the practice). The only two occasions during which I used attorneys for collections have been when I was owed money from companies with whom I had contracted and they terminated the relationship, owing me funds. I used an attorney in both situations and won court orders for payment (clearly written and enforceable contracts prior to the problem helped prevail in court).

2.30.5.1.3 Insurance agent

Although many of the readers will have found the APAIT malpractice to be sufficient, I never thought that it met all of my group's needs. For years, I have had a true group with multiple locations and levels of professional staff, and I have found that I needed a local agent who could sell professional malpractice from a company that also would cover renters, fiduciary, personal property, and liability (non-professional) all in one policy. It made more sense to me to have one company cover everything so that in case of a claim, two or more companies did not simply point fingers and assert that it was the other's responsibility. Therefore, I have always had just one company write all of my insurance for the employees and office on one policy, and have a local agent (only two across a 19 year span) handle any of the details involved therein.

2.30.5.1.4 Support staff

It was once explained to me by a close friend that you cannot do multiple full-time functions such as being a clinician, administrator, or marketer, all within a 40–50 hour week. What has allowed me to find and initiate the projects within the practice has been an individual who has functioned as the "runner of the practice." The Office Manager implements and follows up on all aspects of the practice with both support staff and clinical staff reporting to her for all administrative issues. What has worked exceedingly well has been my "initiator spirit" and her "implementer behavior." The Office Manager has had a number of functions in the practice, all additive until they get delegated to a support staff member who reports directly to her. The Office Manager came from a background of public relations. In addition to the administrator function in overseeing the hiring of all support staff and purchasing all equipment and supplies for the practice, the Office Manager has been intimately involved in all financial aspects of the practice. She has overseen all payroll and payables function in consultation with the accountant. The creation of the general ledger and the type of computer-based accounting system was something that the two of them devised with the awareness of the type of information I believed that I needed to make decisions about the practice. The payroll function that has now been contracted out is still coordinated by the Office Manager who prepares all the data (gross wages) for the payroll company. The Office Manager works closely with the accountant to file all tax payments in a timely fashion.

Personnel issues are all handled through and by the Office Manager. Once clinical staff are hired, they deal directly with the Office Manager to request such things as vacation, sick leave, supplies, and continuing education seminars. These decisions are made and implemented either in consultation with the divisional director, myself, or by herself. In addition, the Office Manager fulfills a strong public relation function, handling all referrals and special needs from attorneys who refer to the practice. This has allowed for a personal relationship between the attorney's office and a single representative of the practice. As we developed a number of state-wide projects (managed care capitated project in 1984–86, our state-wide nursing home business currently ongoing, and our state-wide EAP), the Office Manager has functioned as the liaison with the outlying staff and the contract facilities. There is a Clinical Director for all projects who is always available to the clinical staff if that is the need, but short of that, most requests are for administrative and informational items. The Office Manager typically is not in the field and, hence, is available to those callers. There have been a number of practice consultations that I have been contracted to do that has included the Office Manager. We were hired by a local defense attorney to help in a malpractice suit against a psychologist and his Office Manager. Both of us advised the attorney after doing a site visit and interviewing the psychologist and his Office Manager. Through the Division of Practice Management, I have been to a number of states. Follow-up consultation is done by phone and frequently involves the clinician or staff consulting with the Office Manager around a variety of issues she knows more about than me, for example, computer programs, accounting functions, contract forms. To that end, her time is hired out by the contractor.

Obviously a critical support staff person is the receptionist/intake coordinator. This individual fulfills three major functions in the group. In addition to doing all phone intakes, she also schedules all appointments (save for depositions and court appearances that continue to go through the Office Manager) plus she checks on all incoming clients' benefit plans. Phone intakes in a group practice that bears an individual's name are very tricky. More often than not, the caller asks to speak to or schedule with the principal (typically, that is to whom the client is being referred). The receptionist/intake coordinator is aware of each clinician's area of specialty by training, area of interest, and so on, and so directs the caller to the appropriate clinician. These assignment duties are always done in conjunction with the Director of the clinical practice and never on her own. Scheduling for all clinicians and all locations is done in one master calendar book (not a computer) by the receptionist/intake coordinator. Although I resisted for years, my support staff convinced me that it would be better for the office if we were to check the insurance benefits prior to scheduling clients, informing them of what we were told by the insurance company. This focuses on deductibles and copays and, hence, what our financial expectation is from the client at the first and then each subsequent session. It also avoids the managed care client accessing the office, even having the first appointment, before it is apparent that the client had a particular panel to which they had to go, etc. The receptionist/intake coordinator gets all of the documentation completed for the first visit when it occurs at our main office; the clinicians are responsible for all intake documentation (e.g., Consent to Treat, Fee Agreement, Releases, etc.) when they are working in our satellite offices. The receptionist/intake coordinator is the first line in making available community resources to our EAP clients. She, along with the EAP manager, maintains an updated compilation of available community services, attorneys, financial support systems, and so on. In addition, the receptionist/intake coordinator doubles as the typist for all secretarial functions in the Division of Mental Retardation and Developmental Disabilities (producing hundreds of reports and behavioral programs per year).

We have over the years utilized an individual to function as a secretary/reception support and typist to the remainder of the practice. In addition, she has over the years shared phone duty with the receptionist/intake coordinator, preparing intakes and providing resource information to our EAP clients. She does not schedule new appointments, but does assist in such things as reschedules and cancellations.

Most critical perhaps is the billing department. Over the years, the billing function has evolved from one of the many tasks the Office Manager did to that of a single staff person's job. As the practice became more complicated and as we grew into doing a great deal of Medicare work, we developed the need for a billing department. This staff person needs exceptional computer skills and a curiosity to make a commercial program work maximally for the practice. This individual needs to understand the goals of the billing office to be more than just mailing statements (electronically or by post). The billing office is the arm of the group that has the data by which you, as the owner, will make decisions about future movement. The manner by which this information is maintained and massaged will make the decision-making function of the owner easier. Commercial billing packages can provide more information than simply meets the eye as long as the person working it is inquisitive and daring. In cooperation with the Office Manager, these two individuals can create data presentations that tell "all the news, nothing but the news" about the practice. As noted above, we have begun to spend 50% of our billing time dealing with the fiscal intermediary for Medicare in Ohio. The billing staff person must be capable of negotiating the darkest recesses of an insurance morass; and must be able to understand federal manuals plus carrier regulations, and have the personality to pursue unsatisfactory answers to attempt to guide the billing procedures of the practice.

As an adjunct to this division of the practice, the owner has established and incorporated a separate business that is a billing business for mental health professional practices. The knowledge, hard gained from working within the Medicare arena and over 20 years of insurance business, has presented an opportunity that has been seized and stroked. Remember—never tread water.

2.30.5.2 Clinical Staff

This is probably the most difficult realm to maintain, specifically with the type and style of personnel with whom you want to attract and work. If you believe that your practice has something special to offer employees (e.g., information about professional psychology, business information that you believe is proprietary, procedures and documentation that is special and yours, etc.), you will want to utilize a "covenant not to compete" in each employment contract. Most applicants for a position resist this concept and counter with the argument that they would never "steal" your referral sources, ideas, forms, or client list. The basis of an employment contract is to prohibit that from occurring. The employment status of clinical staff has always been a clear issue according to the IRS, yet seen as murky for convenience sake by our colleagues. Most "employees" (whether licensed or unlicensed) in psychology practices are by convenience treated as "outside subcontractors" ("independent contractors"), but by IRS definition they are indeed employees. This status demands that the employer take out and pay taxes on behalf of the staff. This is a practice that most psychologists have resisted. Malpractice considerations are also important at this point. You need to check with your carrier because frequently an independent contractor cannot be carried on a corporate or supervisor's malpractice. This begins to present complications for contracting and securing work for the group versus the tax and employment status of those performing and billing for the service. Medicare has made it abundantly clear that all providers who are employed by corporate structures for the purposes of contracting and billing and who are currently in the position of supervising another staff member must enjoy employee status.

2.30.5.3 Continued Reading

In addition to the professional journals that we must continue to read throughout our careers, those running "businesses" must be exposed to business publications. Some of these are specific to your locale and others are related generally to the business of running a practice. The former consists of publications such as *Crain's Cleveland Business Weekly* and *The Wall Street Journal*; the latter consists of publications such as *Psychotherapy Finances* and *Behavior Today*. Divisions within the American Psychological Association provide publications with practice information that is relevant to you both from a clinical but also business point of view. As you see new procedures developing, you are confronted by opportunities of new business niches. The information you can access in these publications exposes you to opportunities that you would probably otherwise not see. If your practice has an EAP component to it, you will read about businesses that are expanding or moving into your area. You can be aware of physician group and hospital mergers by reading these papers and see potential opportunities for your practice—all of which can be followed up on, but not all of which will come to fruition. Priortize and then watch your ledger sheets. Frequently, medical practices or hospital programs (e.g., pain and rehabilitation programs, mood disorder clinics, etc.) advertise or put out press releases in these papers, again providing you with an opportunity to expand your services. Many of these programs are in need of a psychology component for the appropriate accreditation. With the mergers and movement of for-profit hospital chains, managed care companies, and other entities entering your geographic region, there are opportunities for you to market your services, expand your scope of practice or simply meet new referral sources. These are opportunities you might not be aware of unless you are exposed to these types of publications. In some areas of the country downsizing or more euphamistically "right-sizing" has provided opportunities for psychologists to create new business ventures and seize the moment.

2.30.6 THE FUTURE

As you read this, there are changes and opportunities going on around you. For example, what began as an excellent and lucrative business venture into long-term care (i.e., nursing home work) has become a much less profitable and questionable venture for those with alternative opportunities. Watching your ledger and consulting with your accountant will tell you when to get out or at least allow you the choice to stick with the project and continue to evaluate the potential therein. The practice owner needs to be one step ahead of the next disaster to be prepared to maintain income flow and profitability. One stays aware of the field by reading and volunteering. Involvement with one's state, local, and national professional organizations is not only a responsibility that we all bear, but it is also an opportunity that is waiting to happen. While on committees or at meetings with other state or local agencies or bureaus, for example, one will see business ventures waiting to happen. While legislative chair of the state association, I was involved and instrumental in having psychologists become providers for the industrial commission of the state. From that time forth, my group has done a great deal of work for that agency. One of my colleagues is positioned on the state association's state and federal agency committee. In that position, she has seen an opportunity with the forthcoming Medicaid HMO and positioned her practice to be a major player in that arena. One gets back multifold from giving if you simply see what is in front of you as opportunities for the growth and development of your practice. After consulting to a large state-wide homehealth agency about issues of managed care, we evolved into a joint venture contractual relationship having nothing to do with managed care. Opportunities abound. The exciting aspect of change and expansion is the opportunity to learn new skills, to meet new people, and create new business opportunities. There is no question that due to outside forces our profession is dynamic and our practices must be prepared to change. To stick with what we used to do because we thought it was a good idea and it was the "right thing" may not pay the mortgage. To be flexible and attempt to work with those empowered to control the marketplace to help them understand appropriate psychological services, ethical, behavioral, and sound clinical practice works to the betterment of the client, clinician, and profession. One can do that alone, in groups, and in organizational ways. You stand a better chance of effecting change if you work through and with your national, state, and local organizations; we are a large and getting to be a loud and effective national profession with which to reckon.

2.31
Technology in Practice

MARK R. McMINN
Wheaton College, IL, USA

2.31.1 INTRODUCTION

The contemporary practice of psychology requires a prudent balance of traditional and emerging communication methods. Interpersonal interactions in the context of human relationship (e.g., speech, emotional expressions, and nonverbal gestures) have been a vital part of emotional healing throughout many centuries, and research findings in the 1990s underscore the importance of relational factors in effective psychological interventions (Whiston & Sexton, 1993). In addition to the time-honored interpersonal communication methods of professional psychology, rapid technological advances have propelled psychologists into another sphere of communication. Today's professional psychologist is increasingly expected to attain mastery in both of these communication methods—the very old and the very new.

It appears likely that technological changes will continue at a rapid or even an accelerating pace in the years ahead. This rapid rate of change suggests an ongoing need for psychologists to keep abreast of technological advances and the implications of these advances for professional practice. To this end, the American Psychological Association (APA) has published three editions of a software directory (Stoloff & Couch, 1992), the APA Practice Directorate has published *Organizing Your Practice Through Automation* (1996), national and international conferences have been established, and many journal articles and books on the topic have been published. Internet discussion groups regarding psychology and mental health practices abound, and the APA has charged the Media Psychology/New Technologies Committee of the Media Psychology Division to consider the implications of virtual reality, artificial intelligence, and other computer technologies. Psychologists are attempting to hold on to the value of established professional practices and communication methods while seeking the advantages available through technological advances.

Previous authors have distinguished between first- and second-wave innovations. First-wave technology allows for efficiency in maintaining records and office procedures but has little direct impact on clinical services. These technologies are now well-established and commonly used in the practice of psychology. They include office management computer software as well as facsimile, telephone answering, and voice mail services. Second-wave technologies have a greater direct impact on patient care and should be considered partially established in that many psychologists already use these technologies, though they will become increasingly prevalent in coming years. These include computerized assessment and interviewing tools, computerized therapeutic applications, telephone consultations, electronic mail, and clinical databases that directly impact patient care. Because of rapid technological changes, a third wave of technological advances must also be considered. This third-wave includes emerging innovations that have only started to affect the practice of psychology. Third-wave advances include teleconferencing, global networking environments (World Wide Web and Internet), virtual reality as a treatment tool, and innovative computer applications in training.

2.31.2 WELL-ESTABLISHED PRACTICE TECHNOLOGIES

A number of technological advances are now well-established as routine (first-wave) resources for professional psychologists. These include computerized office management systems, facsimile capabilities, and telephone answering and voice mail systems. The benefits and potential liabilities of each of these technologies are discussed below and summarized in Table 1.

2.31.2.1 Computerized Office Management

As early as 1987 a surprisingly high rate (90%) of psychologists surveyed in Canada were using computers for tasks indirectly related to clinical services including word processing, billing systems, and database management (Pollock & Maenpaa, 1990). It should be noted that the low response rate obtained in this survey research (23%) may have produced a spurious estimate of the number of psychologists using computers. Nonetheless, a decade has passed since the survey, and it is undoubtedly true that an increasing number of psychologists use computers in routine tasks associated with professional practice.

Word processing software allows a psychologist to reduce the time required for repetitive narrative. For example, a psychologist may use similar language in certain parts of clinical reports or treatment authorization requests. Rather than producing the narrative for each report, a template can be stored on computer disk and adapted for each individual report. Mailing merge options allow for personalized letters to be sent to various addresses for purposes of promotion or information. Also, word processing may improve the accuracy of written correspondence and reports. With tools such as spell checking, electronic thesaurus, and grammar checking, written documents can be scrutinized closely before leaving the psychologist's office. Word processing also allows for the evolving nature of forms and documents: For example, psychologists occasionally need to revise informed consent forms, release forms, or promotional statements. Word processing allows for such changes without requiring retyping.

Electronic billing software allows for the automation of the once tedious process of billing patients and health insurance carriers. Rather than typing or writing the patient's name, address, birthdate, and diagnosis on each bill, this identifying information can be stored electronically and automatically printed on a computer-generated billing form. Standard insurance forms are included in many software programs and printed onto plain paper with an inkjet or laser printer. In other cases the insurance forms are purchased separately and the printer is used to fill in the various fields in the standardized form. Most current billing programs and insurance companies also provide the option of electronic claims filing where the claim is filed via modem and no paper is transferred from the psychologist to the insurance company. Electronic billing promises to reduce much of the paper use traditionally associated with the billing process. Additional practice management software allows psychologists to keep electronic records of patient information, progress notes, financial records, accounts payable, payroll, and appointment scheduling (APA Practice Directorate, 1996).

Table 1 First-wave technologies: benefits and potential liabilities.

Technologies	*Benefits*	*Potential liabilities*
Computerized office management	Reduces time required for repetitive tasks Improves accuracy of written work Allows for evolving forms (e.g., informed consent) Billing efficiency, including reduced paper use Efficient management of patient records	Patient perceptions of increased bureaucracy Ease of duplication may compromise confidentiality and privacy rights In-session use of computers may inhibit patient–psychologist relationship
Facsimile	Immediate transfer of information (e.g., patient records)	Compromised patient confidentiality
Telephone answering and voice mail	Receive phone messages at any time without the expense of added secretarial support or answering services	Compromised patient privacy Technology failure may result in miscommunications

Although the use of first-wave computer software is commonplace in psychological practice, it remains important to consider the potentially negative effects of office computerization for patients. Because patients are generally less concerned about clerical efficiency than the nature of interpersonal interactions and quality of clinical services provided, some may experience highly visible computers as a bureaucratic hindrance or potential violation of privacy. Indeed, with the ease of duplicating electronic records there may be some legitimate basis for concern about violations of privacy and confidentiality. Also, some preliminary evidence from medical practice suggests that it may be important to avoid using computers for record keeping during the consultation itself. Physicians in the UK showed a diminished capacity to relate with patients when using a computer rather than pen and paper to issue prescriptions (Greatbatch, Heath, Campion, & Luff, 1995). Although this finding cannot be directly translated to psychological interventions, it is likely that using a laptop or notebook computer to take notes during a therapy session has an inhibiting effect on the human interactions that play an essential role in services provided by professional psychologists.

2.31.2.2 Facsimile

Facsimile (fax) machines are used to electronically transfer information to or from a remote site. The primary benefit of fax transmission is the immediacy with which information can be transfered. For example, a release form can be faxed to the office of another health care provider before holding a conversation about the patient, or patient records from a previous treatment can be instantly provided to the treating psychologist. Similarly, clinical reports can be faxed from a psychologist's office directly to the hospital floor or the referring professional's office. Contemporary computer software can make such transmissions paperless, with communications flowing from one computer to another.

The primary concern with fax transmission is the risk of compromising patient confidentiality. If a patient report is inadvertently sent to an incorrect fax station, for example, the psychologist has violated the patient's ethical and legal rights to confidentiality. This is especially likely with computer software that allows fax numbers to be stored in an electronic phonebook. Simply selecting the incorrect fax listing on the computer screen (with a single mouse click or keystroke) could result in sending a document to the wrong party and, therefore, in a violation of patient confidentiality. Even if the fax arrives at the correct office, the location and availability of the fax machine to office staff and others may compromise patient records. Because of these concerns, some jurisdictions have passed laws controlling fax transmissions of confidential materials. Thus, it is important for psychologists to know the legal guidelines of their regional or national jurisdictions. If faxing is legally permitted, it is incumbent on the psychologist to double-check the telefax number being used and to have a clear understanding of how the fax transmission will be handled on the receiving end.

2.31.2.3 Telephone Answering and Voice Mail Systems

Telephone answering systems allow callers to leave messages which can later be retrieved at the receiving end. The first generation telephone answering systems, usually depending on a cassette or microcassette recording of the incoming message, have become commonplace in many professional offices. This allows psychologists to receive incoming calls day or night without adding secretarial staff. In some cases psychologists use answering machines in lieu of an answering service. For emergency needs, an alternative phone number or electronic pager number can be left on the recorded greeting message.

The potential liabilities of using an answering machine for incoming messages include problems with patient privacy and technological failure. The patient may leave a message for the psychologist assuming the psychologist is the only one listening, especially if the greeting message is recorded by the psychologist. If a staff member or another professional in the office then listens to the recorded message, the patient may have disclosed information that was not intended for others in the office. Also, because low-cost answering machines have a relatively high failure or error rate, a patient or consulting professional may leave a message which the psychologist never receives. This breakdown in communication, caused by an uninformed faith in technology, can compromise patient care or even result in negligence in urgent situations.

Computerized voice mail systems have helped with both of these potential liabilities. Most voice mail systems have individual voice mail "boxes" which can be selected by the calling party. In addition, these boxes are usually password protected. These innovations reduce the inadvertent violations of patient privacy that frequently occur with low-cost answering machines. Computerized voice mail systems also reduce the likelihood of technological error because they depend on highly dependable digital technology rather than the mechanical and analog technologies used in free-standing answering machines.

2.31.3 PARTIALLY ESTABLISHED PRACTICE TECHNOLOGIES

A second group of technological advances are already used by many psychologists but will become more prominent in professional psychology. These second-wave technologies have more direct impact on clinical services than first-wave technologies, and thus also hold greater benefits and potential liabilities. Second-wave technologies, summarized in Table 2, include computerized assessment tools, computerized interviewing and diagnosis, computerized therapy tools, telephone consultations, electronic mail, and clinical databases.

2.31.3.1 Computerized Assessment Tools

In a survey of members of the Society for Personality Assessment and members of the Clinical Psychology Division of the APA, almost two-thirds of the respondents indicated that they use computers to assist with psychological testing (Ball, Archer, & Imhof, 1994). Over half used computers to help with test scoring and approximately one-third used computers to assist with test interpretation. Fewer than 10% used computers for test administration.

Many software programs are available for automated test scoring and interpretation. Among the most prominent test scoring and interpretation software is the Microtest Q system which generates reports for many tests, including the Minnesota Multiphasic Personality Inventories and the Millon Clinical Inventories. Two Rorschach software products are also widely used: the Rorschach Scoring Program (RSP) and the Rorschach Interpretative Assistance Program (RIAP).

One advantage of computerized test scoring for objective personality tests is improved accuracy. When Allard, Butler, Faust, and Shea (1995) had eight trained technicians and professionals hand score 43 protocols from the Personality Diagnostic Questionnaire-Revised (PDQ-R), they found 53% of the resulting profiles contained errors. Nineteen percent contained errors significant enough to affect clinical diagnosis—an alarming number of hand scoring errors. Hand scoring errors presumably affect other objective personality tests similarly, though it should be noted that the PDQ-R involves more complex hand scoring procedures than many other objective personality tests. In contrast to this high rate of human error, the error rate of computerized scoring is negligible (assuming correct data entry and software development).

Computers may also improve scoring accuracy of projective personality tests. Rorschach software such as the RSP and the RIAP provide algorithms to check for scoring inconsistencies. For example, a person may have coded both a whole blot response and a white space integra-

Table 2 Second-wave technologies: benefits and potential liabilities.

Technologies	*Benefits*	*Potential liabilities*
Computerized assessment tools	Greater accuracy in scoring	Unwarranted perception of interpretive accuracy
	Increases time efficiency	Use among unqualified users
	Access to interpretive expertise through expert system software	Changing professional identity
		Standardization assumptions may not hold with computer-administered tests
Computerized interviewing and diagnosis	More candid responses from patients	Greater difficulty in describing feelings and ideas
	Increases time efficiency	Possibility of excessive false positive diagnoses
	Increases screening of mental health needs in primary care	Must be quickly adapted to DSM changes
Computerized therapy tools	Used as an adjunctive tool for patient education, play therapy, cognitive rehabilitation, and behavior modification	Perceived as dehumanizing and reductive to those who view the human relationship as the essential ingredient of therapy
Telephone consultation	Immediate access to services	Lack of effectiveness data
	Decreases power differential between therapist and patient	Lack of nonverbal cues may inhibit emotional exploration or cause distractibility during session
	Gives privacy (or anonymity) to patient	May add to a sense of social alienation or dehumanization and thereby contribute to psychosocial problems
Electronic mail	As with telephone therapy	As with telephone therapy
		Unclear parameters for professional regulation
Clinical databases	Maintain personal outcome data to demonstrate effectiveness	Expense of equipment and on-line services
	Ready access to literature searches	Time required to input practice data

tion response but neglected to code the higher of the two z-scores. Rorschach software products detect scoring errors such as this and alert the psychologist or technician to the problem.

Computerization also reduces the time required for scoring psychological tests (Alexander & Davidoff, 1990). Whereas it might take 30–45 minutes to hand score a Millon Clinical Multiaxial Inventory, it can be computer scored in approximately five minutes. Similarly, the structural summary calculations for a Rorschach protocol may take almost an hour with a pocket calculator but only a few minutes with the appropriate software.

Test interpretation software provides psychologists with access to the interpretative expertise of test developers. Such software has been labeled "expert system" because it allows the computer to serve as an expert consultant to the psychologist. For example, Dr. John Exner has developed both the Comprehensive System for Rorschach scoring and the RIAP software that helps clinicians interpret Rorschach results. Similarly, Dr. Theodore Millon has been involved in the development of the various Millon tests (Millon Clinical Multiaxial Inventories, Millon Adolescent Clinical Inventory, and others) and in the development of the Microtest Q interpretive software. Automated interpretative systems such as these magnify the availability of experts for each test.

Despite these advantages of computerized test scoring and interpretation, legitimate concerns have been raised about these products and practices, especially regarding interpretative software. First, a computer printout may leave the psychologist with an unwarranted perception of accuracy. Although the scoring accuracy of well-reputed commercial products may generally be assumed, the interpretative accuracy may be suspect because the software developer has neither met the client being assessed nor had access to concurrent test results. Further, the interpretative narratives are often based on an expert clinician's personal experience with a test more than empirically validated results. Second, computerized test interpretation systems may unwittingly encourage the use of psychological tests among unqualified users. For example, a physician, marriage and family counselor, attorney, or social worker may attempt to bypass a psychologist's consulting services by gaining access to test interpretation software for the Minnesota Multiphasic Personality Inventory. To guard against misuse, test publishers closely monitor the qualifications of those who purchase test supplies and software. However, the publishers cannot monitor who actually uses the software once it is sold to the psychologist placing the order. Third, there is some risk that automated interpretative systems may move the identity of the professional psychologist toward that of a technician. At worst, a psychologist might administer tests, use computer-based interpretations, and write a report which includes much of the computer-generated narrative. This might involve little or no critical analysis and consideration of idiographic variables. The psychologist then would sign this report, thus taking legal and ethical responsibility for its contents, yet the computer-generated interpretative report on which the psychologist's report is based is not signed by a professional willing to share responsibility for the psychologist's conclusions and recommendations.

Lively interaction and debate will continue to play an important role in the development of professional standards for using technology in psychological assessment. Psychologists must collectively consider empirical evidence for computerized test interpretation and move forward with technological advances in a prudent manner.

Technological advances have shifted the debate from test interpretation software to automated administration of psychological tests. At the center of this debate is the question of test validity and standardization assumptions when administered by computer rather than pencil and paper.

It is unclear whether tests administered by computer produce comparable results to tests administered with pencil and paper. Sawyer, Sarris, and Baghurst (1991) reported only minor differences in Child Behavior Checklist scores when administered via computer, yet Davis and Cowles (1989) reported a greater tendency to "fake good" on a variety of personality tests administered by computer.

The burden to demonstrate that automated assessments do not significantly violate standardization assumptions rests on the profession of psychology and the individual test users. Under optimal circumstances each test would be restandardized and normative data collected for computer administration. A monumental task such as this would require many years and tremendous financial resources. But even this optimal solution may not completely address the problem because at least one study has found sizable differences among patients in the ways they respond to automated assessments (Spinhoven, Labbe, & Rombouts, 1993). Thus, renorming a test for computer administration may mask the significant individual differences in response styles. Spinhoven et al. (1993) recommend that a preassessment interview be used to determine if a patient is a good candidate for automated assessment.

The limited scope of this chapter does not permit a thorough analysis of other forms of computer-administered psychological testing. Promising areas of automated assessment include computer-assisted functional assessment (Smith, 1993), unobtrusive measurement (Meier & Wick, 1991), and behavioral assessment (Farrell, 1991).

2.31.3.2 Computerized Interviewing and Diagnosis

A variety of innovative diagnostic tools have been developed up to 1997. Some software is designed to be used as an adjunctive tool for diagnosis outside of the actual patient—psychologist interaction. Other software requires the computer to be used directly with the patient as a means for collecting information.

Software designed as an adjunctive tool for diagnosis is developed as an expert system in order to provide a structured algorithm for psychiatric diagnosis. First et al. (1993) report evidence of the effectiveness of the "DTREE: The *DSM* Expert," a computer-based expert system that guides clinicians through a series of decisions based on *Diagnostic and statistical manual of mental disorders* (*DSM*) criteria. Diagnoses obtained through a computerized system were compared with traditional diagnoses made during a case conference, resulting in a high rate of agreement, especially for patients with schizophrenia and major depression.

Software designed for direct patient use involves using the computer as interviewer in a screening interview. The self-administered Computerized Diagnostic Interview Schedule (C-DIS) is an adaptation of the original DIS, a standardized interview administered with pencil and paper. Preliminary research findings suggest that the computerized DIS produces data comparable to the original DIS (Bucholz et al., 1991; Erdman et al., 1992) and that adult

(Erdman et al.) and adolescent (Kight-Law, Mathisen, Calandra, Evans, & Salierno, 1989) patients respond favorably to computerized interviews. Additionally, there is evidence that patients disclose their concerns and symptoms more candidly in a computerized interview than in a traditional interview (Ferriter, 1993) and find a computerized interview less embarrassing (Erdman et al.).

Mini-SCID is a self-administered computerized adaptation of the Structured Clinical Interview for *DSM-III-R* (SCID) that can be used in screening for Axis I disorders. Unlike the C-DIS, Mini-SCID must be used in conjunction with the expert system DTREE (First, 1994).

A computerized version of the Diagnostic Interview for Children and Adolescents-Revised (DICA-R) has also been developed. Initial findings suggest that children find the computerized interview enjoyable and easy to use, and that reliability of results is respectable (Reich, Cottler, McCallum, Corwin, & VanEerdewegh, 1995). Comparability between the original and computerized versions of the DICA-R has not been reported up to 1997.

In addition to the obvious benefit of time efficiency and the benefit of increased patient candor discussed previously, a significant advantage of computer-based psychiatric diagnostic screening interviews is that they may ultimately help identify mental health needs earlier and more thoroughly. For example, if computerized psychiatric interviews were incorporated into primary medical care, it is likely that the mental health needs of patients would be more clearly and readily identified (Lewis, 1992).

One concern about computerized diagnostic interview tools is that patients report being better able to describe feelings and ideas to a human interviewer than to a computer (Erdman et al., 1992). In gaining efficiency with computerized interviews, there is some risk of losing the humanizing factors that have allowed professional psychology to prosper. A second concern is that the comparability of computerized interview data and human interview data has not been definitively established. Whereas two studies have shown comparability between the C-DIS and the DIS (Bucholz et al., 1991; Erdman et al.), a third study suggests that the C-DIS shows poor concurrence with the original (noncomputerized) SCID (Ross, Swinson, Larkin, & Doumani, 1994). Of particular concern is the high rate of false positive diagnoses made by the C-DIS. Finally, it should be noted that computerized interviews must be quickly adaptable to changes in *DSM* criteria. The computerized interviews described here were developed to fit *DSM-III-R* criteria, and will undoubtedly be adapted for *DSM-IV* criteria. Unfortunately, the process of changing the software could render obsolete much of the data supporting their usefulness.

2.31.3.3 Computerized Therapy Tools

Given the complexities of human interaction that are involved in effective psychotherapy, it is unimaginable to some psychologists that computers could ever be used effectively for psychotherapeutic interventions. Nonetheless, computer applications in psychotherapy have been steadily developing since the 1960s and are now used in some therapeutic contexts. The least controversial of these applications involves adjunctive educational programs to help prevent self-destructive behaviors and enhance desirable behaviors (Bloom, 1992). To illustrate, while waiting for an appointment with a psychologist a patient may find it helpful to participate in a educational computer simulation designed to enhance self-esteem, facilitate responsible sexual choices, or reduce alcohol consumption.

Others have found computers helpful to use adjunctively during the therapy session. For example, Kokish (1994) reports using a microcomputer as part of play therapy with children. Similarly, neuropsychologists and rehabilitation psychologists have found utility in using computer rehabilitation programs to restore executive functioning (Gianutsos, 1992; Giaquinto & Fiori, 1992).

Most controversial are the applications designed to replace or replicate part of the therapeutic intervention. Several programs have been designed to deliver behavioral and cognitive behavioral interventions (Bloom, 1992; Kenardy & Adams, 1993). These include the Dilemma Counseling System, designed to help patients choose between two unwanted alternatives, the Therapeutic Learning Program, used to reduce stressful interpersonal problems in the context of an educational group therapy setting, and a variety of specifically focused behavior modification programs used to treat depression, anxiety disorders, behavioral excesses, sexual dysfunction, and other problems. Some of these programs have been used in outcome studies that support their usefulness in providing therapeutic services.

Opinions about computer therapy tools will be partially determined by theoretical orientation. Those who see the human relationship as an essential part of the psychotherapeutic process are not likely to see great value in further developing therapeutic software. Moreover, they express concern that using computers as a substitute for human therapists is dehumanizing and harmful, robbing psychotherapy of the healing interpersonal process. Those who see the delivery of structured techniques as the active ingredient in psychotherapy are likely to be more encouraged by these recent software developments.

2.31.3.4 Telephone Consultation

Although telephones have been commonly available and an integral part of professional psychology for many years, interest in using telephones to deliver clinical services is a relatively recent phenomenon that is quickly gaining the attention of psychologists and professional organizations such as the APA. In a review of the literature, Haas, Benedict, and Kobos (1996) distinguish between telephone use as an adjunctive tool in therapy and telephone-only therapy. With regard to using the telephone as an adjunctive tool, telephones have been used for crisis intervention purposes, referral and screening purposes, and to provide services to established therapy clients when circumstances prevent face-to-face interactions. There is more controversy surrounding telephone-only therapy, which can involve either conventional therapeutic relationships conducted by telephone or pay-per-call services where the client is charged per minute of phone use.

One advantage is that telephone services can be obtained immediately. Rather than calling a psychologist's office to set an appointment several days or weeks in the future, a distressed patient can often make immediate contact with a psychologist offering phone services. Widespread availability of low cost cellular phone services further enhances the psychologist's availability to patients or potential patients. A second advantage is that the power differential between patient and therapist is reduced in a telephone exchange. No diplomas are visible, the patient has the power to hang up at any time, and the emotional intimacy is reduced by the absence of visual cues. Third, telephone therapy adds privacy (or anonymity, if desired) to the therapeutic encounter for those who might be concerned about being seen in the waiting room of a psychologist's office.

Each of these advantages has a corresponding disadvantage. Although there is little or no wait for telephone therapy, one might question the effectiveness of the treatment. Immediate ineffective treatment is no better than waiting for treatment. In the absence of compelling empirical effectiveness data, the question of whether or not telephone therapy works is largely determined by one's theoretical views of therapy. Second, though therapy may reduce the emotional intimacy and power differential of traditional therapy, it does so at the cost of eliminating virtually all nonverbal cues. Distractibility may be a greater problem without visual cues, and neither the therapist nor patient is able to experience the expressions or posture of the other. These factors may limit the emotional depth of exploration as well as understanding of transference and countertransference responses in the therapy process. Finally, although privacy and anonymity may be desirable to clients, one must contemplate the larger sociological dynamics that prompt this preference. Might the desire for anonymity (and the possibility that anonymous therapy can now be purchased) speak to a larger problem of social alienation and dehumanization that contributes to the same emotional problems that telephone psychologists purport to treat?

Several intriguing and promising applications for telephone therapy have been reported, including linking people with AIDS via conference calls (Rounds, Galinsky, & Stevens, 1991), providing support services for older adults (King, 1991), and even doing long-term intensive psychodynamic therapy by telephone (Spiro & Devenis, 1991). However, it is important that psychologists offering services by telephone observe all relevant ethical standards that pertain to providing psychological services. The long-term acceptability of telephone therapy will undoubtedly require persuasive empirical evidence of its efficacy.

2.31.3.5 Electronic Mail

The advent of electronic mail (e-mail), which consists of one person sending a message to another by way of a computer network, raises questions similar to those just discussed regarding telephone services. The Internet has made e-mail communication an easily accessible and global phenomenon. It is conceivable, for example, that a recognized expert in Rorschach interpretation could have a world wide consultation and supervision practice whereby psychologists from all over the world sent Rorschach protocols via e-mail and received interpretative assistance from the expert psychologist. Similarly, a psychologist might keep contact via e-mail with certain patients between therapy sessions, especially in rural settings where the traveling distances between patients and psychologists sometimes necessitate infrequent visits.

Most the advantages and disadvantages pertaining to telephone therapy also apply to e-mail services, except that even fewer cues can be retrieved from e-mail communications than from telephone (i.e., voice tone and inflection can be determined on the telephone). An additional problem, one that also applies to interstate or international telephone therapy, is the problem of professional regulation. When a psychologist in Switzerland offers supervision to a psychologist in the UK or direct services to a patient in the USA, in which country must the psychologist be licensed? To which national and state organizations is the psychologist accountable?

2.31.3.6 Clinical Databases

Although database computer software is commonly used by many psychologists to maintain patient and treatment information, additional clinical applications using database software are increasingly utilized in the practice of psychology. An excellent example is found among psychologists who maintain empirical outcome data for patients they treat (Clement, 1996). Although such databases do not lend themselves to controlled, double-blind outcome studies, they can be very useful in evaluating one's treatment efficacy with various disorders and types of clients. Moreover, as managed health care companies insist on assembling panels of competent therapists, the psychologist with positive outcome results will more likely be included on panels. Literature-based databases, such as PsychLit or various on-line services, are increasingly available for microcomputer use and can be very helpful in searching the literature for previous treatment approaches used for specific disorders. The variety and availability of other clinically relevant databases will expand exponentially as the Internet and World Wide Web grow in coming years. Potential concerns with clinical databases are limited to the expense of equipment plus on-line charges and the time required to input practice data.

2.31.4 EMERGING PRACTICE TECHNOLOGIES

In addition to the technologies discussed thus far, several other emerging technological advances may affect the practice of psychology in coming years. Third-wave technologies, summarized in Table 3, include teleconferencing, global networking environments (World Wide Web and Internet), virtual reality, and training innovations.

2.31.4.1 Teleconferencing

Teleconferencing, also known as videoconferencing, allows for visual and auditory communication through television monitors. Advances in electronics have made teleconferencing equipment increasingly affordable, resulting in experimental uses of teleconferencing among the health care professions. Whereas earlier prototypes required a satellite connection between television monitors, telecommunications can now be transmited much more economically through telephone lines.

Telecommunications are being used to offer medical care to some patients in rural areas of the USA. Technicians lead patients through diagnostic exercises while a physician observes and directs the examination from a remote location. Telemedicine saves travel time and money for many patients and makes medical care available to underserved areas. A similar concept has been developed at the University of Kansas (USA) to deliver neuropsychological services to rural areas. A master's level psychometrician leads a patient through diagnostic procedures while a neuropsychologist at the University observes and supervises the interaction. Patients have expressed satisfaction with the telecommunications services provided (Tröster, Paolo, Glatt, Hubble, & Koller, 1995). A similar strategy has also been used for remote cognitive testing of psychiatric patients in the UK (Ball, Scott, McLaren, & Watson, 1993). Teleconferencing also promises to provide an innovative means for continuing education for professional psychologists.

The primary benefit of telecommunication services is the availability of services and professional expertise to remote areas. Additionally, teleconferencing may enhance the availability of professional expertise around the world. For example, a patient in one part of the world may soon be able to consult with a leading expert in another part of the world about the symptoms he or she is experiencing. Similarly, psychologists throughout the world may participate in continuing education teleconferences with experts in various fields, thus raising the global level of professional expertise.

The main concern with teleconferencing relates to the setup costs. Although the telephone line costs of \$10 to \$35 per hour are not prohibitive, the site setup costs of \$100 000 makes the widespread use of teleconferencing unlikely for most psychology practices, at least until the end of the twentieth century. Also, because most teleconferencing services are not yet covered by health insurance companies, there is little financial incentive for purchasing the necessary equipment.

2.31.4.2 Global Networking Environments

Computer networking allows one computer to communicate with another. The Internet is a

Table 3 Third-wave technologies: benefits and potential liabilities.

Technologies	*Benefits*	*Potential liabilities*
Teleconferencing	Can provide services to remote areas	Setup costs are high
	Will heighten the availability of professional expertise	Not yet covered by most health insurance companies
Global networking environments	May heighten awareness of mental health issues and resources	As with telephone therapy and e-mail (see Table 2)
	May provide mechanism for supervision and consultation with other professionals	
Virtual reality	Provides the experience of *in vivo* exposure for phobias without having to leave the consulting office	Unknown generalizability of symptom relief
Training innovations	Promises to enhance learning and promote technological skills	Need to demonstrate didactic effectiveness

rapidly growing global network that allows communication among computers throughout the world. It is the electronic skeleton that allows for global e-mail communications and for the advent and growth of the World Wide Web. The World Wide Web is made possible by software innovations that allow information to be organized into "pages" which may contain text, graphics, video clips, sound, and connections with other web pages. Connections with other web pages, known as "links," usually appear as standard text printed in a distinct color. Thus, with a single mouse click the user can move from one web page to another. Because it is a global network, the user may (without knowing) be moving from a page in Australia to a page in Germany, then a page in the UK, then the USA and so on. This has led to the terms "web surfing" and "browsing." The software used to access the World Wide Web is called a web browser. Examples of web browsers include Netscape and Explorer.

With the growing use of the Internet and the user-friendly interface of the World Wide Web, many commercial services are now marketed on the Web, including psychological services. For example, Shrink-Link comprises a group of psychologists offering advice over the Internet for $20 per question.

In addition to direct services offered for profit, a number of no-cost resources are accessible through the Web. Newsgroups facilitate discussions among a variety of computers users throughout the world. Here one can find support groups for a variety of problems including depression, loneliness, addictions, and shyness. Professionals can subscribe to newsgroups or e-mail groups (called listserves) to discuss a variety of professional issues such as rural care, research funding, clinical training issues, and professional organizations. PsychNET, a service of the APA, provides free information on a variety of psychological disorders, lists and addresses of mental health organizations, and strategies for choosing a psychologist. Other organizations offer free self-help pages on a variety of topics. Some magazines and journals are available on the World Wide Web as well.

Because of the novelty and rapid growth of the World Wide Web, it is difficult to anticipate all the benefits and potential liabilities that will be forthcoming. What is clear is that the World Wide Web will continue to grow and will be a major technological influence on contemporary societies. Among the benefits for psychologists, it seems likely that the World Wide Web will make mental health information accessible to those who might not otherwise seek it. This heightened awareness of mental health needs may increase utilization of psychological services. Also, the Internet may become a mechanism for supervision and consultation among psychologists and other mental health professionals (Myrick & Sabella, 1995). The greatest liabilities of the Internet will probably be related to those who offer direct mental health services. All the concerns listed previously for telephone and e-mail consultations also apply for Internet consultations.

2.31.4.3 Virtual Reality

Virtual reality combines computer hardware and software to simulate real life experiences by presenting computer-generated graphics and sounds that are responsive to the movements and responses of the individual using the software. When using virtual reality, one wears a helmet that presents a visual field while simultaneously monitoring head movements. Moving one's head to the left, for example, would result in the visual field shifting accordingly. Many virtual reality systems also include gloves to monitor hand movements. In this way the user can pick up objects or move other objects aside while moving through the visual field.

Two reports of using virtual reality to treat acrophobia have recently been published (Rothbaum et al., 1995a, 1995b). By simulating graded exposure to heights, the researchers successfully provided many of the same benefits associated with *in vivo* graded exposure. Unlike *in vivo* interventions, virtual reality allows the treatment to occur in the office or laboratory while giving the psychologist greater control over the stimulus conditions. This appears to be a promising technology for psychology, with the only known liability being the uncertainty of generalizability to real life situations. Other applications of virtual reality in the practice of psychology are likely to be forthcoming.

2.31.5 TRAINING INNOVATIONS

Clinical training in psychology has already been influenced by the technological advances introduced by microcomputers, and it is inevitable that training advances will proliferate in the years ahead. Three types of training innovations are described here, though the list is not comprehensive.

First, one US university has developed a World Wide Web site for psychiatrists planning to take board certification examinations. The site provides sample questions and provides immediate notification of test results. A similar site for the Examination for Professional Practice in Psychology (EPPP) or other certification examinations would be helpful.

Second, a variety of simulations are available in which psychology students observe a situation on interactive videodisk and then are given options of how to best respond (see Engen, Finken, Luschei, & Kenney, 1994; Maple, 1994). Based on the option selected, they are then given more information and more choices. This type of learning environment is private enough to allow students to experiment with questionable options and observe the effects of their actions—something that would not be encouraged in real life practicum training. Many simulations are now available for training purposes, and many more are sure to come by the end of the 1990s. With the ease of newer object-oriented programming languages it is increasingly possible for psychology faculty to develop their own simulations without needing advanced programming expertise.

Third, expert system-based, computer-assisted training programs (ESCATs) utilize artificial intelligence technology to model the decision-making processes of experts in a particular subspecialty. Many aspects of professional training can be facilitated by ESCATs. For example, McMinn and Scanish (1996) developed The Rorschach Trainer, a feedback-rich tutorial program to help students master the scoring variables in Exner's Comprehensive System. There are varying levels of feedback that can be determined by the student or instructor. The Rorschach Trainer allows students to master much of the scoring system outside of the classroom, leaving more classroom time for teaching Rorschach interpretation. Todd (1996) describes the development and validation of an ESCAT to train clinicians to accurately diagnose eating disorders. As additional ESCATs are developed, specialized training may become much more interactive and practical than current lecture-oriented curriculum and continuing education programs. This could be especially important for psychologists practicing in remote areas where continuing education and in-person supervision are not readily obtained.

Appropriate and effective technological methods promise to enhance learning for students while simultaneously equipping them with technological skills to enter the changing mental health marketplace. With the rapid pace of technological advances, the biggest challenge for those developing training software will be to demonstrate the didactic effectiveness of the new training materials.

2.31.6 CONCLUSION

The tools of professional psychology are rapidly evolving in the midst of accelerating technological changes. Many new technologies can enhance the training and professional services offered by psychologists, especially for those who remain commited to the traditional tools, values, and standards of the profession.

2.31.7 REFERENCES

Alexander, J. E., & Davidoff, D. A. (1990). Psychological testing, computers and aging. *International Journal of Technology and Aging, 3,* 47–56.

Allard, G., Butler, J., Faust, D., & Shea, M. T. (1995). Errors in hand scoring objective personality tests: The case of the Personality Diagnostic Questionnaire-Revised (PDQ-R). *Professional Psychology: Research and Practice, 26,* 304–308.

American Psychological Association (1996). *Organizing your practice through automation: Managing information and data.* Washington, DC: Author.

Ball, C. J., Scott, N., McLaren, P. M., & Watson, J. P. (1993). Preliminary evaluation of a low-cost videoconferencing (LCVC) system for remote cognitive testing of adult psychiatric patients. *British Journal of Clinical Psychology, 32,* 303–307.

Ball, J. D., Archer, R. P., & Imhof, E. A. (1994). Time requirements of psychological testing: A survey of practitioners. *Journal of Personality Assessment, 63,* 239–249.

Bloom, B. L. (1992). Computer-assisted psychological intervention: A review and commentary. *Clinical Psychology Review, 12,* 169–197.

Bucholz, K. K., Robins, L. N., Shayka, J. J., Przybeck, T. R., Helzer, J. E., Goldring, E., Klein, M. H., Greist, J. H., Erdman, H. P., & Skare, S. S. (1991). Performance of two forms of a computer psychiatric screening interview: Version 1 of the DISSI. *Journal of Psychiatric Research, 25,* 117–129.

Clement, P. W. (1996). Evaluation in private practice. *Clinical Psychology: Science and Practice, 3,* 146–159.

Davis, C., & Cowles, M. (1989). Automated psychological testing: Method of administration, need for approval, and measures of anxiety. *Educational and Psychological Measurement, 49,* 311–320.

Engen, H. B., Finken, L. J., Luschei, N. S., & Kenney, D. (1994). Counseling simulations: An interactive videodisc approach. *Computers in Human Services, 11,* 283–298.

Erdman, H. P., Klein, M. H., Greist, J. H., Skare, S. S., Husted, J. J., Robins, J. N., Helzer, J. E., Goldring, E., Hamburger, M., & Miller, J. P. (1992). A comparison of two computer-administered versions of the NIMH diagnostic interview schedule. *Journal of Psychiatric Research, 26,* 85–95.

Farrell, A. D. (1991). Computers and behavioral assessment: Current applications, future possibilities, and obstacles to routine use. *Behavioral Assessment, 13,* 159–179.

Ferriter, M. (1993). Computer aided interviewing and the psychiatric social history. *Social Work & Social Sciences Review, 4,* 255–263.

First, M. B. (1994). Computer-assisted assessment of *DSM-III-R* diagnoses. *Psychiatric Annals, 24,* 25–29.

First, M. B., Opler, L. A., Hamilton, R. M., Linder, J., Linfield, L. S., Silver, J. M., Toshav, N. L., Kahn, D., Williams, J. B. W., & Spitzer, R. L. (1993). Evaluation in an inpatient setting of DTREE, a computer-assisted diagnostic assessment procedure. *Comprehensive Psychiatry, 34,* 171–175.

Gianutsos, R. (1992). The computer in cognitive rehabilitation: It's not just a tool anymore. *Journal of Head Trauma Rehabilitation, 7*(3), 26–35.

Giaquinto, S., & Fiori, M. (1992). THINKable, a computerized cognitive remediation: First results. *Acta Neurologica, 14,* 547–560.

Greatbatch, D., Heath, C., Campion, P., & Luff, P. (1995). How do desk-top computers affect the doctor–patient interaction? *Family Practice, 12,* 32–36.

Haas, L. J., Benedict, J. G., & Kobos, J. C. (1996). Psychotherapy by telephone: Risks and benefits for psychologists and consumers. *Professional Psychology: Research and Practice, 27,* 154–160.

Kenardy, J., & Adams, C. (1993). Computers in cognitive-behaviour therapy. *Australian Psychologist, 28,* 189–194.

Kight-Law, A., Mathisen, K. S., Calandra, F., Evans, F. J., & Salierno, C. A. (1989). Computerized collection of mental health information from emotionally disturbed adolescents. *Computers in Human Services, 5,* 171–181.

King, H. (1991). A telephone reassurance service: A natural support system for the elderly. *Journal of Gerontological Social Work, 16,* 159–177.

Kokish, R. (1994). Experiences using a PC in play therapy with children. *Computers in Human Services, 11,* 141–150.

Lewis, G. (1992). Computers in primary care. *International Review of Psychiatry, 4,* 307–310.

Maple, F. F. (1994). The development of goal-focused interactive videodiscs to enhance student learning in interpersonal practice methods classes. *Computers in Human Services, 11,* 333–346.

McMinn, M. R., & Scanish, J. D. (1996). *The Rorschach Trainer.* Lutz, FL: Psychological Assessment Resources.

Meier, S. T., & Wick, M. T. (1991). Computer-based unobtrusive measurement: Potential supplements to reactive self-reports. *Professional Psychology: Research and Practice, 22,* 410–412.

Myrick, R. D., & Sabella, R. A. (1995). Cyberspace: New place for counselor supervision. *Elementary School Guidance & Counseling, 30,* 35–44.

Pollock, N. L., & Maenpaa, M. (1990). How are psychologists using computers? *Canadian Psychology, 31,* 167–171.

Reich, W., Cottler, L., McCallum, K., Corwin, D., & VanEerdewegh, M. (1995). Computerized interviews as a method of assessing psychopathology in children. *Comprehensive Psychiatry, 36,* 40–45.

Ross, H. E., Swinson, R., Larkin, E. J., & Doumani, S. (1994). Diagnosing comorbidity in substance abusers: Computer assessment and clinical validation. *The Journal of Nervous and Mental Disease, 182,* 556–563.

Rothbaum, B. O., Hodges, L. F., Kooper, R., Opdyke, D., Williford, J. S., & North, M. (1995a). Virtual reality graded exposure in the treatment of acrophobia: A case report. *Behavior Therapy, 26,* 547–554.

Rothbaum, B. O., Hodges, L. F., Kooper, R., Opdyke, D., Williford, J. S., & North, M. (1995b). Effectiveness of computer-generated (virtual reality) graded exposure in the treatment of acrophobia. *American Journal of Psychiatry, 152,* 626–628.

Rounds, K. A., Galinsky, M. J., & Stevens, L. S. (1991). Linking people with AIDS in rural communities: The telephone group. *Social Work, 36,* 13–18.

Sawyer, M. G., Sarris, A., & Baghurst, P. (1991). The use of a computer-assisted interview to administer the Child Behavior Checklist in a Child Psychiatry Service. *Journal of the American Academy of Child and Adolescent Psychiatry, 30,* 674–681.

Smith, R. O. (1993). Computer-assisted functional assessment and documentation. *The American Journal of Occupational Therapy, 47,* 988–992.

Spinhoven, P., Labbe, M. R., & Rombouts, R. (1993). Feasibility of computerized psychological testing with psychiatric outpatients. *Journal of Clinical Psychology, 49,* 440–447.

Spiro, R. H., & Devenis, L. (1991). Telephone therapy: Enhancement of the psychotherapeutic process. *Psychotherapy in Private Practice, 9,* 31–55.

Stoloff, M. L., & Couch, J. V. (Eds.) (1992). *Computer use in psychology: A directory of software* (3rd ed.). Washington, DC: American Psychological Association.

Todd, L. K. (1996). A computer-assisted expert system for clinical diagnosis of eating disorders: A potential learning tool for practitioners. *Professional Psychology: Research and Practice, 27,* 184–187.

Tröster, A. I., Paolo, A. M., Glatt, S. L., Hubble, J. P., & Koller, W. C. (1995). "Interactive video conferencing" in the provision of neuropsychological services to rural areas. *Journal of Community Psychology, 23,* 85–88.

Whiston, S. C., & Sexton, T. L. (1993). An overview of psychotherapy outcome research: Implications for practice. *Professional Psychology: Research and Practice, 24,* 43–51.

2.32
The Evolution of Canada's Health-care System and its Implications for the Practice of Psychology as a Health Profession

PIERRE L.-J. RITCHIE and HENRY P. EDWARDS
University of Ottawa, ON, Canada

2.32.1 INTRODUCTION

This chapter discusses the evolution of psychology as an organized profession in Canada, the development and financing of Canada's health-care system, the relationship of health-care policy to the practice of psychology and, in the final section, future directions, with primary care reform as an illustration of trends that will help shape the future of psychology as a major health-care profession in Canada. Professional psychology is presented in historical perspective in relation to Canada's health care system.

There has long been a dichotomy between Canadian psychology as a profession and as an academic/scientific discipline. A cohesive national strategy for the profession has been lacking, due in part to the structure of Canadian society, as well as the nature and functions of national and provincial/territorial psychology associations.

By way of framework, Canada's version of constitutional federalism, which makes this country one of the most decentralized federations in the world, is reviewed in order to show how Canada's health-care system evolved within it. The Canada Health Act of 1984, the legislative cornerstone of Canada's publicly funded national health care system (Medicare), is assessed in this context. Brief comparative reference is made to other modern health-care systems.

Health policy is discussed next in relation to psychology as a health-care profession. For funding purposes, psychology has been associated traditionally with mental health services. Fee-for-service psychological services in private offices have not been funded by Medicare, although psychologists most often are paid from public funds for services provided in public facilities (e.g., hospitals). In general, Canadian health-care policy has not addressed psychological services explicitly. This has limited the public access, especially to primary care services provided by psychologists. Alternative methods of payment for psychological services are under consideration.

The concluding section addresses the future. For all the health professions, primary care reform is already a major issue throughout Canada. A strong emphasis on primary care is of considerable interest to Canadian psychologists, most of whose clinical services fall within definitions of primary care. In addition, the reduction of domestic and international trade barriers will likely prompt greater mobility and lead to greater emphasis on empirically supported approaches and competency-based credentialing.

2.32.2 THE ORGANIZATION OF PROFESSIONAL PSYCHOLOGY IN CANADA

A global review of psychology in Canada was recently provided by Adair, Paivio, and Ritchie 1996). It notes that the development of Canadian psychology as a profession has been distinct from its evolution as a discipline. This dichotomy, which has existed since at least the 1940s, as well as the tensions and debates surrounding it, have been captured in the reports of major discipline reviews (Appleby & Rickwood, 1968; Berlyne, Black, Berry, & Douglas, 1971; Bernhardt, 1961; Ferguson, 1977; Macleod, 1955; Ritchie, Hogan, & Hogan, 1988a; Webster, 1967). It was only in 1994 that the convocation of a national conference devoted exclusively to Canadian professional psychology (Dobson & King, 1995) heralded a new era in its maturation.

Lacking a cohesive national strategy in its organizations and in the realm of public policy, professional psychology has developed piecemeal even though Canadian scholarly contributions to both foundational and applied psychology have been strong and cohesive. Adair et al. (1996) cited the structure of Canadian society as offering a partial explanation. Canada is the world's largest jurisdictionally defined land mass, with a small population base, two official languages, multiple cultures, and a decentralized political system in which the provinces are constitutionally responsible for health services. These features make any national undertaking difficult indeed.

As noted by Adair et al. (1996), events internal to the discipline also contributed to the history and status of Canadian professional psychology. The Canadian Psychological Association (CPA), unlike its counterpart in the United States, largely distanced itself from provincially-based efforts to establish psychology as a human services profession. Only in the 1970s did CPA initiate a slow and difficult shift toward greater involvement in professional issues. Since then, substantial achievements have taken place (Dobson & Dobson, 1993), although tensions between professionals and traditional scientists remain (Craig, 1993; Ritchie & Sabourin, 1992). A promising trend acknowledges the presence of multiple psychologies in Canada, stresses the links of applied psychology to university-based empirical traditions, and advocates for the strengthening of common ground between the practice and science of psychology (e.g., Dobson, 1995; Wand, 1993). This perspective is well anchored in the value that Canadian society attaches to pluralism.

Contemporary professional psychology organizations in Canada are described by Craig (1993). Wright (1971) captured their early history. They may be divided into two types: regulatory organizations with a statutory mandate of public protection, and voluntary societal organizations whose primary mission is to advance the profession. All regulatory bodies are established by and accountable to provincial/territorial legislatures, in keeping with the Canadian constitution. Some have dual regulatory and societal functions. Nationally, there are membership-based societal organizations and consortia or federations of provincial/territorial and national bodies.

2.32.2.1 Provincial/Territorial Organizations

Professional psychology organizations have been established in the 10 provinces and in one of the two territories. In two provinces (New Brunswick, Quebec) and in the Northwest Territories, regulatory and societal functions are combined in the same body. In eight provinces (Alberta, British Columbia, Manitoba, Newfoundland, Nova Scotia, Ontario, Prince Edward Island, Saskatchewan), there are distinct regulatory and societal bodies.

2.32.2.1.1 Regulatory bodies

Approximately 13 000 psychologists and psychological associates are regulated in Canada for the practice of psychology. Statutory professional regulation is decentralized by province/territory. By statute, the regulatory bodies typically exercise five major functions: determination of eligibility criteria for registration (e.g., degree, curriculum, supervised experience, examinations); registration of persons who meet the eligibility criteria; maintenance of a register of regulated psychologists and, where applicable, psychological associates; investigation of complaints against registrants; and discipline for incompetence or misconduct. In addition, they may develop and promulgate guidelines and standards of professional conduct, carry out fitness to practice investigations, monitor individual practices by means of mandatory or voluntary peer reviews, and offer or sponsor continuing education activities. The earliest regulatory board was The Ontario Board of Examiners in Psychology, established in 1960 and renamed The College of Psychologists of Ontario. The most recent regulatory board is Prince Edward Island's, established in 1990.

The most important requirements for initial registration of psychologists are an acceptable graduate university degree, supervised experience, and successful completion of written and oral examinations. A degree in psychology is normally required, although some jurisdictions may accept a degree from a program whose content is primarily psychological, even if the degree title does not include the word "Psychology." Four provinces (British Columbia, Manitoba, Ontario, Saskatchewan) require the doctorate; four (New Brunswick, Newfoundland, Nova Scotia, Prince Edward Island) specify the doctorate but allow registration on the basis of a Masters degree subject to prescribed conditions or for a limited period of time; two (Alberta, Quebec) and one territory (Northwest Territories) require a Masters degree. Specific curriculum requirements are variable.

Supervised experience requirements also vary across jurisdictions. Doctoral entry jurisdictions typically require one or two years of supervised experience, one predoctoral and/or one postdoctoral. Among the Masters entry jurisdictions, Alberta requires 900 hours of supervised postdegree experience; New Brunswick four years; Newfoundland two years postdegree until the year 2001, when the doctoral entry standard becomes effective; the Northwest Territories one year; Nova Scotia six years; and Prince Edward Island two years postdegree. In these jurisdictions, the supervised experience requirements for applicants with doctorates are generally similar to those of doctorate-only jurisdictions. Quebec, however, the province with the largest number of Masters psychologists in Canada, does not specify a supervised postdegree experience requirement. The Examination for the Professional Practice of Psychology is a requirement in all jurisdictions except the Northwest Territories, Prince Edward Island, and Quebec. Oral examinations are also used in all jurisdictions except Newfoundland, the Northwest Territories, and Quebec. In addition to registering psychologists, three provinces (Manitoba, Ontario, Saskatchewan) also register Masters level "Psychological Associates." In Ontario, the psychological associates are autonomous practitioners, except that they may not communicate a diagnosis unless this has been formally and individually delegated. In Manitoba and Saskatchewan, they practice under supervision.

The above picture shows considerable diversity across Canada. Indeed, nowhere is the historic absence of a cohesive national strategy for the development of professional psychology more evident than in the variable education and training entry levels for the practice of psychology across provinces and territories. Despite its repeatedly expressed intent to resolve this problem, organized psychology has been unable to do so. Greater uniformity in entry level criteria for psychologist registration may be achieved, however, due largely to the Agreement on Internal Trade (AIT) and its implications for the regulated professions including psychology. This wide-ranging trade accord was concluded in 1994 by the federal, provincial, and territorial governments. It proposes to eliminate barriers to the free mobility of regulated professionals within Canada, and it outlines processes both for the mutual recognition of professional qualifications and for the development of uniform entry level criteria across the country.

2.32.2.1.2 Societal bodies

The provincial/territorial societal bodies have been vital in promoting the development and advancement of professional psychology in Canada (Adair et al., 1996). The British Columbia Psychological Association was the first to be established, in 1938. World War II precluded further developments, until the Ontario Psychological Association (OPA) was founded almost 10 years later in 1948 (Wright, 1971). Thereafter, voluntary membership-based associations were created throughout Canada, before the advent of regulatory bodies. These associations were most influential in the drive to secure statutory recognition for psychology.

As societal bodies, the associations engage in advocacy and lobbying, provide direct benefits to their members, organize meetings, and offer or organize continuing education and other competence enhancing activities. By mandate, they protect the profession and help to secure its future. Their membership ranges from approximately 40 in the Prince Edward Island Psychological Association to more than 1200 in OPA.

2.32.2.2 National Organizations

2.32.2.2.1 Canadian Psychological Association

CPA was created by 38 founding members in 1939. With 3000 members and 1000 student and other affiliates, it is the oldest national association. Adair et al. (1996) describe six functions provided by CPA: dissemination of original research and informed commentary by means of its three journals, quarterly newsletters, and annual meeting; accreditation of doctoral programs and internships in clinical psychology, counseling psychology, and neuropsychology; sponsorship of member benefits; development and promulgation of a code of ethics as well as several guidelines and standards of practice; advocacy of selected issues pertinent to practitioners and scientists, often in collaboration with other organizations; and attention to the subdisciplines of scientific/academic and applied psychology through formally organized sections and interest groups.

2.32.2.2.2 Council of Provincial Associations of Psychologists

The Council of Provincial Associations of Psychologists (CPAP) consists of both regulatory and societal bodies (Craig; 1993; Wand, 1990). CPAP is a federation that evolved from an advisory committee created within the CPA in 1968 (Berry, Davidson, & Gibson, 1974). It became an autonomous entity in 1983, with the CPA as an affiliate member, and was legally incorporated in 1995. Its primary purpose is to share information and resources among provincial/territorial bodies, and to facilitate national undertakings in the common interest of its member bodies. It fosters understanding, serves as a forum for debate on issues which are ultimately decided elsewhere, and ensures that provincial/territorial matters are duly considered by national organizations.

2.32.2.2.3 Canadian Register of Health Service Providers in Psychology

The establishment of the Canadian Register of Health Service Providers in Psychology (CRHSPP) in 1985 was prompted by two factors, client/patient access and the need for a national credential. In the previous decade, psychologists providing health services were increasingly frustrated in their efforts to secure enhanced access. Funding, particularly of services provided in independent practice settings, was at the source of the accessibility problem. Policymakers in both the public and private sectors increasingly stressed that they would only pursue the possibility of expanded funding once the profession had implemented a credible means of identifying and credentialing those psychologists who had the appropriate training and experience to offer health services. The legal right to practice, while a prerequisite, was an insufficient mechanism since psychologist registration across Canada is typically generic. The fact that the practice of psychology is regulated at the provincial/territorial level highlighted both the need for a national credentialing body for health service providers in psychology and the challenge of developing uniform criteria given varying regulatory standards. The historical development of CRHSPP is reviewed by Wand (1990) and Craig (1993), and the extent to which its purpose and structure were influenced by the National Register of Health Service Providers in

Psychology in the United States is described by Ritchie (1995a). Less than a decade after its establishment, Craig (1993) noted that CRHSPP is being increasingly recognized by governments, insurance companies, and quality assurance agencies.

Unlike its American counterpart, the Canadian Register's governance is determined by its corporate members, the provincial/territorial bodies of psychology, and CPA, each of which is entitled to nominate one person to its Board of Directors. CRHSPP lists more than 3000 psychologists and publishes an annual directory. Eligibility criteria for listing are based on training, experience, and statutory registration or licensure as psychologist in a province, territory, or non-Canadian jurisdiction.

CRHSPP also plays an important role in promoting the public's access to qualified health service psychologists, and it collaborates with its corporate members, other health professions in Canada, and international bodies in furthering the development of the profession. Research on issues related to the delivery of health services and continuing education complement its broader objectives. In this manner, its strategic priorities contribute to Canadian professional psychology as a major health profession (Hurley & Ritchie, 1995).

2.32.3 HISTORY AND CURRENT STATUS OF CANADA'S HEALTH-CARE SYSTEM

Canadian federalism has produced a publicly funded health-care system that is primarily under provincial/territorial control. Nonetheless, the federal government's funding role has enabled it to shape the main features of a national, publicly funded health-care system. This section traces its history, legislation, and the impact of federal funding cuts. It concludes by noting that the mix of private and public financing of the Canadian system often is not well understood.

2.32.3.1 The Broader Context

Canada's health-care system has been the object of much domestic and external scrutiny since the mid-1980s. In the early 1990s, the prospect of health-care reform in the USA generated substantial interest in the Canadian system (e.g., Adams, 1994; Haislmaier, 1992), including mental health issues (e.g., Freeman, 1994; Torrey, Bigelow, & Sladen-Dew, 1993) and factors pertinent to psychological practice (e.g., Wedding, Ritchie, Kitchen, & Baner, 1993). Some assessments have been more critical (e.g., Danzon, 1992; Enthoven, 1990), while others have been more positive (e.g., Barer & Evans, 1992). Similar to other industrialized nations which had developed a substantial publicly funded health-care system, Canada experienced strong internal pressures to embark on its own reforms. In the short-term, this was driven largely by immediate fiscal objectives, especially that of reducing the level of public debt. Longer term perspectives, however, included concern about the sustainability of a publicly funded universal health-care system, particularly in the context of an increasingly aged population.

From an international vantage point, the creation of the UK National Health Service in 1948 is often regarded as a major benchmark in publicly funded health care. Actually, the forerunner of the modern era dates back to 1883, when the Social Sickness Fund was established in Germany. Before the close of the nineteenth century, variations were implemented in Belgium (1894) and France (1898). Luxembourg followed in 1901. Greece, Ireland, Italy, the Netherlands, Portugal, and the UK all had a form of mandatory health insurance prior to World War II. The UK National Health Service, however, introduced universality, central financing, and public administration as features which would be adopted two decades later in Canada.

2.32.3.2 Evolution of Canada's Health-care System

To appreciate the status of the Canadian health-care system as well as to understand psychology's place within it requires some knowledge of how Canada's health-care system evolved. Canada is characterized by a largely confederal system in which substantial powers are held by the constituent provinces. Although executive federalism, exercised by the federal government, has increased greatly since World War II, Canada remains one of the most decentralized federations in the world. Canada's constitutional regime has been the object of continuing intense debate within Canada.

To understand the politics and policies which influence the nature of Canada's health-care system, it is essential to know that the administration of health care is a provincial responsibility under the Canadian constitution. The federal government, however, is unfettered in its authority (known as the federal spending power) to disburse money. Hence, the Canadian federal government can make funds available to the provinces for health care (or other areas within provincial responsibility such as welfare and various social assistance programs). In doing so, it can also set conditions for the use of these funds, notwithstanding that it has no authority to administer or deliver the actual services. The only exception to this constraint applies to persons in the direct employ of the federal government (e.g., members of the armed forces) or whom the constitution has placed under exclusive federal responsibility (e.g., aboriginal Canadians living on federal reservations).

In practice, nationwide programs and national standards have developed in Canada only when the federal government has made it attractive financially for the provinces to agree implicitly to relinquish some of their autonomy. Nonetheless, the provinces always retain regulatory control for areas within their constitutional jurisdiction. Hence they can, and sometimes do, prevent institutions (e.g., hospitals) under their authority from receiving federal funds. To avoid such stalemates, Canada has evolved a form of cooperative federalism whereby the federal and provincial governments typically establish formal agreements concerning the use of federal funds in areas of provincial jurisdiction. An important feature of such agreements is that the funds are typically transferred directly to the provincial governments. These funds may be conditional (i.e., subject to meeting established criteria) or unconditional. The federal government's financial participation in health care has led to the transfer of federal funds to the provinces/territories subject to more specific conditions than in any other area of federal/provincial transfer (e.g., education).

Deber (1992) summarized the early history of the federal government's involvement in health and the initial federal-provincial arrangements which preceded the current system. The federal parliament first investigated and reported on sickness insurance in 1928. In 1935, it made its first legislative attempt to mandate the collection of information on health insurance plans, as part of a broader employment and social insurance act which subsequently was found to be unconstitutional. A health insurance bill was drafted during World War II, and the federal government offered to contribute federal funds toward a comprehensive health insurance plan as part of its Reconstruction proposal to the provinces. A conference was convened to address the Reconstruction proposal, but it could not agree on the fiscal elements of the social security proposals of which health was a part.

The federal government resorted to its spending power in 1948 to fund general health grants. However, some provinces also chose to proceed on their own, especially in establishing hospital insurance plans. Health insurance returned actively to the agenda of the annual Conference of First Ministers (which brings together the federal Prime Minister and their provincial counterparts) in 1955. This culminated in the first major federal health legislation in the modern era, the Hospital Insurance and Diagnostic Services Act (HIDS), which was implemented in 1958. Consistent with the constitution, administration of services remained under the direct or regulatory control of the provinces but receipt of federal funds was made contingent on meeting specified conditions. Eligible services had to meet tests of comprehensiveness (linked to the notion of "medically necessary"), portability, public administration, and universality. Imprecise definitions (especially of "medically necessary," a problem for the interpretation and implementation of all subsequent federal-provincial health funding arrangements), were a feature of the HIDS. Nonetheless, it marked a turning point in moving toward a national health-care system.

2.32.3.3 Cooperative Federalism in Action

The zenith of cooperative federalism regarding a national health-care system (and arguably regarding any federal-provincial matter) was reached in 1965–66 with the passage of the National Medical Care Insurance Act (MCA) which commonly came to be known as "Medicare." It received the support of all provinces and was implemented in 1968. It retained the four criteria of the HIDS but substantially expanded the range of services covered to include virtually all services provided by physicians regardless of setting (inpatient or office based). Problems of interpretation and implementation remained.

Although provinces varied in the flexibility or rigidity of the options offered to physicians for participation in the Medicare system, the outcomes were similar across the country. Overwhelmingly, physicians joined the system. Soon, 98% of all physician services were reimbursed through the various provincial plans set up under the provisions envisioned by the federal legislation, a level which has remained steady since the 1960s, growing to 99% by 1994 (National Forum on Health, 1997). Hospital services also remained largely covered by the public system, varying between 90 and 94% of all costs from the 1970s (Federal, Provincial, and Territorial Advisory Committee on Population Health, 1996).

Other professional services were funded differently. In this respect, psychologists are situated similarly to most health providers other than physicians. Inpatient and outpatient services provided within or through public facilities are covered, although the facilities and the provincial/territorial governments that fund them have full discretion on which nonphysician services they will cover. Furthermore, unlike physicians, other health professionals including psychologists have not been reimbursed through the public purse for community services delivered in their private offices. These have been funded through a range of private mechanisms including extended health plans underwritten by insurance companies.

The last major piece of federal legislation in this area, the Canada Health Act (CHA), was passed in 1984. It was essentially similar to the MCA which it replaced. Its major purpose was to strengthen the enforcement provisions available to the federal government with respect to the five principles set out in the legislation. The four basic historic criteria were retained as well as the more precise definition of accessibility. The CHA is the current legislative cornerstone of the national health-care system.

In the two decades between the MCA and the CHA, important changes occurred in the nature of the federal government's financial participation in health care. It shifted from an open-ended 50–50 shared-cost formula linked to provincial spending to a complex system of cash and tax transfers called Established Programs Financing Arrangements (EPF) introduced in 1977. In principle, two-thirds of this federal-provincial transfer were flagged for health and one-third for postsecondary education.

In the mid-1980s, the federal government introduced increasingly stringent measures to address an escalating level of public debt. These arbitrary measures included a dramatic reduction in the transfers to the provinces under the provisions of the EPF. In concert with the federal government's earlier decision to constrain provincial discretion in the allocation of federal funds earmarked for health when it adopted the CHA, the progressive decrease in the transfer of federal funds has also yielded recurrent discord in federal-provincial relations. The impact is partly reflected in the decrease in gross domestic product (GDP) attributable to health expenditures. After rising from 7.4% in 1971 to more than 10% in the early 1990s, the proportion spent on health declined to 9.5% in 1995 and is projected to decrease a bit further. This proportion is comparable to that spent in several other Organization for Economic Co-operation and Development (OECD) countries (e.g., Austria, France, Germany), but significantly less than that spent in the USA, where it has risen from 7.6% to more than 14% of GDP in the same 25 years. Given that the provinces are the direct payers of facilities and professionals (largely physicians) reimbursed by the public system, it is noteworthy that health accounted for 28.7% of total provincial/territorial government expenditures in 1976 compared to 31.2% in 1996 (Federal, Provincial, and Territorial Advisory Committee on Population Health, 1996; National Forum on Health, 1997; Thomson, 1996).

In 1995, the federal government introduced a new program, the Canada Health and Social Transfer (CHST), which integrated several previously distinct federal-provincial transfer programs into a single system. The decline in federal cash contributions has continued. However, as a function of growing political pressure and the success of its general deficit reduction policies, the federal government has committed itself to maintaining a specified minimum level of support through the CHST for a five-year period. There is little doubt that confidence in the national health-care system has been shaken, but the public's support for the principles on which it was built remains high. Indeed, the political importance of Canada's health-care system was illustrated by the 1997 federal election. Health care was a priority for all five major political parties, reflecting the salience of this issue for Canadian voters. The incumbent government was re-elected in part on its expressed willingness to make a greater commitment to stable health-care funding, including a guaranteed higher minimum level of cash transfers to the provinces/territories.

2.32.3.4 A Public–Private Mixed Model of Health-care Financing

Outside the country, the public–private blend of Canada's health-care financing is often poorly understood. Notwithstanding the generally broad nature of the public component, the Canadian health-care system functions as a mixed economy. Even the publicly funded system operates with a certain duality, since most physicians are reimbursed on a fee-for-service basis for activities provided in their private offices. This led Stoddart (1987) to observe that the Canadian system is characterized by public financing with private management.

Given the decline in public funding described above, it is not surprising to find a trend toward a greater private share of the total health care dollar. The 76%:24% public–private ratio of 1975 shifted to 72%:28% by 1994. With physician services and hospital care largely covered by the public sector (99 and 90%, respectively), private funding is concentrated on prescription drugs and the noninstitutional care provided by most other regulated health professionals (68 and 86%, respectively). To put these numbers into perspective, total health expenditures in Canada were $72 billion in 1994, or $2010 per capita, third highest among OECD countries (National Forum on Health, 1997; OECD, 1996).

The Report on the Health of Canadians (Federal, Provincial, and Territorial Advisory Committee on Population Health, 1996) concluded that Canada generally benefits from a standard of health which is among the best in the world on most indicators (e.g., life expectancy, infant mortality). From the perspective of psychological factors, it is interesting to note that indicators such as quality of life, well-being, impact of health problems on everyday life, as well as measures of mental, social, and emotional health, have been added to traditional indicators of Canadians' health status. This shift underscores the importance increasingly accorded in Canada to psychological and social variables, not only in measuring health, but in setting health policy.

2.32.4 HEALTH-CARE POLICY AND FINANCING IN RELATION TO PSYCHOLOGY

Traditionally, the services of private practice psychologists have not been covered by Medicare, and Canadian health-care policy has been rarely explicit in addressing psychological services. However, the regular salaries of most providers of psychological services are paid from public funds. Alternative public and private methods for the payment of psychologists have been actively considered and promoted by organized psychology since the 1970s.

2.32.4.1 Psychology and Health-care Policy

Canadian health-care policy evolved primarily according to a medical model of health care. Within this model, from the origin of universal-access Medicare, the provision of psychological services was associated with mental health (psychiatric) services. Traditionally, this meant that the services of private practice psychologists were not covered by Medicare. Thus, the vast majority of psychological services providers in Canada have worked as publicly funded full-time salaried employees of provincial/territorial or federal agencies such as general hospitals, psychiatric hospitals, school boards, the military, correctional facilities, and mental health clinics. Private practitioners, working primarily in the large urban centers, have been paid directly by their clients/patients on a fee-for-service basis (Ritchie, Wilson et al., 1988).

Varied psychological services are offered in Canada (Martin, Ritchie, & Sabourin, 1988). Consistent with psychology's emergence as a major health profession, health services represent the largest concentration, in such areas as health psychology (Hearn & Evans, 1993), clinical psychology (Hunsley & Lefebvre, 1990), counseling psychology (Hiebert & Uhlemann, 1993), and neuropsychology (Fuerst & Rourke, 1995). These services are offered in a wide range of settings and characterized by considerable diversity. Focusing only on general hospitals, Hearn and Evans (1993) identified 65 areas of service provided by psychologists. The traditional distinctions among clinical, counseling, and health psychology are being increasingly incorporated into the broader designation of health service psychology (Adair et al., 1996). Cognitive-behavioral and behavioral approaches are the most prevalent among a comprehensive range of theoretical orientations (Hunsley & Lefebvre, 1990; Warner, 1991).

During the 1960s, limited third-party coverage for psychological services appeared in private health insurance plans, usually as an extended benefit. Starting in the 1970s, clinical psychology broadened its scope as a health service profession, a process which has continued to the 1990s, and, although psychological services often remain associated with mental health, psychologists are broadly defined healthcare providers in the Canadian health-care system. With this change in identity, psychologists desire increasingly to be funded in the same manner as other health professionals.

2.32.4.2 Psychology and Health-care Financing

A basic question about the public financing of psychological services is: Why were psychologists not included in Medicare on a basis comparable to physicians? Inclusion of psychologists in Medicare was considered during the 1965–68 development period, but the profession itself declined to pursue such inclusion. Few psychologists shared the view prevailing among physicians that government intervention, if at all, would be limited to the disabled and those on welfare. Professional psychology's provincially based leaders focused on the fact that there were relatively few professional psychologists in Canada at the time, and were concerned about the likelihood that initial inclusion might be limited to diagnostic services.

This failure to respond affirmatively to the opportunity for inclusion in Canada's first national healthcare system has bewildered and dismayed subsequent generations of psychologists. In retrospect, the decision is perhaps best understood in terms of three factors characterizing Canadian clinical psychology in the mid-1960s. First of these was the prevailing emphasis in Canadian clinical psychology on institutionally based public service as opposed to the private practice solo-office model espoused by most physicians. Second, and equally important, was the desire to see clinical psychologists legitimized as comprehensive practitioners. In the previous 20 years, psychologists had faced and increasingly overcome obstacles to move out of the "tester" role in order to assume broader clinical responsibilities, especially as psychotherapists. There was a fear that limiting Medicare inclusion to the diagnostic services provided by psychologists might make it more difficult to consolidate their role as treatment providers. Finally, at the national level, the issue was essentially irrelevant to CPA, given its decision two decades earlier not to support the emergence of psychology as a profession. If anything, Medicare inclusion was inimical to CPA's commitment to maintain psychology exclusively as a scientific discipline without professional aspirations. Hence, there was no national effort either to seek inclusion in Medicare as a goal in itself or within a framework that would secure coverage for both diagnostic and treatment services. Such a strategy would emerge only more than a decade later, by which time provincial governments were wary of adding new providers.

As a result, among the peculiarities of the Canadian system is the reimbursement of "psychotherapy" provided by general practice physicians (many of whom have virtually no training in this field) in their private offices, while similarly situated but well-trained private practice psychologists are ineligible for Medicare reimbursement. This is an excellent illustration of the implication of funding providers and facilities rather than services, something which is increasingly regarded as a flaw in Canada's publicly funded health-care system.

Canadian health-care policy has not been explicit in addressing psychological services, except under the rubrics of mental health and some specialized health services. The absence of broad inclusion in provincial/territorial government funding mechanisms has significantly limited the public's access to primary care services provided by psychologists. Since the late 1980s, downsizing in hospitals and other publicly funded institutions has resulted in a substantial reduction in the number of salaried psychologist positions, further limiting the public's access to psychologists, even for tertiary care. However, the public funding of all health-care services, including those provided by psychologists, is in transition. As discussed below, this situation presents opportunities as well as risks to health service psychology.

Given this context, it is important to articulate the key sources and methods of payment on which Canadian psychologists are most likely to rely in future years (Ritchie, Wilson et al., 1988). The sources of payment are either suppliers or users of psychological services. Suppliers are either private or public agencies, ranging from private clinics to government administered universal health-care plans. The users may be individuals, groups, agencies, corporations, or governments.

Several methods of payment commonly used by professionals are available to psychologists. Ritchie, Wilson, et al. (1988) identified 13 types of payment and 12 generic sources of payment actually or potentially available to Canadian psychologists. The vast majority of psychologists in Canada work in regular salaried positions. In large organizations, their salaries are typically within negotiated scales and include a fringe-benefits package. A significant proportion of salaried psychologists earn additional income from part-time private practice. Since the mid-1980s there have been increasing numbers of psychologists engaging in full-time private practice. Greater reliance on alternative methods of payment is required due to the negative influence of reduced federal transfer payments on the numbers and stability of salaried positions. In addition to government sponsored services, the actual or potential sources of funding are the users themselves, organized groups (e.g., employees, cooperatives), agencies (e.g, schools, clinics, hospitals), and businesses or corporations. Payment modalities include traditional fee-for-service, sessional rates, contracts, *per diem* consultations, retainers, and capitation.

2.32.5 HEALTH-CARE REFORM AND ITS IMPLICATIONS FOR PSYCHOLOGY

2.32.5.1 Elements of a Renewed, Publicly Funded Health-care System

The rapid pace of health-care reform will continue into the twenty-first century. The policy elements which will shape Canada's health-care system from 1997 to 2020 are increasingly clear. They are well captured in the final report of the National Forum on Health (1997), commissioned and chaired by the federal Prime Minister. Future health policy will be driven by a greater emphasis on a systems orientation and by fiscal sustainability. As a result, there will be more focus on defining the services to be funded rather than on simply funding providers. Given the traditional strong emphasis on funding physicians, this change potentially allows for the emergence of a larger number of health service providers, especially in primary care. Organized psychology in Canada is working vigorously to ensure the inclusion of psychologists in a reformed primary care system, discussed further below.

Although health services may become more broadly inclusive, funding will not be open-ended and is likely to be increasingly population-based. Variations on capitation as a basic funding mechanism are under renewed consideration for both public and private sector funding. In the public sector, Canada will almost certainly remain a "single payer" system. Evidence-based decision making is regarded as a key element in making the future health-care system appropriate to meeting health needs and in controlling costs.

The transformation of knowledge into action is essential to the functioning of such a system. Health service psychologists have an uncommon advantage relative to other health professionals. They have not only the capacity to be sophisticated consumers of advanced knowledge, they are also specifically trained to generate scientifically sound data. An implication for graduate education is that applied research skills will be especially important to the future marketability of health service psychologists.

The federal and most provincial/territorial governments have achieved their essential deficit reduction targets after introducing sufficient measures to reduce the public debt in the mid-1980s. Although there is no prospect of a return to large-scale public spending, developments indicate a restabilization of public sector health-care funding. The shift toward greater privatization of health care is unlikely to exceed a 70%:30% public–private ratio in the foreseeable future. Organized psychology will sustain its efforts for enhanced coverage of psychological services in both sectors. In the public sector, efforts will likely concentrate on primary care reform. In addition, focused opportunities such as that afforded by publicly administered "no-fault" auto insurance, with access to psychological services as a benefit, will continue to be pursued in the provinces with such insurance schemes.

2.32.5.2 Private Sector Initiatives

Organized psychology's private sector initiatives are concentrating on the traditional extended health and disability plans of the insurance industry, focusing on cost offsets associated with timely use of psychological care. American-style "managed care" has not been a prominent aspect of private sector thirdparty coverage in Canada, but elements of it have begun to emerge. Cognizant of the experience of American colleagues, there is considerable interest in enhancing the role which consumers and providers can play in determining the characteristics of such plans. OPA, with the active support of CRHSPP, is working on a provider-driven plan that would potentially encompass all nonphysician health professionals authorized by statute to practice autonomously. CPAP has expressed strong interest in the possibility of such a proposal being developed as a national plan.

2.32.5.3 Globalization

The reduction of domestic and international trade barriers brought about by the AIT and the North American Free Trade Agreement (NAFTA), respectively, is emerging as a previously unanticipated influence on the evolution of health care. Considerable concern was expressed when Canada and the United States established the Free Trade Agreement in the late 1980s, an agreement that was superseded by the NAFTA, of which Mexico is also a partner. In the short term, there has been no discernible impact on health-care delivery in any of the three countries. In part, this was due to the strong intervention of the health professions in Canada, and to a more limited degree in the United States, which resulted in each NAFTA country remaining unfettered to maintain its established mechanisms for regulating health-care and health professionals. However, both NAFTA and the AIT are likely to have an impact on the future mobility of health professionals. Mobility has emerged as a central topic for organized psychology in Canada, the United States, and Mexico.

The impact of a world economy characterized by the greater globalization of national and regional economies cannot be predicted with any certainty for psychology and other healthcare professions. Among the implications for health service psychology in Canada, none will present greater challenges than the impetus toward competency-based credentialing. In Canada, medicine and nursing have already devoted substantial resources to this issue, and several other health professions (e.g., physiotherapy) are already working actively in this area. In psychology, CPA, CPAP, and CRHSPP concluded an agreement in principle to mount a multiyear, collaborative effort to address this issue. Given the diversity of regulatory standards in psychology, the task will be difficult. On the other hand, external factors, especially government policies which could ultimately impose solutions insensitive to the interests of the public or the profession, provide the incentive for the profession to achieve appropriate solutions.

2.32.5.4 Determinants of Health

Canada has been a leader in generating public policy that attends to the broader determinants of health. Since the 1970s, two federal Ministers of Health made wellness and well-being, with a population-based focus, cornerstones of major federal government initiatives (Epp, 1986; Lalonde, 1974). The importance of attending to the broader determinants of health was reiterated by the Prime Minister's National Forum on Health (1997). Specific changes in health-care delivery and social policy have yet to match the policy rhetoric, but are likely to be incorporated in the reforms into the twenty-first century. For example, according to the Report on the Health of Canadians (1996), women did not score as well as men on measures of psychological well-being and depressions, and younger women appeared to be particularly vulnerable. The report also noted that much remains to be learned about the interpretation and application of such information. This is an opportunity virtually tailor-made for psychologists, whose knowledge and skills are well suited for the planning, implementation, and evaluation of action-oriented programs with targeted health outcomes.

2.32.5.5 Scope of Health Care

From a systems perspective, the largest and most overriding issue is the determination of what is or should be encompassed by health care. In Canada, this will be determined largely by decisions made in the public sector. Canadians expect that all essential elements of health care should be accessible within the publicly-funded system. Historically, this has been driven by a focus on physicians and hospitals as the fundamental elements of health-care delivery. Now, health-care reform is creating a shift toward greater overall emphasis on the need, appropriateness, and efficacy of health services. This is not occurring without considerable disruption and resistance.

Virtually no one believes that a return to the *status quo ante* is either achievable or desirable. In the future, a larger number of services will be provided in community settings that do not require the capital intensive investment of hospitals and large-scale facilities. However, consumers also want ready access to the range of services typically found in larger facilities. Health-policy planners want to control costs and prompt a shift toward greater emphasis on the maintenance of wellness relative to the treatment of disease and injury. Canadians remain strongly committed to the five core principles on which Medicare is based (accessibility, comprehensiveness, portability, public administration, universality) but are increasingly open-minded about the possibility of changing health service delivery mechanisms in view of economic and other realities, provided that the core principles are respected.

2.32.6 THE FUTURE OF PSYCHOLOGY AS A HEALTH-CARE PROFESSION IN CANADA

Two foci provide the context for assessing the future of psychology as a health service profession in Canada. The recommendations of the 1994 Mississauga Conference on Professional Psychology provide a broad vision. Primary care, as an area of specific application, links psychology to the broader structural and funding reforms which are prompting significant changes in Canada's health-care delivery system.

2.32.6.1 A Global Road Map: The Mississauga Conference

An important global portrait of professional psychology's preoccupations and the means by which it seeks to secure its future is found in the report of the 1994 National Conference on Professional Psychology (Dobson & King, 1995), known as the Mississauga Conference. The conference was initiated and organized by CPA in collaboration with CRHSPP, the National Health Research Development Program (an agency of the federal government), OPA, the Quebec College of Psychologists, and CPA's own sections on Clinical Neuropsychology, Clinical Psychology, and Counseling Psychology.

The conference developed some 50 guiding principles and an equivalent number of specific action plans for training, funding, and advocacy. The conference report stressed that psychologists must respond constructively to the needs and expectations of the Canadian public, especially at a time of fiscal restraint. It urged that the profession's capacity for creativity and flexibility, while remaining faithful to its scientific rigor and service-oriented values, be mediated by its ability to develop greater cohesion as an organized profession. Although encompassing professional psychology as a whole, the outcomes of the Mississauga Conference are especially germane to the future of health service psychology.

The training of future professional psychologists generated stimulating debate. Preparing them for the expectations of the marketplace was established as a legitimate training goal. In this context, Evans (1995) predicted that graduate education in professional psychology would become more focused on entrepreneurial skills and more market-oriented. The conference participants reaffirmed the doctoral degree for entry to practice as a psychologist, but agreed that training models could vary in their relative emphasis on practice and research. Furthermore, the diversity of applied psychology in Canada prompted a call for organized opportunities to support the development of proficiencies associated with specialties, as a complement to education and training for general practice.

The Mississauga Conference legitimized psychology's status as a business, complementary to its standing as a profession (Hearn, 1995). The conference also emphasized that advocacy is anchored in the public interest and must be responsive to public input (Ritchie, 1995b). This is consistent with the view that professional psychology serves a broader purpose than the narrow perpetuation of guild-driven goals. Viewed as a global road map, the approved action plans of the Mississauga Conference will help to shape professional psychology in Canada in the early decades of the twenty-first century.

2.32.6.2 Primary Care: An Illustration of Psychology's Future as a Health Service Profession

Primary health-care reform, being advocated in Canada and elsewhere, will likely have major implications for the practice of broadly defined health service psychology. Driven by broader public policy issues, primary care reform affords psychology a renewed opportunity to offer its unique competencies to the Canadian public.

2.32.6.2.1 Primary health-care reform as a public policy issue

Primary health-care reform is increasingly advocated in Western industrialized countries. Historically, Canada's primary care system, driven by physicians reimbursed on a fee-for-service basis, has encouraged an episodic, medically oriented approach. In Canada, a reformed primary health-care model is recommended, among other reasons, as the continuing entry point into the health-care system and because it can comprise comprehensive, continuing care (Manga & Campbell, 1994). A strong emphasis on such a model of primary care is of interest to psychologists because a comprehensive primary care system has the potential for more efficient primary consultation time (Hart, 1992), continuing rather than episodic care (Manga, 1993), and multidisciplinary teamwork (Fulop & Roemer, 1982).

The reform of primary health care is already a major public policy issue across Canada. The 1995 Conference of Ministers of Health received a report, commissioned from their senior officials who administer the respective provincial/territorial health-care systems, which called for a radical reorganization of primary care and for the introduction of population-based funding (capitation). Psychology was explicitly among the health professionals envisioned for inclusion in the proposed "Primary Care Organizations" (PCOs).

Provincially, Quebec has embarked on an ambitious effort to develop "Local Community Service Centres," blending some elements of primary health care with some social services. However, psychologists have been significantly under-represented in such settings. The inclusion of psychologists in a reformed primary care system has received the most systematic attention in the province of Ontario, where the Minister of Health has set primary care reform as a priority. The health professions, among them psychology, have been asked to contribute to the reform process by describing their role in primary care, their linkages to other professions, and their sources of funding. Several professions, again including psychology, were further invited to collaborate on the development of an interdisciplinary model for the provision of primary care services. Psychology participated under the auspices of OPA, with national support from the CRHSPP. Psychology's proposal established a clear vision and mandate for psychologists in a reformed primary care delivery system (OPA, 1997). The following considerations are based on this proposal.

2.32.6.2.2 Principles for professional psychologists providing primary care

Psychology committed to the establishment of the most appropriate roles for psychological services providers based on the principles of patient choice, rational utilization, and evidence-based decision making. Observance of these principles requires all professionals providing primary care as partners to have access to each other.

Because psychology has a broad scope of practice including the authorized act of diagnosis, its services span primary and tertiary care. Nonetheless, most clinical services provided by psychologists fall within contemporary definitions of primary care. However, some of the services properly construed as primary care have been historically provided in hospitals and other tertiary care settings, and may continue to be so provided in some communities although likely on a reduced scale. Psychologists will also continue to deliver services which are clearly part of tertiary care, such as sophisticated neuropsychological diagnosis of closed head injury patients, in tertiary care settings.

2.32.6.2.3 Competencies brought by psychologists to primary care

The particular competencies that health service psychologists bring to primary care include diagnosis, consultation, treatment, design and implementation of prevention and health promotion programs, as well as applied research.

Psychologists have particular expertise as diagnosticians. In community-based health-care settings, there is a high prevalence of patients with psychological problems or disorders associated with their physical complaints. Contrary to historic practice patterns, cost-effective patient care indicates that, in such cases, psychological diagnosis should be undertaken before other, considerably more expensive, diagnostic procedures. This will be feasible only when psychologists are as readily accessible to patients as physicians and nurses, and when psychologists' community-based services are publicly funded. It is expected that psychologists would both see patients for diagnostic consultation and provide partner health professionals with consultation around relevant diagnostic questions. Where the diagnostic question is primarily psychological, psychologists would be the most effective coordinators of the diagnostic process. This would be particularly important when the level of diagnostic complexity is moderate to high.

Treatment is a second major area of direct and indirect service. In future, the emphasis will likely be on short-term, empirically-supported approaches. Group therapy will be a preferred treatment modality, coupled with timely utilization of individual, couple, or family psychotherapies. Psychologists may provide treatment directly, supervise the treatment provided by other professionals, or provide consultation to other providers concerning the planning and implementation of appropriate treatments.

Psychologists will play a leading role in the design, adaptation and refinement of large-scale community based prevention and health promotion programs. Furthermore, since health-care settings will be expected to conduct in-house applied research, the fact that psychologists are educated as applied scientists will enable them to make a substantial contribution in this area, particularly in the areas of needs assessment, outcome evaluation, program evaluation, and clinical research.

Finally, the linkages of psychologists to other health professionals are expected to be strengthened in primary care agencies. In such settings, psychologists would probably have three types of linkages with other professions. Linkages would begin with day-to-day operations. All health-care providers would work in proximity to each other, and be accessible to their fellow providers and to each other's patients. An emphasis on patient need, rather than established patterns of service delivery, would benefit the patient, promote interdisciplinary collaboration, and enhance cost-effectiveness. The key would be access to the right provider for the most appropriate service at the right time.

Coordination and communication among various health practitioners, and across community agencies and services, are essential to the care of patients presenting with multiple physical and social needs. Primary care agencies would be well placed to play a central coordinating role, with participation from psychologists and other health professionals.

Psychology-specific linkages would likely derive from the health needs and referral patterns that are central to the work of psychologists. For example, psychologists would facilitate access to psychological services in tertiary facilities, and would make direct referrals to the specialized health services of psychiatrists, neurologists, pediatricians, and others.

2.32.6.2.4 Funding for psychologists providing primary care

The absence of province-wide public funding mechanisms across Canada has been the greatest impediment to the appropriate utilization of primary care services provided by psychologists. Traditionally, psychologists have provided some primary care diagnostic and treatment services in the outpatient departments of general hospitals, but downsizing has eliminated many positions and rendered psychological services less accessible.

The shift to a capitation funding system based on formulae driven by the demographics offers potential advantages to psychologists. In particular, funding will not be limited to physician services. However, there are utilization risks which will be borne by the providers rather than by the funder (i.e., provincial/territorial governments). Hence, careful attention to the derivation of capitation funding formulae will be required. Unfortunately, psychologists and other providers have little historic experience and data upon which to draw to bolster their negotiating strength in such negotiations. Governments will also have a stake in demonstrating good faith to ensure the success of primary care agencies to maintain the credibility of primary care reform with the public. When primary care agencies are set up, practitioners who are eligible for some private sector funding for other services may be able to offer an expanded range of services through a blend of public and private funding, provided that services reasonably construed as primary care remain publicly funded.

2.32.7 CONCLUSIONS

The long-standing dichotomy between psychology as a profession and psychology as an academic discipline had a retarding effect on the development of a cohesive national strategy for the profession in Canada. The emergence of stronger provincial/territorial associations, a reversal of CPA's previous antipathy to professional psychology, the creation of the CRHSPP, successful advocacy efforts which strengthened psychology's legitimacy through legislative recognition and the exemption of psychological health services provided by CRHSPP Listees from the federal Goods and Services Tax, have all enhanced Canadian psychology's standing significantly as a major health-care profession since 1980.

Although psychological services have not been covered directly by Medicare, the vast majority of psychologists in Canada have been reimbursed from public funds as regular salaried employees. Parallel services that emerged through private sector funding have improved public access to psychological services for some segments of the population. Full-time private practice remains the fastest growing segment of professional psychology in Canada. The development of innovative funding mechanisms is being pursued by organized psychology and entrepreneurially oriented psychologists across the country. Throughout Canada, health-care psychologists offer an increasingly wide range of high-quality services. Notwithstanding a decade of significant disruption and dislocation in publicly funded health services which has affected all health-care professions, there is in the late 1990s a reasonable likelihood of stable public funding, albeit at a reduced level when compared to historic baselines. The potential inclusion of psychologists in a reformed primary health-care system offers a promising opportunity to remedy limitations on the public's access to community-based psychological services engendered by anomalies in the Medicare program since the 1970s. On balance, after a period of sustained evolution since the 1940s, the realistic prospect for Canadian health service psychologists is bright for those who are prepared to adapt to emerging opportunities.

2.32.8 REFERENCES

Adair, J. G., Paivio, A., & Ritchie, P. (1996). Psychology in Canada. *Annual Review of Psychology, 47,* 341–370.

Adams, D. (1994). The future and long-range planning of health care services: A Saskatchewan perspective. *World Hospitals and Health Services, 30*(1), 25–31.

Appleby, M. H, & Rickwood, J. (1968). *Psychology in Canada: Special Study #3.* Ottawa, ON: Science Council of Canada.

Barer, M. L., & Evans, R. G. (1992). Interpreting Canada: Models, mind-sets, and myths. *Health Affairs, 11,* 44–61.

Berlyne, D. E., Black, A. H., Berry, R. G., & Douglas, V. I. (1971). *The Future of Canadian Psychology. Report to the Canadian Psychological Association and the Science Council of Canada.* Ottawa, ON: Science Council of Canada.

Bernhardt, K. S. (1961). *Training for Research in Psychology.* Toronto: University of Toronto Press.

Berry, R. G., Davidson, P. O., & Gibson, D. (1974). Advisory Council of Provincial Associations of Psychologists. *Canadian Psychology, 15,* 368–175.

Craig, K. D. (1993). The organization of professional psychology in Canada. In K. S. Dobson & D. J. G. Dobson (Eds.), *Professional psychology in Canada* (pp. 11–45). Toronto: Hogrefe & Huber.

Danzon, P. M. (1992). Hidden overhead costs: Is Canada's system really less expensive? *Health Affairs, 11,* 21–43.

Deber, R. (1992). Regulatory and administrative options for Canada's health care system. In *Exploring options for Canada's health care system.* Ottawa, ON: HEAL/ Canadian Nurses Association.

Dobson, K. S. (1995). Psychology in Canada: The future is not the past. *Canadian Psychology, 36*(1), 1–11.

Dobson, K. S., & Dobson, D. J. G. (Eds.) (1993). *Professional psychology in Canada.* Toronto: Hogrefe & Huber.

Dobson, K. S., & King, M. C. (Eds.) (1995). *The Mississauga Conference on Professional Psychology: Final Report.* Ottawa, ON: Canadian Psychological Association.

Enthoven, A. C. (1990). What can Europeans learn from Americans? In *Health care systems in transition. The search for efficiency.* OECD Social Policy Studies no. 7

(pp. 57–71). Paris: Organization for Economic Co-operation and Development.

Epp, J. (1986). *Achieving health for all: A framework for health promotion.* Ottawa, ON: Health and Welfare Canada.

Evans, D. (1995). Proceedings of the training group. In K. S. Dobson & M. C. King (Eds.), *The Mississauga Conference on Professional Psychology: Final Report* (pp. 8–12). Ottawa, ON: Canadian Psychological Association.

Federal, Provincial, and Territorial Advisory Committee on Population Health (1996). *Report on the health of Canadians.* Ottawa, ON: Health Canada.

Ferguson, G. A. (Ed.) (1977) *Report of the Vancouver Conference on the Organization and Representation of Psychology in Canada.* Ottawa, ON: Canadian Psychological Association.

Freeman, S. J. (1994). An overview of Canada's mental health system. *New Directions for Mental Health Services, 61,* 11–20.

Fuerst, K. B., & Rourke, B. P. (1995). Human neuropsychology in Canada: The 1980s. *Canadian Psychology, 36,* 12–45.

Fulop, T., & Roemer, M. I. (1982). *International Development of Health Manpower Policy.* Geneva, Switzerland: World Health Organization.

Haislmaier, E. F. (1992). Northern discomfort: The ills of the Canadian system. *Health Systems Review, 25*(4), 34–38.

Hart, J. T. (1992). Two paths for medical practice. *Lancet, 340,* 772–775.

Hearn, M. (1995). Proceedings of the funding group. In K. S. Dobson & M. C. King (Eds.), *The Mississauga Conference on Professional Psychology: Final Report* (pp. 13–17). Ottawa, ON: Canadian Psychological Association.

Hearn, M. T., & Evans, D. R. (1993). Applications of psychology to health care. In K. S. Dobson & D. J. G. Dobson (Eds.), *Professional psychology in Canada* (pp. 247–284). Toronto: Hogrefe & Huber.

Hiebert., B., & Uhlemann, M. R. (1993). Counselling psychology: development, identity, issues. In K. S. Dobson & D. J. G. Dobson (Eds.), *Professional psychology in Canada* (pp. 285–312). Toronto: Hogrefe & Huber.

Hunsley, J., & Lefebvre, M. (1990). A survey of the practices and activities of Canadian clinical psychologists. *Canadian Psychology, 31,* 350–358.

Hurley, G., & Ritchie, P. L.-J. (1995). Current and emerging strategic priorities of the Canadian Register of Health Service Providers in Psychology. *Register Report, 20*(1), 11–15.

Lalonde, M. (1974). *A New Perspective on the Health of Canadians.* Ottawa, ON: Health and Welfare Canada.

MacLeod, R. B. (1955). *Psychology in Canadian Universities and Colleges.* Ottawa, ON: Canadian Social Sciences Research Council.

Manga, P. (1993). Health economics and health care reform: Contributions and controversies. *Health and Canadian Society, 1*(1), 177–203.

Manga, P., & Campbell, T. (1994). *Health Human Resources Substitution: A Major Area of Reform Towards a More Cost-Effective Health System.* Working Paper. Ottawa, Canada: Queen's University of Ottawa Economic Projects.

Martin, R. M., Ritchie, P. L.-J., & Sabourin, M. (1988). The state of psychological practice in Canada: Current status and directions for the future. In P. L.-J. Ritchie, T. P. Hogan, & T. V. Hogan (Eds.), *Psychology in Canada: The state of the discipline in 1984* (pp. 73–119). Old Chelsea, PQ: Canadian Psychological Association.

National Forum on Health (1997). *Canada Health Action: Building on the Legacy-Final Report of the National Forum on Health.* Minister of Public Works and Government Services, Ottawa: National Forum on Health.

Organization for Economic Cooperation and Development (1996). *Health Data 1996.* Paris: Author.

Ontario Psychological Association (1997). *Psychological Services in Primary Care.* Toronto: Author.

Ritchie, P. L.-J. (1995a). Origins of the Canadian Register and its Relationship to the National Register. *Register Report, 20*(1), 11–15.

Ritchie, P. L.-J., (1995b). Proceedings of the advocacy group. In K. S. Dobson & M. C. King (Eds.), *The Mississauga Conference on Professional Psychology: Final Report* (pp. 18–28). Ottawa, ON: Canadian Psychological Association

Ritchie, P. L.-J., Hogan, T. P., & Hogan, T. V. (Eds.) (1988). *Psychology in Canada: The State of the Discipline, 1984.* Ottawa, ON. Canadian Psychological Association.

Ritchie, P. L.-J., & Sabourin, M. E. (1992). Sous un même toit: Canada's functional-structural approach to the unity of psychology. *International Journal of Psychology, 27,* 311–325.

Ritchie, P. L.-J., Wilson, R. F., Berry, R., Boulay, M., King, M., & Sabourin, M. (1988). The funding of psychological health services. *Canadian Psychology, 29*(2), 187–205.

Stoddart, G. L. (1987). Alternative modes for health care delivery. In *Aging With Limited Health Resources Proceedings of a Colloquium on Health Care* (pp. 68–71). Economic Council of Canada, Ottawa, ON: Supply and Services Canada.

Thomson, A. (1996). *Diminishing expectations: Implications of the CHST.* Ottawa, ON: HEAL/Canadian Nurses Association.

Torrey, E. F., Bigelow, D. A., & Sladen-Dew, N. (1993). Quality and cost of services for seriously mentally ill individuals in British Columbia and the United States. *Hospital and Community Psychiatry, 44*(10), 943–950.

Wand, B. (1990). *The Council of Provincial Associations of Psychologists: 1967–1990.* Ottawa, ON: Council of Provincial Associations of Psychologists.

Wand, B. (1993). The unity of the discipline: A challenge for the profession. *Canadian Psychology, 34*(2), 124–134.

Warner, R. E. (1991). A survey of theoretical orientations of Canadian clinical psychologists. *Canadian Psychology, 32,* 525–528.

Webster, E. C. (Ed.) (1967). *The Couchiching Conference on Professional Psychology in Canada.* Montréal: Canadian Psychological Association.

Wedding, D., Ritchie, P. L.-J., Kitchen, A., & Binner, P. (1993). Mental health services in a single payer system: Lessons from Canada and principles for an American plan. *Professional Psychology—Research and Practice, 24*(4), 387–393.

Wright, M. J. (1971). The psychological organizations of Canada. *Canadian Psychology, 15,* 112–113.

2.33
Changing Health Care Environment in the United States: Steadily Evolving into the Twenty-first Century

PATRICK H. DeLEON and GARY R. VANDENBOS
American Psychological Association, Washington, DC, USA
MORGAN T. SAMMONS
National Naval Medical Center, Bethesda, MD, USA
and
ROBERT G. FRANK
University of Florida Health Sciences Center, Gainesville, FL, USA

2.33.1 INTRODUCTION

The US' health care system is undergoing unprecedented changes which will have a direct impact upon the future of professional psychology. These include: increasing acceptance of managed care, extraordinary technological advances within the computer and communications industries, drastically increasing numbers of psychologists, and the evolution of psychology into the generic health care arena. Advances in telehealth constitute major opportunities and challenges. Obtaining prescription privileges represents an entirely "new frontier." Psychology is one of the "learned professions" and should prosper if the practitioner and academic communities work collaboratively to address society's pressing needs. Is the next generation willing to become involved in the political and public policy efforts that are required?

2.33.2 PROFESSIONAL PSYCHOLOGY: ONE OF THE "LEARNED PROFESSIONS"

The USA is considered to be highly educated. Yet, the reality is that slightly less than 20% of adults possess a baccalaureate degree, and of those entering division one colleges, only half (56%) actually graduate within six years (DeLeon, Sammons, & Sexton, 1995).

Accordingly, it is contended that professional psychology, with its historical emphasis upon doctoral level training, has a truly unique and pressing societal responsibility to act as one of the "learned professions" (DeLeon & Wiggins, 1996). Society's pressing needs must be addressed affirmatively wherever psychological expertise could be deemed relevant. There is a societal obligation to work to ensure that all Americans have access to quality health care, including mental health care. There must be a collective responsiveness to the ever expanding opportunities for the psychology profession as it evolves within the nation's health care and educational arenas. Simply stated, psychologists have a responsibility to demonstrate effective leadership. As one of the "learned professions," psychologists must not "sit on our laurels" and be complacent.

Reflecting on the profession's past, psychology has an impressive history of successfully overcoming numerous obstacles to the establishment and expansion of professional practice. Psychologists are now authorized to autonomously provide psychotherapy in all states, are independently reimbursed for services rendered under nearly every federal and private health program, are routinely granted hospital privileges in the public and private sectors, and provide expert testimony in the courts (Resnick, DeLeon, & VandenBos, 1997). By 1996, 47 states had enacted psychology "freedom of choice" statutes.

The establishment of professional schools has resulted in numbers expanding beyond anyone's expectations. The current estimate being in excess of 70 000 licensed practitioners and an American Psychological Association (APA) total membership, across all categories of members, in excess of 150 000. Psychologist colleagues have been appointed to numerous positions of public trust. Approximately one third of US states have selected psychologists to direct their mental health system. Psychologists have served in numerous positions of high level federal responsibility; including in the US Congress, as Institute directors, head of the Federal Bureau of Prisons, and hospital (facility) commanders. The future should bring similar administrative and legislative recognition, not to mention broader clinical appreciation for the inherent value of the behavioral and psychological sciences throughout the delivery of quality health care (VandenBos, DeLeon, & Belar, 1991).

However, it must also be reported that some senior colleagues have begun raising serious questions about the profession's collective willingness to continue to engage in the administrative and legislative struggles that are required. It is as if the current generation of professional psychologists believes that they are entitled to a comfortable life, rather than being willing to work aggressively to obtain or maintain one. Stated slightly differently, recent graduates do not seem to appreciate the importance to their profession (and to society) of becoming personally involved in the public policy and political process. Interestingly, this phenomenon seems also to be the case within a number of the other nonphysician disciplines. It has further been observed that unlike many colleagues in the other disciplines, very few psychologists truly appreciate the long-term policy implications for practice of fostering viable clinical-training collaborative relationships (DeLeon, 1989).

2.33.3 MANAGED CARE

There can be little question that for most practitioners (and increasingly for those who are employed within academia) the 1990s can be summarized by the dreaded phrases "the advent of managed care" and the "industrialization of health care." Across the nation, many colleagues report that their incomes are being dramatically slashed. Practitioners, and particularly those in solo private practice, have become increasingly vocal in decrying the intrusion of managed care into their lives; allegations are made that the "quality of care" they are now able to provide may no longer even be within ethical boundaries; and that clinicians' complex judgments are simply not valued. In essence, many colleagues sincerely believe that efforts to curtail the costs of health care have supplanted providing necessary and quality health services. It is as if managed care companies are practicing health care, rather than administering a health care benefit (Miller, 1996).

Few would argue that there have not been unconscionable abuses under managed care. And, it is also the case that those who ultimately pay the bill have become increasingly involved in questioning what it is that they are actually receiving for their money. Many colleagues are fierce individualists; it would be an understatement to suggest that they passionately object to having anyone "overseeing" their clinical judgment. And yet, there is also a growing body of evidence which highlights that unnecessary variances exist in health care delivery, particularly in certain geographical areas (Wennberg, 1984). And, further, that credible indications continue to surface that many clinicians (regardless of discipline) always seem able to proffer "reasonable reasons" to provide services, as long as they will be reimbursed.

Notwithstanding the considerable emotional turmoil surrounding managed care expressed by numerous practitioners during the past years, the 1990s has also seen increasing numbers of psychologists working with, or being employed by, credible managed care organizations. Many report that they are very excited about their increasing ability to contribute significantly to improving their patients' overall health status, and that their practices are constantly expanding into entirely new and previously unforeseen arenas. A fundamental policy question that has been raised by the leadership of the Committee for the American Psychological Association of Graduate Students (APAGS) is: Have our training programs really kept up with the evolving changes in health care delivery? Or, is psychology instead training a generation of practitioners who will ultimately not possess the fundamental skills necessary to survive in the changing health care environment?

The practical, financial, and clinical reality is that increasing numbers of Americans are enrolling in managed care. Both the Clinton Administration and the Republican Congress continue to express great faith in the quality of care that is provided by managed care organizations. In 1996, nearly 57% of all Americans were covered by managed care, a doubling of the number from a decade ago. Nearly three-quarters of Americans covered by employer-based health insurance plans are enrolled in managed care plans, compared with only half in 1993. The Administration's Fiscal Year 1998 budget request for the Department of Health and Human Services (HHS) expressly noted that since 1993, the number of Medicare and Medicaid beneficiaries enrolled in managed care plans has experienced unprecedented growth. Focusing specifically upon the delivery of mental health care, it is estimated that 149 million people are insured through managed behavioral health firms (National Health Policy Forum, 1997). Previously enacted psychology "freedom of choice" laws will need to be amended to reflect the changing market place. The Balanced Budget Act of 1997 (P.L. 105–33) provided the states with greater flexibility to require individuals receiving Medicaid to enroll in managed care plans and specifically eliminated the previous statutory requirement that the states first needed to obtain a formal waiver from the federal government (i.e., HHS).

From a public policy perspective, it is evident that many simply do not appreciate that managed care is here, and that it is not a new conceptual entity. Managed care existed during the days of the great depression, and managed care was the cornerstone of President Nixon's health care agenda (DeLeon, Bulatao, & VandenBos, 1994; DeLeon, VandenBos, & Bulatao, 1991). The health programs of the various federal and state agencies (i.e., the Veterans Administration [VA], Indian Health Service, and Department of Defense) have always had to face the realities of providing comprehensive health care, for an identifiable patient population, within finite budgetary constraints (i.e., have been "managed"; Blanck & DeLeon, 1996). A related and equally significant fundamental health policy concept is that many psychologists are just beginning to appreciate that the delivery of psychological services extends far beyond the delivery of only mental health care *per se*; and that from a public policy perspective, psychological care is but a small subset of health care (DeLeon & VandenBos, 1991). Psychologists are health care professionals.

2.33.4 TELEHEALTH–TELEMEDICINE

2.33.4.1 Federal Developments

One of the most exciting and far reaching developments that has occurred within the health care arena since the mid-1980s has been the increased clinical applicability of computer and telecommunications technology. Historically, most Americans (and particularly practitioners) have viewed the process of receiving health care as a highly personal, one-on-one experience between the patient and practitioner (usually a physician or dentist). With the advent of the nurse practitioner and physician assistant movements during the mid-1960s (DeLeon, Kjervik, Kraut, & VandenBos, 1985), the notion and appropriateness of "physician extenders" providing care became increasingly acceptable, if not commonplace, that is, the fact that there might be someone (or something) in between the doctor–patient relationship began to seem normal. In the late 1990s, the unprecedented advances in technology which are occurring are taking this process a significant step further—the actual physical location (i.e., presence) of the practitioner is becoming almost irrelevant.

In 1994, a bipartisan, bicameral *ad hoc* Steering Committee on Telehealth and Health Care Informatics was established in the US Congress. Its objective was to allow interested members to informally explore how these technological advances might best be utilized to improve access to quality health care, particularly in rural America. It seems intuitive that the increasing sophistication and exponential growth of technology must have clinical implications for health care delivery—but exactly in what fashion has yet to be determined.

In many ways, the clinical application of telehealth–telemedicine is still in its developmental stages. Accordingly, it is pleasing to note the extent to which various governmental agencies and private organizations with health policy expertise have begun collaborating to establish a comprehensive policy framework for what might evolve. By the end of the first session of the 105th Congress (1997), impressive reports had already been issued by the Institute of Medicine (IOM, 1996), the former Office of Technology Assessment (US Congress, OTA, 1995), the General Accounting Office (GAO, 1997a), and the US Department of Commerce (1997). The federal government had established a Federal Interagency Joint Working Group on Telemedicine, which among other responsibilities has been tasked with establishing a world wide web-accessible inventory of federally-sponsored telemedicine projects. Note, as an aside, the consistent efforts by organized medicine and the Clinton Administration to utilize the policy phrase "telemedicine," notwithstanding the Congress' statutory preference for the more generic and inclusive term "telehealth."

Some of the highlights from these reports are: by the end of 1996, nearly 30% of rural hospitals were expected to use telehealth to deliver patient care; more than 40% of telehealth programs were in operation one year or less; and the most common clinical uses for telehealth were diagnostic consults, medical data transmissions, and management of chronic illnesses.

The Commerce Department report (1997) expressly addressed the potential applicability of telehealth for mental health services:

> Unlike some specialties such as cardiology, mental health telemedicine applications do not require a high degree of image specificity, thus the technology can be simpler and costs can be lower. Moreover, initial evidence indicates that telemedicine works well for group therapy as well as individual consults. (p. 19)

By the middle of the 105th Congress over 35 federal organizations, 10 state governments, and numerous private organizations had sponsored hundreds of initiatives in over 40 states. According to the Department of Commerce, over a three-year period, the Federal government alone invested more than $646 million, with different agencies developing their own unique priorities. The Library of Medicine of the National Institutes of Health was projected to be providing $42 million, targeting proposals that examined specific use of the technology in health care, whereas the HHS Office of Rural Health Policy was targeting multispecialty networks of care, stressing improving access to care in rural areas.

The Office of Rural Health Policy is the lead telehealth programmatic agency for HHS. In Fiscal Year 1996 it awarded $9.9 million in grants under one particular initiative, in which grantees were to belong to, or propose becoming members of, a network and thereby able to provide a minimum range of services. Each network was to provide a minimum of seven services, one of which was to be the stabilization of patients in emergency services. Although to date psychology has been only tangentially involved, the potential is definitely present since the office has demonstrated an explicit emphasis on encouraging multidisciplinary and community-focused care, with priority being given to projects that proposed providing care in such community-based settings as schools, assisted living facilities, individuals in the home, and so forth. That year, the Office awarded an additional $4.75 million to eight telemedicine projects under its rural health outreach grant program, as well as providing support to two major telemedicine demonstration projects in West Virginia and Iowa. Overall, between 1994 and 1997, the Office awarded approximately $36 million in telehealth funding.

2.33.4.2 Professional Issues

Some of the evolving clinical and public policy issues in telehealth that should be particularly relevant to professional psychology include: confidentiality of patient records, insurance reimbursement, interstate licensure decisions, malpractice liability, and the potential for "cookbook medicine" or requiring predetermined algorithms of care. Many of these policy issues will eventually be debated at the state level, both in the legislature and by administrative agencies. By the end of 1997, 15 states had decided to offer some telemedicine coverage under their Medicaid programs and the states of California and Louisiana had enacted legislation mandating coverage for telehealth consultation services under private insurance plans.

Health policy experts and clinicians can readily appreciate how this advancing technology might work for services that are primarily visual (or physical) in nature; that is, reading x-rays, performing dermatology consults, and transmitting medical records over long distances. For professional psychology the underlying question becomes: how can telehealth capabilities facilitate traditional psychological interventions which may not be as concrete (or physical) in nature? Computerized testing and diagnostic interviews and consultations are possible. What about providing psychotherapy? The more one gets involved, it also becomes clearer that there remains the critical issue of how to facilitate practitioner acceptance of this new technology.

Reflecting again upon the profession's training programs from a national frame of reference, the APA past-President Ron Fox has reported that there are approximately 26 identifiable telehealth programs within medical school environments, but none within psychology's training programs (personal communication, 1997). Fortunately, various elements of the APA governance (the Board of Educational Affairs, the Committee for the Advancement of Professional Practice, the Board of Professional Affairs, and the Committee on Rural Health) have begun addressing the policy and programmatic implications. The Department of Commerce report expressly referenced psychology's efforts. Telehealth is becoming a major factor in the delivery of mental health care. The *American Medical News* (1997, November 10) reported that mental health, constituting 20% of the 1996 consultations, has become telehealth's most common use.

For psychology, the fundamental issues of interstate licensure, privacy/confidentiality concerns, and patient outcome measures must be systematically addressed. Already a number of states (10 by 1997) have decided to require that telehealth practitioners possess multistate licensure. Professional nursing, however, has been considering urging their licensure boards to adopt a "driver's license" approach, under which the practitioner/consultant would only be required to be licensed in one state. Within medicine, the Federation of State Medical Boards is exploring what approach they should recommend as appropriate guidelines to their licensure boards.

The leadership of professional psychology, and in particular the leadership of its professional schools, must collectively become systematically involved in the ongoing HHS demonstrations and policy dialogues. For example, the Health Resources and Services Administration (HRSA) requested policy guidance on:

> the legal barriers to the cost-effective use of telemedicine and specific suggestions for overcoming these barriers. In particular, we seek suggestions for easing licensure barriers to physicians and other health professionals providing telemedicine services across state lines, and comments on specific alternatives, such as those recently proposed by the Federation of State Medical Boards and the Institute of Electrical and Electronics Engineers ... (R)espondents are encouraged to provide comments and suggestions on other legal issues associated with telemedicine such as liability/malpractice ... to identify the particular challenges in assuring privacy, confidentiality, and security in the conduct of telemedicine and provide suggestions for addressing those challenges. Comments will be reviewed and considered for incorporation into the final report to Congress. (*Federal Register*, August 9, 1996, p. 41 640)

We must ask ourselves: what elements of professional psychology, other than the professional schools, might become involved in the actual delivery of health care utilizing telehealth? And, thus, intimately affected by governmental decisions?

To again focus upon the federal government's role as a provider of health care and to give another perspective of the extent to which telehealth has already matured: in 1996, the health officials of the Department of Defense (DoD) testified before the Senate Appropriations Committee (US Department of Defense, 1996, S. Hrg. #104–756). The witnesses described their considerable enthusiasm for the clinical and teaching potential inherent in the technology revolution. Medical digital technology, telemedicine, advanced computer-based medical expert systems, information management—

for combat as well as for day-to-day business and clinical practice—were explicitly addressed. Allowing attending providers on board ships to transmit real-time ultrasound videos and full color images back to specialists at major treatment facilities hundreds of miles away was clearly "doable." It was noted that DoD's telehealth presence in Bosnia was extraordinary.

As we have indicated, the DoD is a major provider of health care. It administers care in 116 military hospitals and 513 clinics for a beneficiary population of over 8.3 million, with a medical budget of approximately $9.6 billion annually. In 1996/97 alone, DoD spent $48 million developing telemedicine infrastructure. What lessons can be collectively learned from military colleagues?

2.33.4.3 Federal Legislative Developments

The Kennedy–Kassebaum health insurance legislation, the Health Insurance Portability and Accountability Act of 1996 (P.L. #104–191), surfaced some very interesting policy implications for professional psychology, not the least of which was the extensive debate surrounding the possibility of enacting mental health parity legislation. The final enacted bill did not include the mental health parity provision but did recognize that advances in health care technology, and specifically telemedicine, will have a major impact upon how health care will be delivered in the future. The conference agreement

> directs the Health Care Financing Administration (HCFA) to complete its ongoing study of Medicare reimbursement of all telemedicine services and submit a report to Congress on reimbursement of telemedicine services by March 1, 1997. The report would . . . include an analysis of the cost of services provided via telemedicine, and include a proposal for Medicare reimbursement of telemedicine services. (H. Conf. Rpt. #104–736, p. 235)

The Balanced Budget Act of 1997 (P.L. 105–33) was subsequently enacted and took the next step by requiring the Secretary of HHS to continue the Department's three-year demonstration project under which Medicare will pay for telemedicine services at 57 Medicare-certified facilities and to make Part B payments under Medicare for telehealth "professional consultation" services available by no later than January 1, 1999. Interestingly, this same legislation also substantially modified the Graduate Medical Education (GME) program (which will be addressed in more depth later in the chapter) in ways which could have a major impact upon psychology as a health profession. Historically, the GME program has stressed hospital based services and has been physician dominated. The Budget Act expanded direct medical education payments to entities that were previously not eligible (and where psychologists are increasingly being employed), specifically to federally qualified health centers, rural health centers, and Medicare + Choice organizations. Most importantly for psychology, the conference report expressly "urges the Secretary to include physician assistants and psychologists under (the allied health) authority" (H. Conf. Rpt. #105–217, p. 822) for determining reimbursement.

During the conference deliberations on the Fiscal Year 1998 Appropriations bill for the Department of Defense (P.L.105–56, 1997), specific language was also included focusing upon telehealth:

> The conferees agree that pursuant to the GAO report "Telemedicine: Federal Strategy is Needed to Guide Investments," DoD Health Affairs should contract with an outside organization, which has previously demonstrated the ability to assess and plan strategic telehealth initiatives, to enumerate current telehealth efforts and recommend coordination activities among the tri-services to prevent duplication and enhance "dual use" telecommunications for health care delivery, education, and related public sector applications. This assessment should also include the worldwide computer-based patient record as a necessary component of telehealth. The resulting report and recommendations shall be provided to the congressional defense committees by April 1, 1998. (P. L. 105–56, 1997, H. Conf. Rpt. #105–265, p. 139)

Clearly major advances are evolving in telehealth within the federal sector. To cite another example, the Senate reports accompanying the DoD and VA appropriations bills for Fiscal Year 1998 also formally recognized this technology's potential for upgrading VA nursing staff professional skills.

> VA/DoD distance learning pilot project. The Committee encourages the DoD to continue the VA/DoD distance learning pilot project to transition clinical nurse specialists to the role of nurse practitioners. This collaborative program with the USUHS Graduate School of Nursing will increase the number of primary care providers. (Sen. Rpt. 105–45, p. 149)

And,

> The Committee encourages VA to continue the VA/DoD Distance Learning Pilot Program to transition clinical nurse specialists to the role of nurse practitioners. This collaborative program

with the Uniformed Services University of the Health Sciences Graduate School of Nursing will add to the number of primary care providers required to care for the projected increase in the numbers of aging and female veterans. (FY 1998 Departments of Veterans Affairs, 1997, Sen. Rpt. #105–53, p. 16)

We would rhetorically ask: are VA psychologists involved in these activities?

2.33.5 PRESCRIPTION PRIVILEGES

The move towards prescriptive authority (DeLeon, Fox, & Graham, 1991; DeLeon, Sammons, & Sexton, 1995) takes place in the context of two major shifts in health care provision and training. The first of these is that organized medicine is gradually losing its monopoly on the provision of health care services. Other health care specialties—such as advanced practice nursing, podiatry, and optometry—are moving into fields which had previously been the sole purview of the physician. In the USA, though not the case globally, control of the prescription pad has long been the *sine qua non* of medicine. American medicine has found that control of prescriptive authority has proven to be an astonishingly potent political tool, and, since the beginning of the twentieth century, considerable effort has been expended by physicians to establish a relative monopoly on this function. Surrendering this authority, which is an emblematic step in the gradual dissolution of medicine's hegemony in health care provision, is the subtext which underlies the opposition by psychiatry and other branches of organized medicine to the acquisition of prescriptive authority by psychologists.

The data illustrating this shift are dramatic. An extraordinary illustration of this trend is revealed by the fact that the number of prescriptions written by nonphysician prescribers more than doubled between 1992 and 1996. In 1992, 0.22% of all prescriptions were written by nurse practitioners or physician assistants; in 1996, this figure was 0.57%. Though still small in comparison to the overall numbers of prescriptions written, this percentage represents over one million prescriptions per month (*American Medical News*, 1996, June 17). Since July, 1995, the Drug Enforcement Administration (DEA) has issued controlled substance prescription numbers to nurse practitioners and physician assistants.

These numbers have been driven by remarkable legislative successes by the various professional groups. In particular, those of advanced practice nurses (APNs) have demonstrated the changing scope of health care provision. In 1975, North Carolina became the first state to provide nursing with prescriptive authority. By 1996, APNs had some form of prescriptive authority in all states except Illinois. In 19 states, they could prescribe from formularies including controlled substances completely independent of physician involvement, a figure which had almost doubled from two years previously, when APNs could prescribe independently in only 11 states. In 1997 it was estimated that there are approximately 75 000 APNs throughout the nation. Optometrists and podiatrists possess prescriptive authority in all states (except the District of Columbia, for optometry). Physician assistants and pharmacists have acquired more limited forms of prescriptive authority, but at a rate which is quickly expanding. In the case of podiatry and optometry, these privileges are granted without physician oversight, and the degree of latitude afforded physician assistants and pharmacists has increased significantly. In the US Army there is a program for physical therapists, ongoing for more than two decades, under which they are granted prescriptive authority in the course of treating neuromuscular complaints (Benson, Schreck, Underwood, & Greathouse, 1995).

Although the medical press frequently implies that nonphysician prescribers imperil patients' well-being (i.e., are "public health hazards"), data have long been extant which demonstrate that nonphysician health care providers prescribe psychotropics at least as well as their medically trained counterparts. Studies in the 1970s demonstrated that nonmedically trained mental health providers, armed only with knowledge acquired during weekly seminars, did not differ from psychiatrists in their prescribing patterns (Platman, Dorgan, & Gerhardt, 1976). In the state of California, over a million patients were seen by nonphysician prescribers with no adverse consequences (State of California, 1982). Interestingly, less than 20% of all psychotropic medications are ordered by psychiatrists.

In addition to the results of demonstration projects and similar efforts, overall differences in safe practices between physicians and nonphysicians can be inferred by using the frequency of successful malpractice actions against both groups. Here, the extant data speaks clearly in favor of the argument that nonphysicians prescribe safely. In general, nonphysician groups are usually more successful than their physician counterparts at avoiding completed malpractice actions. For example, in a study of lawsuits related to failures to diagnose heart attacks, it was discovered that physician extenders were successfully sued least often among a varied group of medical specialties (including cardiologists and general practitioners), accounting for only four of 495 claims in the reporting period (Flannery, 1997).

Figures for prescribing psychologists are, of course, not available, but tangential evidence suggests parallel experiences for psychologists. A 13-year history of malpractice actions against psychologists in California indicated a total absence of successful claims for failure to diagnose medical conditions in patients seen by psychologists (Dorken, 1990). From these data one could reasonably infer that malpractice actions would not be a significant concern for those who prescribed. Further oblique support for this position comes from another interesting study which found that psychologists were as good as general physicians, and slightly (but not significantly) better than a small group of psychiatrists, in detecting Axis III conditions masquerading as Axis I problems (Sanchez & Kohn, 1991).

Patient acceptability of nonphysician prescribers has been good, particularly within organized systems of care. In England, nurses were granted prescriptive authority in 1994. A survey of patients after this change suggested that most patients were comfortable with this new arrangement. The principal benefits seen were that patients no longer had to visit two providers in order to get a prescription, that time was saved, and that patients could get medications from providers with whom they had previously established trusting relationships. No patients expressed opposition to the idea of nurse prescribing (Luker, Austin, Hogg, Ferguson, & Smith, 1997).

Among psychologists, the Psychopharmacology Demonstration Program (PDP) established under the auspices of the Department of Defense has provided a unique laboratory for experimentation in curriculum development for prescribing psychologists (Sammons & Brown, 1997). The program was established during Congressional deliberations on the Fiscal Year 1989 DoD Appropriations bill (P.L. 100–463, 1988) and has now graduated 10 Fellows who are privileged to prescribe at their military facilities. There have been several independent evaluations of the highly controversial program which have confirmed that the Fellows provide high-quality health care. There is disagreement, however, as to whether the program has been cost-effective (GAO, 1997b; Jones, Cohen, Munsat, Dorris, & Berson, 1996).

The second major shift is more specific to organized psychiatry. It is a subset of the first; that is, reflecting the gradual reduction in power of organized medicine. From our vantage point, it is clear that there is growing recognition that psychiatry as a profession has imperiled its existence by excessive reliance on biological models of psychopathology and biological interventions. And perhaps even more significant in the long run, psychiatry has not been able to attract a critical mass of American medical school graduates into its residencies.

A number of psychiatrists are now beginning to understand that the future of their profession as a discipline may depend to a great extent on its ability to combine psychological and pharmacological approaches to treatment. Unfortunately, a history of excessive reliance on ideologically grounded disciplines (first Freudian psychoanalysis, and later psychopharmacology), has limited the clinical evolution of psychiatry. In our judgement, psychology is a much more heterogeneously grounded discipline, and the variety of subdisciplines which make up the field have allowed us to sidestep the trap of falling into a single treatment modality. Nonetheless, it is important that psychologists recognize that, in order to prosper, they must be open to embracing ideologies and methodologies that had previously been regarded as outside their scope of practice. They must be careful not to emulate the mistakes of physician colleagues, who have found that reliance on unimodal treatment strategies quickly leads to obsolescence. Instead, they must develop and utilize the most appropriate investigatory techniques to determine which treatments, and in which combinations, will optimize the science and clinical practice of psychology.

2.33.5.1 Fewer Prescribers, Greater Challenges—Rising Needs

By the year 2020, psychological and behavioral disorders, such as major depression, bipolar disorder, panic disorder, schizophrenia, and alcoholism will have surpassed all but a very few other causes of worldwide morbidity and mortality. On a global level, unipolar major depression is projected to represent the second most significant contributor to disability adjusted life years, and neuropsychiatric conditions in general will contribute 10.5% to disability adjusted life years (Murray & Lopez, 1997). Again, a rhetorical question: what are the training programs doing to target these populations?

2.33.5.2 The Challenge of Psychiatric Residency Training

In 1994, only 3.2% of all US medical school graduates entered a psychiatric residency, the lowest number since 1929 (Sierles & Taylor, 1995). At the same time, the number of international medical graduates (IMGs) entering US residencies has escalated exponentially, and has increased 64.7% since 1990 (Peterson et al., 1997). The influx of IMGs who enter US residencies and then stay to practice medicine (as the majority of IMGs do) is not unique to psychiatry. Nationwide, 25.2% of all medical residency slots are filled by IMGs, but the problem is particularly acute in psychiatry where nearly half (41.8%–49.5%) of all US psychiatry residency programs are dependent on IMGs—that is, over 50% of their first year residents are IMGs (Whitcomb & Miller, 1995). It has been estimated that if Congress merely adopted the recommendations of organized medicine as to how to limit the percentage of GME payments currently going to international medical graduates, psychiatry would experience a 40% reduction of its residency slots the first year alone.

It has been noted that the oft-cited rationale for utilizing IMGs (i.e., that they would provide more services to indigent citizens) was not found to be true, with only a minority of IMGs being engaged in treating the poor and traditionally underserved. Could it be that the high percentages of IMGs in US psychiatry may be a factor in the astonishing utilization of psychotropic medications by their specialty? It has been reported that the percentage of psychiatrists' patients receiving medications rose from 27% in 1975 to 54.5% in 1988. Similar analysis of data from 1988 and 1989 indicated that 61.7% of all psychiatric patients received medication, and that IMGs were disproportionately represented in that group of psychiatrists defined as "high medication practice" (Olfson, Pincus, & Sabshin, 1994). As others have demonstrated, the percentage of psychiatric patients receiving medication continues to climb, with over 90% of patients receiving at least one drug in a 1996 survey of psychiatrists (West, Zarin, & Pincus, 1997).

During the DoD psychopharmacology training program, the Fellows became acutely aware of the relevance of their psychological training to the complex issues surrounding utilization of psychotropic medications. There are a number of prescribing areas in which psychology should be more actively involved; particularly, in asking relevant clinical utilization questions. Gender-specific training in clinical psychopharmacology is an open and challenging field. From a pharmacoepidemiological perspective, differential rates of prescribing for men and women are well recorded. Women are more likely than men to be prescribed psychotropic drugs, and this difference is not entirely explainable by generally higher rates of diagnosis of mental distress in women. In particular, elderly women are more likely than any other segment of the patient population to receive psychotropics. The factors which contribute to these discrepancies are less well understood. Is gender of the patient the sole determinant of differential rates of prescribing? This seems unlikely. It is more likely that an interaction exists between the gender of the prescriber and gender of the patient which can further explain such differences.

Another clinical issue which requires elucidation is the persistence of high risk prescribing patterns, despite the availability of data suggesting safer clinical strategies. It has been noted that this is an especially significant issue for elderly females, who receive disproportionate shares of psychotropic medication. On a more preclinical level, gender specific physiological functions, such as the effects of pregnancy, lactation, menopause, and estrogen levels on both the production of mental disorders and the pharmacokinetic and pharmacodynamic properties of psychotropic drugs, still await extensive investigation.

2.33.5.3 Towards More Rational Prescribing Practices

It is reasonably clear that a medical degree and completion of a psychiatric residency *per se* is not the prime determinant of best prescribing practice of psychotropics. Thus, a question that begs investigation is to clarify the essential components of the knowledge base which underlies skillful prescribing, and perhaps more importantly, what components of education (didactic and clinical) are necessary to allow providers to distinguish when a patient will be more responsive to medication or nonallopathic therapies.

Since the Second World War, the pharmacopoeia for mental disorders has expanded exponentially. The development of effective pharmacological treatments for many forms of mental distress has revolutionized mental health care and eased the suffering of untold numbers of patients. But in spite of advances in drug treatments and greater understanding of neurochemical processes in mental illness, collective insight into the mechanisms of action of almost all psychotropic drugs remains rudimentary. And, decades of clinical experience notwithstanding, there do not as yet exist universally defined, science-based criteria to guide the clinician in the selection and use of specific drugs for the treatment of any mental disorder.

These gaps in knowledge can partly be ascribed to the incomplete maturation of the mental health field. Additionally, a history of what must be considered fairly "shaky research" methods has led to questions regarding generalizability of clinical trials (Healy, 1990; Kraemer, 1995). Certain issues, such as the existence of a large placebo effect in psychotropic drug studies, continue to bedevil researchers in the field. The subject of generalizability has aroused considerable recent controversy, and the question of whether short-term clinical trials of medication can translate to the real-world, clinical environment is being answered with increasing skepticism.

Psychiatry's long tradition of clinical practice based on professional consensus rather than academic (or "hard") science has also served to retard the understanding of true clinical responses to psychotropic drugs. For example, it is common clinical practice to use serotonin reuptake inhibitors (SRIs) for the treatment of most forms of depression, in spite of evidence suggesting that tricyclic antidepressants (TCAs) may be more efficacious in treating severe depressions. In this instance, the negative effects of using consensus based, rather than science based, criteria are in all probability minimal. In other examples, however, consensus based psychiatric treatments have had significant negative repercussions on patient outcomes. The phenomenon of rapid neuroleptization, for instance, a common clinical practice in the past, is thought to have led to increased incidence of the potentially fatal neuroleptic malignant syndrome.

Although unappreciated by many psychologists, the gap between research and clinical psychopharmacology practice remains large. Some have attempted to rectify these disparities by constructing treatment algorithms that guide clinicians as to appropriate drug use. These efforts are still embryonic, and, unfortunately, treatment algorithms themselves may once again be developed on the basis of expert consensus rather than clinical science. Also, drug algorithms only address the pharmacologic aspects of treatment and rarely attempt to include psychosocial or other treatments (Rudorfer, 1995).

It is safe to assume that pharmacotherapy alone is not a sufficient condition for recovery from most forms of mental distress. Although it has been proposed that psychotherapy is an "occasionally indicated, delegatable" function (Klein, 1995, p. 81), examination of available evidence should temper any rush towards sole reliance on pharmacotherapy as an effective treatment strategy. For the most part, this is due to the reality that a substantial placebo effect operates in most psychotropic drug studies. The high rate of placebo responding to antidepressants is a particularly robust finding. Meta-analytic review of a large number of clinical trials of antidepressants indicated, for example, that while 60%–70% of depressed patients respond to drugs alone, approximately 35% displayed a therapeutic response to placebo. As a result, only around 25% of participants could be considered as true drug responders (Preskorn, 1996). Up to 70% of drug response in less severe depressions may be a placebo response. Indeed, the placebo response is so well demonstrated that some have suggested the clinical use of "pill placebo" as an effective intervention for depression (Brown, 1994). Sizable placebo responses have also been observed for other classes of psychoactive drugs as well, a fact which raises not only clinical concern but also methodological issues, as it is possible that many, if not most, patients in clinical trials can detect the differences between active drugs and placebos.

2.33.5.4 Aging Populations—Aging Programs

Although society continues to mature and age, as a profession, psychology continues not to prepare graduate students effectively for the challenges of caring for an older population (VandenBos & DeLeon, in press). Psychology training programs must be in the forefront of developing psychological based treatment programs targeted towards the needs of the elderly. Students in psychopharmacology will require far greater expertise than is currently available in most standard training programs if they are to provide adequately for the psychological and pharmacological needs of older Americans. The high rates of overprescription in elderly Americans has received wide comment. Programs educating physicians and other health care providers regarding rational use of psychopharmacologic agents have resulted in significant reductions in prescriptions written for elders. Given the importance of psychosocial factors in the care of the elderly, we would again rhetorically ask: are any of the professional schools demonstrating an interest in establishing psychology-based teaching programs in nursing homes?

2.33.6 HEALTH CARE COSTS

The growth in psychology reflects changes in health care in the USA. In 1950, the USA spent $13 billion or 4.4% of its gross national product (GNP), on health services. Twenty years later in 1970, the USA spent $75 billion or 7.5% of its GNP on health services. By 1980, this had increased to $250 billion or 9.4% of the GNP. In the 1990s, health spending increased to $740 billion or 13% of GNP, with estimates it would increase to more than 16% by the year 2000 and between 27% and 43% by the year 2030 (Bingaman, Frank, & Billy, 1993; Frank & Ross, 1995).

Increasing costs of this nature cannot be sustained by the US economy. Many believe that the increased cost of health care has been the driving force behind managed care. The federal government represents the largest health care payer in the USA. Federal health care programs (i.e., Medicare and Medicaid) have undergone substantial, uncontrolled growth. The federal government's share of health care spending rose from 28.1% in 1992 to 31.7% in 1993. In the six-year period between 1992 and 1998, Medicaid is projected to grow by 10.5%, and Medicare is expected to grow by 9.4%. This growth in spending stands in sharp contrast to other federal expenditure growth which is estimated, for the same period, to be 2.5% (Frank, Sullivan, & DeLeon, 1994).

2.33.6.1 The National Health Care Debate

Awareness of increasing costs of the health care system led to a national debate on overhauling the health care system in the early days of the Clinton Administration (Frank, 1993; Glueckauf, Frank, Bond, & McGrew, 1996). This debate resulted in no new immediate federal legislation. The functional outcome of the debate, however, was a transition to reform at the state level and reform through private markets. It has become clear that only incremental change is possible at the federal level (Frank & VandenBos, 1994).

Within private markets, fragmented care has often been viewed as a sizeable factor in the escalation of cost. Most patients have multiple providers, practicing in different settings, providing multiple work-ups and multiple prescriptions for treatment. This fragmentation of care leads to diminished accountability for outcomes. In addition, multiple providers create numerous opportunities for overdiagnosis, excessive treatment, and iatrogenic outcomes. Payers, aware of the cost of fragmentation, have focused on streamlining delivery systems that emphasize accountability by restricting access to patients.

Integrated service networks (ISNs) have been touted as an effective ingredient in the implementation of systems focusing on quality and accountability. In the 1993–1994 health care debates, several states considered proposals to legislate ISNs (Frank & Kivlahan, 1997). Although few states were successful in legislating this approach, the combined power of payers has functionally moved many delivery systems in this direction. ISNs are networks of organizations that provide, or arrange to provide, a coordinated continuity of services to a defined population for whom they are clinically and fiscally accountable for outcomes and the health status of the population served. Organized delivery systems may be created through the vertical integration of organizational services or through the virtual integration created through a series of contracts. The goals of organized delivery systems differ dramatically from the goals of single entities practicing in the fragmented health care system. While systems focus on singular patient encounters, ISNs or organized health care systems focus on the health of the community through prevention and health promotion. Integral to the development of these complex organizations is the use of "holographic organizations." In these organizations, constituent parts (i.e., key roles and services) are included in smaller delivery systems so that every aspect of the organization replicates the larger entity.

These evolving changes in organized delivery systems have critical implications for the practice of psychology. As organized delivery systems have become more dominant in the practice landscape, the solo practitioner has become an endangered species. Pressure to combine and to join specialty groups or multispecialty groups has been intense. Payers have used the "power of contracting" to exclude individuals who are not part of larger groups providing discounts and accountability.

It now appears that capitation will evolve differently in unique markets. While some markets will move towards massive levels of capitation as seen on the West Coast and some portions of the Midwest and Rocky Mountain areas, other areas such as the Southeast will be slower to become dominated by managed care. Indeed, there seem to be countervailing trends which suggest that even within high managed-care environments, the move towards capitation may be diminishing. Instead, there seems to be a trend towards point-of-service (POS) plans. In POS plans, participants are charged a slight surcharge in return for access to a wide range of providers. These plans have spread dramatically within California. Consumer demands for "choice" have increased options for broader provider panels. In many states legislation guaranteeing access to certain classes of providers, such as dermatology or OB/GYN, has become common.

There has been increased concern that capitated models place specialists at unreasonable risk. Primary care providers, by referring their most complex expensive cases to specialists, can remain under their cap and "dump" the most complex cases. In several highly penetrated managed-care markets, new trends emphasizing "episode of care" payment have become more apparent. In this model, care is "unbundled" so that the focus is on the individual case or the disease level. The Oxford Health Plan (Norwalk, CT) has committed its future growth to this model. Oxford is developing criteria for the start and completion of each episode of care. All care provided within a designated period is defined as part of this care episode. The practitioner receives a fixed, global price for services and all specialists bid on the provision of services within the disease episode. Importantly, in this model, there is emphasis upon cross-disciplinary teams.

Congruent with this approach is the growth of a number of specialized companies focusing on "disease management." For example, "for-profit" companies specializing in cancer, diabetes, asthma, and rehabilitation have now become common. Within ISNs, care of chronic disease conditions provided by several disciplines has become the method of delivery. Instead of vertical integration, these systems are horizontally integrated across the episode of care.

HealthSouth, a major rehabilitation company headquartered in Birmingham, AL, has often been touted as a classic example of this strategy. In 1982, HealthSouth was founded as an outpatient rehabilitation company. By 1997, it was fully operational in 30 large markets and HealthSouth facilities were located in all 50 states. Operating revenues grew from $25 million in 1991 to $2.4 billion in 1996, with a 28.2% operating margin in 1996.

Changes of this type have important implications for the practice of psychology. Increasingly, it has been recognized that psychology is a health specialty not merely a mental health specialty (DeLeon, Frank, & Wedding, 1995). Interestingly, a number of psychologists have taken another step and now consider themselves "primary care providers," rather than "specialists" of any type.

The slowness of this definitional recognition has come at high cost. During the 1993–1994 Congressional debate psychology mistakenly placed its primary emphasis upon mental health benefits. Arguing that each American was entitled to 52 sessions of psychotherapy per year, organized psychology emphasized an approach that had little likelihood of succeeding. Organized psychology pursued this strategy despite considerable evidence that this proposition would garner little external support. Late in the debate psychologists recognized that the narrow advocacy of mental health benefits, as opposed to suggesting changes in the broader health care arena, limited the ability of the profession to significantly impact the outcome of health reform conversations. This change in position led to recognition that psychology is a health profession. Interestingly, as many as 75% of all members of the APA identify themselves as "health care providers."

While psychologists initially contented themselves with narrow, self-defeating arguments, other groups staked out positions in the larger policy landscape. The American Medical Association, for example, led all other organizations in total contributions to political action committees during the national elections. In contrast, psychologists divided themselves into small, argumentative camps debating the veracity of each others' approach to the profession. The schism between academic psychology and the clinical practice community is marked, and in our judgment is extremely destructive.

2.33.6.2 The Town-gown Split

While American physicians have demonstrated loyalty to their training institutions, such leanings are rare in psychology. Many physicians have lamented the increasing pressure for clinical dollars within medical schools. This trend, however, demands medical school faculties engage in clinical practice and has assured that academic physicians are aware of trends within their profession and remain proficient clinicians. Psychology, in contrast, has followed a more "ivory tower science" approach. In many academic enterprises psychologists have little institutional incentive to be personally involved in clinical practice. Consequently, graduates of these programs who move into the practice community have little subsequent contact with their academic faculty. This creates schisms between the academic and clinical practitioners. Clinical practitioners come to believe that the academics understand little about their day-to-day lives. Such beliefs seem reasonable when few academic psychologists engage in actual clinical practice. Unfortunately, one result is that a true understanding of the drastic changes evolving in the health care delivery system is severely limited among those in many academic departments.

2.33.6.3 Self-identity

The failure of psychologists to identify with their academic training institutions has other implications. As the number of psychologists increase, they are moving into diverse settings. Increasingly, psychologists are moving into policy roles in addition to traditional clinical, academic, or science roles. There are numerous opportunities for psychologists in the public policy area. Behavioral science expertise is critical to health and educational programs. The demand for individuals with knowledge of these areas creates opportunities for psychologists. In addition, the broad purview of psychology training programs guarantees that graduates will continue to be sought for many diverse opportunities (Lorion, Iscoe, DeLeon, & VandenBos, 1996). Unfortunately, a tendency to be divorced from academic homes creates little common identification among psychologists. The tendency for different camps within psychology to devalue colleagues who work in different settings guarantees that a common identity is unlikely for the profession. As psychologists move into more diverse niches, this lack of common identity will continue to result in individual psychologists identifying more with their new opportunities, rather than with their profession in general.

It has been noted that physicians in policy settings identify strongly with their medical training. They assure that opportunities for physicians are developed through their policy positions and promulgated rules and regulations. In contrast, psychologists often seem to use a "scientific" approach to assessing the value of extending psychology into new settings. This approach requires empirical validation of the usefulness of psychologists for each and every niche. The tendency for psychologists within different camps to devalue each other exacerbates this problem.

2.33.6.4 The Congressional Science Fellowship Program

Several programs have created special opportunities for psychologists to learn more about health policy formulation on a "first hand" basis. Although psychology curriculae rarely emphasize either health policy or public health, the broad training psychologists receive is ideal for the evaluation of policy issues.

In 1974, the APA created the Congressional Science Fellowship program. This program has now been responsible for facilitating the involvement of 61 individual psychologists in policy-making and the political process. Through the APA Fellowship, psychology's expertise is systematically applied to society's priorities. The program allows psychologists to spend a year in Washington, DC working in the legislative or administrative branches. Through this "hands on" experience, psychologists have the opportunity to see (and participate in) national public policy being made on a first-hand basis. Upon completing their Capitol Hill experience, approximately half of the Fellows take policy-related positions within various agencies, while the other half return to their previous positions.

Another program that holds tremendous opportunity, but which unfortunately has been only rarely considered by psychologists, is the Robert Wood Johnson Health Policy Fellowship (RWJ). Like the APA Fellowship, this program was created in the mid-1970s to provide mid-career academic health center faculty the opportunity to learn about public policy through actual experiences. The RWJ Fellowship is administered by the Institute of Medicine (IOM) at the National Academies of Sciences. Each year, through a competitive process, a few are selected from academic health centers and invited to spend a year in Washington, DC working within the legislative or administrative branches. Again, most RWJ Fellows choose to work within the Legislative Branch. The program provides an extensive didactic training on health policy prior to the actual Fellowship experience. Fellows are exposed to leaders from virtually every sector of the American health care system. After the didactic sessions are completed, fellows spend 10–14 months working on federal health policy. To date, only two psychologists have taken advantage of the RWJ—Danny Wedding and Robert G. Frank.

Within health care, there are many critical issues which will affect the future of professional psychology. In the late 1990s most psychologists are concerned with those changes in health care delivery that impact their own economic status. Without question, such concerns are vital to the future of individual psychologists in practice. On the larger scale, however, psychology as a profession must be concerned about issues which open up new markets and expand the scope of practice, such as the acquisition of the ability to prescribe medication (DeLeon & Wiggins, 1996). In the 1980s concerns were voiced within the profession regarding whether it should seek authority to admit to hospitals. Each of these professional expansion decisions is critical to the future and vitality of the profession and each reflects the interface between psychology and organized medicine. For each issue, organized medicine has a history of standing between psychology and the ability to achieve the goal. As concerns regarding the number of providers and the level of utilization of health care services have increased, all types of health professionals have found themselves pitted against each other in a battle to win the health care dollar.

Since the 1890s organized medicine has demonstrated that it is the most effective health profession in the public relations arena. Starting at the turn of the twentieth century, organized medicine teamed with hospitals to create the ultimate public relations campaign. These organizations created the concept that health care must be provided by physicians in hospitals to assure the health and well-being of the American people. While there are clearly elements of truth within this premise, the most striking aspect of this partnership was the ability of these two groups to essentially vanquish other competitors such as osteopathic medicine.

2.33.6.5 The Professional School Movement

Organized medicine has been nothing short of remarkably successful at convincing the American public they should, using tax dollars, finance the education of American physicians. Starting with the passage of Medicare in 1965, taxpayers have subsidized the training of each American physician. These subsidies support both medical school education and, to a larger degree, training in residencies. Despite the fact that it now appears there is a clear excess of specialist physicians in the US, since the 1960s Americans have provided extraordinary subsidization for the training of American physicians. In 1997 alone, each American spent $48.91 on graduate medical education (GME). Annually, the federal government spends about $75 000 for each resident in training. The overall cost of the GME program exceeded $6 billion in 1997 (Medicare Payment Advisory Commission [MedPAC], 1997). Provisions included in the Balanced Budget Act of 1997 are expected to begin to curtail the program.

There is an important "reverse psychology" to the marketing support for graduate medical education. Simply put, if Americans spend this much to support the training of their physicians, physicians must be more valuable than any other health professionals. Indeed, if one examines the record of support for other health professions it is negligible in contrast to the monies provided to physician training.

Psychology, in particular, receives a very limited amount of support under Title VII (the Health Professions provisions) of the Public Health Service Act. Although medicine and the other nonphysician health care professions receive support under this initiative, support for psychology's internships or residencies is virtually nonexistent. It is the inclusion of physicians and professional nursing under GME and Title VII (or VIII for nursing) that creates the circular outcome that more money must be spent on physician training and advanced practice nursing and less on other health professions. Since psychologists are not formally included under the various federal government training programs, the limited value of the profession to the health of the nation is continuously demonstrated. Without inclusion, it is unlikely that psychology will become a critical health profession in the USA (Dunivin, 1994). And, since the vast majority of psychology's graduate students are now within professional schools, it is their leadership that must steer this legislative recognition.

2.33.7 OPPORTUNITIES FOR THE FUTURE

As psychologists have transitioned from mental health providers to health care providers, the opportunities have never been greater (Johnstone et al., 1995). Since the 1970s the field of psychology has changed substantially. One simple indication of the magnitude of this change is the increase in the number of psychologists. Between 1974 and 1990, it is estimated that the number of psychologists increased by 300%. This growth was accompanied by a 72% increase in the number of psychology training programs. If these estimates are correct, psychology's overall workforce increased from a ratio of 8.6 psychologists per 100 000 people in 1959 to nearly 22.4 psychologists per 100 000 people in 1989. There are definitely the numbers to be a major player in the legislative and health care arenas.

To cite one concrete example of an evolving opportunity: in the late 1990s, as many as 100 million Americans have chronic health conditions that limit one or more of their activities. Chronic health conditions engender significant cost. Individuals with activity limitations account for only 17% of the population but 40% of all medical expenditures. The per capita cost for individuals with chronic conditions are three times greater than individuals without these conditions.

Psychologists frequently care for individuals with chronic health conditions. Within settings such as rehabilitation hospitals, psychologists perform diverse activities ranging from provision of direct psychological care to the organization and management of all services to individuals with disabilities. In each of these examples psychologists are critical to the well-being of these individuals with chronic health conditions. The overall value of psychologist contributors in these types of health settings is intuitive but not well demonstrated empirically. Undoubtedly, as is reflected by the trend towards disease management models, more attention will be directed toward chronic health conditions in the future. Psychologists have the opportunity to demonstrate their critical role in treating those who are afflicted with chronic conditions.

It is a political and public policy decision as to which profession's training programs will be supported by the federal government. Psychology possesses the numbers, maturation, and clinical value to qualify. The underlying issue is: do psychologists collectively possess the necessary political will? There are many areas within the health care system in which psychological expertise can make a very real difference in the lives of the nation's citizens. The underlying question remains, however: will the next generation of psychologists take up the challenge?

2.33.8 CONCLUSION

Psychology is one of the "learned professions" and as such, possesses the responsibility of effectively addressing society's pressing needs. During the past decade, our nation's health care system has undergone tremendous structural changes which have had direct implications for the profession. These have not been easy times for the profession, especially for those in solo private practice. There has been an unprecedented acceptance of managed care, increasing requirements for professional accountability and the provision of cost-effective services, and a gradual awareness of the clinical potential inherent in technological advances within the communications and computer industries—that is, telehealth. Simultaneously, with the advent of the professional school movement there has been an exponential growth in the number of professional psychologists.

The period to 2010 will provide professional psychology with numerous opportunities and challenges. To survive and flourish, the profession must internally decide what are its strengths and where can it best excel—psychology is no longer merely one of the mental health professions. Psychologists must ensure that their academic and practice communities work together to address society's needs. Concerted efforts, especially by the leadership of the professional schools, must be made to ensure that psychology is expressly recognized as one of the health professions throughout the federal government's reimbursement and health training initiatives (i.e., GME and Title VII). The profession must further systematically seek to ensure that its "scope of practice" reflects advances in training, including obtaining prescription privileges and working collaboratively throughout the health care arena.

The behavioral sciences and specifically psychology have much to offer to the nation's health care struggles. It is unclear, however, whether the next generation of graduates is collectively willing to become personally involved in the necessary political and public policy endeavors.

ACKNOWLEDGMENT

The opinions expressed by Morgan T. Sammons represent his views as a private citizen and in no way represent the official views or positions of the US Navy or the Department of Defense.

2.33.9 REFERENCES

Balanced Budget Act of 1997, Pub. L. No. 105–33, 111 Stat. 251 (August 5, 1997). H. Conf. Rpt. #105–217.

Benson, C. J., Schreck, R. C., Underwood, F. B., & Greathouse, D. G. (1995). The role of army physical therapists as nonphysican health care providers who prescribe certain medications: observations and experiences. *Physical Therapy*, *75*(5), 380–386.

Bingaman, J., Frank, R. G., & Billy, C. L. (1993). Combining a global budget with a market driven delivery system: Can it be done? *American Psychologist*, *48*(3), 270–276.

Blanck, R. R., & DeLeon, P. H. (1996). News from Washington, DC—Managed care: Strongly conflicting views. *Professional Psychology: Research and Practice*, *27*(4), 323–324.

Brown, W. A. (1994). Placebo as a treatment for depression. *Neuropsychopharmacology*, *10*(4), 265–269.

DeLeon, P. H. (1989). New roles for "old" psychologists. *The Clinical Psychologist*, *42*(1), 8–11.

DeLeon, P. H., Bulatao, E. Q., & VandenBos, G. R. (1994). Federal government initiatives in managed health care. In S. A. Shueman, S. L. Mayhugh, & B. S. Gould (Eds.), *Managed behavioral health care: An industry perspective* (pp. 97–112). Springfield, IL: Charles C. Thomas.

DeLeon, P. H., Fox, R. E., & Graham, S. R. (1991). Prescription privileges: Psychology's next frontier? *American Psychologist*, *46*, 384–393.

DeLeon, P. H., Frank, R. G., & Wedding, D. (1995). Health psychology and public policy: The political process. *Health Psychology*, *14*(6), 493–499.

DeLeon, P. H., Kjervik, D. K., Kraut, A. G., & VandenBos, G. R. (1985). Psychology and nursing: A natural alliance. *American Psychologist*, *40*, 1153–1164.

DeLeon, P. H., Sammons, M. T., & Sexton, J. L. (1995). Focusing on society's real needs: Responsibility and prescription privileges? *American Psychologist*, *50*(12), 1022–1032.

DeLeon, P. H., & VandenBos, G. R. (1991). Psychotherapy in managed health care: Integrating federal policy with clinical practice. In C. S. Austad & W. H. Berman (Eds.), *Psychotherapy in managed health care: The optimal use of time & resources* (pp. 251–263). Washington, DC: American Psychological Association.

DeLeon, P. H., VandenBos, G. R., & Bulatao, E. Q. (1991). Managed mental health care: A history of the federal policy initiative. *Professional Psychology: Research and Practice*, *22*, 15–25.

DeLeon, P. H., & Wiggins, J. G. (1996). Prescription privileges for psychologists. *American Psychologist*, *51*(3), 225–229.

Dorken, H. (1990). Malpractice claims experience of psychologists: Policy issues, cost-comparisons with psychiatrists, and prescription privileges implications. *Professional Psychology: Research and Practice, 21*, 150–152.

Dunivin, D. L. (1994). Health professions education: The shaping of a discipline. *American Psychologist, 49*, 868–878.

Fiscal Year 1989 Department of Defense Appropriations Act, Pub. L. No. 100–463, 102 Stat. 2270 (October 1, 1988).

Fiscal Year 1998 Department of Defense Appropriations Act, Pub. L. No. 105–56, 111 Stat. 1203 (October 8, 1997). S. Rpt. #105–45; H. Conf. Rpt. #105–265.

Fiscal Year 1998 Departments of Veterans Affairs and Housing and Urban Development, and Independent Agencies Appropriations Act, Pub. L. No. 105–65, 111 Stat. 1344 (October 27, 1997). Sen Rpt. #105–53.

Flannery, F. T. (1997). Liability in the diagnosis and treatment of myocardial infarction: The physician's insurers association of America study. *Legal Medicine Open File 1997*, 12–15.

Frank, R. G. (1993). Health care reform: An introduction. *American Psychologist, 48*(3), 258–260.

Frank, R. G., & Kivlahan, C. (1997). *The use of information and misinformation in a state health reform initiative*. Washington, DC: National Academy Press.

Frank, R. G., & Ross, M. J. (1995). The changing workforce. The role of health psychology. *Health Psychology, 14*(16), 519–525.

Frank, R. G., Sullivan, M. J., & DeLeon, P. H. (1994). Health care reform in the states. *American Psychologist, 49*(10), 855–867.

Frank, R. G., & VandenBos, G. R. (1994). Health care reform: The 1993–1994 evolution. *American Psychologist, 94*(10), 851–854.

Glueckauf, R. L., Frank, R. G., Bond, G. R., & McGrew, J. H. (Eds.) (1996). *Psychological practice in a changing health care system*. New York: Springer.

Health Insurance Portability and Accountability Act of 1966, Pub. L. No. 104–191, 110 Stat. 1936 (August 21, 1996). H. Conf. Rpt. #104–736.

Healy, D. T. (1990). The psychopharmacological era: Notes towards a history. *Journal of Psychopharmacology, 4*(3), 152–167.

Institute of Medicine. (1996). *Telemedicine: A guide to assessing telecommunications in health care*. Washington, DC: National Academy Press.

Johnstone, B., Frank, R. G., Belar, C., Berk, S., Bieliauskas, L. A., Bigler, E. D., Caplan, B., Elliott, T. R., Glueckauf, R. L., Kaplan, R. M., Kreutzer, J. S., Mateer, C. A., Patterson, D., Puente, A. E., Richards, J. S., Rosenthal, M., Sherer, M., Shewchuk, R., Siegel, L. J., & Sweet, J. J. (1995). Psychology in health care: Future directions. *Professional Psychology: Research and Practice, 26*(4), 341–365.

Jones, C. B., Cohen, S. A., Munsat, P. E., Dorris, J. F., & Berson, B. S. (1996). *Cost-effectiveness and feasibility of the DoD psychopharmacology demonstration project: Final report* (VRI-DSID3-1.08 WP96-1 (R.01)). Arlington, VA: Vector Research.

Klein, D. F. (1995). Psychopharmacological practice and health reform. *Psychiatric Annals, 25*, 79–83.

Kraemer, H. C. (1995). Methodological and statistical progress in psychiatric clinical research: A statistician's perspective. In F. E. Bloom & D. J. Kupfer (Eds.), *Psychopharmacology: The fourth generation of progress* (pp. 1849–1860). New York: Raven.

Lorion, R. P., Iscoe, I., DeLeon, P. H., & VandenBos, G. R. (Eds.) (1996). *Psychology and public policy: Balancing public service and professional need*. Washington, DC: American Psychological Association.

Luker, K., Austin, A., Hogg, C., Ferguson, B., & Smith, K. (1997). Patient's views of nurse prescribing. *Nursing Times, 93*, 51–54.

Medicare Payment Advisory Commission (MedPAC). (1997, October). *Selected medicare payment policies*. Washington, DC: Department of Health and Human Services.

Miller, I. J. (1996). Managed care is harmful to outpatient mental health services: A call for accountability. *Professional Psychology: Research and Practice, 27*(4), 349–363.

Murray, C. H., & Lopez, A. D. (1997). Global mortality, disability, and the contribution of risk factors: Global burden of disease study. *Lancet, 349*, 1436–1442.

National Health Policy Forum (1997). *Issue brief. Mental health parity: Unresolved issues affecting employers, consumers, and insurance companies.* (No. 709). Washington, DC: George Washington University.

Nonphysician prescribing doubles (1996, June 17). *American Medical News, 39*(23), 2.

Olfson, M., Pincus, H. A., & Sabshin, M. A. (1994). Pharmacotherapy in outpatient psychiatric practice. *American Journal of Psychiatry, 151*(4), 580–585.

Peterson, B. D., West, J., Pincus, H. A., Kohout, J., Pion, G. M., Wicherski, M. M., Vandivort-Warren, R. E., Palmiter, M. L., Merwin, E. I., Fox, J. C., Clawson, T. W., Rhodes, K. K., Stockton, R., Ambrose, J. P., Blankertz, L., Dwyer, K. P., Stanhope, V., Fleischer, M. S., Goldsmith, H. F., Witkin, M. A., Atay, J. E., & Manderscheid, R. W. (1997). An update on human resources in mental health. In R. W. Manderscheid & M. A. Sonnenschein (Eds.), *Mental health, United States, 1996* (pp. 168–204). Rockville, MD: US Department of Health and Human Services.

Platman, S. R., Dorgan, R., & Gerhardt, R. J. (1976). Some social and political ramifications of utilizing nonphysicians as chemotherapists. *International Journal of Social Psychiatry, 22*, 65–69.

Preskorn, S. H. (1996). A dangerous idea. *Journal of Practical Psychiatry and Behavioral Health, 1*, 231–234.

Request for comments on legal issues relating to telemedicine. (1996, August 9). *Federal Register, 61*(155), 41640.

Resnick, R. J., DeLeon, P. H., & VandenBos, G. R. (1997). Evolution of professional issues in psychology: Training standards, legislative recognition, and boundaries of practice. In J. R. Matthews & C. E. Walker (Eds.), *Basic skills and professional issues in clinical psychology* (pp. 281–303). Needham Heights, MA: Allyn and Bacon.

Rudorfer, M. V. (1995). Editor's note. *Psychopharmacology Bulletin, 31*, 453–455.

Sammons, M. T., & Brown, A. B. (1997). The Department of Defense psychopharmacology demonstration project: An evolving program for postdoctoral education in psychology. *Professional Psychology: Research and Practice, 28*(2), 107–112.

Sanchez, P. N., & Kohn, M. (1991). Differentiating medical from psychological disorders: How do medical and nonmedically trained clinicians compare? *Professional Psychology: Research and Training, 22*, 124–126.

Sierles, F. S., & Taylor, M. A. (1995). Decline of US medical student career choice of psychiatry and what to do about it. *American Journal of Psychiatry, 152*, 1416–1426.

State of California, Office of Statewide Health Planning and Development, Division of Health Professions Development. (1982, November). *Prescribing and dispensing pilot projects* (Final report to the legislature and to the healing arts licensing boards). Sacramento, CA: Author.

Telemedicine activity triples in one year, survey says (1997, November 10). *American Medical News, 40*(42), 17.

US Congress, Office of Technology Assessment (1995). *Telecommunications technology and Native Americans:*

Opportunities and challenges. (OTA-ITC-621). Washington, DC: US Government Printing Office.

US Department of Commerce (1997, January). *Telemedicine report to Congress.* (#1997–418–626/42023). Washington, DC: US Government Printing Office.

US Department of Defense (1996, June 5). Testimony on Fiscal Year 1997 Department of Defense Appropriations. S. Hrg #104–756. (ISBN 0–16–054069–0). Washington, DC: US Government Printing Office.

US General Accounting Office (1997a, February). *Telemedicine: Federal strategy is needed to guide investments.* (#GAO/NSIAD/HEHS-97–67). Washington, DC: US Government Printing Office.

US General Accounting Office (1997b, April). *Defense health care: Need for more prescribing psychologists is not adequately justified.* (GAO/HEHS-97–83). Washington, DC: US Government Printing Office.

VandenBos, G. R., & DeLeon, P. H. (in press). Clinical geropsychology and US federal policy. In M. Hersen & V. B. Van Hasselt (Eds.), *Handbook of Clinical Geropsychology.* New York: Plenum.

VandenBos, G. R., DeLeon, P. H., & Belar, C. D. (1991). How many psychologists are needed? It's too early to know! *Professional Psychology: Research and Practice, 22*(6), 441–448.

Wennberg, J. E. (1984, November). Testimony before the US Senate Appropriations Committee. Variations in Medical Practice. (S. Hrg. #98–1239). pp. 2–37.

West, J. C., Zarin, D. A., & Pincus, H. A. (1997). Clinical and psychopharmacologic practice patterns of psychiatrists in routine practice. *Psychopharmacology Bulletin, 33*(1), 79–86.

Whitcomb, M. E., & Miller, R. S. (1995). Participation of international medical graduates in graduate medical education and hospital care to the poor. *Journal of the American Medical Association, 274,* 696–699.

2.34
The Evolution of Managed Behavioral Health Care: A Psychologist's Perspective on the Role of Psychology

CLARISSA C. MARQUES
Green Spring Health Services Inc., Columbia, MD, USA

2.34.1 CHANGE AND INSTABILITY: CONTEXT FOR MANAGED BEHAVIORAL HEALTH CARE

The delivery of behavioral health care services can be characterized by a process of continuous, if not at times chaotic, changes in response to a rapidly evolving health care environment and instability in the role of the behavioral health care provider in providing services to consumers. It is easy, if not simplistic, to view the changes as precipitated by the advent of managed care itself, but the evolution of managed behavioral health care lies in the behavioral health service system itself and the economics of providing behavioral health care services (Feldman, 1993; Mechanic, Schlesinger, & McAlpine, 1995). The context for the development of managed behavioral health care was, at least in part, provided by the system for delivering behavioral health services. In particular, four aspects of the delivery system provided context for the development of managed behavioral health care.

(i) Diversity in the professional categories of providers delivering behavioral health care services and the training associated with each category of provider to provide behavioral health care services

(ii) Variety in the therapeutic orientation(s) of the behavioral health care providers even within any given professional category of provider.

(iii) Variance in the modalities of treatment available for individuals with mental disorders with limited information to compare the outcome of care by modality.

(iv) Fragmentation in the continuity of care for individuals across levels of care or between providers within the same level of care.

While these characteristics of the delivery system could have been valuable in generating multiple approaches to the challenges of providing services to individuals with mental disorders, instead these characteristics led to confusion for the consumer and added costs for the payor. There was little in the way of consensus-based decision-making for matching a consumer's behavioral health care needs with a type of provider (or providers) best able to deliver the recommended modality (or modalities) of treatment to achieve the optimal outcome for the individual for the dollar spent on service. Each individual was on his or her own to navigate the delivery system and each payer complained that there must be a better way to attain value for the health care dollar. Managed behavioral health care grew out of an effort to stem the raising costs of mental health and substance abuse services, while rationalizing a delivery system that appeared fragmented and confusing to consumers and payors (Berlant, Trabin, & Anderson, 1994).

2.34.2 CONCEPTS OF MANAGED BEHAVIORAL HEALTH CARE

Managed behavioral health care, as an industry, is frequently characterized as a single program without differentiation. However, the reality is that managed behavioral health care organizations vary by key dimensions in a matrix of the: type of program(s) offered, populations served, service delivery system(s) offered, benefit(s) managed, and funding arrangement(s) offered to purchasers. Each of these characteristics in combination can create a significantly different type of managed behavioral health care program with differing impacts on the consumers and providers of services.

2.34.2.1 Types of Programs

It is difficult to discuss the management of care separately from the delivery system that is providing the care. However, it is an important feature of managed behavioral health care to track where the roles of the manager and provider of care are the same and where these roles diverge. It is equally important to note the ability of the managed behavioral health care organization to direct consumers within the delivery system. The types of behavioral health care management can be seen in three broad categories of patient care management: (i) utilization management, (ii) staff practice management, or (iii) network management.

Utilization management is one of the earlier forms of managed behavioral health care derived from the peer review process. At its core, this form of managed behavioral health care consists of a review of the care, either inpatient or outpatient, conducted prospectively, concurrently, or retrospectively, to determine if the care being recommended or the care being provided meets the criteria of being medically necessary. A variant of utilization management is applying the utilization management principles for individuals with catastrophic or high-risk conditions only leading to intensive utilization management for a circumscribed group of individuals with high-risk conditions. For the consumer, utilization management does little to assist the individual in navigating among the categories of professional providers offering services, evaluating the appropriate treatment options, or monitoring the quality of care received. For the purchaser, utilization management contains the cost of care, but does little to assure that the health care dollar is being spent wisely. For the provider, utilization review entails constantly building a case for the medical necessity of the care being recommended and risking that a reviewer will not make the same determination as the provider putting payment for services at risk. One of the most appealing aspects of a utilization review program, from the consumer and provider perspectives, is that this form of managed care is essentially nondirectional in that the managed behavioral health care organization is not directing the consumer to any particular provider. Instead, the managed behavioral health care organization is making a medical necessity determination regarding the care that is being provided or recommended without directing the consumer to a particular provider. The provider continues to be the provider and manager of care with a peer reviewer overseeing the medical necessity of care for reimbursement purposes.

A staff model delivery of care has long been a mainstay of the publicly funded health care delivery system, but has become more common with staff model health maintenance organizations that delivered managed behavioral health care through a staff model environment (Feldman, 1994). At the core of staff model delivery systems is the delivery and management of most, if not all, of the behavioral health care services needed by a population of members through staff providers. All services required by members are provided through the staff model delivery system and any services needed outside of the staff model delivery system must be preauthorized by a representative of the staff model delivery system. Management of the care continues to rest with the staff model provider.

While this model worked well in areas with high geographic concentrations of members and where mental health care was integrated with other health care, it tended to not work as well for accounts with a wide geographic dispersion of members and where the health care was not well integrated with other health care options. National employers with multiple health care plans tended to not opt for staff models except in selected geographic areas with a high concentration of employees. For consumers their options were limited to receiving care through the staff model delivery system, with the attendant pressure on evening and weekend appointments. For providers there was no access to these consumers unless the provider was a member of the staff delivery system. For purchasers the options were clearer, tighter quality control was possible and costs contained, but the choice and access to providers was limited to the staff model delivery system.

Most staff model delivery systems have evolved into mixed staff and network model delivery systems, partly to respond to consumer need for greater choice and access to providers, but also to respond to the economic need to have providers in geographically distributed areas and to have a range of behavioral health care subspecialists, yet not having enough membership in areas to support a full staff model. Network providers augmented the existing staff model delivery system, providing greater geographic coverage, better access to appointments for consumers, and a wider array of subspecialty expertise. The development of mixed staff and network model delivery systems helped expand the range of health plans within geographic regions, but continued to have difficulty in meeting the needs of the national or regional employers who wanted consistency in the delivery of behavioral health care benefits. With the management of care within mixed staff and network model delivery systems, it became increasingly difficult to ensure that the treatment protocols and guidelines followed by the staff model delivery system were being applied equally and effectively across the panel of network providers. The larger the panel of network providers, the less likelihood of the provider feeling closely affiliated to the culture, the practice, and the economics of the health plan. The provider within the staff model delivery system maintained dual roles as the provider and internal manager of the care and an external manager of care provided within the network.

In response to national and regional employers, managed behavioral health organizations created national networks of participating providers all credentialed to meet standard requirements and included in practice management efforts to ensure some minimal consistency in the management of care. To guide the consumer to the manager of care was a representative of the managed behavioral health care organization, typically a behavioral health clinician, whose task was to assess the immediate needs of the consumer and match the consumer to the provider(s) within the network best able to initiate treatment. In the network model delivery system, the role of the provider and manager of care became truly separate. The manager of care became the consumer advocate coordinating aspects of care delivered through a provider delivery system and became responsible for overseeing the quality and outcome of care delivered by the provider. Purchasers of behavioral health care benefits could solve the dilemma of the diversity of providers, treatment modalities, outcome management methodologies and cost by holding a single managed behavioral health care organization accountable for all the complexity in the field, while retaining control of the quality of services and cost of care. For the consumer, the network model delivered wider access to providers with greater standardization in practice and a consumer advocate to coordinate care. For the provider, the network management model took away a key functional role in the management of care and left the provider struggling with the boundary between providing and managing care.

2.34.2.2 Populations Served

The population of patients to be served by managed behavioral health care organizations can also vary along key dimensions, such as the need for service and utilization of resources, demographic characteristics of the patient population, presence of comorbid medical/health conditions, and previous mental health and/or substance abuse treatment. An understanding of the population to be served provides the basis for the pricing and underwriting assumptions associated with the funding for the cost of care and for the design of the types of programs that will be offered.

2.34.2.2.1 Need for service and utilization of resources

A population-based perspective requires the examination of individuals in five broad clusters:

(i) those who *do not need* mental health and/or substance abuse services and *do not seek* those services;

(ii) those who *do need* mental health and/or substance abuse services and *do not seek* those services;

(iii) those who *do need* mental health and/or substance abuse service and *seek inappropriate* services;

(iv) those who *do need* mental health and/or substance abuse services and *do seek* those appropriately; and

(v) those who *do not need* mental health and/or substance abuse services, *yet seek* the services anyway.

Each cluster has a different impact on the managed behavioral health care organization, the broader health plan, the providers within the managed behavioral health care organization and the health plan organization, the consumer and his/her family, and the society in which the individual resides and the resources needed to sustain public health.

2.34.2.2.2 Demographic variables

Within these broad clusters, there are also the more traditional demographic characteristics of populations, including age, gender, marital status, and geographic location of residence. The demographic characteristics are typically available as part of a membership eligibility database determined at the time that the individual and his or her eligible dependents were enrolled within a health care program. These same membership eligibility databases tend to exclude information that would provide additional insight into the impacted populations, such as racial/ethnic affiliation, educational, occupational, and income level. These are variables that are sometimes inferred, but the absence of data on the broad population limits some of the programming that can be developed to address specific needs.

2.34.2.2.3 Presence of comorbid medical/health conditions

An intersecting population-based variable is the presence or absence of a comorbid medical/health condition. This variable is bidirectional. Individuals with one or more significant comorbid medical/health condition(s) may not have a specific mental health diagnosis, yet may experience an improved outcome with the presence of focused behavioral health intervention (Barlow, 1994a, 1994b). A good example is the improved mortality rate for individuals with breast cancer who receive a focused behavioral health intervention in conjunction with the prescribed treatment regimen as compared to those individuals receiving the treatment regimen without the behavioral health intervention. For individuals with an identifiable mental health diagnosis, the provision of behavioral health services may be complicated by the presence of one or more comorbid medical/health condition(s) (Pallak, Cummings, Dorken, & Henke, 1994). An example would be the difficulty in providing treatment for a reoccurring major depressive disorder with an individual who had recently undergone an organ transplant procedure. While the examples may seem obvious, the population-based variables related to the incidence and prevalence of medical/health conditions within a given population will influence the type of managed behavioral health care program and the funding to make the services available to individuals.

2.34.2.2.4 Presence of previous mental health and/or substance abuse treatment

If past behavior is the best predictor of future behavior, then previous mental health and/or substance abuse treatment is one of the indicators of the presence of serious and/or persistent mental illness. Approximately only one of five people suffering from a mental disorder seeks treatment, suggesting a significant unmet need in services. These individuals are likely to use the general medical delivery system, thereby increasing the overall health care costs (Pallak, et al., 1994).

2.34.2.3 Service Delivery Systems

Behavioral health care services have historically been offered in one of two types of delivery systems, either open access to any licensed provider or through staff model community based treatment programs. Managed behavioral health care organizations brought an array of other options for service delivery systems, including directed access, guided access, delegated access and integrated delivery systems.

2.34.2.3.1 Open access

Open access to any licensed provider had been the delivery system associated with indemnity insurance programs with the only limitation on service being an annual and/or lifetime benefit maximum. For consumers not covered under an indemnity insurance program, community mental health centers and other publicly funded community treatment resources were available for consumers seeking mental health and substance abuse specialty care. Additionally, mental health and substance abuse services were offered through staff model treatment programs associated with many staff model based health plans. The first limitation placed on an open-access delivery system was the establishment of a contracted panel or network of providers. However, most health insurance plans continued to market their traditional indemnity program as having in excess of 95% or more of all available physicians in a geographic area as an incentive for consumers to select their insurance product leading to an essentially open access to almost any licensed provider. These contracted networks, however, were built for a health insurance product, and, for the most part, determined that any licensed provider meant any licensed physician. Many of the contracted networks for indemnity insurance products excluded psychologists and rarely included any other mental health professional types. When psychologists were included, it was not with the intent to include broad participation, but tended to include psychologists in practice with a contracted network physician or psychologists with specific expertise that was not covered by the contracted network physician panel. Consumer access to nonphysician behavioral health care providers was limited to referral by a physician within the contracted network physician panel. Physicians made relatively few referrals, particularly for outpatient-based services, and referrals for inpatient-based services were made when a patient was in acute need of that level of care, which typically meant in need of a psychiatrist. As psychologists, other mental health professionals and consumers applied pressure to health insurance plans to include them as part of the contracted network of providers, health insurance plans turned to managed behavioral health care organizations to manage the diversity of behavioral health care providers and the challenges of credentialing and contracting with a network of specialists in the treatment of mental health and substance abuse disorders.

2.34.2.3.2 Directed access

Managed behavioral health care organizations brought a new twist to the development of contracted networks, the ability to contract with a wide array of behavioral health care providers by having credentialing standards specific to each professional category. Managed behavioral health care organizations also brought the subspecialty expertise needed to differentiate between the types of services offered by the behavioral health care provider and the levels of care available in the treatment continuum. Managed behavioral health care organizations created the network to handle all mental health and substance abuse service needs and created the basis for "carving out" the mental health and substance services from the health plan product. The consumer was offered the opportunity to access services through the managed behavioral health care organization directly rather than exclusively through the contracted network of physicians for the health plan. This development led to what has become known as a "gate-kept" model for service delivery. Because the consumer no longer needed to access services through a network physician for the health plan, access to the specialty mental health care network was directed by a representative, typically a clinician, of the managed behavioral health care organization to the provider (or providers) in the network able to address the consumers needs.

Directed access continues to exist, primarily in programs associated with health maintenance organizations, and where the services are provided within a more defined geographic area. The intent is to have a defined group of quality, multidisciplinary behavioral health care providers who can function as a part of an organized health care system and to discourage consumers from seeking services outside of the organized health care system both for cost and quality of care concerns. The development of directed access delivery systems also led to a significant decrease in the number of providers needed to deliver mental health and substance abuse services.

2.34.2.3.3 Guided access

Managed behavioral health care organizations also needed to address the requirements of purchasers, typically large employer groups, who desired access to a specialty mental health and substance abuse contracted network and wanted to permit consumers the ability to have broad access to providers. Consumer requirements drove the modifications to the directed access model of service delivery. In particular, consumers were concerned about the continuity of care and played an active role in nominating providers to be included in the network to minimize the disruption in care when a managed behavioral health care program was implemented. Consumers also found value in having a clinician at the managed behavioral health care organizations who was able to discuss the consumer's unique needs and able to assist the consumer by providing information about types of providers, types of treatment modalities, and expectations of treatment. The clinician at the managed behavioral health care organization became the consumer's advocate in jointly determining what services were needed, ensuring that the consumer had the referral(s) needed to address the situation, and creating options for flexible case management.

The guided access delivery system is inherently a more expensive program. However, from the consumer's perspective, it reduced the discontinuity of care created by more directed access programs and reduced the fragmentation that plagued the historic delivery system because the care was now more flexibly coordinated. Providers bemoaning the intrusion of managed behavioral health organizations into the treatment planning process would be surprised at the number of questions that consumers have regarding the provision of mental health and substance abuse services that consumers are unwilling or unable to address with a provider directly.

2.34.2.3.4 Delegated access

Perhaps one of the older forms of delegated access has been the community mental health center program. In delegated access delivery systems, a delivery system is designated as the entry point into the array of options offered by the delivery system. With community mental health centers, the designation as the point of entry was based on geographic catchment areas. To enhance access, many community mental health centers also created satellite sites to improve the availability of entry points. As the consumer entered the delivery system, the providers within the system were delegated the responsibility for managing the care within the limits of what was available using other systems, such as the state hospital system, when needed. Just as guided access to the delivery system was driven by consumer needs, delegated access to the delivery system was driven by provider needs, particularly organized group practices.

Many organized group practices have developed expertise in some of the key elements of the management of behavioral health care services and have positioned themselves as being capable of delivering those services with minimal oversight. Purchasers of managed behavioral health care services have also recognized the role that the organized group practices can play in minimizing administrative costs associated with managed behavioral, yet have remained concerned about handing the entirety of the process over to organized group practices who do not have the significant infrastructure found within managed behavioral health care organizations.

Managed behavioral health organizations have, for the most part, developed various programs for assessing the capacities of organized group practices to manage care, delegating key elements of the clinical management process, and overseeing the quality of care within the group practice. The implementation of a delegated access model can occur with or without any difference in the payment or funding methodology. In other words, organized group practices may have delegated access to outpatient services in which the group is paid on a fee-for-servicebasis, a discounted fee-for-service basis, a case rate basis, or a subcapitated basis. The payment methodology does not dictate the delegated arrangement, but may become a component of the arrangement. This is an important point to make in a time when many providers are seeking to take financial risk for care costs to gain control over the management of care. These are indeed separate issues and providers need to carefully evaluate their capacity to assume risk with the possibility of adverse selection across a smaller population base.

2.34.2.3.5 Integrated delivery systems

Integrated delivery system is a complex concept that means many different things depending upon one's perspective within the delivery system. One notion of an integrated delivery system was the concept of placing all the required levels of care within one integrated delivery system which will allow the purchaser and consumer of health care service to receive all the needed services within a seamless delivery system that would facilitate the needed access to the appropriate level of care at the appropriate time. The difficulty for integrated delivery systems within the behavioral health care arena is that relatively few individuals need the full range of integrated delivery system services. Integrated delivery systems do offer advantages under a case rate payment methodology for those individuals who will need the full continuum of services to manage an episode of care (i.e., inpatient hospitalization, partial hospitalization, intensive outpatient treatment, and ongoing outpatient treatment for maintenance and stabilization), but it is more difficult to have all individuals receive services from a single integrated delivery system because of the consumer issues raised under the directed access model.

Another notion of an integrated delivery system is the concept of providing managed behavioral health care services within a broader health care system. In some ways we have come full circle back to the original notion of delivering direct staff model services within a broader health plan delivery system such as a health maintenance program. Most managed behavioral health care organizations have created mechanisms to imbed the behavioral health services within a broader health plan delivery system by offering direct delivery of services (through staff or contracted clinicians) or by creating a subnetwork of specialty providers that function as the behavioral health service division within the broader health plan meeting the requirements of the health plan for integrated care.

The current state of the managed behavioral health care industry is that most managed behavioral health care organizations have some form of all of the options for delivery system access present within their networks. The terminology may vary from organization to organization, but the concept is a tiered network strategy built upon concentric circles. The widest element of the circle is the universe of all providers which is growing at an exponential rate, followed by the universe of contracted network providers, followed by yet smaller subsets of providers who have one or more specialty arrangements with a managed behavioral health care organization to address specific purchaser or consumer needs.

A provider's experience with a managed behavioral health care organization will be strongly shaped by the nature of the delivery system(s) within which he or she is providing services.

2.34.2.4 Benefits Managed

It goes without saying that health care benefits vary widely. But particularly in the area of mental health and/or substance abuse benefits, the variability is enormous. The variability in access to benefits has led to the extension of the Medicaid program to cover the uninsured and to the parity initiatives on the state and federal level.

Managed behavioral health care organizations can only manage an existing benefit. They can work to improve access and accountability for a limited benefit, but cannot change an existing benefit into a better benefit or create a benefit where one does not exist. Many consumers do not separately consider their mental health and/or substance abuse needs when selecting a health plan. Cost is still typically the primary consideration. Instead, the consumer typically becomes aware of a mental health and/or substance abuse benefit when a crisis emerges.

2.34.2.5 Funding Arrangements Offered

The funding arrangements for managed behavioral health care organizations have two components, the cost of care and the cost of the management of the care. There are three basic types of funding arrangements for managed behavioral health care organizations: (i) administrative services only (ASO), (ii) capitation, and (iii) performance-based risk corridor(s). Everything else is variation on a theme.

ASO is a funding arrangement in which the managed behavioral health care organization is paid for the services rendered in the management of the care. It does not include the cost of the care itself, although the services provided by the managed behavioral health care organization can be quite extensive. The services can include the costs associated with building and maintaining a broad national network, paying claims, handling all reporting requirements, providing 24 hour access to members, and coordinating all aspects of patient care.

Capitation is a funding arrangement in which the managed behavioral health care organization is provided the funds for the cost of care and for the services rendered in the management of care. The cost of care is determined by historical utilization of care when that data is available or by comparing the member characteristics and benefit structure with other comparable accounts and estimating utilization. The cost of care equation has two components, the utilization of services and the unit cost per service. Capitation has particularly impacted psychologists in clinical practice because of the cost per unit of service. The master's-prepared therapists have been willing to contract for a lower cost per unit of service. Physicians have been required inpatient and medication management services, which has enabled them to retain greater leverage on the cost per unit of service. Psychologists have been caught between the two.

Performance-based risk corridor funding has been a mechanism used by purchasers for ensuring accountability in managing the behavioral health care benefit. The managed behavioral health care organization places some or all of their administrative fee at risk for performance within a prescribed corridor along any number of dimensions. Corridors can be established around any number of performance indicators, such as utilization, member satisfaction, timeliness of reporting, and accuracy of claims processing. Corridors can also be established around the cost of care, allowing the managed behavioral health care organization to participate in the cost savings associated with containing the cost of care or to share in the risk associated with failing to meet the cost of care expectations.

Managed behavioral health care organizations are judged by the membership and the revenue associated with the membership. The revenue associated with ASO funding and performance-based risk corridor funding is much more limited than the funding associated with capitation because the cost of care is not included in the revenue equation. The risk associated with adverse selection is also embedded in the revenue associated with capitation, particularly in membership populations in which the historical utilization is not completely known or where the benefit has changed.

A survey conducted in 1995 suggested that of 185.7 million Americans with health insurance, over half (58.2% or 108 million) were enrolled in a managed behavioral health care organization. Managed behavioral health care revenues for 1994 were approximately $2.1 billion with approximately 20% of the membership enrolled in risk-based (capitation), network-based programs and 20% enrolled in nonrisk-based networks and the remainder in hybrid programs, including significant numbers of members involved in employee assistance programs (Oss, 1995).

2.34.3 QUALITY AND ACCOUNTABILITY

The value-added promise of managed behavioral health care organizations has been to improve the quality and accountability within the behavioral health care field by providing objective indicators of quality of care (Marques, Geraty, Harbin, Hoover, & Theis, 1994). The challenge lies more in the promise than in the reality. Managed behavioral health care organizations are poised to have all of the elements necessary to make a significant contribution to the quality of behavioral health care service. Poised because managed behavioral health care organizations have:

(i) access to health care data,

(ii) management information systems to support the collection of health-care data,

(iii) opportunities for outcomes measurement, and

(iv) infrastructures to support evaluation and analysis.

To date, the reality, for the most part, has been short of the opportunity.

2.34.3.1 Access to Health Care Data

All of the managed behavioral health care organizations are gathering enormous quantities of data. Expectations for the ways in which the data could be used have risen dramatically over the past five years. The major questions that impact managed behavioral health care organizations revolve around the internal issues related to the availability of the data, the currency of the data, the integrity of the data, the applicability of the data to questions pertaining to the outcome of care. Questions also revolve around the externally focused issues related to the ability to share the data within the concerns for privacy of health care data, the competitive nature of the organizations and the regulatory pressures impacting the industry. The good news is the increasing efforts at standardization of sets of data used by health care systems and managed behavioral health care organizations. The American Managed Behavioral Healthcare Association (AMBHA) established its own performance indicators for managed behavioral health care organizations in its Performance Measures for Managed Behavioral Health Care Programs (PERMS 1.0) initiative which prompted the members of AMBHA to begin capturing data and reporting comparative data in a common format structure (AMBHA, 1995). The bad news is the increasing expectations by purchasers and consumers about the timeliness, user-friendliness, and accessibility of the data. The corresponding expectations and costs to the managed behavioral health care organizations are shared with the providers, increasing the administrative workload on the providers to supply and audit needed data. There has also been another subtle, but significant, shift in the expectations regarding data availability. The shift is away from a retrospective framework to a more continuous, dynamic framework for the applicability of data. An example might help illustrate the shift. Managed behavioral health care organizations have been collecting patient or member satisfaction data for a number of years, yet that data reflects a retrospective evaluation of member satisfaction with a provider during a specified period of time that predates the survey process. The current purchaser and consumer environment places a premium on receiving that member feedback immediately following the receipt of service, incorporating the data into a dynamic provider profiling tool which then guides the next referral to that provider. The expectation in most cases exceeds the reality, however, the trend is definitely for data availability on a continuous or "real time" manner coupled with the expectation that the data will be used to manage providers and direct care (Bengen-Seltzer, 1995).

2.34.3.2 Management Information Systems to Support the Collection of Health Care Data

The search for the management information system optimized to meet the needs of managed care has been akin to the search for the Holy Grail. Most managed behavioral health care organizations are utilizing management information systems that were originally designed for managed health care, in particular, for utilization review programs. These management information systems do not provide the flexibility needed, in general, to address the current and changing needs of the managed behavioral health care environment.

Managed behavioral health care organizations that have grown through acquisition tend to have "legacy" systems that become a part of the system platform. Managed behavioral health care organizations that have grown through adding new membership in the rapid growth environment of the field have not been able to keep their management information systems updated due to the focus on rapid growth and expansion. Managed behavioral health care organizations that have not grown do not tend to have the resources to allocate to management information system infrastructure development.

On the positive side of the equation, managed behavioral health care organizations have placed a premium on flexibility in the design of the management information systems which has led to systems that are less rigid in architecture, more amenable to customization and change, more modular in their ability to connect to other applications, and better able to integrate with multiple claims payment systems. The fact that these management information systems are built from a flexible platform affords a better opportunity to electronically interface with providers than the structured systems used by health insurance plans.

2.34.3.3 Opportunities for Outcomes Measurement

A similar shift is occurring in the outcomes measurement activities. More traditional indicators of outcome had been evaluated against criteria of reliability and validity. Currently, indicators of outcome have the additional pressure of being confronted by business realities. Managed behavioral health care organizations are using outcomes measurement as one key aspect in the management of the network or providers. The demand is stemming from employers and purchasers of health care services to provide meaningful measures of patient improvement and treatment effectiveness and that the data is collected on an ongoing basis and used in decision-making regarding referral and continued care (Bengen-Seltzer, 1995).

2.34.3.4 Infrastructure to Support Evaluation and Analysis

This is the most vulnerable area within managed care organizations and has led to the development of strategic partnerships with academic and research institutions to provide the independence of evaluation and analysis. In the infancy of managed behavioral health care, much of the data was held as proprietary to the organization and not available for independent review. Given the highly competitive nature of the industry, the position was understandable. However, managed care organizations also had difficulty gaining acceptance of their research and evaluation efforts because of the taint of the information being collected for marketing purposes and had not being subjected to peer review processes. Currently the environment is opening up for collaborative approaches to addressing mental health and substance abuse policy issues with federally funded initiatives and through collaboration with research and training institutions.

2.34.4 IMPACT OF THE ADVOCACY AND CONSUMER MOVEMENTS

In evaluating managed behavioral health care organizations, one cannot underestimate the impact of the advocacy and consumer movements. Both forces have place mental health care at the forefront of a powerful political agenda to bring parity to the federal and state legislative bodies and worked to remove the stigma of mental illness. The parity movement itself would have had a more difficult uphill struggle without the real world experience of the managed behavioral health care organizations in managing care within even unlimited benefit environments. Parity, in the absence of methodologies for managing care, would have been a very difficult initiative to convince purchasers of health care services that the costs would not accelerate exponentially. The data from managed behavioral health care organizations currently providing services in states with parity initiatives implemented provided a basis for the cost estimates associated with the federal parity initiative. Increasingly, the coalitions to shape the mental health and substance abuse policies have forged partnerships between the managers of care and the individuals and advocates most interested in the behavioral services available for those most in need of those services.

2.34.5 PROMISE AND CHALLENGE OF PSYCHOLOGY

Training and education. There have been numerous discussions regarding the number of mental health providers who are entering the field each year and whether there is a surplus of providers. There is a perspective that has been shaped by years of working within managed behavioral health care organizations that can be shared. By all indicators, there is indeed a surplus of mental health providers. The more significant variable, though, is where are the providers electing to deliver service. In any major standard metropolitan area, there is a high likelihood that any given managed behavioral health care organization has a surplus of providers and has closed the network to new providers in that area or has restricted access into the network to providers with particular expertise (most frequently child and adolescent psychiatrists). However, the semirural and rural areas of the country continue to be seriously underserved by behavioral health care providers, as are the urban, inner-city areas, where some of the need for behavioral health care services is the greatest. If psychologists are to make a case for the early identification and timely treatment to address the unmet need and to support more equitable access to coverage for mental health and substance abuse disorders as afforded under various state and federal parity initiatives, the profession will need to actively address the distribution of resources to deliver the required services in underserved areas.

The second part of the discussion is focused on whether the training that psychologists receive has prepared them for the environment into which they will enter. Psychologists frequently report feeling professionally "squeezed" in managed behavioral health care networks between psychiatrists, who because of their medical training and licensure are uniquely situated to provide medication management and inpatient hospital based services, and other master's-prepared therapists, who may be more likely to accept a lower rate of reimbursement than psychologists. The concern seems to stem from the perceived lack of differentiation for psychologists relative to other mental health professionals, with the exception of psychological testing as a distinguishing skill. The unfortunate aspect of the discussion is the difficulty that psychologists have in seeing that the training provided to doctoral-level psychologists is unique among the mental health professionals, not just for the provision of behavioral health care services, but also for the management of behavioral health care systems of care. What most psychologists come to learn in professional practice is that the greatest strength is drawn from all of the subspecialty programs within psychology. Each subspecialty area contributes to a different knowledge and skill base, such as industrial and organizational psychology for the management of health care delivery systems, experimental psychology for the methodology needed to assess the outcome of care, statistical psychology for understanding the meaningfulness of data, social psychology for understanding the impact of social and family systems on the individual, and developmental psychology for understanding the staging process of human development. The list could continue, the profession has yet to prepare graduates to embrace the richness of the field and encourage psychologists to apply themselves to all aspects of the health care system.

There are many forces that will reshape managed behavioral health care. The opening of this chapter addressed the forces at work to create an ever-changing health care environment and those forces will continue to drive the managed behavioral health care organization to evolve to meet the needs of consumers and purchasers of behavioral health care services. The question remains whether psychologists, as a professional group representing multiple subspecialties, find a path for understanding and participation in the evolution of behavioral health care services.

2.34.6 REFERENCES

American Managed Behavioral Healthcare Association (1995). *Performance measures for managed behavioral healthcare programs.* Washington, DC: Author.

Barlow, D. H. (1994a). Psychological interventions in the era of managed competition. *Clinical Psychology: Science and Practice, 1,* 109–122.

Barlow, D. H. (1994b). Health care policy, psychotherapy research, and the future of psychotherapy. *American Psychologist, 51,* 1050–1058.

Bengen-Seltzer, B. (1995). *Fourth generation managed behavioral health: What does it look like?* Alexandria, VA: Manisses Communication Group.

Berlant, J., Trabin T., & Anderson, D. (1994). The value of mental health and chemical dependency benefits: more than meets the eye. In E. Sullivan (Ed.), *Driving down health care costs: Strategies and solutions.* Frederick, MD: Panel Publishers, Division of Aspen Publishers.

Feldman, S. (1993). Managed mental health services: Ideas and issues. In S. Feldman (Ed.), *Managed mental health* (pp. 3–26). Springfield, IL: Charles C. Thomas.

Feldman, S. (1994). Managed mental health: Community mental health revisited? *Managed Care Quarterly, 2,* 13–18.

Marques, C., Geraty, R., Harbin, H., Hoover, K., & Theis, J. (1994). Quality and access in the managed behavioral healthcare industry. *Behavioral Healthcare Tomorrow, 3,* 23–29.

Mechanic, D., Schlesinger, M., & McAlpine, D. (1995). Management of mental health and substance abuse services: State of the art and early results. *The Milbank Quarterly, 73,* 19–55.

Oss, M. (1995). *OPEN MINDS: The Behavioral Health Industry Analyst*, January.

Pallak, M., Cummings, N., Dorken. H., & Henke, C. (1994). Medical costs, Medicaid, and managed mental health treatment: The Hawaii study. *Managed Care Quarterly, 2,* 64–70.

2.35
Demographic Characteristics of Psychologists and Supply/ Demand Issues: The Netherlands

PAUL M.G. EMMELKAMP
University of Amsterdam, The Netherlands
and
A. SCHOLING
University of Groningen, The Netherlands

2.35.1 INTRODUCTION

In 1996 there were approximately 20 000 psychologists in the Netherlands, a country which has nearly 15 million inhabitants. Less than one third of them was organized in the Dutch Psychological Association (Nederlands Instituut van Psychologen (NIP)). As far as clinical psychology is concerned, there are two formal professional registrations, that is, the license of "clinical psychologist" provided by the NIP and the license of "psychotherapist" provided by the government, but this situation will change, as will be discussed below. Since 1988, registration as a psychotherapist has been *conditio sine qua non* for registration as a clinical psychologist. Since 1986 formal course requirements and supervised practice have been required in order to be registered as a psychotherapist; since 1989 also for registration as clinical psychologist. The content of these programs are described in this chapter.

The first clinical psychologist in the Netherlands was appointed in 1942. His tasks were limited to diagnostics and he worked under the supervision of a psychiatrist. If there was interest in therapy in the 1940s and 1950s, this was primarily in psychodynamic therapy. With the rise of the nondirective and behavior therapies in the US and in Great Britain in the 1960s, an increasing number of clinical psychologists got involved in psychotherapy in the Netherlands.

There are some studies in the Netherlands which provide figures about the number and characteristics of psychologists who work in mental health settings (Beekman & Heike, 1991; Brunenberg, Neijmeijer, & Hutschemaekers, 1995; Hutschemaekers, Brunenberg, & Spek, 1993; Neijmeijer & Hutschemaekers, 1995; Trijsburg, Duivenvoorden, & Dijkstra, 1988; van Son & van der Staak, 1993). Estimates in this chapter are based on these studies.

2.35.1.1 The Study of Psychology at the University

In contrast to most other countries, in the Netherlands students follow primarily courses in psychology. After approximately one and a half years in which students have to follow courses in all fields of psychology and in methodology and statistics, students specialize in one of the main directions within psychology: developmental psychology, social psychology, psychonomy (general psychology), work and organizational psychology, personality psychology or clinical psychology, and health psychology. For another two and a half years students follow courses in their specialization, have to conduct research in this area, and undertake practice work under supervision.

Eight universities in the Netherlands offer university programs in clinical psychology or health psychology. The total number of graduates in psychology has stabilized since 1990 at about 1025. Clinical psychology has been one of the most popular specializations over the years; 25–30% of the students choose clinical psychology as their specialization.

2.35.2 POSTGRADUATE EDUCATION

After they have graduated from university (i.e., after the first phase of four years), students have several options. Most of them prefer further training in practice or research in the area of clinical psychology, but only few of them actually get the chance to enter one of the formal postdoctoral training programs. This training includes two training programs in clinical practice and one training program in clinical psychology research.

2.35.2.1 Psychotherapy Training Program

Students who want further education in clinical practice have several options. As noted above, until 1998 two formal registrations exist for psychologists working in the field of mental health care: psychotherapist and clinical psychologist. From 1998 this situation will change, as will be described below. First, some information about the contents and the numbers of trainees in the present training programs is given.

Both programs require several years of training after the academic study has been completed. The Psychotherapy Training program involves courses (440 hours) and supervised practice (at least 125 hours supervision over at least 500 hours psychotherapy). Further, trainees have to undergo some form of psychotherapy ("personal therapy," at least 50 hours). This training is accessible for graduates in (clinical) psychology and medicine, provided that they have completed the relevant courses in their university education. Introductory courses in the psychotherapy training program include psychopathology, general aspects of psychotherapy, skills for handling specific situations in clinical practice, systems theory, and introductions to the main psychotherapy orientations: (i) learning theory/cognitive-behavior therapy, (ii) client-centered therapy, and (iii) psychodynamic therapy.

After the introductory courses, students choose one of these three main orientations in psychotherapy. In this area they have to follow two of the following three specializations: children and adolescents, partner/family therapy, and group psychotherapy, both in theoretical work and in supervised practice. The supervised practice must extend over at least four and at most seven years; during this period the trainee must be working for at least two days a week in a mental health institute.

There is no requirement for the psychotherapy trainee to have a salaried appointment for the clinical practice part of the program; in fact, many trainees work as volunteers, while the costs of the courses total up to about $19 000, apart from the costs for personal therapy (about $4000) and the supervision (ranging from US$0 to 8000). Until 1998, no limitations were imposed on the numbers of psychotherapy trainees. In 1996, approximately 2500 people were registered as psychotherapists, while many were still in training. The estimate for 1997 is that 3016 persons will be registered as psychotherapists (Hutschemaekers, Brunenberg, & Spek, 1993).

2.35.2.2 Clinical Psychology Training Program

The Clinical Psychology Training program involves all the elements of the Psychotherapy Training program. Additionally, courses (*in toto* 740 hours) must be followed in clinical assessment, interventions not considered psychotherapy (crisis intervention and consultation, supportive interventions, pharmacotherapy), ethical aspects, and research in clinical practice. In addition to the requirements for psychotherapy training, an additional 140 hours of supervision are required, 70 about psychodiagnostic issues and another 70 about psychological interventions other than psychotherapy and about ethical aspects.

The training is spread over five years, in which students follow courses for one day a week while working in a mental health institute during the other four days. In contrast to the psychotherapy training program, applicants can follow this program only if they have paid employment in a mental health institute. The costs of this program total up to about $28 000, apart from the costs for personal therapy and supervision. In the period 1991–1997, approximately 350 people started the Clinical Psychology Training program.

2.35.3 HEALTH CARE PSYCHOLOGY TRAINING PROGRAM

Changes are taking place in the postgraduate training program. In 1998 the legal registration existed of two basic professions in the field of mental health care: "health care psychologist" and "psychotherapist." The new Psychotherapy Training program will be more or less comparable to the earlier one. However, in the new Psychotherapy Training program, systemic psychotherapy as an additional main orientation is included.

The Health Care Psychology Training program will spread over two years, in which trainees will have to follow courses (440 hours) during one day a week and acquire clinical experience during the other four days. The program is more or less comparable to the first two years of the earlier Clinical Psychology Training program. Some of the registered health care psychologists will be allowed, after completion of their training, to follow further specialization to be clinical psychologist, which will take another three years. For both the health care and the psychotherapy programs, only paid (partly subsidized) training posts will be acknowledged. As a consequence, the numbers of trainees will be drastically limited. In 1998 and 1999, only a total of 82 applicants each year will be allowed to start health care psychologist training and 42 psychotherapist training in the Netherlands.

Apart from these formal training programs, there is a possibility to obtain registration as a member of one of the various therapy associations, such as the associations of (cognitive) behavior therapy, client-centered therapy, psychodynamic therapy, group therapy, etc., but these registrations are not approved officially by the government. One of the "nonlegal" registrations that is becoming increasingly important is registration by the NIP as a "first-line psychologist." These psychologists offer low-threshold brief psychotherapy; a referral via a general practitioner or mental health institute is not required. Gradually more insurance companies pay a (limited) number of treatment sessions provided by these first-line psychologists.

2.35.3.1 Clinical Psychology Research Training Program

The main route to specialization in scientific research is via an appointment as an "assistant in training" ("Assistent in Opleiding" or AIO in Dutch). An AIO is appointed at a university, either for four years full-time, or for five years four days a week. The AIO appointment is a combination of training (including courses) and conducting a research project; in addition, it is customary that AIOs participate in teaching courses in the department where they are appointed.

The aim of the AIO appointment is to conduct, relatively independently, a scientific research project in the area of clinical psychology, resulting in a Ph.D. thesis. A typical AIO thesis consists of four to six (international) publications on a clinically relevant topic, for example, several experimental studies on cognitive processes, attentional bias (in patients and controls), or studies on the etiology, assessment, and treatment of specific anxiety or affective disorders. In the first year of their appointment, the ratio of research to training is supposed to be 55:45, and in the last year 85:15. In practice, most AIOs spend less time following courses than is formally prescribed.

There are no official data available about the numbers of new AIO vacancies; the estimate is that in the field of clinical psychology about 20 postgraduates start this route every year. The AIO appointment offers hardly any possibilities for obtaining formal clinical registrations, although most AIOs are involved in clinical work as part of their thesis.

2.35.4 WORK SETTINGS OF CLINICAL PSYCHOLOGISTS AND PSYCHOTHERAPISTS

In 1996 approximately 1200 people were licenced as clinical psychologists, but many more psychologists work in mental health settings. The chapter will include below figures for the numbers of clinical psychologists and psychotherapists and their respective fields.

2.35.4.1 Psychologists Working in Mental Health Settings

Beekman and Heike (1991) and Brunenberg, Neijmeijer, and Hutschemaeckers (1995) provide an overview of the kind of institutions in mental health care in which psychologists work. Based on these studies, the following estimates have been made of the number of full-time equivalents (FTEs) of psychologists working in mental health care settings (see Table 1).

Table 1 Number of psychologists (FTEs) working in specific settings.

Type of care	*Numbers*
Institutes	
Alcohol and drug centers	20
Psychiatric hospitals	545
Clinical child care: institution	15
Clinical child care: day center	60
Nursing homes	350
Institutes for mental retardates	380
Institutes for deaf and blind, etc.	60
Noninstitutional care	
School guidance	25
Community mental care	900
Centers for alcohol and drug abuse	55
Private practice	480
Other	85
Justice	
Penal institutes	75
Child custody	12

Source: Beekman and Heijke (1991); Brunenburg et al. (1995).

It is, therefore, estimated that 3082 FTE psychologists work in mental health care. These estimates exclude those psychologists working primarily in administrative functions, those who are primarily involved in teaching or research, and those who are employed as a psychotherapist or work in general hospitals (see below). Clearly, not all of the psychologists working in mental health settings are licenced clinical psychologists. The mean age of psychologists working in clinical settings is estimated to be 40 years; approximately 45% are below and 55% are over the mean age. Slightly more psychologists are female (54%) (Brunenberg et al., 1995). Based on the numbers of students enrolled in clinical psychology training programs, it is expected that the number of female clinical psychologists will increase in the future.

2.35.4.2 Psychologists Working in General Hospitals

Since the early 1950s, clinical psychologists have been employed in general hospitals. Although in the early days the emphasis was on assessment, more recently psychologists have been employed in treatment, teaching, and consultation with medical specialists. In 1988, the National Board of Health (Nationale Raad voor de Volksgezondheid, NRV) recommended that in every general hospital at least one psychologist should be employed. In 1995, there were 122 general hospitals in the Netherlands, with a mean of nearly 500 beds per hospital; 101 hospitals (82%) had a department of clinical psychology. The number of licenced clinical psychologists employed in general hospitals was estimated as 194 FTEs. An additional 70 nonlicensed FTE psychologists were also employed in general hospitals: half were trainees in a clinical psychology training program, a few others psychotherapists. In most hospitals clinical psychology is a separate department where clinical psychologists are considered to be "normal" members of the medical staff. Most patients are referred by the department of neurology, followed by the departments of child medicine, internal medicine, psychiatry, and cardiology (Neijmeijer & Hutschemaeckers, 1995).

The figure of the number of psychologists working in general hospitals in Neijmeijer and Hutschemaeckers' study (1995) is less than that in the study of Beekman and Heijke (1991). The higher number of psychologists in general hospitals in the latter study is presumably due to several factors. First, a number of smaller hospitals closed because of government regulations. Second, in the Beekman and Heijke study, psychologists who worked in administrative functions and psychotherapists were also counted as psychologists, which was not the case in Neijmeijer and Hutschemaeckers' study (1995).

2.35.4.3 Psychotherapists

In 1996, approximately 2500 psychotherapists were officially licenced by the Dutch government. Psychiatrists are not included in this figure, since they are not required to be licenced as a psychotherapists. Based on two studies (Hutschemaekers et al., 1993; Trijsburg et al., 1988), the mean age of psychotherapists is estimated as 48 years; nearly 10% are between the ages of 30 and 40 years; 55% are between the ages of 41 and 50 years and 35% are over age 50 years. Approximately half of the psychotherapists are female. Based on the numbers of students enrolled in postgraduate psychotherapy training programs, it is expected that female psychotherapists will outnumber male psychotherapists in the future. Approximately 70% of the psychotherapists have a university degree in psychology (Hutschemaeckers et al., 1993), but this figure will also change in the future. Nearly all students in psychotherapy training programs have a university degree in psychology.

As to the therapeutic schools, most psychotherapists are members of either the association of cognitive-behavior therapy (30%) or the association of family therapy (29%), followed by the associations of group psychotherapy, client-centered psychotherapy, and child psychotherapy. Only 11% are members of one of the three psychoanalytical psychotherapy associations which co-exist in the Netherlands.

Most psychotherapists (60%) work in community mental health centers (RIAGGS); 20% are employed in a psychiatric hospital and 10% in a general hospital. More than half of the psychotherapists also have a private practice (Hutschemaeckers et al., 1993).

2.35.4.4 Relative Numbers of (Clinical) Psychologists, Psychotherapists, and Psychiatrists

Estimates have been made of the relative number of (clinical) psychologists, psychotherapists, and psychiatrists in the Netherlands. For every 10 000 inhabitants there are two psychologists, one psychotherapist, and one psychiatrist available (Brunenberg et al., 1995). The mental health services are spread across the country, but there are relatively more psychotherapists in the western part of the Netherlands where most larger cities are.

2.35.5 JOB PROSPECTS

Until the early 1970s the demands from society equalled the numbers of psychologists available on the market. Nevertheless, at that time gloomy prognoses were given for the future. If one thing has become clear over the past three decades, it is that accurate forecasts are difficult to make. In the 1970s it was predicted that the numbers of psychology students would decrease in the ensuring years, whereas the demands from society were expected to increase. The contrary has proven true. As a consequence, official data from employment offices show increasing numbers of unemployed psychologists: 330 in 1976/77 growing to 1760 in 1985/86 (Van Drunen & Breijer, 1994). Data from employment offices, however, are unreliable. Some authors (e.g., Beekman & Heijke, 1991) have estimated that about half of the those registered as searching for a job are not searching any longer, partly because they had found a job and partly because they had decided to stop searching for work. In addition, these data do not give information about the type of work that is conducted by clinical psychologists, and more specifically, whether they do the kind of work they have been trained for.

Since 1980, several studies have been conducted on demand/supply issues among persons who recently graduated from university. The studies were published between 1981 and 1996, and were reviewed by Brenninkmeijer and Scholing (1996). Most of the studies concerned the graduates from one university only. The percentages of responders varied from 49.4 to 93%. The percentages of persons unemployed varied from 10.2 to 51.3%. The low percentage came from a study with a response rate of 55.1% (Dons, 1992), the highest from a study with a 93% response rate (Dijkstra & Bannenberg, 1986), which might indicate that, in general, nonresponders tend to be more often unemployed. Although the data in these studies lend no clear support for this hypothesis, such selection bias cannot be ruled out.

Beekman and Heijke (1991) studied the job prospects for clinical psychologists in the interval 1990–1995. They estimated the total number of clinical psychologists searching for a job (the recently graduated and the unemployed) at about 4900 for those five years.

Most studies are not designed to reveal trends over the years. Two studies that were conducted at the department of Clinical Psychology in Groningen, however, lend themselves best to a comparison of data over the years, because (i) they refer to students that followed training in clinical psychology at the same university, lived in the same geographical area, in the time intervals 1983–1986 and 1987–1993, respectively, and (ii) almost identical questionnaires were used. The first study of 120 people (Schaufeli & De Vries, 1988) had a response of 75%; of these 78% were employed. The second study, of 250 people (Scholing & Brenninkmeijer, 1995) had a response of 60%; 83.5% were employed. First, it must be noted that in both studies responders were classified as being employed when they had paid work for at least four hours per week. The percentages unemployed are more than twice as high as the mean unemployment rate in the Netherlands (7–8%), but more favorable than the mean unemployment rate of students from other Dutch programs in clinical psychology. The unemployed were over-represented in the recently graduated: from the graduates of 1992 and 1993, 31.5% were unemployed vs. 13.6%, 5.9%, and 11.1% in the years 1987–1989, respectively.

For nearly 36% of the subjects from the Brenninkmeijer and Scholing (1996) study it took at least six months before they got their first paid job; for almost 20% it took at least a year. This implies a slight improvement compared with the situation for the subjects from the Schaufeli and De Vries (1988) study. It seems that it takes some time and effort before new psychologists find a job, but that many of them succeed eventually. In the second study, 30% of the respondents had a full-time job, in contrast with 45% in the first study. This is in line with the general trend in the Netherlands towards more part-time jobs, usually between 17 and 32 hours a week.

The next question concerns the type of work the responders found. In Table 2 a comparison is made between both studies. It shows a shift to more typically clinical work at the expense of research work (mainly at the university).

Table 2 Type of work, in percentages of numbers of responders.

Type	*Study I*[a]	*Study II*[b]
Clinical psychologist	54	68
Research psychologist	16	13
Academic work, but not as clinical psychologist	12	6
Psychologist	8	6
Under academic level	5	5
Other	5	2

Source: Schaufeli and De Vries (1988);[a] Brenninkmeijer and Scholing (1996).[b]

2.35.6 FUTURE DEVELOPMENTS

There are a few areas that will require more psychologists in the future. Most importantly, it is expected that an increasing number of psychologists will be employed in the care of the elderly. Further, an increasing number of psychologists will be working in penal institutes and with juvenile delinquents. Given the relatively few people addicted to hard drugs in the Netherlands, it is not expected that there will be a major increase in the number of psychologists working with addicts. Further, in contrast to most other countries, relatively few people are HIV positive, so special measures to increase the number of psychologists working in this area are not expected.

There are two other areas in which it is expected that there might need to be an increase in the number of psychologists. First, there is a clear need for clinical psychologists to work in firms and factories, for example, providing stress management training. Another growth area is that of behavioral medicine. Given the emphasis in the Dutch health-care system on accountability, it is expected that an increasing number of psychologists will work with stress-related illnesses that were traditionally the domain of medical practitioners.

2.35.7 REFERENCES

Beekman, T. B. J., & Heijke, J. A. M. (1991). Prognoses voor 1990–1995. De arbeidsmarkt voor klinisch psychologen. [Prognoses for 1990–1995. Employment for clinical psychologists]. *De Psycholoog, 26*(4), 187–193.

Brenninkmeijer, J., & Scholing, A. (1996). Werk en werkloosheid onder klinisch psychologen [Work and unemployment among clinical psychologists]. *De Psycholoog, 31,* 31–35.

Brunenberg, W., Neijmeijer, L., & Hutschemaekers, G. (1995). *Beroep: Psycholoog/pedagoog.* [Profession: Psychologist/child psychologist]. Utrecht: Nederlands Centrum Geestelijke volksgezondheid.

Dons, W. J. (1992). *Waar zijn al die psychologen gebleven?* [Where are all those psychologists?]. Unpublished manuscript. Catholic Univerity of Brabant.

Drunen, P. van, & Breijer, M. (1994). Meer en meer, al maar meer. De ontwikkeling van het aantal psychologen in Nederland. [More and more: The development of the number of psychologists in the Netherlands] *De Psycholoog, 28,* 16–20.

Dijkstra, C., & Bannenberg, J. (1986). Er zijn te veel klinisch psychologen. [There are too many clinical psychologists]. *De Psycholoog, 21,* 178–182

Hutschemaekers, G., Brunenberg, W., & Spek, H. (1993). *Beroep: Psychotherapeut.* [Profession: Psychotherapist]. Utrecht: Nederlands Centrum Geestelijke volksgezondheid.

Neijmeijer, L., & Hutschemaekers, G. (1995). *GGZ in het algemeen ziekenhuis.* [Mental health care in the general hospital]. Utrecht: Nederlands Centrum Geestelijke volksgezondheid.

Schaufeli, W., & Vries, A. de (1988). Werk en werkloosheid onder klinisch psychologen. [Work and unemployment among clinical psychologists]. *De Psycholoog, 23,* 399–406.

Scholing, A., & Brenninkmeijer, J. (1995) *Werk en werkloosheid onder afgestudeerden in de richting klinische psychologie van de RUG*. [Work and unemployment among clinical psychologists graduated at the University of Groningen] Unpublished manuscript. University of Groningen.

Trijsburg, R. W., Duivenvoorden, H. J., & Dijkstra, S. (1988). Psychotherapie als beroep. [Psychotherapy as a profession]. *Nieuws voor Psychotherapeuten*, 1–16.

van Son, M. J. M., & van der Staak, C. P. F. (1993). Inleiding. [Introduction] In W. T. A. M. Everaerd et al. (Eds.), *Handboek Klinische Psychologie* (pp. 1–28). Bohn, Stafleu, van Loghum, Houten.

2.36
Demographic Characteristics of Psychologists and Supply/ Demand Issues: United States

JESSICA L. KOHOUT
American Psychological Association, Washington, DC, USA

2.36.1 INTRODUCTION

Clinical psychology has flourished over the past two decades. The number of psychologists in the health service provider subfields has tripled during this time, from approximately 20 000 in 1975 to almost 70 000 by 1995 or about 2500 new doctorates in the health service provider subfields each year (National Science Foundation [NSF], 1996). Equally striking are changes in the "face" of professional psychology. In the 1970s, a newly minted doctorate in clinical psychology would have been white, male, and in his late twenties. More often than not he would have earned a Ph.D. and would be headed, after licensure, toward academic employment or into independent practice. In contrast, today the new doctorate is likely to be a woman and white, although the representation of persons of color has inched up over time. Graduates today are somewhat older than their colleagues two decades ago, with the median age of new Ph.D.s in 1995 at just over 33 years (Henderson, Clarke, & Reynolds, 1996). Increasingly, new graduates may have earned a Psy.D. degree. The new doctorate is less likely to find as many opportunities for academic employment and independent practice as was the case in the 1970s. In fact, clinical psychology may be faced with some tough decisions as it heads toward the twenty-first century, finding work in a system that is searching for the means to confront worsening social problems in light of shrinking financial resources and shifting national priorities.

This chapter begins by discussing the current supply of clinical psychologists and attempts to answer the question "How many are there?" For the most part, this chapter focuses on doctoral-level psychologists, and in some cases, due to limitations of available data, is forced to narrow its focus further on Ph.D. psychologists. However, no discussion of supply or demand can occur without some reference to the supply of master's-level psychological personnel or to the supply of professionals in mental health fields outside psychology.

The next section addresses the demographic characteristics of clinical psychologists, including the gender, racial/ethnic distributions, age, and types of degrees. One of the largest shifts, that of the changing gender composition or the gender "tip" and the implications for the field is given particular attention.

The third section of this chapter presents information about the employment and geographic distributions of clinical psychologists in the USA. What are clinical psychologists doing, in what types of settings and where?

Fourth, the issue of supply and demand is raised. The question of balance is not reducible simply to provider–client ratios but must consider the many recommendations that have urged psychologists to "shift and expand their focus" (Fox, 1994); look at "systems of delivery" (Kiesler & Morton, 1988; Schneider, 1990); explore a "universe of alternatives" (Sarason, 1981); and conduct a "cognitive reappraisal" (Humphreys, 1996). Discussion is worthwhile and, ultimately, encouraging.

The final section incorporates information on the social, economic, and legal milieus in which psychology is embedded and to which the field must respond, and suggests possible future directions for this major subfield of psychology as it moves into its second century. The chapter concludes with a short summary.

2.36.2 HOW MANY ARE THERE?

In order to answer this question as accurately as possible, there must be some agreement about what is meant by "clinical psychologist." As stated in Section 2.36.1, the data are limited to those with doctoral degrees. However, there still is ample room for variability. The answer varies depending upon the purpose driving this question. For example, one may choose to include those with degrees in all health service provider subfields, those with degrees in clinical only, those who are licensed or those with certain degree and licensure combinations. Training in a health service provider subfield does not ensure that the individual is working as a practitioner or provider of health services. Licensure alone does not guarantee preparedness to deliver services and in fact can be used by those with degrees in other psychological subfields such as applied experimental, social psychology or industrial/organizational psychology as an indication of additional "certification" and qualification. This has proven useful to psychologists who are employed in applied or business settings. It is the case that psychologists may be licensed in more than one state and thus may end up being counted more than once in any census activity.

The first count consists of the pool of clinically trained psychological personnel (all those eligible to provide services at the doctoral level). This pool includes:

(i) residents of the USA,

(ii) those with doctoral degrees in clinical psychology as well as other health service provider subfields,

(iii) licensed or not licensed, and

(iv) may or may not currently be providing direct services.

The second count comprises those who are actively providing direct services and consists of US residents with a doctoral degree in a health service provider subfield in psychology, licensed for the independent practice of psychology, and working in psychology as a health service provider. It is important to remember that the majority of doctoral degrees in the health service provider subfields go to clinical psychology and thus the numbers presented here should be highly representative of this specific subfield. Where possible, the numbers are presented separately for the subfield of clinical psychology.

The data for this chapter were derived by using the American Psychological Association (APA) membership numbers and state-by-state data on the number of licensed psychologists. The analyses originally were performed in preparation of a chapter that appears in a National Institute of Mental Health (NIMH) publication called *Mental health United States, 1996* (Peterson et al., 1996). In 1995, there were some 69 817 clinically trained psychologists in the USA. Approximately 76% (53 061) of this number was clinically active. Some 70% of new psychology Ph.D.s in health service provider subfields are granted in clinical psychology specifically (Henderson et al., 1996), which yields an estimate of almost 49 000 trained clinical psychologists and just over 37 000 active clinical psychologists in the USA. These estimates are likely to be conservative since they are based on survey returns rather than census counts and are likely to miss some of the Psy.D. graduates who come from programs outside the accreditation process.

Turning briefly to the master's level, there was a 600% increase in the number of master's-level psychological personnel between 1960 and 1991 (US Department of Education [USDOE], 1994, 1996). The first half of the 1990s witnessed at least 10 000 new master's graduates each year in psychology alone. There were at least 900 terminal master's programs in psychology in 1991 and other data indicate that the number of institutions awarding master's degrees has increased since the mid-1980s (Snyder & Hoffman, 1995; USDOE, 1994). Estimates placed the number of master's-level psychological personnel at 102 945 in 1994 an additional 20 000 by 1996). Data from the National Science Foundation indicate that about 32% (39 342) of the master's graduates were employed in psychology (NSF, 1988). Adding this number to a figure reported in the APA's 1983 Census of psychological personnel (Stapp, Tucker, & Vanden Bos, 1985) yielded approximately 55 551 master's-level psychological personnel working in psychology. At least two-thirds and probably closer to three-fourths of the master's graduates were in the health service provider subfields.

National data reveal two other fields that produced substantially more master's degrees from 1992 to 1993 than psychology. These were counselor education/guidance services in education, and social work (USDOE, 1994), and it is easy to see how the graduates in these fields could be competitors for jobs held by master's-level psychological personnel. Due to changes occurring in the health care delivery system, it also is clear that they could represent a substantial challenge to the full employment of doctoral-level psychologists.

The large numbers of master's degrees granted yearly in psychology, social work, and in counselor education in education; organized psychology's singular focus on the doctoral-level degree as the entry-level degree for the independent practice of psychology; efforts of master's-level providers to organize politically to influence state licensing laws, coupled with shifts in the health care delivery systems and an increasing emphasis on cost containment have pushed the question about the roles and functions of the master's-level psychologist in the provision of health services to the forefront. Increasingly, they are perceived as being in direct competition with doctoral-level providers. This has been called the "master's issue."

2.36.3 WHAT DO THEY LOOK LIKE?

The most obvious shift is in the gender composition of psychology (Pion et al., 1996). Enrolled students and degree recipients at all levels are predominantly female. For example, in 1995, women accounted for 67% of all full-time doctoral students and 74% of full-time master's students in psychology (Williams, 1996). From 1993/94, the most recent year for which data were available, women earned 73% of the bachelor's degrees and 72% of the master's degrees awarded in psychology (USDOE, 1996). Of all new psychology Ph.D.s in 1995, 64% were women, almost doubling the 32% of 20 years earlier (Henderson et al., 1996). The health service provider subfields in psychology have not been immune to this gender tip and it is not surprising that women comprised 44% of the clinically trained pool in 1995, up 5% from 1989 (Dial et al., 1990).

What are the implications of this momentous shift in gender composition, for the field and for services? A thorough discussion of this shift can be found in the Report of the Task Force on the Changing Gender Composition of Psychology available from the Women's Program Office of the APA. Case study findings also were presented in a 1996 *American Psychologist* article (Pion et al., 1996). A summary of the implications addressed in the case study includes the following. The pipeline data indicate that the face of the psychological workforce will continue to change. Rather than imply that these shifts are responsible for any decreases in earnings, or decline in attractiveness or autonomy, the report stresses the fact that the changes that have and are occurring in psychology are the result of external economic and legal forces and not the influx of women into the field.

The representation of persons of color in psychology remained small at about 6% of clinically trained psychologists (Peterson et al., 1996). The population of women was slightly more diverse than was the case for men. The presence of racial and ethnic minorities in psychology was smaller than their representation in the US adult population. Racial and ethnic minorities earned 14% of the Ph.D.s in psychology and 12% of those awarded in clinical psychology in 1995 (Henderson et al., 1996), but they represented 23% of full-time doctoral students in 1995; thus the pipeline is showing some diversification.

The median age of clinically trained psychologists has increased. In 1995 this number was just under 49 years, up somewhat from 1989 when it was just over 44 years. Median years since the doctorate also increased from 12 to 15 years between 1989 and 1995. Generally, women were younger than men and had earned their degrees more recently than men (Peterson et al., 1996).

2.36.4 WHERE ARE THEY FOUND?

The question is interpreted broadly and data are presented for the employment settings and activities as well as for the geographic locations of professional psychologists. In 1995 most of the clinically active psychologists were working full time and at least 50% held two or more positions. Part-time workers were more apt to be working at one position only. Again, most of these data are drawn from the publication by Peterson et al. (1996).

The data indicate that the largest single proportion of clinically active psychologists claimed independent practice as a primary employment setting (52.5%), mostly in individual (41.2%) as opposed to group (11.3%) arrangements. Academic settings were second at 14% and most of the clinical psychologists in these settings were located in higher education (e.g., universities and colleges (11%)), with the remaining 3% in secondary schools and other educational settings. Hospitals were claimed by just over 12%, 6.5% were working in clinics, while nursing homes employed less than 1%. Just over 14% of the practicing psychologists chose a generic "other human service setting" or "other" (see Figure 1).

For the 46% of active professional psychologists specifying a secondary employment setting, independent practice arrangements again were most frequent. Individual private practice was chosen most often (37.4%), while 9.4% specified group practices. Almost 18% were employed in universities and colleges. Hospitals were chosen by 8.9%, clinics by 5.1%, and nursing homes by less than 1%. Schools and other educational settings employed less than 3% and other human service or other settings claimed just over 18%.

A major point of interest in these data is the fact that despite the changes in health care delivery systems, the largest single proportion of practicing psychologists remains in independent practice These findings are supported by data from a 1995 Committee for the Advancement of Professional Practice (CAPP) survey of practicing members of the APA (APA Practice Directorate, 1996) .

Turning from setting to primary activity, just over three fourths of the clinically trained psychologists were involved in patient care and direct service, 9% were teaching, 8% were administrators and 4% were involved in research. Just under 3% indicated some other activity that was not specified (see Figure 2).

The question was asked about extent of involvement in each activity as opposed to primary or most important activity. Again, three-quarters of the clinically trained population was involved in patient care and direct service. This was not a surprise, given the overwhelming presence of professional psychologists in independent practice settings. However, it was interesting to discover that almost two thirds also taught, slightly more than a quarter was involved in administration, and just under one fifth conducted research. The other category climbed to 30% which is sizeable and warrants additional analysis to uncover these activities (see Figure 3).

Taking the setting and activity data together, it appears that clinical psychologists still do consider themselves to be independent practitioners, and that they continue to remain involved in a variety of activities, including teaching, administration and research. The other category is of great interest.

Geographically, where are psychologists located? Regionally, the East and West coasts of the USA held the single largest proportions of clinically trained psychologists, that is, 21% were in the Middle Atlantic region and 17% in the Pacific region. The center of the USA and the South and Mountain regions have markedly lower representation. At the state level, although insufficient to boost the Pacific region on its own to the most populous, California had the highest number of clinically trained psychologists, followed by New York, Pennsylvania, Massachusetts, and Ohio. The same patterns apply to the clinically active subset. A general rule of thumb with respect to understanding the geographic distribution of psychologists in the US is to look to the large metropolitan areas and the areas with numerous graduate programs in professional psychology. The large populations have supported the training programs while the training programs and later, their graduates, have used these concentrations of people for the internships and practices.

2.36.5 ISSUES OF DEMAND: ARE THERE TOO MANY?

When assessing the issue of whether there are too many doctoral psychologists, it depends on what you define as the appropriate scope of practice. It is becoming evident that there likely are a sufficient number of psychologists trained to provide mental health services to individual clients in independent practice settings. At the same time, it is equally evident that wrenching shortages continue to plague other parts of the systems of service delivery. Examples of shortages include rural and frontier areas to which traditionally clinically trained psychologists cannot be recruited and to which they are

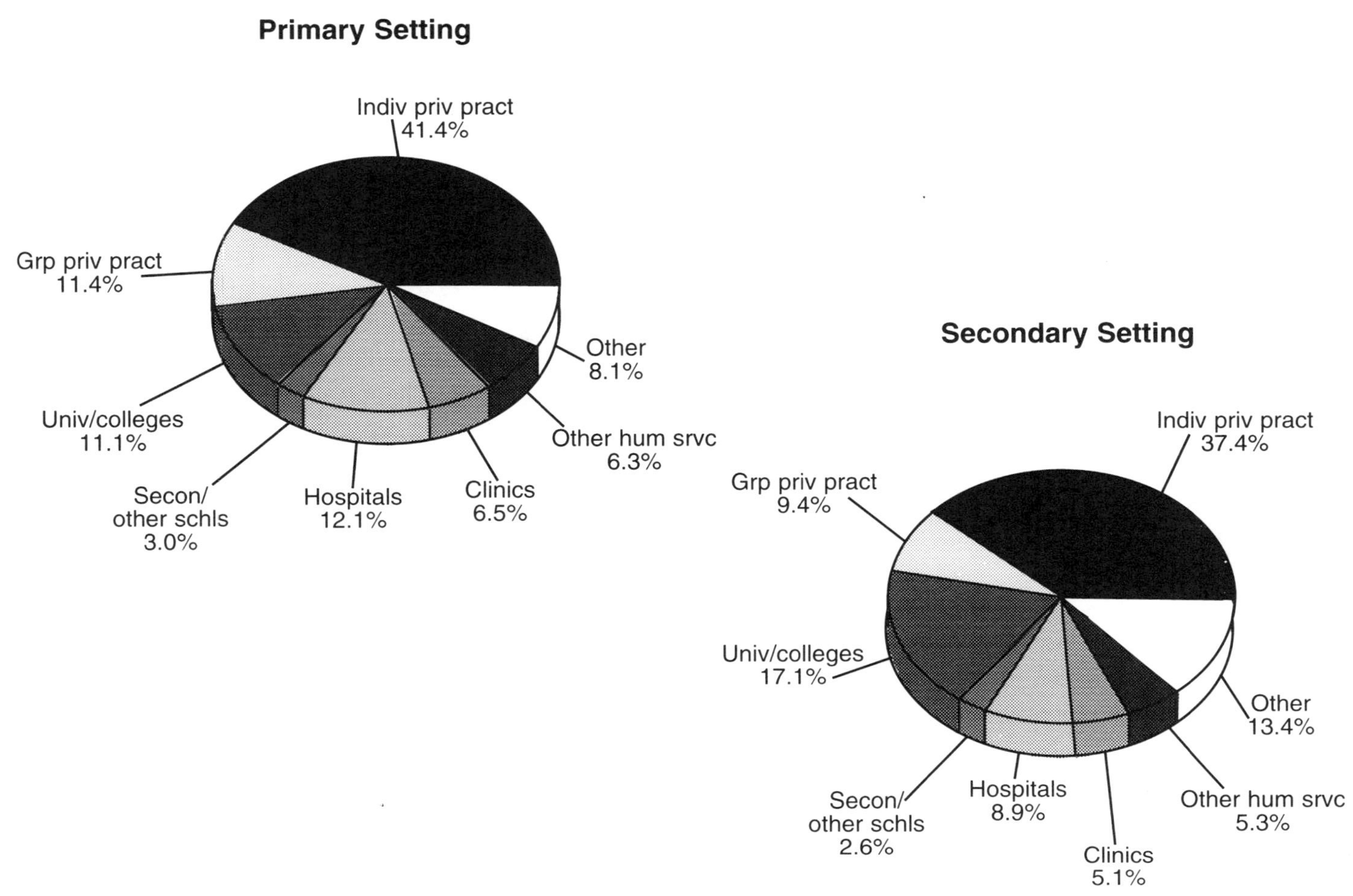

Figure 1 Primary and secondary employment settings of clinically active psychologists: 1995. Note: Percentages may differ slightly from the text due to rounding by the graphics package. Source: Peterson et al. (1996).

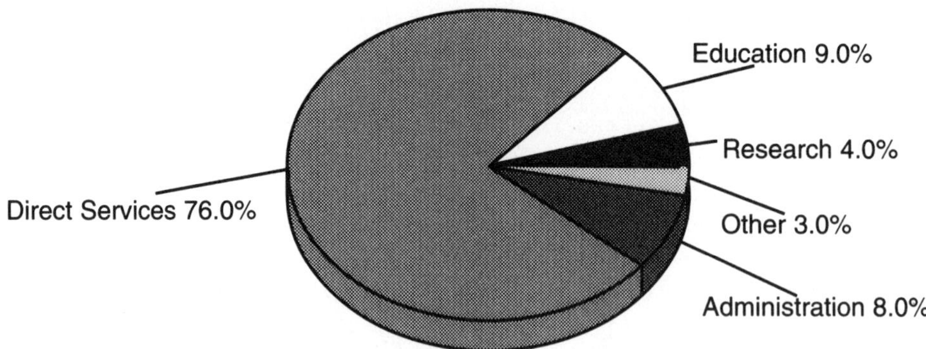

Figure 2 Primary activities of clinically trained psychologists: 1995. Source: Peterson et al. (1996).

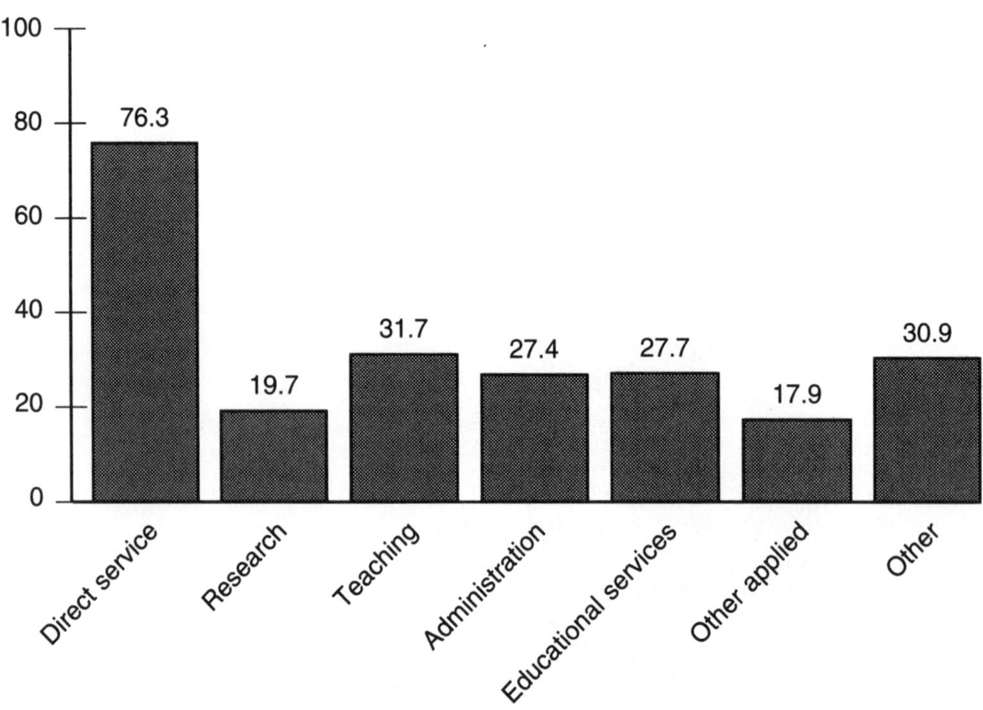

Figure 3 Any involvement in activities, clinically trained psychologists: 1995. Note: Percentages will total more than 100% as respondents could provide more than one response. Source: Peterson et al. (1996).

not attracted. Areas within urban settings that may appear dangerous or not able to support a solo practice also may be underserved. Other shortages can be defined with respect to the clients' needs (e.g., seriously mentally ill adults, seriously emotionally disturbed children, homeless persons, immigrant and minority populations, and the elderly) and organizational settings (clinics, hospitals, state agencies). A common characteristic of these groups of clients, settings, and areas is that they may not fit within the parameters/paradigm of a typical independent practice, and consequently will lack access to services.

Although a perceived oversupply of clinically-trained psychologists and threats posed by the health care revolution to the free practice of psychology may appear to be recent developments, this is not the case. In fact, a number of voices have been raised in common chorus for some time, urging psychology to expand its perspectives on what constitutes an appropriate scope of practice. Sarason (1975, 1981, 1983) has been urging an exploration of the "universe of alternatives" since the mid-1970s. Levy (1984) noted that training and practice in psychology could be more productive if they adopted a human services perspective rather than remaining limited to a focus on the treatment of individual mental health problems. Kovacs (1989) urged that we prepare psychologists to deal with challenges people face across the life span in a variety of settings. In the early 1980s and up to the present, Fox has written and talked about shifting and expanding the focus in professional psychology from an illness driven to a prevention driven model. Kiesler and Morton (1988), VandenBos, Belar, and DeLeon (1991), and Humphreys (1996) have joined the chorus, arguing for a shift to a larger proactive focus on designing systems/interventions/ways to promote healthy behavior and well-being at all levels. Yet, noted Schneider (1990), "it seems that the major practice preoccupations are geared toward a system that is disappearing rather than to the one replacing it."

For the most part the education and training structures in psychology have not changed, and students are not receiving the training they will need to personally succeed in, and effectively contribute to, the evolving health care environment. Despite the many calls for an expansion of the scope of practice and the obvious shifts in health care delivery systems, pessimism among established psychologists and a degree of panic among trainees and new graduates is already evident. At all levels of government and in many business settings, there is a general lack of understanding of what it is that psychologists do and can offer. The depth of understanding appears little better at the level of the individual citizen, where data from the evaluation of the Psychology Traveling Exhibit indicate fairly simplistic and uninformed views of what it is psychologists do. Positively, outcome interviews indicate that people are learning about the variety of research and the practical applications of psychology as a consequence of having attended the exhibit (APA Science Directorate, 1996).

If the educational system does not respond by providing training appropriate to the new health care systems and if clinically trained psychologists continue to establish traditional independent practices in which the client must come to the provider for individual or group treatment, a situation in which the psychologist actually is very passive, it is likely that the judgement will be that there are too many clinical psychologists and that they are irrelevant to the evolving systems and real world problems. This judgement will be held by psychologists, since they will have difficulty making a living, as well as by those responsible for establishing the new systems of health care and by those who are passing the laws and handing out funding for education, training, research, and outreach. The perception of oversupply can be as deadly as actual oversupply, dampening the interest of potential students in psychology as a career and lessening the support for the education and training of psychologists at all levels.

There is no oversupply. In fact, the persistent and worsening nature of many of society's ills and the fact that many of these have behavioral bases lend support to the argument that there are too few clinically trained psychologists. But psychology does appear to have hit a setback in that there is a mismatch between the training that students are receiving and the needs of the society. Suggestions about how to meet these needs is the subject of the next section.

2.36.6 FUTURE DIRECTIONS

Psychology should abandon efforts to model itself after medicine and move toward a proactive and self directing approach in order to define an appropriate scope of practice. This will require the combined efforts of all players within professional psychology. Examples include national, regional and state associations, the education and training structures within psychology, psychologists and students of psychology, and others.

> Professional psychology is that profession which is concerned with enhancing the effectiveness of human behavior. Therefore, a professional psychologist is one who has extensive expertise in the development and application of quality services to the public in a controlled, organized, ethical manner; based upon psychological knowledge, attitudes and skills, in order to enhance the effectiveness of human functioning. (Fox, 1982)

In the future, professional psychology should be prevention driven (Fox, 1994; Sarason, 1975, 1981, 1983) and it should help people to deal with the challenges of daily living across a variety of settings (Kovacs, 1989) and roles (e.g., family, work, parent, etc.). Emphasis is increasing on "designing and implementing interventions that help people pursue healthy behaviors and end or reduce risky behavior" (Humphreys, 1996). Psychology is moving away from a focus on individual-level problems toward the community, social problems, and human services. It will be part of a multidisciplinary effort in many instances in which the psychologist bands together with professionals from other fields to study social problems. The interventions that are designed as a consequence of this elaboration will be stronger by virtue of their multidisciplinary origins.

Defining professional psychology in this way immediately opens up many new avenues for productive and satisfying work. Some of the areas to which psychologists can contribute include human resources management, environmental design, training and supervision, and research on consumer behavior (VandenBos et al., 1991). VandenBos et al. also noted the variety of health related areas in which professional psychologists have made contributions, including: pain management, coping with stressful medical procedures, controlling drug side effects, physical self examination, health monitoring, recovery from illness or surgery, behavioral health, sticking to a health care regimen, and more.

How do we get to this stage? The recommendations that appear below can also be found in the Final Report and Recommendations of the APA Working Group on the Impact of Managed Care and Changes in the Health Services Delivery System on the Education and Training and Continuing Education of Professional Psychologists (American Psychological Association, Education Directorate and Research Office 1996). A copy of this report can be obtained from the APA's Research Office or from the Center For Mental Health Services, Washington, DC.

2.36.6.1 APA Recommendations

The educational system will have to change. Educational institutions will need to target clinical and research expertise to society's real needs (VandenBos et al., 1991). There needs to be greater emphasis on life-long learning and the content and the nature of the training will have to change. Some have called for a common core of general knowledge with specialization occurring postdoctorally. Practical experience or internships will need to be developed outside mental health settings to give trainees some experience with professionals from other fields in a variety of settings. Providing experiences with a diversity of populations and clients will be essential.

Technological literacy is critical to managing one's practice and evaluating and demonstrating effectiveness and efficiency. This involves computer literacy, ability to use information and delivery system technologies and research skills.

The ability to work with and communicate with professionals from other disciplines via interdisciplinary teamwork in multidisciplinary settings will be central to success in the evolving systems. Professional ethnocentrism is to be avoided.

Ultimately, the professional psychologist should be innovative, flexible and able to adapt to nontraditional settings, clients and modes of delivery by offering interventions that have been shown to work.

Practitioners will have to be able to demonstrate the cost effectiveness of psychological services and be able to predict and control costs. They will have to be able to fill public education and advocacy roles and they will need an understanding of the structure of evolving health care systems, including financing, organization, policy, and delivery principles. The ability to market one's services is necessary.

These recommendations and observations from the field indicate that health psychology will have a large role in the future (Cummings, 1995), by providing psychologists with the skills necessary to plan, research, and implement intervention programs for somaticizers and noncompliant chronically physically ill as well as programs for those with unhealthy behaviors (smoking, overeating, etc.) (e.g., Cummings, Dorken, Pallak, & Henke, 1993; Pallak, Cummings, Dorken, & Henke, 1993). Empirical outcomes research is also critical in that it will comprise the basis on which psychological interventions/therapies will rest, most of which are likely to be small group and psychoeducational in nature (Cummings, 1995).

2.36.7 SUMMARY

Clinical psychology has changed noticeably since the 1970s. Post-World War II shifts to a postindustrial society, in which the economy was based largely on the provision of services and an increased dependence on scientific and technical knowledge, brought with it an explosion of opportunities for professional psychology (Howard et al., 1986). The numbers of graduates have grown, tripling between 1975 and 1995 from 20 000 to almost 70 000. Recognizing opportunity, women flocked to psychology. Schools of professional psychology have been established that award a doctor of psychology (Psy.D.) rather than the Ph.D.

Primary employment shifted from organizational or institutional settings to private practice, nudged along by legal changes, increasing acceptance of psychological services and favorable reimbursement policies, and the psychologist was located most often in urban areas, near concentrations of population necessary to support a practice.

Questions about imbalances between supply and demand can be answered a number of ways. If one maintains a fairly limited view of what constitutes practice), then there appears to be an overabundance of practitioners and the supply is greater than the demand. This has negative consequences for the full employment of clinical psychologists. Indeed, data indicate that shifts in the health care delivery system in the USA have had negative impacts on health service providers in independent practice who must try to develop new niches.

Additionally, it is important that organized psychology takes some time to address the master's issue in a reasoned and grounded manner. Perhaps gathering data on the actual content of training at both levels would be a start. Revisiting the frequently mentioned rift between the science and practice of psychology is a needed exercise.

As many have argued, professional psychology must explore alternatives and expand its understanding of what constitutes an appropriate scope of practice. This shift from an "illness" model to a prevention model from a largely passive and reactive stance to one that is positive, proactive and in control—offers many new opportunities for professional psychology. Supply does not exceed demand and unemployment remains low. Above all, the benefits of such a shift extend beyond psychology, to society and individuals, by identifying healthy behaviors and the ways to practice those behaviors.

Although the goal of adopting a prevention approach has been discussed many times and is, from all appearances, a welcome outcome, a critical stumbling block remains. That is that the majority of the education and training systems in the USA have not begun to revise their training to meet the needs of a changing system. As a consequence, students in the health service provider subfields are not learning the knowledge and skills necessary to function effectively in the evolving health care system. The next challenge to reaching the goal of a prevention or human services model is to work with the education and training systems in psychology to design curriculum to meet this need.

2.36.8 REFERENCES

American Psychological Association, Education Directorate and Research Office (1996). *Final report and recommendations of the American Psychological Association working group on the impact of managed care and changes in the health services delivery system on the education and training and continuing education of professional psychologists.* Washington, DC: Author.

American Psychological Association, Practice Directorate (1996). *The Committee for the Advancement of Professional Practice (CAPP) practitioner survey results.* Washington, DC: Author.

American Psychological Association, Science Directorate (1996). Preliminary results of the evaluation of the museum exhibit, Psychology: Understanding ourselves, understanding each other. Unpublished analyses. Washington, DC: Author.

Cummings, N. A. (1995). Impact of managed care on employment and training: A primer for survival. *Professional Psychology: Research and Practice, 26,* 10–15.

Cummings, N. A., Dorken, H., Pallak, M. S., & Henke, C. J. (1993). The impact of psychological intervention on health care costs and utilization: The Hawaii Medicaid project. In *Medicaid: Managed behavioral health and implications for public policy: Volume 2. Healthcare and utilization cost series* (pp. 3–23). San Francisco: Foundation for Behavioral Health.

Dial, T. H., Tebbutt, R., Pion, G. M., Kohout, J., VandenBos, G., Johnson, M., Schervish, P. H., Whiting, L., Fox, J. C., & Merwin, E. I. (1990). Human resources in mental health. In R. W. Manderscheid, & M. A. Sonnenschein (Eds.), *Mental health, United States, 1990.* Center for Mental Health Services and National Institute of Mental Health, DHHS # (ADM)90–1708. Washington, DC: US Government Printing Office.

Fox, R. E. (1982). The need for a reorientation of clinical psychology. *American Psychologist, 37,* 1051–1057.

Fox, R. E. (1994). Training professional psychologists for the twenty-first century. *American Psychologist, 49,* 200–206.

Henderson, P. H., Clarke, J. E., & Reynolds, M. A. (1996). *Summary report 1995: Doctorate recipients from United States universities.* Washington, DC: National Academy Press.

Howard, A., Pion, G. M., Gottfredson, G. D., Flattau, P. E., Oskamp, S., Pfafflin, S. M., Bray, D. W., & Burstein, A. G. (1986). The changing face of American psychology: A report from the Committee on Employment and Human Resources. *American Psychologist, 41,* 1311–1327.

Humphreys, K. (1996). Clinical psychologists as psychotherapists: History, future and alternatives. *American Psychologist, 51,* 190–197.

Kiesler, C. A., & Morton, T. L. (1988). Psychology and public policy in the "health care revolution." *American Psychologist, 43,* 993–1003.

Kohout, J. L. (1993, August). *Employment opportunities in psychology: Current and future trends.* Paper presented at the annual meeting of the American Psychological Association, Toronto, Canada.

Kovacs, A. L. (1989, February). *The uncertain future of professional psychology.* Paper presented at the annual meeting of the Council of Graduate Departments. Tucson, Arizona.

Levy, L. H. (1984). The metamorphosis of clinical psychology: Toward a new charter as human services psychology. *American Psychologist, 39,* 486–494.

National Science Foundation (1988). *Profiles—psychology: Human resources and funding.* (NSF 88–325). Washington, DC: US Government Printing Office.

National Science Foundation (1996). *Characteristics of doctoral scientists and engineers in the United States: 1993.* (NSF 96–302). Arlington, VA: National Science Foundation.

Pallak, M. S, Cummings, N. A., Dorken, H., & Henke, C. J. (1993). Managed mental health, Medicaid, and medical cost offset. *New Directions for Mental Health Services, 59,* 27–40.

Peterson, B. D., West, J., Pincus, H. A., Kohout, J., Pion,

G. M., Wicherski, M. M., Vandivort-Warren, R. E., Palmiter, M. L., Merwin, E., Fox, J. C., Clawson, T. W., Rhodes, K. K., Stockton, R., Ambrose, J. P., Blankertz, L., Dwyer, K. P., Stanhope, V., Fleischer, M. S., Goldsmith, H. F., Witkin, M. J., Atay, J. E., & Manderscheid, R. W. (1996). An update on human resources in mental health. In R. W. Manderscheid & M. A. Sonnenschein (Eds.), *Mental health, United States, 1996*. Center for Mental health Services, DHHS# (SMA) 96-3098. Washington, DC: US Government Printing Office.

Pion, G. M., Mednick, M. T., Astin, H. S., Ijima Hall, C. C., Kenkel, M. B., Keita, G. P., Kohout, J. L., & Kelleher, J. C. (1996). The shifting gender composition of psychology: Trends and implications for the discipline. *American Psychologist, 51,* 509–528.

Sarason, S. B. (1975). Psychology of the Finland Station in the Heavenly City of the 18th century philosophers. *American Psychologist, 30,* 1072–1080.

Sarason, S. B. (1981). An asocial psychology and a misdirected clinical psychology. *American Psychologist, 36,* 827–837.

Sarason, S. B. (1983). Psychology and public policy: Missed opportunity. In R. D. Feiner, L. A. Jason, J. N. Moritsugu, & S. S. Ferber (Eds.), *Preventive psychology: Theory, research and practice* (pp. 245–250). New York: Pergamon.

Schneider, S. F. (1990). Psychology at a crossroads. *American Psychologist, 45,* 521–529.

Stapp, J., Tucker, A. M., & VandenBos, G. R. (1985). Census of psychological personnel. *American Psychologist, 40,* 1317–1351.

Snyder, T. D., & Hoffman, C. M. (1995). *Digest of education statistics.* (NCES 95–029). Washington, DC: US Department of Education.

US Department of Education, National Center for Education Statistics (1994). Earned degrees and completion surveys. Unpublished tabulations.

US Department of Education (1996). Degrees conferred by discipline, sex, and level of study. Unpublished raw data.

VandenBos, G. R., Belar, C. D., & DeLeon, P. H. (1991). How many psychological practitioners are needed? It's too early to know! *Professional Psychology: Research and Practice, 22,* 441–448.

Williams, S. (1996). Race/ethnicity and gender data for graduate students and faculty from the 1995–96 Graduate Study in Psychology survey. Unpublished analyses. Washington, DC: American Psychological Association.

2.37
Psychologists' Work and the Public's Perceptions: A Dichotomy

RAYMOND FOWLER and RHEA K. FARBERMAN
American Psychological Association, Washington, DC, USA

2.37.1 THE PUBLIC'S PERCEPTIONS

2.37.1.1 The Impression

Psychology is a broad discipline, but public understanding of its breadth and what it contributes to society is narrow. Psychologists work in so many settings that it is difficult to identify all of them, but the impression of psychologists many people have is limited to them as professors, researchers, or in the traditional counseling and clinical roles.

A national telephone survey conducted in 1995 by the American Psychological Association (APA) (Penn and Schoen Associates, 1995) found that 45% of all respondents believed that psychologists "generally help people with problems or offer counseling." Others (30%) said that psychologists "analyze people or study human behavior" (see Figure 1).

While it is true that many psychologists engage in clinical and counseling work, the world of psychology is much broader than the public often realizes because the work of psychologists in other settings occurs under other job titles and identities.

2.37.1.2 The Reality

Since the domain of psychology is the study of human and animal behavior, there are very few areas of inquiry which are not of interest to psychologists. In fact, psychological skills and

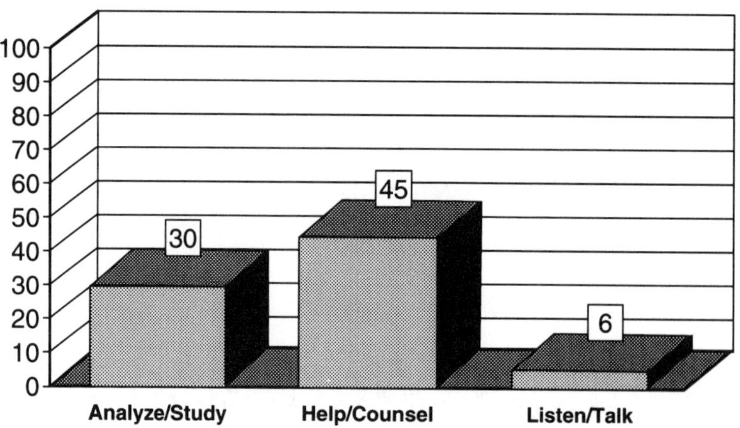

Figure 1 What Do Psychologists Do?
Source: American Psychological Association.

knowledge are relevant to a broad segment of social problems and public policy issues, for example, aging, AIDS, violence, depression, and drug abuse.

Today approximately 80 000 doctoral level psychologists (about half of the psychologists in the world) live and work in the USA. They work in a number of major subfields including clinical psychology, counseling psychology, developmental psychology, educational and school psychology, forensic psychology, health psychology, industrial/organizational and engineering psychology, neuropsychology, quantitative and measurement psychology, rehabilitation psychology, and social psychology. The first two subfields, clinical and counseling psychology, are somewhat familiar to the general public (although studies show that the public has very little understanding of how to differentiate among mental health providers). The remaining subfields, research shows, are unfamiliar to most members of the lay public.

Exact reports of how many professionals work in each of the subfields are difficult to ascertain because many in the field work in more than one role (see Figures 2 and 3). It is estimated however that approximately 20% of the discipline are in academic positions teaching and conducting research. Approximately 50–60% are thought to be primarily engaged in health service delivery (APA, 1996a).

2.37.2 THE HIDDEN CONTRIBUTIONS OF PSYCHOLOGY

There are numerous places where psychologists and psychological data collection and analysis are making contributions behind the scenes (e.g., social welfare, health and medicine, education, and corporate competitiveness) but are unknown to the general public. Some examples are:

(i) *Computer technology*. The computer and electronic communications revolution has benefited from, and continues to need, the input of psychologists. Computer learning and communications require that people learn to use the systems and function comfortably at them. Psychologists help in the design of teaching tools as well as operating systems and work stations that match human minds and bodies. Social psychologists also study the effect that communications via satellites and circuitry rather than face-to-face have on society and the way human beings interact.

(ii) *The new American demographics*. Towards the twenty-first century the world is a smaller place. America is more culturally, racially and ethnically diverse then it has ever been before. Psychology has a role in understanding the needs and ramifications of a more diverse population and helping institutions from governments to business to schools adjust to this new reality.

(iii) *Corporate downsizing*. Industrial/organizational psychologists and engineering psychologists teach corporations and business leaders to do more with less and deal with international economic challenges by finding work efficiencies, streamlining production processes, and promoting good management of human resources.

(iv) *Education reform*. Psychologists study the teaching and learning process and work in schools to make them more effective.

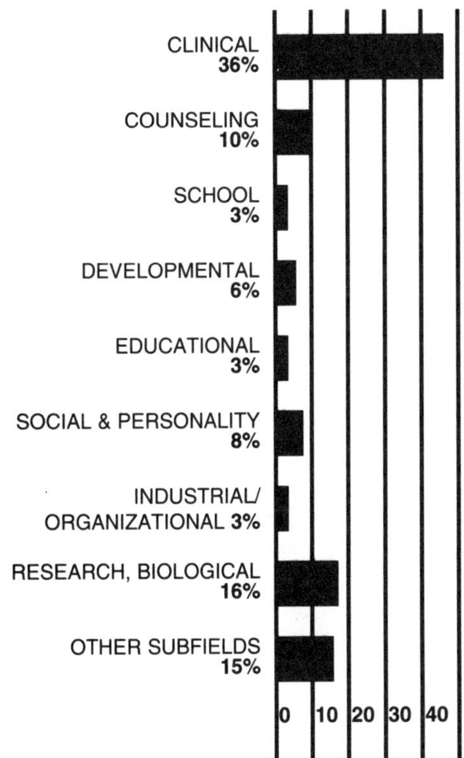

Figure 2 Subfields doctoral psychologists enter. Source: Adapted from 1993 *Survey of Doctorate Recipients*, National Research Council and National Science Foundation, Washington, DC.

2.37.3 THE WORK OF PSYCHOLOGISTS IN NUMEROUS AND VARIED SETTINGS

2.37.3.1 Psychologists in Healthcare Settings

It is estimated that between 50 000 and 60 000 psychologists work in a wide range of healthcare settings such as hospitals, clinics, in individual private practice, and as members of teams of primary care providers. Health psychologists study how biological, psychological, and social factors affect health and illness. In the last two decades clinical psychology has made large strides in evolving from a mental health profession to a health profession that teams with other healthcare providers—from primary care physicians to disease specialists—to provide comprehensive healthcare for patients. While most health disciplines specialize in the physical aspects of illness, psychologists are expert in the behavioral aspects of illness and the coping and adjustment skills needed to recover from illness. The connection between the mind and the body is well-established. Health psychologists understand how emotional illness can have physical ramifications and apply that knowledge to help people get well and stay well.

Psychologists begin to make important contributions to a patient's health at the initial stages of care giving. Psychologists evaluate patients by assessing personality traits and cognitive and motor abilities (memory or reaction time, for example). They work with other specialists to design and implement treatment plans to improve those skills.

Psychologists also help patients deal with the stress or discomfort which can be caused by the medical care, and play a critical role in keeping patients to their treatment regimes and recovery. Cancer patients, for example, often consult psychologists for help with medical decision making, treatment compliance, and the stress and depression that can accompany a cancer diagnosis.

Health psychologists also have an important role to play in preventing illness. They investigate health problems that affect large segments of the population such as smoking, sexually transmitted diseases, and poor diet. They can then design interventions to deal with these problems.

Research has shown that approximately half of all visits to primary care doctors are for symptoms for which psychological rather than physical causes are primary. The health psychologist in the USA therefore has a critical role to play in both the well-being of the American public and in reducing national healthcare expenditures.

Some psychologists have extensive training in psychopharmacology and work closely with physicians in determining appropriate medication for patients. Many psychologists believe that expanding their clinical skills to include prescribing drugs will allow them to better treat their patients. In a 1995 poll of its membership, the APA found that 62.7% of its members agreed with the statement, "appropriately trained psychologists should prescribe medication." Of the membership, 33% disagreed with the statement. No states currently license psychologists to prescribe drugs, but it is being considered by a few state legislatures.

Those who argue for prescription privileges believe that psychologists who prescribe will be better able to provide complete care for patients and will be able to appropriately coordinate medications with the psychotherapy needs of the patient. Opponents of prescribing, however, worry that the need to keep up with new advances in psychopharmacology will rob psychologists of the time necessary to continue to develop their expertise in psychotherapy.

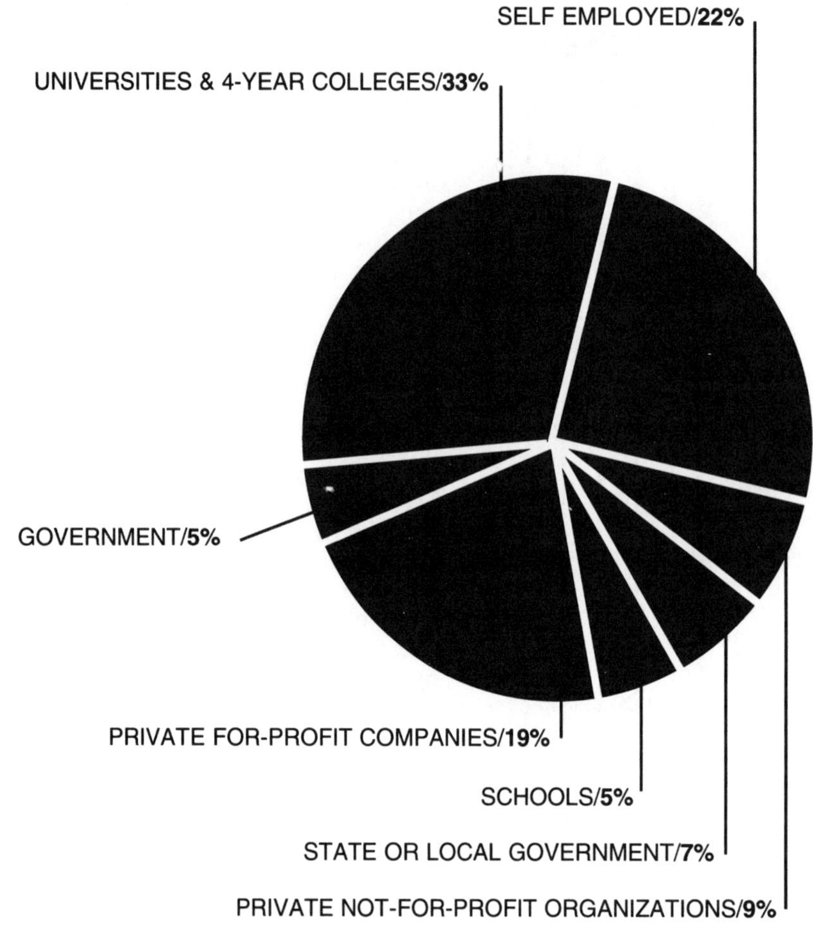

Figure 3 Where doctoral psychologists work.
Source: Data for psychologists working full time for others adapted from *Survey of Doctorate Recipients*, National Research Council and National Science Foundation, Washington, DC. Individual and group practice data are from Research office, APA Central Programs.

Up to 1997, four psychologists have graduated from a special military training program created to test the value of prescribing privileges for psychologists working with military personnel and their families and have been authorized to prescribe drugs. After some initial conflict with their military colleagues in the psychiatric ranks, all report good working relationships with other military doctors. Seven additional psychologists are in the training program in 1997.

2.37.3.2 Public Health Programs

Psychologists are tackling some of the late twentieth century's most troubling public health issues by both studying their root causes and designing interventions to solve them or help people cope with their ramifications.

Psychologists have been at the forefront of the battle to defeat AIDS since the epidemic was first identified. Psychologists are studying how to educate and motivate AIDS patients and those at high risk of contracting the virus to protect themselves against becoming infected. Needle exchange programs, for example, have been studied by many researchers. Psychologists also help patients and their families cope with the challenges of living with AIDS/HIV (Clay 1996; Sleek 1996).

Substances abuse is a problem that robs many people of their livelihoods, families, and even their lives. Psychologists, many specializing in the treatment of drug and alcohol abuse, treat patients with substance abuse. Research psychologists also study why some people become addicted to a substance while others do not, as well as what treatments programs have the greatest success rates.

Violence is a universal problem in the world. Violence takes places in urban centers, in rural communities, in the workplace, and at home. Psychologists have both studied the causes of violence and designed interventions to prevent it. In the workplace, psychologists theorize that violence often erupts as the results of unchecked stress and rage within an employee, but find it difficult to predict who may become violent in the work setting. Psychologists who study workplace violence have found that losing one's job is a better predictor of violence than age, gender, socioeconomic status, ethnicity, or diagnosable mental disorder. But, evidence does show that those who become violent often have a history of aggression, poor self-esteem, are socially isolated, and blame others for their problems (Martin, 1994).

Family violence is another area that psychologists have studied and work to prevent. Violence among family members is not restricted to any cultural or economic groups, but through research, psychologists have ascertained that family violence is circular—that it is passed from generation to generation within a family. Children who are abused and who witness adult members of the family hitting each other are more likely to be both the perpetrators and victims of violence as adults.

Psychologists intervene with families that are having trouble with domestic violence in numerous ways. Often helping people acquire better life skills, such as parenting skills and job skills, will help lessen the violence problem. A program in which psychologists make repeated home visits to families who are experiencing problems with violence has been found to be particularly effective in stemming that violence. The full involvement of many community resources in coping with the family violence problem has also proven to be very important (APA, 1996b).

2.37.3.3 The Workplace

Psychologists can be found in the workplace under a variety of job titles from human resources manager to quality performance director to wellness manager to consultant but most are there with the same basic mission; to make the workplace productive and safe.

Businesses today face numerous human resource challenges; getting the right employee in the right job, getting employees the training they need, making the workplace safe and keeping employees healthy, making the production process (whether the product is a widget or intellectual property) efficient, and keeping non work-related problems from interfering with employee performance.

Psychologists study, design, and implement intervention strategies to keep workers reporting to work healthy, ready to work, and to keep business moving ahead.

Clinical psychologists are also branching out into the fairly new subfield of executive coaching; working with corporate executives to strengthen their management, leadership, and interpersonal skills. Often both corporate leaders and line managers do not have a sufficient understanding of employee morale needs and how to build high functioning workplace teams and resolve conflict. Psychologists teach these skills where needed.

Workplace issues are likely to remain a strong area of work opportunities for psychologists. It is estimated that the direct and indirect costs of stress-related disorders to business in the USA now stands at \$100 billion annually. Furthermore, about 600 000 workers a year are disabled by psychological disorders.

2.37.3.4 Forensic Psychologists

Forensic psychologists work within and for the justice system and attempt to bring psychological knowledge to bear in the search for justice and equitable outcomes in court cases. Psychologists who work in forensic psychology often interview defendants at the request of defense attorneys or the court to judge their competency and state of mind. Psychologists are typically involved in divorce and child custody cases usually offering an opinion about the developmental and emotional health of any children involved in the case.

Other psychologists study jury behavior and help attorneys select juries who will be most likely to side with their clients.

2.37.3.5 Human Factors Research

Designing machinery and manufacturing processes to fit comfortably with the labor force is the expertise of human factors and engineering psychologists.

Human factors psychologists also study human performance and match the limits of human performance to work demands. For example, psychologists working in the NASA Fatigue Countermeasures program are developing a means by which to measure pilot fatigue and its effect on performance. Concerns about pilot alertness especially during long transmeridian flights were first raised in the early 1980s. Today, psychologists working on or with the NASA team use basic behavioral research on sleep physiology and circadian rhythms to design instruments that measure alertnes and performance. They have also taken these instruments into the cockpit to test general theories and countermeasures where pilots actually work (Azur, 1996b).

This research has concluded that allowing pilots to rest during long flights can improve their alertness at the end of that flight. Findings from this research will have important cross over into many other fields that require around the clock schedules such as law enforcement, public safety, and medicine.

Another area in which psychologists are working behind the scenes to protect the public is in the design of medical devices. The US Food and Drug Administration (FDA) must approve all medical devices; FDA approval is based on product safety and effectiveness, although not whether the product is user-friendly. However, these devices are often used by staff in busy hospitals, who are working on severe time constraints, heavy workloads, and at times fatigued.

An added emphasis on good human factors engineering in the design of medical devices began in the early 1990s when the FDA started to ask why so many well-trained professionals were failing to use them properly. Psychologists who work in the area point out that as medical devices become more complex and as more and more healthcare takes place in the home or some other out-of-hospital settings making medical devices more user-friendly is more critical than ever (Azur, 1996a).

2.37.3.6 Psychologists in Schools

Schools mirror the communities in which they exist. Today they are asked to teach children in increasingly difficult circumstances. Psychologists, both by studying the teaching and learning process and by working in schools directly with administrators, teachers, and students, are helping schools fulfill their mission.

School psychologists bring health and social services into schools or expand those services which already exist. Such programs involve a holistic approach to problems which do not have simple solutions such as substance abuse, youth violence, or teenage pregnancy. For school-based health programs to be effective they must be appropriate to student ages and development levels. As schools move to meet the health needs of their students, psychologists are able to help with program design based on their knowledge of how children grow and develop. Psychologists, for example, have studied why teenagers join gangs or take health risks and can therefore develop strategies that will effectively deal with these circumstances.

Many school districts employ psychologists full-time. In other school districts, psychologists are consultants to administrators and teachers.

Educational psychologists concentrate their work on the study of how effective learning and teaching take place. They consider a variety of factors, such as human abilities, what motivates students, and the effect on the class of the diversity of races, ethnic, and cultural backgrounds that makes up most school populations.

The basic question which educational psychologists have sought to answer is what motivates children to learn and what is detrimental to that learning. Psychologists have found that much of the answer lies in showing students the personal stake they have in the learning process and in giving them choice and personalization in their work assignments.

2.37.3.7 Military Psychologists

The work of psychologists has long helped the military improve training programs and study the effects of military operations on soldiers. For example, psychologists completed a large scale study, involving over 10 000 Gulf War veterans, which examines the impact on soldiers and reservists of rapid mobilization, leaving home and family life, as well as exposure to combat and other war-related stresses. Results from this study convinced the US military to make mental health services more available for American troops when they were deployed into Bosnia in December of 1995. Thirty-seven percent of those soldiers interviewed in the Gulf War veterans study were diagnosed with a psychiatric condition, most commonly either depression (11%) and posttraumatic stress disorder (5%).

As it becomes more common for military troops to be called to international trouble spots to act as peacekeepers, psychologists are studying the psychological stresses involved in that assignment which often includes dealing with strict rules of engagement, a hostile local population, and scores of displaced persons.

2.37.3.8 Psychologists Study the Media

Psychologists were pioneers in studying the effects that television would have on its viewers, especially children. Psychological research done over the since the 1950s has shown that children who watch a lot of violent programming on television are:

(i) less sensitive to the pain and suffering of others,

(ii) more fearful of the world around them,

(iii) more likely to behave in aggressive or harmful ways toward other people (APA, 1991).

In the late 1990s, psychologists are at the forefront of the study and applications of the Internet and other forms of electronic communication and information exchange. Psychologists, for example, want to know what effects the Internet will have a person's ability and desire to deal with people on a face-to-face basis. Is teaching over the Internet an effective way for children or adults to learn? These are questions which psychologists who study the media and new media technologies are investigating.

Clinical application of new media technologies is an area of controversy within the profession. The Internet is an example of a new communications technology with numerous potential applications in the mental health arena.

Does psychotherapy via the Internet have value? Is offering therapy via the Internet an ethical thing for a provider to do? Some proponents of psychotherapy via the Internet say that for people who live in rural areas or for other reasons can not get to a mental health provider's office, help through the Internet is better than no help at all. Others say it is valuable as an adjunct to an occasional face-to-face sessions. However, some observers believe that the Internet is a poor replacement for traditional psychotherapy.

2.37.3.9 Sport Psychology

At the 1996 Summer Olympic Games in Atlanta few individual athletes and teams went into the competition without having first worked with a sports psychologist. Two high profile events, women's gymnastics and track and field, especially benefit from the attention of sports psychologists. Both events demand supreme concentration and put years of training and preparation into a few minutes of performance which will separate victory from defeat.

Psychologists who work with athletes help them refine their focus on competition goals and motivation. They also help athletes deal with the anxiety and fear of failure that often accompany competition.

Ground-breaking research by sports psychologists has shown that quality training and mental preparation for competition were the two consistent elements needed for Olympic caliber success. Quality training was characterized by intense focus during practice, clear daily goals, imagery training to perfect skills, athletes who imagine success, prepare for training, and motivate themselves. Mental preparation for competition included having a precompetition plan, having a competition focus plan, evaluating the lessons of competition, and controlling distractions.

2.37.4 FUTURE DIRECTIONS

As the twenty-first century approaches a few demographic realities are clear. The population of the industrialized nations is aging, the world population continues to grow, and the American population is more diverse than ever. Psychologists will have important roles to play in the study and application of knowledge to help individuals and society as a whole cope positively with these changes.

In 1992, the last year for which data is available, 3373 doctorates in psychology were awarded by universities in the USA. Of these graduates 46% said they would pursue work in clinical and counseling psychology and 16% planned to pursue work in psychological research; the rest varied widely. These newcomers to the discipline will comprise the psychology workforce of the twenty-first century. It may also be important to note that during 1992 63 513 students earned their bachelor's degree in psychology and another 10 215 earned a master's degree in the field (Wicherski & Kohout, 1995).

Psychology continues to be a very popular undergraduate major, ranking second as the most common major for undergraduates on many campuses. About 5% of these new bachelors degree holders go on to earn their doctorate. Others join such job fields as social services, sales and service personnel, business management, engineering and computer science (see Figure 4).

Since the 1890s, psychology has grown dramatically and made important contributions to society. The next 100 years holds the same potential for the discipline.

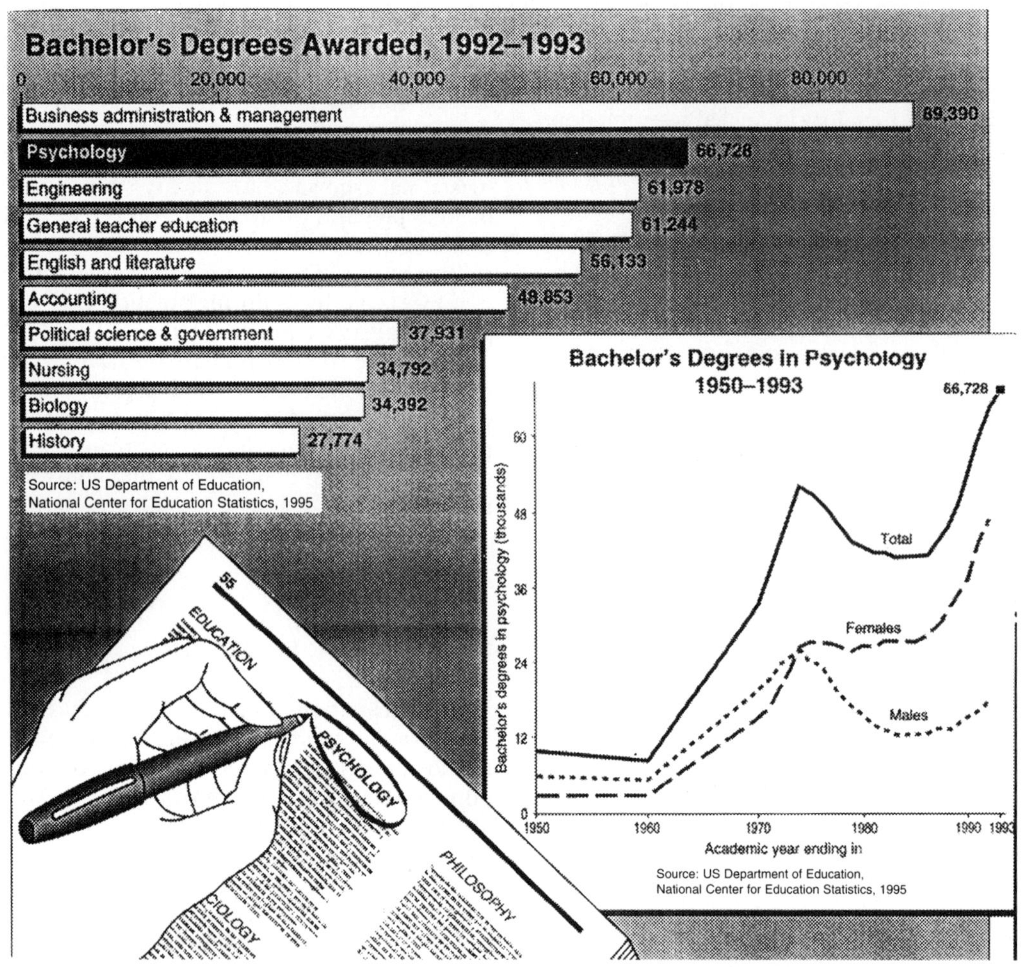

Figure 4 Most popular bachelor's degrees awarded, 1992–1993. Source: American Psychological Association.

2.37.5 REFERENCES

American Psychological Association (1991). *Violence on television: What do children learn, what can parents do?* Washington, DC: Author.

American Psychological Association (1996a). *Psychology: Careers for the 21st century*. Washington, DC: Author.

American Psychological Association (1996b). *Report of the APA presidential initiative on family violence*. Washington, DC: Author.

Azur, B. (1996a, May). FDA calls on psychologists to improve medical devices. *APA Monitor, 23*.

Azur, B. (1996b, May). Naps lead to safer piloting, study shows. *APA Monitor*, 22.

Clay, R. (1996, June). Targeted interventions curb the spread of HIV. *APA Monitor*, 29.

Martin, S. (1994, October). Workplace is no longer a haven from violence. *APA Monitor, 29*.

Penn and Schoen Associates (1995). *Public opinion on mental health issues*. Report to the American Psychological Association, Practice Directorate. Washington, DC: Author.

Sleek, S. (1996, June). AIDS therapy: Patchwork of pain, hope. *APA Monitor*, 1.

Wicherski, M., & Kohout, J. (1995). *1993 Doctorate employment survey*. Washington, DC: American Psychological Association, Research Office.

2.38
The Image of Psychology in the Mass Media: The United States

RHEA K. FARBERMAN and RAYMOND D. FOWLER
American Psychological Association, Washington, DC, USA

2.38.1 INTRODUCTION

The reach and impact of television and films are unquestioned. Of all American homes with children, 99% own at least one television. Movies have been popular leisure time entertainment since the 1930s.

In their book, *Tuning in trouble: Talk TV's destructive impact on mental health*, psychologists Heaton and Wilson (1995) write that "television is at the heart of American culture; its power and influence are unparalleled."

About movies, Sklar (1994) writes in his book *Movie-made America*,

> ever since the peep shows first captivated urban audiences, film has had a revolutionary impact on American society transforming culture from the bottom up, radically revising attitudes toward pleasure and sexuality, and at the same time, cementing the myth of the American dream.

Many professions have been created in the public's mind through their portrayals in film and on television. For a generation of Americans, Marcus Welby set the image of what their family doctor should be. In the 1960s Perry Mason set the image of the laconic lawyer who fought for justice and always got to the truth. That image has been greatly changed by later television portrayals of lawyers on such hit shows as *LA Law* and *Murder One*.

People such as Bob Newhart, Woody Allen, and Nurse Ratched in *One Flew Over the Cuckoo's Nest*, have combined many characters to create the public image of the therapist and the patient; an image that in the movies and on television has revolved more around dysfunction than improved functioning.

Research has shown that the public's ability to differentiate between different types of mental health providers is poor (Woods, Jones, & Benjamin, 1986). What role did the media play in this lack of understanding? There are numerous examples of the media's stereotypical portrayal of mental health professionals. There are also numerous examples of the often poor job the media has done in portraying the therapeutic relationship.

During the 1930s numerous films featured a psychiatrist character. All had central European accents, were comical figures, and often appeared to be in need of treatment themselves. The actor Fritz Feld created the mold with his portrayal of a psychiatrist (complete with a facial tic) in *Bringing Up Baby* (1938).

In the 1947 classic, *A Miracle on 34th Street*, the character Kris Kringle is challenged by the Macy's store psychologist who pronounces Kris "dangerous and psychotic." Again however, the protagonist outwits the mental health provider, a small and nervous man who twists his eyebrows incessantly. This was "therapist as villain" movie-making. When an elderly man believes himself to be Santa Claus, eventually even the lawyers see his humanity and goodwill and begin to root for him. The villain of the film is the psychologist hired to screen new employees, he is a bundle of nervous habits and odd behavior—paranoid and downright mean.

In the 1958 film, *No Time for Sergeants*, Andy Griffith plays a Georgia farm boy who joins the air force and outwits the military psychiatrist. "Well I reckon I love my mother," Griffith tells the psychiatrist. "Don't you love your mother?" he then asks, evoking anger from the doctor.

The 1960s hit television sitcom *I Dream of Jeanie* featured a NASA psychiatrist, Dr Bellows. Poor Dr Bellows was always in a state of befuddlement as the other main characters, Jeanie, Roger, and Major Nelson, hide Jeanie's true identity (see Figure 1).

Probably the most far-reaching of all the television and film characterizations of psychologists and psychiatrists is the television sitcom of the early 1970s, *The Bob Newhart Show*. The Newhart show was extremely popular and held the Saturday evening time slot. The protagonist, Bob Newhart, a psychologist, was a caring but ineffectual therapist. A stream of patients came in and out of his office, each more strange and dysfunctional than the last. This one show, the only network show of the time featuring a psychologist as one of the main characters, left an indelible impression in the TV viewing public's mind—the psychologist as the middle-aged man in a now wildly out of style polyester suit, kind, but bumbling and unable to do much of anything to help his patients cope with their problems. His patients were an odd collection of neurotic souls—caricatures of people rather than real people. A virtual parade of dysfunction on both sides of the therapeutic relationship.

The cable television network, *Comedy Central*, has created a modern day psychotherapist as sitcom example, *Dr Katz: Professional Psychotherapist*. The show's producers describe it as an animated TV show about the funny, lovable psychotherapist who people love to take advantage of. The fact that this show is animated is somehow fitting with the way that the entertainment industry has treated and continues to portray the profession.

The best-selling novel by Pat Conroy and later a hit movie (1991), *The Prince of Tides* created a new portrayal of the psychiatrist—different from earlier characterization but also troubling. In the movie, Barbara Streisand plays a competent, compassionate, very human professional, but one with questionable ethics. The story line takes the Streisand character from psychiatrist to the main character's lover. The problem is the main character, Tom Wingo, who is also the brother of one of Streisand's current patients.

2.38.2 WHAT HAVE ALL THESE IMAGES ADDED UP TO CREATE?

The question is, what effect have these negative and inaccurate portrayals of psychiatrists and psychologists had on the viewers' psyche and health consumer behavior? The provider-character who is "crazy," strange, befuddled, and ill-tempered gets the most laughs and is most common. But is it educative and reassuring for the viewing public?

What has been the effect of the media portrayal of psychologists and other mental health providers? Many studies have shown that the public is not well educated when its comes to mental health issues nor types of mental health specialists. Americans are unsure as to how psychotherapy works and what psychologists and psychiatrists actually do.

In 1994, the American Psychological Association (APA) conducted both a national telephone survey and consumer focus groups to ascertain the public's attitudes towards and understanding of mental health issues and providers. Some important results were as follows:

(i) The public is nearly universally unable to differentiate between the different types of mental health providers.

(ii) Few people understand the educational and licensure requirements to practice psychology. Just 36% of those asked know that a doctoral degree is required to be a psychologist. Additionally, one in five believed that psychologists need a medical degree to practice; these data may reflect people confusing psychologists with psychiatrists.

(iii) Finally, there exists a great deal of confusion about the best way to evaluate and select a mental health provider.

A summary of the findings of the national focus group series reported the following,

Figure 1 The media often portrays therapists as characters and humorous fugures (Source: APA).

"across all the groups there was general confusion about the differences between the various types of mental health care providers. Most had limited experience in using or being exposed to mental health care services. Some made comments about the images of such professions being based on what they had seen in the media, particularly talk shows and programs like *Bob Newhart.*"

Another focus group finding was that the term "mental health" was actually associated with "mental illness" by most people and to these people mental illness meant "being crazy."

This research also identified five primary barriers which prevent people from seeking psychological services. Three seem particularly related to the images created by television and movies—concerns about the treatment outcome (43%), the length of treatment (26%), and about how seeking treatment will affect their career (26%).

Where does the public get the impression that psychotherapy treatment would go on for indefinite lengths of time and the outcome of all of this time would be questionable? A Woody Allen movie comes to mind! "I don't think you ever get cured," said one focus group participant.

2.38.3 WHAT IS LOST?

Have the wrong impressions of the therapeutic process that the public has had an effect on its mental health? Data, again collected by APA, suggests that they have.

The APA found an information gap when it did public attitudes research. Most people knew that psychological health is important to ones' overall well-being, but did not feel that they knew when it was appropriate to seek mental health services or how to go about selecting a provider.

Of even greater concern than a lack of information is the negative impression that the media's handling of the mental health profession has given the public. Research has shown that the therapeutic set, the concept that if the client believes the therapist to be an expert in psychological techniques the client will improve, holds (Turkat, 1977). The question is, if the public generally believes that mental health professionals are incompetent how does that interfere with the therapeutic relationship?

2.38.4 THE TELL-ALL AND TALK SHOW PHENOMENON

While in the past, the mass media helped create a false image of mental health providers, in the 1990s, many media personalities are helping to decrease the stigma around mental health issues through their own public acknowledgments of mental health problems. In 1987, Patty Duke revealed her battle with manic depression in an autobiography and in numerous public appearances on behalf of mental health causes. Newsman Mike Wallace has talked openly about his battle with depression as has columnist Art Buchwald.

Another promising media direction for the discussion of mental health issues was the early television talk shows. The format, pioneered by Phil Donahue in 1967, began as a serious and substantive place to discuss social issues that before were not discussed anywhere else. At their inception, the talk/interview format shows were a breath of fresh air and a new opportunity to discuss issues that affected everyone but that few people talked about, such as domestic violence, family relationships, race relations, and sexuality. Mental health professionals including psychologists were often invited to be part of these shows to comment and add a psychological perspective and knowledge to the discussion. Many hailed these shows as a way to "give psychology away" and help people who might not otherwise seek help.

Phil Donahue's show met with great success and popularity, and not surprisingly was copied. By the early 1990s there were nearly a dozen talk/interview format shows on the airways in America, each trying to outdo the other for ratings by being that much more provocative, outrageous, and obnoxious.

With few exceptions, TV talk shows became little more than organized, electronic bar-room brawls. During the final 60 seconds of the show, the mental health professional was asked to appear on air and solve the guest's problem, be it marriage infidelity (my mother slept with my husband is not an atypical show topic), eating disorders, body image disorders, gambling addictions, or a host of other serious and intensely personal life problems.

Heaton and Wilson (1995) have studied the TV talk show phenomenon and have written about it in their book *Tuning in trouble: Talk TV's destructive impact on mental health.* They write, "TV talk shows make a mockery of the mental health profession by obscuring the fact that change and recovery are most often a long and painful process. Innocent viewers, moreover, succumb to a "copycat syndrome" being persuaded that they too not only have the same problem, but can solve it with similar quick-fix, sound-bite therapy. Television talk shows entertain their enormous viewing audience with a steady stream of wounded guests, self-serving gurus, and manipulative hosts who offer quick

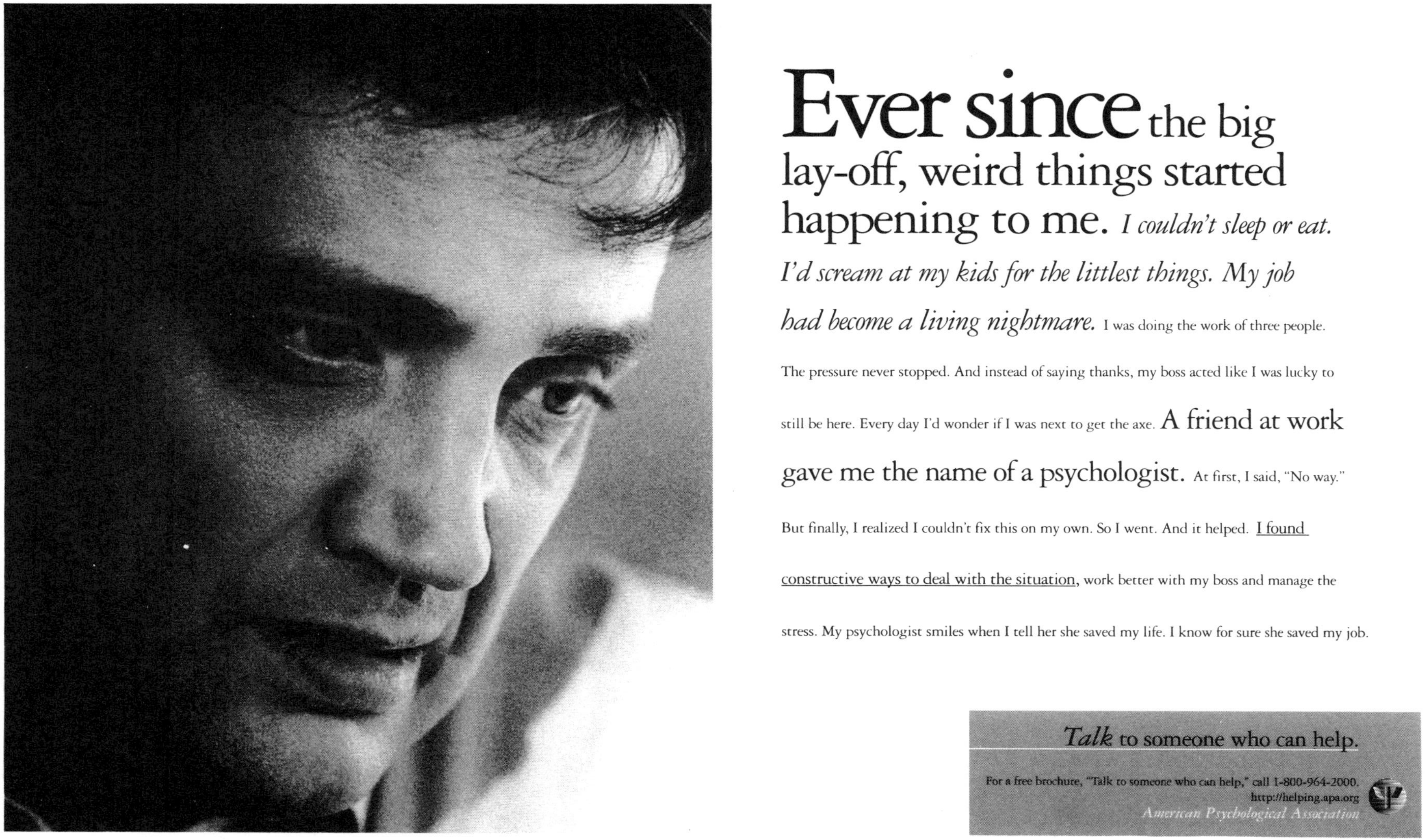

Ever since the big lay-off, weird things started happening to me. *I couldn't sleep or eat. I'd scream at my kids for the littlest things. My job had become a living nightmare.* I was doing the work of three people. The pressure never stopped. And instead of saying thanks, my boss acted like I was lucky to still be here. Every day I'd wonder if I was next to get the axe. A friend at work gave me the name of a psychologist. At first, I said, "No way." But finally, I realized I couldn't fix this on my own. So I went. And it helped. I found constructive ways to deal with the situation, work better with my boss and manage the stress. My psychologist smiles when I tell her she saved my life. I know for sure she saved my job.

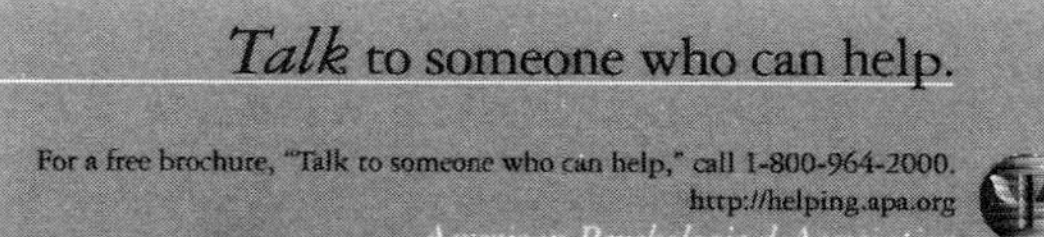

Figure 2 Public Education Advertising (Source: APA).

"You have breast cancer."

In those four words, my whole life changed, from the inside out. *"We'll need to operate, then you'll have radiation."* I sat there stunned. My doctor's words flew past me. He said something about seeing another doctor, a psychologist, to help me through this. He handed me a little white card. I numbly put it in my wallet, never realizing it held the key to my full recovery. The next few weeks were hell. The pain, the fear, the anger. I was lucky. They got all the cancer. But to get better physically, I had to get better emotionally. Then I remembered the card. I pulled it out and called. What a relief to have someone to talk with, someone who is trained to do more than just listen sympathetically.

My psychologist helped me to understand and cope with my feelings. I was surprised to find how much better that made me feel—stronger, able to start living again. I also learned ways to help my husband and kids talk about how scared they were. I lost a breast. But my psychologist helped me gain a stronger sense of what's really important in my life.

Talk to someone who can help.

For a free brochure, "Talk to someone who can help," call 1-800-964-2000.
http://helping.apa.org
American Psychological Association

Figure 3 Public Education Advertising (Source: APA).

Figure 4 Public Education Advertising (Source: APA).

and easy solutions to complex problems. Can we afford to dismiss this drive-by psychology of Donahue, Geraldo, and Ricki Lake as just harmless entertainment?"

In late 1994, as the talk shows' battle for viewers came to fever pitch, the Public Affairs Office of the APA began recommending that psychologists should not appear on the daytime talk shows. The APA stated in a media alert announcing the decision, "No good purpose is served for the viewing audience nor for the profession when a psychologist is associated with a 27 minute screaming match and viewers are offered unrealistic, quick fix approaches to serious life issues."

By the early summer of 1996, the Talk TV phenomenon seemed to be wearing itself out and being replaced by new "old style" programing such as the Rosie O'Donnell show. However, the harm perpetrated on the public's understanding of and expectations of mental health providers (and respect for them) by these trash talk shows is yet to be known.

2.38.5 HOW SHOULD THE PROFESSION RESPOND?

Comical and inaccurate portrayals of mental health providers has created a stereotype image of the profession and has likely added to the stigma around mental health services. These issues challenge the profession to act to provide the public with more accurate information and a more accurate, more professional, more human image of its ranks. "It's critical that psychology communicate its value to many publics; consumers, the media, and policy-makers," says Dorothy Cantor, a past president of APA, "if psychology doesn't communicate about psychology, who will?" she asks.

2.38.5.1 Public Education Campaign

The public image of psychology has been the concern of "lone voices" in the profession for decades. Research studies of consumer information and attitudes have pointed toward the profession's need to better define and market itself to the public (Benjamin, 1986; Schindler et al., 1987; Webb & Speer, 1986).

In 1995, the APA Council of Representatives directed that the association undertake a national public education campaign designed to communicate the value of psychological services. The campaign was unveiled in February 1996 and is expected to be a long-term effort involving not only the national association but state psychological associations, APA divisions, and individual psychologists.

The campaign consists of advertising, news media relations, consumer information, and grass roots activities. The advertising (TV, radio, and print), the campaign's most visual product, carries the tag line "Psychology: Talk to Someone who Can Help" and features vignettes which attach psychological services to issues that Americans worry about, such as serious illness, raising children, and coping with job stress.

The overall goal of the campaign is to close the information gap that APA's research uncovered. In a changing health care marketplace, consumers act to protect their access to those services they understand, are comfortable with, and value. The campaign is designed to call the public's attention to psychology by linking its services to problems people worry about and then to educate the public about what psychologists do, how psychotherapy works, as well as the unique training and skills of psychologists (see Figures 2–4).

2.38.5.2 Psychology's Role in Reporting News Events

Gaining expertise in working with the news media is another important way in which psychology can reclaim its image and its image-making. The news media often call upon psychologists to help interpret or to comment on daily events. As major events unfold, the APA Public Affairs Office gets calls from print and electronic reporters looking for people to go on the air or on the record to help explain events. Examples of such events include the bombings, arrests, aircraft disasters, the controversy of recovered memories, post-traumatic stress disorder in earthquake survivors, and others. Tomorrow's news may be another opportunity for psychology to help redefine its image and display its knowledge of human behavior. However, in order to take advantage of this opportunity, individual psychologists must be prepared for the newsmaker role. The best way to get this preparation is to participate in media training programs (offered at APA's convention every year) and to practice those skills.

Without the resources to produce a new hit movie in which the hero is a competent, professional, sound, and humanistic psychologist, there are other ways in which individual psychologists can help redefine psychology's public image, for example, participation in grass roots public education activities and availability to the news media.

2.38.6 REFERENCES

Benjamin, L. T. (1986). Why Don't they understand Us? A history of psychology's public image. *American Psychologist, 41*(9), 941–946.

Heaton, J. A., & Wilson, N. L. (1995). *Tuning in trouble: Talk TV's destructive impact on mental health.* New York: Jossey-Bass.

Schindler, F., Berren, M. R., Hannah, M. T., Berigel, A., et al. (1987). How the public perceives psychiatrists, psychologists, nonpsychiatric physicians, and members of the clergy. *Professional Psychology: Research and Practice, 18*(4).

Sklar, R. (1994). *Movie-made America.* New York: Vintage.

Turkat, I. D. (1977). Television psychologists and the therapeutic set. *Psychology, 14*(2), 65–68.

Webb, A. R., & Speer, J. R. (1985). The public image of psychologists. *American Psychologist, 40*(9).

Wood, W., Jones, M., Benjamin, L. T. (1986). Surveying psychology's public image. *American Psychologist. 41*(9).

2.39
National Priority Needs: Implications for Clinical Psychologists in the United States

JOANNE E. CALLAN
California School of Professional Psychology, San Diego, CA, USA

2.39.1 INTRODUCTION

Clinical psychology's very roots were planted firmly in its science base, yet also in its promise as a profession responsive to a wide range of human needs. Its essential focus was initially, and remains, on psychological and behavioral aspects of human functioning. Although its earliest foundations lay in general psychology emanating from Wilhelm Wundt's University of Leipzig laboratories in the 1870s, several traditions within psychological thinking are credited as contributing significantly to the development of clinical psychology as it is known today, and, presumably, to directions it will take in the future.

Korchin (1976), writing about major influences on clinical psychology, supported Watson's (1953) earlier identification of two traditions, other than the early European experimental influence, which have had marked impact: psychometrics and dynamic thinking. Rotter (1963), while noting the contributions of experimental and theoretical psychology to clinical psychology, pointed out the significance of clinical psychologists' gradual move from working predominantly in the 1900s–1940s with children and with assessment activities (in particular, intelligence testing) to functioning more as therapists and case managers since the 1950s. Arguably, a time of clinical psychology's greatest consolidation occurred during and just after World War II, when clinical psychologists joined other health care providers in responding to the many psychological needs of America's service men and women. Indeed, several psychologists considering the history of clinical psychology (e.g., Korchin, 1976; Shakow, 1969) relate the evolution of three major professional activities carried out by clinical psychologists—diagnosis, psychotherapy, and research—to World War II's special psychological needs. Korchin referred to these three activities as the "holy trinity of postwar clinical psychology" (1976, p. 45).

Later, fueled by political and social forces of the 1960s, the community mental health movement underscored psychology's importance to public health needs. By that time, clinical psychology was well established as one of the nation's major mental health professions. Just as the Veterans Administration (VA) had been singularly instrumental in advancing the education and training of psychologists to meet service needs following World War II (continuing its support to the present), the National Institute for Mental Health (NIMH) provided major support for the education and training of mental health professionals, including clinical psychologists in the 1960s, 1970s, and 1980s (with decreasing support in the 1980s and 1990s). Accordingly, clinical psychology has been responding to major public needs since the 1940s and, no doubt, will continue its commitment to national needs and priorities in the future.

Parallel developments in education and training also reflected clinical psychology's science and professional bases as well as its responsiveness to public needs. The Boulder Conference, led by American psychologists representing the American Psychological Association, the VA, and the NIMH, was held in 1949 for the purpose of developing standards for educating and training clinical psychologists (Raimy, 1950). One of the most enduring outcomes of the conference was the establishment of the scientist-practitioner training model, a model reaffirmed in several subsequent conferences (Korchin, 1976). In 1973, the Vail Conference addressed a lingering and also growing concern about how psychology could best educate and train clinicians to be responsive to changing and increasing demands for psychological services in both public and private sectors. A central question was how to assure clinical as well as research expertise, and conference deliberations on this matter led to the recognition of a new training model, one that emphasized professional training (Korchin). This recognition did not eliminate the scientist-practitioner model, which, in fact, continues to be observed by many graduate programs; rather, it broadened the ways in which graduate programs in clinical psychology would be designed and implemented.

Since the 1960s, as indicated previously, clinical psychology, both as a science and as a profession, has been recognized as a national player in public health, especially with regard to mental health. The NIMH, for example, has identified four disciplines as essential to addressing national mental health needs: clinical psychology; psychiatry; nursing; and social work. These four disciplines have been included in NIMH's applied and training programs, and as noted above, NIMH-supported clinical training programs provided major resources for several decades to assure an available pool of mental health service providers. Clinical training funding, divided among these four mental health professionals, was at the highest level of \$93 million in FY 1967; regrettably, however, that level dropped to 10.9 million in FY 92 and to 2.9 million in FY 1993 (Callan, 1993).

Clearly, national leadership on mental health needs and services has been influenced considerably by NIMH-sponsored programs and directions. In the late 1980s, for example, NIMH in collaboration with others, including professional and advocacy groups as well as educators and trainers, identified four populations whose urgent mental health needs merited special attention: (i) seriously emotionally disturbed children; (ii) the seriously mentally ill; (iii) ethnic minorities; and (iv) the elderly. Clinical psychology was a central player in the series of conferences held between 1988 and 1992 on the education and training of health care providers for these particularly needy groups.

The mental health challenges of these groups, along with numerous other public problems, constitute a broad array of national needs to which clinical psychology has relevance. Arguably, they are apparent in all major human and social systems: in government, education, health, law and justice, transportation, environmental and community safety, communication, and in the worlds of work, art, and play. Individuals, families, and communities face myriad challenges in everyday living, ranging from meeting basic needs for food and shelter to higher order ones related more to quality of life. When special problems such as those of the underserved, under-represented, or the otherwise needy are also considered, the complexity and urgency are almost overwhelming. Identifying and addressing priorities among them, especially in the context of an increasingly complex and diverse society, are daunting tasks. Moreover, effectively responding to them on a national scale will certainly require the knowledge and skills as well as the caring of many. Not only must clinical psychology play a leadership role in this response, it must become an active, ongoing partner with other psychologists, other professions, and the public.

2.39.2 SELECTED NATIONAL PRIORITIES

In order to provide such leadership and build such partnerships, it is imperative that clinical psychologists become well informed on national needs. This chapter, building on the history of clinical psychology, focuses on selected national priorities, first identifying several key need categories and then elucidating the urgency associated with each and the implications for clinical psychology. Four need categories are presented: (i) health care (including mental health); (ii) education; (iii) work and economics; and (iv) families and communities: relationships, systems, and communication.

Although these categories take into account special populations, such as the four identified by NIMH, they provide a broader context, one identifying the larger human and societal needs that constitute national priorities for the USA as the twenty-first century nears. Reflecting overarching challenges, they highlight the broad scope as well as the complexity of national issues with which clinical psychology can engage in the next few decades and thereby make a real and dramatic difference for humankind. As clinical psychologists become both better informed and actively involved in addressing national priorities, the relevance and promise of clinical psychology as a science and as a practice will achieve heightened visibility and meaning.

2.39.2.1 Health Care

Rapidly escalating health costs since the 1970s as well as diminishing access to health care have mandated health care reform. According to Resnick and DeLeon (1995), cost estimates for health care in 1993 were around \$880 billion; moreover, access to health care is becoming nonexistent for many Americans with almost 40 million Americans lacking health care coverage and an estimated two million losing health care coverage each month. Mental health costs have been spiraling as well. Annual costs of depression exceed \$43 billion (Greenberg, Steglier, Finkelstein, & Berndt, 1993), while the annual overall expenses associated with mental health and substance abuse is \$273 billion (Rice, Kelman, Miller, & Dunmeyer, 1990). Inpatient substance abuse services grew 30% between 1986 and 1988, and adolescent inpatient treatment grew 65% ([see Frank & Salknero, 1990], as reported in Slosar & Lettieri, 1996).

Unquestionably, health care reform is a national priority, and only those disciplines actively engaged in the reform process will influence the directions it takes, an involvement that is critical in the face of such developments as expanding managed care. Indeed, in order to have a viable future, clinical psychology must exercise a leadership position in national health care planning and service delivery. Its leadership must be positioned from the broadest possible base, focusing on health care and not limited to mental health care, with which it has been associated in the past to a large extent. Although psychotherapy remains an established and effective modality (see below), it cannot stand as the *sine qua non* of clinical psychology. The developing trend since the 1980s in which clinical psychologists have been increasingly assuming roles more associated with general health care must persist.

Behavioral health research and service delivery constitute an area of general health care to which clinical psychology has natural relevance. In fact, clinical psychologists as well as health psychologists have become increasingly involved in professional activities related to behavioral health since the late 1970s. Among the many compelling behavioral health problems existing in the USA today requiring both further research and the development of more effective prevention and treatment strategies, one of the most pressing is drug abuse. Indeed, in its different forms and combinations, the abuse of drugs has reached such impressive levels as to have been identified as one of the nation's highest health and social priorities.

Alcohol dependence and abuse are among the most prevalent national disorders within America, for example, as reported in the *Diagnostic and statistical manual of mental disorders* (*DSM-IV*) (American Psychiatric Association [APA], 1994), and at a terrifically high price: in 1988, for example, costing >\$58 billion (National Institute on Drug Abuse, 1990). Of the 73% among the population reporting use of alcohol, >19 million are problem drinkers according to Winick (1992). Also according to Winick, another group, consisting of the approximately 36% of the population who are cigarette smokers, a figure representing a slight reduction from several years ago, actually constitute an especially alarming problem, given the upsurge of smoking among young people (Winick, 1992). A parallel problem involves the increasing number of adolescents and young adults who are using marijuana. Approximately one-third of the population reports the use of marijuana one or more times, making it among the most widely used drugs (APA, 1994). It has been described by Johnson and Muffler (1992) as the most frequently used illicit drug in the nation among those using drugs recreationally or intermittently and also among the most common secondary drugs used by abusers of other drugs, along with alcohol and cigarettes.

The same authors indicate that one of the more recent and threatening illicit drug developments has been the rapid invasion and increased usage of crack cocaine in the USA since 1985. Admissions for cocaine users rose from approximately 2000 in 1983 to >11 000 in 1989 (most for crack cocaine abuse rather than cocaine snorters), and treatment modalities and programs are insufficient to address the increased number of abusers. These authors caution that "much is unclear about how long the crack era will last and how long its effects will persist" and underscore the "crying need for a new treatment approach that is even modestly effective" (p. 127).

Referring to the "terrible tragedies" that arise out of drug abuse, Lowinger (1992) notes that it is among the nation's poorer citizens and also the infants of drug-addicted women that the greatest toll is exacted. His admonition is:

> Society has a stake at least in reducing, even if unable to eliminate completely, such tragedies. If it is to do so effectively, the true issues that must be dealt with are unemployment, poverty, racism, sexism, and feelings of powerlessness and alienation in our society. Every American has the right to hope for a future that can provide healthy sources of self-esteem, pleasure and affiliation. (p. 141)

Preventing and ameliorating costly and painful physical as well as psychological problems associated with such abusive behaviors are clearly critical health care goals. Psychologists are challenged to become professionally involved with interventions that effectively interrupt the addictive cycle, including behavioral as well as other approaches. Clinical psychologists may serve not only as consultants but also as program designers and managers for a variety of health programs and interventions, and, of course, they may continue to make critical contributions through their research expertise, as suggested by Barlow, Hayes, and Nelson (1984). As Nirenburg (1983) indicates, clinical psychologists work effectively in the treatment and management of addictive behaviors such as alcohol abuse, obesity, cigarette smoking, and drug abuse with a variety of treatment techniques including social skills training, problem-solving skills, vocational skills, chemical treatment, aversive conditioning, and relaxation.

Clinical psychologists provide valuable services for other health problems as well, and it is likely that such contributions will be in even greater demand in the future. They provide neuropsychological evaluations and treatment planning for brain-injured patients, for example, clinical services that can be expected to become even more sophisticated and accessible in parallel with anticipated technological advances. Clinical psychologists also contribute creatively by developing and managing prevention programs (Lorion, 1991), one of the most promising clinical efforts, from both cost-saving and disease prevention perspectives.

Even as clinical psychologists are assuming a broader role in general health care, however, they must continue to be skilled psychotherapists. Psychotherapy remains a viable and effective clinical tool, demonstrably a treatment of choice for a wide range of health problems. Even though further research will be helpful in demonstrating its value as a clinical treatment to a broader audience of health service providers and the general public, psychotherapy has already been shown to be an effective intervention for both physical and psychological problems. Reviews of recent research elucidate psychotherapy's efficacious and cost-saving contributions in alleviating or contributing to the cure of both physical and mental illnesses, a particularly critical finding in these times of managed care practices that delimit intensive and long-term psychotherapy. Lazar (1997), for example, identifies several mental health populations who benefit markedly from extended dynamic psychotherapy: patients with anxiety disorders, especially children; depressives, especially adolescents and also those with interpersonal and self-esteem symptoms; and post-traumatic stress disorder, borderline personality disorder, and multiple personality disorder patients as well as schizophrenics. Further, in describing positive outcomes from intensive psychotherapy with patients having certain physical illnesses, Lazar notes such dramatic results as increased survival rates for metastatic breast cancer patients in psychotherapy and points out as well the value of extended group psychotherapy in such health promotion programs as diet and exercise regimens and also refers to the greater stability of diabetic patients in three to four times a week psychotherapy.

It is ironic that a country with such a high degree of expertise in health care—supported by comprehensive research activities resulting in elucidating findings such as those on efficacious treatment noted above—has so many people to whom health care is either minimally provided or absent altogether. In the face of such inequity and, moreover, in the best interests of the general public, clinical psychology is challenged to bring to bear its knowledge and skills, as well as its essential regard for the human condition, as an energetic player in health care delivery. Not only must it address the wide range of health issues for which it has both relevance and promise, clinical psychology must assume energetic and assertive leadership for national health policy development and administration. Indeed, from both research and practice perspectives, clinical psychology has much to offer. Its expertise is key to the success of future health care delivery in this country.

2.39.2.2 Education

The USA's commitment to education is interwoven in its history as a nation. Both before and after the Revolution, leaders such as Thomas Jefferson and Benjamin Franklin were advocates for educating the masses, given what they saw as the "intimate relationship between educational opportunity and social, political, and economic education" (Gutek, 1991, p. 28). Jefferson strove diligently for many years to implement public education at all levels, from the lower grades through higher education; however, he achieved success only in the establishment of the University of Virginia. Although early resistances such as he encountered slowed national efforts to educate the masses, gradually throughout the nineteenth century progress was realized first with the establishment of common schools and then high schools. Cremen (1988), tracing America's commitment to education as reflected in the views of Thomas Jefferson, Horace Mann, and John Dewey, and also through conservative as well as progressive national administrations, pointed to the influential role of education in America:

> The notion of education as holding the key to the achievement of the nation's most fundamental political aspirations—of racial integration or social quality or economic productivity—remained constant, indeed no longer a characteristic progressive idea but increasingly a characteristic America idea, held with the same depth of commitment that had attached to religious belief during an earlier era in American history. As American education went, so would go the American people and the American nation. (p. 155)

Arguments supporting psychology's applications to education can be traced back to Herbart and, from a specifically more American perspective, to William James' *Principles of psychology* (1890) (James, 1952) and his subsequent writings on psychology and education. Indeed, among the many theoretical influences impacting American education in the late nineteenth and twentieth centuries, theories of psychology were among the most influential.

Even with continuing support for public as well as private education up to the present time, education has suffered strong criticism in the last couple of decades, in sharp contrast with the positive regard it enjoyed during the years of the education heyday that followed World War II. In the 1950s, for example, the promise of a high school education for all Americans and the expectation of an opportunity for higher education or training were fostered by the implementation of a number of federal programs, including the GI Bill. After the 1960s, however, not only have both dimmed considerably, but, as reflected in *Education: A nation at risk* (US National Commission on Excellence in Education, 1983), concerns about the overall lack of quality in America's educational programs have increased. As a result, the general public has joined educators and policymakers in demanding education reform. Holtzman (1992) writes that "major reform in public education, perhaps even radical changes that would scarcely have been voiced a generation ago, will be the driving force to ameliorate" many of the social problems such as "community renewal, family preservation, child development, and education" (p. xiv).

From a national perspective, specific priority areas of education reform have been identified and supported in important pieces of legislation, for example, those outlined in *Goals 200: The Educate America Act* (PL 103-227), passed in March, 1994, and *The Improving America's Schools Act of 1994* (IASA, PL 103-382). One section of IASA focuses on safe and drug-free schools and communities, acknowledging and responding to the nation's serious drug abuse and violence problems. Given the prevalence of these problems, especially among youth, and their invasion into the schools, clinical psychologists have a particular responsibility, and are in a special position, to address them. Findings from their research have already been invaluable to policymakers, for example, as in legislative decision-making around such matters as appropriate television programming for children (Wilcox & Kunkel, in press).

Another development which has become a major influencing factor in education reform is the view that early education programs as well as K-12 schools must address emotional and adjustment needs of students as well as content requirements. A related movement has advocated the provision of school-based services, including health care services. These developments are particularly inviting to clinical psychologists, whose research and applied expertise are so relevant to both: (i) the emotional development and adjustment of children and adolescents; and (ii) cognitive and learning strategies. Although this relevance is well established, it has been the case that for a good part of this century, psychologists, apart from school and educational psychologists, have not been consistently involved with schools. Many clinical psychologists, for example, may have worked with patients or clients on school-related problems (e.g., through professional activities with parents and students, including assessment and interventions), but not have spent many professional hours actually in school settings. As a result, they may not have been as informed on national education developments and needs in the past as will be required with anticipated greater state control, as, for example, in the context of school-based services.

A related development in education, the emphasis on early childhood education as well as parent–child development programs, has been of particular interest to psychologists for some years (e.g., Holtzman, 1992; Johnson, 1988; Johnson & Walker, 1987; Walker, Rodriguez, Johnson, & Cortez, 1995, Zigler, 1989; Zigler & Lag, 1991). A good deal of effort has been expended in implementing these programs in high-poverty areas, and both educators and psychologists have been encouraged by initial as well as subsequent reports indicating positive outcomes with respect to both cognitive and emotional development, for example, managing behavioral problems. More recent information, however, suggests that these promising outcomes are not maintained over time unless other kinds of interventions are included as well (D. L. Johnson, personal communication, July, 1996; Johnson & Blumenthal, in press). Specifically, positive gains seem more likely to persist when mothers of the children enrolled in the early education programs are supported through corollary education and training programs. On completion of the two-year Avance program in San Antonio, for example, more mothers went to work, and it is anticipated that this outcome will lead to better economic futures for the families which will, in turn, support a longer-term maintenance of the positive behavioral and academic gains realized by the children in the program (Walker et al., 1995). Results such as these suggest exciting possibilities for psychologists and educators interested in integrating and implementing early childhood education and parent–child development programs. Clinical psychology has much to offer in such efforts to advance early childhood education and development opportunities, and it can be a major player in assuring that these gains, which otherwise might remain only temporary, are maintained.

Other recent and mounting concerns, also related to the emotional needs of K-12 students, have been identified by Claire Ellen Weinstein, then President of the American Psychological Association's Division 15 (Educational Psychology), concerns supported by Gutek (1991) about persistent issues and challenges facing American education. While acknowledging the importance of *Goals 2000*, Weinstein extends the focus she believes educators and psychologists must pursue by identifying three key issues related to the current emphasis on the personal and social development of students: transitions, literacy, and self-system variables (C. E. Weinstein, personal communication, July, 1996). Enthusiastic in the hope that psychologists will more fully address these critical issues in the future, Weinstein stresses the necessity for collaboration between clinical psychologists and both educational and school psychologists. Such urging seems particularly valid, given: (i) the striking demographic and cultural changes taking place in our communities which are impacting our schools; and (ii) the resulting need for integrated responses and services.

Self-system variables are considered here briefly in respect of space limitations; they are selected from the three noted by Weinstein to emphasize the centrality of personal and social adjustment issues to the learning process. Moreover, not only is a focus on self-system variables particularly congruent with clinical psychology's domain, it is also especially relevant to understanding and addressing social and cultural challenges growing out of the increasing ethnic and cultural diversity in both urban and rural populations. Educators are experiencing great need for psychological understanding as they attempt to respond in school settings to the rapidly increasing, nationwide diversity. As children from diverse backgrounds and cultures enter local schools, speaking different languages and reflecting vastly different family as well as cultural values—for example, regarding such basic matters as parenting, religion, gender roles—challenges to educators are impressive. Administrators and teachers must have support in understanding, appreciating, and working in the context of self-system variables as they are reflected by students as well as their families and communities. Equally important, educators must have opportunities to consider how their own values relate to dramatically changing systems.

Student and family beliefs, expectations, and goals, for example, not only determine significantly how students perceive their school environments but also how well they will perform. How such views fit within specific community as well as administrative and teacher cultures can be a major determining factor regarding if and how students become and remain engaged in learning. As clinical psychologists work with families and children experiencing school-related problems, they are likely to find their understanding and interventions informed by determining the nature and fit of self-system variables that are obtained in a specific situation. From a school-based perspective, as psychologists gain greater appreciation for these kinds of interactions, they are likely to have opportunities for supporting an effective rapprochement among students, their families, and their teachers. An integrated and interactive approach on the parts of educators and psychologists seems congruent with Holtzman's view that psychologists can be "in the forefront of bringing about the necessary changes and scientific advancement" for education reform to succeed (Holtzman, 1992, p. xiv).

2.39.2.3 Work World and Economics

Radical changes in the world of work are impacting every family and community unit in our society in one way or another. Not only has the composition of professionals and workers changed significantly with respect to diversity (e.g., gender and ethnicity), the nature of work itself has changed remarkably. Technological advances alone, for example, have made for sea changes in the work setting. Computers and other digital products are used by 50 million workers every day (Cascio, 1995). A more gradual but nonetheless dramatic change in workforce composition is the increasing number of women working outside the home. Not only are more women working, more women are in the professional arena and more are working full-time. The increase of mothers in the workforce increased from 57% in 1980 to 68% in 1994 (Hartmann, Spalter-Roth, & Chu, 1996).

These workforce shifts contribute to major changes not only in the work place but also among families and communities. Included in the national-scale demands created by such changes are child and family care needs; health and safety issues in the work place, both physical and psychological; and job satisfaction and fulfillment, free of excessive stress. Changing standards and expectations on acceptable working conditions and settings as well as expected work place behaviors and relationships are leading to new and interesting developments. Harassment issues, for example, were almost unheard in the 1980s; yet, they are so much in the forefront today that alert human resources offices are conversant in the legal as well as everyday practical implications of such matters. Quite different from expectations a few decades ago, most workers today seek benefits for themselves and their families, and they expect protection from violence and injury in the work setting. Stress in the work place is another pervasive work problem, and clearly it is one to which clinical psychologists can bring considerable relevant research and applied expertise, as are the other critical work-related matters just noted.

Still another development, a key economic matter which has significant psychological ramifications, involves the changing nature and availability of jobs and raises questions about job security, thus, about family security. The fairly recent transition from an industrial society to a technologically driven one has been revolutionary with both positive and negative outcomes. Workers at all levels without computer skills are likely to find themselves unable to gain employment in many future work situations. On the one hand, business can be conducted more quickly and with greater ease as a result of technological advances, and more complex tasks can be completed and integrated than can be accomplished manually. On the other hand, companies and agencies, able to replace people with computers and other technological advances including mechanical operations, are downsizing, one result of which is that individuals who had expected lifetime job security are finding themselves among the unemployed. Tying downsizing to several other factors as well, including efforts to improve productivity, location moves, mergers, and new ways of organizing work, Cascio (1995) notes that seven million layoffs have occurred since 1987, and asserts that downward mobility is now the rule, not the exception.

What about the already unemployed? As expected welfare system changes are initiated in the next few years, communities will be faced with how the currently unemployed, including single mothers, will find employment providing them with a necessary income. Among the disadvantaged living in the USA, the largest group comprises single-mother families. They constitute 60% of all poor families with children, and those living in these families constitute 22% of all poor people (Hartman et al., 1996); or, put another way, in 1994: "44 percent of single-mother families were poor, compared with 8 percent of married-couple families with children and 12 percent of people over age 65" (p. 24). Clinical psychologists, along with others, such as the Institute for Women's Policy Research, surely are challenged to study factors contributing to this regrettable status and develop strategies for assuring upward change.

Based on studies investigating job availability in low-income areas, questions have been raised regarding the assumption that stopping state support will force welfare recipients to "join the labor market and support their children with honest jobs" (Newman, 1996, p. 20). Results indicate that the going may be tough, especially in geographical and target areas that will start from a low point—as in one inner-city neighborhood study, for example, where there was 18% unemployment with 40% below the poverty line and where new jobs were in short supply. One specific finding noted that "the ratio of jobseekers to successful hires in the fast-food restaurants studied in Harlem is approximately 14 to 1; moreover, among those rejected, 73% had not found work of any kind a year later" (p. 21). Those groups most frequently rejected were: younger applicants, especially 18 years and under; African-Americans, as compared with Latinos and others; residents of the neighborhoods, as compared with applicants commuting to work from other neighborhoods (a complicating factor for young mothers who need to work near their children); those without "connections," that is, those outside of friend and family networks; native-born applicants, as compared with legal immigrants; and those without prior work experience.

Such findings underscore the importance of developing and implementing programs to address job training and also those to create new jobs. The former need relates, interestingly enough, to reports on parent–child development programs (e.g., Walker et al., 1995). Although oftentimes in the past, such efforts have been viewed as largely the domain of private industry and business, or of government, it is clear that the development of new approaches informed by psychological understanding is a major economic priority for this country. Among some current views of welfare mothers are depictions of them as "welfare queens," as pathological, and as lazy, whereas others look to socio-cultural problems, including increasing numbers of teenage pregnancies, high divorce rate, lack of education and job training, as the major contributors (Newman, 1996). The resolution of this complex cluster of social and economic problems certainly could be aided by research as well as other expertise from clinical psychology. Moreover, in the context of broad collaboration with other scientists and professionals working closely with local communities as well as state and national policymakers, clinical psychologists could contribute significantly to new and better integrated approaches.

Such national work-related problems have vast implications for clinical psychologists, as they do for the general public. Clearly, considering such factors as emotional satisfaction, stress management, and the promotion of mastery and productivity, there are a number of national priorities which clinical psychology can appropriately address. There exist a number of opportunities involving collaboration with industrial and organizational psychologists, as supported by Cascio (1995): there is "an exciting agenda with large potential payoffs for individuals, organizations, and society as psychology moves into the 21st century" (1995, p. 938).

2.39.2.4 Families and Communities: Relationships, Systems, and Communication

That a central theme of both 1996 national party conventions, Republicans and Democrats, reflected the strong concern of Americans about the health, wealth, welfare, and happiness of the American nation's families and communities appears to be no accident or mere coincidence. Indeed, individuals across the USA openly express a yearning for greater individual opportunity but in the context of healthy and meaningful relationships, particularly those associated with family and community. They seek safe and supportive environments, ones that allow them to pursue their personal, family, and community goals. Clinical psychology is in an especially advantageous position for studying not only the kinds of changes that would respond to this yearning but also interventions which might best facilitate such changes. Outcomes from such programs as the Avance project, for example, are yielding provocative and exciting possibilities for bringing about changes in our communities (Walker et al., 1995). Clinical psychologists are challenged to work, not only with educators and collaboratively with other psychologists from various specialty areas, but also with local communities as well as state and national groups, to develop programs that better support children and their families. They can also serve as advisors to state and national legislators who are struggling to gain relevant, valid information about individuals, families, and communities in their various social, educational, and economic systems that would enable them to make better decisions in all public arenas on behalf of their constituents. Clinical psychologists must continue to be at the ready to provide information and counsel on matters of national priority to families and children, responding with critical leadership as they have in the past on such issues as teenage pregnancies and the negative influence of television violence on youth (Wilcox & Kunkel, in press).

Among the many family and community issues viewed as national priorities by leaders and policymakers as well as the general public, there are three that seem to be among the most pressing: violence, increasing diversity across the nation, and the social and economic problems associated with situations of disadvantage, the latter including poverty and the related high incidence of drug abuse. Again, given space considerations, violence is considered here, as an exemplar of the three, because of the particularly urgent need for relief through effective interventions, and also because, as a matter of national crisis, it has compelling implications for the future work of clinical psychologists.

Arguably, violence is one of the single greatest problems facing the USA and the world today. Possibly the USA's most devastating social and human problem, it strikes and is felt in every context of life: families, schools at all levels (preschool through 12 and on into higher education), the workplace, and in communities. Indeed, because the cost of violent events and actions is so great and the damage so extensive, the prevention of injury is an identified priority for federal and state public health offices. The Center for Disease Control and Prevention in Atlanta, part of the United States Public Health Service, has as one of its major priorities the development of further understanding and strategies for addressing the prevention of intentional and unintentional injuries. Recent violent and highly visible events, such as the April 1995 Oklahoma City bombing of the Alfred P. Murrah Federal Building, the 1995 Simpson trial, the June 1996 Saudi Arabian bombing of the American Marines' housing, and the July 1996 TWA plane crash in New York, have received wide media coverage, drawing attention to the pervasiveness of violence, or suspected violence, in American life. The visibility of these events demonstrates dramatically the destruction and pain that individual dissidents, those who are deeply psychologically disturbed, alienated groups, and others can inflict on families and communities.

Studies on the incidence and patterns of domestic violence indicate that at least half of the injuries sustained by women are related to partner abuse, and in some age groups, more than half of all reported rapes are committed by partners. Women are much more likely to be abused than men. Even though women may have reported injuries multiple times to their physicians and in emergency rooms, the violent causes of their repeated injuries may not be discerned. Recent litigation in several states involved violence to women in the workplace, from sexual harassment to alleged murder.

Every day in America: three children die from child abuse; 15 children die from gunshots, 135 000 children bring guns to school; and 1.2 million latchkey children come home to a house where there is a gun. Recent analyses show that in addition to the high price in psychological anguish paid by individuals, families, and communities as a result of violent behaviors and acts, physical injuries suffered by the victims of violence are increasing in number. The numbers are so staggering that the American Medical Association construes epidemic violence as a leading cause of death. Prevention of injury is an identified priority for federal and state public health offices.

Clinical psychologists are poised advantageously to address violence issues. Not only can they conduct requisite research to better understand the etiology and course of violent behaviors and acts in different contexts, they are already leaders actively involved in the development and implementation of effective interventions (e.g., Cohen & Mannarino 1996). Using their understanding about human motivations and conditions that lead to violence, they are poised to develop strategies and interventions to ameliorate, relieve, and dissipate individual and community violence. Clinical psychologists have a particular responsibility to work in interdisciplinary programs focusing on the development and implementation as well as the evaluation of such strategies and interventions, including interdisciplinary training programs (e.g., see Gallmeier & Bonner, 1992).

2.39.3 SUMMARY

Hubert Humphrey, Vice President of the USA from 1965 to 1969, once said:

> The moral test of government is how it treats those who are in the dawn of life—the children; those who are in the twilight of life—the aged; and those who are in the shadows of life—the sick, the needy, and the handicapped. (quoted in Edge & Groves, 1994, p. 2)

The subtitle of a 1996 publication titled *Psychology and public policy* (Lorion, Iscoe, DeLeon, & VandenBos, 1996), places this quote in an appropriate context with respect to clinical psychology's responsible and effective response to national priorities: "Balancing Public Service and Professional Need." In the foreword to that publication, Fowler says that "psychologists do not operate in a social vacuum" (p.ix), and he goes on to assert that psychologists' "theories must recognize social realities, their methods must allow for differing attitudes and behaviors, and their treatment must respond to socially defined psychological and behavioral problems" (Fowler, 1996, p. ix).

These authors identify a reciprocity between the importance of policy to the profession and that of the profession to policy formulation. As described, this reciprocity makes explicit the imperative that psychologists engage in national policymaking as well as in professional activities directly addressing national needs. Clinical psychologists, of course, are challenged accordingly, if not especially, to engage in clinical research relevant to national priorities and in applied contributions responsive to the country's most pressing social and human problems.

This chapter's focus serves that charge by presenting and elucidating four broad areas reflecting current national priorities and, then, by noting clinical psychology's relevance to, and encouraging its engagement with, them. With an impressive history in this regard and great promise for addressing human need, welfare, and happiness, clinical psychology should do no less.

2.39.4 REFERENCES

American Psychiatric Association (1994). *Diagnostic and statistical manual of mental disorders* (4th ed.). Washington, DC: Author.

Barlow, D. H., Hayes, S. C., & Nelson, R. O. (1984). *The scientist practitioner: Research and accountability in clinical and educational settings.* New York: Pergamon.

Callan, J. E. (1993). APA advocacy eyes scant federal dollars. *Monitor.* Washington, DC: American Psychological Association.

Cascio, W. F. (1995). Whither industrial and organizational psychology in a changing world of work? *American Psychologist, 50*(11), 928–939.

Cremen, L. A. (1988). *American education: The metropolitan experience—1876–1980.* New York: Harper & Row.

Edge, R., & Groves, J. (1994). *The ethics of health care: A guide for clinical practice.* Albany, NY: Delmar.

Cohen, J., & Mannarino, A. (1996). A treatment outcome study for sexually abused preschool children: Initial findings. *Journal of the American Academy of Child and Adolescent Psychiatry, 35*(1), 42–50.

Fowler, R. D. (1996). Foreword. In R. Lorion, I. Iscoe, P. DeLeon, & G. VandenBos (Eds.), *Psychology and public policy* (pp. ix–xiv). Washington, DC: American Psychological Association.

Gallmeier, T., & Bonner, B. (1992). University-based interdisciplinary training in child abuse and neglect. *Child Abuse and Neglect, 16,* 513–521.

Greenberg, P., Steglier, L., Finkelstein, S., & Berndt, E. (1993). The economic burden of depression in 1990. *Journal of Clinical Psychology, 54,* 405–418.

Gutek, G. (1991). *An historical introduction to American education* (2nd ed.). Prospect Heights, IL: Waveland Press.

Hartmann, H., Spalter-Roth, R., & Chu, J. (1996). Poverty alleviation and single-mother families. *National Forum, 76*(13), 24–27.

Holtzman, W. (1992). *School of the future.* Washington, DC: American Psychological Association.

James, W. (1952). *The principles of psychology.* (1890). A *Great books of the Western World 53* publication. Chicago: Encyclopaedia Britannica.

Johnson, B. D., & Muffler, J. (1992). Sociocultural aspects of drug use and abuse in the 1990's. In J. H. Lowinson, P. Ruiz, R. B. Millman, & J. F. Langrod (Eds.), *Substance abuse: A comprehensive textbook* (2nd ed. pp. 118–137). Baltimore: Williams and Wilkins.

Johnson, D. L. (1988). Primary prevention of behavior problems in young children: The Houston parent–child development center. In R. Lorion & J. Ramos-McKay (Eds.), *14 ounces of prevention: A casebook for practitioners* (pp. 44–52). Washington, DC: American Psychological Association.

Johnson, D. L., & Blumenthal, J. (in press). Final report of the parent–child development center follow-up project (unpublished manuscript, received from author July 1996).

Johnson, D. L., & Walker, T. (1987). Primary prevention of behavior problems in Mexican–American children. *American Journal of Community Psycology, 15*(4), 375–385.

Korchin, S., Jr. (1976). *Modern clinical psychology.* New York: Basic Books.

Lazar, S. G. (1997). Epidemiology of mental illness in the United States: An overview of the cost effectiveness of psychotherapy for certain patient populations. In S. G. Lazar (Ed.), *1997 Psychoanalytic Inquiry Supplement (Extended dynamic psychotherapy: Making the case in an era of managed care).*

Lorion, R. (1991). Prevention and public health: Psychology's response to the nation's health care crisis. *American Psychologist, 46*(5), 516–519.

Lorion, R., Iscoe, I., DeLeon, P., & VandenBos, G. (Eds.) (1996). *Psychology and public policy.* Washington, DC: American Psychological Association.

Lowinger, P. (1992) Drug abuse: economic and political basis. In J. H. Lowinson, P. Ruiz, R. B. Millman, & J. G. Langrod (Eds.), *Substance abuse: A comprehensive textbook* (2nd ed., pp. 138–142). Baltimore: Williams and Wilkins.

National Institute on Drug Abuse (1990). *National household survey on drug abuse: Main findings 1988.* Rockville, MD: National Institute on Drug Abuse.

Newman, K. S. (1996). Job availability: Achilles heel of welfare reform. *National Forum, 76*(3), 20–23.

Nirenberg, T. D. (1983). Treatment of substance abuse. In C. E. Walker (Ed.), *The handbook of clinical psychology* (Vol. II, pp. 633–665). Homewood, IL: Dow Jones-Irwin (Dorsey Professional Issues).

Raimy, V. C. (Ed.) (1950). *Training in clinical psychology* New York: Prentice-Hall.

Resnick, R., & DeLeon, P. (1995). News from Washington, DC, the future of health care reform: Implications of 1994 elections (1995). *Professional psychology: Research and Practice, 26*(1), 3–4.

Rice, D., Kelman, S., Miller, L., & Dunmeyer, S. (1990). *Report on the economic costs of alcohol and drug abuse and mental illness: 1985.* US Department of Health and Human Services Public Health Service, Alcohol, Drug Abuse, and Mental Health Administration.

Rotter, J. B. (1963). A historical and theoretical analysis of some broad trends in clinical psychology. In S. Koch (Ed.), *Psychology, a study of a science* (Vol. 5, pp. 780–830). New York: McGraw-Hill.

Shakow, D. (1969). *Clinical psychology as science and profession.* Chicago: Aldine.

Slosar, J. R., & Lettieri, R. (1996). Financing mechanisms in the delivery of mental health care services: Widgets or wisdom? *Psychologist Psychoanalyst, XVI*(1), 11–16.

US National Commission on Excellence in Education (1983). *A nation at risk.* Washington, DC: US National Commission on Excellence in Education.

Walker, T. B., Rodriguez, G. G., Johnson, D. L., & Cortez, C. P. (1995). Avance parent–child education program. In S. Smith (Ed.), *Two generation program for families in poverty: A new strategy* (pp. 67–90). Norwood, NJ: Ablex.

Watson, R. I. (1953). A brief history of clinical psychology. *The Psychological Bulletin, 50,* 321–346.

Wilcox, B. & Kunkel, D. (in press). Taking television seriously: Children and television policy. In E. Zigler, S. L. Kagan, & N. W. Hell (Eds.), *Children, families and government: Preparing for the 21st Century*. New York: Cambridge University Press.

Winick, C. (1992). Epidemiology of alcohol and drug use. In J. H. Lowinson, P. Ruiz, R. B. Millman, & J. G. Langrod (Eds.), *Substance abuse: A comprehensive textbook* (2nd ed., pp. 15–29). Baltimore: Williams and Wilkins.

Zigler, E. F. (1989). Addressing the nation's child care crisis: The school of the 21st century. *American Journal of Orthopsychiatry, 59,* 485–491.

Zigler, E. F., & Lang, M. (1991). *Child care choices: Balancing the needs of children, families, and society*. New York: Free Press.

2.40
National Priority Needs: Implications for Clinical Psychologists in Japan

YOSHIKO SHIMONAKA and KATSUHARU NAKAZATO
Tokyo Metropolitan Institute of Gerontology, Japan

2.40.1 NEEDS OF OLDER ADULTS IN JAPANESE SOCIETY

By 1995, life expectancy in Japan reached 76.5 years for men and 82.98 years for women. Also by 1995, Japanese life expectancy had been the highest in the world for 10 consecutive years for men and 11 consecutive years for women. This trend will continue.

Japan joined the list of nations with great longevity in the 1970s. In the years before World War II, Japan was a developing country, lagging far behind Western countries in terms of life expectancy. In 1935–1936, life expectancies for Japanese men and women were 46.92 years and 49.63 years, respectively, while life expectancies for both men and women of other countries such as Holland and Sweden were over 60 years.

According to World Health Organization (WHO) statistics, a nation is categorized as having an aging society if the ratio of people aged 65 and older exceeds 7% of the entire population. Figure 1 (Japanese Ministry of Health and Welfare, 1994) shows changes in the ratio of people aged 65 and older in major countries between 1950 and 2025. In Japan, the ratio became 7% in 1970 and it took only 25 years for the figure to double, reaching 14% in 1995. Furthermore, it is evident that the aging of Japanese society is proceeding at a drastic speed when compared to an 85 year period for Sweden (7% in 1890 and 14% in 1975), a 70 year period for the USA (7% in 1945 and an estimated figure of 14% in 2015), a 50 year period for the UK (7% in 1930 and 14% in 1980), and a 45 year period for Germany (7% in 1930 and 14% in 1975).

It is also noteworthy that the population of those aged 65 and older in Japan will continue to increase at a rate that will not be observed in any other country, and will reach an estimated figure of 21.3%, the highest in the world, in 2010. An ultra-aging society is expected in Japan by 2020.

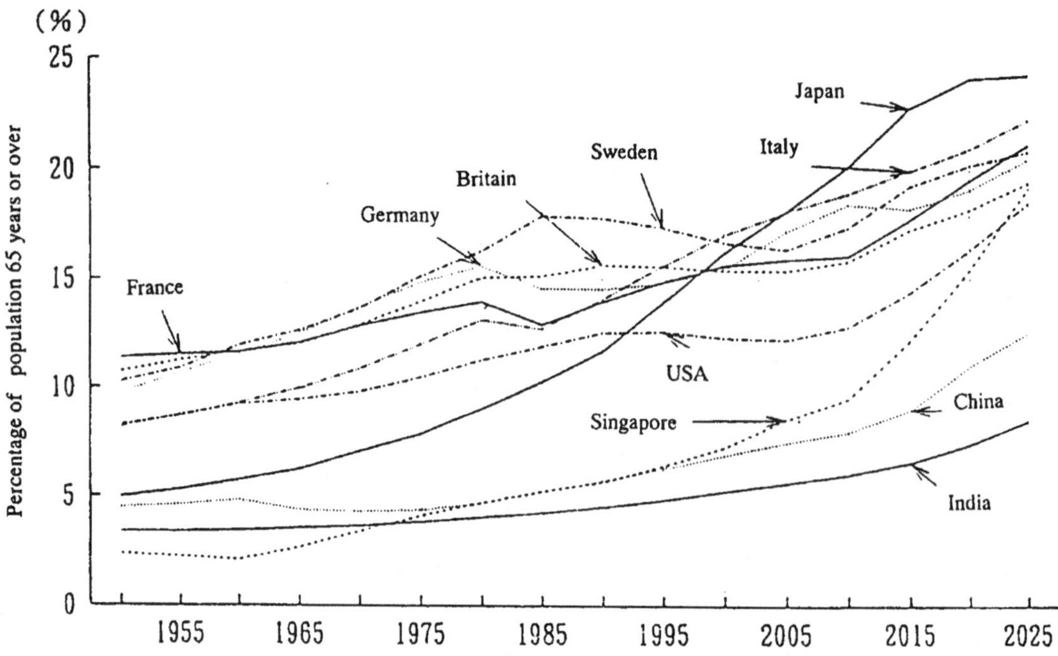

Figure 1 Changes in ratio of people 65 and over in Japan and other countries.

Now that Japan is facing an aging society, various issues concerning the aged are surfacing. One of the important issues is the change in family structure. The traditional Japanese family system (three generations in one household) started to break down after World War II, and "the nuclear family," which had long been common in Western countries, began to take over. The ratio of those aged 65 or older living with a child was 68% in 1975. The figure had dropped to 55.3% by 1994. This figure, however, is still high compared to such Western countries as the USA, the UK, and Sweden.

The ratio of those aged 60 and over who prefer to live with a child or grandchild is 53.6% in Japan, quite a high figure compared to that of Germany (15.4%), the USA (3.4%), and the UK (3.9%) (Japanese General Affairs Agency, 1992). Despite the fact there are more elderly in Japan who live with their family and who prefer to do so than in other countries, the ratio of those who felt lonely was over 50%, much higher than in the USA and the UK. This suggests that there is a wide gap between the expectations Japanese elderly people have of their family and the reality of their daily life. The same can be said about how they feel about work after retirement.

As to how Japanese elderly people feel about having a postretirement job, 35.9% replied that they would "work as long as they are healthy" and 22.7% replied that they would "work until they were about 70." These two figures together show that more than half the population of elderly people in Japan are willing to work (Japanese General Affairs Agency, 1995). In reality, however, the employment rate of those aged 65 years and older had dropped from 38.1% in 1962 to 24.3% in 1994.

The most common motivation for those who wanted to work was "the desire to make friends." The motivations given in other countries such as the USA and the UK were "earning money" or "enjoying work." This difference indicates that elderly people in Japan have little interaction with their community and reveals the fact that they are living with a feeling of loneliness.

Another difficult issue regarding the elderly in Japan in the 1990s is that of frail or demented elderly people. In 1990, there were approximately 1 million cases of senile dementia nationwide, and this figure is expected to climb to 1.5 million by the year 2000, and 2.47 million by 2015. The number of elderly people who are frail or bed-ridden was 810 000 in 1990 and it is estimated that this figure will triple to 2.29 million by 2025 (Japanese Ministry of Health and Welfare, 1992). At present, there are 15 caregivers (careworkers or family members) to one elderly person. By 2025, however, there will be only two caregivers for one elderly person, a very severe reduction.

According to a survey conducted by the Ministry of General Affairs in 1995, 41.5% of the elderly aged 65 and older wish to receive care at home, and 54.8% of those expect their family members to assume this task. But, since 1985, the number of people in the younger generation who consider looking after their aged parents an obligation has been decreasing drastically, and they tend to consider living with their parents and supporting their parents as separate matters (Japanese Ministry of Health and Welfare, 1996).

Despite the fact that this gap between the expectations of the elderly and the consciousness of the younger generation has started to become clear, in reality, one out of four people aged 65 and older who died had received care from their family members while bedridden for more than half a year. Female members of the family are more likely to assume the responsibility of taking care of elderly family members than men in the following order: the elderly person's wife (31.6%), the wife of the eldest son (27.6%), and the eldest daughter (15.5%). Only 5.0% of the elderly persons' husbands assume such responsibilities. It is reported that more than half of those who assumed these responsibilities had jobs and 20.6% of them had given up their work to take care of an elderly family member (Japanese Ministry of Health and Welfare, 1996).

The responsibility of caring for the elderly increases the fatigue and stress of the responsible family member. There have been reports in newspapers, albeit few, regarding elderly abuse and murder of old people. Abuse and murder of the elderly appear to be associated with their caregivers' added fatigue and stress.

2.40.1.1 Clinical Psychological Services Sought in Japan

Since the Japanese Association for Certification of Clinical Psychologists was established in 1989, the number of certified clinical psychologists has been increasing year by year. In 1997, more than 5000 clinical psychologists are working at various institutions or in private practice. The Association of Japanese Clinical Psychology has more than 7000 members, and the number of research papers presented at its annual congress has also been increasing. The Education and Training Committee of the Association of Japanese Clinical Psychology conducted a survey on the content of the clinical psychological services provided by its 2296 new members for a period of six years from 1986 to 1991 (Association of Japanese Clinical Psychology, 1993). Data were obtained by multiple choice responses. 53.6% of the clinical psychologists surveyed were full-time workers, their most common workplaces being hospitals (37.9%), followed by counseling centers in universities and schools (15.7%), and child guidance clinics (15.3%). Almost 70% worked at the aforementioned three workplaces. Other workplaces included welfare facilities for rehabilitation (6.3%), court (6.8%), private clinics (4.8%), research institutions (3.5%), mental health centers and health centers (3.3%), the Ministry of Justice (1.9%), and others (4.5%). 22.3% of the clinical psychologists surveyed were part-time workers.

The ratio of part-time workers working for hospitals was 24.2%, which was lower than that of full-time workers. However, the ratios of part-time workers working for child guidance clinics (29.0%), private clinics (12.4%), and mental health centers and health centers (11.8%) were higher than those of full-time workers.

Regarding the contents of the clinical psychologists' work, psychological therapy was the most common (70.6%), followed by psychological assessments (52.1%), interviews and consultations (50.1%), supervision and training (9.1%), and others (6.7%).

Clients for the services of clinical psychology can be categorized into the following age groups: children and youths (58.7%), middle aged people (55.0%), college students and working youths (41.7%), infants (39.6%), and the elderly (18.4%). Given the large number of the elderly people in Japan, 18.4% is a rather small figure for clinical psychology services, especially when we consider the fact that about 7% of those aged 65 and older are reported to have mental disorders.

Bullying in Japanese schools is a serious problem which has come to light. Due to the increasing number of cases of bullying, a school counseling system has been planned and discussed since 1995 for future implementation by the Ministry of Education. Appreciation for clinical psychology has started to permeate Japanese society owing to this problem. Clinical psychologists have also started tackling the pressing issue of HIV counseling. Furthermore, systems for crisis intervention such as the "Lifeline" system have gradually been put in order. It must, however, be pointed out that only a few elderly are taking advantage of these services. This is because they tend to think that revealing a personal psychological problem to a stranger is shameful. Also, they are not used to paying money for such intangible services as counseling.

2.40.2 SPECIFIC PSYCHOLOGICAL PROBLEMS IN JAPANESE OLDER ADULTS

2.40.2.1 Psychological Disturbance in Old Age

The Ministry of Health and Welfare conducted a survey on outpatients according to the *ICD-9* (*International statistical classification of diseases and related health problems-ninth revision*) in 1993 (Japanese Ministry of Health and Welfare, 1995).

The highest number of older adults sought treatment for senile/presenile organic psychosis (senile dementia) (43%), followed by neurosis (33%), and manic-depressive psychosis (26%). There is a tendency to consider depression as a more serious problem than neurosis among the aged, however it is evident from the above figures that the threat of neurosis should not be ignored (Japanese Ministry of Health and Welfare, 1995).

Figure 2 shows trends of outpatients by age group suffering from neurosis and manic-depressive psychosis. The curves for neurosis show a difference between the numbers of male and female outpatients receiving treatment. The peak for women is in the 70–74 age group, but not much difference among age groups exists in the men's curve. Little difference can be seen between the curves for men and women for manic-depressive psychosis, and the peak for both is in the 70–74 age group.

The results of this survey suggest that there is more chance of suffering from psychological disorders during the period from middle age to old age than at any other time in life. However, clinical services for these people are lagging behind the services available to younger people.

2.40.2.2 Suicide Among the Elderly: Aspects of Suicide Unique to Japan

Figure 3 (Association for Health and Welfare Statistics, 1994) shows trends of the suicide rate

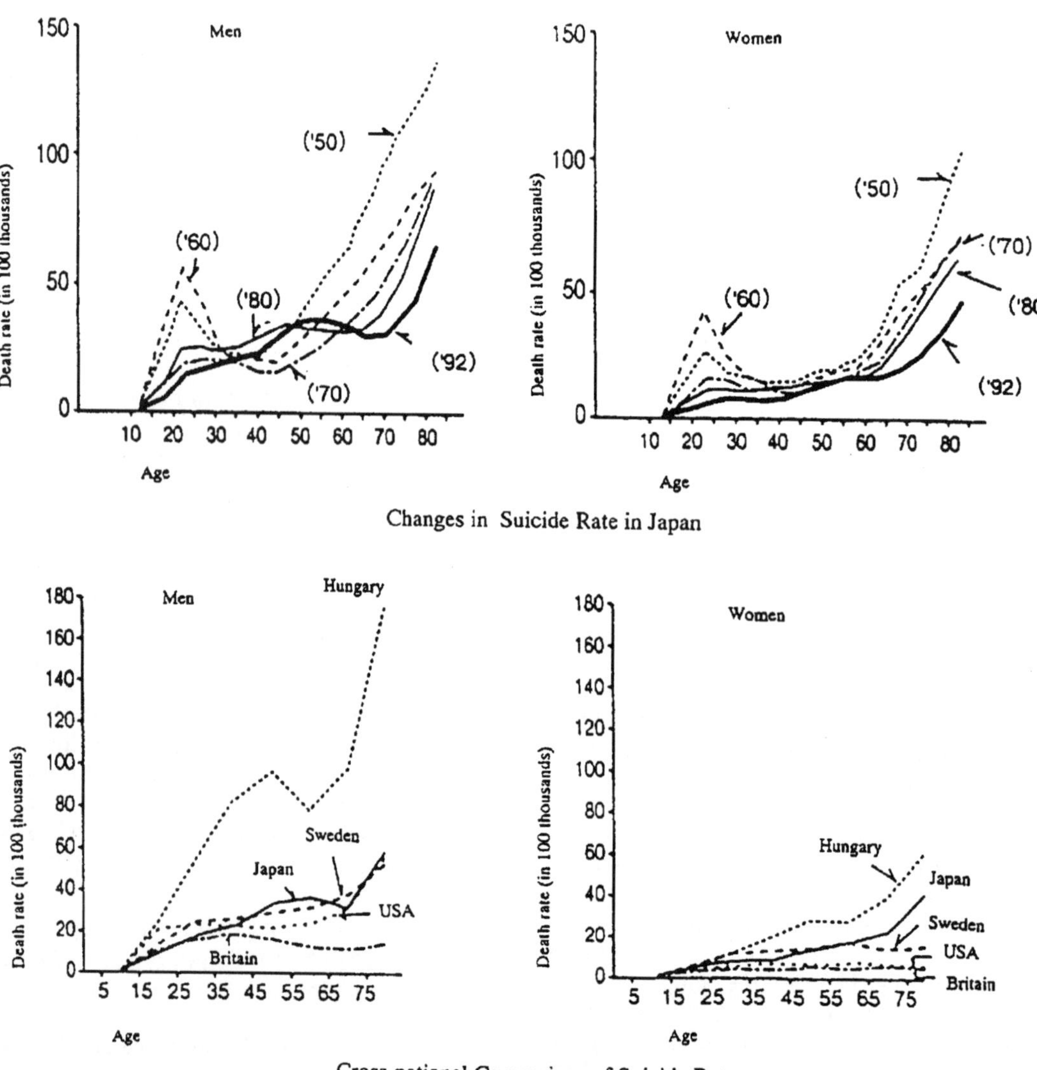

Figure 2 Suicide rate of elderly people: changes in Japan and cross-national comparison.

in different years by age group in Japan as compared to other countries. Although the suicide rate of people aged 65 years and older is declining year by year, it is still the highest among all age groups. The graphs comparing suicide rates of people aged 65 and older in different countries show that Hungary has the highest rate for both men and women, and that Japan has the second highest for both men and women. The leading cause of suicide among the elderly is illness (70%), followed by family problems, alcohol dependency, and psychological disturbance. Few suicides result from financial difficulties. This suggests that many older adults are suffering from illness or facing problems with their family while they are living in relative affluence. Older adults commit suicide because they "don't want to be a nuisance to the family." Committing suicide is not considered a sin in the religious views of most Japanese. The same can be said of double suicides of married couples which are discussed in this section.

What is considered a double suicide of a married couple is not the same in Japan as it is the West. Husband and wife mutually agree to commit suicide, or, in some cases, one spouse kills the other and then commits suicide. It must be understood here that Japanese people do not consider the murder/suicide of a married couple to be any different from a double suicide. Unlike the prevailing views in Western culture, this kind of murder/suicide is classified along with double suicide due to some profound cultural differences between Japan and the West. Older couples in Japan do not consider their spouses as individual persons, but rather as a part of themselves. Together, they are an inseparable whole, or "one flesh." This idea stems from the traditional Japanese concept of the extended family system. Older Japanese couples try to solve their problems by themselves, without outside help. When considering suicide, they tend to think, "It is better for my wife (or husband) to die with me, rather than for me to leave her (or him) alone to suffer." This attitude, while common in Japan, may be difficult for Westerners to understand.

Although cases have been few, murder of elderly people by a family member caregiver has become a social problem. In 1992, for example, there were 20 such cases, 17 of the victims being women. The murders were committed by husband or wife (9 cases), son or daughter (10 cases) and daughter in law (1 case) (Takeda, 1994). In most of the murder cases, the task of caring for the elderly had been done entirely within the family without the help of others or public service organizations, and thus, the caregiver's mental and physical fatigue had reached its limit.

2.40.2.3 Elderly Abuse: Abuse and Neglect

There is little substantiated data on elderly abuse in Japan due to the fact that people have been reluctant to discuss the issue. Tanaka (1994) surveyed 400 At-home Elderly Care Support Centers throughout Japan. These centers act as coordinators between families or older adults and public service organizations. The survey was conducted via mail and 220 replies were received (55%). Seventy-two of the respondants reported elderly abuse as one of their items for consultation.

What seems characteristic in Japan is that if elderly abuse is divided into abuse and neglect, there is more of the latter. The ratio of abuse, as opposed to neglect, was 75.1% in New York, 84.4% in London and 43.1% in Japan nationwide. This means that neglect made up more than half the cases of elderly abuse in Japan. In common with Western countries, more women are abused than men and the abuse rate increases with age. It is unique to Japan that most cases of abuse are committed by family members, and also that the abuse rate increases as the caregiver's age increases. The main cause of abuse is the fatigue associated with caregiving.

2.40.3 PSYCHOTHERAPEUTIC APPROACHES FOR THE ELDERLY IN CLINICAL GEROPSYCHOLOGY

Although the number of research papers presented at the Congress of the Association of Clinical Psychology has been increasing, much less research has been done with elderly people. This is due to the fact that gerontology has only recently been introduced and research into gerontological clinical psychology has not yet been established as a field in Japan.

The first and only gerontological research center in Japan, the "Tokyo Metropolitan Institute of Gerontology," was established in 1972, just before the population of people aged 65 years and older reached 7%. This is when research into the psychological characteristics of the elderly first began. Shimonaka and Nakazato (1980, 1986) compared personality characteristics of elderly people with those of young and middle-aged adults using a sentence completion test. With respect to family relationships, elderly people gave more positive responses to family images. As for self-perception, elderly people perceived their past and present selves as being more positive while the younger

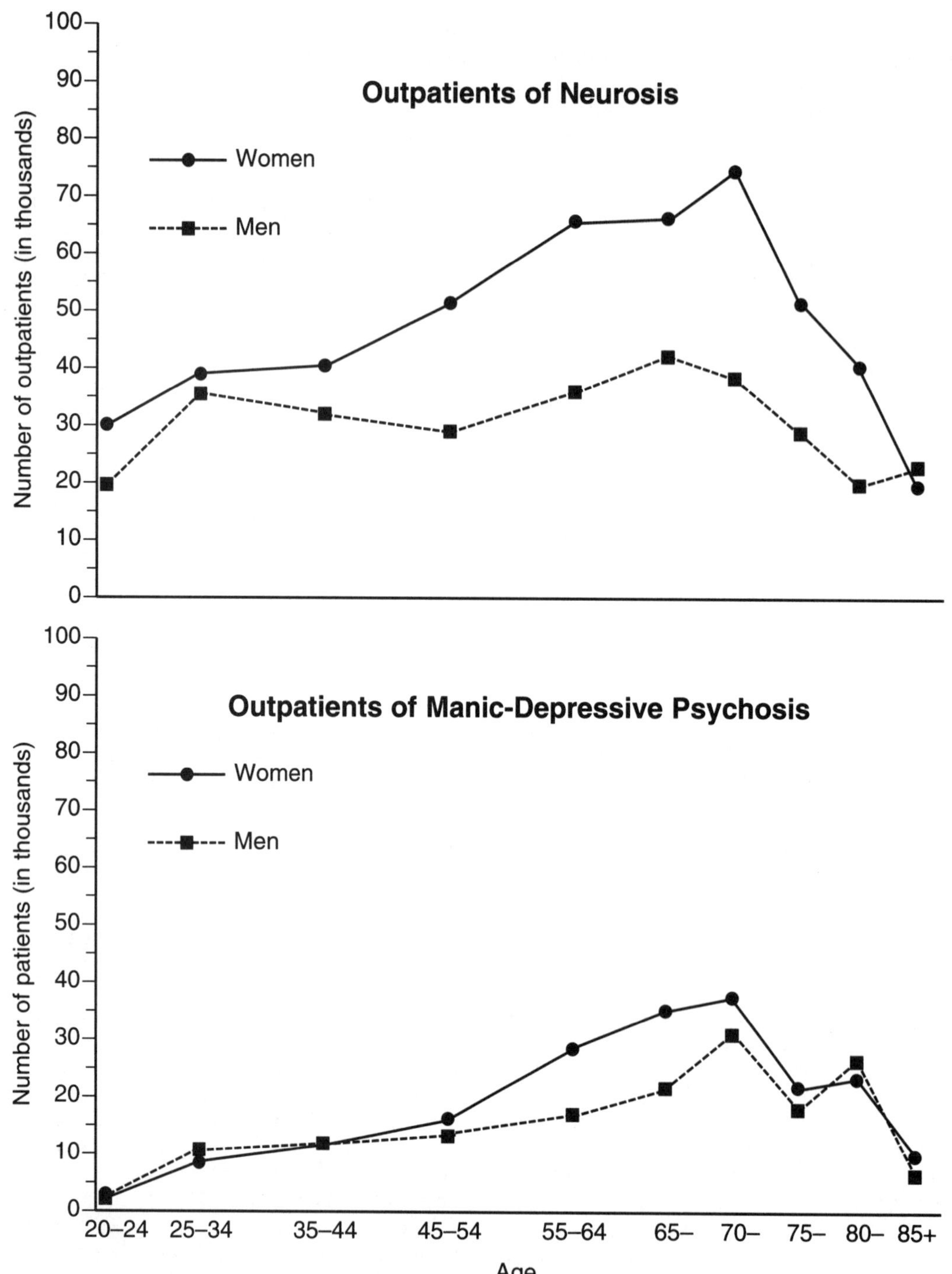

Figure 3 Number of outpatients of neurosis and manic-depressive psychosis according to age group and sex.

generations perceived their future selves as being more positive. However, future self-perception for elderly people was limited by the ultimate finality of death. More young adults viewed death with negative feelings such as fear, sorrow, or distress than did the older adults, who saw death in a neutral manner, as destiny, or a natural phenomenon.

Furthermore, in order to investigate stability or change in personality from young-old age to old-old age, a survey, which had been given to 70 year olds living in the community, was followed up 10 years later (1976–1986). It was revealed that positive family image increased with advancing age. With respect to self-perception, the past self changed from objective to positive. The present self maintained positive responses, while the future self shifted from objective to negative (Shimonaka & Nakazato, 1989).

The Rorschach Inkblot Test has often been used to analyze the personality of the elderly in Japan. Shimonaka and Nakazato (1991) used the Rorschach Inkblot Test six times over a 10 year period to study changes in personality related to aging and to determine whether significant changes in personality precede death.

Age-related changes were observed in the number of responses, responses regarding rejection, shading and popular, poor form level, and content range. Changes in these variables suggest that productivity, creative thinking, cooperativeness, and concern for and interest in society lessen with advancing age. Over the four to six years preceding death, popular responses and content range declined, with the decline accelerating near death. Tests given within two years of death showed less animal movement response, higher form (F(−)%), and higher human content. These results suggest that productivity, vital energy, and ego strength become reduced prior to death, while interest in and sensitivity to others is maintained to the end (Shimonaka & Nakazato, 1991).

People are inclined to have a negative image towards aging. This tendency was especially strong during the 1960s and 1970s. During this time, old age was considered to be a time of much negative change and anxiety (Cattell, 1965; Jarvik & Russell, 1979). However, from the results of the life-span developmental approach regarding anxiety (Costa et al., 1986), it has been suggested that feelings of anxiety decrease as age increases.

The anxiety of Japanese adults aged between 25 and 92 years was measured using a Japanese version of the State–Trait Inventory and found that the level of anxiety lowered linearly as age increased. These results suggest that anxiety about death is not, as expected, especially strong in old age (Nakazato & Shimonaka, 1989).

Psychotherapy for elderly people by clinical psychologists in Japan is quite uncommon. Since the 1980s, however, more effort has been made in this regard at institutions and day care centers for the elderly, as the population of the elderly has been increasing. This has been mainly group therapy, and there has been no reported research on behavior, cognitive, or family therapies yet. Moreover, many of the research papers available use results based on case studies and subjective evaluations by practitioners. Since most subjects of group therapy are those with senile dementia, reality orientation, reminiscence, and therapeutic recreation are the main activities provided. This is probably due to the fact that the drastic increase of people with senile dementia has become a social problem in Japan. Since these group therapy activities had not been used until 1990 in Japan, many research papers mainly examine their effectiveness.

The effectiveness of reality orientation has been examined using as subjects people with moderate senile dementia in a nursing home. Changes in the dementia scale (Hasegana, 1983; Kahn, Goldharb, Pollack, & Peck, 1960) were observed before, just after, and six months after the orientation. The participants showed improvement in the dementia scale scores, unlike the control group, which showed no change.

Furthermore, according to the evaluation of daily behavior in the ward by the charge nurse, improvement was seen in social communication. The improved dementia scale scores were even maintained six months after the orientation. These results suggest that reality orientation is very effective at the early stages of dementia (Shimonaka & Nakazato, 1989; Shimonaka, Nakazato, Habu, Haga, & Mizuno, 1988).

The effectiveness of reminiscence, which is as common as reality orientation in countries other than Japan, was examined with inpatients of a psychiatry ward as subjects, and evaluation was made using the Moses scale. Moses scale scores showed improvement after reminiscence. These results suggest that the psychological state, relationships with others, and the level of independence among people with senile dementia was improved by participating in reminiscence (Kurokawa, 1995).

There have been other reports on the effectiveness of therapeutic recreation incorporating play therapy, art therapy, sports therapy (Kawamuro, 1995; Koike, 1995; Sadaki, 1993), and music therapy (Kitamoto, 1996) which are carried out at geriatric hospitals, day care centers, and nursing homes.

Finally, there has been a unique approach, in which group therapy, provided during day care for outpatients with senile dementia who are receiving care at home from their family, is combined with group counseling provided for the outpatients' family members. This attempt aims to vitalize the residual mental functions of people suffering from senile dementia whose activity is restricted to their homes. At the same time, family members who are exhausted from care giving are provided with rest time and group counseling (Kato et al., 1987).

The various therapies above for people with senile dementia have just been introduced in Japan and they are still at a stage where their effectiveness is being researched. Storandt,

Siegler, and Elias (1978) have pointed out in *The clinical psychology of aging* that there were too few clinical psychologists for people aged 65 and older. Despite the fact that 10% of those aged 65 and over were in need of some kind of mental health services in the US at that time, clinical psychology had long neglected the treatment of older adults. In the mid-1990s Japan is in the very same situation. Although there are few clinical psychologists in Japan, their efforts for proper application of therapies to the aged today will bear fruit and become a touchstone for tomorrow's clinical psychologists for the aged.

2.40.4 REFERENCES

Association for Health and Welfare Statistics (1994). *Trend of national health.* Tokyo: Association for Health and Welfare Statistics.

Cattell, R. B. (1965). *The scientific analysis of personality.* New York: Penguin.

Costa, P. T., Jr., McCrae, R. R., Zonderman, A. B., Barbano, H. E., Lebowitz, B. Z., & Larson, D. M. (1986). Cross-sectional study of personality in a national sample: 2. Stability in neuroticism, extravertion, and openness. *Psychology and aging*, 1, 144–149

Education and Training Committee Association of Japanese Clinical Psychology (1993). Questionnaire to the new members (1986–1991). *Journal of Japanese Clinical Psychology, 11,* 66–78.

Hasegawa, K. (1983). The clinical assessment of dementia in the aged: A dementia screening scale for psychogeriatric patients. In M. Bergener, U. Lehr, E. Lang, & R. Schmitz-Scherzer (eds.), *Aging in the eighties and beyond.* New York: Springer.

Institute of Population Problems, Japanese Ministry of Health and Welfare (1994). *Population trends.* Tokyo: Health and Welfare Statistics Association.

Japanese General Affairs Agency (1992). *Survey on the life and opinion in later years.* Tokyo: Chuohoki.

Japanese General Affairs Agency (1995). *Survey on attitudes among the elderly people.* Tokyo: Chuohoki.

Japanese Ministry of Health and Welfare (1992). *White paper on health and welfare.* Tokyo: Japanese Ministry of Health and Welfare.

Japanese Ministry of Health and Welfare (1996). *White paper on health and welfare.* Tokyo: Japanese Ministry of Health and Welfare.

Jarvik, L. & Russell, D. (1979). Anxiety, aging and the third emergency reaction. *Journal of Gerontology, 34,* 196–200.

Kahn, R. L., Goldharb, A. I., Pollack, M., & Peck, A. (1960). Brief objective measures for determination of mental status in the aged. *American Journal of Psychiatry, 117,* 326–328.

Kato, S., Ikeda, K., Hirata, N., Imai, Y., Ichihara, H., Homma, A., & Hasegawa, K. (1987). Attitudes toward the elderly with dementia among their family caregivers and their changes. *Japanese Journal of Psychogeriatrics, 4,* 779–789.

Kawamuro, Y. (1995). Group psychotherapy. *Japanese Journal of Psychogeriatrics, 6,* 1503–1511.

Kitamoto, F. (1996). An attempt at group music therapy for elderly persons. *Journal of Japanese Clinical Psychology, 14,* 141–151.

Koike, K. (1995). Therapeutic recreation. *Japanese Journal of Psychogeriatrics, 6,* 1497–1502.

Kurokawa, Y. (1995). Reminiscence group with Japanese dementia patients. *Journal of Japanese Clinical Psychology, 13,* 169–179.

Nakazato, K., & Shimonaka, Y. (1989). The Japanese State–Trait Anxiety Inventory: Age and sex differences. *Perceptual and Motor Skills, 69,* 611–617.

Sadaki, T. (1993). An example of a group therapy program for elderly people with dementia. *Journal of Japanese Clinical Psychology, 11,* 53–58.

Shimonaka, Y., & Nakazato, K. (1980). Psychological characteristics of Japanese aged: A comparison of Sentence Completion Test responses of older and younger adults. *Journal of Gerontology, 35,* 891–898.

Shimonaka, Y., & Nakazato, K. (1986). The development of personality characteristics of Japanese adults. *Journal of Genetic Psychology, 147,* 37–46.

Shimonaka, Y., & Nakazato, K. (1989). Personality development among the Japanese elderly: A ten-year longitudinal study on a sentence completion test. *Journal of Cross-Cultural Gerontology, 4,* 347–356.

Shimonaka, Y., & Nakazato, K. (1989). *Effectiveness of reality orientation applied to Japanese elderly with dementia.* Paper presented at the Tenth Biennial Meetings of ISSBD, Jyvaskyla, Finland.

Shimonaka, Y., & Nakazato, K. (1991). Aging and terminal change in Rorschach responses among the Japanese elderly. *Journal of Personality Assessment, 57,* 10–18.

Shimonaka, Y., Nakazato, K., Habu, K., Haga, S., & Mizuno, H. (1988). Effects of group work for dementia in the nursing home residents. *Japanese Journal of Clinical Psychiatry, 17,* 101–109.

Statistics and Information Department, Minister's Secretariat, Japanese Ministry of Health and Welfare (1995). *Patient survey* (Vol. 1). Tokyo: Japanese Ministry of Health and Welfare.

Statistics and Information Department, Minister's Secretariat, Japanese Ministry of Health and Welfare (1996). *Report on the socioeconomic survey of vital statistics.* Tokyo: Association for Health and Welfare Statistics.

Storandt, M., Siegler, I. C., & Elias, M. F. (Eds.) (1978). *The clinical psychology of aging.* New York: Plenum.

Takeda, K. (1994). *Why are elderly women killed by their family member?* Tokyo: Minerva.

Tanaka, S. (1994). *Preliminary study on elderly abuse in Japan.* Tokyo: The Study Group for Casework for the Elderly.

2.41 National Advocacy for Psychology

JILL N. REICH and NINA G. LEVITT
American Psychological Association, Washington, DC, USA

2.41.1 INTRODUCTION

The development of knowledge and its application occurs within a social construct. As such, a discipline is both influenced by the society in which it lives and, when that knowledge is disseminated and applied, it influences that society. This dynamic is especially true for a discipline like psychology, and very particularly clinical psychology, which has so much to contribute to issues of national and global concern. For example, the results of a massive new assessment of the world's state of health, and of the changes it is likely to undergo between 1997 and 2020, underscores the role of behavior in maintaining a healthy citizenry (Murray & Lopez, 1996). This study reports that the most overlooked cause of death and disability is injury, specifically using the word "injury" rather than "accident" in order to communicate that injurious events are avoidable. They note that the most important single variable expected to impact the world's health in 2020 is the use of tobacco. In a ranking of conditions purported to cause the greatest disease burden, severe depression moves from fourth highest in 1990 to second highest in 2020.

These data and their projections suggest that the discipline of psychology, especially through its subfield of clinical psychology, should be at the forefront of healthcare, and through these contributions valued highly by the society in which it lives. A prominent measure of the national status of the discipline is the support of that discipline in the corridors of national governance. For psychologists in the USA, this means looking at the perception, knowledge, and support for the discipline from members of the US Congress: members of the Senate (Senators) who represent their states each term for a period of six years and members of the House of Representatives (Representatives) who represent their districts (within each state) each term for a period of two years (despite much discussion about limiting the number of terms a member may serve, no action has ever been passed to do so). A second source of support and hence a measure of status lies in the Executive branch of government which through its agencies implements the legislation and policies set by Congress. It is through these governing bodies that the larger society identifies its interests, expresses its values, and develops the means to meet its national needs.

The role of advocacy in society's perception of psychology cannot be underestimated. This role is enlarged by the dynamic nature of advocacy which works to recognize psychology's potential to contribute to areas of national need and in so doing further reinforces the need for psychology's contributions to society. By definition, "advocacy" involves "pleading or defending the cause" (Webster; 1995), in this case, the cause of psychology. Thus, when advocating on behalf of psychology, one educates policymakers and implementers about the value of the discipline and hence the need or right of the discipline for support, resources, recognition, status, and the like. At the national level, most often advocacy involves working with policymakers and their staffs in Congress, and/or the implementors of these policies, the staffs in the various federal agencies.

In this chapter, the process of advocacy will be described, with its critical variables, and how these factors, together with existing structures for advocating, serve to enhance or hinder successful advocacy on behalf of psychology, in particular, utilizing examples from advocating for support for education in professional psychology. Moreover, as the advocacy process by its very nature is a changing one, emphasis should be placed on patterns rather than particulars as the specifics can be expected to change quickly and often.

2.41.2 THE NATURE OF ADVOCACY IN THE POLITICAL PROCESS

2.41.2.1 What is Advocacy?

The democratic process is one in which complementary and competing interests must vie for recognition and, through that recognition, for control and resources. Whose interests and which factors are recognized might be thought to be determined logically by the nature of the issue. But whose understanding of the issue and which priority among the many possible will prevail? How the policymaker understands the issue, its component parts, and what interests or factors are thought to be critical to the matter being deliberated necessarily is in the eye of the beholder. Thus, when advocating on behalf of psychology, that is, when pleading the case of the discipline, in effect the listener is being educated about the ways in which psychology can contribute to the issue at hand. To be effective, this must be done in ways that are meaningful, of interest, and value to the listener, and true to the discipline. In the political process, with its broad range of interests and decision making, this means that the job is to demonstrate to the listener, the policymaker, or legislator why and how psychology can serve the national issue being considered. Of course, the particular issue varies. Given the US national legislative agenda with its attention to healthcare, and the potential of clinical psychology to contribute to this agenda, the conversation is most likely to focus on one of the six major areas of health that have been demonstrated to be behaviorally based: violence, substance abuse, smoking, injury, diet, and AIDS. The goal then is to have the listener recognize that psychology has a significant contribution to make, so that when funding is being allocated or professional fields identified for inclusion in a particular practice or intervention, the listener will conclude that psychology should be a part of the policy and so named in the legislation. At the very least, the goal of advocacy is that the legislation should not preclude or deny psychology's participation in the bill being considered.

2.41.2.2 Why is Advocacy Necessary?

Ideally, advocacy is necessary for the same reasons that any education endeavor is necessary; so that the policymaker will have the benefit of the most pertinent information to the task, that is, so that the issues faced by legislators will have the benefit of the contributions of the discipline. In this scenario, the best the discipline has to offer is put forward to a particular cause and the results left to the good judgment of the legislators. But the political process is not always so ideal. There will be many ways to meet the demands being deliberated, many interests involved, and limited resources available for allocation. In these cases, advocacy also serves to bring attention and recognition to psychology. In the US political process, if there is no advocacy on behalf of the discipline, psychology is unlikely to be recognized. Herein lies a particular problem for clinical psychology in the complex and crowded healthcare arena in the 1990s.

This problem arises from the very nature of the discipline being a field with numerous subfields. It is not well understood by the general public. Among those who do know the discipline, some know psychologists as mental health practitioners; others are aware that psychologists are behavioral scientists who conduct research in areas like cognition and neuroscience; and still others remember their psychology professors from undergraduate courses in personality and perception. Yet often these separate parts are not a coherent whole, able to bring the full strength and richness of the discipline to bear on the range of policy matters before Congress. Moreover, in the process of advocating for a particular issue, and needing to keep the message simple, most often only a limited part of psychology will be addressed, for example, the needs of practice or the particular implications for science. Thus, despite the many roles that psychologists actually serve, there remains a limited public understanding of psychology as a whole and the many ways in which the discipline can be applied to real issues of public concern and national need: a fact that unfortunately is as true for policymakers as for the general public.

2.41.2.3 Who Does Advocacy?

There are many answers to this question. On the most general level, while this answer may come as a surprise to the reader, in fact, everyone in the discipline advocates. The problem of course being that psychologists are unaware that in the process of their work, they also serve to educate others about whether or not this work is valuable, deserves public recognition, support, and sometimes even protection. In spite of the lack of awareness, whether in classrooms or offices, how the discipline is presented, to whom, and with what level of respect and value will greatly influence how the listener will view the discipline now and in the future. Perhaps the most misunderstood arena for advocacy are classrooms where the citizens of tomorrow are most likely to be introduced to the discipline and its potential to contribute to areas of national need. If psychologists do not show respect for the discipline as a whole, others can hardly do so. If psychologists do not demonstrate how their knowledge base can contribute to national need, others cannot do so. And if the value and application of their work to areas of national interest are left unspoken, then these citizens, or their representatives, cannot be expected to allocate national resources to support psychologists' education, science, or practice.

On a more direct level, of course, advocacy follows a planned strategy, developed by professional lobbyists working with psychologists and focused on policymakers involved in issues of particular interest to psychologists, whether these be in the areas related to education, practice, science, or public interest. This approach, necessarily focused and targeted, remains dependent on the participation of psychologists at every level and activity as will be delineated as the process of advocacy for psychology is described.

2.41.2.4 What Makes Advocacy Effective?

Effectiveness is based on the same factors that make any human interaction effective: clarity, consistency, context, and credibility. Advocacy is not accomplished through magic nor are advocacy skills acquired through academic study. Advocacy, while a learned behavior, must be expanded through experience and perfected by practice. In other words, if advocacy is examined for its key elements, the most basic skills of human interaction will emerge. These skills then must be augmented by knowledge of the discipline, motivation to succeed, much persistence, and a little bit of good luck.

Some compare the components of successful advocacy to those of actual warfare, in this way placing key factors into the framework of a battle. Whether or not warfare is considered effective human interaction is debatable. However, the analogy serves to focus attention on the importance of reaching a conclusion in a competitive environment. At times, the analogy seems apt; the competition is real and the desire to win is strong. Zorack (1990) reports that the lobbying process parallels those factors developed by British Major-General J.F.C. Fuller during WWI as elements of a successful combat campaign:

(i) objective—clearly define an attainable goal,

(ii) offensive—exploit the initiative, be proactive, not reactive,

(iii) mass—concentrate efforts at optimum time and place,

(iv) economy of force—focus on one initiative at a time,

(v) maneuver—place opposition at disadvantage,

(vi) unity of command—maintain one leader,

(vii) security—know what information to share and what not to share,

(viii) surprise—employ unexpected legislative maneuvering when possible, and

(ix) simplicity—simplify and limit all requests.

The above-mentioned tenets for a successful campaign, regardless of the battlefield, are self-evident if advocacy is conceptualized as a campaign and the delivery of the discipline as the artillery. For this advocacy battlefield, the message is to recognize the need and value of psychology to society thereby establishing its right to support, recognition and involvement in legislation, and its implementation. In this view of the advocacy process, emphasis remains on the importance of communicating effectively, most often to individuals with little knowledge of the message and with great need to act efficiently and effectively for a broad range of very vocal constituents. Psychologists, especially, should be able to utilize their understanding of perception, memory, problem solving, social interaction, motivation, and the like to develop effective strategies for advocacy.

2.41.3 ADVOCACY: IN ACTION

2.41.3.1 Advocacy: Goals and Plans

Successful advocacy requires a plan of action consistent with the goal. As an example, the overarching goal for education is to increase federal funding for education and training programs in psychology. But there are many ways to go after this larger goal: through new legislation, by revising existing legislation to more effectively include psychology, or by changing regulatory language that controls how the legislation is implemented to name the most likely target areas. Careful analysis of the range of legislation that it is possible to effect, the likelihood of success, the ability of the results to benefit the discipline, as well as the more practical factors of time, cost, and resources will determine the particular target initiative. Because advocacy resources can rarely match the range of possible initiatives, priorities must be established. Within the American Psychological Association (APA), priorities are first established for Education by the Board of Educational Affairs with assistance from the Education Directorate and the Public Policy Office. Once the priorities are set for education, they are then tested with those of the other Directorates to achieve oversight, coordination, and priorities for the association as a whole. For example, in 1996, opportunities were available to impact the Higher Education Act and the Public Health Service Act as both were being reauthorized during the 105th Congress. Thus, it was decided to target, as the primary advocacy goals, expanded eligibility and increased participation for psychology in these bills.

Choice of a particular target initiative determines where the strategy will be focused since political combat may take place in either the legislative or executive branches of government. Although education advocacy is focused primarily on Congress and the legislative process, it sometimes targets the Executive Branch around the promulgation of regulations, thereby seeking to establish a positive and productive relationship with agency officials who administer the programs in which psychology participates. The two priority pieces of legislation for education, both in the reauthorization process, focus the strategy on Congress, particularly the members of those committees with jurisdiction over these bills who make final recommendations for action to the full Congress.

With the goals established and targets identified, education advocacy first develops a clear message. An information strategy was employed to educate the chairs and members of relevant committees and subcommittees in the Senate and House of Representatives about psychology's ability to meet national needs. If psychology is seen as important to the nation's well-being, then the education of psychologists should be supported by federal funds. In order to educate and thus garner support from these key legislators, two sources of information are needed. First, clear, databased, and well-presented information is necessary to establish psychology's contributions to national needs. In choosing from among the many possible topics for this information base, areas of interest and meaning to the audience should be sought and found. So, if the Chairperson of the Committee is very interested in health, say cancer treatment, then demonstrating psychology's role in meeting these particular needs is likely to be of great interest. Thus, topics are chosen and data and other relevant information about psychology's contributions to these topic areas are gathered from publications, the APA Research Office, federal agencies, and other sources to develop concise and clear informational materials. In making the case, psychology's ability to contribute in significant ways to the topic area must be demonstrated, but also the value and contribution of psychology must be established through benefit-analysis and cost-effectiveness data. Particularly, but not exclusively, in the 1990s healthcare arena, these two factors are dominant in considering the value of a discipline's ability to contribute.

Further, since psychology is not yet firmly established in the public's mind as a health profession, and certainly not as "primary care," efforts to justify and promote the contribution of psychology to healthcare are critical to successful advocacy. Awareness must be increased about clinical psychology's unique contributions and expanding knowledge, not only as mental health providers, but especially as behavioral health professionals. The reason for this emphasis is twofold. First, it is consistent with the work of many in the field; there is much for psychology to contribute as a behavioral health provider. Just as important is that behavioral health is consistent with the view policymakers have of healthcare in the 1990s and as they expect it to evolve in the twenty-first century. This approach points out that in making the case, it must be understood how listeners understand the issue and fit the discipline's work, worth, and contributions to that perspective.

Fortunately, this fit is often not difficult to make, but it must be remembered to take the time to do so. After all, the sign of a good educator is to begin at the student's level of knowledge and understanding and build from there. Knowing that the policymaker understands and values the role of behavior in healthcare sets the stage for placing clinical psychologists' unique contributions as educators, researchers, and practitioners into that context. In other words, the advocate starts with the perceptions of those making policy, understands how to fit the discipline into their national priorities, and elucidates what they need to know about psychology in order to make the relevant connections to garner their support.

Once the primary message of how the discipline can contribute to the area being considered and the value of psychology as a cost-effective player is established, then the advocate can move on to another essential aspect of the advocacy message which is to educate policymakers about concerns and interests of psychologists. Until this point, the advocate has been educating the policymakers about how the discipline meets their needs. Having achieved that part of the message, advocates move on to explain what the discipline needs in order to be able to continue to make these important contributions. This might be funding for education and training of a new generation of psychologists or new skills for the current cohort; support for continued research and new knowledge, or inclusion as providers of healthcare, eligible to access programs of federal support for healthcare.

2.41.3.2 Advocacy: Making the Connection

With the message developed and packaged, how to present it must be determined, coordinated, and implemented utilizing as many formats as possible, delivered by those most relevant to the audience: their constituents, the voter; their expert constituents, the psychologist voter; and finally national experts, the lobbyists and staff of national associations, in that order of importance and credibility. At the same time, it is the national experts whose full-time job is to advocate. The remaining participants are volunteers working within limitations on time, resources, and advocacy expertise and "the lobbyist who has the access has the best opportunity to wield the most influence" (Zorack, 1990). It is critical to establish rapport and a positive relationship with key legislators and their staff. A positive, ongoing relationship has implications for present and future legislative initiatives. The relationship must be based on honesty and trust, be mutually beneficial, provide expertise (directly or indirectly) and ensure constituent support.

Establishing a relationship with staff and/or legislator is accomplished primarily through visits to policymakers at the national, state, and local levels. Congressional briefings on a particular subject of interest to legislators and their staff, as well as site visits to places of interest in their districts/states, are also helpful in establishing relationships. Keeping in touch with staff by telephone is another important way to maintain ongoing communications. As members of Congress begin to use Internet, that will be another important and far easier method of communication for advocates. The use of fax machines and email, in fact, has revolutionized communication that needs to be timely and efficient. However, too much contact (e.g., phone calls, faxes, or email) can also be a serious nuisance to busy staff and legislators, and at times highly detrimental to one's efforts.

Constituents communicate best through visits, phone calls, and letters. In fact, constituent mail is still the most effective means of influencing how a member of Congress votes. The other is supporting members of Congress in their fundraising efforts to be re-elected, especially members of the House of Representatives who must run for office every two years. When thought of in terms of educating these members, consistency is a worthwhile investment.

Finally, successful connections result from a multifaceted strategy. Especially if the message is a new or unfamiliar one, it will benefit from several hearings, different perspectives, and several messengers. Thus, a successful strategy will depend not only on the ability to know what actions are needed, but ultimately on their implementation. Some initiatives will require working with one or more associations in a coalition, some will involve taking the message directly to the legislator, while others demand working with some or all of the committee staff, and some may need an accompanying public relations campaign while others will require a one time Congressional briefing. Of course, the quantity and quality of activities undertaken to meet an advocacy target initiative must be consistent with the availability of resources and time.

2.41.3.3 Advocacy: Process or Outcome

Following any policy issue in the popular press makes it obvious that legislation and policymaking are ongoing processes. So too is advocacy. Thus, it makes sense that establishing and maintaining relationships with legislators, staff, and agency officials must be a continuous process. This recognition makes the determination of the outcome of a particular advocacy initiative unclear, especially when working with the legislative branch. Therefore, it is unwise to measure the success or failure of a legislative initiative on whether or not a particular advocacy goal is achieved at a specific moment in time.

Indeed, federal legislative initiatives are unpredictable, especially when dealing with enacting or reauthorizing legislation. Even though budget and appropriations legislation occur according to a defined cycle, their underlying legislative processes are unpredictable such that along the way any anticipated outcome is far from certain; it is simply not done until it is done. In fact, as the entire legislative process becomes subject to greater political influences and tensions between the executive and legislative branches of government, it becomes ever less certain what is going to happen or when. For example, during the first session of the 104th Congress, the Republican-controlled House and Senate could not come to an agreement with the Democratic Administration on funding federal programs. As a result, 15 separate Continuing Resolutions were enacted to allow federal programs to continue during this fractious period. However, with each enactment of a Continuing Resolution, programs were targeted for a set percentage reduction in funding with no opportunity to change any other part of the legislation.

Certainly, enacting or reauthorizing legislation is the most uncertain process to effect, as thousands of bills are introduced each session but only a handful are enacted into law. In fact, as demonstrated in the above example, even those bills being reauthorized (i.e., those bills requiring review and extension) are not necessarily acted upon within the term of Congress specified for reauthorization. A good example is the effort to reauthorize the Public Health Service Act during the 103rd Congress. It passed both Houses of Congress, and was approved in conference by both houses. However, at the last minute, only the full House gave the bill its final *pro forma* approval; the Senate did not. Thus, the Public Health Service Act remained unchanged. The Senate Republicans looking to the November 1994 elections, when the Republicans made sweeping victories and took control of both Houses of Congress, did not want to give President Clinton even one small success regarding healthcare legislation. This result was most unfortunate for psychology because the proposed revised Public Health Service Act legislation had contained a hard-won provision to set aside funds for the education and training of minorities in psychology. As a result, this piece of legislation remains a high priority for education advocacy efforts, five years and three sessions of Congress after first beginning this work.

In summary, getting a bill drafted is the easy part, getting it passed is next to impossible. In fact, getting a bill through Congress takes an enormous amount of time and effort. Amending a piece of legislation depends on whether or not the statute is up for consideration (i.e., reauthorization), as well as what the proposed amendment(s) contain. It must be emphasized that the least amount of change, coupled with its degree of simplicity, positively effects its chances of being accepted.

Advocacy efforts regarding federal regulations are the easiest to control, which is not to suggest that they are easy. For instance, providing feedback to the agencies promulgating regulations happens according to a schedule and usually results from a consensus, that is, getting those who have a vested interest to agree with how a program is to be implemented. Working with agencies to direct more funds and attention to a specific field (e.g., psychology), or to place representatives of the field on advisory bodies, is much more challenging and far from certain. An example from education occurred, during the 103rd Congress, when the Bureau of Health Professions (a program authorized by the Public Health Service Act) chose to focus primarily on increasing the number of ethnic minority physicians. With decreasing federal funding, the Bureau of Health Professions was not interested in increasing the number of psychologists in the programs without first receiving an increase in funding. For this reason, education advocacy efforts to work with the agency to include psychology in their programs became a notable challenge. It is pleasing to report that this has met with continued success. This success has been gained in small steps over several years with still some distance to go before the goal will have been reached. Each step has required ongoing connections with the agency's staff, maintaining their attention to psychology's needs and psychology's ability to support their agency's mission and goals. Finally, along the way it is necessary to be sure that the agency's staff is cognizant of the links between Congressional decisions as evident in legislation, psychology's constituents, and agency implementation.

All of this serves to underscore the importance of having a clear and well-marked strategy, one that serves as a road map for a long and at times frustrating journey. Detours along the way must be expected and markers established against which to measure progress and ensure that the journey remains on track. Like any journey, separating process from outcome along the way can be distracting and miss the point. In the advocacy world, advancing the cause of psychology may occur in spite of missing any particular legislative target, and that advance will serve well in the next round of legislation and policymaking.

2.41.3.4 Advocacy: Cost, Competition, and Champions

As has been described, achieving advocacy goals may take years to accomplish during which time consideration of cost, competition, and champions are most relevant. Lobbying is of little consequence if the advocacy plan or activities lack organizational support that translates into real dollars. The more resources available, the more extensive and thorough the advocacy. Unfortunately, there is no consistent relationship between the amount of money spent and the likelihood of success. No matter, it is also always true that without adequate funding, the scope of advocacy goals and expectation for success must be limited from the start. Funding is needed for professional staff to create and prepare information materials, to contact and prepare psychologists' advocates, to organize and assist in the delivery of the advocacy message, to fund the necessary trips, and related support of the myriad of advocacy activities that are part of successful campaigns.

The cost of an advocacy initiative will be dependent not only on the expected activities of the initiative but also on the extent of competition or opposition encountered along the journey. For example, current beneficiaries of existing legislation often do not want to share the limited federal dollars that would result from adding psychology to the recipients of federal support. Also, it is not uncommon to find that there are those who want funds directed to their legislative priorities and away from others. Whatever the reason, the competition must be addressed and that requires more time, effort, and money. For example, opposition from others in the healthcare community during the Public Health Service Act debate resulted from their reluctance to share limited, and dwindling, federal funds. That particular obstacle was removed by forming a coalition with other professionals in the healthcare community to advocate jointly for issues of mutual interest. What was most effective in establishing this coalition was educating the healthcare community about what psychologists do, convincing them that together, better healthcare can be provided, each complementing and supplementing the other professional services. Nevertheless, in the competitive arena of healthcare, opposition from the medical community and others will remain a challenge for psychology to confront; each aspect will need to be addressed and argued one on one, for a long time to come.

Competition and opposition are constant companions of the advocacy process. As outlined, there are many stages in the legislative process. Each one presents an opportunity to block your competitors and likewise to be thwarted by them. Congressional champions are the single most significant factor in meeting these challenges. Especially when the opposition is stiff, a powerful legislator serving as your champion can be the deciding factor. Champions and supporters of the proposed advocacy initiative are critical to advancing the cause: it is extremely difficult, likely impossible, without them. These champions not only bring the message to the floor of Congress but also shepherd the votes of other policymakers in your favor.

2.41.3.5 Advocacy: The Uncontrollable Element of Time

Timing is everything. If one waits too long in the political process before presenting a case, there will not be sufficient time to carry forth the message through letters, visits, and testimony. As the voting nears, legislators, and their staff are frenzied, unwilling, and unable to process new information, especially information that will upset delicate balances built among existing constituents. But if a proposal is presented too early, it may be shelved by the legislators and/or their staff, forgotten in the midst of more pressing matters requiring immediate attention. Lobbyists must monitor their contacts with legislators and staff; no one likes someone who usurps their valuable time. Nevertheless, unless calls are made regularly to legislators and staff, it is easy to miss important opportunities to plead the cause. For example, a hearing on a particular bill provides an excellent opportunity to have a psychologist testify in Congress, in this way publicly making the case for the discipline to all Committee members.

The length of time to accomplish an advocacy initiative is the most uncontrollable of all aspects of advocacy. Indeed, complicated initiatives must be considered for the long haul, that is, more than one session of Congress, often several years (note: one session of Congress covers a two-year period). For example, the Public Health Service Act reauthorization entered the first session of the Congress, approximately five years after the initial efforts to reauthorize that legislation. Moreover, all along the way it is necessary to compromise, increasing the chances of getting less than what you at first wanted, and probably concluding with something quite different from what you first set out to accomplish. Nevertheless, as noted above, there are tangible benefits from the process during these long initiatives: educating policymakers about issue and discipline, establishing a positive relationship with key legislators and their staffs, and through this work garnering their support for psychology that will serve well for future endeavors.

During this time, however, the larger political context will change, a factor directly effecting the political process. Prevailing national priorities do not remain constant. Variables such as fiscal strength and social climate, whether real or perceived, national or international, impact what happens in Congress by influencing the policymakers' receptivity to your ideas, messages, and needs.

2.41.3.6 Summary

Successful advocacy is a complex, multidimensional process requiring discipline and flexibility, vigilance, and strategic action. It requires ongoing involvement by psychologists who often understand neither the reasons for their participation nor the process. Finally, vicissitudes of time act to introduce a level of uncertainty and lack of control particularly frustrating to the uninitiated. In all, for so important an activity, it is fraught with barriers to its success. Coordination, knowledge, experience, and motivation are key to meeting these challenges.

2.41.4 THE ADVOCATES

2.41.4.1 The Constituent

As Tip O'Neill, a legendary Speaker of the House of Representatives for over 15 years, was frequently heard to say: "Politics is people." Without question, the key player in any advocacy initiative is the constituent (individually or collectively). Individually, each constituent is important because they vote to elect the legislator, something that is especially significant to members of the House of Representatives who must stand for election every two years. Understanding this, many psychologists are politically active and play a role in the political process at all levels: local, state, and federal. Collectively, groups of constituents (e.g., state associations) have substantial clout, especially if there is an established network of communication and committed members who have financial and other means of support. Large national associations, such as the APA, are perhaps the "wealthiest" politically because of the number of members nationwide who can give their support.

APA members, like members of other associations, can be involved in advocacy through grassroots activities which are quantitative and qualitative. Quantitative grassroots refers to the broad-based approach aimed at generating as many letters, calls, and visits to legislators as possible. Qualitative grassroots emphasizes the quality of the relationship (or the connection) between individual constituent and their legislators. These relationships require thoughtful interaction about common interests; communication that exists over time, not limited to meeting self-serving causes for either side; and meaningful contributions and responses one to another, that is, contributions that each side acknowledges and values. For legislators, constituents need to know that their concerns have been heard and met in the legislative process. For constituents, legislators look to them as a critical factor in political fundraising. It is a reality of American politics that funds are required to run for office or to be re-elected. Once again, members of the House of Representatives are particularly vulnerable because of their election schedule. For this reason, members of Congress appreciate financial support, regardless of the amount. Further, when there are a number of issues to which they might respond, they will choose those that are popular with their supporters. A clear sign of interest can be communicated through financial support. Thus, in spite of discussions to the contrary, until there is a significant change in the political process, a fact of life remains that constituents and organizations who can contribute funds will very likely have the most influence in the legislative process.

2.41.4.2 The Lobbyist

The lobbyist's three mottos are: (i) tell the truth; (ii) burn no bridges; and (iii) if you don't ask, you don't get (Wolpe, 1990). Lobbyists are conveyors of information. Helpful information is appreciated; information supporting and justifying an issue is essential for accomplishing one's advocacy objectives. Indeed, the main job of the lobbyist is to get decision makers interested and involved in the lobbyist's issues. Communications must be continuous, occurring on a regular and timely basis, through the use of newsletters, newspaper articles, internet, broadcast faxing, phone banks, and 800 numbers. Lobbyists must also educate and train their advocate participants about the process of advocacy: how the legislative process works, how to develop relationships with legislators, how to communicate with legislators, and the like. At APA this is accomplished by special training weekends with a group of psychologists around a particular target goal and culminating in visits. Ideally, in the future, this training will take place throughout the country on a state or regional basis so as to expand the number of psychology constituents/voters effective and knowledgeable about the advocacy process.

Lobbyists also need information themselves. Lobbyists need to know the field they represent, and the issues of their employers in order to be prepared to describe, explain, and justify issues and needs with legislators and their staff. For example, in the area of psychology and healthcare, lobbyists need to know the many ways the discipline contributes to good health, they must be able to answer complex questions, and be able to make the necessary connections between these contributions and the discipline's needs, say in the area of education and training. During each visit to legislators, it is imperative for the lobbyist to know just what they want to accomplish. They need to know the interests and idiosyncracies of their listeners in order to make their case, often during a time of high tension and great demands. Lobbyists, like constituents, need to establish relationships over a period of time, and preferably nurture these relationship during the quiet times afforded by Congressional recesses.

In addition, lobbyists must anticipate the opposition and solidify support from allies. Lobbyists need to be prepared to deal with the opposition, directly and indirectly. Most of all, they need the support of allies. In the political process, there is strength in numbers and relationships built over time on foundations of trust.

2.41.4.3 Third Parties: Organizations/ Associations

Numbers count in the political process as a measure of interest and because they represent votes. Thus, an organization or association has a more powerful voice than an individual and a coalition of many organizations has significantly more power than just one organization. It is especially helpful when organizations can work together toward shared goals of mutual benefit. For this reason, whenever possible in advocacy efforts, organizations are sought with which to coordinate activities, complement and supplement efforts of one another. In some instances, membership in coalitions requires a fee to support paid staff to work on behalf of all the coalition members (e.g., Council on Education Funding). However, working with coalitions is a luxury not always available because of competing interests among groups with similar needs.

2.41.5 FUTURE DIRECTIONS

While the nature of advocacy seems straightforward, its implementation remains complex for the discipline of psychology. To be effective, the discipline must be accepted as a credible player in the legislative arena. People who have participated in national advocacy efforts are likely to have been surprised by the naivety about the discipline by well-meaning professionals in a variety of congressional offices and federal agencies. For example, there is often confusion of psychology with other mental health fields; a common question posed to psychology advocates is to explain how psychology differs from psychiatry, social work, or counseling. If psychology is not recognized as a discipline with important and unique contributions to make, then there is little incentive for policymakers and implementors to support its needs. Moreover, even when the discipline is recognized for its unique qualities in one area, for example, practice, it may be unknown for its potential to contribute to another area, for example, science. Because advocacy for psychology most often occurs within specific and limited interests rather than speaking to the discipline as a whole, the full range of the discipline often remains unknown and its real potential fragmented. For example, if taken as a whole, the discipline could be presented around a particular topic area (e.g., smoking cessation) in terms of the implications for education, research, and practice. In this way, each interest would serve to reinforce the others, the needs could be reinforced optimally and over the long term the message would find a meaningful context to the listener on a variety of issues. Yet, such an approach demands considerable coordination, assumes consistency of interests among psychologists, and requires a common understanding of and involvement in the advocacy process. None of these requirements is being met in the late 1990s. As a result, at best, federal policymakers have an uneven understanding of the field, its potential to contribute to the national good, and its many needs.

In a world of limited resources and a crowded political environment, advocacy is needed more than ever to garner the support of federal policymakers in order to establish psychology as a field of national significance of benefit to all Americans. To do this, all psychologists are needed to participate in the advocacy process. Internally, all psychologists must be educated about why advocacy is important to them and how to participate. Externally, education is needed to bring the benefits of the discipline to the public, to garner their support and, through them, the support of their representatives in Congress. To manage these efforts requires a central organization drawing together the breadth of the discipline. APA, the largest scientific and professional organization representing psychology in the United States, is positioned uniquely to play this role for the discipline. As the world's largest association of psychologists with a membership of over 150 000, the APA includes researchers, educators, clinicians, consultants, and students representing 51 different subfields of psychology and maintaining affiliation with all State Psychological Associations and territorial associations. With a mission to advance psychology as a science, as a profession, and as a means of promoting human welfare, the APA fits well as the focal point for advocacy in psychology. Organized according to the major interests of the discipline, Education, Practice, Public Interest, and Science, these structures also serve to direct its advocacy foci. Such an organization ensures attention to each interest group and its advocacy priorities. At the same time, separating these functions leads to challenging demands for the coordination of activities and priorities.

Given this organization, it is not surprising that the development of advocacy for the discipline mirrors the development of its separate parts. Thus, the more established areas like practice and science have the clearest messages and the greatest influence on the political process, both internally and externally. The newer and broader area of education is just beginning to establish its message to the discipline as well as in Congress. In an environment of relative wealth, these distinctions can work. Each interest group can focus on policy areas of greatest relevance to them, and work with those policymakers involved in their issues. As resources dwindle and the government seeks ways to limit its scope, these distinctions become troublesome; most often confusion develops around priorities.

In this way the discipline of psychology in the advocacy world suffers from its riches. The kind of direct message so central to good advocacy is not easy to achieve. Because it is a field with many subfields, a singular theme is often elusive. Because it is a discipline with at least four major interests: education, practice, public interest, and research, priorities can be difficult to establish. Education seeks to increase funds to educate and train current and future psychologists; Science works primarily with agencies to ensure that support is available for psychological research; so too Practice works most particularly on issues of parity for the psychologist practitioner; and Public Interest focuses on AIDS, Children and Families, Diversity, and like issues of public service. When legislation and policy parallels these as separate interests, work flows smoothly albeit without forcing what could be the benefit of contributions from the other interest areas. When the policy environment overlaps, for example, when the same Committee handles legislation related to two or more of these interests, separate messages can be confusing and the need to meet with the same members of Congress about different initiatives and priorities can appear as an uncoordinated strategy. Such confusion can be further exacerbated by the fact that different organizations, often with similar names, can arrive at the doorstep of the decision maker carrying different messages of needs and requests.

The next step for psychology advocacy is to be coordinated and complementary. The discipline of psychology can and will benefit from advocacy regardless of its focus. Advocacy priorities for the field need to be assessed by each interest group represented by the directorates in APA as well as the association as a whole. This process has begun, but like all collaborations, it takes time as each part learns to work with and trust the others. Further, this path of coordinated advocacy is challenged by the different levels of maturity and resources of each interest group. Whereas Practice advocacy has a long history of work, grass roots development, and active member involvement,

Education is just beginning, has the fewest resources, and a constituent group (i.e., educators) largely unaware of the need of their involvement.

There is much to be done; there is enough work, and enough glory, for everyone to shine. There are great successes on which to build. Successful advocacy must be done by psychologists for psychology.

2.41.6 REFERENCES

Merriam Webster (1995). *Webster's collegiate dictionary*. Springfield, MA: Author.

Murray, C. J. L., & Lopez, A. D. (Eds.) (1996). *The global burden of disease*. Boston: The Harvard School of Public Health, on behalf of the World Health Organization.

Wolpe, B. C. (1990). *Lobbying Congress: How the system works*. Washington, DC: Congressional Quarterly.

Zorak, J. L. (1990). *The lobbying handbook*. Washington, DC: Professional Lobbying and Consulting Center.

Subject Index

Every effort has been made to index as comprehensively as possible, and to standardize the terms used in the index in line with the following standards:

Thesaurus of Psychological Index Terms, APA, Eighth Edition, for the selection of psychological terms.

Thesaurus of ERIC Descriptors, ERIC, Twelfth Edition, for the selection of education terms not covered by the above.

EMTREE Thesaurus for the selection of medical terms not covered by the above.

IUPAC Recommendations for the nomenclature of chemical terms, with trivial names being employed where normal usage dictates.

In general, the index follows the recommendations laid down in BS ISO 999:1996.

In view of the diverse nature of the terminology employed by the different authors, the reader is advised to search for related entries under the appropriate headings.

The index entries are presented in word-by-word alphabetical sequence. Chemical terms are filed under substituent prefixes, where appropriate, rather than under the parent compound name; this is in line with the presentation given in the *Thesaurus of Psychological Index Terms.*

The index is arranged in set-out style, with a maximum of three levels of heading. Location references refer to page number; major coverage of a subject is indicated by bold, elided page numbers; for example,

professional licensing, oral examinations **1234–55**
  and public accountability 266

See cross-references direct the user to the preferred term; for example, character *see* personality

See also cross-references provide the user with guideposts to terms of related interest, from the broader term to the narrower term, and appear at the end of the main heading to which they refer; for example

credentialing
  see also professional certification; professional licensing; recredentialing